MYTHOLOGIZING PERFORMANCE

A VOLUME IN THE SERIES

MYTH AND POETICS II

GREGORY NAGY, EDITOR

LEONARD MUELLNER, ASSOCIATE EDITOR

For a full list of titles in this series,
visit our website at cornellpress.cornell.edu.

A complete list of titles published in the original
Myth and Poetics series is available at the back of this book.

MYTHOLOGIZING PERFORMANCE

RICHARD P. MARTIN

Cornell University Press
Ithaca and London

First published 2020 by Cornell University Press

Library of Congress Cataloging-in-Publication Data

Names: Martin, Richard P., author.
Title: Mythologizing performance / Richard P. Martin.
Description: Ithaca : Cornell University Press, 2020. | Series: Myth and
    poetics II | Includes bibliographical references and index.
Identifiers: LCCN 2017057565 | ISBN 9781501713095 (cloth) |
    ISBN 9781501713101 (pbk.)
Subjects: LCSH: Greek poetry--History and criticism. | Oral
    tradition--Greece. | Literature and anthropology--Greece.
Classification: LCC PA3092 .M37 2018 | DDC 881/.0109--dc23
LC record available at https://lccn.loc.gov/2017057565

For Greg Nagy

CONTENTS

Part III. Hesiodic Constructions

Part IV. The Backward Look

SERIES FOREWORD

Gregory Nagy

As editor of the renewed and expanded series Myth and Poetics II, my goal is to promote the publication of books that build on connections to be found between different ways of thinking and different forms of verbal art in pre-literate as well as literate societies. As in the original Myth and Poetics series, which started in 1989 with the publication of Richard P. Martin's *The Language of Heroes: Speech and Performance in the "Iliad,"* the word "myth" in the title of the new series corresponds to what I have just described as a way of thinking, while "poetics" covers any and all forms of preliterature and literature.

Although "myth" as understood, say, in the Homeric *Iliad* could convey the idea of a traditional way of thinking that led to a traditional way of expressing a thought, such an idea was not to last—not even in ancient Greek society, as we see, for example, when we consider the fact that the meaning of the word was already destabilized by the time of Plato. And such destabilization is exactly why I prefer to use the word "myth" in referring to various ways of shaping different modes of thought: it is to be expected that any tradition that conveys any thought will vary in different times and different places. And such variability of tradition is a point of prime interest for me in my quest as editor to seek out the widest variety of books about the widest possible variety of traditions.

Similarly in the case of "poetics," I think of this word in its widest sense, so as to include not only poetry but also songmaking on one side and prose on the other. As a series, Myth and Poetics II avoids presuppositions about traditional forms such as genres, and there is no insistence on any universalized understanding of verbal art in all its countless forms.

VOLUME FOREWORD

Gregory Nagy

As I write in the series foreword, the driving force that inspired my original project of editing such a series stems from an understanding of *myth* and *poetics* as formulated by Richard P. Martin in his book *The Language of Heroes: Speech and Performance in the "Iliad"* (1989), which was the first volume to appear in the original Myth and Poetics series. That book has been for me the inspiration not only for MP but also for the second phase of the same series, MP II—which I see as Myth and Poetics 2.0, as it were. And now comes Martin's new book, *Mythologizing Performance*, which is just as foundational for the overall project of Myth and Poetics.

Although this book appears chronologically as the third, not the first, in the new series, it takes pride of place in tracing the intellectual genealogy of Myth and Poetics 2.0. That is why I felt the need to write a separate foreword to this particular volume, above and beyond the uniform foreword that I write for all the volumes in the series. The task of writing such a special text is difficult for me, since so much of my own thinking about myth and poetics is indebted to the discoveries and discovery procedures of Richard P. Martin. How can I write, in just one brief paragraph that I have set as my goal, an adequate statement of my indebtedness to Martin's work?

What makes my task even more difficult is that I discovered, as I was reading the page proofs for *Mythologizing Performance*, that the author has actually dedicated his book to me, his editor. That does not seem right, I first thought to myself when I made my surprise discovery of his gracious dedication. But then, on second thought, it all made sense to me: you see, Richard P. Martin was once, long ago, my student. And, I now tell myself, teachers should ideally learn more from their students than the other way around—and such an ideal is, after all, exactly what I have experienced over so many years of intellectual collaboration with my dear colleague Richard.

So, without any further self-consciousness about the inherent difficulties of my task, I proceed with an attempt to capture, in one paragraph, the importance of this new book.

In *Mythologizing Performance*, what Richard P. Martin has given his readers is a dazzlingly concise and yet far-ranging overview of the earliest phases of ancient Greek verbal art. In the course of the seventeen essays contained in this riveting book, Martin delves into the fundamentals for understanding the poetry attributed to Homer and Hesiod, which he analyzes in terms of the traditions that went into the performing as well as the composing of ancient Greek myths in the context of their ritual settings. In addition, he deftly connects Homeric and Hesiodic poetry with the far less well-known poetic and prosaic traditions underlying the kinds of lore that the Greeks attributed mostly to the mystical figure of Orpheus. All along, Martin keeps in mind the *performativity* of ancient Greek verbal art, revealing brilliant new insights about ancient Greek performers known as *citharodes*, that is, singers who accompany themselves on the stringed instrument known as the *kithara*, and *rhapsodes*, that is, reciters of poetry that is musically unaccompanied. And the absolutized model for such performers, as Martin demonstrates most convincingly, is none other than Apollo himself, whose divinity comes to life in his charismatic role as god of mythologizing performance.

PREFACE

In editing and occasionally updating the chapters that follow, I have sought to retain the mindset of the originals, taking care not to import backwards what I learned later. If one might not always detect progress in the varied attempts, at least my grappling with evidence and trying gradually to widen the questions may be helpful to readers. If I had known thirty, twenty, or ten years ago what I know (or at least think I know) now, I would have written differently. In the same spirit, I have not attempted to update references to new translations or editions, assuming the interested reader will find the best of the most recent ones. I have, however, provided at the end of chapters, where appropriate, a longer footnote that refers to a few of the most important works subsequently written on the issue at hand. These notes are emphatically not a compendium of all the books or articles that have mentioned the given problems that I have treated but are simply my reckoning of the truly major advances.

I owe gratitude to all those over the years who invited me to speak, or attended the talks, at which many of these pieces were first tried out, in the US, Europe, and Argentina (Chapters 2, 3, 5, 7, 8, 9, 12, 13, 14, 15). Thanks go also to the patient volume editors for whom I produced Chapters 1, 4, 6, 10, 11, 16, and 17. To four persons in particular I owe more than can ever adequately be expressed: my smart, genial, generous children, Catherine and Thomas; my wife, Anastasia-Erasmia Peponi, whose aesthetic sensitivity is luminous and whose *homophrosunê* has kept me whole; and Gregory Nagy, Hellenist par excellence, friend of forty years, Doktorvater, and ever-inspiring exponent of the traditions handed down by his own teachers, Albert Lord and Roman Jakobson. To him this book is humbly dedicated.

MYTHOLOGIZING PERFORMANCE

INTRODUCTION

To sum up more than three decades of research on the hexameter poetic traditions of archaic Greece is not easy, especially because the problems on which I have worked, and the approaches I have tried, are too varied to treat as a unified whole. Some key texts provide continuity: I have gravitated over the years to the *Homeric Hymn to Apollo*, the *Odyssey*, and the *Works and Days*. But this volume of essays does not attempt to offer anything like a comprehensive reading of those endlessly fascinating poems, articulating, instead, my views on some interesting problems within them. As will become clear, I have often looked to the margins and the marginal (so-called "Orphic" tablets, pulp fiction), as well as to performance traditions beyond geographic and temporal borders for analogies that might spur further thinking (medieval Irish and modern Greek especially, as well as Egyptian, Indic, and African practices). Rather than providing an overall view, therefore, of early Greek verse-making, the following remarks should be taken as a blend of provocation, manifesto, and users' guide; a defense of a particular brand of philology that draws on comparative work and the diachronic study of literary semantics; and a meditation on methods and values in the analysis of culture.

The title *Mythologizing Performance* requires some explanation and expansion. Its second term has, by now, become notoriously capacious. As the folklorist and linguistic anthropologist Richard Bauman points out, "The term 'performance' and its grammatical variants and compound forms cover a lot of ground, and the terrain is far from clearly marked."[1] Bauman's own work (an early influence on mine) is illustrative, ranging from poetics and intertextuality to analysis of folklore genres and study of the speech protocols of seventeenth-century Quakers. It will be convenient, therefore, to list the aspects of "performance" most relevant to the following essays by reference to Bauman's seminal book, *Verbal Art as Performance*.[2] This is not to privilege a single scholar's definition, of course, in an area where dozens

---

[1] Bauman 2011, 707. See also, on the general development of his ideas regarding verbal art in performance, Bauman 2002 and 2013.

[2] Bauman 1977, esp. pp. 9–11.

of writers have carried out meticulous work that clarifies the subject, but merely to provide parameters within which we might make further distinctions. Later in this introduction, I will turn to the particular strain of classical philology that has shaped my body of work thus far, in fruitful dialogue with anthropology, folkloristics, and linguistics.[3]

First, as Bauman's book title makes clear, at issue is a subset of broader possible "performances"—namely "verbal art." By using this phrase (rather than "oral literature" or "oral poetry"), Bauman simultaneously broadens the area of investigation to include stylized ways of speaking that allow for creative variation (greetings, jokes, games, prayers, etc.) alongside more conventionally acknowledged genres (lyric, epic, drama), but narrows the focus to products of language. The notion of verbal-artistic "performance" thus can be viewed as part of a continuum that merges with other, primarily non-verbal, routines and enacted relationships (for instance, ritual and kinship protocols)—phenomena that can decisively affect the conditions for verbal art. But the core of the analysis will remain linguistic communication.

Second, performance offers a distinctive sort of "frame" that puts the literal linguistic content of any communication into a new perspective. Building on the insights of the anthropologist Gregory Bateson and the sociologist Erving Goffman, Bauman analyzes the particular "frame" of verbal-art performance in terms of how it guides interpretation. Within this frame, the essential actors are a "performer" and an "audience"—although these may never be formally or overtly identified as such. The performer assumes responsibility for a "display of communicative competence," in Bauman's words, based on his or her ability to speak in "socially appropriate ways" while being accountable to the audience for the manner in which communication occurs.[4] The audience, meanwhile, assumes the right to evaluate the communication in terms of the performer's ability and effectiveness. Audience members enjoy an enhanced experience based on the inherent qualities of the verbal expression, which in turn are inseparable from the performer's skill. (In a less abstract mode, that one can talk of a "lousy joke-teller," a "brilliant preacher," a "persuasive orator," or a "failed poet"— my examples, not Bauman's—highlights the mutually dependent factors of ambition, evaluation, and aesthetic norms.)

---

[3]   Nagy 1996a has been my essential guide in thinking about performance as it applies to ancient Greek verbal art.

[4]   Bauman 1977.

A third and essential point flows from the notion of "framing": in Bauman's formulation, "Performance becomes *constitutive* of the domain of verbal art as spoken communication" (11). This approach, in sum, solves the bind that can be presented by an "etic" notion of "verbal art," in which some (perhaps arbitrary or unexamined) "universal" notions might wrongly be imposed on a culture's productions.[5] Rather than seeking to identify what is "art" by reference to (culturally specific) formal features (e.g., rhyme or meter as indicative of "poetry"), pinpointing performance by frame-analysis works through contextual cues: when individuals or groups are detected in a "performance" relationship (given the expectations and assumptions outlined above), the substance of their communication is, thereby, "verbal art." The spoken communication involved in purchasing a bus ticket (usually) occurs outside any "performance" frame; a later narration, however, relating to one's friends the sufferings and joys of the bus trip, operates within the frame.

Bauman's delineation of the features of "performance" draws on detailed work in the ethnography of speaking, a field that developed in the mid-1960s and brought folklorists together with linguistic anthropologists.[6] One of the most productive results of this encounter of specialties has been the recognition that materials of interest to folklorists—specific verbal genres varying from one tradition to another among cultures—bear a relationship to broader structures within the languages studied by anthropologists. Taxonomies of the types of speech-acts identified by name within a particular culture can be seen to map onto "genres of speaking." These in turn match, or at least provide the basis for, creative, artistic "genres" central to entertainment and social life. In other words, the verbal arts in a given culture are part of a continuum with the units (lexical and cognitive) organizing a culture's overall understanding of speech behavior.

For example, villagers of the southern central plateau of Madagascar divide their speech modes into, on one hand, *resaka*, a category of "ordinary talk" that covers gossip, requests, discussion, and consultations, among other speech-genres; and on the other, *kabary*, the modes of which include formal speeches at marriages and funerals, at ancestral bone-turnings and circumcisions, and expressions of gratitude or sympathy. In effect, use of *kabary makes* an occasion into a formal or ritual moment.[7] The Western

---

[5] For a concise discussion of "emic" and "etic," see Dundes 1962.

[6] For a representative sample, see Bauman and Sherzer 1989.

[7] Keenan 1989, 126–27.

classically-derived category of "oratory" is only a rough equivalent for *kabary*; a similar approximation would be to call *resaka* "talk," and *kabary* "making a speech." The "marked" category (to use the distinction from Prague School linguistics) is clearly *kabary,* while *resaka* is "unmarked." The techniques of stylization and ornamentation that enrich *kabary* include smaller "genres" such as proverbs and traditional sayings, the appropriate use of which can be judged by an audience during performances (events that sometimes involve two speakers in ritualized dialogues). In Bauman's terms, we can imagine the *kabary* mode as dynamically working in two directions: if a speaker uses the familiar conventions of the mode, he prompts his hearers to assume the "frame" of performance is in play; if a certain performance "frame" (e.g., a wedding) is already in place, the formal speech-events within it will then be held up to the standard of previously audience-tested *kabary* performances.

My interpretation of the *Iliad*, published nearly thirty years ago, made use of a number of studies from the ethnography of speaking to identify a marked category within Homeric Greek, distinguished lexically by the noun *mûthos* and related verb forms, which stands in regular contrast with an "unmarked" category designated by the noun *epos*. That the Greek words in question give us, in the *diachronic* perspective, English "myth" and "epic" respectively, and that these seem to be overlapping categories, rather than complements or contrasts, can cause confusion (Chapter 1 in this volume, "Epic as Genre," attempts to clarify the relationship). But the identification of a mode of speech (*mûthos*) marked (like *kabary*) by fullness of expression and frequent deployment of rhetorical devices gives us a basis *within* the poetry of Homer to pinpoint moments in which the frame of "performance" dominates. In other words, an ancient synchronic and culturally-acknowledged ("emic") system, rather than a modern, imposed "etic" scheme offers contemporary readers of Homer a sort of amplifying device, a means of listening all the more attentively to the key, "marked" utterances in the epics.

A first interpretation, then, of the present book's title might take the word "mythologizing" as adjectival—that is, "performance that acts like a *mûthos*." Inasmuch as *muthoi* can be understood as performances, a complete inventory of the speech-acts designated *mûthos* in archaic poetry would in theory provide us with the parameters of "performance" in early Greek culture. While such a collection remains a desideratum, the essays in this book follow a different path, foregoing simple lexical investigations in favor of treating each poetic production as itself an instantiation of *mûthos*-style speech: that is to say, in Bauman's terms, a performance.

Perhaps a few Classicists might still question the basis for my decision to approach the *Odyssey* or *Works and Days* as performances, given the absence of incontrovertible evidence that these poems, as we have them, represent transcripts of actual live performer–audience interactive events. To such sceptics, at least three sorts of response can be addressed. First, we can adopt an hermeneutic perspective, one that begins from the texts as we have them, spirals outward to fit textual evidence into hypothetical broader patterns, and returns (via the "hermeneutic circle") to re-read the texts with the refined hypotheses in mind. Because it is undisputed that the Homeric and Hesiodic poems, and the *Homeric Hymns*, explicitly depict (and comment on) rhetorical, poetic, or musical actions (or combinations thereof), it makes sense to begin our interpretations with the assumption that these internalized depicted performances (whether or not tagged as *muthoi* in the texts) must bear *some* relationship to the world of discourse experienced by the actual composers and transmitters of the poetry containing them. (The less plausible interpretive option would be to suppose that the pictures of performance within each poem were intentionally unreal, deracinated, or alien to the listeners.)

This is not to say that the acts thus represented match precisely the actions of those making the representations. A well-known case in point concerns the various songs of Phemius and Demodocus in the *Odyssey*.[8] No one can reasonably assert that the *Odyssey*, in terms of style, length, contents, audience, performer, and other aspects, exactly fits any of the songs that Demodocus the court performer produces for his eager listeners on Scheria. The *Odyssey*, as a whole, sung or recited, would take approximately 24 hours; the songs of Demodocus, as depicted, take at most a long evening. The *Odyssey* is built on a complex double-stranded plot-line focused on forty days in the life of its protagonist and his son; the songs of Demodocus focus on brief episodes from the Trojan War or the love-lives of the gods, lasting less than a day. Demodocus and Phemius, the two named singers whose performances we hear of in the poem, appear to be comfortably settled professionals, resident in royal houses, where their job is to entertain and celebrate the king, his guests, and his entourage. No rivals are in sight; yet, from the *Works and Days* we learn that poetic rivalry is actually a paradigmatic instance of "good competition" (*Works and Days* 24–26), while the *Odyssey* itself offers another glimpse of the lifestyle of singers

---

[8] A good review of previous work is contained in Segal 1994.

when it includes *aoidoi* in a list of itinerant "public" craft-experts, called *dêmioergoi* (along with doctors, prophets, and joiners: *Odyssey* 17.383–85). It seems, therefore, that the representations of singers within the *Odyssey*, even in terms of archaic Greek practices, were stylized retrojections of an idealized situation, one that may or may not have existed several generations before the composition of the poem.[9] After all, the *Odyssey* (like the *Iliad*) deals with an overtly distinct and earlier era, a heroic age in which conditions were different (usually, bigger and better). In this regard, the Hesiodic perspective—in explicitly acknowledging the demise of the heroic age (*Works and Days* 176–201)—gives a more realistic glimpse of the situation of actual poets and singers.

To recognize the effects of stylization in the Homeric representation of performance does not undercut the force of the many clear continuities between the concerns and techniques of the fictionalized "internal" performers and those real composers who were responsible for shaping the Homeric poems we now possess.[10] The two levels of composition each draw on such techniques as signaling their topics by a preposed noun phrase and relative clause (cf. *Odyssey* 1.1 *Andra moi ennepe ... hos* and the description of the song of Phemius at *Odyssey* 1.326–27, *noston aeide ... hon*); or punctuating narration with direct mimetic speech (cf. *Odyssey* 8.306–20, in the song about Ares and Aphrodite).

On a broader basis, both the *Odyssey* as a whole and its internal narrators are devoted to the commemoration of heroic *kleos* (fame through poetry). And the poem's hero is himself an itinerant performer (like rhapsodes of the classical period and like Homer as pictured in the *Lives* traditions).[11] His narratives can be compared to a poet's. Alcinous, the king of the Phaeacians, declares as much half–way through Odysseus' artful recounting of his underworld journey (*Odyssey* 11.363–69):[12]

> ὦ Ὀδυσεῦ, τὸ μὲν οὔ τί σ' ἐΐσκομεν εἰσορόωντες,
> ἠπεροπῆά τ' ἔμεν καὶ ἐπίκλοπον, οἷά τε πολλοὺς

---

[9]   De Jong 2001, 191–92 stresses the idealization of the figure of the singer in the *Odyssey*, connecting this with the *Odyssey* poet's desire for self-promotion and implicit rivalry with earlier exponents of heroic traditions. On competition as a performance driver, see below.

[10]   On the differences between representations of singers and the external realities of Homeric performance, using the notion of diachronic skewing, see Nagy 1990, 21–26; on further subtle differentiation of the *Odyssey* narrator from the poem's characters, including singers, in terms of the handling of speech and narrative, see the excellent analysis in Beck 2012, 140–54.

[11]   On the *Lives* see Nagy 2010, 29–47.

[12]   The ironies of this scene and its relation to oral-poetic practices are discussed in Chapter 8 below.

βόσκει γαῖα μέλαινα πολυσπερέας ἀνθρώπους,
ψεύδεά τ᾽ ἀρτύνοντας ὅθεν κέ τις οὐδὲ ἴδοιτο·
σοὶ δ᾽ ἔπι μὲν μορφὴ ἐπέων, ἔνι δὲ φρένες ἐσθλαί.
μῦθον δ᾽ ὡς ὅτ᾽ ἀοιδὸς ἐπισταμένως κατέλεξας,
πάντων τ᾽ Ἀργείων σέο τ᾽ αὐτοῦ κήδεα λυγρά.

> Odysseus, in the first place we do not at all suppose, as we look at
> you, that you are the kind of dissembler and cheat which the dark
> earth breeds in such numbers among far-flung humankind, men
> that fashion lies out of what no man could ever see. But upon you
> is grace of words, and within you is a heart of wisdom, and your
> tale [*mûthon*] you have told with skill, as a minstrel [*aoidos*] does,
> the grievous woes of all the Argives and of your own self. [trans.
> Murray and Dimock 1995]

The *mûthos* of Odysseus (or "performance" as I have been arguing), spoken
so skillfully (*epistamenôs*) and in such detail (*katelexas*), resembles a singer's
in all but the feature of musical accompaniment (missing, in the hero's rendition). Moreover, although the logical link is not stated in so many words,
this *mûthos* as a species of powerful utterance is implicitly truthful, when
contrasted with the lies (*pseudea*) that characterize the speech of the sorts
of "dissembler and cheat" who apparently have made their way to Scheria
before this. The juxtaposition of truth and falsehood in Alcinous' evaluation of the story makes it clear that he treats the ongoing performance as
an extension of the hero's apparent character—a man with a good mind and
shapely rhetoric to match (*morphê epeôn*). In other words, for the king at
least, there is no artificial distinction of the type that later literary critics
made between "poetic" and "prose" discourses—they are of a piece. Lastly,
the observation about the *mûthos* of Odysseus being more reliable than the
fictions of others—due to its status as an eyewitness account that is not based
on "what no man could ever see"—must be compared with the language of
the well-known Hesiodic initiation scene. At *Theogony* 22–28, the poetic
narrator tells how he was first commissioned by the Muses to sing hymns in
praise of them and the other divinities:

> One time, they taught Hesiod beautiful song while he was pasturing
> lambs under holy Helicon. And this speech [*mûthon*] the goddesses
> spoke first of all to me, the Olympian Muses, the daughters of aegis-
> holding Zeus: "Field-dwelling shepherds, ignoble disgraces, mere
> bellies: we know how to say many false things [*pseudea*] similar to
> genuine ones, but we know, when we wish, how to proclaim true
> things [*alêthea gêrusasthai*]."

Thus, an overriding concern with the truth-content of performance is what characterizes both the relationship of the performer with his audience, as represented *internally* in Homeric epic, and the *external* frame for a performance that delivers the divinely-inspired words of the poet Hesiod (who is both the "author" and a character within his own composition, in the terms of the *Theogony*). Once more, the seamless continuity of attitude across generically distinct forms of representation deserves our attention.

Finally, taking the widest panoramic critical view, it has been shown in detail by Anastasia-Erasmia Peponi that the aesthetic vocabulary and narrative tropes describing the ways that musical and poetic performances are apprehended and appreciated within early Greek hexameter poetry are co-extensive with literary depictions of how listeners received Homeric verse and related instances of *mousikê* in the classical period.[13] Whether it is the songs of Hermes, of the Sirens, or of the *Odyssey*'s court-poets, the overwhelming emotional responses elicited by these mythic, fictional performances (from tears to enchantment to catharsis, the sensation of fusing with song, and silence) have precise parallels in scenarios written by Plato, Xenophon, and Aristophanes regarding their contemporaries. Of course, the fifth- and fourth-century depictions are themselves to a certain extent stylized: we cannot claim that they capture "real life" responses in every detail. Nevertheless, such scenes make use of deep-rooted, shared cultural assumptions and practices. That they affirm resemblances and continuity between the performances contained in archaic fiction and actual performances of their own day gives us a strong justification for approaching our texts afresh, not as purely textual products but as the result of full-fledged, living oral and aural experiences.

Plato's dialogue *Ion* offers a second category of response—we might call it semi-historical—to those who question the performance context of hexameter poetry. The single most extensive source of information about the performance of Homeric poetry in the classical period, the *Ion* gives an account of a dialogue between Socrates and a professional performer of Homeric verse, Ion of Ephesus—a "rhapsode" or "song stitcher" who travels the Greek world competing in performance contests (*agônes*). The evidence of the dialogue must be handled with care because Plato, obviously, is a hostile witness: his commitment to the superiority of Socratic discourse means that he must downgrade what he clearly views as the major competing form of education in classical Athens, the traditional teaching of poetry,

---

[13] Peponi 2012.

especially Homeric.[14] Thus, Socrates is shown to undercut the rhapsode's claim to knowledge based on his particular expertise, as the philosopher relegates both the poets and the interpreters of poetry to the category of "inspired" interpreters (*hermênês*)—who by definition are not in control of their own thinking (*ouk emphrones* 534a). This move is accomplished by eliding Homeric poetry with dithyramb, the form of Greek choral lyric in which Athenian tribes competed against one another at the festival of the Dionysia (cf. *Ion* 534a). While this merger cannot withstand careful critical comparison, since the genres possess completely different metrical, dictional, and musical features, it allows Socrates to paint the form of recited, non-choral epic with the vivid colors of melic poetry—moreover, a form of this sung-and-danced verse that was notorious, at the time of the dialogue, for its extravagant, often aerial imagery, its innovative rhythms and instrumental accompaniment, and the evocation of ecstatic enthusiasm on the part of the dithyrambic narrative voice.[15] In short, in the *Ion* "Homer" has been hijacked and held captive to the philosopher's will.

It is clear that the rhapsode Ion, as presented by Plato, is in the habit of reciting established versions of the *Iliad* and *Odyssey*, although no reference is made to a written *text* of either poem. Expressions like "as the poems have them" (535c) are ambiguous, leaving unspecified the form in which the poems exist.[16] The passages quoted by Plato closely resemble (but are not always identical with) the epics as known from later ancient and medieval papyri and manuscripts. The very first passage cited contains a variation, when Ion, apparently recalling Homeric lines from the Funeral Games of Patroclus, uses the adjective "well-planed" to describe the body of the chariot (ἐϋξέστῳ ἐνὶ δίφρῳ: *Ion* 537a7). As it occurs in the "vulgate" text, however, and is printed in modern editions (*Iliad* 23.335), the phrase takes the form "in a well-woven chariot" (ἐϋπλέκτῳ ἐνὶ δίφρῳ), with a different and rarer adjective found only in this scene to describe a chariot-box.[17] The

---

[14] Cf. on Homer's usefulness in education the view expressed (but kept at arm's length) in Plato *Republic* 606e. For similar sentiments: Isocrates *Panegyricus* 159 and Aristophanes *Frogs* 1034–36 and passages analyzed in Ford 2002, 197–208. On the *Ion* and Plato's attempt to discredit traditions of rhapsodic competition, see especially Nagy 2009, 373–86.

[15] LeVen 2014, 152–88; the style is nicely parodied in Aristophanes *Birds* 1387–90.

[16] In my own experience during fieldwork in western Crete involving the heroic romance *Erotokritos*, skilled oral performers who had learned this (originally written) poem by heart from repeated hearings (rather than textual study) referred to it as "speaking" its lines (*to tragoudhi lei*, "the song says"). The neutral phrasing leaves ambiguous the original form of the composition.

[17] Curiously, three of the total of four occurrences of either εὔπλεκτος (with -το-suffix) or the related (s-stem) adjective εὐπλεκής in Homer are confined to *Iliad* 23, where twice they modify

variation in adjective could result from faulty recall of a written text that Ion (or Plato) quotes from memory. It might also, however, reflect another possibility: that Ion re-creates the Homeric passage by combining his memory of a standardized version with supplementation, at some points, that draws on his internalized knowledge of the traditional diction consistently employed by Homeric (and Hesiodic) poetry. In the latter case, it is relevant that the epithet found almost exclusively here in our sources for the *Iliad* 23 passage (ἐϋξέστῳ) does occur twenty-one times in Homeric poetry to describe crafted objects from bath-tubs to chairs, boards, and boxes.[18] In other words, it was available within the poetic *Kunstsprache,* and its identical metrical shape and similar phonic shape facilitated the variation.[19] The larger point remains: there is no explicit evidence that Ion ever acquired his knowledge of Homer from written texts at all. He might as easily have learned by heart (from earlier rhapsodes) a fairly organized sequence of scenes, character speeches, and treatments, and then have *varied* these from one performance to the next, especially under the pressure of competition against other rhapsodes from various city-states.[20]

How "creative" a fifth-century rhapsode like Ion might have been is still a matter for debate. Of course, the answer depends on our definition of creativity when it occurs within a long tradition, such as that of Homeric poetry. Some scholars have sought to establish a firm divide between the "creative" early poet, "Homer," and slavishly imitative later reciters.[21] Others

---

"chariot," (lines 335 and 436) and once "ropes" (line 115); at *Iliad* 2.449, the adjective describes the woven "tassels" of Athena's aegis.

[18] One manuscript of the *Iliad* (D = Laurent. 32.15, dated to eleventh century) has ἐϋξέστῳ, but this could represent a Byzantine correction made on the basis of the Plato text. The adjective εὔξεστος occurs a total of twenty-one times in Homer; all but three instances occupy the same metrical slot as in Plato's version of the line at *Iliad* 23.335. Only once does it describe a chariot-box (*Iliad* 16.402), in the exact phrase that Ion uses for his version of the line from *Iliad* 23.

[19] On similar alternatives as symptoms of the multiformity to be expected in an oral tradition, see Nagy 2004, 25–39.

[20] West 2011 suggests both that the rhapsodes owned texts (on the evidence of Xenophon *Memorabilia* 4.2.10) and that they knew them by heart (Xenophon *Symposium* 3.6), observing that recitation from memory "will have been a prime source of the textual variation characteristic of pre-Aristarchean copies." He fails to note that the variation was more likely generated by the rhapsodes' immersion in the traditional system of diction than by simple slips of memory. On the role of competition in performance of hexameters, see Collins 2001b.

[21] The most persistent version of this view was first expressed by Kirk 1962, 302–24. As his overall discussion reveals, the urge to draw a contrast between "creative" or "true" oral composers and reproductive rhapsodes is wrapped up with views on the dating of Homer, the quality of Homeric language (as opposed to allegedly "later" hexameters), the historicity of the Trojan War, and the date of the introduction of the alphabet. The *aoidos*/rhapsode contrast has most often been used to support

prefer to place Ion on a spectrum of performers that gradually ranges from those whose every poetic production is a newly created "composition-in-performance," to those whose creativity comprises more localized variation on the level of phrase, line, or passage.[22] Although the lack of evidence makes it unlikely that the question will ever see resolution, three points should be made to put it in perspective. First, the few references we have to rhapsodic activity of earlier periods than that depicted in the *Ion*, in particular concerning the sixth century BCE, present us with performers engaged in producing new songs. A hexameter fragment attributed to Hesiod (fr. 357 MW) recalls a time when that poet and Homer together as "singers" (*aoidoi*) made poetry with music (μέλπομεν) in honor of Apollo on his sacred island, Delos, "having stitched together song in new hymns" (ἐν νεαροῖς ὕμνοις ῥάψαντες ἀοιδήν). Not only do these lines portray a collaborative enterprise, which looks like a mythologized retrojection of the collaborative turn-taking in performance that characterized the rhapsodic competition at the Athenian Panathenaea; they also highlight the novelty of the production—a detail that we can compare with the words of Telemachus, concerning the Ithacan singer Phemius, that the newest song (νεωτάτη) is what audiences always celebrate (*Odyssey* 1.351–52).[23] In other words, the joint work of Homer and Hesiod is in this fragment imagined not simply as the recitation of an acknowledged older text, but as a new creation—even if it can still be conceived as the intertwining of two previously performed pieces. The verb *rhaptô*, from which the agent noun *rhapsoidos* ("song stitcher") is derived, easily allows for the latter possibility: a piecing together of segments. At a more fine-grained level, it could also refer to the practice of piecing together formulaic elements (phrases, lines, and scenes).[24]

The same extensive scholium to Pindar that preserves the pseudo-Hesiodic fragment (scholia to *Nemean* 2.1, iii.31 Drachmann) offers further precious detail about a sixth-century rhapsode named Cynaethus, apparently

arguments in favor of a supposed one-time, early fixation of the Homeric text. On the weaknesses of those positions, see Nagy 1996b, 19–27, 93–112.

[22] For the latter (to me, much more plausible) viewpoint, see now the masterful rebuttal in González 2013, 276–83 and 331–44 of those (like Pelliccia, as cited by him) who still hold to the notion of a dichotomy. For an attested rhapsodic variation (the only one mentioned in the scholia to the *Iliad*), see Σ *Iliad* 21.26b "κάμε χεῖρας ἐναίρων": Ἑρμόδωρος ὁ ῥαψῳδὸς χεῖρας ἐναίρων ἤκουε "χειροκοπῶν," κατεχρήσατο δέ. As Cassio (2002, 124) points out, this variant from the rhapsode Hermodorus ("got tired cutting hands" instead of "tired out his hands") sounds ludicrous.

[23] On the idea of joint production, see Chapter 7. On collaborative sequenced performance in the Athenian contest, see Nagy 1996a, 70–77.

[24] The latter explanation is preferred by Kirk 1962, 312.

one of the guild of performers known as the Homeridae ("member of Homer's kin group"). The interpretive trigger for the historical remarks of the scholiast is Pindar's etymologizing reference in *Nemean* 2.1–2 to the Homeridae as "singers of stitched verses" (ῥαπτῶν ἐπέων ... ἀοιδοί) who customarily start their poems with a *proemium* to Zeus (as Pindar is in the act of doing in the poem, and the victor whom he praises has done by winning at a festival of Zeus).[25] We might note, as an aside, that Pindar, as composer of choral song-and-dance pieces, in this epinician ode (circa 485 BCE) makes the same move that Plato's Socrates will make a century later in the *Ion* (circa 380 BCE): an intentional elision of epic hexameter verse with the poetics of melic poetry. That Pindar may consider himself, like the later philosopher, to be engaged in rivalry with Homeric poetry, can be argued from a number of other passages, but only here does he seem to use the strategy of co-opting the competing genre's poetics.[26] Curiously, this melding of types (rhapsodic, epinician, hymnic) by means of their shared proemial trope echoes on a generic level what was reportedly done within hexameter verse by the rhapsode Cynaethus and his circle "who they say made many of the verses and grafted them into the poetry of Homer" (οὕς φασι πολλὰ τῶν ἐπῶν ποιήσαντας ἐμβαλεῖν εἰς τὴν Ὁμήρου ποίησιν). By bringing together some circumstantial evidence with the further information in the scholium (derived in part from the third-century BCE historian Hippostratus) according to which 1) Cynaethus was the first person to perform Homeric poetry as a rhapsode in Sicily, in 504 BCE; and 2) Cynaethus composed the *Homeric Hymn to Apollo*, one can venture that this man worked creatively with traditions at a level well beyond minor variations.[27] If it indeed was he (or his circle) who constructed the *Hymn to Apollo* as we have it—dated, on independent historical grounds, to the late sixth century BCE—his art extended to the yoking of distinctive "Homeric" and "Hesiodic" styles embodied in the two parts of the *Hymn*. This created a structure that replicates the dynamic collaboration we hear of in the pseudo-Hesiod fragment cited above, in which Hesiod and Homer "stitch" a song in tandem.[28]

---

[25] On these lines as imitating the style of a "Hymn to Zeus," see Nagy 2009, 226–32.

[26] This should be considered in the context of the complex generic inter-relationships between the independent traditions represented by Pindaric and Homeric poetry, as explicated in the book-length analysis in Nagy 1990.

[27] As González (2013, 494) puts it, "... in all likelihood both he and those in his circle followed the centuries-old practice of recomposition in performance ... ."

[28] Further on Cynaethus, see Nagy 1990, 73–75 and González 2013, 492–94. On the range of opinions concerning dating of the *Hymn,* see Richardson 2010, 13–16.

To return to Plato's *Ion*. Even if this late sixth-century rhapsode is no Cynaethus and, in the strictest interpretation, recites a memorized, pre-established text verbatim without addition or ornamentation, one cannot deny that Plato still portrays his practice as far more than a "reading." It is instead an emotion-packed, dramatic, visual experience. The poetry is "chanted" (ᾄδετε τὰ ποιήματα 532d8; cf. 535b), even while lacking musical accompaniment; the auditors are also spectators (*theômenous*, 535b; cf. *theatai* 535d) whom the performer Ion can bring to experience *ekplêxis* (the state of being awe-struck: 535b1–3). Most striking, Ion himself presents the epic scenes that he is reciting with all the skill of an actor, transmitting intense emotion and causing his audience to react accordingly (535c–e). He accepts Socrates' assimilation of his professional artistry to that of the *hupokritês* (536a1; cf. 532d7).[29] In sum, Ion's production of the poetry, although it may not have the spontaneity of "composition-in-performance," is nevertheless equally as attuned to, aware of, and interactive with an audience as must have been the supposedly "creative" stage of the medium Ion has inherited. It is, by Bauman's terms, a performance, whether or not we view it as somehow "original."

As if to underline this kinship among the evolutionary stages of the rhapsodic medium, Plato has Socrates refer to Phemius, the Ithacan singer (*aoidos*) within the *Odyssey* as a *rhapsoidos* (533c1).[30] And then there is the elaborate conceit of the magnetized rings, through which Socrates seeks to make Ion understand why he can be so enthusiastically and exclusively dedicated to Homer, while Hesiod, Orpheus, and Musaeus leave him cold.[31] This analogy makes the rhapsode the equivalent of the master-poet whose work he recites: both are "interpreters" (*hermênês*). The notion of interpretation can be taken in two senses that happen to coincide in the contemporary English word. It involves enacting the words (or music, or dramatic art) of another, as when the conductor Michael Tilson Thomas "interprets" Mahler or the cellist Yo Yo Ma "interprets" a Bach suite; and it also denotes providing a parallel exegetic discourse concerning the works (as when we "interpret" a poem by paraphrase and explication).[32] Ion boasts to Socrates that he, in effect, does both superbly well: not only does he bring out all the

---

[29] On the key importance of this concept for our understanding of rhapsodic performance, see González 2013, 297–317 and 521–639.

[30] At *Laws* 658b, Homer is called a rhapsode: cf. West 2011.

[31] On the image of the rings, see Nagy 2009, 374–78.

[32] For the semantics of *hermêneuein* in the *Ion*, see González 2013, 299–302.

emotional impact of the dramatic highpoints in, for example, a speech by Achilles, Andromache, or Odysseus; he also presents "thoughts" about the material that he recites. Ion's habit of providing such *dianoiai* seems to reflect a widespread practice, to judge by (generally ironic) references in Plato, Xenophon, and Isocrates to the rhapsodes' extra-narrative discourses.[33]

The word Ion chooses to describe his manner of giving exegesis or commentary (it is unclear exactly what his *dianoiai* comprise) brings us finally to some noteworthy points regarding the performative nature of this rhapsode's art. To Socrates' observation that a good rhapsode must thoroughly learn to be an interpreter of Homer's own "thought" (*dianoia*), Ion responds proudly that he himself can speak many fine *dianoiai* about Homer, better than the most famous in the business, naming Metrodorus of Lampsacus, Stesimbrotus of Thasos, and Glaucon. Given the chance (an opportunity Socrates politely declines), the rhapsode will perform. "And indeed," Ion asserts, "it is worth hearing, Socrates, how well I have embellished Homer [ὡς εὖ κεκόσμηκα τὸν Ὅμηρον] so that I think I deserve to be crowned with a golden crown by the Homeridae" (530c–d). With the verb *kosmeô*, the rhapsode turns his art of commentary into an extension of the poetic art depicted within the *Odyssey* itself: as Jose González has shown in detail, the idea of *kosmos* (which covers both "ordering" and "adornment") is a key concept *within* epic for describing correctly formed and sequenced narrations—the ideal of style to which the epics aspire.[34] In other words, recitation ("interpretation") of the epics and "embellishment" through *dianoiai* about them are two aspects of one and the same process, in the rhapsode's ideology.

Ion's "embellishment" can itself be understood in two ways. Drawing on accounts of modern singers of heroic epic, some critics have proposed that the *kosmos* Ion brings to the poems refers not to the "thoughts" but to actual poetic expansion by means of his own ornamentation, in the form of new phrases and new lines.[35] Such a reading makes Ion resemble the twentieth-century *guslar* Avdo Međedović of Montenegro, famed for his ability to expand a composition using formulaic resources in the course of oral composition-in-performance, so that an epic song of a few thousand lines would

---

[33] See R. L. Hunter 2011 and Ford 2002, 72–73.

[34] González 2013, 194–200, 281. Centrally important is the *Odyssey*'s description of Demodocus' song of the Wooden Horse as *kosmos* (*Odyssey* 8.492).

[35] Boyd 1994, 116–21; but see the skepticism of Hunter 2011, 36.

grow into more than 12,000 lines in his own rendition.[36] But it is not necessary to overstate the creative additions of Ion (which most likely would have been given more notice in the dialogue, and not tied to *dianoiai*) in order to understand what he does in more vivid terms of enactment. From accounts of Indic epic recitation, specifically of the *Rāmcaritmānas* of Tulsidas, we learn that the dual arts of reciting a text and providing commentary are treated equally (and judged critically by audiences) as necessary components of live performance events that attract thousands of listeners.[37] We do not know whether the judging criteria at the Panathenaic rhapsodic contests took into account the quality of Ion's *dianoiai*, of his histrionic performance, or of his faithfulness to a text (either as notional script or actual prompt-text). At any rate, bringing *kosmos* to Homer need not have involved something disposable or parasitic on the "text"; comparative study shows that such adornment forms an authentic and valuable part of an overall performance.

To sum up at this point: we have seen two bodies of evidence (song and *mûthos* performances as given in the poems; lore about rhapsodes) that impel us to treat archaic hexameter poems as performances. The analysis of this evidence (from hermeneutic and historical angles, respectively) raises the broadest question of all: what *difference* does it make to treat these as performances rather than texts? A third body of evidence—this time, built into the very medium of hexameter poetry—will help me to articulate an answer. It should be stressed at the outset that this third body represents a complementary and inherently *diachronic* set of facts to juxtapose with the *synchronic* evidence we have catalogued thus far.

The distinctive aspects of Homeric style—repeated phrases, recurrent scenes, a mix of dialects—had by the early decades of the twentieth century long been subjects of analysis.[38] The discovery of the metrically-sensitive and systematic nature of the Homeric "art-language" (*Kunstsprache*) had previously been noticed at the level of individual word-endings or pronoun usage: for example, the existence of five different forms of the genitive case for the word *ego* ("I") had been explained by earlier scholars as the reflex

---

[36]   On Avdo, see Lord 1991, 57–71; on multiformity expressed in thematic expansion and contraction during composition-in-performance, see Lord [1960] 2000, 99–123. On ornamentation as an important aspect of Bosnian and Homeric oral poetics, see Elmer 2010.

[37]   Lutgendorf 1991.

[38]   A concise account of the preceding philological work of Witte, Düntzer, Ellendt, and others is available in Foley 1988, 6–19. The paragraphs that follow retain some material from my longer introduction to the translation of Hélène Monsacré's book *The Tears of Achilles* (Center for Hellenic Studies, 2018).

of the necessity imposed by the hexameter (each form having a different metrical shape). That the epics consisted almost entirely of formulas—lines and phrases re-used in whole or part, involving all kinds of words, not just proper nouns—had been proposed but not demonstrated in 1923 by Antoine Meillet (1866–1936) in *Les origines indo-européennes des mètres grecques.*

Shortly after the publication of Meillet's book, the young American scholar Milman Parry (1902–1935) initiated the systematic study of the techniques of oral-traditional heroic song while studying in Paris. A native of Oakland, California, Parry began his doctorate at the Sorbonne soon after obtaining his M.A. from Berkeley with a thesis on the diction of early Greek epic poetry, directed by George Calhoun. His doctoral work comprised a comprehensive analysis of the formulas in Homeric poetry, focused on recurrent combinations of proper nouns and attached epithets. Parry attempted to explain why, for instance, Achilles at certain moments is "swift-footed" and Odysseus "of much cunning," but in other lines the same heroes are described, respectively, as "glorious" or "of many devices." His major thesis, published in 1928 as *L'épithète traditionnelle dans l'Homère*, demonstrated for the first time that formulaic phrases provided, for each major character throughout the epics, one and (with very few exceptions) *only* one adjective to accompany any given proper noun, varying with the standard metrical segments of the epic hexameter line. Such an economical and extensive system, Parry concluded, could only have arisen over generations of poetic production, developed by epic poets who passed down their art within a continuing tradition. No one composer could, or would have reason to, devise such a system.

The diachronic perspective provided by the first phase of Parry's investigations of the Homeric texts made it possible to view the epics as products of long-term evolution, rather than the work of a single gifted poet. If it shifted the spotlight away from the lone genius composer, Parry's pathbreaking demonstration of the traditional nature of the formula compensated at the same time by enabling interpreters to claim access to deeper structures of thought and cultural knowledge shared over generations. Poetic formulae persist because they encapsulate themes, images, and motifs of enduring importance to many audiences. In short, the epics are not the one-time artistic inventions of a single person whose relationship to any broader culture is impossible to determine: Homeric poetry *is* the broader culture. The all-important diachronic dimension, in the form of formulaic diction, exists as a testament to *multiple* performances, although it does not yield information about any *single* performance event.

Nor, at first, did the system discovered by Parry reveal the reasons for its own existence. Not until the second phase of his research, when he carried out fieldwork in the Bosnian-Muslim region of Novi Pazar in the early 1930s, did he realize, while making live recordings, that similar extensive and convenient dictional systems were employed by demonstrably illiterate performers of traditional South Slavic heroic poetry. By a powerful analogy, Parry suggested that Homeric poetry, too, must have been the product of oral composition-in-performance. Albert Lord (1912–1991), who had accompanied him on his second expedition, continued after the tragic early death of Parry in 1935 to work along similar lines in the Balkans, eventually publishing in 1960 the landmark presentation of their work, in his Harvard dissertation-book, *The Singer of Tales*. That volume made the first sustained case for the proposition that Homeric poetry was oral poetry, composed anew every time that a singer performed, through the creative use of formulas at the level of verse, as well as larger passages and episodes. Rather than memorize and recite a fully formed epic, the South Slavic singers of traditional heroic songs created something original each time they sang. Of course, these original compositions bore a family resemblance to all the previous performances, inasmuch as they used the same basic building blocks. But individual shapings could be detected even within this traditional process, in terms of expansion of scenes and re-deployment of conventional language.

Let us return to the question posed above: what the factor of performance means for early Greek hexameter poems. Given the work of Parry, Lord, and the scores of scholars who have built on their insights (analyzing more than a hundred poetic traditions), we can appreciate the impact of performance in terms of a combination of external pragmatic factors (how performers and audiences interact) and internal poetic factors. The latter, represented especially but not exclusively by the traditional formula, provide a way for audiences to understand a given passage or line through a sort of metonymic *pars pro toto* process. That is to say, a traditional formula summons up all the contexts and situations in which it has customarily been deployed in previous performances. It is redolent of generations of tale-telling and singing.[39] To call Odysseus *polumêtis* ("having much cunning intelligence") evokes all the legendary episodes in which he has put his wits to use. To call Achilles "swift-footed" evokes his race around the walls of Troy pursuing Hector, and perhaps other events in his mythic biography. (Given the number of epics lost to us but known to have existed in archaic times, we

---

[39] J. M. Foley 1991 and 1999 provide illustrations of the phenomenon.

can only speculate.) Formulaic language is traditional, and therefore able to produce powerful resonances, even at the level of recurrent patterns made by prepositional phrases and conjunctions (as I show in Chapter 16). Formulae are the currency that enables the crucial performer-audience exchange. Variations and creative, even catachrestic, redeployments of formulae shape meaning for listeners of the poems.[40] The *diachronic* word-hoard represented by traditional diction and its related narrative techniques (especially similes and type-scenes) thus underwrites the *synchronic* moments in which poets engage with their public.

These internal effects will be noted many times in the chapters of this book. At this point, rather than list instances of such smaller-scale effects, I shall attempt to summarize the types of external performance factors shaping the poems about which I have written. But first it is worth circling back once more to the intellectual genealogy that led to these parallel explorations of performance that I have been tracing—both performance writ large and on the microscopic dictional level, the synchronically vivid and the diachronically durable. One finds surprising points of contact.

In Parry's study of Homeric diction and in the directions in which it took him one can detect (at one remove) the influence of Ferdinand de Saussure, the brilliant linguist whose lectures in Geneva were posthumously reconstructed from student notes and published in 1916. Saussure was the most influential teacher of Antoine Meillet, who had taken courses from him in Paris during the period 1885–89. From him, Meillet clearly learned the value of studying the living, synchronic state of a language. When Parry defended his Sorbonne thesis, it was Meillet, as chairman of the jury, who invited to the *soutenance* of May 31, 1928 Matija Murko (1861–1952), a linguistics professor at the University of Prague, then visiting Paris to deliver a series of lectures on his specialty, the folk poetry of Yugoslavia. It was at Meillet's urging that Parry later absorbed Murko's works and decided to carry out his own fieldwork, during periods of leave from his position in the Harvard Department of the Classics.

Two decades later, when Parry's co-worker Albert Lord defended his Harvard dissertation in 1949, the Slavist and linguist Roman Jakobson (1896–1982) was on the committee. Not only had Jakobson come to know Murko in Prague in the 1920s, he had made use of his early field recordings as he began his own career. Jakobson, like Meillet, also drew on the work of Saussure to

---

[40] For a full-scale demonstration of the enrichment enabled by traditional diction, within one *Iliad* book, see Kelly 2007.

develop key concepts in his studies in structural linguistics. His early work with Nikolai Trubetzkoy, a fellow member of the informal Linguistic Circle of Prague, used Saussurean concepts to lay the foundation for an approach to language as a system in which basic elements, like phonemes, possess meaning only through a systematic and contrastive relationship to other elements. During the Second World War, Jakobson taught at the New School in New York City. There, another émigré scholar, the French anthropologist Claude Lévi-Strauss (1908–2009) attended his lectures on structural phonology, and with Jakobson's encouragement began work on what would become his landmark 1949 study *The Elementary Structures of Kinship*.

Dell Hymes, the linguistic anthropologist, first met Jakobson and Lévi-Strauss in the summer of 1952 during a conference at Indiana University. After hearing Jakobson at a subsequent conference there (in 1958) deliver his classic paper on "Linguistics and Poetics," Hymes re-oriented his own work toward the functions of language, eventually developing the field known as the ethnography of speaking.[41] His colleague in this area, Richard Bauman, with whose remarks on performance I began this introduction, also credits Jakobson:

> In the process of attempting to refine and specify more clearly my developing notion of performance in the writing of *Verbal Art*, I was strongly inspired by Prague School poetics in the work of Roman Jakobson and his colleagues in prewar Prague, especially Jan Mukarovský, and by Erving Goffman's frame analysis, to which I was introduced by Goffman's lectures and by conversations with him even before the publication of *Frame Analysis* in 1974. Prague School poetics, especially as developed in Mukarovský's and Jakobson's writings on the poetic function, and Jakobson's writings on the metalingual function, parallelism, and shifters, rests centrally on dimensions of linguistic reflexivity, the capacity of language to refer to itself, to treat itself as an object.[42]

It emerges, then, that two intertwined strands are woven into the fabric of the twenty-first-century study of traditional poetry and performance: one anthropological, one linguistic, both leading back to Saussure (although with a number of further interactions along the way), one via Meillet, the other via Jakobson (who binds the two strands together). One cannot omit mention of a further twist: Parry himself, as John García has shown, was influenced as a student at Berkeley by the three courses he took from A. L. Kroeber

[41] Hymes 1983.

[42] Bauman 2002, 94.

(1876–1960), a linguistic anthropologist and leading scholar in American Indian studies.[43] The importance of recovering the cultural artifacts of non-literate peoples; of the key role of tradition in culture; and of the notion of "the genius of the people" as opposed to the cultural dominance of individual artists—clearly these themes are common to the work of Kroeber and Parry. The latter may well have inherited a passion for them from his teacher.

What stands out as we survey this intellectual heritage is the crucial role that anthropology plays in broadening our understanding of individual cultural productions. This is worth stressing, because for many classical scholars, both upon the first appearance of *The Singer of Tales* and in later decades, the work of Parry and Lord seemed to raise disturbing questions about authorship and the perceived superiority of certain cultural epochs. Did the discovery of a systematic set of conventions for producing epic diminish or abolish the genius of an individual poet Homer? And did the textualization of Homeric verse signal an irreversible total shift from "oral" to "literate" culture? The last decades have seen much needed nuancing of such questions, so that crude oppositions of "orality" and "literacy" are no longer taken as plausible explanatory devices in cultural studies, while the question of "authorship" has itself been historicized as part of a late-Romantic obsession that unhelpfully obscures the ways in which traditional verbal arts operate.[44] Yet one wonders how much more progress might have been made had Classicists readily appreciated and adopted broad-minded anthropological approaches to language, poetry, myth, and culture as early as 1960 (the year Lord's book was published, and the year of Kroeber's death). As it turned out, proponents of oral-traditional poetics within Classics often had to fight a rear-guard action against more reactionary views. Some scholars appeared to suspect that ethnographic work would subvert their vision of a Western tradition built (so it seemed) on the hegemony of Homer.[45]

It is time to turn to specifics, in relation to the question of what literary interpretation gains from a performance perspective on hexameter poetry. Although the chapters that follow were never planned as part of an organized

---

[43] García 2001.

[44] On the second issue, see Martin 2017; on various anthropologically inflected approaches that have enriched Classics since the 1970s, see Martin 2008.

[45] On the reactionary stance taken to oral-traditional poetics, see especially Nagy 1996b, 6–11. Of the many dismissive comments that could be quoted, especially directed at Albert Lord, I content myself with one by Arieti (1992, 88) on my own 1989 book: "Martin affords to anthropological investigators of exotic tribes a reverence he does not share for his colleagues in Classics ... ." The failure to place "exotic" in scare quotes is revealing.

exposition of the approach, in retrospect one can view them as structured around three major recurrent phenomena related to performance. Allow me to call these "awareness," "competition," and "impersonation." At times, these are overtly thematized in the poems—Chapter 16, on the chariot race of *Iliad* 23, illustrates how that competition can be extended into a meta-poetic meditation (while not losing any of its amazing vigor and suspense). In most cases, however, the phenomena need to be understood as external framing attitudes: if we read, for instance, the performances of Odysseus in *Odyssey* 8 (Chapter 12) and *Odyssey* 11 (Chapter 8) as framed by a latent understanding that his words are meant to evoke rival poetic traditions, our appreciation for the artistry of the scenes in question increases: the poetry gets deeper, and becomes (even more) multidimensional. That, to me, is what a philologically honest literary criticism should accomplish. To turn to these three aspects, then:

Awareness

In its simplest form, we might describe awareness in performance as "phatic," like those utterances or intonations whose purpose is to keep alive an interaction between speaker and addressee: "you know," "see," "right?" or, in Modern Greek, "katalaves?" and so on. In terms of the ethnographic approach to verbal art, a recent formulation puts it concisely: "the esthetics of performance are tightly bound up with the issue of reflexivity—the perform-er's awareness of him- or herself as a participant in an interaction, his or her signaling of this awareness, and the reciprocal phenomena experienced by the audience."[46] In early Greek hexameter compositions, remarkably few directly "phatic" signals survive, by which an audience is recognized, let alone addressed. (One moment might be the narrator's request that the Muse in *Odyssey* 1.10 "tell also to us".) But there exist other ways through which the poetry itself communicates its awareness of being a stylized medium and privileged means of exchange between the speaker (poet, singer, reciter) and audience. A "set toward the message" (in Jakobson's terms)—that is, a focus on the "poetic" function of language—can also become (though Jakobson did not develop this connection) a "phatic" function, serving to communicate to an audience "we are sharing verbal art now." It is a matter of subtle shifting. If the medium of hexameter verse and formulaic diction is the default for

---

[46] Berger and Del Negro 2002, 63.

communicating about the world of gods and heroes, or ethical instruction, then a shift in register *within* that medium (while basic hexameter style is maintained) can bring about a sharper awareness of the stylized, poetic nature of the exchange, resulting in the audience's heightened awareness of the possibilities for fictionalizing and impersonation with which the poetry constantly plays. In Chapters 2 and 3, I detect two essential shifts in performance key, of the sort that would be easily recognizable to oral audiences in living exchanges, but are much harder to hear in our silent reading of the texts. That similes are lexically, linguistically, and even metrically distinct, sounding much more like our surviving fragments of archaic Greek lyric, leads me in Chapter 2, after a survey of comparative non-Greek traditions, to suggest that they were performed in a different manner than the surrounding narrative—perhaps even sung as opposed to recited.[47]

A similar intratextual discovery is at the core of Chapter 3: that the phrasing of speeches draws on a distinctly different set of formulaic resources than does narrative, at least in a subset of speeches in the *Odyssey*. Notably, this does not just occur in cases where one would normally expect changes of tense or ending (presents or futures in speeches, second-person addresses, etc.), but in what we might consider straightforward expressions often used in narrative—which, however, turn out to be restricted to speeches in Homer. As with similes, this minor key modulation can be paralleled through a survey of comparative folk traditions, especially in Central and Southeast Asia, in which character-speech is actually performed in a different manner (or even, different dialect). A third example of modulation within the default mode of hexameter is examined in Chapter 4. Nestor's autobiographical speech, often dismissed as rambling and misplaced, on closer examination can be seen as a relic form of an older way of narrating heroic experience (a fine example of characterization by style). To an audience immersed in the default style of Homeric verse, Nestor's self-mythologizing performance must sound different, as though composed in a minor key. Not only would an audience's awareness of its changed style make the speech stand out; the placement of the speech, as well, within the *Iliad*'s narrative draws on a less diffuse awareness, the remembrance of the oddly disturbing night raid carried out in Book 10, in which Nestor played a controlling role. In sum, the stylistic and narratological shift evident in Nestor's autobiography intensifies and

---

[47] On similes as malleable components of living performances, even stylizing agonistic relations, see now Ready 2011.

complicates an emotional reaction to the dramatic ambush by Odysseus and Diomedes in the preceding episode.

While such key modulations function to re-focus the audience during a performance, drawing attention to the very medium in which they are absorbed, another technique draws on an audience's awareness of different "genres of speaking" in order to create or deepen the meaning of a poetic scene. I have tracked various examples of this effect in Chapters 6, 9, 12, and 14. Accustomed as we are to read poems—rather than hear or imagine them as living performances—it is easy to assimilate this technique to the realm of "intertextuality." But to do so risks being reductive and misleading. When in *Odyssey* Book 8 Odysseus, in a rebuke to a young Phaeacian mocker, uses tropes and formulae that we can find also in a passage of the *Theogony*, it cannot be presumed that an ancient audience is meant to hear an intertextual "quote" of that specific Hesiodic text (or vice versa, hears the *Theogony* somehow "recalling" the *Odyssey*). More importantly (as I show in Chapter 12), and in accordance with the findings of oral-traditional poetics, Odysseus makes use of a genre of discourse (didactic material about the good king) that can be identified as a free-standing traditional genre outside Greek (in this case, in Old Irish, Avestan, and Sanskrit texts). In other words, comparative literary analysis here allows one to transcend false dilemmas of relative chronology or borrowing, by pointing to a common generic (rather than textual) source.

The so-called "Orphic" tablets that I explore in Chapter 9, using detailed comparisons with several Homeric scenes, pose a similar challenge to text-based "intertextual" analysis. Here, too, the possibility must be left open that the composers of these miniature sets of instructions for the deceased bearer's behavior in the Underworld operated with the resources of traditional poetry. This corpus would have been well known to their local audiences, but was not necessarily in the form of our *Iliad* and *Odyssey*. The "performance" of reading such instructions—both the performance by the living initiate, when first instructed by an Orphic or Dionysiac *peritus*, as well as his or her projected posthumous "re-performance"—gained authority from the user's familiarity with epic conventions and episodes, and the initiate's awareness of underworld scenes in much longer narrative works.

Two other essays here attempt to read Greek poetic texts using our awareness of a specific globally-attested genre (lament, Chapter 14) or of particular tag-lines (*exodia*, Chapter 6) that, according to ancient lore found in Byzantine handbooks, marked the actual performances by rhapsodes, citharodes, and composers (or actors) of comedy and tragedy. Once more, the key factor for interpretation is an audience's awareness that the language they are hearing, complete with a certain set of images, phrasings, and rhetorical stances, "belongs" to a genre *other* than that of the dominant narrative. To hear the underlying tone of Helen's speeches within the *Iliad* requires awareness of the poetics of Greek laments (a topic about which we are informed by a continuous tradition lasting more than two millennia). It is true that a modern audience, even when unequipped with such deep local knowledge, can still feel the impact of Helen's words. But the awareness generated by reference to the dynamics of lament performance provides a more historically authentic interpretation. Good philology and intellectual honesty require the reconstruction of contexts nearest to antiquity, rather than the privileging of our own thought-worlds.

Competition

An awareness of other ways of speaking, singing, and performing clings to any audience, ancient or modern. In a culture where certain genres have evolved continuously over generations, thick webs of association, built on recollection of virtuosos, remembrance of the most powerful (or failing) compositions and the contexts in which they first appeared, along with marked likes and dislikes, are to be expected. Film fandom, in contemporary life, offers a rough parallel. In the context of ancient poetic production, a further factor, quintessentially Greek, must be taken into account: performance is most often competitive. Many of our surviving texts are known to have originated in, or been subject to judgment in, formal settings like that of the Athenian *mousikoi agônes*. These most prominently featured, at the Panathenaea, rhapsodic recitation and contests in playing instruments, or singing to accompaniment; and at the Dionysia, contests in the performance of tragedy, comedy, satyr-play, and dithyramb. Again, the film world with its festivals (Cannes, Thessaloniki) and awards (Oscars, Golden Globes) provides something akin. It is not difficult to detect in a number of movies the urge to emulate winning (or high-grossing) recent films (Hollywood's notion of success). The hidden world of writers, agents, and producers, fully aware of the evolving medium's hits and flops, shapes the films we see. What did the equally intense competition mean for ancient poetic composition? In the case of comedy and tragedy, we have some clear examples: Aristophanes' relationship to Euripides is a case in point.[48] But, once again, hexameter poems reveal less.

---

[48] See most recently Zuckerberg 2014 with further bibliography.

Six of the following chapters trace hints of rivalry, competition, and the clash (or uneasy accommodation) of poetic genres. Chapter 7 reads the *Homeric Hymn to Apollo* in the light of biographical traditions about a contest between Homer and Hesiod (lore that originated in some form in the sixth century BCE). Here, the analysis relies on close readings of formulae and metrics, concluding that the two parts of the *Hymn* that have most often been analyzed as separate compositions were meant to imitate the stylistic voices of the two commanding figures of hexameter production. That hymnic poetry was itself most likely the object of recitation in rhapsodic contests lends another dimension to the substructure of generic rivalry that I uncover in the *Hymn*. Chapter 5 also originated, like Chapter 7, in a conference at the University of La Plata, Argentina (a decade later). It places the *Hymn to Apollo* in yet another competitive framework, with help from a reading of the stylistically cognate *Hymn to Hermes*. Here, the question is one of rhapsodic performance as opposed to the art of the citharode (singing to the accompaniment of a large and resonant concert-style stringed instrument). Since each art was legendarily associated with competitors at a leading festival (citharody at Delphi, rhapsody in Athens—although the Panathenaea also accommodated citharodic contests), one can imagine the mutual maneuverings of Hermes and his older half-brother Apollo regarding Hermes' invention the lyre as being based in performer-oriented assertions about the values of their own respective arts. To do so opens up new perspectives about the aesthetic effect of each performance genre. The coda in Chapter 5 on Poseidon's "crash-test" at Onchestus in Boeotia brings together the notions of competition with those of ritual and the act of judging (*krisis*). It is a reminder that Greek competitive events—athletic, musical, or other— were inevitably held under the aegis of heroes and gods.

Chapter 16 focuses on another scenario involving narrow escapes and the wreckage of chariots (like the rite for Poseidon in his Boeotian shrine). Not only is competition thematized overtly in Book 23 of the *Iliad*; it is clearly related to issues of poetic rivalry and endurance. The poem about Achilles was constructed to outpace others, aided by the poem's own assertions about "unwithering fame." Within that framework, the highlighted competition (a chariot-race), as I argue, reflects the poem's awareness of a number of other contests, from the Trojan War itself to its disputed longer-term impact on the landscape (e.g., the Achaean Wall, doomed to destruction, but kept intact in poetic memory).

Chapters 8 and 13 revolve around another form of competition, stemming from the repertoires of actual rhapsodic reciters. On the basis, once more, of Plato's *Ion*, as well as from reports about Athenian ritual practitioners, we have evidence that compositions attributed to Orpheus were in general circulation, and performed rather than kept as esoteric documents. If we imagine that an audience for the *Nekuia* of *Odyssey* Book 11 has an awareness of such performances, and that the "Orpheus" repertoire included the famous visit of the mythical Thracian singer to the Underworld, the eye-witness account of his own *katabasis* given by Odysseus gains in depth and importance, since we must hear it as rivaling another singer's. The further irony—that Odysseus performs his autobiographical *mûthos* narrative explicitly "like a singer" (*Odyssey* 11.368), in close proximity to the professional court-poet Demodocus—underlines the theme of competition.

The *Shield of Heracles* attributed to Hesiod, the authorship of which was already disputed in the Hellenistic period, represents another relic of competitive composition, on my reading. From indications that such an extended *ekphrasis* could be performed as a stand-alone piece (a performance possibility known also from other oral traditions), we can imagine a three-way dynamic of emulation: the evolving Homeric *Iliad* embeds the extended device within Book 18 (describing Achilles' new armor); a version with a different aesthetic ("pulp," in my analysis) occupies most of a heroic narrative about Heracles; and the first portion of the *Shield of Heracles* is embedded in the Hesiodic *Catalogue of Women*. As with the intriguing similarity between *Odyssey* 8.166–77 and *Theogony* 79–93 (examined in Chapter 12), chronological relations are impossible to establish. More relevant is the clear stylistic differentiation, of a sort that could arise in competitive contexts, as a way of swaying highly aware and experienced audiences. Finally, the slippery notion of "epic" as applied to ancient Greek verbal arts, and investigated in Chapter 1 in this volume, emerges as, at best, a retrospectively applied label. The study of poems as performances, which at one or more points were subject to the strains and stresses of agonistic composition-in-performance or recitation, justified considering even metapoetic genre classifications like "epic" as contested and negotiable, part of an ongoing shaping of Greek verbal art by its practitioners and audiences. As I formulate this situation, with reference to such competition: "The genre inhered in its performers. Neither formal nor thematic boundaries prevented rhapsodic cross-pollination."

Impersonation

Reading an early Greek hexameter poem—or any piece of verbal art, for that matter—we search out clues to help construct the figure of a narrator. The idea that a communication must have a specific speaker is the norm. With texts read in private, distanced from a performer, the construction of a speaker will vary according to the individual reader. In performance, on the other hand, an audience faces a living embodiment of the communication. The question for it then becomes: who does the person facing us pretend to be? We cannot affirm that rhapsodic reciters of Homer impersonated "Homer," although they must have advertised, in the various discourses surrounding their performances, some affiliation to the traditional mastersinger. As both actor and narrator, the Homeric reciter or poet slips in and out of many characters—now Odysseus (himself a master impersonator of other characters), now a god. More directly, the speaker of the *Hymn to Apollo* (line 172) poses as the "blind man" from rocky Chios, as he instructs a chorus of young women on Delos to speak of him in this manner, recommending him as the sweetest singer in whom they take pleasure, should someone ever ask (167–71).[49] It is the Hesiodic corpus, however, that offers the most fruitful opportunities for performers to make meaning by impersonation, and I have drawn out the implications of this in Chapters 10 and 11. While not openly declaring that the author of the *Theogony* is the singer or reciter appearing before an audience *hic et nunc*, the poem artfully elides its present narrator with that "Hesiod" whom the Muses once taught on Mt. Helicon (cf. *Theogony* 22 with *Hêsiodon* as object, shifting in line 24 to the apparently appositive *me*). The listeners and viewers of a performance of the *Works and Days*, finally, are led to believe (or make-believe) that the narrator is a small-scale farmer from Ascra who has had a quarrel over inheritance with a brother Perses. And yet the audience at a festival where rhapsodes "do" Hesiod surely knows they are judging a professional reciter of hexameter. Much as the rhapsode Ion's total involvement in re-presenting the heroic deeds within Homeric epic is aimed at engaging the audience on an emotional level, the various impersonations embedded in the hexameter corpus make possible a direct and dramatic impact. Keeping in mind the

[49]   On the riddling self-identification, see Nagy 2009, 205–6.

dynamic bond between the audience as a group and the lone performer who addresses them, we may not find it accidental that the *Odyssey* as we have it, with its preposed "Telemacheia," in effect positions the audience as impersonating the suitors of Penelope (the epic-internal group whom we first encounter as they are being entertained by a singer). I explore similar metapoetic possibilities in Chapter 15. (The coda formed by Chapter 17 might be viewed as folding together competition and impersonation: Apollonius imitating Homer and Orpheus, while turning his new epic into a worthy rival of the works attributed to those older figures.)

To come full circle: if the first meaning of my title *Mythologizing Performance* can designate the sort of authoritative communication that commands attention—performance as *mûthos*—the second meaning (taking "mythologizing" as gerund instead of adjective) captures an essential further phenomenon. The effect in question must have arisen precisely from the nature of hexameter verse-making as a traditional, oral, performative art. The performer in a very tangible way embodies all earlier performers. (In this regard, the model for citharodic performance at Delphi, in which singers even dressed so as to imitate Apollo, is a template: see Chapter 5.) "This" poetic moment is like "that." These figures of "myth" are creatures of the here-and-now. The power of poetry to make them come alive is the same force that enables the re-creators—"Homer," "Hesiod," and the rest—to locate their own origins in the legendary past, their performances effectively mythologized.[50]

---

[50] Nagy's formulation of this effect (1996a, 223), slightly re-wording a sentence by T. S. Eliot, sums it up perfectly: "the most individual parts of his performance [Eliot: "work"] may be those in which the dead poets, his ancestors, assert their immortality most vigorously."

I

Epic Genre and Technique

1

EPIC AS GENRE[1]

I. Introduction

If "epic," ancient or modern, represents a "genre" in any meaningful sense, our first task should be not to enumerate the characteristics of a classification, but to ask what might be the ultimate usefulness, whether to literary criticism or cultural studies, of such categorizing. What do we gain from calling something an epic? Should the category therefore be as wide as possible or bounded and narrow? To answer fully, we need to look at the historical roots of our own taxonomy of genres in classical Greek sources (Part II, below), as well as at a broad range of contemporary comparative evidence from non-Western societies in which traditions seemingly comparable with classical "epic" exist (Part III).

The circularity in the latter procedure will be immediately apparent. If the first rule of the comparative method is to know what to compare, there will always be the chance that we do not know *enough*: that our initial selection of epic-like material from India, Africa, the Middle East, and Central Asia somehow omits highly important poetry or prose that a Eurocentric mindset, raised on classical epic, cannot grasp as relevant. Even to divide verbal art into "poetry" and "prose" might turn out to be misleading, from the standpoint of non-Western traditions (as Dennis Tedlock and others have argued, focusing on native American works). But since every investigation needs to start somewhere, the critic's hope is that the "hermeneutic circle" morphs into a spiral: that the initial selection prompts re-thinking of old classifications, and even leads to productive reactions by others working in different fields. Although this volume is concerned primarily with ancient

---

[1]   Originally published in *A Companion to Ancient Epic*, ed. J. M. Foley (Oxford: Blackwell, 2005), 9–19.

epic, from regions near the Mediterranean, it might lead to fresh analyses of compositions from many periods and places.

To enable this dialogue, and to prevent a premature canonization of "genre" that only impedes further understanding, we should begin with the assumption that "epic" is a contingent and culture-bound category. It may be "poetry" or "prose" or some *tertium quid*, by our reckoning. It may even look like what we would call "drama" or "lyric." Despite such *formal* differences, many societies may share a *functionally* similar category. What this chapter will argue is that "epic," applied to similar categories across cultures, plays a necessary role that *transcends* genre (thus making fruitless the attempt to pin it down as any single genre). In other words, "epic" stands out precisely by presenting itself, time after time, as the "natural" state of speech, the pre-existent mode, the word-before-genre, the matrix of other forms. And this consistent tendency can in turn best explain the semantic development and assumptions that have given us the very term that we are undertaking to analyze.

Ultimately, any concept of genre that underwrites the specific classification of "epic" should stress, above all, two *communicative* functions. First, as a means of channeling and clarifying communication between authors and readers (or performers and audiences), a shared genre acts as an agreement concerning the horizon of expectation, whether about the language, motifs, characterizations, themes, or even length of a given work. (We do not expect a "novella" to be 700 pages long. We might expect an "epic" performance to last at least an evening.) It is an implicit signaling device for senders and recipients of verbal art. Second, for those, like ourselves, removed in time from the immediate experience, genre forms an essential piece of cultural information. Knowing a culture's genre system, and its network of associations, is as significant as learning about its history, geography, economy, or languages. Once the native system is elicited, we can compare it with those of other societies, just as we can compare languages. And as with any such anthropological explorations, the knowledge thereby gained only counts when taken further, as a means of fostering human communication. To put it negatively, we should not define "genre" or "epic" simply as an ideal Platonic form for static contemplation. Definitions need to be dynamic aids to learning and social integration.

Modern handbooks of literary terms, in defining "epic," inevitably mention features of content, such as a cosmic scale; a serious purpose; a setting in the distant past; the presence of heroic and supernatural characters;

and plots pivoting on wars or quests. The presence or absence of any such features should not be decisive, however, in defining a genre. Nor because they happen to be common to both oral and written (or "primary" and "secondary" epic), can these features be seen as proof that a natural or universal "epic" form exists, since "secondary" epics are of course explicitly modeled on the former. Recent scholarship, by contrast, has deconstructed the wall between written and oral modes, and all but abandoned notions (going back to the early twentieth-century) of "primary" epic (supposedly, Homeric poetry, *Beowulf*, and most non-Western poems) as opposed to "secondary" epic (Apollonius of Rhodes' *Argonautica*, Vergil's *Aeneid*, the works of Milton, Spenser, Tasso, etc.). The match between "primary" and "oral" was never satisfactory, anyway, since most of the compositions available to readers had long been texts, whatever their performance history. A better solution has been the recognition of "transitional texts" in the formulaic style typical of composition-in-performance. In addition, modern ethnographers can attest to the fluidity of the very idea of "text" in many cultures that are most productive of "epic." Finally, the distinction between "primary" and "secondary" has been seen more recently to encode more insidious contrasts between "primitive" song produced by underdeveloped, often tribal groups and "cultivated" writing done by elite males, usually in the service of a developing nation-state. At its worst, the contrastive pair was just a polite substitute for the chauvinistic opposition of "pre-art" vs. "high art."

What has led handbook writers to associate as "epics" such disparate compositions as *Beowulf* and *Paradise Lost*, over and above the features of content just mentioned, are roughly comparable formal features: the length of a poem; the very fact of poetic form ("heroic" verse lines); musical accompaniment or song style; highly rhetorical speeches by heroic figures; invocations or self-conscious poetic proems; similes; and "typical" or recurrent scenes and motifs. These formal features are usually treated rather clinically as isolated textual markers, rather than as intertwined relics of possible performances. For instance, length of composition is often considered an absolute, apart from possibly variable contexts of audience interaction. Was *Beowulf* ever longer or shorter and still, for medieval English hearers, the "same" poem? Does performance length depend on where the "epic" was shared (during work or festivals, in a royal hall or tavern)? Could a fifty-line version still be "*Beowulf*"? Does cosmic scale demand extreme length? By the same token, can the Old English *Seafarer* be "epic" (and if not, what genre is it?)? Such questions arise especially with ancient texts for which we have multiple versions, such as *Gilgamesh*. They can be approached, if not positively answered, by examining such Indic traditions as *Rāmcaritmānas*, of which even a brief song session by women at local shrines is still regarded as "epic" recitation. To take another example, long similes—seemingly the stock-in-trade of "epic" composition—turn out in many cultures to be poetic interludes consciously imported from companion traditions (what one might call "lyric"). In these cases, as in many others, contemporary performances force us to question traditional handbook definitions. "Epic" emerges as a notional instead of normative term.

II. Defining "Epic" in Ancient Greece

Thematic and formal features are inevitably joined in the handbook "epic" definitions by reference to the *Poetics* of Aristotle (384–322 BCE). As a wide-ranging scholar with access to written sources later lost, as well as to living traditions of composition and commentary, Aristotle must have first place in any discussion of ancient literary criticism. But one problem in treating him as an authority on ancient "epic" is that he is relentlessly literary. By his era, the tradition of Homeric poems had most likely passed through two if not three stages of crystallization, in oral and textual phases, with relative degrees of fixity and vastly different conditions of audience reception. Thus a fourth-century Athenian intellectual's perception of "epic" gives no guarantee of resembling an eighth-century Ionian performer's sense of his or her poetic repertoire. Paradoxically, performers of Homeric epic even in Athens, two centuries before Aristotle, may not have known that they were singing or reciting "epic." That is to say, we can no more posit a cohesive and unchanged "Greek" notion of epic than we can a universal definition.

From the surviving early texts in hexameter (Homer, Hesiod, Homeric Hymns, Epic Cycle), it is clear that the word for the production of entertaining tales of heroes or gods to the accompaniment of a stringed instrument (*phorminx*) is "song" (*aoidê*) and the performers are "singers" (*aoidoi*): see, for example, the descriptions of the Ithacan bard Phemius (*Odyssey* 1.325–52) and the Phaeacian singer Demodocus (*Odyssey* 8.43–46, 469–521). But a synonym for long narrated stories can be *mûthos* (plural *muthoi*; in Homer, the word usually denotes "authoritative utterances"). For example, the heroes Nestor and Machaon "took delight in tales [*mûthoisi*] speaking in detail [*enepontes*] to one another" (*Iliad* 11.643). A minor variation of the same poetic verse introduces the night-long narrative session shared by Odysseus and Penelope upon his return (*Odyssey* 23.301—note that the concluding portion of the hero's tale is called *epos*, 23.342). The main distinction between *aoidê* and *mûthoi* seems to be whether music is involved, and whether the performer is a professional. Both Odysseus and Achilles straddle the line by being expert at *mûthos*-speech and also like bards (Achilles when he plays the *phorminx* at *Iliad* 9.186–91, Odysseus when compared to an enchanting singer at *Odyssey* 17.518–21). In fact, as we shall see, "epic" is most comparable to "myth" (the word derived ulti-mately from *mûthos*), both in archaic Greek terms and in the contemporary non-Eurocentric world.

For Aristotle in the *Poetics*, *mûthos* has what appears to be a completely different meaning than our word "myth." He uses it to mean something like "plot" or more broadly "narrative" (see *Poetics* 1449b5–8). As we shall see below (part IV), this development is not unexpected given the earlier semantic range of *mûthos* before the fifth-century BCE. The further reach of the concept, as we see it in the *Poetics*, actually accords well with a similarly broad reach of "epic" both in classical sources and later. Yet despite the exten-sive cultural spread of both myth and epic in Greece, Aristotle significantly chooses as his centerpiece for an all-inclusive poetics the Athenian genre of tragedy. This has several implications. First, it means that he nowhere tries to define "epic" as a closed category distinct from other genres. Instead, because Aristotle always seeks to articulate the larger components in the construction of verbal art, he comments on features that usually overlap epic and tragedy, such as plot-structure, recognition, diction, and reversals of fortune (see, e.g., *Poetics* 1455b16). For Aristotle, drama is as self-evident and singular an experience as film is for us; opposing it to *epopoiia* (his word for "epic-verse-making" or "epic") is more akin to contrasting film and "the novel" taken as a whole—without regard to particular sub-genres like romance, western, techno-thriller, mystery, or other. The smaller-scale features that might be used to separate out sub-categories of poetry are, for Aristotle, less impor-tant than the matter of imitation (*mimêsis*, his overarching concern in the *Poetics*). *Epopoiia* is one of six named types of performance—a mixed group we would consider untidy in its inclusion of musical arts such as pipe-playing and concert lyre-playing with tragedy, comedy, and dithyrambic poetry. All are supposed by him to be forms of "imitation," but differing in their means, manners, or objects of representation (1447a). What distinguishes "epic" in this connection is its representation of characters who are "noble" or "people of quality" (*spoudaios*: see *Poetics* 1449b10), a point to which we shall return. The mimesis is done by means of a particular meter ("heroic" verse, i.e., dactylic hexameter); at considerable length; with many episodes; through a combination of narrative and character speeches; and using elevated vocabulary and unusual words (1459b9–18). But these features are only noted by way of making the contrast with tragic drama, not in order to capture the essence of "epic."

A second important implication of choosing tragedy as his model is that the spirit of competitive dramatic production in Athens infiltrates Aristotle's own analysis. The habit of making value judgements must have been normal for Athenians of several generations, accustomed as they were to see one playwright each year awarded first place at the Dionysiac festival, by the decision of a citizen panel. Thus, though starting with a purely descriptive examination of the aspects of poetic mimesis, Aristotle in the *Poetics* shifts into a prescriptive and critical stance. He describes only partially "tragedy" or "epic," before taking up the *best* way of making both. For the latter, this means that Homeric poetry eclipses any discussion of the genre as a whole, for Homer is judged best, by Aristotle, given his use of diction and "thought" (*dianoia*), of focused plots, and of plausible fictions (see *Poetics* 1459a17–1460a19). In short, Homeric poetry is best because it most closely approaches tragic drama.

We have dwelt on Aristotle's treatise because, consciously or not, every writer and critic of Western epic since the fourth-century BCE has been influenced by its choices and assumptions. Although the elevation of Homeric epic to a place of primary importance, overriding numerous other hexameter poems in Greek, began most likely at a specific socio-political stage in sixth-century Athens, the reasoned approval of Aristotle ensured this canonization. When we peer around this brilliant spotlight of attention, trying to see within the shadows it has created, even the *Poetics* can provide tantalizing glimpses of a lost world of poetic art. That world, had it survived, might have radically altered later and modern notions of "epic" as a genre. A starting point for imagining this rich and varied archaic verbal tapestry comes from Aristotle's own notion that Homer was not the composer of the *Iliad* and *Odyssey* exclusively; he also authored the *Margites*, a poem (now almost entirely lost) using a mixture of hexameter and iambic meter to narrate the ridiculous adventures of a numbskull, the title figure. Aristotle places this composition within the category of "blame" or "lampoon" (*psogos*) and speculates that there must have been many such poems before Homer, although the *Margites* was the earliest to survive to his own day. As with his general elevation of Homeric art, he finds the *Margites* to be far beyond the personal invective characteristic of *psogos*, and as much a model for later dramatic comedy as the Homeric epics were for tragedy (1448b38). The fourth-century philosopher clearly distinguishes this comic piece from the more serious compositions, mostly on the basis of its tone and object of *mimesis*. Whether the same generic distinction would occur to a performer or audience two or three centuries earlier is an open question.

Another way into the lost world of "epic"-like works, which may help us extract a definition of "epic" from Aristotle, is via meter. He himself uses the term *hêrôikon* to denote the meter of Homeric epic, but indirectly shows awareness that others (whom he does not name) call the same verseform *epos* or *epê* (plural of *epos*); this much we can extrapolate from his corrective words (1447b15–18) chiding those who talk of *epopoioi* ("*epos*-verse-makers") while referring only to the meter they use, not to the sort of imitation they pursue. In Aristotle's view, this approach leads to absurdities, such as putting Homeric poetry into the same category as the verses of the philosopher Empedocles, although "there is nothing common to Homer and Empedocles except the meter" and the latter should be called "scientist" (*physiologos*) rather than poet. Reading this comment together with his further remarks on mimesis, one can see, first, that Aristotle intends to use the term *epopoiia* more circumspectly, bringing it closer to what "epic" has meant since his time. Essentially, he defines it in terms of an attitude and style—high-language praise of the "serious." But the second observation to be made—an interesting corollary—is that *some* of his contemporaries or predecessors were willing to elide such differences among poems as lay in content or attitude. For these anonymous others, *epopoiia*, inasmuch as it signified the body of work in hexameters, composed by *epopoioi*, would have extended far beyond the circumference of Homeric or Aristotelian "epic." It would most likely have included those poets (again, lost to us) whom Aristotle distinguishes from Homer on the basis of how they represented characters, whether like the norm (as did Cleophon) or worse (as did Hegemon of Thasos, the first to compose "parodies" (1448a13). Only in smug retrospect, however, can we say that these unnamed, all-embracing non-Aristotelians, embedded in their own historical periods and performance cultures, were wrong and Aristotle right.

As it turns out, we may have an interesting reference to such a broader sweep in the work of the historian Herodotus, who flourished a century before Aristotle. On one hand, Herodotus seems to share Aristotle's view that *epopoiiê* ("epic-verse-making," in his Ionic dialect form) demands a certain selectivity and seriousness. Significantly, Herodotus retrojects this view onto Homer himself (who, he believes, lived around the ninth-century BCE). Speaking of a version of the Trojan saga in which Helen with her paramour Paris visits Egypt on her way to Troy, the historian concludes (*Histories* 2.116.1): "And, in my opinion, Homer knew this story, too; but seeing that it was not so well suited [*euprepês*] to epic poetry [*epopoiiê*] as the tale of which he made use, he rejected it, showing that he knew it" (trans. Godley). After citing verses that he claims show Homer's knowledge of the alternate version (*Iliad* 6.289–92, *Odyssey* 4.227–30, 351–52), Herodotus remarks on an inconsistency with yet another version to argue that "the Cyprian verses [*Kupria epea*] are not the work of Homer but of someone else" (*Histories* 2.117.2).

The poem he alludes to—now known as the *Cypria* and surviving only in a few quotations—was clearly "epic" in having thematic and formal features found in the *Iliad* and *Odyssey*. Yet the historian's phrase can denote either "epic poetry" or "hexameter verses." This ambiguity, frequent in the classical period, on the other hand makes it possible that a poem decidedly *non*-Homeric in its themes might also have been "epic" to Herodotus and his audiences. The composition in question, cited for its ethnographic details, is referred to as "the epic/hexameter verses [*epea*] now called by the Greeks *Arimaspea*" (4.14.3) and attributed to one Aristeas of Proconnessus, a Greek town in Asia Minor: "This Aristeas, possessed by Phoebus, visited the Issedones; beyond these (he said) live the one-eyed Arimaspians, beyond whom are the griffins that guard gold, and beyond these again the Hyperboreans, whose territory reaches to the sea" (trans. Godley). The mention of divine possession by Apollo and mythical wonders already marks a great gulf between this archaic poem and the generally more realistic Homeric epic, although Herodotus does say that Aristeas got his stories of one-eyed men and griffins as hearsay from the Issedones (4.16.1). More astounding is the biography of the poet: according to tales Herodotus has heard, Aristeas dropped dead in a fuller's shop, vanished before burial, and reappeared alive seven years later, at which point he composed the poem about his wanderings. He vanished again, turning up 240 years later in a Greek settlement in southern Italy, where he announced (before his final disappearance) that Apollo had blessed the townspeople with a divine visit and that he himself had followed the god in the form of a crow.

Scholars have rightly seen in this weird tale a memory of age-old shaman-istic practices, involving out-of-body experiences and animal transformation. How could such a poem, though *epea* (i.e., hexameter verses) be "epic"?

Before we too quickly eliminate it from the category or narrow our definition, it is worth recognizing the strong family resemblances between the *Arimaspea* and another travel narrative, the *Odyssey*. We might especially be reminded of the first-person wonder-tales of Odysseus in Books 9–12 of the *Odyssey*. Those adventures, in turn, resemble what we know of at least one hexameter poem attributed to the mythical Orpheus, telling of his descent to the Underworld. Orpheus, the magical singer, able to move trees and animals with his song, bears more than a passing resemblance to a shaman, as many have seen; his association with the initiatory-quest epic, the *Argonautica*, draws us closer to more familiar "epic" territory. Finally, the stories of the shaman-like adventures of the philosopher-priest Pythagoras, to whom hexameter verses were also attributed, fit into this expanded "wonder epic" category.

The usefulness of such a broadened class, within Greek tradition, becomes clear when we look once again at the Homeric *Iliad* and *Odyssey*. The audiences for both epics surely obtained additional meanings from the way in which these poems drew on material with an oblique connection to their more obvious "heroic" themes. Just as the *Odyssey* can be seen as expanding itself by way of the poetry of shamanic quest, the *Iliad* can be observed complicating its plot through the inclusion of a quest and trickster figure, Odysseus. Such a lateral, relational approach might even lead us at this point to formulate a further definition of genre: a set of allowable intertexts (oral or written), embracing all those compositions that communicate through consistent mutual allusivity. (It should be noted that the set also allows for "null allusion"—that is, for producing a point precisely by refusing to make overt reference to one or another contemporary and related tale or poem-type.) If the *Iliad* cannot be fully appreciated without the figures, themes, or diction of other Trojan War sagas, in whatever form these existed, these others qualify for inclusion in the genre. The Epic Cycle, a series of poems in hexameter that gained shape in the eighth through fifth centuries BCE, would, for example, fit this definition. So would the *Theogony*, the *Shield of Heracles*, and the *Catalogue of Women* attributed to Hesiod. The *Theogony*, a poem of about 1000 lines telling of Zeus' rise to power, has even been read as the heroic biography of the chief god, although the story is framed by the first-person introduction of the poet himself, singing of his initiatory encounter with the muses on Mt. Helicon. As Jenny Strauss Clay and Leonard Muellner have shown, the long narrative Homeric hymns also form a close bond with the fore-mentioned compositions. Both these and the shorter hymns in the collection seem to have functioned, at some stage, as preludes to longer "epic" compositions.

If we continue to open the field to admit such verses, how then does one prevent a notional "genre" of epic, even within Greek, from becoming too unwieldy a tool? More bluntly, what is *not* epic? How, for instance, would we account for another long hexameter poem, the *Works and Days*, which includes a narrative of conflict (Hesiod and his brother Perses, apparently feuding over an inheritance), but also includes proverbs and maxims, fables with a political point, and advice on farming and ritual? What of those diverse (now fragmentary) compositions that seem to have been swept together and placed under the name of the Boeotian "peasant" poet—the *Instructions of Cheiron, Bird-Prophecy, Marriage of Ceyx, Descent of Theseus to the Underworld, Astronomy*, etc.? Such apparently non-"epic" verse can have a mutually allusive interconnection with what became, in time, mainstream Homeric epic. For example, the Hesiodic *Works and Days* in its lengthy meditation on "right" justice (*dikê*) makes an indispensable poetic counterpart to the central themes of both the *Iliad* (the disputes between Agamemnon and Achilles, Achaeans and Trojans) and the *Odyssey* (the vengeance on the hubris of the suitors). By the same token, the *Theogony* puts in dogmatic form the key points, in similar formulaic phrases, that Odysseus uses to instruct the Phaeacian nobility in Book 8 of the *Odyssey*. Again, the *Odyssey* features an extended "catalogue" of heroic women in the Underworld scene of Book 11, which even in antiquity was matched with the Hesiodic *Catalogue*. Clearly, generic interplay and expansion, allusion and multiformity, were essential to the art of *epopoiia* in archaic Greek. It does not make sense to isolate only some of the resultant multilayered compositions as "epic."

A straightforward assumption can account for the tight bonds among all these hexameter poems: namely, the existence, from at least the sixth-century BCE, of travelling reciters or singers, called "rhapsodes" ("song-stitchers"), at least some of whom traced their ancestry to the master singer Homer himself. These shapers of the canon in any given generation could define "epic" simply as the substance of their repertoire. They could also explicitly cross-reference, and explain to audiences, the complex ways in which the mythological, heroic, and "folk" lore of their poems fit together. We know, from depictions in Plato's *Ion, Republic*, and *Laws* (among other sources) that the rhapsodic repertoire included poetry attributed to Homer and Hesiod, as also Orpheus, Musaeus, and other shadowy earlier poets. In sum, the genre inhered in its performers. Neither formal nor thematic boundaries prevented rhapsodic cross-pollinization. Our notion of "epic" will not be too large if it expands to fit the performance repertoire of these important figures and, by extension, the cognitive and aesthetic capabilities of their audiences.

III. "Epic" Cross-Culturally

"Epic"—or any other literary genre—cannot be classified apart from the performers who transmit it. One can even argue, as Gregory Nagy does, that the invention of "genre" as a system of categories in Greek literary history only occurs when the oral-traditional performances of the archaic period are reduced to writing, mostly during the fifth century BCE, and the originating events lost or forgotten. "Genre," in this regard, is a tool for scholars and librarians. This is not to say that poets themselves never had an awareness of technical and thematic distinctions among, for example, verses to honor gods, tell of heroic deeds, mock social offenders, or accompany religious processions. But this was a matter of implicit poetics, both performers and audiences following what tradition suggested.

A review of contemporary verbal art in sub-Saharan Africa, India, and Egypt will show that the fluidity of early Greek modes—and, as far as we can tell, that of Near Eastern ancient epic—is the norm in traditional societies. At the same time, we shall see:

- that while something resembling "epic" *can* be distinguished *from* other forms, it is even more significant to see it *in relation to* its accompanying genres in performance
- that the specifics of textual or performance style cannot be used to determine whether or not a performance is "epic"
- that the epic "genre" has symbiotic ties with folktale, myth, and especially praise-poetry
- that, above all, epic stands out as the most pervasive, "unmarked' genre, in terms of when and where it can be performed, while at the same time it is the culturally most significant and "marked" form in terms of its ambitions and attitudes.

These observations, brief as they are, can help us to re-think the classical and Western notion of "epic," while leading us to a deeper sense of the limits and possibilities of genre definitions.

Let us begin with the issue of boundaries. Daniel Biebuyck places the *Mwindo* narrative from the Congo within an array of other distinct verbal art-forms practiced by the Nyanga people. Significantly, the sequenced singing and recitation of long narratives (*kárisi*) incorporates these other genres of discourse: proverbs, riddles, and prayers in poetic form, eulogistic recitations, formulas used by diviners and medicine men, personal songs, animal tales, instructions, and political advice, all find a place within *Mwindo*. Such generic inclusiveness is common throughout African epic narrative. A crucial further point can be adduced from the work of Dwight Reynolds on the *Sirat Bani Hilal*, as performed in northern Egypt. Reynolds points out that the urge to treat as the "epic" the pure story-line of one Bedouin tribe's exploits must be resisted, if one is to appreciate the full impact of the performance. The Egyptian bard always dovetails his singing with two other equally important and formally different components, the praise of Mohammad (*madih*) and proverbial advice in lyric form (*mawwal*). More surprisingly, even when *within* the epic a character is about to speak, the same canonical sequence of genres occurs. In short, the "epic" must be taken as total social event including audience interaction, instrumental music, and these framing genres, not just the "text" we might want to cull from it.

We know that epic recitation was preceded by proems resembling the Homeric hymns (see Thucydides *History of the Peloponnesian War* 3.104). As mentioned above, Homeric and Hesiodic poems could be recited by the same rhapsodic performers. The Hesiodic corpus encompasses proverbial lore in diction and structures that have been compared to Greek lyric. In short, one can imagine an ancient Greek performer sequencing exactly the same functionally similar genres as the Egyptian bards—praise (*humnoi*); wisdom (*gnômai*), and "epic" (narrowly conceived). Furthermore, it can be argued that Greek epic not only can be *framed by* but itself consciously *embeds* such sub-genres as praise and blame poetry, maxims, and lyric similes (see further part IV).

Such fluid genre boundaries relate to the wide range of "epic" performance styles, both in the course of one composition and across regions. Mande hunters' epics comprise three genres—narrative, song, and praise proverbs—and hence three performance styles. In Central African epic traditions, it is common for the main reciter to be accompanied by backup singers performing melodic portions organic to the tale (often the character's "speech" as song). The Nyanga bard dances and dramatically mimes parts of *Mwindo*, even taking on the hero's role, while select respondents repeat his verses (compare the narrative and dance event described at *Odyssey* 8.255–369). In contrast to Central African multi-media productions, West

African performances, such as the widespread *Sunjata* epic, often feature a solitary reciting *griot*. (There are many local indigenous names for this role, which combines historian, praise-poet, herald, and arbitrator.) One such, the Maninka *jeli*, recites the epic at high speed, accompanying himself on a small four-string instrument.

Joyce Flueckiger's research in northern and central India shows not only that "epic" can be done in widely different styles, but that even the same long, heroic narrative, like the Dhola-Maru tradition, sung in communities a few hundred miles apart, qualifies as "epic" in one but not the other. Community self-identification, caste ambitions, and local religious cult all determine whether a people views the epic as its own defining narrative.

If content or consistent style fail to demarcate contemporary "epic," neither do the Eurocentric contrasts with "folktale" or "myth." For example, the *mvet* narrations of the Fang (southern Cameroon, Gabon) recount episodic struggles between two clans, a mortal and immortal. There is no central protagonist; magical elements abound, along with romance or folk-tale motifs. Yet the night-long narrations function like other Central African epics to address the society's abiding concerns. Their human quest stories are simply a strand in a much larger tapestry of cosmic issues—how plants, animals, and social hierarchies came to be. In Greek, we might at first perceive fewer cosmic issues in the martial or adventure epics. But the Hesiodic corpus, especially the *Catalogue of Women*, is clearly related to local concerns, rites, and tales; the *Theogony* embodies an entire cosmology. The investigations of Georges Dumézil have been especially useful in illustrating how "epic" in Greece, and even more so in the related languages of Iceland, Ireland, India, and Rome, is often a matter of cosmic myths, historicized and secularized.

Myth and folktale might be considered the deeper roots of epic, yet they can just as easily be synchronic and interactive with epic. It is perhaps best to think of them along a spectrum, with audience interest the determining factor in how unspecified, as to time and place, a story can be, and what belief it engenders. A different dynamic exists between epic and praise poetry. As described by Africanists, praise-poetry is an allusive, highly compressed, and non-narrative evocation of the genealogies and successes of chieftains. Marked by often obscure, riddling names, brief references to events, and a repetitive, incantatory style, this genre is more widespread than epic, especially in southern and eastern Africa. Instead of a range on a spectrum, the praise-poem is a telescope: what is compressed in a style that imitates the instantaneous exultation of a client before his patron, in epic is expanded to fill out chronology, cause, and characterization. While praise (often in second-person address) is more direct and more lucrative, epic (usually third person) is more lucid. The dynamic interaction of praise and epic should make us think of such poetic forms as ancient Greek *epinikia* and *enkômia*, as preserved mainly in the work of Pindar (circa 518–438 BCE), often noted for the same features—allusive, elliptical, gnomic, and narrative only in a kernel form. Medieval Irish bardic verse and prose sagas exhibit a similar kernel-and-expansion relationship. Whether or not we construct a diachronic development from praise poetry to epic, the synchronic reality of their interdependence must be kept in mind.

In brief, contemporary "epic" stands in at least three typological relationships to other types of verbal art. It can (1) incorporate *smaller* forms (proverbs, songs, etc.). It can (2) embody an entire *deep* form, providing epic skin for the bones of myth or folktale concerns; and it can (3) expand a socially functional *kernel* form, praise-poetry. Furthermore, all three relations can occur simultaneously, as in the *Sunjata*. The many versions available (1) feature songs of *griots* and wise sayings; (2) embody a folktale type of the boy's success story, about a marginalized mother-son dyad and its rise to power; and (3) contain frequent formulaic praises of the hero as founder of the kingdom of Mali (and of his griot as ancestor of modern singers). Perhaps, indeed, we should define epic as that form that consistently represents all three of the above relations.

The *expansiveness* of epic as "super-genre" brings us, finally, to observe a matching *pervasiveness* on the level of performance. From the accounts of numerous ethnographers, it is clear that "epic" events are unconfined in contrast to most other stylized verbal art, and not pinned to authorized occasions, rituals, or audiences, such as initiatory groups. Epic can be sung in almost every setting, by professionals or amateurs. Just as epic as *actual* performance functions as a soundstage, an environment for setting off all sorts of smaller genres, so epic as *possible* performance is equivalent to the cultural environment itself, ready to be instantiated and evoked at any moment. As dozens of field studies show, the total "epic" is, in fact, never performed unless elicited by an outsider, such as the folklorist. Yet even when it is brought forth, as usually, in shorter episodic form, the performance depends on an audience and performer's unspoken awareness of the *totality* of a story and its conceivable permutations. In potential size, epic is hugely ambitious, undertaking to articulate the most essential aspects of a culture, from its origin stories to its ideals of social behavior, social structure, relationship to the natural world and to the supernatural. The scope of epic is matched by its attitude: as Aristotle noted, it dwells on the serious. (Even its meter, says Aristotle, is "most stately and weightiest": *stasimôtaton kai onkô-destaton, Poetics* 1459b34–5.) Epic, the ultimate metonymic art-form from the perspective of its *pars pro toto* performance, is on the level of ideology a metonymy for culture itself.

IV. Coda

At this point, we might return to a significant conundrum within ancient Greek semantics, one already alluded to above. *Mûthos*, the word that gives us "myth," denotes in Homeric epic an authoritative utterance. It marks usually a long and detailed speech most often performed before a critical audience, expecting assent, and in the sub-genre mode of a command, an insult, or a detailed act of memory-recitation. This might sound like a good synonym for "epic" itself, which, as we have seen, in scope and ambition is homologous with "myth" in the societies where it flourishes. Oddly enough, the word that gives us "epic" is, in fact, *contrasted*, within our oldest Greek poetry, with *mûthos*. It can be described, within the synchronic system of Homeric diction, as unmarked. *Epos* usually refers to short utterances; non-public "sayings"; brief ordinary remarks; or intimate communication, as between husband and wife or hero and companion. Later, the plural *epea* comes to mean, as we have seen, "hexameter verses" or "epic," whereas within Homer this plural (but not the singular) can be a synonym for *mûthos*. How does this transformation occur? Are we dealing with an historical development or something deeper, embedded in the very nature of an art-form? In the light of the Greek evidence above, particularly about the status of *epos* as both *marked* (in literary history) and *unmarked* (in Homeric diction), we might notice that "epic" as a genre, as seen from a non-Western stance, illustrates exactly this paradoxical bifocal relationship. On the one hand, it is as pervasive as everyday speech—intimate, simple, potential in any utterance. It can happen at any time; it can embody any matter and make it significant. On the other, "epic"—like the plural *epea* and especially its most famous occurrence, in the formulaic phrase describing speech as *epea pteroenta* "winged words"—is a mode of total communication, undertaking nothing less than the ideal expression of a culture. If the usefulness of "genre" is to provide a heuristic tool for honing inter-cultural communication, the good of "epic" lies in its power to craft, through generations of performers and audiences, larger harmonies, in which the discrete pieces of the individual's life fit and make sense.[2]

---

[2]   For surveys and analyses of contemporary epics, see Beissinger et al. 1999; Hatto and Hainsworth 1980/1989; Oinas 1978; Okpewho 1992; and Reichl 1992. On larger questions of genre in ancient texts: Depew and Obbink 2000. On genres in performance: Bauman 1992; Bynum 1976. On native genre categories: Bauman and Sherzer 1989. For the poetry/prose distinction: Tedlock 1983 and Fine 1984. The notion of transitional texts is examined in Lord 1995; J. M. Foley 1990 and 1991. Key explorations of the formation of Greek notions about epic are: González de Tobia 2014; Ford 1997; and Nagy 1999a. On Aristotle's contribution: Halliwell 1986 and Richardson 1992; on the Epic Cycle: Burgess 2001; and on other Greek epics: Huxley 1969. On *mûthoi* as "tales," see Edmunds 1997. For the semantics of *mûthos* and *epos*: Martin 1989. On the relationship between lyric and epic traditions: Nagy 1990; on rhapsodes and text fixation: Nagy 1996a, 1996b, 2002; on shifts in performance style and genres: Phillips 1981. Valuable analyses of "epic" cross-culturally are Belcher 1999 and Stone 1988 (African); Biebuyck and Mateene 1969 (*Mwindo* epic of Nyanga); Austen 1999 (*Sunjata*); Reynolds 1995 and 1999; and Slyomovics 1987 (Egyptian); and Flueckiger 1989 and 1999 (Indic).

2

SIMILES AND PERFORMANCE[1]

The linguist Michel Bréal, better known as a semanticist than Homerist, had been a teacher of Antoine Meillet, the great comparatist who succeeded him in the chair in comparative grammar of the Collège de France.[2] Bréal's little book *Pour mieux connaître Homère* is actually cited once by Meillet's student Milman Parry in *L'Épithète traditionnelle*, to the effect that the fixed epithet provides not only a rest to the singer but a pause for the audience.[3] It is not his view on the formula, however, that seems to me an appropriate introduction to this paper, but Bréal's remarks on the simile:

> These comparisons, which the poet draws out pleasantly, where he often adds several verses not at all necessary, are completely the opposite of popular poetry, which, if it sees a resemblance, says it in a word without dwelling on it. To enjoy these models of descriptive style would require an audience with time to spare, and, moreover, one with a taste for little tableaux.

Similes, he continues, are "pieces which are apparently out of place, which have the look of borrowings from another literary genre."[4] This pronouncement will serve nicely to summarize my argument: in short, I will suggest that Bréal is wrong when it comes to similes in oral poetry but quite right in speculating on another genre as their source. I want to show that similes in Homeric poetry play a role that we can only fully appreciate after examining living oral performances from a range of cultures, performances which feature a number of compositional devices, including similes. I will argue that a major effect of similes in performance has been neglected

---

[1] Originally published in *Written Voices, Spoken Signs: Tradition, Performance, and the Epic Text*, ed. E. J. Bakker and A. Kahane (Cambridge, MA: Harvard University Press, 1997b), 138–66.

[2] See Meillet 1966, 440–53.

[3] Parry 1971, 171; Parry cites the 1906 edition.

[4] Bréal 1911, 107; my translations.

thus far in Homeric studies, but that this effect is, in fact, analogous to the one achieved in non-Western performances by other genres interacting with epic. Finally, I will attempt to show through linguistic analyses that similes are affiliated with, and may be taken from, the epic performers' prior knowledge of *non-epic* Greek poetic genres. In the end, I believe we can come away from such an exploration with a new appreciation for the component arts that went into the complex craft of Homeric verse-making.

As in any comparative enterprise, we must begin with an internal analysis. What do similes accomplish *within* the Homeric poems? Given the tendency in Classics for interpretive modes to drop from sight and return generations later unchanged by subsequent advances in literary theory, it will be more efficient to sketch out the three basic modes of answering this question, rather than attempt a chronological history of critical stances. These can be characterized as *rhetorical, thematic,* and *rhythmic.* It is not surprising that there is a correlation between these modes and varying historically conditioned views on the nature of Homeric poetry. When the text is still imagined, in some dim way, as a sort of performance, the rhetorical interpretation of similes prevails; once the poems are taken up as artifacts rather than as enactment, especially in the early part of the twentieth century, thematic and ultimately structural criticism holds sway.[5]

The rhetorical critique of similes permeates the ancient hermeneutic tradition, in which similes are primarily interpreted as affective devices. Our sources for this mode comprise mainly the scholia to the poems, themselves deriving in turn largely from Peripatetic treatments both of Homeric *cruces* (such as Aristotle's *Homeric Problems*) and more generally of discourse (such as his *Rhetoric* and *Poetics*).[6] Using Erbse's index to the *Iliad* scholia, one can survey the words *homoiôsis* "likening" and *parabolê* "comparison" to gain some idea of this rhetorical mode.[7]

Most noticeable in such a survey of the scholia is the concern of the commentator with the appropriateness of the comparison to the specific narrative moment. For example, at *Iliad* 5.487, when Sarpedon uses a simile in his rebuke to Hector, and says "watch out that you do not become prey and a find for the enemy, like ones caught in the mesh of an all-catching net," the scholiast remarks "the *homoiôsis* is apt [*oikeia*] as of many different

[5]   Two more recent books now examine and illustrate in depth diverse modern approaches to the similes: the performance-centered (Ready 2011) and the text-thematic (Scott 2012).

[6]   On the Peripatetic roots of Hellenistic criticism see Richardson 1992 and Porter 1992.

[7]   Erbse 1988.

men being surrounded and caught like fish."[8] Equally important for the ancient commentators are the ways in which similes bring a scene vividly before the eyes.[9] Of the simile that compares the Trojan onrush at 15.381 to waves swamping a boat, the scholiast says, "The poet always surpasses himself in comparisons—for what could be more vivid, more emphatic, or altogether more concordant [*sumphonôteron*]?"[10]

The usefulness of the simile for heightening emotion and for creating *pathos* is commonly noted by the scholiasts.[11] We should realize, also, what the scholiasts *do not* do: there are no attempts at "symbolic" interpretation or cross-referencing to similes in other books of the poems, no attempt to treat these devices as part of a larger pattern. The mode can be called rhetorical because the interpreter is mainly concerned with the immediate role that a particular trope plays in persuading an audience of the reality of the narrative. Richardson remarks that it is easy to disparage the scholiasts' approach to similes, but more valuable to see "how often the scholia do in fact appreciate more fully than we do the way which the similes enhance the poem."[12] One could expand on this to observe that the ancient interpretive tradition even in its late "scholiastic" form preserves in this rhetorical mode more of a sense of the poem as performance—albeit something more akin to oratory—than do subsequent interpretive modes. Though Richardson does not make much of the fact, he points out that the Townleian scholiast to *Iliad* 16.131 even comments on how this section of the *Iliad*, the arming of Patroclus, should be performed: "It is necessary to recite [*propheresthai*] these verses in a rush [*speudonta*] expressing the yearning for the end." The phrasing, "*epipothêsin tês exodou mimoumenon*," could also be translated as "representing" or "imitating" the "desire for the end." Of course, we might think first of all of rhapsodic performance, which, in Plato's *Ion*, resembles a kind of dramatic representation. But the further point to make here is that the representation involved is actually triplicate: the performer's desire to bring about an effective *exodos*; the desire of Patroclus, the character he represents, to achieve an end to battle; and finally, the *audience's* desire to see and feel the most satisfying conclusion. "Miming a desire" is a beautifully apt way of describing what we know happens in interactive oral performances of epic, where performers enact what

---

[8]   Erbse 1971, 73.

[9]   Richardson 1980.

[10]   Erbse 1975, 91.

[11]   Griffin 1976.

[12]   Richardson 1980, 80.

audiences want, using all the poetic and musical resources at their disposal.[13] It is stunning that the scholiast preserves a sense of this interaction.

The scholiasts do in fact consider Homer to be thus engaged with his narrative, almost in the manner of a participant on one side. On *Iliad* 11.558–62, the bT scholia notice the simile comparing Ajax to a stubborn donkey whom the Trojans, like boys with sticks, try to dislodge from a field: "The *parabolê* is to show contempt of the Trojans [*pros kataphronêsin tôn Trôôn*] because he [Ajax] flees Zeus not them." By means of the simile Homer scores a point against the adversary. This agonistic language appears in an explicit reference to poetics, in the bT scholia to *Iliad* 12.278–86, a simile comparing flying weapons to a snowfall. The poet had used a more compact version of the image earlier in the book, at line 156:

> They threw as they defended themselves and the huts
> and the swift ships.
> They flew like snowflakes [*niphades ... hôs*] to the ground, which the
> blowing wind, whirling the dark clouds, sheds thick
> on the nourishing earth.

When the poet expands the image and applies it to a shower of rocks at lines 278–86, the scholiast says, "The poet seems to hold a contest with himself regarding the comparison. He elaborates it more magnificently." To sum up, the ancient mode of interpreting similes in the scholia imagines something like the conditions of oral performance, even down to the milieu of contest and poetic heroics.

In describing the more familiar, second mode, the thematic, I want to focus on a paradox. We might have imagined that the study of similes would change radically after Parry and Lord's work became assimilated by a generation of classicists. Instead, what happened shows how a dominant intellectual paradigm redirects new advances. For the work of Moulton, published in 1977, can be seen to rely essentially on the same interpretive strategies as the well-known book by Hermann Fränkel, brought out by the same press fifty-six years before. This, despite the publication in 1974 of William Scott's book, a reworking of the dissertation he completed at Princeton ten years before.[14]

Scott had shown that the style of repetition–plus–variation visible in the similes marked it as an oral art form parallel in its workings to the deployment

---

[13] Some fine recent accounts include Blackburn, Claus et al. 1989; Lutgendorf 1991; Mills 1990; Basso 1985; Moyle 1990; Connelly 1986.

[14] Scott 1974; Fränkel 1921.

of epithets and the construction of type-scenes. But his useful lists and typol-
ogies seem not to have produced new work specifically focused on the *implications* of an orally generated simile.[15] Moulton in his introduction, after
acknowledging Scott's approach, argues for subtle patterning of similes in
relation to narrative structure, characterization, and themes. In this project,
Moulton is largely successful. But he is also simply returning to the path that
Fränkel trod. In both, the interpretive strategy is to group together similes by
content and then analyze each as the expression of a larger theme. Fränkel,
discussing the snow similes in Book 12, first finds all the other examples of
the image and contrasts the somber, threatening mood of these (as far as
can be determined from the contexts) with the modern reader's responses,
our *Schneegefühle*.[16] Where Moulton makes an advance over Fränkel is in his
demonstration that the *succession* of similes forms a running commentary on
the action within the narrative. Similes are "synergetic" with narrative. Of
course, this interpretation depends on a prior assumption about the mood of
an individual simile, sometimes, for instance, at the level of a diffuse fire and
light imagery.[17] The strategy is static because it insists on the text as a closed
set of tropes, balanced against or connected to one another, but appreciated
fully only in retrospect, not at the moment of performance but in the leisure
of re-reading. If the discussion of fire imagery in such a framework reminds
us of Cedric Whitman's brilliant chapter on the same topic, and Moulton's
charts begin to resemble the famous outline of the Geometric *Iliad*, it is
not, I think, coincidental.[18] The resemblance goes to the heart of the critical method shared by most Anglo-American literary critics, especially classicists, until recently.[19] The dominant mode of close (and closed) reading
directs them away from the full implications of oral poetics. Their shared
method can be characterized by the summing-up statement in the chapter on
image in Wellek and Warren's *Theory of Literature*, that *vade mecum* of New
Criticism: "Like meter, imagery is one component structure of a poem. In
terms of our scheme, it is part of the syntactical, or stylistic, stratum. It must

---

[15] On similar lags in modern Homeric criticism, see Martin 1989, 1–4 and 1993, 222–28.

[16] Fränkel 1921, 32.

[17] Moulton 1977, 76–86.

[18] Whitman 1958, 249–84.

[19] On the persistence of this method see de Jong and Sullivan 1994, 1–8. The method is still at work
in Lonsdale 1990.

be studied, finally, not in isolation from the other strata, but as an element in the totality, the integrity, of the literary work."[20]

Rather than denigrating either rhetorical or thematic approaches, I am urging a marriage of the two. We have to consider for any given simile both the local immediate affective strategies at work, and the wider-reaching thematic purposes. But these are not the whole story. There is room for, and I would hold, a need for, a third approach, which we might call the "rhythmic." Let us imagine the similes as they would come to the ear of an audience during the performance of Homeric epic. The most noticeable feature of similes, when we do this, is the way in which they punctuate the narrative, giving it an almost musical rhythm and providing episodic definition. In fact, in the midst of the *Iliad*'s battle books, we begin to expect similes; Tilman Krischer has shown that they are an intimate part of the technique, not simply a relief from what modern readers consider tediously boring slaughter.[21]

To illustrate the rhythmic function of the similes, and explain why we come to expect them, I provide below a sample analysis of one of the *Iliad*'s longer books, with similes marked in relation to episodes. I have done the same for a number of other books, with similar results. A look at the breakdown here will show what I consider to be the key performance factor in the uses of similes—namely, the way in which they demarcate narrative segments:

Interaction of similes and episodes in *Iliad* 11.

1–14	Zeus sends Eris, who rouses Achaeans
15–46	Agamemnon arms
47–61	Both sides prepare for battle
62–66	*Hector = star, his armor = lightning*
67–73	*Troops = rows of reapers, wolves*
73–83	Disposition of the gods (omitted by Zenodotus, athetized by Aristophanes and Aristarchus)
84–90	*Timing of conflict=woodcutter's day*
91–112	Killings by Agamemnon
113–21	*Agamemnon = lion, Trojans = deer*
122–29	Agamemnon pursues two Trojans until they stop
129–30	*Agamemnon stands against them like a lion*
131–55	Speech of suppliant warriors
136–42	Agamemnon refuses them
143–46	Agamemnon kills them

[20] Wellek and Warren 1962, 211. This approach appears even in a theoretically sophisticated book, Nimis 1987, which is still mainly interested in semantic associations and long-distance thematic bundling.

[21] Krischer 1971, 36–75.

147	*He rolls one like a holmos*
148–54	General chase
155–58	*Agamemnon = fire in forest*
159–62	Description of aftermath
162–71	Chase goes to Skaian gates
172–78	*Fleeing ones = cows, pursuers = lions*
179–217	Aftermath and Zeus' promise to Hector
218–263	Agamemnon's opponents
264–68	Agamemnon's pain worsens
269–72	*His pain = woman's in labor*
273–83	Agamemnon leaves battle
284–91	Hector urges on the Trojans
292–98	*Hector = hunter, gust of wind*
299–304	Hector's opponents
305–9	*Hector = west wind*
310–23	Diomedes and Odysseus begin killings
324–27	*The heroes = boars among dogs*
328–35	They take sons of Merops
336–67	Hector vs. Diomedes
368–95	Diomedes vs. Paris
396–400	Diomedes retreats wounded
400–10	Odysseus' soliloquy
411–13	Trojan ranks close in
414–19	*Trojans = dogs around boar*
420–55	Odysseus' killings, fight with Sokos
456–73	Odysseus calls for help, Ajax and Menelaus respond
474–84	*Trojans = jackals*
485–91	Ajax attacks Trojans
492–97	*Ajax = rushing river*
498–509	Hector battles near the river
510–20	Nestor leads away Machaon
521–42	Kebriones urges Hector to aid others; he does
543–47	Ajax in fear
548–57	*Ajax in retreat = lion from cattle*
558–65	*Ajax = donkey beset by boys*
566–74	Ajax slowly retreats under attack
575–95	Eurypylos going to help is wounded
596	*All fight like fire*
597–618	Achilles sees Nestor coming back and summons Patroclus
619–44	Nestor refreshes Machaon
645–803	Nestor welcomes Patroclus with story and advice
804–48	Patroclus returns, treats Eurypylos

Another way to describe the principle governing the use of similes can now be ventured: similes do not occur in the middle of an action; they either draw attention to the start of an action or to its finish. Put another way, similes are not like freeze frames or slow-motion sequences in film, but like transition shots, often accompanied by theme music. To point out that the similes are devices to regulate the flow of narrative is not to deny that they also mark emotional peaks; it happens that, as in most dramatic narratives, these two, the episodic boundary and the emotional peak, occur together. The underlying principle, in its respect for the integrity of the narrated episode, might be compared with what has been called Zielinski's Law, the tendency for Homeric epic to present, as sequential, events that are actually imagined as happening simultaneously.[22] Both the placing of similes at boundaries and the narrating of simultaneous events as if they were consecutive work to focus the audience on one event as they propel the narrative forward.

I am not suggesting that the similes came first and Greek epic poets built a narrative around them, although techniques of this kind are not unheard of in oral art: Harold Scheub's book on the Xhosa *ntsomi* shows how the technique of "core-images" allows experienced women who narrate this genre to compose in performance.[23] A closer poetic parallel to the combined rhythmic/thematic function of similes in narrative might be the function of the chorus in Athenian drama. If we go somewhat farther afield, however, it turns out that there are even more relevant comparanda to this episode-framing function of the simile. The comparative material I shall cite comes from a wide range of cultures, but from specifically *heroic* traditions within each culture, thus from traditions parallel in content to the Greek epic. In each of the traditions, which I shall survey briefly at this point, episodic boundaries and emotional peaks are emphasized, and this is done by a shift in performance mode, either from prose to verse, from chant to melodic song, or from one type of song to another. In a number of cases, the songs are the locus for simile and metaphor, though this is not obligatory in all the traditions that I shall mention. The main point is that we must recognize in living oral performances the feature of performance shifts and layerings: rarely if ever is a performance "text" uniform in its texture. My argument is that these shifts are functionally akin to the rhythmic function played by similes in Homer.

---

[22]   On this phenomenon, see esp. Krischer 1971, 91–121.

[23]   Scheub 1975.

Within the past decade or so, we have gained from folklorists and anthropologists excellent transcriptions of complex oral performances. For instance, in her book *Dried Millet Breaking*, Ruth Stone shows how in the highly interactive Woi epic of the Kpelle people of Liberia three levels of performance exist simultaneously.[24] First, there is epic framing, in which metatextual comments are made by the performer, either casual asides to the audience ("my kneecaps are hurting") or stylized phrases. An example of the latter category are the formulaic calls by the performer to his chorus and to the designated audience member who is "answer-giver."[25] With a very demanding audience, interested in "vividness" and "trustworthiness," the metatextual can include such exchanges as that which occurs after a rather strange episode—when the hero rubs newly-forged iron on his buttocks and flies off. The designated audience spokesman asks, "Were you there?" to which the narrator answers, "Very near."[26] Sometimes this sort of exchange is actually built into the next performance level, the story-telling that takes place in normal prose: the audience/questioner will say, "Don't lie to me" to which the narrator might report the speech of the hero by way of proof.

These first two levels are, of course, completely absent from our Homeric texts. The third level of performance in the Woi epic is that of song produced by the narrator. In Stone's words, "Here we find the most esoteric and abstract ideas. Proverbial phrases and formulas, some that are found in other Kpelle music, lace this text." She goes on to observe that, in the tunes, sung by the narrator and then repeated by a chorus, the narrator "inserts the heart and soul of the epic, the proverbs and other nuggets of 'deep' Kpelle."[27]

In the Woi epic, one item regularly associated with song is proverbs: these play a generalizing role, placing the situation in terms of larger cultural entities, while also highly developed in terms of set diction and useful in placing characters in relation to one another. A sung phrase like "the large large rooster, the hen's voice is sweet, the rooster crows the dawn" emphasizes the paradox of a lesser character trying to outdo a superior, while it also restates a general cultural maxim.[28] Although these are not similes, it has been remarked by many that similes in Homer perform just such functions as generalizing experience and incorporating acknowledged cultural views

---

[24] Stone 1988, 12–61.

[25] Stone 1988, 13.

[26] Stone 1988, 27.

[27] Stone 1988, 12–13.

[28] Stone 1988, 21.

of both the civilized and natural worlds. Less often noticed about Homeric similes is their frequent concentration on the *sound* of an action (e.g., *Iliad* 3.1–9), another performance feature over and above the rhythmic that the Woi epic brings to light.[29]

Turning to other cultures in Africa, we can note that Igbo epic performance features four distinct and shifting styles: (1) narrative in ordinary voice; (2) three kinds of lyric song, used respectively to comment on emotional states of characters, make appeals to a hero as if he were present, and give a hero's own lyrical outburst at peak moments; (3) invocative style to declaim hero lists and praise epithets; and (4) oratorical style, in the singer's own voice, giving the audience moralizing or prophetic advice.[30] Once again, I do not claim that similes are found exclusively in one of these voices, but rather that the epic shows *functionally conditioned performance shifts*. The Igbo tradition has formalized and made distinctive in performance a pragmatic feature that has caused considerable discussion in Homeric studies, the direct address of characters in the poems.[31]

For epic in Central Asia, we are lucky to have Karl Reichl's recent guide to Turkic oral poetry, giving us an expert collection of techniques and tales. From his rich material, I select just one: the use of verse in the *Book of Dede Qorqut* to contrast with the usual epic prose.[32] One function of the verse is in "catalogue of beauty" passages. "My wife with the body of a cypress, my wife with joining eyebrows like a drawn bow—with red cheeks which are like autumn apples" runs one that continues in this lyrical mode to make a number of other comparisons. Praise and lament are done in a similar style, also in verse. Here we have not only a contrastive device (verse vs. prose) to highlight peaks in the narrative; in addition, we see how the tradition, dating back to the thirteenth century, also employs similes in lyric portions.

In Sumatra, Nigel Phillips has recorded performances of *sijobang*, the singing of a narrative about the hero Anggun Nan Tungga, which can be performed either by soloists with musical accompaniment or by dramatic troupes of fifteen to twenty male actors who mime the story as the narrator

---

[29]   Often the song features onomatopoetic portions as a rhythmic device, and these are most subject to contemporary influences: at one point in the story, the narrator imitates an airplane noise while describing how Woi's house will go up into the sky. An onomatopoetic formula for ending episodes is the singer's "Dried millet" *wese* (sound of breaking), and the chorus response, "Wese."

[30]   Azuonye 1990, 53–60.

[31]   Martin 1989, 234–36.

[32]   Reichl 1992, 47–49.

sings.[33] *Sijobang* features a prose story-line that is framed and interrupted by a verse form called *pantun*, in which the singer can introduce comic touches, refer to love stories, or even talk about audience members. In the metaphorical system of the performers, these verse segments are known as "flowers" and the song is said to blossom most fully in certain social situations (e.g., when the audience is not well known to the performer, thus allowing him to expatiate on topics otherwise prohibited). Not only do *pantun* verses have a rhythmic function, punctuating episodes; they play the role of meta-performance comment, of deixis pointing to the *hic et nunc* of the song's production. Interestingly, it is in these "flowers" of song-segments that one also finds similes, as occurs in Phillips' transcript B: "I tried to tell it but I could not, it is like felling a *sampie* tree ... I tried to stop you but I could not, it is like stopping water flowing downstream: what is the good of suffering?"[34] Admittedly, there is nothing as detailed or as rich in narrative elements as the Homeric simile here, but the *sijobang* similes, like the Homeric, can be readily extended in length, mainly through the use of parallelism.

My final examples are from Southeast Asia. Even greater varieties of textural elaboration occur here in traditions I have sampled. In the Tamil performances of the Palavecamcervaikkarar story, Stuart Blackburn identifies no fewer than five musical and song styles above and beyond the ordinary speech style that is used to represent the narrative line.[35] A first style is reserved for marking dramatic tension at births, marriages, and deaths in the story; a second performance marker, involving the addition of a particle "*e*" to key words, is used for most crucial events.[36] A third marker consists of audience ululation at certain moments. Again, there is an extra-epic dimension to this stylistic variation: the same behavior occurs ritually at births and marriages, yet it is not reserved for these events in the epic performance. Finally, two musical and rhythmic effects exclusively mark such events as the imminent death of the hero. I will return shortly to the analogue within Greek epic for the sort of genre-embedding evident in the Tamil tradition.

Let me conclude this rough survey by singling out the work of Susan Wadley, who set out to find the significance of performance shifts within the North Indian *Dhola* epic. She shows, first, that scenes or episodes are

---

[33] Phillips 1981, 1–6.

[34] Phillips 1981, 116 (transcript B lines 428–34).

[35] Blackburn 1986.

[36] The existence of such performance-discourse particles is perhaps not irrelevant to the problems of augmented verbs in Homeric and Vedic narrative.

demarcated by "verbal strategies that involve the use or nonuse of music"—
that is to say, one cannot disentangle text from performance in this tradition.[37] One of these strategies, called *dhola dhar* is a long song run used
for ending episodes. It can be filled with simile: "When destruction comes
to man, first lightning falls on the brain, one's own mother is like a lion,
and father seems like Yamraj [the god of death]."[38] Using speech-act terms,
Wadley differentiates informing talk (the prose narrative) from situating
talk—the song-sections, of which she finds at least six styles. These, in turn,
are associated with song genres, often employing similes. For instance,
the *alha* section—"and he rose immediately from his room, think of a lion
moving in the forest, as he went his boots thumped loudly and his shield
clanked on his shoulder"—is done in a performance style associated by its
tune and rhythm with martial epic, but embedded here in the larger narrative text to create characterization. From her fieldwork Wadley concludes, "...
in Indian epic singing, the moods and characters of events and persona are
conveyed by changing voices and situations through shifts in song genres."
Narrative, and especially character development, is achieved "through the
conscious choice of symbolically-charged melodies, textures, and rhythms
borrowed from the regional pool of genres."[39]

It is time now to take the comparative evidence and make a hypothesis
that can be tested in terms of Greek poetry. Given that similes in Homer
have a rhythmic performance function, and that this function is filled by
song or other genre shifts in *actual* oral epic, we should allow for the possibility that similes develop from or are related to a separate performance
style within Greek. From the comparative and typological viewpoint, similes
in fact belong with the elevated "song" portions of performance, while the
narrative functions like the lower-register, explanatory "prose" sections of
performance.

Having suggested this possibility of a distinct genre origin for similes on
the basis of typology, I note now that a supporting argument is available from
a completely independent study of Homeric language.

Starting with work published in 1953, and more fully in the second
edition of his *Studies in the Language of Homer*, G. P. Shipp found that
linguistic features that had independently been established by Pierre
Chantraine as "late" developments appear in similes in a much greater

[37] Wadley 1991, 201.

[38] Wadley 1991, 220.

[39] Wadley 1991, 217.

proportion than in the rest of Homer's text.[40] More than half the similes include late forms, according to Shipp. The implications of his finding have been taken two ways: Shipp himself thought that this meant similes were either composed later than the narrative of the poems or interpolated.[41] Meanwhile, T. B. L. Webster and Geoffrey Kirk saved the integrity of the poems by assuming that the monumental composition of the epics was as late as the time of the composition of the similes. Of course, "late" is a relative term in this discussion; no absolute dating is possible.[42]

Logically, the "lateness" of the similes could be interpreted on the surface as a simple reflection of the performer's situation. Those portions that one can imagine must change from year to year or even one performance to the next—the asides, digressions, and similes—since they refer to the "real" world of the audience, are more likely to be in less standardized, "later" language of a form more contemporary with the poet. Hainsworth puts it this way: "It is certainly the case that contemporary language was freely admitted to the less traditional parts of the diction, such as similes, comments by the poet, and anecdotes."[43] There is, however, more complication to be considered. The rediscovery of the work of Mikhail Bakhtin, for one thing, has helped us remember that there is really no such thing as unmediated "natural" language in texts.[44] The same might be said *a fortiori* for traditional performance media. If indeed the language of similes was simply an example of a poet's contemporary, later Ionic dialect intruding on a poem expressed in an earlier, delimited *Kunstsprache*, we would have no problem agreeing with those who see in the "late" similes a simple sign of recent composition. As it is, however, the similes contain features *not* to be identified with any one dialect and, moreover, some that are definitely *not* Ionic as we know it.

To test my hypothesis, let us make use of Shipp's extensive analysis, in which he matched items throughout Chantraine's grammar to their occurrence in specific Homeric narrative segments. My analysis of this material compares the "late" and rare items that Shipp found in similes with the other surviving Greek song traditions, especially those of Pindar's choral lyric and of Theognidean elegy. We can conclude that there is a relation between the

---

[40]   Shipp 1972, esp. 208–22.

[41]   Shipp 1972, 215–18.

[42]   Webster 1964, 223–38; Kirk 1965, 144.

[43]   Hainsworth 1989, 22.

[44]   Bakhtin 1981.

sub-genre of similes, on the one hand, and the genres of lyric performance, on the other. Notice that the correlation of many of Shipp's "late" features with Pindaric choral art tells against the simple solution of making similes "contemporary" Ionic, because Pindar's quite specialized medium is almost exclusively Doric and Aeolic in its makeup.[45]

In what follows, I have listed more than a dozen places, hitherto unremarked, where Pindar and/or Theognis and Hesiod use the "late" features that Shipp and critics before him found problematic in Homeric similes. A full-scale analysis would no doubt produce many more. These examples will suffice to show the range of phenomena involved in the correlation.

- At the least complex level, that of morphology, we can see that a word for "milk" takes an unusual form only once, in a repeated simile. The other Homeric instances of the word show a *t*-suffix (cf. *Odyssey* 4.88, 9.246), as does the Latin cognate *lac, lact–is*. But in the simile there appears the nominative of a neuter-s-stem (*Iliad* 2.471 = 16.643):[46]

    In spring when milk (*glágos*) moistens the pails

In a Pindaric hyporcheme (fr.106.4 SM) the genitive of this s-stem form is incorporated in a longer poetic trope, a priamel, in which goats from Skyros are said to be best for milking.[47]

- Still on the level of morphology, let us look at two words that are apparently later formations competing with earlier forms even within Homeric diction. At *Iliad* 4.424–26 the battle-lines of the Achaeans are compared to relentless waves cresting about the headlands:

    On the deep, first, it rises to a crest [*korussetai*] but then
    broken on the land it roars greatly, and around the cliffs
    curling, it comes to a head [*koruphoutai*] and spits sea spume.

The verb *koruphoutai* stands out as one of a handful of present stems of its kind derived from nominal stems other than o-stems.[48] Pindar uses the same word in the figurative phrase "the farthest point forms a peak [*koruphoutai*]

---

[45] On Pindaric dialect, see Forssman 1966.

[46] On the forms: Shipp 1972, 193 and Risch 1974, 18, 80.

[47] Mss. C and E have the more common genitive *galaktos*.

[48] Risch 1974, 330; Shipp 1972, 98.

for kings" (*Olympian* 1.113).[49] Pindar and Homer also share *korussetai*, a denominative verb of a commoner morphological type that seems to have developed a similar meaning "rise to a crest," but primarily means "put a crest [of a helmet] on," and by extension, "arm."[50] This latter verb (ultimately from the same root) is used in the same simile at *Iliad* 4.426, where we can read a metaphorical force, and thus perhaps detect a locus of diffusion for the secondary denotation. If *korussetai* means primarily "arms itself" (like a hero—cf. *Iliad* 19.364, 7.206) the application to a wave—which "gets its crest up"—in this line brilliantly elides two aggressive phenomena characterized by high threatening "crests" and destructive encounters with whatever stands in their way. Notice that even though the overt point of comparison within this simile turns on the *frequency* of waves whipped up by Zephyrus and the movement of multiple lines of Greek troops (cf. 423 and 427), the immediately preceding object of the poet's gaze, nevertheless, has been an armed hero, Diomedes, leaping into action with a crash of bronze (420–21) and the simile begins by sounding as if it is meant to elaborate on *this* movement rather than the general troop advance (cf. 422–23 *Hôs d'ot '... ornut'*). Therefore, the choice of *korussetai* to describe the wave is even more apt in context.

We may note, in addition, that the use of the verbal metaphor in the simile does what good poetry always does, recovering the radical vividness of the language itself. For *korussetai* here takes us back to the original metonymy underlying the semantic extension of the verb; that is to say, the etymological sense "put on a helmet" has already been watered down elsewhere in Homeric diction to mean "put on arms" in a more general sense (thus even spears can be "helmeted"—cf. *Iliad* 3.18 *kekoruthmena*). The formulaic quality of expressions with the broader semantic range shows that this is already traditional. But in the simile, the wave/warrior comparison is most exact if we assume the verb means literally "put on a crest" rather than the more extended "arm oneself." In short, the simile (an allegedly "late" feature) seems to preserve an *earlier* state of the language in this case. At the same time, it could be argued that the odd shift in comparison—from what first appears to be a description of Diomedes to a general characterization of waves of troops—occurs because this radical meaning of *korussetai* has by this

---

[49] On this interpretation of the line, see Kirkwood 1982, 58. It could be that the metaphor is more striking in Pindar: the horizontal axis—what is farthest—is pictured as a vertical ascent—what stands tall like a mountain.

[50] Cf. *Iliad* 2.273, 4.495.

time become obscure to poet and audience, though the motif of waves in a martial comparison remains important.

- In the next example of shared diction, we find an adjective meaning "power-ful," with a distinctive formation, used in the simile at *Iliad* 11.119:

  rushing, covered with sweat, under attack from the powerful beast
  [*krataiou thêros*]

As Shipp points out, the masculine *krataios* is secondary to the inherited *u*-stem adjective *kratus*, having been formed by analogy to the inherited feminine *krataiê*.[51]

Pindar used this later-formed masculine in describing Telamon, father of Ajax, who once took Troy (*Nemean* 4.25–26). The Pindar passage shows no sign elsewhere in its context of borrowing a strange word from Homer; this is not allusion.[52] The most we can say is that Pindar and Homer share diction that is unusual from the Homeric standpoint. Although the masculine *kratus* is not common in Homer, the usual adjective form in epic is *krateros*.

- "Late" or rare features found by Shipp in similes can be detected in the diction of Theognidean poetry as well as Pindaric. For example, the word *smi-kros* for "little" (instead of the more common *oligos* and *tutthos*) occurs in Homer only in the simile at *Iliad* 17.755–57:[53]

  As a cloud of starlings or daws comes
  shrieking destruction when they catch sight of a hawk
  on its way, that brings the little [*smikrêisi*] birds death ...

The phrase "little bird," with the non-epic adjective, recurs at Theognis 579–82:

  I hate a bad man, and having veiled myself I pass by
      with the empty mind of a little bird [*smikrês ornithos*].
  And I hate a woman who runs around and a greedy man
      who wants to plow someone else's field.

---

[51] Shipp 1972, 196. A similar analogical formation and its poetic implications have been analyzed in Nagy 1999b, 349–54.

[52] Of course, Pindar can on occasion make use of recognizable Homeric phrases for conscious effects: Forssman 1966, 86–100.

[53] Shipp 1972, 197.

This intriguing small dialogue seems to use the phrase in question within lines spoken by a female (as the participle shows), with a reply spoken by a male.[54] The whole exchange has the sound of a traditional insult duel: the exactly structured pair of couplets is formally equivalent to modern-day Cretan *mandinadhes*, which are also used extensively in negotiating male-female relations.[55] It could be that the word *smikros* for "little" enters epic through a pre-existing lyric tradition that features encounters involving gender clashes. In this connection I observe that in the Homeric simile we are examining, the *kirkos* is masculine, and the little birds (like the first speaker in Theognis), feminine. A further stylization of the lyric *topos* that I am postulating might be the bird-to-bird talk we find in Hesiod's fable of the hawk and nightingale (*Works and Days* 202–12), where the clash is also along gender lines, but one bird, the nightingale, also clearly represents the poet. Finally, it is not impossible that Pindar, in *Pythian* 3, combines this set of poetic associations (bird = small; female, opposed to male) with the other well-known *topos*, of poet as bird, when he asserts towards the poem's end (107–9):

> I will be little among the little [*smikros en smikrois*], big with the big,
> and the divinity ever at my mind I shall honor,
> doing service according to my own device.[56]

Of course, I am not claiming that any of the lyric associations of this trope affect the simile in the *Iliad*, but I note that the non-epic adjective does fit comfortably into a *systematic* series of related themes outside epic, another indication perhaps that this is where the generic origin of the diction is to be sought.

- Still on the lexical level, we find several substantives, uncommon in Homeric diction but used in similes, deployed within a more fully articulated set of themes in lyric poetry. The following simile (*Iliad* 15.410–13) contains the

[54]   Commentators on the lines since von Leutsch in 1871 have read them as dialogue: see Garzya 1958, 224; Harrison 1902, 196–97. West 1974, 156 assumes it is one poem, but not a dialogue; van Groningen 1966, 228–30 goes so far as to see two unrelated poems. The emendation by West 1989, 201 (changing the participle to masculine accusative in line 580) destroys the ironic effect that Garzya had detected.

[55]   A good example of such *mandinadha* duelling is analyzed by Herzfeld 1985, 144–46. See also the extensive collection of Droudakis 1982, esp. 123–30.

[56]   On the topos of poet as bird, see Gow 1965, 143 on Theocritus *Idylls* 7.47. Note that the *makhana* of Pindar, synonymous with his poetry, is elsewhere styled "winged" (*Pythian* 8.34), and that Pindar can refer to rivals (his or the victor's) as birds (*Olympian* 2.87).

only occurrence in Homer of the word *sophiê*, "wisdom," the only abstract noun formation of this type in Homer.[57]

> But as a chalk-line makes straight ship's wood
> in the hands of a skilled carpenter, one who knows
> all wisdom [*sophiês*] well, by Athena's suggestions,
> Thus was their war and battle made evenly taut.

Pindar uses the word twenty times, and Theognis ten, but most interesting is the further context in Theognis 1003–9:

> This virtue, this prize is best among men
> and fairest for a wise man [*sophôi*] to bear;
> A common good is this, for the *polis* and all the people:
> The man who stays firmly standing at the front.
> In general for men I shall advise [*hypothêsomai*]: with youth's
> glorious flower he who thinks noble thoughts
> should enjoy his own possessions well ...

The speaker's promised advice to the wise man here comprises an elegiac imperative contrasted with the martial poetic ideal.[58] The *Iliad* passage in a similar manner mentions the advice of Athena (*hypothêmosunêisin*) alongside the recipient's own wisdom. But whereas wisdom is only touched on briefly in epic, it is unmistakably a topic appropriate to lyric and epinician advising; poetic direction on how to obtain it constituted a recognizable genre distinct from epic but interacting with that form.[59]

- In the simile at *Iliad* 15.381–84, the word *toikhos*, which elsewhere means "wall of a house," in Homer, is applied to the sides of a ship that waves are swamping:

> As a great wave of the broad-wayed sea
> goes down above the ship's side [*toikhôn*] whenever the force
> of the wind drives it on—for that's what most swells waves—
> the Trojans with a great shout went down upon the wall

---

[57]   Risch 1974, 116.

[58]   Young 1971, 61 sharpens the contrast by placing in quotation marks lines 1003–6 (except *sophôi*), citing Tyrtaeus 9.13ff. and 7.29ff.

[59]   On such *hypothekai* poetry, see Martin 1984a.

This shift from "wall" to "hull" has been thought to represent a later semantic development; in the absence of other attestations we cannot be sure.[60] I note only that, within this simile, there is a contrast between the ship's "walls" and the famous Achaean wall (cf. the related word, *teikhos*, at line 384). This is followed by a sort of reification of the simile, as the Trojans pour over the defensive wall and threaten the *actual* Achaean ships: the simile of the waves describes a flood of men, yet the objects of both metaphorical and real inundations are the same. Rather than representing a catachresis of the regular meaning of *toikhos*, I suggest further that the simile at *Iliad* 15.381–84 taps into an independent series of tropes visible in such lyric forms as Theognis' lines (673–76) on the "ship of state":

> They do not care to bail, and the sea dashes over
>   both sides [*toikhôn*]. With difficulty, to be sure,
> is any one saved, such things do they do. They stopped
>   the good helmsman, who kept watch knowledgeably.

We could say that these lines are reminiscent of the Homeric simile. But, put the other way, it could be that the simile makes use of an emotionally intense song-moment in which one can lament the total loss of civil order in a *polis*. It is easier to believe that Homeric art redeploys traditional diction (including the nautical meaning of the otherwise unusual *toikhos*) in this way, just as the *Dhola* epic borrows freely from a regional genre pool. At the moment of describing the worst disorder in the Achaean camp, the poet would then be eliciting in his audience all the associations entailed by an allegory of the Theognidean type. The alternative is to think that Theognis borrowed specifically from the one Homeric simile where the word *toikhos* meant ship hulls and developed his own allegory from there. That the elegiac lines embody a carefully elaborated, enigmatic utterance, artful in the extreme, is made clear from lines 681–82, characterizing the verses as an *ainigma*, hidden from all but those of an in-group skilled in poetic wisdom.[61] This sort of characterization applies more to a complex reworking of a traditional extended poetic metaphor than to a random borrowing from Homeric hexameters. If anyone "borrows" here, it is the Homeric composer.

- Sometimes, the least obvious word leads one onto a rich vein of shared diction and motif indicating lyric/epic interaction in similes. The adverb *exaiphnês*

---

[60]   Chantraine 1968–80, 1099.

[61]   See especially Nagy 1985.

"suddenly" is a "late" rarity in a simile that compares fighting to a fire that rises up suddenly (*Iliad* 17.736–39):[62]

> Thus they speedily bore the corpse from the war
> to the hollowed ships. But war was tense for them
> like a wild fire that starting up suddenly [*exaiphnês*], attacks
> and burns a city of men, and houses get ruined.

Pindar (*Olympian* 9.52) uses the same adverb once, precisely in a scene of natural disaster, when speaking of a primordial flood:

> They say that water's strength had flooded the black earth but then,
> by Zeus' devisings,
> an ebb-tide suddenly [*exaiphnâs*] took the bilge.

The phrase *ormenon exaiphnês*, "starting up suddenly," occurs in another simile (*Iliad* 21.14), which describes the Trojans fleeing Achilles as locusts flee to a river when they are set aflutter by flames. The contrast is ironic: the river is relief for the locusts, but in this case will be death for the Trojans, and in fact is about to flood the plain, in this poetic rendition of a clash of the elements outside Troy. If we imagine that the primordial flood scene alluded to in Pindar recapitulates some mythic narrative, and does so with a conventional signal (the adverb *exaiphnês*), then we can speculate that the similes about sudden fire key the Homeric audience to similar mythic descriptions of cosmic disaster, over and above the explicit martial conflict in the similes. At any rate, it is worth noting the closeness and specificity of contexts surrounding this seemingly banal adverb.

- A simile at *Iliad* 16.384–88 presents a similarly complex case of intertextual (or, as I now prefer, meta-performative) poetics:

> As the whole black earth is pressed hard by a hurricane
> on an autumn day, when Zeus pours torrential rain
> the time he is angered at men who by violence
> render crooked judgements in the agora
> and drive out justice,
> not respecting the regard of the gods [*theôn opin ouk alegontes*].

Shipp, citing Chantraine, observes that the verb *alegô* takes an accusative rather than the usual genitive object only when used in the simile line *theôn opin ouk alegontes*, "not respecting the regard of the gods." Meanwhile, it has

---

[62] Shipp 1972, 195.

long been seen that this simile resembles a motif in Hesiod (*Works and Days* 248–51):[63]

> O kings, you yourselves take notice of this justice,
> for close by, among men, immortals note
> how many grind down one another with crooked judgements
> not respecting the regard of the gods [*theôn opin ouk alegontes*].

The Homeric simile containing this line thus apparently recasts as an allusion the juridical and theological message of the Hesiodic lines, adding to them the meteorological details of Zeus' wrath, but omitting the reference to kings, while the Hesiodic passage fails to mention the signs of the gods' displeasure. We should not assume borrowing in either direction; both passages partially articulate a larger shared complex of ideas and images.[64] Even more interesting is Pindar's use of the verb *alegô*, again with the unusual accusative, as he explains his motives for praise (*Olympian* 11.11–15):

> Child, Hagesidamos, for your boxing
> I shall sing a sweetsung ornament upon your crown of gold olive
> respecting the race of the Zephyrian Lokrians [*genean alegôn*].

It is worth noticing that the grand opening priamel of Pindar's poem foregrounds his choice of sweet-sounding hymns by contrasting it with other human needs, specifically for wind and rain—exactly the two cosmic threats in the Homeric simile about Zeus' justice (*Olympian* 11.1–3):

> Sometimes men need winds the most, sometimes waters
> from the heavens, watery children of cloud.

Pindar's respect for the victor's homeland, embodied in the form of this choral song, will by implication reinforce the cosmic order (*dikê*) so conspicuously absent in the world described by Homer and Hesiod. The choral poet by his song ensures that the injustice imagined in the Iliadic vignette (16.384–92) never happens. The verb *alegô* with its rare accusative object is a dictional peculiarity specifically associated with this theme, a theme embedded, in turn and independently, in the poems of Hesiod, Homer, and Pindar.[65]

---

[63] For recent discussion, see Janko 1992, 365 and Schmidt 1986, 109–10.

[64] The same phenomenon underlies other Hesiodic lines: see Martin 1984a.

[65] Against possible objections that such small details cannot evoke such large themes, I offer the evidence gathered from actual fieldwork with living traditional poetics, as summarized by J. M. Foley 1991, 1–60.

The place of Pindaric poetry in these examples needs to be put into perspective. We are really talking about two phenomena. First, there is the diachronic priority that praise poetry of the type represented by Pindar seems to have over epic of the type represented by Homer.[66] Second, Pindaric art may appear diachronically "older" than Homer because for its own compositional reasons it preserves ideologies either forgotten, suppressed, or barely alluded to by Homeric epic. We have seen one such case in the motif of Zeus' justice and the flood. Another such topic may have been life after death, on which Pindar has been thought to preserve traces of Orphic ideas.[67] In that case, it is significant that one proof-text for Pindar's "Orphic" view of the afterlife contains the adjective *apalamnos* "helpless; hard to deal with" (*Olympian* 2.57). The word appears once in Homer, in a simile at *Iliad* 5.597, describing a traveller who stands helpless before an impassable river. The expected form of the adjective, *apalamos*, is found in Hesiod *Works and Days* 20.[68] Shipp's comment on the word is worth quoting, as it reveals much about his assumptions: "As *apalamnos* and also *palamnaios* are common in early poetry including Doric and tragedy, it is more likely that the simile has the word from such a source than that it has an epic origin." He therefore imagines a very late stage of composition for this simile, because it contains a word found otherwise in later poetry.[69] But if we take into account the way in which living oral poetic traditions function, we can reformulate the solution without recourse to problematic late datings and interpolations: given its context in Pindar, it is likely that the word comes from another genre of poetry, of the Orphic-hymnic type. Part of that tradition made its way down into the work of Pindar and other lyric poets, while Homeric poetry independently made contact with Orphic themes and diction.[70]

In this case and in others, of course, it is not the actual words of the fifth-century Boeotian poet, but the art of his lyric forebearers that has been deployed by the epic composer. Most of that earlier lyric tradition is lost to us. When we do have it, interesting questions of mutual shared themes and diction arise. A centerpiece for the investigation must remain two similar passages about the effects of midsummer, Hesiod *Works and Days* 582–88

---

[66] Nagy 1990 offers persuasive metrical and dictional details to support this argument. To my knowledge, his account has not been challenged.

[67] West 1983, 110.

[68] Risch 1974, 54.

[69] Shipp 1972, 245.

[70] West 1983, 120 notes points of contact with regard to theogonic material.

and Alcaeus fragment 347 LP. Recently, J. C. B. Petropoulos has convincingly explicated the link between these in terms of their recasting of functional, local song traditions still attested in modern rural Greece. The two passages, long considered in standard literary terms as the result of "borrowing" by one poet of another's work, "may well be independent manifestations derived from the same stock of thematic material," Petropoulos concludes.[71]

I want to extend this finding in terms of Homeric poetry and the relationship that I have been outlining between lyric traditions and similes. The well-known passage describing the Trojan elders on the walls of their city compares them to cicadas (*Iliad* 3.150–52):

> γήραϊ δὴ πολέμοιο πεπαυμένοι, ἀλλ' ἀγορηταὶ
> ἐσθλοί, τεττίγεσσιν ἐοικότες οἵ τε καθ' ὕλην
> δενδρέῳ ἐφεζόμενοι ὄπα λειριόεσσαν ἱεῖσι·

> Stopped from warring by old age, but talkers,
> good ones, like cicadas which in the wood
> sitting on a tree emit a slender voice.

The late feature noted by Chantraine and Shipp is at line 152: *dendreôi ephezomenoi* has a rare synizesis reflecting the loss of an original intervocalic digamma (*dendrewôi*).[72] Shipp believes the synizesis is produced under pressure from an Attic form *dendros* (dative *dendrôi*), which is itself a reinterpretation back-formed from the plural *dendrea*, by analogy. If the Homeric simile, as well as the Hesiodic scene (which has the same phrase, at *Works and Days* 583), compress a traditional poetic motif that is expanded in the Alcaeus song, the traditional *type* represented by Alcaeus 347 could be the source for the hexameter treatments. Furthermore, if the phrase *dendreôi ephezomenoi* was originally in a different generic context, it may not have been metrically intractable—as it appears to be in Homer and Hesiod.[73] I leave for another time further exploration of the thematic implications of *Iliad* 3.150–52 in the light of the passage's apparent relationship to traditional lyric motifs.

---

[71] Petropoulos 1994, 82. For different comparative evidence tending towards the same conclusion concerning Hesiodic poetry, see Martin 1992a.

[72] Shipp 1972, 12. Kirk (1985b, 284) accepts the linguistic lateness of the feature but attributes it to "the most developed phase of the language of oral epic; that is, it is likely to be by Homer himself."

[73] An older phrase without synizesis, *dendrewôi ephezomenos*, would form a choriambic dimeter, the lyric meter attested in, for example, Anacreon 349 PMG.

- Following up the notion that lyric forms may have affected the diction of similes, we might attribute some other metrical irregularities within Homeric verse to the differing demands of lyric meter; seemingly aberrant diction may have been precut to fit another mold. This seems to be the case in *Iliad* 23.226–28:

> When the Dawnstar [*Heôsphoros*] goes to utter light upon the earth
> after whom saffron-robed Dawn spreads over the sea
> then the fire was dying down and the flame stopped.

Shipp notices the harsh synizesis in the initial syllable of the word for Dawnstar, *Heôsphoros*.[74] We can add that a similar synizesis must occur at Pindar *Isthmian* 4.24 (also a simile):[75]

> But, awakened, has a sheen on its skin
> like the wondrous Dawnstar [<*Ao*>*sphoros*] among other stars.

The Pindaric form might, in fact, be restored as *Asphoros*, a form featuring the expected West Greek contraction instead of synizesis.[76] In sum, the poet of *Iliad* 23.226 uses this word metrically as if it had its Doric contracted form and may do so under the influence of local western Greek non-epic lyric.

- Finally, a similar argument might help us explain at least one "acephalic" line, which occurs in a simile at *Iliad* 9.4–7:

> As two winds stir up the fish-filled sea,
> Boreas and Zephyrus, which blow from Thrace
> coming on suddenly, and the black wave gathers
> in a crest, and spreads much seaweed alongside the sea.

The short initial vowel of *Boreês* causes the irregularity.[77] As it happens, we have in Pindar a context in which these two wind names are fitted with other dictional elements in such a way that the syllables retain their natural quantity (*Parthenia* 2 [fr. 94b Sn-M] 16–18):

> κεῖνον, ὃς Ζεφύρου τε σιγάζει πνοὰς
> αἰψηράς, ὁπόταν τε χειμῶνος σθένει

---

[74] Shipp 1972, 9.

[75] <Ἀο>σφόρος with synizesis is Bergk's emendation (ἐωσ–, ἀωσ–, codd.), necessary for meter.

[76] This was suggested in a note by Bury 1892, 68, although he prints Bergk's emendation in the text.

[77] Leaf 1900, 372 notes that one class of mss. reads Attic *Borras* here.

φρίσσων Βορέας ἐπι-
σπέρχησ᾽ ...

That one, that calms the quick winds of Zephyr
and when Boreas bristling with storm's strength rushes ...

If Homeric poetry is here assimilating a non-hexameter poetic motif, one perhaps appropriate to seasonal or hymnic material, then it acquires along with the motif the diction and meter of the source tradition. In this connection, then, it is a pleasant surprise to find in the same Pindar passage another peculiarity of the language of Homeric similes, namely the unusual deployment (from a Homeric standpoint) of a compound of *sperkhô* in the active, rather than middle form, used intransitively to mean "rush."[78]

In sum: starting from the internal evidence of the rhythmic punctuation provided by similes within the *Iliad*, we then find by comparison that this corresponds *functionally* to that of distinctive song-genres in the performance of epics in a number of cultures. Returning to non-epic song-texts from ancient Greek tradition, we further find a number of *formal* congruences between similes and lyric poetry, at the level of diction and even meter. An analogy to the process would be the way that Homeric speeches stylize elements of actual "sociopoetic" performance genres.[79] As with those embedded speech-acts, the "lyric" similes are "sub-genres" only if we take the viewpoint of the all-encompassing Homeric performer; but we know that even as late as the fifth century a poet like Pindar, as Gregory Nagy has elegantly shown, can hold a quite different view about the priority and value of Homeric art.[80]

We shall probably never know whether similes were ever perceived by an ancient audience as having a different performance register. But one thing this investigation of Homeric epic can tell us: once more, the genius of this ambitious super-genre appears to be its inclusion of every other form of song-making. Like the art of the *Hymn to Apollo*'s Delian maidens, which they learned from the man of Chios, it is polyphonic and therefore marvelous.[81]

---

[78] Shipp 1972, 199; cf. *Iliad* 13.334.

[79] Martin 1989, passim.

[80] Nagy 1990, 199–214, 414–37.

[81] Nagy 1990, 375–81 on the multiple personifications involved in *Hymn to Apollo* 156–68. For intensive analysis and new interpretation, see now Peponi 2009.

3

FORMULAS AND SPEECHES
THE USEFULNESS OF
PARRY'S METHOD[1]

In the entire output of his writing on the art and craft of Homeric verse-making, Milman Parry never alluded to what seems a crucial difference in the epics: the distinction between the poet's narrative and the speeches attributed to characters in that narrative. It seems this should matter: if more than half the lines in Homer are the direct speech of mortals and gods, either these *are* formulaic in some sense, or they are not. If they *are*, it can hardly be that they are composed solely of the type of noun-epithet formula to which Parry, in *The Traditional Epithet in Homer*, devoted most of his discussion.[2] On the other hand, if they are not formulaic, doesn't this place a serious stumbling block in the way of the notion that Homeric epic verse was the medium of oral performance? Can it be that Homeric speeches might betray the *non*-oral composition of the poems? Are formulas the preserve of tradition, and speeches the space for spontaneity in this art form? Should we give up trying to construct a poetics different from that applied to written verse?

I will argue that this is not the case: when gods or mortals speak in Homer, the diction is as formulaic as that of the narrative segments of the poems. But, beyond this reassuring fact, certain other conclusions can be drawn when we look at the *ways* in which speeches are formulaic. Here, Milman Parry's methods of analyzing Homeric diction, with some important extensions, can lead us to new insights about much larger compositional issues, such as the construction of scenes and the development of character-ization. I hope to offer several such insights during the course of explicating

---

[1]   Originally published in *Hommage à Milman Parry: le style formulaire de l'épopée homérique et la théorie de l'oralité poétique*, ed. F. Létoublon (originally Amsterdam: Gieben, now Leiden: Brill, 1997), 263–73.

[2]   Translated in Parry 1971, 1–190.

one portion of a speech from the *Odyssey*. Although these arise from a straightforward application of the study of formulas, I have not found any of the points I shall make in *Odyssey* commentaries, including the recent joint enterprise of Heubeck and others.[3] Therefore, I am encouraged to think that there is still much work to be done by those who take Parry's scholarship seriously. The workings of formulas in speeches are still largely unexplored, although Parry 65 years ago pointed the way, perhaps without himself realizing it.

We are all familiar with the progress of the argument in Parry's thesis: the extension and economy of formulaic expressions—not merely the fact of their repetition—meant for Parry that Homeric diction represented a medium that could not have been developed by any single poet and was therefore traditional. We know, too, that the linkage between traditional verse and oral composition was made by Parry later on, and does not affect his demonstrations in *The Traditional Epithet*.[4] But what seems not to have been realized, judging from recent criticism, is that Parry *by no means* restricted the idea of formula in the way that his most cited definition would indicate.[5] His definition, the "expression regularly used, under the same metrical conditions, to express an essential idea" certainly describes the sort of phrases he studied in detail: the series of adjectives connected with the proper names of heroes, which showed economy and extension in the most-needed places, especially the nominative case.[6] Yet, when we re-read the early portions of *The Traditional Epithet*, it is clear that Parry focused on noun-epithet formulas after considering a number of other possibilities, all of which he thought too complex to be capable of demonstrating economical use.[7] In fact, he uses the word "formula" to describe the combination of pronoun, particle, and noun, conjunction, and verb, and several other patterns.[8] Only in the case of preposition and proper noun did he go beyond the combination of noun and epithet, but not because he thought only these were true formulas: rather, as he put it, "outside of noun-epithet formulae and epithets of heroes we are compelled to forgo quantitative analysis" (*Traditional Epithet* 105).

---

[3]   Heubeck et al. 1988–92.

[4]   For a recent restatement of these key points, see Lord 1991, 73–103.

[5]   Typical of the misunderstandings on this point is Shive 1987; see the review by Nagy 1988.

[6]   Parry 1971, 13.

[7]   Parry acknowledges the limitations imposed by his choice of data at Parry 1971, 20–21.

[8]   See for example the discussion at Parry 1971, 16.

This focus on quantitative analysis made *The Traditional Epithet* such a powerful work. Its wider connections with the positivist trends in intellectual life in the early 20th century, and in the history of Classical Philology, are worth investigating. Unfortunately, the urge to quantify the so-called "formulaic content" of poems and then use this as a litmus test of "oral composition" came to distract a number of subsequent investigators. We are, thankfully, through with that era in which the very possibility of interpreting Homeric poetry was thought by some to be threatened by Parry's work. But we face a different threat nowadays, from those who dismiss Parry's discoveries as ultimately irrelevant to the interpretation of the poetry. What do we have to offer those who believe that the true genius of Homer, the alleged individual creativity of a great poet, lies in those elements of the *Iliad* and *Odyssey* which cannot be easily labeled formulaic? In other words, those who notice formulas in Homer only to be able to rescue the poet from their clutches? The devotee of traditional poetry would like to assert that the poetry is precisely in the formulas, and furthermore that the formulas are everywhere, even in those portions of the poems that might seem at first sight most spontaneous and "untraditional," the speeches. But to do this we must return to that labyrinth of formulas outside the pale of the noun-epithets, the realm that Parry skirted as being unquantifiable.

If we begin at the level of the passage, rather than the level of the individual phrase, the task of finding what is in some way "formulaic" might appear less hopeless. The beauty of Milman Parry's method, overall, is that it takes everything into account and refuses to discard evidence. This same ideal should guide us in determining what is formulaic in speeches. This is to say that we need a close word-by-word analysis of as many Homeric speeches as one can examine. But in conjunction with such an undertaking, we need to have at least a tentative notion of how far the term "formula" can be extended. Professor Hainsworth, in his recently published *Iliad* commentary, observes that consensus has still not been reached on the definition of formula. He proceeds to list seventeen phenomena that a formula definition should take into account. These include the fact that certain words and word-shapes have a preferred location in the verse; that phrases recur, which often conform to the cola of the verse; that sentences are patterned in specific ways; that phrases agglomerate; and that phrases become obsolete, and are replaced by others.[9]

---

[9]   Hainsworth 1993, 1–5.

At this point we should perhaps ask: if a definition of the formula could be made that would include such phenomena, what would we do with it? How could it aid interpretation of the poetry? Or should it be thought of as an end in itself? It is clear that one's definition of the formula depends ultimately on what it is to be used for. When counting formulas to prove orality, a clear rule—say, a phrase repeated once in the same metrical position—will do. But once we move beyond raw statistics, a more flexible instrument is needed. Hainsworth himself has given us the most flexible definition so far, stemming from his detailed studies over the past twenty-five years: as he puts it in the introduction to his *Iliad* commentary, "A formula is a group of two or more words that are associated with each other."[10] However, this definition can still not immediately account for such things as the tendency of certain words to prefer one location in the line. I would like to suggest an addition to this formulation. My addition is ultimately inspired by Parry's observation that conjunctions, prepositions, pronouns, and even particles are used in recognizable but hard to quantify patterns within Homer. The unified field theory that I am proposing was sketched out in my book, *The Language of Heroes*, several years ago, but I now take the opportunity of offering to a critical audience a refined version, together with my thoughts on how this unified field theory of the formula can be employed in interpretation.[11]

I believe that we can account for almost all the aspects of dictional behavior in Homer by taking a structural linguistic view of the formula. In this view, the formula can be seen as consisting of two levels: we can call them the syntagmatic and paradigmatic. Or, to use Roman Jakobson's terms, the formula, like language, comprises an axis of selection and an axis of combination.[12]

By the syntagmatic I mean essentially what Hainsworth calls the formula: two or more words associated with each other. At the most rigid level, these are the phrases upon which Parry concentrated, phrases that the poet can employ with confidence to fill out a number of metrically different verses: such things as *dîos Odusseus* and *podas ôkus Achilleus*. Hainsworth's path-breaking book on the flexible formula has shown how these can be separated, inverted, inflected, expanded, and collapsed, and how similar manipulations apply to common nouns as well.[13] The key aspect of the syntagmatic formula

---

[10]   Hainsworth 1993, 18.

[11]   Martin 1989, 162–70.

[12]   See the influential conference paper Jakobson 1960.

[13]   Hainsworth 1968.

is that there are at least two words to be considered: usually in proximity, usually noun and adjective or verb and adverb.

Paradigmatic formulas can be explained with reference to the metrical structure of the line. It is well known that the noun–epithet formulas match up with the breaks between cola in the hexameter. Without approaching the question of priority, whether the phrase or rhythm came "first," I can say, however, that this one fact, i.e., that syntagmatic formulas and the cola are so often identical in shape, militates against the notion recently proposed by Edzard Visser, which would have it that the poet composes on the basis of *single words* of appropriate metrical shapes.[14] If single words alone lie at the heart of the compositional technique, there is absolutely no reason for the colon breaks to have ever developed in the first place in their attested positions or to have been preserved. But the focus on single words *can* be useful. For instance, if we look more closely at the hexameter, it can also be conceived as a series of metrical slots, smaller than cola, but larger than the dactyl/spondee foot, ready to accommodate words of one to five or six syllables. Eugene O'Neill, Jr. drew attention to the tendency of certain metrical word-shapes to come at certain positions in the verse: an unusual thing, if we consider the range of possible places into which words could theoretically fit into the verse. As you recall, O'Neill shows that word-types are not spread evenly in all the possible places. "Localization" instead takes place.[15] But we can go further than this and notice that not only certain word shapes, but certain lexical items appear regularly only in a few places in the line. When a single word, be it noun, verb, conjunction, or particle, occurs by itself, regularly in a particular slot in the line, I call this a "paradigmatic formula." To put this another way, in terms of composition: whenever the poet composes a line, he can rely on not one but two types of knowledge to complete the verse: 1) what phrases fit which cola ("syntagmatic formulas") but also, even more important when we come to talk about speeches, 2) what single words can regularly come at what point in the verse.

Under the heading of paradigmatic formulas, we can account for other phenomena: for example, where similar sounds or similar syntactic patterns or even morphemes crop up at the same points in different lines. Two well-known attempts to describe these phenomena are those by Joseph Russo,

---

[14]   Visser 1988. Nagy has convincingly explained the development of the hexameter from shorter lyric meters, and traced the enormous implications of this fact, first in Nagy 1974, with expansions in Nagy 1990.

[15]   O'Neill 1942.

regarding the "structural formula," and by Michael Nagler, who argued for
the role of a "pre-verbal Gestalt" underlying the surface diction.[16] My notion
of paradigmatic formulas differs from the earlier descriptions, however,
because I wish to restrict the definition of paradigmatic formula to mean
only the appearance of the same *word* in the same metrical slot (allowing
for inflection), rather than a word-shape or morphological type. My idea
of paradigmatic formula will cover Visser's single-word theory, as well, and
bring it into line with these other earlier attempts. It is important to point
out, however, that neither the paradigmatic nor syntagmatic type alone can
be taken as defining the formula: both are needed and must be understood
as interacting.

Some paradigmatic formulas, in fact, come from the ossification of
syntagmatic formulas, which lock words into particular slots because they
must accommodate entire phrases. A number of these lexical items reap-
pearing in particular slots do so because they reflect the syntax of the
language. As far as one can tell, the unmarked Indo-European sentence had
subject + object + verb word-order, so that in the Homeric line it is natural
that the verb so often comes at the end of the verse when the verse is equivalent to a whole sentence. Another tendency within Indo-European syntax,
so-called Wackernagel's Law, accounts for the appearance of particle strings
near the front of the verse, since enclitic and unemphatic pronouns and
particles came second in the Indo-European sentence.[17]

Prepared with this unified field theory of the formula, we can finally look
at a speech to see what its formulaic background can teach us. Let us begin
with *Odyssey* 2.40–54. Using the Thesaurus Linguae Graecae CD-ROM text
of Homer, and an Ibycus searching program to look at every word and collocation, and compare with contexts elsewhere in the poem, I was able to
stratify the text as follows:

> "ὦ γέρον, οὐχ ἑκὰς **οὗτος ἀνήρ, τάχα** δ᾽ **εἴσεαι αὐτός**,   40
> ὃς λαὸν ἤγειρα· **μάλιστα** δέ μ᾽ **ἄλγος** ἱκάνει.
> **οὔτε τιν᾽** ἀγγελίην στρατοῦ **ἔκλυον** ἐρχομένοιο,
> **ἥν** χ᾽ ὕμιν **σάφα εἴπω**, ὅτε πρότερός γε **πυθοίμην**,
> **οὔτε τι** δήμιον ἄλλο πιφαύσκομαι οὐδ᾽ ἀγορεύω,
> **ἀλλ᾽ ἐμὸν αὐτοῦ** χρεῖος, **ὅ μοι κακὰ** ἔμπεσεν **οἴκῳ**,   45

---

[16]   Russo 1966; Nagler 1974, 1–26. Parry himself, in his use of the term "formula-type," acknowledged from the start something akin to the structural formula, and in this was followed by Lord and
Notopoulos.

[17]   See Collinge 1985, 217–19.

δοιά· τὸ μὲν πατέρ' <u>ἐσθλὸν</u> ἀπώλεσα, ὅς ποτ' ἐν **ὑμῖν**
τοίσδεσσιν **βασίλευε, πατὴρ δ' ὣς ἤπιος ἦεν·**
νῦν δ' αὖ καὶ **πολὺ μεῖζον,** ὃ δὴ τάχα <u>οἶκον ἅπαντα</u>
πάγχυ διαρραίσει, βίοτον δ' ἀπὸ πάμπαν ὀλέσσει.
μητέρι μοι **μνηστῆρες** ἐπέχραον **οὐκ ἐθελούσῃ,**   50
<u>τῶν ἀνδρῶν φίλοι υἷες</u> οἳ ἐνθάδε γ' εἰσὶν ἄριστοι,
οἳ πατρὸς μὲν ἐς **οἶκον** ἀπερρίγασι νέεσθαι
Ἰκαρίου, **ὅς κ' αὐτὸς** ἐεδνώσαιτο **θύγατρα,**
δοίη δ' ᾧ κ' ἐθέλοι καί οἱ κεχαρισμένος ἔλθοι·

Note that I differ from Parry in that I display differences between *speech* and *narrative* formulas. Those expressions in **boldface italicized type** occur elsewhere in Homer with some regularity in the metrical slot in which they appear here, within speeches (but not exclusively in speeches). They are paradigmatic formulas in speeches. This means that if one has a string of such words, as in line 40 οὗτος ἀνήρ, τάχα, they do *not* occur together with enough regularity to justify calling them a syntagma. οὗτος occurs with ἀνήρ, a few times, but more often a form of this word simply comes in this slot, and the same goes for ἀνήρ, on its own.

The **boldface non-italicized** expressions occur *together* regularly enough for one to claim that this is not accidental. A good example of such a syntagma is line 47 πατὴρ δ' ὣς ἤπιος ἦεν.[18] A few times, it is hard to tell whether we are dealing with accidental collisions of paradigmatic formulas, or with real syntagmata that appear in broken-up form (see for example, line 44 πιφαύσκομαι οὐδ' ἀγορεύω, the elements of which occur separately several times in these slots). These ambiguous cases are indicated in <u>wave underlined</u> type here.

Comparing the **boldface non-italicized** (syntagmatic formulas in speeches) with the *plain faced, underlined* (also syntagmatic, but narrative mainly) formulas will show that there are quite few "narrative" formulas, but a good many "speech" formulas, even on this one axis of our definition. This means, from the point of view of characterization, that Telemachus at this point is not sounding like a narrator: he does use a phrase in line 51 (φίλοι υἷες) that occurs only one other time in this form of the plural, but a number of times in the singular (mainly in narrative, to describe persons fallen in battle, in the format "X the dear son of Y"). At line 46, notice that the poet has combined the two categories: πατέρ' ἐσθλόν is usually a narrative

---

[18]   Cf. *Iliad* 24.770, *Odyssey* 2.234, 5.12, 15.152.

syntagma; but ἐσθλὸν ἀπώλεσ- comes mostly in speeches.[19] It is interesting further that the most clearly identifiable narrative syntagmata here are those featuring the theme of father and son; this theme, on the macro level, can be thought of as generating the entire *Telemachy*. I will return to another narrative formula, λαὸν ἤγειρα, later, to see its deeper narrative roots.

One should notice, in looking at the stratified text above, the large amount of boldfaced type. The boldfacing in either Roman or Italic type indicates formulaic expressions found elsewhere in Homer *within speeches*— the distinction Parry did not choose to make. Those phrases that are underlined and *not* boldfaced are formulaic primarily in narrative. The proportion tells us at a glance that most of this speech is formulaic, *in its own genre of speeches*. There is little cross-over from narrative. Thus we can tentatively conclude that we are dealing with not one but two traditions of Homeric verse-making: one for *diegesis*, with a separate but equal one for *mimesis*. Conclusive proof will have to await a jointly undertaken, full-scale analysis of all the speeches in Homer. From my work thus far on both poems, it appears to me that this holds good as a rule for Homeric speeches—they employ a distinct set of formulas, showing the same sorts of ossification and flexibility as the narrative portions of the text.[20] The final thing to notice are those words in plain face type that are not underlined, which are not, in any way that I can discover, formulaic. They occur rarely, but in groups, like islands stranded in a sea of formulas. I stress that we can only identify such "islands" by the use of a dual definition of the formula. To switch metaphors for a moment, we might think of the result of our search for paradigmatic and syntagmatic formulas as resembling the weaving of a net: if this heuristic procedure replicates the poet's compositional technique, it is perhaps not accidental that weaving is one of the oldest Indo-European metaphors for verse-making. By constructing this net or sieve, we can strain out segments that are neither formulaic in the sense of repeated syntagmata or in the sense of repeated single words in a metrical slot. Of course, we should not leap to the conclusion that such portions of the verse are Homer's unique contribution to the epic. Instead, these non-formulaic portions show us the seams in the construction of the scene, probably indicating where slightly new handling of old poetic themes is being mapped out. The innovation,

---

[19]   *Iliad* 23.280, *Odyssey* 4.724–26, 4.814–16.

[20]   The apparent results fit well with the comparative evidence from Central Asian and Southeast Asian folk traditions, in which speeches comprise a separate, marked form of discourse within larger epic or dramatic structures, to the extent that they can even form their own *Kunstsprache*, distinct from that of the larger performance medium: details in Martin 1989.

of course, is not necessarily to be attributed to one man called Homer; it could already have occurred at some stage in the preceding generations of performers.

Now that I have isolated formulaic portions of this speech, I would like to illustrate a few of the gains thereby reached for understanding the epic. The test of a formula definition is its usefulness in interpretation. In this passage, we can see that syntagmatic formulas lead us to several larger observations, provided we take time to study all the other scenes in which the syntagmata appear. On the other hand, the paradigmatic formulas help one as a negative influence: they point out areas of possible innovation; then, through study of surrounding expressions, formulas or not, we can discover some of the compositional logic of the scene. This is to say that the syntagmata can be compared directly with other expressions, whereas the paradigmatic expressions do not lead us directly to comparable passages.

Let us return to the expression λαὸν ἤγειρα in line 41. The only other time that the augmented singular aorist is used comes in this same scene, at *Odyssey* 2.28. It happens to occur in the same metrical slot in the question there: νῦν δὲ τίς ὧδ' ἤγειρε; Telemachus' reply to this question is unusual because it is unmetrical. As Stephanie West observes in her commentary, his line (*Odyssey* 2.41) has an anomalous lengthening of the second syllable in λαόν.[21] However, she fails to mention the reason for the anomaly. It is clear that the lengthening is caused by displacement of a familiar formula from its usual place at the end of the line, in which the verb appears, unaugmented, six times. The formula is inflected but always has the shape of an adonic: e.g., λαὸν ἀγείρας (*Iliad* 2.664, 4.377 etc.).

To sum up at this point: the poet has Telemachus answer a question that was posed with a simple interrogative and verb by using the same verb attached to its formulaically associated noun, λαόν. The tendency in a Homeric answer to mirror the syntax of the question produces here a metrical anomaly. Speeches, which so often respond to previous speeches, are much more complex than narratives in Homer. While in narrative the λαὸν ἀγείρας formula sits comfortably at the end of the line, in this speech the speaker must augment the verb to answer the augmented form of the question-verb; but doing so destroys the metrical shape of the syntagmatic formula, turning it into a cretic, which is then obviated by lengthening the final syllable of λαόν.

---

[21] Heubeck et al. 1988, 132.

But we can go a step further. The phrase λαὸν ἀγείρας is the embodiment of a typical scene—the mustering of troops—that we can see dramatized
many times in the *Iliad*. The mustering has its own array of conventions,
as is well known. There is no doubt that the typical scene is traditional at
the narrative level. But there is something unusual in the deployment of
the formula λαὸν ἀγείρ-. When we examine all the contexts in which this
formula occurs, it emerges that the phrase is not always in Homer's voice,
but in fact five out of six times occurs within a speech made by a character,
most often by Nestor (four times).[22] But even though it is in this environment, we must recognize further that the formula occurs in the character's
retelling of a story from the past: in other words, in a narrative *within* the
speech. To take two examples, Nestor at *Iliad* 11.716, recalling his boyhood
deeds, says that a messenger came and roused the troops; Agamemnon in
Iliad 4.377, in provoking Diomedes to fight, recalls that the hero's father
Tydeus went to Mycenae once λαὸν ἀγείρων. This opens up perspectives
on a complex of narrative possibilities: in Homer, we have actual dramatization of the typical scene of mustering the troops (for instance, in *Iliad*
Books 2 and 4). Second, we have characters who *recall*, using the formula
in its line-end form, such typical scenes in the past—this sort of usage is a
clear signal, from the native informants, that the scene itself is traditional,
for *they* remember it as happening long ago. And there are two further ways
of handling this theme.

A passage at *Odyssey* 3.140, again by the master of recollection, Nestor,
tells us that after the fall of Troy, an assembly was held and the leaders
said "why they assembled the *laoi*" (τοῦ εἵνεκα λαὸν ἄγειραν). Notice that
this verse also uses the line-end formula, but is a description of a dramatic
moment within the actual type-scene of mustering the troops. We do not
need to speculate about whether the "explanation" of why a commander
called together troops is or is not part of the type-scene. Investigation shows
that it regularly *is* featured this way (e.g., *Iliad* 2.110–41, Agamemnon's
speech). So Nestor's recollection of a *past* event accords with the way Homer
dramatizes the same type of event in *present* time. We have a traditional
scene on two levels, in *diegesis* and *mimesis*.

Now, by checking all the syntagmatic formulas involving λαόν and
ἄγειρ- forms, and not just the line-end, rigidified formula, but the flex-
ibly used examples as well, we discover that the fourth way of handling the
"troop mustering" scene is unique to our passage in Book Two of the *Odyssey*.

---

[22]   *Iliad* 2.664, 4.377, 11.716, 11.770, 16.129; *Odyssey* 3.140.

Nowhere else in Homer does a character both explain *why* he gathered the troops *and* use the formula λαόν + ἄγειρ-. And yet these two strategies, separated, are well attested, and we should call them traditional. So the construction of the line (*Odyssey* 2.41), in which we have seen a metrical anomaly, is in fact completely sensible and intuitive for a poet pushing the tradition ever so slightly beyond its previous embodiments. Not only does he represent Telemachus explaining himself, but does so having him use the formula used to describe great troop musterings of the past. This sort of hyper-dramatization—making past narrative formulas refer to the immediate dramatic scenario—must finally carry some quantum of characterization for a listening audience. If we consider the effect here, Telemachus, whose own status is ambiguous, impetuously uses an old warrior's way of talking. I suggest that we see here some true characterization by style.

I will conclude with one example discovered through examining *paradigmatic* formulas. In looking at these one-word items, many times one finds surprising but rather random results. Sometimes, we can make further use of them. Take, for example, line 52, and the phrase οἳ πατρὸς μὲν ἐς οἶκον. By examining the paradigmatic formulas involved here, we learn, first, that *only* here, out of 121 occurrences of the genitive πατρὸς in Homer, does it occur in this metrical slot. Our suspicions are heightened by the similarly unique appearance of the particle + preposition μὲν ἐς. Such short words could conceivably come together in the verse almost anywhere. But in fact the combination μὲν ἐς, which is attested seven times altogether, occurs everywhere else in just one position in the line, that ending at the first long of the second foot.[23] This may be a sign that a conventional narrative pattern (contrastive particle + phrase indicating direction) is being remade at this point.

We may notice next that the combination ἐς οἶκον occurs in only two other places, both in the *Odyssey* (14.318 and 17.84), where it is at line-end. This combination could only have arisen after the loss of digamma in οἶκον. The usual way to say "into the house" in Homer is with *postposition* οἶκον ἐς, which avoids the problem of digamma altogether.[24] The difference from the usual Homeric usage led Bentley to emend the preposition to πρός, but this usage is equally rare in Homer.[25] We should keep ἐς οἶκον in the text, while seeking to discover what caused the unusual phrasing, through a consideration

---

[23] See *Iliad* 5.788, *Odyssey* 1.284, 5.460, 9.72, 15.37, 131.

[24] *Odyssey* 5.42, 115; cf. *Odyssey* 7.77.

[25] It occurs twice, in a repeated line: *Iliad* 9.147 = 9.289.

of formulaic expressions. Remembering that every phrase develops associations with context through its repeated use in particular situations, we must go about explicating by reviewing all relevant passages in order to establish the contextual register of any given phrase. All these paradigmatic irregularities are symptomatic of larger changes at the levels of theme and scene construction. What has pushed words out of their usual positions here? We may find a clue in the phrase οἶκον ... νέεσθαι, which represents a version of a widely used syntagmatic formula. The full formula is in fact οἰκόνδε νέεσθαι, which is regularly line-final and also features yet another, older way of expressing direction, by means of the accusative of the goal without preposition. Most important is that this fuller, line-final phrase maintains a quite narrow range of associations, centered on the essential theme of return *from Troy*.[26] The traditional nature of this theme is attested in several ways: the existence of an epic sub-genre of *Nostoi*, represented both within the *Odyssey* (the song of Phemius, *Odyssey* 1.326) and in a composition recognized as part of the so-called Cycle. Second, as the work of Douglas Frame has shown, the very concept of *nostos* is so traditional within epic poetry that it has already by Homer developed a nexus of further associations (especially with *noos*) that in turn structure much of the *Odyssey*.[27] Finally, there is Calvert Watkins' discovery in Anatolian tradition of the second millennium BCE an instance of the specific theme of return from Troy.[28] The theme encapsulated in the phrase οἰκόνδε νέεσθαι thus stands a good chance of being embedded in the oldest stratum of Homeric epic.

When we turn to the passage under consideration, however, we see immediately that this phrase is used in a strikingly different connection. For here reference is made to the suitors who are said to shrink from *going to the house* of Penelope's father, Ikarios, to ask for her in marriage. To an audience familiar with the conventional link between the formula οἰκόνδε νέεσθαι and heroic *nostoi*, this reapplication must seem highly ironic. Further implications affect characterization: either Telemachus at this point is shown to be badly misusing conventional language, or—I think more likely—he is depicted as one who has already the rhetorical skill to deform traditional formulas precisely in order mock his opponents. After all, it is Telemachus who is so fond of hearing heroic *nostoi* that he prevents his mother from halting a poetic rendition thereof at *Odyssey* 1.326–59. Presumably he

[26]   E.g., *Iliad* 2.290, 354, *Odyssey* 1.17; see *Iliad* 5.716 for a related formula.

[27]   Frame 1978.

[28]   Watkins 1986.

knows the language of this sub-genre. To return to the formulaic level: let us note that the innovative use of the syntagmatic formula οἰκόνδε νέεσθαι, which is remade at *Odyssey* 2.52 into ἐς οἶκον ... νέεσθαι, is highlighted for us by the attendant disruption in paradigmatic positions. This is merely a surface manifestation of the newly pointed use of an ancient theme. A further examination, for which there is no time at the moment, would show that the unique occurrence here of πατρός in this metrical slot is a similar surface marker of a shift on the larger compositional level. For the traditional thematic focus, as far as the *Odyssey* is concerned, must be the house of *one's own* father—a topic that Telemachus addresses in several important speeches. But here the linking of the two nouns, house and father, applies to *Penelope*'s family. In short, we can see here yet another level of the poet's narrative craft: the minor change in conventional phraseology, detectable through my proposed formula definition, relates to a shift in a Homeric figure's represented point-of-view. Telemachus speaks of his mother's situation rather than his own; he transfers phrasing normally referring to the speaker's situation (e.g., one's own father) to a third person (her father). The act of imaginative projection by a character adds another dimension to the already rich poetic narrative. We might consider such extensions and re-applications, proceeding from the highest levels of narrative and plot-shaping, to be the true generators of change in Homeric diction. The novelty of a shift in viewpoint, in this case, can be seen through the rips that we have examined in the formulaic texture.[29]

---

[29]   Although almost every modern interpretation of a Homeric passage will assign meaning to repeated diction, analytical studies of the Homeric formula as a pervasive poetic phenomenon have not been frequent since the date of this contribution (originally written for a conference in Grenoble, France, September 1993). Sale 1996 offers a cautious overview of types of formulas (but fails to take into account the proposals of Martin 1989). Bakker 1997 integrates formulaic expressions into a broader study of Homeric speech using Wallace Chafe's approach to narrative discourse. Minchin 2007 extends the comparison with features of natural language usage. Further new perspectives are provided by the essays in Antović and Cánovas 2016.

4

WRAPPING HOMER UP
COHESION, DISCOURSE, AND
DEVIATION IN THE *ILIAD*[1]

I. Theories and "Texts"

Among the many works of ancient verbal art that might fruitfully yield to intratextual readings, the Homeric epics stand out, not necessarily because they are the most complex (Ovid and Apuleius are far beyond them), but because, unlike later works, their very status as "texts" has always been, and remains, uncertain. Of course, this has only increased, not discouraged, criticism of the poems, so that the number of texts bent on denying textual status to the *Iliad* and *Odyssey* takes up ten times the shelf space of the poems:

> Homer was poor. His scholars live at ease
> making as many Homers as you please.
> And every Homer furnishes a book.
> Though guests be parasitic on the cook
> the moral is: *It is the guest who dines.*
> I'll write a book to prove I wrote these lines.[2]

Misguided notions of what constitutes *any* text have taken their toll on the criticism of Homer, as they have on Greek lyric.[3] In the case of the *Iliad* and *Odyssey*, moreover, the growing realization that what we read on the page could be anything from a transcript to a distant mimesis of an oral performance has complicated the interpretive task. Then again, too many who

---

[1] Originally published in *Intratextuality: Greek and Roman Textual Relations*, ed. A. Sharrock and H. Morales (Oxford: Oxford University Press, 2000), 43–65.

[2] Cunningham 1960, 35.

[3] For a sensitive critical review of the interpretation of lyric, see Johnson 1982, 4–95.

posed as Homeric literary critics have, in fact, been would-be historians, tangled up in the circular business of settling the "Homeric Question" while simultaneously making judgment calls on what "belongs" in the poems.[4] The genetic fallacy—that knowing the sources can take the place of interpreting the work—fastened tightly onto Homeric verse. Added to all this, there is the long history of Homer-abuse—what other ancient author, after all, has gained readers with nicknames like *Homêromastix* (Homer-whipper) and *Homêropatês* (Homer-trampler)?[5] While some critics, from Plato on, labored to save their innocent audiences from the wickedness or absurdity of Homer, others (moderns as well as ancients) tried to save the Poet from himself, in the form of his contradictions, "mistakes," or the alleged defacements of later versifiers. Both types of corrective effort meant manhandling the text as it was known, whether in the 4th century BCE or the nineteenth century. Allegorizing, athetizing, expurgating, slicing, suturing, willful revision— each has had its day, with the longest spate occupying almost the entire last century, from Lachmann to Wilamowitz.[6]

I do not intend to rehash the story of the critical reception of Homer. Yet it is necessary, before undertaking what I hope is a theoretical and practical advance in reading part of the *Iliad* intra-textually, to map the broad features of contemporary Homeric criticism, not only to spotlight the sort of entrenched positions that still pockmark the landscape and hinder forward movement, but also to inventory methodologies and salvage what remains useful. Basic considerations, concerning which text one uses and which commentaries, also demand this sort of caution. To take one prime example: the most recent text edition of the *Iliad* (and the only electronic edition freely available) has been produced by Helmut van Thiel.[7] What may escape the notice of inexperienced users is the editor's underlying ideological position, which has remained unchanged since his earlier work, *Iliaden und Ilias*.[8] As

---

[4]   Page (1955b and 1963) embodies this tendency, which has not yet died out: the recent attempt by Powell 1991 to revive Wade-Gery's implausible speculation correlating the origin of the alphabet and the fixation of the Homeric text similarly bypasses complex poetry in favor of simplified history.

[5]   Applied, respectively, to the grammarian Zoilus (Galen *De methodo medendi* 10:19) and the proto-philosopher Xenophanes (Diogenes Laertius *Lives of the Philosophers* 9.18). On modern misuses of Homer, see Morris 1986.

[6]   For a convenient sampling of expurgations (on moral grounds) see Murray 1934, 122–23. On the methods of Aristarchus and Zenodotus, see Nagy 1996b with bibliography. Useful histories of Homeric interpretation: Clarke 1981; Myres 1958; and Adam Parry's preface in Parry 1971. On the theory of individual songs, see Lachmann 1874.

[7]   Van Thiel 1996.

[8]   Van Thiel 1982, 28–29.

stated there, and reiterated in the prefaces to his editions, van Thiel believes that the Alexandrian critics of Homer did not have access to authentic variants from any sources; rather, all the readings attributed to them in the exegetical tradition are in fact conjectures, on a par with, say, the conjectures of Bentley. Thus, van Thiel feels it necessary to cite them only occasionally in his *apparatus criticus* (while vilifying the much fuller apparatus of T. W. Allen's *editio major*).[9] In fact, van Thiel claims that a selection of fewer than a dozen "good" manuscripts is sufficient to establish the *Iliad* text.[10] Thus, in the interests of typographical clarity at the bottom of the page, the reader is prevented from considering a number of ancient alternatives to the text as printed.

This may seem like a minor problem, not worth objecting to, were it not that van Thiel (as the title of his earlier book indicates) is one of the last of the Lachmannian *Liederjäger*, convinced that he can find the exact outlines of no fewer than four separate "poems" in the *Iliad* as we have it. Furthermore, van Thiel asserts that the *Iliad* is the product of a massive merging of these pre-existing texts by an "editor" who is one and the same as the "composer."[11] Although it is not made explicit in his text of the *Iliad*, the complex system of notations therein referring the reader to "associated" lines is meant to coincide with the editor's earlier work, in which such iterations are interpreted as the traces of unassimilated double treatments of the narrative, the "Frühilias" and "Spätilias" being detectable in this way.

Had he not put forth a widely available edition, van Thiel's work on "*Iliad*s" might be treated by contemporary Homerists as a monstrous revenant, its 700 pages devoted to a critical stance thought to have been buried long ago.[12] The stance depends on an aesthetic that refuses to take seriously the techniques of oral poetry, especially repetition in all its forms; the demands of genre and tradition; or the possibilities afforded by multiple

---

[9]   Van Thiel 1996, vii–ix; cf. Allen 1931.

[10]   He would do well to read Housman's Juvenal preface on the subjects of superstition and blind faith in editing: Housman 1961, 53–62. For a balanced view of the edition, see West 1998.

[11]   See van Thiel 1982, 24–30.

[12]   Although another irruption, also massive (879 pages), appeared as recently as 1993: Dawe's translation and "analysis" of the *Odyssey*, prefaced with a bizarre extended comparison of the text with the body of a dead girl (p. 8) undergoing a post mortem exam, and by snide remarks concerning Milman Parry. Were it not that the author had established a reputation as editor before this, a reader might be forgiven for thinking the entire work either an obsessive's delusions or an ingenious self-parody.

re-performances in interactive settings.[13] It is an aesthetic nicely satirized by Tzvetan Todorov in an essay from thirty years ago, on the quest for "primitive narrative" according to which stories must follow "laws" of verisimilitude, stylistic unity, "the priority of the serious," non-contradiction, non-repetition, and non-digression.[14] In order to envision an intratextual reading of the *Iliad*, we should reject the genetic/Analyst approach embodied by van Thiel and his adherents, precisely so that we can investigate the prematurely suppressed, messier aspects of the text in all their manifestations. In my view, contradictions, repetitions, digressions and other anomalies (for example, Book 10 of the *Iliad*, more on which below) are rich with meaning and should not be erased from our texts in the process of a misguided search for the "real" Homer.[15] That is to say, the Homeric poems *are* texts, in the sense of cohesive discourses, rather than compilations of sentences from various other texts. They happen to show features more characteristic of spontaneous, unrevised discourse, features that highly literate culture tends to reject. But this does not mean we should force them to fit a modern literary-critical mold.

Before examining the opportunities opened by this discourse-perspective, it is worth pointing out two other obstacles to the sort of intratextual reading I have in mind. Both grow out of a reaction to Analyst critical methods, and both take notice of work on oral poetics, but leave us with an *Iliad* either too "loose" or "tight" to handle as discourse. On one side lies what I shall call "structural" dogma, the belief that finding responsion between passages and lines within the *Iliad* and *Odyssey* attests to unitary, monumental composition, and therefore to one controlling intelligence, that of the genius poet Homer. One variety of this approach uses the demonstrable complexity of the poems to wrest them from the hands of "oralists," the standard line

---

[13]   A sample: van Thiel finds traces (p. 19) that the death of Patroclus must at one time have been carried out solely by Apollo, and then in another version with Hektor added, because the treatment in the existing *Iliad* violates reason: Apollo would not have been engaged in battle in Book 16 if he had heard Zeus' prohibition against gods fighting, which we have at the beginning of Book 8. For the continuing disdain of anti-oralists, see Dawe 1993, 13–19.

[14]   Todorov 1971. The article was written in 1967. On the continuing assumption by some Hellenists that works of literature ought to conform with modern criteria for coherence, see the salutary review by Lynn-George 1982.

[15]   I do not wish at this point to enter into the recent debate on the status of Alexandrian readings, on which see most fully Nagy 1998. I note only that the approach of van Thiel, Janko, and Powell requires an interlocking set of questionable assumptions, such as an early, once-and-for-all fixation of an oral performance, subsequently immune to significant variation; the possibility for precise dating of oral-formulaic texts; early widespread literacy; and the figure of a "master" composer (or editor). I address this constellation of flawed hypotheses in a work in progress.

being that, even though the epics show signs of traditional composition, no oral poem could be so structured.[16] This dogma derives, in modern times, from New Criticism, as appears most clearly in Cedric Whitman's version of the argument, *Homer and the Heroic Tradition*.[17] Whitman also brought into play two tropes that would become common in such arguments from design, the (allegedly related) patterning of early Greek vase painting and the outlining of the poem by means of elaborate, symmetrical charts.[18] The most recent versions of this approach, those of Taplin and Stanley on the *Iliad*, illustrate both the tenacity of critical fixations on structure, and the subordination of literary criticism to "real" history. Thus, Stanley's book, after 250 pages meant to delineate complicated parallels and patterns, culminates in a quite positivist chapter, "Structure and the Homeric Question," and concludes that the *Iliad* is "distanced from its inherited medium" in attaining "literary form."[19] One gets the impression that the structures are explicated mainly to argue the historical point (a sixth-century textualization of the poem). "Framing" and "ring-composition" are the devices most favored by his version of the approach; no attention is given to how an audience or reader would assimilate and react to such structures; we are meant to marvel; but some may want to ask, *cui bono*? Taplin's book appeared just a year before that of Stanley, so that they run on parallel lines, mutually unaware. By contrast with Stanley, Taplin imagines a poem that is conscious of its audience at all times. His argument, as well, heads towards a historical conclusion (that the *Iliad* was designed for performance at a three-day festival), and thus stresses structural components (a tripartite shape for the poem). But Taplin, perhaps from his experience as a critic of ancient drama, is more attuned to the effects of narrative movement throughout the composition, asking, for instance, what the effect of accumulated parallels (e.g. visit scenes) might have been on an audience. Instead of frames and rings, he works with notions of "stored allusions" and "resonances." He explicitly rejects the "scripsist" notion that only the employment of writing could have produced such effects.[20] Nevertheless there is in the book a strong tug towards

[16] Skafte Jensen (1980, 28–45) effectively rebuts arguments that cite "quality" as proof of a written text.

[17] For a fair critique of Whitman, see Tsagarakis 1982, 3–6.

[18] The reverse side of the dust cover to Whitman's book contained the whole "geometric structure of scenes in the *Iliad*," suitable for framing.

[19] Stanley 1993, 296.

[20] Taplin 1992, 36.

tight-lacing and an interest in *Fernbeziehungen*, which are then interpreted as a sign of masterly composition.[21] "It is part of the *Iliad*'s greatness, and one of the ways it rewards an attentive audience," says Taplin, "that such detailed and powerful connections are made across such huge narrative distances." Once again, the dominant, authorizing image of the structural approach is monumentality. Whether or not the distant connections are used to argue for an *Iliad* composed in writing, their existence seems to be regarded as more important than the narrative flux within the poem. We might ask: what about *near* relations? What can the immediate juxtapositions of passages, styles, and motifs, or even disjunctions, reveal?

If such approaches are laced too tight to allow one to appreciate the flow and texture of the poem, another set of responses fails to satisfy because it directs attention to "looseness" of construction, only in the service of a larger, historicizing argument about parataxis in oral poetry. This is the approach associated primarily with James Notopoulos, an early adherent of the work of Milman Parry and Albert Lord; it gained prominence later through the writings of Ong, Havelock, and other less scholarly exponents of the notion of "oral" mentality, a concept that arguably set back the study of Homeric style as much as it advanced recognition of the culturally different aspects of an archaic social context.[22] Notopoulos contrasted what he called the "paratactic and inorganic flexible unity" of Homer with later, Aristotelian ideals of poetic unity. One could easily agree with his protest against the tyranny of the *Poetics* in critical discussions of epic, however, without necessarily accepting the further step, in which Notopoulos seems to conceive of the *Iliad* and *Odyssey* as comprising nothing *but* digressions. In his reaction against the Aristotelian-inspired Analysts, he flees to the other extreme, arguing that Homeric narrative as a whole resembles the structure of its frequent paratactic clauses, the *lexis eiromenê* identified by Aristotle on the level of the sentence. Digressions, he argued, "far from being like Homer's similes, for purposes of relief, are actually the substance of the narrative, strung paratactically like beads on a string."[23]

Several questions arise from this appraisal. If digressions are in fact organic, in this new definition of the term, then why not similes as well? Why

---

[21] On "distant relations" in the poem, see now Reichel 1994, with full bibliography and critique of earlier studies.

[22] It is significant that Havelock 1963 cites Notopoulos (eight times) more than he does either Lord (five times) or Parry (three times) in his list of modern authorities, p. 328. For a critique of this school and for further bibliography, see now Bakker 1997.

[23] Notopoulos 1949, 6.

should they be "relief" any more or less than "digressions"? Why should we assume that a work displaying a heavy use of parataxis syntactically should do so at higher narratological levels? Is this not a kind of primitivist determinism? Surely Aristotle, in the discussion cited by Notopoulos (*Rhetoric* 3.9), applies his notion of additive style only to sentences; it is simply misleading for Notopoulos to claim the philosopher's "pregnant remarks" on the first sentence of Herodotus "show that he is conscious of *a type of literature*, of which Herodotus is a late survival" (my emphasis). For Aristotle's own definition of *lexis* in the *Poetics* proves that it does not extend beyond sentential syntax. He does not articulate anything like a discourse grammar, let alone a theory of "types" of literature distinguished by their different *lexeis*. Notopoulos' calculated misreading of Aristotle is only compounded in Havelock's generalizations, which verge on attributing *Urdummheit* to Homer's audience. In parataxis, he finds the expression of a "law" applicable "to all that 'knowledge' which the tribal encyclopedia may contain," i.e., discrete, isolated bits of information, all that the short attention span of pre-Classical Greeks can comprehend.[24]

Most important for what follows, this "loose" construction of epic style neglects the actual scene-by-scene interpretation of the poems, albeit in a different way than that of "tight" interpreters. While the latter focus on static, rigid structures, the former privilege an alleged *lack* of structure, only for purposes of reconstructing some sort of cognitive evolution. Both brands of theory undervalue the dynamic movement of the *Iliad* and *Odyssey*. What is wanted now, it seems, is a processual method, one that would account for the shaping of the poem in performance, and one that takes account of a generation's linguistic work in discourse analysis. The recent work of Bakker represents something in this mode, as one workable approach to outlining the rhetoric of Homeric passages through the study of deictics and discourse particles; it also offers a powerful refutation of earlier critics' resort to "parataxis."[25] But as he deals with stretches of text involving no more than a few connected sentences, Bakker's focus necessarily bypasses the level of the episode.[26] It is at this narrative level that the notion of *intra-textual*

---

[24] Havelock 1963, 185. Also involved in this view are relics of Romantic notions on Homeric primitivism, on which see now McLane and Slatkin 2011.

[25] Bakker 1997, esp. 35–53, 86–122.

[26] Other recent approaches based on structures of plot or point-of-view are quite useful but less concerned with the intratextual flow of the poem. De Jong 1997, in focusing exclusively on what she calls "focalization," sidesteps texture, pace, and order, among other key narratological aspects. Schein 1997 accommodates the idea of symmetry to an appreciation of the linear progress of narrative, at

reading, I believe, bears investigating within Homeric criticism. As a test case, *Iliad* 11.655–803 will offer us a longer narrative, the interpretation of which has several consequences for our reading of the text as also for constructing theory.

II. Tales and Texts

As the tide of battle turns against the Achaeans, and the heroes Odysseus, Diomedes, and Agamemnon are wounded, Patroclus is summoned by Achilles and sent to find out the identity of the latest casualty, whom he has glimpsed Nestor escorting from the field. A quick look into the old man's hut tells Patroclus that it is Machaon who has been hit; as he starts back to report this to Achilles, Patroclus is detained by Nestor, who proceeds to instruct him by means of a long autobiographical tale about his youthful exploits in Pylos (lines 664–762). "This lifelike picture of a little border raid," observed Leaf, "is in itself inimitable, and we may well be grateful for it. But yet, if we take it with its context, we are forced to admit that it has no bearing on the situation, and is grotesquely out of place at a moment when Patroclus has refused even to sit down, in order that he may return with all speed to Achilles."[27] As typical as this Analyst critique is, nevertheless we must resist a response that would seek to argue for the relevance of the episode: that would mean being trapped in the same interpretive mode, being forced to read the poem as though only passages that made an immediate and direct impact on advancing the plot were the ones that mattered.

Let us admit, instead, that this speech of Nestor strikes a modern listener as digressive. An "emic" poetics of the sort I am advocating would next question this very category: in ancient Greek terms, is there even an equivalent for the critical judgment embedded in "digression"?[28] Is there a value attached to the phenomenon of speaking off-topic? Norman Austin pointed the way to a less culturally biased perception of "digression" by showing that

---

a higher structural level. Morrell 1996 offers an important perspective on a "fractal" non-linear compositional style, while Minchin 1992 makes use of recent work from cognitive psychology in evaluating oral-poetic conventions.

[27] Leaf 1900, 465. He notes the "Odyssean" character of language in the episode, the use of the four-horse chariot, and the composer's supposed ignorance of western Peloponnesian topography as further evidence of lateness.

[28] Cf. J. M. Foley (1997, 2) on the project of ethnopoetics to recover the "endemic" expressive structures of narratives. Although he is speaking about a compositional, rather than evaluative, mode, the point applies equally.

this device works in two key ways within Homeric poetry: to encapsulate stories that are paradigmatic for heroic behavior and to highlight crucial moments of the plot. As Austin notes: "In paradigmatic digressions the length of the anecdote is in direct proportion to the necessity for persuasion at the moment."[29] In the case of Nestor, his anecdotal speech "is long precisely because the situation is desperate."[30]

We could build on this insight in several ways. First, while it may seem contrary to our notions of poetry, which are a late Romantic inheritance, epic is itself a form of rhetoric and so prizes persuasive speech, the more so as that speech reaches monumental proportion.[31] Furthermore, embedded in Greek syntax, morphology, and poetic diction we find traces of a different attitude than ours, one that seems to present the *highly* relevant as being "aside." Consider the noun *paradeigma*, which designates a standard, most often in the context of an overt or implied speech-act where an authority points to, shows, or mentions a different standard to an observer. Socrates in the *Apology* (23b) points out to the jury that Apollo had thus meant him to be a *paradeigma*, "as if he should say that 'this one of you, humans, is the wisest—the one who like Socrates recognized that he has no value, really, when it comes to wisdom.'" It is in the nature of *paradeigmata* to be, literally, "sideshows," with the qualification that the "side" concern is, for a time, the essential. I suggest that this paradoxical semantic field of the preverb *para-* can be explained by assuming that it is structured around the shifting nature of discourse, as it alternates between the points-of-view of speaker and addressee. That is, what appears to the *addressee* as "aside"— something requiring attention to be diverted—is from the *speaker's* viewpoint "beside"—something brought into discussion and placed quite close to the person addressed. We can extend this structure to explicate the semantics of at least three related terms describing speech-acts that form the core of important Greek discourse-genres: *parabasis* (the "step aside" of the Old Comic chorus); *parabolê* (the comparison, later "parable"—cf. Aristotle *Rhetoric* 2.20.4); and *parainesis*. The lattermost can be seen as a key genre,

---

[29] Austin 1966, 306.

[30] Austin 1966, 312. On the central importance of so-called digressions, see also Friedrich 1975, 102–7.

[31] I examine some implications of the analogy between represented speech and epic discourse in Martin 1989.

one that frames the discourse of didactic, elegiac, and even dramatic poetry in Greece.[32]

There is a wider theoretical point to be made here. By now, it should be clear that such intra-textual features as cohesion, continuity, and unity *cannot be textually* determined. Instead, they flow from a speech community's sense of appropriate, genre-bound behaviors.[33] Without a sense of these internal boundaries, i.e., a cultural poetics, we are working in the dark. Yet, even if we see that "digressions" such as Nestor's are integral to the societal speech-habits enshrined in epic, and determine that the "aside" of *Iliad* 11.656–803 is culturally and poetically essential, it remains to examine the texture of his speech. Somewhat paradoxically, that texture turns out to be distinctively different from the rest of the poem. Of course, this is not cause to delete it; by being different, it draws attention with subtle irony to the gap between Nestor's paradigm of the past and the present reality: although it is fitting for the old warrior to mark this dramatic moment with a long story, the story itself does not quite fit.

To begin at the level of theme, the story from his youth that Nestor chooses to relate hardly matches the present situation. Mabel Lang has remarked that "cattle and wars about cattle-raiding are highly irrelevant to Homer's purpose and could even be embarrassing as parallels for the war over Helen, so Homer's use of such stories despite their possible awkwardness suggests that they played a major role in Pylian tradition."[34] Although the themes might seem incongruent, we should not resort too quickly to an extra-textual solution—an alleged necessity to feature local Pylian traditions—without evidence of similar exceptions, and before exhausting intra-textual considerations. Since Homeric poetry tends towards quite the opposite tack, leveling local traditions in favor of Panhellenic narrative, an intra-textual approach seems the wiser option.[35] We should ask instead what meaning might inhere in such thematic clashes.

Another set of differences emerges when one compares Nestor's clearly paradigmatic speech with other examples of the genre within Homeric poetry. Victoria Pedrick finds not only that the *paradeigma* is unsuitable to

---

[32]   On the poetics of *parainesis,* see Chapter 12 below; Latacz 1977; and Kurke 1990. Hubbard 1991 shows that *parabases*, rather than offering mere asides, are integral sites for intertextual allusion in Aristophanes.

[33]   Létoublon 1990, 181–82 makes a similar point about repetition of messages in the *Iliad*.

[34]   Lang 1987, 334.

[35]   On epic's Panhellenic preference, see Nagy 1999b, 139–41.

the point the aged hero apparently is trying to make, but also that, unlike the seven other *paradeigma*-speeches in the *Iliad* (including three by Nestor, at 1.254–84, 7.124–60, 23.626–50), this long speech in Book 11 is not addressed to the person for whom it is meant; contains an implicit rather than overt message; and lacks details that would tailor it to the ultimate addressee.[36] "Ironically the *paradeigma* works," notes Pedrick, "on the wrong hero. Patroclus does not pass on the lesson to his friend; instead he attempts his own *aristeia*."[37]

Introducing the concept of irony into the discussion of this passage is an important first step that can take us even further. For there are several layers of irony underlying Nestor's seemingly off-target advice. Pedrick has pointed to what we might call dramatic irony: an event turns out differently than characters in the poem might have predicted; Patroclus fights in Achilles' stead, though the message of Nestor seems to have been meant for the latter. But at least two other layers emerge here, of ironies built into characterization, and it is difficult to decide which, if either, is basic. Nestor can be seen as a well-meaning adviser, an acknowledged authority and speaker, whose wisdom nevertheless is ultimately exposed as dangerously irrelevant. Or, he can be viewed, more cynically, as the villain of the piece, whose autobiographical anecdote is calibrated precisely to rouse Patroclus to fight, even beyond his mandate (with predictable results).

Parallels for either prospect occur elsewhere in Homeric verse; significantly, they also involve Nestor. Thus, in the *Odyssey*, we hear the old king hinting broadly to Telemachus that he should eliminate the suitors by imitating Orestes, who avenged his father's death (*Odyssey* 3.195–200). The heroic paradigm is clearly wrong, as even the young addressee, in this case, seems to realize, when he replies that the gods have not given *him* such strength. Nestor's misapplication of the paradigm is all the more visible to an audience because it repeats the advice of Athena/Mentes (1.289–302), but is noticeably less careful. Whereas she had told Telemachus to play Orestes' role *after* determining that Odysseus is dead (1.289), Nestor attaches no such precaution. Athetizing lines 3.199–200, as Aristophanes of Byzantium and Aristarchus did, avoids some awkwardness, but at the cost of eliminating the irony that may have been integral to traditional conventions for representing Nestor in epic. In this case, the critical response that seeks to help a Homeric character appear smarter could be bleaching out opposing

---

[36] Pedrick 1983, 57.

[37] Pedrick 1983, 68.

but subtle dramatic effects within the compositions. As for the other view, that Nestor may represent an authoritative force both irresistible and of ambiguous intent, we have the odd picture of Nestor both embodying (*Iliad* 2.20–22) and approving (2.80–83) the deceptive dream sent to Agamemnon by Zeus: a preternatural manipulator.

In the sort of critique just mentioned, the Alexandrian scholars' low tolerance for intra-textual dissonance anticipates Analyst objections. Thankfully, athetesis, as far as can be seen, did not lead to the deletion of verses in later editions, so that rich poetic material survives, even if shadowed by Hellenistic critical suspicions.[38] The case is somewhat different with variant readings, where the efforts of modern, reductive editing (see Part I above) can obscure the very details of difference and disjunction that give a varied texture to Homeric mimesis. Nestor's speech provides a good example in its first line (11.656):

τίπτε **τ'ἄϱ'** ὧδ' Ἀχιλεὺς ὀλοφύϱεται υἷας Ἀχαιῶν

Why, then, does Achilles feel pity for the sons of Achaeans ...

The OCT (Monro and Allen) and van Thiel print the particle string (which I have boldfaced and translated "then") and supply no variants in the apparatus. Allen's later *editio maior* of the *Iliad*, however, reveals that at least one family of manuscripts has, instead, at this point the word τάϱ, an enclitic conjunction that Herodian said should be read at several places in Homer.[39] In the light of recent work by Watkins, arguing that the Greek conjunction is formally and functionally matched by a cuneiform Luvian locatival particle, one might imagine that this is indeed a very old piece of Homeric Greek; further work by Katz demonstrates the degree to which it is embedded in a few restricted formula classes.[40] One of these is its use to make more forceful

---

[38]   We can only conjecture about what additional verses may have been dropped, leaving no trace in the scholia regarding the early critical opinions about their status. Recently, awareness has grown that "plus-verses" attested in Homeric papyri (but not by medieval mss.) are textually valuable and even necessary; see, for example, Natalucci 1996.

[39]   See LSJ[9] s.v., where, however, the information on mss. attestation needs updating. Mazon 1937 prints τάϱ in his text at 11.656, and translates "*pourquoi ... pleure-t-il donc tant ... .*"

[40]   Watkins 1995, 150–51. I wish to thank Joshua Katz, who kindly showed me the text of his 1996 paper delivered at the meeting of the American Philological Association, detailing the deployment of this word within Homer (now published as Katz 2007). For a sceptical appraisal of Watkins' suggestion, see Dunkel 2008. As an alternative to the view that Homeric language preserves an inherited older particle *tar, diachronically distinct in meaning and etymology from τ'ἄϱ', one could imagine the synchronic co-existence of a semantically distinct univerbated form (τάϱ) alongside the

interrogatives (who/where/why *in the world*), an effect that makes sense in Nestor's question. What deserves notice, in line with my argument, is the uniqueness of this rare particle: of the seventeen times that τίπτε occurs in the *Iliad*, only here is it followed by the archaic form τάρ. I suggest that this usage fits an attempt to make Nestor's language and style *sound old*, as though coming from a different generation.[41]

Such a micro-level stylistic feature, by itself, might seem a matter of coincidence. Therefore, it is worth remarking that the same speech contains a larger structure that also sounds like a rare archaism, a fragment of Mycenaean Greek discourse. Lines 677–81 tote up the stock netted in the Pylians' retaliatory raid on the people of Elis:

> ληΐδα δ' ἐκ πεδίου συνελάσσαμεν ἤλιθα πολλὴν
> πεντήκοντα βοῶν ἀγέλας, τόσα πώεα οἰῶν,
> τόσσα συῶν συβόσια, τόσ' αἰπόλια πλατέ' αἰγῶν,
> ἵππους δὲ ξανθὰς ἑκατὸν καὶ πεντήκοντα
> πάσας θηλείας, πολλῇσι δὲ πῶλοι ὑπῆσαν.

> We rustled together booty from the plain, a great hoard:
> fifty herds of cattle, as many flocks of sheep,
> as many herds of swine, as many broad goat-herdings,
> and as for tawny horses: one-hundred fifty,
> all mares, many with foals alongside.

The triplex τόσα ... τόσσα ... τόσ'... in this miniature catalogue is unparalleled within Homer. But the structure and the function of the list bear a close resemblance to Linear B texts, contemporary with the probable era of the Trojan War, discovered on tablets from what has been called Nestor's own "palace" at Pylos. Though dealing with grain rather than livestock, the lists of goods within a palace economy in this way pinpoint each item with "so much" (*Documents in Mycenaean Greek* 114 = PY En 609.1–3):

> Pa-ki-ja-ni-ja **to-sa** da-ma-te DA 40
> **to-so-de** te-re-ta e-ne-si: (men 14)

---

non-lexicalized particle sequence, parallel to the co-existence of γάρ and γ' ἄρ', as proposed by Nagy 2004, 73-4 and n.130, updated in the online version of 2017: http://nrs.harvard.edu/urn3:hul.ebook:CHS_Nagy.Homers_Text_and_Language.2004..

[41] One of the few Iliadic instances of interrogative *tis* + *tar* comes in the speech of an old man, Priam at *Iliad* 3.226, while two are in the poet's request formula to the Muse (1.8, 2.761—another old man's voice?).

wa-na-ta-jo-jo ko-to-na ki-ti-me-na **to-so-de** pe-mo (wheat 2) [42]

There are so many *acreages* belonging to Pakija
and there are so many fief-holds upon them: 14 men.
The private plot of ?Wanataios: so much seed ...

In sum, Nestor here is speaking exactly in the manner of Bronze Age Pylian palace officials. Such archaic—or archaizing—touches are bound to make his rhetoric stand out in the flow of the poem.[43]

At a higher stylistic level, Nestor's speech also draws attention to itself as different, at least in the high degree to which it uses a device merely glimpsed elsewhere in the *Iliad*. This is the backward-moving style of exposition that has been called "lyric narrative," a style that involves the starkest contrast between "story"—in the Formalist sense of the actual chain of events—and "discourse"—the order in which the teller recounts events.[44] When the old hero summons up his memories, it is not through a simple recollection of a raid, retold in flashback style. Instead, we are carried back through a series of narrative nodes, each prompting a chronologically earlier point (marked here as PR) to explicate motivation and cause:

> 671–72 There was a *neikos* with Elis, when I killed Itymoneus.
> (PR) 674 He was guarding his cattle.
> 675–88 His death; return and division of spoils among Pylians.
> (PR) 688 Elis owed many.
> (PR) 689 Because we had been few and in bad shape.
> (PR) 690 For Heracles had killed all but
> one son.
> 694–95 So Elis mistreated us.
> 696–97 Neleus took his share of spoils.
> (PR) 698–99 Because Elis owed him a chariot and team.
> (PR) 701–2 It went there to compete and Augeias
> kept it.

[42] See Ventris and Chadwick 1973, 241–45 on #114–16 (= PY En 609, 74, 659); also, Bennett and Olivier 1973, 112–13. For another close parallel between a Pylos Mycenaean text and Homeric poetry, see Lang 1987, 334 on social structure as reflected in PY Cn3 and *Odyssey* 3.4–8. *Prima facie*, it is not impossible for such discourses to survive embedded in Homeric diction: for evidence that a major syntactic feature, so-called "tmesis," survives from *pre*-Mycenaean Greek in Homeric diction, see Horrocks 1980.

[43] The scholia (T ad 11.678–81) sense a stylistic difference: "one did not say these things any differently even in prose (*pezôi ... logôi*).

[44] On the complex structure and its similarity to Pindaric narrative, see Schadewaldt 1966:83–84. On the notions of story and discourse, Chatman 1978.

703–5 So Neleus had his share and made fair division of the rest.
706–61 Counter-raid by Elis, Nestor's *aristeia*.

Nestor's paradigmatic discourse about his youthful exploits steps back from its story-line three times; two of these involve further back-tracking. Whether or not the Iliadic narrator has aimed here at capturing an archaic discourse style, there can be no doubt that Nestor's way of describing his past is clearly different, at the structural level, from the poet's own mode of narration.[45] But it does not necessarily follow that Nestor's way is worse, or that, as Slater has suggested, "it must be meant to illustrate the deliberate bumbling of Nestor."[46] We could, after all, define Homeric style as deviating from an older norm represented by the mellifluous Nestor.[47]

Differentiation of the type we have been analyzing occurs as well in the content of Nestor's tale. While it is true that the description of his triumph resembles the typical Iliadic *aristeia*, complete with helpful divinities, a crisis (750–51), battlefield biographies (739–41), and even a simile (747), Nestor's narrative also contains conspicuous features at variance with the surrounding epic.[48] He moves across a wider range of terrain and time, signposting each stage with geographical or temporal formulaic markers:

711 ἔστι δέ τις Θρυόεσσα πόλις αἰπεῖα κολώνη
There is a city Thryoessa, a steep hill ...

722 ἔστι δέ τις ποταμὸς Μινυήϊος εἰς ἅλα βάλλων
There is a river Minueios running to the sea

725 ἔνθεν πανσυδίῃ σὺν τεύχεσι θωρηχθέντες
From there with all speed, armed with gear ...

753 ἔνθα Ζεὺς Πυλίοισι μέγα κράτος ἐγγυάλιξε·
Then Zeus granted great power to the Pylians

[45] A point that is missed by Dickson 1995, who stresses the similarities between Nestor and narrator. If a style shared with much lyric is, indeed, marked as sounding "older," and therefore appropriate to Nestor, this would accord with Nagy's findings (1990) regarding the relative antiquity of lyric meter vs. Homeric hexameter.

[46] Slater 1983, 122.

[47] For appreciation of the persuasive artistry of Nestor's speech here, see Minchin 1991 and Dickson 1995, 173–79.

[48] On the similarities, see Pedrick 1983: 63–66; also, Fenik 1968, 113 who notes that "Nestor relates everything much more hurriedly than the poet himself normally does"; Hainsworth 1993, 298; and Dickson 1995, 173.

759   ἔνθ' ἄνδρα κτείνας πύματον λίπον· αὐτὰρ Ἀχαιοὶ
           Then having killed the last man I left him ...

Similar phrases structure the poem's wider narrative, but never occur bunched in such small compass. The conclusion of the battle, also, is unlike anything in the *Iliad* in its elevation of the young hero to divine status:

761   πάντες δ' εὐχετόωντο θεῶν Διὶ Νέστορί τ' ἀνδρῶν.
           They all prayed to Zeus, among gods, and Nestor among men.[49]

Most striking, however, is the unique generic complexion of the tale, for the battlefield *aristeia* is only half the story; the episode starts with a nighttime raid that is clearly a warrior's initiation (11.683–85):

           καὶ τὰ μὲν ἠλασάμεσθα Πύλον Νηλήϊον εἴσω
           ἐννύχιοι προτὶ ἄστυ· γεγήθει δὲ φρένα Νηλεύς,
           οὕνεκά μοι τύχε πολλὰ νέῳ πόλεμον δὲ κιόντι.

           And we drove them into Pylos, Neleus' town,
           by night. And Neleus was glad at heart
           because much fell to me when I went new to war.

The traditional nature of this raid story can be detected even within Homeric diction: the name of Achilles' son, Neoptolemus, "new to war," encapsulates the theme of Nestor's tale. In its only two appearances within epic (*Iliad* 19.327, *Odyssey* 11.506), the name occupies exactly the metrical position (after the trochaic caesura) that the phrase νέῳ πόλεμον fits here. And the *Odyssey* passage reflects the same narrative movement: Achilles in the underworld rejoices (γηθοσύνη, *Odyssey* 11.540) on hearing Odysseus relate the story of young Neoptolemus' wartime exploits, as Neleus rejoiced (γεγήθει) over his son. Comparative evidence from the early literature of Ireland and India (cultures with traditions cognate to Greek) shows that initiatory raid stories, with similar details, are a very old genre.[50] It is the occurrence of this theme, and not any alleged "late" compositional traits that accounts for the similarity between Nestor's tale and the *Odyssey* at the level of diction. The appearance of a number of words only here in the

---

[49] Schadewaldt 1966, 86.

[50] See Bader 1980; also Athanassakis 1992, with further bibliography. Frame 1978, 86–115 brilliantly recovers the mythopoeic resonances of Nestor's cattle-raid in Indo-European terms. His findings concerning the story in *Iliad* Book 11 are expanded and further solidified in Frame 2009, 48–49, 105–21, 728–33.

Iliad, but with parallels in the *Odyssey*, does not mean that an "*Odyssey-Poet*" composed Nestor's speech.[51] It does alert us, however, to a shift in style within the *Iliad*, as if the nighttime and fantastic world of the other epic, in which a solitary hero lives by his wits, bubbles up into Nestor's memory. The *Odyssey*, of course, is framed by a detailed initiation story, that of Telemachus, like Nestor (11.693) a lone son.[52] Formally and functionally, the initiation tale reminds us of the famous "digression" concerning the scar of Odysseus (*Odyssey* 19.393–466).[53] That story of first-blood precedes a heroic epiphany, as does Nestor's the epiphany of Patroclus, albeit the latter story, as Pedrick saw, ironically substitutes the telling of an old *aristeia* just when a new, live version is demanded.[54]

Thus, the deep mythic past and a temporally closer epic expression of theme in the *Odyssey* offer two "intertexts" of Nestor's raid story.[55] But intratextually, it seems to stand, like its protagonist, alone. It marks itself out as different. Raids and booty are mentioned in the poem, in connection with the earlier deeds of Achilles: his sack of Lurnêssos (20.187–94) and Thêbê (1.366–69, 6.414–28), the latter being the ultimate cause of his quarrel with Agamemnon. These, however, remain off-stage; like the Fall of Troy (also described in terms of booty—cf. 9.138, 18.327), raids are never dramatized in the poem. There is one significant exception: the *Doloneia* of Book 10.

If it seems that comparing Book 11 with 10 is to analyze *obscurum per obscurius*, this is mainly because the episode describing the night-raid of Diomedes and Odysseus has suffered the same critical dismissal as Nestor's tale. Burnt with the brand of "late," "unIliadic," and "interpolated," it has failed to attract attention for its poetic qualities. This is unfortunate; whatever its origins, Book 10 *has* been integrated into the *Iliad*. As the latest commentator says, "although since antiquity opinion has been virtually universal among Homerists that the Book does not form part of the design

---

[51] For the list, see Cantieni 1942, 12.

[52] See Martin 1993 on the poetic implications of this framing.

[53] It is interesting that 11.677 ἤλιθα πολλὴν, found only here in the *Iliad*, occurs in the scar-story (*Odyssey* 19.443).

[54] Pedrick 1983, 66.

[55] For a cogent analysis of how the term might apply to Greek oral traditions, see Edmunds 1995, 4–7. I do not mean to imply that the *Iliad* refers to other written texts; it may make reference to fairly fixed *themes*.

of the *Iliad* ... the Book is not an *Einzellied*."[56] I suggest that it is precisely at such junctures—when a passage is judged "different"—that intratextual criticism proves most useful. All that we have learned from the continuing study of intertextuality can aid us in making more fine-scale and sophisticated internal analyses: "In principle, the same forces of cohesion and disintegration are in operation within a text as between texts."[57]

The apparent "disintegration" caused by Book 10 must be seen in close relation to the following episode. Diction provides signals towards this reading: for example, "Odyssean" language has been seen to characterize Book 10, like Nestor's story.[58] Athena plays a major role, and receives offerings, in both episodes (10.460, 11.729). More pointedly, it is Nestor who devises the spy-mission (10.204–17), and Nestor who waits to welcome them back joyfully (10.532–53), as his father did long ago for him. In short, any attempt to dismiss Book 10 from our *Iliad* must be constrained by the appearance of this raid theme, in stylized remembrance, in Book 11. As much as Nestor's, Diomedes' raid is a *rite de passage*.[59] They are mutually reinforcing, shared attempts to vary the texture of the poem. To put the critical situation more positively, Nestor's story is clearly all one piece: a raid and distribution (11.671–707) followed by a pitched battle (708–61), both within an initiatory setting. There is no reason why the *Iliad*, as a larger-scale discourse, should not then include both night raid (Book 10) and day battles. To represent the entirety of heroic experience, the poem, in fact, *must* include both sides.[60]

To conclude, we can go further into the poetics of the *Iliad* as a whole by paying attention to three devices interacting here, all of which are central to intratextual analysis. First, framing. Nestor's story with stress laid on the proper compensation that resulted from his raid (11.696–705) is thematically relevant to the outer story, the initial conflict of the *Iliad*, centered on the theme of fair division.[61]

---

[56] Hainsworth 1993, 151; on the arguments for separate authorship, see his summary of the controversy, pp. 151–55. Further on Book 10: Fowler 2000.

[57] Kolarov 1992, 35.

[58] Hainsworth 1993, 154.

[59] On this see Schnapp-Gourbeillon 1982.

[60] Another excursive passage, on the Shield, seems to make an effort to combine the two types of fighting, by *dolos* and by *biē*: 18.516–40. These may be emblematized within the passage by the unusual cooperation of Ares and Athena (18.516).

[61] The theme is embodied in the formula *dais—eisê*: cf. *Iliad* 1.468, 602; 2.431 and esp. 9.225 (with Hainsworth 1993, 94–95) and cf. 11.705: δαιτρεύειν, μή τίς οἱ ἀτεμβόμενος κίοι ἴσης.

The strategy of valorizing what might otherwise seem like intrusive or extraneous episodes by relating them to a frame-narrative relies on the recognition of similarity.[62] The same happens, to some extent, with the second phenomenon involved here: the *mise en abyme*, a text-within-text that functions as a microcosm or mirror of the text itself.[63] I propose that Nestor's narrative in Book 11 is precisely such a mirror, but that it is a distorting device. As the *mise en abyme* in modern fiction has been found to suggest other possibilities for the narrative, "to fill in 'blanks' when abundant, form them when scarce, or hollow them out by filling them," in Dällenbach's words, so Nestor's autobiography works to heighten our sense of difference within the poem's world. It draws our attention precisely because it is itself so different in texture and style from what precedes. The battle at Troy is not the same as a Pylian raiding expedition; Patroclus is not a young initiate, nor is Achilles (if anyone, it is Diomedes); Helen is not the same as stolen cattle. To the *Iliad*'s propensity for depicting faulty communication (cf. Agamemnon's Dream), surely we should attribute the contrast between Nestor's paradigm about booty and Achilles' already-stated rejection, during the Embassy, of exactly this model (9.406–9):

> Cows and sturdy flocks can be got by raids [*lêistoi*]
> Tripods are to be had, and tawny horses' heads,
> But a man's *psykhê* cannot return or be taken as booty [*lêistê*] ...

Achilles already realizes that glory at Troy can only mean his death, not the start of a glorious career. Nestor's paradigm does *not* fit, and is meant to be *seen* not fitting. If it succeeds, it is only because a more gullible audience hears the old man's Siren song.[64] I leave to critics with a more deconstructive bent the conclusions to be drawn from such a representation of rhetoric and reception. At any rate, I believe this effect is all the more highlighted by the third intratextually charged feature: juxtaposition. The *Doloneia*, after all, did not have to precede so closely Nestor's paradigmatic persuasion, nor did it have to come so close on the heels of Achilles' rejection of the raid-mentality. The process of performance, however, that singer-audience proximity that must underlie the *Iliad* at some point, produces meaning and coherence from

---

[62]   Frangoulidis 1997 is a good illustration of this sort of reading.

[63]   On the role of *mise en abyme* in enabling a reading of the larger text, see Dällenbach 1986, 9–23, and Fowler 2000.

[64]   See Dickson 1995, 195–97 on Nestor as Siren. To my mind, he does not account for Nestor as an even more sinister figure.

this very device of close "bundling" of episodes that are meant to be felt as related.[65] I stress this device because it gives value to a poetic phenomenon that is at the opposite extreme from the long–distance, structural connections often favored by those who defend Homeric artistry.

What results for our interpretation from the combination of these poetic strategies? At one level, the *Iliad* appears to offer a sobering view of its own constructedness: the poetic description of individual *aristeiai*, the art that occupies much of the poem itself, is revealed to have its roots in highly contingent, rhetorically slanted autobiography. Even the management of war, if we consider Nestor's choreography as central to the plot of Book 10, is seen to stem from a commander's memory of his own youthful raiding experience. On another level, the poem clearly makes a point of transcending personal experience, of deriving its narrative not from human *kleos* but from divine autopsy (*Iliad* 2.484–93), as if the poet realizes thoroughly the persuasive perils of stories like Nestor's. Then again, paying heed to the order in which Books 10 and 11 unfold—which is to say, processing the poem, like an audience, intratextually, with all its bumps and fissures—action precedes meditation. We feel the excitement, *first*, of the raid and kill (Book 10) before we realize, in the *next* episode, that Nestor has staged it all, perhaps even in a misguided attempt to relive his own youth. That realization is itself a bitter message, but no more acidic than the rest of the *Iliad*'s careful dissection of the mechanics of glory. In this intratextual reading, finally, the *Iliad* understands itself far better than did many of its future listeners and critics; its composer, one senses, would understand the lament of a much later writer (and ex-Marine), the late André Dubus: "I have always known that writing fiction had little effect on the world; that if it did, young men would not have gone to war after the *Iliad*."[66]

---

[65]   See the essays in Gernsbacher and Givón 1995 on the phenomenon within natural language.

[66]   Dubus 1991, 87.

II

MYTHIC HYMNISTS,
HISTORICAL PERFORMERS

5

APOLLO'S KITHARA AND POSEIDON'S CRASH-TEST

RITUAL AND CONTEST IN THE EVOLUTION OF GREEK AESTHETICS[1]

The concepts of verbal articulation (*logos*) and material craft-ability (*tekhnê*) are related in the ancient Greek imaginary. This relationship has played a major role in shaping the ways in which we still understand aesthetics and performance, as well as the aesthetics of performances. Some important features in the early Greek development of this intellectual matrix form the core of what follows, as I examine two specific examples in order to highlight the bonds among craft, art, ritual, and performances (verbal, as well as other) in the ancient Greek *mentalité*. As with so many Greek performance traditions, those that I shall analyze have been "mythologized" through consistent references to the functions and typical behaviors of certain divine figures: here, Apollo and Poseidon.

What unites the mythopoetic examples that we shall examine is the presence of the contest (*agôn*) and the crucial notion, arising from this quintessential Greek idea, of *krisis*, which we can translate "judgment under pressure."[2]

As an indication of their enduring importance as well as the high stakes involved in these concepts, we should take note of the semantic shading of their English derivatives: "agony" and "crisis." It seems, in other words, that for mortals to make an impact through *logos* and *tekhnê* is potentially fraught

---

[1] Some material in this essay also appears an article published in Spanish as "Apolo, el ejecutante," in *Mito y performance: De Grecia a la modernidad*, ed. A. M. González de Tobia (La Plata, Argentina: Editorial de la Universidad Nacional de La Plata, 2010), 17–41.

[2] Fundamental for the discussion of *agôn* is Nagy 1990, 385–87, also 118–22; for *krisis* 61–63; in relation to *agôn* 402–3.

with dangers, rendering the outcomes—expressions and arts of all types—all the more precious. This attitude toward verbal and material craft, arising from a specific context of rituals and festivals, may be said to mark the classical tradition in literature and art for all of subsequent Western culture.

Once we have acknowledged the prejudice encapsulated in our typical application of the adjectives "humble" to craft, versus "intricate" to art, we might ask how we can escape the attitudes fostered by industrialization, technology (a word to which I shall return), elitist education, post-Enlightenment privileging of the "rational" and the closely related Romantic equating of "traditional" with "primitive." The philologist's instinct is to delve into the earliest texts and pay attention to the nuances of usage and diction regarding *logos* and *tekhnê*. This is not the place for a full-scale analysis.[3] Instead, let us observe that the most striking result of such investigations, in terms of the cultural attitudes they indicate, is that material and verbal skills (those that we can tentatively assign, respectively, to *tekhnê* and *logos*) are not in a relationship of subordination (one low and the other higher). Weaving, carpentry, metalworking, painting, sculpture, embroidery—all of these *tekhnai* are by no means humble. They are instead quite literally divine.

From our earliest sources in Mycenaean Greek, it is obvious that such crafts and their practitioners are not only of highest value to the palace economies of Pylos, Knossos, Thebes, and Chania. They are also intimately tied to the religious rituals of the Mycenaean kings. Weaving women and shining cloth, well-shaped chariots, their wheels, poles, and chassis, subject to collection and redistribution by the central palaces, are not only the prerogatives of the elite but are integral to the display of power and control. And that display, in turn, is crucial for the mediating role of Mycenaean kings, between the gods and their subjects.[4] Of course, the bureaucratic texts in Mycenaean, such as we have them preserved on thousands of accidentally baked clay tablets in Linear B script, narrowly represent an entire culture that flourished between circa 1600–1200 BCE. They offer evidence for the organization and transfer of people and objects, but can tell us nothing of what the elites and their subjects *thought* about crafts. For the latter, the historian of ideas must rely on the testimony of a later era, the hexameter poetry of the archaic period (circa 750–500 BCE) that is attributed to Hesiod, along with the epics

---

[3]   For debates concerning the developing notions of *logos*, see the essays in Buxton 1999.

[4]   On Mycenaean palace economies and religious functions, see Lupack 2008. On the redistribution of luxury and other goods, see Killen 2008.

attributed to Homer (whom later ages supposed contemporary with Hesiod), and the "Homeric" hymns to various divinities. Once one focuses on notions of craft in this body of verse (something we tend to gloss over while reading for character and plot), an abundance of scenes and connections emerges. Let me mention just a few that can underscore the importance of craftwork to religion, and its "religious" status.

We can start with the most obvious, the employment of craft-workers to decorate and amplify the specific performances of worship. A bull to be sacrificed, for instance, could have its horns gilded. The *Odyssey*, describing how Telemachus is welcomed to a magnificent feast in Nestor's city of Pylos, takes care to include mention of a *khalkeus* or bronze-worker, named Laerkês, who also handles gold (*Odyssey* 3.432–38):

> ἦλθε δὲ χαλκεὺς
> ὅπλ᾽ ἐν χερσὶν ἔχων χαλκήϊα, πείρατα τέχνης,
> ἄκμονά τε σφῦράν τ᾽ εὐποίητόν τε πυράγρην,
> οἷσίν τε χρυσὸν εἰργάζετο· ἦλθε δ᾽ Ἀθήνη
> ἱρῶν ἀντιόωσα. γέρων δ᾽ ἱππηλάτα Νέστωρ
> χρυσὸν ἔδωχ᾽· ὁ δ᾽ ἔπειτα βοὸς κέρασιν περίχευεν
> ἀσκήσας, ἵν᾽ ἄγαλμα θεὰ κεχάροιτο ἰδοῦσα.

> There came the bronze-worker, with bronze tools in his hands,
> the essentials of his craft [*tekhnê*],[5] anvil and hammer and well-made tongs,
> with which he worked gold. Athena came also to participate in the rites.
> The old horseman Nestor gave the gold. And the smith then working it,
> sheathed the bull's horns, so that the goddess might take delight seeing the dedication.

As the language makes clear, the mediation of a craftsman transforms the natural object into an art-object, an attractive, pleasing dedication (like a cult statue: *agalma* can also mean this).[6] At the same time, the explicit transfer of the precious gold from the king's palace to the craftsman makes clear that the success of a pleasing, beneficial ritual for the community depends on the intervention of the royal house.

---

[5] Note that *peirata tekhnês* can also be honorific: the "ultimate limits" of craft—as if the tools *embody* his *tekhnê*. On the complex semantics of *peirar*, see Bergren 1975.

[6] For *agalma* as cult statue, see Nagy 1990, 364.

The same passage, with its mention of Athena (who is disguised as Mentor, an older man guiding Telemachus on his journey) should remind us that crafts have divine patronage as well. Athena *Erganê*, the "worker," is connected with the arts of cloth-production, especially as they relate to the making of fabrics that are dedicated to gods—like herself.[7] At the Panathenaea (depicted on the Parthenon frieze), one such woven article, the *peplos* for Athena's great statue on the Acropolis, is carried in a dedicatory procession.[8] Hephaestos, on the other hand, is connected with the working of metal. It is Athena who is linked further, by her very genealogy, with the kind of thinking characteristic of "craft": *Mêtis* or "cunning intelligence," her mother, was a goddess swallowed by Zeus to enable the chief god to control this potentially dangerous and deeply female "way of knowing." *Mêtis* as common noun denotes as well non-linear, intuitive, on-the-spot, in-a-pinch capacities, the kind of peripheral mental vision and know-how that characterizes the helmsman of a ship and the driver of a chariot.[9] The latter is especially relevant to the scenario I shall examine shortly.

In all the employments of *mêtis*, what we discover is that "craft" is a totalizing and honorific concept inclusive of "art" in the senses that the West has tended to use since the eighteenth century (as in "the fine arts"). Craft is at times closer to "craftiness," at other times to "artfulness." The key point is that *tekhnê* does not distinguish those ways of acting that will later be sorted out, contested, at times opposed to one another, as varied and divergent skills.

This is a good point at which to remind ourselves that *logos* is equally rich and broad in ancient usage. Sometimes interpreted as an overarching concept that covers the range represented by the Latin pair of terms *ratio* and *oratio*, *logos* is both mental skill (reason, intelligence—even *cunning intelligence*) and the product thereof (an account, verbal art). In the later sense, as becomes clear, it will tend to overlap with *tekhnê*, rather than be its polar opposite. For the making of well-shaped, appropriate, reasonable speech is as much a craft (or art) as is the weaving of cloth or the fashioning of useful objects in wood. It is emblematic of this association that the art/craft of poetry is presented within Greek poetry metaphorically in terms of weaving (*huphanas humnon*, "having woven a song": Bacchylides 5.9–10) and carpentry (*tektones kômôn*,

---

[7]   On the goddess under her Athenian cult-title, see Pausanias *Description of Greece* 1.24.3.

[8]   See for a full description of this event and perspectives thereon, Neils 1992.

[9]   On "cunning intelligence," see Detienne and Vernant 1978.

"shapers of celebration songs": Pindar *Nemean* 3.4–5).[10] In modern Greek, the word for literature—*logotekhnia* ("wordcraft")—perfectly encapsulates a point of view that can already be detected in Greek texts from two and a half millennia earlier.[11]

Time now to turn to the first of two case-studies.

Crash Test

In the *Hymn to Apollo* (circa 500 BCE?), which Thucydides, at least, attributed to Homer (3.104), the god is celebrated as the divine patron of two supremely important cult sites in Greece: the island of Delos and the mountain shrine at Delphi. The hymn narrates his birth in Delos, and then, in a very compressed *Bildungsroman*, his voyage to Delphi to establish the Pythian cult-center there. I will concentrate in the second part of this paper on the "crafts" united in Apollo's divine repertoire—specifically music and poetry (taken as a unitary pair) and archery. These he possesses from his birth onward. But there is a mysterious episode, on his foundational journey, that involves another god and another craft. While journeying through Boeotia in his progress toward Parnassus, the young god Apollo stops at Onchestus, about twenty-five kilometers northwest of Thebes (which, the *Hymn* stresses, is not yet a city). The grove of Poseidon appears to have occupied the narrow pass (at modern Stení) on the road overlooking the Teneric Plain to the east and the Kopaic basin to the west.[12] The poet of the hymn provides a brief and intriguing digression about the place (230–38):

> Ὀγχηστὸν δ' ἷξες Ποσιδήϊον ἀγλαὸν ἄλσος·
> ἔνθα νεοδμὴς πῶλος ἀναπνέει ἀχθόμενός περ
> ἕλκων ἅρματα καλά, χαμαὶ δ' ἐλατὴρ ἀγαθός περ
> ἐκ δίφροιο θορὼν ὁδὸν ἔρχεται· οἱ δὲ τέως μὲν

---

[10] The metaphors are both of Indo-European date: see Durante 1976 and Nagy 1996a, 74–76.

[11] It is worth noting that another compound-noun—*tekhnologia*—containing the same lexical elements, in reverse order, points to the importance of verbal expression in relation to material skill: successful "technology" requires giving a reasoned account of craft; the ability to persuade (through diagram, theory, and proof) is central even to fields that seem at the furthest remove from verbal art; or, to speak gnomically: *tekhnologia* needs *logotekhnia*.

[12] Schachter 1986, 207–20 provides details of archaeological and inscriptional finds at the site, indicating a Bronze Age occupation and later cult activity dating to at least the sixth century BCE. The age of the cult is uncertain; it may continue practices of the second millennium. Teffeteller 2001 points to similar Near Eastern chariot rites of that era.

κείν' ὄχεα κροτέουσιν ἀνακτορίην ἀφιέντες.
εἰ δέ κεν ἅρματ' ἀγῇσιν ἐν ἄλσεϊ δενδρήεντι,
ἵππους μὲν κομέουσι, τὰ δὲ κλίναντες ἐῶσιν·
ὡς γὰρ τὰ πρώτισθ' ὁσίη γένεθ'· οἱ δὲ ἄνακτι
εὔχονται, δίφρον δὲ θεοῦ τότε μοῖρα φυλάσσει.

You reached Poseidon's glorious grove, Onchestus,
where the new-tamed colt takes a breather, burdened as it is
pulling the beautiful chariot, and on the ground goes the driver, even
a good one,
having leapt from the chariot. Meanwhile, the horses
casting off his lordship rattle the empty vehicle.
If the chariot breaks in the wooded grove,
they take care of the horses, but they leave the chariot tilted up.
For thus first of all was the sacred rite. And they pray to the lord,
but the god's dispensation then guards the chariot.

What does this strange ritual mean?[13] Why is it even mentioned in the hymn? With religious rites, a linear interpretation is less persuasive—I would say, less possible—than an attempt to appreciate the multiple meanings, latent and overt, generated by a series of actions in the sacred sphere. The rite surely re-affirms and celebrates the commanding role of Poseidon when it comes to horses and horsemanship. Why the sea-god who is also the earth-quake god (a scientific accuracy, tsunamis being no doubt known to the ancients) should be Hippios—Poseidon of Horses—has always been a matter for speculation. At an abstract level, the mystical association of sea-god with horse-god might well depend on the uncontrollable nature of both elements: in other words, horses are like the sea, and he who rules one can control the other. By extension chariots are like boats—and there is ancient evidence for this association.[14] A wonderful image bringing the two together is that of Poseidon guiding his gold chariot from his sea-cave at Aegae across the sea on his way to aid the Greeks in their battle at Troy (*Iliad* 13.25–30):

γέντο δ' ἱμάσθλην
χρυσείην εὔτυκτον, ἑοῦ δ' ἐπεβήσετο δίφρου,
βῆ δ' ἐλάαν ἐπὶ κύματ'· ἄταλλε δὲ κήτε' ὑπ' αὐτοῦ

---

[13] The latest assessment, with a good summary of previous scholarly attempts, is Teffeteller 2001. Opinions range from seeing it as soliciting an augury to considering it as a test for horses and chariot–driving warriors.

[14] See Nestor's "hymn" to *mêtis* in *Iliad* 23.313–18, which associates woodcutters, helmsmen, and charioteers as those who use this intelligence.

πάντοθεν ἐκ κευθμῶν, οὐδ' ἠγνοίησεν ἄνακτα·
γηθοσύνῃ δὲ θάλασσα διίστατο· τοὶ δὲ πέτοντο
ῥίμφα μάλ', οὐδ' ὑπένερθε διαίνετο χάλκεος ἄξων·

... he took his golden whip, well-made, and mounted the platform of his chariot, and drove over the waves, and sea creatures
played about beneath emerging from their lairs, nor did they fail
to recognize their lord [*anakta*]. In gladness the sea parted and
the horses flew fast and beneath the chariot the bronze axle did
not moisten.[15]

Compare the associations of this scene of godly ease and control with
the ritual of Poseidon at Onchestus, in which a *failure*, a chariot crash is
commemorated. In the logic of divine–human relations that applies as well
to the celebration of heroes in ancient Greece, the human element, even
in failure, can stand as a signal token of the god's superhuman power and
success. There is a power, a *mysterium tremendum* in Poseidon's grove. The
ritual calls for a human to surrender control: even one who is a good driver
(*elatêr agathos*, line 232) must leave his comfort zone, his place of special
power and control. The charioteer then goes on the ground like his opposite, the foot soldier, while his horses and chariot continue without him. It is
important that he is said to "leap" out of the chariot (233) in what must itself
be a conspicuous display of courage and skill, as well as a useful maneuver
for battle.[16]

The loss of control by the charioteer who jumps from his moving vehicle
has a different meaning for a second category of participants in the rite, the
horses (or perhaps at least one horse, the newly-trained colt).[17] This horse,
no longer driven, gets to draw breath (*anapneei*). The diction is that which
is used in the *Iliad* to describe the rare moment of refreshment that occurs
for fighters in the heat of battle (e.g., *Iliad* 16.42, 18.200). Significantly,
such moments in the *Iliad* are provided by the heroic fighting of others or
by the intervention of a god (like Poseidon himself in Book 13). We could
imagine this refreshing pause for the horse as a gift from its heroic human

---

[15]   On this scene and its congeners in epic, see Nagy 2009, 1§148.

[16]   Those with a West Coast, New Age religious bent will see precisely this gesture as spiritual
wisdom, abandonment to the divine—probably not exactly what the Greek action signified. On
another Californian note, I would compare the similar, albeit illegal, display of manhood known in
some Oakland neighborhoods as "ghost-riding," in which tricked-out street-racers replace horse-
drawn chariots, and drivers jump out of their moving cars.

[17]   For the debate over the number of horses involved, see Teffeteller 2001. I assume that the colt
can be metonymic for the paired horses involved.

charioteer, as if from a fellow-fighter. Or, in a more competitive spirit, we can think of this as something the horses wrest from their controlling human master. Slightly in favor of the latter interpretation is the language of release: the horses proceed into the grove "casting off their lordship" (*anaktoriên aphientes*). The moment is one of liberation. One of the interesting further features of the ritual, whether we think collaboration or competition, is what happens with the now driverless chariot. As the poem says, "They rattle the empty chariot along." The verb *kroteousin* has the sense of hitting (cf. the derived noun *krotala* "cymbals"), as if the horses are aggressively trying to lose the last vestige of the human culture that has been attached to them. On the one hand, to wax more abstract for a moment: we have the *phusis* of the horses, as it were on cruise control, without a human at the reins, but under the superhuman observation (or even control) of Poseidon. The god, I would argue, like the horses, is both symbol and embodiment of *phusis* "nature," as contrasted with human *nomos* ("law, custom, habit")—that is to say, all the arts, crafts, and technology that make culture possible. The artifice of humans is here abandoned almost on an experimental basis, or as a gamble, an odd sort of horse race.[18] And the experiment, like the athletic event of leaping from the moving chariot, is in itself very modern sounding. It is, in brief, the ultimate crash test (without dummies). That is to say, the rattling, jostled, driverless car is subjected, through this yielding of *nomos* to *phusis*, to all of the unpredictable shocks and bumps that a new Volvo is given in a Swedish automobile-manufacturing torture chamber. As the poem continues, "if the chariot breaks in the wooded grove, on the one hand they take care of the horses, but on the other hand they leave it [the chariot] having tilted it up. For this was the holy rite at the very first. And they pray to the lord and then the portion/lot of the god [*moira*] guards the chariot." There is no doubt that what we witness in the *Hymn to Apollo* is a long-standing ritual practice, within the very terms of the poem. While we do not know of the relationship in absolute terms of the establishment of Poseidon's cult versus that of Apollo, in narrative terms, the brief digression places the one prominently before the other, just as Poseidon is older than his nephew Apollo. It is proper to note in this connection that chariot-rituals are crucial components of kingship inaugurations in ancient India and medieval Ireland, a commonality that argues for an Indo-European cultural practice underlying

---

[18] Pindar *Isthmian* 1.32–33, 52–54 and *Isthmian* 4.19–23 imply that real horse-races were conducted at the shrine of Poseidon in Onchestus.

the whole complex.[19] So the presentation (at least in poetic narrative) of the chariot-ritual along the young Apollo's way to his new seat of power may have significance as a marker of his own inaugural moment. In the immediate context of the Onchestus ritual, there is no explicit mention of kingship, it is true. And yet, as we noted, the poem's language recalls something not far from it. "Lordship" (*anaktoriê*) is the quality of being an *anax*. From Mycenaean texts, it appears that this term (in older form *wanax*), in fact, indicates a status higher than that of the "king" or *basileus* (appearing in Linear B as *qa-si-re-u*).[20] Dictionally, the charioteer is a *(w)anax* "lord" but so is the god, indicated, it appears, by *(w)anakti* ("to the lord") at line 237 (cf. *Iliad* 11.28 above, where *anakta*, also in line-final position, is referring to Poseidon). The now-abandoned chariot is in the god's field of control (*moira*: "lot" or "apportionment"). From the point of view of human culture, it has lost its usefulness and is left behind, but from the god's point of view, it is an acquisition, in the form of a dedication. The logic of sacrifice works the same way.[21]

The odd rite at Onchestus demands further unpacking, since we have not yet tackled the distinctive feature of this action sequence, the crash. What is signified in the dedication to the god of the unsuccessful vehicle? One might think of dedications as usually indicative of successful outcomes. For example, the small silver votive plaques clustered around almost every icon in a Greek Orthodox church are meant to show thanks to God, the

---

[19] Teffeteller 2001 notes, in addition, Hittite and Babylonian analogues, one of which is quite specific in reference to an *empty* chariot in a god's precinct.

[20] On relative status of the two, see Shelmerdine 2008, 127–29 and 135. It is of interest that the lower-ranked *qa-si-re-u*, as she notes, is several times associated with work-groups of craftsmen, such as bronze-workers at Pylos. Could the later *basileus* have evolved from the "master" of a guild? Further bibliography at Salis 1996, 115–16.

[21] A more radical possibility here, that at least deserves consideration, is that we should interpret *(w)anakti* to mean the *human* charioteer, whose *anaktoriê* has been mentioned a few lines before. From the perspective of later worshippers at Onchestus, he would be prayed to in his role as heroic warrior or celebrated king of the past, who had once subjected himself and his vehicle to Poseidon's rite. To say that "they pray" at the moment of dedication to a human would then blend the perspective of heroic age with that of the later worshippers in hero-cult. For a similar pairing of god and human hero in worship, see *Iliad* 11.761 (the conclusion of Nestor's initiatory raid): πάντες δ' εὐχετόωντο θεῶν Διὶ Νέστορί τ' ἀνδρῶν, "They all prayed to Zeus, among gods, and Nestor among men." Note that Nestor at the time is very much alive, having just completed a successful and spectacular feat in a chariot (jumping *onto* a vehicle and then taking fifty chariots of the enemy, 11.743–50). On Nestor's tale, see Chapter 4 above. In regard to initiatory chariot events, we should also keep in mind the elaborate race of *Iliad* 23, at Patroclus' funeral games, in which Antilochus the son of Nestor is a featured driver (see further Chapter 16 below). Klymenos, a mythical hero, is said to have died in a race at the grove (Pausanias *Description of Greece* 9.37.1); his heroic *exemplum* could be part of an unattested *aition* of the myth.

Virgin, and the saints for timely intervention in cases of illness, trouble, or want. Exactly the same dedicatory habit was ubiquitous in ancient Greek and Roman temples. One can still see the amazing array of models of human body parts dedicated at Corinth and read the testimonies of healings at Epidaurus. In these cases, the dedicatory objects are visible expressions of needs met, or in some instance, of wants to be addressed in the future. But the broken chariot (basket, pole, and other gear: I take *diphron* as metonymic for the whole vehicle) is *not* like that. Rather than comparing it to the wheel-chairs and crutches that festoon the walls of Christian healing shrines from Lourdes to Knock, we can compare the chariot, leaning against the shrine wall, to notches on a gunslinger's belt or crosses on a fighter pilot's fuselage. They are victor's trophies, commemoration of power. Here the commemoration would be of Poseidon's power in contrast to human weakness. The logic of hero-cult applies, however. At the same time as the failure (in this case, of the driverless car) is displayed, the heroic leap may have been recalled (perhaps even in oral-traditional praises). A three-dimensional, dramatic rendition of a similar scene is available to us in the story of Hippolytus, the "horse-loosened," a grandson of Poseidon, recounted most memorably by Euripides (*Hippolytus* 1198–1248). He dies, tangled in the reins of his chariot that Poseidon caused to crash (in obedience to the wish of his son Theseus, father of Hippolytus). We can read his end as the consequence of *not* leaping in time. Yet his death shows the power of the god, and his devotion to at least one human, his son. And so, in the Onchestus ritual as presented in the *Hymn to Apollo*, Poseidon is granted the ultimate visible recognition of his superior skills at chariot control, through the dedication of uncontrolled and broken human vehicles.

Do these vehicles, however, really signify an oppositional stance? Is it a case of Poseidon Hippios, master of driving, showing up the would-be human masters of his art, who fail to control their chariots? Clearly not. Nor is it a story, like that of the young Pelops, of Poseidon protecting a driver and bringing him to success in a race.[22] There *are* no drivers when it comes to the heart of this test. The *Hymn to Apollo*, instead, gives us a quite different scenario, involving a four-way multi-faceted *krisis* or "judgment under pressure." To recap the elements: we have, first, the presiding god to whom broken chariots will be dedicated (while presumably the unbroken vehicles escape being frozen in time as ritual objects in a shrine and instead continue

---

[22] The story is told in an explicit hero-cult context in the epinician ode *Olympian* 1 of Pindar, for Hieron's victory of 476 BCE.

in human use). Second, we have a human driver who bails out, leaving his horses (the third element) to rattle and jostle his chariot, dragging it along uncontrolled. The fourth element now deserves mention: the chariot itself. The Greek *plurale tantum* noun *harmata* means literally "joinings." The very notion focuses on construction (as if one were to call a car "car-parts"). If the crash-test of the ritual does not invoke successful driving, then what exactly *is* being tested, or in other words, what is subjected to the *krisis*? In a word: craft. Put simply, on display when the chariot enters the wooded grove of the god, whether to crash or survive intact, is the skill of whatever "joiner" (for which the Greek is *tektôn*, sharing a root with *tekhnê*) made the chariot, crafting its careful *harmata*. It is not impossible that the driver himself was that "joiner" (though he need not have been). He would thus not only race his own car, but show how good a car-maker he could be. Craftsmen—like the goldworker in Nestor's Pylos—are perfectly able to achieve independent epic commemoration.[23]

The scenario I have sketched is not overt in the *Hymn*, which, we must admit, treats the whole rite in passing, as a sort of religiously inclined traveller's tale, based on learned local lore, like those found centuries later in Pausanias.[24] But it must have been obvious in the rite itself: the better-made chariot would not rattle into pieces. Preserved in the highly visible line of broken chariots is a sort of anti-victor list. One would like to know whether the dedications were anonymous or inscribed.[25] In any event, the string of damaged vehicles says silently to the god "you won," even if it does not say overtly to the viewers "so-and-so lost." Despite the somewhat unusual nature of the ritual, we must recognize in it a format that characterizes Greek art and craft for centuries. The "performance" of the highly crafted chariot (in our own sense of vehicle "performance") is carried out:

---

[23] This construction skill may itself be a part of the expected heroic repertoire: see the *Iliad* in its several mentions of heroes (like Lykaon: 21.35–38) who are captured while cutting wood for their vehicles. In Irish saga, as well, the hero Cú Chulainn is thus represented, as are some of his enemies: see Bernhardt-House 2009. We should also remember that Epeius, maker of the Wooden Horse, is an Iliadic hero, not just a carpenter.

[24] On the characteristics of Pausanias' religious narratives, see Pirenne-Delforge 2008.

[25] Worth closer attention in this connection is the dedication by Arcesilas of his *winning* chariot at Delphi (in a cypress-grove), as commemorated by Pindar *Pythian* 5.34–42, who stresses how the victor did *not* break the "daidalic" work of the craftsmen who made his vehicle. I intend to take up this point in a later study.

1. in a religious setting;
2. involving an explicit or implicit contrast and contest with other perform-
    ers (here, other chariots, driver-leapers, and carpenters);
3. for the ultimate purpose of glorifying a divinity; and,
4. in the process, providing implicit or explicit *criteria* (*kritêrion*, that which
    enables the *krisis*) whereby one can judge further performances.

This four-part definition of a craft-contest, based on an archaic poetic
description of an obscure Boeotian ritual, will easily be seen to apply to the
best-known aesthetic events from classical Athens: the musical, dramatic,
and rhapsodic contests of the Panathenaea and Dionysia festivals, the soil
from which our texts of Homer, Sophocles, Aristophanes, and hundreds
of other (fragmentary) poets grew. Recitations of epic, the playing of pipe
(*aulos*) and concert lyre (*kithara*), singing to these instruments, the staging
of tragedy, comedy, satyr-play, and dithyramb—all fit into this format of
"craft-contest." (We even hear of "art" contests—in painting, for example—
to which the format equally applies.[26]) It may not be irrelevant, given this
context, that the very medium of the Homeric hymn is known to be a
contest-performance medium. The *Hymn to Apollo*, which preserves the
fascinating Onchestus episode, may itself have been the result of a contest
in rhapsodic hymn composition-in-performance. At the very least, as I have
argued elsewhere, it can be interpreted to represent such a contest in a stylized way.[27] Ancient traditions about the life of Homer have him competing
at Delos in the composition of a hymn to Apollo; some evidence even names
Hesiod as his rival, and/or collaborator, in such a contest.

Now that we have uncovered in one small passage of the *Homeric Hymn
to Apollo* the parameters and ideology of a small-scale, highly archaic contestation of aesthetic craft, it is time to turn to a second case-study, which
examines, as it were, the ideology surrounding the other end of the process:
the *criteria* and attitudes arising from an event dedicated to Poseidon's sometime rival, Athena—the festival of the Panathenaea.

---

[26] On contests in painting and sculpture, see Hurwit 2015, 153–56. On the agonistic settings for
Greek performance, see Martin 2015.

[27] See Chapter 7 below.

Apollo's Kithara

Apollo represents the ideal of a male who has passed through an initiatory period and appears at the height of his powers. We see this initiatory celebration and its aftermath, in compressed form, in the *Hymn to Apollo*.[28] The Homeric *Iliad* dramatizes the antagonism of this god (on the level of myth) to two humans who are (unfortunately for them) similar to him: the god-like Achilles and his beloved companion Patroclus.[29] But outside the world of heroic epic, Apollo's status is brought out, in typical ancient Greek fashion, through iconographic and poetic representations that evoke a structural juxtaposition of Apollo to another god, his younger half-brother and sometime rival, Hermes.

The field of their rivalry is a contestation-by-craft, taking place within the realm of the Muses, *mousikê*. A key component of the mythology surrounding Apollo is his involvement with singing, dancing, and playing string instruments. The lattermost, an extremely important aspect of Apolline musical culture, has most recently been meticulously explored and presented in the magnificent work of Timothy Power, *The Culture of Kitharôidia*, which covers just about everything connected to the art of singing to the *kithara* (forerunner, in word and artifact, of our "guitar").[30] I wish to examine just two moments in the ancient depiction of Apollo as a singer to this large stringed instrument.

Apollo the Citharode is more than just an incidental portrayal of the god with a proto-guitar. He is instead a mythic construction that benefited certain groups within archaic Greek culture. I consciously use these words, "myth" and "mythic" with an awareness of the usage, in the earliest surviving Greek poetic texts, of the word *mûthos*. As I have explained in an earlier work, the word *mûthos* in Homer does not immediately refer to what we might call myths—that is stories about gods and heroes—but rather to a particular kind of speech-act. It signals the use of speech when making a command, or a rebuke or a long act of remembrance. Put another way, a *mûthos* is, in the earliest usage, an utterance seeking authority, an assertion of identity, and

---

[28]   On Apollo as initiator and initiated, see Burkert 1985, 260–64 and Graf 2009, 90–91.

[29]   The god-hero antagonism at work is analyzed in detail by Nagy 1999b.

[30]   Power 2010.

a strategic positioning.[31] I believe that these same characteristics actually do continue into later usages of the word to mean something more like our modern word "myth." We should not be misled by the apparent anonymity of "myths," as they are so often presented in this later meaning. Every myth started as a *mûthos* by some person or persons, as a way to represent and manipulate the world.

I maintain that the *mûthos* of Apollo the Player (and Singer) stems from a method of self-presentation by the very performers who themselves transmitted "myths"—that is to say, actual human players and singers of epics and hymns. Their mythic self-presentation, or "mythologizing" of performance, can in turn be seen as regionally determined within Greek culture. In other words, the stories of Apollo the Citharode represent in large part a stylization of the type that is called "epichoric"—existing in a particular land.[32] But the particular localization, as I shall argue, is that of a very specific *festival*, as opposed to the rites of other cult-centers (as was the case with Onchestus, above). We shall see that "criteria" for performance—the aesthetic notions that we might think universal—are in fact determined, and even over-determined, by highly local conditions. Any genealogy of modern aesthetics has to start with the *realia* of such localized rites.

Let us start with verbal art. The *Homeric Hymn to Apollo*, which gave us our first example, the rite of Poseidon at Onchestus, spends much more of its narrative proclaiming Apollo as the Citharode. After his mother, Leto, has convinced the island of Delos that acting as a divine maternity ward will be an economic benefit in future years, Delos makes the pregnant Leto swear an oath that Apollo will indeed build a glorious temple on the small rocky island (lines 51–92). In labor for nine days and nine nights, Leto grasps a palm tree, kneels on the ground, and, surrounded by nymphs and goddesses, brings forth the twins Apollo and Artemis. The young god is so powerful he bursts his swaddling bands. His first words in the poem proclaim his future areas of expertise (lines 131–32):

εἴη μοι κίθαρίς τε φίλη καὶ καμπύλα τόξα,
χρήσω δ' ἀνθρώποισι Διὸς νημερτέα βουλήν.

---

[31]   Martin 1989, 10–88. On the later development of the word's semantics, in which it comes to approximate (but is not co-extensive with) more familiar meanings attached to the modern "myth," see Martin 2013.

[32]   On the power of epichoric attachment in performance, see now Fearn 2011 and Boterf 2012.

> May the *kithara* [or "*kithara*-playing"] be dear to me and the bent
> bow,
> and I will utter to mortals the unerring will of Zeus.

He presents himself as one who can play a stringed instrument, called in the Greek of the poem, the *kitharis* (a by-form of the more common noun *kithara*). He will also be an archer and a prophet. I cannot enter here into the connection between the first two skills, music-making and archery, but it is most likely very old. Philippe Montbrun has recently shown in detail that the hunting bow and one-stringed musical instrument are, indeed, one and the same physical object among many peoples of Africa, South America, and Oceania.[33] As for the connections between musical performance and prophecy, the work of Lisa Maurizio and others has demonstrated that oral poetics has a key role in the production of prophetic hexameters at the Delphic oracle. It may even be the case that the Pythia, the prophetess of Apollo, spoke in verse.[34] In short, the three skills that Apollo professes might be thought of simply as three aspects of *one* powerful super-craft, a skill that boils down to *inerrancy*—whether of getting the right note in musical performance, the right target in athletic and martial performance, or the right prediction in talk of the future. Such an abstract but unifying concept should right away make us withhold judgment about the exact criteria for any one of those performances. It opens a world of strange possibility (from an aesthetic view): is a string-player better when he is more athletic, "bowing" with a vengeance, "hitting" the right notes precisely? Or when the music seems to us sweeter, more expressive, more moving and sensitive? We cannot assume that there is one correct, culturally transcendent answer.

The instrumental aspect is just one part of this craft of *citharody* (singing to the accompaniment of the *kithara*). But the choice of instrument to accompany song is, it turns out, a key signifier when it comes to drawing attention to such features as status, audience, occasion, and even the auditory volume of actual performances. We must, therefore, keep clear the distinction between *kithara* (or *kitharis*), and on the other hand, "lyre" (*lura*), which is often casually but misleadingly misapplied to the stringed instrument of Apollo. (Indeed, most translations of *Hymn to Apollo* line 131 write "lyre" for the Greek word *kitharis*.) It is worth emphasizing the differences between

---

[33] Montbrun 2001.

[34] Maurizio 2001. See, in addition, González 2013, 284–90, with further bibliography.

these ancient Greek stringed instruments, both in terms of their material construction and their semantic associations in broader cultural terms.[35]

First, the kithara. This large seven-stringed instrument with a sizable wooden sound-box required physical strength to hold it up for any length of playing time.[36] In classical times, it was handled by professional musicians, often in the competitive environment of musical contests, at major festivals. Those festivals included, most conspicuously, the Pythian Games held at Apollo's shrine at Delphi. In relation to the *kithara*, I must first make some further observations on vocabulary, lest it be thought I am taking diction at face value in arguing that Apollo is, in a strictly technical sense, a *citharode*. Within the *Homeric Hymns*, one must admit, the terms used for instrumental playing are somewhat ambiguous. That is, one could argue that the noun *kitharis*, cited above (*Hymn to Apollo* 131), might be used in an unmarked way to mean *any* stringed instrument. It might even be used, as it is in most of the few occurrences in Homeric poetry, as a *nomen actionis* to mean "instrument-playing" rather than an instrument.[37] The noun *kithara* (rather than *kitharis*) is first attested in Theognis (line 778).[38] The default noun for the instrument that is played by singers in the Homeric epics is yet another term: *phorminx*.[39] In the *Hymn to Apollo*, this noun alternates with *kitharis*. Furthermore, the verbs derived from either noun, *phormizein* and *kitharizein* appear to be interchangeable.[40] All this means that the diction of hexameter

---

[35]   For a parallel sociocultural analysis of the equally marked *aulos* (double-pipe), see Martin 2003b.

[36]   On the instrument, see Comotti 1989, 63, and Maas and Snyder 1989, 53–78, with illustrations. On the endurance involved, see Power 2010, 52, 107, 121.

[37]   As denoting an action rather than physical instrument in Homer, see *Iliad* 13.731 (paired with *aoidê* "art of song," as gifts of a god). A similar pairing at *Iliad* 2.599–600 employs the suffixed noun form *kitharistus* to denote the art of playing (rather than the actual instrument) that the Muses took away from Thamyris along with his *aoidê*, "art of song." More ambiguous are *Odyssey* 1.159, 8.248, and *Iliad* 3.54, where *kitharis* could be construed either as the instrument or as a metonym for the art of playing. Meanwhile, the noun as used at *Odyssey* 1.153 obviously denotes the actual instrument placed in the hands of the singer Phemius.

[38]   In the context of paean-performance for Apollo.

[39]   It occurs twenty-one times in the *Iliad* and *Odyssey*, in connection with just a few distinct performances, almost exclusively executed by professional musicians: by Apollo (two different occasions, *Iliad* 1.603 and 24.63); by Demodocus (sequence of three songs, *Odyssey* 8.67, 99, 105, 254, 261, 537; cf. 8.266 [verb *phormizôn*]); by Phemius (*Odyssey* 17.262, 270, 21.430, 22.332, 340, 23.133, 144; cf. 1.155 [verb *phormizôn*]); by Achilles (*Iliad* 9.186, 194); by an unnamed player at a Spartan wedding (*Odyssey* 4.18 [verb *phormizôn*]); in a simile, referring to a generic expert player (*Odyssey* 21.406); and in two celebrations on the Shield (*Iliad* 18.495 and 569, on which see below).

[40]   Note especially *Iliad* 18.569–71 (describing a young man who plays and sings on the Shield of Achilles):

poetry has a good deal of flexibility in describing instrumental performance. The words "to play the *phorminx*" and "to play the *kithara*" can be taken in their semantically broad, unmarked sense, and in this way even applied to the playing of the small tortoise shell lyre—a completely different instrument. Or, the words can be taken in a semantically *narrow*, marked sense to mean precisely playing the larger, wooden box instruments, the *kithara* and its forerunner, the *phorminx*. Such flexibility proves useful as poets engage in mythologizing their own art-forms.

Let me also suggest that we may be seeing in this flexible system of descriptive terms the strata of generations of actual performance practices. In this connection I am reminded of an observation by the folklorist Dwight Reynolds, a scholar who has also undergone training as an Egyptian oral epic poet. He notes that even when a bard of the contemporary Hilali oral epic is obviously playing on a twentieth-century violin, with several strings, he says to his audience, in his verses, "I sing to you as I play on my *rabāb*"—although the *rabāb* is a much older, one-string instrument, clearly *not* what he is using in his act of performance. The text and the context, thus apparently dissonant, are seamlessly joined through the willing suspension of disbelief.[41] And in fact, the fiddle does function, for poet and audience, as the spiritual and practical descendant of the *rabāb*. The *ideology* of traditional performance remains the same despite the practical upgrade and shift in the form of accompanying instrumentation.

As we return to the *Hymn to Apollo*, therefore, we should keep in mind that the poem might be describing either Apollo using a lyre, or Apollo using the professional contest instrument, the *kithara*. I shall contend that the *Hymn to Apollo* points to the latter scenario. In fact, the *kithara*—the big-box instrument—is for Apollo the *default* instrument. Another Homeric hymn, the *Hymn to Hermes*, as we shall see, insists on the latter scenario, his use of the *lyre*. It is this primeval contrast that will lead us to some

---

τοῖσιν δ' ἐν μέσσοισι πάϊς <u>φόρμιγγι</u> λιγείῃ
ἱμερόεν <u>κιθάριζε</u>, λίνον δ' ὑπὸ καλὸν ἄειδε
λεπταλέῃ φωνῇ·

Conversely, Phemius' playing on the *kitharis* is described with the verb derived from the noun *phorminx* at *Odyssey* 1.153–55 (see note 38, above):

κῆρυξ δ' ἐν χερσὶν <u>κίθαριν</u> περικαλλέα θῆκε
Φημίῳ, ὅς ῥ' ἤειδε παρὰ μνηστῆρσιν ἀνάγκῃ.
ἦ τοι ὁ <u>φορμίζων</u> ἀνεβάλλετο καλὸν ἀείδειν ...

[41]   On this reference to the older instrument, see Reynolds 1989, 67; for detailed study of the Hilali performance tradition see Reynolds 1995.

conclusions about the mythic meanings of kithara vs. lyre in terms of performance practices, social semiotics, and aesthetics.

In order to explore the further implications of Apollo as a player and singer, a citharode, let us start with the following lines (*Hymn to Apollo* 156–64):[42]

> There is also a great wonder the fame of which will never perish,
> the Delian maidens, the servants of the far-shooter.
> Who, after first hymning Apollo
> and then in turn Leto and arrow-pouring Artemis,
> commemorating men and women of old
> sing a hymn and enchant the races of humans.
> The voices and the rhythmic patterns of all humans
> they know how to represent; each one might think
> that he himself is speaking, so beautifully is their song fitted
> together.

The immediate context is a description of the Ionian festival at Delos in honor of Apollo. Along with other events, it includes, in the poet's rendition, a chorus of maidens of Delos who charm the assembled festival crowd on the sacred island with their astounding vocal performance. The speaker of the *Homeric Hymn* at this point appears to introduce himself, as well as a second man, a foil figure. Bidding the Delian maidens farewell, just after these lines, the speaker says: "If a stranger should ask, 'Who for you is the sweetest of singers frequenting this place, in whom do you take most delight?' tell him this:—'A blind man, he lives in rocky Chios. That man's songs, all of them, are best ever after'" (lines 168–73). This scripted response seems to be an artful if rather indirect self-advertisement on the part of the performing poet. In the form in which it is scripted for the Delian maidens, it resembles a contract: the parties are marked out by the contrasting line-intial *humeis* and *hêmeis* ("*you*" plural and "*we*"). "*You* give this answer," says the anonymous speaker, "and *we* in turn will spread your poetic fame [*kleos*] as far as we wander on earth to the well-peopled cities of men. And I will never cease to praise far-shooting Apollo, god of the silver bow, whom rich-haired Leto bore."

Since the time of Thucydides, this passage from the *Hymn to Apollo* has been taken as evidence for the history of performance practices. Most often, the mysterious blind man of Chios has been interpreted as a reference to

---

[42] See most recently on the exact interpretation of these lines, Peponi 2009, with further bibliography. The translation given here is hers (2009: 67n74).

the figure of Homer. What is not always stressed is the open-ended wording of these lines: there is no direct assertion that the speaker of the *Hymn to Apollo* is, in fact, the same as the *tuphlos anêr*, the blind man. The identity of the hymn performer is instead elided—we are meant to *associate* him with Homeric traditions, with all who have ever wandered around performing songs of Homer, but it may or may not be "Homer" who speaks to the Delians.[43]

I would add that the Homer figure here most closely resembles that of the wandering poet found in the *Lives of Homer* and in the *Contest of Homer and Hesiod*. These traditional stories appear to go back to the sixth century BCE, a time when the texts of the poems of Homer and Hesiod were being crystallized and set down in some form or other. As we see Homer mythologized in those traditions, he represents a much more expansive repertoire than the composer of our *Iliad* and *Odyssey*. The Homer of the *Lives of Homer* stories composes curses, magical spells, epigrams, and hymns, as well as what we might call epic. He comes into town and gets himself advertised, stays at cobblers shops or men's gathering spots, even makes up small-scale epics about the history of the city in which he finds himself. The Homer of the *Lives* traditions is an ornery character as well, who will curse a town if he feels that he has been disrespected—in good poetic fashion of course.[44] Now, if we acknowledge that the speaker of the ancient *Hymn to Apollo* associates himself with such an expansive, multi-generic repertory for the poetry of Homer—from curses to praise poems to epigrams and spells—the next claim in my argument becomes a bit more likely: namely, that the performer of our *Hymn to Apollo* himself wants to pose as a *citharode*—or, at least, to strongly suggest the possibility. This might be surprising since it is clear that the Homeric hymns as a group must have been *rhapsodic* compositions meant for competitive recitation, like the *Iliad* and *Odyssey* in their sixth-century formats.[45] By "rhapsodic," I mean recited, without musical accompaniment or melody. We have a picture of such recitation in the dialogue of Plato titled *Ion*, after the wandering rhapsode or "song-stitcher" of that name. Ion the rhapsode goes from place to place competing as a reciter of the *Iliad* and *Odyssey*. Let me stress the difference once more. Our evidence for actual

---

[43] For the fullest recent treatment, taking into account earlier discussions, see Sbardella 2012, 34–36 and 85–99.

[44] On the *Lives* and Homer's technique as wandering poet, see Martin 2009 and Nagy 2010, 29–47.

[45] On the variety of performance contexts for the *Homeric Hymns*, see Clay 2011b; on *Hymns* specifically in rhapsodic performance, see Collins 2001b.

performance of Homeric poetry and, by extension, *Homeric Hymns*, tells us that they were *recited* in competitions, not *sung*. Yet the internal picture given us by the *Hymn to Apollo* suggests that the composer of such poetry is a *singer*, specifically a *citharode* or singer to the kithara.

What are the signs of this hymnist's imagined citharody? Most clearly, it comes in what I shall call "emblematic melding." To explain this, I refer to another passage. Several critics have noted that the transition in line 177 and following of the hymn is abrupt.[46] Most attribute this to an alleged gap or seam between the so-called Delian and Pythian parts of the *Hymn*. It is true that the first part of the *Hymn to Apollo* dwells on the career of the young god near the time of his birth on Delos, while the second highlights his acquisition of Delphi as a place for a temple from which to issue oracles. Since the eighteenth century, critics have insisted that the *Hymn to Apollo* is, in fact, two poems clumsily stuck together, one originally designed for performance on Delos, the other for performance at Delphi. I do not believe this explanation.[47] At any rate, in the passage at hand, after promising to spread the fame of the Delian maidens, the speaker—who previously referred to himself with a plural pronoun *hêmeis*—says at line 177, "but I [*singular* pronoun] will not cease making a *humnos* about far-shooting Apollo." He then makes good on his claim, breaking into what we can identify as high-style hymnic rhetoric in the Greek poetic tradition (*Hymn to Apollo* 179–93):

> O Lord, Lycia is yours and lovely Maeonia and Miletus, charming city by the sea, but over wave-girt Delos you greatly reign your own self. Leto's all-glorious son goes to rocky Pytho, playing upon his hollow lyre, clad in divine, perfumed garments; and at the touch of the golden key his lyre sings sweet. Thence, swift as thought, he speeds from earth to Olympus, to the house of Zeus, to join the gathering of the other gods: then straightway the undying gods think only of the lyre and song, and all the Muses together, voice sweetly answering voice, hymn the unending gifts the gods enjoy and the sufferings of men, all that they endure at the hands of the deathless gods, and how they live witless and helpless and cannot find healing for death or defense against old age.

In this miniature praise section, the very first image the poet offers us is, significantly, of Apollo, seen in all his glory as *citharode*. Not only are both the mortal and divine hymnists juxtaposed in this manner. The description interconnects details, as well. We see Apollo as he strides toward an assembly

---

[46]   Opinions given in Càssola 1975, 498.

[47]   For my alternative view, see Chapter 7 below.

of the gods (*homêgurin*), surely a match for the picture we have just seen of the Homeric poet, the blind man of Chios, as travelling around. Both man and god are hymnists on the move. The epiphany of Apollo on Olympus prompts divine delight in *kitharis* and *aoidê*, instrumental playing and singing, and leads to further song and dance among the gods. That comes in a description that many have observed closely replicates the features of the human musical events on Delos mentioned earlier in the poem.[48] In the earlier passage, the poem refers to the gathering of Greeks from all over the islands and adjacent coast, and speaks of how they are transfixed by the virtuoso performance of a set of human girls who can imitate the voices and movements of all.[49] Schematically, we have a chiasmus:

Delian maiden / mortal singer (Homer)

divine singer Apollo / Olympian maidens

The emblematic melding here accomplishes in almost tactile fashion the sort of analogizing by which myth as a whole functions. The assertion embedded in this juxtaposition is: just as Apollo is *Musagetês*, leader of the *Muses*, so the blind man of Chios—or his representative—is choral leader of the *Delian* chorus, the one who provides them with songs. This matching detail is further underlined by the line–final occurrence of the word for song, *aoidê* at 173 (referring to "Homer") and at 188 (referring to Apollo). To repeat, no matter what the actual performance conditions were over the years for this *Hymn to Apollo*—including recitation in performance, without music of any kind—the text itself insinuates that the *Hymn to Apollo* is exactly like Apollo's *own* song. Let me put it more pointedly: the human singer worships the god by modeling himself on this divine patron of song.[50]

---

[48] Clay 1989, 53–56; cf. Power 2010, 442–43.

[49] On the meaning of the "imitation," see now Peponi 2009.

[50] The late-antique lexicon of Hesychius yields some surprising and remarkably detailed information about what appear to be actual performance habits from an earlier period. The lexicon tells us that the phrase "But, lord ..." (*all'anax*) was known to be a conventional closing phrase, or *exodion*, within the performances of actual *citharodes*. By contrast, the phrase "But now the gods" functioned as an *exodion,* or signoff phrase, for *rhapsodes*. I submit that we see exactly this closing strategy, but in a split-up and expanded version at lines 177–79 of the *Hymn to Apollo*. Here the poet says *autar ego*—(compare *alla* of the *exodion*) and then says *o ana* (compare *anax* of the *exodion*). See

There is one further emblematic melding to examine in the Apollo hymn. As the poem proceeds, Apollo realizing the need for priests for his newly founded temple in Delphi, goes out and hijacks a boat. Specifically, he takes the form of a dolphin, leaps into a ship manned by Cretan sailors and proceeds to flop around and rock it. While Apollo the Dolphin lies there, the boat starts steering itself toward the place he desires (388–439). When it reaches his goal, Apollo resumes his divine form and tells the Cretans they will be his servants. He then leads them in a high-spirited but formal procession up the mountain to his shrine, playing his *phorminx* as he goes (452–516). The Cretans follow, singing a victory song or *paean* "just like the *paeans* of the Cretans, for whom the Muse has placed in the heart honey-voiced song" (518–19). If the hymnist of this poem is being likened to Apollo, so the Cretan sailors—his newly found priests—are likened to Cretan *paean* singers. The victory song or thanksgiving song to Apollo called the *paean* was normally sung to the *kithara*. By mythic calculation, the hymnist of the *Hymn to Apollo* is like Apollo who in turn is like the leader of Cretan *citharode* singers. Hence once again, the *Hymn* performer comes out looking like a *citharode*. I shall return to the Cretans in a moment, in formulating my final thoughts about the role of ritual and contest in developing the aesthetics of performances.

For now, we should note that this very artful and careful merging of performers within the *Hymn to Apollo* gains even more resonance when placed next to the evidence from iconography and literary-historical traditions. A key to this broader complex is the lore passed down to us by the second-century CE travel writer Pausanias. In his section on the Pythian games, we must note several key points. Before the reorganization of the Pythian games in the sixth century BCE, as we learn from other sources, the only contest was in citharody. Pausanias says this took the form of singing a hymn to Apollo. The first winner was Chrysothemis of Crete. The passage is worth quoting in full:

> The oldest contest and the one for which they first offered prizes was, according to tradition, the singing of a hymn to the god. The man who sang and won the prize was Chrysothemis of Crete, whose father Carmanor is said to have cleansed Apollo. After Chrysothemis, says tradition, Philammon won with a song, and after him his son Thamyris. But they say that Orpheus, a proud man and conceited about his mysteries, and

---

Hesychius A 3113 (Latte); and cf. Gostoli 1990, 54, 146–48. For extensive analysis of this usage, see Chapter 6 below.

Musaeus, who copied Orpheus in everything, refused to submit to the competition in musical skill.

They say too that Eleuther won a Pythian victory for his loud and sweet voice, for the song that he sang was not of his own composition. The story is that Hesiod too was debarred from competing because he had not learned to accompany his own singing on the harp. Homer too came to Delphi to inquire about his needs, but even though he had learned to play the harp, he would have found the skill useless owing to the loss of his eye-sight.[51]

There are a number of fascinating and relevant aspects to Pausanias' collection of observations on Delphic performance history. We can note, first, how the character and biography of various "authors" are obviously tied to the local traditions about whether or not they were fit to participate in a particular event. Thus Orpheus and Musaeus are too proud, Hesiod too unskilled in music, and Homer, paradoxically, skilled but unable to make use of his skill due to blindness—which sounds like a crudely manufactured excuse.

We should note further that Chrysothemis, the first victor, had a living connection with Apollo, since his father had performed *katharsis* for the god. The ritual context, therefore, is doubled—the citharode sings a hymn *and* is the son of one who provided ritual cleansing. By the way, the very name Chrysothemis or "Golden Rule" would make an appropriate epithet for the god himself. In the *Hymn to Apollo*, the baby god is resplendently dressed in gold, with gold belt and gold dagger. The very first divinity to feed the baby Apollo is not his mother Leto, but instead the goddess *Themis*—"Proper Rule, or Custom." She gives him nectar and ambrosia—the perfect pablum for an immortal (lines 123–24). What I am suggesting is that calling oneself "Chrysothemis" in the context of Apolline cult and festival evokes images of the very origin of the god Apollo. Let us add to Pausanias' information at this point a further piece of lore. According to a tradition passed down by the Byzantine scholar Photius (*Bibliotheca* 320b), this mortal singer Chrysothemis was the first to wear expensive clothing and to take up the *kithara* to sing a solo *nomos* or traditional song-pattern in *imitation* of Apollo (*eis mimêsin Apollonos*). The anecdote is nothing less than an aetiological story to explain the customary dress of both competitive citharodes and their instruments (also by the way, elaborately clothed, as we shall see).[52]

---

[51] Pausanias *Description of Greece* 10.7.3; trans. W. H. S. Jones.

[52] See further Power 2010, 28–29.

The other points in Pausanias' passage are all worth pondering, but we must pass quickly over them. Essentially, this lore retrojects a division of repertoires, perhaps originating in the sixth century BCE. The Pythian games tradition of competitive singing to the accompaniment of the kithara, interestingly, includes in its list of victors (and thus, in the contemporary repertoire) Philammon, Eleuther, and best of all the mythic performer Thamyris, who, the *Iliad* tells us, was once defeated by the Muses in a contest (*Iliad* 2.591–600).[53] But it *excludes* Orpheus, Musaeus, Homer, and Hesiod. These latter, it can be argued, are all to be associated with *rhapsodic* performance, although the passage does not state this. In stressing Homer's skill at playing an instrument, and then veering away from this by excluding him, the Pythian lore seems to mirror inversely what the *Hymn to Apollo* presents: a *citharodic*, singing-and-playing Homer, in the actual context of a *rhapsodic* hymn. It is as if the keepers of Pythian lore, perhaps the priests and operators of the games, acknowledge a tradition of Homeric citharody, but take pains to reject it. Within the terms of the Pythian lore reported by Pausanias, such a rejection would make most sense if citharodic ideology—collaborating with the rules of the games, as set by Apollo's proponents—*requires* from its performers the ability to *see* the god in order to proclaim his glory—you do not acquire such details from what other people tell you. You must see for yourself.[54]

Let me return to the essential conclusion we can draw from the passages we have just reviewed. The origin myths and ideology of citharodic performance at the games in Delphi, the Pythian games, pivot around imitating the god *in his role as citharode*. The *Homeric Hymn to Apollo*, as I am suggesting, promotes that very ideology, although it seems that the Pythian contests *excluded* from competition all that was considered to be Homeric poetry—yet another indication of how what were primarily ritual events shaped the very canon of Greek literature.[55] At this point, we could expatiate on the function of such divine mimesis. It seems to have played a specific role within the broader area of male initiation. In this connection, we need to recall that Apollo is the god of clan membership, as attested especially in Dorian lands (like Crete) but also in Athens. As a young god, with characteristic long hair,

[53] For the competing traditions at work in this myth, see Martin 1989, 29–30 and Wilson 2006–07.

[54] An analogy might be made with the powerful force of *darśan*—pious religious viewing of the sites and images of gods—in Hinduism, on which see Eck 1998.

[55] In the sixth century BCE, the corpus of "Homeric" verse was certainly much more extensive than the *Iliad* and *Odyssey* and *Hymns*, and included large portions of what was later called "Cyclic" poetry: Nagy 2010, 69–78.

he is the embodiment of that stage in a young man's life when he is called an ephebe—"on the verge of full youth." Apollo does not get old; he remains the eternal ephebe. To be a full man, the mortal Greek passes through the ephebic stage, learning the craft of the warrior, but also learning the other relevant skills of being an aristocratic male. These skills include the production of music and song—embodied in Apollo the Citharode. This whole ancient Greek social-mythic complex can be characterized in the anthropologist Michael Herzfeld's phrase, as the "Poetics of Manhood"—to borrow the title of his important book about the late-twentieth century inhabitants of an upland village in western Crete.[56]

And now it's time for us to talk further of Cretans. It must not be accidental that the first citharodic winner, a generation after the god himself, according to the ancient lore, was from Crete. I submit that the reason Apollo in the mythic narrative preserved in the *Hymn to Apollo* has to choose *Cretan* merchant pirates to be his priests is simply because the traditions and lore concerning *actual* citharodic performance at Delphi have pre-determined that ethnicity to be the operative one. The stories and practices of real performers, in other words, have moved quietly into the *mythic* representations, retrojecting a number of details from the present age, about what singers really do (or their own stories about what they do), into a distant Golden Age. Nor should we be disturbed by the odd combination of priests and singers in this picture—the mythic Cretan sailors becoming sacrificial officiants at Apollo's temple, while the Cretan performers are good at singing. At Delphi, as at Athens, where the Eumolpidae or "good-singer" family had ritual functions, and further afield, in the cults and poetic traditions of Vedic India, priests and singers are quite often one and the same persons.[57]

Two semi-historical figures can help fill in the picture that I have been drawing of the ideology of "emblematic melding." Terpander, a citharode from Lesbos, who flourished around 680 BCE, established the first citharodic contest at the Carneia in Sparta—and proceeded to win the contest.[58] Since the Carneia was a long-standing Apollo festival, we see once again the close relation between citharody and the god. But in the stories that tell us how Terpander invented the seven-string lyre, and the set of tunes to be sung

---

[56] Herzfeld 1985. On Apollo, poetry, and initiatory practices, see Johnston 2013, who highlights the god's paradigmatic role in the *Hymn to Hermes*. On musical components of Apolline training, in festival contexts, see Pettersson 1992.

[57] Eumolpidae: Graf 1974, 59–65, 93–100; Vedic India: Winternitz 1981, 150–55.

[58] Pseudo-Plutarch *De musica* 1131a–1132e; Gostoli *ad loc.* 1990, 84–85.

to the kithara, we see also the melding of human musician with divine. For Apollo, too, is a first-founder, discoverer of institutions and inventor of *nomoi* in several senses. (The word *nomoi* can mean both "tunes" and "laws").[59] The second figure, whose names is Thaletas or Thales, is a sort of shamanic alternative to Terpander; the traditional dating puts him, too, in the seventh century BCE, when he is credited with founding another Spartan institution, the Gymnopaidia.[60] Thaletas or Thales also is said to have prevented war or cured plague with his songs, which included paeans and a kind of processional song call *huporkhêma*.[61] If Terpander imitates the divine model Apollo in his innovations, Thaletas does so by his healing and harmonizing activities. Looked at another way, both of these historical citharodic biographies reflect the emblematic melding of performer and patron. What is more, Thaletas comes from an interesting town (one that we associate with one of the earliest surviving Greek law codes on stone): Gortyn, in southern Crete.

The literary evidence about Apollo as citharode is dwarfed by the visual, which would require a long book and a good deal of art-historical expertise to analyze in full.[62] Let me summarize for the sake of brevity: from a sample data set comprising the 536 vases for which the online Beazley archive at Oxford provided images in a keyword search, as well as the *Lexicon Iconographicum* section on Apollo with kithara, it emerges that the kithara accompanies Apollo in a fairly restricted set of scenes—ones that are ritual, public, and celebratory.[63] The god plays in processions, especially divine weddings, like that depicted on a well-known sixth-century *dinos* by Sophilos.[64] Apollo also plays at altars flaming for sacrifice, or during libations; and Apollo leads the Muses in song. Such type-scene attestations capture the marked nature of public performance on this instrument, the very same marked and ritually grounded performance that one sees in the human citharodic contests at the Carneia and the Pythia. A related point is that Apollo himself in vase depictions looks like a human citharode contestant, and vice versa. We

[59] Power 2010, 215–23 has an extended discussion of the multiple meanings of *nomos*.

[60] The name of the festival, at least, is familiar to the modern world through the music of Erik Satie, *Les Gymnopedies*; see Pettersson 1992.

[61] Barker 1984, 214–16.

[62] On statues of Apollo Citharode, see Flashar 1992. On vase depictions, see now Power 2010, 249, 286–87, 425–30. A slightly fuller version of the visual evidence is in Martin 2010, from which I have borrowed some material for this portion of the current essay.

[63] *Lexicon Iconographicum Mythologiae Classicae* 2:1 (1984) 199–213 (#82–238).

[64] British Museum 1971.11–1.1.

have established the close "emblematic melding" of human citharodes and divine player. I have argued that this goes back to the actual practices and ideology of the citharodes, specifically in the contest situation at Delphi, in the Pythian games. Now is the time to turn at last to a third place, triangulating, as it were, between Apollo's sites of Delphi and Delos, and the aesthetics of its contests, and those honoring another divinity, Athena, in the Panathenaea. I will take a slight detour, however, reaching Athens through Arcadia, at least in mythic terms.

A companion poem to the *Hymn to Apollo* is the hymnic composition that celebrates the birth and adventures of his half-brother, the god Hermes. While we cannot dwell on the *Hymn to Hermes* at the same length as Apollo's hymn, it is worth noticing how the poem embodies a suggestive and discordant transgression against Apolline harmonies. The *Hymn to Hermes* is a comic masterpiece, a rags-to-riches tale, telling how the god's mother Maia gave birth to him in a cave far distant from the house of his father Zeus. Soon after being born, Hermes decides to steal the cattle of his brother Apollo. Cattle-raiding, like being skilled at chariot-driving, is known as an ancient form of proving manhood, connected with initiation stories in Greek, Indic, and Irish.[65] In the world of modern Crete—as Michael Herzfeld's book shows in detail—it has been replaced as an initiatory experience by the stealing of sheep from one's older male neighbors, fulfilling a key function in the Poetics of Manhood.[66]

So the *Hymn to Hermes*, in its basic plot, enacts a transgression, with a baby doing the deed of a young man, not unlike the way Apollo himself, in the *Hymn* dedicated to him, is instantly depicted as maturing. Yet the *Hymn to Hermes* goes a step further. Not only is it about a legal and ritual transgression (Hermes, in fact, invents a new kind of sacrifice: lines 110–36); it also encapsulates a musical transgression. After being caught and threatened with punishment by his older brother, Hermes charms Apollo by singing a hymn to the gods while accompanying himself on his own invention, the tortoise-shell lyre (*Hymn to Hermes* 418–33):[67]

---

[65] See Walcot 1979 and Melia 1979. Note that the biography of Nestor, as recounted by him at *Iliad* 11.670–761, tells of a cattle-raid followed by a battle in which Nestor seizes an opponent's chariot and, using it, cuts down 100 enemies in the fray; see further Chapter 4 above.

[66] Haft 1996 makes use of Herzfeld 1985 to illuminate the *Hymn to Hermes*.

[67] Translation from West 2003a, 147–49. For full analysis of the aesthetic being espoused here, see Peponi 2012.

Having taken it on his left[68] arm, he tried it out with a plectrum in a tuned scale, and it rang out impressively under his hand; and Phoibos Apollo laughed for pleasure, the lovely sound of its wondrous voice invaded his senses, and sweet longing captivated his heart as he listened. Playing delightfully on the lyre [λύρῃ δ᾽ ἐρατὸν κιθαρίζων], the son of Maia stationed himself unafraid on Phoibos Apollo's left, and soon, with the lyre's clear accompaniment [λιγέως κιθαρίζων], he was striking up his song, and his voice came lovely: he spoke authoritatively of the immortal gods and of dark Earth, how they were born originally and how each received his portion. Remembrance first of the gods he honored in his song, the mother of the Muses, for she had Maia's son in her province, and then the rest of the immortal gods Zeus' splendid son honored according to seniority and affiliation, relating everything in due order, and playing the lyre that hung from his arm [ὑπωλένιον κιθαρίζων].

Before proceeding further, we should note at this point that the word "lyre" is used just once (line 423), while further references to the instrument (lines 425 and 433) simply use the line-final participle *kitharizon*. West's translation here (and those of others) seeks to clarify and supplement the text by intruding "lyre" into each of the latter two references, but it is more important, for my argument, that any noun that would specify the instrument is actually suppressed. We understand the object to be "lyre," but the sense is carried along by the poet's choice of the ambiguous term that means, literally, "playing as on a kithara" but (as we have seen above) can mean more neutrally "strum."

After Apollo expresses his amazement at this novel form of music-making, asking what the *tekhnê* ("craft, skill") and *mousa* (either "Muse" or "type of music") might be (line 447), he reminds Hermes of his own involvement in song and dance as a follower of the Muses (lines 450–54), but significantly, makes no mention of his kithara-playing abilities, which are so prominent in the *Hymn to Apollo*.[69] Indeed, his astonishment seems to imply that stringed instrument playing, the art of the *kithara*, has not yet been invented. Therefore, it is something of a jolt when Apollo refers to Hermes' lyre-playing using the verb derived from the noun *kithara* (455):

---

[68] Note that the object-noun is omitted altogether: some editors (e.g., Càssola [1975, 536] and others there cited) replace the transmitted reading *labôn* ("having taken") with the name of an instrument, either *lurên* or *kitharin*, but I believe that the text of 418, as it stands with its direct object elided, is exactly right.

[69] The only instrument mentioned is the double-pipe, *auloi*, at line 452.

θαυμάζω, Διὸς υἱέ, τάδ᾽ ὡς ἐρατὸν <u>κιθαρίζεις</u>.

Once more, West's translation, intruding the noun "lyre," seeks to avoid any possible cognitive dissonance prompted by the verb:

> I am amazed, son of Zeus, how beautifully you can *play such things on the lyre.*

Further blurring of the referent occurs in the scene of exchange that soon follows. Hermes graciously allows Apollo to practice his own invention, while craftily implying that Apollo might in return instruct him in the prophetic arts (lines 464–73; again, there is no mention of pre-existing Apolline musical knowledge):

> You can help yourself to the knowledge you want. But as your heart is set on playing the lyre [θυμὸς ἐπιθύει <u>κιθαρίζειν</u>], play it [<u>κιθάριζε</u>], make music [μέλπεο], and be festive, accept it from me; and you, dear friend, give me prestige [κῦδος] in turn.

What I have called "dissonance" continues: handing over the lyre so that his half-brother can try it, Hermes refers, twice, to the act of playing it using the verb *kitharizein*. When Apollo takes it, a peculiar transformation occurs, as can best be seen by juxtaposing West's normalizing translation with the odder Greek original. The key phrases are highlighted below (lines 496–502):

> With these words *he held out the lyre* [<u>ὣς εἰπὼν ὤρεξ᾽</u>] and Phoibos Apollo took it; and he willingly handed Hermes the shining goad and enjoined on him the care of cattle, which Maia's son accepted gladly. Then, *taking the lyre* [<u>κίθαριν δὲ λαβών</u>] on his left arm, Leto's glorious son, the far-shooting lord Apollo, tried it out with a plectrum in a tuned scale, and it rang out enchantingly below, while the god sang beautifully to its accompaniment.

As can be easily seen, in the first phrase the object-noun has been gapped out: the Greek says simply "So speaking he held out," in line with a strategy of avoidance we have now seen earlier (cf. line 418). But, more disturbingly, in the second highlighted phrase that object that the audience has known to be a lyre is explicitly named *kitharis* (an equivalent to *kithara*). In other words, the instrument has undergone a metamorphosis, at least at the verbal level, from lyre to *kithara/kitharis*. To complicate the picture even more, a third term occurs in the next lines describing the now reconciled gods as they approach Zeus (505–6):

Zeus' two beautiful children themselves went prancing back to snowy Olympus, entertaining themselves *with the lyre* [τερπόμενοι φόρμιγγι].

West translates it as "lyre"—in accord with the drift of the poem's action thus far—but the noun in question is *phorminx*. As we have seen, this noun regularly is correlated with professional playing and with the forms *kithara/kitharis/kitharizô*, in the Homeric epics.[70]

In the poem's remaining two references to the tortoise-shell instrument, formerly owned by Hermes, it is called *kitharis* (lines 509, 515). In short, the same instrument takes on a different identity depending on the god who plays it: a lyre for Hermes, a kithara for Apollo.

As if to underline the metamorphosis of lyre to kithara, Hermes on handing over the instrument delivers an extended piece of advice to Apollo (lines 478–88) that relies on a crucial verbal transformation, a metaphor in which the lyre is fully equated with a female companion (*hetaira*):

> Be a fine musician, fondling this clear-voiced girl friend [λιγύφωνον ἑταίρην] who knows how to talk fine and fittingly. Take her confidently to the banquet [δαῖτα θάλειαν] and the lovely dance [χορὸν ἱμερόεντα], and the bumptious revel a source of good cheer day and night. If one questions her with skill and expertise, she speaks all kinds of lessons to charm the fancy, easily tickled [ἀθυρομένη] with tender familiarity, avoiding tiresome effort. But if a novice questions her roughly, then she will utter useless, discordant rubbish.

This fanciful conceit, in turn, brings to mind the earlier episode in the *Hymn to Hermes* centering on the infant god's crafting of the lyre by killing a tortoise and making its shell into a sound box (lines 22–59). There are parallels between the diction used by Hermes when seducing the tortoise into his cave, and that which he later uses to instruct Apollo about the proper handling of the female *organon* that the tortoise became at his hands (31–32):

> Hello, my lovely, my dance-beat dinner companion, welcome apparition! [χαῖρε φυὴν ἐρόεσσα χοροιτύπε δαιτὸς ἑταίρη]
> Where did you get this fine plaything [τόδε καλὸν ἄθυρμα] this blotchy shell that you wear, you tortoise living in the mountains?

I would argue that such seemingly dissonant shifting, through which the tortoise-shell lyre is so markedly transformed into a *kithara*, is at the heart of this composition, directing the audience toward the poem's striking

---

[70] See above, especially footnotes 40–41.

theological and musical assertion: that without Hermes, Apollo would never have learned his famous art. To repeat: in the *Hymn to Apollo*, the god was clearly depicted as a citharode, as we have seen. Playing on the large concert instrument, the *kithara*, is his special sphere of action, declared at birth. Yet the *Hymn to Hermes* conspicuously represents Apollo as completely taken with an attraction to the *lyre* and to the art of intimate song accompanied by this smaller, lighter instrument. Why does the *Hymn to Hermes* show Apollo acquiring from his thievish younger brother not the *kithara* (his canonical instrument) but rather a *lyre*?

As is well illustrated by images on vases, as well as from surviving archaeological remains, kitharas are to lyres as concert harps are to banjos. There is a considerable difference between them in the practicalities of playing, but even more in the semiotic associations of the two stringed instruments. The latter, in fact, can be aligned in terms of a structural opposition that I shall now attempt to articulate.

The tortoise-shell lyre represents a set of associations very much on the surface in the *Hymn to Hermes*, associations that are opposed to those accompanying the *kithara*. Take, for example, the passages that describe the first song-performance of the infant Hermes. He strikes up the instrument and then sings to it in accompaniment "trying things out on the basis of improvisation (*ex autoskhediês*, line 55). We know, however, that singing to the *kithara* in actual contests required the playing of set patterns or *nomoi*.[71] One did not just pick up a *kithara* and improvise, at least not in the most frequent situations that called for kithara-playing: when praising the god, competing in contests (either of singing to kithara or of kithara playing, solo), or accompanying sacrifice. Furthermore, whereas Apollo's followers sing the formal and public genre of *paeans* in the hymn praising him (the kind that Cretans are famous for), Hermes' song instead resembles the improvised off-hand insult contests of young men at feasts (*Hymn to Hermes* 55–56).[72] The association of the lyre with eating, dancing, and the type of woman who attends parties (*hetaira*) could hardly be more marked: at the major poetic transformation points, as we have just observed (tortoise to lyre, lyre to *hetaira*), the same images are highlighted. Finally, the content of Hermes' song is purely autobiographical. The baby singer gives us a first-person view of his

---

[71]   Power 2010, 500–6.

[72]   The informality and bantering tone remind me of another modern Cretan parallel, the duels between men (and sometimes women) who compose rhyming-couplets called *mandinadhes*. Such informal contests can arise in any number of situations: see Martin 2017.

environment, including maids and pots (*Hymn to Hermes* 46–62). This might remind us of another sort of ancient Greek poetry, the often obscene, highly personalized verse attributed to Archilochus, the soldier-poet from the island of Paros. Perhaps it is not accidental that Archilochus was said to have been initiated into poetry as a young man by some sarcastic Muses whom he met on the road, and who gave him, in return for his cow, the gift of a lyre (note—*not* a kithara).[73]

While the instrument depicted in the *Hymn to Hermes* is clearly a tortoise-shell lyre, the audience knows that, in order to be the appropriate accessory for the mature god Apollo, it has to be a *kithara*. It must, in effect, cross the semiotic divide. Therefore, not only does the poet help the suspension of disbelief by refusing to foreground *either* lyre or kithara in their marked forms (as we have seen above); the poet also depicts Hermes with his *lyre* miming the contexts in which one would expect a *kithara*. That is to say, he plays with the underlying structural opposition of the instruments. Hermes' second song-performance is to the accompaniment of his home-made lyre in an agonistic and legalistic setting, something we might expect from a more formal, judged performance. His composition (422–32) is a theogony, a ritual composition of the sort attributed to the primeval mortal singer Orpheus. Yet, whether or not Apollo is meant to indicate that he has never heard stringed music before, his comment on Hermes' newly produced art relates it to sympotic festivity (*euphrosunê*), love, and sleep (447–49). In other words, this music is underlined as being private, non-ritual, and consolatory—the opposite of *kithara* music on all three counts. Just as the first song-performance of Hermes was compared to the impromptu bantering of young men (lines 55–56), so Apollo compares his second song to the sympotic custom of "passing to the right" at young men's feasts (454: οἷα νέων θαλίης ἐνδέξια ἔργα πέλονται).[74] In other words, Hermes' lyre-playing and singing remains firmly within the associative sphere of informality, privacy, and play, even though it might have looked, at first sight, more like a formal theogony appropriate to a professional and publicly competing citharode.

The moment of exchange between Hermes and Apollo, generated by Hermes' second performance, reverses the sort of contract made between

---

[73] On the tale, see D. Clay 2004.

[74] Perhaps youths singing casual table-songs or *skolia*, if that is what *endexia* refers to: the habit of making songs go round the table in a certain direction, to the right; cf. Càssola 1975, 537, Bowie 1993, 360–61, and Martin 2017.

the Delian maidens and the poetic figure with whom they interact in the *Hymn to Apollo.* "*I* will give you this instrument; *you* give me glory," says Hermes (*Hymn to Hermes* 475–77), whereas the Homer-figure, the blind man of Chios said in effect, "*You* use my words, *I'll* give you fame" (*Hymn to Apollo* 171–75). Apollo, agreeing to the bargain, grants Hermes power over some lesser types of prophecy and ends up gaining a lyre. Yet the verbal transmutation effected by the hymn's composer has elevated that lyre to the high-status instrument of the god, known elsewhere as the *kithara*—as if a ukelele has been changed into a Stradivarius.

In analyzing myths of performance, one must always ask: *cui bono?* That is to say, which singers of tales would benefit from suggesting, transgressively, that Apollo's instrumental art was a) the product of a plea-bargain, b) the music of drinking parties, and c) the result of playing on a loosely-strung, lightly resonant instrument that probably could not be heard farther than the end of the table in someone's house, let alone in a huge crowd at a concert competition? The answer is quite clear. This is precisely the sort of depiction we would expect to be crafted by performers who were themselves *non*-musical, not accompanying themselves on the kithara, reciters rather than singers—which is to say, the *rhapsodes*.[75] It is not accidental, I suggest, that the exchange in which Apollo gets his instrument involves his counter-gift to Hermes of a *rhabdos* (line 530–32):

> Moreover, I will give you a beautiful wand [*rhabdos*] of wealth and fortune, made of gold, trefoil; it will keep you safe from harm, fulfilling all the dispositions of good words and events that I claim to know from the utterance of Zeus.

The staff or wand, symbol of the rhapsodes (from which their name is sometimes derived), makes Hermes resemble another semi-mythic singer, Hesiod, famously given a marvelous *skêptron* in his initiation into poetry by the Muses (*Theogony* 30–31).[76] Moreover, Hermes' staff, alongside its magico-talismanic functions to grant fertility, is tied to prophecy, although in what is apparently a mediating manner, dependent on the oracular power of Apollo. Hesiod's gift, too, involves the ability to proclaim future events as well as celebrate the past (*Theogony* 32).

---

[75] Here I would stress the serious intent of the *Hymn to Hermes* depiction, *pace* Power (2010, 434) who sees in it a less fraught presentation of "a playful allegory for Athenians' own enthusiastic integration of the music of the lyre and *kithara* into their civic and sympotic musical lives."

[76] On the derivation of *rhapsoidos*, see González 2013, 336–38, with earlier literature.

In the social world of ancient performer culture, just as in the contemporary world of celebrity musicians (especially rappers), various groups must have characterized one another in an effort to distinguish themselves. Some performers might claim an affiliation between their own art and the genre of citharody, an assertion that makes itself visible in the *Hymn to Apollo*. Others, on the other hand, must have chosen to belittle that very assertion, claiming (as does the *Hymn to Hermes*) that Apollo in fact prefers the sort of privatized, aristocratic, non-ritualized and—most important—*non-agonistic* music associated with the younger boy's instrument, the lyre. Either way, performers lay claim to a divine ancestry and authorization for their own current practices, whether song or recitation. But at the same time, they contested primacy in that sphere.

The under-cutting of citharodic performance, by way of the assertion of the primacy of Hermes' lyre over Apollo's *kithara*, is on one level a kind of inversion joke, the younger initiate (Hermes) making fun of the older initiate model (Apollo). Just as Apollo is the eternal ephebe, Hermes is the eternal trickster, a figure of parody and adolescent play. But these are mythopoeic universals. At the historical level, we can most plausibly pinpoint the context for this competition between musical ideologies within the developing institution of the Panthenaic games at Athens. One key fact distinguishes the Delphic Pythian (and probably the Spartan Carneia) musical contests from the Athenian, as the latter games came to be organized by the Peisistratid tyrants in the sixth century BCE. The Panathenaea featured *rhapsodic* competitions. The Pythian festival did *not*. Even after reorganization in 582 BCE, the Pythian musical contests featured only: citharody (the originating event); playing the kithara without singing; playing the aulos; and singing to the accompaniment of the aulos. That is to say, there was no rhapsodic recitation. Gregory Nagy has shown in a magisterial series of works how the Panathenaic complex and its ideology shaped the rhapsodic treatment of Homer.[77] As he points out in his book, *Plato's Rhapsody and Homer's Music*, even in the fourth century, rhapsodic competition, in terms of prize money, took second place in comparison to citharody, for which one could win, at least in 380 BCE, 1000 drachmas.[78] What the prize scale was in the sixth century is hard to tell. At any rate, at some point, the Homeric hymns, too, must have been in the orbit of the rhapsodic competitions,

---

[77]   On the key importance of the Panathenaic context for Homeric recitation, see Nagy 2002 and 2010.

[78]   Nagy 2002, 38–40.

probably at Athens, and most likely at other cities as well. At the same time, singers would be competing, perhaps with similar material, in singing to the kithara. The testimonia about the citharode Terpander indicate that he sang his own material but also set Homeric verse to music.[79] From the point of view of the evolution of poetic forms, this is interesting; from the point of view of a rhapsode, it is downright *dangerous*. Walter Burkert suggested some years ago that the rhapsodic format was itself in a sort of competition with emerging poetry of the type we see in the choral poet Stesichorus.[80] For choral lyric, I would now substitute as the nemesis of the rhapsodes, at least in mythic terms and the manipulation of myth, the art of citharody. The *Hymn to Hermes* asserts that *Apollo is no citharode*. If this strategic move succeeds, the god is safely marginalized as a lyre-player: Apollo remains a musician, but the citharodes lose a patron—to the conspicuous public benefit of their rivals or descendants, the rhapsodes, reciters in public of hexameter verses without music. Since there is no standard contest in the singing of *lyric* verse, elevating Hermes and his instrument does not pose a risk to the rhapsodes. They have simply, through compositions like the *Hymn to Hermes*, mythologized away the threat.

The more general point that we might take away from this twin study of the inter-relations of craft and the rhetoric about it, as well as the craft of talk, the *logos* of *tekhnê*? It is the pressure of Greek agonism, of contests, of judgment (*krisis*) within a ritual situation—the Pythian games on the one hand, and the Panathenaea on the other—that have encouraged the growth of an entire body of myth, lore, and explanation to undergird a set of rules and regulations. *Out of krisis come kriteria*. The aesthetics we innocently associate with both lyre or kithara playing, and naively, perhaps, fail to disambiguate when looking at representations of Apollo, are an expression of contestation, social and artistic clashes reaching back at least to the sixth century BCE. But, by the same token, *all* aesthetic values in the classical tradition, we should realize, emerge from specific settings of parameters in taste, bound up with the realities of social practice, religious affiliations, class and ethnic ties. Let us not be lured back into Neo-Classical assumptions that Greek aesthetics was the pure product of unfettered disinterested thought. In the same spirit, I would suggest that we should recognize and make use of such parallels or potential continuities as the modern Greek poetic and musical scene can offer, especially but not only in more traditional areas, in order

---

[79] Gostoli 1990, 18–22. See Power 2010 passim, for the most complete analysis of Terpander.

[80] Burkert 1987.

to discover, in precise ethnographic terms, how the pressure of competition shapes authors and authority, contexts and content.

The fate of Apollo's craft, then, is like the result of Poseidon's crash-test, writ large. Compared to the meager fragments of citharodic verse that we still possess, the rhapsodic epics attributed to Homer are massive monuments. They are the vehicles that got through the grove. Yet Apollo's kithara, like the losers' chariots, survives and is celebrated even when silent, suspended in dedication.[81]

---

[81] This paper took its final shape as a contribution to the Athens Dialogues of the Onassis Foundation, Athens (November 24–27, 2010). Its second section originated as a talk at Delphi in the conference on Apolline Politics and Poetics in 2003, and was later expanded and modified in a talk at the International Symposium on Myth and Poetics in La Plata, Argentina in June 2009 (subsequently published as Martin 2010). This chapter represents my continued reflection on the various problems involved, and is significantly changed from the earlier versions.

6

THE SENSES OF AN ENDING
MYTH, RITUAL, AND POETIC
EXODIA IN PERFORMANCE[1]

Citharodic Closings

Rare and unusual information about ancient performance traditions is contained in a fragment attributed to a scholar of the Hadrianic period, Aelius Dionysius the Atticist. He is probably the same man whose voluminous works on the history of music are mentioned in the *Suda* and several other sources, for these included much information on auletes, citharodes, and poets, and the lexicon shows similar familiarity with technical terms of *mousikê*.[2] For example, Aelius Dionysius preserves for us the term *epiporpama* (a kind of jacket worn by citharodes), which he quotes from Plato the comic poet (PCG 10):

> ἐπιπόρπαμα· ἡ τῶν κιθαρῳδῶν ἐφαπτίς. Πλάτων ἐν Ταῖς ἀφ' ἱερῶν
> "δότω τὴν κιθάραν τις ἔνδοθεν καὶ τοὐπιπόρπαμα."

[1] Originally published in *Donum natalicium digitaliter confectum Gregorio Nagy septuagenario a discipulis collegis familiaribus oblatum: A Virtual Birthday Gift Presented to Gregory Nagy on Turning Seventy by His Students, Colleagues, and Friends*, ed. V. Bers et al. (Washington, DC: Center for Hellenic Studies, 2012), http://nrs.harvard.edu/urn-3:hul.ebook:CHS_Bers_etal_eds.Donum_Natalicium_Gregorio_Nagy.2012.

[2] On the historian of music, see Suda δ 1171: Διονύσιος, Ἁλικαρνασεύς, γεγονὼς ἐπὶ Ἀδριανοῦ Καίσαρος, σοφιστής, καὶ Μουσικὸς κληθεὶς διὰ τὸ πλεῖστον ἀσκηθῆναι τὰ τῆς μουσικῆς. ἔγραψε δὲ Ῥυθμικῶν ὑπομνημάτων βιβλία κδ´, Μουσικῆς ἱστορίας βιβλία λς´· ἐν δὲ τούτοις αὐλητῶν καὶ κιθαρῳδῶν καὶ ποιητῶν παντοίων μέμνηται· Μουσικῆς παιδείας ἢ διατριβῶν βιβλία κβ´, Τίνα μουσικῶς εἴρηται ἐν τῇ Πλάτωνος Πολιτείᾳ βιβλία ε´. Schwabe (1890, 6) is agnostic on the question of whether the Atticist was the same man as the musicologist, but cites Müller's belief that they were. On the lexicographical work in relation to other such work, see Erbse 1950.

Epiporpama: The citharodes' uppergarment. Plato in *The Women from the Temples*. "Let someone from inside give the *kithara* and the epiporpama."

The following fragment on musicians and poets is transmitted by the Byzantine scholar Photius (*Lexicon* α 987):

Ἀλλ᾽ ἄναξ· ἐξοδίου κιθαρῳδικοῦ ἀρχή, ὥσπερ κωμικοῦ μὲν (adesp. fr. 48 Dem.) ἥδε "καλλιστέφανος," ῥαψῳδῶν δὲ "νῦν δὲ θεοὶ μάκαρες τῶν ἐσθλῶν ἄφθονοί ἐστε."

"*But, lord.*" The beginning of a citharodic *exodion* [exit song], just as of the comic [*exodion*] there is this: "having a beautiful crown" and of the rhapsodes: "Now, blessed gods, be unstinting in fine things."

Although he does not attribute it directly in his *Lexicon* to Aelius Dionysius, Photius elsewhere speaks of the utility of the Atticist's specialized lexicon, *Attika Onomata,* and recommends it—in both its first and second *ekdoseis*— to all who would care to learn Athenian epichocric terms for lawsuits and festivals, among much other useful information (Photius *Bibliotheca* Cod. 152–53). Several other late sources enable us to fill out further this intriguing bit of antiquarian lore. The fullest version of the information, and the only to trace it directly back to Aelius Dionysius, comes in the twelfth-century Homeric commentary by Eustathius, in partial explanation of a line in Book 2 of the *Iliad* (Eustathius *ad Homeri Iliadem* 1:364, line 6):

(v. 360) Ἰστέον δὲ ὅτι ἐκ τοῦ "ἀλλ᾽ ἄναξ," ὅπερ ἐνταῦθα παρὰ τῷ ποιητῇ κεῖται, ἀρχή τις ἐξοδίου κιθαρῳδικοῦ τὸ "ἀλλὰ ἀλλ᾽ ἄναξ," ὡς ἱστορεῖ Αἴλιος Διονύσιος, ὥσπερ, φησί· κωμικοῦ μὲν ἥδε· "καλλιστέφανος", ῥαψῳδοῦ δὲ αὕτη· "νῦν δὲ θεοὶ μάκαρες τῶν ἐσθλῶν ἄφθονοί ἐστε," τραγικοῦ δέ "πολλαὶ μορφαὶ τῶν δαιμονίων."[3]

Note that from "but lord" which is here found in the poet, there is a beginning of a citharodic *exodion*, the [phrase] "but [other things?] lord," as Aelius Dionysius relates, just as, he says, there is this of the comic [*exodion*]: "having a beautiful crown," and this of the rhapsodes: "Now, blessed gods,

---

[3]   I disagree with the punctuation provided by the latest editor, Theodoridis 1982, 106 (lemma #987); he includes ἥδε within the quoted *exodion*. The correct syntax (and thus punctuation) is clear from the otherwise similar Eustathius passage (κωμικοῦ μὲν ἥδε vs. ῥαψῳδοῦ δὲ αὕτη). Schwabe (1890, 102) prints the phrase correctly and notes further (103 n2) that lexicographers also collected proemial phrases, e.g., Hesychius α 3944 ἀμφὶ ἄνακτα· ἀρχὴ νόμου κιθαρῳδικοῦ (cf. Terpander. fr. 2 Gostoli = PMG 697).

be unstinting in fine things." And of the tragic [*exodion*]: "many are the shapes of the divine."[4]

Zenobius the paroemiographer (*Centuria* 5.99) appears to give a faulty version of the rhapsodic tag-line, but usefully adds a phrase to the citharodic closing:

Σὺν δὲ θεοὶ μάκαρες. τοῦτο ἐπιλέγουσιν οἱ ῥαψῳδοί· ὡς καὶ οἱ κιθαρῳδοί, "Ἀλλ' ἄναξ μάλα χαῖρε."

In addition [reading *sun*, rather than the more plausible *nun*] the blessed gods: the rhapsodes make a formal close with this [*epilegousin*]. In the same way, too, the citharodes "but lord, rejoice/farewell, indeed."[5]

Diogenianus (*Centuria* 6.88), another collector of proverbs, attests to the more plausible phrasing "Now [*nun*] blessed gods," although his version (missing the particle *de*) is unmetrical for inclusion in hexameter verses. He indicates further that the phrase had a usage—perhaps outside of any poetic context—"said of those worthily avenged for what they did" (ἐπὶ τῶν ἀξίως τιμωρουμένων ἐφ' οἷς ἔπραξαν). An entry in the *Suda* (σ 1454) employs the Zenobian phrasing (Σὺν δὲ θεοὶ μάκαρες), identifies it as rhapsodic, then gives a slightly shorter form of the citharodic signature line (ἀλλ' ἄναξ χαῖρε), and ends by explaining "these are finishing phrases (ἐπιφωνήματα) among the old-time poets." No doubt the traditions of stylistic ornamentation among the teachers of rhetoric have influenced this description, as they may also have helped preserve the details about closing phrases, in the first place. We can note, for example, that the essay of Demetrius on style devotes a section to the definition and use of the *epiphônêma* (*De elocutione* 106–111)—although he expands the idea to cover ornamental passages unneeded by the immediate argument (such as a phrase used to fill out a Homeric simile, or a gnomic utterance added to the narrative description of the arms in the hall of Odysseus).[6]

While we can see that the theorists of prose writing, as often, sought models in epic usage, and may have tacitly acknowledged the poetic performance practice of rhapsodes, citharodes, and others singing a stylized endpiece—the *exodion*—there is no sign that any of them (including Dionysius

---

[4]   On the evidence of the other attestations, I assume the repetition in Eustathius (ἀλλὰ ἀλλ' ἄναξ) is a garbled transmission of an original ἀλλ' ἄναξ, although van der Valk 1971 ad loc. does not entertain this possibility.

[5]   For *epilegô* as "make formal close," I rely on the usage of such later genres as Attic oratory, in which *epilogos* was a recognized and stylized final portion of the defense speech; see LSJ s.v.

[6]   Cf. Hermogenes *De inventione* 4.9, for an even more expansive definition.

of Halicarnassus, whom the *Suda* [δ 1174] identifies as an ancestor of Aelius Dionysius the Atticist) elaborated on the specific form of these four types of poetic *exodia* or their wording.[7] But, then again, there are very few signs that the poetry itself, in the form that we now have it, featured any of the phrases that we find preserved by the lexicographic and paroemiographic traditions.

We might initially take comfort in seeing the lore about *exodia* confirmed by extant tragedies that do in fact end with the tag-line "many are the shapes of the divine." The full tragic *exodion*, as found in the *Alcestis* of Euripides, runs (1159–63):

> πολλαὶ μορφαὶ τῶν δαιμονίων,
> πολλὰ δ᾽ ἀέλπτως κραίνουσι θεοί·
> καὶ τὰ δοκηθέντ᾽ οὐκ ἐτελέσθη,
> τῶν δ᾽ ἀδοκήτων πόρον ηὗρε θεός.
> τοιόνδ᾽ ἀπέβη τόδε πρᾶγμα.

> There are many shapes of divinity, and many things the gods accomplish against our expectation. What men expect is not brought to pass, but a god finds a way to achieve the unexpected. Such was the outcome of this story. [trans. Kovacs]

Three other tragedies by Euripides end with these exact lines (*Andromache, Helen, Bacchae*). Encouraged by this confirmation, we might then look at verses that are associated with rhapsodes or citharodes to see whether the conventional verse tag-lines assigned to their respective performers are found in our surviving texts. By extension, we could even hope to identify some compositions as having been part of certain genres or repertoires given the occurrence of the conventional *exodia* in them. But hopes of finding an exact repetition of either sort of rhapsodic or citharodic *exodion* are soon shattered by experiment. On the other hand, the pursuit becomes all the more interesting when we open up the possibility that our extant texts, while they may not quote *exodia* tag-lines, stylize, allude to, or present family resemblances to these apparently well-known phrases. It could be that performers, indeed, avoided direct use of the phrases precisely to undermine audience expectations, while still providing a touch that would recall to mind the poetic convention. Then, too, we can imagine the possibilities for signalling genre-crossing that such tacitly shared audience-performer knowledge could generate. All this requires us to think beyond the

---

[7] On the employment in later analysts of rhetorical practice, especially Aristotle, of Homeric poetry, see now Knudsen 2014.

immediate *text* and to incorporate the *context* of live performance—which is itself a sort of text—into our interpretations.[8]

Let us begin with the alleged citharodic *exodion*, in the fullest form that we can reconstruct *ἀλλὰ ἄναξ μάλα χαῖρε.[9] Two details of my reconstruction are worth pausing over. Although the sources transmit only the elided form ἀλλ' ἄναξ, this combined with the rest of the phrase (preserved only in Zenobius) would be unmetrical for a hexameter.[10] It could of course be argued that citharodic *nomoi* were *not* regularly composed in hexameters. Our picture is complicated by the innovations of Timotheus and other proponents of the New Music at Athens in the later fifth century.[11] The testimonia do tell us that Terpander, the alleged seventh-century BCE inventor of the names of the *nomoi*, and a composer of them, put Homeric hexameters, as well as his own hexameter verses, to melodic accompaniment (test. 27 Gostoli = Heraclides Ponticus fr. 157 Wehrli). But as Gregory Nagy and others have pointed out, lyric meters, some related to the hexameter, are also attested for such *nomoi*.[12] A second point to keep in mind is that an unelided form *ἀλλὰ ἄναξ would be linguistically older; Eustathius, offering what must be a mangled form of the phrase in the sequence "ἀλλὰ ἀλλ' ἄναξ" (difficult to understand unless the second word represents a neuter plural object of some unexpressed verb), might nevertheless be preserving a memory of an original *unelided* phrase *ἀλλὰ ἄναξ in citharodic use. (I shall return shortly to Eustathius and this phrase, as it does appear unelided in the Homeric context upon which he comments.) Poets of a generation no longer aware of the original initial digamma in *wanax (as we see it attested in Mycenaean) would naturally avoid the apparent hiatus and elide to ἀλλ'

---

[8]   I am inspired by Reynolds 1995, a meticulous ethnographic study stressing the need to view "context" as the real "text" (and vice versa) in oral performances.

[9]   Power (2010, 188–89) assumes the phrase was dactylic, but interprets it as more likely "the lead-off verse ... of the end of the prooimion rather than of the song proper," comparing it to the conclusion of many *Homeric Hymns* (e.g., 21.5, 31.17).

[10]   See also for the elision Hesychius α 3113: ἀλλ' ἄναξ· ἐξόδιον κιθαρῳδῶν τοῦτο, καθάπ<ερ ῥαψ>ῳδῶν καὶ τὸ "νῦν <δὲ θεοί ..>"

[11]   Power (2010, 336–50) looks at the testimonia concerning Terpander and other early figures in the light of Timotheus and the New Music.

[12]   It is worth quoting Nagy (1990, 89 n.36) regarding a prime source of our information, [Plutarch] *On Music* (1132de): "In this source, the *nomoi* of Terpander are understood anachronistically as equivalent to the *nomoi* of Timotheus of Miletus, a virtuoso composer of the late fifth century, who is said to have composed his earliest *nomoi* in dactylic hexameters: "Plutarch" *On Music* 1132e. At 1132de (see Barker 1984:209 n. 25) the source infers that Terpander too composed primarily hexameters (though it would be more accurate to say, on the basis of Terpander PMG 697, that Terpander composed in meters related to the hexameter: Gentili and Giannini 1977:35–36)."

ἄναξ. At any rate, in looking for traces of this phrase, I have searched for both elided and unelided forms over the whole range of Greek epic and lyric verses, using as a basis of comparison both the short and long versions of the alleged *exodion*. There are some interesting results.

The logical place to look first is among verses identified as citharodic, meager as they are. Timotheus of Miletus, in his famous *nomos, The Persians* (PMG 791), uses the word ἀλλ᾽ at the very end of his citharodic composition, in combination with the *sphrêgis* that gives his name and polis affiliation (234–40):

> Μίλητος δὲ πόλις νιν ἁ
> θρέψασ᾽ ἁ δυωδεκατειχέος
> λαοῦ πρωτέος ἐξ Ἀχαιῶν.
> ἀλλ᾽ ἑκαταβόλε Πύθι᾽ ἁγνὰν
> ἔλθοις τάνδε πόλιν σὺν ὄλβῳ,
> πέμπων ἀπήμονι λαῷ
> τῶιδ᾽ εἰρήναν θάλλουσαν εὐνομίᾳ.

> It was the city of Miletus that nurtured him, the city of a twelve-walled people that is foremost among the Achaeans. Come far-shooting Pythian, to this holy city and bring prosperity with you, conveying to this people, that they be untroubled, peace that flourishes in good civic order. [trans. Campbell]

Admittedly, it is not followed by ἄναξ or the rest of the full citharodic tag-line. Yet the line does contain a vocative addressing the god Apollo as Pythios and formulates a prayer for peace and prosperity.[13] (In this latter point, it resembles the rhapsodic *exodion*, which is overtly a prayer for similar good things: *esthla*.)

Of course, it might be objected that almost all Greek hymns feature a send-off formula of some sort, even if ἀλλ[ὰ] ἄναξ μάλα χαῖρε never occurs verbatim. As Hordern points out (2002, 246), in connection with the end of the Timotheus poem, "a short prayer is a common feature at the end of hymns," adducing epigraphically attested poems by Isyllus, Ismenius, Philodamos, Limenius, and Aristonous. In effect, we are dealing with normal Greek prayer-style, of the sort represented even in a lower register by the writer of mimiambic verses, the Hellenistic poet Herodas, as in the opening

---

[13] Gostoli 1990, 147 notes the dictional resemblance between these lines and the *exodion*, but prefers to see the similarity as the result of widespread, traditional formulaic closings and salutations.

of his poem about the visit to the shrine of Asclepius by two women wishing to sacrifice a cock (*Mimes* 4):

{ΚΥΝΝΩ}

χαίροις, ἄναξ Παίηον, ὃς μέδεις Τρίκκης
καὶ Κῶν γλυκεῖαν κἠπίδαυρον ᾤκηκας,
σὺν καὶ Κορωνὶς ἥ σ' ἔτικτε κὠπόλλων
χαίροιεν, ἧς τε χειρὶ δεξιῇ ψαύεις
Ὑγίεια, κὠνπερ οἵδε τίμιοι βωμοί
Πανάκη τε κἠπιώ τε κἰησὼ χαίροι ...

Hail, Lord Paieon, you who rule over Trikka
And have made Kos and Epidauros your dwelling-place;
Koronis, too, who bore you and Apollo,
May they fare well, and she whom you touch with the right hand,
Hygieia,
And those for whom altars are revered, Panake and Epio and
Ieso—Hail.

Because "fare well" (*khaire*) can be used at the start or end of any exchange in Greek, we hear it as the potential worshipper enters the sanctuary, or when the worshipper leaves the divinity's space. A lyric poem from the shrine of Asclepius at Epidaurus makes explicit the departure of the speaker (the Mother of the Gods, in this narrative) and joins this to the "send-off" formula and an address using the word ἄνασσα (PMG 935 = IG IV² 131):

καὶ οὐκ ἄπειμι εἰς θεούς,
ἂν μὴ τὰ μέρη λάβω,   20
τὸ μὲν ἥμισυ οὐρανῷ,
τὸ δ' ἥμισυ γαίας,
πόντω τὸ τρίτον μέρος
χοὖτως ἀπελεύσομαι.
χαῖρ' ὦ μεγάλα ἄνασ-   25
σα Μᾶτερ Ὀλύμπου.

"I shall not go off unless I get my portions, half of the heaven and half of the earth and a third portion, half of the sea: only then shall I go off." Greetings, great Mother, queen of Olympus! [trans. Campbell]

So the individual elements of the alleged citharodic *exodion—khaire*-forms, forms of **wanak*—are hardly surprising in a hymnic context. In addition to the examples above, and in several epigraphic hymns, it is worth noting that *every one* of the collection of Homeric hymns contains a *khaire* formula.[14] A few employ a multiform line that is quite close in wording to the citharodic *exodion*, as the following examples show:

> In Herculem, line 9:
> Χαῖρε ἄναξ Διὸς υἱέ· δίδου δ᾽ ἀρετήν τε καὶ ὄλβον.

> In Solem, line 17:
> Χαῖρε ἄναξ, πρόφρων δὲ βίον θυμήρε᾽ ὄπαζε·

> In Lunam, line 17:
> Χαῖρε ἄνασσα θεὰ λευκώλενε δῖα Σελήνη

Whether such lines are meant to actively summon up *citharodic* practice, in a medium that might have been recited rather than sung (see below), or whether the resemblance is a reflex of a more general hymnic-prayer rhetoric, it is hard to deny that the placement of these verses underlines their similarity with the citharodic *exodion*.

It may be slightly more surprising that citharodic compositions (so it would appear, if the information about the *exodion* is correct) were at some time period explicitly connected with a singer's farewell to a god—a markedly hymnic closing for a genre that we might not immediately associate with hymns. If we take them at face value (perhaps unwisely), the words of Plato's Athenian in the *Laws* (700b) make it clear that at some (perhaps irrecoverable) point, hymns were distinct from *nomoi*, and citharodic were distinct from other sorts:

> Among us, at that time, music was divided into various classes and styles: one class of song was that of prayers to the gods, which bore the name of "hymns"; contrasted with this was another class, best called "dirges"; "paeans" formed another; and yet another was the "dithyramb," named, I fancy, after Dionysus. "Nomes" also were so called as being a distinct class of song; and these were further described as "citharodic nomes" [νόμους τε αὐτὸ τοῦτο τοὔνομα ἐκάλουν, ᾠδὴν ὥς τινα ἑτέραν· ἐπέλεγον δὲ κιθαρῳδικούς].

---

[14] Cf. also the *Paean Erythraeus in Aesculapium*, lines 19–20 (Χαῖρέ μοι, ἵλαος δ᾽ ἐπινίσεο τὰν ἐμὰν πόλιν εὐρύχορον) and the *Paean in Apollinem et Aesculapium* (= IG 3.1.171b), lines 23–24 (Χαῖρε, βροτοῖς μέγ᾽ ὄνειαρ, δαῖμον κλεινότατε, ὦ [ἰὲ Παιάν]), both in Powell 1925.

Then again, paeans and dithyrambs, which Plato's speaker places apart from *humnoi*, are clearly directed towards gods (Apollo and Dionysus, usually), just like hymns. Because the texts of identifiable citharodic nomes are so meager, the lore about citharodes must be consulted. It yields a number of details that do connect performance to the god Apollo. First of all, Apollo as depicted in the *Hymn to Apollo*, and in visual art, is himself the archetypal citharode.[15] Second, the chief festival at his shrine in Delphi had as its centerpiece in the *mousikoi agônes* a citharodic competition.[16] Before the reorganization of the Pythian games in the sixth century BCE, the *only* contest was in citharody, which according to Pausanias, took the form of singing a hymn to Apollo. The first winner was Chrysothemis of Crete (Pausanias *Description of Greece* 10.7.3):

> The oldest contest and the one for which they first offered prizes was, according to tradition, the singing of a hymn to the god. The man who sang and won the prize was Chrysothemis of Crete, whose father Carmanor is said to have cleansed Apollo. After Chrysothemis, says tradition, Philammon won with a song, and after him his son Thamyris. But they say that Orpheus, a proud man and conceited about his mysteries, and Musaeus, who copied Orpheus in everything, refused to submit to the competition in musical skill.
>
> They say too that Eleuther won a Pythian victory for his loud and sweet voice, for the song that he sang was not of his own composition. The story is that Hesiod too was debarred from competing because he had not learned to accompany his own singing on the harp. Homer too came to Delphi to inquire about his needs, but even though he had learned to play the harp, he would have found the skill useless owing to the loss of his eye-sight.

A supplement to Pausanias' information at this point comes from a tradition passed down by the Byzantine scholar Photius (*Bibliotheca* 320b) that the mortal singer Chrysothemis was the first to wear expensive clothing and to take up the kithara to sing a solo *nomos* or traditional song-pattern in *imitation* of Apollo (*eis mimêsin Apollonos*). This anecdote is nothing less than an aetiological story to explain the customary dress of both competitive citharists and their instruments. In sum, we can rest assured that the

---

[15] See Nagy 1990, 353 on "the archetypal virtuoso performance of Apollo"; in this volume, see further Chapters 5 and 7.

[16] On the Pythian *agôn* see Power 2010, 371–78.

citharodic nomes featured a strong tie to Apollo as addressee, performance model, and probably theme.

Before turning to non-hymnic—or, at least, possibly *covert* hymnic—allusions to the citharodic art, we should note that the seemingly least important word of the *exodion* we have thus far been examining—ἀλλ'—is actually quite highly marked, in and of itself, as indicating a turn away from the narrative of a hymn and toward closure.[17] Consider, for example, the ending of the *Homeric Hymn to Demeter* as it turns from narrating the blessings of the older goddess, to a direct address to the immortal pair (Demeter and her daughter Persephone):

> Ἀλλ' ἄγ' Ἐλευσῖνος θυοέσσης δῆμον ἔχουσαι   490
> καὶ Πάρον ἀμφιρύτην Ἀντρωνά τε πετρήεντα,
> πότνια ἀγλαόδωρ' ὡρηφόρε Δηοῖ ἄνασσα
> αὐτὴ καὶ κούρη *περικαλλὴς* Περσεφόνεια
> πρόφρονες *ἀντ' ᾠδῆς* βίοτον θυμήρε' ὀπάζειν.
> αὐτὰρ ἐγὼ καὶ σεῖο καὶ *ἄλλης* μνήσομ' *ἀοιδῆς.*

> So come, you that preside over the people of fragrant Eleusis, and seagirt Paros and rocky Antron—Lady, bringer of resplendent gifts in season, mistress Deo, both you and your daughter, beautiful Persephone: be favorable, and grant comfortable livelihood in return for my singing. And I will take heed both for you and for other singing. [trans. West 2003]

Through phonic resonances the key indicator of the send-off (ἀλλ') echoes twice (see *italicized* words above) as the poet begs for livelihood in exchange for the song—a perfect example of the *do ut des* economy in which ancient hymnic poetry operated. The final echo in ἄλλης ... ἀοιδῆς functions to forecast future performances of this or a similar song; but at the same time, as has been pointed out by Gregory Nagy, this ending allows the rhapsodic "hymn" to segue into a performance of another type of *hymnos*—namely Homeric epic. We can do no better in attempting to articulate this state of the evidence than quote at some length Nagy's own elegant formulation in *Pindar's Homer*:

---

[17] This would seem to be a long-lasting convention: cf. the ending of a Sibylline Oracle of the Imperial period (Geffcken #11, lines 322–24), which is even closer to the citharodic *exodion* (and also embeds a final phrase from the shorter *Homeric Hymn to Aphrodite*):
 ἀλλά, ἄναξ, νῦν παῦσον ἐμὴν πολυήρατον αὐδήν
 οἶστρον ἀπωσάμενος καὶ ἐτήτυμον ἔνθεον ὀμφήν
 καὶ μανίην φοβερὰν, δὸς δ' ἱμερόεσσαν ἀοιδήν.

That these Hymns are morphologically preludes, with the inherited function of introducing the main part of the performance, is illustrated by references indicating a shift to the performance proper, such as *metabêsomai allon es humnon* 'I will shift to the rest of the song [*humnos*]' at *Homeric Hymns* 5 (verse 293), 9 (verse 9), and 18 (verse 11). To sum up the essence of the prooimion, I quote the wording of Quintilian (*Institutio oratoria* 4.1.2): *quod oimê cantus est, et citharoedi pauca illa, quae antequam legitimum certamen inchoent, emerendi favoris gratia canunt, prooemium cognominaverunt...* 'that *oimê* is song and that the *kitharôidoi* refer to those few words that they sing before their contest proper, for the sake of winning favor, as *prooimion* ...'. Quintilian's reference to 'those few words' sung by the *kitharôidoi* 'lyre [*kithar*â] singers' is belied by the proportions of some of the larger *Homeric Hymns*, which had evolved into magnificent extravaganzas that rival epic in narrative power, as in the case of the *Hymn to Apollo*. It is in fact legitimate to ask whether the *Homeric Hymns*, especially the larger ones, were functional preludes ..."

Nagy concludes that "the medium of the *Homeric Hymns*, which is poetry recited in dactylic hexameter, is several stages removed from the medium of *kitharôidiâ*, that is, song."[18]

With the mention of the mode for performance of the *Homeric Hymns*, in view of their citharodic relations, we need to pause for a moment to recognize a more complex interpretive situation than that involved in tracing prayer tropes and "sacral" language within hymns. Or, more accurately, we need to face the problem of explicating multiple speech-genre and song-related layers in early Greek poetry. That is to say, it is possible to foreground—but not to extricate—diction and rhetorical tropes that we can imagine being shared with non-poetic prayer (greetings to a god; the *hypomnesis* of a prayer, in which the god's past intercession or the worshipper's past invocations are recalled; the final wish for some boon; and send-off formulas). In fact, our earliest "prayers" in Greek are already all in poetic form—that is to say, literary representations of prayer—and it would be difficult in practice to distinguish "poetic" prayer from "actual." Except for a few scattered notices, we do not have anything in Greek like the corpus of Latin prayers preserved by the elder Cato in *De Agricultura*. Another way of approaching this problem is to admit the possibility that all prayers in early Greek were in high style, with formal metrical and phonic means that kept them distinct from "prose"—that, in fact, "poetry" was the medium with

---

[18] Nagy 1990, 353–54.

which to pray. It is a short step from here to the assertion that prayer and hymn in early Greek are in fact indistinguishable.

With Homeric hymns, however, we meet two degrees of further complexity. First, the hymnic function, as it is represented by the *Hymn to Apollo* and *Hymn to Hermes,* is unmistakably equivalent to citharodic performance, as Nagy has demonstrated. It features one performer, master of an instrument and singing to its music. Chronologically, the instrument moves from Hermes to Apollo (if we credit the tale of the *Hymn to Hermes,* itself highly colored with a particular musical ideology). I have argued that the pairing of the *Hymn to Apollo* and *Hymn to Hermes* allows us to trace a significant symbolic transfer that must be related to the relative standing of archaic Greek performance traditions, in which not only are sympotic lyric forms, accompanied with either *barbitos* or tortoise-shell lyre, set apart from public, citharodic competitive performances, but also citharodic performances of the agonistic type familiar at Delphi and Athens were distinguished from rhapsodic recitations—the latter, significantly, a feature of the Athenian Panathenaea but not the Delphic Pythia.[19] (As we shall see below, similar competing versions must undergird the lore about Archilochus and his acquisition or lack of instruments.)

However—a second point of complexity—Homeric hymns were themselves in all probability not just several stages removed from citharody, but had become embedded in the *rhapsodic* competition repertoire. One telling passage suggesting this comes at the end of the shorter *Hymn to Aphrodite* in the corpus, where the poet—using the *khaire*-diction familiar from the citharodic *exodion*—asks for victory "*in this contest*":[20]

> Χαῖρ' ἑλικοβλέφαρε γλυκυμείλιχε, δὸς δ' ἐν ἀγῶνι
> νίκην τῷδε φέρεσθαι, ἐμὴν δ' ἔντυνον ἀοιδήν.   20
> αὐτὰρ ἐγὼ καὶ σεῖο καὶ ἄλλης μνήσομ' ἀοιδῆς.

> I salute you, sweet-and-gentle one of curling lashes: grant me
> victory *in this competition*, and order my singing. And I will take
> heed both for you and for other singing. [trans. West 2003]

---

[19] Chapter 5 above; see also Martin 2011. Power (2010, 468–75) discusses the "lyric politics" underlying the depiction of the transfer in the *Hymn to Hermes*. His analysis of the *Hymn's* melding of sympotic with competitive citharody does not cover the contrast I would draw between Athenian (Panathenaic) and Delphic (Pythian) festival contexts, as they are ideologically expressed in the *Hymn to Hermes* vs. the *Hymn to Apollo*. Elsewhere (250–57), Power does note the rivalry between citharodes and rhapsodes expressed variously in ancient sources. I would simply extend this insight to the contrastive stances of the two *Homeric Hymns* just mentioned.

[20] See further Chapter 7 below.

The deployment of the unmarked word "song" (ἀοιδῆς) here and elsewhere in hexameter verse that was most likely *recited* allows the competing poet to elide the actual conditions of performance and to affiliate himself with a tradition of musically accompanied verse, whether or not he himself plays or is accompanied by a musician. To put this another way, one type of poetry shaped for competitive performance in *recitation* (hexameter long narrative, including Homeric style hymns) clearly asserts a genealogical link to another type of poetry meant for *singing* (again, in competition) to the accompaniment of a kithara. What is the upshot? In short, we have a perfect setting for intertextual, inter-generic, and inter-performative hybridization. Recall once more that the Panathenaea featured *both* rhapsodic *and* citharodic competitions: it was only natural that performers of one type would listen to and learn from those of the other, and that audiences for both would appreciate strategies, tropes, and even phrasings borrowed and shifting (in inter-generic competition) from one to the other. We might label this speculative, but—as with most philological work beyond the most basic steps—a certain amount of imaginative "reconstruction forward" has to be indulged in if we are to make progress.

To return to the analytical problem at a slightly more abstract level: any occurrence of sacral, prayer diction (*khaire*, *anax*) might be "hymnic" in a general application of that term. If we take seriously the evidence of Aelius Dionysius, at least one specific "sacral" usage was associated with *citharodic* songs (or, if we extrapolate from other lore about Delphic traditions, citharodic hymns *to Apollo* in particular). But, as I have noted already, the citharodic use must further be viewed within the framework of competitive citharoidia, at Athens, Sparta, and Delphi (to name just three of the premier venues for this contest). I propose now that the *exodion* ἀλλ[ά] ἄναξ μάλα χαῖρε was a sign and a product of that very competition. As a convention, it was by definition well-known, part of the audience's horizon of expectation. Here we have the parallel of the tragic *exodia* to guide us. They must have developed at Dionysiac competitions in Athens and probably served the same function of indicating to judges and audience that the play was over— a curtain, as it were, in a theater that lacked such devices.

Given the conventional quality of citharodic *exodia*, I propose further that the "hymnic" or prayer style address (or elements thereof) involving address to a *wanax* or the verb *khaire* might crop up even in *rhapsodic* usage—that is to say, in the performance of Homeric, Hesiodic, or other recited poetry—and, when it did, could carry with it the distinct trace of a dual heritage—not just as (generic) "prayer" or "hymn" but as the sort of language used in citharodic contestation. In other words, it might repay the effort of hearing a few instances of such language within rhapsodic poetry played against a "citharodic" sound-track, to see whether these already rich texts might yield even more meaningful resonances.

In a previous work, I have pointed out briefly how one "rhapsodic" text that strives to assert its "citharodic" relationships makes use of the language found in the citharodic exordia.[21] This is the *Hymn to Apollo*, at lines 165–81:

> ἀλλ' ἄγεθ' ἱλήκοι μὲν Ἀπόλλων Ἀρτέμιδι ξύν,   165
> χαίρετε δ' ὑμεῖς πᾶσαι· ἐμεῖο δὲ καὶ μετόπισθε
> μνήσασθ', ὁππότε κέν τις ἐπιχθονίων ἀνθρώπων
> ἐνθάδ' ἀνείρηται ξεῖνος ταλαπείριος ἐλθών·
> "ὦ κοῦραι, τίς δ' ὕμμιν ἀνὴρ ἥδιστος ἀοιδῶν
> ἐνθάδε πωλεῖται, καὶ τέῳ τέρπεσθε μάλιστα;"   170
> ὑμεῖς δ' εὖ μάλα πᾶσαι ὑποκρίνασθαι ἀφήμως ·
> "τυφλὸς ἀνήρ, οἰκεῖ δὲ Χίῳ ἔνι παιπαλοέσσῃ,
> τοῦ πᾶσαι μετόπισθεν ἀριστεύουσιν ἀοιδαί."
> ἡμεῖς δ' ὑμέτερον κλέος οἴσομεν ὅσσον ἐπ' αἶαν
> ἀνθρώπων στρεφόμεσθα πόλεις εὖ ναιεταώσας   175
> οἱ δ' ἐπὶ δὴ πείσονται, ἐπεὶ καὶ ἐτήτυμόν ἐστιν.
> αὐτὰρ ἐγὼν οὐ λήξω ἑκηβόλον Ἀπόλλωνα
> ὑμνέων ἀργυρότοξον ὃν ἠΰκομος τέκε Λητώ.
> ὦ ἄνα, καὶ Λυκίην καὶ Μῃονίην ἐρατεινὴν
> καὶ Μίλητον ἔχεις ἔναλον πόλιν ἱμερόεσσαν,   180
> αὐτὸς δ' αὖ Δήλοιο περικλύστου μέγ' ἀνάσσεις.

But now, may Apollo be favorable, together with Artemis, and *hail, all you Maidens!* Think of me in future, if ever some long-suffering stranger comes here and asks, "O Maidens, which is your favorite singer who visits here, and who do you enjoy most?" *Then you must all answer with one voice* (?), "It is a blind man, and he lives in rocky Chios; all of his songs remain supreme afterwards." *And we* will carry your reputation wherever we go as we roam the well-ordered cities of men, and they will believe it, because it is true. *And myself, I shall not* cease from hymning the far-shooter Apollo of the silver bow, whom lovely-haired Leto bore.

---

[21] The idea was expressed in one paragraph in my paper on "Apollo Citharode" delivered at Delphi in the conference on *Apolline Politics and Poetics* in July 2003. This was later reworked and modified in a talk at the International Symposium on Myth and Poetics in La Plata, Argentina in June 2009, which resulted in the publication of Martin 2010. A longer English version was delivered at the Athens Dialogues in November 2010 and is reworked in this volume as Chapter 5.

> *O Lord*, Lycia too is yours, and lovely Lydia, and Miletus the
> beautiful town by the sea; and you again, none other, are the
> great lord of wave-washed Delos. [trans. West 2003]

Clearly, all four elements of the citharodic *exodion* appear in these lines:
(ἀλλ' at 165; ἄνα, 179; μάλα, 171; χαίρετε, 166). In retrospect, I now see
more clearly that the conventional citharodic *exodion* has been dispersed
and re-cast in two ways. First, there is an internal expansion (lines 166–78)
that arises from the hymnist's elaborate presentation of a dialogic episode
within the narrative, in which the poet-speaker ("the man from Chios")
addresses the Delian maidens and contrasts their epichoric choral performance (marvelous for its fascinating imitative qualities) with his own mobile
song-making—perhaps, Panhellenic in ambition.[22] If we did not have the
intricate pronominal play of *hûmeis/hêmeis/egôn* (lines 166, 171, 174, 177),
which is generated by this interplay (itself a vivid genre-contrast), and could
in effect collapse the passage, suppressing the lines that intervene and that
describe the respective musical accomplishments and tasks of the performing
entities, line 165 would meet up with 179:

ἀλλ' ἄγεθ' ἱλήκοι μὲν Ἀπόλλων Ἀρτέμιδι ξύν,	165
ὦ ἄνα, καὶ Λυκίην καὶ Μῃονίην ἐρατεινὴν	179

That is, a version of the citharodic *exodion* would be prominently displayed,
one element of it at the start of each line. I am not suggesting that any sort
of mechanical expansion did, in fact, ever occur; rather, the entire idea of
the *Hymn to Apollo*, with its multiple innovations and pairings, embodies an
expansion aesthetic that has been organically employed to make a long and
interesting narrative, the fruit of generations of reworking various traditions.
Such an expansion might even have occurred in the context of rhapsodic
contests, as I suggested some years ago.[23] A second sort of expansion in this
particular passage of the *Hymn* takes the conventional sign-off formula with
ἀλλ' and lengthens it into a pivot passage: what sounds to be, at first hearing,
a sign-off tag (at line 165) is then, after the internal expansion I have just
outlined, re-doubled by the formulaic line αὐτὰρ ἐγὼν οὐ λήξω ἑκηβόλον

---

[22] For full analysis of the Delian maidens' performance, see Peponi 2009.

[23] Martin 2000b.

Ἀπόλλωνα. Note that this, too, sounds at first like an *exodion*-style close; compare in the very same *Hymn to Apollo* the last lines:[24]

> Καὶ σὺ μὲν οὕτω χαῖρε Διὸς καὶ Λητοῦς υἱέ·
> αὐτὰρ ἐγὼ καὶ σεῖο καὶ ἄλλης μνήσομ' ἀοιδῆς.

To sum up: the *Hymn to Apollo*, in its pursuit of a conscious modelling of its protagonists (Apollo and the Chian poet) on citharodes, makes "citharodic" sounds at the key switch-over point in the middle of the composition, which is both an ending and a beginning. It is further worth noting that αὐτὰρ in this use is a perfect formulaic complement for ἀλλ(ά), because, while both are isosyllabic and of the same metrical shape, the latter ends with a vowel and can thus fit a range of line-initial metrical situations that cannot be accommodated by the former. The *Hymn to Apollo* passage shows us both complementary formulas at work, one backing up the other.

This is one passage, then, of a rhapsodic composition that gains highly relevant thematic resonance from a citharodic "feel" and rhetorical strategy. Before leaving the hymns to examine an epic moment, it is worthwhile pointing out another passage that may feature similar latent associations. In the *Hymn to Aphrodite*, the goddess encounters Anchises on Mt. Ida, alone in the cattle pen, while the other cowherds are out on the range. The goddess of love stands before him, disguised as a *parthenos*; as *eros* grips the young man, captivated by her wondrous shining beauty, he greets her and runs through a litany of possible divinities she resembles, ending with a promise to build an altar, and a prayer that he might receive from her fame, long life, and descendants. In light of the prayer and the divine interlocutor, it is unremarkable that Anchises begins his speech with the words Χαῖρε ἄνασσ' (92–99):

> Χαῖρε ἄνασσ', ἥ τις μακάρων τάδε δώμαθ' ἱκάνεις,
> Ἄρτεμις ἢ Λητὼ ἠὲ χρυσέη Ἀφροδίτη
> ἢ Θέμις ἠϋγενὴς ἠὲ γλαυκῶπις Ἀθήνη
> ἤ πού τις Χαρίτων δεῦρ' ἤλυθες, αἵ τε θεοῖσι   95
> πᾶσιν ἑταιρίζουσι καὶ ἀθάνατοι καλέονται,
> ἤ τις νυμφάων αἵ τ' ἄλσεα καλὰ νέμονται,
> [ἢ νυμφῶν αἳ καλὸν ὄρος τόδε ναιετάουσι]
> καὶ πηγὰς ποταμῶν καὶ πίσεα ποιήεντα.

---

[24]   See similar phrasing at the end of the long *Hymn to Demeter* (495) and *Hymn to Hermes* (580) and at the end of nine of the shorter *Hymns* in the collection (Pan; Muses and Apollo; Artemis, etc.).

Hail, Lady, whichever of the blessed ones you are that arrive at this dwelling, Artemis or Leto or golden Aphrodite, high-born Themis or steely-eyed Athena; or perhaps you are one of the Graces come here, who are companions to all the gods and are called immortal; or one of the nymphs, who haunt the fair groves and the waters of rivers and the grassy meads. [trans. West 2003]

But an echo of the citharodic *exodion* would be perfectly apt, since the audience at this stage already knows what Anchises was doing when first approached by Aphrodite—namely, playing the kithara (76–80):

> τὸν δ' εὗρε σταθμοῖσι λελειμμένον οἷον ἀπ' ἄλλων
> Ἀγχίσην ἥρωα θεῶν ἄπο κάλλος ἔχοντα.
> οἱ δ' ἅμα βουσὶν ἕποντο νομοὺς κάτα ποιήεντας
> πάντες, ὁ δὲ σταθμοῖσι λελειμμένος οἷος ἀπ' ἄλλων
> πωλεῖτ' ἔνθα καὶ ἔνθα *διαπρύσιον κιθαρίζων*.   80

> ... and found him left all alone in the steading, the manly Anchises who had his beauty from the gods; the others were all following the cattle over the grassy pastures, while he, left all alone in the steading, was going about this way and that, playing loudly on a kithara. [trans. West 2003; slightly modified]

That is to say, the first words of Anchises to the goddess are also the *last* words of his song—his *exodion*. Perhaps, in a *mise en abyme* effect not unfamiliar to archaic Greek composers (one thinks of *Iliad* 9.186–91—Achilles singing to the phorminx while Patroclus waits), Anchises can be imagined as in the process of breaking off from singing to his kithara something like the *Homeric Hymn to Aphrodite*. He is, after all, as a rustic singer who encounters a goddess in the wild (like Hesiod or Archilochus), himself a multiform; perhaps he performs a tale of one, as well.

Does Homeric epic ever echo the citharodic *exodion*—and why? Word-searches of the relevant diction turn up only one passage, but a particularly interesting one. The stylistic background has to be stated, first, in order for us to appreciate the peculiarity foregrounded by the scene in question. Of the ninety-three times that ἄναξ appears in Homeric poetry, only seventeen times does it function as vocative (i.e., as in the citharodic *exodion*). Seven out of those seventeen occur in addresses to Agamemnon (not surprising in view of his regular epithet ἄναξ ἀνδρῶν Ἀγαμέμνων).[25] The only other

[25] Unusual as is the sequence ἀλλὰ ἄναξ, it might have been generated formulaically on the basis of two relevant templates (or their "preverbal Gestalt" to use Nagler's helpful concept). The phrase "But, up now" occurs four times in Homer (e.g., *Iliad* 6.331: ἀλλ' ἄνα μὴ τάχα ἄστυ πυρὸς δηίοιο

mortals thus addressed are his brother Menelaus (*Iliad* 23.588), Odysseus (*Odyssey* 11.71), Teiresias (*Odyssey* 11.144), and Ajax (*Odyssey* 11.561). Six times gods are called upon with ἄναξ (Apollo: *Iliad* 16.514 and 523, *Odyssey* 8.339; Hypnos: *Iliad* 14.233; an unknown river god: *Odyssey* 5.445 and 450). Only in one passage in all of Homeric verse is this vocative introduced with the word ἀλλά (as in the *exodion*). This occurs as Nestor offers his advice to his leader (*Iliad* 2.360–68):

> ἀλλὰ ἄναξ αὐτός τ' εὖ μήδεο πείθεό τ' ἄλλῳ·   360
> οὔ τοι ἀπόβλητον ἔπος ἔσσεται ὅττί κεν εἴπω·
> κρῖν' ἄνδρας κατὰ φῦλα κατὰ φρήτρας Ἀγάμεμνον,
> ὡς φρήτρη φρήτρηφιν ἀρήγῃ, φῦλα δὲ φύλοις.
> εἰ δέ κεν ὣς ἔρξῃς καί τοι πείθωνται Ἀχαιοί,
> γνώσῃ ἔπειθ' ὅς θ' ἡγεμόνων κακὸς ὅς τέ νυ λαῶν   365
> ἠδ' ὅς κ' ἐσθλὸς ἔῃσι· κατὰ σφέας γὰρ μαχέονται.
> γνώσεαι δ' εἰ καὶ θεσπεσίῃ πόλιν οὐκ ἀλαπάξεις,
> ἦ ἀνδρῶν κακότητι καὶ ἀφραδίῃ πολέμοιο.

> Come, my lord: yourself be careful, and listen to another.
> This shall not be a word to be cast away that I tell you.
> Set your men in order by tribes, by clans, Agamemnon,
> and let clan go in support of clan, let tribe support tribe.
> If you do it this way, and the Achaians obey you,
> you will see which of your leaders is bad, and which of your people,
> and which also is brave, since they will fight in divisions,
> and might learn also whether by magic you fail to take this
> city, or by men's cowardice and ignorance of warfare. [trans.
> Lattimore 2011]

θέρηται). This association would have provided a familiar sound-sequence upon which an innovative ἀλλὰ ἄναξ might be composed in performance, especially since the ἀλλ' ἄνα phrase features a homonym (ἄνα) of the rarer vocative form of ἄναξ (ἄνα), which occurs three times in Homer (always as vocative of Zeus, e.g., *Iliad* 3.351: Ζεῦ ἄνα δὸς τίσασθαι ὅ με πρότερος κάκ' ἔοργε). A more immediate source for the unique expression in *Iliad* 2.360 may be lines of the type attested twice in the *Odyssey*, in which the feminine form is used, addressing a goddess. At *Odyssey* 3.380, Nestor (again) is the speaker, in a prayer: ἀλλά, ἄνασσ', ἵληθι, δίδωθι δέ μοι κλέος ἐσθλόν. At *Odyssey* 6.175, Odysseus uses the same vocative phrase to address Nausicaa, whom he has compared to a goddess. In neither scene is a citharodic flavor detectable (although the entire scene is undoubtedly colored by poetry about choruses of young women, and Alcman may have composed a similar scene: cf. scholia HQ ad *Odyssey* 6.244ff [Dindorf]: αἱ γὰρ ἐμοὶ—ἐνθάδε ναιετάων] ἄμφω μὲν ἀθετεῖ Ἀρίσταρχος, διστάζει δὲ περὶ τοῦ πρώτου, ἐπεὶ καὶ Ἀλκμὰν αὐτὸν μετέβαλε παρθένους λεγούσας εἰσάγων "Ζεῦ πάτερ, αἲ γὰρ ἐμὸς πόσις εἴη").

It is remarkable that this passage, which can be pinpointed nowadays through searching digitized texts, on the basis of its otherwise unattested sequence ἀλλὰ ἄναξ, was already singled out for comment in the twelfth century (perhaps recalling earlier, no longer extant analyses) by Eustathius. For this is the precise point in his massive commentary when the Homeric scholar chooses to make the remark with which I began this paper:

> (v. 360) Ἰστέον δὲ ὅτι ἐκ τοῦ "ἀλλ' ἄναξ," ὅπερ ἐνταῦθα παρὰ τῷ ποιητῇ κεῖται, ἀρχή τις ἐξοδίου κιθαρῳδικοῦ τὸ "ἀλλὰ ἀλλ' ἄναξ," ὡς ἱστορεῖ Αἴλιος Διονύσιος.

> Note that from "but lord" which is here found in the poet, the beginning of a citharodic *exodion* [comes], the [phrase] "but [other things?] lord," as Aelius Dionysius relates …

Perhaps as both bishop and master rhetorician, Eustathius was hypersensitive to forms of address and prayer-style. Or, it could be that his well-trained literary ear detected the unusual combination. He does not give an opinion as to whether the strong resemblance to the citharodic *exodion* in this (and only this) line in all of Homer means anything. But I believe we can indeed make a claim for several latent associations. First, it should be recognized that the overall structure of Nestor's speech (*Iliad* 2.336–68) places the vocative appeal at the proper location for an *exodion*-like close. Eight lines from the end of his intervention, it comes as he turns from comments more generally aimed at the reluctant troops of the Achaeans toward a final address to Agamemnon. The first part of his speech, moreover, functions like the *hypomnesis* of a prayer. The content, as well, has an overtly religious dimension, as the aged warrior reminds the Achaeans of the vows they undertook, with solemn libations, to conquer Troy. If they return to Argos now, it will be a denial of faith in the promises of Zeus, sealed with his own signs of thunder and lightning as they set out on the expedition (348–53). Unlike the usual prayer-style, Nestor does not match the *hypomnesis* with a wish for future blessings: rather than saying simply "just as you promised … so now act," he expands on the rhetorical formula to say "so now do not go until requiting Helen's woes" (354–56). The final prayer or wish is then directed to Agamemnon (not the troops): he should marshall the troops, marking them off (κρῖν') by tribe and clan. This, too, has a religious function, for in this manner it will be possible to tell, says Nestor, whether failure to succeed comes through a divinity's will (θεσπεσίῃ) or human insufficiency.

Kirk in his commentary notes that Nestor's frequent tactical advice "tends to be expressed in untraditional language" (1985, 154). One wonders whether Nestor's style is *generically* different, and if that reflects in turn an affiliation with a different mode of singing the tales of past generations—something more akin to citharody. Nestor is, after all, a survivor of battles that are for the current Trojan War warriors the events of long ago; with these tales he entertains and instructs his most recent hearers.[26] Another angle of vision would allow us to see in the content and style of Nestor's instructions to Agamemnon in Book 2 a more specifically Apolline directivity. The god who points out how things should be, whether the route of roads or the places for colonies, is also the quintessential god of *nomos* and properly honored with citharodic *nomoi*, just as he plays them himself while leading the chorus (cf. Pindar *Nemean* 5.24–25).[27] In the *Hymn to Apollo* the functions of leader of a chorus, giver of orders (to the Cretan sailors, his intended priests), and player of the kithara converge (*Hymn to Apollo* 513–43). Apollo's concern for the *phula* of mortals who will come to his temple (cf. identical line-end formula in *Hymn to Apollo* 537 and 538: φῦλ' ἀνθρώπων) is not quite the same as Nestor's for the *phula* of the army that he would order into place, but the overlap in diction, given the other contextual markers, is interesting.

Also of interest is the afterlife of such language in similar religious contexts. Several centuries after the period in which the Homeric hymn likely crystallized into the form in which we have it, another Apolline figure—Isyllus of Epidaurus—undertook to order the worship for Apollo Maleatas and Asclepius. In the hexameter portion of his foundational paeanic hymn, the diction of the Nestor's advice in the passage we have been analyzing comes together with instructions for the proper celebration of his god:

> Τόνδ' ἱαρὸν θείαι μοίραι νόμον ηὗρεν Ἴσυλλος   10
> ἄφθιτον ἀέναον γέρας ἀθανάτοισι θεοῖσιν,
> καί νιν ἅπας δᾶμος θεθμὸν θέτο πατρίδος ἁμᾶς,
> χεῖρας ἀνασχόντες μακάρεσσιν ἐς οὐρανὸν εὐρύ[ν·
> οἵ κεν ἀριστεύωσι πόληος τᾶσδ' Ἐπιδαύρου
> λέξασθαί τ' ἄνδρας καὶ ἐπαγγεῖλαι κατὰ φυλὰς   15
> οἷς πολιοῦχος ὑπὸ στέρνοις ἀρετά τε καὶ αἰδώς,
> τοῖσιν ἐπαγγέλλεν καὶ πομπεύεν σφε κομῶντας

---

[26] On the depths of tradition hidden in the stories by and about Nestor, see now Frame 2009.

[27] On the ancient associations between the two meanings of *nomos* ("law" and "musical mode"), see Ford 2002, 260.

Φοίβῳ ἄνακτι υἱῷ τ' Ἀσκλαπιῷ ἰατῆρι
εἵμασιν ἐν λευκοῖσι δάφνας στεφάνοις ποτ' Ἀπόλλω,
ποὶ δ' Ἀσκλαπιὸν ἔρνεσι ἐλαίας ἡμεροφύλλου   20
ἁγνῶς πομπεύειν, καὶ ἐπεύχεσθαι πολιάταις
πᾶσιν ἀεὶ διδόμεν τέκνοις τ' ἐρατὰν ὑγίειαν,
εὐνομίαν τε καὶ εἰράναν καὶ πλοῦτον ἀμεμφῆ,
τὰν καλοκαγαθίαν τ' Ἐπιδαυροῖ ἀεὶ ῥέπεν ἀνδρῶν,
ὥραις ἐξ ὡρᾶν νόμον ἀεὶ τόνδε σέβοντας·   25
οὕτω τοί κ' ἁμῶν περιφείδοιτ' εὐρύοπα Ζεύς.[28]

This law, sacred by divine Fate, Isyllus composed, an imperish-
able, everlasting gift to the immortal gods; and all the people,
lifting their hands to the wide heaven, to the blessed gods, set it
up as a binding rule of our fatherland: to select and to summon
by tribes whichever men may be best in this city of Epidaurus,
those who have in their hearts virtue and reverence that safeguard the city; to summon them and to have them lead a procession to lord Phoebus and to his son Asclepius, the physician,
dressed in white raiment and with flowing hair; to lead a solemn
procession to the temple of Apollo bearing garlands of laurel and
then to the temple of Asclepius bearing branches of tender olive
shoots; to pray them to grant forever to all citizens and to their
children fair health and to grant that the noble character of the
men of Epidaurus always prevail, together with good order and
peace and blameless wealth from season to season so long as they
revere this law. So may Zeus the far-seeing spare us.

Obviously a careful student of epic-style hexameters, Isyllus may have heard
in the unusual phrasing that the Homeric poet gives Nestor at *Iliad* 2.360–63
a reminiscence of Apolline citharodic ethos.

Rhapsodic Practice—An Intermezzo

As we turn to the alleged rhapsodic *exodion* (νῦν δὲ θεοὶ μάκαρες τῶν
ἐσθλῶν ἄφθονοί ἐστε) preserved by Photius and Eustathius, it is not necessary to dwell on its similarity to hymnic or prayer formulations. The same
strictures apply as with the citharodic: that is, more contextual clues need
to be sought in order to face the objection that certain dictional items are

---

[28] IG IV²128; Furley and Bremer 2001, 180–92; translation by Edelstein and Edelstein 1945. For
an analysis of the innovations in this poem, see LeVen 2014, 312–28.

generally hymnic, and not specifically attached to resonances of rhapsodic practice. We can, however, make one perhaps noteworthy distinction right off, in contrasting it with the citharodic closing. Whereas that tag-line called on one god (probably Apollo, given the lore about citharodic contests) and bade him "rejoice/farewell" (*khaire*), leaving unspecified the further prayer for benefits, the rhapsodic *exodion* calls on *all* the gods (θεοὶ μάκαρες) and embeds in the same hexameter line the request for good things (*esthla*) in abundance. It is purely speculative to imagine that the context of rhapsodic contests called for a less specialized appeal, spreading out the set of addressees and pluralizing it as "blessed gods" rather than one. Of course, we might expect the Panathenaea to inspire poets to end their contest-pieces with appeals specifically to Athena—but these are not, to my knowledge, attested, apart from the two short *Homeric Hymns* addressed to her (#11 and #28, Allen-Sikes-Halliday). On the other hand, the very existence of such a varied range of hexameter prooimia as we find in the *Hymns* is itself a kind of confirmation that travelling, competing rhapsodes needed to be prepared for whatever divinity was most prominent in the cities they visited—a picture that fits well with that of the widely-ranging "Chian" bard in the *Hymn to Apollo*, as also with the portraits of Homer and Hesiod in the *Lives* and the *Certamen*.

It must be noted immediately that, just as with the citharodic *exodion*, the rhapsodic is in fact never attested verbatim in those extant texts that we have reason to believe rhapsodes may once have performed. This includes not just Homer and Hesiod, but also Archilochus, Stesichorus, and other "lyric" poets. By itself, the formula θεοὶ μάκαρες is a common one, occurring thirty times in Homeric poetry and sixteen times in Hesiod (including transformations into other grammatical cases). Here there are some revealing details. Only four times does it occur (as in the *exodion*) in the vocative, all in the same formulaic line in the *Odyssey* (Ζεῦ πάτερ ἠδ' ἄλλοι μάκαρες θεοὶ αἰὲν ἐόντες). At *Odyssey* 5.7, Athena uses this line to preface her call for the gods to aid Odysseus; at *Odyssey* 8.306, Hephaestus calls the gods to witness his errant wife with Ares in bed; and at *Odyssey* 12.371 and 377, Helios calls for Odysseus' crew to be punished for devouring his cattle. The usage is strikingly specific and consistent: in each passage, one divinity seeks justice from the rest of the community of gods.[29] Thinking of the possible resonances if we import *into* the poem what we know of this framing *exodion*,

---

[29]   The context reminds us that Diogenianus (*Centuria* 6.88), mentioned above, cites as proverbially said in the case of vengeance the phrase νῦν θεοὶ μάκαρες.

it is difficult to see in specific passages any tonal connection with the rhapsode's closing call for *esthla* from the blessed gods. On the other hand, if we *export* to the rhapsodic *exodion* the specific tone and situation found through *internal* analysis of the epic, it could be significant that the call νῦν δὲ θεοὶ μάκαρες τῶν ἐσθλῶν ἄφθονοί ἐστε places in the mouth of a human singer what the audience will have recognized, at least in poems known to us, as divine speech. If this is the register of the line, then the competing rhapsodic poet will have elevated himself to a level above his audience, in what might be a relic of (or aspiration to) a vatic or sacral poetic function.[30]

Only once in hexameter verse before the late antique poet Nonnus does the adjective ἄφθονος appear. This occurs not in adjacency to the formula θεοὶ μάκαρες but in a telling passage that does have a relationship to gifts of the divine. The passage, I shall argue, takes on new shades of meaning, when we recall that the Hesiodic *Works and Days* was regularly performed by rhapsodes.[31] The description of the Golden Age emphasizes the abundance of grain available to the χρύσεον γένος that enjoyed a god-like existence under the reign of Cronus (*Works and Days* 109–12). Their death was like sleep, and the earth bore for them an *unstinting* harvest (116–26):

> θνῆσκον δ᾿ ὥσθ᾿ ὕπνῳ δεδμημένοι· ἐσθλὰ δὲ πάντα
> τοῖσιν ἔην· καρπὸν δ᾿ ἔφερε ζείδωρος ἄρουρα
> αὐτομάτη *πολλόν τε καὶ ἄφθονον*· οἳ δ᾿ ἐθελημοὶ
> ἥσυχοι ἔργ᾿ ἐνέμοντο *σὺν ἐσθλοῖσιν πολέεσσιν*.   119
> ἀφνειοὶ μήλοισι, φίλοι μακάρεσσι θεοῖσιν.
> αὐτὰρ ἐπεὶ δὴ τοῦτο γένος κατὰ γαῖα κάλυψε,
> τοὶ μὲν *δαίμονές* εἰσι Διὸς μεγάλου διὰ βουλὰς
> *ἐσθλοί*, ἐπιχθόνιοι, φύλακες θνητῶν ἀνθρώπων,
> οἵ ῥα φυλάσσουσίν τε δίκας καὶ σχέτλια ἔργα
> ἠέρα ἐσσάμενοι πάντη φοιτῶντες ἐπ᾿ αἶαν,   125
> *πλουτοδόται*· καὶ τοῦτο γέρας βασιλήιον ἔσχον.

... and they died as if overpowered by sleep. They had all good things: the grain-giving field bore crops of its own accord, much and unstinting, and they themselves, willing, mild-mannered, shared out the fruits of their labors together with many good things, wealthy in sheep, dear to the blessed gods. But since the earth covered up this race, by the plans of great Zeus they are

---

[30] Cf. Mondi 1978 for comparative evidence concerning Indic masters of speech (heralds) and their function as sacrificial officials.

[31] The main evidence for rhapsodic performance of Hesiod is Plato *Ion* 531.

fine spirits upon the earth, guardians of mortal human beings:
they watch over judgments and cruel deeds, clad in invisibility,
walking everywhere upon the earth, givers of wealth; and this
kingly honor they received. [trans. Most 2007]

As Gregory Nagy eloquently argued thirty years ago, the Golden generation
(along with the Silver) represents a poetically stylized version of heroes as
they appear in cult.[32] Let us note, in relation to the rhapsodic *exodion* and
the specific association we have seen of the vocative θεοὶ μάκαρες with just
vengeance in the *Odyssey*, that the Golden Age *daimones* as presented by
Hesiod are specifically called defenders of justice (124). They are marked,
further, by *having* good things and *being* good themselves (119, 123). In
other words, we have overt or latent associations within this short passage of
the Golden Age heroes, with the "gods," givers of abundance and *esthla*, as
addressed in the vocative of the *exodion*.[33] Finally, it is worth noting that—as
Nagy has once more shown—the Golden Age is described in terms that make
it a multiform of the Age of Heroes a few lines later in Hesiod (170–73):[34]

> καὶ τοὶ μὲν ναίουσιν ἀκηδέα θυμὸν ἔχοντες   170
> ἐν μακάρων νήσοισι παρ' Ὠκεανὸν βαθυδίνην,
> ὄλβιοι ἥρωες, τοῖσιν μελιηδέα καρπὸν
> τρὶς ἔτεος θάλλοντα φέρει ζείδωρος ἄρουρα.

... and these dwell with a spirit free of care on the Islands of the
Blessed beside deep-eddying Ocean—happy heroes, for whom
the grain-giving field bears honey-sweet fruit flourishing three
times a year. [trans. Most 2007]

The lucky heroes of this latter, fourth age, also beneficiaries of abundant
crops, dwell blissfully in the Isles of the Blessed (also under the rule of
Cronus).[35] In this multiform of the Golden Age, we therefore have the
specific verbal link with θεοὶ μάκαρες of the *exodion*. What is to be made of
these indications?

I submit that we can now distinguish the citharodic *exodion* more sharply
from the rhapsodic, in a way that takes into account, and makes more sense

---

[32] See Nagy 1999b [1979], 151–222 for the extended argument.

[33] For gods (generally) as givers of good things, see *Hymn to Demeter* 224: καὶ σὺ γύναι μάλα χαῖρε,
θεοὶ δέ τοι ἐσθλὰ πόροιεν (the ironic reply of the goddess to Metaneira).

[34] Nagy 1999b, 167–73.

[35] On the positioning here and import of the lines concerning Cronus found in some mss., see West
1978, 195–96.

of, performance contexts and the relative expressive positionings of the poet (singer or reciter). The citharodic *exodion* clearly calls upon a god—as we have seen, most likely Apollo, and probably was used in the context of festivals like the Pythia at Delphi and Karneia at Sparta. By extrapolation, the negotiation of the poetic performance is like that of sacrifice, prayer, and hymn: once praised, the god now should rejoice (and, implicitly, be favorable). The rhapsodic *exodion*, by contrast, is more specific about the overt request for abundance of good things, and its addressee is plural—the θεοὶ μάκαρες. But I suggest that these "blessed" ones are in fact *the heroes whose exploits are described within epic*. Functionally, citharodic and rhapsodic compositions work in a quite similar manner, to fashion a verbal *agalma* that attracts attention and triggers generous repayment from divinities (and perhaps from patrons—another dimension). But formally, the citharodic compositions will have focused on the exploits of the *god*—just as the *polukephalos nomos* that was a required contest-piece at the Pythia narrated the initiatory and foundational exploit of Apollo's killing of the Python.[36] In contrast, the rhapsodic poems thematize mortal, *heroic* exploits—that is, the deeds of heroes notionally "before" they become immortalized in song or cult. But the framework for performance of such epics is, naturally, the post-epic world of the Iron Age in which the epic heroes, the *daimones*—in the form of θεοὶ μάκαρες— can be worshipped and asked for blessings in abundance: νῦν δὲ θεοὶ μάκαρες τῶν ἐσθλῶν ἄφθονοί ἐστε. From the standpoint of the Greek audience for rhapsodic performances, the heroic protagonists of epic narrative exist still, as real cultic presences in the landscape, πλουτοδόται—"wealth-providers." To recite their exploits is to gain their favor. (A number of close parallels from ancient and modern Indic epic tradition might be adduced here.[37]) Even if a city-state sponsors the recitation (as at the Panathenaea), the heroic boon, now extended to a broader community, is still the aim and endpoint. As Nagy continually reminds us—myth and poetry in ancient Greece are inextricable from ritual performance. In a very real sense, reciting Homeric epic is itself a ritual act. The long-neglected *exodion* of the rhapsodes encapsulates this fact.

---

[36]   Details in West 1992, 213–15.

[37]   See, e.g., Claus 1989 and Kothari 1989 on the relation of local epics, within the Tulu and Rajasthan traditions, to communication with the deified dead.

End-Piece: The "Komic" *Exodion*

As we have seen, the citharodic and rhapsodic *exodia* preserved by the lexicographical tradition are never found verbatim in poetic compositions, but
tracing fragments of them can help us to see more links between text and
context, ritual and performance. The *exodion* identified as "comic" offers
at first sight a bleaker prospect for philological progress. To begin with, by
both Photius and Eustathius, we are given only one word as a clue, "having
a beautiful crown":

ὥσπερ κωμικοῦ μὲν ἥδε "καλλιστέφανος," ῥαψῳδῶν δὲ "νῦν δὲ θεοὶ
μάκαρες τῶν ἐσθλῶν ἄφθονοί ἐστε." [Photius *Lexicon* α 987]

ὡς ἱστορεῖ Αἴλιος Διονύσιος, ὥσπερ, φησί· κωμικοῦ μὲν ἥδε·
"καλλιστέφανος," ῥαψῳδοῦ δὲ αὕτη· "νῦν δὲ θεοὶ μάκαρες τῶν ἐσθλῶν
ἄφθονοί ἐστε," τραγικοῦ δέ "πολλαὶ μορφαὶ τῶν δαιμονίων." [Eustathius
Ad Homeri Iliadem 1:364.6]

In our extant comic texts (from the 152 authors compiled in the *Canon*
of the *Thesaurus Linguae Graecae*), the adjective appears once—or so it
seems. Actually, the citation from Demianczuk's *Supplementum Comicum*
(1912) printed as #48 of his *Fragmenta incertae comoediae* and reading "ἥδε
καλλιστέφανος" is, of course, derived from the lexicographers, so we end
up in a perfect textual circle. Furthermore, the old *supplementum* citation
perpetuates a misunderstanding of the lexicographers' syntax (a construction that may have stemmed from Aelius Dionysius himself), a misconstrual
also found in editions of Photius (but not Eustathius), by intruding into the
quoted *exodion* the deictic ἥδε, which clearly was part of the scholars' own
prose transmitting the poetic tag-line, rather than a piece of the *exodion*.[38] So
we are left empty-handed.

There are plenty of crowns in comedy—the noun *stephanos* (uncom-
pounded) and related verb forms occur at least 100 times—but these, too,
offer barely a foothold for analysis. As one of the most abundant and visible
semiotic markers in ancient social life, crowns crop up at symposia, as signs
of festivity, at sacrifices, as dedicatory objects, and even as funeral bier
adornments. Worshippers at the Thesmophoria, the Dionysia, and Eleusinian
mysteries, were said to wear crowns of myrtle. The Pythia's tripod at Delphi
was adorned with a laurel crown. Brides and grooms wore crowns: since
comedy sometimes ends with a wedding, should we look to such final

---

[38] Kassel and Austin correct the error: PCG vol. 8 (1995) 67, #181.

marriage scenes? (Unfortunately, even if crowns were part of the actors' costumes at, for instance, the wedding marking the end of the *Birds*, the word is never used in the text and we would have to fill in stage directions ourselves.) And of course winning athletes wore crowns. This last context, given the competitive nature of all the poetic events featuring *exodia*, deserves further investigation.

As it turns out, in three Aristophanic passages, the connection of crown and victory can help us explore more relevant background. It has to be admitted, however, that only two are *exodia* passages, while only one features a crown (not the passage in the *exodion* position). The one involving a send-off that features a crown and a victory song comes in the *Knights* some 200 lines before the play's end. The Sausage-Seller has finally defeated Paphlagon to become the new favorite of the Demos, who in turn regrets having ever crowned and endowed his previous demagogic favorite and tells him to surrender his *stephanos* (*Knights* 1225–28). After some further comic exchange about the fulfillment of a fatal oracle, Paphlagon exits on the *ekkuklema* in paratragic fashion (*Knights* 1250–56):

Paphlagon:
ὦ στέφανε, χαίρων ἄπιθι· καί σ' ἄκων ἐγὼ   1250
λείπω· σὲ δ' ἄλλος τις λαβὼν κεκτήσεται,
κλέπτης μὲν οὐκ ἂν μᾶλλον, εὐτυχὴς δ' ἴσως.
Sausage-seller:
Ἑλλάνιε Ζεῦ, σὸν τὸ νικητήριον.
Slave:
ὦ χαῖρε, καλλίνικε, καὶ μέμνησ' ὅτι
ἀνὴρ γεγένησαι δι' ἐμέ·

Paphlagon:
Begone and farewell my crown; against my will do I abandon you.
Some other man will take you as his own, no greater thief but luckier
        perhaps.
Sausage-seller:
Zeus of the Hellenes, yours the prize of victory!
Slave:
Hail, fair victor, and bear in mind that you became a big shot thanks to me.
        [trans. Henderson]

The Acharnians ends with a similar scene of defeat, when Dicaeopolis (*Acharnians* 1224–25) calls to be taken to the judges of the Choes drinking-contest (and by metatheatrical extension, those judging the Lenaea competition in the *hic et nunc* of performance), while his opponent Lamachus is taken offstage. He returns triumphant, having drained his cup first, and breaks into a victory cry (1227-34):

Δι.   ὁρᾶτε τουτονὶ κενόν. τήνελλα καλλίνικος.
Χο.   τήνελλα δῆτ᾽, εἴπερ καλεῖς γ᾽, ὦ πρέσβυ, καλλίνικος.
Δι.   καὶ πρός γ᾽ ἄκρατον ἐγχέας ἄμυστιν ἐξέλαψα.
Χο.   τήνελλά νυν, ὦ γεννάδα· χώρει λαβὼν τὸν ἀσκόν.   1230
Δι.   ἕπεσθέ νυν ᾄδοντες· "ὦ τήνελλα καλλίνικος."
Χο.   ἀλλ᾽ ἑψόμεσθα σὴν χάριν
        τήνελλα καλλίνικον ᾄ-
        δοντες σὲ καὶ τὸν ἀσκόν.

Dicaeopolis   Look, this pitcher's empty cup! Hail the Champion!
Chorus   Hail then—since you bid me, old sir—the Champion!
Dicaeopolis   And what's more, I poured the wine neat and chugged it
                 straight down!
Chorus   Then Hail, old chap! Take the wineskin and go.
Dicaeopolis   Then follow me, singing "Hail the Champion"
Chorus   Yes, we'll follow in your honor singing "Hail the Champion"
                 for you and your wineskin. [trans. Henderson]

Dicaeopolis announces his victory with the traditional cry that we have already heard accompanying the transfer of the crown in the *Knights*. There is no crown mentioned at this moment in the *Acharnians* (although we might imagine that Dicaeopolis as a symposiast at the Anthesteria is wearing one). What starts as a triumphal interjection is then turned by both the protagonist and the chorus into a song as they exit the orchestra (1231: ᾄδοντες). This same song-phrase τήνελλα καλλίνικος also concludes the *Birds*, as Peisetaerus leads his bride Basileia (beautifully crowned?) offstage to the triumphal paean of the chorus (*Birds* 1763–65):

Χο.   ἀλαλαλαί, ἰὴ παιών,
        δαιμόνων ὑπέρτατε. τήνελλα καλλίνικος, ὦ

Thus far we have seen three send-off scenes, two of them at the position of an *exodion*, all marked with the language of the victory song (and one— although not an *exodion*—with an overt reference to crowning). But such circumstantial evidence does not seem quite enough to make a firm connection with the alleged *exodion* phrase καλλιστέφανος. The scholia to the end of the *Birds*, however, provide some further information that can help narrow the gap between our texts and the lexicographic evidence. From the commentary (*Scholia ad Aves* 1764) we learn—with some confusion—the deeper history of the τήνελλα καλλίνικος song:

> Τὸ *τήνελλα* μίμησίς ἐστι φωνῆς κρούματος αὐλοῦ ποιᾶς ἀπὸ τοῦ ἐφυμνίου οὗ εἶπεν Ἀρχίλοχος εἰς τὸν Ἡρακλέα μετὰ τὸν ἄθλον Αὐγέου
>> "τήνελλα ὦ καλλίνικε,
>> χαῖρε ἄναξ Ἡράκλεες,
>> αὐτός τε κιόλαος, αἰχμητὰ δύω."
> δοκεῖ δὲ πρῶτος Ἀρχίλοχος νικήσας ἐν Πάρῳ τὸν Δήμητρος ὕμνον ἑαυτῷ τοῦτον ἐπιπεφωνηκέναι.

> "Tenella" is an imitation of a type of sound from the playing of the pipe, from the hymn-refrain [*ephumnion*] that Archilochus addressed to Heracles after the Augean contest:
>> "Tenella, O fair-victory
>> Hail lord Herakles
>> Yourself and Iolaos, two spear-fighters."
> It seems that Archilochus first having been victor in the Demeter hymn in Paros added this interjection for himself.

Worth noting, first off, is the detail that the τήνελλα song is marked as having a double performance heritage, even in this compact rendition of its history. It was both a declaration celebrating personal victory in a hymn contest (a scenario similar to its use by Dicaeopolis in *Acharnians*) and part of a praise-song for Heracles. The time dimensions, relative and absolute, are vague. Is Archilochus imagined to have been present at the victory of Heracles, or simply to have recalled it? And was he the *first ever* to win the Demeter hymn-contest (as Chrysothemis had been first at Delphi to win the Apollo-hymn event)? Or, did he win the hymn-contest *first*, and then compose the praise verses? And do we get here a glimpse of an Archilochus as citharode? (If so, the phrase χαῖρε ἄναξ might recall the citharodic *exodion*.) The association of Archilochus with the Parian Demeter cult is attested in other sources, as well, so this may be the place to note that the second-earliest occurrence of the rare adjective καλλιστέφανος is as an epithet of Demeter in the *Homeric Hymn* dedicated to her (*Hymn to Demeter* 251, 295). (The very earliest would be the late eighth-century BCE Nestor's Cup inscription, where the epithet modifies the name of Aphrodite.) If we can imagine Archilochus's own hymn to Demeter as featuring this epithet, then the phrase καλλίνικε applied to himself would have been a nice compliment and ending to the body of the hymn, in effect playing on *her* crown within the narrative to draw attention to *his own* (crowned?) victory after singing the praise narrative.

The scholia to Pindar present us with even more dizzying possibilities. They comment extensively on the first lines of Pindar's *Olympian* 9, which begins with a reference to the Archilochean composition:

> Τὸ μὲν Ἀρχιλόχου μέλος
> φωνᾶεν Ὀλυμπίᾳ,
> καλλίνικος ὁ τριπλόος κεχλαδώς
> ἄρκεσε Κρόνιον παρ' ὄχθον ἀγεμονεῦσαι
> κωμάζοντι φίλοις Ἐφαρμόστῳ σὺν ἑταίροις·

> The resounding strain of Archilochus,
> the swelling thrice-repeated song of triumph,
> sufficed to lead Epharmostus to the hill of Cronus,
> in victory-procession with his dear companions. [trans. Svarlien]

In addition to what we have learned from the scholia to the *Birds*, the Pindaric poem pins down the place of performance to Olympia, refers to a triplex singing, and uses the apparently impromptu short song as a foil for Pindar's own epinician praises. Note also that the short song is said to be sufficient for the victor Epharmostus as he celebrates in a *kômos* with his friends. We shall return to this setting shortly.

Clearly the song was of great interest to ancient scholars whose notes were absorbed into the Byzantine commentary tradition. The key information contained within the *scholia vetera* to *Olympian* 9.1 can be summed up as follows, with my further notations in brackets, pointing to some curious gaps:

Archilochus having come to Olympia made the verses to Heracles [unstated: why and when]. Because he lacked a citharode, Archilochus spoke the word τήνελλα and thereby imitated the tune (or rhythm and sound) of the kithara in the midst of the chorus, while the chorus said the rest of the words καλλίνικε χαῖρε ἄναξ Ἡράκλεις; therafter anyone lacking a citharode used the τήνελλα [this assumes that normal celebratory song at Olympia was citharodic]. Alternatively: during an evening *kômos* celebrating the victor, if an aulete could not be found, one of the victor's companions would sing τήνελλα [the confusion over which instrument was imitated recalls the use in the *Birds* scholion of the term *krouma* for the sound of the aulos, a term usually applied to kithara playing]. The victor acted as *exarchos* for the song, as he processed in *kômos* with friends to the altar of Zeus. The phrase and short song came to be used to celebrate all victors.

A few more lines in the *scholia vetera* attribute to Eratosthenes (apparently, the Alexandrian librarian: p. 226 Bernhardy) more specific information about genre. The Hellenistic scholar said that the melos of Archilochus was not an epinikion but a hymn to Heracles; that Pindar called it *triploos* because the phrase *kallinike* used to be repeated three times; and that the word τήνελλα was said by the exarchos "apart from the tune" (ἔξω τοῦ μέλους), whenever either citharist [note: not citharode] or aulete was not present. The chorus of komasts then added their "fair-victory" cry so that the whole line was created through this collaboration: τήνελλα καλλίνικε. The actual *arkhê* of the hymn was the next line (χαῖρε ἄναξ Ἡράκλεες). It seems that Eratosthenes is trying to reconcile competing claims about exactly which instrumental sound was replaced by τήνελλα, the *epiphônêma* of Archilochus. I would add the suggestion that these competing claims most likely went back to performers' lore about the invention of their own repertoires, and were shaped further by the competing claims of festivals such as the Pythia, Karneia, and Panathenaea. We know about the Pythia, for instance, that stories circulated concerning why certain major poets could not compete: Hesiod, for example, had not learned how to sing to the kithara (Pausanias *Description of Greece* 10.7.3—see also above). In short, a pre-Hellenistic genre-sorting process that must have aligned *recited* verse (Hesiodic, Archilochean) in contradistinction to *sung* poetry probably underlies the "evolution" of Archilochus in lore from (apparently citharodic) hymn singer to impromptu *kômos* leader lacking an instrument to accompany himself. At the same time, as the Hellenistic-era Mnesiepes inscription commemorates, Archilochus could be remembered as a lyre-player and singer, who acquired his instrument directly from the Muses.[39]

Let us return to the problem of the "comic" *exodion*. By now it has taken a slight twist. Tracing the roots of the καλλίνικε song segment that marks a turning point in the *Knights* and provides an *exodion*-like moment for the end of *Acharnians* and *Birds*, we can see that—even without mentioning crowns—the song-event thereby evoked within comedy is, in fact, komastic. To put this another way, we might read into the wording of Aelius Dionysius and the lexicographical tradition (κωμικοῦ μὲν ἥδε· καλλιστέφανος) the root-meaning "belonging to the *kômos*." Of course, in context, the "comic"

---

[39]   Clay 2004, 14–16.

is meant (clearly contrasted with the "tragic" closing also mentioned in the lexica), but this καλλίνικε-song practice, when we put it into the context of Olympian competitive culture with its musical and poetic traditions, reveals itself to be, rather, "komic." It is as if, in the use of the καλλίνικε-ending, Aristophanic comedy—at least in some productions (just as Euripides confined the "tragic" *exodion* to a few plays, of which we know)—gestured toward the pre-dramatic origins of his own art-form, affirming the affiliation between Archilochean iambus and Old Comedy.[40]

At the same time, we need to consider whether the καλλίνικε-ending always carried with it a latent association with athletic games—specifically (as far as the sources tell us) the Olympian. Does it mean something for characters in an Aristophanic comedy—Dicaeopolis and Peisetaerus—to be escorted from the orchestra at play's end by a komastic chorus to the sound of a victory-song that the audience must have known well to be for Olympic victors? Or for the Sausage-Seller to be greeted as if he had won the pancration or other event? Once more, we face the analytical dilemma of how to prioritize layers, as when we dealt with hymnic language above: were certain phrasings, like καλλίνικε, more vaguely triumphal, and only thought of as athletic when an obvious Olympic context called for it? We might flip the question the other way round: could it be that the proclamation by Dicaeopolis, after his victory in the compulsory drinking contest of the Choes, points to a genre-specific transmission of the καλλίνικε formula, *without* reference to the Olympic games? Even in that case, there would still be an interesting overlay of meanings. The Anthesteria (the Dionysiac wine festival in which the "Pots" segment, Choes, took place on the second day) is in this way being consciously melded into the Dionysia and Lenaea (distinct festivals at Athens), and the "pre-dramatic" but highly komastic rites of the former are being signaled, stylized, and incorporated through the snatch of the *exodion*-like triumph-song, into the *hic et nunc* of dramatic production (in the case of *Acharnians*, at the Lenaea of 425 BCE).

A third layering of signification cannot be ruled out. Indeed, there is one remaining body of evidence that may prove relevant to the question of the missing καλλιστέφανος *exodion* for comedies. It might, in fact, bring together the komastic, Olympic, and dramatic celebrations, with an Athenian focus. One fact that can be discovered though an otherwise unrewarding search for significant uses of καλλιστέφανος in the corpus of Greek literature has to do with an unusually specific naming practice, reported by scholiasts,

---

[40] Rosen 1988 remains fundamental for this connection.

Pausanias, and Aristotle. The scholion (1d Drachmann) to Pindar's *Olympian* 8, glossing the word *khrusostephanos*, informs us that the olive tree from which leaves were used to crown Olympic victors was named "fair-crown": ἡ διδομένη τοῖς νικῶσιν ἐλαία *καλλιστέφανος* καλεῖται. Similar information comes from Pausanias, who further provides the exact location of the famous tree (*Description of Greece* 5.15.3):

> κατὰ δὲ τὸν ὀπισθόδομον μάλιστά ἐστιν ἐν δεξιᾷ πεφυκὼς κότινος· καλεῖται δὲ ἐλαία *Καλλιστέφανος*, καὶ τοῖς νικῶσι τὰ Ὀλύμπια καθέστηκεν ἀπ' αὐτῆς δίδοσθαι τοὺς στεφάνους. Τούτου πλησίον τοῦ κοτίνου πεποίηται Νύμφαις βωμός· *Καλλιστεφάνους* ὀνομάζουσι καὶ ταύτας.

> About opposite the rear chamber [of the Temple of Zeus] a wild olive is growing on the right. It is called the *Olive of the Beautiful Crown*, and from its leaves are made the crowns which it is customary to give to winners of Olympic contests. Near this wild olive stands an altar of Nymphs; these too are styled *Nymphs of the Beautiful Crowns*. [trans. Jones and Ormerod]

We should note at this point that tree and nymphs share the epithet—just as we have seen it applied to a goddess (Demeter in the *Hymn* to her). In the work attributed to Aristotle called *On Marvellous Things Heard*, an account is given of the progenitor of this Olympic sacred olive tree (51):

> Ἐν τῷ Πανθείῳ ἐστὶν ἐλαία, καλεῖται δὲ καλλιστέφανος· ταύτης πάντα τὰ φύλλα ταῖς λοιπαῖς ἐλαίαις ἐναντία πέφυκεν· ἔξω γὰρ ἀλλ' οὐκ ἐντὸς ἔχει τὰ χλωρά. ἀφίησί τε τοὺς πτόρθους ὥσπερ ἡ μύρτος εἰς τοὺς στεφάνους συμμέτρως. ἀπὸ ταύτης φυτὸν λαβὼν ὁ Ἡρακλῆς ἐφύτευσεν Ὀλυμπίασιν, ἀφ' ἧς οἱ στέφανοι τοῖς ἀθληταῖς δίδονται. ἔστι δὲ αὕτη παρὰ τὸν Ἰλισσὸν ποταμόν, σταδίους ἑξήκοντα τοῦ ποταμοῦ ἀπέχουσα· περιῳκοδόμηται δέ, καὶ ζημία μεγάλη τῷ θιγόντι αὐτῆς ἐστιν. ἀπὸ ταύτης δὲ τὸ φυτὸν λαβόντες ἐφύτευσαν Ἠλεῖοι ἐν Ὀλυμπίᾳ, καὶ τοὺς στεφάνους ἀπ' αὐτῆς ἔδωκαν.

> In the Pantheon there is an olive-tree, which is called that of the beautiful crowns. But all its leaves are contrary in appearance to those of other olive-trees; for it has the pale-green outside, instead of inside, and it sends forth branches, like those of the myrtle, suitable for crowns. From this Heracles took a shoot, and planted it at Olympia and from it are taken the crowns which are given to the combatants. This tree is near the river Ilissus, sixty stadia distant from the river. It is surrounded by a wall, and a severe penalty is imposed on any one who touches it. From this the Eleians took the shoot, and planted it in Olympia, and from it they took the crowns which they bestowed. [trans. Dowdall]

This story fits, in general outline, with the myth attested in Pindar's *Olympian* 3, that Heracles was the first to plant olive trees at Olympia. But the remarkable feature of this report, a bit of lore not found attested elsewhere, is that the famous Olympian olive was actually a transplanted shoot of an older tree that grew *in Athens*. In the Pindaric ode, Heracles travels to the land of the Hyperboreans to get saplings. As Pavlos Sfyroeras has pointed out, however, there are signs that Pindar in *Olympian* 3 appears to be manipulating traditions about the birthplace of the olive tree in an indirect challenge to Athenian claims about their polis having been the first place such trees grew, as gift of Athena.[41] If this is right, then the erasure in non-Athenian literature might have extended to epichoric Athenian stories about which spot the Olympian Καλλιστέφανος supposedly originated from. The site of the "Pantheon" near the Ilissus is not discussed elsewhere, as far as I can find, in the ancient descriptions of Athens. (The building called "of all the gods" in Pausanias is a later Hadrianic construction, near his Library and the Agora.) The foundations of a few as yet unidentified temples have been found near the Ilissus, southeast of the Olumpieion. Further complication is introduced by the version of the story in pseudo-Aristotle that we find in the scholion to Aristophanes *Plutus* 586: in an otherwise very similar account, the tree is said to be near the Ilissus, yet some distance from a temple σταδίους ξ' τοῦ ἱεροῦ ἀπέχουσα. It is unclear whether the commentator had in mind a different temple, or placed the tree apart from the so-called Pantheon. Another scholiast, on Pindar *Olympian* 3, elucidates line 12 with a note that conflates the *alsos* at Olympia with an (otherwise unattested) Pantheon in Olympia itself: πρὸς αὐτὸ τὸ τῆς Πίσης ἄλσος διαλέγεται· ἢ πρὸς τὸ Πάνθειον, ὅπου αἱ ἐλαῖαι φύονται.

Let me conclude this string of lore and extrapolations with the possibility that once upon a time Attic comedies did, in fact, end with καλλιστέφανος. If this was actually just the first word of a longer utterance, the whole might have run "Fair-crowned is Demeter" or even Athena, or Dionysus. But even the single word might have evoked deeper associations. Like καλλίνικε, it would make audiences think of victory—dramatic or komastic. In regard to the latter, it is not amiss to recall that the Anthesteria itself was held at the shrine of Dionysus "in the Marshes" (another site presumably near the marshy verge of the Ilissus, also unidentified at present). To have the chorus and actors shout καλλιστέφανος with a gesture toward the southeast of the Theater of Dionysus would once more merge pre-dramatic ritual

---

[41] Sfyroeras 2003; see also Pavlou 2010.

for the wine-god with the highly evolved Dionysiac celebrations centered around tragedy, comedy, and the dithyramb. Finally, this *exodion*—comic or "komic" as it may have been—will have been a proud assertion that even Olympia, the ultimate site of victory in the Panhellenic world, owed its coveted crowns to an ancient sacred olive tree growing not far from an archetypal Athenian river.

7

SYNCHRONIC ASPECTS OF HOMERIC PERFORMANCE
THE EVIDENCE OF THE
HYMN TO APOLLO[1]

Here I will discuss neither the prehistory of Homeric epic, nor its transmission after these poems achieved a fixed form.[2] Instead, my focus will be on two moments of *synchronicity*, one modern and one archaic. Our own modern moment at the end of the millennium gives us a unique angle of vision from which to view the *Iliad* and *Odyssey*. For the past few generations, the most important question in Homeric studies has been: are the poems better understood and interpreted as texts or as performances? Although there is not absolute consensus as we near the end of the century, most would agree that the insights of Milman Parry, Albert Lord, Gregory Nagy, and several other pioneering scholars into the nature of oral-traditional poetic performances must be central if we are to understand the art of Homeric composition.[3]

It may seem that our distance from the poems poses an insurmountable obstacle to imagining the circumstances and techniques of Homeric performance. How can we overcome centuries of diachronic change to re-constitute an archaic *synchronic* viewpoint on Homeric poetry? For if this art form is, indeed, one shaped by and continually renewed through performances,

---

[1] Originally published in *Una nueva visión de la cultura griega antigua hacia el fin del milenio*, ed. A. M. González de Tobia (La Plata, Argentina: Editorial de la Universidad Nacional de La Plata, 2000), 403–32.

[2] For indications of the long prehistory of the compositions we call Homeric, see, e.g., Durante 1976; on the later transmission, Lamberton 1997.

[3] For an evaluation of the claims that we can continue to read Homer without perspectives from oral poetics: Martin 1989. Recent formulations of the key insights about Greek poetry as performance: Lord 1995; Nagy 1996a; J. M. Foley 1995.

the synchronic axis should be our focus. As Gregory Nagy puts it in his recent book *Homeric Questions*, "Fieldwork in the study of oral poetry as it is performed requires a synchronic perspective, for purposes of describing the actual system perpetuated by the tradition."[4] How, then, can we perform Homeric "fieldwork"?

In *The Language of Heroes*, I attempted to explicate "Homer out of Homer" by analyzing the speeches of characters in the poem and applying the internal poetics that I discovered to the external composition itself, the *Iliad*. I now continue this sort of fieldwork by examining a composition that has been attributed to Homer since at least the time of Thucydides, the *Homeric Hymn to Apollo*. The analysis of the hymn that I am about to propose can enable us to understand more clearly not just the composition of this artful poem but at least one larger aspect of Homeric poetry as performance: how poems begin.

In 1782, David Ruhnken (1723–98) wrote in the second edition of his critical letter on the *Homeric Hymns* that the *Hymn to Apollo* as we now have it is the result of an editorial decision, the later connection of two hymns that were originally independent compositions.[5] It is now known that Ruhnken, in fact, repeated, as his own words, almost the very words of a learned Frisian physician, Adrian Heringa, who in 1753 had communicated this idea to Ruhnken in a letter, now in the University Library at Leiden.[6] The idea became known as Ruhnken's, so I too shall refer to it that way, while acknowledging that some more complicated ventriloquism underlies this notation—not the last such miming to be found in connection with this hymn.[7]

Ruhnken's reason for splitting the hymn in two was quite straightforward: he said that line 165 gives the usual epilogue and closing to a hymn (*solitum Hymni epilogum et finem*), while line 179 is the beginning of another hymn.[8]

---

[4] Nagy 1996b, 17.

[5] Ruhnken 1782, 7; A. Miller 1986, 111.

[6] Van der Valk 1977, 441; Förstel 1979, 21–22.

[7] Yet another fiction clings to the man: he gained some notoriety in England from the ditty penned by Richard Porson—"I went to Strasburg, where I got drunk / With that most learned Professor, Brunck; / I went to Wortz, where I got more drunken / With that more learned professor, Ruhnken"—but, in fact, Porson never left England: M. Clarke 1937, 16.

[8] Cited in A. Miller 1986, 111.

ἀλλ' ἄγεθ' ἱλήκοι μὲν Ἀπόλλων Ἀρτέμιδι ξύν   165
ὦ ἄνα, καὶ Λυκίην καὶ Μηονίην ἐρατεινὴν   179

His supporting arguments were circumstantial:first, the testimony of Thucydides (*History of the Peloponnesian War* 3.104), who quotes the *Hymn to Apollo*, calling it a prooimion. Runhken claimed that Thucydides' introduction to his (variant) version of lines 165–72 (τὸν γὰρ Δηλιακὸν χορὸν τῶν γυναικῶν ὑμνήσας ἐτελεύτα τοῦ ἐπαίνου ἐς τάδε τὰ ἔπη) meant not that Homer "was ending his praise of the Delian women" but "he was ending the *Hymn to Apollo*." As corroboration, Ruhnken offered the words of Aelius Aristides concerning Homer's apparent self-description in the poem (*Orations* 34.35 = Dindorf 2.559):

διαλεγόμενος γὰρ ταῖς Δηλιάσι καὶ καταλύων τὸ προοίμιον, εἴ τις ἔροιθ' ὑμᾶς, φησὶν "Ὦ κοῦραι, τίς δ' ὕμμιν ἀνὴρ ἥδιστος ἀοιδῶν ..."

He interprets this also as a reference to a conclusion; thus, for Ruhnken, two ancient authorities attested to a hymn to Apollo ending about one-quarter of the way through the composition that we now possess in medieval manuscripts.[9]

Ruhnken's "discovery" anticipated by thirteen years the *Prolegomena to Homer* by Friedrich Wolf, the book that began the passion for dissecting Homeric epic.[10] The same Analytic tendencies proceeded to beset the *Hymn to Apollo*.[11] By 1840 Lehrs was seeing no fewer than six hymns underlying the poem. By 1908, Ludwich in his *Homerischer Hymnenbau* had divined the structure of the whole composition as consisting of seventy-eight heptads— Apollo's sacred number—duly represented with proper spacing in his edition. In this critical atmosphere, Wilamowitz in 1916 sounded like the voice of cool reason, when he reaffirmed that the hymn comprised two parts and argued that the second, the so-called "Pythian" hymn, was a continuation modeled on the Delian hymn.[12] An Analyst view of the poem as comprising two parts was effectively canonized by his authority and thus survives two

---

[9]   It is worth stressing that the alleged break has no manuscript authority: Thalmann 1984, 65. On Thucydides' citation as a traditional formulaic variant, see Janko 1982, 2–3.

[10]   See the translation and essay on historical context: Wolf [1795] 1985. The book was dedicated to Ruhnken, whom Wolf praised (chap. 31) for his opinions on the recently discovered *Hymn to Demeter*. In Wolf's own account of the book's genesis, however, Ruhnken's work does not figure: Wolf [1795] 1985, 232–35.

[11]   Förstel 1979 recounts the numerous Analytic proposals.

[12]   Wilamowitz 1920, 440–62.

centuries after Ruhnken in Janko's 1982 book on epic diction.[13] Long after most people have given up "analyzing" the Homeric epics into constituent parts and critics have begun treating them as artistic unities, this way of splitting up the *Hymn to Apollo* still persists.[14] The question is whether the persistence stems from neglect, or from sensitivity.

For one familiar with oral poetics, Analyst argumentation can be seen to depend on a hermeneutic model of texts, copies, and editions that simply is anachronistic in the society of archaic Greece.[15] This is why the explication by Andrew Miller in his monograph on the hymn is considerably more appealing. Among others, Kakridis, Dornseiff, and Floratos preceded Miller in Unitarian interpretation of this hymn as one composition.[16] But Miller succeeds in particular because he wisely draws on the treasure-house of Pindaric hymnic rhetoric as a resource, thereby discovering a close relationship among the poem's parts.[17] Building on his work, Jenny Strauss Clay's scene-by-scene Unitarian interpretation has the added advantage of incorporating the thematic thrust of the poem, as a whole, into the larger realm of theogonic myth-making, which she sees as the central role of the major hymns.[18] Clay believes that a single poet aimed in the poem to press local Delian or Pythian traditions into the service of a more embracing Panhellenic ideology.[19] Again, the Unitarian picture is inherently more appealing in its respect for social context and poetic nuance. Furthermore, methodologically, the Unitarians are on safer ground: after all, varied content hardly need betoken a difference in authorship.[20] Moreover, Ruhnken's circumstantial evidence tottered as critics pointed out that both Thucydides and Aristides more likely meant that the poet at line 165 ended his direct praise of the Delian girls, not the hymn.[21]

---

[13] Janko 1982, 27–29, 99–119.

[14] See, e.g, Kirk 1985a, 113–14 in what some regard as the current standard literary history.

[15] See Nagy 1989 on the social staging for early Greek poetics; G. P. Edwards 1971, 33–39, 167–89 offers a closely reasoned critique of older "model/copy" argumentation.

[16] Kakridis 1937; Dornseiff 1935; Floratos 1952; cf. Baltes 1982.

[17] A. Miller 1986, 1–9.

[18] Clay 1989, 17–94.

[19] A similar observation had been made already by Nagy 1999b [1979], 6–7.

[20] For a history of Unitarian readings: Förstel 1979, 43–50, Drerup 1937.

[21] See Drerup 1937, 101. Aloni 1980 shows that the wording of Aelius Aristides does not imply that the hymns ends here; Heubeck 1966, 229–30 demonstrates that Thucydides does not use *epainos* as a synonym for *humnos*. Moreover, he shows in a later article (Heubeck 1972, 138–40) that lines

In addition to the growth of a sceptical outlook towards such things as ambiguous external evidence, another change has tilted the balance in favor of the Unitarian reading. The appreciation of oral-formulaic style that began with Milman Parry's work has made it hard to argue for separate poems on the basis of diction. Since Parry, scholars have had the means to realize that repetition or redeployment of a word or phrase can never by themselves be evidence for such phenomena as interpolation; cannot be used to claim priority for one or the other line; and are not a reliable guide to detecting the tracks of different composers.[22] Kirk attempted the lattermost project, through a good deal of impressionistic reading but the most that such diction-based analyses can accomplish is to show that both parts of the *Hymn to Apollo* use the phrasing of epic, more or less successfully.[23] Neither Hoekstra nor Cantilena, in analyses much more thorough-going than Kirk's, finds significant difference between the Delian and Pythian segments, from the point of view of formulaic diction.[24]

Despite these negative findings, it appears that the case for dividing the hymn *can* still seek support from linguistic stylistics. Janko, looking at such things as employment of movable-nu, finds that the Delian hymn (which he believes *was* a separate hymn) employs movable-nu before a consonant to make a long syllable in the verse about four times as often as the Pythian hymn, and sees in this a confirmation of the Delian part's East Greek origin.[25] A related phenomenon, metrical observance of digamma, similarly

---

179–81 are an artful transformation of the usual ending formulae, but do not signal a finale. Much of the argument could have been avoided if earlier critics had possessed the "new" Simonides poem on the battle of Plataea, *P.Oxy.* 3965, fr. 1 + 2 ed. Parsons, which begins with a hymn to Achilles, followed by a break-off formula and then a new narrative, yet is obviously conceived as one composition; cf. West 1993, 4. Note especially the similar structure of the respective transitions: line 15 of the Simonides poem bids farewell to Achilles (*khaire*), and line 16 highlights the poet's shifting attention—*autar egô*; cf. *Hymn to Apollo* 166 *khairete* and 177 *autar egôn*.

[22] See the detailed critique in G. P. Edwards 1971, 33–39, 167–89.

[23] See Kirk 1981; also his later remarks (1985a, 114) on the "relaxed and ample expression" of the Delian portion vs. the alleged "crabbed and prosaic" style of the Pythian. Frolíková 1963 notes minor differences in the use of epithets for Apollo, but fails to take account of formulaic flexibility and ends up conceding that both portions have non-Homeric as well as Homeric traits in diction. De Hoz 1964 more reasonably finds that the hymns represent a dictional tradition independent of epic.

[24] Hoekstra 1969, 25–34; Cantilena 1982. Notopoulos 1962, 358 using a definition that includes formula-*like* phrasing finds the Delian part 87% formulaic, the Pythian 94%.

[25] Janko 1982, 65–66; on some problems in Janko's approach: Thalmann 1984, 205 n. 88.

distinguishes the hymn's sections, with the "Delian" markedly less observant than the "Pythian."[26]

The point to which the studies of the last two hundred or so years have brought us has been recently best formulated by Susan Shelmerdine, who characterizes the *Hymn to Apollo* as "an intentional blend of two separate traditions which has kept the language of each (Delian and Pythian) distinct in many places, yet consciously structured the narrative to connect the most important themes and events of the two."[27] She does not ask what circumstances would have produced precisely this compositional intention. In what follows, I would like to propose an answer to this question.

Two features of this hymn have not been fully appreciated. I stress that the features are not at the level of diction, which, being tied to content, must inevitably be different whenever different topics—the birth of Apollo, or his travels, or the foundation of Delphi—are sung about. Instead of relying on diction, I will focus first on the structure of the hymn, then on metrics, next will review the limited information about the origin of this hymn (or hymns), and, finally, will suggest how my analysis can clarify the vexed beginning of this hymn, as well as the function of the proems to the surviving Homeric epics.

My point on structure involves the poetic status of parallelism. Connoisseurs of Near Eastern, especially Biblical, poetry, would never denigrate the role of parallelism as a constitutive device.[28] Much of the intellectual history of Classics, however, was until recently marked by efforts to distinguish Greek culture and poetry from its eastern predecessors; parallelism, viewed as un-classical, was in studies of the *Hymn to Apollo* a target of the Analysts. The point is crystallized in the running debate between Dornseiff and Jacoby early in this century: wherever Dornseiff, the Unitarian, wanted to see an expansion, by the same poet, of an earlier motif—for instance, the expansion in lines 207–99 of the opening travel motif of the hymn—Jacoby, the Analyst, claims to find a sorry imitation by some later poet—in this case,

---

[26] West 1975, 161 calculated the rate of observance to neglect of initial digamma as Delian 1.6/1 vs. Pythian 3.6/1.

[27] S. Shelmerdine 1995, 59.

[28] On the pervasive parallel structures in Hebrew poetry: Watson 1994.

copying of the opening section of the poem.[29] While at odds over the status of parallel passages, both Analysts and Unitarians agree on their existence.[30] Consider the following paired affiliations in theme:

- 1–13 & 186–206: Apollo amidst the other gods
- 19–24 & 208–13: consideration of ways to hymn Apollo
- 20–50: Apollo's sway/Leto's journey
  & (doubled motif) 216–28 Apollo's journey
  421–39 journey with Cretans
- 52–60 Leto's promise & 525–44 Apollo's promises
- 61–82 Delos afraid & 239–76 Telphusa afraid
- 83–88 oath-taking & 331–39 cursing
- 95–101 & 305–30 jealousy of Hera
- 115–26 birth of Apollo & 340–55 birth of Typhaon
- 147–64 Ionian festival
  & (doubled motif) 189–206 Olympian festival
  502–24 Delphic celebration

The question is, of course, whether these are conscious, artistic echoes intended by one poet or mechanically composed repetitions made by a later poet using a pre-existing smaller hymn as a model—either the Delian or Pythian portion.[31] I lean towards the former explanation, with one difference, which I shall explain later. But first I must draw attention to what I consider an unrecognized feature: the Pythian hymn's consistent expansion of the Delian's material (see above). In other words, we are not dealing just with reuse of a motif, but with significantly ornamented and magnified appropriations. The Pythian hymn, that is to say, operates in terms of what I have elsewhere called the "expansion aesthetic."[32] In the *Iliad*, this aesthetic can be seen at work in pairs of speeches. He who talks bigger talks better. The Glaucus and Diomedes exchange, and especially the speeches of Achilles (to Agamemnon, to the embassy, to Lykaon, to Aeneas, and to

---

[29] Dornseiff 1935; Jacoby 1933. Note that Dornseiff was aware of the role of parallelism in ancient Near Eastern verse: 1959, 379–93. On his role as an early defender of the text's unity, see Floratos 1952, 290.

[30] On the parallels within the hymn, see West 1975, 162; Altheim 1924, 441; Förstel 1979, 51–52; Thalmann 1984, 65–73. Baumeister 1860, 107 describes the hymn's structure as "antistrophic"; cf. Burkert 1979, 58: "both parts are parallel in structure to such an extent that, if they are not by the same author, one part is modeled on the other."

[31] Wilamowitz 1920 argued that the Pythian section was a continuation by a lesser poet, West 1975 that the poet of the Delian part copied the Pythian.

[32] Martin 1989.

Hector) all show this consistent use by a second speaker of the first speaker's phrases and topics, but with the added feature—that the person who speaks second outdoes the first. Sheer size is a criterion. Furthermore, the paired speeches are carefully matched in structure.[33] I have argued that this aesthetic is at work in the composition of the *Iliad* itself, a poem that outdoes competing epics such as the Heracles poems through its sheer mass. If we apply this aesthetic to the parallel and expanded structure of the *Hymn to Apollo*, what is the result? The Pythian part of the hymn should be seen as competing with, and besting, the Delian.[34]

Whatever their earliest origins, the *Homeric Hymns* as we have them fulfill more than a religious function: they were apparently preludes to epic performance and—most significant here—can *themselves be used in performance* contests.[35] The ending of *Hymn 6* in our collection asks the addressee, Aphrodite, specifically for "victory in *this agôn*" (lines 19–20):

> δὸς δ' ἐν ἀγῶνι
> νίκην τῷδε φέρεσθαι, ἐμὴν δ' ἔντυνον ἀοιδήν.

Grant me to win victory in this contest and fit out my song.

Of course, in hymn-contests, the context for the request does not have to be made explicit, any more than it does in the speeches of the *Iliad*, as the immediate context of the performance makes clear to a listening audience what the event and reward were to be.[36]

Given this agonistic function of hymns, I now propose that our *Hymn to Apollo* comprises an unusual combination intentionally paired by one composer or performance tradition to represent, or re-enact, a contest of two poets, one trying to beat the other, with a hymn, in an *agôn*. I shall go further and identify the two poets: the "Delian" is Homer and the "Pythian"

---

[33] Lohmann 1970, 30–40, 96–112.

[34] Already Baumeister 1860, 116 imagined this situation but in a diachronic sense, when he noted that the Pythian section seemed intended to overcome the fame of the pre-existing Delian; as will become clear, I imagine instead a *synchronic* symbiotic relationship between the hymns, although of course their traditional *material*—themes and phrases—existed before the composition-in-performance of the *Hymn*.

[35] Other evidence for hymn-contests: Archilochus' victory with a Demeter hymn in a Parian contest, mentioned by the scholiast to Aristophanes *Birds* 1764 (Rutherford 1896, 591); Pausanias *Description of Greece* 10.7.2 on the ancient Delphic hymn contest, from which Hesiod was excluded; Hesiod *Works and Days* 650–54 on his victory at Khalkis.

[36] For agonistic impulses as a primary shaping factor in Greek poetry generally: Griffith 1990.

is Hesiod.[37] In the creative rhapsodic tradition that surely shapes all surviving archaic hexameter, it makes little sense to assert that a Homer or Hesiod "actually" composed any given verses; instead, what is important is that certain compositions are attributed to these poets by audiences and performers.[38] It will suffice to call the *Hymn* singers "Homer" and "Hesiod." All that is missing to make the *Hymn to Apollo*'s setting an explicit contest is a single poetic line—and I must point out that several such single lines are indeed missing from our manuscript tradition.[39] The line would have read (in the vicinity of *Hymn to Apollo* 176): "Then Hesiod in turn began to sing." Exactly such a narrative break in the representation of a poetic contest is, in fact, present in a comparable Greek hexameter poem, *Idyll* 6 of Theocritus (line 20):

Τῷ δ' ἐπὶ Δαμοίτας ἀνεβάλλετο καὶ τάδ' ἄειδεν.

The Hellenistic poets knew the hymn tradition well; the example of Callimachus stands out, but Aratus, Apollonius, and Theocritus clearly imitated them.[40] It may not be too drastic to assume that Theocritus knew a hexameter poetic contest using hymnic material (either in texts or in his own experience); at any rate, it is interesting that Damoetas, the herdsman in *Idyll 6*, performs by assuming a *persona*, that of the Homeric Cyclops. In the *Hymn to Apollo*, the passage concerning the marvelous Delian maidens (156–72) contains two instances of *personae*: the poet, addressing them, names himself as the "blind man of Chios," while the maidens themselves are said to know how to imitate the voice and movement (*krembaliastus*) of every kind of person.[41] At the very least, we can say that the singer of the Delian portion assumes the mask of Homer.[42]

---

[37] I find after writing this paper that Pfister 1928, 9 made in passing the suggestion that ancient lore had linked the two parts of the *Hymn* with the contest mentioned in Hesiod fr. 265 Rzach = 357 MW, on which see below. He offers no further arguments for this.

[38] On the role of rhapsodes in the evolution of our Homeric text: Nagy 1996b, 84–86, 110–11; González 2013 passim.

[39] In the text of Allen-Sikes-Halliday (1936), there are lacunae after *Hymn to Apollo* 81, 317, and 539.

[40] R. L. Hunter 1996, 46–52 sees this familiarity partly as a reflex of the unbroken chain of rhapsodic transmission into the third century BCE.

[41] For *krembaliastus* as specifically *dance* movement, see the analysis by Peponi 2009 of visual evidence featuring women who play on percussive *krotala*.

[42] Of course, if it really was Homer who thus "signed" his work, rather than a rhapsode giving a stylized representation of the master singer, it is *less* likely that the details of lines 172–78 would

Having made this proposal—that *our Hymn to Apollo* is the representation of a poetic contest between Homer and Hesiod—I must turn towards two tasks: showing how some of the pieces of this puzzle had been put together before me; and showing how the new data that I have collected make this all the more likely a conclusion.

Baumeister's edition of 1860 first raised the notion, soon forgotten, that the Delian hymn was composed by one of the Homêridai and the Pythian by a follower of Hesiod.[43] He suggested this on internal evidence (knowledge of topography and local traditions of Boeotia; non-Homeric phrasing), as well as external evidence, primarily the key testimony of the scholion to Pindar *Nemean* 2.1, which mentions rhapsodizing of Homeric and Hesiodic compositions. In addition, the scholia to *Iliad* 2.523 refer to what we now read as *Hymn to Apollo* 241 as coming from Hesiod (fr. 70.18 MW, from the *Catalogue of Women*). Another piece of external evidence was drawn into discussion by Otto Crusius a century ago: the lines from the *Contest of Homer and Hesiod* (the *Certamen*) that tell how Homer sang a hymn to Apollo at the horn altar in Delos, a hymn that was thereupon written on a tablet and dedicated in the temple of Artemis; the first line, the only one given, matches that of the existing *Hymn* (*Certamen* lines 315–20 Allen)—evidence that, at least this part, was attributed to Homer.[44]

As we have it, the *Certamen* dates to Hadrian's era. But papyrus finds early in this century have made it clear that the fourth-century sophist Alcidamas, pupil of Gorgias, is responsible for most of the surviving version, as the young Friedrich Nietzsche had divined.[45] The *Certamen* gives us interesting glimpses of forms of poetic dueling—for example, the exchange of "amphibolic gnomes" in which Hesiod gives a line that seems to offer an impossible conclusion, to which Homer must reply with a verse that gives good sense and syntax, while avoiding the absurdity towards which Hesiod had been steering him. For instance, when Hesiod says, "they took dinner then, the meat of cows and the necks of horses ... ," Homer jumps in to give the second accusative a different governing verb, enjambed in the completion-verse:

---

be included. He doth protest too much. It is significant that late features of language and diction cluster in this very passage: Gladstone 1876, 116 speaks of "such a crowded appropriation of marked Homeric phrase as could not have been due to Homer" here; cf. Hoekstra 1969, 25.

[43] Baumeister 1860, 115 *a poeta ... e disciplina Hesiodi*.

[44] Crusius 1895, 718; *Certamen* text from Allen 1912:237.

[45] Nietzsche 1870–73; for full details and bibliography, including views that the work contains archaic material, see now O'Sullivan 1992, 63–105.

"... they unhitched, sweating when they had their fill of war."[46] This section of the *Certamen,* in particular, displays what must have been the skills of some hexameter performers at intricate variation. Comparative evidence from modern Turkey shows that such complex variation need *not* be text-based (i.e., in the *Certamen* need not be an invention of Alcidamas), but flourishes specifically in actual minstrel contests.[47] In this connection, it is interesting that at least two lines from the "Pythian" hymnic section have been identified as having a similar "amphibolic" structure.[48]

After a seemingly arbitrary royal decision to award Hesiod the victory (because he sang of peace), Hesiod dedicates his tripod to the Muses, inscribing on it "that he defeated divine Homer by a hymn at Khalkis" (*Certamen* 210–16). He then proceeds to Delphi, where the Pythia warns him about his death. The *Certamen* places the poetic contest in Euboea, at Khalkis. This is apparently an old tradition, though in the actual Hesiodic lines that seem to refer to the same event the poet does not say whom he defeated, only that it was by a *hymnos* (*Works and Days* 656–58):

> ἔνθα μέ φημι
> ὕμνῳ νικήσαντα φέρειν τρίποδ' ὠτώεντα.
> τὸν μὲν ἐγὼ Μούσησ' Ἑλικωνιάδεσσ' ἀνέθηκα

The *Certamen* lines may seem odd, because nothing in the narrated contest between the two poets resembles a "hymn" in the narrower sense; the word seems to be used in this event as synonymous with *epic verse.*[49] Shortly after this point, the *Certamen* features the *hymn* performance, but by Homer, and *not* (at least overtly) in a contest. After defeat by Hesiod and a period of wandering about performing epics and composing epigrams, he comes at last to Delos, where he performs the Apollo hymn. Thus the *Certamen* seems to imagine a complementary distribution: *Hesiod* wins a contest, but not with a hymn in the narrow sense; *Homer* is rewarded for a hymn in the narrow sense, but not because he sang it in a contest.

---

[46] *Certamen* 102–37. Kakridis 1980, 133–34 cites a modern Greek folk example of amphibolic gnome. For the technique, see in detail Collins 2004.

[47] Erdener 1993 attests to similar, and even more complex, poetic entrapments in contemporary Turkish song contests.

[48] Kirk 1981,174, who identified this, finds it "non-traditional," by which he means non-*Homeric.*

[49] On the semantics of *humnos* "song," see Nagy 1990, 353–57.

Both Crusius in 1895 and Janko in 1982 (apparently unaware of the earlier work) adduce another testimonium, the fragment attributed to Hesiod (357 MW):[50]

ἐν Δήλῳ τότε πρῶτον ἐγὼ καὶ Ὅμηρος ἀοιδοὶ
μέλπομεν, ἐν νεαροῖς ὕμνοις ῥάψαντες ἀοιδήν,
Φοῖβον Ἀπόλλωνα χρυσάορον, ὃν τέκε Λητώ.

We can notice that this passage, from the scholia to *Nemean* 2.1 concerning rhapsodes, fills a gap in the story: the speaker "Hesiod" says that he and Homer first sang at Delos. He does *not* say that this was a contest, but he uses the phrase ἐν νεαροῖς ὕμνοις ῥάψαντες ἀοιδήν, "in new *hymnoi* stitching a song." This description could fit a kind of cooperative enterprise in which the two poets "stitch together" their songs synchronically. The fragment clearly represents two poets working at the same time, not just two pre-fabricated poems sung anonymously. Nagy has recently explicated the metaphor underlying *rhapsôidia* as follows: "Many various fabrics of song, each one already made ... become remade into a unity, a single, new continuous fabric, by being sewn together."[51] While he does not refer to the *Hymn to Apollo*, I must point out that Nagy's description fits exactly the situation that I envision as being represented both by the poem and by this Hesiodic fragment that refers to the cooperative composition of the two great hexameter poets. One may question how jointly "stitching" a song, as in fragment 357 MW, can be reconciled with competitive singing, and I will return to this problem in my conclusion. But at this juncture, we must turn to the new evidence regarding the second feature of the *Hymn*, its metrics, in order to see that two poetic *personae* are, in fact, aurally distinguished in the *Hymn to Apollo*.

As the following analysis of lines 176–203 shows, there is an unusual stylistic feature that occurs in a marked way soon after Ruhnken's alleged break between the two portions of the hymn:

οἱ δ' ἐπὶ δὴ πείσονται, ἐπεὶ καὶ ἐτήτυμόν ἐστιν.
αὐτὰρ ἐγὼν οὐ λήξω ἑκηβόλον Ἀπόλλωνα
ὑμνέων ἀργυρότοξον ὃν ἠΰκομος τέκε Λητώ.
ὦ ἄνα, καὶ Λυκίην καὶ Μῃονίην ἐρατεινὴν
καὶ Μίλητον ἔχεις ἔναλον πόλιν ἱμερόεσσαν,   180

---

[50] Crusius 1895, 718; Janko 1982, 113 is led by this to observe "at some period hymns called 'Homeric' and 'Hesiodic' were recited together on Delos in Apollo's honor," but does not see in this a direct allusion to our *Hymn*.

[51] Nagy 1996b, 86.

αὐτὸς δ' αὖ Δήλοιο περικλύστου μέγ' ἀνάσσεις.
εἶσι δὲ φορμίζων Λητοῦς ἐρικυδέος υἱὸς
φόρμιγγι γλαφυρῇ πρὸς Πυθὼ πετρήεσσαν,
ἄμβροτα εἵματ' ἔχων τεθυωμένα· τοῖο δὲ φόρμιγξ
χρυσέου ὑπὸ πλήκτρου καναχὴν ἔχει ἱμερόεσσαν   185
ἔνθεν δὲ πρὸς Ὄλυμπον ἀπὸ χθονὸς ὥς τε νόημα
εἶσι Διὸς πρὸς δῶμα θεῶν μεθ' <u>ὁμήγυριν ἄλλων</u>·
αὐτίκα δ' ἀθανάτοισι μέλει κίθαρις καὶ ἀοιδή.
Μοῦσαι μέν θ' ἅμα πᾶσαι ἀμειβόμεναι ὀπὶ καλῇ
ὑμνεῦσίν ῥα θεῶν δῶρ' ἄμβροτα ἠδ' ἀνθρώπων   190
τλημοσύνας, ὅσ' ἔχοντες ὑπ' ἀθανάτοισι θεοῖσι
ζώουσ' ἀφραδέες καὶ ἀμήχανοι, οὐδὲ δύνανται
εὑρέμεναι θανάτοιό τ' ἄκος καὶ γήραος ἄλκαρ·
αὐτὰρ ἐϋπλόκαμοι Χάριτες <u>καὶ εὔφρονες Ὧραι</u>
Ἁρμονίη θ' Ἥβη τε Διὸς θυγάτηρ τ' Ἀφροδίτη   195
ὀρχεῦντ' ἀλλήλων ἐπὶ καρπῷ χεῖρας ἔχουσαι·
τῇσι μὲν οὔτ' αἰσχρὴ μεταμέλπεται οὔτ' ἐλάχεια,
ἀλλὰ μάλα μεγάλη τε ἰδεῖν καὶ εἶδος ἀγητὴ
Ἄρτεμις ἰοχέαιρα ὁμότροφος Ἀπόλλωνι.
ἐν δ' αὖ τῇσιν Ἄρης καὶ εὔσκοπος Ἀργειφόντης   200
παίζουσ'· αὐτὰρ ὁ Φοῖβος Ἀπόλλων ἐγκιθαρίζει
καλὰ καὶ ὕψι βιβάς, αἴγλη δέ μιν ἀμφιφαείνει
μαρμαρυγαί τε ποδῶν καὶ ἐϋκλώστοιο χιτῶνος.

At issue is the metrical feature known as Hermann's Bridge, the noted avoidance of word-break after the trochee of the fourth foot in the hexameter. In Homeric verse, this rule is violated very rarely: counts range from 1 per 200 verses to 1 per 1000.[52] But in the *Hymn to Apollo* (546 lines), word break after the fourth trochee occurs nine times (or 1 per 60 verses). Three occurrences, the most densely clustered, are underlined in the above passage. The others are:

Ἴμβρος τ' εὐκτιμένη καὶ Λῆμνος <u>ἀμιχθαλόεσσα</u>   36
ἂψ περιτελλομένου ἔτεος <u>καὶ ἐπήλυθον ὧραι</u>   350

καὶ Θρύον Ἀλφειοῖο πόρον <u>καὶ ἐΰκτιτον Αἶπυ</u>   423

καὶ σπεῖσαι μακάρεσσι θεοῖς οἳ <u>Ὄλυμπον ἔχουσιν</u>   498 = 512

ῥηΐδιον ἔπος ὕμμ' ἐρέω <u>καὶ ἐπὶ φρεσὶ θήσω</u>   534

---

[52] On the lack of agreement over violations, see Appendix below.

Clearly, eight of these nine breaks occur after line 165, the spot that marks the division of hymns according to Ruhnken.[53] In addition, the violations that occur in the second part of the hymn are part of a larger stylistic feature, noted by underlinings above: five of the eight "Pythian" cases of violation occur when the word *kai* is correpted next to a word beginning with *e-* (3x) or *eü-* (2x). Correption, of course, is widespread in all hexameter verse; in this position (*kai* before the second short of the fourth foot), it is less common, but still can be found, 68 times in the *Odyssey* (an average of 1 per 178 verses), for example.[54] Only once in the *Iliad* and *Odyssey* combined, however, does the constellation of correpted *kai* plus disyllabic *eü-* occur in the fourth foot, at *Iliad* 2.592 (= *Hymn to Apollo* 423):

> Οἳ δὲ Πύλον τ᾽ ἐνέμοντο καὶ Ἀρήνην ἐρατεινὴν
> καὶ Θρύον Ἀλφειοῖο πόρον καὶ ἐΰκτιτον Αἰπὺ
> καὶ Κυπαρισσήεντα καὶ Ἀμφιγένειαν ἔναιον
> καὶ Πτελεὸν καὶ Ἕλος καὶ Δώριον, ἔνθά τε Μοῦσαι
> ἀντόμεναι Θάμυριν τὸν Θρήϊκα παῦσαν ἀοιδῆς   595
> Οἰχαλίηθεν ἰόντα παρ᾽ Εὐρύτου Οἰχαλιῆος·

The line comes in the sentence describing Thamyris' *poetic contest* with the Muses as he returned from Oichalia—an interesting contextual analogue to the possible *agôn* represented by the *Hymn*.[55] It may be that the same rhapsodes interested in stylizing a hymn-competition between Homer and Hesiod also had a hand in composing this *Iliad* scene.

For the deeper significance of the specific stylistic feature illustrated in the "Pythian" portion, whereby fourth-foot trochee breaks coincide with correpted *kai*, I draw attention to the following lines from Hesiod's *Theogony*:[56]

---

[53]   If one takes line 179 as the start of the "Pythian" hymn, then two violations occur before the break. The division that best fits my reading of the poem occurs after 176. It should be pointed out that purely numerical averages do not capture the actual *density* of violations, that is, the number of lines *between* violations. In a random sample of 546 Homeric lines *Odyssey* 5.1–493 plus 6.1–53, I find the following intervals between "violations" in the broadest sense—see Appendix: 5.225, 5.476, 6.9, 6.10. My impression from reading similar stretches of text is that the longer intervals of approximately 200 lines are most common.

[54]   My calculation was done using a concordance to van Thiel's *Odyssey* text, Tebben 1994. I have not been able to analyze the *Iliad* in this way.

[55]   On the assertion, embedded in this passage, of Homeric authority vs. other poetic traditions, see Martin 1989, 229.

[56]   See also fragments 33.18 and 123.2 MW.

74   ἀθανάτοις διέταξε νόμους   καὶ ἐπέφραδε τιμάς.
122   δάμναται ἐν στήθεσσι νόον   καὶ ἐπίφρονα βουλήν.
237   αὖτις δ᾽ αὖ Θαύμαντα μέγαν καὶ ἀγήνορα Φόρκυν
896   ἶσον ἔχουσαν πατρὶ μένος   καὶ ἐπίφρονα βουλήν,

Works and Days

6   ῥεῖα δ᾽ ἀρίζηλον μινύθει   καὶ ἄδηλον ἀέξει,
7   ῥεῖα δέ τ᾽ ἰθύνει σκολιὸν   καὶ ἀγήνορα κάρφει
25   καὶ πτωχὸς πτωχῷ φθονέει   καὶ ἀοιδὸς ἀοιδῷ.
44   ὥστε σε κεἰς ἐνιαυτὸν ἔχειν   καὶ ἀεργὸν ἐόντα·
67   ἐν δὲ θέμεν κύνεόν τε νόον   καὶ ἐπίκλοπον ἦθος
78   ψεύδεά θ᾽ αἱμυλίους τε λόγους καὶ ἐπίκλοπον ἦθος
183   οὐδὲ ξεῖνος ξεινοδόκῳ   καὶ ἑταῖρος ἑταίρῳ
208   τῇ δ᾽ εἶς ᾗ σ᾽ ἂν ἐγώ περ ἄγω   καὶ ἀοιδὸν ἐοῦσαν·
493   Πὰρ δ᾽ ἴθι χάλκειον θῶκον   καὶ ἐπαλέα λέσχην
574   φεύγειν δὲ σκιεροὺς θώκους   καὶ ἐπ᾽ ἠόα κοῖτον
602   θῆτά τ᾽ ἄοικον ποιεῖσθαι   καὶ ἄτεκνον ἔριθον
674   μηδὲ μένειν οἶνόν τε νέον   καὶ ὀπωρινὸν ὄμβρον

It is safe to say that this is a noticeable feature of Hesiodic verse. Most striking is the *Works and Days*, with a ratio of 1 occurrence per 69 lines—nearly three times the *Odyssey* average—and especially the high density in the first 200 lines. Let me stress: I am not arguing that Hesiod composed the Pythian part of the *Hymn to Apollo*. In fact, it is odd that this "Hesiodic" feature is so prominent right after the break. This fact leads me to suggest that we have here an *impersonation of Hesiod*, which seeks, as do modern impersonators, to establish the personality being mimicked through an immediate heavy emphasis on the most characteristic traits of its target.[57]

Now we can return to the speaker who was identified in antiquity as "Hesiod" in fragment 357 MW. Notice in these lines exactly the same rare word-break conjoined with the same sort of correption of *kai*:

ἐν Δήλῳ τότε πρῶτον ἐγὼ καὶ Ὅμηρος ἀοιδοί

This stylistic fingerprint suggests that either there existed a Hesiodic hexameter version of the *Certamen* at an early period—or more likely, that whoever composed the *Hymn to Apollo* as we have it made these lines as part of its framing narrative, to introduce the great imaginary contention of the bards.

---

[57]   Also in favor of the "Hesiodic" sound of the Pythian portion are the greater proportion of observed digamma and a contrastive lack of Hesiodic features in the Delian portion compared with the other hymns in the collection, which would make the first section sound more "Homeric": Janko 1982, 106.

My conclusion does not necessarily contradict the scenarios produced by several scholars who have attempted to situate the *Hymn's* composition in historical terms. The invaluable scholion to *Nemean* 2.1 (3.29.9–18 Drachmann) asserts that the *Hymn* was written by one Cynaethus of Chios "who first rhapsodized Homer's epics in Syracuse" and attributed by him (*anatetheiken*) to Homer.[58] Taking this cue, Burkert and Janko independently suggested that the performance occasion for the *Hymn* was the unique Delian-Pythian festival staged by Polycrates on Delos, most likely in 522 BCE.[59] Neither imagines a contest, but rather a performance of hymns that had been spliced for the occasion. We do not, however, require a datable contest-situation; on my reading, the *representation* of a contest would still explain better the preserved stylistic differences. After all, if we assume as these scholars do that one rhapsode composed in or for performance a hymn meant to be his own, or in his own voice, even with materials drawn from distinct traditions, the metrical and linguistic differences noted above should *not* occur: his own style should permeate the composition. On the other hand, we know from Plato's *Ion* (531a2) that some rhapsodes did perform the verses of *both* masters (and Archilochus as well): thus it would not be impossible for one performer to "do all the voices."[60]

So much for my argument that a specific performance context is being represented by the *Hymn to Apollo*, a context that can explain the seeming stylistic anomalies between the two portions, through reference to characterization by style. In this light, the citation by Thucydides (*History of the Peloponnesian War* 3.104) of the lines from this hymn, the passage that first led Ruhnken to his radical proposal, should be given one more look. Only Heubeck seems to have appreciated the great care with which the ancient historian supported his argument that there had been musical and gymnastic contests on Delos before the Athenians revived them after the "katharsis" of

---

[58] Note that the verb is also *vox propria* for dedication; for application to a hymn, cf. the event discussed above, *Certamen* 320–21 Allen: the Delians wrote Homer's lines on a tablet and dedicated it (*anethēkan*) in the shrine of Artemis. To my knowledge, this sentence is universally interpreted in the way Burkert 1979, 54 reads it "and he wrote, among the works attributed to Homer, the hymn to Apollo and *fathered it on Homer.*" Yet I fail to see why we cannot take the syntax and semantics more simply to read "and dedicated it to *him* [*autôi* = Apollo]." I intend to examine the interpretation of the entire scholion more closely in a separate article.

[59] Burkert 1979, 59; Janko 1982, 113–14; Aloni 1989 expands and elaborates the argument drawing historical parallels with Peisistratid initiatives; cf. De Martino 1982, 52.

[60] This would give even further metadramatic point to the praise of the Deliades' mimetic ability. It is interesting that of the three poets mentioned as *objects* of rhapsodic performance, Hesiod and Archilochus are also depicted in tradition as hymnic competitors, perhaps another indication that their biographies stem from rhapsodes, who retrojected onto them their own habits. On Homer as competitor, see below.

426/5 BCE. As Heubeck points out, lines 146–50, cited at 3.104.4, attest only to the existence of athletic and *choral* performances (ὀρχηστυῖ καὶ ἀοιδῇ), while 165–72 (cited at 3.104.5) constitute for Thucydides the proof of the *mousikês agôn*.[61] It is in these lines that "Homer" proposes the poetic contract with the Delian maidens.[62] (In performance, these were either the "back-up singers" for a rhapsodic/citharodic performance or participated in a separate choral *agôn*.[63]) Clearly, Thucydides read the poet's riddling advice (that the girls should tell others they like the blind man's songs best) as agonistic self-advertisement.

If, finally, we extend this analysis and imagine that our "Homeric" poems—epics and hymns—at some point in their long evolution were *composed* (rather than simply "recited") in just such contest situations, what can we learn?[64]

A number of things might be noted, but I shall focus on one. It is well known that the beginning of the *Hymn to Apollo* presents many problems, especially in the seemingly arbitrary variation of verb tenses. Is the description of Apollo's entrance onto Olympus the narration of a one-time event in the past, at his coming of age, properly belonging later in the narrative? Or is it a description of an eternal present, in which Apollo is continually posing a threat to the Olympian order?[65] In any case, this is a powerful passage, a poetic tour de force as sudden as Apollo's entrance.

If we imagine that the *Hymn* represents a poetic contest, it is not unlikely that the ambiguity in the opening lines captures a feature of actual performance practice by those who composed as they sang: namely, the urge to

---

[61] Heubeck 1966, 227–28, who points out that Thucydides' version of line 150 with *kathesôsin* vs. the *Hymn to Apollo stêsôntai* refers to the act of gathering, not setting up a contest. He voices doubt as to whether lines 165ff. prove Thucydides' point and wonders if he got the idea of a contest of singers from later rhapsodic practice. In my reading of the *Hymn*, the lines prove the point; Thucydides' conception about Homer performing in an agonistic setting may reflect the ideology of rhapsodes whom he could interview, rather than his own retrojection.

[62] For this scene as "contract," see D. Miller 1986, 62, who, however, sees it as *not* "overtly agonistic." I would claim it is.

[63] Aloni 1993 suggests that the *Hymn* was designed to *introduce* such a choral competition, rather than serve as a proem to an epic performance at Delos.

[64] No one doubts that rhapsodic contests figured in the *transmission* of these poems; in arguing for an effect on *composition*, I am aligning myself with Nagy's perspective on the evolution of the Homeric text, as outlined most recently in Nagy 1996b, 29–112. I note especially his conclusion (p. 110) that it was Panathenaic rhapsode performance that led to the "achievement of a near-textual status of the Homeric poems." I take this to mean that we should imagine a certain degree of flexibility and fine-tuning in the actual performances: they are much closer to "composition-in-performance."

[65] On the problems of the opening, see West 1975,163; Càssola 1975, 486; Janko 1982, 100; J. S Clay 1989, 22–29.

seize on the most captivating and exciting episode first, before a competitor might get the chance to elaborate the episode in its correct chronological position in the tale. "Homer," anticipating that his opponent would relish elaborating the splendid arrival of the god on Olympus, beat him to the punch, although he had not even told yet of the god's birth, and tried to "universalize" the eventual epiphanic moment.

Such a (hypothetical) practice—preemptive poetic strikes—would provide a motivation for the rule, which we find attributed to Hipparchus the son of Peisistratus concerning Homeric rhapsodic competition at the Panathenaea, that each performer pick up the story where the previous one left off (*ex hypolêpseôs*).[66] We should distinguish effect from intent here. From the diachronic perspective, such a rule would eventually have the effect that long epic compositions would become crystallized and comprehensive. But from the *synchronic* perspective, on which I have dwelt, the rule would function differently: by forcing rhapsodes to perform in order, no one singer is given a competitive advantage over any other.[67] The superb management of athletic games to assure equity could easily have been extended by the promoters of the Panathenaic games in this way.[68] To put this another way, the contest that I find represented in the *Hymn to Apollo* gives us a glimpse of a "pre-Peisistratid" *agôn*. Perhaps we should call it a poem from the age of the "lamb-singers," *arnôidoi*. The *Nemean* 2.1 scholion (on the authority of Dionysius of Argos) identifies these men as predecessors of the rhapsodes and contrasts them specifically by mentioning the former group's propensity for singing whatever section of the poetic tradition each one chose to (*hekastos ho ti bouloito meros êide*).[69] Whether this is an authentic memory or an archaizing fiction, the scenario brings us finally to a fuller understanding of the importance *for competitors* that the proems of epic, too, be artful and arresting.[70] If our Homeric epics in their present form date from before the Peisistratid period in the later sixth century,

---

[66]   On the sources for this rule, see Allen 1924, 227.

[67]   Nagy 1996b, 75–84 identifies the intent of the rule as being to enforce the "even weighting" of episodes in epic; I am fully in agreement. As the *Iliad* and *Odyssey*, however, represent the ultimate crystallization, the end-product of such weighting, we would be less likely to see signs of competitive pre-emptive poetic strikes within them.

[68]   De Martino 1982, 36–41 in the course of a difficult argument that "Homer's" self-praise eliminated him from contests metaphorically (i.e., severed the *Hymn* from the Homeric corpus) refers to the rule (cf. Herodotus *Histories* 8.59) that those who tried to get a head-start in athletic events were penalized. I suggest the rule would have applied to poetic contests as well.

[69]   Nagy 1996b, 84 cites the passage in discussing the Panathenaic "rule."

[70]   It may explain why the proem of the *Odyssey*, e.g., poses so many problems for interpreters: see the careful reading by Pedrick 1992.

we might read at *Odyssey* 1.10 a relic of the period when poets could and did begin their composition where they wanted—stylized as the Muse's choice: "tell us, also, about these things, daughter of Zeus, starting from whatever place [*hamothen*]." But perhaps, as in the heavily emphasized allusion to the Homeric persona in the *Hymn to Apollo*'s first portion, the command that the Muse begin the story "at any point" is also a convenient synchronic fiction. It is an even more effective and persuasive way to begin a composition when there is a rule in existence that one *cannot* just start anywhere in the story.

I conclude with some comparative evidence that clarifies the methods and implications of the sort of agonistic composition that I have proposed for the *Hymn to Apollo*. The folklorist Yildiray Erdener reports, after observing some 500 song duels in northeastern Turkey during 1982, that each singer (*ashik*) involved in these organized contests at coffee-houses has devised a number of strategies for embarrassing and defeating his opponents. In one technique, singers entrap their challengers by forcing them into absurd or obscene rhymes within the required rhyme-scheme. This may remind us of the amphibolic gnomes of the *Certamen*. Erdener does not record encountering agonistic production of long poems, such as I am proposing. But one detail of the sociology of Turkish song-contests remains suggestive: each *ashik* not only secretly observes his audience just prior to performance in order to prepare verses that will praise the specific group each night; he also *confers* at length, prior to the performance, with that night's competitor. In other words, competition induces *collaboration*. It is in this light, ultimately, that fragment 357 MW makes most sense: "Homer" and "Hesiod" stitch together their song through collaborative competition of the type still attested in living oral traditions.[71] In this light, as well, the praise of the Delians by the blind man of Chios is more than merely a compliment to the local chorus; it is part of a broader strategy to capture the good will of his voting audience by working it into his act: like every oral performer, he adjusts his composition to suit the immediate situation.[72] Nationally-known

---

[71] Such a context would explain the seamless matching that is articulated by Ballabriga 1990, 19: "Tout semble donc se passer comme si la première partie de l'hymne prévoyait la seconde." "Homer" can in fact know fairly well ahead of performance what "Hesiod" will sing; in the event, "Hesiod" can of course re-adjust his verses to match the previous performer's. W. Knight 1941, 312–13 came closest to this notion in his interpretation of fr. 357 MW as representing a joint Homeric/Hesiodic composition by a process of "epic combination." He imagines, however, something like the "agglutinative" method envisioned by Notopoulos as resulting in this hymn (1962, 348); neither scholar is thinking of live contest performance as real or represented context for the *Hymn*.

[72] Cf. De Martino 1982, 67 on "Homer's" words at 165–73 as the equivalent of "un agonistico curriculum vitae."

Turkish singers compete in annual festivals where the best performers gather and their prestige is placed on the line. It seems likely that our *Hymn to Apollo* re-enacts and reflects a long Greek tradition of similar contests.[73]

Appendix: On Hermann's Bridge

I base part of the preceding argument on a stylistic feature involving the fourth-foot trochaic caesura. It would be easier to argue tangible stylistic variation between Homer and Hesiod if we had: 1) a precise definition of when Hermann's Bridge (hereafter HB) is violated; and 2) reliable statistics of the entire hexameter corpus, keyed precisely to this definition. These remain desiderata. A third (3) consideration is whether metrical variation at this level could have been perceived by an audience so as to produce characterization by style. In the interest of clearing the ground, I offer the following observations:

1. *Definitions.* Hermann (1805, 692–96) in first noting the rarity of word-break after the first short in the fourth foot (hereafter tr4) cited 18 examples (p. 692) without immediate further categorization, including such lines as *Iliad* 9.394, 21.483, 21.575 and *Odyssey* 5.400, 5.476, 7.192. He made no claim to have counted all the examples. At the same time, he proceeded to introduce several qualifications that would make the rare caesura more "tolerable":

   a. if a caesura occurs after the first syllable of the fifth foot as well (as in *Iliad* 6.2, 24.60; this eliminates *Odyssey* 7.192 from his preliminary list on p. 692, although Hermann at no point explicitly re-evaluates the list).

   b. if the word after the caesura is *not* amphibrach (he cites *Iliad* 9.482 and 10.317, but in fact this constraint would seem to make tolerable almost all instances and also eliminates from his preliminary list on p. 692 all but *Iliad* 21.483, 21.575, *Odyssey* 5.400 = 6.294 = 12.181, 7.192 [but see rule "a" above], 8.554, 12.47, 18.150). In other

---

[73] Since the original publication of this article, the most probing further structural and thematic analysis has been by Heiden 2013, whose conclusion (p. 8) accords with the view offered here of the overall unity of the poem: "The meticulously comprehensive analogousness of ... specific, extensive, and arbitrary sequences of topics indicates intentional planning particular to the hymn." I wish to offer my warmest thanks to Prof. Ana Maria González de Tobia for the invitation to present this material as a paper at the University of La Plata, Argentina during the excellent Coloquio that she organized. I owe special thanks to Prof. Dora Pozzi, who graciously and speedily translated my paper into Spanish for the event and chaired the session. For advice concerning its arguments I am indebted to many participants in the Coloquio, as also to audiences at Stanford, UCLA, Yale, and Princeton.

words, at this point only six different lines, from his original exempla, remain. However, since Hermann never constructs or enumerates an airtight category of "violations," the paring down has no consequences.

c. Most important for our purposes, he refuses to identify as any sort of violation lines such as *Iliad* 1.33, *Odyssey* 4.677, in which a monosyllable joined in sense to the next word *precedes* tr4: "Haec minime rara sunt exempla" (p. 693). This means that Hermann did not focus on the *kai + correption* lines that I identify in this paper as a "stylistic fingerprint."

Hoekstra (1969, 62) seemingly generalizes this mitigating factor to include any monosyllable, but does not specify whether he is speaking of the word before or after the caesura. West (1982, 38 n18) offers the more efficient formulation: word-division after prepositive or before postpositive is disregarded for the purposes of identifying violations. (I thank Fred Naiden of Harvard for pointing out West's version to me.)

Solomon (1985) taking what he calls the "softening" effects (p. 25) into account (*a* through *c*, in my list) adds to them several mitigating circumstances suggested after Hermann's work (mainly by Monro and van Leeuwen):

d. if the final word of the hexameter = 5 syllables (e.g., *Iliad* 10.317).

e. if the "violation" follows an elision.

As he notes, by these criteria *Theogony* 319 is the only line in Hesiod to offer an unmitigated violation of HB. He does not subject Homer to such an examination.

2. *Statistics.* As with studies concerning the Homeric formulae, every scholar seems to have used his or her own implicit definition when counting "violations" of HB. As is already clear from #1 above, even the notion of violation expresses a rigidity that Hermann himself avoided in noting the phenomena surrounding tr4. Obviously, what one wants is a graded list telling, for each hexameter composition, how tr4 occurs, in terms of the categories *a* through *e* above (and any not so "mitigated"). Only then can we make accurate comparative statements. Note further that such an account would ideally examine textual traditions, formula usage, and higher narrative features in the vicinity of each "violation" (in sum, a potential dissertation). This much said, I present a range of statistics that have already been somehow compiled regarding HB and have a bearing on the *Hymn to Apollo*:

- The oft-cited figure that violations (undefined) of HB occur 1 per 1000 lines in Homer was put forward by Maas (1962, para. 87) without citation of source. West (1966, 94–95) criticized it as low, claiming instead that HB violations (constraints unstated) occur 1 per 550 lines in Homer and 1 per 370 lines in Hesiod. Solomon (1985, 22–23) in turn claims West used inaccurate information from van Leeuwen 1890, but does not say exactly where the inaccuracies lie and offers no new figures of his own.

- O'Neill (1942, 158), compiling figures on the basis of 1000-line segments (NB: *not* randomly selected, as they match book-divisions), found that tr4 marks 1.2% of *Iliad* lines, 0.9% *Odyssey*, 1.1% Hesiod. If these figures are compared with West's, above, and we assume no vast inaccuracies, then 1/6 to 1/5 of Homer's tr4 violate HB; 1/4 of Hesiod's do. Compare van Raalte (1986) who gives more comprehensive figures on tr4: *Iliad* 4.2%, *Odyssey* 3.3%, Hesiod 6%. Clearly either criteria or accuracy have shifted from the earlier analysis; in any event, seen proportionally, differences between Homeric and Hesiodic practice do not seem significant.

- Athanassakis (1970, 139) ignores constraint *c* and finds that HB violations occur in 5% of Hesiodic lines. This produces an absurd result if O'Neill's figure concerning tr4 is accurate (it may be that he ignored enclitics in counting tr4): there would be four times more HB violations than there are tr4. Athanassakis contrasts a figure he finds in Sturtevant alleging that 2.2% of the first 500 lines of the *Iliad* violate HB. Of course, we do not know the latter scholar's definition of HB.

- Sicking (1993, 78) says 0.47% of the *Iliad* lines violate HB. No source or definition given.

In sum, depending on often unstated criteria for counting and defining HB, violations range from a low 0.1% (Maas), through 0.18% (West) and 0.47% (Sicking) to Sturtevant's 2.2%. It would be fruitless to compare any figures I have found regarding Hesiod and the *Hymn*, given the lack of clear-cut criteria.

3. *Results for stylistic analysis.* One now understands why Janko (1982, 37) thought it "unwise" to draw conclusions from violations of HB. Nevertheless, I am prepared to defend my interpretation of the metrical features included in the body of my argument, while conceding that no purely statistical evidence has yet been adduced to distinguish Homer from Hesiod in terms of HB. What matters is that 1) the feature *kai* + correption at HB position occurs densely in Hesiod, sparsely in Homer, and is split along Delian/Pythian lines in the *Hymn* and 2) the feature clusters in the Pythian portion right after what I call the performance break (or as previous scholars had it, the textual break). Can an audience appreciate such features? Hermann (1805, 694) seems to imply that *someone* would recognize, but may take himself as the model audience: "quo quis praestantior

fuit poeta, eo diligentius ab ista caesura abstinuit." Solomon (1985, 25), in the course of a persuasive defense of the artistry of Hesiod *Theogony* 319, argues that it is "not impossible that Homer occasionally intended violations of Hermann's Bridge." Of his leading examples, *Iliad* 2.246 and 2.250, he notes "perhaps it is no accident that Homer here violates Hermann's bridge twice in five lines, the context of which refers to Thersites' 'skill' in speech." I would add that this finding concerning characterization and style is precisely in line with my own independent conclusions regarding the abnormally high amounts of correption in Thersites' speech (Martin 1989, 112). Solomon's fine-scale analysis leads him to suggest that at 2.250 Odysseus' "violation of the 'normal' mode of metrical speech ... is meant to reflect an ironic mimicry of Thersites' crude speech ... ," exactly when Odysseus is describing his enemy's speech-habits. Surely if the performer of the *Iliad* can *represent* Odysseus at this point *representing* in turn the speech habits of *his* opponent, the same performer (or one pretending to be him, or an entire rhapsodic tradition of performing) can mimic the "opponent," proletarian Hesiod.

8

RHAPSODIZING ORPHEUS[1]

Orpheus—we know him as a poet, a musician, and a myth. Yet we must recall that all three of these media—poetry, music, and myth—arise, at some point, out of an act of performance. The last-mentioned, *mûthos*, can, in fact, be described from Homer on as the very paradigm for performance in archaic Greece: a public utterance that seeks through persuasive means to negotiate authority before a critical audience.[2] In this connection, it should be worth asking: exactly what sorts of performances originated and transmitted the figure of Orpheus?[3]

To begin with, it is clear that, in archaic Greece, cult and ritual provided a site for audiences and performers to comment on this multivalent figure. Such occasions even made use of hymnic poetry that had been attributed to the Thracian singer. There are a number of testimonia, such as the report by Pausanias (*Description of Greece* 9.27.2; cf. 9.30.12) that the Lykomidae of Phlya sang Orphic hymns to accompany rituals. Fritz Graf has thoroughly investigated the interrelation of Orpheus, Musaeus, and the Eumolpidae at Eleusis.[4] We might be misled by the ancient evidence into thinking that private gatherings, *thiasoi*, or initiate groups were the only or even the major locus to feature Orphic poetic performances.[5] This need not be the full picture, however. I will argue instead that Orphic poetry, whatever its private affiliations, formed part of the rhapsode's repertoire. If we assume Orphic poems played a part in this very public kind of performance, it can

---

[1] Originally published in *Kernos* 14 (2001): 23–33.

[2] See Martin 1989; Calame 1998; Nagy 1996a, 113–52.

[3] This paper originated as a contribution to the annual gathering of the Coralie consortium, held May 24–26, 2000 at the University of Lausanne. It is a pleasure to thank Claude Calame and the members of this continuing scholarly *thiasos* for advice and encouragement.

[4] Graf 1974.

[5] On these, see West 1983, 79, 260–63.

help clarify and explain several hitherto unconnected phenomena in ancient myth and poetics.

To sharpen the point about performance, let me first juxtapose two quotations, one from Martin West, the other from Plato. While discussing the apparently unusual status of the Derveni commentator, West makes the following more general statement: "While not secret, Orphic poems seem to have had a very limited circulation. They were not a matter of general public interest. They were not taught in school or recited for public or social entertainment."[6] West, of course, approaches the Orphic material from a relentlessly literary point-of-view. He thinks in terms of texts, in terms of circulation of scrolls, and in terms of copying and borrowing from books. Even his imagined historical sketch for the intrusion of messy Asiatic rites into Greece calls to mind descriptions of the advent of a genteel neo-paganism in prim Edwardian Britain. Perhaps we need to apply a somewhat less anachronistic model. If, as West argues, Orphic poetry was so private, we must then ask: how can Plato describe it in terms of a broad audience's competence to judge performances? For this is what Plato seems to be saying at *Ion* 533b–c:

> Ἀλλὰ μήν, ὥς γ᾽ ἐγὼ οἶμαι, οὐδ᾽ ἐν αὐλήσει γε οὐδὲ ἐν κιθαρίσει οὐδὲ ἐν κιθαρῳδίᾳ οὐδὲ ἐν ῥαψῳδίᾳ οὐδεπώποτ᾽ εἶδες ἄνδρα ὅστις περὶ μὲν Ὀλύμπου δεινός ἐστιν ἐξηγεῖσθαι ἢ περὶ Θαμύρου ἢ περὶ Ὀρφέως ἢ περὶ Φημίου τοῦ Ἰθακησίου ῥαψῳδοῦ, περὶ δὲ Ἴωνος τοῦ Ἐφεσίου [ῥαψῳδοῦ] ἀπορεῖ καὶ οὐκ ἔχει συμβαλέσθαι ἅ τε εὖ ῥαψῳδεῖ καὶ ἃ μή.

> But surely, I think, you never saw a man, when it came to aulos-playing, kithara-playing, singing to the kithara, or rhapsodizing, who is clever at performing an explanation [*exêgeisthai*] about Olympus or Thamyris or Orpheus or Phemius the Ithacan rhapsode, yet is clueless about Ion of Ephesus and cannot find anything to say concerning what he rhapsodizes well and what not.

Are we meant to assume that Socrates in the *Ion* is talking about a much more elite esoteric art of proto-literary criticism? If so, how do we reconcile his comment with the obvious point he is making—that Ion, a public rhapsodic performer, who acts in front of perhaps 20,000 people, can be judged on the same level as the legendary stars of citharodic and aulic art? It is far easier to interpret this passage as an allusion to the practices within contemporary "performances" by players and singers who attributed their

---

[6]   West 1983.

materials—however they might have creatively changed them—to the big-name artists of the mythic past. The inclusion of aulos performance in Socrates' comment is the key piece of evidence for this argument, for even if musical notation existed, how could anyone in the late fifth century BCE have judged the performance of a given player, unless this performance continued to be something *live*, that is to say a *re*-performance that projected itself back onto an Olympus, Orpheus, or Thamyris? We shall return to this point at the end of this chapter, when I come to talk of other mythic projections.

It may be true that we lack direct evidence that tells us unequivocally how rhapsodes included Orphic poetry in their performances. But this does not prevent us from interrogating the indirect evidence that exists. In what follows, I shall take an oblique approach to the problem, by looking first at poetry we certainly know was in the rhapsodic repertoire—Homeric and Hesiodic verse. I will be focusing, in particular, on the "catalogues of women" that appear in both corpora, and on some related codicological evidence. Then we might return to Orpheus, the performer and the myth.

The indirect approach forces us to touch briefly on a larger theoretical issue: intertextuality. The problems and delights arising from intertextuality, so familiar from later literature, appear within archaic Greek poetry as well, although this poetry in all likelihood is the result of oral composition-in-performance. Unfortunately, two modes have dominated the criticism of such poetry and affected especially the issue of intertextual relations. In the specific cases where Homer and Hesiod show close resemblances we can find: 1) a positivist, "genetic" approach that insists on reconstructing influences and uses textuality as its paradigm (Homer "read" Hesiod or vice versa) and 2) a generic approach—for example, one could claim that Homer and Hesiod both made use of pre-existing "catalogue poetry."[7]

Both approaches, of course, have a perfectly legitimate ancestry within our discipline—these are, after all, the working assumptions behind stemmatology and dialectology. In the study of poetics they leave something to be desired. While the second method is a good deal better than the first, it is still not as fruitful as a third possible avenue of approach, which I propose now—i.e., the study of intertextual effects via performance. Or, if we need a more appropriate term, "performance interaction." By this I mean that, even in the context of live oral composition, it is possible for one performer to "allude" to and even "quote" other traditions known to him and recognized

---

[7] Examples of the first abound in Analyst critiques of Homer; I have tried the second, "generic," approach in order to resolve a problem in Hesiod *Works and Days* and *Odyssey* Book 8: see Chapter 12 below with further bibliography on both methods.

by the audience. Furthermore, it is possible in such situations to make a point by the use of the "quoted" material in question. Again, I am arguing that all this can be done without any textualization.[8]

In *Odyssey* 11.225ff. generations of critics have seen resemblances to the style of the Hesiodic *Catalogue of Women*. Some passages match scraps of the *Catalogue* verbatim. Take, for example, the conversation between Poseidon and his lover Tyro (fr. 31 MW = P. Tebt. 271, ed. Grenfell-Hunt):

> ....].[.]..Ποσειδάων λ[
> τέξεις δ' ἀγλαὰ τέκ]να, ἐπεὶ οὐκ ἀποφώ[λιοι εὐναὶ
> ἀθανάτων· σὺ δὲ τ]οὺς κομέειν ἀτιτα[λλέμεναί τε.
> ....]. ἵν' ἀγλαὰ τέκνα τ[εκ-
> ....].τανεμεσσητοι τε[
> ὣς εἰπὼν ὃ μὲν αὖτις] ἀγαστόγωι εμ[
> ....]η ἔβη οἰκόνδε [νέεσθαι

Grenfell and Hunt, the original editors of the papyrus, thought, in fact, that this was a scrap of prose commentary on the *Odyssey*; Vitelli believed it was a piece of cyclic epic; in 1937, Pfeiffer identified it on the basis of content and style as coming from the Hesiodic *Catalogue*. Already in 1884, however, Wilamowitz, working from other transmitted fragments and some Berlin papyri, had seen the resemblances between the Hesiodic and Homeric *Frauenkataloge* and had begun the game of assigning priority: he favored Hesiod as the source for Homer since he claimed that the *Catalogue* was not motivated within the *Odyssey* episode and had no inherent connection with the hero.[9]

We cannot enter into the century-long debate that ensued. Given the methods implicit in priority-hunting (subjective evaluation based on impressions of style, dating by assumptions about content and attitude, etc.), we can expect indefinite results. And that is what we are given in Heubeck's contribution to the Oxford *Odyssey* commentary. In brief, he thinks the catalogue is probably an interpolation, but to remove it would require deeper cuts into the fabric of the narrative.[10]

If we shift methodology, however, and follow a performance approach, the catalogue style in Odysseus' recounting of his *katabasis* becomes something

---

[8]   Further work on this set of issues includes Pucci 1987; Martin 2001b; Korenjak 1998. Less confident about the sort of procedure I am sketching is Dowden 1996.

[9]   Wilamowitz-Moellendorff 1884; Pfeiffer 1937. In general, see West 1985 ad loc.

[10]   Heubeck et al. 1989, ad loc.; see also Page 1955b, 20–51.

rather new. Instead of a sign of textual untidiness, to be excused or mopped up, it is a key moment where the poet characterizes his own performance at the same time as he represents the ability and cunning of his internal narrator, Odysseus. And this will be relevant to our view of Orphic poetry, as well.

No one, it seems, has asked what it means that the character/narrator Odysseus *is represented as performing* precisely this kind of catalogue poetry within the *Odyssey*. Some excellent work has been done, however, on the pragmatics of the so-called "intermezzo." Lillian Doherty makes the point that the catalogue of heroines is calculated to please the Phaeacian queen Arete; Odysseus' interruption of his narrative, and his suggestion that it is time for all to go to bed, prompts her (rather than her husband) to get the Phaeacians to offer more guest gifts. Doherty compares *Odysseus* to Scheherezade. There are no dire consequences in this version, but the hero does end up playing on the audience's curiosity precisely to reap rewards; because Odysseus knows his audience is a gendered one, he slyly produces a story with special emphasis on the fates and virtues of women.[11]

William Wyatt makes a similar point: he further adduces evidence from nineteenth-century Istanbul about wandering minstrels, the *mettagh*, who collect their money just when the action of the narrative is becoming intense—to see whether the audience is seriously interested in getting to the really good stories. We might view this behavior as a classic hustle. For Wyatt, the enthralling material comprises the coming encounter with Trojan War veterans; the *Catalogue* itself is more of a tease. Both he and Doherty recognize that the nice detail of a storyteller getting paid inside the poem has a certain resonance for a real audience facing a real performer.[12]

More details could be added from comparative studies to show how closely Odysseus' strategy resembles an oral poet's.[13] But let us explore the contextual hints a bit further here. When we take into consideration the precise deployment of motifs and their timing within *Odyssey* Book 11, it emerges that Odysseus resembles not just any generic oral poet: he works like a *rhapsode*. For Odysseus uses a *Catalogue of Women* in the way that real rhapsodes must have been using the genre in actual performances, probably around the end of the sixth century. In referring to rhapsodes as creative

---

[11]   Doherty 1991.

[12]   Wyatt 1989; see also on the thematics of the *Catalogue*, Houlihan 1994.

[13]   Most relevant are Reynolds 1995 and Slyomovics 1987.

interpreters and re-performers of a poetic tradition, I am following the lead of Gregory Nagy, who has examined the evidence in full.[14]

We know that catalogue material in general had a sort of optional status for some later scribes. A small group of *Iliad* papyri and manuscripts, for instance—but one that includes the important *Townleianus*—omits the Catalogue of Ships altogether; three manuscripts place it after Book 24 of the poem.[15] The *Townleianus*, meanwhile, preserves a scholion that indicates some versions of the *Iliad* segued into the *Aithiopis*.[16] Closer to the texts at hand in this discussion: the Hesiodic *Theogony* in at least a few manuscripts does not end sharply, but instead continues with what we recognize as none other than the *Catalogue of Women* (lines 1021–22 in West's edition). In the case of the *Theogony*, West wants to see this as a mechanical importation, perhaps from a scholion or ancient book tag.[17] But I suggest instead that in all these cases what we are seeing is neither scribal nor editorial practice (which, at any rate, it would be hard to motivate). These segues and omissions bear the marks of actual performance conditions; they could well be remnants of rhapsodic practice, the live-performance "stitching together" of songs that is alluded to in the contest of Homer and Hesiod, and to which fragment 357 MW must refer:[18]

> ἐν Δήλῳ τότε πρῶτον ἐγὼ καὶ Ὅμηρος ἀοιδοὶ
> μέλπομεν, ἐν νεαροῖς ὕμνοις ῥάψαντες ἀοιδήν,
> Φοῖβον Ἀπόλλωνα χρυσάορον, ὃν τέκε Λητώ.

> In Delos, then, first Homer and I as singers
> made music, stitching a song in new compositions
> concerning Apollo of the golden dagger, whom Leto bore.

I am proposing the following scenario: just as some performers of the *Theogony* could prolong their singing or recitation with the *Catalogue of Women* (as the textual evidence suggests), so Odysseus the performer creates suspense in the midst of *Odyssey* 11 using precisely this kind of catalogue material. The intertextual effect attunes an audience to yet another external resemblance. For at this point in the poem, rather than looking like an

---

[14] On rhapsodes as recomposers-in-performance, see Nagy 1990, 21–29 and 1996b, 59–86.

[15] See the apparatus in Monro and Allen's Oxford *editio minor* (1920) *ad Il.* 2.484ff.

[16] Monro and Allen 1920, *ad Il.* 24.804.

[17] West 1966, *ad loc.*

[18] On the implications of this fragment and on the stitching of verses, see Chapter 7 above, with further bibliography.

itinerant storyteller or poet, Odysseus, to an audience that knows rhapsodic repertoires, looks like a rhapsode. If, as seems likely, the performer of our *Odyssey* was *also*, at some stage in the transmission, a rhapsode, the ironic mirroring effect would be all the more striking.

At this juncture, we are enabled to circle back to Orpheus. It is well known that at least one poem called *Descent to Hades* was associated with his name—perhaps several. In these compositions, which West thinks stem from the late sixth century, it appears the poet recounted, in the first person, all that he saw on the trip down to recover his dead wife.[19] Obviously, the Odyssean *Nekuia* offers parallels in terms of theme. Wilamowitz long ago, followed more recently by Böhme, asserted that the entire *Nekuia* was an interpolation by an editor interested in Orphism.[20] By contrast, we can imagine a case of "performance interaction" that would not depend on a scribe copying a pre-existing text, but on the fact of one performer responding to contemporary and *competing* repertoire traditions.[21] If the *Orphic Descent to Hades* circulated not just privately, but in public rhapsodic performance, the very existence of the *Nekuia* in Book 11 may well represent a response to this competitive pressure. The much-noticed incongruities that have led Analysts to see massive interpolation might then be the result of an *Odyssey* performer's attempt to appropriate the latest popular performance topics in his community.

While we have no *direct* evidence for such an appropriation (even though it is a common occurrence in comparative oral traditions), the dynamic of the *Odyssey* episode again provides a lead. In Book 11, Odysseus' "catalogue" of women features one crucial difference that brings it closer to a sacred narrative by a poet who has made a descent to the underworld (as in the supposed Orphic accounts). From the proem of the Hesiodic *Catalogue* (fr. 1 MW = P. Oxy. 2354, ed. Lobel) we can see that the performer calls on the Muses in language similar to that in *Iliad* 2.484–87, the introduction to the Catalogue of Ships:

> Νῦν δὲ γυναικῶν ⌊φῦλον ἀείσατε, ἡδυέπειαι
> Μοῦσαι Ὀλυμπιάδε⌊ς, κοῦραι Διὸς αἰγιόχοιο,
> αἳ τότ' ἄρισται ἔσαν [
> μίτρας τ' ἀλλύσαντο .[
> μισγόμεναι θεοῖσ[ιν
> ξυναὶ γὰρ τότε δαῖ⌊τες ἔσαν, ξυνοὶ δὲ θόωκοι

---

[19] On the *katabases*, see West 1983.

[20] See Böhme 1970, 31–59 with reference to earlier work.

[21] For other indications of such responsiveness, see Martin 1989, 225–30.

ἀθανάτοις τε θε⌊οῖσι καταθνητοῖς τ' ἀνθρώποις.
οὐδ' ἄρα ἰσαίωνες ομ[
ἀνέρες ἠδὲ γυναῖκες ε[
ὀσσόμεν[ο]ι φρ[εσὶ] γῆρ[ας
οἳ μὲν δηρὸν ε.[..]κ.[
ἠΐ[θ]εοι, τοὺς δ' εἴθ[αρ] ε.[
ἀ[θ]άνατοι [νε]ότητ[
τάων ἔσπετε Μ[οῦσαι
ὅσσ[αι]ς δὴ παρελ[έξατ' Ὀλύμπιος εὐρύοπα Ζεὺς

And now sing of the tribe of women, sweet-voiced
Olympian Muses, daughters of aegis-holding Zeus,
those who were the best at that time [
and they loosened their girdles [
mingling with gods [
or at that time the feasts were in common and in common the councils
for the immortal gods and for mortal human beings;
and yet not equally long-lived [
men and women [
seeing in their spirit old age [
the ones for a long time [
youths, but the others at once [
immortals youthfulness [
Of these women tell [Muses:
all those with whom lay [the Olympian, wide-voiced Zeus

(trans. Most 2007, adapted)

Iliad 2.484–87:
Ἔσπετε νῦν μοι Μοῦσαι Ὀλύμπια δώματ' ἔχουσαι·
ὑμεῖς γὰρ θεαί ἐστε πάρεστέ τε ἴστέ τε πάντα,
ἡμεῖς δὲ κλέος οἶον ἀκούομεν οὐδέ τι ἴδμεν·
οἵ τινες ἡγεμόνες Δαναῶν καὶ κοίρανοι ἦσαν·

Tell me now, you Muses who have your homes on Olympos.
For you, who are goddesses, are there, and you know all things,
and we have heard only the rumor of it and know nothing.
Who then of those were the chief men and the lords of the Danaäns?

(trans. Lattimore 2011)

Contrast the opening of Odysseus's list, with its stress on the autobiographical "I" (*Odyssey* 11.225–37):

νῶϊ μὲν ὣς ἐπέεσσιν ἀμειβόμεθ', αἱ δὲ γυναῖκες
ἤλυθον, ὤτρυνεν γὰρ ἀγαυὴ Περσεφόνεια,

ὅσσαι ἀριστήων ἄλοχοι ἔσαν ἠδὲ θύγατρες.
αἱ δ' ἀμφ' αἷμα κελαινὸν ἀολλέες ἠγερέθοντο,
αὐτὰρ ἐγὼ βούλευον, ὅπως ἐρέοιμι ἑκάστην.
ἤδε δέ μοι κατὰ θυμὸν ἀρίστη φαίνετο βουλὴ   230
σπασσάμενος τανύηκες ἄορ παχέος παρὰ μηροῦ
οὐκ εἴων πίνειν ἅμα πάσας αἷμα κελαινόν.
αἱ δὲ προμνηστῖναι ἐπήϊσαν, ἠδὲ ἑκάστη
ὃν γόνον ἐξαγόρευεν· ἐγὼ δ' ἐρέεινον ἁπάσας.
ἔνθ' ἦ τοι πρώτην Τυρὼ ἴδον εὐπατέρειαν,   235
ἣ φάτο Σαλμωνῆος ἀμύμονος ἔκγονος εἶναι,
φῆ δὲ Κρηθῆος γυνὴ ἔμμεναι Αἰολίδαο·

"Thus we two talked with one another; and the women came, for august Persephone sent them, all those that had been the wives and the daughters of chieftains. These flocked in throngs about the dark blood, and I considered how I might question each; and this seemed to my mind the best plan. I drew my long sword from beside my stout thigh, and would not allow them to drink the dark blood all at one time. So they drew near, one after the other, and each declared her birth, and I questioned them all.

"Then, you must know, the first that I saw was highborn Tyro, who said that she was the daughter of flawless Salmoneus, and declared herself to be the wife of Cretheus, son of Aeolus."

[trans. Murray and Dimock 1995]

With his repeated insistence on sight throughout the passage (11.235, 260, 266, 271, 281, 298, 306, 321, 326), Odysseus makes the claim of autopsy that the *Iliad* performer, in the splendid *recusatio* of *Iliad* 2.484–87, declines to make, and that the Hesiodic performer also foregoes. In other words, Odysseus trumps both strategies. He has been to Hades and back, and lived to tell. He has seen what others only hear about.

The phenomenon would be parallel, in my understanding, to the assertions that the *Iliad* in Book 2 (N.B.: within another catalogue) makes about the fate of the poet Thamyris. In the terms of Homeric poetry, in competition with Heracles traditions, the bard Thamyris, and by implication poets who claim to recite his words, is defective, a loser to the Muses.[22] For the evidence that there must have existed such later performers of poetic traditions attributed directly to Thamyris, we can refer once more

---

[22] See Martin 1989, 229–30.

to the passage of Plato's *Ion* with which I began. It is worth noting that the gigantic Underworld painting by Polygnotus in the Cnidian Lesche at Delphi, dating to the mid-fifth century BCE, portrayed Thamyris as blind and dejected, with a broken lyre at his feet. In the same part of the painting, says Pausanias, Orpheus was depicted playing a kithara, with an attentive group of hearers nearby.[23] This representation, I suspect, produced a similar message of poetic denigration concerning Thamyris, but this time with Orpheus instead of Homer as the privileged poet of the pair.

We know that Hesiodic poetry was in the rhapsodic repertoire; I have argued that the Homeric catalogue in Book 11 responds to the Hesiodic form of *catalogue* narrative in a challenging, competitive way. My suggestion now is that the *Odyssey* also responds and rises to the challenge of Orphic material—the autobiographical descent of the poet—although the full range of performance contexts for such poetry is hidden from our view. The other evidence to support my idea that Orphic poetry was rhapsodic is circumstantial. Leaving aside the question of the late "rhapsodic" *Theogony* as a puzzle with an intriguing attribution, we might focus instead on an individual first, the infamous Onomacritus. Several testimonia associate him with Orphica, as also with a Peisistratean project to fix Homeric poetry.[24] The question is: was he also a rhapsode? That he was a poet, at least, is argued by Gregory Nagy who observes that the story of Onomacritus being caught while forging oracles fits with the assumption that he was a professional rival of the poet Lasus of Hermione.[25] In addition to this, I note that Onomacritus is explicitly associated by Plutarch with another character, the mysterious Cynaethus. From the precious scholion to Pindar *Nemean* 2, we know that Cynaethus was certainly a rhapsode:

Ὅθεν περ καὶ Ὁμηρίδαι. Ὁμηρίδας ἔλεγον τὸ μὲν ἀρχαῖον τοὺς ἀπὸ τοῦ Ὁμήρου γένους, οἳ καὶ τὴν ποίησιν αὐτοῦ ἐκ διαδοχῆς ᾖδον· μετὰ δὲ ταῦτα καὶ οἱ ῥαψῳδοὶ οὐκέτι τὸ γένος εἰς Ὅμηρον ἀνάγοντες. ἐπιφανεῖς δὲ ἐγένοντο οἱ περὶ Κύναιθον, οὕς φασι πολλὰ τῶν ἐπῶν ποιήσαντας ἐμβαλεῖν εἰς τὴν Ὁμήρου ποίησιν. ἦν δὲ ὁ Κύναιθος τὸ γένος Χῖος, ὃς καὶ τῶν ἐπιγραφομένων Ὁμήρου ποιημάτων τὸν εἰς Ἀπόλλωνα γεγραφὼς ὕμνον ἀνατέθεικεν αὐτῷ. οὗτος οὖν ὁ Κύναιθος πρῶτος ἐν Συρακούσαις ἐραψῴδησε τὰ Ὁμήρου ἔπη κατὰ τὴν ξθ΄ Ὀλυμπιάδα, ὡς Ἱππόστρατός φησιν.

---

[23]   Pausanias *Description of Greece* 10.30; see Kebric 1983 for full details and bibliography.

[24]   See Stoessl 1939.

[25]   Nagy 1990, 172–74 and 1996b, 104–5.

"Whence the Homeridai": In the ancient period, they called the Homeridai those of the family of Homer, who also sang his poetry by handed-down tradition. After that, these were the rhapsodes, no longer tracing their lineage from Homer. Cynaethus and those around him were pre-eminent, those who, they say, having composed many epic verses inserted them into Homer's poetry. Cynaethus was a Chian, and was the one who wrote the *Hymn for Apollo* (among the poems assigned to Homer) and credited it to him. This Cynaethus was the first who rhapsodized the epic verses of Homer in Syracuse, during the 69th Olympiad, as Hippostratus says.

From the point of view of later generations, even in the fifth century, by which time rhapsodizing had been standardized and subject to further rules, the expansion and experimentation on traditional material as done by a Cynaethus and an Onomacritus could only be branded as forgery or falsification—hence the tone of the testimonia. It is significant that the one interpolation attributed to Onomacritus within the text of Homer as we have it is precisely in the *Odyssey* 11 underworld scene, as mentioned in the scholia to *Odyssey* 11.604 (Dindorf):

παῖδα Διὸς μεγάλοιο] τοῦτον ὑπὸ Ὀνομακρίτου ἐμπεποιῆσθαί φασιν. ἠθέτηται δέ. ἔνιοι δὲ οὐ τὴν οἰνοχόον Ἥβην, ἀλλὰ τὴν ἑαυτοῦ ἀνδρείαν.

"Child of great Zeus": They say this was inserted by Onomacritus, but it has been athetized. Some say Hêbê is not the wine-pourer but his own manly vigor."

It would make sense if Onomacritus, *as a rhapsode* of Orphic material, would have had an interest in fine-tuning a scene of *katabasis*. This does not imply, however, that Onomacritus as an "editor" interpolated the *Nekuia*.

A second piece of circumstantial evidence for the widespread, rhapsodic performance of Orphica is one of the most obvious: the Orphic theogonic passage of Aristophanes *Birds* (lines 693–702).[26] If such theogony material was in fact only in limited circulation for a literary elite, of the sort West hypothesizes, how could Aristophanes have expected the audience of his comedy to get the point? Even if it is, as West argues, a question of borrowed motifs—how did people know the motifs? Rhapsodizing Orpheus—assuming that Orphic material was public, performed, and popular—could provide the answer.

The final piece of circumstantial evidence brings us to myth, and especially mythic projection of performances. It has been convincingly argued by Nagy that much of what we know from the testimonia and poetry about

[26] See Dunbar 1995, 437–47.

Homer and Hesiod is, in fact, a retrojecting strategy employed by the very rhapsodic tradition that transmits their poetry.[27] It so happens that we have several intriguing stories about Orpheus as well, specifically about his role as poet. Aside from the stories that attest to the power of his kithara playing while he lived (and which are probably connected to the lore and ideology of actual kithara-performers) there are the post-mortem tales. His severed head keeps on singing; a shepherd who sleeps by his tomb sings with the voice of the dead poet; the dead Orpheus or his head is credited with oracular powers.[28] As well as being a powerful image of the survival of oral tradition, one with rich comparative connections in Irish and Indic lore, this myth complex can equally be a rhapsodic construct, the obverse of the way in which Homeric poetry tends to denigrate Thamyris. It is a strategy for giving status and a patina of prestige to one's performances. To say that Orpheus' head keeps on singing is another way of expressing a sociopoetic fact, that audiences and performers kept on singing and performing "Orpheus" stories and poems attributed to him. In fact, this was the claim that Terpander, a key figure in the development and performance of citharodic epic, must have made in his own work, perhaps in the seventh century. Pseudo-Plutarch *De Musica* (5.1132f) cites Alexandros (*Fragments of the Greek Historians* 273 F 77) to the effect that Terpander "took as models [*ezêlôkenai*] the hexameter verses of Homer and the melodies of Orpheus." Again, there is no absolutely direct evidence; one might object that Terpander is not a rhapsode, but in this story, it seems he is quite close to being one. As an inventor of citharodic nomes, and singer of hexameters, he might even be considered a genetic link between older poets and sixth-century performers. To make a mimesis of Orpheus, as Terpander did, is to perform at the outer limits of influence, in effect to be a first imitator: Orpheus mimed no one, we are told (*De musica* 5.1132f). That sense of reconnecting with a distant past, an aboriginal song, in turn must have cast a glow over the *mûthos*-making public performances of rhapsodes in archaic Greece. If a performer could manage to reproduce Orpheus, miming his melodies, then an audience, no matter how stolid, might respond as though charmed—surely a wish that any Ion might cherish.[29]

---

[27] Nagy 1996a, 59–86.

[28] For full details and comparative materials, see J. Nagy 1990.

[29] On the phenomenon of "intertextuality" in an oral-traditional milieu, see now Tsagalis 2008. On the figure of Orpheus as a proto-citharode sometimes in contestation with rhapsodic traditions, see Power 2010, 268–73, 355–66.

9

GOLDEN VERSES
VOICE AND AUTHORITY
IN THE TABLETS[1]

While our understanding of the so-called "Orphic" tablets continues to improve thanks to the scrutiny of many learned proponents of *Religionswissenschaft*, the appreciation of these texts from a literary stand-point has lagged somewhat behind. What follows, therefore, are some tentative thoughts on the poetic heritage and environment of the Gold Tablet texts. The broader study of Greek poetry will be seen to advance their explication; by the same token the tablets significantly increase the available stock of Greek poetic reality—whatever their religious functions may have been.[2]

As the first rule of comparative studies is to know what to compare, we should begin by assuming that texts written in Greek hexameters of any time or place can and should be compared with one another.[3] As a matter of practice, one can extend this principle to cover as well medieval and modern Greek texts in the *dhekapendasyllavos* meter that became the inheritor of the hexameter.[4] The second rule of comparative studies—that one proceeds

[1] This essay is based on a paper delivered at the Ohio State University Conference *Ritual Texts for the Afterlife* (April 2006), organized by Fritz Graf and Sarah Iles-Johnston. It was also published as part of the Princeton/Stanford Working Papers in Classics (2007), http://www.princeton.edu/~pswpc/pdfs/rpmartin/040701.pdf.

[2] I am grateful to Fritz Graf and Sarah Iles Johnston for the generous invitation to their 2006 Ohio State conference on the tablets, for which this paper was originally produced. For rigorous questioning and helpful comments I owe thanks to attendees on that occasion, as also to the audience (of a Spanish version) at the *XIX Simposio nacional de estudios clásicos*, Universidad Nacional de Rosario (October 2006).

[3] This maxim, often cited by Calvert Watkins, guides the precise analyses in his masterwork (Watkins 1995) including his chapter on the poetics of the tablets (pp. 277–91).

[4] On the history of this meter with recent bibliography see Letsios 2005. For a point of poetic diction in the tablets, on which medieval Greek verse can help, see below.

from an internal analysis of any given text to external comparisons—will be invoked here to require that we discover the internal structures of the tablet texts and compare them with other structures; one-off, random word equivalences are not useful unless they lead to analysis of larger rhetorical and literary structures.

Thanks to the meticulous work of Alberto Bernabé, Richard Janko, and several others, the first desideratum for studying the tablets—a thorough internal analysis—has been accomplished. Janko's useful "archetype" of the longer texts offers us a hermeneutic tool for discussing those tablets, although I would insist that this archetype should *not* be reified into a datable, written ancestor of our lamellae.[5] It could just as easily—and more likely—always have been a mental template underlying oral composition and transmission, one never itself textualized in the full "archetype" form. Furthermore, it represents the sum total of hexameter lines, in what we imagine as the full scenario underlying these tablets. Yet no one tablet has this entire set of lines, as can easily be seen. Instead, as is typical in oral tradition, only a portion is "recited" or "performed" on any one gold leaf.

So much for the state-of-play concerning *internal* analysis. The *external* comparison with the appropriate sphere of hexameter poetics remains to be carried out in detail. This can be done on several tiers. In what follows, the focus will be on two levels of detail. First, I shall look at type-scenes comprising a few dozen lines, especially from the *Odyssey*, in which instruction and direction are the ruling motifs. Second, I'll explore formulaic diction at the level of individual hexameter lines or half-lines, tracing a series of resemblances, parallels, and resonances between tablet texts and a wider range of Greek epic poetry. After a few illustrations of these levels at which the small and large poems interact, I shall narrow the focus to one tablet and then conclude by making some suggestions about the authority of the narrative voice that we hear emanating from it and from its congeners.

Following Milman Parry's breakthrough work, the discussion of type-scenes in Homeric poetry burgeoned and flourished for several decades, as shown by the master-bibliography compiled by Mark Edwards, whose own work was central in this growth.[6] The study of one sub-category of type-scenes, those involving speech, has not progressed so far. My own interest

---

[5]   This key article (Janko 1984) has now been updated in Janko 2016; the original article predated the publication of some important tablets, at least one of which gives a previously unattested line. Janko's analysis here dovetails with my own in several ways and I am largely in agreement with his conclusions on details.

[6]   Edwards 1992.

in this sort of study some years ago focused on the *Iliad*, but the present investigation will make use of its sister epic, the *Odyssey*, to analyze some comparanda.[7] Speech type-scenes, as we may call them, differ from the usual runs of recurrent verses that describe arming, dining, getting up, and going to bed—those comfortable Hemingwayesque topics that sink into the hearer's mind and embody "Homer." Speech-type scenes represent more flexible but recurrent modes of handling a situation. They occur in character-voice instead of narrator-voice, although there are interesting overlaps (for instance in the *Iliad*, Achilles talks like Homer and vice versa).[8] We might think of these scenes as rhetorical topoi, but they are not necessarily or usually in the form of arguments or Aristotelian enthymemes. Their usefulness as a hermeneutic tool when it comes to the lamellae derives from their being a node or two higher up on the narratological tree. That is to say, instead of being constituted by content and its treatment (armor, chariots, food, drink, or bed) at a particular point, the speech type-scenes are built on syntactical and pragmatic frameworks. In other words, instead of restricting us to hunting for comparable content between lamellae and epic—something that is almost by definition bound to fail given the genre differences—the employment of speech type-scenes enables us to carry out a more fine-grained approach. Thanks to the *Thesaurus Linguae Graecae*, we can easily pin down co-occurrences of adverbs, imperatives, deictics, and other speech markers, so that one can compare types of speech (commands, giving directions, assertions) that are relevant to the types of speech contained in the lamellae.

How might the corpus of tablet texts look from the angle of speech-type scenes? The neat A/B text typology that goes back to Zuntz in the 1970s broke down with the publication of more recent texts from Pelinna and elsewhere.[9] The 2001 Spanish edition and commentary by Bernabé and Jiménez outlines a more flexible articulation of the corpus of the tablets. Using the divisions there established, one can label the shared content (according to the editors' analysis) that marks each group of lamellae.[10] Their numbers shall be matched to the following shorthand phrases representing my own speech type-scene scheme:

- L1 through L6 (= Bernabé [2004] fr. 474–84): "map and script"

---

7   Full analysis in Martin 1989.

8   Martin 1989, 146–205. Further on speech type-scenes, see Chapter 3 above.

9   On the evolving complexity of the corpus, see Bernabé 2000 and now Janko 2016.

10   See the chart, with comparative numbering, at Bernabé & Jiménez 2001, 257–58.

- L7a–b (= Bernabé [2004] fr. 485–86): "point of death"
- L8 (= Bernabé [2004] fr. 487): "greeting"
- L9–11 (= Bernabé [2004] fr. 488–91): "arrival and boast"

(Bernabé and Jiménez numbers #L12–16 are not included in my typological inventory since they are much closer to sumbola or magical formulae and do not seem to give us a foothold in terms of narrative or speech-act beyond the performative utterance.)

The first set ("map and script") are those that deal with negotiating the intricate, dark landscape of the underworld. This is the most verbally rich type. It involves a set of instructions about topography concerned with finding the right spot for drinking of the Spring, and then a second strategy—what to say when you get there (hence my designator for it). We shall return to this major division later, after a brief survey and some comments on the others.

Tablets L7 a–b ("point of death" in my scheme), the famous gold leaves from Pelinna in the shape of ivy, certainly recall no specific scene in Homeric poetry.[11] By the very nature of the sentiment on them—"now you have died [*ethanes*] and now you have been born [*egenou*]"—they are excluded from an epic art form that gains its power from a relentless focus on death and dying, instead of on regeneration. And as one might expect, a survey of the ninety-one poets listed in the TLG canon under the generic label "epic" reveals no co-occurrence of these verbs, or even an instance of the single second-singular *ethanes*. However, there is one curious scene of virtual rebirth in the *Iliad* that can lead us on to a speech-type that is relevant, I believe, to this second tablet group. In Book 21, before all heaven breaks loose in the battle of the gods, Achilles encounters a man named Lycaon, whom he had captured and sold into slavery on Lemnos, some twelve days before. He reacts with amazement (*Iliad* 21.53–59):

> ὀχθήσας δ' ἄρα εἶπε πρὸς ὃν μεγαλήτορα θυμόν·
> "ὢ πόποι ἦ μέγα θαῦμα τόδ' ὀφθαλμοῖσιν ὁρῶμαι·
> ἦ μάλα δὴ Τρῶες μεγαλήτορες οὕς περ ἔπεφνον   55
> αὖτις ἀναστήσονται ὑπὸ ζόφου ἠερόεντος,
> οἷον δὴ καὶ ὅδ' ἦλθε φυγὼν ὕπο νηλεὲς ἦμαρ
> Λῆμνον ἐς ἠγαθέην πεπερημένος· οὐδέ μιν ἔσχε
> πόντος ἁλὸς πολιῆς, ὃ πολέας ἀέκοντας ἐρύκει."

In anger, then, he addressed his braveheart spirit:
"Indeed, a great miracle here I see before my eyes:

---

[11] Tsantsanoglou and Parássoglou 1987.

braveheart Trojans whom I slew
get themselves back up from beneath the gloomy dusk.
Look how this one fled the pitiless day
bound up and shipped to holy Lesbos. But the sea of grey
did not detain him, though it hold many, despite their will."[12]

Undeterred by this *mega thauma*, Achilles shifts into killer mode and although piteously supplicated by Lycaon, rejects his pleas with harsh words: before Patroclus died, the hero says, I would have spared you, but now no enemy can escape death at my hands (*Iliad* 21.106–7):

ἀλλὰ φίλος θάνε καὶ σύ· τί ἦ ὀλοφύρεαι οὕτως;
κάτθανε καὶ Πάτροκλος, ὅ περ σέο πολλὸν ἀμείνων.

But *philos*, die—you too. Why blubber this way?
Even Patroklos died—so much your better.

The tone is interesting: *philos* is like hard-bitten battle-field talk: "sorry, pal—you die." Not ironic, it is instead indicative of the mix of pathos and horror that is the *Iliad*. For our purposes of comparison, the follow-up speech is equally important, for after Achilles proceeds to slay Lycaon and toss him into the river, he then offers a vision of his enemy's post-death experience (*Iliad* 21.122–27):

Lie there now with the fish to lick your wounds
and get the blood off, little do they care:
your mother will not lay you on the bier and wail;
Scamander, in its whorls, will bear you to the sea's broad gulf.
Leaping up [*thrôiskôn*] with a rush and rippling the black wave
some fish will eat Lykaon's shining flesh.

Compared with the tablet verses, this is obviously the reverse of that emblem of bliss, "falling into the milk." Curiously, there are still some verbal parallels. Lycaon ("Wolfie") who will lie with the fishes (their licking an anti-type of the ritual cleansing of the corpse), instead of finding a safe harbor or spring, will get plenty of salt water, in the wide gulf of the sea. The Pelinna tablets use *thrôiskô* for the leap of ram and bull into the milk; the leaping fish will nibble the deceased. As well as counter-pointing the happy-death scenario detail by detail, this little speech is in effect an *anti*-lament: Achilles explicitly says that his victim's mother will *not* place him on the bier and

---

[12] All translations mine unless otherwise noted.

weep over him. We should remember that the lamellae texts are also, after all, anti-laments. Rather than the frequent lament strategy about how the deceased has left his kin bereft (cf. the elaborate wake for Hector at *Iliad* 24.718–75), the "point of death" tablets in particular declare that everything gets *better* after one has died. The focus, as in Achilles' speech, is on the experience of the deceased, not as in lament on the feelings of the bereaved.[13]

Turning more briefly to the other groupings, we might detect speech type-scenes even in these shorter lamellae texts. The "greeting" group actually comprises one tablet, Bernabé's #L8 = fr. 487 from Thurii. It begins in good hexameter fashion (with Doric coloration), "whenever the soul leaves the light of the sun," and after a line of somewhat obscured direction, breaks into direct address: "Hail, having suffered the experience [*pathêma*] that you had not before suffered. A god, out of a man, you have become." The single word *khaire*, at line-initial position, draws us into a speech-type that is familiar not just from many greeting scenes in Homeric poetry and later epic, but also, more relevant, from the tradition of hexameter hymns. This is a fairly obvious parallel. The implications, however, might bear further investigation. John García has recently shown how the *khaire*-formula functions at the heart of kletic hymns as a way of pinpointing the epiphany of a god amid the longer third-person narratives that surround the formula.[14] I would add that in the context of the tablets, the word *khaire* cues us to the transformation of mortal into immortal even before we are explicitly told that *anthrôpos* has become *theos*. An audience or composer may well be drawing on Panhellenic or local hymnic traditions in the composition and reception of this tablet text.

My fourth group, labeled "arrival and boast," may be seen as an amalgam of two speech types. In point of fact, a check of the TLG shows that nowhere in epic does one find the verb *eukhomai* ("I pray or boast") attested within a few lines of the verb *erkhomai* ("I arrive or go"), despite the neat phonic figure made by the pairing of the two verbs, which, to use a linguistics term, form nearly a "minimal pair." This independent poetic feature of the lamella when it comes to combinations of formulaic phrases is worth keeping in mind. We are

---

[13]   On the tropes of lament in Homeric epic, see Chapter 14 below and Dué 2002. The speech type-scene of words directed to the dying in the *Iliad* recurs when Achilles kills Hector, but without the extended forecast about the treatment of Hector's corpse. Hector *himself* envisions that he will be eaten by dogs near the tents of the Achaeans, and Achilles does not relieve his mind of such terrors before dispatching him (*Iliad* 22.335–36). This becomes, of course, the primary suspense mechanism until the end of the poem. On the theme and its expressions in the *Iliad*, see Segal 1971.

[14]   García 2002.

never dealing with mere imitations of the poetic language of epic in reading the tablets. The tradition, passed down by whatever means, is in touch with epic or other techniques of hexameter composition, but is not subservient to them. As a sign of contact, observe the recurrent positioning of *erkhomai* outside the tablet texts: it is always line-initial in hexametric verse. As a sign of compositional independence, on the other hand, we should immediately notice that the verb in the tablets (Bernabé's L9–11 = fr. 488–91) must, in fact, mean "I am coming" in the set phrase *erkhomai ek katharôn kathara* ("I come, clean from the clean"). By contrast, in the epic tradition the verb most often means "I am going," as when Patroclus (*Iliad* 11.839) says to the wounded fighter Eurypylus, "I am going to tell Achilles the *mûthos* that Nestor commanded." The same deictic positioning characterizes other prominent Homeric examples: a warrior goes out to get a lance (*Iliad* 13.256); Hera goes to see the edges of the earth (*Iliad* 14.301); and Eumaeus says he is not in the habit of going to town (*Odyssey* 14.373). Within epic poetry, only in medieval Greek have I found a clear usage of the verb *erkhomai* to mean "I am coming" (as it does still in Modern Greek), in a fifteen–syllable verse from the Byzantine *Achilliad* (Cod. Napol. BN III.B27, line 1584):

> Take me in, Frangkos, take me in [*dhexou me*]: it is to you I come
>   [*erkhomai pros esena*].[15]

The "arrival and boast" tablets of my fourth category follow the deceased person's announcement "I am here" with a heroic-sounding phrase, "I assert that I am yours when it comes to my blessed heritage" (*kai gar egôn humôn genos eukhomai olbion einai* = L9.3, L10a.3). Of course, the line-final formula (without *olbion*) is the most frequent way for an Iliadic hero to establish his genealogy on the field of battle. Leonard Muellner's monograph on Homeric *eukhomai* and its meanings provides a full explication of the bi-valence of this old semantic item.[16] The formula is used in specific type-scenes of extended verbal combat (often designated *mûthos*).[17] What resonance, if any, does that provide when juxtaposing epic with "Orphic" texts? Perhaps we are meant to hear an authoritative utterance on the part of the newly–dead speaker who encounters Persephone, the *khthoniôn Basileia* prominent in this tablet group. The fuller scenario that we can imagine has the speaker implying, as

[15] Note the co-occurrence of "come" [*erkhetai*] and "take" [*dekhesthe*, as restored by West] in tablet L.11.1–2 (= fr. 491).

[16] Muellner 1976.

[17] See Martin 1989, 67–86.

it were that "The ritual has worked. I belong here." This heroic proclamation is followed in the texts of the "arrival and boast" division by phrasings that clearly recall heroic death in the *Iliad*. For instance, we have *alla me Moir' edamasse*.[18] Finally, the boast that the deceased has made it successfully to the heart of the underworld is addressed to divinities with significant names: good counselor (Eubouleus) and good fame (Euklees). The latter name is especially pertinent in a context of heroic identify and self-presentation. After all, as we shall see a bit further, the dead who bore these tablets in the grave were in every technical religious sense *heroes*.[19]

Let us now return to the first category, mentioned briefly above, which deserves more attention: "map and script," describing the topography of Hades and what to do there. The *Odyssey* is more fruitful for comparisons when it comes to this category. Two scenes in particular come to mind. As indicated earlier, this tablet group, the largest thus far, is complicated by the co-existence of two tropes, the pointing out of landmarks and then the instructions concerning what the deceased bearer of the gold tablet should say. Have we anything like this in epic?

The most obvious place to look for intertexts is the journey of Odysseus to the underworld. As I have argued elsewhere, the *Odyssey*, given the evolving elaboration and textualization of the Homeric poems, was most likely already aware of and responding to a long Orphic narrative of the *katabasis* type. In generic terms, in other words, *Odyssey* Book 11 and the *katabasis* traditions are roughly related.[20] But let us look at the speech-type elements to explore what else might be parallel. It emerges that the *Nekuia* of *Odyssey* Book 11 is actually less productive of parallels than other passages. We have to back up a bit, to the end of *Odyssey* Book 10, to see how the entire episode of the hero's descent features one set of instructions framing another, Circe's advice surrounding that of Teiresias, and in fact supplementing it in crucial ways.

After telling him he must find the blind prophet whose wits are still with him, even when dead, Circe directs Odysseus to the edge of the world and tells him what to do on arrival (*Odyssey* 10.508–47). Some of the parallels

---

[18]   Compare *Iliad* 16.849, the words of Patroclus at his death; see also Calame 2006, 264–65. In a complementary view, De Jáuregui 2011 now persuasively examines the boast-formula in its relation to epic type-scenes of supplication.

[19]   On the heroic status of the deceased in terms of their positioning between sky and earth, see the analysis of Calame 2006, 246–48

[20]   Martin 2001a.

to the tablet texts L1–6 are rather obvious. There is, first, the insistent use of *entha* in initial position to mark both temporal and spatial stages in the *Odyssey* passage (10.513–17):

> ἔνθα μὲν εἰς Ἀχέροντα Πυριφλεγέθων τε ῥέουσι
> Κώκυτός θ', ὃς δὴ Στυγὸς ὕδατός ἐστιν ἀπορρώξ,
> πέτρη τε ξύνεσίς τε δύω ποταμῶν ἐριδούπων·   515
> ἔνθα δ' ἔπειθ', ἥρως, χριμφθεὶς πέλας, ὥς σε κελεύω,
> βόθρον ὀρύξαι ὅσον τε πυγούσιον ἔνθα καὶ ἔνθα ...

There Puriphlegethon flows into Acheron
and Cocytos, which is an offshoot of Styx water—
and a rock and joining of two roaring rivers—
In *that* spot, hero, after drawing close, as I command
Dig a pit a cubit square—this way and that.

Cf. 10.526–30:

> αὐτὰρ ἐπὴν εὐχῇσι λίσῃ κλυτὰ ἔθνεα νεκρῶν,
> ἔνθ' ὄϊν ἀρνειὸν ῥέζειν θῆλύν τε μέλαιναν
> εἰς Ἔρεβος στρέψας, αὐτὸς δ' ἀπονόσφι τραπέσθαι
> ἱέμενος ποταμοῖο ῥοάων· ἔνθα δὲ πολλαὶ
> ψυχαὶ ἐλεύσονται νεκύων κατατεθνηώτων.

But once you beseech the famous races of the dead
then sacrifice sheep: one male, one female; black;
twisting them toward Erebus, but yourself away
toward the river's streams. Then many souls
of those struck down with death will come.

and 10.538:

> ἔνθα τοι αὐτίκα μάντις ἐλεύσεται, ὄρχαμε λαῶν,

Then immediately will come the seer, o host-leader.

This resembles the pragmatic locating function of the "archetype" phrase *entha katerkhomenai* (L1.4, L2.6) although the tablet text uses *entha* only to mark place, rather than time. Interestingly, the *Odyssey* instructions that most resemble this part of the tablet's text come at lines 529–30 ἔνθα δὲ πολλαὶ / ψυχαὶ ἐλεύσονται νεκύων κατατεθνηώτων. But that is exactly where the *Odyssey* poet uses *entha* in a *non*-initial position and in the meaning "then" rather than "there." Once again, it is clear that we are not dealing with a simple phenomenon of poetic models and copies. In both tablet and epic texts, the underlying formula can be identified as *psukhai nekuôn* "souls of the dead." The *Odyssey*, on the one hand, expands this phrase (529–30) with two modifiers: *pollai* and *katatethneôtôn*. The anonymous poet who composed the verse on the tablets, however, chooses to make a pun with the verb for "be refreshed; become alive": "There, coming down, souls [*psukhai*] of the dead take solace [*psukhontai*]." The tablet verse employs the preverb *kata*—in the *Odyssey* version attached to a different verb (10.530)—by describing the souls "coming *down*" instead of "struck *down* dead." Of course, in both the epic and tablet texts, we are dealing with trees, water, and drinking. Circe's elaborate description does not mention the cypress tree that is so commonly featured in the tablets, but instead speaks of poplars and willows (*Odyssey* 10.510). She also gives a vivid picture of a confluence of underworld rivers. The *entha* locating that spot and the same word repeated to pinpoint where Odysseus should dig are co-relative, framing *Odyssey* 10.513–16: *there* where the waters flow, *there* dig the libation pit. In essence, the procedure parallels the tablet scenario, but in the tablet this initial refreshment stop that one encounters (like the pit Odysseus digs, both of them near trees: e.g., L1.3, L2.5) is the stop that one is told to *pass by*. It is as if the tablet poets have out-performed Circe or Homeric epic tradition by providing *two* stops rather than just one. I admit that there are distinctions in function within these proposed intertexts. The epic hero of the *katabasis* is, after all, not dead, and is seeking directions home, rather than trying to make a name for himself in the underworld. But it is significant that we can see in both epic and tablets some shared formulas, shared rhetorical strategies (the *entha* trope), and shared motifs (drinking, inclusion, and exclusion), even though these are applied to different narrative contexts.

If there is a certain predictability to finding tablet texts that are parallel to the *Odyssey*'s underworld scene, resonances are less expected in one of the poem's more realistic episodes, the hero's meeting on the beach with the young girl Nausicaa. Just emerging from a near-death experience, Odysseus entreats the princess and is given a bath, clothes, and finally, directions (*Odyssey* 6.255–315). Nausicaa is wonderfully talkative: she tells Odysseus that he will have to walk to town, lest people gossip about her involvement with a strange man. She says that they will pass a double *limên* (*Odyssey* 6.263, a harbor, rather than the lake as in the *limnê* of Memory in the tablet). She also fears that one of the rough sailors might mock them asking who the "fine big stranger" is who accompanies the girl. If she did not get him off a boat, perhaps he is a god come down from heaven to answer her prayers (*Odyssey* 6.276–80). The phrase *ouranothen katabas* tempts us to think at this point of the "arrival and boast" phrase concerning the deceased person's *genos ouranion*. It might not be so fanciful to think in terms of *katabasis* throughout this Phaeacian scene, especially when we hear from the royal princess a topographical excursus (*Odyssey* 6.291–94). There is a grove of poplar trees (*alsos ... aigeirôn*) with a spring (*krênê*). Odysseus is supposed to wait there. For the listening audience, the details about trees and water are pleasant enough, but that is because we have not yet experienced the details of Books 10 and 11. In "real time"—considering the chronology of the journey rather than the re-telling—Odysseus has already been to the realm of Hades and has stopped at precisely such a grove, not of Athena but of Persephone (cf. *Odyssey* 10.509–10: *alsea ... aigeiroi*). He is perhaps a bit perturbed by all this *déjà vu* instruction.

Afterwards, Odysseus is supposed to go to the city and make inquiries about the location of the palace (*Odyssey* 10.298: *ereesthai*). We can compare the "map and script" tablet L1.9, on which the guardians are said to ask what the deceased is seeking (*hot<t>i de exereeis*). Further details seem to tally. When her father's house "conceals" him (6.303 *kekuthôsi*), says Nausicaa, Odysseus is to proceed through the hall to her mother Arêtê, who is seated at the hearth. He is to beseech her to be assured of a homecoming. The framing verb is ominous, as it is often used in mention of Hades or earth "concealing" the dead (cf. *Iliad* 23.244, *Odyssey* 3.16). Apart from this, the scenario might sound oddly familiar. To paraphrase Nausicaa's directive more abstractly: "Go to a royal maiden; do not stop at the first place I shall tell you; go to the second place (and there pray to a female). Then you will be safe and sound." At the risk of opening a contentious debate, I suggest that the *Odyssey* scene, while it is perfectly comprehensible by itself, would sound all the more intriguing and amusing if an audience already knew something associated with the dead and resembling our "map and script" texts. Of course, that would mean, in practical terms, some down-dating of the epics and/or earlier projections of "Orphic" tablet materials. As it stands, not much more than a century separates a possible Peisistratean text and our earliest tablet. In short, it is not impossible that the remarkable entry of Odysseus into the palace of Alcinous has been fashioned on instructions for a trip to the dead.[21]

---

[21]   As regards relative dating, I am in agreement with the position now articulated by De Jáuregui 2011, 273 that in the sixth and fifth centuries BCE, "... the oral epic tradition was not yet completely fossilized and wholly dependent on the *Iliad* and the *Odyssey*." He does not, however, explore the

It is time to turn for a few minutes to the larger picture that might help orient us in thinking about the interaction of poetic compositions going on in the archaic period and later. As mentioned earlier, it seems possible that Orphic saga material in poetic form was, in fact, available in the century that the Homeric poems were taking their near-final shape—the sixth century BCE.[22] I would like to sketch out how that phenomenon—the availability of Orphic poetry in rhapsodic performances—might relate to other kinds of compositions. Then we can finish off with something smaller—in fact, with a single point of shared diction—for which the larger picture should prepare us and which might illuminate a context for the tablets.

How are we to imagine that the parallels originate between Homeric epic and the Orphic lamellae? As borrowings of well-known verses? Or is there something more complex going on here? The latter seems more likely. One interesting example of several can suffice to remind us once again of the independence of the tablet-text poetic tradition, when compared with the Homeric text. The "map and script" tablets consistently retain the archaism of uncontracted a-stem genitive in the noun *Aidao*, "of Hades," at L1.2 (*Aidao domous*), L3.1 (*Aidao domôn*) and L4.1 (*Aidao domois*). The formula "house of Hades" using this archaic genitive occurs seventeen times in Homeric verse; another seventeen instances of the genitive occur in other phrases.[23] But the *Odyssey* also has, twice, the "house of Hades" formula with the newer, contracted genitive *Aideô* (metrically trisyllabic: *Odyssey* 10.512, 23.322).[24] One of the instances comes in the passage already analyzed, Circe's instructions (*Odyssey* 10.511–12):

νῆα μὲν αὐτοῦ κέλσαι ἐπ᾽ Ὠκεανῷ βαθυδίνῃ,
αὐτὸς δ᾽ εἰς Ἀΐδεω ἰέναι δόμον εὐρώεντα.

The ship [μέν] beach on the spot, at deep-whirling Ocean,
But yourself [δ᾽] go into Hades' moldering house.

---

poetic effects in the *Odyssey* of the overlaying of thematic and formulaic materials that could still occur within such a fluid performance tradition. I would insist that the resonances travel both ways, from "epic" to tablets, but also vice versa.

[22] On the "crystallization" of Homeric epic in this period, see Nagy 1996b and Nagy 2010.

[23] The Homeric instances of the formula cluster in a few books: *Iliad* 15.251, 22.52, 482, 23.19, 103, 179; *Odyssey* 4.834, 10.175, 491, 564, 11.69, 12.21, 14.208, 15.350, 20.208, 24.204, 264.

[24] Two other times the newer genitive *Aideô* modifies another word: *Iliad* 8.16, *Odyssey* 12.17.

The modification of a traditional formula—in this case the replacement of the older genitive by the contracted form—can often be attributed to compositional pressures brought on by the rhetorical structure of a given passage. We might venture to think that the addition of line-initial *autos* in *Odyssey* 10.512 has forced the composer to use the newer style phrasing. And if we further ask why the emphasis on *autos* was needed, part of the answer has to lie in the preposed-topic style of this couplet, contrasting Odysseus (*de*) and his ship (*men*), although it is admittedly a rather ordinary juxtaposition. This sort of compositional pressure, in turn, arises when a poet attempts more complex narratives while juggling a traditional stock of formulae. The tablet text, not needing a contrastive verbal device within its smaller narrative scope, can retain the older, longer formula with *Aidao* (the focus is on the deceased auditor; there is no boat nearby). The point is that the compositional practice of the tablet poems is, in at least some places, as old or older than that of the epics.

I would urge us to think of the lamellae, therefore, as participating in a rich synchronic and diachronic context of hexameter verse production, coupled with varied performance contexts. What I am suggesting might be pictured as a four-cornered cultural configuration. Let us think of a square with its top two corners representing "performance" genres and the lower corners representing what we may designate "performative" genres. The top line of the square connects two "long" forms, poetry that comes to us in connected texts of anywhere from 200 to 15,000 lines. Another name for these would be "rhapsodic" genres. In my suggested configuration, one corner would be occupied by poetry that we believe was subject to public performance by rhapsodes starting from at least the sixth century BCE. This corner would include Homeric epic in the broadest sense (including compositions attributed to Homer besides the *Iliad* and *Odyssey*); the Hesiodic corpus—again with such things as the *Ornithomanteia* and the *Melampodia*; the so-called Homeric hymns; and the poems of the Epic Cycle.

The other corner for "performance" poetry is allotted to Orphic "epic" or saga literature—essentially the *Argonautica* and *katabasis* traditions. This body of poetry of course is much harder to evaluate; we are forced to argue from testimonia of later date and from the much later existence of hexameter poems ascribed to Orpheus, such as the Orphic *Argonautica* and the *Lithica*. Yet we can characterize this body of compositions as "rhapsodic" in the sense of available for competitive and repeated public performance, because it is clearly associated with *rhapsoidia* already in Plato's *Ion* (533b–c):

Ἀλλὰ μήν, ὥς γ' ἐγὼ οἶμαι, οὐδ' ἐν αὐλήσει γε οὐδὲ ἐν κιθαρίσει οὐδὲ
ἐν κιθαρῳδίᾳ οὐδὲ ἐν ῥαψῳδίᾳ οὐδεπώποτ' εἶδες ἄνδρα ὅστις περὶ μὲν
Ὀλύμπου δεινός ἐστιν ἐξηγεῖσθαι ἢ περὶ Θαμύρου ἢ περὶ Ὀρφέως ἢ περὶ
Φημίου τοῦ Ἰθακησίου ῥαψῳδοῦ, περὶ δὲ Ἴωνος τοῦ Ἐφεσίου [ῥαψῳδοῦ]
ἀπορεῖ καὶ οὐκ ἔχει συμβαλέσθαι ἅ τε εὖ ῥαψῳδεῖ καὶ ἃ μή.

But surely, I think, you never saw a man, when it came to *aulos*-playing,
kithara-playing, singing to the *kithara* or rhapsodizing, who is clever at
performing an explanation [*exêgeisthai*] about Olympus or Thamyris or
Orpheus or Phemius the Ithacan rhapsode, yet is clueless about Ion of
Ephesus and cannot find anything to say concerning what he rhapsodizes
well and what not.

The simplest reading of this passage would see it as confirming the existence of two related discourse habits. First, it must have been a part of performance ideology and practice in the later fifth century BCE for contemporary
players, singers, and reciters to attribute their materials to mythical founders
of their medium.[25] Otherwise, why would an exegete be said to give an
opinion on works by these long-dead men, just as one might do concerning
the painter Polygnotus or sculptors, for whom one could still point to artifacts
in naming the artist (cf. *Ion* 533a)? Of course, rhapsodes like Ion were doing
the same sort of attribution in alleging that their materials descended from the
Chian bard. In the absence of a publicly accessible text or score, however, the
verbal and musical arts differ crucially from the visual arts, to which Socrates
smoothly analogizes them in the *Ion*: they have existence only in performance and so there is much greater leeway for creative attribution. Indeed,
we could say that the discourse about Homeric or Orphic art (or Olympic
or Thamyrian) transmitted by performers of those genres must have been a
fruitful source of the varied and contradictory lore that later shows up in our
"biographical" testimonia, as in pseudo-Plutarch *De musica*. Another sort of
discourse, intersecting with such performer-based genealogizing, was clearly
an exegetical tradition carried on by the very performers and itself a matter
of implicit, if not explicit, competition. Ion prides himself on speaking better
than Stesimbrotus or any other commentator about Homeric art; dramatic
"interpretation"—how to perform Homer—thus led seamlessly into critical
interpretation—*why* one recited what one did, what "Homer" meant.[26] If, as
the *Ion* passage most likely indicates, Orphic poetry was recited or sung in

[25]   See Martin 2001a, 24–25.

[26]   For a detailed examination of this and related phenomena spurring the rise of Greek literary
criticism, see Ford 2002, especially 68–72.

public, the respective sequence of attributions in the passage indicates that its medium was probably *kitharôidia*. It is worth pointing out, however, that the "bard" Phemius, whom Socrates alludes to as a rhapsode at *Ion* 533c, is in fact presented in the *Odyssey* as singing while playing the phorminx (*Odyssey* 1.153–55). In other words, he is typologically a citharode.[27] The further example of Terpander, inventor of "citharodic nomes" in hexameter, shows that material could easily jump the species divide, from song to recitation, in either direction.[28] At any rate, whether sung or recited, it is not inconceivable that Orphic material and epic material traveled on the same public performance circuits, with bards and citharodes performing at festivals from Chios to Delos to Epidaurus—perhaps even at Eleusis.[29] This would have led to interaction between the two types of poetry at the upper "corners" of our performance square. It would also, naturally, have meant that performers of "Orpheus" were also Orphic interpreters. Consequently, it would not be far-fetched to imagine the composer of the exegesis of Orphic cosmogony found in the Derveni papyrus as himself an Orphic bard.[30]

Such interaction between brands of public poetry could have led to the parallels we have noted between the *Odyssey* and *Iliad*, on the one hand, and specific tropes in the Orphic tablets. The imagined long-form, public Orphic compositions like the *Argonautica*, may have been the mediating locus. One possibility, for example, is that the short-form tablet texts fed into narrations of a *katabasis* type. One can imagine a katabatic poem in which Orpheus enacts (in the manner of Odysseus) the "directions" found in our tablet texts. By the same token, the tablet texts might echo formulas and content once found in an Orphic long-poem about an underworld visit. The key hypotheses are, first, that this exchange of ideas and phrases was most likely an

---

[27] On Phemius as proto-citharode, see Power 2010, 185, 210. For the synonymity of phorminx and *kithara*, see Chapter 5 above.

[28] Glaucus of Rhegium in his historical work *On Poets* apparently located Homer chronologically between Orpheus and Terpander, perhaps reflecting late fifth-century thought about the affiliations of the recited and sung hexametric modes: see Ford 2002, 139–42.

[29] Again, for details see Martin 2001a. On the Orphic poetic heritage as it relates to Eleusis, see the fundamental work of Graf 1974. One could speculate that such traveling "Orphic" performers (artistic and/or religious figures), parallel to rhapsodes, provided to local communities or believers the poetic materials that appear on the widely dispersed tablets.

[30] Ford 2002, 76 notes that the Orphic exegesis of the Derveni papryus "replicated the esoterism of the songs themselves," but stops short of conjecturing that the author of the former was also a singer of the latter. On various rhapsodes (such as Stesimbrotus) who have been proposed as possible authors of the Derveni commentary, see Janko 1997. Calame 2014, by contrast, distinguishes between "rhapsodic" voice and exegetical style in the papyrus.

oral, rather than script-based process; and, second, that it was not a one-way process. From what we know of cultures where stylized, formulaic texts are used for both ritual and entertainment purposes (for example, in India and south Asia, with regional employments of "epic"), there is a constant and highly productive interplay among the various expressions of mythic material—short and long, poetry and song, ritual, lore, anecdote, monuments, festivals, and tomb-cult.[31]

This brings us to the bottom line of the proposed square. Here I would place two short forms that were crafted, as far as we can tell, for a functional purpose. These are the gold tablets—to ensure a smooth transition into the afterlife—and another form of hexameter poetry, unjustly neglected: the Delphic oracles. Despite the skepticism of Fontenrose and some others, there is no good reason to doubt that those who sought advice from Apollo could be given actual poetic responses.[32] At the same time, there is of course evidence that oracular responses were also made in short non-poetic forms, as short as a word or two. The lead tablets at Dodona come to mind. It is worth noting, in this regard, that a similar bifurcation marks the Orphic tablet tradition, some featuring poems that are about the length of oracular responses, others with single words. I would want to pull into this orbit, as well, the astragaloi found at Delphi and on display in the museum at the site. These bone dice are inscribed with a few letters or, in some cases, short words: *Gê* ("earth"); *Nux* ("night"), Thetis, and Akhilleus, among others[33] If one accepts a possible parallel to another laconically inscribed set of markers, the Olbian Orphic ivory tokens, we may want to push the analogy and think of games (sacred or profane) in both locales, or even funeral customs.[34] But the main point is this: just as it has been shown that the hexameter *oracle* tradition forms a coherent corpus and, most importantly, one that is independent of Homeric verse in diction and technique, so the hexameter "Orphic" tablets might easily form a tradition independent from that of either Homeric epic or even long Orphic poems. This is not to say that there is no contact between the corners: the figure of the square should suggest four communicating corners, rather than random points in space.

---

[31] Among the richest recent descriptions of such interactions is Hiltebeitel 1999.

[32] For an argument in favor of original poetic oracles, see Maurizio 1997 with further bibliography.

[33] Of the more than 25,000 knucklebones found in the Corycian cave, thirty-one are inscribed with names: see Amandry 1984, 370–78. For the use of astragaloi in divination ritual, see the study by Graf 2005 and on similar finds in other sanctuaries, see Bundrick 2014, 681–82.

[34] On the tablets, see Zmud' 1992.

The square as a hermeneutic device can also make us think about the parallels between Orphic tablet texts and hexameter oracle texts at the level of phrase and diction. This is a project for further investigation at length. Initial probing, however, turns up a few curious resemblances, one of which brings us back to the notion of the *hêros*. Consider Fontenrose Q69, a "quasi historical response" according to his typology, which was transmitted through Plutarch's *Life of Solon* (9.1) and that, Fontenrose thinks, may have come from Hermippus or directly from Androtion.[35] It gives authoritative directions for hero cult: specifically, to propitiate the heroes of Salamis:

> ἀρχηγοὺς χώρας θυσίαις ἥρωας ἐνοίκους
> ἵλασο, τοὺς κόλποις Ἀσωπιὰς ἀμφικαλύπτει,
> οἳ φθίμενοι δέρκονται ἐς ἠέλιον δύνοντα·

> Leaders of the land, the resident heroes, with rites
> propitiate, whom the Asopian plain hides in its bosom,
> those who, having perished, look toward the setting sun.

The Plutarch story presents Solon as proceeding to sacrifice to Periphemus and Cychreus, two local insular heroes, secretly at night, as a way of ensuring his success in eventually taking over the island. Compare the text of the tablet from Entella (L2 = fr. 475 Bernabé). The first partial lines from this tablet refer mysteriously to *m]emnême<n>os hêrôs*, a "mindful hero" and then mention "darkness to embrace." The syntax is somewhat unclear. It is worth pointing out the occurrence, in the oracle response to Solon, of similar diction within two lines, with forms of the verb *amphika-lupsai* in the same metrical slot. In context, the tablet differs from the oracle inasmuch as one instructs the dead, and the other instructs the living about how to worship the dead. But going a bit further, we can say they both really deal with the same topic: the proper behavior associated with underworld divinities.

Here we can finally return from the big picture of the sociology of archaic performance to the smaller scale of poetic diction. It seems not to have been suggested that *memnêmos hêrôs* is a direct address to the recipient of the Entella tablet: "Mindful of this, hero—you should do the following ... before—or after—darkness embraces [you]."[36] A modest proposal that we

---

[35] Fontenrose 1978, 326.

[36] For a different rendering, supplying a third-person verb ("let the hero get this written down"), see Janko 2016, 109, who, however, does not take into account the epic parallels I have cited. Restoration of a third person would not be necessary if we assume the opening of the Entella tablet

should, in fact, read the line in this way is based on two additional speech habits found in hexameter poetic traditions.

First, it is clear that the participle *memnêmenos* can function most often with a genitive or infinitive in a command to "be mindful" of some important fact or action: woodcutting, plowing, and so forth (cf. Hesiod *Theogony* 562, *Works and Days* 422, 616, 623). The essence of Hesiod's advice to his brother Perses is summed up with the participle in *Works and Days* 641–42:

τύνη δ', ὦ Πέρση, ἔργων μεμνημένος εἶναι
ὡραίων πάντων, περὶ ναυτιλίης δὲ μάλιστα.

You must be mindful of all works in their season,
Perses—especially when it comes to seafaring.

Note that in this and several other verses, *memnêmenos* is precisely in the metrical slot where Frel's restoration puts the word on the Entella lamella.[37]

Second, we can see from the Homeric examples that there are speech situations in epic where the word *hêrôs* functions as a vocative. At *Iliad* 11.838, Patroclus asks his companion Eurypylus "how shall this be? What shall we do?"

πῶς τὰρ ἔοι τάδε ἔργα; τί ῥέξομεν Εὐρύπυλ' ἥρως;

In most of its occurrences, the vocative *hêros* comes at line-final position, just as in the text from Entella (e.g., *Iliad* 10.416, 11.819). Even more significant are the addresses of the god Apollo to the hero Aeneas (*Iliad* 20.104), given the relative status of the interlocutors; and that of Menelaus to Telemachus (*Odyssey* 4.312), which like the Entella tablet involves a question-and-answer structure, the older man asking "what need led you here?" followed by the vocative (τίπτε δέ σε χρειὼ δεῦρ' ἤγαγε, Τηλέμαχ' ἥρως). Compare, without the vocative, the question of the *phulakes* to the deceased in text L4.6 (= fr. 477 Bernabé, lamella from Pharsalus): *ho ti khreos eisaphikaneis*. Nor should we forget that the vocative *hêrôs* is also used in at least one *Odyssey* directive passage already analyzed (Circe to Odysseus at *Odyssey* 10.516) and

---

ran something like "When he is on the point of death, *say this* … ." It seems impractical at best for the afflicted individual to consider having a tablet engraved only at death's door.

[37] Frel 1994, 184. The word also occupies the slot before the final foot of the hexameter in Hesiod *Theogony* 562 and *Works and Days* 616.

possibly another (Nausicaa to Odysseus at *Odyssey* 6.303).[38] Apart from the Homeric tradition, it is interesting that the *Thebais*, a lost epic of the archaic period, combined instructions (apparently by the mantis Amphiaraus) with this vocative (fr. 4):

> πουλύποδός μοι, τέκνον, ἔχων νόον, Ἀμφίλοχ' ἥρως,
> τοῖσιν ἐφαρμόζειν, τῶν κεν κατὰ δῆμον ἵκηαι,

> Child, adapt to those whose town you come to,
> having the disposition of the octopus, hero Amphilochus.

The late poems attributed to Orpheus might have been considered a prime source of parallels for the diction and rhetoric of the tablet texts, but they turn out to provide fewer speech parallels than one wishes. The *Lithica* (line 404) uses the vocative *hêrôs* to introduce a new section of didactic material, while slightly later verses have the word at the line-end (Ἀλλὰ σύ γ' ἥρως, 418) modified by and in close proximity to the participle πεφυλαγμένος "protected" (419). For this deployment, compare the tablet L8.2 from Thurii (fr. 487 Bernabé), which has the same participle in the same position. The context is about directions to go out "well protected as to all things" in both the Orphic *Lithica* and the Thurii text, although the former is talking about snake-protection through the potency of siderite.

Where, then, do these parallels take us? What can we conclude on the level of cultural practice after working up the philological analysis? I have argued that a close reading by way of type-scenes and poetic diction produces interesting parallels. I have further constructed a hypothetical performance "square" to suggest how the longer poetic genres and the shorter sub-genres (including the tablets), the composers and their techniques, can all fit together. Let me end with an observation about the "voice" behind these texts that we can begin to hear if we listen closely.

There has been some consensus that the "voice" speaking the tablet texts is none other than that of Orpheus. He was after all the heroic survivor of descent to the underworld and also was known as a poet of hexameters.[39] Who would be better placed to speak such wisdom? However, I would like

---

[38] Commentators attempt to read *hêrôs* in *Odyssey* 6.303 as genitive, with the preceding name *Alkinooio*, although this would involve an unparalleled form. The situational parallel with the Circe episode, in which the undoubted vocative at 10.516 occurs, may well motivate a *vocative* at 6.303; the scholiasts *ad loc.* interpret *hêrôs* as vocative, to Hainsworth "a desperate expedient" (Heubeck et al. 1988, 312).

[39] See Riedweg 1998.

to question somewhat this monophonic position, attractive as it may be. Looking back at the pragmatics of the speaking situations—who is using which words in what situations—when we compare epic and other hexameters, it seems that the evidence provides us with a series of speakers who can instruct their listeners not so much because they are divine authorities as because they are (or are *also*) close acquaintances: Nausicaa, for example, in the *Odyssey*, or Circe, the lover of Odysseus. Those who use the *memnêmos* or *hêrôs* formulas are Hesiod to his brother Perses, Patroclus to his companion, and Amphiaraus to his young addressee. In sum, the speech exchange in these examples does depend on one person knowing more, but the knowledge is presented on a deeply human level, *not* from an unbending authority. We are hearing in the tablet texts the voice of intimate persuasion, that sort of talk that Homer calls *pukinon epos*.[40] This is the sort of talk whispered in the ear of a friend or spoken in a small intimate circle, the *epos* that Andromache had hoped in vain to hear from her husband before his death (*Iliad* 24.744). It is advice, not dogma. Orpheus could have been imagined as singing these tablet verses to his followers. But just as easily, I propose, Pythagoras could have spoken them. We do, after all, have gnomic directions ascribed to the mysterious philosopher.[41] Nor should we forget that one ancient tradition dating back to Ion of Chios in the fifth century BCE claimed that Pythagoras made the poems that were attributed to Orpheus (Diogenes Laertius *Lives of the Philosophers* 8.8). If we believe Clement of Alexandria (*Stromata* 1.131.4), a Pythagorean was actually responsible for the "Orphic" poem describing a descent to Hades. Given these hints about voices and texts, authorship and authority, is it unreasonable for us to conclude that the famous Golden Verses of Pythagoras were not simply a Golden Rule, in which the adjective is a dead metaphor, but Golden because they resembled—or were—these very verses from the tombs of the ancient dead, inscribed on fragile sheets of gold?

[40] On the semantics of this formula, see Martin 1989, 35–37.

[41] For a summary and further bibliography, see Riedweg 2002, 120–23.

III

HESIODIC CONSTRUCTIONS

10

HESIOD AND THE DIACTIC DOUBLE[1]

Tu le connais, lecteur, ce monstre délicat,
Hypocrite lecteur—mon semblable—mon frère—

That didactic poetry is as complex as other literary forms has become an acceptable proposition. Now it is time to explain how this complexity operates, how the pragmatics of the form entwine with the intricacies of cultural contexts, what this quintessentially "engaged" poetry aims at, how genre-mixing and tonal shifts can create as highly textured a surface as those of epic, dramatic, or lyric poetry. The *Works and Days* of Hesiod, the crystallization of an ancient Greek "advice" tradition, should give pause to those who like their Greek literature to evolve nicely out of the primitive.[2] Already at the head of the stream of didactic in European literature, Hesiodic poetry displays the high style of epic, the stylized first-person of lyric, and—the focus of this chapter—a dramatic structure enacted as a two-way conversation

---

[1] Originally published in *Synthesis* 11 (2004): 31–53. Translations of Hesiod are based on the translation by G. Most, with some modifications.

[2] Primitivist assumptions about Hesiod's inability to be strictly logical underlie Havelock 1966 and West 1981. I hesitate to use the term "didactic" for several reasons: the other surviving poems closest to Hesiod are clearly more interested in giving moral and political advice, rather than technical instruction (Theognis, Solon, Tyrtaeus); even closer are passages within Homeric "epic" (another problem term; see Chapter 1 above) in which *paraenesis* is represented. In short, we are dealing with a genre of discourse rather than an identifiable literary type; on this, see Martin 1984a.

of which we are privileged to hear just half, but meant to know the rest.[3] Why not read it with at least the same attention one gives Baudelaire?[4]

Of course, the Eurocentric viewpoint is limiting. Long before Hesiod, didactic fictions figured in the verbal art of Sumerians, Akkadians, and Egyptians.[5] As has been shown in the case of Hesiod's theogonic poetry, this flourishing Near Eastern art influenced Greek. There is, however, little point in tracing parallels unless they can tell us something further about the idiosyncratic inscapes of the works themselves. I shall make use of some parallels to highlight such differences further on. But to catch the distinctive quality of Greek didactic poetry we must first step back into the extra-literary and step aside, for a comparative perspective.[6] From this angle, the complexity of didactic finds its closest analogue in the poetics of myth. Limited only by the previous experience of real audiences and the capability of performers, both didactic and myth make use of fictive audiences and tellers to explore the ethical alongside the metaphysical and cosmological, while locating all three in the ordinary. Perhaps this is not accidental; just as there appear to be no societies without some form of socially embedded narratives that we can identify, at some level, as stories of belief, none seems to lack didactic traditions. Often the two combine. Sometimes the didactic moment emerges in a fleeting line within a mythic poem:

> The hummingbird is good and big.
> So that's the way it is;
> there were workers in hot country.
> They were burning bean pods.
> The fire could be seen well, it was so tall.
> The hummingbird came,
> it came out
> it came flying in the sky.
> Well, it saw the fire;

---

[3]   For a careful analysis of the structural features of passages involving the addressee, see Schmidt 1986, who is, however, not interested in the literary pragmatics of the problem. For fuller comparison to lyric, see Arrighetti 1975, 5–36. This is not the place to rehearse all the arguments in favor of Hesiod, his brother, and their proceedings as fictional constructs, on which see especially Nagy 1992, 36–82. Suffice it to say that whether or not the poem has an historical basis, while fascinating in itself, has no relevance for interpretation. All we have is the text.

[4]   Perhaps we do not think of Baudelaire as "didactic," yet the poem he chooses to introduce *Les Fleurs du Mal* is a catalogue, in excellent Cynic diatribe style, of *la ménagerie infâme de nos vices.*

[5]   See, e.g., Longman 1991 and the survey of Near Eastern material in West 1978, 3–15.

[6]   I am encouraged in taking this comparative approach, since we have no evidence for an explicit native poetics for "didactic": see Schuler and Fitch 1983.

> its eyes were snuffed out by the smoke.
> It came down
> it came down
> it came down, so that they saw it was big
> Don't you believe that it is little, it is big.

This portion of a simple-sounding poem from Zinacantán (a *municipio* in the state of Chiapas, Mexico) opens with description: the hummingbird is good and big. This is "the way it is," a fact about the cosmos—albeit counter-intuitive, we might think, to anyone who has seen hummingbirds. Following the fact, which is put in "constative" form, comes a miniature story of the unspecified past that functions at the same time as an argument.[7] How do we know the bird's size? Once upon a time "they saw it was big." And then a "directive," the expected form of didactic utterance: "Don't you believe that it is little ... ." Belief, proof, teaching—all are so artfully blended that it is impossible to pin down the poem with a genre label.

One thing Mesoamerican anthropologists can relate about this composition is its symbiotic relation with myth.[8] The hummingbird is associated with the god Huitzilopotchtli, who is in turn an image of the sun during spring and summer. Furthermore, hummingbirds are known for their fierce territoriality and thus, in local belief, represent warriors: a Zinacantecan man is advised to eat the heart of the bird before fighting. But the sun god is also a warrior, whose irridescence—like the bird's coloring—changes under different conditions. And the hummingbird is "hot"; the gift of a dead bird, tied with green ribbon, can warm your lover's heart. And so on. The deeper one pursues this associative logic beneath the Zinacantecan poem, the less surprising does it seem that the hummingbird is so emphatically "big." As Eva Hunt demonstrates in her monographic explication of this little composition, the line in the poem represents the enduring worldview of a pre-Hispanic ritual and agricultural calendar that celebrates and observes the waxing of the sun/god/bird during a specific time of year.

How does this ethnographic perspective help us read Hesiod? Most importantly, it allows one to broaden the area of analysis: not just the overtly "directive" but the "constative" descriptive and narrative portions of poems

---

[7] I choose these speech-act terms in an attempt to bring more specificity to stylistic analysis. For further illustrations, see Martin 1989; for an extension into social history, see Ober 1989. A minimal typology of speech-acts can provide an anchor and organizing principle when exploring art-forms that make the variation of surface expression into an aesthetic ideal.

[8] See E. Hunt 1977, 52–111; the full text of the poem is on pp. 29–30.

like the *Works and Days* and the *Theogony* can be examined as didactic, because all the segments of these poems collaborate in the transmission of cultural norms: teaching is more than reeling off imperatives. We can go further: didactic becomes compelling precisely through its affiliation with an underlying contemporary narrative. If the narrative becomes part of the directive message of the poem, as happens with the *Works and Days*, then it has the same status as myth within its poem. It is, in effect, myth in the making, a conscious display of the themes and motifs one finds in stories about *illud tempus*, but crafted into the frame of the *hic et nunc*. These are not, in other words, narratives skewed in some way by their time difference, but beautifully complementary tellings of the same basic story, featuring variations in addressee and deixis such as one can notice between epic and lyric expressions of the same story.[9]

It is the foundation narrative—or, in these terms, "myth"—of the *Works and Days* which will be my focus: namely, the story, only partially explicit, of the poet's ongoing relationship with his brother Perses, the poem's addressee. Though often noticed, the unusual nature of this story remains unexplained. It is uniquely Hesiodic: when compared with other wisdom texts from traditional cultures, the *Works and Days* frame-narrative stands out because it does not represent the message of the poetry in the form of instructions by a father to a son, king to prince, or tutor to pupil.[10] The poem never envisions such asymmetrical, generational transmission. Jenny Strauss Clay approaches this interpretive question but leaves it open in a footnote to her recent study of the poem: "The more equal fraternal relationship between speaker and addressee (we do not even know whether Hesiod was older than Perses) may be significant: what is the basis for Hesiod's authority to instruct his brother?"[11] My answer, in brief, will be that the "myth" of Perses *is* the message. Vastly richer than the bumper-sticker message ("Question Authority"—to which one must instantly reply "Says who?"), the poem nevertheless empowers in the same way. By the conclusion of his performance, the speaker of the poem has not only constructed his authority as equal to that of Zeus, but also ironized it nearly

---

[9]   For the fundamental distinction between *mythopoiia* (reshaping of received myths) and *mythoplasia* (invention of new poetic myth) I am indebted to the precise and illuminating work of Anastasia-Erasmia Peponi, particularly her study of Sappho 16 LP in Peponi 1995. On the lyric background of the *Works and Days*, see Chapter 11 below.

[10]   See West 1978, 34.

[11]   J. S. Clay 1993. Stein 1990, 26 notes the oddity of the brother figure but takes it as confirmation that Hesiod really had a brother, who is not a persona.

out of existence. Consequently, the addressee can more realistically have the chance of becoming like his advisor, and does not have to wait for years to test his wisdom (the long-range assumption of the generational model). The poem's lyric technique, and its dialogic format, require change and assent in the here-and-now.

The choice of "brother" to stand for the Other of the didactic addressee is thus far from arbitrary. Indeed, it would appear in the poem's terms to be inevitable; or, at least, the poet has structured this composition in such a way that the cosmos itself emerges as ineluctably double (with consequent dilemmas). After exploring this theme of doubles as it shapes the preliminary myths of the poem and affects some later portions, I shall address the dramatic function of the merging of the pragmatic frame (an argument between brothers) with the poem's narratives about twosomes. Finally, I shall take up a few extra-dramatic questions about the further affiliations of Hesiodic verse, in order to speculate on Hesiod's *real* brothers.

Trio for Doubles

The poem proper begins with what sounds like a correction (*Works and Days* 11–12):

> Οὐκ ἄρα μοῦνον ἔην Ἐρίδων γένος, ἀλλ' ἐπὶ γαῖαν
> εἰσὶ δύω ...

> So, there is not just a single race of Strifes: there are two on earth.

If we cared neither for voice nor subtlety, it would be enough to read this as a footnote to the *Theogony*, or a clumsy way of expressing what the poet *really* wanted to say.[12] More to the point is the tone created in the text at hand by the joining of particle and imperfect tense, a usage that Denniston describes as "denoting that something which has been, and still is, has only just been realized."[13] This is, first of all, a conversation, and one that is on-going, with an edge to it. Homeric examples of the speech strategy occur, significantly, at tense moments when one speaker wants to vent his anger: Achilles replies to Odysseus (*Iliad* 9.316), "So, there is no

---

[12] West 1978, 142 says Hesiod had the idea of saying, "There is such a goddess as Emulation" but then realized this was not the same as the Eris mentioned in *Theogony* 225ff, and so thinks aloud while correcting himself.

[13] Denniston 1950, 36.

gratitude for fighting always"; Achilles in a troubled reply to the "great fool" Patroclus (*mega nêpios Iliad* 16.46 and *meg' okhthêsas* 16.48) bitterly recalls Agamemnon's theft but concedes, "so, it's not possible to be angry forever" (16.60); Glaucus berates Hector (*Iliad* 17.141 *khalepôi ênipape muthôi*), "so, you fall far short of battle-power" (*Iliad* 17.142). Thus Hesiod (as I shall call the speaker of the *Works and Days*) begins by bristling. "So [contrary to what I, or you, used to think] there is *not* just a single *genos* of Eris." The undertone here: someone has made me realize differently and I do not like it. Hesiod's response—I shall not call it "teaching"—is to complicate: things are not as simple as they might have seemed. In fact, they are relentlessly duple, as the text proceeds to illustrate, and does so not just when it comes to Strife, but in a mythic sequence that is triple.

First, the two Erides. At this early point in the poem, perhaps the traditional audience knows Hesiod is arguing with a brother, perhaps not (line 10 is not revealing). We do know, however, that this is a conversation in which one speaker claims the authority to attempt speaking truth to another, who bears the ominous name "Wrecker."[14] Furthermore, we soon get the sense that the addressee resembles one of the Strifes. The tone of voice that I have just mentioned is, after all, that which one uses to blame somebody. The first detail about the double Strife concerns precisely this topic: the good is praiseworthy "if one notices" (νοήσας, 12) while the bad is to be blamed (ἐπιμωμητή, 13). The bad Eris, in addition, fosters evil war and increases conflict (δῆριν ὀφέλλει, 14). Within a short space, the phrase is repeated with reference to the idle behavior of Perses, who neglects work in order to be on the sidelines at public wrangling and disputes (29).[15] Once his livelihood is assured, says the poet, Perses might "increase conflict" in this way (33). But for now, he should pay attention to settling the *neikos* within the family (διακρινώμεθα νεῖκος, 35). The contrast is doubled: alongside the traditional distinction in blame-discourse between useless talk and necessary action (see, e.g., Aeneas to Achilles on *neikea, Iliad* 20.251-57), there is the contrast between quarrels over other people's goods (κτήμασ' ἐπ' ἀλλοτρίοις, 34) as opposed to the in-house fraternal dispute. The implied directive to Perses is therefore two-fold: don't listen to disputes; work; but (first) pay attention to *this* dispute. The further implication, expressed by the initially puzzling line "for you there will no longer be a second time to act this way"

[14]   On the mythic and poetic resonances of the name, see Nagy 1992, 74–75. For another resonance, see the last section of this chapter.

[15]   Lardinois 1995, 202 has noted the parallel phrasing.

(34–35), is that proper attention to the internal settlement will soon convince him of the value of working rather than disputing. There is nothing illogical about the train of thought.[16] The key lies in the assimilation of Perses to the "bad" Eris that keeps him from listening to the serious advice of his brother. The adviser, as we might expect, is at the same time assimilated to the praise-worthy Eris. For both of them rouse men to work (20), the good Eris by inspiring emulation of its farm-centered wealth (21–22). Competition is a good thing, for potters, craftsmen, beggars—and poets (24–26). Given the last-named example of beneficial agonistics, an audience cannot help but identify Hesiod with good Eris. In this light it is significant that "good" Eris is rooted in the land and is better (ἀμείνω) for mortals (19), characteristics that mark the speaker's discourse (about land management *passim*, and what is "better," specifically at, e.g., lines 314, 320, 776). In sum, the talk of Eris which opens the poem is a rhetorically artful "indirect directive" that works by matching the feuding brothers of the moment with their mythic and theo-gonic template (given a change of gender). The implicit message is also good therapeutic discourse: these disputes have *always* happened in families. This strategy is part of Hesiod's effective *pre*-didactic rhetoric, aimed at solving a would-be adviser's first problem: getting the hearer to listen.[17]

Let us move now to the second and third set of doubles, which are embedded in the story of Pandora. Like the story of the dual Eris, this myth takes us back to the early constitution of the world. Humans labor to get a living because Prometheus once tricked Zeus (42–48). But their ultimate punishment, in the form of pains, ills, and disease from Pandora's jar, only spread through the world because Epimetheus failed to heed Prometheus' warning about accepting a gift from Zeus (83–89). The audience is not told that Epimetheus is the brother of Prometheus. Then again, at this point we have not heard in so many words that Perses is Hesiod's brother. The parallel omissions of this known detail of sibship function to draw the pairs closer in the composition. Again, the myth as presented does more than give

---

[16] I disagree with West 1978, 37 on the logic involved and with his interpretation of lines 34–35 (ad loc.), which he apparently takes as a reference to Perses' potential for prolonging the *fraternal* conflict. The point is not that Perses likes dispute, but that he is not directly involved in the one dispute that can help him. Hesiod's is a protreptic argument saying why Perses should *become* a direct addressee in the first place.

[17] Another double lurks here, inasmuch as this appeal to Perses is represented as the result of an apparently failed intervention by the "kings" whom Perses allegedly bribed by skimming something in addition to his take of an original division (lines 37–39). The legal status of the earlier proceeding is of less interest than its rhetorical role in this text, as a foil to focus attention on the absolute neces-sity for listening *now*.

us background for Hesiod's gnomic utterances; it has a rhetorical function, too. If the Eris explanation worked to focus Perses' attention on the present *neikos*, the tale of Prometheus takes the next step, warning of catastrophe if a brother's word is not taken. This connection to the frame-narrative can explain why the role of Epimetheus is incorporated prominently in the telling of the Pandora story within the *Works and Days*, while in the *Theogony* it is restricted to an allusion within a genealogy (*Theogony* 511–12), although the creation of Pandora is told also in that poem (570–90).

Epimetheus thus enjoys a reputation as much as his brother, albeit the reverse. Neither is found blameworthy. The rough equality between them characterizes the third set of doubles as well, Zeus and Prometheus. It is legitimate to fill out the myth with details from the *Theogony*, as we can assume an audience for this poetry would draw on a similar knowledge of tradition. In this light, the further resemblances to the pairing of Perses and Hesiod become clearer. The original deception by Prometheus occurs at a division (*Theogony* 537 *dassamenos*); the *Works and Days* dispute originates the same way (37 *edassameth'*).[18] The elaborate competition carried out with gift and deceptive counter-gift finds a parallel in the "real" story's detail about Perses' bribe, another flawed exchange (*Works and Days* 38–39).[19] It would seem, then, that the passage presents a two-sided trickster: smarter than his brother (like Hesiod) but conniving to win (like Perses). Most important, however, is the broader picture of Zeus and Prometheus as co-equal creators, for this gives a glimpse of hierarchy subverted, then solidified, in mythic time. I stress their creating role because there is some reason to assume that yet another mythic detail of the Prometheus story, his shaping of mankind out of clay, underlies the text in lines 47–104. Specifically, the next segment of the text, the Myth of the Ages, begins "If you want, I shall sum up *the other* story" (Εἰ δ' ἐθέλεις, ἕτερόν τοι ἐγὼ λόγον ἐκκορυφώσω, 106). In epic usage the adjective *heteros* can regularly have the full etymological meaning "the other of two," rather than simply "another," whether or not the demonstrative is present (cf. *Iliad* 4.502, 5.258). In this poem, *heteros* (21) without article clearly refers to one other in the context of pairs (see 23, 25–26). If this strong reading of *heteros* is followed, the emphasis of the Myth of Ages on the divine creation of each race becomes understandable: the point is not

---

[18] On the deeply traditional theme of strife over a division, see Nagy 1999b, 127–39, 213–21, 314–16.

[19] Note *Theogony* 548, Prometheus' address to Zeus as *kudiste megiste* and *Works and Days* 38, Perses *kudainôn basilêas*.

that the Gold, Silver, and other races came to be, but that Zeus or other gods produced them: the first two are made by immortals (110: ἀθάνατοι ποίησαν Ὀλύμπια δώματ' ἔχοντες, cf.127), the second two specifically by Zeus (143, 158; perhaps also the last: 173d). Stressing this feature of the Ages would then allow us to make better sense of line 108, as we can now see that the story is meant to illustrate "how gods and mortals are born from the same source." The usual force of the adverb is considerably watered down if we read, with West, "they started on the same terms."[20] In this *heteros logos*, gods produce people; in the Prometheus story, the son of a Titan makes them as his private amusement. Although the latter story is nowhere on the surface here, the frequent reference to the involvement of humans in the myth (49, 51, 56, 82, 88, 90, 100) makes it sound as if they were the stakes being contested. Furthermore, Zeus' design of Pandora from clay (60–61) would be most appropriate if she is meant to compete and consort with Promethean products of the same stuff. To sum up: this juxtaposition of stories, far from being random, can be read as a diptych about alternative models of creation. Nothing less than the Olympian order is brought into question thereby: whereas the Promethean creation is spoiled by a brother's one failure of foresight, the attempts by Olympians multiply, degenerate, and end in entropy. If these two stories are united in an overall tale of competition between creator-craftsmen, we have yet another rendition attesting to the pervasiveness of strife.[21] But we have moved one further step in the implicit argument of the composition: the eventual loser, Prometheus—like Perses, an addressee in this poem (54–58) but never a speaker—is nevertheless given his due; so shall Perses, it is suggested. We are not far from the *Prometheus Bound* and its somewhat blunter equal-time anti-Olympian script: Question Authority.

Metals, Birds, and Maidens

G. B. Conte, whose notion of the addressee as *prefigurazione di lettore* has influenced recent readings of Hesiod, among other ancient poets, also works with the idea that didactic as a genre is "open," "*un contenitore aperto a svariate*

---

[20] West 1978, 178 notes that the word is used properly of blood-relationship; he has no parallels for the weaker meaning.

[21] Typological analogues for such competitive creation can be found in Native American Coyote tales: see "In the beginning of the world" in Shipley 1991, 18–43.

possibilità."[22] Thus far, I have tried to show that the bewildering variety of material in the early portion of the *Works and Days* is united by the prominence given in each "myth" to differentiations of power between apparent equals—brothers, Strifes, creators. An inherent tension exists between, on one hand, the intentional surface variety, which gives an authentic sound of "talk" to this poetic monologue and, on the other, the practical message, constant in the *Works and Days*, that one should practice *dikê*. But the varied expressions are more than just an interesting cover for the unchanging precept. The "myths" proceed in fugue form, developing the theme while revealing new aspects of it. The addressee, this reader in the text, is educated by virtue of the effort he must make to follow the theme in its increasingly ornate and allusive mythopoeic forms. Most essential, the "doubles" that we have traced thus far serve to reinforce the instruction all along: this is not simply authoritative truth handed down, as in the generational transmission of wisdom; it is wisdom that invites debate, an "open" format that is stylized, in the *Works and Days*, as a continuing *neikos*.

In the open-ended nature of the composition's form we can find a perfect match for the thematic concern with *dikê* that becomes so prominent in the Myth of the Ages. For dealing fairly, practicing justice, is, as Hesiod sees it, a habit, not an acquisition. Humans like Perses are always poised between *hubris* and *dikê*; the choice is open. By the same token, the Iron Age in which we live is, in fact, a future state, as the tenses of lines 177–96 emphasize repeatedly. The time-frame and events of this mythic passage make a close fit with the earlier myths of Strife and Pandora. The good Eris draws persons together in competitive effort, a feature iconically represented by the syntax and word order at lines 25–26:

καὶ κεραμεὺς κεραμεῖ κοτέει καὶ τέκτονι τέκτων,
καὶ πτωχὸς πτωχῷ φθονέει καὶ ἀοιδὸς ἀοιδῷ.

And potter is angry with potter, and builder with builder,
and beggar begrudges beggar, and poet poet.

But unbridled *hubris* in the Iron Age will split them apart as a negatived example of the same figure highlights at 182–84:

οὐδὲ πατὴρ παίδεσσιν ὁμοίιος οὐδέ τι παῖδες
οὐδὲ ξεῖνος ξεινοδόκῳ καὶ ἑταῖρος ἑταίρῳ,
οὐδὲ κασίγνητος φίλος ἔσσεται, ὡς τὸ πάρος περ.

---

[22] Conte 1991; for the influence of these notions, see Schiesaro et al. 1993 passim.

> Father will not be like-minded with sons, nor sons at all,
> nor guest with host, nor comrade with comrade,
> nor will the brother be dear, as he once was.

The implication of the narrator's choice of tense must be that we can escape the nightmare future by preferring *dikê* in the present.[23] As we saw in the positioning of the *aoidos*—i.e., the speaker—in the Eris passage (26), here the role of brother—i.e., addressee—is saved for the key last mention. The future scenario is in one other way a rewrite of the Pandora myth's message: if a brother does right, this time, all might go right. If *dikê* is not done, however, the beneficial women who inhabit earth now, Aidôs and Nemesis, clothed in white, will then return to the gods, a precise reversal of the original descent from Olympus of the tricked-out, harmful female, Pandora.

As Vernant showed in his explication of the Myth of the Ages, the five-part temporal progression in the story represents a simpler collocation of *dikê* vs. *hubris*, which in turn is relevant to the larger thematic structure of the poem.[24] In this way, the seemingly digressive myth becomes completely relevant to the plea made to Perses. But we might go further, as we trace the appearances of didactic doubles, to consider the relevance of particular details within the first contrasting pair, the Gold and Silver Ages. J. S. Clay suggests that Perses may be meant to see himself mirrored in the *mega nêpios* of the Silver race (131).[25] Certainly, the use of the phrase to address him elsewhere (e.g., 633) points to this association. If we consider the context, the scene can also be read as a negative exemplum in relation to the outer frame of the *Works and Days*, a case of the implied failure of didactic. Not only do the Silver people fail to mature properly, staying home with mother for a century; when grown, they fail to sacrifice (135–36: *athanatous therapeuein; erdein*). Yet this is exactly what defines the human condition, as we learn from the *Theogony*; moreover, the instruction to sacrifice was apparently the primary lesson presented by a didactic composition attributed to Hesiod. The opening lines of this poem, the *Kheirônos Hypothêkai*, as preserved in the scholia to Pindar, tell the addressee (perhaps Achilles), "first, when you reach home, sacrifice [*erdein*] fine offerings to the immortal gods" (fr. 283.2–3 MW). In other words, an audience familiar with such traditional instructional verse (similar to verses in the *Works*

---

[23] Vernant 1981, 13–41.

[24] Vernant 1981, 13–41.

[25] J. S. Clay 1993, 27.

and Days itself: cf. 336) would see in the behavior of the hubristic Silver race a deviation from the model of properly matured heroic youth. If Perses is like the Silver men, it is because he is always in danger of ignoring instruction. The symmetry that we noted between the Strifes and the brothers is here repeated, inasmuch as the poet himself has, by contrast, something in common with the Golden Age: both are connected with agricultural abundance, Hesiod through his knowledge of farm lore, the Golden Age by its characteristic automatic profusion (lines 116–17).

We have seen that Perses as brother duplicates the poet's figure more closely than could an addressee from a younger generation. With the myth of the hawk and nightingale, we are reminded that Perses is himself one part of a dual audience, the other being the "kings" for whom Hesiod now makes his "coded" message, the *ainos*.[26] As the story is told here, the hawk has seized the smaller bird and tells it, when it cries, not to fight against the stronger, as its woes will only be increased. Clearly, the tale relates to the rapacity of the "bribe-devouring" kings (38–39) whom Hesiod called "fools" (*nêpioi*) for their inability to recognize that gain does not come so easily in the post-Promethean world (41–46). What we should notice here is the separation made between Perses and the kings, his would-be former allies. At the earlier mention (37–38), Perses is given equal if not greater blame, for having snatched additional goods in order to influence a legal decision. But now, it is the kings alone who are excoriated. When the short tale is over, Perses is addressed with positive encouragement, not blame (213):

Ὦ Πέρση, σὺ δ' ἄκουε δίκης μηδ' ὕβριν ὄφελλε·

As for you, Perses, give heed to Justice and do not foster Outrageousness.

The subtle shift from the earlier passage marks another stage in the gradual rehabilitation of the brother: we are meant to notice that he does not require harsh words. Kings, on the other hand, have a different look to them, now that we have heard about the contest of Zeus and Prometheus in the meantime. Still, the moral of the bird fable can be taken to apply to both audiences, in slightly different ways, because it speaks of equalizing differences in power. In this fable, the powerful kings will be seen to lose, while the weaker bird wins.

---

[26] On semantics of the term and characteristics of the genre, see Nagy 1990, esp. 147–50, 309–15.

Given the allusive artistry of the *Works and Days*, which I have wanted to see as part of its function in educating listeners, we should not expect the text to offer an overt interpretation of the type "the hawk is the bad king, the nightingale is the singer"; furthermore, interpretation is not needed because meaning is already embedded in the culture, where myth provides enough association for what these birds represent. As with the Zincantecan poem with which this piece began, what is *not* said is equally if not more important than the explicit textual signals. Thus the *ainos* by itself, without an interpretive framework constructed by the poet, carries weight. Apart from the "message" however—that one should not be predatory like a hawk—the *ainos* has a higher rhetorical function in the composition of the *Works and Days* since it functions as a foil: Perses is *not* the kings, therefore not the hawk. He can hardly be the nightingale, either, but at least he can be associated with it, as we shall see shortly. This interpretation goes counter to that of West, who says Hesiod fails to make effective rhetorical use of the story. It worries West that the fault of the hawk is not expressed directly: "The hawk's *hubris* matches the king's without putting it in a ridiculous light or showing it to be ill-advised."[27] But just as the Zinacantecan poem runs counter to our culture's ideas about hummingbirds, the Hesiodic *ainos* demands more than European "common-sense" analysis. Aerodynamically, nightingales are no match for hawks; mythically, they can best them every time, though only a Greek audience, attuned to the mythopoeic convention, might know this. In other words, we do not need to be told that the nightingale is the good bird, or will win this match. On the level of poetic diction, we have a good example of how local knowledge influences interpretation. West notes *ad loc.* that the adjective *poikilodeiron*, "dapple-necked," is inappropriate for the bird in question and better suits the thrush. Good ornithology, but it ignores the far-reaching mythopoetic associations of *poikilos* in Greek. Chief among these is the connection between the "variegation" represented by *poikilos* and the realms of craft and song.[28] In view of the rich background of themes to which the word points, we know that the bird's craft consists in the ability to change its song progressively; its endurance is marked by the ability to sing continuously; and its craftiness emerges from the combination of strength and changefulness. This is, in short, an Odyssean bird; it is not

---

[27]   West 1978, 204.

[28]   On the poetic themes associated with the nightingale and specifically with this adjective, see now the explication in Nagy 1996a, 30–65.

accidental that the epic hero is characterized as *poikilomêtês*, "with variegated cunning" (e.g., *Odyssey* 13.293).

Two more reasons that an audience would read this story as a victory of nightingale over hawk, even though this is never stated, become clear from the text. First, we can read this tale as being about communication. Here it is worthwhile noting a purely linguistic point, the force of *su d'* at line 213. This rare emphatic use makes the personal pronoun in the nominative a contrastive. What the hawk did *not* do is listen. *You*, Perses, should. The hawk does not understand because he and his victim speak different ways: she mourns pitifully (*eleon ... mureto* 205–6), which he misinterprets as "you screeched," *lelêkas*.[29] In effect, the hawk cannot "hear" the nightingale; for the space of the story, the text uses the hawk as focalizer of the action, as we get his view. What he hears, the voice of the nightingale, is never enunciated and gets interpreted by him as something that we know it is not, because he cannot comprehend, knowing as he does only fear and not pity. His rational argument, masked as persuasion—"it's madness to fight against the stronger"—is just as irrational as the nightingale's lament. But lament in the realm of Greek poetry has the advantage of being a powerful shaper of individual reputation and is thus placed in the mouths of the Muses themselves (e.g., *Odyssey* 24.60–62, Achilles' funeral).

Second, as Puelma and others have pointed out, it matters that the bird is specifically called a singer (208), for this key word unites it with the poet performing the poem.[30] I would add that in the pragmatics of oral performance—the performance context that this poem at least mimics, whatever the circumstances of its composition—the singer standing before an audience has unmistakable authority and power. He or she can curtail or expand performance, telling the story this way, now, whatever other versions an audience may have heard. The audience, for the duration of performance, is in the grip of the *aoidos*, as the descriptions of poetic performance in Homer tell us time and again. In purest form, song is overpowering desire, a Siren enchantment.[31] In sum, Hesiod *qua aoidos* does not need to make an overt assertion of his or the nightingale's power: the hawk has already lost, no matter what the fate of the nightingale—because the singer clearly survives in front of us, a sign that "nightingales" and what they say must be right.

---

[29]   A sound better suited to hawks: West 1978 ad loc. cites *Iliad* 22.141.

[30]   Puelma 1972; also, Nagy 1990, 256 and 1992, 66–67.

[31]   This in turn is characterized in images suitable for bird-song: see, e.g., the iconographic tradition of bird-Sirens, on which Neils 1995.

Ultimately, Hesiod's refusal to make an explicit condemnation of the hawk's *hubris* can be read as a magisterial dismissal of hawk and kings, a *damnatio*, from the standpoint of the more clever nightingale/singer.[32]

There is yet more to be found in the deployment of this artful *ainos* that can bring us closer to the distinctiveness of this poem. The detail just mentioned, that the hawk does not listen, is meant, as I said, to sway Perses. Behind this lies the threat of praise and blame, the traditional power of the poet: the *aoidos* will always be around to settle your reputation in the future, no matter what you do to him now. But the Hesiodic strategy is more subtle here, even as it depends on this authority to destroy the authorities. For Hesiod does not now say "listen to *me*" but "listen to *dikê*." It might seem like a sudden jolt to move from the bird's lamenting voice in the *ainos* to some previously unheard and abstract *Dikê*, but the poem makes the metaphorical shift easier for us. *Dikê* is a victimized woman, as we begin to hear at lines 220 ff., and there is a "clamor" (ῥόθος) when she is manhandled. The syntactical parallelism of 208/220 clarifies the bird/woman parallel:

τῇ δ' εἷς ᾗ σ' ἂν ἐγώ περ ἄγω καὶ ἀοιδὸν ἐοῦσαν   208

You are going wherever I shall carry you, even if you
are a singer

τῆς δὲ Δίκης ῥόθος ἑλκομένης ᾗ κ' ἄνδρες ἄγωσι   220

there is a clamor when Justice is dragged where men
carry her off [trans. Most 2006]

To summarize at this point: Hesiod has first used the *ainos* as a foil to separate one audience (Perses) from another (the kings) and encourage his primary addressee by means of the blame he attaches to the secondary group. Then, through the association of nightingale and *Dikê*, he turns his primary addressee into a listener with two functions. On one hand, the command "listen to *Dikê*" means "pay attention to this composition." As we have seen, the method of the poem has been to involve Perses in the message from the start, plunging him into a *neikos*. This equation of the poet's talk with the voice of *Dikê* is made emphatic shortly after the description of the social and natural effects of *dikê* and *hubris* (lines 225–47). For we learn (lines 256–60) that *Dikê* is not only a woman, but a *parthenos*, daughter of Zeus, who reports to him about human injustice. Furthermore, the verb used to

[32]   On this technique in Homeric exchanges, see Martin 1989, 142–43.

describe her speech (γηρύετ') is the same that characterizes the speech of the Muses themselves at *Theogony* 28 (ἀληθέα γηρύσασθαι).[33] On the other hand, now "listen to *Dikê*" has an even more urgent sense, which we can paraphrase: "hear the cry of a woman [*Dikê*] being raped and do something about it." How can Perses fail to respond? By doubling his role (poet/*Dikê*) and that of Perses (listener/rescuer), Hesiod empowers his brother, crediting him with the potential to become a heroic figure of just dealing, like the good king whose land flourishes. More than this, by imagining his addressee as the person who listens to *Dikê*, Hesiod places him on a level with the king of the gods. For it is Zeus who ultimately hears out the complaints of his daughter.

With this elevation, we come full circle to the proem, which I have delayed discussing until now. Again, a marked contrastive provides an entrance into the technique of doubling. Hesiod's hymnic praise of Zeus has concluded with the mention of the god's power to straighten what is crooked and wither the arrogant. Then, in a shift to the imperative, this "constative" description becomes "directive," as Hesiod tells Zeus to fulfill the role he has just outlined (9–10):

> κλῦθι ἰδὼν ἀίων τε, δίκῃ δ'ἴθυνε θέμιστας
> <u>τύνη· ἐγὼ δέ</u> κε Πέρσῃ ἐτήτυμα μυθησαίμην.
>
> Heed, when you have seen and heard, by justice keep straight the ordinances,
> *You*, for your part. But *I* would like to tell Perses the truth.

If Perses, in the sequence that I have outlined, is gradually brought to the point where he can become like Zeus, it is only, at last, to become like his brother, who has already asserted from the start an authority on the level of the supreme arbiter.[34]

You, Too

It is easier to be like a brother than like a father. One already is, genetically. Nothing should come closer, not even a *hetairos*, as Hesiod will say (*Works and Days* 707–12):

---

[33] Compare Hesiod's intent in *Works and Days* 10: ἐγὼ δέ κε Πέρσῃ ἐτήτυμα μυθησαίμην.

[34] On the assertion of authority in this proem, see Nagy 1990, 256–58.

μηδὲ κασιγνήτῳ ἶσον ποιεῖσθαι ἑταῖρον·
εἰ δέ κε ποιήσῃ, μή μιν πρότερος κακὸν ἔρξεις,
μηδὲ ψεύδεσθαι γλώσσης χάριν· εἰ δέ σέ γ᾽ ἄρχῃ
ἤ τι ἔπος εἰπὼν ἀποθύμιον ἠὲ καὶ ἔρξας,
δὶς τόσα τείνυσθαι μεμνημένος· εἰ δέ κεν αὖτις
ἡγῆτ᾽ ἐς φιλότητα, δίκην δ᾽ ἐθέλῃσι παρασχεῖν,
δέξασθαι·

Do not treat a comrade in the same way as your brother: but if you
do, then do not harm him first, nor give him a lying grace with
your tongue; but if he begins, telling you some word contrary to
your spirit or even doing some such thing, then be mindful to
pay him back twice as much. But if he is led once again towards
friendship and decides to offer requital, accept it ...

"We are no longer conscious of Perses as the recipient of this advice," notes
West in his commentary (p. 330). But why not? This brotherly wisdom,
impersonally given, is an effective marker of the hard-won assent of the
addressee to become a listener who can now deal with the "true things" on a
level of abstraction, removed from the distorted world of the *neikos* in which
he had been trapped previously. And it is a sign of Hesiod's confidence in the
conversion that he can risk telling Perses to take double the vengeance on a
brother-like friend who says or does anything wrong. Finally, it is a further
pledge that this fraternal supporter of *dikê* will not, in fact, act wrongly, for,
in the terms set up, to do so would be to curse himself with instant and two-
fold retribution.

I have argued that the choice of the brother-figure enables the poet to
approach as an equal, and persuade, his addressee in a way that the more
familiar guise of tutor or father-figure prevents. We see the poet's persuasion
as it succeeds within the poem because by line 298 it is obvious that he is
able to move on to the specific precepts telling Perses *how* to work, instead
of dwelling on the *need* to work rather than bribe kings or grab goods.[35] The
break is signaled by a three-part coda that once more works as a pair of foils
(lines 293–97):

οὗτος μὲν πανάριστος, ὃς αὐτῷ πάντα νοήσει,
φρασσάμενος τά κ᾽ ἔπειτα καὶ ἐς τέλος ᾖσιν ἀμείνω·
ἐσθλὸς δ᾽ αὖ καὶ κεῖνος, ὃς εὖ εἰπόντι πίθηται·

---

[35]   J. S. Clay 1993, 32–33 is less optimistic about the representation of a successful learning experience on the part of Perses.

ὃς δέ κε μήτ᾽ αὐτὸς νοέῃ μήτ᾽ ἄλλου ἀκούων
ἐν θυμῷ βάλληται, ὁ δ᾽ αὖτ᾽ ἀχρήιος ἀνήρ.

The man who thinks of everything by himself, considering what
will be better, later and in the end—this man is the best of all.
That man is fine too, the one who is persuaded by someone who
speaks well. But whoever neither thinks by himself nor pays heed
to what someone else says and lays it to his heart—that man is
good for nothing.

Of the three characters—the man who thinks independently vs. one who
obeys a good speaker vs. one who does neither—Perses can now be assumed
to have chosen the middle role, encouraged by the ideal of the first and
dissuaded by the last.

To this rhetorical strategy that works on its object by saying "you, too,
can be like me," two further aspects of the *Works and Days* must be compared
in conclusion. Both emerge most clearly in the passage on sailing. First, the
seemingly ironic tone. After detailing the proper storage of gear and seasonable time for sailing (618–32), Hesiod reminds Perses that their father took to
the sea for want of sufficient livelihood and left Aeolian Cyme, "not fleeing
wealth nor riches and happiness" (637)—a wry understatement—only to land
up in Ascra, "bad in winter, wretched in summer, and never good" (640).
More ironic is the admission, after promising to tell of "the *metra* of the sea,"
that Hesiod himself is "not a bit sophisticated when it comes to sailing and
boats" (649: οὔτε τι ναυτιλίης σεσοφισμένος οὔτε τι νηῶν). His only sea experience came from crossing the 65-meter channel over to Euboea. One could
interpret these as testimonia to the power of inspiration, as Hesiod seems to
indicate that we should at 661–62: despite his limited knowledge, the Muses'
teaching allows him to tell the mind of Zeus. At the same time, there is some
humor to the scenario of Perses' being invited to learn sailing from such a self-
confessed landlubber. Whichever way we read these lines, their effect depends
on the *captatio* principle that has characterized the creation of personae all
along in this poem. If the adviser is to be trusted, it is because he, too, has been
there, at the low level of his advisee; starting from nothing, he can now tell all.

From a careful study of diction in this and related passages, Ralph
Rosen has argued that the sailing episode is nothing less than "an *ainigma*
that compares the poetics of *Works and Days* to the poetics of the Homeric
epic."[36] In Rosen's reading, the comparison situates the poetic medium of

---

[36] Rosen 1990, quote on p. 113; see also Nagy 1992, 78–79.

Hesiod at a level below the Homeric, but the right level. Hesiod, in this version, acknowledges that epic poetry can be dangerous, like spring sailing. It is better to be "seasonable" when launching onto the poetic sea. Hesiod, as he represents his craft, has had some success (witness his victory in the funeral games of Amphidamas) in his own small venture.

The strategy that I have been tracing—the self-deprecating, equalizing stance towards a "brother"—may, however, help us read the metapoetic reference of the sailing passage in a somewhat different manner. Note that Hesiod does not directly deprecate the contest itself, only the size of his sea voyage in getting to the games, which is in explicit contrast to the epic voyage of the Achaeans from Aulis (lines 651–53). Nor does he identify the other contestants for the tripod that he brought back to Helicon. But another tradition, which is attested in the *Contest of Homer and Hesiod*, makes it clear that the meeting at Chalcis is a showdown between the exponents of epic and didactic.[37] We have seen already, in the *ainos* of the hawk and nightingale, that certain facts do not require mention in an attuned audience and that *refusal* to mention someone, in this medium, can be a powerful strategy for showing one's superior power. In other words, we need not read Hesiod's "autobiography" here as part of a humble concession that his poetry is second to the ambitious scope of epic. The *Certamen* shows us a performer who is every bit as good as Homer at extemporizing and capping lines. Interestingly, it is the content of Hesiod's song, rather than his versifying, that wins him the tripod, as the judge, King Paneides, decides to make the award to one who sang of peaceful agriculture rather than wars and slaughters (*Certamen* p. 233 Allen). If this thematic division, war vs. peace, has any claim to antiquity (and the design of the shield of Achilles in *Iliad* 18 would suggest so), we are left with two related prospects. First, there is the possibility that the "myth" of Hesiod and his brother Perses, the structural and rhetorical principle for the first part of the *Works and Days*, may itself be a reflection of the traditions of rhapsodic competition that we find stylized in such representations as that in the *Certamen*.[38] It is noteworthy that the *Certamen* story is explicitly opposed to other configurations of literary history in which Homer was said to be younger or older than Hesiod (*Certamen* pp. 226–27 Allen). If either were true, then one poet would inevitably have to be considered the pupil

---

[37] The composition is Hadrianic, but has an excellent claim to contain material from at least the sixth century BCE: see Richardson 1981 and Chapter 7 above.

[38] There may be a similar inscribing of performance traditions into the narrative of the *Iliad* in the mention of Thamyris in *Iliad* 2.594ff., as argued at Martin 1989, 229–30.

or imitator of the other, a relation congruent with the more familiar picture of didactic transmission. If the *Works and Days* was itself composed or at least re-performed in rhapsodic competitions (as appears from Plato's *Ion* 531–32), it would have been all the more powerful if presented as a direct address to a "Perses" who represented not only a "brother" and a general audience in need of instruction, but also the "other" major mode of hexameter performance.

This brings us to a concluding suggestion, again based on the realities of rhapsodic performance. Imagine the live presentation of character that rhapsodes like Ion, certainly (and I suspect composers like "Homer," probably) practiced. Whoever performed the *Odyssey* in something like the form that it now has must, for the space of four books, "become" the *persona* of Odysseus, the hero who sacked Troy ... Τροίης ἱερὸν πτολίεθρον ἔπερσε. Perses, "Wrecker," would be an appropriate nickname for this character; *ptoliporthos* was a generic epithet for Iliadic heroes as well as for Odysseus.[39] Indeed, the entire genre of epic about Troy's fall may be represented metonymically as a tradition about a "sack" (cf. *Iliou Persis*). The beauty of this didactic strategy of creating the brother-as-other is that, in the end, anyone can be adopted by Hesiod—perhaps even his epic-rhapsodic *semblable*.

---

[39] Nagy 1992, 74–75 takes the connection to the destruction of cities in terms relevant to the internal themes of the *Works and Days*, in particular the destructive power of *hubris* in the *polis*. I regard our readings as complementary.

11

HESIOD'S METANASTIC POETICS[1]

The received wisdom about Hesiod's poetics is simple: he is no Homer. His poetry is supposedly rough, awkward, unsophisticated, repetitive, disjointed, a second-best versifier's striving after effect.[2] Too often the rhetoric even of those who respect Hesiodic poetry damns it with faint praise. Readers of the second edition of the *Princeton Encyclopedia of Poetry and Poetics*—to take just one easily available reference that students might consult—learn that Hesiod's "didactic epics" were meant for "the peasant of Boeotia rather than the Ionian aristocrat, being concerned with the morality and beliefs of the small farmer toughly confronting a life of ceaseless labor and few rewards. While they cannot be compared to Homer's works in scope or genius, they often display much poetic power."[3]

It is worth pausing over such influential criticism because essential concerns of poetics are recognized, if only superficially, therein. First, the problematic notion of "genius." What does it mean to identify any poet in this way? And does it make sense at all in the case of Homer, about whom we know nothing, and whose poetic predecessors have left only names? Let us admit that calling Homer a "genius" is, at the least harmful level, merely literary-critical shorthand, and at its least helpful, a dangerous retrojection

---

[1] Originally published in *Ramus* 21, no. 1 (1992): 11–33.

[2] Lamberton 1988b, 144 has a choice selection of such judgments from Kirk and West, which he rightly dismisses. Unfortunately, Solmsen, who edited the widely used Oxford Classical Text (1983), was highly susceptible to such opinions. He questions the authenticity of *Theogony* 775–806, for example, because the passage has to his ear "a smooth elegance quite alien to the genuine Hesiod": see Solmsen 1982, 16.

[3] Trypanis 1974, 326. The revised article on "Greek Poetry" in the most recent edition of this reference work (Greene et al. 2012, 578) reprints, in lieu of Trypanis' paragraphs on Hesiod, the third edition's (1993, 483) only slightly less condescending words by C. J. Herington: "The Hesiodic works show nothing of the architectonic skill of Homer or of his genius for realizing character through speech. They are essentially episodic codifications of ancient lore."

of Romantic ideology.[4] Such language reifies and personalizes certain qualities one associates with the poetry transmitted under Homer's name. Furthermore, the qualities are usually identified impressionistically (a mode of criticism hallowed by Matthew Arnold's essay *On Translating Homer* and practiced by most English critics since).[5] But how do we explain or quantify the "nobility," "plainness," and "rapidity" that Arnold found? Traditional aesthetic appreciation of Homer simply refused, since it was built into Romantic notions that "genius" productions are by definition unanalyzable.

We might next notice how "genius" and "scope" are coordinated in the traditional criticism of Hesiod—which, since antiquity, has always been a by-product of the vexed critical reception of *Homer*. If Homer is somehow "best" because his epics try to enshrine heroic exploits within heroically long poems and to make heroic careers the expression of cosmic struggles, then *of course* Hesiod will never attain Homeric "scope." What is missing in such traditional criticism is a sense of genre. Hesiodic poetry is *not* Homeric epic, or even "epic" at all (a word derived from post-archaic systematizing).[6]

When one says Hesiod composed for peasants, at least it is acknowledged that ancient as well as modern poetry had audiences. Of course, this acknowledgement is employed most often to explain or excuse the poetry's allegedly infelicitous style. But notice the slippage between mention of this imagined ancient audience and talk of "poetic power." Power to affect whom? Us, surely, not Boeotian peasants; which is to say a long line of audiences *like* us, back to antiquity, since we would presumably not even possess any Hesiodic verse were it not transmitted by those who valued it. Yet from what we know about ancient scholarship, such transmission depended on learned poet-critics who resembled Ionian aristocrats much more than Boeotian peasants. What we do know is that these same Alexandrians experimented with the peasant *persona*. If we had no more of Theocritean poetry than the pastoral idylls, no real biographical traditions about the poet, and no Vergil to imitate him, I suspect at least a few modern critiques would denigrate Theocritus' Coan inelegance.

---

[4]   H. Clarke 1981 traces the intricate interplay between such Homer criticism and wider literary critical trends.

[5]   As Warren Anderson points out (1965, 82–86), Arnold's impressions were based on a number of inaccuracies. Goodheart 1984, 3–4 shows how New Criticism continued to stress an Arnoldian reliance on literary "judgment," resulting in an "antitheoretical animus" that "persists in certain English critics who can't resist a sneer every time they utter the word 'theory'."

[6]   For attempts at definition, see Chapter 1 above.

So, either there was a clean cultural break within antiquity, making it possible for sophisticated audiences suddenly to appreciate "rough" Hesiodic poetry (like the Romantic discovery of "Ossian" perhaps?); or the original audience for Hesiodic poetry should no longer be so naively imagined. We have to begin a study of Hesiodic poetics starting with these largest questions, sorting out the several possible "audiences" for Hesiod and following up the leads given by those who have stressed that "Hesiod" himself is largely a traditional *persona*. I believe this will gain us a sense of the distinctiveness and value of Hesiodic poetics.

First, we might point to the audience that the poetry, in the form we have it, *represents* as listening to the performance. In the *Works and Days*, the "kings" and Hesiod's brother Perses have been taken as this audience, because they are directly addressed, but already the picture is more complicated: the voice that gives us the poem is not directly described as a *poetic* voice at all, if we understand the proem to set the pragmatic terms, the audience-listener relations, for the composition (*Works and Days* 1–2):[7]

> Muses of Pieria, who spread fame by songs [ἀοιδῇσι κλείουσαι],
> come here, narrate in detail about [ἐννέπετε] Zeus, making a
> *hymnos* about your father [ὑμνείουσαι] ...

The marked term *ennepete*, as we see from more extensive use in Homeric diction, applies to a speech-act in which one *narrates* something at length and in detail. This important verb is systematically coordinated with another marked term, *mûthos*, "authoritative speech-act," as in the Homeric formula *ennepe mûthon*, which describes how Iris transmitted a warning from Zeus to Hera and Athena (*Iliad* 8.412).[8] Given this precise usage, there is no reason to take the verb at *Works and Days* 2 as a simple synonym for "sing" (*aeidein*), although this activity also is attributed to the Muses in the previous line.[9] The emphasis of *ennepete* is different, more specific; it calls attention to the content, the length, and the authority of a performance. This is to say that the "audience" of the *Works and Days* is, in the first place, all those who hear the Muses' praise of Zeus, including Hesiod and an implied general audience, which may or may not include Perses and the "kings" about whom

---

[7] I shall address in my conclusion the implications of the relative dating of this proem, which Robert Lamberton 1988a has recently argued is late.

[8] For the semantics of *ennepe*, see Martin 1989, 238; for *mûthos*, Martin 1989, 1–42. Other forms of this formula describe commands of Zeus (*Iliad* 11.186) and Nestor (*Iliad* 11.839).

[9] Nagy 1990, 21 makes the same point, contra West, with reference to debate on the development of actual epic performance.

we learn later. Moreover, the audience is not hearing a song so much as a narrative.

Compare the way in which the mutual *story-telling* enjoyed by Nestor and Machaon is described in the *Iliad* (11.642–43):

> When those two, drinking, put off the parching thirst,
> with *mûthoi* they found pleasure narrating [*enepontes*] to one
> another.[10]

Finally, the narrative tells us first about a chief god who himself authorizes the Muses' celebratory singing, their ability to give fame-through-poetry (*kleos*), for it is Zeus who makes mortals famous or obscure (*Works and Days* 3–4). At this point in the proem, Zeus becomes the second "audience" of the poem (9–10):

> κλῦθι ἰδὼν ἀίων τε, δίκῃ δ' ἴθυνε θέμιστας
> τύνη· ἐγὼ δέ κε Πέρσῃ ἐτήτυμα μυθησαίμην.

> Listen, seeing and hearing, by justice make straight the judgements,
> *you.* But *I* would like to make a *mûthos* [*mûthêsaimên*] of true things
> for Perses.

The first few lines, then, of the poem that has been read repeatedly as straightforward Hesiodic autobiography offer a far from simple picture of the poet's audience or function. Hesiod commands the Muses (in contrast with their tart instructions *to him* in the *Theogony* proem, lines 23–35). At the same time, the poet associates Zeus with poetry but distances himself from it, since, as *mûthos*, his composition introduces itself not as musical speech but as authoritative talk, or more exactly, instruction. Now it is worth pointing out that the *Iliad* and *Odyssey* can be similarly contrasted, the former beginning "Sing [*aeide*] goddesss, of the wrath," the latter "Narrate [*ennepe*], Muse, about the man ... ." In this regard, it is interesting that of the two Homeric poems it is the *Odyssey* that contains many close parallels to instructional verses found in Hesiod.[11] We should pay attention to such proemial lexical distinctions because they are our only internal clues to

---

[10] See Martin 1989, 39, where I use the same translation of *mûthoi*. One of the several erroneous claims by Arieti in a review (1992, 87–90) is that I identified *mûthoi* as "set speeches" instead of stories in this scene.

[11] E.g., *Odyssey* 17.347 = *Works and Days* 317; also, the phraseology shared by *Odyssey* 8.170–73 and *Theogony* 88–92, on which see Chapter 12 below; and cf. other examples cited by Edwards 1971, 166–89 and Cantarella 1931, 12–13.

genre-patterning, with no independent ancient testimony obliging us to read all hexameter as "epic" or "song."

Once we thus place at either extreme of the spectrum of Greek hexameter poetry Hesiod's *Works and Days* and Homer's *Iliad*, and contrast their poetics, other differences emerge. (Note that this is *not* to claim priority for one genre or text, or explicit cross-references on the part of either genre.) Most striking is the way in which Hesiodic poetry assumes the stance of an outsider who happens to be allowed inside, exposing the narrator as one who has learned intimately the language of the group but still speaks with the viewpoint of one whose special experiences, emerging from a certain solitude and isolation, locate him on the margin of the community. Paradoxically, from this point he has a clearer view of the center. Thus, the figure of Hesiod embodies the most authoritative source (as in the *Theogony*) but also critic (as in the *Works and Days*) whom one could imagine. I shall argue that this status as "exterior insider," which we see dramatized in the poetry of the *Works and Days* especially, made it possible for ancient traditions, already operative in the *Works and Days*, to represent Hesiod as a *metanastês*, one who has moved into a new community. Herodotus and others would later use the figure of Anacharsis the Scythian "sage" who visited Greece, for the same effect.[12] "Metanastic" poetics is the voice of the immigrant; but it is also the technique of the mystic who returns, as a stranger in his own land, to tell about what he knows. In what follows, I shall concentrate on the poetics of the *Works and Days*, showing how the "metanastic" stance helps us to understand such smaller-scale features as the poem's rhetorical structures, sub-genres, and even diction and dialect variations. Once the poetics of this most distinctive Hesiodic composition are sketched, we can compare the results with the poetics of the *Theogony*.[13]

This century's rediscovery of a rich ancient Near Eastern literature in Sumerian, Akkadian, Hittite, Ugaritic, and several other languages has made it easier to identify the genre of the *Works and Days* as a "wisdom" composition. Yet, as one can discern in Martin West's helpful (though incomplete) survey of such literature, the form of wisdom compositions varies so widely that assignment to the genre by no means settles all the questions regarding

---

[12] On the usefulness of Anacharsis, see Hartog 1988, 64–82 and Kindstrand 1981.

[13] To extend the argument to the *Scutum* would require a demonstration that the poem is as much "Hesiod's" as the *Works and Days* and *Theogony*, an assertion I am not prepared to make: see further Chapter 13 below.

the poetics of a given work.[14] The most obvious gain for interpreting the *Works and Days* is oddly enough, an advance that many Hellenists, including West, still adamantly resist: that we should consider the poem's narrator and addressee to be entirely fictional conventions inextricable from the genre. The positivist historicism that refuses to acknowledge the *persona* in Hesiod feeds on the old genius/peasant dichotomy that I mentioned above.[15] It also relies on misuse of comparative typology: West follows Nicolai and others in asserting that, because the *Works and Days* narrator addresses his brother, rather than a son or prince (the usual generic addressees), Perses must be a "real" person.[16] This conclusion further props up several exercises of faulty logic. One favorite argument is along the lines of West's comment that "it would be exceptional for a pretend person to be addressed by one who is just what he seems to be, namely Hesiod—and no one supposes Hesiod himself to be an assumed character."[17] So Perses, on this account, is not a *persona* because brothers are not conventional in the genre and Hesiod is not a *persona* because Perses isn't. Another version comes from Bernard Knox, who thinks "no one has gone so far as to doubt the existence" of Hesiod's father "and it seems unlikely that Hesiod would add a fake brother to a real father." Yet another twist is Peter Green's assertion that "no one supposes that Hesiod invented himself; and since his personal relationships stand at the heart of the *Works and Days*, it is hard to believe, from the circumstantial evidence he offers, that he has saddled himself with a fictitious father and brother for the occasion."[18]

---

[14] West 1978, 3–22. I miss in his listing any compositions from the Americas and East Asia. In what follows, if I should seem to confront most often West's positions, it is because he is usually a learned and recent formulator of any Hesiodic problem. As an example of complications suggested by comparative material, note West 1978, 7 on genre-crossing within hymnic and admonitory compositions.

[15] This is linked to the Idealist strain in modern German classical criticism and thus again ultimately to Romantic views: see Griffith's excellent analysis, 1983, 37–41.

[16] West 1978, 34; yet even West 1978, 15 cites *Mahabharata* 3.148–49 without claiming that Hanumat or his brother, whom he there advises, is "real." Signs of the usual father-figure/"son" dramatic frame are evident in the *Works and Days'* use of *nêpios*-addresses: see Pellizer 1972, 38–42. Griffith 1983, 55–57 treats the brother-motif as a subtle innovation in the traditional dramatic framing of wisdom works.

[17] West 1978, 34.

[18] Green 1984, 22; Knox 1989, 7. Stein 1990, 26 uses the "real" father argument to claim that Perses is real, then on p. 44 claims that if Perses is a *persona*, the father has to be real because Hesiod (who is not a *persona*) would not have doubled *personae* by making the father one. Similar logic bedevils Zanker 1986, 26–36, who argues (p. 26 n. 4) that Hesiod relies on the Muses for instruction

Rather than play this desperate game to defend a "real" Hesiod, a few modern critics have returned to explore the possibilities of interpretation arising from reading Hesiod and his kin as *personae*, a suggestion as old as Friedrich Welcker's 1826 edition of Theognis. Certainly the evidence of the Theognidean corpus, along with what we know of no longer extant "advice" (*hupothêkai*) compositions, which put wisdom in the mouths of Cheiron the Centaur, Nestor, or ancient sages, points toward fictional dramatization in this genre *within Greek*, just as in the Near Eastern works.[19] Gregory Nagy's further demonstration that the very name Hesiod means "one who emits the voice," (1982b) leads one to see the poet as a generic figure who embodies the singing power of the Muses. Once we are allowed to compare Hesiod and Hesiodic dramatization not with other "authors," but with other traditional characters and situations within Greek literature, avenues of approach open up to rich thematic parallels, such as the presentation of the "beggar" Odysseus in his quarrel (*eris*) with Eurymachus at *Odyssey* 18.366–75.[20] The story of how Hesiod's father left Cyme in Asia Minor and settled in Boeotia can be reinterpeted in terms of its appropriateness to the themes of wealth, outrage (*hubris*), and justice (*dikê*), which lie at the heart of the *Works and Days*.[21] The advice on seafaring given by Hesiod at *Works and Days* 618–94 can be read as a highly artful, even enigmatic expression of one genre's self-presentation vis-à-vis Homeric epic.[22] The prominence of the "Hymn to Hecate" (*Theogony* 411–49) need no longer be attributed to some personal cult of a historical Hesiod's family; its function, as poetry that highlights and completes the praise of Zeus's reign, can now emerge.[23]

In short, abandoning the positivists' search for the "real" Hesiod is crucial if we are to put poetics first. Then we might appreciate Hesiod as "a mask for many anonymous voices, all trained, and trained well, over generations to sound the same, to speak with the same identity, and to pass on the same traditions," and we might explore further the way in which the

---

in navigating (his only experience in sailing being the 65-metre crossing from Aulis to Euboea), but does not talk of the Muses' help for farming-instructions, therefore must have been a farmer.

[19]   West 1978, 24–25 has a list, now expanded and interpreted by Kurke 1990.

[20]   Nagy 1992, 37–82, esp. 47–41, 70–71.

[21]   Nagy 1992, 72–76. Griffith 1983, 61–62 notes the father's function as a negative paradigm, thus an innovation vs. the usual father-function in the wisdom genre.

[22]   As Rosen 1990, 99–113 has shown.

[23]   See Griffith 1983, 53–55.

"autobiographical" remarks of the poet "always serve a specific and necessary function within the contexts in which they occur."[24]

Actually, we do not have to go beyond early Greek poetry to find analogies to the sort of wisdom composition represented by the *Works and Days*. A number of critics have found in the long speech of Phoenix to Achilles in the *Iliad* (9.434–603) a close parallel to the mixture of direct personal address, exhortations to listen to wisdom, and persuasive rhetoric one sees in Hesiod.[25] Phoenix, like Hesiod, narrates elaborate mythical exempla (Meleager: *Iliad* 9.524–99; compare *Works and Days* stories of Prometheus, Pandora, and the Five Ages). He vividly represents the wrinkled, lame Prayers (*Litai*) and swift-footed Destruction (*Atê*) in allegories that recall the mistreated Justice (*Dikê*) at *Works and Days* 220–24 and 256–63, as well as personifications of Destruction, Hunger, Shame, and Retribution, among others (cf. *Works and Days* 200–37 generally). And he prefaces his speech with a personal story, the quarrel he had with his father over a mistress, which drove him to flee his country.[26] It is this last feature that I wish to concentrate on, for I believe it helps us find a tighter link between Hesiodic poetics and the Hesiodic persona than has been recognized previously.

Let us grant that the general function of such autobiographical recollections, in both the speech of Phoenix and the *Works and Days*, parallels that of the *hypomnêsis* in Greek and Latin prayer-style as "a reminder of a special connection between speaker and addressee."[27] If his rhetoric contains such striking resemblances to Hesiod's, what should we make of the specific details of Phoenix's career? The point of his story is to reaffirm the close affection he has with Achilles. Thus, he positions himself in lines 438–41 as a father-figure, recalling that he was sent by Peleus to watch over Achilles because the young hero is *nêpios* "ignorant" and untried in war and speaking-assemblies (*agoreôn*). At this point we can notice two parallels already to Hesiod. The poet of the *Works and Days* brings up an "autobiographical"

---

[24] The first of these elegant formulations is by Lamberton 1988, 35, the second by Griffith 1983, 38.

[25] Jaeger 1945, 66 notes in passing that the *Works and Days* is a "huge admonitory speech" and thus uses myths as Homeric speeches do; I do not agree, however, with Jaeger's view that Hesiod borrows the technique from Homer, since it is more likely a genre of discourse used independently by both composers: see the model given in Martin 1984a. The assumption of borrowing detracts from the careful analysis of the passages by Schmidt 1986, who discusses the earlier studies by Diller and Munding.

[26] André Lardinois points out (personal communication) that this story also is paradigmatic and mirrors the quarrel between Achilles and Agamemnon over Briseis, contra Schmidt 1986, 96–124.

[27] Griffith 1983, 56.

reminiscence about a father both he and his addressee knew. Speaking of the need to wait for the right sailing season, he recalls (*Works and Days* 633–34):

ὥς περ ἐμός τε πατὴρ καὶ σός, μέγα νήπιε Πέρση,
πλωίζεσκ' ἐν νηυσί, βίου κεχρημένος ἐσθλοῦ·

Thus my father and yours, very ignorant [*nêpie*] Perses,
used to sail in ships, lacking a noble livelihood.

Moreover, the addressee is described as "ignorant" (*nêpios*), although in the *Iliad* scene the description fits a former stage of Achilles' life, whereas Perses is even now in need of instruction about proper behavior.

Phoenix does not call to mind only Achilles' father. As the exhortation continues, he shifts to the recollection of his own father, Amyntor, who once cursed him with infertility because, at the urging of his aggrieved mother, Phoenix slept with the older man's mistress (*Iliad* 9.448–61). Having broken out from his father's guarded house, Phoenix made his way to Phthia and Peleus, he recalls. Significantly, Achilles' father "received me eagerly and loved me as a father loves his son, his only son [*mounon*], last-born, to many possessions." With this detail, we might compare the ideal household envisioned by Hesiod's precept (*Works and Days* 376–77):

μουνογενὴς δὲ πάις εἴη πατρώιον οἶκον
φερβέμεν· ὣς γὰρ πλοῦτος ἀέξεται ἐν μεγάροισιν·

May there be an only-born son to care for the paternal home.
That way wealth grows in the halls.

Within the *Works and Days*, of course, this ideal of preserving familial property makes sense in the speech of one who has had a bitter dispute about patrimony with his brother. If we read the Phoenix story with this in mind, it appears that the old advisor experienced the situation that the Hesiodic viewpoint can only wistfully recommend. Or, put another way, Phoenix describes his personal biography in rhetoric that uses the themes of a *Works and Days* desideratum.[28] Furthermore, in his flight into a new country, Phoenix finds the wealth that Hesiod's father failed to get. "He [Peleus] made me rich

---

[28] Nagy 1992, 76–77 connects the *mounogenes* theme with the figure of Hecate in the *Theogony* (only-born daughter of another "Perses") and the story of the two Erides. It is clear that the theme was important enough to create a nexus of mythical representations, which makes it more likely that an audience would appreciate its appearance in the Phoenix story.

[*aphneion*] and gave me a great troop," he says (9.483). Contrast *Works and Days* 635–40:

ὅς ποτε καὶ τῆδ' ἦλθε πολὺν διὰ πόντον ἀνύσσας,
Κύμην Αἰολίδα προλιπὼν ἐν νηὶ μελαίνῃ,
οὐκ ἄφενος φεύγων οὐδὲ πλοῦτόν τε καὶ ὄλβον,
ἀλλὰ κακὴν πενίην, τὴν Ζεὺς ἄνδρεσσι δίδωσιν.
νάσσατο δ' ἄγχ' Ἑλικῶνος ὀιζυρῇ ἐνὶ κώμῃ,
Ἄσκρῃ, χεῖμα κακῇ, θέρει ἀργαλέῃ, οὐδέ ποτ' ἐσθλῇ.

The one who arrived here crossing a great sea
after leaving Kyme in Aeolia by black ship,
not fleeing wealth [*aphenos*] or riches and prosperity
but evil poverty, which Zeus gives men.
He settled near Helicon in a wretched village
Ascra, bad in winter, rough in the heat, and never good.

Phoenix is technically a *metanastês*. Therefore, it is appropriate that he lives not in the center but at the margin of Peleus' realm, as he says (*naion eskhatiên Phthiês*) in a comment coming immediately after his mention of his new riches. Structurally, his description of his flight and settlement thus parallels Hesiod's description of his father's move from Asia Minor. (Compare line-initial *naion* "I was living" at *Iliad* 9.484 with *nassato*, "he lived," same position, *Works and Days* 639.)

Many readers, from Aeschylus on, have been charmed by the remarkable appeal that Phoenix makes in the last lines (485–95) of his "autobiography," in which he recalls his care for the toddler Achilles and acknowledges the emotional compensation he derived from the boy.[29] Ironically, this beloved substitute son, Achilles, seems also to have constructed an image for his *own* condition based on his acquaintance with Phoenix, just as Phoenix defines himself here in terms of his relation to Achilles. For Achilles is the only speaker in Homeric poetry to use the word *metanastês* and does so first in this scene. He begins his reply to the last embassy appeal by Ajax by alluding to his anger (*kholos*) at the way Agamemnon has mistreated him, "like some sort of honorless immigrant" (*metanastês—Iliad* 9.646–48). The dramatic situation adds to the force of Achilles' words, since the first character in the poem to have described himself as a true *metanastês* (albeit without using the term) is sitting within earshot.

---

[29]   Cf. the nurse's speech in *Choephoroe* (lines 748–62).

The word appears only one other time in Homer, in a repetition of this line addressed by Achilles to Patroclus (16.59). Is it a coincidence that Patroclus happens to be the only other *metanastês* to tell his immigration story in the poem? We learn it later, when his *psûkhê* visits Achilles to appeal for funeral rites; the discourse situation is thus like that of Phoenix's speech, as Patroclus begs not to be left alone after death, but to have his bones mingled with Achilles' in one urn (23.83–84, 91; cf. 9.437-38). This emotional appeal forms a ring-composition around its rhetorical "proof," the "autobiography" in which it emerges that Patroclus fled his own country because he killed a boy—"the son of Amphidamas"—in anger over a dice-game (*Iliad* 23.85–90). Like Phoenix, Patroclus recalls his own father (Menoitios, who brought him as a boy to Phthia), the kindness of Achilles' father (who received him and made him Achilles' *therapôn*), and the theme of "ignorance" (his own at the time of the manslaughter: *nêpios*, 23.88). In sum, we are dealing here with an archaic poetic *topos*.[30] Phoenix and Patroclus supplicate Achilles by establishing their bond with him, made possible by his father's behavior when they had emigrated to Phthia. Their extra-legal status at the time offered an extreme test case; as we can discern from Achilles' phrase, the *metanastês* was typically and understandably "without honor" (*atimêtos*). Part of the implicit message to Achilles is that he should now, like Peleus, gracefully meet the challenge of similar extreme cases. Achilles' use of the word *metanastês*, on the other hand, shows that he elicits sympathy by conjuring up his addressee's worst fears: if not for his father, they, too, might have been scorned.

What does this *topos* mean for Hesiod's composition? I am suggesting, first of all, that even in its smallest details, especially that of his father's career, the *persona* of Hesiod is a *traditional* way of framing the type of "exhortation to wisdom" poetry embodied in the *Works and Days*. More evidence of the traditional associations of this *topos* helps us appreciate the integral nature of other parts of Hesiod's poem. Strabo (9.5.18) attributes to Demetrius of Scepsis a tradition that Phoenix chose to flee to Phthia

---

[30] "Archaic" not just because it already shows formal patterning in Homer, like a type-scene, but also because it shows signs of affiliation with the Indo-European institution of fosterage. Appeals made to the hero Cúchulainn in the Old Irish *Cattle-Raid of Cooley* use fosterage-ties as a similar basis for appeals. Mühlestein 1981, 85–91 notices the generic appropriateness of the names of Phoenix's kin for a figure who "rouses" (cf. Ormenos) Achilles to "ward off" (cf. Amyntor) attack. Bannert 1981, 91 notes the parallels in the careers of Phoenix and Patroclus without attributing importance to their metanastic status. Ephorus (FGrHist F 100) said that Hesiod's father left Cyme after killing a kinsman, a tradition resembling that attached to Patroclus and to yet another advisor-figure, Theoclymenus (*Odyssey* 15.224). And Odysseus, as well as being the prototypical outsider on his *nostos*, was said to have fled to Italy after being condemned by the Ithacans for manslaughter of the suitors: Aristotle fr. 507 Rose = Plutarch *Quaestiones Graecae* 14.

because his grandfather Ormenos had founded it. The story goes that Ormenos had two sons, Amyntor (father of Phoenix) and Euaemon, father of Eurypylus. The shared right to succession (*diadokhê koinê*) was given over to Phoenix's cousin *because* Phoenix left his country. In other words, the lore about Phoenix combines the equivalents of Hesiod's father (as *metanastês*) and Hesiod himself (dispossessed of his rightful share).[31] This suggests to me that these two themes within the *Works and Days* have an underlying link: it is the disaster of immigration that problematizes patrimony. Some might object that Hesiod is, in fact, not himself a *metanastês*.[32] While it is true that he never tells whether he is a first-generation Boeotian or not, another piece of lore concerning this theme reminds us that the consistent Greek representation of father-son bonds puts the question in a different light. Pausanias, explaining why before the return of the Dorians only those Peloponnesians in Argos and Sparta were called Achaeans, reports that it was because Achaeus' sons Archander and Architeles emigrated from Phthiotis to Argos, where Archander stayed. And Archander, the actual immigrant (who came *from* the precise area that Phoenix fled *to*) gave the name *Metanastês* to his *son*, an event which Pausanias reads as Archander's claim to settle the new land (*Description of Greece* 7.1.6). Whether Hesiod is first or second-generation off the boat is thus moot.

We have seen that the metanastic perspective unites themes that are not overtly connected in Hesiodic poetry. The themes did not *have* to be, if we believe that these were traditionally related and that an audience was used to their mutual relation. For a later audience of Athenians, a people whose local mythology affirmed that they alone of Greeks were not immigrants (μοῦνοι δὲ ἐόντες οὐ μετανάσται Ἑλλήνων, Herodotus *Histories* 7.161.18–19), the metanastic perspective formed an integral part of dramatic, historical, and oratorical conceptualizations of "Greekness."[33] The work of Herodotus can be read, in part, within this framework, especially when we consider the thematic force of the final scene of Book 9 (122.5). In this carefully placed anecdote, Cyrus, the Persian king, is remembered as having once resisted his advisors. When they complained of inhabiting a small, rough country

---

[31] The detail about Eurypylus opens new perspectives on *Iliad* 11.809–48, the scene in which he is healed by Patroclus (who resembles Phoenix, as we have seen) using medical skills that Cheiron (another wisdom-poetry narrator) taught Achilles. One could read the scene as a vindication of Phoenix by proxy.

[32] But note the *Vita* by Tzetzes and the *Suda* entry (s.v. "Hesiodos") assume he emigrated with his family: texts in Jacoby 1930, 112, 114.

[33] As can be seen from the passages cited in Welskopf 1985, cols. 1166–72.

and suggested moving to a better (μεταναστάντες ἐκ ταύτης ἄλλην σχῶμεν ἀμείνω), he advised them (παραίνεε) that to do so would mean eventual subjection to others, since "soft" men came from soft places. At first glance, the pragmatics of this exchange may appear to be the reverse of what I have been sketching, since the advisor-figure, here himself a king, speaks to his own people and refuses to be a *metanastês*, even though his advice closely resembles the immigrant Hesiod's preference for restraint instead of appropriation, as in the poet's characterization of the greedy "kings" as fools who do not know "how much more is half than the whole or how much benefit comes in mallow and asphodel" (*Works and Days* 40–41). But of course this criticism of Persian expansion is an indirect praise of a traditional Greek sense of limit and "Cyrus" is a Herodotean persona, a wise advisor who *is* foreign to the intended *external* audience of the composition.

Looking briefly at the lore surrounding a similar Herodotean metanastic persona, Anacharsis the Scythian, we might see, first, that there are even more themes in the *Works and Days* appropriate to the generic "outsider," and second, that the speech-habits associated with such wise immigrants can help us understand the poetic structure of Hesiod's didactic composition. Anacharsis, son of a royal Scythian and Greek mother, spoke both languages and thus could criticize either culture.[34] His critique of Greek behavior at many points resembles the Hesiodic stance: his caution against the tongue, for example, as the "best and worst" part of a person can be compared to Hesiod's depiction of language at *Works and Days* 719–21, where the tongue is called the "best storehouse" for humans when used sparingly.[35] Like Hesiod, he was said to have written about simplicity of life.[36] More intriguing are the quite specific parallels between the stories about these two moralists. Both have problems with their brothers: Anacharsis was said to be the brother of the king of Scythia and was killed by him while they were out hunting together, because his brother did not like his newly acquired Hellenism. Some reported that he was slain while performing Greek rites (Herodotus *Histories* 4.76, Diogenes Laertius *Lives of the Philosophers* 1.102).[37] Again, like the Hesiodic persona (*Works and Days* 618–49), Anacharsis has a low opinion of sailing: he said the hull's four-finger width showed how

---

[34] Herodotus *Histories* 4.76–77 is the earliest source; full testimonia are in Kindstrand 1981.

[35] See Kindstrand 1981, 53–54; cf. *Works and Days* 321–26.

[36] Kindstrand 1981, 61–65, detailing a tradition found from Ephorus on.

[37] Kindstrand 1981, 10–11 explores the evidence. The Herodotean account may place the death near a grove of Hecate, reminding one of the close relation between poet and goddess in the *Theogony*.

close was death for passengers and called those vessels safest that had been hauled ashore (Diogenes Laertius 1.103–4). The Scythian's suspicion about sailing is probably tied to a negative view of mercantile trading in the *agora*, which Anacharsis is represented (Diogenes Laertius 1.105) as equating with mutual deception. We can compare once again the Hesiodic preference for subsistence farming over the dangers of sea trading (and also against hanging about the *agora—Works and Days* 28–32).[38]

If Anacharsis gives us another evolutionary stage, as it were, of an essentially similar mode of moral critique, it becomes more interesting that this figure brings with him a traditional verbal style. Here the representations of narrative lore and the conventions of poetics meet. Diogenes Laertius (1.101) records that the manner of Anacharsis gave rise to a proverb—"speech from the Scythians"—because he was outspoken (διὰ τὸ παρρησιαστὴς εἶναι). "Outspokenness" or "free-speaking" (*parrhesia*) was, of course, well known as a valued concomitant of Athenian democracy.[39] The association between this style of speaking and "outsiders" like Anacharsis originates in the special stance that certain figures on the margin are enabled, by their position, to assume. Within the *Iliad*, the blame-filled Thersites, marginalized by his ugly appearance and hate-relationship with the major heroes (*Iliad* 2.215–20), functions as a constant critic of the Achaean leadership. The harsh treatment he receives at the hands of Odysseus nevertheless does not disguise the essential truth, albeit exaggerated, of his denunciation of Agamemnon. For our investigation it is important to notice that his outspoken speech, viewed by epic as abuse (cf. *neikee—Iliad* 2.224) matches at several points the advice-poetry of Hesiod: both Hesiod and Thersites offer unwelcome remarks to kings; both are described as verbally adept (Thersites as "clear-voiced speaker," *ligus agoretês, Iliad* 2.246; cf. the comparison of poet and nightingale in fable at *Works and Days* 208); both are defeated by a stronger opponent on the side of the kings.[40]

Phoenix, another *metanastês*, as we have seen, also is permitted *parrhesia* on the grounds of his close relationship with Achilles; the scholiast on *Iliad*

---

[38] For explication of the way in which this Anacharsis story represents an old aristocratic *Greek* ideal, seen also in advice poetry of Theognis, see Kurke 1989. She notes (p. 538 n. 9) that Hesiod, unlike Anacharsis, does not denigrate trade so much as warn against dangers of the sea.

[39] See Ober 1989, 296–97, 322 with further bibliography there.

[40] For extended comparison of the poet of *Works and Days* and Thersites, see Puelma 1972; also, remarks of Zanker 1986, 33. The similarities make sense when we realize that the Thersites figure fits the conventions of an old tradition of blame-poetry, seen elsewhere in Archilochean *iambos*: see Nagy 1999b, 253–64. Hesiod would then be employing the poetics of a widely known genre.

9.496 refers to his use of "the frankness of upbringing" (ἡ τῆς ἀνατροφῆς παρρησία) in persuading his ward. His freedom of speaking on the basis of his outside status is thus doubly determined, as Phoenix is neither a full member of the local in-group nor of Achilles' family. Different as these two Iliadic characters may appear, blamer of kings on one hand, advisor of heroes on the other, the depiction of their *parrhesia* allows us to apply an archaic, native poetic model to Hesiod.

"Outspokenness," I suggest, is actually both a social phenomenon and a Greek literary style. As the latter, it best describes the open-ended, all-embracing structure of Hesiodic verse. The overriding structural fact of Phoenix's speech at *Iliad* 9.434–605 is its blend of several distinct narrative genres: personal appeal based on a shared memorate (434–45), autobiography (435–95), allegory and personification in an *ainos* (495–514), mythic narrative (524–99). I pointed out above that the *Works and Days* happens to feature a similar genre mix. Now I return to this point having offered an explanation in terms of larger themes within Greek literature and having given this speaking strategy a name: the quality that critics have noticed in Phoenix's advice and Hesiod's poem is not an *accidental* similarity, but a basic convention of the *parrhesia* that both speakers are entitled to by reason of their metanastic status. In other words, "free-speaking" implies that the speaker is so impassioned as to use every available mode of persuasion. If this speech happens to be criticism and is viewed from the unwilling recipient's standpoint, we see it described as *neikos* "blame," but its fullness and seeming haphazardness still persist: Thersites knew "many words in his mind, disorderly, random, not according to order (ἄκοσμά τε πολλά τε ᾔδη μάψ, ἀτὰρ οὐ κατὰ κόσμον) for contending with kings" (*Iliad* 2.213–14).[41]

We should compare this epic description of Thersites' rhetoric with some evaluations made of Hesiod's own style. The alleged lack of overt logical connection in the *Works and Days* that Eric Havelock attributed variously to Hesiod's entrapment by familiar formulas, partial memory of the *Iliad*, or pre-philosophical thought is characterized by another critic, Martin West as "mental hops, skips, and jumps," and a "hotchpotch," while B. M. W. Knox adduces Hesiod's lack of an architectonic quality he claims to find in Homeric epic and complains, regarding Hesiodic use of arguments, "if one

---

[41] It is significant corroboration that Old Comedy, which describes itself in terms of *parrhesia*, presents a similar generic mix (lyric, invective, myth) and creates similar interpretive problems for critics uncomfortable with its open-ended structure.

doesn't fully explain the facts, he will give us two."[42] The Homeric poet's critique of Thersitean *parrhesia* makes sense from the aristocratic standpoint of the genre; but modern criticism of the closely related Hesiodic speaking style has failed to understand that fullness, apparent digressiveness, and genre mixing are *positive* poetic values, virtual identification marks that cue an audience into an important genre of speaking. The problems—if there are any—of Hesiodic "structure" have to be read within the demands of a genre that may have had more in common with Roman satire than Greek epic.[43]

The most important poetic strategy for constructing such an open-ended advice composition as the *Works and Days* is the inclusion of a number of other genres. One such type, the coded message of the fable (*ainos*), has been the focus of much good work recently and needs no further explication here.[44] Instead, I wish to point out how we might discover pervasive adaptations of two other separate genres in the *Works and Days*—songs and proverbs—once we allow that the poem's own generic conventions make room for such re-shapings. The only other prerequisite for an appreciation of Hesiod's technique is that one understand how a poet working in a traditional oral medium can adapt diction and meter, interweaving genres at will, with virtuosic skill and flexibility. The detailed study of living oral poetries convinces one that this is the case.[45] Investigation of how generic adaptations take place in actual oral performances can thus converge with the growing critical awareness that Hesiodic poetry represents an oral art.[46]

In at least one dimension, the representation of himself within his poem, Hesiod is more like a lyric poet than Homer.[47] It is especially interesting,

[42] Havelock 1966, 62–63; West 1976, 385; West 1981, 65; Knox 1989, 5, 18. An important exception is the work of Broccia 1969, 41–51, which shows the subtle topical critique accomplished by this sort of Hesiodic "doubling" rhetoric. Recently, Hamilton 1989, 77 has explicated a "subtle but noticeable series of echoes articulating the main parts of the *Works and Days*."

[43] See R. Hunt 1981.

[44] See Nagy 1990, 57, 256 and 1999, 222–41.

[45] From the rich recent scholarship demonstrating this flexibility, I single out in particular Connelly 1986; Slyomovics 1987; J. M. Foley 1991.

[46] For the first fully developed demonstration of this discovery, see Edwards 1971; also Hoekstra 1957. Peabody 1975 offers a detailed attempt at reading *Works and Days* as oral poetry on the level of the structure of the "song" as a whole. On the level of phrasing, see Minton, 1975. As another oralist, Patrizia Mureddu, notes (1983), Parry 1930, 90–91 had already suggested that Hesiod as well as Homer composed in oral style. Delay in following up this insight has stemmed partly from critical disagreement over the value of formula-counting, and indeed, the definition of a formula. There is still much work to be done on evaluation of repeated diction in Hesiod: see Fernández Delgado 1982.

[47] Stein 1990, 1 notes the resemblance, but it does not necessarily follow that this seemingly personal voice reflects use of writing by Hesiod and also a later stage of composition than Homeric

then, to find close verbal resemblance between parts of the *Works and Days* and lyric poetry actually attested. A prime example of this overlap comes in the description of the height of summer (*Works and Days* 582–88):

> Ἦμος δὲ σκόλυμός τ' ἀνθεῖ καὶ ἠχέτα τέττιξ
> δενδρέῳ ἐφεζόμενος λιγυρὴν καταχεύετ' ἀοιδὴν
> πυκνὸν ὑπὸ πτερύγων, θέρεος καματώδεος ὥρῃ,
> τῆμος πιόταταί τ' αἶγες, καὶ οἶνος ἄριστος,   585
> μαχλόταται δὲ γυναῖκες, ἀφαυρότατοι δέ τοι ἄνδρες
> εἰσίν, ἐπεὶ κεφαλὴν καὶ γούνατα Σείριος ἄζει,
> αὐαλέος δέ τε χρὼς ὑπὸ καύματος ... .

When the artichoke flowers and the shrill cicada
perched on a tree pours down clear song
dense, from its wings, in the time of tough heat,
then goats are fattest, wine is best,
women most wanton, men most weak,
since Sirius parches head and knees,
And from the heat the skin is dry ...

Hesiod goes on at 589–96 to construct a picture of a *locus amoenus*, where one can relieve the day's heat with breeze and shade, food and wine. The drinking motif and other details link this passage with Alcaeus F 347 (Voigt), as noticed by commentators from the time of Proclus (iii 281 Gaisford):

> τέγγε πλεύμονας οἴνῳ, τὸ γὰρ ἄστρον περιτέλλεται,
> ἀ δ' ὥρα χαλέπα, πάντα δὲ δίψαισ' ὑπὰ καύματος,
> ἄχει δ' ἐκ πετάλων ἄδεα τέττιξ ...
> ἄνθει δὲ σκόλυμος, νῦν δὲ γύναικες μιαρώταται
> λέπτοι δ' ἄνδρες, ἐπεὶ < > κεφάλαν καὶ γόνα Σείριος   5
> ἄσδει

Drench the lungs with wine, for the star returns.
The season is harsh, all is thirsty from the heat,
the sweet cicada shrills from the leaves.
The artichoke flowers and now women are most damnable,
and men weak, since Sirius parches the head and knees.

The poems' shared diction need not, however, mean that one poet copied the other; as J. T. Hooker has seen, both can draw independently on a store

---

epic; nor do I think we must immediately assume that Hesiodic verse is "gattungsmässig völlig anders" than lyric (p. 3). For fuller comparison, see Arrighetti 1975, 5–36.

of related phrases and themes.[48] In fact, I believe we can go a step further. On a comparative basis, such detailed elaboration about the dangers and delights of a season is not easy to parallel in other didactic poems, but it does have a congener in song traditions: we might think of the Middle English poem "Somer is i-comen in, loude syng cuckow ..." (MS Harley 978). A more extensive parallel is provided by folk poetry from Russia, where a strong tradition of seasonal folk songs and "calendar-songs" (*koljadki*) has survived into the twentieth century and been widely collected. The Russian songs are marked by often enigmatic language and by a relationship to folk rituals: they are the texts for performances involving traditional actions as well as words. The mention of idealized seasonal conditions—abundance of cattle and grain, prosperity of the house—occurs in a context of "wish-incantation," according to specialists.[49] In brief, I propose that Hesiod incorporated into his hexameter verse the language of a seasonal *song* he knew, one that survived in another stylization by Alcaeus, in what may have been an older metrical and linguistic shape.

Another section of Hesiod's poem might be further interpreted through comparison with folk song, specifically the Rhodian swallow song attested in Athenaeus (PMG 848). The Hesiod passage (*Works and Days* 504—25) delineates the rigors of the month Lenaion, when all the days are "ox-flaying" cold and Boreas blows through trees and glens, hide and hair, but does not affect a desirable girl at home (519–25):

> καὶ διὰ παρθενικῆς ἁπαλόχροος οὐ διάησιν,
> ἥ τε δόμων ἔντοσθε φίλῃ παρὰ μητέρι μίμνει,   520
> οὔπω ἔργα ἰδυῖα πολυχρύσου Ἀφροδίτης,
> εὖ τε λοεσσαμένη τέρενα χρόα καὶ λίπ' ἐλαίῳ
> χρισαμένη μυχίη καταλέξεται ἔνδοθι οἴκου,
> ἤματι χειμερίῳ, ὅτ' ἀνόστεος ὃν πόδα τένδει
> ἔν τ' ἀπύρῳ οἴκῳ καὶ ἤθεσι λευγαλέοισιν·   525

And he does not blow through the tender-skinned girl,
who stays in her house with her dear mother,
not yet aware of golden Aphrodite's works,

---

[48] Hooker 1977, 80–81. Nagy 1990, 462–63 notes that the metrical variation reinforces Hooker's argument. The old view of Page 1955, 305–6 and others that Alcaeus "translated" Hesiod is unfortunately continued in Meyerhoff 1984, 158–60.

[49] For texts in Russian, see Poltoratzky 1964, 27–40. On the function of *koljadki*, see Sokolov 1950, 180–85 and Chicherov 1975, 113–22. Erren 1990, 190–91 sees the *Works and Days* as a new blend of political rhetoric and a type of calendar poetry that he traces to Sumerian literature.

> her soft skin well bathed, anointed with oil,
> she lies down in the inner room of the house
> on a winter's day, when the boneless one gnaws
> his own foot, in his fireless house and miserable haunts.

The drama of this Hesiodic vignette might result from the poet's transformation of details from a real dramatic *song* situation into a third-person narration. In a Rhodian custom (performed in Boedromion), boys solicit food and wine while singing, "She's come, she's come, the swallow, bringing fine seasons." If not treated, they claim, their trick will be to break in and take the woman sitting inside, since "she's a little one and we will easily carry her" (lines 15-16). Without claiming that the poet of the *Works and Days* knew this song, we can still imagine that similar seasonal poetry was available to him. The safe inner space of the *oikos*, source of wealth and fertility, is contrasted, in both Hesiod and the folk song, with the violent exterior where hungry males threaten to invade; the parallel is closer when we recall Boreas' mythical role as abductor of women (Plato *Phaedrus* 229c–d). Furthermore, if we consider the deep antiquity of the sexual imagery of *Works and Days* 507–25, evident from the poetic cognates of the deprived "boneless one," in Old Irish and Old English, it appears likely that Hesiod's poem reshapes, in a new setting, words most appropriate to a ritual performance.[50]

Kennings, like the "boneless one" of *Works and Days* 524, have often been remarked as distinctively Hesiodic, but, as I have suggested, may also be taken as arising within the smaller song-genres that the *Works and Days* has absorbed in order to fulfill its larger purpose as instructional (rather than ritual) verse. Again, a modern instance may illustrate how such enigmatic language acquires its own native interpretation through a folk-ritual enactment. In another Rhodian composition, a modern folk remedy for erysipelas, these words are repeated seven times while burning bits of cotton and wood are flicked off the infected area:

> *kato sto gialo stin ammo/ oi spanoi zevgari kanoun/*
> *vazoun tis psoles ton aletri/ kai t'archeidia ton zevgari*
> *mi osporos ton matiasei/ miti fokio na rizosi*

> Down on the beach, on the sand,
> the beardless ones are mating,
> they use the penis like a plough

---

[50] Watkins 1978, 231–35. Again, I would compare Russian *koljadki*, with their clear fertility functions. For exhaustive treatment of the "boneless one," see now Bader 1989.

and their testicles like a pair of oxen.
Let not the Evil Eye fall on the seeds
nor the erysipelas take root.[51]

In this sort of composition, then, condensed narrative and incantation coexist. In Hesiod, ritual has fallen away; the parallel is rather between "narratives" (like the calendar vignettes) and another genre, precepts. In this second embedded genre, distinction is not formally made between such precepts as "Do not make a companion equal to a brother" (707) and "Do not cross the fair water of ever-flowing rivers before praying" (737–38): ritual and ethics converge.[52] Proverbial expression as a genre of social speech was probably a contemporary phenomenon for the poet of the *Works and Days*, as it is in most traditional societies. In late nineteenth-century Moscow, Roman Jakobson recalls, "Children strenuously practised the Russian art of interspersing their discourse with proverbial saws and thus learned to alternate and coordinate their individual experience with established maxims."[53] My point is that Hesiodic stylization of this social genre results in changes in the "texture" of the poem, which make it sound quite un-Homeric. The primary difference between his poetic proverbs and the everyday speech-genre is that the latter are not accumulated: one "performs" them as isolated items to point up an argument. Proverbs have their own poetic markings—internal rhymes, assonance, alliteration, binary structure, paronomasia. These, along with positive-negative expressions (cf. *Theogony* 551 *gnô rh'oud' êgnoiêse*, "he knew and did not fail to know") and compulsive etymologizing can be seen as extending throughout Hesiodic technique (yet not Homeric) from an original function as devices to make memorable *proverbial* expression.[54] Once proverbs are joined, as in the *Works and Days*, the poetic possibilities multiply. Couplets and triplets built around one word or root and varying

---

[51]   Cited by Lawrence Durrell 1960, 195–96, quoting from a paper by A. R. Mills contributed to the *Bulletin for the History of Medicine* (n. d.).

[52]   On the homology of moral and ritual correctness in Theognis and Hesiod, see Nagy 1992, 69.

[53]   Jakobson 1966, 638. Compare M. L. West's note (1981, 61): "The Russian traveller Valikhanov encountered a sultan of one of the Kazakh tribes whom he took to be an imbecile, because his intermittent utterances consisted of rhymed couplets of rather general import, accompanied by alarming rollings of the eyes. Probably the man was simply making conversation in the most formal and polite way he knew."

[54]   On internal marking of proverbs, see Russo 1983, 121–30. Examples of the techniques and comparison with other archaic poetic traditions are in Campanile 1977, 105–6; also, Cantarella 1931. In archaic Irish poetic texts and in the *Mahabharata*, there occur maxims of legal, medical, religious content, similar to Hesiod's and also marked by emphatic poetic features: see Campanile et al. 1974, 239–44. See Durante 1976, 131, 142, 149 for useful parallels in Vedic poetry.

the series of end-stopped, one-line precepts, make a more dramatic performance, artful in its own terms. When runs of proverbs occur, we can hear
the hexameter break up, as if the poet were shifting rhythm using a different,
more rapid meter. Emphasizing word-breaks, we find such syntactically
bipartite lines as the following (*Works and Days* 308–13):[55]

> ἐξ ἔργων δ' ἄνδρες
>   πολύμηλοί τ' ἀφνειοί τε,
> καί τ' ἐργαζόμενος
>   πολὺ φίλτερος ἀθανάτοισιν …
> ἔργον δ' οὐδὲν ὄνειδος,
>   ἀεργίη δέ τ' ὄνειδος.   310
> εἰ δέ κεν ἐργάζῃ,
>   τάχα σε ζηλώσει ἀεργὸς
> πλουτεῦντα· πλούτῳ δ'
>   ἀρετὴ καὶ κῦδος ὀπηδεῖ.

> From works are men
>   cattle-rich and wealthy
> and the working man
>   is dearer to the gods …

> Work is no shame
>   worklessness is shame.
> If you work,
>   soon, the workless one will envy
> you making fortune. On fortune
>   follows excellence and glory.

The claim that such Hesiodic verse is somehow less elegant than Homer's
cannot be sustained if one considers metrical variety. More than a century
ago, Paulson showed that Hesiod's verse constantly changes hexameter
shapes (by varying the number and position of spondees in each line): the
longest passage formed of identical metrical sequences in Hesiod comprises
only five lines (*Theogony* 745–49) and even these lines feature word-breaks
in different places, when compared with one another.[56] What may give a
different, slower sound to Hesiodic verse is its higher proportion of verses

---

[55] Pellizer 1972a suggests that proverbs functioned as pre-constituted metrical units (paroemiac-
shaped) for the poet of the *Works and Days*. This would explain the patterning exhibited, but there
is still a certain amount of joining, enjambment, and breaking of the metrical frame, which I take to
be the poet's innovatory art.

[56] Paulson 1887, 1.

containing one or more spondees.[57] A further distinctive touch is the combination of the spondaic type with proverbial language falling into balanced clauses, or using positive-negative expressions. An extreme illustration for several of these tendencies comes at *Works and Days* 354 (here spaced to show the major word-breaks, with underlines to show spondaic phrases):

> *kai domen* hos ken dôi kai *mê domen* hos ken mê dôi

To capture the balance and rhyme we might break up the line graphically in translation:

> And give to one who gives; and don't
>   give to one who won't
>   give.

Similar phrase structure underlies *Works and Days* 353, where there is only one spondee, but an important one, coming at the spot where a conjunction stitches the two line-halves together:

> *Ton phileonta philein,   kai tôi   prosionti proseinai.*

> The befriender befriend and the approacher approach.

From such examples, one can soon see that Hesiodic poetry in this one, seemingly small feature differs from Homeric because the meter is symptomatic of a more pervasive rhetorical strategy, that of embedding proverbs, with their pre-existing metrical and poetic values, into a larger composition.[58]

Now that we have been led by Hesiod's metanastic stance to consider genre-inclusiveness and thus explore small-scale features like meter, it is time to connect the "immigrant" persona with one more puzzling aspect of this poetry that also makes it both like and unlike Homeric verse: its dialect. Despite the autobiographical detail in the poems, it remains indisputable that Hesiod's language is more Ionic than Homer's.[59] He even uses an Ionic

---

[57]   See Paulson 1887, 4–6 for the statistics on spondees: 45% of verses in *Works and Days* have two or more spondees vs. 31% in, e.g., Book 1 of the *Iliad*; see also West 1966, 93.

[58]   Fernández-Delgado 1982 after reviewing theories of the development of the hexameter out of shorter lines, proposes that these preforms were mainly used for *gnomic* expressions of Hesiodic type.

[59]   Edwards 1971, 195–96 summarizes the linguistic features involved, e.g., distribution of genitive plural *-eôn/-ôn* as opposed to *-aôn*. Pavese 1972, 52–54 admits that some elements are organic Ionisms, e.g., neglect of digamma (conserved late in actual Boeotian) is much more frequent in Hesiod. Nagy 1992, 61 points out that Hesiodic poetry's "self-proclaimed Boeotian provenience would be nearly impossible to detect on the basis of language alone."

month name, Lenaion, when a different, Boeotian name existed.[60] Some have suggested historical solutions, such as the presence of Ionian singers on the mainland in the eighth century.[61] Others point to the Ionic heritage of hexameter verse, while assuming this was the poetic *koine* in Boeotia as well. And it is true that "We should look to Ionia rather than to Dark Age Boeotia for the precursor of the *Works and Days*."[62] But rather than emphasize the chronologically later character of Hesiodic diction vs. Homeric, I suggest that we put the question in performance terms. If Hesiod "sounds" markedly Ionic to an audience, which means the poet chooses expressions involving known Ionisms instead of traditional unmarked phrases, what message does an audience get?[63] The same message, I believe, that a stand-up comedian transmits in doing "dialect" jokes: i.e., this speaker is a foreigner and the discourse has something to do with his foreignness.[64] The "foreign" dialect of Ionia is overemphasized to shore up the persona of the "outsider." In other words, Hesiod's metanastic fiction is sustained even into details of phonology. Another strategy complements this. West notes, "there is nothing in Hesiod which need be Boeotian," but he also observes that besides the highly Ionic coloring of the poems there are undisputed Aeolisms.[65] Three of these occur in the *Works and Days* passage on seafaring. And one affects the very word "I advise," a key term for the entire composition—here (*Works and Days* 683), *ainêmi*, rather than Ionic *aineô*. In choosing this, Hesiod is not simply mimicking his father's speech, but identifying himself with Aeolic Cyme, speaking the language of the old country, as he performs in the new.

What might this mean for the interpretation of the *Works and Days* as a whole? I suggest that it further allows us to read the poem in conjunction with Ionic elegiac poetry (much of which is composed by a "Megarian" Theognis!). There is no need to take Hesiodic poetry as the product of

---

[60] See Nagy 1992, 63. Hoekstra 1957, 199 suggests the name can be used because the public in Boeotia knew Ionic poetry so well.

[61] Hoekstra 1965, 25 n. 3.

[62] West 1978, 26.

[63] Edwards 1971, 38 believes Hesiod "shows himself acquainted with the hexameter tradition in a later phase, as is evident not only from the general Ionic appearance of his language ... , but also from particular expressions with these features ... ."

[64] Lamberton 1988, 111 finds the same analogy to stand-up comedy congenial for explaining how the seemingly haphazard texture of the *Works and Days* occurs when the poet consciously makes his organization *sound* like the "explicitly free and arbitrary choice of a highly individualized speaker." On the loosely connected style of the *Works and Days,* see further Chapter 10 above.

[65] West 1966, 90.

Boeotia, or concerned with a Boeotian audience, at all. We might instead read its context as the *eris* within the Ionic city-state and its topics as relevant to the struggles of oligarchs and tyrants on the eastern side of the Aegean. The mask of the Boeotian peasant in the *Works and Days* becomes protective coloring for an Ionian poet, or any other who might wish to adopt it.

Finally, it is through this image of the Hesiodic author as authoritative outsider that we can understand more clearly the poetic framework of the *Theogony*. The enigmatic words of the Muses to the poet at *Theogony* 26–28, whatever the deeper meaning of the divine claim to be able to tell "lies like the truth," have the force of a prohibition; their "we know" is exclusive.[66] The line that the Muses draw between the shepherds and themselves stands as a sign of Hesiod's status, as much as does his pastoral life on the physical margin of the community. Even when he appears to cross the line, through the Muses' gift of song, his standing remains paradoxically that of the outsider, as he proceeds to commemorate those with higher authority: Zeus, the Muses, the well-speaking kings (*Theogony* 36–93). We could speculate on deeper origins for this stance, perhaps going back to shamanistic extra-body experiences as necessary for theogonic knowledge, a combination familiar from Orpheus lore.[67] The similarities in tone between Hesiodic poetry and Biblical prophetic poetry have been noticed by Wilamowitz, Dornseiff, Sinclair, Detienne, and others.[68] The scholiast to the *Theogony* proem (*ad* 32, 38) noted its mantic language. We hear a clearly prophetic voice in the style of *Works and Days* 182–201, where Hesiod decries the Iron Age dearth of *kharis* and *philia* and projects it into the future.

Equally compelling, but less obvious, are Hesiodic lines in both major poems that bear a striking dictional resemblance to Delphic hexameter oracles. At line 286 of the *Works and Days*, for example (Σοὶ δ' ἐγὼ ἐσθλὰ νοέων ἐρέω, μέγα νήπιε Πέρση), Hesiod uses the same vocative expression, *mega nêpie*, as the Pythia does to Croesus (Herodotus *Histories* 1.85.2). The Hesiod line just before this, on the survival of the just man's race, was attributed by the paroemiographer Apostolius to the Pythia herself. There are many other such overlaps.[69] The poet to whom were attributed the

---

[66] I am convinced by Ferrari's argument (1988) that the Derridean reading of this scene by Pucci and Arthur is unsupported by the text. Griffith 1983, 48–49 recognizes a traditional statement of divine power vs. mortal in the song of the Muses.

[67] On which see West 1983, 4–6.

[68] Bibliography in Pellizer 1972a, 29–31.

[69] Cf. *Works and Days* 285 with Herodotus *Histories* 3.86.3; in part, *Works and Days* 648 = oracle at Herodotus 1.47; see Pellizer 1972b, 40 and Cantarella 1931, 5–10, who notes Waltz had already seen

Melampodia, Khresmoi, and *Ornithomanteia,* all concerned with divinatory acts, might well have posed as a *mantis* himself. Whether as travelling religious poet or spokesman for Delphi, Hesiod in this stance inevitably fits the metanastic persona, as Delphi was by definition the extra-polis sanctuary. Nor is "outsider" status coincidental to mantic functions: "where divination is by trance-mediumship the prophet is often a stranger, a person deemed free from partisan interest," as Robert Parker reports.[70] This is to say, then, that the apparently diverse poetic personae of the adviser-critic in the *Works and Days* and the praiser of divinities in the *Theogony* are united on a higher level: as *metanastês* Hesiod suits both.

If the metanastic fiction underlying these personae survived, perhaps it was because it also suited the needs of later rhapsodes as well as it may have a composer from an earlier generation. Gregory Nagy has observed that the transcendental, Pan-Hellenic stance of the poet is "facilitated by the historical fact that the figure of Hesiod has no native city to claim him, since Askra was destroyed by Thespiai."[71] I would add that travelling rhapsodes could integrate this lore with their own self-presentation as authoritative outsiders. This may explain why the prooimia and some autobiographical passages seem not to have been available in local Boeotian versions of Hesiod texts: their usefulness is precisely in the context of performance elsewhere and may conceivably have been developed by rhapsodes who never set foot on mainland Greece.[72] At any event, the epitaph for Hesiod's tomb in Orchomenus, as we find it embedded in the *Contest of Homer and Hesiod,* a composition that undoubtedly owes much to rhapsodic performance and lore, depicts Hesiod as even in death a man without his own country, the eternal metanastic (lines 250–53 Allen):[73]

Ἄσκρη μὲν πατρὶς πολυλήιος, ἀλλὰ θανόντος
ὀστέα πληξίππων γῆ Μινυὰς κατέχει

---

how *Works and Days* 235 relates to the curse of the Amphissians in Aeschines *Orations* 3.33; see also McLeod 1961. Fernández-Delgado (1985) shows that the corpus of hexameter oracles represents a distinct, old tradition, which may have influenced Hesiodic and Homeric diction.

[70] See Parker 1985, 30. Again, I am reminded of the *Odyssey's* metanastic mantic Theoclymenus.

[71] Nagy 1992, 52.

[72] On the problem, see Lamberton 1988b, 46–48, who posits a Hellenistic date for fixation of the autobiographical traditions. I agree but would stress their earlier oral performance function. Similar traditions must underlie the old lore in the *Certamen,* datable to the fourth century but probably stemming from lost sixth-century versions: see Richardson 1981.

[73] On the story about Hesiod's bones being brought to Orchomenus (or Ozolian Locris, in another tradition) see Nagy 1992, 49.

Ἡσιόδου, τοῦ πλεῖστον ἐν ἀνθρώποις κλέος ἐστὶν
ἀνδρῶν κρινομένων ἐν βασάνῳ σοφίης.

Ascra is his fatherland, rich in grain, but now the land
    of Minyans who goad the horse holds the bones
of the dead Hesiod, he whose renown is greatest
    of men who are judged in the test of wisdom.

12

HESIOD, ODYSSEUS, AND THE INSTRUCTION OF PRINCES[1]

It should no longer be necessary to point out the futility of any attempt to determine, from the texts alone, which passage was composed first: the lines of the *Theogony* proem that concern the Muse's gifts to kings (*Theogony* 79-93) or Odysseus' reply to the inhospitable taunt of the Phaeacian youth Euryalus (*Odyssey* 8.166-77). Priority-hunting, based on subjective notions of what is artful in archaic Greek poetry, has failed to answer the dilemma. New methods of approach are needed.[2]

The two passages in question are the following:

> ξεῖν᾽, οὐ καλὸν ἔειπες· ἀτασθάλῳ ἀνδρὶ ἔοικας.
> οὕτως οὐ πάντεσσι θεοὶ χαρίεντα διδοῦσιν
> ἀνδράσιν, οὔτε φυὴν οὔτ᾽ ἆρ φρένας οὔτ᾽ ἀγορητύν.
> ἄλλος μὲν γὰρ εἶδος ἀκιδνότερος πέλει ἀνήρ,
> ἀλλὰ θεὸς μορφὴν ἔπεσι στέφει· οἱ δέ τ᾽ ἐς αὐτὸν   170
> τερπόμενοι λεύσσουσιν, ὁ δ᾽ ἀσφαλέως ἀγορεύει,
> αἰδοῖ μειλιχίῃ, μετὰ δὲ πρέπει ἀγρομένοισιν,
> ἐρχόμενον δ᾽ ἀνὰ ἄστυ θεὸν ὣς εἰσορόωσιν.
> ἄλλος δ᾽ αὖ εἶδος μὲν ἀλίγκιος ἀθανάτοισιν,
> ἀλλ᾽ οὔ οἱ χάρις ἀμφιπεριστέφεται ἐπέεσσιν,   175
> ὡς καὶ σοὶ εἶδος μὲν ἀριπρεπές, οὐδέ κεν ἄλλως
> οὐδὲ θεὸς τεύξειε, νόον δ᾽ ἀποφώλιός ἐσσι.

(*Odyssey* 8.166–77)

Stranger, you have not spoken well; you seem like a man blind
with folly. So true is it that the gods do not give gracious gifts

---

[1] Originally published in *Transactions of the American Philological Association* 114 (1984): 29–48.

[2] For the most complete bibliography on the problem, see Neitzel 1977, to which add Braswell 1981. On the problems of "borrowing" and "imitation" in an oral tradition see Janko 1982, 225.

to all alike, not form, nor mind, nor eloquence. For one man is inferior in looks, but the god sets a crown of beauty upon his words, and men look upon him with delight, and he speaks on unfalteringly with sweet modesty, and is conspicuous among the gathered people, and as he goes through the city men gaze upon him as upon a god. Another again is in looks like the immortals, but no crown of grace is set about his words. So also in your case your looks are preeminent, nor could a god himself improve them, but in mind you are stunted. [trans. Murray and Dimock 1995]

Καλλιόπη θ'· ἡ δὲ προφερεστάτη ἐστὶν ἁπασέων.
ἡ γὰρ καὶ βασιλεῦσιν ἅμ' αἰδοίοισιν ὀπηδεῖ.   80
ὅντινα τιμήσουσι Διὸς κοῦραι μεγάλοιο
γεινόμενόν τε ἴδωσι διοτρεφέων βασιλήων,
τῷ μὲν ἐπὶ γλώσσῃ γλυκερὴν χείουσιν ἐέρσην,
τοῦ δ' ἔπε' ἐκ στόματος ῥεῖ μείλιχα· οἱ δέ νυ λαοὶ
πάντες ἐς αὐτὸν ὁρῶσι διακρίνοντα θέμιστας   85
ἰθείῃσι δίκῃσιν· ὁ δ' ἀσφαλέως ἀγορεύων
αἶψά τι καὶ μέγα νεῖκος ἐπισταμένως κατέπαυσε·
τούνεκα γὰρ βασιλῆες ἐχέφρονες, οὕνεκα λαοῖς
βλαπτομένοις ἀγορῆφι μετάτροπα ἔργα τελεῦσι
ῥηιδίως, μαλακοῖσι παραιφάμενοι ἐπέεσσιν·   90
ἐρχόμενον δ' ἀν' ἀγῶνα θεὸν ὣς ἱλάσκονται
αἰδοῖ μειλιχίῃ, μετὰ δὲ πρέπει ἀγρομένοισι.
τοίη Μουσάων ἱερὴ δόσις ἀνθρώποισιν.

(Theogony 79–93)

... and Calliope—she is the greatest of them all, for she attends upon venerated kings too. Whomever among Zeus-nourished kings the daughters of great Zeus honor and behold when he is born, they pour sweet dew upon his tongue, and his words flow soothingly from his mouth. All the populace look to him as he decides disputes with straight judgments; and speaking publicly without erring, he quickly ends even a great quarrel by his skill. For this is why kings are prudent, because when the populace is going astray in the assembly they easily manage to turn the deeds around, effecting persuasion with mild words; and as he goes up to the gathering they seek his favor like a god with soothing reverence, and he is conspicuous among the assembled people. Such is the holy gift of the Muses to human beings. [trans. Most 2006]

The passages share two and one-half verses. If we rule out the chance occurrence of such similar diction and the notion of borrowing, one possibility remains: parallel inheritance from a single common source. There is a way to agree with the Analysts that the resemblances here are not coincidental, while avoiding the critical traps of "imitation," "adaptation," or "borrowing." As G. P. Edwards concludes, "We can never rule out the existence of an older place X, which provided a common source for both A and B at the lines in question, so making their chronological relationship impossible to determine."[3] I cannot claim to have discovered a poem which serves as the common source for the *Theogony* and *Odyssey* passages, but I can go beyond Edwards's essentially negative conclusion: the two passages under consideration can be said to share a common genre, which generates the similar phrases in each place. By analyzing Greek and Old Irish texts, I propose to pinpoint the genre from which both Homer and Hesiod draw.

The generic elements to which I refer are best understood as belonging to "genres of discourse," to use the phrase of the critic Tzvetan Todorov.[4] He insists, first, that a genre is an institution of society, and so should interest historians and anthropologists as well as literary critics; the link between genre and social life will be important for the problem at hand.[5] Second, Todorov points out that genre is simply the "historically attested codification of discursive properties" such as setting, addressee, speaker, diction, rhythm, and theme, the variables of any speech-act; in literature, these variables happen to be more rigidly defined and selected than they are in ordinary discourse. It is useful to think of genre, then, as a type of selective coding.[6] I will return to this notion later in this paper. Suffice it to say for now that genre, because it is related to discourse, is implicit in

---

[3]   Edwards 1971, 189. Several scholars are careful to point out the possibility of common borrowing from tradition as regards these two passages: cf. Duban 1980, 12 n. 11; Walcot 1963, 11–12 and 1966, 124–25; West 1966, 183; the tradition involved is not specified by them. Concerning the *Theogony* passage, Edwards 1971, 168–69, while not denying the possibility of common inheritance, accepts earlier arguments for Homeric priority.

[4]   Todorov 1978 applies the notion to a range of modern works; see 1978, 51 for his definition of the term; and, for further comparison of rules of discourse with those of genre, see Todorov 1975, 362–63. Other useful work might be done, using Todorov's notion, to recover the themes and diction appropriate to an archaic Greek system of genres. For a working model in one genre, see Pavese 1979.

[5]   Todorov 1978, 49. On genre as convention and institution, see the analysis of Raible 1980, 326.

[6]   Raible 1980, 325, 335–43 notes that genres, like texts and words themselves, are characterized by selection and abbreviation of elements in a system. From the perspective of a semiotician, Raible defines genre as a set of distinctive marks drawn from as many as six dimensions, including communication-situation.

any literary production: behind the words of a poem lie unspoken assumptions regarding the context and manner of communication proper to a given location, occasion, and interlocutors.

At times, this generic affiliation might be marked out by diction or syntax; the use of vocatives, for instance, is a traditional element in Greek poetic *paraenesis* ("advice") from Homer on. At other times, the dramatic context by itself can mark a discourse as properly belonging to a certain genre, since the presence of speakers with a particular status naturally arouses generic expectations. The marking of a discourse as appropriate for a particular genre can occur even though the discourse is embedded within a composition of an entirely different genre. Thus, in the medium of Homeric poetry, where changes of speaker occur frequently, it is theoretically possible that each speaker's discourse shows signs of belonging to a particular genre. Nestor and Phoenix, for instance, are not just advisors: they become conduits for the genre of paraenetic poetry; Andromache, Hecuba, and Helen are not just lamenting women, but speakers *within* epic-poetry of lament poetry, which has a long and old tradition *outside* epic as well, a tradition most likely as old as epic, with its own conventions and stylizations of language, as Alexiou has shown.[7] Although it may seem mechanical to describe epic characters in terms of their poetic affiliations in this way, such a view might help us to understand how such massive compositions as the *Iliad* and *Odyssey* attained their bulk: by the introduction of pre-existing or contemporary non-epic genres. This mode of composition is exactly what gives both Homeric poems their convincingly realistic tone, producing in the audience the sense that actual words are being reported by the Muse (as the poet's ideology would declare). Stylized discourse, be it lament, advice, praise, or blame, is incorporated and preserved in the medium of Homeric hexameter verse.[8]

One more thing needs to be emphasized before I return to pinpoint the genre of *Odyssey* 8.166–77 and *Theogony* 79–93. It is a working principle of oral poetics that theme creates diction and similar themes create similar diction.[9] By attributing certain themes to genres of discourse, I am adding

---

[7]   Alexiou 1974, 4–13, 161–84. Mawet 1975, 42ff. also traces elements of distinct genres within epic laments, raising the possibility that epic evolved from laments.

[8]   On the versatility of Homeric poetry in integrating various traditions, see Nagy 1999b, 6. Sinos 1980, 75 and n. 5 illustrates some ways in which the *Iliad* subsumes other traditional genres. Further on problems of genre-interaction in early Greek poetry: Latacz 1977, 1–20; Diller 1962, 44–46, 58; Puelma 1972, 86–87 (on genre *ainos*); Nagy 1999b, 235–41.

[9]   See Lord 1960, 49: "Formulas are, after all, the means of expressing the themes of the poetry." Nagy 1999b, 1–6 is a concise statement of the interworking of theme and diction in archaic Greek

another level to the hierarchy of traditional modes of expression in archaic Greek poetry. The lowest level of this hierarchy—the word or phrase—is often labeled *formula*, but one might call any one of these levels of expression "formulaic."

With reference to the problem with which we began, then, I would claim that similar themes produce the resemblances. The themes are generated by a common source, an ancient genre of discourse, which has a basis in social fact of considerable antiquity, the discourse between a king (or advisor) and a prince. This genre has long been called "Instruction of Princes" (or *speculum principum*); its wide attestation is surveyed by West in his edition of the *Works and Days*, the best surviving reflection of the genre in Greek. We know that similar compositions in Greek once existed, especially from the fragments of a poem called the *Instructions of Cheiron* attributed to Hesiod (fr. 283–85 MW). The high status of the *Kheironos Hupothekai* as a source for instruction-poetry is evident in Pindar's "citation" of the poem at *Pythian* 6.19–26:

> σύ τοι σχεθών νιν ἐπὶ δεξιὰ χειρός, ὀρθὰν
> ἄγεις ἐφημοσύναν,   20
> τά ποτ' ἐν οὔρεσι φαντὶ μεγαλοσθενεῖ
> Φιλύρας υἱὸν ὀρφανιζομένῳ
> Πηλεΐδᾳ παραινεῖν· μάλιστα μὲν Κρονίδαν,
> βαρύοπα στεροπᾶν κεραυνῶν τε πρύτανιν,
> θεῶν σέβεσθαι·   25
> ταύτας δὲ μή ποτε τιμᾶς ἀμείρειν γονέων βίον
> πεπρωμένον.

> Truly, by keeping him at your right hand, you uphold the precept, whose words of advice they say Philyra's son once gave to the mighty son of Peleus in the mountains, when he was away from his parents: above all gods to revere Cronus' son, loud-voiced lord of lightning and thunder, and never to deprive of like honor one's parents during their allotted lifetime. [trans. Race 1997]

Both the extant *Works and Days* and the fragmentary *Instructions of Cheiron* accord with other examples of this genre, in many literatures, in their concern with transmitting the rules for proper legal, religious, political, and social

---

material. I have sketched the relationship of theme to motif and phrase, within several European traditions, in Martin 1984b. The shared verses of the passages at hand are not "formulaic" in terms of phrase repetition (except for *Odyssey* 8.173 = *Theogony* 91, a fairly frequent phrase: cf. Krafft 1963, 69 n. 1).

behavior.[10] While the *Works and Days*, along with similar poetry such as the elegiacs of Theognis, has long been recognized as *hupothêkai*, commentators on the *Theogony* have treated the poem as a compendium of lore about myth and cosmology, rightly noting its links with other theogonic texts but neglecting the frame-narrative, which includes the proem.[11] To my knowledge, the possibility of an embedded genre of instruction-poetry within the *Theogony* or the *Odyssey* has not been addressed.

To turn to the passages: what specifically marks these portions of the *Odyssey* and the *Theogony* as appropriate to a shared Instruction of Princes genre? Three elements occur in both that are closely similar in phrasing or situation. The first two are thematic and generate the shared diction; they comprise the theme of faultless speaking ability (*asphaleôs agoreuei*: *Odyssey* 8.171 and *Theogony* 86) and that of "honey-sweet respect" (*aidôi meilikhiêi*: *Odyssey* 8.172 and *Theogony* 92). The third element is dramatic context, which generates the "looking on" motif (*Odyssey* 8.173 and *Theogony* 85, 91). I shall discuss this later. The first two elements can be traced within poetry explicitly designated as "instructions"—the speaking-theme in the cognate Indo-European tradition of Old Irish poetry and the *aidôs*-theme within Greek tradition.

First, the speech theme. The Old Irish literary genre called *tecosc* ("instruction") comprises five principal compositions, the earliest of which, *Audacht Morainn* (*AM*), dates from 700 CE and is therefore the earliest Western European specimen of the *speculum* genre. The *Audacht Morainn* ("Testament of Morann") purports to be the death-bed instructions of the mythical first Irish lawmaker, Morann, to Neire, his foster-son, for transmission to the young king Feradach Find Fechtnach. Irish tradition itself casts this poetry as an inheritance from deep antiquity; in fact, the *Audacht* contains nothing but pre-Christian material, and, in the words of Calvert

---

[10] See West 1978, 7, 14–18. In terms of the definition of genre in Raible 1980, one could describe prince-instruction as set in a particular communication-situation (older man advising younger, usually at a point of crisis or initiation), with an open-ended structure (e.g., strings of injunctions), presented as either direct conversation or as a testament, governed by hierarchical order (injunctions in order of importance), with a "real" purpose (i.e., the genre presents itself as factual and necessary for world order). On the contents of the *Kheironos Hupothêkai*, see Schwartz 1960, 241 and Nagy 1982b, 61–62.

[11] Friedländer 1913, 558-616 outlines the similarities. On the inadequacy of the commonplace description of the *Works and Days* as merely "instructions" or "wisdom literature," see R. Hunt 1981. An exception to the usual treatment of the *Theogony* is Detienne's analysis (1967, 17–18) of the work as a praise-poem directed to Zeus as king.

Watkins, is a "window on a genre of Indo-European literature."[12] The core of the *Audacht Morainn* deals with the notion of the Ruler's Truth, a force brought into life by the king's verbal behavior, which ensures the prosperity and abundance of a society. This notion has exact cognates, both in semantics and syntactical expression, in Indo-Iranian and in Greek poetry, as Watkins shows, citing for the latter literature the *Works and Days*, wherein the fable of the hawk and the nightingale (*Works and Days* 203–12) is explicitly directed to the kings and has as its main concern the contrast between "straight" and "crooked" *dikê*.[13] Straight *dikê* leads to an ideal state of plenty (*Works and Days* 225–35):

οἳ δὲ <u>δίκας</u> ξείνοισι καὶ ἐνδήμοισι διδοῦσιν   225
<u>ἰθείας</u> καὶ μή τι παρεκβαίνουσι δικαίου,
τοῖσι τέθηλε πόλις, λαοὶ δ' ἀνθεῦσιν ἐν αὐτῇ·
εἰρήνη δ' ἀνὰ γῆν κουροτρόφος, οὐδέ ποτ' αὐτοῖς
ἀργαλέον πόλεμον τεκμαίρεται εὐρύοπα Ζεύς·
οὐδέ ποτ' <u>ἰθυδίκῃσι</u> μετ' ἀνδράσι λιμὸς ὀπηδεῖ   230
οὐδ' ἄτη, θαλίῃς δὲ μεμηλότα ἔργα νέμονται.
τοῖσι φέρει μὲν γαῖα πολὺν βίον, οὔρεσι δὲ δρῦς
ἄκρη μέν τε φέρει βαλάνους, μέσση δὲ μελίσσας·
εἰροπόκοι δ' ὄιες μαλλοῖς καταβεβρίθασι·
τίκτουσιν δὲ γυναῖκες ἐοικότα τέκνα γονεῦσι·   235

But those who give straight judgments to foreigners and fellow-citizens and do not turn aside from justice at all, their city blooms and the people in it flower. For them, Peace, the nurse of the young, is on the earth, and far-seeing Zeus never marks out painful war; nor does famine attend straight-judging men, nor calamity, but they share out in festivities the fruits of the labors they care for. For these the earth bears the means of life in abundance, and on the mountains the oak tree bears acorns on its surface, and bees in its center; their woolly sheep are weighed down by their fleeces; and their wives give birth to children who resemble their parents. [trans. Most 2006]

---

[12] Watkins 1979, 182. Further on the antiquity of this text: F. Kelly 1976, xv and Henry 1982, 35 (on the relation of Morann to the Vedic figure of Varuna). On the relation between early Irish kings and judges, including Morann, see Wagner 1970, 1–45 and Binchy 1970, 4–16. Note that the Irish instruction is specifically to a foster-son, in the *AM* and elsewhere, a detail identical with the tradition that Cheiron instructed Achilles, Jason, et al. in a type of fosterage. The motif of Achilles' fosterage is an Indo-European relic, according to Campanile 1981, 32–34.

[13] Watkins 1979, 183, 192–93.

This opposition of good and bad justice is mirrored in Old Irish instruction poetry, where one is told the many results of *fírbretha* as opposed to *góbretha* (true and false judgments). The results of the latter are often painfully elaborated; the true judgments lead to increased yields of milk, fish, corn, and fair children.[14]

Watkins also mentions the other striking appearance of the Ruler's Truth notion in archaic Greek poetry: the words of Odysseus to Penelope in which he details the results of an ideal king's good rule (*Odyssey* 19.106–14):[15]

> τὴν δ' ἀπαμειβόμενος προσέφη πολύμητις Ὀδυσσεύς·
> ὦ γύναι, οὐκ ἄν τίς σε βροτῶν ἐπ' ἀπείρονα γαῖαν
> νεικέοι· ἦ γάρ σευ κλέος οὐρανὸν εὐρὺν ἱκάνει,
> ὥς τέ τευ ἢ <u>βασιλῆος ἀμύμονος</u>, ὅς τε θεουδὴς
> ἀνδράσιν ἐν πολλοῖσι καὶ ἰφθίμοισιν ἀνάσσων   110
> εὐδικίας ἀνέχῃσι, φέρῃσι δὲ γαῖα μέλαινα
> πυροὺς καὶ κριθάς, βρίθῃσι δὲ δένδρεα καρπῷ,
> τίκτῃ δ' ἔμπεδα μῆλα, θάλασσα δὲ παρέχῃ ἰχθῦς
> ἐξ εὐηγεσίης, ἀρετῶσι δὲ λαοὶ ὑπ' αὐτοῦ.

> Then resourceful Odysseus answered her, and said: "Lady, no one among mortals upon the boundless earth could find fault with you, for your fame goes up to the broad heaven, as does the fame of some blameless king, who, with the fear of the gods in his heart, is lord over many valiant men, upholding justice; and the black earth bears wheat and barley, and the trees are laden with fruit, the flocks bring forth young unceasingly, and the sea yields fish, all from his good leading; and the people prosper under him." [trans. Murray and Dimock 1995]

This passage, apparently a digression in the interview between husband and wife on Ithaca, will turn out to be a key element in Odysseus' revelation. We have seen, then, that Old Irish and Greek instructional poetry— the *Audacht Morainn* and the *Works and Days*—both contain one inherited theme concerning the abundance resulting from the power of a good king, and that the same theme appears in the *Odyssey*. The point that I wish to

---

[14] See sections 12–21 *AM*, apparently the oldest section in the text, according to F. Kelly 1976, 6–7.

[15] Watkins 1979, 192; cf. F. Kelly 1976, xvii. For evidence concerning the high antiquity of Greek kingship traditions as reflected in the *Odyssey* 19 passage, see Mondi 1980, 203–16; on kingship as a relic institution at the composition of Homeric epic, see Drews 1983, 105–6, 144; on the heritage of Greek kingship, see Detienne 1967, 42–50.

make involves the same spread of attestation, with the substitution of the *Theogony* proem for the *Works and Days* passage.

In *Audacht Morainn*, it is implicit that the *fír flathemon* is verbally expressed by the king. There is evidence, in fact, from the twelfth century that a king actually recited or assented to the proverbial statements and injunctions of a *tecosc* during his inauguration ceremony. It may help us to appreciate the social parallels in the Greek and Irish situations for instruction-poetry if we note that such Irish inaugurations involved the passing of a rod, symbol of sovereignty, from a poet to the new king: the rod thus resembles the *skêptron*, not only in its close connection with kingship, but also in its relation to authoritative poetic speech. The Irish king is certified by the poet; reciprocally, the poet is maintained by the king and tribe. A similar relationship lies behind the proem to the *Theogony*, a poem resembling an inauguration ode for Zeus and detailing (as did Irish odes) the king's genealogy and battle prowess. Hesiod's gift of a *skêptron* from the Muses (*Theogony* 30) is a gift from their father, Zeus, and gets as its recompense the gift of the *Theogony* itself, which authorizes the divine king.[16]

Explicitly as well, the *Audacht* presents instructions on the role of speaking in kingship. After discoursing on the prosperity that the Ruler's Truth accomplishes, Morann gives Feradach a string of admonitions (*AM* sect. 55, ed. Kelly):

> *Apair fris*, (a) *bad trócar*, (b) *bad fírión*, (c) *bad chosmuil*, (d) *bad chuib-sech*, (e) *bad fosath*, (f) *bad eslabar*, (g) *bad garte*, (h) *bad fíalainech*, (i) *bad sessach*, (j) *bad lessach*, (k) *bad éitir*, (l) *bad inric*, (m) *bad suthnge*, (n) *bad foruste*, (o) *bad fírbrethach*.

> Tell him, let him be (a) merciful, (b) just, (c) impartial, (d) conscientious, (e) firm, (f) generous, (g) hospitable, (h) honourable, (i) stable, (j) beneficent, (k) capable, (l) honest, (m) well-spoken, (n) steady, (o) true-judging.

The final three are of particular interest here: "let him be well-spoken, steady, true-judging." For, semantically, we have here the exact pairing of the Greek phrase *asphaleôs agoreuei*.[17] The notion of true judgment, central to the

---

[16]   On the Irish inauguration ceremonies and other king-rituals, see F. Kelly 1976, 14; Dillon 1973, 1–8; and Byrne 1973, 7–27, esp. 15ff. On the meaning of Hesiod's *skêptron*, see Duban 1980, 7 and Puelma 1972, 94, both of whom also notice the parallel action of poets and kings in the description of the Muse's gifts (*Theogony* 79–103).

[17]   The adverb *asphaleôs* is especially important because, in the diction of the *Theogony*, only Gaia and Ouranos bear the adjective form as epithet: as Duban notes (1980, 19), this implies that "the king's 'unerring' pronouncements are the moral safeguard to the universe's physical stability"; he

Hesiodic description of ideal kingship in the *Theogony* passage (cf. especially *Theogony* 85–90), in *AM* immediately follows the phrases concerning speech—as is proper for the ideology of a culture in which tribal king and judge are closely allied.[18]

Examples can be multiplied to show that speaking well and truthfully is traditionally important advice in Irish Instruction of Princes. The *Senbríathra Fithail* ("proverbs" of the pagan judge Fithal), another *tecosc* text, has among its formulas the following: *adcota miltenga brithemnacht* ("A sweet tongue begets judgment"). We can note in this formula the association, as in the *Theogony* proem, of the king's speech with judgment. Furthermore, the word *miltenga*—literally "honey-tongue"—appears to contain the exact notion found in *meilikhios*, a key adjective in the Greek passages in question.[19]

The "Battle of Airtech" (*Cath Airtig*) contains the *tecosc* given by Conall Cernach to Cuscraid Mend Macha, as the latter assumes the kingship. After the instructions concerning proper gift-bestowal and assembly-holding, the new king is enjoined as follows:[20]

---

parallels the king's effectiveness in *Odyssey* 19.109–14, a passage that we have already seen is derived from archaic prince-instruction material. Old Irish *foruste*, the word translated here as "steady," might be further glossed "unmoved because rooted in tradition," as the noun *forus*, from which the adjective is derived, has particular reference to abstruse knowledge, especially of legal precedents and lore: cf. *Dictionary of the Irish Language* (Dublin 1913–76) "F," col. 373 s.v., sections *b* and *c*. On the importance of such "steadiness" in the context of kingship, cf. the evidence of a third cognate tradition (ancient India) as seen in, e.g., *Rig Veda* 10.173.4, noted by Schlerath 1960, 118. The lack of cognate linguistic expressions for these identical themes in the three traditions cited (Irish, Greek, Indic) should not be taken as proof that the complex of ideas regarding kings developed late and independently in each dialect of Indo-European, as semantic structures are often retained despite surface lexical renewal: cf. Watkins 1981, 764–99, esp. 780, 794.

[18] The *Audacht* presents the ruler not only as possessing the mystical *fír flathemon*, upon which justice is based, but also as setting legal precedents in the matter of fees, obligations, honor-price, and so forth (cf. *AM* sections 47–52). At the same time, the existence of independent judges appears to be acknowledged (cf. section 23, "Let him not exalt any judge unless he knows the true legal precedents," F. Kelly 1976, 8–9).

[19] On this formula, see Smith 1928, 14. Although *meilikhios* is probably not related to the Greek word for "honey" (*meli*), as Chantraine showed (1937, 169–74), there is no doubt that an association between the two word-groups had developed by the time of the composition of the *Theogony* proem (cf. lines 83–84: the Muses pour dew on the king's tongue and his words pour forth *meilikha*). Compare also the Homeric description of Nestor's voice at *Iliad* 1.249, a poetic detail that may be of Indo-European date, on which see Schmitt 1967, 256. Finally, on the association of honey and true speech, see Scheinberg 1979; and on the symbolic value of honey in the *Theogony* in relation to speech, see Pucci 1977, 19–21.

[20] Best 1916, 173. The obscure word *tethrai* may mean "paragons": cf. *Dictionary of the Irish Language* (above, note 16) s.v. 2 *tethra*. Compare the similar injunction, also in a context of judging, contained in *Tecosca Cormaic* ("Instructions of Cormac"): *eolas cech berla*, "knowledge of each language," is one of the essentials for the tribe's welfare (text in Sullivan 1983, 343c13).

> *Bat eolai in gech berlae ar narbat ainfis i nnach dán conruidfe a fritacra*
> *friut.*
> *Bat fíren fírbrethach cen forbrisiu n–indsciu etir tethrai trén (ocus) trúg.*

Be skilled in every tongue, so thou be not ignorant in any art that one will speak in argument with thee. Be just and righteous in judgment, not supressing speech between the *tethra* of the strong and the weak.

As in *Audacht Morainn*, instruction on speech is immediately followed by advice concerning judgment (with the same word used: *fírbrethach* = "true-judging"). It should be pointed out that in both the *Audacht* and the *Battle of Airtech*, the instructions to the king are embedded in a narrative, as I believe is also the case in the *Odyssey*. In my final Irish example, the embedded *tecosc* is less well integrated with its narrative, a sign that the story-teller is, indeed, borrowing from another genre to fill out his tale. In a section of the *Wasting Sickness of Cú Chulainn (Serglige Con Culainn)*, the hero instructs his foster-son Lugaid, who has been chosen as next king of Tara by an unusual bull-feast divination ceremony (278–82):[21]

26. *Ní fresnesea co labur.*

> *Ní aisnéisea co glórach.*
> *Ní fuirse.*
> *Ní chuitbe.*
> *Ní faithchither senóri.*

Be not haughty in contradiction.
Be not loud in telling.
Do not play the buffoon.
Do not mock.
Do not threaten old men.

This portion of Cú Chulainn's instructions centers, once more, on the proper verbal behavior for kings. Although the contexts differ in the *Wasting Sickness* and the *Odyssey* passages, both Cú Chulainn and Odysseus instruct their young prince interlocutors to speak in a respectful, restrained manner. In Greek terms, this means having *aidôs*; this brings us to the second theme shared by the *Odyssey* and *Theogony* passages with which we began.

---

[21] Dillon 1975, 9; translation in Dillon 1951, 57, who notes uncertainties *ad loc*. Once again, the addressee is a foster-son; cf. n. 11 above.

Aidôs is an important topic of Prince Instruction, as can be seen more clearly when we turn from the shame culture of ancient Ireland to that of archaic Greece. Hesiod's *Works and Days*, as we have seen, is an explicitly instructional composition. It is significant, given this context, that the poem dramatizes the negative exemplum of the Fifth Age in terms of *aidôs*: the era is to be marked by a complete failure of reciprocal relationships (*Works and Days* 182–91) usually observed between family members, *xeinoi*, and parties to oaths (*Works and Days* 192–94):

> δίκη δ' ἐν χερσί· καὶ αἰδὼς
> οὐκ ἔσται, βλάψει δ' ὁ κακὸς τὸν ἀρείονα φῶτα
> μύθοισι σκολιοῖς ἐνέπων, ἐπὶ δ' ὅρκον ὀμεῖται.

> Justice will be in their hands, and reverence will not exist, but the bad man will harm the superior one, speaking with crooked discourses, and he will swear an oath upon them. [trans. Most 2006]

Aidôs is clearly a matter of proper verbal behavior here; the man who lacks this quality speaks "crooked words" in harming his betters. The description of the Fifth Age closes with another reference to *aidôs*, this time in the symbolic departure from earth of the goddess, accompanied by Nemesis (*Works and Days* 199–200). Finally, before proceeding to the specific instructions of the poem's latter part, Hesiod directs to his brother Perses a short exhortation concerning *aidôs* (*Works and Days* 317-19):

> αἰδὼς δ' οὐκ ἀγαθὴ κεχρημένον ἄνδρα κομίζει,
> αἰδώς, ἥ τ' ἄνδρας μέγα σίνεται ἠδ' ὀνίνησιν·
> αἰδώς τοι πρὸς ἀνολβίῃ, θάρσος δὲ πρὸς ὄλβῳ.

> Shame is not good at providing for a needy man—shame, which greatly harms men and also benefits them: for shame goes along with poverty, and self-confidence goes along with wealth. [trans. Most 2006]

In contrast to the preceding portions of the poem, in which *aidôs* is a virtue, these lines present the other side of the notion, by a particularly Hesiodic splitting of the abstract qualities into "good" and "bad" (cf. the section on Eris, *Works and Days* 11–26; also, Nemesis, at *Theogony* 223, is a pain for mortals, whereas at *Works and Days* 200, it is implicitly good). But this contrast is not a contradiction: the problem arises when some people have *aidôs* while others lack it; the very existence of the notion means that it can be used for good or ill (just as an oath "does harm" to humans in general, when someone swears falsely: *Theogony* 231–32). Hesiod is not urging Perses to dispense with *aidôs*; to the contrary, his discussion ends with a reference to the disastrous consequences of "shamelessness" (*anaideiê*) overpowering *aidôs* (*Works and Days* 324ff.): the gods diminish the life and wealth of that man who gets *olbos* with violence. In the light of this conclusion, *Works and Days* 319, αἰδώς τοι πρὸς ἀνολβίῃ, θάρσος δὲ πρὸς ὄλβῳ, should be read as a bitterly ironic piece of advice: "*aidôs* for poverty, boldness for wealth." Hesiod is on the side of *aidôs*; boldness (*tharsos*) is synonymous in this context with "taking *olbos* by force" in line 321, the short-term worldly success with long-term disadvantages. This portion of the *Works and Days*, then, is just as much prince-instruction on *aidôs* as is the preceding description of the Fifth Age.

The poetic genre that I have posited as the source of the similar passages from the *Theogony* proem and from *Odyssey* Book 8 is continued after Hesiod's time in the instructional poetry of Theognis of Megara.[22] It should not be surprising, then, to find that the theme of proper *aidôs* bulks large in the later tradition. Even though Theognidean poetry is addressed to the polis of Megara, through the foil-figure Cyrnus, the connection with the old tradition of prince-instruction is maintained through such formal characteristics of Theognidean poetry as the exhortations to remember (e.g., Theognis 27–30), the aphoristic style (e.g., 143–54), and, over all, the communication situation (an old man advises a young one) that frames the poetry.

Just as in the *Works and Days*, *aidôs* in Theognis' verse is conspicuous by being absent. Compare with *Works and Days* 192–94 this description of the *present* day in Theognis (289–93):[23]

> Νῦν δὲ τὰ τῶν ἀγαθῶν κακὰ γίνεται ἐσθλὰ κακοῖσιν
> ἀνδρῶν· ἡγέονται δ᾽ ἐκτραπέλοισι νόμοις·
> αἰδὼς μὲν γὰρ ὄλωλεν, ἀναιδείη δὲ καὶ ὕβρις
> νικήσασα δίκην γῆν κατὰ πᾶσαν ἔχει.

---

[22] See Friedländer 1913. My view of the poetic relationship among Cyrnus, Theognis, and Megara owes much to the work of Nagy 1982a.

[23] The opposition *aidôs* vs. *hubris* is traditional in Homeric diction: Cheyns 1967, esp. 9–10. Cheyns further compares Euryalus with Thersites, another reviler of kings: both can be said to embody *hubris*.

Now what the noble consider vices are deemed virtues by the base, and they rejoice in perverted ways [laws?]. For respect is lost and shameless outrage, having overcome justice, prevails in all the land. [trans. Gerber 1999]

More important for the present question, in Theognis as well, *aidôs* is regularly associated with proper speech. The famous lines promising immortality to Cyrnus conclude with a complaint in which the boy's lack of *aidôs* is equated precisely with the wrong verbal behavior, deceptive speech (253–54):

αὐτὰρ ἐγὼν ὀλίγης παρὰ σεῦ <u>οὐ τυγχάνω αἰδοῦς</u>,
    ἀλλ' ὥσπερ μικρὸν παῖδα <u>λόγοις μ' ἀπατᾷς.</u>

And yet I do not meet with a slight respect from you, but you deceive me with your words, as if I were a small child. [trans. Gerber 1999]

In exchange for immortality, Theognis' poetry elicits the properly mature use of respectful speech, bestowing a gift of words on the listener in two ways: externally (through *kleos*, 245–46) and internally through an instruction in proper speech.

The connection between speech and *aidôs* is made even more clearly in lines 83–86:[24]

Τούτους οὔ χ' εὕροις διζήμενος οὐδ' ἐπὶ πάντας
    ἀνθρώπους, οὓς ναῦς μὴ μία πάντας ἄγοι,
οἷσιν <u>ἐπὶ γλώσσῃ. τε καὶ ὀφθαλμοῖσιν ἔπεστιν</u>
    <u>αἰδώς,</u> οὐδ' αἰσχρὸν χρῆμ' ἔπι κέρδος ἄγει.

Not even if you searched among all men would you find so many that a single ship could not carry them all, men on whose tongue and eyes there is a sense of shame and whom profit does not lead to a disgraceful act. [trans. Gerber 1999]

Finally, the similarity of diction between the lines just quoted and the following piece of Theognidean instruction justifies us in treating as nearly synonymous *aidôs* and *to meilikhon* (365–66):

---

[24] Lines 85–86 exhibit the traditional association of *aidôs* and sight, on which see Gould 1973, 88 n. 74. Compare also the role of sight in both *Theogony* 85 and *Odyssey* 8.173, in which the respectful "looking-on" is generated by *aidôs*.

Ἴσχε νόῳ, γλώσσης δὲ τὸ μείλιχον αἰὲν ἐπέστω·
δειλῶν τοι τελέθει καρδίη ὀξυτέρη.

Hold back on your thoughts, but let there always be sweetness on your tongue; a heart that is too quick to show emotions is assuredly a mark of the base. [trans. Gerber 1999]

Thus, Theognis is operating with the same concepts and poetic diction as Homer and Hesiod: recall the recurring phrase *aidôi meilikhiêi*, which joins the two concepts that are complementary in Theognis, each concept having a special association with speech.[25]

We have seen so far that *aidôs* is a proper topic for instructional poetry, as both the *Works and Days* and Theognis show; that *aidôs* has a special association with speech; and that there is an established traditional diction surrounding instruction on *aidôs*. The relevance of these points to the discussion of *Odyssey* 8.166–77 and *Theogony* 79–93 should be clear: in both of the passages *aidôs* arises precisely in the context of a speech-act, one which involves, explicitly, an audience and a speaker.

Now the dative of manner, *aidôi meilikhiêi*, has long been seen to function differently in each passage: in *Odyssey* 8.172 it certainly describes the speaker's behavior, whereas in *Theogony* 92 it describes audience reaction. To my mind, this is simply a powerful confirmation of the essentially reciprocal quality of *aidôs*, not a mistake on the part of an adapting poet, as critics hunting the "original" passage would have it.[26] As J. P. Gould has noted, *aidôs* is one of many Greek words "where reciprocity of usage implies reciprocity of behavior and attitude in the situation of which the word is used: the feeling of *aidôs*, we may say, is common to both parties in the encounter, or … characteristic of the encounter itself."[27]

It is easy to see how a speaker uses *aidôs*—in knowing when and how to speak. At *Odyssey* 8.166–77, Odysseus upbraids Euryalus precisely because the younger man has spoken without *aidôs*. Odysseus then goes on to

[25] The phrase *aidôi meilikhiêi* thus resembles formulaic phrases of the type *aithomenon pur*, in which the adjective expresses the essential quality of the noun. In light of the semantics of *aidôs* (quintessentially reciprocal), I suggest that *meilikhios* (etymology unknown: see n. 18 above) is related to the IE root **mei-* (cf. Lat. *munus*, Skt. *Mitra*), the semantics of which are analyzed by Benveniste 1966a, 315–26, esp. 322–23.

[26] Cf. von Erffa 1937, 46: he claims Homer is the original because *Theogony* 92 is unusual in its use of the dative. Interpretation varies according to how critics assign *aidôs* at *Theogony* 92: to the king or to the audience; Neitzel 1977, 39 summarizes earlier views.

[27] Gould 1973, 87; further on the reciprocal quality of *aidôs*: Turpin 1980.

exhibit the quality himself in deftly turning a personal attack into a general comment that yet has a pointed, hidden message for the young prince. This same episode on Phaeacia can help us to understand how the audience in the speech-act, the *laoi*, show *aidôs* (as the Hesiodic description says they do). At *Odyssey* 7.69–72, the queen, Arete, is described:

> ὡς κείνη περὶ κῆρι τετίμηταί τε καὶ ἔστιν
> ἔκ τε φίλων παίδων ἔκ τ' αὐτοῦ Ἀλκινόοιο
> καὶ <u>λαῶν, οἵ μίν ῥα θεὸν ὣς εἰσορόωντες</u>
> <u>δειδέχαται μύθοισιν, ὅτε στείχῃσ' ἀνὰ ἄστυ.</u>

> So heartily is she honored, and has ever been, by her children and by Alcinous himself and by the people, who look upon her as upon a goddess, and greet her as she goes through the city. [trans. Murray and Dimock 1995]

It obviously shares the Homeric and Hesiodic motif of "looking on one as a god." The reference to greeting with words (*deidekhatai muthoisin*) contains the same idea as *Theogony* 91 *hilaskontai aidôi meilikhiêi*: the *laoi*, inspired by *aidôs*, know how and when to make their requests. Once again, speech and *aidôs* are closely related; the phrase *aidôi meilikhiêi* refers to both the form and the content of speech, and is an ellipsis for "*aidôs*, which expresses itself in *epea meilikhia*."[28]

A consistent association in Greek poetry between *aidôs* and kings is further evidence that instruction concerning *aidôs* belongs in discourse between princes and advisors. Witness the regular collocation of *aidoios* with *basileus* (e.g., *Theogony* 80 above).[29] Moreover, the link between *aidôs* and kingship is explicit in the *Hymn to Demeter*, as shown in Metaneira's words to the disguised goddess (*Hymn to Demeter* 213–15):

> Χαῖρε γύναι, ἐπεὶ οὔ σε κακῶν ἄπ' ἔολπα τοκήων
> ἔμμεναι, ἀλλ' ἀγαθῶν· <u>ἐπί τοι πρέπει ὄμμασιν αἰδὼς</u>
> <u>καὶ χάρις, ὡς εἴ πέρ τε θεμιστοπόλων βασιλήων.</u>

---

[28] *Meilikhios* most commonly modifies *epea*: Cunliffe 1963, 260; cf. the scholiast's comment at *Theogony* 92, that the adjective is an epithet of *audê*: DiGregorio 1975 *ad loc.*

[29] *Xenoi* and *parthenoi* are the only other social groups regularly associated with the adjective: see Gould 1973, 87–88.

"Greetings, lady, for I do not expect you come from low parents,
but ones of standing; your eyes have a striking modesty and
charm, as might come from lawgiver princes." [trans. West 2003a]

A good example of the reciprocal nature of this *aidôs* occurs at *Iliad* 10.237–
39. "Pick the best companion," says Agamemnon to Diomedes, "and do not
yield to *aidôs* and pick the worse, even though he be kinglier":

> μηδὲ σύ γ᾽ <u>αἰδόμενος</u> σῇσι φρεσὶ τὸν μὲν ἀρείω
> καλλείπειν, σὺ δὲ χείρον᾽ ὀπάσσεαι <u>αἰδοῖ εἴκων</u>
> ἐς γενεὴν ὁρόων, <u>μηδ᾽ εἰ βασιλεύτερός ἐστιν</u>.

The king is implicitly deserving of *aidôs* and possessor of it. In this way, we
can align the complementary roles of *aidôs* as follows:[30]

aidôs—of the sender	*aidôs*—of the receiver
Odyssey 8.172 (speaker)	*Theogony* 92 (*laoi* vs. king)
HHDem. 214–15 (kings)	*Iliad* 10.237–39 (prince vs. king)

Agamemnon's words to Diomedes, by their tone and in their dramatic
context, make clear that *aidôs* is not just associated with kings, but also a
fit subject on which to instruct young kings, such as Diomedes. Homeric
epic offers other episodes in which there is similar mention of *aidôs* but no
explicit reference to the status of the respective speakers and listeners; on
close examination, these episodes, too, share the characteristic situation of
prince-instruction (old adviser to young prince). The Embassy of *Iliad* 9, for
instance, can be viewed as an extended dramatization of prince-instruction,
with Phoenix holding the central role. The old man's instructions concerning
the *Litai* conclude with the advice to practice *aidôs* (*Iliad* 9.508-9):

> ὃς μέν τ᾽ αἰδέσεται κούρας Διὸς ἆσσον ἰούσας,
> τὸν δὲ μέγ᾽ ὤνησαν καί τ᾽ ἔκλυον εὐχομένοιο·

> Now him who will respect the daughters of Zeus, when they draw
> near, him they greatly benefit, and hear him when he prays ...
> [trans. Murray and Wyatt 1999]

---

[30]   For this model of the speech-event, see Jakobson 1960, 353. For the following analysis of *Odyssey*
8 and *Odyssey* 19, I rely on Jakobson's distinction of code and message as constituent factors in any
speech-event.

(Note that Ajax's speech concludes on the same notion, with a call for *aidôs*, directed towards the *hetairoi* this time: *Iliad* 9.640.) Some episodes reverse the direction of communication but nevertheless focus on the theme of *aidôs*. One particularly interesting example is at *Odyssey* 3.96–97, where the young prince Telemachus addresses Nestor, urging him to dispense with respectful reticence and to tell him straight out about Odysseus. Telemachus' words contain a verbal transformation of the key noun phrase discussed above, *aidôs meilikhiê*:

μηδέ τί μ᾽ αἰδόμενος μειλίσσεο μηδ᾽ ἐλεαίρων,
ἀλλ᾽ εὖ μοι κατάλεξον ὅπως ἤντησας ὀπωπῆς.

And do not out of consideration or pity for me speak soothing words, but tell me truly what evidence you came upon. [trans. Murray and Dimock 1995]

Nestor, as a king, possesses *aidôs*, which he exercises in his manner of speaking. We recall, also, that Nestor is more than just a careful speaker concerned with the content of his talk; in Homeric epic he qualifies as the ideal speaker, whose words "flow forth sweeter than honey" (*Iliad* 1.249):

τοῦ καὶ ἀπὸ γλώσσης μέλιτος γλυκίων ῥέεν αὐδή·

... he from whose tongue speech flowed sweeter than honey. [trans. Murray and Wyatt 1999]

Compare *Theogony* 84 on a king's speech:

τοῦ δ᾽ ἔπε᾽ ἐκ στόματος ῥεῖ μείλιχα·

his words flow soothingly from his mouth. [trans. Most 2006]

In addition, Nestor as an ideally long-lived king, who survives three generations, is constantly seen as instructing the rest of the Achaeans, from Agamemnon to Patroclus. We may therefore characterize the ideal Homeric king as both practitioner of the genre of prince-instruction and exemplar of its precepts. Finally, Nestor's dramatic role in the *Iliad* is to reconcile Agamemnon and Achilles: in other words, to solve a *neikos* in the *agora*;[31]

---

[31] On Nestor as ideal king: Detienne 1967, 73 n. 133; on the *Iliad* theme of *neikos* in the *agora*: Havelock 1966, 70 and Nagy 1999b, 311–13.

this underlies his actions from the mediating speech in Book 1 (254–84) to his interview with Patroclus in Book 11.

It appears, then, that we can find in Homeric epic not only references to a king's proper behavior and perquisites, but also dramatization of what, in the *Theogony* description of ideal kings, is merely abstract description. In the latter, kings are said to prompt *aidôs*, speak well and with powerful effect, and solve *neikea*; in the former, they actually *do* so. In fact, the *Iliad* in particular can be seen as a poem almost wholly about kingship and its abuse.[32] But, as I shall show now, the *Odyssey* as well has much to do with the theme of kingship, more than is generally acknowledged by critics who dwell on the adventure sequence to the neglect of the larger "frame" narrative of Books 1–8 and 13–24. We must bear in mind Odysseus' kingly status in order to appreciate the full resonances of the portions of the poem in which he plays beggar. In the same way, in Book 8, it is crucial that the audience recall Odysseus' status. Only then does one perceive that Odysseus is signaling his kingship to the audience within the poem, the Phaeacians. He does so by means of prince-instruction to Euryalus. Presumably, an audience familiar with archaic Greek compositions in the genre—such as the *Kheirônos hupothêkai*—would delight in Homer's creation of dramatic ironies throughout this scene. For Odysseus the stranger yet speaks like a king, to those who know.

We have seen that Odysseus' words to Euryalus contain two themes prominent in prince-instructions elsewhere, which account for the presence of similar phraseology. But the dramatic context itself in *Odyssey* 8 marks Odysseus' discourse for what it is. Stanford, noting the apparent digression in the speech to Euryalus, compares it to a "short sermon on the diversity of gifts" (adducing 1 *Corinthians* 12:4ff.) and his emphasis on the authoritative tone of the speech is correct: Odysseus is delivering the archaic Greek equivalent of quoting St. Paul, using the topic and tone of traditional instructional poetry.[33]

---

[32] The abuse of kingship in the *Iliad* is specifically related to Agamemnon's lack of *aidôs*: cf. *Iliad* 1.22–24 (his failure to honor Chryses) and *Iliad* 1.149 (Achilles' charge of *anaideia*). On the wider connections of this *Iliad* theme (the inferior king vs. superior warrior), see Davidson 1980, 197–202. Irish tradition also includes a number of tales in which the generating circumstance is a king's faulty behavior or failure to observe taboos (*geasa*) attached to kingship: see Draak 1959, 653.

[33] Stanford 1959, vol. 1 *ad loc.* In fact, Odysseus in the *Iliad* is a regular sermonizer about kingship in particular: of the four examples of gnomic verses that mention the role of *basileus* in the *Iliad*, Odysseus speaks three (*Iliad* 2.196, 2.204ff., 19.182–83; the fourth is by Calchas, *Iliad* 1.80); for the collection, see Ahrens 1937, 12ff. Only in the *Odyssey* are Odysseus' pronouncements disguised.

What is explicit in *Theogony* 86ff.—that it is the king who speaks fault-lessly, winning *aidôs* and solving a *neikos* in the *agora* thereby—is acted out in the *Odyssey*. Odysseus makes a general statement to his opponent (8.176–77), whom the poet has already characterized as being the best looking of the nobles (8.116). Although the contrasting character in Odysseus' short speech, the anonymous man to whom the gods have given the gift of speech, appears to be simply a foil, we must see that it is none other than *Odysseus himself*. This is disguised self-reference.[34] Odysseus does not have to say that he (unlike Euryalus) can speak well and with *aidôs*: he demonstrates this in his reply. If Odysseus conceals the reference to the identity of the good speaker, we recall that at this point in Scheria he still masks his own identity. The two hidden facts are significantly intertwined. Odysseus the faultless *speaker* is Odysseus son of Laertes, *king* of Ithaca.

In other details as well, the *Odyssey* passage offers a dramatic version of the abstract king-ideal of the *Theogony* (again, this is not to say that Homer "dramatizes" a pre-existing text of Hesiod, but that both use common themes in different modes). For the contest between Odysseus and Euryalus is actu-ally described by Alcinoos as a *neikos* during an *agôn* (8.238–39); the poet calls it a *neikos* as well (8.158 *neikese*). By winning, Odysseus acts to solve the *neikos*.[35] Note that *agôn* is a formulaic variant for *agora* in epic diction, and that the scene of the contest has in fact been described twice already in Book 8 as the *agora* (8.109, 156).

Not only are all the terms of the *Theogony* description thus acted out (speaking, *aidôs*, solving *neikos* in the *agora*); the poet of the *Odyssey* has prepared his audience to view the contest with Euryalus as being related to kingship. What I have called the "looking on" motif, prominent in the two passages under discussion (*Theogony* 85, *Odyssey* 8.173) is also used to introduce Telemachus' arrival at the Ithacan *agora* and Odysseus' own arrival at the Phaeacians' *agora* (*Odyssey* 2.10–13 and 8.16–19):[36]

---

[34] Cf. Berres 1975, 134, who views Odysseus' self-reference as evidence for an adapting *Odyssey*-poet's desire for self-portraiture. Since Odysseus, the king, refers to himself, the arguments of West and Wilamowitz (that the *Odyssey* description does not fit a king, therefore Hesiod is prior) are not valid: cf. West 1966, 183; Wilamowitz-Moellendorff 1916, 478–79. Also insupportable is Solmsen's contention (1954, 10) that the *Odyssey* passage leaves out all reference to kings (a point used to argue Homeric priority). Ancient critics, conscious of social roles, noted Odysseus' kingly status: the scholiast to *Theogony* 86 (DiGregorio 1975) selects Odysseus as the prime example of a king (citing *Odyssey* 4.693) to elucidate the Hesiod passage on ideal kingship.

[35] See Martin 1983, 65–76 on the Greek notion of contest as solution to difficulties.

[36] The primary and most extended expression of this "looking-on" motif comes at *Iliad* 12.312 (the people look on Glaucus and Sarpedon as gods). It is part of a larger theme, that of the "honor

βῆ ῥ᾽ ἴμεν εἰς ἀγορήν, παλάμῃ δ᾽ ἔχε χάλκεον ἔγχος,
οὐκ οἶος, ἅμα τῷ γε δύω κύνες ἀργοὶ ἕποντο.
θεσπεσίην δ᾽ ἄρα τῷ γε <u>χάριν</u> κατέχευεν Ἀθήνη·
<u>τὸν δ᾽ ἄρα πάντες λαοὶ ἐπερχόμενον θηεῦντο.</u>

Telemachus went to the assembly, holding in his hand a spear of bronze—not alone, for along with him two swift dogs followed; and wondrous was the grace that Athene shed upon him, and all the people marveled at him as he came. [trans. Murray and Dimock 1995, slightly modified]

καρπαλίμως δ᾽ ἔμπληντο βροτῶν <u>ἀγοραί</u> τε καὶ <u>ἕδραι</u>
ἀγρομένων· <u>πολλοὶ δ᾽ ἄρα θηήσαντο ἰδόντες</u>
<u>υἱὸν Λαέρταο δαΐφρονα.</u> τῷ δ᾽ ἄρ᾽ Ἀθήνη
θεσπεσίην κατέχευε <u>χάριν</u> κεφαλῇ τε καὶ ὤμοις.

Speedily the place of assembly and the seats were filled with gathering men. And many marveled at the sight of the wise son of Laertes, for wondrous was the grace that Athene shed upon his head and shoulders. [trans. Murray and Dimock 1995]

In the first passage, the context is concerned with the uncertainty as to whether the young prince will be king of Ithaca and gain a permanent place on the throne of his father, which he now temporarily occupies (2.14). Interestingly, his speaking ability is singled out for mention as the characteristic that most marks him for the position of king. Antinoos says (*Odyssey* 1.384-87):

Τηλέμαχ᾽, ἦ μάλα δή σε διδάσκουσιν θεοὶ αὐτοὶ
ὑψαγόρην τ᾽ ἔμεναι καὶ θαρσαλέως ἀγορεύειν.

---

of gods": one is honored (*Iliad* 9.155), repaid (*Iliad* 9.302–3), welcomed (*Iliad* 22.435) like "a god." Other instances of the theme: at *Iliad* 22.394 Hector is prayed to "like a god"; at *Odyssey* 7.11—a scene preparatory to the passage under discussion—Alcinoos, clearly a king, is said to be heard "like a god" by the *dêmos*. Note that, in the two passages cited in the text, the pouring of *kharis* by Athena is closely associated with the audience's favorable reaction to the figures of Telemachus and Odysseus. This accords precisely with the association of *kharis* and *aidôs* in *Hymn to Demeter* 214–15, quoted above: the possessor of *kharis* transmits *aidôs* (and therefore receives it also). Finally, let me cite Pindar *Olympian* 1.30: Χάρις δ᾽, ἅπερ ἅπαντα τεύχει τὰ μείλιχα θνατοῖς, in order to indicate the traditional nature of the dictional equivalences among terms which describe reciprocal behavior:
   aidôs + *kharis* (*Hymn to Demeter* 214–15)
   kharis + *ta meilikha* (*Olympian* 1.30)
   to meilikhon + *aidôs* (Theognis 85–86, 365)
   aidôi meilikhiêi (*Theogony* 92, *Odyssey* 8.172).

μὴ σέ γ' ἐν ἀμφιάλῳ Ἰθάκῃ βασιλῆα Κρονίων
ποιήσειεν, ὅ τοι γενεῇ πατρώϊόν ἐστιν.

"Telemachus, surely the gods themselves are teaching you a lofty
style, and to speak with boldness. May the son of Cronus never
make you king in seagirt Ithaca, which thing is by birth your
heritage." [trans. Murray and Dimock 1995]

So too in Scheria there is the possibility that the new arrival will knock
the islanders out of contention and become Nausicaa's husband. The poet
plays with the resonances of a folklore motif, the royal marriage test.[37] Royal
marriage seems far from connected to the topic of prince-instruction, but
as it turns out, in the *Odyssey* marriage and kingship have everything to do
with one another. Penelope and the rule of Ithaca are indissociable. I pointed
out earlier that *Odyssey* 19 contains an extended fragment of the Ruler's
Truth ideology, in form resembling something directly taken from prince-
instruction poetry. Who gives this apparent digression within the poem?
None other than the disguised king again, Odysseus.

Both in his talk with Penelope and in his reply to Euryalus, Odysseus
allows his interlocutor to know that he is the king—provided the interlocutor
recognizes the genre in which Odysseus is speaking.[38] In Book 8, he seals
his coded signal with a clear sign consisting of a spectacular discus-throw.
As if to contrast with the final revelation of his status, Odysseus begins the
throw while still wrapped in his *pharos* (8.186); the throw literally lowers the
status of the Phaeacians as it reveals Odysseus' own: they cower to the ground
beneath the flung discus (190), which flies "past all the *sêmata*." While the
discus surpasses these "distinguishing marks," the result of the throw is *itself*
a *sêma*, one which Athena validates in person with a proclamation containing
a double meaning (*Odyssey* 8.195–98):

καί κ' ἀλαός τοι, ξεῖνε, διακρίνειε τὸ σῆμα
ἀμφαφόων, ἐπεὶ οὔ τι μεμιγμένον ἐστὶν ὁμίλῳ,

---

[37] Such resonances were certainly possible for an ancient audience: witness the multiform, attested
in cult, in which Odysseus competes in a foot-race to win Penelope and makes dedications to Athena
for his victory: Pausanias *Description of Greece* 3.12.4, discussed in Detienne 1981, 24–25. Further on
such folktale elements in the competition for Penelope: Hoelscher 1978.

[38] Odysseus' parallel role as poet, manipulating genres of discourse, once more makes it easy to lose
sight of the artful composer Homer, who puts the genre of instruction-poetry into Odysseus' mouth
for purposes of the wider composition. The layering evident in Odysseus' speech at *Odyssey* 8.167ff.
is thus another piece of evidence (like Odysseus' lies and his adventure-telling) for the theory that
the *Odyssey's* overriding concern is with the practice of narrative per se: see Todorov 1977, 53–65.

ἀλλὰ πολὺ πρῶτον. σὺ δὲ θάρσει τόνδε γ᾽ ἄεθλον·
οὔ τις Φαιήκων τόν γ᾽ ἵξεται οὐδ᾽ ὑπερήσει.

"Even a blind man, stranger, could distinguish this mark, groping
for it with his hands, for it is in no way confused in the throng
of the others, but is far the first. You may take confidence from
this throw, at any rate: no one of the Phaeacians will reach this,
or surpass it." [trans. Murray and Dimock 1995]

The key to the riddle is contained in an unusual catachresis, for only here
(196) in Homeric poetry is *homilos* used to refer to inanimate objects rather
than to a throng of persons, usually warriors. The significance of the usage
becomes clearer when we note that *homilos* can be used to describe the
spectators at a contest (as at *Iliad* 23.804, 813) and actually is used of the
Phaeacian onlookers in this very contest at *Odyssey* 8.109.

Athena's brief *epinikion* commemorating Odysseus' throw can be
decoded to mean that Odysseus stands out from the "crowd" just as his
discus is "not mixed in with the *homilos*." The message of Athena is exactly
that which Odysseus transmits concerning himself (the "speaker") in his
words to Euryalus: cf. 8.172, μετὰ δὲ πρέπει ἀγρομένοισιν. "Even a blind
man" can distinguish Odysseus' sign, says Athena; the statement is ironically
half-fulfilled soon after the contest when Demodocus, the blind bard, tells
the story of Odysseus in the Trojan Horse. but does not recognize the person
who requested the tale, Odysseus (8.487ff.). This "sign" that has "surpassed
all others," then, is iconic for Odysseus' status as surpassing speaker, athlete,
and king.

In Book 19, a *sêma* again follows Odysseus' coded use of prince-
instruction in the conversation with Penelope. This time the sign that alerts
the audience to the presence of other coded messages is the brooch that
Penelope recognizes from Odysseus' description.[39] Following Nagy's recent
demonstration that poetry itself can be a *sêma* in epic, I now suggest that in
both the *Odyssey* 8 and 19 episodes, Odysseus is delivering *two* semata: those
designated as such (the discus-throw, the brooch) and the undesignated use
of a genre of discourse as a code to his listener.[40]

---

[39] On the ironies of this entire scene see Fenik 1974, 20–25; on Odysseus' clothes as a coded
message, see Nagy 1983, 36–37.

[40] On poetry as *sêma*: Nagy 1983, 51. The general symmetry between the Phaeacian and Ithacan
recognition scenes is outlined by Fenik 1974, 53–55.

In Scheria, only keen-minded Alcinoos succeeds in interpreting the sign, though the audience of the poem appreciates its meaning: it requires a king to know one. In Book 19, suspense arises from the use of the hidden *sêma*: will Penelope accomplish the task of reading Odysseus' genre? But the queen, clever woman, king's proper wife (herself *like* a good king: *Odyssey* 19.108–9), must no doubt have already understood the speaker for what he is—not beggar but king, instructor of princes.[41]

[41] A shorter version of this paper was first delivered at the American Philological Association meeting in Philadelphia (December 1982). Useful suggestions for the initial publication came from the anonymous *TAPA* referees and Gregory Nagy, whom I thank. On the early recognition of Odysseus by Penelope (hinted at in the final paragraph) see now Vlahos 2007.

13

PULP EPIC

THE *CATALOGUE* AND THE *SHIELD*[1]

"All normal people need both classics and trash." George Bernard Shaw's adage, comforting to those whose personal preferences lean toward rap music rather than *Rigoletto*, can also apply to the professional realm. Trash and classics go hand in hand. Mutually self-defining as these are, however, one rarely finds them brought together in the same critical discourse, any more than one finds them embodied in a single writer (apart from rarities like the noir novelist Raymond Chandler, who took top marks in the Civil Service Classics exam of 1907).[2]

In this paper I propose to re-read a problematic classical (if not classic) text, the *Shield of Heracles* attributed to Hesiod, by using a "trash aesthetic." Explicit reference to this aesthetic has increasingly played a role in the analysis of a wide range of artistic productions and cultural forms, from trailer parks to New Jersey hairstyles to Bill Clinton's girlfriends. Film bulks largest in the aesthetic consideration of trash, and vocabulary and examples from movies will be useful in this analysis. The subcategory of trash analysis centering on verbal narrative (called "pulp theory" after the novels—like Chandler's—once thought to be worth less than the cheap paper they were printed on) will also prove helpful.[3]

The discovery of a likeness between pulp film and written narrative is, of course, nothing new, as the media have always been symbiotic in production as in reception. Brendan Behan tells of Borstal Boys passing the time in

---

[1]   Originally published in *The Hesiodic Catalogue of Women: Constructions and Reconstructions*, ed. R. Hunter (Cambridge: Cambridge University Press, 2005), 153-75.

[2]   On the formative influence of Chandler's classical education at Dulwich College, London, see Hiney 1997, 15–16, 21, 24 and Bloom 1996, 48–49.

[3]   Useful introductions centered on film are Cartmell et al. 1997; Schaefer 1999; Mendik and Harper 2000. For the trash mode in literary analysis, see Hawkins 1990.

custody by telling what they called "pictures"—that is, stories they could all piece together from remembered gangster films.[4] At another level, Quentin Tarantino's brilliant trash masterpiece *Pulp Fiction* asserts the essential likeness of trashy novels and trashy films. This exploration of the trashiest piece of ancient Greek heroic poetry is in homage to him.[5]

Who says the *Aspis* (as I will call the poem, to distinguish it from the description of Achilles' shield in the *Iliad*) is trash? Just about every Hellenist who bothers to mention it. The poem has the worst reputation accorded any piece of surviving hexameter poetry. Albin Lesky says: "A poet of limited gifts has tried to elevate and ennoble a standard feature of epic but has merely defaced and distorted it."[6] For Thalmann, "the poem's execution is not worthy of the underlying conception," though he grants that even as mediocre a poet as the composer of the *Aspis* could milk some meaning out of the standard technique of scenic juxtaposition.[7] Professors Barron and Easterling in the *Cambridge History of Classical Literature* call the *Aspis* "a weak and muddled account of the fight between Herakles and Cycnus," which "lacks the strength and wit of Hesiod" and "depends for its effects on sheer accumulation of detail, preferably detail of a sensational kind."[8] On the whole, they conclude, it is clumsily adapted from Homer. Martin West, in the second and third editions of the *Oxford Classical Dictionary*, concurs: "Disproportion is characteristic of the work; the Homeric apparatus of arming, divine machination, brave speeches, and long similes is lavished on an encounter in which two blows are struck in all. Parts of the description of the shield betray a taste for the macabre."[9]

For nineteenth-century appreciations, we can turn to Paley who in turn approves the colorful views of Welcker's nemesis, Colonel Mure. "Wild and fantastic, without originality, and turgid without dignity" is the Colonel's judgment; "not only is the poetical law against rude collisions of heterogeneous elements completely set at naught, but the text is often, to all appearances, purposely so disposed, that the same line contains the conclusion of one and the commencement of another image of the most offensively opposite character. The joyous is suddenly converted into the pathetic, the

---

[4] Behan 1959, 334.

[5] On the development of Tarantino's aesthetic, see Woods 1996.

[6] Lesky 1966, 104.

[7] Thalmann 1984, 62–64.

[8] Barron and Easterling 1989, 62.

[9] West 1970, 511. The view is repeated in his article for the third edition of the *OCD* (1996).

tender into the terrible, with an almost burlesque effect."[10] J. P. Mahaffy, at
the end of the century, was somewhat kinder in his appraisal, noting that
"had we lost the *Iliad*, we should doubtless admire many of its features in
the copy" (by which he means the *Aspis* ekphrasis). But fortunately, he goes
on to say, "we are not reduced to this extremity."[11] Where the *Iliad* shield
is exciting and picturesque, says Mahaffy, the *Aspis* is "merely terrible and
weird." Which makes one think that perhaps Mahaffy's most famous student,
Oscar Wilde, would have made the perfect translator of the miniature epic.[12]

On those occasions when the Classicist does not choose to vent his
disapproval of the style of the *Aspis*, the dismissal is done discreetly, with
a charge of copying. Thus, T. W. Allen refers to "the palpable imitation" of
Iliad 18 by the *Aspis*.[13] Even Richard Janko lapses into the language of model
and copy when it comes to this poem, claiming that it is one of a class of
"late" compositions that imitates a fixed text of the *Iliad*.[14] We shall return
to this highly debatable notion later. The critical disparagement of the *Aspis*
has deep roots in antiquity. Value judgments are entangled with questions of
authenticity and authorship, when it comes to Homer versus Hesiod versus
pseudo-Hesiod. Aristophanes of Byzantium, as we learn from the following
ancient *hypothesis* to the *Aspis*, suspected that the poem was not by Hesiod
but by an imitator of Homer. Others defended its authorship:

> The beginning of the *Shield* is in circulation [φέρεται] in the fourth book of
> the *Catalogue*, extending to line fifty-six.[15] And for this reason Aristophanes
> has suspected that it does not belong to Hesiod, but to someone else
> choosing to imitate [μιμήσασθαι] the Homeric shield. The Athenian
> Megacleides knows the poem to be genuine, but censures Hesiod; for he
> says it is illogical for Hephaestus to make armor for his mother's enemies.
> Apollonius of Rhodes in the third book says it belongs to him [Hesiod]
> both from its style [ἐκ τοῦ χαρακτῆρος] and from finding that Iolaus again

---

[10]   Paley 1883, xxii.

[11]   Mahaffy 1891.

[12]   Mahaffy greatly influenced the young Wilde, whom he escorted to Greece and Italy; cf. Ellmann 1987, 27–28, 55, 70.

[13]   Allen 1924, 92; see Thalmann 1984, 64.

[14]   Janko 1986.

[15]   For this technical sense of φέρεσθαι in reference to literary attestation (frequent in scholia), see LSJ, ninth ed., *s.v.* VIII.

acts as the charioteer for Heracles in the *Catalogue*. And Stesichorus too says that the poem is Hesiod's.[16]

Apparently, Aristophanes based his reasoning first on the assumption that Hesiod *did* compose the *Catalogue of Women*, and second that Hesiod would *not* repeat fifty-six of his own lines (contained in Book 4 of the *Catalogue*) in composing another poem, the *Aspis*. One of the few other ancients to voice an opinion about the poem is pseudo-Longinus (*On the Sublime* 9.5). Comparing a few lines from this poem about Achlys, the mist of war-death, with the Homeric depiction of Eris (*Iliad* 4.442), he observes:

> Quite unlike this is Hesiod's description of Gloom [ἀχλύς], if indeed we are right in adding the *Shield* to the list of Hesiod's works; 'rheum from her nostrils was running' [*Aspis* 26]. He has not made the image terrible [δεινόν], but offensive [μισητόν].[17]

The critical attitude at this stage is not far from that of Friedrich Wolf, who undertook in 1817 to edit the *Aspis*, only to show, as he says, how in a few decades heroic verse had degenerated from the Homeric type.[18] Two more recent critics have resisted the usual line. Andrew Becker, in a sophisticated book on *ekphrasis*, devotes some pages to the complex self-reflexive character of the *Aspis*, its constant directing of our attention toward the indescribable and unspeakable qualities of the very things it describes and speaks of.[19] Robert Lamberton, in his general introduction to Hesiod, is not afraid to use "parasitic" in a value-neutral sense when speaking of the *Aspis*. He also speaks of its "outrageousness that is both satisfying and liberating," and brilliantly compares the poem to the art of Goya and to the Old Irish saga *Táin Bó Cúailnge*. Only Lamberton strikes one as actually liking this composition.[20]

Has the *Aspis* failed so disastrously or have its interpreters? Could it be that terms like "failure" applied to archaic Greek poetry are themselves problematic? Before examining the specific verses that provoke the hottest criticism in the *Aspis* and trying to come up with a different critical idiom, we should draw back for a moment to recall the critics' criterion: Homer—as "Longinus" makes explicit. But whose Homer? The aesthetics of the

---

[16] For the text, cf. Solmsen 1983, 86.

[17] Translation by Fyfe 1932, 145–47.

[18] On Wolf's edition, cf. Ranke 1840, v.

[19] Becker 1995, 36–40, a condensation of Becker 1992.

[20] Lamberton 1988b, 138–44.

later critical tradition about epic are shaped by Aristotle. In the *Poetics*, he famously denigrated episodic narratives—for instance, poems united only because they dealt with Heracles—in favor of the μῦθος εἷς, the organic plot, of the Homeric epics.[21] While we can admire Aristotle's awareness of the uniqueness of Homer, we need not toss out the non-Homeric simply because it did not suit Aristotle's austere tastes.

Contemporary ethnophilology can broaden our scope. Study of heroic oral traditional literature in other cultures, whether Indic, Irish, West African, Central Asian, or South Slavic, will easily show that the single episode, lasting a few hours in performance, and chosen by the singer to fit the mood and politics of his immediate audience, is the basis for live composition in performance.[22] Or in other words, the 480-line, single-episode *Aspis* looks much more like an oral poem than does the *Iliad*. Still, one may object, even if we restrain an Aristotelian appetite for the big-ticket organic epic, the *Aspis* does not satisfy. One can value the episodic and still find the *Aspis*, in its diction and structure, a mess—not to say, trash. I *want* to call it "trash" but I shall employ the term (and its affiliate, pulp) in a different register, as the name of a heuristic device rather than as a term of abuse. My intent in employing the trash aesthetic is not to reverse the terms, to plump for pulp, or to subvert canons of taste (by now a quaint archaism). It is a more neutral aim, to analyze techniques and stylistic traits common to the creation of pulp and to the pseudo-Hesiodic verses. We could simply rest content with the amusing irony that it took the world two millennia and millions of Hollywood dollars to catch up with the aesthetic of the *Aspis*. But it is better if we look for a critical payoff. After an analysis of the categories of pulp technique that match the strategies of the *Aspis*, the payoff will emerge first in the way of an internal stylistic analysis and then in a complete re-evaluation of the part this poem plays in relation to the Hesiodic *Catalogue of Women*.[23]

We need to specify what characterizes the pulp aesthetic. Clive Bloom in *Cult Fiction* offers a range of features.[24] First among them, interestingly, is episodic narration—as he notes, it is good for serialization. Next, purposive, teleological movement in the plot is to be expected; so is a focus on outward

[21] *Poetics* 1451a.

[22] On the episode as unit, see Blackburn et al. 1989, 11; Belcher 1999, 27, 51; Flueckiger 1999, 133–34.

[23] It may not be amiss to view the *Catalogue*, in movie terms, as the ultimate chick-flick from antiq-uity: on the female-directed framing of a cognate passage, the "catalogue" in *Odyssey* 11, see Doherty 1991 and Martin 2001a.

[24] Bloom 1996, 132–55.

appearances and an avoidance of psychologizing action. Consistency of character is elevated over complex plot. Readers of pulp desire consistency, just as they constantly desire that a given narration will go the limit. Five modern genres can be said to operate by "pulp" rules—science fiction; horror; private eye; western; and superhero. I would place the *Aspis* on the cusp of the latter two categories. The poem features a superhero Heracles, son of Zeus, who is depicted battling it out with a bad character, Cycnus, son of Ares, in a shoot-'em-up scene reminiscent of the showdown at the OK Corral. At the same time, the pictures on the shield of Heracles give us plenty of horror touches, including vampirism. The term episodic fits the *Aspis*, as we have already said; so does lack of psychological realism. Perhaps it requires a long poem like the *Iliad* to articulate inner character and monumental composition of the Homeric type might thus represent a breakthrough for oral-poetic art. At any rate, it should be borne in mind that the practicalities of short, episodic length probably account for several of the other pulp features.

Although the title Bloom chooses for his chapter on the rules of pulp is "Living In Technicolor," his main concern is verbal narrative, not movies. Comic books are as close as he gets to the visual. They happen to crystallize the critical issues especially well, because public outrage in the 1950s led to the creation of a voluntary Comics Code, and, as Bloom points out, simply reversing the proscriptions gives us a neat definition of pulp. The Code rules that "all scenes of horror, excessive bloodshed, gory or gruesome crimes, depravity, lust, sadism or masochism shall not be permitted."[25] Delete the negative and you have the recipe for a bestseller. For cinematic strategies equivalent to the pulp rules, I am taking into account the above-mentioned, all of which seem to apply to the *Aspis*. In addition, the following more technical feature can be matched with passages from the poem.

First, *noise*. The trashier the movie, the louder it is. Fans of David Lynch's highly disturbed *Eraserhead* will recall the screech level. Merchant and Ivory films, by contrast, are as silent as the tomb; classic Bergman is near soundless. The *Aspis* on the other hand is loud: it has been calculated that sound words occur nearly twice as often in the pseudo-Hesiodic as in the Homeric shield.[26] Lines 57–65 are not untypical. They describe Heracles' discovery of Cycnus and his father Ares standing in a chariot:

[25]   Bloom 1996, 142–43.

[26]   Picot 1998, 50 n. 13; see also Lamberton 1988b, 142 on noise in the *Aspis*.

Ὃς καὶ Κύκνον ἔπεφνεν, Ἀρητιάδην μεγάθυμον.
εὖρε γὰρ ἐν τεμένει ἑκατηβόλου Ἀπόλλωνος
αὐτὸν καὶ πατέρα ὃν Ἄρη’, ἄατον πολέμοιο,
τεύχεσι λαμπομένους σέλας ὣς πυρὸς αἰθομένοιο,   60
ἑσταότ’ ἐν δίφρῳ· χθόνα δ’ ἔκτυπον ὠκέες ἵπποι
νύσσοντες χηλῇσι, κόνις δέ σφ’ ἀμφιδεδήει
κοπτομένη πλεκτοῖσιν ὑφ’ ἅρμασι καὶ ποσὶν ἵππων·
ἅρματα δ’ εὐποίητα καὶ ἄντυγες ἀμφαράβιζον
ἵππων ἱεμένων. κεχάρητο δὲ Κύκνος ἀμύμων ...   65

And he slew Cycnus, the gallant son of Ares. For he found him in the precinct of far-shooting Apollo, him and his father Ares, never sated with war. Their armor shone like a flame of blazing fire as they two stood in their chariot: their swift horses struck the earth and pawed it with their hoofs, and the dust rose like smoke about them, pounded by the chariot wheels and the horses' hoofs, while the well-made chariot and its rails rattled around them as the horses plunged. And blameless Cycnus was glad ...[27]

The staccato sounds of line 59—αὐτὸν καὶ πατέρα ὃν Ἄρη’, ἄατον πολέμοιο—provide a drumbeat. Light effects—flashing armor in the grove—are followed by horses beating the ground, scratching hooves, dust flying up, more beating (κοπτομένη, 63), and then the rumble of the chariot wheels (ἀμφαράβιζον, 64), all of which occurs before anyone even thinks of fighting. Noise surrounds the auditor of the *Aspis*. More often, it is coupled with spectacular sights and colors—the equivalent of animated special effects in film. Three passages might be adduced in this connection. The first (191-96) comes from the shield description:

Ἐν δ’ Ἄρεος βλοσυροῖο ποδώκεες ἔστασαν ἵπποι
χρύσεοι, ἐν δὲ καὶ αὐτὸς ἐναρσφόρος οὔλιος Ἄρης,
αἰχμὴν ἐν χείρεσσιν ἔχων, πρυλέεσσι κελεύων,
αἵματι φοινικόεις ὡς εἰ ζωοὺς ἐναρίζων,
δίφρου ἐπεμβεβαώς· παρὰ δὲ Δεῖμός τε Φόβος τε   195
ἔστασαν ἱέμενοι πόλεμον καταδύμεναι ἀνδρῶν.

And on [the shield] stood the fleet-footed horses of grim Ares made of gold, and deadly Ares the spoil-winner himself. He held a spear in his hands and was urging on the footmen: he was red

---

[27] Translations throughout are based on Evelyn-White 1914, with minor changes.

with blood as if he were slaying living men, and he stood in
his chariot. Beside him stood Fear and Dread, eager to plunge
amidst the fighting men.

Unlike the dynamic of the *Iliad* shield's arming, we are not looking over
the god's shoulder as he manufactures the inlays. This artifact is completed
already and the *en* phrases are static, not part of a larger phrase "he made
on it" (contrast, e.g., *Iliad* 18.483, 490). Even so there is movement and
color. Fear and Dread stand straining to enter the fray. Ares is urging on
the fighters, stepping onto the chariot. His golden horses contrast with the
bloody god (αἵματι φοινικόεις, 194). If we imagine the polished shield as
both depicting and reflecting, it is interesting that the same god is facing
Heracles at this very moment, as if his picture were caught on the lens of the
shield surface.

The next two passages to contemplate are more complicated combinations of color, or of color and sound, featuring extensive synaesthesia. At line
139, Heracles picks up the shield, described as "all-glancing" (*panaiolon*).
This initial appearance is then developed further in lines 141–48:

πᾶν μὲν γὰρ κύκλῳ τιτάνῳ λευκῷ τ' ἐλέφαντι
ἠλέκτρῳ θ' ὑπολαμπὲς ἔην χρυσῷ τε φαεινῷ
λαμπόμενον, κυάνου δὲ διὰ πτύχες ἠλήλαντο.
ἐν μέσσῳ δ' ἀδάμαντος ἔην Φόβος οὔ τι φατειός,
ἔμπαλιν ὄσσοισιν πυρὶ λαμπομένοισι δεδορκώς·   145
τοῦ καὶ ὀδόντων μὲν πλῆτο στόμα λευκαθεόντων,
δεινῶν, ἀπλήτων, ἐπὶ δὲ βλοσυροῖο μετώπου
δεινὴ Ἔρις πεπότητο κορύσσουσα κλόνον ἀνδρῶν...

For its whole orb shimmered with enamel and white ivory and
electrum, and it glowed with shining gold; and there were zones
of cyanus drawn upon it. In the center was Fear worked in
adamant, unspeakable, staring backwards with eyes that glowed
with fire. His mouth was full of teeth in a white row, fearful and
daunting, and upon his grim brow hovered frightful Strife who
arrays the throng of men ...

If we disregard Heyne's rejection of 143, we can add dark blue to the
palette. Perhaps the reason he rejected the line and Solmsen continues to
bracket it in the Oxford text is this very garishness. The lights come up,
as Phobos, in the center, looks back with fire-gleaming eyes. And then we
are back to colors, with his white gleaming teeth (146). Strife is apparently

floating above his face, described as βλοσυρός, an adjective of uncertain meaning, much beloved by the *Aspis* poet. The second passage (228–37) has even more of this effect:

αὐτὸς δὲ σπεύδοντι καὶ ἐρρίγοντι ἐοικὼς
Περσεὺς Δαναΐδης ἐτιταίνετο· ταὶ δὲ μετ' αὐτὸν
Γοργόνες ἄπλητοί τε καὶ οὐ φαταὶ ἐρρώοντο   230
ἱέμεναι μαπέειν· ἐπὶ δὲ χλωροῦ ἀδάμαντος
βαινουσέων ἰάχεσκε σάκος μεγάλῳ ὀρυμαγδῷ
ὀξέα καὶ λιγέως· ἐπὶ δὲ ζώνῃσι δράκοντε
δοιὼ ἀπῃωρεῦντ' ἐπικυρτώοντε κάρηνα·
λίχμαζον δ' ἄρα τώ γε, μένει δ' ἐχάρασσον ὀδόντας   235
ἄγρια δερκομένω· ἐπὶ δὲ δεινοῖσι καρήνοις
Γοργείοις ἐδονεῖτο μέγας φόβος. ...

> Perseus himself, the son of Danae, was at full stretch, like one who hurries and shudders with horror. And after him rushed the Gorgons, unapproachable and unspeakable, longing to seize him; as they trod upon the pale adamant, the shield rang sharp and clear with a loud clanging. Two serpents hung down at their girdles with heads curved forward; their tongues were flickering, and their teeth gnashing with fury, and their eyes glaring fiercely. And upon the awful heads of the Gorgons great fear was quaking.

The scenery—Perseus chased by the Gorgons—was common in archaic art. This and other details led archaeologically-minded critics, such as Myres and Cook, to date the *Aspis* to the sixth century BCE.[28] I am more interested in the sound effects that tart up the action here. As they tread on the pale adamant of the shield, the pursuing Gorgons make the metal shriek and clang (233), sharp and shrill. We then get a visual moment (dual snakes dangling from their belts), followed by more noise: the snakes are sticking out their tongues (presumably hissing) and clashing their teeth. We are not meant to pause and ask whether snakes actually have teeth, since to an audience it doesn't matter—it is over the top, scary, and therefore great.[29]

This passage, with its snakes in tight focus, shows us something of the effect of the camera dollying in. Extreme close-up is a staple of trash cinema,

---

[28]   Cook 1937 and Myres 1941.

[29]   Part of the project of trash aesthetics is "taking audiences and their pleasures seriously": Cartmell et al. 1997, 1. The frequency of violent scenes, especially Gorgon-slaying, in sixth-century vase-painting should tell us something about tastes in poetry as well

as it is of porn, a related genre. Knives, bullets, or other invasive instruments more tellingly hit a nerve the closer you see them. In the *Aspis*, the hero's body is never really glimpsed, sheathed as it is in various pieces of armament and armor. The constituents, however, are celebrated visually, in synecdochic homage to the hero within. One item gets an especially close camera shot (128–38):

θήκατο δ' ἀμφ' ὤμοισιν ἀρῆς ἀλκτῆρα σίδηρον,
δεινὸς ἀνήρ· κοίλην δὲ περὶ στήθεσσι φαρέτρην
κάββαλεν ἐξόπιθεν· πολλοὶ δ' ἔντοσθεν ὀιστοὶ   130
ῥιγηλοί, θανάτοιο λαθιφθόγγοιο δοτῆρες·
πρόσθεν μὲν θάνατόν τ' εἶχον καὶ δάκρυσι μῦρον,
μέσσοι δὲ ξεστοί, περιμήκεες, αὐτὰρ ὄπισθε
μόρφνοιο φλεγύαο καλυπτόμενοι πτερύγεσσιν.
εἵλετο δ' ὄβριμον ἔγχος, ἀκαχμένον αἴθοπι χαλκῷ.   135
κρατὶ δ' ἐπ' ἰφθίμῳ κυνέην εὔτυκτον ἔθηκε,
δαιδαλέην, ἀδάμαντος, ἐπὶ κροτάφοις ἀραρυῖαν,
ἥ τ' εἴρυτο κάρη Ἡρακλῆος θείοιο.

> Over his shoulders the fierce warrior put the steel that saves men from doom, and across his breast he slung behind him a hollow quiver. Within it were many chilling arrows, dealers of death which makes speech forgotten: in front they had death, and trickled with tears; their shafts were smooth and very long; and their butts were covered with feathers of a brown eagle. And he took his strong spear, pointed with shining bronze, and on his valiant head set a well-made helm of adamant, cunningly wrought, which fitted closely on the temples; and that guarded the head of god-like Heracles ...

The deadly arrows of Heracles are transformed into tripartite beasts, like Geryon or the Chimaera, at lines 131–34. They bring the chill of doom; they are dealers of death that makes one forget how to talk. The way in which the weapon, lovingly described in close-up, captures the essence of the killer Heracles, recalls such pulp classics as *The Maltese Falcon*. Compare the way in which the essence of Dashiell Hammett's hero is captured as he rolls tobacco:

> Spade's thick fingers made a cigarette with deliberate care, sifting a measured quantity of tan flakes down into a curved paper, spreading the flakes so that they lay equal at the ends with a slight depression in the middle, thumbs rolling the paper's inner edge down and up under the outer

edges as forefingers pressed it over, thumbs and fingers sliding to the paper cylinder's ends to hold it even while tongue licked the flap, left forefinger and thumb pinching their end while right forefinger and thumb smoothed the damp seam, right forefinger and thumb twisting their end and lifting the other to Sam's mouth.[30]

Spade's cigarette may have more erotic potential than Heracles' arrows, but the extravagant desire of the camera for the object, the extreme close-up, is the same as in the *Aspis*. Slow motion is obtained both in Homeric narrative and in the *Aspis* by the device of the simile, which acts like a freeze-frame, pausing the action as the poet develops another, analogical argument to interpret the scene within the scene. One thinks of such trash effects as the use of split screens in Quentin Tarantino's *Jackie Brown*—itself a parodic use of the technique developed by B-grade movies and TV in the 1960s. What makes the *Aspis* different, trashier than the *Iliad*, is a matter of degree: the simile overload, the complexity and action of the similes themselves, and the subsequent time-lag this brings about. Consider lines 374–92:

ὡς δ' ὅτ' ἀφ' ὑψηλῆς κορυφῆς ὄρεος μεγάλοιο
πέτραι ἀποθρώσκωσιν, ἐπ' ἀλλήλαις δὲ πέσωσι,   375
πολλαὶ δὲ δρῦς ὑψίκομοι, πολλαὶ δέ τε πεῦκαι
αἴγειροί τε τανύρριζοι ῥήγνυνται ὑπ' αὐτέων
ῥίμφα κυλινδομένων, ἧος πεδίονδ' ἀφίκωνται,
ὡς οἳ ἐπ' ἀλλήλοισι πέσον μέγα κεκλήγοντες.
πᾶσα δὲ Μυρμιδόνων τε πόλις κλειτή τ' Ἰαωλκὸς   380
Ἄρνη τ' ἠδ' Ἑλίκη Ἄνθειά τε ποιήεσσα
φωνῇ ὑπ' ἀμφοτέρων μεγάλ' ἴαχον· οἳ δ' ἀλαλητῷ
θεσπεσίῳ σύνισαν· μέγα δ' ἔκτυπε μητίετα Ζεύς,
κὰδ δ' ἄρ' ἀπ' οὐρανόθεν ψιάδας βάλεν αἱματοέσσας,
σῆμα τιθεὶς πολέμοιο ἑῷ μεγαθαρσέι παιδί.   385
οἷος δ' ἐν βήσσῃς ὄρεος χαλεπὸς προϊδέσθαι
κάπρος χαυλιόδων φρονέει θυμῷ μαχέσασθαι
ἀνδράσι θηρευτῆς, θήγει δέ τε λευκὸν ὀδόντα
δοχμωθείς, ἀφρὸς δὲ περὶ στόμα μαστιχόωντι
λείβεται, ὄσσε δέ οἱ πυρὶ λαμπετόωντι ἔικτον,   390
ὀρθὰς δ' ἐν λοφιῇ φρίσσει τρίχας ἀμφί τε δειρήν·
τῷ ἴκελος Διὸς υἱὸς ἀφ' ἱππείου θόρε δίφρου.

As when rocks leap forth from the high peak of a great mountain, and fall on one another, and many towering oaks and pines

and long-rooted poplars are broken by them as they whirl swiftly
down until they reach the plain; so did they fall on one another
with a great shout: and all the town of the Myrmidons, and
famous Iolcus, and Arne, and Helice, and grassy Anthea echoed
loudly at the voice of the two. With an awful cry they closed: and
wise Zeus thundered loudly and rained down drops of blood,
giving the signal for battle to his dauntless son. As a tusked boar,
fearful for a man to see before him in the glens of a mountain,
resolves to fight with the huntsmen and whets his white tusks,
turning sideways, while foam flows all round his mouth as he
gnashes, and his eyes are like glowing fire, and he bristles the
hair on his mane and around his neck--like him the son of Zeus
leaped from his horse chariot.

Cycnus and Heracles have just dismounted—their charioteers drive the
horses off, with obligatory sound effect. The heroes are about to go to it,
when a simile intervenes: just as when rocks leap from a high peak and fall on
one another, and no fewer than three varieties of trees are crushed as these
boulders rumble down the hill to the plain—such is the way the men fell on
one another (with a scream, for good measure). It takes a long time for those
rocks to drop. The sound resounds, introducing in artful fashion various
place names, all the towns that reverberate to the spreading noise.[31] Two
more noises (a war cry and Zeus' thunder) delay the clash even more—the
enemies still have not engaged, as far as we hear. And then a meteorological
tour de force, bloody rain: not, as in the *Iliad*, to mourn a hero's imminent
death, but a sign from Zeus that his son is going to win.[32] We still have not
arrived at the first punch, when a second simile takes over: the gnashing,
bristling, foaming boar. Like many other "real" parts of the combat, this
finds its analogue on the shield—recall the image of white-toothed, flaming-
eyed Phobos. A glance at the further text of this passage reveals that nine
lines of seasonal description (setting the time of this combat) and two more
similes, of eleven lines in total, are yet to come. Only then does Cycnus
make the first spear-cast. This is not incompetence on the part of the poet,
but simply a different aesthetic, privileging manipulation and suspense, the
sort of sustained slow motion that commands the viewer to look while it
refuses to reward the gaze. Striptease may be the apt trash analogy.

---

[31]   The technique (following a sound in order to further a narrative) resembles that of the "shouting
in prison" theme of South Slavic epic: cf. J. M. Foley 1990, 288–327.

[32]   Contrast *Iliad* 16.459 and cf.the *Aspis* scholiast's comment in Ranke 1840 *ad loc.*

Overblown or awkward dialogue is often a component of pulp, as it is of the *Aspis*. This is a consequence of the mode's overriding orientation toward action. One speech that seems out of all proportion contains the words of Iolaus to Heracles at lines 103–14. In a run-on fashion, with everything mentioned in pairs, the younger hero says: "Good friend, indeed the father of men and gods honors your head, as does bull-like Earth Shaker, he who holds the veils of Thebe and protects the city. Such a mortal as this tough and big, are they leading into our hands, so you can win fine *kleos*." He urges Heracles to arm and concludes that "Ares shall not frighten the unshakeable son of Zeus or make the son of Iphicles run away. I think he is the one who will flee the two sons of the blameless son of Alcaeus, who are close upon him eager for war, and combat which is dearer to them than a banquet." This is probably not characterization by style—the younger warrior spouting whatever comes into his head—but rather the poet loading on every cliché he can come up with. Pulp likes to spell things out: important scene coming up.

If the modern examples so far seem common and the *Aspis* examples unexceptional or hackneyed, perhaps it is precisely because we are awash in pulp, which has become the default mode. Sexploitation, blaxploitation—even now, in Italian film, nunsploitation—all overwhelm the sensibilities. Yet they are just the logical endpoint of a marked tendency within the medium. As Doris Wishman, the director who brought us *Nude on the Moon* and *Bad Girls Go To Hell*, once said, "Let me tell you something—all movies are exploitation movies."[33] Saturation raises the ante—the next trash movie will have to be that much trashier. Tarantino goes from *Reservoir Dogs* to *Pulp Fiction* to *Four Rooms*—quite conscious that his audience dares him to do the next bad thing.[34] One suspects ancient epic audiences experienced the same proliferation. For every Kurosawa—the best directorial analogue for the Homeric poet—there were a dozen would-be Doris Wishmans, composing *Aspis*–like combats for a hungry crowd.[35]

---

[33] Quoted in Mendik and Harper 2000, 157.

[34] Tarantino, quoted in Woods 1996, 108, about the possibility of making further spin-offs of *Pulp Fiction*: "I like the idea that I'm taking a genre that already exists and reinventing it, like Leone re-invented the whole Western genre. I think I've taken on an established genre like the pulp thriller and made it challenging to myself *and to my audience*" (emphasis mine).

[35] Acting in unison are the sophistication of a trash-conscious audience, a steady rate of consumption and production, and a high degree of formulaic construction and thus expectation. Worth re-examining from this sociopoetic perspective is Roger Corman's series *The Student Nurses* (1970), *Private Duty Nurses* (1972), *Night Call Nurses* (1972), *The Young Nurses* (1973), and *Candy Stripe Nurses* (1974), on which see McGee 1988, 83.

Pulp poetics depend on a simple overriding rule: more is more. When we turn finally to the category of excess and some illustrative passages, it may seem redundant to speak of this principle. After all, the entire *Aspis* is excessive and that is essentially what makes it distinct from Homeric epic. I would, however, like to articulate a bit further *how* this poem makes itself more. The technique involves both the accumulation of detail and the type of detail piled on. There is a crescendo effect, apparently: a sort of *Gesetz der wächsenden Schrecklichkeit*. At the level of verse and phrase, the accumulating details are detachable. That is, they most often are loosely connected syntactically, added subjects or noun modifiers unnecessarily enjambed or strung along in *lexis eiromenê*. Finally, the heaping up of detail has its own rhythm. Most favored is the triplet, or triplets within triplets. Consider lines 149–67:[36]

σχετλίη, ἥ ῥα νόον τε καὶ ἐκ φρένας εἵλετο φωτῶν
οἵτινες ἀντιβίην πόλεμον Διὸς υἷι φέροιεν.   150
τῶν καὶ ψυχαὶ μὲν χθόνα δύνουσ' Ἄιδος εἴσω
αὐτῶν, ὀστέα δέ σφι περὶ ῥινοῖο σαπείσης
Σειρίου ἀζαλέοιο κελαινῇ πύθεται αἴῃ.
ἐν δὲ Προΐωξίς τε Παλίωξίς τε τέτυκτο,
ἐν δ' Ὅμαδός τε Φόνος τ' Ἀνδροκτασίη τε δεδήει,   155
ἐν δ' Ἔρις, ἐν δὲ Κυδοιμὸς ἐθύνεον, ἐν δ' ὀλοὴ Κὴρ
ἄλλον ζωὸν ἔχουσα νεούτατον, ἄλλον ἄουτον,
ἄλλον τεθνηῶτα κατὰ μόθον ἕλκε ποδοῖιν·
εἷμα δ' ἔχ' ἀμφ' ὤμοισι δαφοινεὸν αἵματι φωτῶν,
δεινὸν δερκομένη καναχῇσί τε βεβρυχυῖα.   160
Ἐν δ' ὀφίων κεφαλαὶ δεινῶν ἔσαν, οὔ τι φατειῶν,
δώδεκα, ταὶ φοβέεσκον ἐπὶ χθονὶ φῦλ' ἀνθρώπων
οἵτινες ἀντιβίην πόλεμον Διὸς υἷι φέροιεν.
τῶν καὶ ὀδόντων μὲν καναχὴ πέλεν, εὖτε μάχοιτο
Ἀμφιτρυωνιάδης· τὰ δ' ἐδαίετο θαυμ'τὰ ἔργα·   165
στίγματα δ' ὣς ἐπέφαντο ἰδεῖν δεινοῖσι δράκουσι·
κυάνεοι κατὰ νῶτα, μελάνθησαν δὲ γένεια.

Pitiless she, for she took away the mind and senses of poor wretches who made war against the son of Zeus. Their souls passed beneath the earth and went down into the house of Hades;

---

[36] The juicier pulpy excess in Solmsen's *Oxford Classical Text* of the poem is often found within brackets, iconic for the chaste editor's hands blinkering his eyes at the scarier parts of the movie.

but their bones, when the skin is rotted about them, crumble away on the dark earth under parching Sirius. Upon the shield Pursuit and Flight were wrought, and Tumult, and Panic, and Slaughter. Strife also, and Uproar were hurrying about, and deadly Fate was there holding one man newly wounded, and another unwounded; and one, who was dead, she was dragging by the feet through the tumult. She had on her shoulders a garment red with the blood of men, and terribly she glared and gnashed her teeth. And there were heads of snakes unspeakably frightful, twelve of them; and they used to frighten the tribes of men on earth who made war against the son of Zeus; for they would clash their teeth when Amphitryon's son was fighting; and brightly shone these wonderful works. And it was as though there were spots upon the frightful snakes; they were dark blue on their backs, but their jaws were black.

This section picks up after the description of Strife (see above): "Hard to deal with, that one; whosoever makes war with the son of Zeus, she takes their mind away." The *Aspis* poet is nothing if not methodical. So much for the enemy mind; now what about their bodies and souls? A *men*/*de* does it: the souls go under the earth, while the bones, when the skin rots around them, putrefy on the black earth with Sirius parching them. That gives us the whole picture. It may seem too much that, next, alongside Pursuit and Flight, we have Hubbub, Murder, and Manslaughter. Editors desperately hit the delete key when, in line 156, Strife, Moil, and Fate join this fray. But look at the architecture before you take out the airbrush. Lines 154–56 (unbracket the last) make a nice triple crescendo: ἐν + τε + τε (two items); then ἐν + τε + τε + τε (three items); then ἐν + ἐν + ἐν (three items), and an adjective for good measure. This triplet trips another wire. *Kêr* has three victims, nicely arranged in waxing style (157–58). And a third triplet completes the set of three. For Fate wears a bloody garment (159), glares terribly (160), and is gnashing her teeth (160)—as most beings in this poem eventually do (compare the twelve blue-black unspeakable serpents in line 164, who gnash whenever Heracles works out). Enough with excess, you may say. But as more is more in this poem, so there is more to say. The following passage would make the perfect box-office poster, were the *Aspis* a movie. By now, we are used to the blue Fates with white teeth and βλοσυροί foreheads. We yawn, perhaps, as they do battle to suck the blood of the newly fallen (250ff.), clamp corpses in their claws, and toss back the bodies when they have sated themselves with gore. The female-wrestling match among Klothô and her sisters should definitely remain in our texts.[37] And then arrives the poster child, Achlys, the internal audience for all these shenanigans (264ff.). Terrible, mournful, pale, shriveled and reduced by hunger, with swollen knees and long fingernails, she is the ideal Boogy Woman. From her drip snot, blood, and tears (another triplet), which mingle with the dust on her shoulders—about as good as it gets.

Where does all this analysis ultimately lead us? It hardly takes talent to perceive that the *Aspis* is, by most people's standards, gross and over-written. Can the trash aesthetic as delineated and illustrated here help us to resolve weightier questions of composition and literary history? I would argue that it can, in fact, ease, if not resolve, long-standing dilemmas posed by the poem, both internal and external. The internal first. Wilamowitz first systematically analyzed what he called "dittography" in this poem. He drew attention to the recurrent phenomenon visible, for example, in lines 282–83 within the following passage:

> αἳ δ' ὑπὸ φορμίγγων ἄναγον χορὸν ἱμερόεντα.   280
> ἔνθεν δ' αὖθ' ἑτέρωθε νέοι κώμαζον ὑπ' αὐλοῦ.
> τοί γε μὲν αὖ παίζοντες ὑπ' ὀρχηθμῷ καὶ ἀοιδῇ
> τοί γε μὲν αὖ γελόωντες ὑπ' αὐλητῆρι ἕκαστος
> πρόσθ' ἔκιον· πᾶσαν δὲ πόλιν θαλίαι τε χοροί τε
> ἀγλαΐαι τ' εἶχον.

And the girls led on the lovely dance to the sound of lyres. Then again on the other side was a rout of young men revelling, with flutes playing; some frolicking with dance and song, and others were going forward in time with a flute player and laughing. The whole town was filled with mirth and dance and festivity.

What produced these apparently interchangeable lines? According to Wilamowitz, they arose from variation originating in different rhapsodic performances of the poem.[38] In other words, the texts of the *Aspis* that reached the Alexandrians were texts produced or used by professional reciters. Richard Janko, eighty years later, flirted with a similar conclusion about this poem, but he has shied away from this finding when it comes to

---

[37] An inversion of *Vampirella* (1996), one of the brilliant Roger Corman's more than 500 productions: on his horror/parody aesthetic see Corman 1990 and McGee 1988.

[38] Wilamowitz 1905, 122: "Was nach Alexandreia kam, also Handschriften des 4. Jahrhunderts, waren Rhapsodenexemplare."

the text of Homer.[39] And yet it should be remembered that Aristophanes of Byzantium employed a critical sign to indicate interchangeable consecutive lines within Homer, showing us that what appears to be exactly the same phenomenon was once detectable there as well.[40] Speaking of the *Aspis*, Janko, wedded to a notion of rigidly fixed texts and relying on the methodology of his Cambridge dissertation, calls this "rhapsodic interpolation," a phrase that would suggest a rather different phenomenon. Janko's term assumes a fixed text of the *Aspis* (and in fact, he dates the poem on historical grounds quite precisely to the years between 591 and 570 BCE).[41] Furthermore, it postulates rhapsodes who possess and then wish to tinker with that text.

A simpler, and I believe more plausible, treatment of this situation can start from a consideration of the other rough spots of alleged "dittography." Wilamowitz' model would posit a redactor attempting for some reason to record alternate versions of the text. Janko's interpolation theory is an even more text-oriented way of putting the same case. But what is remarkable about these so-called doublets is that only one of the several pairs simply cannot make sense as they stand: with lines 282–83, one has to choose one verse over the other. The other doublets reflect an attempt by somebody, apparently a person knowledgeable about traditional diction, to stitch lines together. Take, for example, the description of the harbor on the shield at lines 207–15:

> Ἐν δὲ λιμὴν εὔορμος ἀμαιμακέτοιο θαλάσσης
> κυκλοτερὴς ἐτέτυκτο πανέφθου κασσιτέροιο
> κλυζομένῳ ἴκελος· πολλοί γε μὲν ἂμ μέσον αὐτοῦ
> δελφῖνες τῇ καὶ τῇ ἐθύνεον ἰχθυάοντες   210
> νηχομένοις ἴκελοι· δοιὼ δ' ἀναφυσιόωντες
> ἀργύρεοι δελφῖνες ἐφοίβεον ἔλλοπας ἰχθῦς.
> τῶν δ' ὕπο χάλκειοι τρέον ἰχθύες· αὐτὰρ ἐπ' ἀκτῆς
> ἧστο ἀνὴρ ἁλιεὺς δεδοκημένος, εἶχε δὲ χερσὶν
> ἰχθύσιν ἀμφίβληστρον ἀπορρίψοντι ἐοικώς.   215

---

[39] Janko 1986, 39-40. This is not the place to enter the debate on the importance, in the case of variant readings, of the rhapsodic heritage underlying the Homeric texts: for opposed viewpoints, see Janko 1998 and Nagy 1998. I point out, however, that the *Aspis* evidence has not previously been employed in the discussion. An interpretation along the lines sketched by Wilamowitz, with the modifications I offer, adds further weight to the plausible arguments of Nagy.

[40] Pfeiffer 1968, 178.

[41] Janko 1986. On his methodology, see Taplin 1992, 33 n. 39. The statistical arguments for dating based on the attestation of certain "late" morphological features fail to take into account repeated elements of diction. Furthermore, there is no criterion for distinguishing "false" archaisms from authentic ones.

> And on the shield was a harbor with a safe haven from the irre-
> sistible sea, made of refined tin wrought in a circle, and it seemed
> to heave with waves. In the middle of it were many dolphins
> rushing this way and that, fishing; and they seemed to be swim-
> ming. Two dolphins of silver were spouting and devouring the
> mute fishes. And beneath them fishes of bronze were trembling.
> And on the shore sat a fisherman watching: in his hands he held
> a casting net for fish, and seemed as if about to cast it forth.

There is nothing syntactically offensive about the curving harbor, made
of tin, with its swell of waves. Dolphins, like swimmers, sport in it. Lines
209–11 have been bracketed as too close in meaning to 211–12. But the
technique of this poet calls for close-up shots, as we have seen: thus, the latter
lines focus us on two dolphins, who spout off and chase the fish. Another
camera shift (213) tracks the fish as they dart off in fear. Finally, the camera
pulls back to show us a fisherman, playing the role of internal audience for
this scene (as was Achlys in her scene), just as he is about to do his own
fish-catching.

This, and other such passages (e.g., 203–5; 293–95), are neither smooth
nor elegant, but do reward efforts to understand them. If we are willing to
make such efforts for Aeschylus, Stesichorus, and Apollonius, whose styles
all engage the same "pulp" mode on occasion, then we should give the *Aspis*
the benefit of the doubt.[42] The key to a sympathetic understanding is to
admit that the composer of the *Aspis* wanted at every turn to make a bigger,
more detailed, often gorier, usually livelier poem. And if that meant hauling
out his best lines and puffing them up with good lines from other rhapsodes he had heard, all the better: no expansion is too bad to venture.[43] If
trash demands it, live performance encourages it. A glance at run-of-the-
mill epics, episodic and oral, as transcribed from live performance, can show
one exactly the same "mistakes" that occur when a singer or reciter takes
risks and plays up a theme, sometimes to excess, for an eager audience. The
virtuosos of a tradition, whether Indic Ram recitations, Egyptian Hilali epic,
or the Sunjata of West Africa, think well on their feet and can telescope as
well as expand. For the majority of oral bards, however, expansion is the

---

[42] It is not accidental that ancient traditions associated Hesiod and Stesichorus, even to the point of
naming the latter a son of Hesiod: see Mazon 1928, xiii.

[43] On the expansion aesthetic as operating in the *Iliad*, see Martin 1989. The difference with the
Aspis once again is merely quantitative.

easier option.[44] A cognate Greek illustration can be found in a so-called "wild" papyrus (PBerol. 9771, first century BCE) featuring the *ekphrasis* of Achilles' shield in the *Iliad*.[45] Allen and West print these "plus" lines, not attested in the mainstream manuscript tradition, in the apparatus as *Iliad* 18.608a–d:

> ἐν δὲ λιμὴν ἐτέτυκ[το] ἐανοῦ κασσιτέρ[οιο]
> κλυζ[ομ]ένωι ἴκ[ελ]ος δοιὼ δ' ἀναφυσιόω[ντες]
> ἀργύ[ρεοι] δελφῖνε[ς ἐ]φοίνεον ἔλλοπας [ἰχθῦς]
> τοῦ δ' [ὕπ]ο χάλκε[ιοι τρέον ἰ]χθύες α[ὐ]τὰ[ρ ἐπ ἀκταις]

And on the shield was a harbor made of refined tin and it seemed to heave with waves. Two dolphins of silver were spouting and killing the mute fishes. And beneath this fishes of bronze were trembling. And on the shores ...

When we compare them with the *Aspis*, lines 207–13, the following pattern emerges (underlined phrases showing matches between the lines, italicized bold showing near matches):

> <u>Ἐν δὲ λιμὴν</u> εὔορμος ἀμαιμακέτοιο θαλάσσης
> κυκλοτερὴς <u>ἐτέτυκτο</u> πανέφθου <u>κασσιτέροιο</u>
> <u>κλυζομένῳ ἴκελος</u>· πολλοί γε μὲν ἂμ μέσον αὐτοῦ
> ***δελφῖνες*** τῇ καὶ τῇ ἐθύνεον ἰχθυάοντες   210
> νηχομένοις ἴκελοι· <u>δοιὼ δ' ἀναφυσιόωντες</u>
> <u>ἀργύρεοι δελφῖνες</u> ***ἐφοίβεον*** <u>ἔλλοπας ἰχθῦς</u>.
> <u>τῶν δ' ὕπο χάλκειοι τρέον ἰχθύες·</u> αὐτὰρ ἐπ' ***ἀκτῆς***...

And on the shield was a harbor with a safe haven from the irresistible sea, *made of* refined *tin* wrought in a circle, *and it seemed to heave with waves.* In the middle of it were many *dolphins* rushing this way and that, fishing: and they seemed to be swimming. *Two dolphins of silver were spouting and devouring the mute fishes. And beneath them fishes of bronze were trembling. And on the shore* ...

From the point of view of the *Aspis*, the *Iliad* plus-verses—albeit already an "expansion" on the commonly attested way of narrating the Achilles

---

[44] For examples of such "mistakes" that reflect convergence of themes in the poet's memory, see Lord 2000, 94–95 and 1991, 29; on metrical "errors" as indicating thematic or formulaic seams, see J. M. Foley 1999, 72–74.

[45] For the most recent analysis of the papyrus, see Natalucci 2000, who considers it a valid representative of a once fuller, pre-Aristarchean version of the *Iliad* scene and not a product of cross-interpolation.

shield scene—have telescoped an even longer way of narrating. Vice versa, we could say that the *Aspis* version expands on an already "expansive" version of the *Iliad* scene. Doubters and "scripsists" will say that this is proof the brackets at lines 209–11 belong where they are, that those verses are "interpolated," since the *Iliad* papyrus at line 608b seems to be the equivalent of *Aspis* 209 (first segment) with line 211 (final segment).[46] Yet this is to make the hazardous assumption that the *Aspis* is copying a specific text of the *Iliad*, and yet doing so from a perspective that took account of a para-Iliadic tradition at the same time as it expatiated on the "text." If one maintains a more flexible (and ethnographically more plausible) hermeneutic, the two passages in question are simply big and small variants of the same theme, subjected to the sort of free-wheeling expansion or telescoping typical of live performance.[47] The point is that the *Aspis*, in such a situation, will always choose to go large.

Now we can turn to the question most relevant to broader literary history: just who was this composer of an always-over-the-top *Aspis*? I would risk asserting that it was the same person who composed the *Catalogue of Women*, and not just the individual *ehoie* about Alcmene, which, according to the *hypothesis*, contained the first fifty-six lines of the *Aspis*, but the entire poem. My suggestion is built on four kinds of evidence, which I shall conclude by explaining.

First, there is the evidence of separability. By this, I mean the scattered remarks indicating how portions of hexameter verse that we moderns may consider organic in a poem were once treated by some ancient scholars as detachable. The A-scholia to *Iliad* 18.39–49 record that Zenodotus first athetized the description of the Nereid chorus because it had a "Hesiodic *kharaktêr*." (Recall that the *kharaktêr* of the *Aspis* was cited by Apollonius Rhodius, according to the *hypothesis*, in his defense of its attribution to

---

[46] On "scripsists," see Taplin 1992, 35–37. Revermann 1998, for example, wants to see the plus-verses in the *Iliad* at this point as "a peculiar interpolation of a condensed version" of the *Aspis* verses. He leaves open the possibility that the *Iliad* lines are due to "rhapsodic intervention and amplification," yet it is clear from his further remarks that he has in mind a textual phenomenon, in which individual rhapsodes are mere conduits allowing verses to leach from one *recorded* poem into another. Orality, in this model, is incidental. By way of contrast, I propose that what we see in the *Aspis* and *Iliad* overlap is much messier and closer to a true recomposition-in-performance. The poet whose work made its way into the Berlin papyrus has produced a different way of ornamenting the scene, which happens to bear a family resemblance to the *Aspis*. But as we can see, the lines do not present a simple transposition of pre-existing *Aspis* lines inserted into a pre-existing *Iliad*. For performer and audience, the version of P51 is plausible, traditional in diction, and interesting.

[47] Lord 2000, 99–123 first traced this in South Slavic heroic poetry. A number of subsequent studies have reported the same phenomenon.

Hesiod.) Two points of interest arise from this brief notice: that Alexandrian connoisseurs thought themselves capable of detecting stylistic differences within hexameter poetry and based their decisions about authorship on this; and that they did not feel bound by other considerations of structure or artistry when they suggested that certain lines did not belong in a poem. Note that this is far different from claiming that Zenodotus and his successors were proto-Analysts in any way. For their decisions about such atheteses, as far we can track them through the evidence of scholia, appear to have been shaped with a keen appreciation of the *types* of passage or scene that could contain such "other" material. This is to say that the connoisseurs (poets, critics, and often poet-critics) carried with them a native sense of where one might expand or contract, a sense equal to—perhaps directly derived from—rhapsodic performers themselves.[48] In the case of separability, therefore, we should treat the intuition of Zenodotus with some respect. In this connection, it is highly significant that the same critic athetized the entire *Shield of Achilles* from the *Iliad* (A-scholia *ad Iliad.* 18.483), as he was satisfied with "the summary preface" (κεφαλαιώδης προέκθεσις)—apparently lines 18.478–82, which mention that Hephaestus made a stout shield and decorated it with δαίδαλα πολλά. We do not know whether the two scholia just cited should be harmonized—that is, whether Zenodotus athetized the *Iliad* shield *because it too was Hesiodic*. But even if that was not his motive, it remains clear that an Alexandrian could treat a long shield description as separable from its surrounding context.

This brings us to the second category of evidence, the creative habits of rhapsodes. What, after all, would one have done with a separable *Shield of Achilles*? Martin Revermann, in an article on the textual transmission of that *Iliad* passage, suggests that the Iliadic shield may, in fact, have been used for separate recitation in performance, as a show-piece or an encore.[49] Though he does not refer to them, the practice of performing such an individual episode is well attested in other oral poetic traditions.[50] The *Certamen* of Homer and Hesiod presents the two battling bards "self-segmenting," as it were, their own poetry, in the interest of pleasing an audience and

---

[48] On the possible interaction between rhapsodes and critic-poets, see Hunter 1996, 50–52.

[49] Revermann 1998.

[50] This can apply either to segmenting of plot elements or to long runs of description. On Indic, see Flueckiger 1999. One can find parallels from Mongol, Kirghiz, Egyptian, and West African epics; from my fieldwork in Sphakia and Selinos, Crete in 1996 and 2002, I can attest to the practice of segmenting the *Erotokritos* and *Daskaloyiannis* epics.

judge.[51] The much-controverted evidence concerning the performance of Homer at the Panathenaea can show us at least this much, that no one rhapsode ever recited an entire poem.[52] By definition, then, rhapsodes delivered time-constrained segments. These could either be rounded off, or allowed to dangle with a loose thread, which a succeeding rhapsode might then pick up to stitch the foregoing to his own performance. At any rate, a shield description like that in the *Aspis* or *Iliad* would seem to be the right length for live performance.[53]

Whatever one's aesthetic judgment on the relative value of the two shield *ekphraseis*, it seems highly likely that the *Iliad* poet has simply expanded his or her already massive performance by embedding this traditional, separable sub-genre. The shield of Heracles is much more functional in its episode than is that of Achilles. One can easily imagine there being in the repertoire of the rhapsodes a class of such expansions; the genius of the Homeric composers is to vacuum up the sub-genres that naturally occur on their own in the oral poetic surroundings, and put them to new and pointed use. I have argued elsewhere that this is precisely what happens in the case of the "catalogue of women" in *Odyssey* Book 11, or with the genre of speaking to be identified as Instruction of Princes in both the *Odyssey* and the *Theogony*.[54] What this means, once again, is that the Hesiodic *Aspis* stands a good chance of being an authentic continuator of an older way of performing. On the larger scale, I would assert that what we call Hesiodic poetry is—like the epic cycle and Orphic poetry as well—the unmarked remnant of rhapsodic repertoires. After the rise of Homer as epic *par excellence*, anything non-Homeric could well have been homogenized, in opposition to the marked poetic category, as "Hesiodic." Of course, as G. P. Edwards and others have shown, the verse itself has every claim to be as old or older than the Homeric poems as we have them.[55] The structures of motif, plot, and even diction can be best viewed as that material which the homogenizing Homeric composers had to

---

[51] See now for a sophisticated evaluation of this work, Graziosi 2002. For the techniques employed in the *Certamen* and their relation to verse-composition patterns, see Collins 2001b.

[52] On the interpretation of the evidence for sequenced recitation, see Nagy 2002, 9–22, 43–50.

[53] Homeric "books" could also fit a convenient one to three-hour performance slot: on the interrelations of book division, performance, and textual transmission, see the debate in Skafte Jensen 1999.

[54] See Chapters 8 and 12 above.

[55] Edwards 1971; Nagy 1992.

work with. Not by accident is *Homêros* the "fitter-together."[56] The *Aspis*, by these terms, is most likely akin to the Iliadic shield not as an inferior copy to a superior model, but as two instantiations of a *tour de force* that rhapsodes could choose to do in performance: the "extended armament-*ekphrasis*." I now want to propose that the strategy of expanding by means of a shield *ekphrasis* is not just what we see in our version of the *Iliad*. It is exactly what is happening in our version of the *Catalogue of Women* attributed to Hesiod. In other words, I want to suggest that the *Aspis* was a part of the *Catalogue* just as much (and as separably) as Achilles' shield was within the *Iliad*.

Of course, there is no positive proof in the way of manuscript evidence. But there is no real negative proof either. The Oxyrhynchus finds edited by Lobel (fr. 195) do not support a claim either way. They simply confirm a part of what the transmitted *hypothesis* says.[57] Most critics have automatically assumed that the *Aspis* was composed by some poetaster, who copied or borrowed the Alcmene biography in the *Catalogue* and clumsily pegged onto this the story of Heracles' fight against Cycnus.[58] Wilamowitz was the only critic willing to see the situation the other way round: he thought that a separate *Aspis* poet inserted his poem *into* the *Catalogue* (a view which West has tried to rebut, to my mind unsuccessfully).[59] To my knowledge, no one has suggested that the *Aspis* and *Catalogue* composers were one and the same. An immediate objection might be the following: if the *Aspis* was as integral to the *Catalogue* as the shield to the *Iliad*, why do we have ancient references to them as separate? My response is that one can refer to a portion of any epic by its own episode-name. Thus, in the *Iliad*, we get the *Peira*, the *Teikhoskopia*, or—for the shield—the *Hoplopoiia*. In this light, the *Aspis* would be what rhapsodes and their near relations, the critics, called that part of the

---

[56] Nagy 1990, 373. The creation (probably in rhapsodic lore) of Homer and Hesiod as two primeval poetic figures accords with later critical practice, whereby what was not by one had to be by the other. It worked both ways: Aristarchus (like Zenodotus, it seems) condemned as un-Homeric any passages he suspected of having a Hesiodic character: see Pfeiffer 1968, 220.

[57] Glenn Most, pointing to the specification in the *hypothesis* that the first fifty-six lines of the *Aspis* were in the *Catalogue*, argued in the May 2002 Craven Seminar at Cambridge that the remainder of the *Aspis* as we have it therefore could *not* have been in the poem. More cautiously, we might say that a version of the *Catalogue* as known to the composer of the *hypothesis* writer only featured part of the *Aspis*. What was said above concerning telescoping and expansion applies here as well: just as some *Iliad* copies omitted the Catalogue of Ships—and might have copied performance habits in so doing—some instances of the *Catalogue of Women* may have featured an extended, others a shortened, *Aspis*.

[58] Allen 1924, 79, for example, who says, "the *Aspis* has no allusion to determine the date of the *Catalogue* (from which its first portion was taken)."

[59] Wilamowitz 1905; Merkelbach–West 1965, 300 n. 3.

Catalogue where one went all out and did a 400-line riff. Then again, there is the role of Zenodotus. Why did his successor Aristophanes of Byzantium need to worry about whether the *Aspis* was or was not "Hesiodic," unless earlier scholars had brought up the issue? If the earlier critic Zenodotus decided, as he did with the Iliadic shield, that the *Catalogue* version, too, was separable, the tradition of treating the *Aspis* as a free-standing composition could have begun just before the time of Aristophanes.

Now the problem will be to show how the poetry of the *Aspis* is like the rest of the *Catalogue* and therefore could have fitted inside it. Here, my third category of evidence comes into play, that with which I began this paper—the trash aesthetic and its preferences in theme and structure. (The dating of the two pieces, by the way, is not a problem, since critics have independently placed the *Catalogue* and the *Aspis* in exactly the same decades, the first quarter of the sixth century BCE, on the basis of historical and genealogical details, including traces of Delphic propaganda.)[60] West, who provides good arguments for the *Catalogue* dating, is also the one to whom we can turn for support for the notion that the whole composition must have been a rather pulpy poem. Each of its five books seems to have comprised around 1,100 verses. And—given its mythic material—the poem's narration will have included, at the very least, a god-defier (Salmoneus), Siamese twins, at least two shape-shifters (one of whom, in bee-form, gets nailed by Heracles in classic B-movie fashion, just when he alights on a chariot-yoke), a man who devours himself, and raving mad girl gangs.[61] From the scrappy remains of the *Catalogue* we can see, first, that Heracles flitted in and out constantly, reminding one of his continual present-absence in Apollonius' epic.[62] A number of episodes expanded into digressions about Heracles. Second, we see that episodes can be quite long and complex. For instance, the Suitors of Helen section, as we have it, is already 180 lines long and the whole may have been much larger.[63] This section also seems to come at book-end. The *Aspis* would have made a fine ending, as well, in its case to Book 4. As West notes, the *Catalogue* poet likes to finish off books expansively.

Turning now to the fourth and final sort of evidence, the texture of the respective texts, we can glance at the now famous description of the seasons

---

[60] For details, see Janko 1986.

[61] A poem you could pitch to Ms. Wishman in a New York minute, seeing as she already did the movie version of a kind of *Catalogue*: *Bad Girls Go to Hell*.

[62] On Heracles in the *Catalogue*, see Haubold 2005.

[63] Cf. Cingano 2005.

and the behavior of snakes with which our text of the *Catalogue* ends (fr. 204.124–42). The natural lore has a specific role: it pins down the time of events through reference to the occurrences of seasons, in the style of the *Works and Days*. The event that this passage refers to has to do with the punishment of a *hubristês* (see line 137—the snake itself?). Compare *Aspis* lines 393–401:

> ἦμος δὲ χλοερῷ κυανόπτερος ἠχέτα τέττιξ
> ὄζῳ ἐφεζόμενος θέρος ἀνθρώποισιν ἀείδειν
> ἄρχεται, ᾧ τε πόσις καὶ βρῶσις θῆλυς ἐέρση,   395
> καί τε πανημέριός τε καὶ ἠῷος χέει αὐδὴν
> ἴδει ἐν αἰνοτάτῳ, ὅτε τε χρόα Σείριος ἄζει,
> τῆμος δὴ κέγχροισι πέρι γλῶχες τελέθουσι
> τούς τε θέρει σπείρουσιν, ὅτ' ὄμφακες αἰόλλονται,
> οἷα Διώνυσος δῶκ' ἀνδράσι χάρμα καὶ ἄχθος·   400
> τὴν ὥρην μάρναντο, πολὺς δ' ὀρυμαγδὸς ὀρώρει.

And when the dark-winged whirring grasshopper, perched on a green shoot, begins to sing of summer to men—his food and drink is the dainty dew—and all day long from dawn pours forth his voice in the deadliest heat, when Sirius scorches the flesh (then the beard grows upon the millet which men sow in summer), when the crude grapes which Dionysus gave to men—a joy and a sorrow both—begin to color, in that season they fought, and loud rose the clamor.

Not only is this a digression on nature-lore; it too, unusually, pins down the time of a single event—Heracles' fight with Apollo's enemy, Cycnus, a *hubristês* if ever there was one. The diction surrounding the *Catalogue* snake (fr. 240.135–37) resembles closely *Aspis* snake descriptions (cf. 160–7); there may be only so many ways to put skin on a snake, but given other patterns so far, this counts.

Do I overrate the *Aspis* by finding for it a home in the *Catalogue of Women*? Or am I trashing the *Catalogue* by smuggling into it this debased product of the rhapsodic imagination at its bloodiest? The classic contradiction of the study of pop culture raises its head. Maybe we should let the *Aspis* lie and not any further suck the flamboyancy out of it. After all, as Clive Bloom puts it: "Pulp never went to school and hates the academy."[64]

---

[64] Bloom 1996, 134.

IV

THE BACKWARD LOOK

14

KEENS FROM THE ABSENT CHORUS
TROY TO ULSTER[1]

I.

What experimentation is to science, comparison should be to philology—a way to test hypotheses and produce new ones that account for more of the data, more economically. What one chooses to compare, of course, will affect the results. On one end of the spectrum lies the tracing of curious resemblances among otherwise isolated words, motifs, or customs, and the urge to weave around these an intriguing narrative, either of primitive origins, long-distance cultural contact, or deep genetic relationship.[2] The nineteenth century's fascination with atomistic and often obscure comparanda gave way in the twentieth century to a more dependable tendency to compare total structures, linguistics leading the way to the other end of the spectrum, with anthropology trailing some decades later.[3] Neither method was specifically designed for the study of verbal art, although Frazer's great work was prompted by a scene in Vergil's *Aeneid* and Lévi-Strauss' best-known

---

[1] Originally published in *Western Folklore* 62, no. 1 (2003): 119–42. Also reprinted with additional notes in *Lament: Studies in the Ancient Mediterranean and Beyond*, ed. A. Suter (Oxford: Oxford University Press, 2008), 118–38.

[2] Frazer is of course the major figure. "He could always find a minor superstition among frolicking harvesters or New Year celebrants to match any more grandiose theme. The switches of scale give us a sense of flippancy": Douglas 1982, 284. Her article offers a balanced assessment of Frazer's continuing importance (even after Wittgenstein's critique). Ackerman 1987 well analyzes the connection between the scholar's anthropology and his Classical philology. Hyman 1959 shows how Frazer's intellectual roots tangled with those of a number of other Victorian figures. On the aims and methods of Frazer's contemporaries, see Stocking 1987.

[3] A well-known story, concisely told by Culler 1975, 3–54 and Donato 1972. Detienne 2000 traces the concomitant narrowing of the range of comparanda that this involved.

article starts with the *Oedipus Rex* of Sophocles. Yet the philologist studying ancient or medieval texts has much to gain from a controlled use of ethnographic comparisons of both types—those based on telling Frazerian detail (now once again in fashion), as well as those concerned with global structures.[4] In fact, a twenty-first-century philology *without* strong affiliations to social anthropology, folkloristics, and performance study is increasingly untenable and in danger of exhausting itself on hermetic quests into the endlessly intertextual.[5]

An explication of two puzzling passages, one ancient Greek, the other medieval Irish, can illustrate the advantages of comparing old texts and modern cultures. My approach in this paper will be quadrilateral: modern Greek evidence illumines the Homeric *Iliad* and *Odyssey*; ancient Greek social practices can shed light on the medieval Irish *Scéla Muicce Meic Dathó*; and a famous modern Irish poem might be fruitfully reconsidered along the way. Underlying this approach is one key assumption: that typologically similar institutions often generate similar rhetoric and poetics.[6] That is to say, the details of the individual document or performance (the object of one sort of ethnography) can be brought into touch with larger structures (objects of a different sort of anthropology) so that we do not lose sight of either end of the data spectrum and we end up clarifying both in the process. Where our evidence from pre-modern periods is patchy and unsure, as is often the case with Greek and Irish materials, we can still look to mutually illuminating models for performances, ancient, medieval, and modern.[7]

---

[4]   On the rediscovery of Frazer's rich (if not "thick") description and resemblances to Geertzian practice, see Boon 1982.

[5]   For an incisive evaluation of intertextuality studies in Classics, see Edmunds 2001. Responses to the sterility of pure intertextuality, within my discipline, have gone in two directions: toward questioning the ways in which we construct any individual text (see Sharrock and Morales 2000) and toward broadening the text's boundaries by way of attention to social context (whether through New Historicism or the slightly softer "cultural poetics," on which see Kurke and Dougherty 1993). On the modern relationship between anthropology and Classics, see Martin 2008.

[6]   For an illustration of the principle in connection with a different pairing of Greek and Irish texts, see Martin 1984a with further bibliography on the approach. Masterly demonstrations of the method can be found in Nagy 1990 and 1999b; Watkins 1995; and Benveniste 1969/1973. On finishing this article, I came across McCone 1984, 27, whose formulation, applied to Greek and Irish as well, nicely fits the view expressed here.

[7]   I find an encouraging defense of my sort of intellectual poaching in Guneratne 1999: "To be a successful fieldworker, one must be at least a little uninhibited about being conspicuous and unwittingly violating local norms, because the nature of fieldwork makes this virtually inevitable." She contrasts with this the diffidence she felt accompanying her husband during fieldwork in Nepal. As a para-ethnographer and part-time Celticist, I was honored yet abashed to have been included in the UCLA conference on performance models (February 2001) organized by Józsi Nagy. I wish to thank

Such models do not "prove" anything about the texts in question, but might provide better hypotheses—all that one can ask of most investigations.

First, the ancient Greek conundrum, a passage that was controversial already in the third century BCE.[8] In Book Four of the *Odyssey*, the hero Menelaus, now safely home from the Trojan War, reminisces, for the benefit of his young guest Telemachus, about the exploits of Odysseus in the final days of the siege. He recalls how his own wife, the exquisite Helen, nearly ruined Odysseus' plan of the Trojan Horse through a strange feat of ventriloquism—or so it seemed—enacted on the night that the Greek heroes lay hidden inside, waiting to make their sneak attack (*Odyssey* 4.277–79):

> τρὶς δὲ περίστειξας κοῖλον λόχον ἀμφαφόωσα,
> ἐκ δ' ὀνομακλήδην Δαναῶν ὀνόμαζες ἀρίστους,
> πάντων Ἀργείων φωνὴν ἴσκουσ' ἀλόχοισιν·

> Three times you walked around, handling the hollow ambush;
> you called by name the best of the Danaans,
> in voice resembling all the Argives' wives.[9]

Only the determination of Odysseus, claims his old friend, prevented the warriors with him inside the Horse from crying out in response to Helen's near-fatal provocation. This extremely odd behavior by the Spartan queen has usually been connected with Helen's alleged resemblance to a sorceress, as scholars attempt to translate her adeptness at drug administration into something more sinister. Yet there is no other evidence to point the audience in that direction.[10] Then again, one can anachronistically psychologize Helen's character to ask why she nearly betrayed the Greeks (fear of her new Trojan relatives by marriage, Stockholm syndrome, etc.).[11] But if we wish to base our explications on the immediate and more appropriate level of traditional conventions within archaic Greek poetry, it is important to inquire

---

him for the kind invitation to that fascinating event, at which my position was often more that of the anthropologist's spouse.

[8] It appears that the Alexandrian critic Aristarchus questioned the authenticity of several lines in the passage, including the detail of Helen's mimetic behavior: see Heubeck et al. 1988, 211–12, where it is suggested that "there may be more to this curious detail than meets the eye."

[9] Translations of all Greek and Irish passages in this paper are my own unless otherwise noted.

[10] Just before Menelaus tells his rather pointed story about her, Helen spikes the party's drinks with a powerful Egyptian pain-killer (*Odyssey* 4.220–32). Austin 1994, 77–81 removes the first scene from the realm of sorcery but reads lines 277–79 as celebrating Helen for her "daimonic powers"; see further Suzuki 1989, 66.

[11] For bibliography and discussion see Suzuki 1989, 69.

first what other scenes this passage resembles in motif or diction. This is to ask, in another way: what might have resonated with a traditional Greek audience of oral-poetic craft, one aware of multiple performances that repeatedly featured the same characters, tales, and phrases? A close resemblance has sometimes been noted with the similar ventriloquist abilities of the maidens of Delos in the *Hymn to Apollo*, an anonymous composition in epic hexameter style, perhaps dating from the sixth century BCE. The marvel created by these young women is described as part of a longer passage celebrating the central festival of Apollo on his rocky sacred island, an event attended by travelers from all the Ionian city-states (*Hymn to Apollo* 160–64):[12]

μνησάμεναι ἀνδρῶν τε παλαιῶν ἠδὲ γυναικῶν
ὕμνον ἀείδουσιν, θέλγουσι δὲ φῦλ' ἀνθρώπων.
πάντων δ' ἀνθρώπων φωνὰς καὶ κρεμβαλιαστὺν
μιμεῖσθ' ἴσασιν· φαίη δέ κεν αὐτὸς ἕκαστος
φθέγγεσθ'· οὕτω σφιν καλὴ συνάρηρεν ἀοιδή.

Calling to mind men of old and women
they sing a hymn and charm the tribes of mankind.
The voices and rhythm of all people they know to imitate;
each might say that he himself was speaking:
that is how fine their song fits together.

At the risk of explaining *obscurum per obscurius*, we can note that both performances, Helen's and the maidens', involve miming another's voice. But the lone figure of Helen is said in the *Odyssey* specifically to have imitated the voices of women, the wives of the Greek heroes inside the wooden horse. By contrast, the chorus of Delian women sings *about* a plurality, both men and women of an earlier age. Theirs is an epicizing act, overtly referring to distant heroic characters, yet their performance apparently represents the voices of all kinds of people actually present. The magic of the Delians' song lies in its ability to involve the audience so completely that each listener feels the closest affinity with the speaker—a beautiful image of the ultimate merging

---

[12] On the controversies surrounding this complex poem, which seems to offer a glimpse of epic song performed by female choruses, as well as a stylized reference to the (mythologized) Homeric poet himself, see Lonsdale 1995; Nagy 1995; and Martin 2000b; for more on the vocal abilities of the Delian maidens, see Martin 2001b with further bibliography. For the translation "rhythm" of Greek *krembaliastus* in line 163 (usually taken as "chattering" or "clacking"), I am indebted to Anastasia-Erasmia Peponi's work (2009) concerning dance-concepts in this passage.

of singer and rapt audience.[13] That the stress falls on the *choral* nature of the maidens' performance can be deduced from the verb *sunarêren*, "fits together," which denotes a joint production at the same time as it emblematizes, in context, the perfect "fit" between performers and listeners. In this highly charged scene, a distinctly Greek poetic ideology finds its summation: choral song has the power of modeling and enabling community cohesion.[14] This force of the preverb *sun*, "together," can be paralleled with reference to musical and vocal performance, in a number of compound words, such as the verb *sumphônein*, which ultimately gives us "symphony."

The differences between these two vocal events strike one as much as the similarities: Helen's seems not to be a canonical performance, but a spooky sort of improvisation. After all, the only "audience" is either the fearful concealed Greeks, or Helen's latest husband, the Trojan Deiphobus, who accompanied her to see the Horse. And where is the pleasure one expects, the regular concomitant of women's singing in Greek poetry? Furthermore, is it not perverse that one woman becomes a chorus? Then again, we might recall that Helen is herself a singular being, a divinity, outside epic, and a multiform of the Indo-European dawn goddess. Her abilities and practices have the right to be oddly different.[15]

The closest parallel for women's "choral" performance of this type within Homeric epic takes us to the end of the *Odyssey*. There it is not mortal women, however, but the Muses who once sang an antiphonal lament over the body of Achilles, toward the end of the war. As the shade of Agamemnon recounts the scene to Achilles, his companion now in Hades (*Odyssey* 24.58–62):[16]

> ἀμφὶ δέ σ' ἔστησαν κοῦραι ἁλίοιο γέροντος
> οἴκτρ' ὀλοφυρόμεναι, περὶ δ' ἄμβροτα εἵματα ἕσσαν.
> Μοῦσαι δ' ἐννέα πᾶσαι ἀμειβόμεναι ὀπὶ καλῇ
> θρήνεον· ἔνθα κεν οὔ τιν' ἀδάκρυτόν γ' ἐνόησας
> Ἀργείων· τοῖον γὰρ ὑπώρορε Μοῦσα λίγεια.

---

[13]   Archaic Greek myth and poetics, from the stories of Orpheus to depictions of court bards in the *Odyssey*, fantasize in a number of ways about the power of song: good recent examinations of the topic are Segal 1994 and Aloni 1998.

[14]   On the concept, see Calame 2001, 207–63 and Nagy 1995. The civic importance of choruses for an ancient city-state was repeatedly acknowledged by Plato in the *Laws* (e.g., 796b–c). On the institution in fifth-century Athens, see Wilson 2000.

[15]   On the ambiguous status of Helen, as mortal and/or goddess, see Clader 1976 passim and Austin 1994, 10–12.

[16]   This is another passage subjected to critical doubts since antiquity.

> Around you stood the daughters of the Old Man of the Sea,
> pitifully wailing, and clothed you in immortal clothes.
> The Muses, all nine, with responsive lovely voice
> made the lament. Then you might have seen
> no Argive tearless—in such a way did the clear-toned Muse arouse
> them.

Some critics have tried to explain the singular Muse of line 62 as a type of abstraction or even an (unparalleled) metonymy for "music," but the more functional explanation, through ethnopoetics, would interpret the scenario differently. One Muse leads the group and responds to them, as they respond to her and to one another, *ameibomenai opi kalêi.*[17] In this interpretation, the divine performance recounted in *Odyssey* 24 would match lament performance as attested in medieval and modern, as well as other ancient texts.[18] It might show, in addition, a performance context (responsive song) whereby "one" and "many" are enabled to exchange roles, so that the boundaries of personality are blurred. But how can this lament at the death of Achilles help us to understand the original object of attention, Helen's weird imitative powers as she circles the Trojan Horse?

To take stock thus far: the Delian maidens present us with a chorus that can imitate the voices of others; so can Helen, but she is not a chorus. The Muses, on the other hand, operate in such a way that individual and choral voice naturally alternate; the vocal relation is symbiotic. If Helen is conceptualized as an *exarkhousa*—a chorus-leader—we might be able to imagine that she crystallizes the power of choral song, within her own individual performance, in effect imitating call *and* response. But this suggestion seems to lead us into a further speculation, namely that Helen is somehow connected with the performance, specifically, of lament, for that is the precise context— indeed, the only context—in which call-and-response is seen to function

---

[17] Russo et al. 1992, 366–67 traces the interpretive genealogy and proposes tentatively that the singular Muse is an *exarkhousa* or chorus-leader. Following them, I read *hupôrore* as transitive, but would submit that the understood object is *the lament of the other Muses*, as fellow chorus-members (not the Greek heroes who observed this lament). Compare *Iliad* 24.760 (of Hecabe's lament), Ὣς ἔφατο κλαίουσα, γόον δ' ἀλίαστον ὄρινε ("So she spoke, weeping, and raised incessant lamentation"), where the same verb takes as explicit object the noun *goos* (a non-musical, non-professional lament, as opposed to a *thrênos*, which the Muses performed over Achilles in *Odyssey* 24.61). The introduction to Hecabe's words significantly specifies that she is the *exarkhousa*, leader of the performance: *Iliad* 24.747: τῇσιν δ' αὖθ' Ἑκάβη ἁδινοῦ ἐξῆρχε γόοιο ("For them, Hecabe started out the pulsing lament"). The proposal is in line with the dynamics within modern lament, as sketched further below.

[18] Choral responsion to a single female leader is well documented: see Alexiou 1974 passim.

in Homeric descriptions of song. I suggest that, odd as it may seem at first sight, Helen, as we see her in Homeric verse, possesses a close affinity for lament. Furthermore, it can be demonstrated that the diction and rhetoric used by the Homeric poet to depict her in several key passages are permeated with markers of the lament genre. In addition, if we observe modern rural Greek practices of lament, as ethnographers have recorded them, a number of other puzzling features of Helen's character and story cohere in a new way. If Helen is thought of as an expert lamenter, a professional keener, her ambiguous status, mantic abilities, and ghostly double can start to make sense. Finally, we can begin to understand what she was doing that dark night outside the Horse. Once we acknowledge the key role of choral poetry in the art of lament, we can understand the Irish material, even without reverting to reconstructions of Indo-European institutions, much as those have their attractions.

II.

To establish Helen as keener, we need to work from both ends, drawing on traditional philological analysis of the ancient text (especially by comparing phraseology) but, equally, on contemporary examinations of a social-poetic genre, the *moiroloyia* (literally "fate-saying"), an enduring folk tradition on which there is now much careful ethnographic work. Scholarship of the past twenty-five years seeks to analyze Greek laments in terms of social categories and gender relationships; the role of performers in village life; and the attitudes towards kin, death, religion, and work that these songs embody. I rely in particular on the work of Nadia Seremetakis; among others studying lament and grief within Greek culture whose work has influenced me are Loring Danforth, Neni Panourgia, Gail Holst, Margaret Alexiou, and Ioannis Tsouderos.[19] For analysis of the ancient text, as will become clear, I rely on the fundamental insights of Milman Parry, Albert Lord, and the scholars who have followed in their tracks in treating Homeric epic as the product of an oral-traditional art.[20]

[19] I take this opportunity to thank the last four scholars named here for personal communications over the past few years on various aspects of Greek lament. Helpful also on the lament tradition are: Caraveli-Chavez 1980; Kassis 1985; Morgan 1973; Motsios 1995; and Skopetea 1972. [Update 2017: on lament, see further Dué 2002; Tsagalis 2004; Fishman 2008; and the essays in Suter 2008.]

[20] The deeply traditional and precise nature of Homeric diction has been most fruitfully demonstrated by Gregory Nagy in a series of books and articles (see especially 1999b, 1990, 1996a). See

Helen makes one overt formal lament in the *Iliad*.[21] In a striking poetic moment, at the very end of the poem, the woman who caused the Trojan War weeps over the body of Hector, her brother-in-law (*Iliad* 24.761–75):

τῇσι δ᾽ ἔπειθ᾽ Ἑλένη τριτάτη ἐξῆρχε γόοιο·
Ἕκτορ ἐμῷ θυμῷ δαέρων πολὺ φίλτατε πάντων,
ἦ μέν μοι πόσις ἐστὶν Ἀλέξανδρος θεοειδής,
ὅς μ᾽ ἄγαγε Τροίηνδ᾽· ὡς πρὶν ὤφελλον ὀλέσθαι.
ἤδη γὰρ νῦν μοι τόδε εἰκοστὸν ἔτος ἐστὶν   765
ἐξ οὗ κεῖθεν ἔβην καὶ ἐμῆς ἀπελήλυθα πάτρης·
ἀλλ᾽ οὔ πω σεῦ ἄκουσα κακὸν ἔπος οὐδ᾽ ἀσύφηλον·
ἀλλ᾽ εἴ τίς με καὶ ἄλλος ἐνὶ μεγάροισιν ἐνίπτοι
δαέρων ἢ γαλόων ἢ εἰνατέρων εὐπέπλων,
ἢ ἑκυρή, ἑκυρὸς δὲ πατὴρ ὣς ἤπιος αἰεί,   770
ἀλλὰ σὺ τὸν ἐπέεσσι παραιφάμενος κατέρυκες
σῇ τ᾽ ἀγανοφροσύνῃ καὶ σοῖς ἀγανοῖς ἐπέεσσι.
τὼ σέ θ᾽ ἅμα κλαίω καὶ ἔμ᾽ ἄμμορον ἀχνυμένη κῆρ·
οὐ γάρ τίς μοι ἔτ᾽ ἄλλος ἐνὶ Τροίη εὐρείη
ἤπιος οὐδὲ φίλος, πάντες δέ με πεφρίκασιν.   775

Helen, the third, began to lead their lamentation.
"Hector, dearest to my heart of all my brothers-in-law,
truly, Alexandros the godlike is my husband
who led me to Troy—I should have died before then!
Already now this is the twentieth year for me
since I came from there and left my native land;
But never did I hear from you an ill, degrading word.
Instead, if anyone else in the palace would curse me
a sister-in-law, brother-in-law, or one's long-robed wife,
or my mother-in-law (father-in-law was gentle as a father),
it was you who restrained them with words you spoke aside,
with your gentle-minded way and gentle words.
So I weep for you and at the same time, myself—luckless one!—
grieved at heart.
For there is no one else for me, in broad Troy, mild or friendly:
all are bristling in fear at me.

---

also Benveniste 1969/1973, and for a clear presentation of the theory underlying such analyses, the several works by J. M. Foley 1988, 1991, 1999.

[21] For full analysis of the differences in Homeric rhetoric between formal and improvised laments, see Tsagalis 1998.

Helen has the right to lament publicly at this moment because she is kin by marriage to the murdered Hector. But by the time we see her in this official role of mourner at the end of the poem, Helen's language sounds familiar. The reason emerges when we go beyond an analysis restricted to speeches specifically designated as laments (*goos* or *thrênos*) and look instead at the language of Helen elsewhere in the poem. Her other speeches, even though they are not called laments, more often than not contain the strategies and phrases of that genre. In other words, Helen in her appearances earlier in the *Iliad* would sound very much like a lamenting woman to the ears of a traditional audience aware of the deployment of speech motifs.[22] Primary evidence comes from Book 3, when Helen first makes her entrance in the *Iliad*. At the moment she is called to come to the walls of Troy to see her present husband Paris battle her former husband Menelaus, Helen is weaving a story-cloth depicting the sufferings that the warriors have already undergone for her sake (*Iliad* 3.125–28). Thus, even before she utters a word, Helen is placed in the context of lamentation.[23] When she reaches the wall and begins to respond to Priam's questions about the Greek warriors whom they view on the plain below, the speech has an unmistakable tone that derives from lament phrasings (underlined below) found elsewhere in Homeric epic (*Iliad* 3.171–80):

> Τὸν δ' Ἑλένη μύθοισιν ἀμείβετο δῖα γυναικῶν·
> αἰδοῖός τέ μοί ἐσσι φίλε ἑκυρὲ δεινός τε·
> ὡς ὄφελεν θάνατός μοι ἀδεῖν κακὸς ὁππότε δεῦρο
> υἱέϊ σῷ ἑπόμην θάλαμον γνωτούς τε λιποῦσα
> παῖδά τε τηλυγέτην καὶ ὁμηλικίην ἐρατεινήν.   175
> ἀλλὰ τά γ' οὐκ ἐγένοντο· τὸ καὶ κλαίουσα τέτηκα.
> τοῦτο δέ τοι ἐρέω ὅ μ' ἀνείρεαι ἠδὲ μεταλλᾷς·
> οὗτός γ' Ἀτρεΐδης εὐρὺ κρείων Ἀγαμέμνων,
> ἀμφότερον βασιλεύς τ' ἀγαθὸς κρατερός τ' αἰχμητής·
> δαὴρ αὖτ' ἐμὸς ἔσκε κυνώπιδος, εἴ ποτ' ἔην γε.   180

---

[22] On the notions of speech-motifs and speech-genres as structuring devices within Homeric mimesis, see Martin 1989 and 1997a.

[23] The word *aethlous*, "trial" is not only used to describe prize-contests, but is a formulaic complement for *algea* in the phrase *algea paskhein* "to undergo griefs." On the polyvalence of the scene, see Austin 1994, 37–41 with further bibliography. He does not note lament associations, however.

Helen, glorious among women, answered him with strong words:
"Dear father-in-law, you are revered and inspire awe.
Evil death should have been my pleasure when I followed your son
here, leaving marriage-chamber, kin, dear daughter, my age-mates.
But that was not to be. I melt with weeping for it.
This, though, I'll tell you—which you ask and inquire:
Over there is the wide-ruling son of Atreus, Agamemnon—
good king and strong fighter, both. And as well, to me,
shameful bitch, he was brother-in-law—if all that ever happened."

In line 180: Helen refers to Agamemnon as one "who used to be" (with marked iterative-imperfect form ἔσκε) and adds "if he/it ever was"— a formulaic phrase regularly used of the absent or dead. Both recur in *Odyssey* 19.315 when Penelope recalls Odysseus, who she thinks has perished:[24]

οἷος Ὀδυσσεὺς <u>ἔσκε</u> μετ' ἀνδράσιν, εἴ <u>ποτ' ἔην</u> γε

The way Odysseus used to be among men, if ever he was ...

Although Agamemnon is very much alive and in view, Helen's diction treats her own past, and its figures, as the dead object. We can hear in this a brilliant poetic re-working of a traditional speech-motif from another genre (lament), an innovatory enrichment pushing the poetic system to new expressiveness and characterizing Helen in the process.

In line 172: Helen's use of vocatives, *phil<u>e</u> (*sw)ekur<u>e</u> d(w)einos te*. The hexameter meter can only be scanned correctly here if we assume that the necessary long syllabic quantities (underlined above) were generated by the earlier presence of consonants that were lost in most dialects before the earliest possible fixation of any portion of the Homeric text (approximately 750 BCE). In other words, this double vocative, "dear father-in-law and held in awe," must have been already an old phrase in some ancient poetic tradition. What does this have to do with lament? Although it is certainly possible that such frozen archaic phrases were preserved in a number of contexts, one is struck by the predominant occurrence of designations of kin within the genre of lament as it is now practiced in Greece, especially among the women of Inner Mani. From fieldwork, Gareth Morgan and Nadia Seremetakis report that lament sessions regularly begin with highly conventionalized traditional greetings exchanged among kin, using kin-titles—some of them not in common speech

---

[24] See also Priam about the dead Hector, *Iliad* 24.425–28. On the resonance of the phrase, see Kirk 1985b, 290–91.

usage—rather than proper names. Thus *kafí mou*—or *adhelfoúla mou*—can be used not just for blood sisters (the literal meaning in modern Greek) but any female kin. Indeed, the lament performance arising in these modern occasions is a primary way of establishing and articulating the speaker's exact sentiment for degrees of kin affection, precisely through such designations. This is a striking case of social poetics in action.[25] In this regard, it is worth noting that Helen's single overt speech of lament (cited above) specifically singles out Priam as her "good" in-law: "father-in-law was gentle as a father" (*Iliad* 24.770). The theme of Helen's relationship to Priam, which emerges fully in her lament for Hector at the poem's finale, revolves around the same phrase that we see in a highly traditional occurrence earlier in the poem. To put it pointedly, "dear father-in-law—*phile (*sw)ekure*—may well have arisen in a formal lament like the Book 24 example and have been reused innovatively in the scene of Helen and Priam on the wall.

Rather than continue the dense philological demonstration to show that Helen is *always* using lament language within the *Iliad* and thus would sound like a constant and even professional mourner to an attuned audience, I turn now to three implications of the picture I have been drawing, of Helen as keening woman.[26]

1. Helen's mantic abilities can be understood if we retroject to archaic Greek times a belief found today concerning modern Greek lament experts. The modern Greek lore on lamenters makes them also consistently adept at interpreting signs that warn of imminent death. In the view of Seremetakis and others, they are the modern equivalent of diviners. Turning to *Odyssey* 15.172–73, let us imagine that an ancient lamenter might also have been credited with this capacity. Helen says:

"κλῦτέ μευ· αὐτὰρ ἐγὼ <u>μαντεύσομαι</u>, ὡς ἐνὶ θυμῷ
ἀθάνατοι βάλλουσι καὶ ὡς τελέεσθαι ὀΐω."

---

[25] Seremetakis 1991, 86–92; Morgan 1973.

[26] Cf. further *Iliad* 6.343–58: Helen denigrates Paris in front of Hector in a speech filled with obvious mourning imagery applied to her own wished-for death. The blame elements in a "lament" speech are even clearer at *Iliad* 3.426–38, when she hurls a *mûthos* at Paris and wishes that he had died in his recent duel with Menelaus. A solution to the somewhat disturbing co-occurrence of blame and lament elements can flow from the evidence of modern Maniot laments, about which Holst-Warhaft 1992, 75–97 reports that movement between the themes of grief and revenge often occurs in the same song; see also Seremetakis 1991, 126–58 on violence as a topic in *moiroloyia*. Even in cases where death has been natural, the widow can blame the deceased for abandoning her to the cruelties of life without his protection. Death is figured as desertion; cf. Caraveli-Chavez 1980, 137–38.

"Listen—I will act as prophet [*manteusomai*], the way
the gods put it in my spirit and I think it will turn out."

Odysseus will come home, she says, and punish the suitors just as an eagle
has appeared and snatched a goose in the sight of all. Helen's ability to
foresee the future and the persuasive ability she has at this, may well stem
from her role as the paradigmatic lamenter for the heroic age. What I am
suggesting can contribute to an economy of explanation. There is no need
to resort to the rather *ad hoc* explanations that have depicted Helen as a
witch. Knowing the poetics of a social institution and retrojecting them, we
can explain two aspects of Helen's characterization through one assumption.

2.   A second worrisome passage in the *Odyssey* can also be clarified in this
way. The following lines have remained enigmatic, despite being a center
of scholarly attention in recent years.[27] On her first entrance in the epic,
Helen notices the newly-arrived Telemachus with Nestor's son Peisistratus
and says (*Odyssey* 4.138–40):

"ἴδμεν δή, Μενέλαε διοτρεφές, οἵ τινες οἵδε
ἀνδρῶν εὐχετόωνται ἱκανέμεν ἡμέτερον δῶ;
ψεύσομαι ἦ ἔτυμον ἐρέω; κέλεται δέ με θυμός.

Menelaus, god-nourished, do we know who these claim
to be, among mortals and who have reached our home?
Shall I tell a lie, or speak the truth? My heart commands me.

As the lines that immediately follow these show, Helen has already
divined, from his looks, that the guest is the son of her old acquaintance
Odysseus. But what is the force of "Shall I tell a lie ..."? The words have
inevitably prompted comparison with those of other enigmatic females, in
a passage that shares similar poetic diction—the Muses' own declaration to
Hesiod in the beginning of the *Theogony* (27–28):[28]

"ἴδμεν ψεύδεα πολλὰ λέγειν ἐτύμοισιν ὁμοῖα,
ἴδμεν δ' εὖτ' ἐθέλωμεν ἀληθέα γηρύσασθαι."

Here, the Muses, less tentatively, assert: "We know how to say many lies
like true things, and when we want, we know how to sing truths." But do

---

[27]   Heubeck et al. 1988, 203.

[28]   Ferrari 1988 is the most sensible view of the debate over the alleged deconstructive import of this
couplet.

they tell the truth to Hesiod? And what does Helen's heart command her? Why is the disjunction of truth or fiction even made problematic in both passages? It is in connecting these apparently isolated puzzles in archaic Greek poetry that the value of a "performance model" attested from field-work in modern Greece can be shown. In a Maniot Greek lament recorded by Nadia Seremetakis in the mid-1980s we hear:

> E, Alogháko, éla kondá
> na ze ta léou na t'aghrikás,
> *alíthia léou ni psémata?*
>
> Alogako, come near,
> so I can tell you, so you can hear:
> *am I speaking the truth or lies?* [29]

What the modern ethnographer can make clear, however, is what we can never directly recover from the ancient text: the context and force of this trope in actual performance. "Am I telling truth or lies," she shows, is a rhetorical convention of the modern lament. It is a powerful, idiomatic expression that simply *asserts the truth* of what the speaker says: i.e., the lamenter is *not* telling lies.

3.   But we should not characterize this as merely an assertion. To quote Seremetakis on the full force of the lament and its choral patterning: "The truth claims that arise from the ritual ... depend on the emotional force of pain, and the *jural force of antiphonic confirmation* [my emphasis]. By stating that they cannot properly sing laments without the help of oth-ers, Maniot women reveal that pain, in order to be rendered valid, has to be socially constructed in antiphonic relations. Antiphony is a jural and historicizing structure." In other words, the assertion of truth is the prime marker for what the entire ritual undertakes to accomplish. Lament, in the words of the fieldworker, "has a built-in record keeping function."[30] Once we realize, with the help of ethnography, that choral performance is not purely an aesthetic choice, but of the essence in lament, we can return to the passage with which we began: Helen "doing all the voices," as she circumambulates the Trojan Horse. It has not to my knowledge been noticed that the closest formulaic line to the description of Helen's action (*Odyssey* 4.278: ἐκ δ' ὀνομακλήδην Δαναῶν ὀνόμαζες ἀρίστους, "You

---

[29] Seremetakis 1991, 103. Note that even surface lexical expressions (from *alēthes* and *pseudos*) remain constant over 2500 years of Greek performances.

[30] Seremetakis 1991, 120.

called by name the best of the Danaans") occurs in *Iliad* 22.415, precisely when Priam laments Hector:

ἐξονομακλήδην ὀνομάζων ἄνδρα ἕκαστον

calling out each man by name

There, the "calling out" of individual names is a chilling part of the very public performance of Priam's grief by the old man himself. The comparative evidence of Maniot lament, meanwhile, shows that this calling out, either of living or dead, is an expected, conventional part of a lament performance.[31] What was Helen doing that dark night? Perhaps what she did was staged as a lament. This would fit the character that she had constructed already for her Trojan audience (recall her speech behavior in *Iliad* Book 3) and that she needed to maintain. At the same time, this would have been a frustrating and excruciating performance for another audience, the Achaean warriors hidden inside the horse. I suggest that in Helen's command performance, she becomes the keener *and* chorus, a lone choral-leader calling out the dead. She provides the voices that would actually have lamented individual heroes had their wives been present (and were they already dead). But in this case the lament *for* the dead, like the call of the Sirens, is a summons *to* death unless one resists it.

To put it briefly, Helen is so closely associated with lament in Greek tradition that she becomes its metonym. I would submit that this phenomenon can be extended into a principle for traditional poetics as a whole: one character can embody a genre. It happens that lament, this antiphonal, foundational speech-act, can be represented in archaic Greece as the original authorizing act that lies behind *all* poetry of commemoration.[32] That may be why the Muses are women, for only women regularly take the professional role of praising and mourning the dead. It should not surprise us, then, that the Muses in Hesiod (*Theogony* 26), on the verge of declaring their powers, bandy about blame expressions, assaulting the shepherds as "mere bellies, wretched shames."[33] As we have seen, the rhetoric of ancient and modern lament resorts to exactly this, to spur the living to act or express the survivor's aporia.

---

[31] Caraveli-Chavez 1980 shows how call-outs structure lament.

[32] On the varied mythic sources of song, see Nagy 1990.

[33] For bibliography and a new solution to the meaning of the first phrase, see Katz and Volk 2000.

A final conclusion for Homeric poetics, emerging from this experiment in socio-philology, is that because Helen represents lament, which in turn can be taken as the source of a community's truth-telling, its ranking of relations among dead and living, the place of Helen as the last person to utter a lament, at the very end of the *Iliad*, is entirely appropriate. She is the female Muse who counter-balances the Muse invoked at the poem's beginning. As another sort of goddess, she is the true inspiration for the Trojan War—and thus also for the stories told about it.

III.

In most comparisons of Greek and Irish literature known to me, the transitional trope usually involves invoking a distant common source, a genetic relation based on shared Indo-European origins.[34] This is by no means to devalue such work, which stands as a monument to the finest controlled philological comparatism. Rather, my Helleno-Hibernian *coda* is an attempt to make connections at a broader typological level, without the precise matching of lexical items that is crucial to the Indo-Europeanist's demonstrations, but with attention to cultural structures.[35] Two conclusions will flow from the comparison I propose: first, that ancient non-Homeric myths concerning the Greek Helen can be explicated by reference to Irish folklore on lamenters; and second, that the essential choral nature of lament in Greece can be used, by way of analogy, to clarify passages in medieval and modern Irish poetry.

The Greek myths have to do with Helen's infamous *eidolon* ("phantom" or "image"—the word gives us ultimately "idol"), which, according to a tradition attested in Stesichorus (sixth-century BCE lyric poet) and Euripides (fifth-century tragedian) was formed by the goddess Hera and sent to Troy as a substitute, while the real Helen innocently sat out the war in Egypt.[36] Whether or not Homer knew about this story and suppressed it is debatable. Yet the close connection between lament and Helen, which we can see in the Homeric representation of her, leads me to the following suggestion, taking

[34] McCone 1984 offers a good critique of the sometimes less productive ways of constructing such origins in the case of Irish materials.

[35] For this method, the work of J. Nagy 1990 on "talking heads" in Greek and Irish mythic traditions has been an inspiration.

[36] Sources are analyzed in T. Gantz 1993; for further bibliography and discussions see Suzuki 1989, 13–14.

account of the sorts of lore that surround the social poetry of lamenting in modern Greece and (earlier) modern Ireland. In Inner Mani, it is thought that a vision of a dying person comes to his or her kin at the time of death, something like a ghost but more vital and convincing than such an apparition. Thus, expert lamenters—the *miroloyistres*—have been known to set out for the funeral rituals before they even get word, through normal channels, that someone has died. They simply realize, from their interpretation of signs, that someone has expired and they are needed as professional mourners. The presence of these elderly professional mourners on the roads is taken as a bad omen and people try to avoid them.[37]

In Modern Greek lore, the lamenter herself, although she may be avoided and seen as a harbinger of death, is *not* seen in a vision. That is the communicative mode of the deceased. But in Irish tradition, as is well known, she is—or, perhaps more often, is heard, as an unseen presence. Both medieval and modern Irish keeners do unusual things, as Angela Partridge's analysis shows.[38] There are stories of the woman who hears about a death and then takes three leaps, upon which she arrives at the scene of the demise—not as good as bilocation, but close. Even more relevant is the tradition of the *bean sídhe*, "woman of the otherworld people." Hearing or seeing her fearsome lamentation is thought to forebode death or disaster in a community.[39] If we assume that a traditional poetic role of Helen as a constant lamenter might have intersected with now lost Greek folk traditions that resembled the surviving Irish traditions, then the stories of her *eidolon* can be interpreted as emerging from a keener's banshee-like apparitions.[40]

Finally, the choral requirements of lament, which were used above to explicate odd moments in Helen's biography, can help us reconsider Irish women's performances in this genre. Although keening is a well-known and widely studied phenomenon in Irish culture and literature, it seems that its potential choral features have been neglected or misunderstood.[41] The quite literary focus on the "authorship" or ownership of lament encourages

[37]   Seremetakis 1991, 46–63.

[38]   Partridge 1980. An example occurs in the *Caoineadh Airt Uí Laoghaire* discussed below (lines 53–55, Ó Tuama and Kinsella 1981).

[39]   Lysaght 1986; Ó hÓgáin 1991, 45–46.

[40]   A glimmering of such a folk tradition can be seen in the episode at *Odyssey* 4.795–841, where an *eidolon* of the sister of Penelope comes to tell her to stop grieving, that her son is alive. Since the scene occurs in a section of the poem which has a artful innovations in narrative, it may be that the tradition of a ghostly *eidolon* coming to tell of a death has here, too, been stylized and varied.

[41]   Ó Buachalla 1998, with analysis and recent bibliography.

such readings. Thus, the most celebrated Irish lament, the *Caoineadh Airt Uí Laoghaire,* has to my knowledge always been taken as the solitary cry of a distraught wife, whose husband was shot dead by a sherriff's man in Macroom, Co. Cork on May 4, 1773.[42] Attention should be drawn, however, to the odd "interruption" that occurs several times in the poem. The sister of Art breaks in, apparently scolding the wife, Eibhlín, while addressing the dead man:

> (Art's sister): Mo chara is mo stór tú!
>   Is mó bean chumtha chórach
>   ó Chorcaigh na seolta
>   go Droichead na Tóime
>   do tabharfadh macha mór bó dhuit
>   agus dorn buí-óir duit,
>   na raghadh a chodladh 'na seomra
>   oíche do thórraimh.

> "My friend and my treasure!
> Many fine-made women
> from Cork of the sails
> to Droichead na Tóime
> would bring you great herds
> and a yellow-gold handful,
> and not sleep in their room
> on the night of your wake."

To this the mourning wife reacts:

>   Mo chara is m'uan tú!
>   is ná creid sin uathu,
>   ná an cogar a fuarais,
>   ná an scéal fir fuatha,
>   gur a chodladh a chuas-sa.

> "My friend and my lamb!
> Don't you believe them
> nor the scandal you heard
> nor the jealous man's gossip
> that it's sleeping I went."

---

[42] Text and translation from Ó Tuama and Kinsella 1981, 200–19. I have also consulted the commentary in Ó Tuama 1961.

She goes on to explain that she had only left the room to settle the young children to sleep. The rhetorical dynamic can be compared with that in the modern Greek examples cited. Blame here elicits a confirmation that the closest kin is, indeed, doing what she must: the antiphonal mode works to stage and underline the assertion of proper ritual.

If we can see traces of a dramatized, interlocutory style in Irish lament in the eighteenth century, what of earlier periods? The songs that have made their way into our surviving manuscripts do not seem to offer help. I think especially of such poems as the lament of Créide for Dínertach.[43] A distinctive element, something we do not have, strictly speaking, in ancient Greek examples, emerges in such compositions: the lament is combined with expressions of passionate love. Créide's quatrains can be taken either as a love poem or a lament. The combination is beautifully shaped metaphorically so that the arrows that slew her beloved are transformed into thoughts that keep her awake:

> It é saigte gona súain
> cech thrátha i n-aidchi adúair
> serccoí, lia gnása, íar ndé
> fir a tóeb thíre Roigne...

> Lamenting love are the arrows that kill sleep
> each hour of the freezing night,
> from being with him, at end of day,
> the man from beside Tír Roigne.

Just as Eibhlín O'Leary's lament is filled with terms of endearment, recollections of her husband's appearance and their conversation, so Créide's words elide the realms of death and eros—a combination to which we shall return in a moment. For now, it is enough to note that such a focus on the loving association of the speaker with the object of her lament militates against the use of a choral voice, for how could many women, even in a stylized version, explicitly affirm this more intimate bond?

Yet there are situations in which this can be imagined. Créide's lament includes one quatrain (7) that seems to allude to choral praise—whether in lament or for the live hero, is hard to tell: "In the land of glorious Aidne ... singing goes on [*canair*] about a glorious flame, from the south of Limerick of the graves, whose name is Dínertach." I note that, although Murphy translates the verb as "men sing," its impersonal-passive force leaves the gender

<hr>

[43] Murphy 1998, #36.

of the subject unstated. I suggest that women might have been the singers, and if so we would have a parallel here for a strange passage from Irish saga.

Like the Greek, Irish tradition is immensely long and vigorous. Going back to the *Scéla Muicce Meic Dathó* (about 800 CE), we encounter a scene evocative of choral performances by women. The lines come at the end of the brawling story of the struggle between the men of Ulster and those of Connaught over the dog of Mac Dathó, which his owner has promised to both sides. In a shift ripe for structuralist myth analysis, the marvelous hound is temporarily trumped by a pig in a pot. The escalating contention for the Champion's Portion (*verbal, interior, spear-fighting, Leinster-centered, cooked*) breaks into a free-for-all chariot-chase across Ireland (*physical, exterior, chariot-fighting centrifugal, raw*).[44] The poor canine at the heart of the battle is carted around Ireland half-impaled on a war-chariot until he gradually disintegrates, thus naming a number of topographical features—"Dog-head," "Dog-tail," and so forth. Women frame the tale. At the opening, we hear Mac Dathó in a dialogue with his wife, who urges him to adopt the plan of giving the hound to both parties. The tale ends with a mysterious passage concerning a group of women and a bit of cinematic plot business worthy of John Ford at his best. Ailill's Connaught charioteer, named Fer Loga, manages to leap onto the hurtling chariot of Conchobar, the Ulster king, taking him by surprise in a chokehold. Asked what he will take to spare the king's life, Fer Loga replies: "Nothing great: bring me with you to Emain Macha and let the single women of the Ulstermen [*mná óentama*] and their maiden daughters of an age to bear young [*a n-ingena macdacht*] perform a choral song [*do gabáil chepóce*] around me every hour saying 'Fer Loga is my darling' [*Fer Loga mo lennán-sa*]."[45] And so it happened, the tale concludes, "since they [the women] did not dare do otherwise." At the end of a year, Fer Loga was let go back west at Athlone, taking a pair of Conchobar's horses with him. The Rawlinson manuscript version (probably fifteenth century) adds a strange retraction at this point, after saying that Fer Loga's wish was granted: "and he did not get the choral songs though he got the horses" (*ní*

---

[44] Recent treatments of the tale do not attempt such an overall reading, although McCone 1984 provides an interesting structural interpretation in terms of other hound-and-hero tales. On other facets of the story, see Buttimer 1982; B. K. Martin 1992; and Sayers 1982 and 1991.

[45] Text as in Thurneysen 1935, 19, lines 9–13, from the *Book of Leinster* version (circa 1160 CE). The somewhat expanded version in Rawlinson B.512 omits the adjective *óentama* but adds a mark after the initial song-verse to indicate "and so forth"—as if other verses had once been known to the scribe or his audience: see Meyer 1894, 56 and 64.

ruc na cepóca cé ruc na heocha).[46] Both Classicists and Celticists realize these days that such manuscript variants are usually loaded: no reading is without its politics. In this case, the stakes are quite clear. A version of the *Tale of Mac Dathó's Pig* asserting that the good women of Ulster spent a year in daily singing of a choral love-song addressed to a Connaught hostage-taker is unlikely to be generated by Ulster tale-tellers. The counter–assertion (he never got the songs) surely represents the remnant of an *Ulster* version struggling to defuse this insulting narrative.

But is there even more at stake? What harm after all is a one-time accession to the musical whim of a terroristic Connaughtman, even an act so clearly charged with erotic overtones (which we might view as a verbal substitute for the conquest and rape of his enemies' women)? The mythistorical threat, I submit, must lie in the assertion, through this minor saga detail, that Fer Loga thereby established in enemy territory a *continuing institution* to embarrass and taunt the Ulstermen, a recurrent song event that Ulster would rather deny. Furthermore, we should view that institution— even in a medieval, Christianized text—as alluding to something closely akin to ancient Greek hero-cult.

To start at the lexical level: the uncommon word *cepóc* has been glossed as "panegyric sung in chorus ('possibly of an erotic character')."[47] But the lexicologists go on to note that the word is used frequently "of the eulogy of the dead." And as O'Curry's collection of material illustrates (although he does not make a point of this), the subjects of this choral performance are not just anyone.[48] A gloss on a fragment of an elegy for Colum Cille defines *cepóc* as a Scottish synonym for Irish *aidbsi*—the term used for the great choral song in the saint's honor, performed by the assembled poets of all Ireland in 590. In addition, the glossator cites a poetic tag showing that *cepóc* was used for praise of a king. Finally, the poem made on behalf of his peers by the chief-poet Amergin on the death of his fellow-poet and teacher Aithirne at the hands of the Ulstermen, contains the quatrain:[49]

---

[46]   Meyer 1894, 56.

[47]   RIA Dictionary s.v., citing Chadwick *Scottish Gaelic Studies* (6) 190. It is clear that the definition has been devised to fit our passage, the first cited after the lemma. The dictionary interestingly adds, from O'Mulconry's glossary, an etymology for *cepóc* (alleged to be "Greek," *graece*): *cae + bo* "i. *laus*." Apparently the author of this gloss took *cepóc* as a compound of which the first element was *coí* "lamenting" (cf. *serc-coí* in the lament of Créide, above).

[48]   O'Curry 1873, 371–74.

[49]   O'Curry 1873, 374 translating *Book of Ballymote* fol.142a. Cf. Stokes 1903:284–85, who translates the word in this passage as "death-chant," as he does earlier (282) when it is applied to lament

> "I will make a *cepóc* here
> and I will make his lamentation
> and here I will set up his tombstone
> and here I will make his graceful grave."

While O'Curry sees the song for Fer Loga and for Colum Cille as expressions of joy, he acknowledges that the other two early attestations center on grief. Comparing the performance to the wide-ranging crooning called *cronán*, he speculates that "the Irish funeral cry, as it is called, of our times, is a remnant (though perhaps only a degenerate uncultivated remnant) of the ancient *Aidbsi* or *Cepóc* of the Gaedhil," and ends with a personal note: in his own day, men and women sang choral laments at funerals in parts of the south of Ireland.[50]

The funeral context of *cepóc* might seem to be contradicted in some cases by the fact that the addressee is alive. Yet we need to allow for stylization. The poetic praise of Colum Cille in 590 may just as easily be a retrojection, a "live" version, of what we know became an elegiac post-mortem performance by 597, the *Amra Choluim Chille*. Similarly, I suggest, the song "Fer Loga is my darling" might be a stylized "live" version of what had become a choral song in Ulster or elsewhere, a lament for a long-dead warrior whose story might gain annual, renewed relevance in the context of a (pagan or Christian) women's ritual. In effect, Fer Loga lives again each time the performance is renewed. To represent the song as one dedicated to a notorious *living* man is to acknowledge this institutional continuity. As we have seen above, the erotic coloration is not foreign to lament (cf. the notion underlying *serc-coí*). The obvious Frazerian analogue would be to the cult of Adonis, which we know was represented poetically by Sappho in the sixth century BCE and practiced in Athens through the fifth.[51] But an even closer comparandum brings us to notice the specific groups selected to sing the song: single (unmarried or widowed?) Ulsterwomen and the (or their) maiden daughters of marriageable age. Compare the explanation for the women's rites for Hippolytus, which the radical antiquarian Euripides enshrines at the end of the tragedy named for this hero. Hippolytus, the object of his stepmother's love, spurned her, only to be falsely denounced as a seducer in her suicide note. Cursed by his father,

---

over Luaine's death caused by Athirne's satire. It is worth noting that this tale features a male dialogic lament over the maiden Luaine, by Conchobar and Celtchair.

[50]   O'Curry 1873, 374.

[51]   Women lament the hero and grow quickly dying grasses as part of the ritual complex; see Detienne 1994 and more recently Reitzammer 2016.

he races away in a chariot, which is then caused to crash. Artemis, *dea ex machina*, promises compensation for the hero's tragic death, as she addresses him in his last moments of life (1423–30):[52]

σοὶ δ᾿, ὦ ταλαίπωρ᾿, ἀντὶ τῶνδε τῶν κακῶν
τιμὰς μεγίστας ἐν πόλει Τροζηνίαι
δώσω· κόραι γὰρ ἄζυγες γάμων πάρος   1425
κόμας κεροῦνταί σοι, δι᾿ αἰῶνος μακροῦ
πένθη μέγιστα δακρύων καρπουμένῳ
ἀεὶ δὲ μουσοποιὸς ἐς σὲ παρθένων
ἔσται μέριμνα, κοὐκ ἀνώνυμος πεσὼν
ἔρως ὁ Φαίδρας ἐς σὲ σιγηθήσεται.   1430

To you, long-suffering man, I shall give
in return for these evils the greatest honors in Troizen.
Girls, unyoked before their marriages, will cut
their hair for you, through long ages, as you harvest
from their tears the greatest griefs. On you forever
there will be the song-making thought of maidens,
and Phaedra's passion will not fall nameless and be hushed.

Hippolytus will, in one sense, never die. His commemoration is, significantly, both erotic (it will concern Phaedra's love for him) and elegiac in tone. We might wonder whether the maidens re-enact in some way their mythic counterpart, the woman who "died " for love as they move (ritually) into the next world—that of their marriages.[53] Their choral song about love is civic and bears a social message: the necessity for passion, the requirement for women their age to enter the sphere of Aphrodite. That the Ulster women who are to hymn Fer Loga are specifically "single" and ready for marriage appears to put their performance into the same initiatory category. This is not to say that some "archaic" ritual is just vaguely recalled, for certainly the scene in the *Scéla Muicce Meic Dathó* functions synchronically on its own as a fit ending to the tale. Yet in both—ritual origin and rhetorical stylization—at the same time as it revivifies memory, performance encodes power, whether that be the force of Aphrodite, emblematized by her young victim, or the aggression of Connaught, planting its hero through maiden songs across the border.

[52] This view of archaic Greek hero-cult and its complex poetic stylizations is deeply indebted to Nagy 1999b.

[53] On the homology between women's marriage and death, see Rehm 1994. It is well known that change of status in initiation rites is stylized as a death: see Burkert 1985, 260–64.

15

TELEMACHUS AND THE LAST HERO SONG[1]

> In the *Odyssey*, it is evident that Telemachus, the exemplary son, will never equal his cruel, restless father. Nor will the astronauts, for all their lonely voyaging, stir us as deeply as Dillinger.
>
> —Paul Zweig, *The Adventurer*[2]

If epics are products of an elegiac urge for touching heroic ages past, the *Odyssey*, that greatest nostalgic poem, cannot but be already a metatext.[3] The protagonist's desire to return to his past, to all that Ithaca and Penelope represent, is counterpointed throughout the poem by a second desire, on the part of Telemachus and other audiences, to hear the past, a desire enacted, challenged, and, once in a while, satisfied, in scenes of elaborate design, from Phemius' song of the Achaean *nostoi* (*Odyssey* 1.325–59) to the stories of Nestor, Menelaus, and Helen in Books 3 and 4, reaching a climax in Odysseus' narrative in Book 11 about his encounters among the dead and an anticlimax in his hurried rehash of his adventures for Penelope (*Odyssey* 23.306–43).[4] By extension, this desire is ours as hearers of the *Odyssey*. To some degree, this latter desire can be identified with an audience's needs and expectations: a poem performed without divagations would be abrupt and inartistic, completely contrary to the expansive style at which both Homer

---

[1]   Originally published in *Colby Quarterly* 29, no. 3 (1993): 222–40.

[2]   Zweig 1974, 46.

[3]   This self-reflexivity of the poem enables it to blend easily with early Greek philosophical thought: see Lachterman 1990.

[4]   For outstanding treatments of the depiction of such narratives and audiences, especially in Book 11, see the two recent articles by Doherty (1991 and 1992). Wyatt 1989 sees in the expansions here a reflection of actual audience-poet interactions.

and the performers within his compositions are masters.[5] A poem about Odysseus *polutropos* is even more so in its essence diverse. Part of the fascination of the *Odyssey* comes from the tension between narratives performed within the poem and the course of the external plot; sometimes they conflict openly, as when Odysseus' *apologoi* on Scheria delay his homecoming. Of course, only a perverse sort of nostalgia for a "primitive narrative" stripped of digressions would want to do away with the *apologoi* of Books 9–12.[6] A more subtle attack, however, on the texture and structure of the *Odyssey* is still carried out in some quarters these days, prompted apparently by the quest for the "primitive," and it is this which the present paper attempts to counter, by taking seriously the metapoetic meanings of one figure in the poem, Telemachus.

The first four books of the *Odyssey*, the so-called "Telemacheia," provide the clearest example of the remarkably fractured contemporary critical reading of Homeric poetry. On one side, classicists such as Reucher and van Thiel continue to produce readings in which these introductory episodes are treated as additional, extraneous, marked by a second hand, that of a postulated "T-poet" who had different goals than the "O-poet," the master credited with what they call the main body of the poem, the story of Odysseus.[7] On the other side, scholars like Pucci, Peradotto, Katz, and Murnaghan approach the *Odyssey* as a unity, and work from an informed literary-critical perspective, but focus their attention on smaller problems of character or theme and so avoid two issues: why the poem is shaped, overall, in the way it is, and how the poem relates to the world of oral composition-in-performance.[8] In other words, these modern "Unitarians" (to use the terms of an older Homeric debate), while managing to escape the pitfalls of "Analyst" dissection of Homer, in embracing attractive deconstructive reading and modernist thematics have nevertheless neglected or misunderstood the most important body of critical work on Homer in this century,

---

[5]   I deal with this shared style at length in Martin 1989.

[6]   This perversity in *Odyssey* studies is brilliantly analyzed by Todorov 1977, 53–65.

[7]   Reucher 1989, on which see my review Martin 1992b; van Thiel 1988 uses less personalized notions of *Früh-* and *Spätodysseen*. For the history of the Analytic treatment of the Telemachy, see Heubeck 1974, 87–113. Patzer 1991 offers a concise critique of Analyst procedure regarding the Telemachy. S. West in Heubeck et al. 1988, 1:53–54 appreciates the importance of the Telemachy for the poem as a whole, but still is tempted to think this section originated as an independent narrative.

[8]   Unless otherwise noted, the citation of the authors' names in this paper will refer to the following books: Peradotto 1990; Pucci 1987; Katz 1991; Murnaghan 1987.

the context-based approach of those who discovered in Homeric poetry the product of a living, oral folk art.

A study of the *Odyssey* starting from the figure of Telemachus might wed the insights of both sides in the critical schism by moving discussion to a different level, that of folk epic performance and the social situations it entails. But beginning with a figure, rather than a theme, involves the critic in one difficulty right away: there is probably no more contested area in literary study than characterization. Recent trends in explicating literature, and especially narrative, have not managed to do justice to this crucial part of the tale-teller's art. Theory has not been able to help the readers of Homer go beyond our instant and strong impression that character construction in the Homeric poems is brilliant, subtle, and cunning. What is more, all too often sophisticated analysis of narrative actually has impeded any appreciation of characterization, whether in epic poetry or elsewhere. As Robert Alter, the comparatist and critic of Hebrew literature, wrote recently, "the narratologists have scarcely any critical vocabulary for encompassing the mimetic dimension of character."[9]

We can trace this state of affairs fairly well. The Russian formalists of the 1920s and 1930s, with their total emphasis on plot as the determinant of character, tended to reduce characterization to a question of function: the model underlying their work is most explicit in Vladimir Propp's well-known *Morphology of the Folktale*, published in 1928, in which he illustrates how a small set of functions and agents from magic helpers to villains can generate a large corpus of Russian wonder tales.[10] Later structuralists of the 1960s and 1970s, including Barthes, Greimas, and Todorov, built onto Formalist narratology.[11] While Todorov acknowledges that there are novels constructed around character (those of Henry James, for example) as well as around plot, he devotes more interest to the techniques and theory behind the latter category.[12] More recently, social and political commitments have turned the focus of contemporary literary theory to popular, noncanonical, and often anonymous works, in other words, precisely those fictions that privilege structuralist interpretation. Subtle characterization is not what audiences most value in television soap opera or popular fiction; of more interest is the genre's virtuosic manipulation of pure plot elements.

[9]   Alter 1989, 51.

[10]   Propp 1958. On his place in Formalist theory, see Birch 1989, 124–25 and Steiner 1984, 80–95.

[11]   The lines of development are sketched by Culler 1975, 230–38.

[12]   Todorov 1977, 66–79.

Finally, nonliterary "character," the notion that we can identify a subsisting, consistent set of behaviors all deriving from some inner force, sounds too transcendental for our grittier *fin de siècle*.

It is significant for Homeric studies that a state-of-the-art book like Marylin Katz's *Penelope's Renown* problematizes the very notion of character, reading into the figure of Penelope the radical indeterminacy of the poem's plot possibilities.[13] For this strategy, although deconstructive in nature rather than structuralist, still privileges event over person, plot over character, by viewing the latter as a reflex of the former.[14] It represents a valuable mode of investigation but leaves us, partly by its very sophistication regarding the ontological, with the more practical critical problem of how figures in the *Odyssey* are represented in this sort of poetry to begin with: how we perceive "character" and, more to the point, how an audience for a performance, rather than readers of text, accumulate knowledge of the actors within the dramatic narrative. These questions require one to grapple with oral poetics, the possibilities of which are still largely undeveloped among classicists.

A decade ago Jasper Griffin found it necessary to start from scratch when he tried to talk about characterization in the epics: "I hope that it will prove possible," he wrote, "to establish some general points about the existence in the poems of characterization, and to see how it is used, rather differently in the two epics, towards the same goals."[15] Griffin must resort to such tentative phrasing because he has read the history of criticism on Homeric characters, from Wilamowitz to Kirk, a history marked by two trends: the perfection of Analyst techniques in the last quarter of the nineteenth century and the development of oral-formulaic techniques for reading Homer in the mid-twentieth century. For the Analysts, including Wilamowitz, there could never be consistent characterization in the epics because the poems themselves were patched together by rhapsodes, interpolators, Redaktors, and Bearbeiters, who willfully transferred words appropriate to one scene—or worse, one character—to another. The work of one of

---

[13]   Katz 3–19 is most explicit about this procedure, which, as she acknowledges, is also prominent in the *Odyssey* books by Pucci and Peradotto. Cf. Peradotto 153–54 who elaborates on the viewpoints of Barthes and Bremond regarding the instability of the notion of "character."

[14]   Cf. Peradotto 122–23 who rightly criticizes "standards of verisimilitude derived from the nineteenth-century novel," but explains apparent inconsistencies in Odysseus' character as deriving from "functional goals to be achieved in the ensuing narrative" (122 n. 1), thus seeming to introduce an equally rigid and time-bound standard of plot efficiency.

[15]   Griffin 1980, 50. In his chapter on characterization he sets himself the modest goals of showing that Homeric characters can differ from one another, have implicit intentions, and be complex (cf. p. 52).

the last of the old-time Analysts, Denys Page, overlaps the second trend, the oral-formulaic. Page, in his *Homeric Odyssey*, can at least explain the alleged mistakes on which earlier Analysts had fastened. The "muddled" instructions of Athena to Telemachus, in Book 1, Page attributes to an oral performer, either a creative poet or an oral reciter, who allegedly mixed things up, transferring to Athena language that belongs properly to the suitors. In Page's solution the poet here becomes the careless botcher, a position formerly reserved for the Analysts' obtuse editors.[16]

The second trend that affected studies of Homeric character should not be attributed solely, or even mainly, to Milman Parry, although his work doubtless provided the impetus. In his groundbreaking thesis on the traditional epithet, Milman Parry defined the formula as "an expression regularly used, under the same metrical conditions, to express an essential idea."[17] This way of looking at the formula was coupled, in Parry's analysis, with the well-known demonstration of the economy and extension of the formulaic systems: the notion that there existed one, but generally only one, formulaic phrase for each grammatical case of a given name and epithet. He concluded that such systematicity meant no one descriptive adjective was invented for the individual passages in which we might find it in the poems of Homer. Epithets were a reflex of the necessity for creating compositions in performance.[18] Parry's thesis, it can be seen in retrospect, traces the same theoretical path, on the level of diction, that the Russian Formalists trod in dealing with character. Like them, Parry was not necessarily against the view that any one element in a composition had deeper meaning. He was merely concerned to show that there was a functional basis for the appearance of epithets. Parry himself did not extend his theory as far as the problem of characterization in Homer. He did, however, recognize so-called "isometric" formulas. For example, Odysseus is described twice as *polutropos*, "having many turnings." This happens in the first line of the poem and again at 10.330. But Parry notes there existed another epithet, equivalent in meter, namely *diiphilos*, "dear to Zeus," which the poet could have used for Odysseus at the two places where he chose *polutropos* instead. Thus, Parry leaves open the possibility that Homer can employ "particularized" epithets.[19] We would expect that these particularized epithets, few as they might be, would form the basis

---

[16] Page 1955b, 52–64.

[17] Parry 1971, 1–190, hereafter *MHV*; quote on p. 13.

[18] A review of the thesis and subsequent alterations can be found in Martin 1989, 149–52.

[19] *MHV* 153–58.

of an examination of Odysseus' character. Parry does not undertake such an exercise. Yet he is not against it: the proper sphere for investigating character in this type of poetry simply seemed to lie outside the system he had discovered. He claims that "we learn the characters of men and women in the *Iliad* and the *Odyssey* not from epithets but from what they do and from what they say."[20]

Unfortunately, Parry's quite elegant theory, with its tremendous value for arguing that Homeric poetry was meant originally for oral performance, led in the next generation after Parry to a severely reductionist reading of Homeric poetry.[21] Again, Denys Page was one of the more authoritative and articulate proponents of what we might call the determinist view of poetic composition. Page in his 1959 book on the *Iliad* wrote that Homer used ready-made phrases "extending in length from a word or two to several complete lines, already adapted to the metre and either already adapted or instantly adaptable to the limited range of ideas which the subject matter of the Greek Epic may require him to express."[22] It does not take much reflection to realize that such a squint-eyed view of Homer blocks out any possibility that the poet can create rich, resonant characters, indeed, can create anything aesthetically satisfying at all. In this view, either there are unlimited formulas—many of which we cannot even identify as such, on the basis of the texts we have—or Homer is bound by his art to sketch two-dimensional figures instead of rounded characters.

Since the late 1950s, Homerists, when they have chosen to focus on character at all, have generally done so by skirting the issue of formulaic composition. Oral theory created an embarrassing dilemma. One knew at first reading that Homeric poetry contained three-dimensional, deeply felt characters. At the same time, the poet's formulaic technique—at least as far as it had been described—should not have resulted in anything at all like good characterization. The more literary Homerists tended to finesse the problem: Cedric Whitman, for instance, wanted very much to believe both Parry's thesis and his own acute sensibility. In a chapter of his 1958 book entitled "Homeric Character and the Tradition," Whitman starts with the observation that "Homeric epic differs radically ... even from the most sophisticated

---

[20] *MHV* 152.

[21] For overviews of this process, see J. M. Foley 1985; Lord 1986; and the annotated bibliography by M. Edwards 1986.

[22] Page 1959, 222.

evolvements of oral poetry found anywhere."[23] When he notices slightly changed repetition of motifs, or embellishments, in arming scenes or *aris-teiai*, Whitman is careful to suggest that such characterizing touches are the mark of a brilliant creative poet moving *beyond* the formulaic tradition. Homer, in this view, turned out to be an exception, the kind of poet one could just barely imagine within an oral tradition: "With singleness of vision and real mastery of the rudiments, a poet might so dispose and deploy his material that the generalized motifs, crystallized phrases, and traditional imagery fall into contextual groupings of great specific significance."[24] Thus, Whitman accounted for both greatness and technique by saying, in effect, that Homer outgrew his own art. Jasper Griffin, in *Homer on Life and Death*, also manages to provide some examples from the *Iliad* of characterization by means of slight change in a type-scene or by verbal repetitions.[25] But he, too, refuses to place the fact of characterization within the Parry model of oral-formulaic composition. In fact, he prefaces the book by saying that he has serious doubts about the utility of much oral-formulaic analysis for interpretation of the poems. We are left with a finely written belle-lettristic appreciation and Griffin's commitment to taste and sense as the standard for judging our literary impressions.[26] If all this is a helpful corrective to the abuses of a mechanistic approach to literature, it still provides no usable understanding of technique, or any explication that would aim for a much needed "unified field" theory of Homeric poetics.

The *Odyssey* itself begins with an extended focus on Telemachus; this by itself justifies an investigation of his character, which, in turn, requires one to face the practical poetic problem of character construction. Only in this way can we understand the hero's son from the inside out, as it were, on the level of the poet's own technique. In what follows I shall outline several ways of employing the tools of oral-formulaic analysis in the study of characterization. Clearly, there is material enough for a book-length study. But the brief examination of Telemachus' characterization in Book One will suffice to show that we can consider Homer a master poet without abandoning our belief that he works within a traditional performance medium. Furthermore, it will lead us to reconsider the shape and intent of the entire *Odyssey*.

---

[23] Whitman 1958, 154.

[24] Whitman 1958, 180.

[25] Griffin 1980, 53–56.

[26] Griffin 1980, xiii–xiv.

First, a word about method. The more we learn about actual oral poetries, from Central Asian to Arabic and African to South American Indian,
the more obvious it becomes that the traditional audience of an oral performance, the "native speakers," as it were, of the poetry, have, all of them, the
mental equivalent of a CD-ROM player full of phrases and scenes. Reading
Homer with the aid of a computerized lexical searching program enables
one finally to replicate the average experience of the audience Homer had
in mind. Modern hearers of a traditional epic in cultures where the song
making survives are observed to comment appreciatively on the smallest
verbal changes, not in the ways a three-year-old demands the exact words
of a bedtime text, but with a full knowledge of the dozens of ways the teller
could have spun out a line at a given point in the narrative. In a living oral
tradition, people are exposed to verbal art constantly, not just on specific
entertainment occasions, which can happen every night in certain seasons.
When they work, eat, drink, and do other social small-group activities, myth,
song, and saying are always woven into their talk. Consequently, it is not
inaccurate to describe them as bilingual, fluent in their natural language
but also in the *Kunstsprache* of their local verbal art forms.[27] In other words,
when we compare every use of every word in Homer with every other use, we
are doing what the listener to an oral poem in a strong native tradition does
naturally. I would go further and say that the full "meaning," and the full
enjoyment, of traditional poetry come only when one has heard it all before
a hundred times, in a hundred different versions. Unfortunately, we are left
with only one version of the *Odyssey*, but this still means: to read Homer is
to have read Homer.[28] In reading the *Odyssey*, we must first identify a range
of "meaning" for both phrases and type-scenes, then use the dictionary of
this poetics to interpret the individual items as they occur chronologically in
the narrative of the poem. The method may seem counter-intuitive when an
argument for the meaning of a scene in Book 1 is based on a repetition of a
few phrases in, say, Books 20 and 24. But in fact this is precisely the point
where oral poetics must differ from standard literary criticism. The reader
of a modern novel, for instance Joseph Conrad's *Nostromo*, only gradually
learns, page by page, in temporal order, just how ironic are certain epithets
applied to the stevedore or the English mine owner. That is because each

---

[27] A wealth of examples may be found in the following sample of excellent studies: Blackburn et al.
1989; Lutgendorf 1991; Mills 1990; Chadwick and Zhirmunsky 1969; Basso 1985; Moyle 1990.

[28] This is one of the ways in which an "oral poetics"—dismissed by Griffin 1980—differs significantly from methods applied to purely written texts. On the differences for our interpretive strategies, see Russo 1987.

novel creates its own language within a genre that makes a demand, even by its title, for something completely new. It is true that Telemachus, in Book One of the *Odyssey*, tells off his mother by pointing out that listeners always are delighted by the newest song—in this case the return of the Greeks from Troy (*Odyssey* 1.351–52). But his remark is ironic in several ways, as I shall show later. Homeric epic does not work like a novel; the "character" of any given person is not constructed anew in each performance, but neither is it a set value known to all in the audience. Thanks to its traditionality and flexibility—the two aspects seen by Parry in the formulaic system—Homeric epic can accomplish characterizing effects that prose fiction cannot bring about.

The characterization of Telemachus occurs in at least four different modes in Book One, all of which function specifically by means of formulaic style and oral performance. Briefly, they are: first, the epithets with which the poet describes him; second, the way the poet frames Telemachus' speeches using formulaic language; third, Telemachus' stylized rhetorical strategies within the nine speeches the poet allots him in the book; and fourth, the way in which the poet focalizes the *Odyssey* narrative through Telemachus.

The first mode, the epithet system, brings us back of course to the nub of the problem of characterization within oral-formulaic poetry. Since Milman Parry's demonstration that the epithet is economically useful, a few literary critics have interpreted his conclusions to mean that epithets are semantically empty. Some Homerists have felt compelled to defend the appropriateness to context, and the resonance, of such famous epithets as grain-bearing earth (*phusizoos aia*), used by Homer at *Iliad* 3.243 to describe the earth that covers Helen's brothers, the Dioscuri, whom she pathetically thinks are still alive.[29] This is not really a counter-argument to Parry's position. In such cases, there is nothing to prevent our saying that the epithet is *both* metrically functional *and* poetically beautiful. No one, to my knowledge, has yet tried to argue that every time each epithet for a hero is used in Homer it is somehow just as apt, in its immediate context, as *phusizoos aia* in *Iliad* 3. And yet there is evidence that the consistent use of certain epithets for certain heroes and not others is meaningful within the formulaic system. William Whallon in 1969, Norman Austin in 1975, and most recently Richard Sacks in his 1987 study of epithets for Hector show this.[30] Sacks can demonstrate that Hector's epithets *phaidimos* "shining" and *androphonos* "man-killing" are indeed deeply significant in terms of the theme of the *Iliad*, but not

[29] This is one of the prime examples among many used to this point by Vivante 1982.

[30] Whallon 1969; Austin 1975, 11–80; Sacks 1987.

necessarily significant at a narrative level in terms of the immediate scene in which they occur. With Telemachus in Book One we can go a step further. Not only is the use of epithets with his name significant on a deeper thematic level: the poet's use of epithet is also sensitive to the context of a particular scene.

Consider the first time we see Telemachus, at *Odyssey* 1.114. Athena in the guise of Mentes has just arrived at the palace in Ithaca. Telemachus sees her first. The line runs:

τὴν δὲ πολὺ πρῶτος ἴδε Τηλέμαχος θεοειδής·

Telemachus, in appearance like a god, saw her first.

A lexical search reveals that the *polu prôtos* phrase "by far the first" is itself a formula used a half-dozen times in the *Iliad* in scenes where one warrior either volunteers first for a test of skill or wounds his enemy first (*Iliad* 7.162, 8.256, 14.442, 23.288, etc.). Within the *Odyssey*, lines beginning *ton / tên de polu prôt-* occur two other times, both in Book 17, which we will turn to examine later. But let us pause over the epithet for a while. *Theoeidês*, "in appearance like a god," at first glance occurs here because the predicate phrase, from *tên* to *ide* in the line, leaves a certain metrical slot for the subject phrase. It happens that of the four noun–epithet formulas attested for Telemachus in the nominative case, only this one will fit this metrical slot: it is an economic system, in other words.[31] The main weakness of this sort of explanation has been exposed by Austin, who pointed out that most of the time the name Telemachus, when we consider all grammatical cases, does not even have an epithet: the poet could have made a line here without an epithet at all.[32] More recently David Shive has gone a step further to show exactly what sorts of other lines Homer could have made up without using certain epithets when he did.[33] Such arguments chivalrously defend the freedom of the poet (although it does not follow that we must agree with Shive's contention that Homer, thus liberated, therefore has to be a *literate* composer). But what is the payoff for our reading of an individual scene such as this?

Once we admit that the epithet use is not merely mechanistic, three possibilities for interpretation arise:

---

[31] The other epithets for this case are *hierê is*; *pepnumenos*; and *hêros*: see lists in Austin 1975, 55.

[32] Austin 1975, 58–61.

[33] Shive 1987. For reaction from an oralist perspective, see Nagy 1988.

1. That Homer even used an epithet for Telemachus here, when we first see him, signals that the scene immediately following is important for our understanding of Telemachus' character. In this regard, the epithet is like a single musical note sounded at the start of a composition.

2. The epithet *theoeidês*, "like a god in appearance," has a deeper significance in terms of its connection with an essential theme of the *Odyssey*, namely the obscure dividing line between humans and mortals.[34]

3. The epithet is significant *in contrast to* any of the other three epithets for Telemachus that Homer might have used had he shaped the line a bit differently. In other words, the epithet has as great a role, or greater, in determining the line's shape as does the verbal phrase. *Theoeidês* is used because it best fits the narrative moment at *Odyssey* 1.114.

An explanation of these three points will show that they are not mutually exclusive. All the effects mentioned can operate at once. We might get a better angle of vision on the first phenomenon by first looking at archaic poetry in a related poetic tradition, that of Old Irish. A number of praise poems survive in Old Irish, written to commemorate local warrior kings by their tribal poets in the sixth century CE and later.[35] One of these archaic alliterative poems purports to praise a mythical king, Móen:

> 1. Móin óin, ó ba nóid, ní bu nós ardríg,
>   oirt ríga, rout án, aue Luirc Labraid.
> 4. Gríb indrid íath n-anéoil aue Luirc Lóiguiri
>   arddu dóinib acht nóibrí níme.
> 5. ór ós gréin gelmair gabais for dóine
>   sceo déib, día óin as Móin macc Aini óinríg.

> Móen the only one, since he was a child—
> not as a high king—slew kings, a splendid throw,
> Labraid grandson of Lorc.

> A griffin who overran unknown countries was the grandson
> of Lóegaire Lorc,
> higher than all men except the holy king of heaven.

> Gold brighter than the sun, he became lord of men and gods,
> the one god is Móen son of Ane the only king.[36]

---

[34] On this Homeric theme, see especially Nagy 1999, 151–73 and J. S. Clay 1983, 159–83.

[35] On this poetry, see Williams and Ford 1992, 40–44.

[36] Translation in Dillon 1969, 18. Text from Meyer 1913, 10–11. Prof. Donnchadh Ó Corráin points out to me that the phraseology of the poem indicates that it is probably an archaizing composition

It is clear that the basic pattern of such praise poetry is to make predications about the subject. This is done in old Indo-European syntactical style by nominal sentences in which the copula "be" is not expressed, as in the third line printed here, which reads literally "A griffin who overran countries unknown—the grandson of Lóegaire Lorc."[37] Other such praise poems have even less narrative. They resemble strings of predicates. Consider this one on a trio of heroes called the three Fothads. The proper names come first in each clause in the first couplet, last in the second:

> *Find* a poet; *Russ* red-haired;
> *Fergus* fiery; lord of the sea.
> A princely champion Nuadu Necht;
> a bright poet phrase are the three Fothads.[38]

One could argue from verse like this and from Sanskrit parallels that such praise poetry is, in fact, the ultimate ancestor of epic diction. Gregory Nagy has demonstrated a related point most fully in his book *Pindar's Homer*, which shows how the very basis of Homeric verse, the unique hexameter meter, could have arisen from shorter meters as found in lyric poetry of archaic Indo-European languages.[39] If we extend the argument now to the structure of the formula as well as the meter in Homer, we can say that such phrases as *Têlemakhos theoeidês* could have started as complete sentences forming a full eight-syllable verse in an archaic praise poem. The phrase, as a nominal sentence, would mean "Telemachos is in appearance like a *god*." Similar sentences really do survive in Greek poetry, specifically in a praise context: for instance in Pindar's *Pythian* 10, which begins Ὀλβία Λακεδαίμων, μάκαιρα Θεσσαλία, two nominal sentences meaning "happy *is* Lakedaemon, blest *is* Thessaly." This is to say, then, that Homeric epic fills out the story implicit in each noun-epithet formula. Epic treats these units as noun phrases, rather than complete sentences, and epic provides each with another verb, as here, so that the adjective becomes attributive rather than predicative: "Telemachus, in appearance like a god, first by far saw him." What must be stressed is that the very use of a name with an epithet

---

by a Christian poet. The stylistic point still stands, however.

[37] On this syntactic style, see Benveniste 1966b.

[38] Meyer 1913, 14.

[39] Nagy 1990, esp. 439–64. The argument is made at greater length, with Sanskrit dictional comparanda, in Nagy 1974.

in Homer conserves the poetic function of the old nominal sentence, if not the syntactic function. Such phrases occur in the narrative at key moments. Notice that this is contrary to the view, often put forward by some readers of Parry, that epithets occur as padding, somehow filling out the line at the unimportant moment when the harried oral poet just wants to get through his sentence and on to the next one and does not pause to think up a novel adjective but simply throws in one that he knows will fit. Turning that view on its head, we see that here the key moment is the introduction of a character we have not encountered before in this performance. *Theoeidês* then functions like the applause from the audience when a well-known actor walks on stage, even if it is in a new role on opening night. Homer and his long praise poetry tradition is making a statement about Telemachus.

What is the statement? Here we can turn to my second observation. The content of the epithet does not necessarily relate to the content of the immediate context. But it does tie in to a very important underlying theme of both the *Iliad* and the *Odyssey*, namely the distinction between gods and mortals. The *Iliad* offers us scenarios in which heroes overstep the limit, fighting even against the gods. And the *Iliad*, as well, in the character of Paris, also called Alexandros, examines the gap between appearance and reality, opening up the possibility that one can have an astoundingly good appearance and still be a coward. Hector berates his brother Paris in Book 3 (*Iliad* 3.39–45):

> Evil-Paris [*Duspari*], best in appearance, mad for women, beguiler:
> you should have stayed unborn and died unmarried.
> I'd prefer that; it would be a lot better
> than to be a mockery like this and despicable [*hupopsion*].
> No doubt the long-haired Achaeans are cackling,
> saying you're the most conspicuous fighter because you've got a good
> appearance, but there's no force in your guts and not a bit of strength.

Hector uses the noun *eidos*, "appearance," three times in this one speech, all to the effect that it is not any guarantee of martial craft. In fact throughout the *Iliad*, mentioning another's *eidos* can be a way of implying that the warrior in question has not got the mettle to survive. In this scene of Book 3, it is thus ironic that the poet Homer, within narrative, consistently denotes Paris with the phrase *Alexandros theoeidês*, as in the line just before the speech I have translated (*Iliad* 3.37). The *Odyssey*, too, dwells on the theme of appearance versus real ability in several places. In a way, the entire action of the poem is predicated on the ability to disguise one's *eidos*, as Odysseus is so successful at doing.[40] Ironically, it is Odysseus in disguise who sermonizes on "appearances" after being mocked during the games of the Phaeacians (*Odyssey* 8.167–77). After instructing Euryalus about the diversity of the gods' gifts, he notes (apparently in self-reference):

> One man is of less account in appearance [*eidos*]
> but the god puts a crowning shape on his words,
> and the people look on him and take delight.

In the dramatic situation of this passage, having a good *eidos* implies that one is neither a good speaker nor, in fact, very bright. It is significant that the young man Euryalus, who has athletic ability but no rhetorical graces, is the object of Odysseus' admonishing words.[41] In the course of the Phaeacian episode, we see the young man learn. By the end of Book 8 he has the wit and poise to offer Odysseus a sword and an apology. This process of education is precisely what happens to Telemachus in the course of the *Odyssey* as a whole, as many critics have remarked.[42] My point is that the use of the formula *theoeidês* marks out Homer's handling of this traditional theme, which we can call "the hero grows up." When an audience keyed into the traditional formulaic system first hears Telemachus described as "having the appearance of a god," it receives a package of thematic messages, as it were, a box of potential narrative directions. This character, the son of Odysseus, could turn out to be like Paris, *Alexandros theoeidês*, all *Schein* and no *Sein*, an indolent golden boy who relies on looks to get by. Or he could be like Euryalus—arrogant, but essentially educable. In fact, each of these two thematic alternatives is displayed in the course of the *Odyssey*. The adjective *theoeidês* is used three times to describe one or other of the pair of chief suitors on Ithaca, the arrogant young men Eurymachus and Antinous (*Odyssey* 4.628, 21.186, 21.277). They are the Paris types, whose behavior clashes with that of Telemachus. The repentant type is also described in the figure of the seer Theoclymenus, to whom the epithet is applied five times, and whose very name "god-hearing" fits the meaning of *theoeidês*. When this young man, a fugitive because he slew a kinsman, encounters Telemachus (*Odyssey* 15.256–81), we see an important stage in the growth of the latter: without questioning, he takes in the outlaw, thus showing how he has assimilated the code of guest-friendship—precisely the skill that the

---

[40] Murnaghan 1987, 3–55.

[41] See my analysis in Martin 1984a, 29–48.

[42] See, with further bibliography, Tracy 1990, 3–26 and J. H. Finley 1978.

suitors conspicuously failed to learn. The meeting of characters who are described with the epithet *theoeidês* therefore encapsulates a key theme in the poem, as it also characterizes Telemachus.

To sum up my first two observations on characterizing by epithets: the very occurrence of an epithet signals the presence of an important theme when Telemachus first comes into view. The theme, in turn, comes to be more explicitly examined in the course of the poem, before the action returns to Ithaca. At that point, Homer's poetic art has a way of wrapping up the theme by a ring composition. When we see Telemachus again in the hall in Book 17, the poet describes him with a line identical to this line in Book 1, except for the initial object pronoun (*Odyssey* 17.328). The line refers to Telemachus' noticing Eumaeus before anyone else does. He nods to the swineherd and arranges a private conversation (*Odyssey* 17.330–34). Repetition here works in a slightly different way than does the recurrent epithet. An audience gets more meaning from the second occurrence of the line because the audience recalls the first use and its context. By Book 17 Telemachus has matured, and the repeated line enables us to juxtapose this scene with the earlier one. In Book 1, when Telemachus receives Mentes, who is actually the disguised Athena, he leaps nervously to the door; after seating his guest, he bombards him with a breathless account of his own sorry state before even asking where Mentes comes from (*Odyssey* 1.158–71). By contrast, Telemachus in Book 17 does not rush to talk; he barely talks at all; a single nod accomplishes all he wants. When Telemachus does speak, it is only to utter a laconic three-liner: "Give the stranger this food; tell him to beg from all the suitors. For a man in need, a sense of shame's no good" (*Odyssey* 17.345–47). The characterization of Telemachus thus works through a process of careful differentiation. The formulaic element—whether the word *theoeidês* or a repeated line—provides the core that enables us to think of Telemachus as a consistent character at all. On the other hand, the repetition in different contexts of the formulaic elements lets us construct a three-dimensional picture of the hero. He is not, after all, just godlike in appearance; he is a person who notices things, who gets the point, before all others, *polu prôtos*.

Does it make a difference that Telemachus is called *theoeidês* when we first see him in the *Odyssey*, rather than one of his other epithets in the nominative: *hierê is, pepnumenos,* or *hêrôs*? I think it does, precisely because we first *see* him. This is my third observation on the epithet. His three other epithets all assert some knowledge on the part of the poet of Telemachus' inner state: his "holy strength" or "prudence" or that he is a "hero." But when we the audience first see Telemachus, we don't yet know what he is like. Therefore, in this all-important curtain-raising epithet, Homer takes the part of his audience. He refers to Telemachus' appearance only. When Telemachus speaks later in Book 1, he can be called "prudent" (*pepnumenos*), because at that point we hear as much from his own words.[43] Finally, there is the clever etymological play in this single line that introduces Telemachus. The young man saw (*ide*) Mentes: we see *him* precisely at the moment when he sees someone else. And to add to this, we see that he has a certain look (*theo-eid-ês*—built on the root *wid* "to see"). To complete this *tour de force* introduction, Homer tells us that Telemachus, until he catches sight of the visitor, had been viewing mentally (*ossomenos*) another prospect: that his father would return and scatter the suitors to the winds. It is significant that we cannot see Telemachus without instantly hearing of his father. Part of the interest of the rest of the plot will come from seeing how far Telemachus can distinguish himself from his father; the process has not yet started when we first see him. Such self-conscious mirroring, the reflecting of our gaze in that of the young hero, is hardly an accident of a mechanistic application of formulas. Instead, this initial scene works as an elegant piece of exposition and intentional characterization. Possible confirmation that Homer here builds up a motif complex of *seeing well / looking good* comes from Book 17 again. Just before the line that repeats this introductory line (*Odyssey* 17.328) comes the most famous and pathetic scene of gazing in the poem, when poor flea-bitten Argos notices the master who left him twenty years ago, strains his ears, wags his tail, and dies (*Odyssey* 17.301–27). The Homer who so ironically named this dog "Flash" (Argos) could well have played again on the fascination with sight and appearances generated out of the single epithet *theoeidês*.

The epithet system's importance in characterization has justified the effort thus far to show just how much we can use it. With the other three elements of characterization in which oral-formulaic technique plays a part, I will more briefly show how they build up the specific theme of Telemachus' growth into authority. I have already alluded to the second mode of the technique: the way in which Homer frames speeches. The epithet system comes into play here, since the adjective *pepnumenos*, as Austin recognized, only occurs when the poet uses it to say "Telemachus spoke" in some form.[44]

---

[43] Austin 1975, 75–78 well draws out the complimentary associations of this epithet, but does not notice the narrative sequencing of epithet usage.

[44] Austin 1975, 74.

Beyond this, however, there is another speech-framing device that characterizes the hero even more explicitly. This is Homer's employment of the
word *mûthos*. I have come to the definition of this word as "authoritative
utterance" after close reading of the formulaic expressions in which the word
appears in Homer. To summarize the system, which I outline fully in *The
Language of Heroes*: of the two main words for speech in Homer, *mûthos*
is the marked term and *epos* the unmarked. *Mûthos* refers to important
speeches that accomplish something, or to performative utterances. *Epos*
can be used for any utterance.[45] In other words, by naming some speech act
mûthos Homer foregrounds the particular words. In terms of this system it
is highly significant that Telemachus is shown to exercise with increasing
authority the type of speech called *mûthos*. The first example comes in Book
1. Towards the end of the scene in the hall, Telemachus' mother descends
from her quarters to tell the bard to stop singing that sad song about the
return of the Achaeans from Troy. Telemachus, somewhat intemperately it
may seem, comes to the defense of Phemius the poet with an apology worthy
of any beleaguered broadcast network (*Odyssey* 1.347–52):

> Poets are not responsible; Zeus, somehow, is responsible
> who gives to bread-winning men, to each, what he wants.
> There is no reason to fault the singing of the Danaans' bad fate.
> People celebrate more the song that comes latest to the hearers.

When this little speech is over, Homer describes it while mentioning
Penelope's reaction to it (*Odyssey* 1.361): "Marveling, she went back to the
house / for she put her son's prudent *mûthos* in her heart." With this one
touch, Homer characterizes the speaker Telemachus as an important rhetorician and a power in the house. The next speech by Telemachus reinforces the
sense we get of his increasing power. Now that Athena has put strength in his
spirit, as she promised, Telemachus can speak with a *mûthos*, an authoritative utterance. At *Odyssey* 1.367 Homer frames Telemachus' speech to the
suitors, saying "Telemachus the prudent began the *mûthoi*." The topic of this
public rhetoric actually focuses on a further *mûthos*, as Telemachus says that
tomorrow all will sit in assembly; at that time, he will make another speech
(*mûthos*) "telling you off without regret" (*Odyssey* 1.373). Once again, a sense
of the formulaic nature of Homeric art can lead us to larger conclusions here.
For the phrase just translated, *mûthon apêlegeôs apoeipô*, is found only one
other place in all Homer. Achilles introduces his magnificent speech to the

45   Martin 1989, 1–42.

Embassy in *Iliad* 9 with these words (*Iliad* 9.309). Rather than seeing this as a borrowing by the *Odyssey* poet from the *Iliad*, it makes more sense to say that both occurrences of this half-line expression shed light on one another. This is the language of a young hero making a crucial pronouncement to an audience that wants him to do something else. We may recall that there are other resemblances as well between Achilles and Telemachus. In the speech in Book 2 that Telemachus forecasts here, he will end up throwing a scepter to the ground, just as Achilles does in *Iliad* 1. Again, characterization happens by means of slight differences between otherwise similar scenes. For Telemachus on throwing the scepter bursts into tears; Achilles precedes his gesture with an image-packed speech, but never cries. We might wonder whether the gesture is itself a stock one in archaic rhetoric. Perhaps it is planned by Telemachus, or even resembles the art of Homer in being both spontaneous and yet formulaic. At any event, it punctuates and sets off Telemachus' speaking ability, the art that Homer has made us focus on by calling it *mûthos*.

The third category of the technique of characterizing Telemachus within this medium of oral-formulaic poetry has to do with the rhetoric of his actual speeches. To examine even a single speech of one character takes a long time because one finds that every word has significant patterning attached to it, formulaic uses that could remind an audience of a number of associations.[46] One example from the speech just cited will suffice to show how what one can call "speech type-scenes" help us understand a character. Just as we see more meaning in an arming scene or a feasting scene by comparing it with all the other instances of the type-scene, so too we can learn by examining repeated speech strategies that depend on the same sort of utterances. One can compare, for example, speeches that tell someone to do something or prayers or insults. Of course, the patterning in these genres can come from actual sociolinguistic use as much as from poetry. Homer tends to stylize strategies that we can note in the rhetoric of everyday life.[47] When we hear someone utter the formulaic phrase words, "Let me handle this," we begin to construct the character of the speaker (e.g., s/he is the take-charge sort) and evaluate the appropriateness of the utterance to the situation at hand. A similar opportunity for imagining character arises at *Odyssey* 1.358–59: Telemachus concludes his speech to Penelope by saying "go back to your quarters and do your own work and tell the maids to do theirs; big talk

[46]   Martin 1989, 167–205.

[47]   Martin 1989, 43–88.

[*mûthos*] will be a care to men, to all of them, especially me. For the power in the house belongs to this one." His words sound like those of an authoritative character, or one who strives to be. Yet when we compare this strategy of speaking with its occurrence in two other places, it appears that Telemachus is less the big man than he seems; or at least the issue is more complicated. At *Odyssey* 11.352–53, Alcinous, the king of the Phaeacians, asserts that the arrangement of Odysseus' trip home will be his doing: "the send-off [*pompê*] will be a care to men, to all of them, especially me. For the power in the *dêmos* belongs to this one."

But why does he feel compelled to say this? Because his wife Arete has anticipated his utterance just before this, when she elicits even more gifts from the Phaeacians (*Odyssey* 11.336–41) by reminding them of their wealth and the guest's needs. It takes the intervention of an old retainer, Echeneos, to readjust protocol. Arete does not speak authoritatively (*mûtheitai*) off the mark, he says (*Odyssey* 11.344–45), but Alcinous is in charge here; at this point the king asserts his power. Given what we know about the Phaeacians from Books 6 through 8, we can say that Arete *is*, in fact, the power on this island; Nausicaa, the princess, has pointedly told Odysseus to bypass the jovial but ineffectual king and go straight to Arete when he wants to beg his way home (*Odyssey* 6.310–12). This means that, in context, the formulaic speech strategy "X will be a care to me: I have the power" has overtones of being attached to one who is in fact still powerless. We can read this association as well in the most famous occurrence of this speaking strategy, at *Iliad* 6.490–93. Hector has ended his tender meeting with Andromache, who has tried to restrain him from reentering the fight on the field. "Go home; war [*polemos*] will be a care to men, especially me," he concludes. He cannot say, "for I have the power" since technically Priam is still in charge, it seems, so the line ends instead "who [the men] have been born in Troy." If we read these words with his previous statement in mind—"no one can escape his fate" (6.488)—we hear not an assertion of actual authority but once more a more desperate attempt to wrest some power from position, *precisely when* the speaker knows he does not have the authority. Alcinous and Hector are both upstaged; coming back to *Odyssey* 1, we can now expect that a traditional audience familiar with this speaking mode would hear irony in Telemachus' words. He *thinks* he can handle the situation on Ithaca, but he still has a lot to learn.[48]

---

[48] The last occurrence of the "leave it to me" trope in the *Odyssey* combines features of the interactions in *Odyssey* Books 1 and 11. After Penelope has skillfully rejected attempts by Antinous and Eurymachus to block the disguised Odysseus from trying the great bow (*Odyssey* 21.311–42),

The fourth feature that effects characterization admittedly occurs in any narrative fiction. However, the precise use of this feature, which has been called narrative focalization, as we see it in the *Odyssey* emerges from the particular setting of oral-performance poetry.[49] Focalization has to do with the way in which information is selected and channeled from the viewpoint of the author, character, or characters who implicitly "see" (as distinguished from narrate) the action. An internal focalizer is a figure within the tale whose privileged viewpoint determines the flow of the narrative. With the constraints of focalization in mind, we might notice now that our *Odyssey* opens with a conspicuous gap when it comes to the situation on Ithaca.

The only hint that there is anything untoward happening on the home island comes just after the proem when Odysseus' homecoming is alluded to (*Odyssey* 1.18):

οὐδ' ἔνθα πεφυγμένος ἦεν ἀέθλων

Not even there had he escaped contests.

A bit further on, the description of Odysseus that Zeus gives early in Book 1 is an apt example of how the suitor problem on Ithaca is elided (*Odyssey* 1.65–67):

πῶς ἂν ἔπειτ' Ὀδυσῆος ἐγὼ θείοιο λαθοίμην,
ὃς περὶ μὲν νόον ἐστὶ βροτῶν, περὶ δ' ἱρὰ θεοῖσιν
ἀθανάτοισιν ἔδωκε ...

How could I forget Odysseus the godly
who excels mortals in consciousness and to the gods
immortal gave sacrifices beyond the rest?

The only hint of what is happening on Ithaca then comes in Athena's words to Zeus at lines 1.88–91:

Telemachus dismisses her with lines exactly matching his earlier rebuke (*Odyssey* 1.356–59 = *Odyssey* 21.350–53), except for the substitution of *toxon* "bow" for *mûthos* at *Odyssey* 21.352, *and* she complies as in Book 1. As in Scheria, the issue involves the authority to give orders. That Telemachus is still not as fully heroic as his father is, however, ironically clear from the anticlimactic phrasing of his opening assertion (*Odyssey* 21.344–45): "Mother, as for the bow, no one of the Achaeans besides me is stronger ... at giving [it] and denying it to whomever I want." We might instead have expected Telemachus to claim that he is the best at stringing and shooting the weapon, not just at controlling access.

[49] On the term and its uses, see Genette 1980, 189–94 and Prince 1987, 32.

αὐτὰρ ἐγὼν Ἰθάκηνδε ἐλεύσομαι, ὄφρα οἱ υἱὸν
μᾶλλον ἐποτρύνω καί οἱ μένος ἐν φρεσὶ θείω,
εἰς ἀγορὴν καλέσαντα κάρη κομόωντας Ἀχαιοὺς
πᾶσι μνηστήρεσσιν ἀπειπέμεν ...

But I shall go to Ithaca, so that I might rouse
his son and place *menos* in his heart
so that once he has called the long-haired Achaeans to assembly
he might order away all the suitors.

Athena introduces the mention of the suitors as if who they are and whom they are wooing *were already well known*. But there has been absolutely no mention of *mnêstêres* up to this point. It is a discourse universal that one needs to know certain things in a narrative; first-mentions are crucial; narrative figures are not simply intruded without identification. What happens in the *Odyssey* is different from the expected convention of a well-constructed narrative opening, for some artful reasons.

First, this narrative gap can be explained if we assume the audience knows the story of Odysseus through a number of versions, which is to say, if we assume a *traditional oral-performance* audience. They know who the suitors are even if we, the uninitiated readers, do not. Let me tease out the implications of this point. The shape of the narrative makes us imagine an audience that has heard the story before. But this goes against precisely the thing that Telemachus has identified as the key quality of a poetic narrative—its novelty. This remark was earlier in this analysis deemed "ironic." We could get around this awkward disagreement over the art of narrative, the difference between Homer vs. Telemachus, by saying that Telemachus is referring to the *style* of a narrative; but it is clear from the language of his speech at *Odyssey* 1.336–44 that he is thinking about information content, poetry as news. He says people like the "newest" story; but the *Odyssey* itself, at least the part about suitors wooing Penelope, has to be an *old story*. In fact, as many have pointed out, the themes of the *Odyssey* make it look like a very old story indeed.[50] After all, it shares motifs with a number of earlier ancient Near Eastern texts, especially the Gilgamesh epic. The most one can say at this stage is that there is a tension between the professed ideology of poetry that we see displayed in Telemachus' speech and the compositional realities of the *Odyssey*. Or perhaps Telemachus, not yet being fully perceptive, does not know how poetry works; in the words of Pietro Pucci, he is an

---

[50]   See J. M. Foley 1987.

"intoxicated reader" who values poetry on the basis of its power to charm.[51] If Homer is silently showing us a young man with a bad head for literary criticism, then we have yet another touch of characterization that seems to fit the earlier picture of Telemachus as a learner. If, on the other hand, we read Telemachus as claiming that the best songs are completely new compositions, in a larger sense, then what he says is in perfect accord with what Lord and others have taught us about oral performance: every composition, no matter how old its themes and expressions, is a brand new work because it has a different shape based on the ever-changing relation between audience and performer.[52]

In the "gap" just mentioned—the failure to introduce the suitors properly as a plot element—there is a further point relevant to characterization. If we look at what is happening here in terms of literary pragmatics, it appears that only one person *in the narrative* can be assumed to know about the suitors without introduction. Only one character is keyed in to the action on Ithaca enough that he can recognize who the suitors and their object are without being told. That character is, of course, Telemachus. In other words, the *Odyssey* as it starts is filtered to us through the eyes and ears of Telemachus, even before we begin the adventures of the young hero within the Telemachy. In narratological terms, he is the internal focaliser of the action: although he is not the narrator, we still see the action as he would see it. This is the most important although least obvious device for Homer's characterization of Telemachus. Not only is he godlike in *eidos*, an apprentice at learning *mûthos* skills, and still somewhat in his mother's control in Book 1. He is like us, and we are like him, both in the position of audience for the heroic past. It has been noticed before that just as Telemachus only now learns about his father, so too we must pick up hints through the journey of Telemachus to gain an understanding of Odysseus.[53] But I want to stress how firmly embedded this conditioning is in terms of the narrative's point of view. If we take this focalization process seriously, we can explain also why Eumaeus the swineherd is the only person addressed consistently in the second person by the poet: "O my swineherd" (*Odyssey* 14.165, etc.). He has been, after all, the closest male to Telemachus on Ithaca. Even the suitors are represented as thinking that if Telemachus is missing from town he must be out at the swineherd's hut (*Odyssey* 4.640). The use of the second-person

---

[51]   Pucci 1987, 201–8.

[52]   Lord 1960 passim, esp. 148–57.

[53]   See with further bibliography Apthorp 1980, esp. 12–16.

address to Patroclus in the *Iliad* can be explained as the reflex of focalization through Achilles, which in turn is attested by the dictional overlaps between the *Iliad* poet and his main hero.[54] So too here the use of second-person address goes hand in hand with Telemachus as focalizer. *He* is the person within the narrative most likely to address Eumaeus this way, in ordinary discourse; *his* point of view then gets extended to the telling of the narrative itself, as the poet and the focalizer of narration often coincide.

I want to conclude by returning to the "last hero song" of my title and speculating about what it means in terms of the *Odyssey*'s overall thematics to have Telemachus, the gateway to this poem, characterized as he is in the formulaic ways I have shown. We receive the poem filtered through an internal audience who desires and listens to Odysseus' story. This audience of one, Telemachus, has his own small adventure story, the goal of which is to gain fame as well as information (cf. *Odyssey* 1.94–95). But we cannot fail to notice that Telemachus at the end of the poem is back in a subordinate position. As in a pedimental sculpture, he flanks his father along with his grandfather Laertes in Book 24. Even if he has grown, he is still not the power in the house. Furthermore, even by the end of the poem, Telemachus has not filled the role of his father in one crucial respect: while *pepnumenos*, he is not *polumêtis*. Odysseus descends from tricksters, is a trickster in this poem, and continues to be one in the long tradition of Western literature.[55] His son never has the opportunity: the trickster's only son has failed to follow the tradition.

If we join this observation to a series of other oddities about the *Odyssey*—for example, its ethical stance—it becomes clearer that the poem itself speaks of the end of a tradition.[56] One can see this most clearly in the underworld scenes of Book 24, a send-off to the entire heroic world of Troy. The heroes are all gone. In the beginning of the poem the Telemachy exists, I think, because the *Odyssey* dwells thereby on the problem of its own transmission. How can oral poets compose if the audience is made up of young men like Telemachus? Can stories change the hearer? Can Telemachus be educated? Yes, the *Odyssey* seems to say tentatively; but then Telemachus becomes different and the old world that made the stories

---

[54] Martin 1989, 235–36.

[55] On Odysseus as trickster, see Russo 1993. I thank Prof. Russo for having let me see the page proofs of his chapter ahead of publication.

[56] On the problems of Odyssean ethics, see the convincing arguments of Nagler 1990 in favor of reading the poem partly as ancient ideological justification for domestic violence.

passes away with his father's last voyage outward.[57] To a traditional audience, such as we can reconstruct by extensive reference to comparative folk materials, the omission of a trickster's career or heroic story for Telemachus must be extremely significant; these gaps say something important about the story. By preposing the Telemachy and thus foregrounding the whole problem of father-son relations, the poet of the *Odyssey* made a conscious attempt to perform a poem about the *end* of tradition. Moreover, to speak of the end of heroic tradition, tailing out with the quite ordinary Telemachus, is also to comment on the end of a poetic tradition, epic verse as practiced by the poet of the *Odyssey* itself, for the two are symbiotic. The point is perhaps not as clear for modern audiences. Yet what we know of the sociology of oral performance transmission can show that the usual mode of a singer's development depends on learning traditional epic songs from his (or her) father.[58] It becomes more significant in this specific regard that the *Odyssey* sets up, then dashes, audience expectations about the character of the hero's son. We never see Telemachus perform; he never tells his story; our attention is shifted from son to father, who then outdoes even the poet Homer (so it seems) by holding audience attention for the space of four books narrated by himself. Rather than being an adventure story with an extra bit tacked on the beginning (as Analysts view it) or a meditation on ambiguity, disguise, language, and the Text (as modern Unitarians would construe it), the *Odyssey*, thus, in this metapoetic reading, is a much more context-bound and specific performance by a poet concerned about the very social conditions that might (but eventually, in fact, failed to) allow epic art to grow. Telemachus is the emblem of that ending.[59]

---

[57] In placing the theme of father-son relations in this framework, I seek to explore yet another layer of the theme recently discussed, in its relation to Hesiodic ideology, by Arrighetti 1991.

[58] Cf. Zygas 1974, which documents the shrinking of the performers' knowledge of epic over four generations. See also Lord 1960, 22–26 on learning epic songs from the father in Serbo-Croatian traditions.

[59] The most important work on Telemachus published in the years since this chapter was written is Petropoulos 2011, a full-scale and elegant analysis of the figure and its poetic resonances. The latest critical approach to the problematic of characterization in Homer is Kozak 2017.

16

UNTIL IT ENDS
VARIETIES OF ILIADIC
ANTICIPATION[1]

What is the *Iliad* waiting for? As we ponder various pathways that any long poem might have taken, the question of epic proportion grows into musing on meaning and technique. What is gained by having the *Iliad* end when it does? How does it finally manage, after more than 15,000 lines, to reach its goal? Until then, how does the poem keep its audience engaged?[2]

Like most mysteries of Homeric verbal art, such questions lure the critic into a garden of forking paths. One route, as regards the question of Iliadic massiveness, leads through—perhaps ultimately, only *into*—the tangled undergrowth of situated performance. The narrative arc of the *Iliad* may have evolved over generations to fit extended composition-in-performance or recitation at a festival, plausibly an event lasting three days and thereby accommodating (if not requiring) a poem of heroic proportion, divisible into three performance segments. The core of the idea can be traced back to Wade-Gery, whose theory, as is frequent with such attempts, led him to a more positivist solution, fixing the place and time of the composition of the *Iliad* as the Panionion at Mycale, sometime in the eighth century.[3] Oliver Taplin's sensitive poetic analysis supported the notion that the poem could have been performed in a non-competitive festival context over three successive days, with suspenseful breaks marking off the action at two major junctures.[4] In the latest and most historically grounded scenario for the role of

---

[1]   This essay will also be published in a forthcoming festschrift for Philippe Rousseau, Lille.

[2]   It is a pleasure to dedicate this brief meditation to Philippe Rousseau, whose provocative works on time, plot, and structure in the *Iliad* have long enlightened and inspired me.

[3]   Wade-Gery 1952.

[4]   Taplin 1992, 11–41.

a non-Athenian festival in crystallizing the *Iliad*, Douglas Frame has postulated a division of the two major epics into six rhapsodic performance units apiece, corresponding to the number of *poleis* in the Ionian Dodecapolis.[5]

Meanwhile, Gregory Nagy has developed a detailed argument over the past twenty years illustrating the primary importance of the Panathenaic competitions in Athens for the crystallization of our Homeric texts.[6] The Panathenaic connection is surely of the highest significance. It helps explain, among other phenomena, the persistent notices of a "Peisistratean" recension of Homeric texts, the Attic coloration of the Homeric *Kunstsprache*, and references to cults of heroes and divinities (Athena, Erechtheus) that would have the most resonance within Athens. Without going deeply into the disputed details of rhapsodic procedure, or the vexed question of time limitations, we can at least acknowledge that the "monumentality" of the *Iliad* owes more to the external conditions of its shaping and transmission in performance than it does to the romanticized ambitions of a single genius composer "Homer." That such a figure may have existed is not ruled out; that he is at least a compelling imaginative construct is certain; that he had anything to do with the *Iliad* as we have it is more doubtful.[7]

The other pathway branching off this particular fork in the road leads us into a slightly less contested area, offered by internal analysis of the devices of epic, for which the rigorous analysis of formulaic diction carried out by Milman Parry in his Sorbonne *thèses* still provides the most illuminating scholarly model.[8] The flurry of work centered on Homeric diction, which flourished from the 1960s through 1980s, has tapered off somewhat. Or, put another way, we might say that the demonstration by Parry and later Albert Lord of the oral-traditional character of Homeric diction has now become canonical. The results that shocked and disturbed scholars fifty years ago are now taken for granted. Nevertheless, it bears repeating that the medium of Homeric formulaic art, due to its conservative nature, affords the interpreter of the *Iliad* access to a bundle of systems along which signification in the epic flows—the synapses, as it were, of the performing poetic brain. Most familiar, of course, are those systems represented by the noun and epithet combinations that Parry originally organized and analyzed. But, as

---

[5]   Frame 2009, 515–620.

[6]   Most recently in Nagy 2010. A useful summary with reference to his earlier work can be found in his recent review (Nagy 2014) of Skafte Jensen's *Writing Homer* (2011).

[7]   On the imaginary projections of this figure, see Graziosi 2002, and also J. M. Foley 1998.

[8]   Parry 1971 contains the translated *thèses* and other papers.

has become increasingly clear, systematicity of meaning and expression at the micro-level of the phrase extends much further.[9] In brief, it becomes easier with each passing year to appreciate Meillet's challenging dictum from 1923 (in *Les origines indo-européennes des mètres grecs*): everything in Homer is formulaic.[10]

My attempt to answer the questions with which I began, concerning the goal of the *Iliad* and the narrative means of attaining it (or putting it off), involves two sorts of internal analysis based on recurrent phraseology. The first, of a more global literary-semantic nature, examines expressions for eventuality, specifically those headed by the repeated phrase *eis ho ke* ("until the point that; until such time as"). The phrase, as much as any noun-epithet combination, has the status of a formula within Homeric usage, whatever its character might have been in ordinary unmarked Greek speech. Collecting and ordering such examples will reveal the range of situations that the *Iliad* conceptualizes as possible outcomes to waiting in all its forms (suspended action, retardation, prevention, and suppression). At the same time, it can give us an idea of the time-range within which the fulfillment of such outcomes is imaginable. Finally, it illustrates the crescendo effect produced by a series of anticipations, each as it were itself a foreshadowing of the final goal, which then will turn out to lie beyond the edges of the Iliadic plot. The second internal analysis is localized: a close reading of the chariot race in Book 23 will show that it offers an analogue to the shaping and thematic concerns of the *Iliad* as a whole, as well as the clearest articulation of the poem's final goal.

"Until Such Time"

Twenty-five times in the *Iliad*, a character (and one time, the poetic narrator) uses the prepositional phrase *eis ho* with an immediately adjoined particle *ke* and the subjunctive mood. This occurs pragmatically with a dual focus, to speak of an action that is to be completed in the future, but from the standpoint of the speaker who is highlighting his own present time. We might call these clauses "final," inasmuch as they anticipate results, and "temporal" because they map out a span of time stretching from a deictic center, the *hic*

---

[9]   Rather than list the dozens of relevant publications, I refer to one compelling and extensive demonstration featuring much further bibliography: Kelly 2007.

[10]   On the history of Meillet's view and controversy surrounding it, see de Lamberterie 1997.

et nunc, to a second locus of interest. Given this basic syntactic structure, presumably available for describing any sorts of situations and activities, the *Iliad* poet carefully constrains and stylizes the number of events that are actually described or predicted within a limited sphere of narrative or speech situations. We observe immediately that this poetic restriction is further constrained to occur almost always in character-speech: that is to say, the poet-narrator only once independently refers to an action with limitations of the type "X takes place until Y occurs." Put another way, this accords with the recognition that the *Iliad* poet rarely *foretells* events in his own voice, choosing instead to have characters speak of the future in foreshadowing speeches.[11] When the poet *does* speak of the future, it is not as a limited span, in the manner marked out by *eis ho ke* + subjunctives, but instead through positive assertions with present or future indicatives. Consider, for example, the moment when Achilles, having watched with concern the ebb and flow of battle, summons his companion Patroclus to discover who has been carried off the field (11.601–3):[12]

> αἶψα δ' ἑταῖρον ἑὸν Πατροκλῆα προσέειπε
> φθεγξάμενος παρὰ νηός· ὃ δὲ κλισίηθεν ἀκούσας
> ἔκμολεν ἶσος Ἄρηϊ, κακοῦ δ' ἄρα οἱ πέλεν ἀρχή.

> At once he spoke to his own companion in arms, Patroklos,
> calling from the ship, and he heard it from inside the shelter, and came out
> like the war god, and this was the beginning of his evil.

Unlike his fictional speakers, the poet can range confidently in vision over all time periods; what, to his characters, is only a dim anticipation or possibility is, for the narrator, always already established as an event known for having taken place (or not). But this capacious view means paradoxically that the epic poet is more narrowly restricted, unable to speak about a series of temporary end-points in talking about the future. The poet cannot, for instance, say prospectively that anything will take place "until such time as" something else happens. Everything, for the Homeric narrator, has already happened.

A further mark of the stylized formulaic nature of the character-expression *eis ho ke* is its restricted range within the hexameter verse. The twenty-six occurrences are attested at only three positions: line-initial (six

---

[11] On poetic manipulation of the technique, see J. V. Morrison 1992.

[12] All translations are from Lattimore 2011, unless otherwise indicated.

times); occupying the second foot (eight times); and, most often, occupying the fifth foot, after the bucolic diaeresis (twelve times). As we might expect, this constraint accompanies a compositional restriction on the semantic range of such expressions and fits with a certain amount of repetition of dictional elements. Three central types of discourse account for almost all the ways in which characters enunciate, through this expression, their sense about future goals: reference to decisions made under pressure (sometimes embedded in speech-acts of reproach); reference to the eventual fall of Troy; and reference to reaching a goal of motion.

A cluster of examples in Book 7 illustrates the function of this formulaic expression in scenes of decision-making. At the coming of night and the urging of the herald Idaeus, Hector and Ajax agree to postpone their inconclusive duel. As Hector formulates the terms of this temporary pause, conflict will resume the next day until a god makes clear which is the winning side (7.290–92):

> νῦν μὲν παυσώμεσθα μάχης καὶ δηϊοτῆτος
> σήμερον· ὕστερον αὖτε μαχησόμεθ' <u>εἰς ὅ κε δαίμων</u>
> <u>ἄμμε διακρίνῃ,</u> δώῃ δ' ἑτέροισί γε νίκην.

> "let us now give over this fighting and hostility
> for today; we shall fight again, until the divinity
> chooses between us, and gives victory to one or the other."

Significantly, the process is envisioned as distinguishing (διακρίνῃ) the two sides. This notion, while not inherently tied to the idea of anticipation, will appear toward the end of the poem in close relation to the act of waiting for an ultimate outcome.

Not long after this agreement in Book 7, Priam proposes another shorter period of waiting, repeating the original denotation of the relevant time frame, the grant of victory by a *daimon* (7.375–78):

> καὶ δὲ τόδ' εἰπέμεναι πυκινὸν ἔπος, αἴ κ' ἐθέλωσι
> παύσασθαι πολέμοιο δυσηχέος, <u>εἰς ὅ κε νεκροὺς</u>
> <u>κήομεν·</u> ὕστερον αὖτε μαχησόμεθ' <u>εἰς ὅ κε δαίμων</u>
> <u>ἄμμε διακρίνῃ,</u> δώῃ δ' ἑτέροισί γε νίκην.

> "and to add this solid message, and ask them if they are willing
> to stop the sorrowful fighting until we can burn the bodies
> of our dead. We shall fight again until the divinity
> chooses between us, and gives victory to one or the other."

A neat example of hexameter expansion, this formulation inserts the secondary specification of a waiting-period (until the burning of corpses) within the primary concern—at which point are the opposing forces to begin battle once more? (Note that the one-on-one duel to which the phrase applied earlier at 7.290–92 is now expanded in context to refer to the clash of both sides in the war.) In other words, with legal-sounding precision the primary pause is defined by exactly how long the secondary pause will take: after the dead are burnt on their pyre, war will resume; that, in turn, will last until one side can manage to claim (god-given) victory.[13] Once again, the motif will be found in amplified form toward the end of the *Iliad*, where pyre-construction and care of the dead punctuate the increasingly intense rhythm of the war.

In contrast to the legalistic tone of these passages in Book 7, another variety of anticipatory passages is more highly colored. At *Iliad* 3.408–10, Helen replies with indignation to Aphrodite, who has appeared to her in semi-disguised form in order to encourage her to watch Paris fight Menelaus. Helen says that the goddess herself should care for the Trojan:

> ἀλλ' αἰεὶ περὶ κεῖνον ὀΐζυε καί ἑ φύλασσε,
> εἰς ὅ κέ σ' ἢ ἄλοχον ποιήσεται ἢ ὅ γε δούλην.
> κεῖσε δ' ἐγὼν οὐκ εἶμι· νεμεσσητὸν δέ κεν εἴη·

> "but stay with him forever, and suffer for him, and look after him
> until he makes you his wedded wife, or makes you his slave girl.
> Not I. I am not going to him. It would be too shameful."

The future imagined by Helen for the goddess is, of course, a fantasy of revenge, based on her own experience of anger and regret. While Aphrodite, as a punishment by the Olympians whom she has distressed, might consort with members of the Trojan extended royal family (e.g., Anchises, in the *Hymn to Aphrodite*), we know she will never be the wife or slave of Paris. In effect, Helen attempts to lay a formal curse on the goddess who has brought her to Troy. But Aphrodite's reply ("do not tease me lest in anger I forsake you and grow to hate you as much as now I terribly love you") forces her to fall silent.

A similar tone of reproach marks the words of the god Ares to the Trojan fighters at *Iliad* 5.465–66:

---

[13]   The expanded form is repeated in Idaeus' repetition of Priam's instruction at *Iliad* 7.395–97.

ἐς τί ἔτι κτείνεσθαι ἐάσετε λαὸν Ἀχαιοῖς;
ἦ εἰς ὅ κεν ἀμφὶ πύλῃς εὖ ποιητῆσι μάχωνται;

" ... how long will you allow the Achaians to go on killing your
people?
Until they fight beside the strong-builded gates?"

Here we might note the repetition of questions, the first unmarked and open-
ended ("until which point?"), the second marked by a hypothetical endpoint ("until the point that they are fighting?"). Furthermore, the second
question draws into finer focus the rather general action of the first: instead
of asking how long the killing will go on, it transforms the temporal dimension into a spatial equivalent, by adding a visually powerful deictic specification (fighting *at the gates*). In brief, this hortatory speech, with its overtones
of frustration and disbelief, does in miniature what the *Iliad* as a whole enacts
as the poem turns a tale of seemingly endless siege-warfare into a cinematic
representation of a few days of movement back and forth across the plain of
Troy: time becomes spatialized.[14]

The battlefield exhortation (*Kampfparänesis*) is a well-known sub-genre
within Homeric poetry. Alongside the example just cited we might add an
indirect version, Nestor's words to Patroclus at *Iliad* 11.666–67, which the
elder hero trusts will be transmitted to the true object of his appeal, Achilles:

ἦ μένει εἰς ὅ κε δὴ νῆες θοαὶ ἄγχι θαλάσσης
Ἀργείων ἀέκητι πυρὸς δηΐοιο θέρωνται,

"Is he going to wait then till the running ships by the water
are burned with consuming fire for all the Argives can do ... ?"

Finally in this vein are the much more brutally direct words of Achilles
to the Trojans, as he flings the corpse of Lycaon into the river Scamander
(*Iliad* 21.133–34):

ἀλλὰ καὶ ὣς ὀλέεσθε κακὸν μόρον, εἰς ὅ κε πάντες
τίσετε Πατρόκλοιο φόνον καὶ λοιγὸν Ἀχαιῶν

"And yet even so, die all an evil death, till all of you
pay for the death of Patroklos and the slaughter of the Achaians"

---

[14] On the power of the *Iliad* poet to make possible such visualization, see J. S. Clay 2011a.

Like the words of Helen in Book 3, the tone is characterized by desire for revenge, which is here explicitly conceived as collective punishment for the death of his companion Patroclus.

The same speech contains another example of the phrase *eis ho ke* that leads us to the second category of usage, reference to the fall of Troy. A few lines before his promise to avenge his companion's slaying, Achilles shifts from the address to a single victim (the dead Lycaon) to his fellow Trojans and allies, saying "perish until we reach Troy" (*Iliad* 21.128–29):

> φθείρεσθ' εἰς ὅ κεν ἄστυ κιχείομεν Ἰλίου ἱρῆς
> ὑμεῖς μὲν φεύγοντες, ἐγὼ δ' ὄπιθεν κεραΐζων.

> "Die on, all; till we come to the city of sacred Ilion,
> you in flight and I killing you from behind ... "

He then remarks parenthetically that the river to which the Trojans have sacrificed will not be a sufficient defense for them and concludes with the threat of lines 21.133–34. Taken together, the two occurrences of the phrase in one rhetorical act produce an equation: his inescapable advance toward the city, slaughtering all in his path, is the beginning of the fulfillment of revenge. The completion of the first stage, however, will be a visible sign of the process of total revenge for Patroclus and the other Achaeans slain at the ships: there is no promise, however, that it will mark the totality of that vengeance. Instead, Achilles, while making the first "until such point" phrase refer to a topographical fact, chillingly leaves open the second anticipatory marker, so that we do not know whether he will exact a numerically precise tit-for-tat or some even greater, psychologically fulfilling counter-attack.

The goal of taking Troy has, of course, structured the entire story of the war, in the mythic materials surrounding the Homeric poems. Within the epic *Iliad* itself, however, this goal appears and recedes, often being occluded by the intra-Achaean strife between Achilles and his comrades. Curiously, it is once more in Book 7 that we find a cluster of clauses headed by *eis ho ke*, this time mentioning the future capture of the city. At *Iliad* 7.29–31 Apollo says to Athena that they should stop the war for now:

> νῦν μὲν παύσωμεν πόλεμον καὶ δηϊοτῆτα
> σήμερον· ὕστερον αὖτε μαχήσοντ' εἰς ὅ κε τέκμωρ
> Ἰλίου εὕρωσιν, ἐπεὶ ὣς φίλον ἔπλετο θυμῷ

"For this day let us put an end to the hatred and the fighting
now; they shall fight again hereafter, till we witness the finish
they make of Ilion, since it is dear to the heart of you ... "

As we saw above, the same diction is used when the mortal speakers discuss
the plan to put the war on hold (compare 7.291 with 7.30). In effect, the
mortals are only dimly aware that some unnamed god will eventually grant
victory and this vagueness of expression contrasts with the divine language
that actually names the end of Troy (*tekmôr* being both goal and terminus) as
the ultimate point. Slightly later, when Hector issues the challenge to a duel,
he traces the failure of the previous oath-taking between enemies in Book 4
to Zeus' ill will (*Iliad* 7.69–72):

ὅρκια μὲν Κρονίδης ὑψίζυγος οὐκ ἐτέλεσσεν,
ἀλλὰ κακὰ φρονέων <u>τεκμαίρεται</u> ἀμφοτέροισιν
<u>εἰς ὅ κεν ἢ ὑμεῖς Τροίην εὔπυργον ἕλητε</u>
ἢ αὐτοὶ παρὰ νηυσὶ δαμείετε ποντοπόροισιν.

"Zeus, son of Cronus, who sits on high, would not bring to fulfillment
our oaths, but is found to be of evil intention toward both sides
until that day when you storm Troy of the strong towers, or that day
when you yourselves are broken beside your seafaring vessels."

Instead of one side "finding the *tekmôr* of Troy," in Hector's version the
most that can be said is Zeus "is found to be" blockading success. The verb
tekmairetai in this context appears to be semantically weakened, meaning "gives
signs" but its derivation (as denominative) from *tekmôr* highlights the further
nuance of investigation, of "getting to the end" in discovering reality. After
specifying what he views as the eventual alternative outcomes for the besieging
Achaeans—overcoming the city or being overcome—Hector goes on to make a
formal declaration (μυθέομαι, line 76) about a more complex set of alternatives
relating to his own possible fate. If he should be killed by the opponent in the
upcoming duel, his armor may be carried back as a prize to the Achaean side,
but his body must be returned to Troy; if he himself kills the opposing man, says
Hector (*Iliad* 7.82–86),

"I will strip his armor and carry it to sacred Ilion
and hang it in front of the temple of far-striking Apollo,
but his corpse I will give back among the strong-benched vessels
so that the flowing-haired Achaians may give him due burial
and heap up a mound upon him beside the broad passage of Helle."

Thus far, the alternative pathways result in a comparative balance: armor is retained, bodies are returned. Yet Hector's rhetorical spin on the future scenario of his own death artfully seizes the final advantage (*Iliad* 7.87–91):

> "And some day one of the men to come will say, as he sees it,
> one who in his benched ship sails on the wine-blue water:
> 'This is the mound (*sêma*) of a man who died long ago in battle
> who was one of the bravest, and glorious Hektor killed him.'
> So will he speak some day, and my glory will not be forgotten."

The remaining three instances of our target phrase, applied to the fall of Troy, come in close association one with the other. After Agamemnon's disastrously mismanaged "test" of his fighters in Book 2, Odysseus saves the day, urging the Greek troops to stay by recalling in detail the optimistic interpretation by Calchas of a divine sign given to the expedition when it initially gathered at Aulis (*Iliad* 2.331–32):

> ἀλλ' ἄγε μίμνετε πάντες ἐϋκνήμιδες Ἀχαιοὶ
> αὐτοῦ <u>εἰς ὅ κεν ἄστυ μέγα Πριάμοιο ἕλωμεν</u>.

> "Come then, you strong-greaved Achaians, let every man stay
> here, until we have taken the great citadel of Priam."

A markedly similar practical and rhetorical situation leads to the use of the *eis ho ke* phrase (twice) at the start of Book 9. Diomedes responds to Agamemnon's suggested abandonment of the expedition with a rousing speech dismissing the commander, while pledging that he will remain to see out the end of war (*Iliad* 9.45–49):

> ἀλλ' ἄλλοι μενέουσι κάρη κομόωντες Ἀχαιοὶ
> <u>εἰς ὅ κέ περ Τροίην διαπέρσομεν</u>. εἰ δὲ καὶ αὐτοὶ
> φευγόντων σὺν νηυσὶ φίλην ἐς πατρίδα γαῖαν·
> νῶϊ δ' ἐγὼ Σθένελός τε <u>μαχησόμεθ' εἰς ὅ κε τέκμωρ</u>
> <u>Ἰλίου εὕρωμεν</u>· σὺν γὰρ θεῷ εἰλήλουθμεν.

> "and yet the rest of the flowing-haired Achaians will stay here
> until we have sacked the city of Troy; let even these also
> run away with their ships to the beloved land of their fathers,
> still we two, Sthenelos and I, will fight till we witness
> the end of Ilion; for it was with God that we made our way hither."

Diomedes in effect picks up and continues the logic of Odysseus as expressed in the earlier passage of Book 2: although the younger hero does not overtly re-state the reason, the Greeks have come to Troy "with a god" because it was Calchas who implied as much. Thus it is appropriate that Diomedes' speech is received in almost exactly the same manner as the earlier authoritative utterance (*mûthos*) by Odysseus. Compare *Iliad* 9.50–51:

> Ὣς ἔφαθ', οἳ δ' ἄρα πάντες <u>ἐπίαχον</u> υἷες Ἀχαιῶν
> <u>μῦθον ἀγασσάμενοι</u> Διομήδεος ἱπποδάμοιο.

with *Iliad* 2.333–35:

> Ὣς ἔφατ', Ἀργεῖοι δὲ <u>μέγ' ἴαχον</u>, ἀμφὶ δὲ νῆες
> σμερδαλέον κονάβησαν ἀϋσάντων ὑπ' Ἀχαιῶν,
> <u>μῦθον ἐπαινήσαντες</u> Ὀδυσσῆος θείοιο[15]

The first two categories of poetic deployment, as we have seen, of the phrase *eis ho ke* in the *Iliad* are narrowly limited to certain speech-acts and speech-situations. The third, while more broad-ranging in terms of the situations to which it applies, is nevertheless strictly kept within a small semantic range, relating to motion toward a goal. It is this final category that will lead us into the longer interpretation of an important passage from the end of the poem.

The relevant lines are easily grouped around the verbs employed in the anticipatory clauses. For the verb "come" we find the following formulaic set, with varying subjects of the verb:

Iliad 10.62 (Menelaus to Agamemnon):

> αὖθι μένω μετὰ τοῖσι δεδεγμένος <u>εἰς ὅ κεν ἔλθῃς</u>,
> ἦε θέω μετὰ σ' αὖτις, ἐπὴν εὖ τοῖς ἐπιτείλω;

Iliad 14.77 (Agamemnon to Nestor):

> ἕλκωμεν, πάσας δὲ ἐρύσσομεν εἰς ἅλα δῖαν,
> ὕψι δ' ἐπ' εὐνάων ὁρμίσσομεν, <u>εἰς ὅ κεν ἔλθῃ</u>
> <u>νὺξ ἀβρότη</u>, ἢν καὶ τῇ ἀπόσχωνται πολέμοιο

Iliad 21.231 (Scamander to Apollo):

> εἰρύσαο Κρονίωνος, ὅ τοι μάλα πόλλ' ἐπέτελλε
> Τρωσὶ παρεστάμεναι καὶ ἀμύνειν, <u>εἰς ὅ κεν ἔλθῃ</u>
> <u>δείελος ὀψὲ δύων</u>, σκιάσῃ δ' ἐρίβωλον ἄρουραν.

---

[15] On the speech of Odysseus and its reception see now Elmer 2013, 98–102.

Iliad 21.531 (Priam to Trojan guards):

> πεπταμένας ἐν χερσὶ πύλας ἔχετ' <u>εἰς ὅ κε λαοὶ</u>
> <u>ἔλθωσι</u> προτὶ ἄστυ πεφυζότες· ἦ γὰρ Ἀχιλλεὺς
> ἐγγὺς ὅδε κλονέων· νῦν οἴω λοίγι' ἔσεσθαι.

A related set of lines centers around the verb "arrive," which functions deictically in context as the complement to "come," since it refers to arrival at a place apart from where the speaker stands:

Iliad 16.455 (Hera to Zeus concerning Sarpedon):

> πέμπειν μιν θάνατόν τε φέρειν καὶ νήδυμον ὕπνον
> <u>εἰς ὅ κε δὴ Λυκίης εὐρείης δῆμον ἵκωνται</u>,
> ἔνθά ἑ ταρχύσουσι κασίγνητοί τε ἔται τε

Three passages use closely related diction that features both verbs "arrive" and "come":

Iliad 11.193 (Zeus to Iris concerning Hector) = 11.208 (Iris) = 17.454 (Zeus, with ἀφίκωνται):

> εἰς ἵππους ἅλεται, τότε οἱ κράτος ἐγγυαλίξω
> κτείνειν <u>εἰς ὅ κε νῆας ἐϋσσέλμους ἀφίκηται</u>
> δύῃ τ' ἠέλιος <u>καὶ ἐπὶ κνέφας ἱερὸν ἔλθῃ</u>.

Only two passages fail to fit the configurations thus far remarked on. In *Iliad* 12.149–50, the epic narrator describes the resistance of two Lapith heroes against the Trojan onslaught, comparing them to two wild boars. The passage is unique in being the only simile to employ *eis ho ke* and the only time the phrase is used in diegetic, rather than mimetic, speech:

> πρυμνὴν ἐκτάμνοντες, ὑπαὶ δέ τε κόμπος ὀδόντων
> γίγνεται <u>εἰς ὅ κέ τίς τε βαλὼν ἐκ θυμὸν ἕληται·</u>

and as they go tearing slantwise and rip the timber about them
to pieces at the stock, the grinding scream of their teeth sounds
high, until some man hits them with his throw and takes the life from
them;

In *Iliad* 14.5–7 Nestor comforts the wounded Machaon:

> ἀλλὰ σὺ μὲν νῦν πῖνε καθήμενος αἴθοπα οἶνον
> <u>εἰς ὅ κε θερμὰ λοετρὰ ἐϋπλόκαμος Ἑκαμήδη</u>

θεϱμήνῃ καὶ λούσῃ ἄπο βϱότον αἱματόεντα·

"Now, do you sit here and go on drinking the bright wine,
until Hekamede the lovely-haired makes ready a hot bath
for you, warming it, and washes away the filth of the bloodstains,"

Both of these passages, however, do speak of the treatment of the body, which itself becomes the goal of motion and activity, whether for good or ill. In this way, they resemble the very last, and most important, application of the trope "until such time." Knowing that his death is to come shortly after that of Hector, whom he has now slain, Achilles transcends his manic anger as he arranges the funeral games for his companion Patroclus. So far has he transcended anxiety about his own fate that at *Iliad* 23.244, before he initiates the first of the athletic events, Achilles calmly directs the Achaeans concerning the proper arrangements for his own cremation and the treatment of his bones (*Iliad* 23.236–44):

"Son of Atreus, and you other greatest of all the Achaians,
first put out with gleaming wine the pyre that is burning,
all that still has on it the fury of fire; and afterward
we shall gather up the bones of Patroklos, the son of Menoitios,
which we shall easily tell apart [εὖ διαγιγνώσκοντες], since they are
conspicuous
where he lay in the middle of the pyre and the others far from him
at the edge burned, the men indiscriminately with the horses.
And let us lay his bones in a golden jar and a double
fold of fat, until I myself am hidden in Hades [εἰς ὅ κεν αὐτὸς ἐγὼν
Ἄϊδι κεύθωμαι]."[16]

How does this employment of the phrase fit into the preceding analysis? From the examples of the first two categories, we have seen that *eis ho ke* introduces two major modes of speaking: the hortatory or reproachful, in which a future event, sometimes repugnant, is anticipated verbally in order to convince the addressee of a course of action in the present. Thus Odysseus and Diomedes urge their fellow Greeks to stay on fighting at Troy until it falls (a desired goal); Nestor and Ares urge martial action to prevent worse outcomes (undesired ends, such as more Trojans or Greeks being killed). Even Helen's attempt to dismiss Aphrodite alludes to an unattractive goal (from the goddess' point-of-view): being erotically dominated by Paris. In sum, the discourse usages of the first two sets of categories are distinctly

---

[16] Lattimore translation modified in line 244 to reflect the reading κεύθωμαι.

conative to use the well-known distinction introduced by Roman Jakobson. By contrast, the passages listed in our third category (attaining a goal of motion) are what Jakobson might call referential, or a speech-act critic might identify as constative. Specifying *when* certain actions are scheduled to take place (when day or night comes; when a bath is ready; when persons reach the ships or gates or Lycia), these expressions are more like a narrator's directions for how the plot of a given passage unfolds. To make the point sharper: while some characters (almost always mortals) use *eis ho ke* to try to persuade addressees, others (usually immortals) use the phrasal trope to set the parameters for action.

At another level, we could distinguish the first two categories from the third by labeling the former *character-centered* and the latter *narratological*. Most importantly, Achilles falls squarely in the latter. Furthermore, his command to keep the bones of Patroclus in a golden vessel until his own should be hidden away with them in Hades presents us with the ultimate framing boundary of the saga of Troy. It is a boundary that is still somewhat ambiguous, as it depends on the fall of Troy, to be followed by a burial for the combined bones of Achilles and his beloved friend. Like other Iliadic scenarios we have seen, it thus embeds one goal within another. At the same time, the existence of a tomb that is to be a temporary cenotaph, from the poem's description, is filled out by extra-Iliadic information that Achilles was finally buried in the tumulus at the Hellespont, making it a real tomb. This is the tradition to which the *Odyssey* adheres (*Odyssey* 24.80–84). Despite some uncertainty (where will Achilles' bones lie until final construction of the larger tomb?), there can be no doubt that Achilles' use of *eis ho ke* provides the most capacious, all-embracing viewpoint when contrasted with the other speakers' speech strategies we have seen.[17]

Meanwhile, from a narratological perspective, we can sum up at this point by observing that the *eis ho ke* formula illuminates one key manner through which the poetic voice controls and retards action. Through the frequent setting up of internal goals, both as imaginative markers of ultimate actions ("until they sack Troy") or practical markers of intermediate movements ("until they reach the gates"), both varieties being projected through the voices of characters, the narrator of the *Iliad* constructs a nested, modular tale, each segment pointing toward a future time when it will be completed, even as the individual episode slows down progress toward the ultimate

---

[17] On the traditions of Achilles' burial, both poetic and myth-historical, see Burgess 2009.

end of the poem.[18] We can, through studying formulaic use of conjunction phrases, thus make finer-grained analyses in support of the valuable observations of such interpreters as Cedric Whitman, Keith Stanley, and Bruce Heiden, who have labored to unpack the "geometric" and related large-scale orderings of this remarkable epic.[19]

The Poem as Race

At this juncture, it is necessary to return to the longer Book 23 passage headed by Achilles' precise command about burial arrangement. The examples we have looked at, of anticipatory *eis ho ke* specifying a period of waiting, have been shown to operate within a narrow spectrum of situations and meanings. I would now push further and propose that this delimited range is closely tied, in terms of image and diction, to that of a race. Without resorting to allegory, we can observe that the elements of duration, marked goal, determination, and decision-making (as to who comes first, who wins what) are shared by both the war for Troy and the athletic event.[20] Therefore, it is entirely appropriate that the *Iliad* as it nears its denouement features a spectacular race, the chariot event sponsored by Achilles. The race is, in short, synecdochic for the poem as a whole.

In recent decades, scholars have articulated more fully the artistry and purposes of this unexpected poetic event, the games for Patroclus.[21] Chief among the interpreters has been Philippe Rousseau, in a series of articles.[22] His brilliant analysis of the ways in which the race precisely reflects the two major death scenes in the poem, those of Patroclus and Hector, is the most powerful reading of the event within its broader Iliadic context, while his delineation of the inherent failings in the racing strategy of the young Antilochus remains the most convincing and detailed explication of a puzzling aspect of the episode.[23]

---

[18] The technique thus enacts on a smaller scale the combination of closure and anticipation that Taplin 1992, 26 identifies as the structuring device for the large, three-part composition, in which markers of narrative-time also serve as signals for performance time.

[19] Whitman 1958; Heiden 2008; Stanley1993.

[20] On the key theme of duration, see now García 2013.

[21] Taplin 1992, 251–60 provides a good summary. See also the perceptive remarks in Alden 2000, 17–21.

[22] Rousseau 1992, 2001, and 2010.

[23] Rousseau 2010, 29–43.

The importance of the episode for broader, even metapoetic, concerns of sign-reading and interpretation has been stressed by Gregory Nagy.[24] Following up on its synecdochic qualities, a longer and more detailed narratological analysis of the chariot race might use it as a heuristic device for reflecting on Homeric technique in the larger structure of the *Iliad* as a whole. How are events described in order and simultaneously? What is the *telos* of any given episode and how is this signaled? How are transitions made? What determines how long something (a race or an episode) lasts? Put another way, the ekphrasis of a race might be read as a primer of Homeric narratological principles, in miniature. This work remains to be done. Alex Purves has made a good start with her remarks on the significance of "overtaking" as a window into the key themes of speed and timing in both the *Iliad* and *Odyssey*.[25] It would be worth exploring whether the description of a complex spectator event such as the chariot-race can function as a mirror for the epic's description of another closely watched contest, the to-and-fro of war.

While not going into such full technical detail here, we might nevertheless observe over a broader expanse how one central theme, allied to a character-type, provides the complicating factor for the race, just as a cognate character generates the major disruption required for the plot of the *Iliad*. Antilochus, out of youthful confidence, ambition, and reckless disregard, disturbs the "proper" order of the race by trying to overtake his elder Menelaus in a narrow defile, a dry river course. Philippe Rousseau has shown in detail how the behavior of Antilochus goes against the advice of his father Nestor concerning the proper employment of "cunning intelligence" (*mêtis*) and is intentionally made conspicuous by its failure.[26] While he contrasts this behavior, within the immediate context of the race, with that of Achilles, it is worth pointing out that the Achilles of Book 23 is a changed man. In the overall plot of the *Iliad*, it was his former self, the hot-headed young man with ambitions for god-like honor, who disturbed the "natural order" of the hierarchy of command with similar near-disastrous results. It was Achilles, now the calm presider over the games, who forced his Achaean companions to the brink of destruction by not harnessing up his chariot team; nevertheless his resolve to wait out the war presents as much of a threat as if he had personally intervened to drive the Greeks into a ditch.

---

[24] Nagy 1983.

[25] Purves 2011.

[26] Rousseau 2010, 29–43.

Even the topographical markers of war and chariot-race, respectively—the Trojans surging toward the Achaean ships and the sea, just as the chariots race from the sea and then back toward it (23.374–75)—present a clear similarity.[27] Details of diction and motif reinforce the homology between the *Iliad* and the race, as if the latter were simply the former replicated in smaller, fractal form.[28] From the moment when Achilles brings out prizes for the competing horsemen, we are reminded of his own role in the poem, because the men are described as "swift-footed" (ἱππεῦσιν ... ποδώκεσιν, 23.262), with the epithet otherwise almost exclusively reserved for the son of Peleus and memorably enacted in his death-dealing race against Hector (*Iliad* 22.137–223).[29] That event from the previous book of the poem, we recall, was itself described by way of explicit comparison to a race of horses at funeral games, clear anticipation of Book 23 (*Iliad* 22.162–64):[30]

> No, they ran for the life of Hektor, breaker of horses.
> As when about the turnposts racing single-foot horses
> run at full speed, when a great prize is laid up for their winning,
> a tripod or a woman, in games for a man's funeral ...

Even though he does not compete, the race at Patroclus' funeral is indirectly expressive of Achilles himself, and not just because he sets its parameters. As he remarks, were he to enter this race, the first prize would inevitably be his, since his horses are immortal, a gift from Poseidon to Peleus (*Iliad* 23.274–79). Thus, Achilles embodies the standard against which all others must rank themselves lower, or in terms of a race metaphor, later. The long "Hymn to Mêtis" delivered by Nestor to Antilochus (*Iliad* 23.311–25) might also summon up recollections of the career of Achilles. He is, after all, the most prominent hero who, we hear elsewhere in the poem, benefited from direct paternal instructions, as recalled by Odysseus and Nestor (*Iliad* 9.252–59, 11.783–84). Phoenix, too, plays the role of mentor, guardian, and father-figure for Achilles (*Iliad* 9.437–43), so that his appointment to be the course

---

[27] Reading ἂψ ἐφ' ἁλὸς with Aristarchus and most MSS.

[28] On "fractals" as an analogue for the technique of the Homeric medium, see Morrell 1996.

[29] The single exception is the Trojan spy Dolon: *Iliad* 10.316.

[30] On the simile, see further Rousseau 2010, 55. Moulton 1977, 80 notes the relationship of this simile to the earlier lines at *Iliad* 22.22–24 comparing Achilles himself to a swift horse with racing chariot.

observer in the chariot race (*Iliad* 23.360–61), while logistically useless (and thus puzzling to many critics), is thematically most apt.[31]

The preparations for the race contain other miniaturized versions of larger *Iliad* narrative strategies. In the listing of champions presenting themselves as contestants, we hear once again snatches of the Catalogue of Ships in *Iliad* Book 2. For example, Eumelus is singled out at *Iliad* 23.289 as one who "excelled at horsemanship" (ὃς ἱπποσύνῃ ἐκέκαστο), with the same diction applied in the Catalogue of Ships to Oilean Ajax (*Iliad* 2.350: ἐγχείῃ δ' ἐκέκαστο). This "lesser" Ajax, the only man thus described in the Catalogue, is the hero featured in an inset exchange of angry words with Idomeneus during the race episode (23.473–98). Significantly, apart from the chariot-race, the only other point in the *Iliad* at which we hear of Eumelus is during the same Catalogue, once when his contingent from Pherae in Thessaly is mentioned (2.714) and once when his horses are named best of those that came to Troy (2.763–67). The brief equine biography is worth lingering over, as it perfectly complements the re-appearance of these same mares in the chariot-race of Book 23:

> Best by far among the horses were the mares of Eumelus
> Pheres' son, that he drove, swift-moving like birds, alike in
> texture of coat, in age, both backs drawn level like a plumb-line.
> These Apollo of the silver bow had bred in Pereia,
> mares alike, who went with the terror of the god of battle.

The audience for the race—external and internal—knows the reputation of the horses, so that this does not need to be mentioned in the episode itself (where we might expect, at 23.289). In the latter scene, we are told that Eumelus excels at horsemanship, but not that his horses are themselves the best (having been raised by Apollo), while in the earlier mentions of Eumelus within the Catalogue, there is no hint of his surpassingly good equestrian skill, only a reference to his horses' powers. The two pieces of information fit neatly together without overlap. Commentators have noticed that Apollo's role as breeder of the mares, alluded to in the Catalogue passage, can explain his anger at Diomedes in the race, at the point when the son of Tydeus is outdistancing Eumelus (*Iliad* 23.383).[32] The bond between these two passages becomes even closer when we hear of the mares "flying" (*Iliad* 23.381

---

[31]   On objections to the role of Phoenix here, see Leaf 1900 ad loc. and Rousseau 2010, 45 n. 80. An oddly subliminal reminder of the presence of Phoenix appears at line 454, when the leading horse seen by Idomeneus is described as being *phoinix* (reddish-brown) with a white *sêma* on its forehead.

[32]   E.g., Leaf 1900, 499 ad loc.

petesthên) neck-and-neck with Diomedes' stallions, a description reminiscent of the comparison of the very same mares to birds at 2.764 (ὄρνιθας ὥς). It is true that nine other times in the poem, a pair of horses is described through the use of this line-end dual verb form, but in all the other cases except one, there is no explicit basis for taking the verb "fly" almost literally.[33] The exception goes further to prove the significance of the comparison. At *Iliad* 16.149, Xanthus and Balius, the immortal horses of Achilles, are yoked together to pull the chariot of Patroclus into his final battle. These "flew with the breezes" (ἅμα πνοιῇσι πετέσθην), a detail immediately juxtaposed to the recital of their blood-line: the Harpyia Podargê, grazing in a meadow near Oceanus was impregnated by Zephryus. Little wonder that this pair race as if levitating, since their parents were both winds.

Yet the mares of Eumelus, for all their promise, are poetically outpaced. No sooner do we learn of their status as "by far the best" (μέγ' ἄρισται, 2.763) than the narrator shifts focus and backtracks slightly. Answering in reverse order the double question about the best of men and the best of horses (2.761–62), he elevates Ajax son of Telamon, but only against the background of the *mênis*-plot as it has by now evolved (2.768–70):

> Among the men far the best was Telamonian Aias
> while Achilleus stayed angry, since he was far best of all of them,
> and the horses also, who carried the blameless son of Peleus.

This is to say that the excellence of both Eumelus' mares and the hero Ajax is limited by time, constrained by an unexpressed but all-controlling anticipation, the universal wait for the return of Achilles. At that future point, the temporary "best" performers will fall back into second place. But even the truly best, Achilles, we are reminded, will not ultimately be borne back safely by his team. The return of Achilles' immortal horses to the battle is singled out by the haunting passage in which one of them, Xanthus, foretells his master's death (*Iliad* 19.400–24). They will return—after all, they cannot die—but Achilles, who has accused them of "leaving" Patroclus (19.403 ὡς Πάτροκλον λίπετ'), will himself be left behind.

In one further detail of equine behavior, the introduction to the chariot-race underlines the tragic shift that has taken place since Book 2. It forms both a minor ring-composition and a stark refusal of the consolation that such a closure device might possibly imply. When the mares of Eumelus were ranked next to Achilles' horses, the latter were said to be standing at

---

[33]   The other examples are 5.366 and 788, 8.45, 10.530, 11.281 and 519, 16.149, 22.400, 23.506.

pasture, grazing on clover and parsley, unemployed because their master lay idle (2.775–77). The Myrmidons, meanwhile, moved about aimlessly, but missed their leader (2.778: ἀρχὸν ἀρηΐφιλον <u>ποθέοντες</u>/φοίτων ἔνθα καὶ ἔνθα). At 23.283, Achilles' horses are once more immobile, but this time it is because they themselves are grieving for the missing Patroclus (τὸν τώ γ' ἑσταότες <u>πενθείετον</u>). Instead of returning for a final victory-lap where their immortal powers would be impossible to ignore, Xanthus and Balius are still out of action, foreshadowing the eventual loss that the *Iliad* itself awaits but will never depict.

Part of the brilliance of the race narrative in Book 23 is the poet's cinematic approach. Instead of the bird's-eye wide-angle omniscience of the sort that an off-track spectator typically gets from video feeds, in which all horses and riders are kept in constant view and we can see relative standings throughout the event, the *Iliad* narrator zooms in on segments, creating a montage of three different close encounters. First, we are made to focus on the race between Diomedes and Eumelus (23.375–400). This turns out to be a vengeful duel between their respective patrons, Apollo and Athena, the latter enabling Diomedes to take the lead by smashing his opponent's chariot, after the former god tried to snatch away Diomedes' whip.[34] Next, the camera moves to a second pairing, Menelaus pursued by Antilochus (23.401–46), which features the reckless passing maneuver that will embroil the two men in post-race disputes. Finally, the focus moves to a spectator-duel: Idomeneus and Oilean Ajax argue about which team is in the lead (23.450–98). This last clash offers something of a meta-*agôn*, as it represents a dispute *about* a dispute, a verbal wrangling concerning the athletic action on the race-course. As with the previous two close encounters (the gods in opposition; the post-race opposition of Antilochus and Menelaus), this, too, contains its own further secondary contest—a proposed wager between the principals, the outcome to be determined (ominously, in terms of the *Iliad*'s earlier action) by Agamemnon (23.485–87). Only the intervention of Achilles, who urges the quarreling heroes to await the results, prevents an escalation of anger.

Now one might object that the Homeric poet only "knows" one way to depict conflict: through the description of individual clashes. That is why, the argument might run, we see in the chariot-race such a conspicuous dyadic narrative technique, the whole story of five competing chariots told in the

---

[34] On the motivations for divine intervention and the thematic connections with the rest of the poem, see Rousseau 2010, 48–54.

form of three competing pairs, only two of which are actually racing (while Meriones is largely ignored). Yet there are enough instances in the poem of the skilled depiction of mass movements of men and horses that we need not credit such limiting critiques.[35] Instead, the dyadic focus in the chariot-race can be seen as yet another way in which the race englobes the rest of the *Iliad*. The homology between racing and running for one's life has already been established imagistically by the time of Book 23, as we have seen; now the resemblance is heavily underlined by the poetic camera-technique usually employed for mortal one-on-one combats.

The Last Lap

If the chariot-race is an artful totalizing summation of the themes and techniques of the *Iliad* itself, counter-balancing in its tight space near the poem's *telos* the global vision of the Catalogue of Ships, we can extend the homology to include the protagonist of the poem and the poet.[36] For the poet, composition-in-performance is itself a race against time—both the synchronic time ticking away as he persuades audiences on any given occasion to keep listening, and the diachronic stretch of time that the poem must endure in order to maintain heroic *kleos* for more than one generation. Homeric epic, in its own terms, is already winning the diachronic contest: its objects of praise are still alive in verse centuries after their deaths. In its own terms, as well, the *Iliad* presents those heroic figures as having desired the very fame through song that keeps their memory alive.[37] Such concentration on its own semi-divine powers of long-term commemoration must have functioned to keep audiences enthralled through the *thelxis* of a powerful poem-in-performance: the Muse-directed medium carried with it the guarantee of ancient tradition, miraculously surviving through the generations and conveying Nestorian authority about the past.[38]

---

[35] E.g., the opening of Book 3: the return of Myrmidons to war in Book 19.

[36] For other indicators of the symbiosis between poet and hero, see Martin 1989, and for comparative evidence of the same phenomenon, see Reynolds 1995.

[37] The most enlightening and thorough analysis of memory in the poem is in Bouvier 2002.

[38] On the central importance of Nestor to the Homeric epics, especially prominent through the Book 23 race, see Frame 2009, 131–72 and passim.

From the internal point-of-view, Achilles the hero is also Achilles the athlete, but paradoxically, one who does not finally compete.[39] When we see him in Book 23, it is not long before he himself will become, like his companion Patroclus, the dead hero celebrated by games, rather than the competitor. His mother Thetis will, at his funeral, lay out god-given prizes for the winners (*Odyssey* 24.85–90). In the underworld, he will be reminded of other funeral games he had attended while alive (*Odyssey* 24.87–89), just as Nestor recalls the athletic events that he as a younger man won and lost (*Iliad* 23.630–45). In this way, epic constructs the funereal athletic event as a site for the proper recognition of honor (*timê*, 23.649) and shared memories (23.619, 648)—in other words, as an analogue for epic itself.[40] If epic, heroic funerals, and the accompanying athletic events alike award and preserve honor and glory (*kleos esthlon*, *Odyssey* 24.94), we should not be surprised to hear in the words of Achilles, as he instructs his companions about his own funeral arrangements, just before he prepares the chariot-race, a metaphor (hitherto, it would seem, unremarked) that metamorphosizes his own death into the ultimate victory (*Iliad* 23.245–48).[41]

> τύμβον δ' οὐ μάλα πολλὸν ἐγὼ πονέεσθαι ἄνωγα,
> ἀλλ' ἐπιεικέα τοῖον· ἔπειτα δὲ καὶ τὸν Ἀχαιοὶ
> εὐρύν θ' ὑψηλόν τε τιθήμεναι, οἵ κεν ἐμεῖο
> δεύτεροι ἐν νήεσσι πολυκλήϊσι λίπησθε.

"And I would have you build a grave mound which is not very great
but such as will be fitting, for now; afterward, the Achaians
can make it broad and high—such of you Achaians as may be
left to survive me here by the benched ships, *after I am gone*."

The words "left … after me" may seem to lack any figurative reference. Yet, in the context of the upcoming race, they turn out to be technically precise and remarkably vivid. Compare for λίπησθε in 23.248 the language used by Antilochus as he urges on his team of horses at 23.407:

[39]   On the association of hero and athlete, see Nagy 1990, 136–45 and 199–214.

[40]   Cf. Rousseau 2010, 45 n. 81. On hero-tombs used for turning-points in the races at historical Panhellenic games, see Nagy 1990, 210 with further bibliography.

[41]   Richardson 1993, 199 notes merely that *deuteros* with a genitive appears only here in epic. Significantly the usage in Herodotus 1.23 (cited by Richardson and Leaf 1900 ad loc.) applies to the ranking of a performer in terms of his excellence: Arion, the citharode, second to none (ἐόντα κιθαρῳδὸν τῶν τότε ἐόντων οὐδενὸς δεύτερον). I would claim the same sense at work in *Iliad* 23.248.

ἵππους δ' Ἀτρεΐδαο κιχάνετε, μὴ δὲ <u>λίπησθον</u>,

"But make your burst to catch the horses of the son of Atreus
nor let them leave you behind."

And compare for δεύτεροι in the same line (23.248) the reference to horses
as coming in "second" at 23.497–98

... τότε δὲ γνώσεσθε ἕκαστος
ἵππους Ἀργείων, οἳ <u>δεύτεροι</u> οἵ τε πάροιθεν.

"Then you each can see for himself, and learn which
of the Argives' horses have run first and which have *run second*."

In other words, to capture the full force of Achilles' metaphor at *Iliad*
23.248 we must translate "such of you Achaeans as will *come in second to
me* [in the race to death and immortality]." Achilles is using the terminology
of the track. From the point of view of both poet and hero, all his Achaean
comrades—by virtue of being *not* the "best of the Achaeans"—rank second,
like so many chariot-teams who have not yet crossed the finish-line behind
him.[42] In order to win the war at Troy, they must wait—the ultimate Iliadic
anticipation, beyond the poem's narration—for the hero Achilles to "win" by
dying. Ironically, the first shall be last: it is Achilles the dearly departed who
will be left behind by his departing friends, localized permanently on the landscape of the Troad, while the Achaeans with their ships (cf. 23.248 ἐν νήεσσι
πολυκλήϊσι) will be left mobile, to find (most of them) their ways home.

---

[42] The centrality of the theme is traced brilliantly in Nagy 1999, esp. 26–41. I would note that
this image of Achilles as metaphorical chariot-racer fits nicely with that of Achilles as *apobatès* as
explicated by Nagy 2010, 170–77. I would also venture that, like the apobatic Achilles, the "racing"
Achilles of *Iliad* 23.245–48 would have most resonance for audiences at the Panathenaea, in which
both four-horse and two-horse chariot-races (alongside the rhapsodic contests performing Homeric
epic) were major events: see Neils, 1992, 91–93.

17

DISTANT LANDMARKS
HOMER AND HESIOD[1]

The *Argonautica* demands to be read as a latter-day Homeric epic that constantly draws attention to un-Homeric and para-Homeric themes and techniques. Recreating the aesthetic tastes of Apollonius and his audience means that we must explore a more complex hermeneutic negotiation than the static notions of "imitation" or "playfulness," "intertextuality" or *emulatio* can encompass.[2] Instead, it may help to imagine the poem dynamically miming what it celebrates—a voyage, a vessel, and a crew of characters. It forges through a sea of traditions, deftly sailing between the clashing rocks of Homer and Hesiod, sighting the smaller (at least to us) islands like Antimachus and the Cyclic epics, skirting the shores of drama and lyric, even stopping off at exotic prose genres. From every such landfall this *Argo*-like poem takes on a self-conscious awareness of its own simultaneous belatedness and innovation.

Consequently, the most important overarching technique in the poem is double vision: that is, the reader's experience is enriched through being made constantly to observe similarities and contrasts, especially, although far from exclusively, with Homeric and Hesiodic verse.[3] Or, to continue the nautical metaphor: every landmark—speech expression, descriptive phrase, even prepositional use—brings into view yet another, more distant, enabling the reader to get a sense of relative depth and distance, along the moving

---

[1]   This essay is previously unpublished.

[2]   Within the ever-accumulating work on intertextuality in Classical literature, I have made most use of these key volumes that articulate and advance theory: Barchiesi 1984; Conte 1991; Bonanno 1990; Hinds 1998; Thomas 1999; Edmunds 2001; and Tsagalis 2008.

[3]   Stephens 2003 examines a different and equally fertile sort of double vision involving Greek literary traditions and Egyptian realities in the Hellenistic period. Combining these perspectives, perhaps we should speak of Apollonian "vision squared."

line of the literary horizon. The total effect of such calibrations makes one sense just how new the *Argonautica* is. This novelty can be analyzed in terms of two essential categories: the crafting of a particular narrative *voice*, and the manipulation of *expectation* by way of major and minor narrative components.

Before examining in brief many of the landmark types that went into this creation, as a sort of mariner's guide to the epic, we must first pause to recollect how wide the literary prospect stretched for Apollonius and his audience, lest we rush into mapping limited one-to-one correspondences between the poem and the full-scale archaic compositions that happen to survive to our era. The possibility must remain open that any apparent imitation or allusion was intended to evoke not primarily our *Iliad, Odyssey,* or *Theogony,* or *Homeric Hymns,* but some other significant poetic moment or monument now vanished. Apart from the works now attributed to Homer and Hesiod at least three sorts of hexameter poetic materials were accessible to Apollonius. First, there existed epics on the Theban saga, including the stories of Oedipus and his descendants, on Heracles, and on the heroic generation of Argos, Corinth, northwestern Greece, and the Peloponnese. Some of these were later labeled "Cyclic" epics, a title whose exact meaning and valence for later generations of Greek authors has been disputed.[4] Second, there existed a number of poetic treatments of the Argonaut story. Some of these, whether oral traditions in poetry or (less likely) written accounts, were already available to audiences before the composition of the Homeric *Odyssey,* judging by the reference at *Odyssey* 12.70 to "the Argo, of interest to all" (*Argô pasi melousa*).[5] The category of Argonaut tales overlaps somewhat with the "Cyclic" tales, since individual crew members for the expedition led by Jason featured as protagonists in further adventure stories.[6] As far as attested hexameter poetry goes, we have evidence that "Argonautic" material existed in the *Corinthiaca* of Eumelus (mid-sixth century BCE); the *Carmen Naupactium* (fr. 3–9 West); and a 6500-line epic attributed to the legendary Cretan sage Epimenides.[7] Third, there existed epics from the

---

[4] For texts, see West 2003b. On the importance of "Cyclic" poems, see Hunter 2008, 144–46; Huxley 1969, 39–50, 165–72; Burgess 2001; Fantuzzi 1988, 7; and Sistakou 2007. For treatment of the Cycle in Alexandria, see Severyns 1928, esp. 254–59 (on *Argonautica* 4.866–79).

[5] See Scherer 2006, 12–22.

[6] The *Carmen Naupactium* (seventh century BCE?) seems to have been of this sort, dealing extensively with genealogical but also Argonautic traditions. See Matthews 1977; Huxley 1969, 69–75; and Scherer 2006, 19–20.

[7] On these, see West 2005, 40–41.

classical period and later that were themselves highly imitative of archaic poems. The works of Antimachus of Colophon (fl. 400 BCE) are a prime example.[8] Pisander and Panyassis, Choerilus of Samos, Philitas of Cos, and Simias of Rhodes also wrote hexameters—only fragments survive—that could have been imitated by Apollonius.[9] Nor should we forget that even the authoritative names "Homer" and "Hesiod" signified quite different accumulations of poetry in the Hellenistic period: the former was often taken as author of the comic poem *Margites* (even by Aristotle: *Poetics* 1448b28–38) and of various heroic epics such as the *Sack of Oichalia*, *Thebaid*, and *Epigoni*, as well as poems of the Trojan cycle, while the latter became a cover term for disparate hexameter poetic traditions ranging from mantic poetry to didactic.[10] A consolation for modern interpreters faced with so much missing material is that Hellenistic poets themselves at least appear to have privileged Homer and Hesiod as their major influences, as is made clear by well-known programmatic statements from Theocritus (*Idylls* 16.20):

> "τίς δέ κεν ἄλλου ἀκούσαι; ἅλις πάντεσσιν Ὅμηρος.
> οὗτος ἀοιδῶν λῷστος, ὃς ἐξ ἐμεῦ οἴσεται οὐδέν."

"Who would wish to listen to anyone else? Homer's enough for everyone; The best poet is the one who will get nothing from me." [trans. Hopkinson 2015]

and Callimachus (*Epigrams* 29 = *Palatine Anthology* 9.507):

> Ἡσιόδου τό τ᾿ ἄεισμα καὶ ὁ τρόπος· οὐ τὸν ἀοιδῶν
> ἔσχατον, ἀλλ᾿ ὀκνέω μὴ τὸ μελιχρότατον
> τῶν ἐπέων ὁ Σολεὺς ἀπεμάξατο. χαίρετε, λεπταὶ
> ῥήσιες, Ἀρήτου σύμβολον ἀγρυπνίης.

The rhythm and the manner are Hesiod's. He of Soli took as a model not the worst of poets, but, I am afraid, the most honeyed of his verses. Hail! delicate phrases, the monument of Aratus' sleepless nights. [trans. Paton 1917]

Even in the scanty remains of the other hexameter works that we do possess, it is possible to find unusual phrases or word-forms resembling those

---

[8] Scherer 2006, 34–35; Matthews 1996.

[9] On Philitas, e.g., see Spanoudakis 2002. The rare word ὄμπνιον appeared in his poetry and philological work: see Dettori 2000, 113–24; Spanoudakis 2002, 142–44; Apollonius employs it at *Argonautica* 4.989.

[10] Pfeiffer 1968, 43–44; Lamberton 1988b, 134–44.

in Apollonius, making it probable that the author of the *Argonautica* cast his net very wide. It is *a priori* likely that he deployed phrases from the pre-existing Argonaut stories—either for reminiscences or for stark contrasts—as much as he did Homeric or Hesiodic material, and here the quite learned scholia to Apollonius are helpful in pointing out the poet's innovations or borrowings at the level of individual words, characters, motifs, or other plot elements. Several examples will be cited under the appropriate headings below.

To begin at the most elementary poetic level: *metrical practice* would seem to be the least likely medium for distinguishing Apollonius's work, as the sea of dactylic hexameter—from Homeric poems through to Nonnus—at first sight looks uniform. Exhaustive metrical studies beginning with early ninteenth-century critics, from Gottfried Hermann on, have shown how uncannily consistent the artificial art-language of the poetic hexameter has remained, even while the Greek language itself changed drastically from tonal to stress-accented.[11] Nevertheless, we can detect small differences between archaic and Hellenistic usage, and furthermore, between Apollonius and contemporaries, that point to more significant ways in which the verses of the *Argonautica* create a different flow and sound.

If one takes account of the distribution of spondees vs. dactyls in the five feet of the hexameter where dactyls are allowed (i.e., all but the last foot), *Argonautica* lines, with an average of 3.85 dactyls per verse, are more rapid than Homeric (average 3.7). A similar rapidity can be detected in the relative numbers of lines containing three spondees (7.95% *Iliad* vs. 4.52% *Argonautica*) and, less commonly, four spondees (0.58% *Iliad* vs. 0.12% *Argonautica*). There is also a significant difference in the localization of spondaic feet within poetic lines: Homeric practice allows more in the fourth foot (22.8% of the total number of spondees, contrasted with 15% in Apollonius), while Apollonius favors *versus spondaici* (i.e., verses with fifth-foot spondees): 7.6% of his spondees are thus located vs. 3.8% in Homer.[12]

---

[11] O'Neill 1942 provides a good review of earlier studies. A thorough analysis of metrical habits from Homer through Tzetzes in twelfth-century Byzantium is Rzach 1882. Wifstrand 1933 shows how metrical habits of Callimachus were retained even by Nonnus, six centuries later, with some adjustments made for linguistic changes. Mooney 1912, 411–28 surveys the major metrical and prosodic peculiarities in the poem.

[12] Figures from Sicking 1993, 72–74. Callimachean hexameters average 3.91 dactyls, have three spondees in 3.53% of lines, place 17.7% of the total number of spondees in the fourth foot of the line and 6.3% in the fifth foot. By the last measure, Apollonius thus stands out even among Hellenistic contemporaries. At the same time, he sounds more Homeric than Callimachean by neglecting the niceties of preserving third-foot caesura and bucolic diaeresis when there exists a diaeresis after the

While it is risky to extrapolate a poetic ethos from stylometrics, it is remark-able that a poem so bound thematically to movement over the sea might have itself moved more quickly in recitation, and when it did slow down its verses with spondaic sequences, was more likely to do so toward the close.

A quirk possibly related to this notable fondness for *spondaici* is Apollonius's unusual deployment of certain metrical word-shapes. From the 1000-line samples of archaic and post-Classical hexameters analyzed by Eugene O'Neill, Jr., it emerges that the *Argonautica* has the highest number of words (294) with the shape of a choriamb (⁻ ˘ ˘ ⁻), the most (104 words) shaped as an adonic (⁻ ˘ ˘ ⁻ ˣ), and the most words of two related shapes: ˘ ⁻ ⁻ ⁻ ˘ (63 in Apollonius as opposed to 31 in the *Iliad* sample) and ˘ ⁻ ˘ ˘ ⁻ ˘ (30, contrasted with once in the *Iliad* sample). These two latter-most metrical word-types are functional variants of the same underlying metrical segment, that which occupies the slot in the hexameter after the "trochaic" caesura (the word-break after the first short of the third foot) and leaves a three-syllable space at the end of the line.[13] Of course, it is implau-sible that either the archaic or Hellenistic poets worked consciously at local-izing certain shapes within the line: instead, bare abstract statistics like these reflect poetic choices made at the level of formula and phrasing, which in turn are mostly determined by the shaping of discourse over a run of several lines (or "paragraphs," if we think in terms of topic and content). Yet statis-tics, when they show such wide variations across authors, potentially point us to significant higher-level stylistic devices. In the case of Apollonius, the device in question is most likely his frequent four-word lines. Consider the following lines near the start of the Catalogue of Argonauts, which cap the mention of the first and most significant recruit, Orpheus (1.32–34):

Ὀρφέα μὲν δὴ τοῖον ἑῶν ἐπαρωγὸν ἀέθλων
⁻ ˘ ˘ ⁻   ⁻ ⁻ ˘ ˘ ⁻ ⁻ ˘ ⁻ ⁻ ⁻

Αἰσονίδης Χείρωνος ἐφημοσύνῃσι πιθήσας

---

third foot ("Bulloch's Law"); and in his more frequent violations of "Meyer's Law" regarding word-end in the second foot (0.9% of lines vs. 0.06% in Callimachus); see Bulloch 1970 and Magnelli 1995.

[13] O'Neill 1942, 147–49. Hagel 2004 updates O'Neill's tables using full-text data, but his more precise breakdown of the results in terms of "appositive groups" and surrounding metrical environ-ments is somewhat more cumbersome for stylistic analysis. If we take as a control one shape listed by Hagel (˘ ⁻ ⁻ ˘ ⁻ ˣ), it appears that Apollonius uses it 43 times as contrasted with 85 times in the *Iliad* and *Odyssey* combined, or, proportionately to the size of the corpora, once every 135 lines vs. once every 325 Homeric lines.

¯ ˘ ˘ ¯ x

δέξατο, Πιερίῃ Βιστωνίδι κοιρανέοντα·

Line 33 contains the metrical word-type that, as we have seen, is much more frequent in Apollonius than in Homer (˘ ¯ ˘ ˘ ¯ ˘), in the midst of a four-word hexameter. The following line (1.34) is also formed of only four words and features another frequent metrical type in Apollonius, a single word filling the adonic segment (after the bucolic diairesis, the word-break between the fourth and fifth feet). Even though the lines are mostly dactylic, their construction lends a stately solidity and closure appropriate for the narrative moment. Line 33 further echoes another four-word line, from the proem, featuring the same diction and theme, obedience to the command of another (1.3):

> Ἀρχόμενος σέο Φοῖβε παλαιγενέων κλέα φωτῶν
> μνήσομαι οἳ Πόντοιο κατὰ στόμα καὶ διὰ πέτρας
> <u>Κυανέας βασιλῆος ἐφημοσύνῃ Πελίαο</u>
> χρύσειον μετὰ κῶας ἐύζυγον ἤλασαν Ἀργώ.

> Beginning with you, Phoebus, I shall recall the famous deeds of
> men born long ago, who, at the command of King Pelias, sailed
> the well-benched Argo through the mouth of the Black Sea and
> between the Cyanean rocks to fetch the golden fleece.[14]

Meanwhile, between lines 3 and 33 comes a couplet with another heavy four-word hexameter, describing the instructional role of Athena in crafting the Argonauts' ship (1.19):

> Νῆα μὲν οὖν οἱ πρόσθεν ἔτι κλείουσιν ἀοιδοί
> <u>Ἄργον Ἀθηναίης καμέειν ὑποθημοσύνῃσι·</u>

> As for the ship, the songs of former bards still tell how Argus
> built it according to Athena's instructions.

Thus, a series of metrically similar lines swiftly highlights the major figures directing the expedition. Such patterning is hardly accidental.[15]

---

[14] All translations of Apollonius are from Race 2009.

[15] Two more four-word hexameters occur in the biography of Orpheus: 1.24, 31. Further clustering of four-word lines occurs in Book 2, for example (list not exhaustive): 3–4; 72, 80, 100, 129, 170, 224; 626, 667, 677, 700, 706, 758; 968, 988, 1060; 1249. According to Bassett 1919, the *versus tetracolos* occurs in 200 verses of the *Argonautica* (once per 29 lines) as contrasted with 431 verses of Homer (once every 64 lines).

Aside from their utility in drawing attention to poetic content at key points, the frequent four-word verses provide Apollonius with a more archaic architecture, like Cyclopean walls of massive stone. It is significant, as well, as Hermann Fränkel observed, that such lines most clearly articulate the four major segments of the Greek hexameter.[16] Bearing in mind this distillation of essential metrical structure, it is worth observing that the greatest frequency of such *tetracolos* verses occurs in the collection of Orphic Hymns (first–third centuries CE).[17] The hymnic aggregation of praise adjectives produces such lines as these from the Orphic *Hymn to Hecate* (4–5):

> Περσείαν, φιλέρημον, ἀγαλλομένην ἐλάφοισι,
> νυκτερίαν, σκυλακῖτιν, ἀμαιμάκετον βασίλειαν.
>
> Daughter of Perses, haunting deserted places, delighting in deer, nocturnal, dog-loving, monstrous queen. [trans. Athanassakis and Wolkow 2013]

We shall return to this stylistic device at the conclusion of the chapter when we attempt to identify more closely the narrative voice behind the poem.

Tightly bound to the meter of the epics is *diction*. Since the path-breaking studies by Milman Parry, the "formula"—although it eludes exact definition—has been increasingly recognized as an essential component of Homeric artistry, capable of bearing "immanent" meaning, so that the occurrence of even a few words triggers reminiscence of entire narrative scenes, situations, and plot-outcomes.[18] One sort of familiarity, on which such recollection depends, is established by repetition of phrases, whether at the level of noun plus epithet ("cloud-gathering Zeus") or more loosely connected "flexible" formulae, where nouns and adjectives regularly co-occur but are not necessarily contiguous.[19] For the latter type, one gets the sense from the frequent appearance of common-noun-and-epithet pairings that the *Argonautica* is "formulaic" at this level, but closer examination shows how novel the poet's combinations actually are. A test sample of

---

[16] Fränkel 1968, 4, 10; his remarks come in an expanded discussion of his widely followed earlier analysis (1926) of hexametric cola.

[17] Bassett 1919, 230 observes that one out of eight hymn verses is of this type.

[18] On formulas in Apollonius, see the basic study by Fantuzzi 1988 updated and expanded in Fantuzzi 2008. For an overview of Parry's work and the concept of "immanent" meaning, see J. M. Foley 1988 and 1991.

[19] On which see Hainsworth 1968.

the first fifty lines of Book 2, for instance, shows fourteen common nouns with adjectives, only two of which are attested in Homer, Hesiod, or the Homeric *Hymns* (*Argonautica* 2.18 κρατερῇ ... ἀνάγκῃ, cf. *Iliad* 6.458; and 2.32 δίπτυχα λώπην, cf. *Odyssey* 13.224). A third pair (2.40–41 οὐρανίῳ ... ἀστέρι) echoes a frequent Homeric formula (*ouranos asteroeis*, *Iliad* 5.769 etc.) but reverses the roles of adjective and noun.

As for the former phrase-type, Apollonius clearly does not employ a dictional system marked by the oral-traditional characteristics of economy and extension, providing for every major figure in each metrical *sedes* one and only one epithet. In fact, Parry chose Apollonius to illustrate exactly this difference between Homeric and later written hexameters.[20] It is generally acknowledged that such systems evolved for the sake of rapid spontaneous composition in performance (of a type subsequently observed in fieldwork). A more nuanced contrast between archaic and Apollonian usage would see the latter as *partially* formulaic, not because the *Argonautica* was orally composed but because the poet desired a certain patina—"Homeric" at the same time as it is obviously not. Whereas Homeric epic is filled with repetitions, those in the *Argonautica* stand out for their scarcity.[21] The scores of formulaic systems within Homeric poetry produce for its audiences a type of predictability that can be summoned—and even violated—to produce special effects. The *intratextual* relationships within Homeric epics are themselves already quite complex, given the working of "traditional referentiality" (to use J. M. Foley's term).[22] Reading Apollonius, then, adds another dimension, the *intertextual*, to an already dense configuration of meanings in his source texts.

Since the crew of the Argo flourished a generation before the heroes of the Trojan War, we would not expect to find the Homeric *epithet system* transferred as a whole to them; these are different characters with names of differing metrical shapes, in a different plot. Teasingly, the two times that the future hero Achilles is named in the *Argonautica*, he is given resonant Iliadic epithets: "son of Peleus" (*Argonautica* 1.558 Πηλεΐδην Ἀχιλῆα; cf. *Iliad* 23.542 and frequently elsewhere, usually in this *sedes*), at the moment when the toddler watches from a hillside the departing ship of his Argonaut father;

[20] Parry 1971, 18–30, 264–75.

[21] Fantuzzi 1988, 61–77 meticulously analyzes the most formulaic of lines—speech-introductions—in terms of their variation from Homeric models.

[22] J. M. Foley 1991. For magisterial analysis of intra- and inter-textual formulaic connections see Muellner 1996.

and "glorious" (4.868 Ἀχιλῆος ἀγαυοῦ; cf. *Iliad* 17.557) in a flashback to the near-immortalization of the infant Achilles by his mother Thetis (which Peleus aborted). Apollonius thereby forecasts and confirms the Homeric glories of the next generation. Since the gods, however, remain the same through all generations, in describing them Apollonius might have chosen to play up continuity by conspicuously using Homeric epithets. Instead, he draws on this system only partially, and—characteristically—in order to introduce subtle variations. A detailed accounting remains to be done of the later poet's re-purposing of the entire divine-epithet system. But even a preliminary analysis of two divinities illustrates the technique in operation.

Homeric epic has twenty-three different epithets that are applied exclusively to Zeus. Of these, Apollonius uses only one, the patronymic *Kronidês* "Son of Cronus." What might be thought the blandest way to designate the father of the gods is, in fact, a means of emphasizing the theogonic past, keeping the audience in mind of the divine struggle for succession (a theme embedded also in the poem's allusions to Prometheus). As a result of this epithetic narrowing, however, the impressive Homeric picture of an authoritative sky-god Zeus who is cloud gatherer, aegis-bearer, clever-deviser, and wide-voiced is abandoned; in the *Argonautica*, Zeus is "Olympian" precisely once, at 4.95 (vs. twenty-eight times in Homer).

Closer analysis of how the poet does employ his chosen Homeric epithet for Zeus reveals some patterned variations on the older epics. For example, Apollonius uses the dative form of the epithet twice:

Argonautica 2.524:

> ἱερά τ' εὖ ἔρρεξεν ἐν οὔρεσιν ἀστέρι κείνῳ
> Σειρίῳ αὐτῷ τε Κρονίδῃ Διί. τοῖο ἕκητι
> γαῖαν ἐπιψύχουσιν ἐτήσιοι ἐκ Διὸς αὖραι

> and [he] duly performed sacrifices on the mountains to that star Sirius and *to Zeus himself, son of Cronus*. And for this reason the Etesian winds sent by Zeus cool the land ...

Argonautica 2.1147:

> τὸν μὲν ἔπειτ' ἔρρεξεν ἑῆς ὑποθημοσύνῃσιν
> Φυξίῳ ἐκ πάντων Κρονίδῃ Διί· καί μιν ἔδεκτο
> Αἰήτης μεγάρῳ, κούρην τέ οἱ ἐγγυάλιξεν

> That ram, by its own instructions, he afterwards sacrificed *to Cronus' son Zeus*, the God of Fugitives, above all other gods. And

> Aeetes received him into his home and betrothed his daughter
> to him

Intratextually, this is constructed to sound "formulaic," inasmuch as the phrase repeats exactly within the space of one book, in the same metrical slot (between the penthemimeral caesura and bucolic diaresis). But *intertextually*, the Apollonian "formula" is subtly unlike its Homeric predecessor: in the three passages where the older epics use the dative, once it is coupled with the name *Diï* (as in Apollonius), but in a verse that switches the order of noun and epithet and uses a different metrical *sedes*:

Iliad 9.172:

> ὄφρα <u>Διὶ Κρονίδῃ</u> ἀρησόμεθ᾽, αἴ κ᾽ ἐλεήσῃ.

> so we may pray to *Zeus, son of Cronus*, if he will have pity.[23]

The other two times, the metrical positioning of the dative *Kronidêi* is the same as in Apollonius, but the epithet accompanies a line-initial *Zêni* (a morphologically "newer" dative of the name Zeus) and a further epithet "of the dark cloud":

Odyssey 9.552 (=13.25):

> <u>Ζηνὶ κελαινεφέϊ Κρονίδῃ</u>, ὃς πᾶσιν ἀνάσσει.

> to *Zeus of the dark clouds son of Cronus*.

Diachronically, we could describe this method of Apollonus as "splitting" the older Homeric phrases and re-assembling the pieces in semi-Homeric manner. Yet it may be more interesting to imagine Apollonius synchronically, as a creative poet working with complete control within an established epic tradition, executing the same sort of formulaic innovation that occurs even *within* the Homeric corpus, as we saw in the examples just cited (morphological and metrical variants *Zêni* / *Dii*; word-order variation). Homeric formulaic practice was itself not monophonic; or, put more paradoxically, Apollonius is most "Homeric" when choosing to be *para*-Homeric in such ways.[24]

---

[23] Translations of the *Iliad* are from Lattimore 2011 unless otherwise noted.

[24] For more examples of the handling of Homeric formulae, see Fantuzzi 2008.

At times, Hellenistic cleverness turns even the level of formulaic diction into an occasion for erudite display. In another line employing the "son of Cronus" epithet (this time in the nominative case), Apollonius tells how Zeus gave the bronze giant Talos to be warder of Crete. The poet places the god's patronymic next to the proper name of the recipient, Europa (*Argonautica* 4.1643):

> Εὐρώπῃ Κρονίδης νήσου πόρεν ἔμμεναι οὖρον.

> he had been given to Europa by Cronus' son to be the island's guardian.

Though probably not related in etymology, Eurôpa closely resembles in sound *euruopa*, "having a wide-sounding voice"—with twenty-three occurrences, one of the most frequent particularized epithets for Zeus in Homeric poetry. What is more, several Homeric lines juxtapose this epithet with his patronymic, e.g., *Iliad* 15.152 (cf. 1.498, 24.98):

> εὗρον δ᾽ εὐρύοπα Κρονίδην ἀνὰ Γαργάρῳ ἄκρῳ

> [they] found the wide-browed son of Cronus on the height of Gargaron.

In short, Apollonius while conspicuously omitting the epithet *euruopa* throughout his composition manages to smuggle in a close facsimile, in a *callida iunctura* that echoes Homeric phrasing. Like Argonauts glimpsing the slightest traces of Heracles, we see a ghost of the older poet in an unlikely place.

Both Zeus and Apollo several times bear distinctive epithets that never occur in Homer. Zeus is "of flight" (*Fuxios* 2.1147), "cleansing" (*Katharsios* 4.708), "kind to guests" (*Euxeinos* 2.378), and "overseeing" (*Epopsios* 2.1123), while Apollo is known as "of embarkation" (*Embasios* 1.359, 404), "prophetic" (*Manteios* 2.493), and "ship-saving" (*Nêosoos* 2.927) among other titles. Through this strategy, Apollonius binds the gods more closely to cult, on the one hand, and on the other to the lineaments of his own plot, which actualizes and gives aetologies for the titles in terms of the Argonauts' varied encounters. This close relationship of epithets to religious ritual within the poem might offer a starting-place for further analysis regarding the generic affiliations of Apollonius' diction. To take one example: the poet uses seventeen times the name *Phoibos* for Apollo, but, quite jarringly in comparison with Homer, only once as an epithet. By contrast, in the *Iliad*,

Odyssey, and Homeric *Hymns* taken together, Phoibos occurs eighty-one times; out of this number, it is paired with *Apollôn* sixty-one times, most often in the familiar line-end formula Φοῖβος Ἀπόλλων (e.g., *Iliad* 1.43). It is significant that the single place in which Apollonius adheres to the usual Homeric pairing comes in the elaborate description of divinities depicted on Jason's cloak (*Argonautica* 1.759–60):

> Ἐν καὶ Ἀπόλλων Φοῖβος ὀιστεύων ἐτέτυκτο,
> βούπαις, οὔπω πολλός, ἑὴν ἐρύοντα καλύπτρης

> And on it was wrought Phoebus Apollo as a mighty youth, not yet fully grown, shooting [at enormous Tityus], who was boldly pulling Apollo's mother by her veil.

In other words, the formal, formulaic style of conjoined Φοῖβος Ἀπόλλων, appearing in a reversed word-order also found formulaically in Homer (*Iliad* 16.700, 20.68, 21.515), highlights the god's appearance in the most highly-crafted artistic creation within the *Argonautica*, as if acknowledging the traditional "art-language" use of the epithet in older epic (even at the precise moment the *younger* Apollo οὔπω πολλός is being described). What does it signify, meanwhile, that Apollonius in the other sixteen instances of *Phoibos* uses it without the god's proper name? Here, too, older hexameter poetry provides clues. The bare *Phoibos* occurs twenty times in Homer and the *Hymns*; thirteen of these are vocatives and more than half (seven) of that number come from the *Hymns*. In other words, in Apollonius we can expect the repeated use of *Phoibos* (alone) to create the sound of sacral language— fittingly in a poem so concerned with ritual establishments.[25]

Just as one cannot disentangle metrical factors from dictional, so these cannot be separated entirely from linguistic changes, prompting further questions of dialect, archaisms, and by-forms. On the level of *morphology and syntax*, we can find interesting differences that make Apollonius sound less archaic. To appreciate these fully, we have to highlight again the general principle that, as a whole, the background of his verse does sound almost uncannily Homeric and/or Hesiodic. In general linguistic usage, he copies the older epics as closely as possible.[26] Uncontracted forms, for example, appear

---

[25] This also fits with evidence for the epithet of Zeus examined above: the uncontracted genitive *Kronidao* (*Argonautica* 2.1211, 4.753, 4.520) occurs nowhere in Homeric epic, but is in the *Homeric Hymn to Demeter* (408) and in the opening invocation to the Muses at Antimachus fr. 1.1 Wyss, on which see Matthews 1996, 80.

[26] See examples in Rzach 1878, 8–30; La Roche 1899.

alongside contracted—*aethlon* (1.15) and *athlôn* (1.1304) *hieron* (1.960) and *hiron* (4.1691), just as in Homer. He widely uses apocope of prepositions and preverbs, e.g., of *ana* in *Argonautica* 1.1061: ἂμ πεδίον Λειμώνιον (cf. *Iliad* 5.96); has old epic forms with initial *pt-* (*ptolin, ptoliethron*) or double *-pp-* (*hoppote*); uses uncontracted endings such as *-âo* for masculine genitive singular and *-aôn* for feminine genitive plural; employs dialect variants such as Aeolic *pisures* (1.671) alongside Ionic *tessares* (1.946); and Aeolic *ummi* along with Ionic *humin*; omits verb augments when metrically convenient; often resorts to epic infinitive endings in *-menai* and subjunctive third-person singular *–si*; and in general, only uses tense formations of particular verbs if they have already been attested in Homer or Hesiod.[27]

The nearly pitch-perfect imitation even extends to frequent lengthening of an otherwise short syllable in places where a once existent digamma in a following word had combined with a second consonant. This feature marked archaic verse where the digamma sound (/w/) had been recently alive in poetic tradition (and was still spoken in many dialects other than Ionic and Attic). By the time of Apollonius the effect was a learned archaism. He gives the preposition *epi* a long second syllable before *d(w)eos* "fear" in such lines as 1.639:

ἄφθογγοι, τοῖόν σφιν ἐπὶ δέος ἠωρεῖτο

entirely in accord with what the linguistically correct treatment found in Homer (e.g., *Iliad* 1.515 οὔ τοι ἔπι δέος). Similarly, he lengthens *gar* "for" at 1.969 (and elsewhere) before *hoi* "to/for him," which originally had the initial w- sound:

μῆλά θ' ὁμοῦ. δὴ γάρ οἱ ἔην φάτις, εὖτ' ἂν ἵκωνται.

This is an exact imitation of Homeric phrases like *Iliad* 5.188: ἤδη γάρ οἱ ἐφῆκα βέλος ("for I have shot my shaft already").[28] As often, Apollonius is here following a tradition of archaizing, since already Panyassis in the fifth century used the same lengthening (fr. 14.6).[29]

---

[27] Full listings and analyses in Rzach 1878.

[28] See further data in Rzach 1882.

[29] Noted by Rzach 1882, 372; on the Panyassis fragment, see Matthews 1974, 76–87. Archaizing lengthening in such phrases also permeates later Greek poetry, into the Byzantine period.

On the other hand, a fine-grained analysis discovers significant differences. There are enough new forms in his poetry, new extensions of old forms no longer understood, and new applications of familiar words, that an experienced reader of archaic poetry would have perceived a continual undertone of novelty. At the level of morphology, Apollonius uses, for example, in lieu of the regular Homeric -*oiato* the more familiar Classical third-plural present optative form in -*ointo* (only once in Homer, in the suspect line *Iliad* 1.344).[30] He freely extends the use of the middle voice—without apparent semantic difference—to many verbs that in Homer appeared only in the active, and uses the dative case with a greater number of verbs, and more often without prepositions.[31] Apollonius often extrapolates from existing Homeric forms, creating futures (such as *damassei* 3.353) or presents (e.g., *ameiro*, 3.186) on the basis of (sometimes false) analogies derived from other verb stems.[32] New noun forms are scattered throughout the poem, such as the word for "child" in *Argonautica* 1.276 (πάιν) and for ship 1.1358 (νῆυν) vs. inherited *paida* and *nêa*.[33] Paradoxically, at times the innovations of Apollonius seem intended to make his poetic texture look older, by over-developing formations that he apparently considered archaic. Thus, the widespread use of adverbs in -*dên* (e.g., 2.826 αἴγδην; 1.1017 ἁρπάγδην).[34] Putting prepositions after the nouns they modify (postposition) reflects archaic syntax, but Apollonius does this once for every nine occurrences of a preposition, whereas Homer was more restrained (once out of thirteen times).[35] Such a longing for archaic patina may explain the poet's indiscriminate deployment of prepositional forms like *h(e)os* that are properly restricted to the third person in older epic usage: Apollonius, liking their antique ring, uses them for *all* persons (e.g., for first person in 3.99: ἀτεμβοίμην ἑοῖ αὐτῇ, "I would have only myself to blame").[36] His fondness for adjectives in -*aleos* and

---

[30] See Boesch 1908,12.

[31] Boesch 1908, 18–21; on cases, Linsenbarth 1887, 48–56.

[32] Marxer 1935, 8–13: the new *ameiro* is by analogy with *keiro*, the aorist of which (*kersai*) resembled an attested aorist (*amersai*).

[33] Marxer 1935, 22.

[34] Marxer 1935, 32.

[35] Haggett 1902, 71, who notes also (p. 36) the poet's fondness for certain compound prepositions (*diek, parek*) used in un-Homeric ways.

[36] Marxer 1935, 61.

abstract nouns in -*sunê* also overextends distinctive but fleeting epic usages, although this may have resulted from imitating tragic poetic diction.[37]

Emblematic of this schizoid approach are his infinitives. Apollonius copies archaic epic usage only half the time, the other half of these forms being variations, sometimes widely different, and often reflecting tragic or lyric poetic habit.[38] In a prominent passage, for instance, he uses *kleiô* to introduce an accusative and infinite construction (1.18–19):

> Νῆα μὲν οὖν οἱ πρόσθεν ἔτι <u>κλείουσιν</u> ἀοιδοί
> <u>Ἄργον</u> Ἀθηναίης <u>καμέειν</u> ὑποθημοσύνῃσι·

> As for the ship, the songs of former bards still tell how Argus
> built it according to Athena's instructions.

The verb existed in Homer, but the closest Homeric syntactical equivalent occurs with a slightly different verb, *aeidein* (*Odyssey* 8.516).[39] Other infinitive constructions imitate instances that occur only once in all Homeric poetry (e.g., the use of *mûtheomai* with infinitive at *Argonautica* 2.458–60; cf. *Iliad* 21.462). In short, the voice being represented through such syntactic choices is both deeply epic-sounding but also conspicuously speaks like other times and genres.

Appreciation of the ways in which Apollonius manipulated Homeric diction must recognize that he was refining a poetic habit begun at least a century earlier, as evidenced by the fragmentary extant works of Antimachus. A Homeric scholar, like Apollonius, this author of a *Thebais* in hexameters and of the long elegiac poem *Lyde* sought out rare words from archaic epic to lend the air of antiquity to his own verses.[40] To take one example: in all of Homer the word *kalaurops* ("herdsman's crook") occurs only once, near the end of the *Iliad*, in lines comparing a heroic iron-toss to the bucolic instrument thrown to separate cattle (23.845): ὅσσόν τίς τ' ἔρριψε <u>καλαύροπα</u> βουκόλος ἀνήρ ("as far as an ox-herd can cast with his throwing stick"). The scholiast to the passage preserves a line in which Antimachus copied this *hapax legomenon*, in the same metrical position (schol. bT Erbse):

---

[37] Redondo 2000, 135–41.

[38] McLennan 1973, categorizing all occurrences, notes that epexegetic infinitives after adjectives in the *Argonautica* are almost always un-Homeric.

[39] See further on *kleiô* and related verbs Linsenbarth 1887, 24.

[40] For the activity of Antimachus as Homeric scholar, see Wyss 1936, fr. 131–48 and Matthews 1996, 373–403. For Apollonius' use of Antimachus, extending even to conjunction usage, see Matthews 1996, 88–91.

καὶ Ἀντίμαχος "πάντες δ' ἐν χείρεσσι καλαύροπας οὐατοέσσας"

[fr. 91 Wyss = 64 Matthews]

Antimachus also [has] "and all in their hands throwing-sticks with handles"

Given this background, when Apollonius twice uses the word in his epic, again in the same *sedes* (2.33, 4.974), we imagine that he depends on a connoisseur audience knowing not just Homer but also the Homeric *imitators* of the intervening centuries. The absence of context in the Antimachus fragment prevents us from assessing what poetic overtones the double reminiscence might have carried.[41] Perhaps significantly, Amycus, who throws down his olive-wood *kalaurops* in 2.33, is about to *lose* a boxing contest, while the Homeric occurrence appeared in an image celebrating athletic *success*. Whether this similarity is conscious or accidental, it illustrates one type of flashback recollection triggered by the subtle repetition of rare words.[42]

Such compressed notes from the margins of medieval manuscripts also are a rich source of observations about the ways in which Apollonius varies Homeric usage. When the narrator at 1.919 declines to speak further of the Samothracian mysteries, τῶν μὲν ἔτ' οὐ προτέρω μυθήσομαι, "of these things, however, I shall speak no further," a scholiast explains that the adverb means "forwards" εἰς τοὔμπροσθεν, citing *Odyssey* 9.64, where it describes the movement of ships. But Apollonius, the commentator adds, has misapplied it to speech (καταχρηστικῶς ἐπὶ τοῦ λόγου: *Schol. Ap. Rhod.* p. 78.20 Wendel). Even more importantly, it is the scholia, both to Homer and Apollonius, that enable us to appreciate how the poet made use of the most exacting critical work on the text of Homer. To take one telling example: at *Argonautica* 1.1081, a line describes how "the other" Argonauts were sleeping:

ὧλλοι μέν ῥα πάρος δεδμημένοι εὐνάζοντο

the rest of heroes, long since overcome by sleep, were slumbering.

The scholiast observes that because the combined form ὧλλοι (*hoi allo*i) is "newer Ionic," the Homeric scholar Zenodotus was criticized for seeking to read this form in place of Ἄλλοι (i.e., without definite article *hoi*) at *Iliad* 2.1: Ἄλλοι μέν ῥα θεοί τε καὶ ἀνέρες ἱπποκορυσταὶ / εὖδον παννύχιοι,

---

[41] A cattle-raid? Matthews 1996 tentatively ties the line to fr. 55 (= 49 Wyss). If this were the case, *Argonautica* 2.33 would then fuse athletic (Homeric) with martial (Antimachean) potential reminiscences, a typically Apollonian destabilizing allusion.

[42] Kyriakou 1995 offers detailed readings of the effects of Homeric *hapax legomena* in Apollonius.

"now the rest of the gods, and men who were lords of chariots, slept night long." The line in Apollonius is clearly modeled on the opening of Book 2 of the *Iliad*, a similar sleep-scene. But the choice of the "un-Homeric" ὤλλοι, insignificant as it might seem, was in context actually a bold statement, showing Apollonius conspicuously taking sides in what must have been ongoing text-critical debates. The poetic payoff from the form itself is unclear—did the poet mean to highlight the belatedness of his text, or was his (and Zenodotus') choice based on the fact that by their time, normal Greek (as in classical Attic) used definite articles (a rarity in Homer)?[43] In another passage from the scholia (to *Argonautica* 2.1005), we learn that Apollonius uses an adjective describing "hard" land (στυφελήν) that Zenodotus in a monograph on unusual words (*Glossai*) had identified as coming from the archaic dialect of the Arcadian city Clitor.[44] It is clear that Apollonius was abreast of the latest work being carried out by scholars whom he knew personally in Alexandria or had read. Zenodotus, after all, preceded him in the post of Librarian at Alexandria; Apollonius himself is said to have written a book "against Zenodotus," as well as critical works on Archilochus and Hesiod.[45]

The extent to which the poet's composition was permeated with references not just to Homeric poetry, but to the specific scholarly works thereon has been increasingly recognized.[46] This can occur at several levels of artistry. Individual rare words, as we have seen, can signal to audiences a fruitful textual relation with archaic epic. Apollonius not only uses more than 100 words attested only once each in Homer (*hapax legomena*), but also drops into his poem—precisely two times apiece—another 50 words attested only *twice* in the older poet (*dis legomena*), and, in another fit of ingenuity, employs *once* in his own poem yet another 157 words that Homer used just *twice*.[47] If nothing else, the poet displays to his contemporaries admirable counting

---

[43] See *schol. Ap. Rhod* p. 95.20 Wendel. Cf. *schol. Iliad* 2.1 (A): ἄλλοι: ὅτι Ζηνόδοτος γράφει "ὤλλοι," which suggests further that Zenodotus acknowledged the psilotic nature of Ionic (loss of intial *h-* , so that *hoi* was pronounced /*oi*/), even as he sought to import the definite article into the Homeric text.

[44] Many more such dialect words might be detectable in Apollonius, had we more of the *Ataktoi Glossai* of Philitas (teacher of Zenodotus), on which see the editions of Dettori 2000, esp. 20–38 and Spanoudakis 2002, 347–400.

[45] Pfeiffer 1968, 144–48; on the fragments of *Pros Zenodoton,* see Mooney 1912, 50–51 and Rengakos 2008, 256–61.

[46] The leading analyst is Rengakos 1994, 2008.

[47] Rengakos 1994, 174 n. 31 and 2008, 252 n. 43.

skill. At a slightly higher level of scholarly comment, Apollonius employs a "lexicographic technique" with scores of more obscure Homeric words by using them in his own poem with varied significations, each of which represents a meaning assigned to the lexical item by one or another ancient critic.[48] Thus, to take just a single adjective, the exact meaning of Homeric *têlugetos*, as we can gather from the scholia, was disputed. Apollonius uses it in the course of one book to mean "born to a father in old age" (1.99), "beloved" (1.149), and "only-begotten" (1.719)—exactly the range of possible meanings discussed in antiquity.[49] This technique turns the *Argonautica* into "a kind of poetic dictionary of Homer."[50] At yet another level, the arming of Aeetes (*Argonautica* 3.1225–34), with its sequence of breastplate-helmet-shield-spear, has been seen to parallel not the standard Homeric arming protocol (in which shield precedes helmet), but the revised version of *Iliad* 3.330–39 (Paris arming) attributed to the textual activity of Zenodotus.[51] Finally, and most striking, it has long been acknowledged that the final line of the *Argonautica*, announcing the crew's return (*Argonautica* 4.1781):

> ἀσπασίως ἀκτὰς Παγασηίδας εἰσαπέβητε

> you gladly set foot on the shores of Pagasae

echoes the going to bed of Odysseus and Penelope (*Odyssey* 23.296):

> ἀσπάσιοι λέκτροιο παλαιοῦ θεσμὸν ἵκοντο·

> gladly they came to their old bed's proper place.

While the latter does not conclude the *Odyssey* as we have it, the line was notoriously an object of critical discussion in Alexandria, with the scholia reporting that Aristophanes of Byzantium and Aristarchus (Homeric scholars flourishing later than Apollonius) considered it the end of the epic.[52] Apollonius would seem to be in favor of such a romantic denouement for the

---

[48] Rengakos 1994, 175–78, crediting Livrea with the term.

[49] See Mooney 1912, 75; Rengakos 1994, 154; cf. on other examples Seaton 1890, 7–9. Zacco 1996 is a fine case-study.

[50] Rengakos 2008, 253.

[51] Rengakos 2008, 259.

[52] See Heubeck 1992, 342–45 on whether this reflects the state of the Homeric *Odyssey* in the early Hellenistic era and whether *telos* should mean "end" rather than "conclusion of the main action." Apollonius could allude to more radical critical treatments known later but not approved by Aristophanes or Aristarchus. For evidence that the Peripatetic scholar Demetrius of Phalerum

earlier adventure poem. Given such exacting employment of Homeric scholarship on his part, an interpretive puzzle remains concerning the "voice"
of the *Argonautica* narrator. To what extent does the generalized use of
familiar Homeric diction and motifs harmonize with this fussy attention to
epic *hapax legomena* and arcane (at least to us) allusions to text-critical or
linguistic controversies in third-century Alexandria? Is there an intentional
dissonance? Or should we attune ourselves to hear not one voice, but something more polyphonic—a naïve "Homeric" (or even more archaic) bardic-
narrator in concert with a sophisticated, opinionated scholar-poet—Ossian
ventriloquized by Nabokov?[53]

This navigation of the vagaries of "voice" has bypassed thus far the
conventional starting-point for most examinations of Apollonius's intertextuality—the *episode*. Relations of specific scenes to Homeric precedents
are often semi-transparent and have been extensively studied. More helpful
might be a summary of the modes of this technique and how they interact,
rather than an attempt to inventory resemblances.[54]

First, episodes can be brought into suggestive relation by the recurrence
of a single detail of description, plot, or character. As the *Argo* reaches Lemnos
(*Argonautica* 1.601–10), the island is called "Sintian" (*Sintêida Lêmnon,* 608),
offering a reminder to the audience of an earlier mythical landing at sunset
there, when Hephaestus, hurled from Olympus, was taken in by the "Sintian
men" (*Iliad* 1.594). The newcomers will be cared for, as was the god, but
the sense of danger animated by the past textual and mythical example is
not far off, especially when the story of the intervening homicide by the
Lemnian women is now narrated (1.609–32).[55] Related to this sort of recall
is a second mode, the use of *hapax legomena* to lend dramatic overtone to
an episode. The Homeric participle *amphipesousa* (*Odyssey* 8.523) occurs

---

already in the late fourth century had discussed this line as the thematic culmination of the *Odyssey*,
see Montanari 2012, 345–47.

[53] The total amount of these familiar phrases in Apollonius may have been increased somewhat
through bias on the part of those copying the text toward Homeric over non-Homeric diction: see
Haslam 1978, 55 for examples of such "invasion." As he shows, scribal preference for more common
Homeric forms (or even Homeric–sounding nonce formations) sometimes ousted from later MSS
the original use of a *hapax legomenon* by Apollonius (e.g., at 1.1300, where a Milan papyrus preserves
the Homeric hapax *anamormurousin*; cf. *Odyssey* 12.238).

[54] See work by V. Knight 1995; Clare 2002; Hunter 1993; Levin 1971; and the useful phrase inventory by Campbell 1981.

[55] For a full explication, see Clauss 1993, 103. A similar resonance provided by small detail comes
in the epiphany of Apollo at Thunias (*Argonautica* 2.676–79; cf. *Iliad* 1.46), on which see Feeney
1991, 75.

once, describing how a wailing woman embraces her husband's corpse, in a simile about Odysseus' tears upon hearing the bard sing the sack of Troy. In the *Argonautica* (1.270), the word, in the same form and *sedes*, occurs in a simile about a distraught girl clutching at her nurse, which in turn describes the posture and emotion of Jason's mother Alcimede. The linkage thus produces a multi-dimensional reference: Odysseus resembles Alcimede (one returned almost home, after leaving his own mother in the underworld; the other watching her son leave); but the mother, in turn, is shifted into other imaginary roles—widow, orphan—that we will soon see made real during Jason's battle at Cyzicus (1.1053–77) and that inevitably recall Andromache and Penelope, among other Homeric grieving women. A further resonance of this departure scene is triggered by another *hapax*, the line-initial *entupas* (*Argonautica* 1.264), describing the grief-stricken father of Jason, "wrapped tightly" in his bed: ἐντυπὰς ἐν λεχέεσσι καλυψάμενος γοάασκεν. The description of Priam, ἐντυπὰς ἐν χλαίνῃ κεκαλυμμένος, in public self-abasement over the death of his son Hector (*Iliad* 24.163) provided the template. The result is a darker coloration for what otherwise might have been a less ominous event.[56]

A third mode involves Homeric type-scenes. These function differently from the *hapax*-enhanced episodes, inasmuch as the creation of meaning pivots upon frequently repeated sequences (arming, embarking, feasting, etc.), rather than on a unique source passage in earlier epic. Using his audience's awareness of such scenes, Apollonius can craft significant changes. When the Argonauts sacrifice to Apollo at 1.402–38, the extended ritual actions, along with their placement within the poem, recall similar scenes at *Odyssey* 3.32–66 and *Iliad* 1.446–74, albeit with dictional variants. The divinity's approving reaction, however, prominent in the Homeric version (*Iliad* 1.457, 474; cf. *Odyssey* 3.62) is conspicuous by its absence.[57] A related technique characterizes the most expansive narrative of battle and its aftermath in the *Argonautica*, 1.1026–78. The poet synthesizes a number of typical Iliadic scenes, complete with similes to mark the start and the conclusion, description of wounds, a run of killings (with typical *variatio* of verbs), flight, and the death of the lead fighter.[58] All this a reader of Homer might expect, but the abrupt nature of the telling makes for an epic *reductio* that

---

[56]   On the entire scene, see Clauss 1993, 40–47 and Cusset 1999, 270–72 with further bibliography.

[57]   The scene is well analyzed by Feeney 1991, 69–70; cf. Cusset 1999, 264–66; on this episode and type-scene intertexts in general, see V. Knight 1995, 49–91.

[58]   Detailed references in V. Knight 1995, 84–93.

reads more like a parody of Homeric style, while the heroization of the dead Doliones through cult lends the passage an aetiological distance completely foreign to the *Iliad*.[59]

The mode of imitation-with-difference perhaps most difficult to articulate is what we may call "multiple overlay," through which two or more Homeric scenes are subtly combined to produce multiple possibilities for interpreting a given Apollonius passage.[60] For instance, the boxing match between Amycus and Polydeuces (2.67–97) gestures both toward the funeral games of Patroclus (*Iliad* 23.683–99) and the fight of Odysseus with the beggar Iros (*Odyssey* 18.25–109), making the Argonautic version teeter between an heroic event and a boorish entertainment. The reception at the palace of Aeetes (3.210–74) carefully combines elements of Odysseus's approach to the house of Alcinous (*Odyssey* 7.4–138) with his arrival on Ithaca (*Odyssey* 13.189–91; 18.86, 374), thus teasing out through phrasal and situational reminiscence the simultaneous opportunity and threat posed to Jason.[61] The cosmogonic song of Orpheus (1.496–511) manages to combine key themes from all three of the songs of Demodocus in Book 8 of the *Odyssey*.[62] The technique tempts the poet to be kaleidoscopic—the speech by the goddesses of Libya to the hopeless crew (*Argonautica* 4.1318–29) overlays no fewer than four Odyssean subtexts: Ino to Odysseus (5.339); the description of Calypso (5.60–70); the song of the Sirens (12.184–91); and the instructions of Teiresias (11.110).[63] In this case, almost cinematic montage aims at a cumulative effect, signaling one outcome (survival) rather than heightening the suspense.

At yet another level, epic source-texts are diffused more broadly throughout the *Argonautica* and the *déja vu* thereby induced establishes more general narrative directions. A series of resemblances has been seen to link Book 3 of the *Argonautica* with Book 10 of the *Odyssey*, staging as it were Jason as an Odysseus, Aeetes as his sister Circe, Eros as a Hermes figure, and, ultimately, Medea as her own enchantress aunt (a meeting that will take place later in the poem).[64] The Lemnian episode is tethered to varied

---

[59] For this reading, see Goldhill 1991, 317–18.

[60] Cusset 1999, 276 suggests the term *surimpression*; others speak of multiple hypotexts or *contaminatio*.

[61] See Bettenworth 2005, who stresses the enriching rather than destabilizing force of the overlay.

[62] Nelis 1992.

[63] Clare 2002, 154.

[64] Correspondences worked out in V. Knight 1995, 176–78.

Odyssean predecessor texts at different points, letting us glimpse Hypsipyle as Nausicaa, as Alcinous, and even as Telemachus, vulnerable inheritor of his father's island state.[65] At the highest level, of course, and particularly in Book 4 of the poem, the shape of the entire *Odyssey* provides the coastline along which the Argo travels and from which it veers away. Critical responses tend to fall on either side of that navigational divide, with some scholars cataloguing the dozens of similar elements that link Jason's voyage with that of Odysseus, while others highlight the bold departures from the Homeric script.[66] Typically, even on the choice of sailing directions, "Apollonius treads a fine line between adaptation of an Odyssean itinerary and rejection of the geographical implausibility of such a route."[67] The *Argonautica* "*Odyssey*" merges fantasy islands with the down-to-earth perspective of Hellenistic *periplous* literature.

Intertextual references of the types listed above operate just below the surface of each episode, with the occasional *hapax* or familiar Homeric phrase jutting up to orient the reader. By contrast, three other closely related categories of epic imitation overtly proclaim their relationship to earlier poetry: the catalogue, *ekphrasis*, and similes. Through these poetic devices, audiences are explicitly invited to compare the art of Apollonius with his models. All three are highly self-conscious supplements, pausing the forward movement of the narrative while calling attention to its literariness. As three distinct techniques aimed at *enargeia*—the urge for precise and vivid description so prized by ancient critics—they create meaning through their conspicuous placement, their links to the action of the poem, and their obvious divergence from Homeric and Hesiodic congeners.

The *Catalogue* of *Argonautica* 1.23–233 immediately distinguishes itself from the renowned Catalogue of Ships (*Iliad* 2.484–760) by giving a list of young warriors rather than a roll-call of regional contingents. It thus naturally flows from the narrator's stated goal of recalling the expedition to Colchis that brought fame to "men of long ago" (*palaigeneôn ... phôtôn*). Two aspects of this personalization stand out: the equal status of the crew members (unlike the Homeric warriors, these are not leaders but Jason's *summêstores* "co-devisers," 1.228); and the individuality of their motives and fates (e.g., Idmon wanting not to be deprived of fame [141], Augeas wishing to see exotic

---

[65]   Bulloch 2006.

[66]   V. Knight 1995, 122–266 tends toward the former, Clare 2002, 125–42 the latter.

[67]   Clare 2002, 139. Dufner 1988 remains unsurpassed for detailed analysis of the Odyssean geographic intertexts.

lands [175], Mopsus and Canthus doomed to die [77–80]). The *Iliad* reserves mention of future fates for the catalogue of Trojan warriors (*Iliad* 2.860–61, 874–75). While both the Iliadic and Argonautic catalogues appear near the start of their respective poems (i.e., in narrative time), they are at opposite ends of the spectrum in narrated time: the gathering at Iolcus happens, as it were, in real time, at the Argo's departure, whereas the Homeric listing comes when ships have been beached for nine years (a vexing conundrum for later Analyst critics of the *Iliad*). The *Iliad* catalogue spirals outward geographically, from Boeotia; that of the *Argonautica* is also structured by place, closely mapped onto the Thessalian segment of the Catalogue of Ships.[68] But atop this topographical layer is placed a binary structure, not found in Homer, with Orpheus and Heracles dominating their respective halves of the list.[69] Finally, the rhythm of the two catalogues, through a similar crescendo effect, highlights a difference in content. Toward the end of the Catalogue of Ships, pain and loss are thematized by a triad of figures missing-in-action (Achilles 2.687–88, Protesilaus 698–702, Philoctetes 721–26). Apollonius responds with a quartet of magical warriors, who see through earth (Lynceus, 1.154–55), run on water (Euphemus 179–82), change shape (Periclymenus, 159–60), and fly (the Boreads, 219–23). This contrast alone speaks volumes about the tone of either epic.[70]

The extended *ekphrasis* of Jason's cloak (1.721–67) reverses the protocols of digressive placement, in comparison with the Iliadic description of Achilles' shield, for the latter is a natural entailment of the plot (the hero has lost his own armor) and a brilliant prologue to the poem's concluding movement. Jason's artifactual equivalent makes him a lover, rather than a fighter; focuses us on the moment when his is still untried, even at this art; and is functionally superfluous. Thematically, on the other hand, the cloak makes richly suggestive connections to its immediate context and the rest of the poem, and has rightly drawn the attention of many interpreters. The reflexive nature of the finely woven work is clear in many ways, starting with the underlying metaphor of poetry as textile.[71] That this is a textual moment to be gazed upon is hinted at through the third of its seven vignettes,

---

[68] See Scherer 2006, 57–134 for the most detailed analysis of narrative and structuring devices, including a study of geographic intertexts. Also useful is the typological study by Sistakou 2001. Antimachus may have composed his own catalogue of Argonauts: Matthews 1996, 71 n. 34.

[69] For further details of this structure see Clauss 1993, 26–34.

[70] On the "destabilizing" function of catalogues in Apollonius, see Clare 2002, 264. For the key subtext of the Homeric "catalogue of women" (*Odyssey* 11.225–330), see Bulloch 2006, 59–67.

[71] Hunter 1993, 56.

Aphrodite's alluring image reflected on Ares' shield (neatly embedding the Homeric model for this very ekphrasis: 1.745–46).[72] At the same time, as Simon Goldhill acutely observed, the cloak raises questions of the deceptiveness of appearances, the difficulty of viewing, the gap between the visual and verbal, and the possibilities of disconnection, through its apparently unstructured sequence of scenes.[73] Like the ram of Phrixus standing at the distant origin of the expedition (1.764–67), the episode seems to speak, but one would wait in vain to understand. Here, the most obvious Iliadic intertext might itself be a red herring, since the cloak's Empedoclean pairing of love and strife, programmatic for the *Argonautica*, is closer to Odyssean concerns, as in Demodocus' song of Ares and Aphrodite (*Odyssey* 8.266–366), already evoked by the song of Orpheus (*Argonautica* 1.496–511). The resemblances to the garb of Odysseus (*Odyssey* 19.225–35), like Jason's in its attractiveness to women, make this secondary Homeric model all the more resonant.[74]

Similes, the third epic device for producing "vividness," take new, sometimes strange, directions at the hands of Apollonius. As with his use of formulas, word-forms, and type-scenes, just enough familiarity is established to make the innovations stand out all the more. Similes occur at a rate near that of the *Iliad* (1 per 71 lines vs. *Iliad* 1 per 76; cf. 1 per 271 lines in the *Odyssey*), but are more evenly spread throughout the poem. Half of them begin with such typical Homeric introductions as *hôs hote*—but half use non-Homeric framing devices. Seven similes extend syntactically into the line resuming the "real" narrative as at 1.575–79:

> ὡς δ' ὁπότ' ἀγραύλοιο κατ' ἴχνια σημαντῆρος
> μυρία μῆλ' ἐφέπονται ἄδην κεκορημένα ποίης
> εἰς αὖλιν, ὁ δέ τ' εἶσι πάρος σύριγγι λιγείῃ
> καλὰ μελιζόμενος νόμιον μέλος—ὣς ἄρα τοίγε
> ὡμάρτευν· τὴν δ' αἰὲν ἐπασσύτερος φέρεν οὖρος

> And *as when* countless sheep follow in the footsteps of a rustic shepherd to the fold after having had their fill of grass, and he goes in front, beautifully playing a shepherd's tune on his shrill

---

[72] Cf. Feeney 1991, 70 on the oddity of this representational *mise en abyme*.

[73] Goldhill 1991, 308–11, with a penetrating survey of earlier interpretations.

[74] Yet another resonance comes from the phrasal recollection of Helen's web (*Iliad* 3.125–28) in *Argonautica* 1.722: see Cusset 1999, 281–82. On the complex thematic ties of the cloak as well as the "amatory" context for the cloak of Odysseus, see Hunter 1993, 52–55. On the parallels with the song of Demodocus—allegorized in antiquity as concerning love and war—see Nelis 1992.

pipes—*thus then* did the fish accompany the ship, and a steady
wind bore it ever onward.

This is an effect that occurs only once in Homeric epic (*Odyssey* 10.414) and
emblematizes the permeable boundary between this device and flow of the
epic action in the *Argonautica*.[75] Of the two primary roles played by similes
in Homer—rhythmic punctuation of extended narrative and emotional highlighting—Apollonius most often chooses the latter.[76] After Jason dons his
cloak and starts out for the city of the Lemnian women, the poet compares
him to a shining star (1.774–81):

> Βῆ δ' ἴμεναι προτὶ <u>ἄστυ</u>, φαεινῷ <u>ἀστέρι</u> ἶσος,
> ὅν ῥά τε νηγατέῃσιν ἐεργόμεναι καλύβῃσιν   775
> νύμφαι θηήσαντο δόμων ὕπερ <u>ἀντέλλοντα</u>,
> καί σφισι κυανέοιο δι' αἰθέρος ὄμματα θέλγει
> καλὸν <u>ἐρευθόμενος</u>, γάνυται δέ τε <u>ἠιθέοιο</u>
> παρθένος ἱμείρουσα μετ' ἀλλοδαποῖσιν ἐόντος
> ἀνδράσιν, ᾧ κέν μιν μνηστὴν κομέωσι τοκῆες—   780
> τῷ ἴκελος προπόλοιο κατὰ στίβον <u>ἤιεν ἥρως·</u>

> He went on his way toward the city like a shining star, which
> young brides, confined in newly made quarters, gaze upon as it
> rises above their houses, and enchants their eyes with its beau-
> tiful red luster through the dark sky, and the maiden rejoices as
> she yearns for the young man who is away among foreign people,
> for whom her parents are keeping her to be his bride. Like that
> star the hero followed in the footsteps of the servant.

Immediately, the simile places other viewers within our ken—young brides
(*numphai*) whose eyes are enchanted by the rising red star (clearly, but
tacitly, Hesperus, with all its erotic associations), and a young maiden,
who longs for her distant husband-to-be. Not only does this dual reference
suggest an evolving relationship, from unwed to married, relevant to the
hero's encounters with Hypsipyle and Medea, but the simile as a whole also
overflows its immediate signified (Jason's appearance) to recall the brightness
of his cloak (red, like a rising sun: 1.725–27) and to gesture proleptically
to his welcome by marriageable women (1.784), including their blushing
queen (1.791: παρθενικὴ <u>ἐρύθηνε</u> παρηίδας). The Homeric background

---

[75] See Carspecken 1952, 60–67 for specifics on all these points. In general on Apollonius' similes,
see Hunter 1993, 129–37; Reitz 1996; Cusset 1999, 117–257; and Matone 1999.

[76] On these roles in relation to the history of Homeric simile interpretation, see Chapter 2 above.

darkens the picture, as most star similes in the *Iliad* are baneful harbingers
(cf. *Iliad* 22.26–32: Priam viewing the approaching killer of his son).[77] The
audience must recall this image when, later on, Medea's anxious weeping is
described (3.656–64) as like that of a *numphê* (newly married or betrothed)
who laments her recently dead love.[78] The vision of ruddy celestial glow
recurs in a simile at the moment Jason seizes the Fleece (4.125–26). Distant
recall of an originating simile like that in 1.774–81 is further enabled by the
exquisite care with which Apollonius carves such lyric gems, even phonically
(note ἄστυ ... ἀστέρι and the meaningful echo of ἠιθέοιο by ἦιεν ἥρως).

The evocation of mixed emotions and viewpoints by way of simile is, of
course, not missing from Homeric art: one thinks of *Iliad* 16.7–11 (Patroclus
compared to a small girl) or *Odyssey* 5.394–98 (Odysseus's sight of land
like children's sight of their recovered father). Nor does Apollonius make
longer similes. Instead, his are marked by a density and breadth of allusion
and atunement perceptible in the finer details. Thus, the Homeric Nausicaa,
leading her age-mates in song, is like Artemis (*Odyssey* 6.102–9):

> οἵη δ' Ἄρτεμις εἶσι κατ' οὔρεα ἰοχέαιρα,
> ἢ κατὰ Τηΰγετον περιμήκετον ἢ Ἐρύμανθον,
> τερπομένη κάπροισι καὶ ὠκείησ' ἐλάφοισι·
> τῇ δέ θ' ἅμα Νύμφαι, κοῦραι Διὸς αἰγιόχοιο,   105
> ἀγρονόμοι παίζουσι· γέγηθε δέ τε φρένα Λητώ·
> πασάων δ' ὑπὲρ ἥ γε κάρη ἔχει ἠδὲ μέτωπα,
> ῥεῖά τ' ἀριγνώτη πέλεται, καλαὶ δέ τε πᾶσαι·
> ὣς ἥ γ' ἀμφιπόλοισι μετέπρεπε παρθένος ἀδμής.

And even as Artemis, the archer, roves over the mountains, along
the ridges of lofty Taygetus or Erymanthus, joying in the pursuit
of boars and swift deer, and with her sport the wood-nymphs, the
daughters of Zeus who bears the aegis, and Leto is glad at heart—
high above them all Artemis holds her head and brows, and easily
may she be known, though all are fair—so amid her handmaidens
shone the maid unwed. [trans. Murray 1919]

The description of Medea is a highly conscious imitation, prompting many
resonances (*Argonautica* 3.876–86):

---

[77] On the simile, see Reitz 1996, 16–19 with further bibliography.

[78] Cf. Hunter 1989, 168–69 on this simile. For a similar linking to actions outside the simile, see
Feeney 1991, 74 on *Argonautica* 2.600 (ship like an arrow) picking up 2.591–92 (oars bent like
bows).

οἵη δέ, λιαροῖσιν ἐν ὕδασι <u>Παρθενίοιο</u>
<u>ἠὲ</u> καὶ Ἀμνισοῖο λοεσσαμένη ποταμοῖο,
χρυσείοις Λητωὶς <u>ἐφ᾽ ἅρμασιν ἑστηυῖα</u>
ὠκείαις κεμάδεσσι διεξελάῃσι κολώνας,
τηλόθεν ἀντιόωσα πολυκνίσου <u>ἑκατόμβης·</u>   380
<u>τῇ δ᾽ ἅμα νύμφαι</u> ἕπονται ἀμορβάδες, <u>αἱ μὲν</u> ἀπ᾽ αὐτῆς
ἀγρόμεναι πηγῆς Ἀμνισίδες, <u>αἱ δὲ</u> λιποῦσαι
ἄλσεα καὶ σκοπιὰς πολυπίδακας, ἀμφὶ δὲ θῆρες
κνυζηθμῷ σαίνουσιν ὑποτρομέοντες ἰοῦσαν—
ὣς αἵγ᾽ ἐσσεύοντο δι᾽ ἄστεος, ἀμφὶ δὲ λαοί   385
εἶκον <u>ἀλευάμενοι</u> βασιληίδος <u>ὄμματα κούρης</u>.

And as when by the warm waters of Parthenius, or after bathing in the Amnisus river, Leto's daughter stands in her golden chariot drawn by swift deer and drives through the hills, coming from afar to partake of a savory hecatomb, and with her follow nymphs in attendance—some gathering from the very source of the Amnisus, others having left groves and peaks with many springs—and all around wild animals fawn on her, cowering with whimpers as she makes her way; thus did they hasten through the city, and all around them the people gave way as they avoided the eyes of the royal maiden.

But the differences are telling. Leto is the viewer within the Odyssean simile and Artemis/Nausicaa is an object of the gaze, "easily recognizable" (ἀριγνώτη), while at the same time essentially like her beautiful companions. In the *Argonautica*, Artemis/Medea is Leto's daughter, but the would-be viewers of the girl (as the simile melts into narrative) conspicuously *refuse* to look, out of fear for her gaze. Unlike the choral ethos of the Homeric scene, the Apollonius version celebrates a divine power dynamic: nymphs from all over gather, animals fawn, and the goddess herself is driving to receive her hecatomb. This theme extends to the mention of rivers, for we are not far from the dangers associated with Artemis bathing, as developed in the myths of Teiresias and Actaeon (and Hellenistic versions thereof). Furthermore, the *Argonautica* simile packs in at least two other hypotexts featuring the jubilant arrival of gods and animal reactions: Poseidon (*Iliad* 13.27–28) and Aphrodite (*Homeric Hymn to Aphrodite* 69–74)—the latter a typically ironic gesture toward the erotic charm of this particular *parthenos*.[79]

---

[79] On these connections and further analysis of this simile, see Hunter 1989, 194–96.

Character construction remains an under-theorized area of study regarding epic, archaic as well as Hellenistic. Unlike readers of nineteenth-century novels, we must look to features beyond realistic psychological depiction, since the hexameter poets in their creation of fictional persons worked within more formal conventions—traditional diction, type-scenes, set speeches. Even simile, as we have seen, can aid in implying character traits. Through situational and dictional echoes, Medea can be characterized as another Nausicaa, but also a Circe, Penelope, Andromache, or Helen.[80] A related form of overlay applied to the erring seer Phineus conflates Circe and Teiresias, leading the audience to assemble his "character" through reminiscence of these Odyssean roles.[81] When Apollonius at other times employs an already complicated Homeric template, the layering produces a more convincing (albeit exasperating) protagonist. Not only is Jason, as we piece him together from other appearances, "jealous of honor but incapable of asserting it, passive in the face of crisis, timid and confused before trouble,"[82] he also bears the scars of earlier imperfect heroes. Thus, Jason's peculiar blend of hesitation, anxiety, and confidence as encapsulated in his "test" of the crew after their passage through the Clashing Rocks (2.621–47) is shadowed by the behavior of Agamemnon and his nearly disastrous *peira* of the troops in *Iliad* 2.56–154.[83] When Jason and Medea do finally settle on action (e.g., the latter at 3.751–824), it is never represented in the clear-cut Homeric schema of decision-making, but rather after a succession of random ideas, flustered thinking, and even discussion with other people about various alternatives, a departure from the tradition made all the more striking by a sprinkling of typical phrases from the older model.[84]

Apart from these techniques, flowing from intertextual awareness, the primary means for constructing character in Homeric epic was direct speech. Even though Apollonius can employ with deft awareness the two main Homeric words distinguishing speech (*epos* and *mûthos*) to create meaningful allusions to the dynamics of the Ptolemaic court, his reporting of a character's words throughout the composition is radically reduced: 71% of the lines in the *Argonautica* are in the poet's voice, as contrasted with 55%

---

[80] V. Knight 1995, 181–84.

[81] Hunter 1993, 90–95; cf. Clare 2002, 75.

[82] Carspecken 1952, 101.

[83] Hunter 1988, 445–47; Kyriakou 1995, 122–31.

[84] Fine analysis in Rosenmeyer 1992.

in the *Iliad*.[85] This alone conduces to the sense that a very different sort of narrator lurks behind the poem's facade. Or, to put it in terms used in this essay, the overarching *expectation* created by all the levels of epic imitation in this poem—that the narrator, given his uncanny ventriloquism, will behave like his Homeric counterpart—turns out to be frustrated by the distinctively un-Homeric *voice*.

It is a more dominating, more interactive, and more emotionally involved voice than that heard in the *Iliad* or *Odyssey*. Indeed, it is most like that of a character within the epic, rather than an all-knowing distant narrator's.[86] Individual words that encode attitudes in Homer, primarily if not exclusively within character-speech (*oloos* "baneful," *stugeros* "hateful"), are used by the narrator in the *Argonautica*.[87] Homeric speakers can call each other or the gods "merciless" or "headstrong" (*skhetlios*, e.g., *Odyssey* 13.293), but in Apollonius it is part of the narrator's vocabulary (as at *Argonautica* 2.1028, where it means "unfortunate").[88] At the level of discourse habit, the voice that tells the tale exhibits the sort of avoidance strategies seen in the speeches by Homeric characters, whether it is vagueness about naming particular gods as responsible for action, or failure to pinpoint the source of changes in wind and weather.[89] Even at the level of discourse particles, the emotional tone and approach of a Homeric speaker is reflected in the use of *pou* "somehow, no doubt" and related forms, as the narrator speculates on the motives and feelings of his characters. Cyzicus is slain "doubtless [*pou*] thinking he was free from cruel destruction" (1.1037). The effect is as if the narrator "engages in a pervasive and variegated dialogue with his narratees."[90] Such staging of the narrator's thoughts and feelings accords with the frequent use of moralizing maxims, as in the same passage: "for mortals can never escape fate"(1.1035).

And so we are encouraged to wonder: *who does* voice the *Argonautica*? The self-constrained nature of the narrator's performance has led to comparisons with the figure of the seer Phineus within the poem, who warns his listeners that they are not permitted to know everything "exactly" (*atrekes*,

---

[85] On *epos* and *mûthos*, see Mori 2001; for the relative rates of speech, see Hunter 2008, 141.

[86] On interactivity of Apollonius' narrator with his characters and audience, see Morrison 2007, 271.

[87] Hunter 1993, 110–11.

[88] Morrison 2007, 284.

[89] Feeney 1991, 87–89 on, e.g., 3.540 *theoi*.

[90] Cuypers 2005, 35 for the quote; passim for examples.

2.312), thus aligning himself with the selective and even misleading revelations by Zeus through oracles. Just so, the narrator eschews full disclosure, especially of sacred or magic ritual: he will not "make a *mûthos*" of the rites of Samothrace (1.919–21) nor sing of Medea's propitiatory sacrifices to Hecate (4.247–50).[91] At the same time, this narrator is remarkably knowledgeable, throughout the poem, in detailing the aitiologies of cult sites and practices.[92] We are initiated into this lore, just as the Argonauts were instructed by Orpheus: the mantic voice of the narrator could well be that of the musician-hero. A near-identification does, after all, take place in the sudden break-off that marks Orpheus' paean to Apollo *Heôios* (2.706–10):[93]

> Δελφύνην τόξοισι πελώριον ἐξενάριξεν,
> κοῦρος ἐὼν ἔτι γυμνός, ἔτι πλοκάμοισι γεγηθώς
> (ἱλήκοις· αἰεί τοι, ἄναξ, ἄτμητοι ἔθειραι,
> αἰὲν ἀδήλητοι, τὼς γὰρ θέμις, οἰόθι δ᾽ αὐτή
> Λητὼ Κοιογένεια φίλαις ἐνὶ χερσὶν ἀφάσσει).

> ... the god killed monstrous Delphynes with his arrows, when he
> was still a naked boy, still delighting in his long locks—*be gracious*,
> lord, may your hair always remain unshorn, always unharmed,
> for such is right; and only Leto herself, Coeus' daughter, strokes
> it with her dear hands.

Furthermore, an Orphic voice would harmonize with the overall hymnic framing of the poem, as marked out even in the invocation of 1.1–2:[94]

> Ἀρχόμενος σέο Φοῖβε παλαιγενέων κλέα φωτῶν
> μνήσομαι ...

> Beginning with you, Phoebus, I shall recall the famous deeds of
> men born long ago ...

The often remarked failure to begin with the Muse can be taken several ways, among them as an assertion of authority equaling that of the daughters of Mnemosyne (and Orpheus himself is the offspring of a Muse, as we are told immediately after the proem: 1.23–34). That Orpheus has divine gifts is implied even syntactically, when his name is conjoined, in the genitive, with

---

[91]   Clare 2002, 274, and Feeney 1991, 61, 64–65, 94.

[92]   On aitiologies in the poem, see Köhnken 2010, 136–37.

[93]   On the complex merging, see Goldhill 1991, 297–98, building on Fränkel 1968, 227–28.

[94]   On hymnic influence in the proem, see Clare 2002, 21 and Hunter 2008, 115; also Clauss 1993, 16–19; Goldhill 1991, 287.

the verb "let us recall": Πρῶτά νυν Ὀρφῆος μνησώμεθα, for which the first line of the *Homeric Hymn to Apollo* offers the closest model (Μνήσομαι οὐδὲ λάθωμαι Ἀπόλλωνος ἑκάτοιο).[95] Orpheus as Muse-substituting narrator can even be detected in the parallel functions assigned in this passage, with the Muses (belatedly and indirectly) invoked as "interpreters" (Μοῦσαι δ' ὑποφήτορες εἶεν ἀοιδῆς, 1.22) and the Muse's son commemorated as "helper" (ἐπαρωγὸν ἀέθλων, 1.32).[96] The gradual occlusion of the narrator's authority in favor of the Muses' can then ironically be read as a type of *agôn* between divine and human singers, in which the latter loses (yet escapes the fate of Thamyris).[97] That a similar *agôn* has already been depicted in the poem, when Orpheus drowns out his cousins the Sirens (4.891–911), adds to the plausibility.

These mythopoeic multiforms bring us finally to a coda that deserves a treatise to itself: the relation of Apollonius to Hesiod. The formulation by Frederick Griffiths contrasts this succinctly with the Homeric influence: "Apollonius' *alter ego* Orpheus is more a Hesiod than a Phemius."[98] In the Alexandrian milieu, the archaic Boeotian was a crucial figure for imitation, as is clear from the *Aitia* and *Hymns* of Callimachus, as well as the *Phainomena* of Aratus.[99] As model for a divinely inspired poet not entangled with human kings and wars, the proem to the *Theogony* was epecially good for Alexandrians to think with, even as they further mythologized it: a version of Hesiod's encounter with the Muses underlies the Argonautic meeting with the Libyan *hêrôssae* (4.1312–36).[100] The Hesiodic model, like the Homeric, was mediated through the contemporary scholarly activity of Alexandria, traces of which remain.[101] Significantly, Apollonius was one of those who wrote on Hesiod: his opinion that a line is missing in the proem after *Theogony* 26 is mentioned in the *scholia vetera ad loc.* (diGregorio).[102]

---

[95] The syntax of 1.1–2 offers ironic contrast, as the genitive is governed by *arkhomenos* "starting from you," but the verb *mnêsomai* "I will recall" this time aims at humans, taking the accusative phrase *klea phôtôn* "the glories of men."

[96] Morrison 2007, 288–95 summarizes the debate over the meaning of 1.22 *hupophêtores*.

[97] On the slippage of the narrator's of authority, see Feeney 1991, 90–91; Goldhill 1991, 292–93; Morrison 2007, 272.

[98] Griffiths 1995, 188.

[99] Hunter and Fantuzzi 2004, 51–60, 351–55; Stephens 2003, 253–56.

[100] Feeney 1991, 92, noting the relevance of the dream-like atmosphere in both scenes.

[101] On Zenodotus' edition of the Hesiodic text, see Schroeder 2009.

[102] On Apollonius' scholarly work on Hesiod, see Pfeiffer 1968, 144 and Cusset 1999, 17.

Equally tantalizing is the information from an ancient *hypothesis* that he considered the [pseudo]-Hesiodic *Aspis* (*Shield of Heracles*) to be genuine, on the basis of its stylistic *kharaktêr*. That at times bizarre composition provides at least one decoration (a chariot race) for his own *ekphrasis* of Jason's cloak (*Argonautica* 1.752–58; cf. *Scutum* 305–13).[103]

Given the epic ambitions of the *Argonautica* one might anticipate a weaker intertextual bond with this non-epic source, but Hesiod's magnetism might, in fact, account for some of the distinctive qualities that differentiate the Alexandrian epic. In terms of structure, the Hesiodic *Catalogue of Women*—as much as emerges from the extant fragments—was a prime hypotext for the Catalogue of Argonauts: Pero, mother of Talaus and Areius (1.118–21) and Periclymenus (cf *Argonautica* 1.156–60), featured in both texts (cf. *Catalogue* frr. 33.11–36, 37). The Apollonian version blazons its generic connection at 1.230–32 by pointing to a matriarchal genealogical bond uniting the Minyans. The Catalogue-like list of the "race of goddesses" ending the *Theogony* includes the mother of Aristaeus (*Theogony* 977), yet another figure found prominently in Apollonius (in the embedded aetiology for the etesian winds: 2.506–52).

Human blood-ties in the poetry of Hesiod flow easily from theogonic materials. The inclusion of Orpheus among Jason's crew opens up the most opportunities for the latter genre to take root. The calming cosmogonic song of Orpheus (1.496–511) is the poem's most obvious debt to Hesiod, but strikingly deviates both in its philosophical beginning ("earth" and "sky" seeming to be unpersonified natural elements), as well as its subsequent "Orphic" lines of succession (Ophion and Eurynome as first inhabitants of Olympus). Only in its closing verses about the Cyclopes and young Zeus does the song align itself with our *Theogony* (*Theogony* 139–46; 477–506); even then the Hesiodic narrative is still in the future, in terms of this Orphic time-frame.[104]

The *Theogony* narrative haunts the *Argonautica* the closer the heroes approach Colchis. Events from deep time—the rise of Zeus—are here horizontally displayed, so that "early" and "far" coincide. As we progress, Amycus is compared to the *Theogony*'s Typhoeus, offspring of Gaea (*Argonautica* 2.38–40; cf. *Theogony* 820–68); another challenger, the snake that guards the

---

[103] Hunter 1993, 55–56; see further Cusset 1999, 20, and on the stylistic character of the *Shield*, see Chapter 13 above.

[104] Clare 2002, 55; cf. Feeney 1991, 67–68, who also adduces the Cyclopean scene on Jason's cloak (1.730–34).

Fleece, was nourished by Gaea with the blood of Zeus's monstrous enemy Typhaon (2.1209–13). The *Argo* sails past the spot where, before the rise of Zeus, Cronus mated with Philyra, begetting the centaur Cheiron (2.1231–41). Prometheus, though his fate elapsed generations ago, is still a living presence in this landscape (2.1248–59). The liver-gnawing eagle is a daily sight and the root nourished by his bloody *ichor* will go toward protecting Jason in his great trial (3.851–57). The Cyclopes of Orpheus' song were "earth-born" (*gêgenees*, 1.510), just as the story ran in Hesiod (*Theogony* 139, though without this adjective). But it is the other Hesiodic offspring of Gaea—Typhoeus, the Erinyes—that we are reminded of while moving east: the six-armed men of Bear Mountain (*Argonautica* 1.943) and ultimately the teeth-sprung warriors of Aeetes (3.499). Jason, in effect, struggles still with theogonic time; it is not accidental that his own contest to subdue the fire-breathing oxen (3.1299–1305, 1326–29) resonates with diction from the *Theogony*'s conquest of the Titans (689–700) and Typhoeus by Zeus (853–68).[105] Although the terms of that struggle are reversed—it is Zeus who smites with burning fire, like the oxen Jason must overcome—this only underlines the hero's own heritage: he comes from the territory of Zeus's rival Prometheus (as he tells Medea: 3.1086–95), from whom he himself can claim descent.

Jason's vanquishing of the oxen enables him to plow and sow, as if moving immediately from a *Theogony* to the *Works and Days*. Words from a central section of that poem (*Works and Days* 415–73) spring up in his cutting of furrows (3.1330–45) and in the imagery used to describe Jason's harvesting of the earth-born warriors (3.1386–90 cutting unripe crop; 1396–1403 crop damaged by rain).[106] Perhaps such diction is only to be expected in a scene related (if weirdly) to agricultural life, yet it reminds us that the "realism" of Apollonius had already been exploited in the poetic tradition by the Boeotian bard whose many wisdom works (whether *Astronomy*, *Bird-Signs*, or *Precepts of Cheiron*) presented "an archaic model for a poetics of information."[107]

---

[105] The defeat of Typhoeus is followed by a description of the threatening winds that arise from the monster (*Theogony* 869–79); the last fiery gasp of the oxen prompts a wind simile (cf. 3.1327 *epipneionte* and *Theogony* 872 *epipneiousi*.

[106] Compare *Argonautica* 3.1381 and *Works and Days* 431 *histoboei*; 1325 and *Works and Days* 467 *ekhetlê*; 1331 and *Works and Days* 463–64 *neios*; cf. also *Scutum* 286–90; 1347 and *Works and Days* 439, 443 *aulaka*; 1399 and *Works and Days* 415 *ombrêsantos*.

[107] Lamberton 1988b, 151.

The image of the farmer with a newly sharpened sickle (3.1388) that describes Jason at work in this Hesiodic context might summon up the *Theogony*, and the *harpê* of Cronus, given to him by his oppressed mother Gaea (*Theogony* 175, 179). The bloody episode might have remained deep beneath this text, were it not for the explicit evocation of it by the *Argonautica* narrator in the next book of the poem (*Argonautica* 4.982–87):

> Ἔστι δέ τις πορθμοῖο παροιτέρη Ἰονίοιο
> ἀμφιλαφὴς πίειρα Κεραυνίη εἰν ἁλὶ νῆσος,
> ᾗ ὕπο δὴ κεῖσθαι δρέπανον φάτις (ἵλατε Μοῦσαι,
> οὐκ ἐθέλων ἐνέπω προτέρων ἔπος) ᾧ ἀπὸ πατρός
> μήδεα νηλειῶς ἔταμε Κρόνος οἱ δέ ἑ Δηοῦς
> κλείουσι χθονίης καλαμητόμον ἔμμεναι ἅρπην·

> There is a fertile, expansive island at the entrance of the Ionian strait in the Ceraunian sea, under which is said to lie the sickle— *forgive me, Muses, not willingly do I repeat my predecessors' words—* with which Cronus ruthlessly cut off his father's genitals. Others, however, say it is the *reaping scythe* of indigenous Demeter.

This remarkable apology for repeating "the *epos* of those who came before" clearly refers to the castration episode at *Theogony* 176–82. In classic Hellenistic fashion, the narrator recalls the story only to counteract the myth by another, in which people "repeat as *kleos*" (*kleiousi*) that the island is actually associated with the scythe of Demeter, who taught the Titans to cut grain. Furthermore, the island is home to the Phaeacians, who boast a very un-Hesiodic (and un-Homeric) origin, as descendants of the blood of Uranus (4.992). Whereas the *Theogony* knows of Erinyes, Giants, and nymphs called *Meliai* emerging from the bloody droplets off the severed genitals (and Aphrodite from the organ itself), this version would ally Jason with protectors who, like him, are connected to powerful figures before or outside the Olympian regime—Uranus and Prometheus. In other words, the apparently innocent alternative version is, politically and poetically, subversive. We could say that Apollonius here treats the martial side of Hesiod— his cosmogonic woundings and slaughters—to a challenge from the agricultural—the celebration of Demeter and her works. The terms of such a contestation were long familiar to Greeks at a metapoetic level. A traditional generic split is contained in the view of Aeschylus, as staged by Aristophanes (*Frogs* 1030–36): Hesiod teaches men the working of the earth, harvest, and plowing; Homer teaches troop formation, armings, and glorious exploits. The later *Contest of Homer and Hesiod*—a second-century CE composition with roots going back to the sixth century BCE—has Hesiod proclaimed the winner in his singing match against Homer, since his lines speak of land-working (*georgia*), not wars and slayings.[108] Given the danger in assuming that Apollonius was governed by a binary opposition—if not Homer, then Hesiod—it is perhaps best, as with so many features of this astounding poet, to triangulate.[109] Orpheus has a contest with the Sirens and, perhaps by implication, with the Muses in the *Argonautica* (if it is indeed his "voice" that we hear behind the narrator). That Homer and Hesiod can abide in such close complementarity in this new epic, rather than be drawn up according to their traditional opposition, shows a compositional skill akin to that of the singer of cosmogonies (1.496–515), the man who by his all-encompassing craft enchants his listeners and puts to rest their quarrels.

---

[108] Allen 1912, lines 205–10. On the fourth century BCE and earlier forms of the story see Richardson 1981.

[109] Morrison 2007, 11.

WORKS CITED

Ackerman, R. 1987. *J. G. Frazer: His Life and Work.* Cambridge.

Ahl, F., and H. M. Roisman. 1996. *The "Odyssey" Re-Formed.* Ithaca.

Ahrens, E. 1937. *Gnomen in griechischer Dichtung.* Halle.

Alden, M. 2000. *Homer Beside Himself: Para-narratives in the "Iliad."* New York.

Alexiou, M. 1974. *The Ritual Lament in Greek Tradition.* Cambridge.

Allen, T. 1912. *Homeri Opera.* Vol. V. Oxford.

———. 1924. *Homer: The Origins and the Transmission.* Oxford.

———. 1931. *Homeri Ilias.* Oxford.

Allen, T., E. Sikes, and W. Halliday, eds. 1936. *The Homeric Hymns.* 2d ed. Oxford.

Aloni, A. 1980. "*Prooimia, Hymnoi,* Elio Aristide e i cugini bastardi." *Quaderni Urbinati di Cultura Classica* 33:23–40.

———. 1989. *L' aedo e i tiranni.* Rome.

———. 1993. "La *performance* di Cineto." In *Tradizione e innovazione nella cultura greca da Omero all' età ellenistica,* vol. 1, ed. R. Pretagostini, 129–42. Rome.

———. 1998. *Cantare glorie di eroi: comunicazione e performance poetica nella Grecia Arcaica.* Turin.

Alter, R. 1989. *The Pleasures of Reading in an Ideological Age.* New York.

Altheim, F. 1924. "Die Entstehungsgeschichte des homerischen Apollon-hymnus." *Hermes* 59:430–49.

Amandry, P. 1984. "Os et coquilles." *Bulletin de Correspondance Hellénique,* supplement no. 9, 347–80.

Anderson, W. 1965. *Matthew Arnold and the Classical Tradition.* Ann Arbor.

Antović, M., and C. P. Cánovas, eds. 2016. *Oral Poetics and Cognitive Science.* Vol. 56. Berlin.

Apthorp, M. 1980. "The Obstacles to Telemachus' Return." *Classical Quarterly* 30:1–22.

Arieti, J. 1992. Review of Martin 1989. *American Journal of Philology* 113:87–90.

Arrighetti, G. 1975. "Esiodo fra epica e lirica." In *Esiodo: letture critiche,* ed. G. Arrighetti, 5–36. Milan.

———. 1991. "Eoikota tekna goneusi: etica eroica e continuità genealogica nell'epos greco," *Studi italiani di filologia classica* 9:133–47.

Athanassakis, A. 1970. "Hiatus, Word End, and Correption in Hesiod." *Hermes* 98:129–45.

———. 1992. "Cattle and Honor in Homer and Hesiod." *Ramus* 21:156–82.

Athanassakis, A., and B. Wolkow, trans. 2013. *The Orphic Hymns*. Baltimore.

Austen, R. 1999. *In Search of Sunjata. The Mande Oral Epic as History, Literature and Performance*. Bloomington, IN.

Austin, N. 1966. "The Function of Digressions in the *Iliad*." *Greek, Roman and Byzantine Studies* 7:295–312.

———. 1975. *Archery at the Dark of the Moon*. Berkeley.

———. 1994. *Helen of Troy and her Shameless Phantom*. Ithaca.

Azuonye, C. 1990. "Kaalu Igirigiri: An Ohafia Igbo Singer of Tales." In *The Oral Performance in Africa*, ed. I. Okpewho, 42–79. Ibadan.

Bader, F. 1980. "Rhapsodies homériques et irlandaises." In *Recherches sur les religions de l'antiquité classique*, ed. R. Bloch, 9–83. Paris.

———. 1989. *La langue des dieux ou l'hermétisme des poètes indo-européens*. Pisa.

Bakhtin, M. 1981. "Discourse in the Novel." In *The Dialogic Imagination: Four Essays*, trans. C. Emerson and M. Holquist, 229–442. Austin.

Bakker, E. 1997. *Poetry in Speech: Orality and Homeric Discourse*. Ithaca.

Ballabriga, A. 1990. "La question homérique: pour une réouverture du débat." *Revue des études Grecques* 103:16–29.

Baltes, M. 1982. "Die Kataloge im homerischen Apollonhymnus." *Philologus* 125:25–43.

Bannert, H. 1981. "Phoinix' Jugend und der Zorn des Meleagros." *Wiener Studien* 15:69–94.

Barchiesi, A. 1984. *La traccia del modello: Effetti omerici nella narrazione virgiliana*. Pisa.

Barker, A. 1984. *Greek Musical Writings*. Vol. 1, *The Musician and His Art*. Cambridge.

Barron, J., and P. Easterling. 1989. "Hesiod." In *The Cambridge History of Classical Literature*. Vol. 1, part 1, *Early Greek Poetry*, ed. P. Easterling and B. Knox, 51–64. Cambridge.

Bassett, S. 1919. "Versus Tetracolos." *Classical Philology* 14:216–33.

Basso, E. 1985. *A Musical View of the Universe*. Philadelphia.

Bauman, R. 1977. *Verbal Art as Performance*. Rowley, MA.

———. 1992. *Folklore, Cultural Performances, and Popular Entertainments*. Oxford.

———. 2002. "Disciplinarity, Reflexivity, and Power in Verbal Art as Performance: A Response." *Journal of American Folklore* 115:92–98.

———. 2011. "Commentary: Foundations in Performance." *Journal of Sociolinguistics* 15:707–720.

———. 2013. "Discovery and Dialogue in Ethnopoetics." *Journal of Folklore Research* 50:175–190.

Bauman, R., and J. Sherzer, eds. 1989. *Explorations in the Ethnography of Speaking.* 2nd ed. Cambridge.

Baumeister, A. 1860. *Hymni Homerici.* Leipzig.

Beck, D. 2012. *Speech Presentation in Homeric Epic.* Austin.

Becker, A. S. 1992. "Reading Poetry Through a Distant Lens: Ecphrasis, Ancient Greek Rhetoricians, and the Pseudo-Hesiodic 'Shield of Herakles'." *American Journal of Philology* 113:5–24.

———. 1995. *The Shield of Achilles and the Poetics of Ekphrasis.* Lanham, MD.

Behan, B. 1959. *Borstal Boy.* New York.

Beissinger, M., J. Tylus, and S. Wofford, eds. 1999. *Epic Traditions in the Contemporary World.* Berkeley.

Belcher, S. 1999. *Epic Traditions of Africa.* Bloomington, IN.

Bennett, J., and J.-P. Olivier. 1973. *The Pylos Tablets Transcribed.* Part 1. Rome.

Benveniste, E. 1966a. "Don et échange dans le vocabulaire indo-européen." In *Problemes de linguistique generale*, vol. 1, 315–26. Paris.

———. 1966b. "La phrase nominale." In *Problemes de linguistique generale,* vol. 1, 151–67. Paris.

———. [1969] 1973. *Indo-European Language and Society.* Trans. E. Palmer. Coral Gables, FL.

Berger, H., and G. Del Negro. 2002. "Bauman's Verbal Art and the Social Organization of Attention: The Role of Reflexivity in the Aesthetics of Performance." *Journal of American Folklore* 115:62–91.

Bergin, O. 1970. *Irish Bardic Poetry.* Dublin.

Bergren, A. 1975. *The Etymology and Usage of PEIRAR in Early Greek Poetry.* New York.

Bernabé, A. 2000. "Nuovi frammenti orfici e una nuova edizione degli Ὀρφικά." In *Tra Orfeo e Pitagora: Origini e incontri di culture nell' antichità,* ed. M. T. Ghidini, A. S. Marino, and A. Visconti, 43–80. Naples.

———. 2004. *Poetae Epici Graeci.* Pars 2, fasc. 1, *Orphicorum et Orphicis similium testimonia et fragmenta.* Leipzig.

Bernabé, A., and A. I. Jiménez San Cristobal. 2001. *Instrucciones para el Más Allá: las laminillas órficas de oro.* Madrid.

Bernhardt-House, P. 2009. "Warriors, Words, and Wood: Oral and Literary Wisdom in the Exploits of Irish Mythological Warriors." *Studia Celtica Fennica* 6:5–19.

Berres, T. 1975. "Das zeitliche Verhältnis von Theogonie und Odyssee: Ein Verborgenes 'Selbstporträt' des Odysseedichters." *Hermes* 103:129–43.

Best, R. I. 1916. "The Battle of Airtech." *Ériu* 8:170–90.

Bettenworth, A. 2005. "Odysseus bei Aietes: primäre und sekundäre intertexte bei Apollonios Rhodios." In M. A. Harder and M. Cuypers 2005, 1–17.

Biebuyck, D., and K. Mateene, eds. 1969. *The Mwindo Epic from the Banyanga (Congo Republic)*. Berkeley.

Binchy, D. A. 1970. *Celtic and Anglo-Saxon Kingship*. Oxford.

Birch, D. 1989. *Language, Literature and Critical Practice*. London.

Blackburn, S. 1986. "Performance Markers in an Indian Story-Type." In *Another Harmony: New Essays on the Folklore of India*, ed. S. Blackburn and A. Ramanujan, 167–94. Berkeley.

Blackburn, S., P. Claus, J. Flueckiger, and S. Wadley, eds. 1989. *Oral Epics in India*. Berkeley.

Bloom, C. 1996. *Cult Fiction: Popular Reading and Pulp Theory*. New York.

Boedeker, D. 1974. *Aphrodite's Entry into Greek Epic*. Leiden.

Boesch, G. 1908. *De Apollonii Rhodii elocutione*. Göttingen.

Böhme, R. 1970. *Orpheus: Der Sänger und seine Zeit*. Bern.

Bonanno, M. G. 1990. *L'allusione necessaria, ricerche intertestuali sulla poesia greca e latina*. Rome.

Boon, J. 1982. *Other Tribes, Other Scribes: Symbolic Anthropology in the Comparative Study of Cultures, Histories, Religions, and Texts*. Cambridge.

Boterf, N. 2012. *Lyric Cities: Poet, Performance, and Community*. Ph.D. diss., Stanford University.

Bouvier, D. 2002. *Le sceptre et la lyre*. Grenoble.

Bowie, E. 1993. "Greek Table-Talk before Plato." *Rhetorica* 11:355–73.

Bowra, C. 1952. *Heroic Poetry*. London.

Boyd, T. W. 1994. "Where Ion Stood, What Ion Sang." *Harvard Studies in Classical Philology* 96:109–21.

Braswell, B. K. 1981. "*Odyssey* 8.166–77 and *Theogony* 79–93." *Classical Quarterly* 31:237–39.

Bréal, M. 1911. *Pour mieux connaître Homère*. 2d ed. Paris.

Broccia, G. 1969. *Tradizione ed esegesi*. Brescia.

Bulloch, A. 1970. "A Callimachean Refinement to the Greek Hexameter." *Classical Quarterly* 20:258–68.

———. 2006. "Jason's Cloak." *Hermes* 134:44–68.

Bundrick, S. 2005. *Music and Image in Classical Athens.* Cambridge.

———. 2014. "Selling Sacrifice on Classical Athenian Vases." *Hesperia* 83:653–708.

Burgess, J. S. 2001. *The Tradition of the Trojan War in Homer and the Epic Cycle.* Baltimore.

———. 2009. *The Death and Afterlife of Achilles.* Baltimore.

Burkert, W. 1979. "Kynaithos, Polycrates, and the *Homeric Hymn to Apollo.*" In *Arktouros: Hellenic Studies Presented to B. M. W. Knox*, ed. G. Bowersock et al., 53–62. Berlin.

———. 1985. *Greek Religion.* Trans. J. Raffan. Cambridge, MA.

———. 1987. "The Making of Homer in the Sixth Century B.C.: Rhapsodes versus Stesichorus." In *Papers on the Amasis Painter and His World*, ed. M. True et al., 43–62.

Bury, J. B., ed. [1892] 1965. *The Isthmian Odes of Pindar.* Reprint ed. London.

Buttimer, C. 1982. "Scéla Mucce Meic Dathó: A Reappraisal." *Proceedings of the Harvard Celtic Colloquium* 2:61–69.

Buxton, R., ed. 1999. *From Myth to Reason? Studies in the Development of Greek Thought.* Oxford.

Bynum, D. 1976. "The Generic Nature of Oral Epic Poetry." In *Folklore Genres*, ed. D. Ben-Amos, 35–58. Austin.

Byrne, F. 1973. *Irish Kings and High Kings.* London.

Calame, C. 1998. "Muthos, logos et histoire." *L'Homme* 147:127–49.

———. 2001. *Choruses of Young Women in Ancient Greece: Their Morphology, Religious Role, and Social Function.* Revised ed. Trans. D. Collins and J. Orion. Lanham, MD.

———. 2006. *Pratiques poétiques de la mémoire.* Paris.

———. 2014. "The Derveni Papyrus between the Power of Spoken Language and Written Practice: Pragmatics of Initiation in an Orpheus Poem and its Commentary." In *Poetry as Initiation: The Center for Hellenic Studies Symposium on the Derveni Papyrus*, ed. I. Papadopoulou and L. Muellner, 165–86. Hellenic Studies 63. Washington, DC.

Cameron, A. 1995. *Callimachus and His Critics.* Princeton.

Campanile, E. 1977. *Ricerche di cultura poetica indoeuropea.* Pisa.

———. 1981. *Studi di cultura celtica e indoeuropea.* Pisa.

Campanile E., et al. 1974. "Funzione e figura del poeta nella cultura celtica e indiana." *Studi e saggi linguistici* 14:228–251.

Campbell, M. 1981. *Echoes and Imitations of Early Epic in Apollonius Rhodius.* Leiden.

Cantarella, R. 1931. "Elementi primitivi nella poesia Esiodea." *Rivista Indo-greco-italica* 15:105–49.

Cantieni, R. 1942. *Die Nestorerzählung im XI. Gesang der Ilias (V. 670–762).* Zurich.

Cantilena, M. 1982. *Ricerche sulla dizione epica.* Rome.

Caraveli-Chavez, A. 1980. "Bridge Between Worlds: The Greek Women's Lament as Communicative Event." *Journal of American Folklore* 93:129–57.

Carspecken, J. F. 1952. "Apollonius Rhodius and the Homeric Epic." *Yale Classical Studies* 13:33–143.

Cartmell, D., et al. 1997. *Trash Aesthetics: Popular Culture and its Audience.* London.

Cassio, A. C. 2002. "Early Editions of the Greek Epics and Homeric Textual Criticism in the Sixth and Fifth Centuries BC." In *Omero tremila anni dopo*, ed. F. Montanari and P. Ascheri, 105–36. Rome.

Càssola, F. 1975. *Inni Omerici.* Milan.

Chadwick, N., and V. Zhirmunsky. 1969. *Oral Epics of Central Asia.* Cambridge.

Chantraine, P. 1937. "Grec meilikhios." In *Mélanges Émile Boisacq.* Vol. 1, 169–74. Brussels.

———. 1968–1980. *Dictionnaire étymologique de la langue grecque.* Paris.

Chatman, S. 1978. *Story and Discourse.* Ithaca, NY.

Cheyns, A. 1967. "Sens et valeurs du mot αἰδώς dans les contextes home-riques." In *Recherches de philologie et de linguistique*, ed. M. Hofinger, 3–33. Louvain.

Chicherov, V. 1975. "Some Types of Russian New-Year Songs." In *The Study of Russian Folklore*, ed. F. Oinas and S. Soudakoff, 113–22. The Hague.

Cingano, E. 2005. "A Catalogue within a Catalogue: Helen's Suitors in the Hesiodic Catalogue of Women (frr. 196–204)." In Hunter 2005, 118–52.

Clader, L. L. 1976. *Helen: The Evolution from Divine to Heroic in Greek Epic.* Leiden.

Clare, R. J. 2002. *The Path of the Argo: Language, Imagery and Narrative in the "Argonautica" of Apollonius Rhodius.* Cambridge.

Clarke, H. 1981. *Homer's Readers: A Historical Introduction to the "Iliad" and the "Odyssey."* Newark, DE.

Clarke, M. 1937. *Richard Porson: A Biographical Essay.* Cambridge.

Claus, P. 1989. "Behind the Text: Performance and Ideology in a Tulu Oral Tradition." In S. Blackburn et al. 1989, 55–74.

Clauss, J. 1993. *The Best of the Argonauts. The Redefinition of the Epic Hero in Book One of Apollonius' "Argonautica"*. Berkeley.

Clay, D. 2004. *Archilochos Heros*. Hellenic Studies 6. Washington, DC.

Clay, J. S. 1983. *The Wrath of Athena: Gods and Men in the "Odyssey"*. Princeton.

———. 1989. *The Politics of Olympus. Form and Meaning in the Major Homeric Hymns*. Princeton.

———. 1993. "The Education of Perses: From 'Mega Nepios' to 'Dion Genos' and Back." In *Mega Nepios: Il destinatario nell'epos didascalico*. Materiali e discussioni per l'annalisi dei testi classici 31, ed. A. Schiesaro, P. Mitsis, and J. S. Clay, 23–33. Pisa.

———. 2003. *Hesiod's Cosmos*. Cambridge.

———. 2005. "The Beginning and End of the Catalogue of Women and its Relation to Hesiod." In Hunter 2005, 25–34.

———. 2011a. *Homer's Trojan Theater: Space, Vision, and Memory in the "Iliad"*. Cambridge.

———. 2011b. "The Homeric Hymns as Genre." In *The Homeric Hymns. Interpretative Essays*, ed. A. Faulkner, 232–53. Oxford.

Collinge, N. E. 1985. *The Laws of Indo-European*. Amsterdam.

Collins, D. 2001a. "Improvisation in Rhapsodic Performance." *Helios* 28:11–27.

———. 2001b. "Homer and Rhapsodic Competition in Performance." *Oral Tradition* 16: 129–67.

———. 2004. *Master of the Game: Competition and Performance in Greek Poetry*. Hellenic Studies 7. Washington, DC.

Comotti, G. 1989. *Music in Greek and Roman Culture*. Trans. R. Munson. Baltimore.

Connelly, B. 1986. *Arab Folk Epic and Identity*. Berkeley.

Conte, G. B. 1986. *The Rhetoric of Imitation: Genre and Poetic Memory in Virgil and Other Latin Poets*. Ithaca, NY.

———. 1991. *Generi e lettori: Lucrezio, l'elegia d'amore, l'enciclopedia di Plinio*. Milan.

Cook, R. 1937. "The Date of the Hesiodic Shield." *Classical Quarterly* 31: 204–14.

Corman, R. 1990. *How I Made a Hundred Movies in Hollywood and Never Lost a Dime* (with Jim Jerome). New York.

Crusius, O. 1895. "Zur Kritik der antiken Ansichten über die Echtheit homerischer Dichtungen." *Philologus* 54:710–34.

Culler, J. 1975. *Structuralist Poetics*. Ithaca, NY.

Cunliffe R. [1924] 1963. *A Lexicon of the Homeric Dialect.* Reprint ed. Norman, OK.

Cunningham, J. 1960. *The Exclusions of a Rhyme.* Denver.

Cusset, C. 1999. *La Muse dans la bibliothèque. Réécriture et intertextualité dans la poésie alexandrine.* Paris.

Cuypers, M. 2005. "Interactional Particles and Narrative Voice in Apollonius and Homer." In M. A. Harder and M. Cuypers 2005, 35–69.

Dällenbach, L. 1986. *Mirrors and After: Five Essays on Literary Theory and Criticism.* Ed. T. S. Evans. New York.

Danek, G. 2009. "Apollonius Rhodius as an (Anti-)Homeric Narrator: Time and Space in the *Argonautica.*" In *Narratology and Interpretation. The Content of Narrative Form in Ancient Narrative,* ed. J. Grethlein and A. Rengakos, 275–91. Berlin.

Danforth, L. 1982. *The Death Rituals of Rural Greece.* Princeton.

Davidson, O. M. 1980. "Indo-European Dimensions of Herakles in *Iliad* 19.95–133." *Arethusa* 13:197–202.

———. 1998. "Epic as a Frame for Speech-Acts: Ritual Boasting in the *Shâhnâma* of Ferdowsi." In *New Methods in the Research of Epic,* ed. H. Tristram, 271–85. Tübingen.

Davies, D. R. 1992. *Genealogy and Catalogue: Thematic Relevance and Narrative Elaboration in Homer and Hesiod.* Ph.D. diss. University of Michigan.

Dawe, R. 1993. *The "Odyssey": Translation and Analysis.* Sussex.

De Hoz, J. 1964. "Poesia oral independiente de homero en hesiodo y los himnos homericos." *Emerita* 32:283–98.

De Jáuregui, M. H. 2011. "Dialogues of Immortality from the *Iliad* to the Gold Leaves." In *The 'Orphic' Gold Tablets and Greek Religion: Further along the Path,* ed. R. G. Edmonds, 271–90. Cambridge.

De Jong, I. 1997. "Homer and Narratology." In Morris and Powell, 1997, 305–25.

———. 2001. *A Narratological Commentary on the "Odyssey".* Cambridge.

De Jong, I., and Sullivan, J., eds. 1994. *Modern Critical Theory and Classical Literature.* Leiden.

de Lamberterie, C. 1997. "Milman Parry et Antoine Meillet." In *Hommage à Milman Parry: Le style formulaire de l'épopée et la théorie de l'oralité poétique,* ed. F. Létoublon, 9–22. Amsterdam.

De Martino, F. 1982. *Omero agonista in Delo.* Brescia.

Demianczuk, J. [1912] 1967. *Supplementum Comicum.* Reprint ed. Hildesheim.

Denniston, J. D. 1950. *The Greek Particles*. 2d ed. Oxford.

Depew, M. and D. Obbink, eds. 2000. *Matrices of Genre: Authors, Canons, and Society*. Cambridge, MA.

Detienne, M. 1967. *Les maîtres de vérité dans la Grèce archaïque*. Paris.

———. [1977] 1994. *The Gardens of Adonis: Spices in Greek Mythology*. Trans. J. Lloyd. Princeton.

———. 1981. "The Sea-Crow." In *Myth, Religion and Society: Structuralist Essays by M. Detienne, L. Gernet, J.-P. Vernant and P. Vidal-Naquet*, ed. R. Gordon, 6–42. Cambridge.

———. 2000. *Comparer l'incomparable*. Paris.

Detienne, M., and J.-P. Vernant. 1978. *Cunning Intelligence in Greek Culture and Society*, trans. J. Lloyd. Sussex.

Dettori, E. 2000. *Filita grammatico. Testimonianze e frammenti*. Rome.

Dickson, K. 1995. *Nestor: Poetic Memory in Greek Epic*. New York.

Dictionary of the Irish Language. Dublin, 1913–76.

DiGregorio, L., ed. 1975. *Scholia Vetera in Hesiodi Theogoniam*. Milan.

Diller, H. 1962. *Die dichterische Form von Hesiods Erga*. Mainz.

Dillon, M. 1951. "The Wasting Sickness of Cú Chulainn." *Scottish Gaelic Studies* 7:47–88.

———. 1969. *The Archaism of Irish Tradition*. Reprint ed. Chicago.

———. 1973. "The Consecration of Irish Kings." *Celtica* 10:1–8.

———, ed. 1975. *Serglige Con Culainn*. Dublin.

Dimock, J. E. 1989. *The Unity of the Odyssey*. Amherst.

Dodds, E. R. 1951. *The Greeks and the Irrational*. Berkeley.

Doherty, L. E. 1991. "The Internal and Implied Audiences of *Odyssey* 11." *Arethusa* 24:145–76

———. 1992. "Gender and Internal Audiences in the *Odyssey*." *American Journal of Philology* 113:161–77.

———. 1995. *Siren Songs: Gender, Audiences, and Narrators in the "Odyssey"*. Ann Arbor.

Donato, E. 1972. "The Two Languages of Criticism." In *The Structuralist Controversy: The Languages of Criticism and the Sciences of Man*, ed. R. Macksey and E. Donato, 89–97. Baltimore.

Dornseiff, F. [1935] 1959. "Nochmals der homerische Apollonhymnos, eine Gegenkritik." In *Kleine Schriften*. Vol. 1, *Antike und Alter Orient*, ed. J. Werner, 413–48. Leipzig.

Douglas, M. 1982. "Judgments on James Frazer." In *In the Active Voice*, 272–91. London.

Dowden, K. 1996. "Homer's Sense of Text." *Journal of Hellenic Studies* 116:47–61.

Draak, M. 1959. "Some Aspects of Kingship in Pagan Ireland." In *The Sacral Kingship*, 651–63. Leiden.

Dräger, P. 1997. *Untersuchungen zu den Frauenkatalogen Hesiods*. Stuttgart.

Drerup, E. 1937. "Der homerische Apollonhymnos: eine methodologische Studie." *Mnemosyne* 4:81–134.

Drews, R. 1983. *Basileus: The Evidence for Kingship in Geometric Greece*. New Haven.

Droudakis, A. 1982. *Mantinades tes Kretes*. Khania.

Duban, J. 1980. "Poets and Kings in the *Theogony* Invocation." *Quaderni Urbinati di Cultura Classica* 33:7–21.

Dubus, A. 1991. *Broken Vessels*. Boston.

Dué, C. 2002. *Homeric Variations on a Lament by Briseis*. Lanham, MD.

Dufner, C. 1988. *The "Odyssey" in the "Argonautica". Reminiscence, Revision, Reconstruction*. Ph.D. diss., Princeton University.

Dumézil, G. 1968–73. *Mythe et épopée*. 3 vols. Paris.

Dunbar, N., ed. 1995. *Aristophanes, "Birds"*. Oxford.

Dundes, A. 1962. "From Etic to Emic Units in the Structural Study of Folktales." *Journal of American Folklore* 75:95–105.

Dunkel, G. E. 2008. "Luvian -tar and Homeric τ' ἄρ." In *Studies in Slavic and General Linguistics*. Vol. 32.1, *Evidence and Counter-Evidence: Essays in Honour of Frederik Kortlandt*, ed. A. Lubotsky, J. Schacken, and J. Wiedenhof, 137–49. Amsterdam.

Durante, M. 1976. *Sulla preistoria della tradizione poetica greca II: Risultanze della comparazione indoeuropea*. Rome.

Durrell, L. 1960. *Reflections on a Marine Venus*. London.

Eck, D. L. 1998. *Darśan: Seeing the Divine Image in India*. New York.

Edelstein, E., and L. Edelstein. 1945. *Asclepius: A Collection and Interpretation of the Testimonies*. Baltimore.

Edmunds, L. 1995. "Intertextuality Today." *Lexis* 13:3–22.

———. 1997. "Myth in Homer." In Morris and Powell, 1997, 415–41.

———. 2001. *Intertextuality and the Reading of Roman Poetry*. Baltimore.

Edwards, G. P. 1971. *The Language of Hesiod in its Traditional Context*. Oxford.

Edwards, M. 1986. "Homer and Oral Tradition: The Formula, Part I." *Oral Tradition* 1:171–230.

———. 1992. "Homer and Oral Tradition: The Type-Scene." *Oral Tradition* 7:284–330.

Ellmann, R. 1987. *Oscar Wilde*. New York.

Elmer, D. 2010. "Kita and Kosmos: The Poetics of Ornamentation in Bosniac and Homeric Epic." *Journal of American Folklore* 123:276–303.

———. 2013. *The Poetics of Consent: Collective Decision Making and the Iliad*. Baltimore.

Erbse, H. 1950. *Untersuchungen zu den attizistischen Lexika*. Berlin.

———, ed. 1971. *Scholia Graeca in Homeri Iliadem* (scholia vetera). Vol. 2. Berlin.

———, ed. 1975. *Scholia Graeca in Homeri Iliadem* (scholia vetera). Vol. 4. Berlin.

———, ed. 1988. *Scholia Graeca in Homeri Iliadem* (scholia vetera). Vol. 7. Berlin.

Erdener, Y. 1993. "Turkish Minstrels in Song Duel: Strategies for Gaining Prestige." *International Folklore Review* 9:55–61.

Erren, M. 1990. "Die Anredestruktur im archaischen Lehrgedicht." In *Der Übergang von der Mündlichkeit zur Literatur bei den Griechen*, ed. W. Kullmann and M. Reichel. ScriptOralia 3. Tübingen.

Evelyn-White, H., ed. and trans. 1914. *Hesiod, The Homeric Hymns and Homerica, Shield of Heracles*. Cambridge, MA.

Fantuzzi, M. 1988. *Ricerche su Apollonio Rodio*. Rome.

———. 2008. "'Homeric' Formularity in the *Argonautica* of Apollonius of Rhodes." In Papanghelis and Rengakos 2008, 221–42.

Fantuzzi, M., and R. L. Hunter. 2004. *Tradition and Innovation in Hellenistic Poetry*. Cambridge.

Fantuzzi, M., and R. Pretagostini, eds. 1995-1996. *Struttura e storia dell'esametro Greco*. 2 vols. Studi di metrica classica 10. Rome.

Farrell, J. 1999. "Walcott's *Omeros*: The Classical Epic in a Post-Modern World." In Beissinger et al. 1999, 270–96.

Fearn, D. 2011. "The Ceians and their Choral Lyric: Athenian Epichoric and Pan-Hellenic Perspectives." In *Archaic and Classical Choral Song: Performance, Politics and Dissemination*, ed. L. Athanassaki and E. Bowie, 207–34. Berlin.

Feeney, D. C. 1991. *The Gods in Epic: Poets and Critics of the Classical Tradition*. Oxford.

Felson, N., and L. M. Slatkin. 2004. "Gender and Homeric Epic." In Fowler 2004, 91–114.

Fenik, B. 1968. *Typical Battle Scenes in the "Iliad"*. Wiesbaden.

———. 1974. *Studies in the "Odyssey"*. Wiesbaden.

Fernández Delgado, J. 1982. "La poesia sapiencial de grecia arcaica y los origenes del hexametro." *Emerita* 50:151–73.

———. 1985. "Poesia oral mantica en los oráculos de Delfos." In *Symbolae Ludovico Mitxelena*, ed. J. Melena, 153–66. Vitoria-Gasteiz.

———. 1987. "Remarks on the Formular Diction of the *Homeric Hymns.*" *Museum Philologum Londiniense* 8:15–29.

Ferrari, G. 1988. "Hesiod's Mimetic Muses and the Strategies of Deconstruction." In *Poststructuralist Classics*, ed. A. Benjamin, 45–78. London.

Fine, E. 1984. *The Folklore Text: From Performance to Print*. Bloomington, IN.

Finley, J. H., Jr. 1978. *Homer's Odyssey*. Cambridge, MA.

Fishman, A. 2008. "*Thrênoi* to *Moirológia*: Female Voices of Solitude, Resistance, and Solidarity." *Oral Tradition* 23:267–95.

Flashar, M. 1992. *Apollo Kitharodos: statuarische Typen des musischen Apollon*. Cologne.

Floratos, Ch. 1952. "Ho Homêrikos humnos eis Apollona." *Athena* 56:286–309.

Flueckiger, J. 1989. "Caste and Regional Variants in an Oral Epic Tradition." In Blackburn 1989, 33–54.

———. 1999. "Appropriating the Epic: Gender, Caste, and Regional Identity in Middle India." In Beissinger et al. 1999, 131–51.

Flueckiger, J., and L. Sears, eds. 1991. *Boundaries of the Text: Epic Performances in South and Southeast Asia*. Ann Arbor.

Foley, H. P. 2005. "Women in Ancient Epic," In J. M. Foley 2005, 105–18.

Foley, J. M. 1985. *Oral-Formulaic Theory and Research: An Introduction and Annotated Bibliography*. New York.

———. 1987. "Reading the Oral Traditional Text: Aesthetics of Creation and Response." In *Comparative Research on Oral Traditions: A Memorial for Milman Parry*, ed. J. M. Foley, 185–212. Columbus, OH.

———. 1988. *The Theory of Oral Composition. History and Methodology*. Bloomington, IN.

———. 1990. *Traditional Oral Epic: The Odyssey, Beowulf, and the Serbo-Croatian Return Song*. Berkeley.

———. 1991. *Immanent Art: From Structure to Meaning in Traditional Oral Epic*. Bloomington, IN.

———. 1995. *The Singer of Tales in Performance*. Bloomington, IN.

———. 1997. "Oral Tradition into Textuality." In *Texts and Textuality: Textual Instability, Theory, and Interpretation*, ed. P. Cohen, 1–24. New York.

————. 1998. "Individual Poet and Epic Tradition: Homer as Legendary Singer." *Arethusa* 31:149–78.

————. 1999. *Homer's Traditional Art.* University Park, PA.

————. 2005. *A Companion to Ancient Epic.* Malden, MA.

Fontenrose, J. 1978. *The Delphic Oracle. Its Responses and Operations, with a Catalogue of Responses.* Berkeley.

Ford, A. 1992. *Homer: The Poetry of the Past.* Ithaca, NY.

————. 1997. "Epic as Genre." In Morris and Powell 1997, 396–414.

————. 2002. *The Origins of Criticism: Literary Culture and Poetic Theory in Classical Greece.* Princeton.

Forssman, B. 1966. *Untersuchungen zur Sprache Pindars.* Wiesbaden.

Förstel, K. 1979. *Untersuchungen zum homerischen Apollonhymnos.* Bochum.

Fowler, D. 2000. "Epic in the Middle of the Wood: *Mise en Abyme* in the Nisus and Euryalus Episode." In *Intratextuality: Greek and Roman Textual Relations*, ed. A. Sharrock and H. Morales, 89–113. New York.

Frame, D. 1978. *The Myth of Return in Early Greek Epic.* New Haven.

————. 2009. *Hippota Nestor.* Hellenic Studies 34. Washington, DC.

Frangoulidis, S. 1997. "Intratextuality in Apuleius' *Metamorphoses*." *L'Antiquité classique* 66:293–99.

Fränkel, H. 1921. *Die homerischen Gleichnisse.* Göttingen.

————. [1926] 1968. "Der homerische und der kallimachische Hexameter." In *Wege und Formenfrühgriechischen Denkens,* 3rd ed., 100–156. Munich.

————. 1968. *Noten zu den Argonautika des Apollonios.* Munich.

Frel, J. 1994. "Una nuova laminella 'orfica'." *Eirene* 30:183–84.

Friedländer, P. 1913. "Hypothêkai." *Hermes* 48:558–616.

Friedrich, R. 1975. *Stilwandel im homerischen Epos.* Heidelberg.

Frolíková, A. 1963. "Some Remarks on the Problem of the Division of the Homeric Hymn to Apollo." In *GERAS: Studies Presented to G. Thomson,* ed. L. Varcl and R. F. Willetts, 99–109. Prague.

Furley, W., and J. Bremer. 2001. *Greek Hymns.* Vol. 2, *Greek Texts and Commentary.* Tübingen.

Fyfe, W. 1932. *Aristotle, The Poetics. "Longinus," On the Sublime. Demetrius, On Style*, ed. W. R. Roberts. Cambridge, MA.

Gantz, J. 1981. *Early Irish Myths and Sagas.* Harmondsworth.

Gantz, T. 1993. *Early Greek Myth: A Guide to Literary and Artistic Sources.* Baltimore.

García, J. F. 2001. "Milman Parry and A. F. Kroeber: Americanist Anthropology and the Oral Homer." *Oral Tradition* 16:58–84.

———. 2002. "Symbolic Action in the *Homeric Hymns*: The Theme of Recognition." *Classical Antiquity* 21:5–39.

Garcia, L. F., Jr. 2013. *Homeric Durability: Telling Time in the "Iliad"*. Hellenic Studies 58. Washington, DC.

Garzya, A. 1958. *Teognide Elegie. Libri I–II*. Florence.

Geffcken, J. 1902. *Die Oracula Sibyllina*. Die griechischen christlichen Schriftsteller 8. Leipzig.

Genette, G. 1980. *Narrative Discourse: An Essay in Method*. Trans. J. Lewin. Ithaca, NY.

Gentili, B., and Giannini, P. 1977. "Preistoria e formazione dell'esametro." *Quaderni Urbinati di cultura classica* 26:7–37.

Gerber, D. E., trans. 1999. *Greek Elegiac Poetry: From the Seventh to the Fifth Centuries BC*. Cambridge, MA.

Gernsbacher, M., and T. Givón, eds. 1995. *Coherence in Spontaneous Text*. Amsterdam.

Ghidini, M. T., A. S. Marino, and A. Visconti, eds. 2000. *Tra Orfeo e Pitagora: Origini e incontri di culture nell'antichità*. Naples.

Gladstone, W. 1876. *Homeric Synchronism*. London.

Godley, A. D. 1926. *Herodotus, with an English Translation*. 4 vols. Cambridge, MA.

Goldhill, S. 1991. *The Poet's Voice: Essays on Poetics and Greek Literature*. Cambridge.

González, J. M. 2013. *The Epic Rhapsode and His Craft: Homeric Performance in a Diachronic Perspective*. Hellenic Studies 47. Washington, DC.

González de Tobia, A. M. 2014. "¿Cómo y cuándo definieron los antiguos griegos la épica como género?" In *Som per mirar: Estudis de filologia grega oferts a Carles Miralles*, vol. 1, ed. E. Vintró, F. Mestre, and P. Gómez, 247–262. Barcelona.

———, ed. 2010. *Mito y performance: De Grecia a la modernidad*. La Plata, Argentina.

Goodheart, E. 1984. *The Skeptic Disposition*. Princeton.

Gostoli, A. 1990. *Terpandro*. Rome.

Gould, J. 1973. "Hiketeia." *Journal of Hellenic Studies* 93:74–103.

Gow, A. S. F., ed. 1965. *Theocritus*. Vol. 2. Cambridge.

Graf, F. 1974. *Eleusis und die Orphische Dichtung Athens in vorhellenistischer Zeit*. Berlin.

———. 1996. "Orphic Literature, Orphism." In *The Oxford Classical Dictionary*, ed. S. Hornblower and A. Spawforth, 3rd ed., 1078–79. Oxford.

———. 2005. "Rolling the Dice for an Answer." In *Mantikê: Studies in Ancient Divination*, ed. S. I. Johnston and P. T. Struck, 51–97. Leiden.

———. 2009. *Apollo*. London and New York.

Graziosi, B. 2002. *Inventing Homer: The Early Reception of Epic*. Cambridge.

Green, P. 1984. "*Works and Days* 1–285: Hesiod's Invisible Audience." In *MNEMAI: Classical Studies in Memory of Karl K. Hulley*, ed. H. Evjen, 21–39. Chico, CA.

Greene, R., S. Cushman, C. Cavanagh, et al., eds. 2012. *The Princeton Encyclopedia of Poetry and Poetics*. Princeton.

Griffin, J. 1976. "Homeric Pathos and Objectivity." *Classical Quarterly* 26:161–187.

———. 1980. *Homer on Life and Death*. Oxford.

Griffith, M. 1983. "Personality in Hesiod." *Classical Antiquity* 2:37–41.

———. 1990. "Contest and Contradiction in Early Greek Poetry." In *Cabinet of the Muses: Essays on Classical and Comparative Literature in Honor of T. R. Rosenmeyer*, ed. M. Griffith and D. Mastronarde, 185–207. Atlanta.

Griffiths, F. T. 1995. Review of Hunter 1993. *Classical Philology* 90:187–91.

Guneratne, K. 1999. *In the Circle of the Dance: Notes of an Outsider in Nepal*. Ithaca, NY.

Haft, A. 1996. "The Mercurial Significance of Raiding: Baby Hermes and Animal Theft in Contemporary Crete." *Arion* 4:27–48.

Hagel, S. 2004. "Tables beyond O'Neill." In *Autour de la césure. Actes du colloque Damon des 3 et 4 novembre 2000*, ed. F. Spaltenstein, 135–215. Bern.

Haggett, A. 1902. *A Comparison of Apollonius Rhodius with Homer in Prepositional Usage*. Baltimore.

Hainsworth, J. B. 1968. *The Flexibility of the Homeric Formula*. Oxford.

———, ed. 1989. *Traditions of Heroic and Epic Poetry*. Vol. 2. London.

———. 1993. *The Iliad: A Commentary. Books 9–12*. Cambridge.

Halliwell, S. 1986. *Aristotle's Poetics*. London.

Hamilton, R. 1989. *The Architecture of Hesiodic Poetry*. Baltimore.

Harder, M. A., R. F. Regtuit, and G. C. Wakker, eds. 2000. *Apollonius Rhodius*. Leuven.

Harder, M. A., and M. Cuypers, eds. 2005. *Beginning from Apollo: Studies in Apollonius Rhodius and the Argonautic Tradition*. Caeculus 6. Leuven.

Harrison, E. 1902. *Studies in Theognis*. Cambridge.

Hartog, F. 1988. *The Mirror of Herodotus: the Representation of the Other in the Writing of History*. Trans. J. Lloyd. Berkeley.

Haslam, M. W. 1978. "Apollonius Rhodius and the Papyri." *Illinois Classical Studies* 3:47–73.

Hatto, A., and J. Hainsworth, eds. 1980/1989. *Traditions of Heroic and Epic Poetry.* 2 vols. London.

Haubold, J. 2005."Heracles in the Hesiodic *Catalogue of Women.*" In Hunter 2005, 85–98.

Havelock, E. 1966. "Thoughtful Hesiod." *Yale Classical Studies* 20:59–72.

Hawkins, H. 1990. *Classics and Trash: Traditions and Taboos in High Literature and Popular Modern Genres.* London.

Heiden, B. 2008. *Homer's Cosmic Fabrication: Choice and Design in the "Iliad".* New York.

———. 2013. "Coordinated Sequences of Analogous Topics in the Delian and Pythian Segments of the *Homeric Hymn to Apollo.*" *Trends in Classics* 5:1–8.

Henry, P. 1982. "The Cruces of Audacht Morainn." *Zeitschrift für celtische Philologie* 39:33–53.

Herington, C. J. 1993. "Greek Poetry." In *The New Princeton Encyclopedia of Poetry and Poetics.* 3rd edition, ed. A. Preminger and T. V. F. Brogan, 481–91. Princeton.

Hermann, G. 1805. *Orphica.* Leipzig.

Herzfeld, M. 1985. *The Poetics of Manhood: Contest and Identity in a Cretan Mountain Village.* Princeton.

Heubeck, A. 1966. "Thukydides III 104." *Wiener Studien* 79:148–57.

———. [1972] 1984. "Gedanken zum homerischen Apollonhymnos." *Kleine Schriften zur griechischen Sprache und Literatur,* 171–86. Erlangen.

———. 1974. *Die Homerische Frage.* Darmstadt.

Heubeck, A., and A. Hoekstra. 1989. *A Commentary on Homer's "Odyssey".* Vol. 2. Oxford.

Heubeck, A., J. Russo, and M. Fernández-Galiano. 1992. *A Commentary on Homer's "Odyssey".* Vol. 3. Oxford.

Heubeck, A., S. West, and J. B Hainsworth. 1988. *A Commentary on Homer's "Odyssey".* Vol. 1. Oxford.

Hiltebeitel, A. 1999. *Rethinking India's Oral and Classical Epics: Draupadi among Rajputs, Muslims, and Dalits.* Chicago.

Hinds, S. 1998. *Allusion and Intertext: Dynamics of Appropriation in Roman Poetry.* Cambridge.

Hiney, T. 1997. *Raymond Chandler: A Biography.* London.

Hoekstra, A. 1957. "Hesiode et la tradition orale." *Mnemosyne* 10:193–225.

———. 1965. *Homeric Modifications of Formulaic Prototypes.* Amsterdam.

———. 1969. *The Sub-Epic Stage of the Formulaic Tradition.* Amsterdam.

Hölscher, U. 1978. "The Transformation from Folktale to Epic." In *Homer: Tradition and Invention,* ed. B. Fenik, 51–67. Leiden.

———. 1988. *Die Odyssee: Epos zwischen Märchen und Roman.* Munich.

Holst-Warhaft, G. 1992. *Dangerous Voices: Women's Laments and Greek Literature.* New York.

Hooker, J. T. 1977. *The Language and Text of the Lesbian Poets.* Innsbruck.

Horrocks, G. 1980. "The Antiquity of the Greek Epic Tradition: Some New Evidence." *Proceedings of the Cambridge Philological Society* 206:1–11.

Houlihan, J. 1994. "Incorporating the Other: The Catalogue of Women in *Odyssey* 11." *Electronic Antiquity* 2.1.

Housman, A. 1961. *Selected Prose.* Ed. J. Carter. Cambridge.

Hubbard, T. 1991. *The Mask of Comedy: Aristophanes and the Intertextual Parabasis.* Ithaca, NY.

Hunt, E. 1977. *The Transformation of the Hummingbird: Cultural Roots of a Zinacantecan Mythical Poem.* Ithaca, NY.

Hunt, R. 1981. "Satiric Elements in Hesiod's *Works and Days.*" *Helios* 8:29–40.

Hunter, R. L. 1988. "'Short on Heroics': Jason in the *Argonautica.*" *Classical Quarterly* 38:436–53.

———, ed. 1989. *Apollonius of Rhodes. Argonautica. Book III.* Cambridge.

———. 1993. *The "Argonautica" of Apollonius: Literary Studies.* Cambridge.

———. 1996. *Theocritus and the Archaeology of Greek Poetry.* Cambridge.

———, ed. 2005. *The Hesiodic Catalogue of Women: Constructions and Reconstructions.* Cambridge.

———. 2008. "The Poetics of Narrative in the *Argonautica.*" In Papanghelis and Rengakos 2008, 115–46.

———. 2011. "Plato's *Ion* and the Origins of Scholarship." In *Ancient Scholarship and Grammar: Archetypes, Concepts and Contexts,* ed. S. Matthaios, 27–40. Berlin.

Hurwit, J. M., 2015. *Artists and Signatures in Ancient Greece.* Cambridge.

Hutchinson, G. O. 2006. "Hellenistic Epic and Homeric Form." In *Epic Interactions. Perspectives on Homer, Virgil, and the Epic Tradition presented to Jasper Griffin by Former Pupils,* ed. M. J. Clarke, 105–29. Oxford.

Huxley, G. 1969. *Greek Epic Poetry from Eumelos to Panyassis.* London.

Hyman, S. E. 1959. *The Tangled Bank: Darwin, Marx, Frazer and Freud as Imaginative Writers.* New York.

Hymes, D. 1983. "The Pre-War Prague School and Post-War American Anthropological Linguistics." In *Essays in the History of Linguistic Anthropology*, ed. D. Hymes, 331–44. Amsterdam.

Jacoby, F., ed. 1930. *Hesiodi Carmina*. Berlin.

———. 1933. "Der homerische Apollonhymnos." *Sitzungsberichte der preussischen Akademie der Wissenschaften* 15:682–751.

Jaeger, W. 1945. *Paideia*. Vol. 1. 2nd ed. Trans. G. Highet. New York.

Jaillard, D. 2007. *Configurations d'Hermès: Une'théogonie hermaïque'*. Liège.

Jakobson, R. 1960. "Linguistics and Poetics." In *Style in Language*, ed. T. A. Sebeok, 350–77. Cambridge, MA.

———. 1966. *Selected Writings IV: Slavic Epic Studies*. The Hague.

Janko, R. 1982. *Homer, Hesiod and the Hymns: Diachronic Development in Epic Diction*. Cambridge.

———. 1984. "Forgetfulness in the Golden Tablets of Memory." *Classical Quarterly* 34:89–100.

———. 1986. "The Shield of Heracles and the Legend of Cycnus." *Classical Quarterly* 36:38–59.

———. 1992. *The Iliad: A Commentary*. Vol. IV, *Books 13–16*. Cambridge.

———. 1997. "The Physicist as Hierophant: Aristophanes, Socrates and the Authorship of the Derveni Papyrus." *Zeitschrift für Papyrologie und Epigraphik* 118:61–94.

———. 1998. "The Homeric Poems as Oral Dictated Texts." *Classical Quarterly* 48:1–13.

———. 2016. "Going Beyond Multitexts: The Archetype of the Orphic Gold Leaves." *Classical Quarterly* 66:100–127.

Johnson, W. R. 1982. *The Idea of Lyric: Lyric Modes in Ancient and Modern Poetry*. Berkeley.

Johnston, S. I. 2013. "'Initiation' in Myth, 'Initiation' in Practice." In *Initiation in Ancient Greek Rituals and Narratives: New Critical Perspectives*, ed. D. Dodd and C. Faraone, 155–80. London.

Kahn, L. 1978. *Hermès passe ou les ambiguïtés de la communication*. Paris.

Kakridis, I. 1937. "Zum homerischen Apollonhymnos." *Philologus* 92:104–8.

———. 1980. *Proomêrika, Homêrika, Hesiodeia*. Athens.

Kassel, R., and C. Austin, eds. 1989. *Poetae Comici Graeci (PCG)*. Vol. 7. Berlin.

———, eds. 1995. *Poetae Comici Graeci (PCG)*. Vol. 8. Berlin.

Kassis, K. D. 1985. *Tragoudhia notias Peloponnesou (Mani, Taygetos, Parnonas)*. Athens.

Katz, J. 2007. "The Epic Adventures of an Unknown Particle." In *Greek and Latin from an Indo-European Perspective*, ed. C. George et al., 65–79. Cambridge.

Katz, J., and K. Volk. 2000. "'Mere Bellies?': A New Look at *Theogony* 26–8." *Journal of Hellenic Studies* 120:122–31.

Katz, M. 1991. *Penelope's Renown: Meaning and Indeterminacy in the "Odyssey"*. Princeton.

Kebric, R. 1983. *The Paintings in the Cnidian Lesche at Delphi and their Historical Context*. Leiden.

Keenan, E. 1989. "Norm-Makers, Norm-Breakers: Uses of Speech by Men and Women in a Malagasy Community." In Bauman and Sherzer 1989, 125–43.

Kelly, A. 2007. *A Referential Commentary and Lexicon to Homer, Iliad VIII*. Oxford.

Kelly, F., ed. 1976. *Audacht Morainn*. Dublin.

Killen, J. T. 2008. "Mycenaean Economy." In *A Companion to Linear B*, ed. Y. Duhoux and A. Morpurgo Davies, 159–200. Louvain-la-neuve.

Kindstrand, J. 1981. *Anacharsis: The Legend and the Apophthegmata*. Uppsala.

Kirk, G. 1962. *The Songs of Homer*. Cambridge.

———. 1965. *Homer and the Epic*. Cambridge.

———. 1981. "Orality and Structure in the *Homeric Hymn to Apollo*." In *I poemi epici rapsodici non omerici*, ed. C. Brillante et al., 163–82. Padua.

———. 1985a "The Homeric Hymns." In *The Cambridge History of Classical Literature*. Vol. 1, *Greek Literature*, ed. P. Easterling and B. Knox, 110–116. Cambridge.

———. 1985b. *The Iliad. A Commentary*. Vol. 1. *Books 1–4*. Cambridge.

Kirkwood, G., ed. 1982. *Selections from Pindar*. Chico, CA.

Knight, V. 1995. *The Renewal of Epic: Responses to Homer in the Argonautica of Apollonius*. Leiden.

Knight, W. 1941. "Integration and the *Hymn to Apollo*." *American Journal of Philology* 62:302–13.

Knox, B. M. W. 1989. *Essays Ancient and Modern*. Baltimore.

Knudsen, R. A. 2014. *Homeric Speech and the Origins of Rhetoric*. Baltimore.

Köhnken, A. 2010. "Apollonius' *Argonautica*." In *A Companion to Hellenistic Literature*, ed. J. Clauss and M. Cuypers, 136–50. Malden, MA.

Kolarov, R. 1992. "A Work and Oeuvre: Intra/Intertextuality." In *Poetics of the Text*, ed. J. Andrew, 35–42.

Korenjak, M. 1998. "Homerische Intertextualität ohne Formeln?" *Materiali e discussioni per l'analisi dei testi classici* 40:133–43.

Kothari, K. 1989. "Performers, Gods, and Heroes in the Oral Epics of Rajasthan." In Blackburn et al. 1989, 102–17.

Kozak, L. 2017. *Experiencing Hektor: Character in the Iliad.* London.

Krafft, F. 1963. *Vergleichende Untersuchungen zu Homer und Hesiod.* Göttingen.

Krischer, T. 1971. *Formale Konventionen der homerischen Epik.* Munich.

Kurke, L. 1989. "*Kapêleia* and Deceit: *Theognis* 59–60." *American Journal of Philology* 110:535–44.

———. 1990. "Pindar's Sixth Pythian and the Tradition of Advice Poetry." *Transactions of the American Philological Association* 120:85–107.

Kurke, L., and C. Dougherty, eds. 1993. *Cultural Poetics of Archaic Greece. Cult, Performance, Politics.* Cambridge.

Kyriakou, P. 1995. *Homeric Hapax Legomena in the "Argonautica" of Apollonius Rhodius: A Literary Study.* Stuttgart.

Lachmann, K. 1874. *Betrachtungen über Homers Ilias.* 3rd ed. Berlin.

Lachterman, D. 1990. "*Noos* and *Nostos:* The *Odyssey* and the Origins of Greek Philosophy." In *La naissance de la raison en Grece*, ed. J.-F. Mattéi, 33–39. Paris.

Lamberton, R. 1988a. "Plutarch, Hesiod, and the Mouseia of Thespiai." *Illinois Classical Studies* 13:491–504.

———. 1988b. *Hesiod.* New Haven.

———. 1997. "Homer in Antiquity." In Morris and Powell 1997, 33–54.

Lang, M. 1987. "Pylos Polytropos." In *Studies in Mycenaean and Classical Greek presented to John Chadwick*, ed. J. Killen, J. Melena, and J.-P. Olivier, 333–41. Minos 20–22. Salamanca.

Lardinois, A. 1995. *Wisdom in Context: The Use of Gnomic Statements in Archaic Greek Poetry.* Ph.D. diss., Princeton University.

LaRoche, J. 1899. "Der Hexameter bei Apollonios, Aratos und Kallimachos." *Wiener Studien* 21:161–97.

Latacz, J. 1977. *Kampfparänese, Kampfdarstellung, und Kampfwirklichkeit in der Ilias, bei Kallinos und Tyrtaios.* Zetemata 66. Munich.

Lattimore, R., trans. 1967. *The Odyssey of Homer.* New York.

———. 2011. *The Iliad of Homer.* Introduction and notes by R. P. Martin. Chicago.

Leaf, W. 1900. *The Iliad.* 2 vols. London.

Lesky, A. 1966. *A History of Greek Literature.* Trans. J. Willis and C. de Heer. New York.

Létoublon, F. 1990. "Le circuit de la communication et la composition de *L'Iliade.*" *Lalies* 8: 177–88.

Letsios, V. 2005. "The Life and Afterlife of Political Verse." *Journal of Modern Greek Studies* 23:281–312.

LeVen, P. A. 2014. *The Many-Headed Muse: Tradition and Innovation in Late Classical Greek Lyric Poetry.* Cambridge.

Levin, D. N. 1971. *Apollonius' "Argonautica" Re-examined: The Neglected First and Second Books.* Leiden.

Linsenbarth, O. 1887. *De Apollonii Rhodii casuum syntaxi comparato usu homerico.* Leipzig.

Lohmann, D. 1970. *Die Komposition der Reden in der Ilias.* Berlin.

———. 1998. *Kalypso bei Homer und James Joyce: Eine vergleichende Untersuchung des 1. und 5. Buches der Odyssee und der 4. Episode (Calypso) im Ulysses von J. Joyce.* Tübingen.

———. 2001. "Ροδοδάκτυλος Ἠώς: Typisches, Untypisches und Erotisches um den Sonnenaufgang." In *Proceedings of the 9th International Symposium on the "Odyssey"*, ed. M. Päisi-Apostolopoulou, 285–303. Ithaka.

Longman, T. 1991. *Fictional Akkadian Autobiography: A Generic and Comparative Study.* Winona Lake, IN.

Lonsdale, S. 1990. *Creatures of Speech: Lion, Herding, and Hunting Similes in the "Iliad".* Stuttgart.

———. 1995. "Homeric Hymn to Apollo: Prototype and Paradigm of Choral Performance." *Arion* 3:25–40.

Lord, A. B. 1986. "Perspectives on Recent Work on the Oral Traditional Formula." *Oral Tradition* 1:467–503.

———. 1991. *Epic Singers and Oral Tradition.* Ithaca, NY.

———. 1995. *The Singer Resumes the Tale.* Ed. M. L. Lord. Ithaca, NY.

———. [1960] 2000. *The Singer of Tales.* Ed. S. Mitchell and G. Nagy. Cambridge, MA.

Louden, B. 1999. *The "Odyssey": Structure, Narration, and Meaning.* Baltimore.

Ludwich, A. 1908. *Homerischer hymnenbau.* Leipzig.

Lupack, S. M. 2008. *The Role of the Religious Sector in the Economy of Late Bronze Age Mycenaean Greece.* Oxford.

Luppe, W. 1986. "Epikureische Mythenkritik bei Philodem—Götterliebschaften in *PHerc.* 243 II und III." *Cronache Ercolanesi* 14:109–24.

Lutgendorf, P. 1991. *The Life of a Text: Performing the Rāmcaritmānas of Tulsidas.* Berkeley.

Lynn-George, M. 1982. Review of J. Griffin, *Homer on Life and Death. Journal of Hellenic Studies* 102:239–45.

Lysaght, P. 1986. *The Banshee: The Irish Supernatural Death-Messenger.* Dublin.

Maas, M., and J. Snyder. 1989. *Stringed Instruments of Ancient Greece*. New Haven.

Maas, P. 1962. *Greek Metre*. Trans. Hugh Lloyd-Jones. Oxford.

Magnelli, E. 1995. "Le norme del secondo piede dell'esametro nei poeti ellenistici e il comportamento della 'parola metrica'." *Materiali e discussioni per l'analisi dei testi classici* 35:135–64.

Mahaffy, J. 1891. *A History of Classical Greek Literature*. 3rd ed. London.

Malkin, I. 1998. *The Returns of Odysseus: Colonization and Ethnicity*. Berkeley.

Marks, J. 2008. *Zeus in the "Odyssey"*. Hellenic Studies 31. Washington, DC.

Martin, B. K. 1992. "The Medieval Irish Stories About Bricriu's Feast and Mac Datho's Pig." *Parergon* 10:171–93.

Martin, R. P. 1983. *Healing, Sacrifice and Battle: Amechania and Related Concepts in Early Greek Poetry*. Innsbruck.

———. 1984a. "Hesiod, Odysseus, and the Instruction of Princes." *Transactions of the American Philological Association* 114:29–48.

———. 1984b. "The Oral Tradition." In *Critical Survey of Poetry*, ed. F. Magill, 1746–68. La Canada, CA. Reprinted with update in R. Reisman, ed. 2011. *Critical Survey of Poetry*, 4th ed. Vol. 1, 214–31. Pasadena, CA.

———. 1989. *The Language of Heroes: Speech and Performance in the "Iliad"*. Ithaca, NY.

———. 1992a. "Hesiod's Metanastic Poetics." *Ramus* 21:11–33.

———. 1992b. Review of T. Reucher, *Der unbekannte Odysseus*. *The Classical World* 86:151–52.

———. 1993. "Telemachus and the Last Hero Song." *Colby Quarterly* 29:222–40.

———. 1997a. "Formulas and Speeches." In *Hommage à Milman Parry. Le style formulaire de l' épopée homérique et la théorie de l'oralité poétique*, ed. F. Létoublon, 263–74. Amsterdam.

———. 1997b. "Similes and Performance." In *Written Voices, Spoken Signs: Tradition, Performance, and the Epic Text*, ed. E. Bakker and A. Kahane, 138–66. Cambridge, MA.

———. 2000a. "Wrapping Homer Up: Cohesion, Discourse, and Deviation in the *Iliad*." In Sharrock and Morales 2000, 43–65.

———. 2000b. "Synchronic Aspects of Homeric Performance: The Evidence of *The Hymn to Apollo*." In *Una nueva visión de la cultura griega antigua hacia el fin del milenio*, ed. A. González de Tobia, 403–32. La Plata.

———. 2001a. "Rhapsodizing Orpheus." *Kernos* 14:23–33.

———. 2001b. "Just Like a Woman." In *Making Silence Speak: Women's Voices in Greek Literature and Society*, ed. A. Lardinois and L. McClure, 55–74. Princeton.

———. 2003a. "Keens from the Absent Chorus: Troy to Ulster." *Western Folklore* 62:119–42.

———. 2003b. "The Pipes are Brawling: Conceptualizing Musical Performance in Classical Athens." In *The Cultures within Greek Culture*, ed. L. Kurke and C. Dougherty, 153–80. Cambridge.

———. 2004. "Hesiod and the Didactic Double." *Synthesis* 11:31–53.

———. 2005a. "Epic as Genre." In J. M. Foley 2005, 9–19.

———. 2005b. "Pulp Epic: The Catalogue and the Shield." In Hunter 2005, 153–75.

———. 2008. "Myth, Performance, Poetics—The Gaze from Classics." In *Ethnographica Moralia: Experiments in Interpretive Anthropology*, ed. N. Panourgia and G. Marcus, 45–52. New York.

———. 2009. "Read on Arrival." In *The Wandering Poets of Ancient Greece: Travel, Locality and Pan-Hellenism*, ed. R. Hunter and I. Rutherford, 80–104. Cambridge.

———. 2010. "Apolo ejecutante." In *Mito y performance*, ed. A. González de Tobia, 17–41. La Plata.

———. 2011. "Poseidon's Crash Test and Apollo's Cithara." http://athensdialogues.chs.harvard.edu/cgi-bin/WebObjects/athensdialogues.woa/wa/dis?dis=39

Martin, R. 2012. "The Senses of an Ending: Myth, Ritual, and Poetic Exodia in Performance." In *Donum natalicium digitaliter confectum Gregorio Nagy septuagenario a discipulis collegis familiaribus oblatum*. http://nrs.harvard.edu/urn-3:hul.ebook:CHS_Bers_etal_eds.Donum_Natalicium_Gregorio_Nagy.2012.

———. 2013. "The 'Myth Before the Myth Began'." In *Writing Down the Myths*, ed. J. Nagy, 45–66. Cursor Mundi 17. Turnhout.

———. 2015. "Festivals, Symposia, and the Performance of Greek Poetry." In *A Companion to Ancient Aesthetics*, ed. P. Destrée and P. Murray, 17–29.

———. 2017. "Crooked Competition: The Performance and Poetics of Skolia." In *Authorship and Greek Song: Authority, Authenticity, and Performance*, ed. E. Bakker, 61–79. Studies in Archaic and Classical Greek Song 3. Leiden.

Marxer, G. 1935. *Die Sprache des Apollonios Rhodios in ihren Beziehungen zu Homer*. Zürich.

Matone, C. 1999. *The Heart on the Sleeve. Image and Emotion in the "Argonautica"*. Ph.D. diss., Columbia University.

———. 1977. "Naupaktia and Argonautika." *Phoenix* 31:189–207.

Matthews, V. J. 1996. *Antimachus of Colophon: Text and Commentary*. Leiden.

———. 1974. *Panyassis of Halikarnassos: Text and Commentary*. Leiden.

Maurizio, L. 1997. "Delphic Oracles As Oral Performances: Authenticity and Historical Evidence." *Classical Antiquity* 16:308–34.

———. 2001. "The Voice at the Centre of the World: The Pythia's Ambiguity and Authority." In *Making Silence Speak*, ed. A. Lardinois and L. McClure, 38–54. Princeton.

Mawet, F. 1975. "Epigrammes, thrènes et dithyrambes: les lamentations funèbres de l'épopée." In *Le Monde grec: Hommages à Claire Preaux*, ed. J. Bingen et al., 33–44. Brussels.

Mazon, P., ed. 1928. *Hésiode: Théogonie, Les travaux et les jours, le Bouclier*. Paris.

———. 1937. *Homère, Iliade*. Vol. 2. Paris.

McCone, K. 1984. "Aided Cheltchair Maic Uthechair: Hounds, Heroes, and Hospitallers in Early Irish Myth and Story." *Ériu* 35:1–30.

McGee, M. 1988. *Roger Corman: The Best of the Cheap Acts*. Jefferson, NC.

McLane, M. N., and L. M. Slatkin. 2011. "British Romantic Homer: Oral Tradition, 'Primitive Poetry' and the Emergence of Comparative Poetics in Britain, 1760–1830." *English Literary History* 78:687–714.

McLennan, G. 1973. "The Employment of the Infinitive in Apollonius Rhodius." *Quaderni Urbinati di Cultura Classica* 15:44–72.

McLeod, W. 1961. "Oral Bards at Delphi." *Transactions of the American Philological Association* 92:317–25.

Meillet, A. [1930] 1966. "Michel Bréal et la grammaire comparée au Collège de France." In *Portraits of Linguists: A Biographical Source Book for the History of Western Linguistics 1746–1963*, ed. T. Sebeok, vol. 1, 440–53. Bloomington, IN.

Melia, D. F. 1979. "Some Remarks on the Affinities of Medieval Irish Saga." *Acta Antiqua Hungarica* 27:255-61.

Mendik, X., and G. Harper. 2000. *Unruly Pleasures: The Cult Film and its Critics*. Guildford, Surrey.

Merkelbach, R., and M. L. West. 1965. "The Wedding of Ceyx." *Rheinisches Museum* 108:300–17.

Meyer, K., ed. 1894. *Hibernica Minora*. Anecdota Oxoniensia, Medieval and Modern Series. Vol. 3, part 8. Oxford.

———. 1913. *Über die älteste irische Dichtung, ii.* Abhandlungen der Königlich Preussischen Akademie der Wissenschaften. Philosophisch-historische Classe 10. Berlin.

Meyerhoff, D. 1984. *Traditioneller Stoff und individuelle Gestaltung.* Hildesheim

Michel, C. 2008. "Hermes in der *Odyssee.*" *Würzburger Jahrbücher für die Altertumwissenschaft* 32:11–34.

Miller, A. 1986. *From Delos to Delphi: A Literary Study of the Homeric Hymn to Apollo.* Leiden.

Mills, M. 1990. *Oral Narrative in Afghanistan: The Individual in Tradition.* New York.

Minchin, E. 1991. "Speaker and Listener, Text and Context: Some Notes on the Encounter of Nestor and Patroklos in *Iliad* 11." *Classical World* 84: 273–85.

———. 1992. "Scripts and Themes: Cognitive research and the Homeric Epic." *Classical Antiquity* 11:229–41.

———. 2007. *Homeric Voices: Discourse, Memory, Gender.* Oxford.

Minton, W. 1975. "The Frequency and Structuring of Traditional Formulas in Hesiod's *Theogony.*" *Harvard Studies in Classical Philology* 79: 25–54.

Mondi, R. J. 1978. *The Function and Social Position of the Kêrux in Early Greece.* Ph.D. diss., Harvard University.

———. 1980. "Skeptoukhoi Basileis: An Argument for Divine Kingship in Early Greece." *Arethusa* 13:203–16.

Monsacré, Hélène. 2018. *The Tears of Achilles.* Trans. Nicholas J. Snead. Introduction by Richard P. Martin. Hellenic Studies 75. Washington, DC.

Montanari, F. 2012. "The Peripatos on Literature. Interpretation, Use and Abuse." In *Praxiphanes of Mytilene and Chamaeleon of Heraclea. Texts, Translation and Discussion,* ed. A. Martano et al., 339–58. New Brunswick, NJ.

Montbrun, P. 2001. "Apollon: de l'arc à la lyre." In *Chanter les dieux,* ed. P. Brulé and C. Vendries, 59–96. Rennes.

Mooney, G. 1912. *The Argonautica of Apollonius Rhodius.* Dublin.

Moreau, A. 2000. "Petit guide à l'usage des apprentis sorciers." In *La Magie I. Actes du colloque international de Montpellier, 25—27 mars 1999,* ed. A. Moreau and J.-C. Turpin, 5–39. Montpellier.

Morgan, G. 1973. "The Laments of Mani." *Folklore* 84:265–98.

Mori, A. 2001. "Personal Favor and Public Influence: Arete, Arsinoë II, and the *Argonautica.*" *Oral Tradition* 16:85–106.

Morrell, K. 1996. "Chaos Theory and the Oral Tradition: Nonlinearity and Bifurcation in the *Iliad*." *Helios* 23:107–34.

Morris, I. 1986. "The Use and Abuse of Homer." *Classical Antiquity* 5:81–138.

Morris, I., and B. Powell, eds. 1997. *A New Companion to Homer*. Leiden.

Morrison, A. 2007. *The Narrator in Archaic Greek and Hellenistic Poetry*. Cambridge.

Morrison, J. V. 1992. *Homeric Misdirection: False Predictions in the "Iliad"*. Ann Arbor.

Most, G. W. 2006. *Hesiod I: Theogony, Works and Days, Testimonia*. Cambridge, MA.

———. 2007. *Hesiod II: The Shield, Catalogue of Women, Other Fragments*. Cambridge, MA.

Motsios, I. 1995. *To Elliniko moirologi*. Athens.

Moulton, C. 1977. *Similes in the Homeric Poems*. Göttingen.

Moyle, N. 1990. *The Turkish Minstrel Tale Tradition*. New York.

Muellner, L. 1976. *The Meaning of Homeric* Eukhomai *through its Formulas*. Innsbruck.

———. 1996. *The Anger of Achilles: Mênis in Early Greek Epic*. Ithaca, NY.

Mühlestein, H. 1981. "Der homerische Phoinix und sein Name." *Živa Antika* 31:85–91.

Mureddu, P. 1983. *Formula e tradizione nella poesia di Esiodo*. Rome.

Murnaghan, S. 1987. *Disguise and Recognition in the "Odyssey"*. Princeton.

Murphy, G., ed. and trans. 1998. *Early Irish Lyrics: Eighth to Twelfth Century*. Reprint ed. with new foreword by T. Ó Cathasaigh. Dublin.

Murray, A. T., and Dimock, G. 1995. *Homer. The Odyssey*. Vol. 1 and 2. 2d ed. Cambridge, MA.

Murray, A. T., and W. Wyatt. 1999. *Homer. The Iliad*. Vol. 1 and 2. 2d ed. Cambridge, MA.

Murray, G. [1934] 1960. *The Rise of the Greek Epic*. 4th ed. New York.

Myres, J. L. 1941. "Hesiod's Shield of Herakles: its Structure and Workmanship." *Journal of Hellenic Studies* 61:17–38.

Myres, J. L. 1958. *Homer and His Critics*. Ed. D. Gray. London.

Nagler, M. 1974. *Spontaneity and Tradition: A Study in the Oral Art of Homer*. Berkeley.

———. 1990. "Odysseus: The Proem and the Problem." *Classical Antiquity* 9:335–56.

Nagy, G. 1974. *Comparative Studies in Greek and Indic Meter*. Cambridge, MA.

———. 1982a. "Theognis of Megara: The Poet as Seer, Pilot, and Revenant." *Arethusa* 15:109–28.

———. 1982b. "Hesiod." In *Ancient Writers*, ed. T. J. Luce. Vol. 1, 43–74. New York.

———. 1983. "Sêma and Noêsis: Some Illustrations." *Arethusa* 16:35–55.

———. 1985. "Theognis and Megara: A Poet's Vision of His City." In *Theognis of Megara: Poetry and the Polis*, ed. G. Nagy and T. Figueira. Baltimore.

———. 1988. Review of D. Shive, *Naming Achilles. Phoenix* 42:364–66.

———. 1989. "Early Greek Views of Poets and Poetry." In *The Cambridge History of Literary Criticism*. Vol. 1, *Classical Criticism*, ed. G. Kennedy, 1–77. Cambridge.

———. 1990. *Pindar's Homer: The Lyric Possession of an Epic Past*. Baltimore.

———. [1990] 1992. "Hesiod and the Poetics of Pan-Hellenism." In *Greek Mythology and Poetics*, 36–82. Ithaca, NY.

———. 1995. "Transformations of Choral Lyric Traditions in the Context of Athenian State Theater." *Arion* 3:41–55.

———. 1996a. *Poetry as Performance: Homer and Beyond*. Cambridge.

———. 1996b. *Homeric Questions*. Austin.

———. 1998. "Aristarchean Questions." *Bryn Mawr Classical Review* 98.7.14.

———. 1999a. "Epic as Genre." In M. Beissinger et al., 21–32.

———. [1979] 1999b. *The Best of the Achaeans*. 2d ed. Baltimore.

———. 2001. "Eléments orphiques chez Homère." *Kernos* 14:1–9.

———. 2002. *Plato's Rhapsody and Homer's Music*. Hellenic Studies 1. Washington, DC.

———. 2004. *Homer's Text and Language*. Urbana, IL.

———. 2009. *Homer the Classic*. Cambridge, MA.

———. 2010. *Homer the Preclassic*. Berkeley.

———. 2014. Review of M. Skafte Jensen, *Writing Homer. Gnomon* 86:97–101.

Nagy, J. 1990. "Hierarchy, Heroes and Heads." In *Approaches to Greek Myth*, ed. L. Edmunds, 199–238. Baltimore.

Natalucci, N. 1996. "Il problema dei 'plusverse' e il P.Sorb.2245." *Bollettino dei Classici* 17:101–115.

———. 2000. "*P. Berol.* 9774: lo scudo di Achille e lo scudo di Eracle." In *Poesia e religione in Grecia*, ed. M. Cannatà Fera and S. Grandolini, 487–97. Naples.

Neils, J., ed. 1992. *Goddess and Polis: The Panathenaic Festival in Classical Athens*. Princeton.

———. 1995. "Les Femmes Fatales: Skylla and the Sirens in Greek Art." In *The Distaff Side*, ed. B. Cohen, 175–84. Oxford.

Neitzel, H. 1977. "Zum zeitlichen Verhältnis von *Theogonie* (80–93) und *Odyssee* (8, 166–77)." *Philologus* 121:24–44.

Nelis, D. 1992. "Demodocus and the Song of Orpheus." *Museum Helveticum* 49:153–70.

Newman, J. 1993. "Epic." In *The New Princeton Encyclopedia of Poetry and Poetics*, ed. A. Preminger and T. Brogan, 361–75. Princeton.

Nietzsche, F. 1870–1873. "Die Florentinische Tractat über Homer und Hesiod, ihr Geschlecht und ihren Wettkampf." *Rheinisches Museum für Philologie* 25:528–40 and 28:211–49.

Nimis, S. 1987. *Narrative Semiotics in the Epic Tradition: The Simile.* Bloomington, IN.

Notopoulos, J. 1949. "Parataxis in Homer: A New Approach to Homeric Literary Criticism." *Transactions of the American Philological Association* 80:1–23.

———. 1962. "The Homeric Hymns as Oral Poetry: A Study of the Post–Homeric Oral Tradition." *American Journal of Philology* 83:337–68.

Ó Buachalla, B. 1998. *An Caoine agus an Chaointeoireacht.* Dublin.

Ó hÓgáin, D. 1991. *Myth, Legend & Romance: An Encyclopedia of the Irish Folk Tradition.* New York.

Ó Súilleabháin, S. 1967. *Irish Folk Custom and Belief.* Dublin.

Ó Tuama, S., ed. 1961. *Caoineadh Airt Uí Laoghaire.* Dublin.

Ó Tuama, S., and T. Kinsella, ed. and trans. 1981. *An Duanaire, 1600–1900: Poems of the Dispossessed.* Mountrath, Portlaoise.

O'Curry, E. 1873. *On the Manners and Customs of the Ancient Irish.* Vol. 3. Ed. W. Sullivan. London.

O'Neill, E., Jr. 1942. "The Localization of Metrical Word-Types in the Greek Hexameter: Homer, Hesiod and the Alexandrians." *Yale Classical Studies* 8:102–76.

O'Sullivan, N. 1992. *Alcidamas, Aristophanes, and the Beginnings of Greek Stylistic Theory.* Stuttgart.

Obbink, D. 2004. "Vergil's *De pietate*: From Ehoiai to Allegory in Vergil, Philodemus and Ovid." In *Vergil, Philodemus, and the Augustans*, ed. D. Armstrong, J. Fish, P. A. Johnston, M. Skinner, 175–209. Austin.

Ober, J. 1989. *Mass and Elite in Democratic Athens.* Princeton.

Oinas, F., ed. 1978. *Heroic Epic and Saga.* Bloomington, IN.

Okpewho, I. 1992. *African Oral Literature: Backgrounds, Character, and Continuity.* Bloomington, IN.

Osborne, R. 2005. "Ordering Women in Hesiod's Catalogue." In Hunter 2005, 5–24.

Otto, B.-C. 2011. *Magie: Rezeptions- und Diskursgeschichtliche Analysen von der Antike bis zur Neuzeit*. Berlin.

Page, D. 1955a. *Sappho and Alcaeus*. Oxford.

———. 1955b. *The Homeric "Odyssey"*. Oxford.

———. 1959. *History and the Homeric "Iliad"*. Berkeley.

Paley, F. A. 1883. *The Epics of Hesiod*. London.

Panourgia, E. Neni. 1995. *Fragments of Death, Fables of Identity: An Athenian Anthropography*. Madison, WI.

Pantelia, M. C. 2002. "Helen and the Last Song for Hector." *Transactions of the American Philological Association* 132:21–27.

Papanghelis, T., and A. Rengakos, eds. 2008. *Brill's Companion to Apollonius Rhodius*. 2nd rev. ed. Leiden.

Parker, R. 1985. "Greek States and Greek Oracles." In *CRUX: Essays presented to G. E. M. de Ste. Croix*, ed. P. Cartledge and F. Harvey, 298–326. Exeter.

Parry, M. 1930. "Studies in the Epic Technique of Oral Verse-Making. I. Homer and Homeric Style." *Harvard Studies in Classical Philology* 41:73–147.

———. 1971. *The Making of Homeric Verse: The Collected Papers of Milman Parry*. Ed. A. Parry. Oxford.

Partridge, A. 1980. "Wild Men and Wailing Women." *Éigse* 18:25–37.

Paton, W. R. 1917. *The Greek Anthology. Volume III, Book 9: The Declamatory Epigrams*. Cambridge, MA.

Patzer, H. 1991. "Die Reise des Telemach." *Illinois Classical Studies* 16:18–35.

Paulson, J. 1887. *Studia Hesiodea I: De re metrica*. Lund.

Pavese, C. O. 1972. *Tradizioni e generi poetici della grecia arcaica*. Rome.

———. 1979. *La lirica corale greca*. Rome.

Pavlou, M. 2010. "Pindar *Olympian* 3: Mapping Acragas on the Periphery of the Earth." *Classical Quarterly* 60:313–326.

Peabody, B. 1975. *The Winged Word*. Albany, NY.

Pedrick, V. 1983. "The Paradigmatic Nature of Nestor's Speech in *Iliad* 11." *Transactions of the American Philological Association* 113:55–68.

———. 1992. "The Muse Corrects: The Opening of the *Odyssey*." *Yale Classical Studies* 29:39–62.

Peersman, J. 1993. "Plisthene et sa famille dans les genealogies de la tradition hesiodique." *L'Antiquité Classique* 62:203–212.

Pellizer, E. 1972a. "Metremi proverbiali nelle 'Opere e i giorni' di Esiodo." *Quaderni Urbinati di cultura classica* 13:24–37.

———. 1972b. "Modelli compositivi e 'topoi' sapienziali nelle 'Opere e i giorni' di Esiodo." In *Studi Omerici e Esiodei* 1:38–42.

Peponi, A.-E. 1995. "Lirikes tropes tis epikis Elenis." In *EUXHN ODUSSEI*, ed. M. Päisi-Apostolopoulo, 315–28. Ithaka.

———. 2009. "*Choreia* and Aesthetics in the *Homeric Hymn to Apollo*: The Performance of the Delian Maidens (lines 156–64)." *Classical Antiquity* 28:39–70.

———. 2012. *Frontiers of Pleasure: Models of Aesthetic Response in Archaic and Classical Greek Thought.* Oxford.

Peradotto, J. 1990. *Man in the Middle Voice: Name and Narration in the Odyssey.* Princeton.

Perceau, S. 2002. *La parole vive: Communiquer en catalogue dans l'épopée homérique.* Leuven.

Petropoulos, J. C. B. 1994. *Heat and Lust: Hesiod's Midsummer Festival Scene Revisited.* Lanham, MD.

———. 2011. *Kleos in a Minor Key: The Homeric Education of a Little Prince.* Hellenic Studies 45. Washington, DC.

Pettersson, M. 1992. *Cults of Apollo at Sparta. The Hyakinthia, the Gymnopaidiai and the Karneia.* Stockholm.

Pfeiffer, R. 1937. "Hesiodisches und Homerisches." *Philologus* 92:1–18.

———. 1968. *History of Classical Scholarship: From the Beginnings to the End of the Hellenistic Age.* Oxford.

Pfister, F. 1928. "Die Hekate-Episode in Hesiods Theogonie." *Philologus* 84:1–9.

Phillips, N. 1981. *Sijobang: Sung Narrative Poetry of West Sumatra.* Cambridge.

Picot, J.-C. 1998. "Sur un emprunt d'Empédocle au Bouclier hesiodique." *Revue des études Grecques* 111:42–60.

Pirenne-Delforge, V. 2008. *Retour à la source. Pausanias et la religion grecque.* Liège.

Poltoratzky, M. 1964. *Russian Folklore.* New York.

Porter, J. 1992. "Hermeneutic Lines and Circles: Aristarchus and Crates on the Exegesis of Homer." In *Homer's Ancient Readers*, ed. R. Lamberton and J. Keaney, 67–114. Princeton.

Powell, B. 1991. *Homer and the Origin of the Greek Alphabet.* Cambridge.

Powell, J. U., ed. 1925. *Collectanea Alexandrina.* Oxford.

Power, T. 2010. *The Culture of Kitharôidia.* Hellenic Studies 15. Washington, DC.

Prince, G. 1987. *Dictionary of Narratology.* Lincoln, NE.

Propp, V. 1958. *Morphology of the Folktale.* Bloomington, IN.

Pucci, P. 1977. *Hesiod and the Language of Poetry*. Baltimore.

———. 1987. *Odysseus Polutropos: Intertextual Readings in the "Odyssey" and the "Iliad"*. Ithaca, NY.

———. 1998. *The Song of the Sirens: Essays on Homer*. Lanham, MD.

Puelma, M. 1972. "Sänger und König: Zum Verständnis von Hesiods Tierfabel." *Museum Helveticum* 29:86–109.

Pugliese Carratelli, G., ed. 2001. *Le lamine d'oro orfiche*. Milan.

Purves, A. 2011. "Homer and the Art of Overtaking." *American Journal of Philology* 132:523–51.

Race, W. H. 1982. *The Classical Priamel from Homer to Boethius*. Leiden.

———, trans. 1997. *Pindar. Olympian Odes, Pythian Odes*. Cambridge, MA.

———. 2009. *Apollonius Rhodius. Argonautica*. Cambridge, MA.

Raible, W. 1980. "Was sind Gattungen? Eine Antwort aus semiotischer und textlinguistischer Sicht." *Poetica* 12:320–49.

Ranke, C. F., ed. 1840. *Hesiodi quod fertur Scutum Herculis*. Ex recognitione et cum animadversionibus Fr. Aug. Wolfii. Quedlinburg.

Ready, J. L. 2011. *Character, Narrator, and Simile in the "Iliad"*. Cambridge.

Redondo, J. 2000. "Non-Epic Features in the Language of Apollonius Rhodius." In M. A. Harder et al., 129–54.

Rehm, R. 1994. *Marriage to Death: The Conflation of Wedding and Funeral Rituals in Greek Tragedy*. Princeton.

Reichel, M. 1994. *Fernbeziehungen in der Ilias*. Tübingen.

Reichl, K. 1992. *Turkic Oral Epic Poetry*. New York.

Reitz, C. 1996. *Zur Gleichnistechnik des Apollonios von Rhodos*. Frankfurt am Main.

Reitzammer, L. 2016. *The Athenian Adonia in Context: The Adonis Festival as Cultural Practice*. Madison.

Rengakos, A. 1994. *Apollonios Rhodios und die antike Homererklärung*. Munich.

———. 2008. "Apollonius Rhodius as a Homeric Scholar." In T. Papanghelis and A. Rengakos, 243–66.

Reucher, T. 1989. *Der unbekannte Odysseus: Eine Interpretation der Odyssee*. Bern.

Revermann, M. 1998. "The Text of *Iliad* 18.603–6 and the Presence of an *aoidos* on the Shield of Achilles." *Classical Quarterly* 48:29–38.

Reynolds, D. 1989. "Tradition Replacing Tradition in Egyptian Epic Singing: The Creation of a Commerical Image." *Pacific Review of Ethnomusicology* 5:1–14.

———. 1995. *Heroic Poets, Poetic Heroes: The Ethnography of Performance in an Arabic Oral Epic Tradition*. Ithaca, NY.

———. 1999. "Problematic Performances: Overlapping Genres and Levels of Participation in Arabic Oral Epic-Singing." In Beissinger et al., 155–68.

Richardson, N. J. 1980. "Literary Criticism in the Exegetical Scholia to the *Iliad*: A Sketch." *Classical Quarterly* 30:265–287.

———. 1981. "The Contest of Homer and Hesiod and Alcidamas' Mouseion." *Classical Quarterly* 31:1–10.

———. 1992. "Aristotle's Reading of Homer and Its Background." In *Homer's Ancient Readers*, ed. R. Lamberton and J. Keaney, 30–40. Princeton.

———. 1993. *The Iliad: A Commentary*. Vol. 6. Cambridge.

———. 2010. *Three Homeric Hymns: To Apollo, Hermes, and Aphrodite*. Cambridge.

Riedweg, C. 1998. "Initiation-Tod-Unterwelt." In *Ansichten griechischer Rituale*, ed. F. Graf, 359–98. Stuttgart.

———. 2002. *Pythagoras. His Life, Teaching, and Influence*. Trans. S. Rendall. Ithaca, NY.

Risch, E. 1974. *Wortbildung der homerischen Sprache*. 2nd ed. Berlin.

Rosen, R. M. 1990. "Poetry and Sailing in Hesiod's *Works and Days*." *Classical Antiquity* 9: 99–113.

———. 1988. *Old Comedy and the Iambographic Tradition*. Atlanta.

Rosenmeyer, T. 1992. "Apollonius Lyricus." *Studi italiani di filologia classica* 10:177–98.

Rousseau, P. 1992. "Fragments d'un commentaire antique du récit de la course des chars dans le XXIIIème chant de l'*Iliade*." *Philologus* 136:158–80.

———. 2001. "Rewriting Homer: Remarks on the Narrative of the Chariot Race in Sophocles' Electra." In *Antiquities: Post-War French Thought*, ed. N. Loraux, G. Nagy, and L. M. Slatkin, 395–405. New York.

———. 2010. "L'oubli de la borne (*Iliade* XXIII, 262–652)." In *La philologie au présent: pour Jean Bollack*, ed. C. Koenig and D. Thouard, 27–56. Villeneuve-d'Ascq.

Ruhnken, D. 1782. *Epistola critica I. In Homeridarum Hymnos et Hesiodum ad virum clarissimum L. C. Valckenarium*. 2nd ed. Leiden.

Russo, J. 1966. "The Structural Formula in Homeric Verse." *Yale Classical Studies* 20:219–40.

——— 1983. "The Poetics of the Ancient Greek Proverb." *Journal of Folklore Research* 20:121–30.

———. 1987. "Oral Style as Performance Style in Homer's *Odyssey*: Should We Read Homer Differently after Parry?" In *Comparative Research on Oral Traditions: A Memorial for Milman Parry*, ed. J. M. Foley, 549–65. Columbus, OH.

———. 1993. "Formulaic Repetition and Narrative Innovation: *Odyssey* 19.440–443, the Boar in the Bush." In *Tradizione e Innovazione nella Cultura Greca da Omero all'Età Ellenistica*, ed. R. Pretagostini, 51–59. Rome.

———. 2000. "Athena and Hermes in Early Greek Poetry: Doubling and Complementarity." In *Poesia e religione in Grecia: Studi in onore di G. Aurelio Privitera*, vol 2, ed. M. Cannatà Fera and S. Grandolini, 595–603. Naples.

Russo, J., et al., eds. 1992. *Commentary on Homer's "Odyssey"*. Vol. 3. Oxford.

Rutherford, I. 2000. "Formulas, Voice, and Death in *Ehoie*–Poetry: The Hesiodic *Gunaikon Katalogos* and the Odysseian *Nekuia*." In *Matrices of Genre: Authors, Canons, and Society*, ed. M. Depew and D. Obbink, 81–96. Cambridge, MA.

———. 2012. "The Catalogue of Women within the Greek Epic Tradition: Allusion, Intertextuality and Traditional Referentiality." In *Relative Chronology in Early Greek Epic Poetry*, ed. O. Andersen and D. Haag, 152–67. Cambridge.

Rutherford, W. G., ed. 1896. *Scholia Aristophanica*. London.

Rzach, A. 1878. *Grammatische Studien zu Apollonios Rhodios*. Vienna.

———. 1882. "Neue Beiträge zur Technik des nachhomerischen Hexameters." *Sitzungsberichte Wien* 100: 307–432.

Sacks, R. 1987. *The Traditional Phrase in Homer*. Leiden.

Sale, W. M. 1996. "In Defense of Milman Parry: Renewing the Oral Theory." *Oral Tradition* 11:374–417.

Salis, T. 1996. *Lexiko Mykênaikon Tekhnikôn Orôn*. Athens.

Sammons, B. 2010. *The Art and Rhetoric of the Homeric Catalogue*. New York.

Sayers, W. 1982. "Conall's Welcome to Cet in the Old Irish *Scéla Mucce Meic Dathó*." *Florilegium* 4:100–8.

———. 1991. "Serial Defamation in Two Medieval Tales: The Icelandic *Ölkofra Þáttr* and the Irish *Scéla Mucce Meic Dathó*." *Oral Tradition* 6:35–57.

Sbardella, L. 2012. *Cucitori di canti: studi sulla tradizione epico-rapsodica greca ei suoi itinerari nel VI secolo aC*. Rome.

Schachter, A. 1986. *Cults of Boiotia*. Vol. 2, *Herakles to Poseidon*. Bulletin of the Institute of Classical Studies Supplement 38.2. London.

Schadewaldt, W. 1966. *Iliasstudien*. 3rd ed. Darmstadt.

Schaefer, E. 1999. *Bold! Daring! Shocking! True!: A History of Exploitation Films, 1919–1959*. Durham, NC.

Schein, S. 1997. "The *Iliad*: Structure and Interpretation." In Morris and Powell 1997, 345–59.

Scheinberg, S. 1979. "The Bee Maidens of the *Homeric Hymn to Hermes*." *Harvard Studies in Classical Philology* 83:16–23.

Scherer, B. 2006. *Mythos, Katalog und Prophezeiung. Studien zu den Argonautika des Apollonios*. Stuttgart.

Scheub, H. 1975. *The Xhosa Ntsomi*. Oxford.

Schiesaro, A., P. Mitsis, and J. S. Clay, eds. 1993. *Mega Nepios: Il destinatario nell'epos didascalico*. Biblioteca di Materiali e discusioni per l'analisi dei testi classici 31. Pisa.

Schlerath, B. 1960. *Das Königtum im Rig- und Atharvaveda*. Wiesbaden.

Schmidt, J.-U. 1986. *Adressat und Paraineseform. Zur intention von Hesiods Werken und Tagen*. Hypomnemata 86. Göttingen.

Schmitt, R. 1967. *Dichtung und Dichtersprache in Indo-germanischer Zeit*. Wiesbaden.

Schnapp-Gourbeillon, A. 1982 "Le lion et le loup: Diomédie et Dolonie dans *l'Iliade*." *Quaderni di Storia* 15:45–77.

Schroeder, C. M. 2009. "Zenodotus' Text of Hesiod." *Classical Quarterly* 59:271–74.

Schuler, R., and J. Fitch. 1983. "Theory and Context of the Didactic Poem: Some Classical, Medieval and Later Continuities." *Florilegium* 5:1–43.

Schwabe, E. 1890. *Aelii Dionysii et Pausaniae Atticistarum Fragmenta*. Leipzig.

Schwartz, J. 1960. *Pseudo-Hesiodea*. Leiden.

Scott, W. 1974. *The Oral Nature of the Homeric Simile*. Leiden.

———. 2012. *The Artistry of the Homeric Simile*. Hanover, NH.

Seaton, R. 1890. "On the Imitation of Homer by Apollonius Rhodius." *Journal of Philology* 19:1–13.

Segal, C. 1968. "Circean Temptations: Homer, Vergil, Ovid." *Transactions of the American Philological Association* 99:419–42.

———. 1971. *The Theme of the Mutilation of the Corpse in the "Iliad"*. Leiden.

———. 1994. *Singers, Heroes, and Gods in the "Odyssey"*. Ithaca, NY.

Seremetakis, N. 1991. *The Last Word: Women, Death, and Divination in Inner Mani*. Chicago.

Severyns, A. 1928. *Le Cycle epique dans l'ecole d'Aristarque*. Liège.

Sfyroeras, P. 2003. "Olive Trees, North Wind, and Time: A Symbol in Pindar, Olympian 3." *Mouseion* 3:313–24.

Shapiro, H. A. 1992. "Mousikoi Agones: Music and Poetry at the Panathenaia." In *Goddess and Polis. The Panatheniac Festival in Ancient Athens*, ed. J. Neils, 53–75. Princeton.

Sharrock, A., and H. Morales, eds. 2000. *Intratextuality: Greek and Roman Textual Relations*. Oxford.

Shelmerdine, C. 2008. "Mycenaean Society." In *A Companion to Linear B*, ed. Y. Duhoux and A. Morpurgo Davies, 115–58. Louvain-la-neuve.

Shelmerdine, S. 1995. *The Homeric Hymns*. Newburyport, MA.

Shipley, W. 1991. "In the Beginning of the World." In *The Maidu Indian Myths and Stories of Hanc'ibyjim*, ed. W. Shipley, 18–43. Berkeley.

Shipp, G. P. 1972. *Studies in the Language of Homer*. 2nd ed. Cambridge.

Shive, D. 1987. *Naming Achilles*. Oxford.

Sicking, C. 1993. *Griechische Verslehre*. With M. van Raalte. Handbuch der Altertumswissenschaft, 2. Abt., 4. Teil. Munich.

Sinos, D. 1980. *Achilles, Patroklos, and the Meaning of Philos*. Innsbruck.

Sistakou, E. 2001. "Paradosê kai neoterikotêta ston katalogo tôn Argonautôn (Apoll. Rhod. *Arg.* 1.23–233)." *Hellenika* 51:231–64.

———. 2007. "Cyclic Stories? The Reception of the *Cypria* in Hellenistic Poetry." *Philologus*. 151:78–94.

Skafte Jensen, M. 1980. *The Homeric Question and the Oral-Formulaic Theory*. Copenhagen.

———. 1994. "Homer's Portrayal of Women: A Discussion of Homeric Narrative from an Oralist Point of View." In *Contexts of Pre-novel Narrative: The European Tradition*, ed. R. Eriksen, 27–44. Berlin.

———, ed. 1999. "Dividing Homer: When and How were the *Iliad* and *Odyssey* Divided into Songs?" *Symbolae Osloenses* 74:5–91.

Skempis, M., and I. Ziogas. 2009. "Arete's Words: Etymology, Ehoie-Poetry and Gendered Narrative." In *Narratology and Interpretation: The Content of Form in Ancient Narrative Literature*, ed. J. Grethlein and A. Rengakos, 213–40. Berlin.

Skopetea, S. 1972. *Ta maniatika moirologia*. Athens.

Slater, W. 1983. "Lyric Narrative." *Classical Antiquity* 2:117–132.

Slatkin, L. M. 2011. *The Power of Thetis and Selected Essays*. Hellenic Studies 16. Washington, DC.

Slyomovics, S. 1987. *The Merchant of Art: An Egyptian Hilali Oral Epic Poet in Performance*. Berkeley.

Smith, R. 1928. "The *Senbriathra Fithail* and Related Texts." *Revue Celtique* 45:1–92.

Sokolov, Y. 1950. *Russian Folklore*. Trans. C. Smith. New York.

Solmsen, F. 1954. "The 'Gift' of Speech in Homer and Hesiod." *Transactions of the American Philological Association* 85:1–15.

———. 1982. "The Earliest Stages in the History of Hesiod's Text." *Harvard Studies in Classical Philology* 86:1–31.

———. 1983. *Hesiodi Theogonia, Opera et Dies, Scutum.* 2nd ed. Oxford.

Solomon, J. 1985. "In Defense of Hesiod's *Schlechtestem* Hexameter." *Hermes* 113:21–30.

Spanoudakis, K. 2002. *Philitas of Cos.* Leiden.

Stanford, W. B. 1959. *The Odyssey of Homer.* 2 vols. Edinburgh.

Stanley, K. 1993. *The Shield of Homer: Narrative Structure in the "Iliad".* Princeton.

Stein, E. 1990. *Autorbewusstsein in der frühen griechischen Literatur.* ScriptOralia 17. Tübingen.

Steiner, P. 1984. *Russian Formalism: A Metapoetics.* Ithaca, NY.

Steinrück, M. 2005. "Le Catalogue des femmes pseudo-hésiodique et les rares amantes héroïques des déesses." In *Κορυφαίῳ ἀνδρί. Mélanges offerts à André Hurst,* ed. A Kolde et al, 293–302. Geneva.

Stephens, S. 2003. *Seeing Double. Intercultural Poetics in Ptolemaic Alexandria.* Berkeley.

Stocking, G. 1987. *Victorian Anthropology.* New York.

Stoessl, F. 1939. "Onomakritos." *RE* vol. 18, cols. 491–93.

Stokes, W. 1903. "The Wooing of Luaine and the Death of Athirne." *Revue Celtique* 24:270–87.

Stone, R. 1988. *Dried Millet Breaking: Time, Words, and Song in the Woi Epic of the Kpelle.* Bloomington, IN.

Sullivan, A., ed. 1983. *The Book of Leinster.* Vol. 6. Dublin.

Suter, A., ed. 2008. *Lament: Studies in the Ancient Mediterranean and Beyond.* Oxford.

Suzuki, M. 1989. *Metamorphoses of Helen: Authority, Difference, and the Epic.* Ithaca, NY.

Taplin, O. 1992. *Homeric Soundings: the Shaping of the "Iliad".* Oxford.

Tebben, J. 1994. *Concordantia Homerica, Pars I: Odyssea.* Hildesheim.

Tedlock, D. 1983. *The Spoken Word and the Work of Interpretation.* Philadelphia.

Teffeteller, A. 2001. "The Chariot Rite at Onchestos: *Homeric Hymn to Apollo* 229–38." *Journal of Hellenic Studies* 121:159–66.

Thalmann, W. 1984. *Conventions of Form and Thought in Early Greek Epic Poetry.* Baltimore.

Theodoridis, C. 1982. *Photius Lexicon.* Vol. 1. Berlin.

Thomas, R. F. 1999. *Reading Virgil and his Texts: Studies in Intertextuality.* Ann Arbor.

Thurneysen, R., ed. 1935. *Scéla mucce Meic Dathó.* Dublin.

Todorov, T. 1975. "La Notion de litterature." In *Langue, discours, société,* ed. J. Kristeva, 352–64. Paris.

———. [1971] 1977. "Primitive Narrative." In *Poetics of Prose,* trans. R. Howard, 53–65. Ithaca, NY.

———. 1978. *Les Genres du discours.* Paris.

———. 1990. *Genres in Discourse.* Trans. C. Porter. Cambridge.

Tracy, S. 1990. *The Story of the "Odyssey".* Princeton.

Treu, M. 1957. "Das Proömium der hesiodischen Frauenkataloge." *Rheinisches Museum* 100:169–86.

Trypanis, C. A. 1974. "Greek Poetry." In *Princeton Encyclopedia of Poetry and Poetics,* ed. A. Preminger, enlarged ed., 326–32. Princeton.

Tsagalis, C. 1998. *The Improvised Laments in the "Iliad".* Ph.D. diss., Cornell University.

———. 2004. *Epic Grief: Personal Laments in Homer's "Iliad".* Berlin.

———. 2008. *Oral Palimpsest: Exploring Intertextuality in the Homeric Epics.* Hellenic Studies 29. Washington, DC.

———. 2009. "Poetry and Poetics in the Hesiodic Corpus." In *Brill's Companion to Hesiod,* ed. F. Montanari, 131–77. Leiden.

———. 2011. "Towards an Oral, Intertextual Neoanalysis." *Trends in Classics* 3:209–44.

Tsagarakis, O. 1982. *Form and Content in Homer.* Hermes Enzelschriften 46. Wiesbaden.

Tsantsanoglou, K., and G. Parássoglou. 1987. "Two Gold Lamellae from Thessaly." *Hellenika* 38:3–19.

Tsouderos, I. 1976. *Kretika moirologia.* Athens.

Turpin, J. 1980. "L'Expression *aidos kai nemesis* et les 'actes de langage'." *Revue des études grecques* 93:352–67.

van der Valk, M. 1971. *Commentarii ad Homeri Iliadem Pertinentes ad Fidem Codicis Laurentiani Editi: Praefationem et Commentarios ad Libros A–D Complectens.* Vol 1. Leiden.

———. 1977. "A Few Observations on the *Homeric Hymn to Apollo*." *L'Antiquité classique* 46:441–52.

van Groningen, B. A. 1966. *Théognis: Le premier livre.* Amsterdam.

van Leeuwen, J. 1890. "Homerica." *Mnemosyne* 18:265–99.

van Raalte, M. 1986. *Rhythm and Metre: Towards a Systematic Description of Greek Stichic Verse.* Assen.

van Thiel, H. 1982. *Iliaden und Ilias*. Basel.

———, ed. 1988. *Odysseen*. Basel.

———, ed. 1996. *Homeri Ilias*. Hildesheim.

Ventris, M., and J. Chadwick. 1973. *Documents in Mycenaean Greek*. 2nd ed. Cambridge.

Vernant, J.-P. [1965] 1981. "Le mythe hésiodique des races." In *Mythe et pensée chez les Grecs*, 13–41. Paris.

Visser, E. 1988. "Formulae or Single Words? Towards a New Theory on Homeric Verse-Making." *Würzburger Jahrbücher für die Altertumswissenschaft* 14:21–37.

Vivante, P. 1982. *The Epithets in Homer: A Study in Poetic Values*. New Haven.

Vlahos, J. B. 2007. "Homer's *Odyssey*, Books 19 and 23: Early Recognition; a Solution to the Enigmas of Ivory and Horns, and the Test of the Bed." *College Literature* 34:107–31.

von Erffa, C. 1937. *AIDOS und verwandte Begriffe in ihrer Entwicklung von Homer bis Demokrit*. Philologus Suppl. 30.2. Leipzig.

Wade-Gery, H. T. 1952. *The Poet of the "Iliad"*. Cambridge.

Wadley, S. 1991. "Why Does Ram Swarup Sing? Song and Speech in the North Indian Epic Dhola." In *Gender, Genre, and Power in South Asian Expressive Traditions*, ed. A. Appadurai et al., 201–23. Philadelphia.

Wagner, H. 1970. "Studies in the Origins of Early Celtic Civilisation." *Zeitschrift für Celtische Philologie* 31:1–45.

Walcot, P. 1963. "Hesiod and the Law." *Symbolae Osloenses* 38:5–21.

———. 1966. *Hesiod and the Near East*. Cardiff.

———. 1979. "Cattle Raiding, Heroic Tradition, and Ritual. The Greek Evidence." *History of Religions* 18:326–51.

Watkins, C. 1978. "Anosteos hon poda tendei." In *Étrennes de septantaine: travaux de linguistique et de grammaire comparée offerts à M. Lejeune*, 231–35. Paris.

———. 1979. "*Is tre fír flathemon*: Marginalia to *Audacht Morainn*." *Ériu* 30:181–98.

———. 1981. "Aspects of Indo-European Poetics." In *Indo-European Studies* IV, ed. C. Watkins, 764–99. Cambridge, MA.

———. 1986. "The Language of the Trojans." In *Troy and the Trojans*, ed. M. Mellink, 45–62. Bryn Mawr.

———. 1995. *How to Kill a Dragon in Indo-European: Aspects of Indo-European Poetics*. Oxford.

Watson, W. 1994. *Traditional Techniques in Classical Hebrew Verse*. Sheffield.

Webster, T. B. L. 1964. *From Mycenae to Homer*. New York.

Wellek, R., and A. Warren. 1962. *Theory of Literature.* 3rd ed. New York.

Welskopf, E. C. 1985. *Soziale Typenbegriffe im alten Griechenland und ihr Fortleben in den Sprachen der Welt.* Vol. 2. Berlin.

Wendel, C. 1935. *Scholia in Apollonium Rhodium Vetera.* Berlin.

West, M. L., ed. 1966. *Hesiod. Theogony.* Oxford.

———. 1970. "Hesiod." In *The Oxford Classical Dictionary*, 2nd ed., ed. N. G. L. Hammond and H. H. Scullard, 511. Oxford.

———. 1974. *Studies in Greek Elegy and Iambus.* Berlin.

———. 1975. "Cynaethus' *Hymn to Apollo.*" *Classical Quarterly* 25:161–70.

———. 1976. Review of B. Peabody, *The Winged Word. Phoenix* 30:382–86.

———, ed. 1978. *Hesiod: Works and Days.* Oxford.

———. 1981. "Is the *Works and Days* an Oral Poem?" In *I poemi epici rapsodici non omerici e la tradizione orale*, ed. C. Brillante et al., 53–67. Padua.

———. 1982. *Greek Metre.* Oxford.

———. 1983. *The Orphic Poems.* Oxford.

———. 1985. *The Hesiodic Catalogue of Women: Its Nature, Structure, and Origins.* Oxford.

———. 1989. *Iambi et Elegi Graeci.* Vol 1. *Archilochus, Hipponax, Theognidea.* Oxford.

———. 1992. *Ancient Greek Music.* Oxford.

———. 1993. "Simonides Redivivus." *Zeitschrift fur Papyrologie und Epigraphik* 98:1–14.

———. 1998. Review of van Thiel 1996. *Classical Review* 48:1–2.

———, ed. and trans. 2003a. *Homeric Hymns. Homeric Apocrypha. Lives of Homer.* Cambridge, MA.

———, ed. and trans. 2003b. *Greek Epic Fragments from the Seventh to the Fifth Centuries BC.* Cambridge, MA.

———. 2005. "*Odyssey* and *Argonautica.*" *Classical Quarterly* 55:39–64.

———. 2011 "Rhapsodes." In *The Homer Encyclopedia*, ed. M. Finkelberg, 3:745–46. Chichester.

Whallon, W. 1969. *Formula, Character, and Context.* Washington, DC.

Whitman, C. H. 1958. *Homer and the Heroic Tradition.* Cambridge, MA.

Wifstrand, A. 1933. *Von Kallimachos zu Nonnos. Metrisch-stilistische Untersuchungen zur späteren griechischen Epik und zu verwandten Gedichtgattungen.* Lund.

Wilamowitz-Moellendorff, U. v. 1884. *Homerische Untersuchungen.* Berlin.

———. 1905. "Lesefrüchte." *Hermes* 40:116–53.

———. 1916. *Die Ilias und Homer*. Berlin.

———. 1920. *Die Ilias und Homer*. 2nd ed. Berlin.

———. 1962. *Kleine Schriften: Lesefrüchte und Verwandtes*. Ed. K. Latte. Berlin.

Williams, J. E. C., and P. Ford. 1992. *The Irish Literary Tradition*. Cardiff.

Wilson, P. 2000. *The Athenian Institution of the Khoregia: The Chorus, the City, and the Stage*. Cambridge.

———. 2006–2007. "Thamyris of Thrace and the Muses of Messenia." *Mediterranean Archaeology* 19/20:207–12.

Winternitz, M. 1981. *A History of Indian Literature*. Vol. 1. Trans. V. Srinivasa Sarma. New Delhi.

Wolf, F. [1795] 1985. *Prolegomena to Homer*. Trans. with Intro. by A. Grafton et al. Princeton.

Woods, P. 1996. *King Pulp: the Wild World of Quentin Tarantino*. New York.

Wyatt, W. 1989. "The Intermezzo of *Odyssey* 11 and the Poets Homer and Odysseus." *Studi micenei ed egeo-anatolici* 27:235–53.

Wyss, B. 1936. *Antimachi Colophonii Reliquiae*. Berlin.

Young, D., ed. 1971. *Theognis*. Leipzig.

Zacco, A. 1996. "Sull'uso di "*apêlegeos*" nel racconto omerico e nelle *Argonautiche* di Apollonio Rodio." *Aevum* 9:151–75.

Zanker, G. 1986. "The *Works and Days*: Hesiod's *Beggar's Opera*?" *Bulletin of the Institute of Classical Studies* 33:26–36.

Zmud', L. 1992. "Orphism and Graffiti from Olbia." *Hermes* 120:159–68.

Zuckerberg, D. G. 2014. *The Oversubtle Maxim Chasers: Aristophanes, Euripides, and their Reciprocal Pursuit of Poetic Identity*. Ph.D. diss., Princeton University.

Zuntz, G. 1971. *Persephone. Three Essays on Religion and Thought in Magna Graecia*. Oxford.

Zweig, P. 1974. *The Adventurer*. Princeton.

Zygas, E. V. 1974. "The Problem of Father-Son Transmission in Russian Heroic Epics." Senior honors thesis, Harvard University.

INDEX OF ANCIENT PASSAGES

INDEX OF SUBJECTS

MYTH AND POETICS

A SERIES EDITED BY

GREGORY NAGY

CPSIA information can be obtained
at www.ICGtesting.com
Printed in the USA
LVHW090206040920
664880LV00007B/107

The Bloomsbury Companion to
Holocaust Literature

Also Available from Bloomsbury:

Eclipse of Reason
Max Horkheimer

Language of the Third Reich
Victor Klemperer

The Bloomsbury Companion to Holocaust Literature

Edited by
Jenni Adams

Bloomsbury Academic
An imprint of Bloomsbury Publishing Plc

B L O O M S B U R Y
LONDON · NEW DELHI · NEW YORK · SYDNEY

Bloomsbury Academic
An imprint of Bloomsbury Publishing Plc

50 Bedford Square	1385 Broadway
London	New York
WC1B 3DP	NY 10018
UK	USA

www.bloomsbury.com

Bloomsbury is a registered trade mark of Bloomsbury Publishing Plc

First published 2014

British Library Cataloguing-in-Publication Data
A catalogue record for this book is available from the British Library.

ISBN: HB: 978-1-4411-2908-6
ePDF: 978-1-4411-1809-7
ePub: 978-1-4725-8744-2

Library of Congress Cataloging-in-Publication Data
A catalog record for this book is available from the Library of Congress.

Typeset by Newgen Knowledge Works (P) Ltd., Chennai, India
Printed and bound in Great Britain

Contents

Contents

Acknowledgements

Many thanks to Leonard Orr, Michael Rothberg, and two anonymous readers for insightful input into this project while it was at the proposal stage. For much-appreciated advice, guidance and encouragement, a huge thank you to Sue Vice, Adam Piette, Jonathan Ellis and Nicky Hallett at the University of Sheffield. Gratitude is also due to the staff of the British Library for assistance in locating and obtaining research materials, and to the editorial team at Bloomsbury, particularly David Avital and Mark Richardson, for all of the assistance provided during the process of completing this volume. Much gratitude is also due to the contributors for showing such patience and good humour during the editing process.

The editor and contributors are grateful for permission to reproduce the following:

Sherman Alexie, 'The Game between the Jews and the Indians Is Tied Going into the Bottom of the Ninth Inning' and 'Inside Dachau', reprinted from *First Indian on the Moon* (1993) and *The Summer of Black Widows* (1996) by Sherman Alexie, by permission of Hanging Loose Press.

Dan Pagis, 'Written in Pencil in the Sealed Railway-Car', reprinted from *The Selected Poetry of Dan Pagis* ([1989] 1996), by permission of the University of California Press.

Gerhard Richter, 'Uncle Rudi' (1965), oil on canvas, Lidice Memorial, Czech Republic, reproduced by permission of Gerhard Richter.

W. G. Sebald, image from W. G. Sebald, *Vertigo* (1990), reproduced by permission of the estate of W. G. Sebald.

Notes on Contributors

Victoria Aarons holds the position of OR and Eva Mitchell Distinguished Professor of Literature and Chair of the English Department at Trinity University. She is the author of *A Measure of Memory: Storytelling and Identity in American Jewish Fiction* and *What Happened to Abraham: Reinventing the Covenant in American Jewish Fiction*, recipients of the CHOICE Award for Outstanding Academic Book, and the forthcoming anthology *The New Diaspora: The Changing Landscape of American Jewish Fiction*. She has published over 70 articles and book chapters and serves on the editorial boards of a number of journals. She is currently completing a book manuscript on post-Holocaust writing, *Third-Generation Holocaust Representation: Trauma, History, and Memory*.

Jenni Adams is the author of *Magic Realism in Holocaust Literature: Troping the Traumatic Real* (2011) and the co-editor, with Sue Vice, of *Representing Perpetrators in Holocaust Literature and Film* (2013). She has published articles and essays on writers including Jonathan Safran Foer, Anne Michaels, Bruno Schulz, Jonathan Littell and Yann Martel, with the overriding preoccupation in her work being the relationship between ethics and aesthetics in Holocaust fiction.

Michael Bernard-Donals is the Director of the Mosse/Weinstein Center for Jewish Studies and the Nancy Hoefs Professor of English at the University of Wisconsin-Madison. He is the author of several books, including *Between Witness and Testimony: The Holocaust and the Limits of Representation* (2001), *An Introduction to Holocaust Studies: History, Memory, and Representation* (2006) and *Forgetful Memory: Jewish Remembrance after Auschwitz* (2009). He is currently at work on two projects: an introduction to Jewish rhetoric (with Janice Fernheimer) and a book on the rhetorical shape of memory at the United States Holocaust Memorial Museum.

Matthew Boswell is a Research Fellow in the School of English at the University of Leeds. Since completing his Ph.D. on Holocaust poetry at the University of Sheffield, his research has focused on Holocaust fiction, taboo forms of Holocaust representation and 'hybrid testimony'. His monograph, *Holocaust Impiety in Literature, Popular Music and Film* (Palgrave Macmillan, 2012), considers irreverent and controversial representations of the Holocaust by non-victims. He is currently working with partners in South Africa and Australia on a range of projects relating to transnational memories of the Holocaust.

Stef Craps teaches English at Ghent University, Belgium, where he also directs the Centre for Literature and Trauma. He is the author of *Postcolonial Witnessing: Trauma Out of Bounds* (Palgrave Macmillan, 2013) and *Trauma and Ethics in the Novels of Graham Swift: No Short-Cuts to Salvation* (Sussex Academic Press, 2005), and has guest-edited special issues of *Criticism: A Quarterly for Literature and the Arts* (2011; with Michael Rothberg) and *Studies in the Novel* (2008; with Gert Buelens) on the topics of, respectively, transcultural negotiations of Holocaust memory and postcolonial trauma novels.

Richard Crownshaw is Senior Lecturer in the Department of English and Comparative Literature, Goldsmiths, University of London. He is the author of *The Afterlife of Holocaust Memory in Contemporary Literature and Culture* (Palgrave Macmillan, 2010), co-editor, with Jane Kilby and Antony Rowland, of *The Future of Memory* (Berghahn, 2010, in paperback 2013), and editor of a special issue of the journal *parallax* on the topic of transcultural memory (2011). He is currently writing a monograph on memory, contemporary fiction and environmental catastrophe.

Fernando Herrero-Matoses received his Bachelor's degree in Spanish Literature and Critical Theory at the University of Valencia, then studied at the Independent Studies Program (PEI) at the Contemporary Museum of Art in Barcelona (MACBA). He received his MA and Ph.D. from the University of Illinois, Urbana-Champaign, where he studied in the Department of Art History. His research examines Spanish contemporary art, and the intersections between art, literature and memory.

Brett Ashley Kaplan received her Ph.D. from the Rhetoric Department at the University of California, Berkeley and is now Professor and Conrad Humanities Scholar in the Program in Comparative and World Literature and the Program in Jewish Culture and Society at the University of Illinois, Urbana-Champaign. Her books, *Unwanted Beauty: Aesthetic Pleasure in Holocaust Representation* (2007) and *Landscapes of Holocaust Postmemory* (2011), examine the Shoah's intersections with art and space. Her current projects are *Jewish Anxiety and the Novels of Philip Roth* (forthcoming) and *The Aesthetic Solution* (in progress).

Adrienne Kertzer is Professor of English at the University of Calgary. She is the author of *My Mother's Voice: Children, Literature, and the Holocaust* (Broadview, 2002) which received the Canadian Jewish Book Award and the Children's Literature Association Honor Book Award. Working on issues of Holocaust representation and the depiction of historical trauma in young adult fiction, she has recently published essays on M. T. Anderson's *The Astonishing Life of Octavian Nothing: Traitor to the Nation*; Terry Pratchett's *Nation*; Sherman Alexie's *The Absolutely True Diary of a Part-time Indian* and Patrick Ness's *Chaos Walking* trilogy.

Erin McGlothlin is Associate Professor of German and Jewish Studies at Washington University in St Louis. Her research interests include German-Jewish literature, the literature of the Holocaust, the graphic novel and narrative theory. She is the author of *Second-Generation Holocaust Literature: Legacies of Survival and Perpetration* (2006) and articles on Claude Lanzmann's *Shoah*, Edgar Hilsenrath's *Der Nazi und der Friseur*, Ruth Klüger's *weiter leben*, Art Spiegelman's *Maus* and other fictional and non-fictional works of Holocaust literature and film. She is currently working on a book titled *Constructing the Mind of the Holocaust Perpetrator in Fictional, Autobiographical, and Documentary Discourse*.

David Miller is a senior lecturer in the Department of English Literature at Manchester Metropolitan University and is the general editor of the *Journal of Literature and Trauma Studies*. His publications include a monograph on poetry and philosophy and articles dealing with critical theory and poetry. His most recent publication is a study of the poetic undercurrents in the work of Ernst Bloch for Duke University Press (SIC Series). He is currently working on a monograph on poetry, trauma and memory and is the editor of the forthcoming *Routledge Companion to Literature and Trauma*.

Sue Vice is Professor of English Literature at the University of Sheffield. Her most recent books are *Shoah* (2011) and *Representing Perpetrators in Holocaust Literature and Film* (2013), co-edited with Jenni Adams. She is currently completing *Textual Deceptions*, a study of false memoirs and literary hoaxes.

Traces, Dis/Continuities, Complicities: An Introduction to Holocaust Literature

The term 'Holocaust literature' encompasses a diverse body of work, from testimony and other writing by survivors through to poetry, fiction, drama and memoir by those who did not experience the events themselves but who nevertheless feel compelled to engage with the long shadow they continue to cast over twentieth- and twenty-first-century culture. The task of precisely delineating 'Holocaust literature' and its key properties is further complicated by the extent to which significant issues in the understanding and interpretation of Holocaust texts differ across geographical, temporal and cultural contexts, as Hilene Flanzbaum notes. Flanzbaum comments, for example, on the lack of relevance of the concept of uniqueness to her own students of Holocaust literature, who 'for their entire lives . . . had been seeing genocides both real and imagined from all media sources' (2011, p. 75).[1] Such debates highlight the degree to which critical and readerly interpretative values and expectations of Holocaust literature are not stable in time despite the solidification of certain formations of responsive rhetoric (e.g. the imperative to contemplate the Holocaust so as not to repeat history's mistakes). Considering the ways in which the critical reception of Holocaust literature has changed over time[2] and across contexts suggests an important qualification of any attempt to definitively map its significance and particularities. Coupled with the diverse and continually evolving nature of Holocaust literature itself, such specificity speaks powerfully against a totalizing approach which might schematize this body of literature in ultimately restrictive and reductive ways.

Bearing in mind the specificity of literary and literary–critical discourses on the Holocaust to the particular place and time of their utterance, this Introduction does not, hence, attempt to present an overarching schematization or theorization of this literature. Instead, it aims to discuss a number of different texts, with a particular focus, for reasons of manageability, on the short story, grouping these together loosely in order to draw out through mutual illumination a provisional problematics of Holocaust literature – here understood broadly as literary works for which the historical context of the Holocaust is of major significance – tentatively charting some of the pertinent issues in Holocaust

1

representation which echo in different ways through the various sections of this Companion, while remaining cognizant of the provisionality of such a mapping. The grouping of the stories into three overlapping sections – 'Traces', 'Dis/Continuities' and 'Complicities' – that intersect and also point outwards into a range of other representational issues and concerns thus aims to strike a middle path between a totalizing approach to this literature that would, perhaps, be deceptively useful in suggesting a stance of omniscience and interpretative closure I cannot and would not wish to claim, and an ideal (yet impossible) Introduction which would echo the proliferating particularities and ever-shifting points of focus within the evolving body of work of Holocaust literature itself. After thus providing a tentative mapping of some of the key issues in the field and linking these to the material that will follow, I then proceed to an explicit discussion of the contents of this volume, which offers a cross-section of current critical approaches to a variety of different aspects of Holocaust writing internationally.

Traces

The first section in this provisional mapping will focus on a number of linked issues concerning alterity and the trace, exploring the ways in which this forms one of the central preoccupations of much writing about the Holocaust. By way of introducing the question of traces, I open with a discussion of Ida Fink's short story of that name from the collection *A Scrap of Time*, originally written in Polish by an author who survived first ghettoization and subsequently in hiding during the war. 'Traces' is a brief narrative concerning a witness's response to a photograph displaying an unnamed ghetto immediately after the inhabitants were taken away to their deaths. She is able to locate the image in time due to the fact that it contains traces of the inhabitants' footprints in the snow, footprints which were erased by the weather later that same day when the ghetto's inhabitants were shot. The witness is initially reluctant to testify, but changes her mind in order to memorialize a group of children who, discovered hiding in the attic of the *Judenrat*, refused to reveal the identity of their families when discovered by the Nazis and were subsequently killed:

> The people are gone – their footprints remain. Very strange.
>
> 'They didn't take them straight to the fields, but first to the Gestapo. No one knows why, apparently those were the orders. They stood in the courtyard until the children were brought.'
>
> She breaks off: 'I prefer not to remember . . .' But suddenly she changes her mind and asks that what she is going to say be written down and preserved forever, because she wants a trace to remain.

'What children? What trace?'
A trace of those children. And only she can leave that trace, because she alone survived. (Fink, 1989, pp. 136–7, ellipsis in original)

The witness then testifies in order to preserve such a trace – a testimony that is for the most part reported in free indirect discourse – though the story ends before the conclusion of this tale: 'In a calm voice she asks for a short break. With an indulgent smile she rejects the glass of water they hand her. After the break she will tell how they were all shot' (ibid., p. 137).

One key issue raised by the story is precisely the relationship between Holocaust narrative and the trace. In the story we find at least three different forms of trace – the footprints themselves, as the physical trace of the victims' former presence and subsequent absence; the photograph, which maintains the visibility of the footprints over time; and the testimony, which enables the other traces to signify by indicating the absent events and individuals encoded within and outside of their content. The story's phrasing of these evocations of the absent dead within a vocabulary of 'traces' calls to mind Emmanuel Levinas's notion of the 'trace of the other', the 'signifyingness' of which 'consists in signifying without making appear . . . . Disclosure, which reinstates the world and leads back to the world and is proper to a sign or a signification, is done away with in this trace' (Levinas, 1996, pp. 61–2). Thus the trace does not make the other present, or claim to do so; it instead offers a locus for the disruptive manifestation of the other's alterity, their lack of availability to our 'grasping', coupled with a decentring awareness of the ethical obligation we bear them, ideas explored further in Michael Bernard-Donals' chapter in this volume. In its emphasis on the task of the witness as the preservation of 'traces' rather than the rendering of the event immediate and present, Fink's story arguably echoes Levinas's vigilance around the parameters of our relationship to absent others, and the capacities of narrative in this respect. That the path through which the absent inhabitants of the ghetto are 'traced' is a difficult and multiply mediated one – the footprints, recorded in the photograph, must then be interpreted in the witness's narrative in order to achieve their 'signifyingness' – at once indicates the precarious nature of such signifying and demonstrates a tentative faith in literature as the mechanism through which the place of absent events and individuals might be indicated – it is narrative, after all, which enables the trace to retain its limited legibility.

The story embodies a broader concern in Holocaust writing with the degree to which the written word is able to preserve a trace both of history itself and of the particular losses the history of the Holocaust entails. Comparisons might be made here to a work like Dan Pagis's poem 'Written in Pencil in the Sealed Freightcar' (Pagis, 1989) (cited in full in Victoria Aarons' chapter in this volume), a poetic fragment which finishes with a broken-off sentence, likewise emphasizing the fragility of the trace yet imbuing this with signifying potency. Similarly, Georges Perec, a member of the 1.5 generation, as Susan Rubin Suleiman defines it,[3] describes at once the inability of the autobiographical sections of his novel *W* to recapture the reality of his parents' lives and deaths ('I know that I am saying nothing . . . what I say is blank, is neutral, is a sign, once and for all, of a once-and-for-all annihilation') and the function of such writing nevertheless as a form of trace: 'I write because they left in me their unbearable mark, whose trace is writing. Their memory is dead in writing; writing is the memory of their death and the assertion of my life' (Perec, [1988] 1996, p. 42). Perec's ambivalence about writing is embodied in the hinge of the second sentence here, in which the semicolon, both an opening and a closing, joins writing's incapacities with the limited signifyingness detailed by Levinas in both a mourning of writing's inability to revivify or make present the lost, and an emphasis of the significance even of this failure.

Fink's 'Traces' in this way offers a route into a more broadly applicable question concerning the capacities and incapacities of narrative in relation to the dead, suggesting that it enables at most a 'signifying without making appear' yet may, at the same time, fulfil the ethical imperative of memorialization. The mode of Holocaust literature to which such questions most obviously pertain is testimony, the referentiality of which is further explored in Sue Vice's chapter in this volume, yet the implications remain resonant for other forms of Holocaust literature, which might be read as offering experiential encounters with the Holocaust were not the irrecoverability of history's absent contents made clear. Issues of genre and witnessing are, indeed, significant to the story itself in that while Fink herself survived the Holocaust, *A Scrap of Time* is a collection of short fiction. As a related point, given that the protagonist in 'Traces' describes the events without making her own subject position clear or definitively claiming to have witnessed the events first-hand, it might be argued that the story leaves an open question regarding the possibility of preserving traces (but traces alone) through positionalities other than that of first-person witness. This blurring of the parameters of the witnessing subject is heightened by the unusual use of indirect speech at key moments in the testimony, such as the description of the children's interrogation (Fink, 1989, p. 137), which has the effect of allowing the voice of witness to infiltrate the third-person narrative, appearing in the process to surpass the boundaries of the individual witnessing subject.

Questions of the degree to which narrative can bear the trace of history, whether one's own or that of others, are further complicated by another of the narratives I wish to briefly focus on here, Charlotte Delbo's 'Morning', from the collection *Auschwitz and After*, which explores in both prose and poetry her experiences as a French political prisoner in Auschwitz and Ravensbrück. While more obviously categorizable as a testimonial vignette than a 'short story', 'Morning' might nevertheless be read as a 'story' in the same sense as the earlier vignette 'One Day', which is interrupted by the aside 'Presently I am writing this story in a café – it is turning into a story' (Delbo, 1995b, p. 26), particularly given its focus on the reconcilability of Holocaust experience with narrative form, the possibility of transparent testimony, and the impact of generic and narratological features on the content and referentiality of Holocaust narrative. The narrative 'Morning' describes the suffering and mutual support of the female prisoners during the morning roll call, yet the possibility of evoking the actual experience of this moment is simultaneously called into question, as in this passage, in which both the ability to convey one's experience to another and the very possibility of selfhood during the Holocaust are radically undermined:

> I am standing amid my comrades and I think to myself that if I ever return and will want to explain the inexplicable, I shall say, 'I was saying to myself: you must stay standing through roll call. You must get through one more day. It is because you got through today that you will return one day, if you ever return.' This is not so. Actually I did not say anything to myself. I thought of nothing. . . . I was a skeleton of cold, with cold blowing through all the crevices in between a skeleton's ribs. (Delbo, 1995a, p. 64)

The critic Jeremy Hawthorne comments that while this passage could be read as a self-conscious highlighting of the artifice of the testimonial account, it might also be read as 'having been written in good faith, with the qualification that follows it the result of brutally honest self-revision on Delbo's part', adding that 'having that possibility in mind serves to alert the reader to the enormous difficulty faced by the survivor who attempts after the event to narrate his or her experience as a victim' (2012, p. 151). These comments recall Dori Laub's theorization in *Testimony* of the Holocaust as 'an event without a witness', in part due to the logic of dehumanization prisoners were forced to internalize, as a result of which 'one [could not] say "thou" even to oneself' (1992, p. 82). Such implications arguably complicate the possibility of bearing witness given the events' capacity to eclipse the subjectivity of the victim, asking questions about the capacity of the autonomous self implied by the act of literary expression to invoke rather than obscure the trace of one's own and others' desubjectivization during the event.[4]

Holocaust history thus poses questions for literary expression in terms of its ability to preserve or convey the site of such experience's resistance to recuperation, its capacity to evoke or approximate traces of alterity rather than invite a misleading 'grasping', and sense of presence concerning, the suffering and assaulted subjectivity of historical others. Such questions are perhaps most keenly felt by those who did not experience these events first-hand, and it is to such a writer that I now turn in the final example of this section. 'The Shawl', by the American novelist Cynthia Ozick, focuses on three characters: Rosa, her baby daughter, Magda, and her niece, Stella. The story depicts a forced march to a concentration camp, during which the characters become weaker, Rosa runs out of milk with which to feed Magda, and Magda instead takes nourishment (or the illusion of such) by sucking on a corner of the titular shawl. In the camp, the teenage Stella removes the shawl to warm her own body, and Magda wanders out into the open, where she is killed by an SS guard. Rosa, having recovered the shawl, then places it in her own mouth in order to avoid reacting audibly to Magda's death.

Such a summary is perhaps a misleading one in attributing to the story a coherence that in actuality is not one of its primary concerns. The exact place and time of the narrative's setting are never clarified, nor is the nature of the march, and the imagistic aesthetic emphasizes privileged moments of subjective perception – as in the opening: 'Stella, cold, cold, the coldness of hell' (Ozick, 1991, p. 11) – rather than an objective sense of events and their continuity. Ozick's decision to focus imagistically on flashes of subjective experience, eschewing at times a clarity and full contextualization of plot and setting, could be read as authorial irresponsibility – particularly if one follows Berel Lang's assertion that 'Holocaust genres are bound (*anchored*) historically, in part because they set out from a particular historical point, but more importantly, because historical authenticity is also what they purport to realize' (Lang, 2000, p. 19); nevertheless, in the context of the issues explored earlier, Ozick's narrative stance might alternatively be read as an intervention into debates about the ethics of Holocaust representation. Katalin Orbán has commented, on the issue of plotting, that:

> If the narratives take risks to not dispose of the other, their narration is always and inescapably under pressure by the apparent impossibility of 'plotting' narrative trauma. How can this problem of plotting be addressed as a writerly project without erasing the ethicity of response, its opening to the traumatic violence that takes it in unforeseen directions? (2005, pp. 31–2)

To impose a coherent and schematic plot upon Holocaust narrative thus risks a totalizing approach through which an openness to the 'other' (in the sense of the human other whose experience finds articulation in the narrative, and the otherness of the experience itself, which resists narrative recuperation) may be foreclosed. In a slightly different register, these are issues that have troubled the project of historiography as well, with such figures as Dan Stone (2003) noting the problematic nature of an application of historiography's formal methodological structures and tools in this context. From this perspective, Ozick's privileging of subjective image over factual precision and plot cohesion may be read as an insistence on her narrative's opening to the other, with the story's opacities marking such alterity, and its focus on the often confused and disorientated experience of individuals rather than the clear perspective of objective knowledge an ethical decision to emphasize the partial and contingent rather than the total.

An analysis of 'The Shawl' thus draws to the fore such significant issues in Holocaust representation, as regards alterity and the trace, as the importance of historical precision (and the contrary role of opacity) and the ethics of plotting. One further point to highlight concerns the depiction of Magda's voice in 'The Shawl'. Magda becomes silent as Rosa's milk dries up, and only emerges into speech in the moments preceding her death, when she wanders out of the barracks where she has been hidden and into the sunlight outside:

> Magda, in the sunlight, swaying on her pencil legs, was howling. Ever since the drying up of Rosa's nipples, ever since Magda's last scream on the road, Magda had been devoid of any syllable; Magda was a mute. . . . Magda was defective, without a voice . . . . But now Magda's mouth was spilling a long viscous rope of clamor. (Ozick, 1991, pp. 15–16)

The sounds uttered by Magda, like the 'scribblings' of her 'pencil legs', are incomprehensible, yet her eruption into speech serves to place a profound emphasis on the silencing the story culminates in, the silencing of a life but also of the story of that life, except where memorialized by others. The episode recalls the narrative of Hurbinek in Primo Levi's *The Truce*, a child of around three described as 'a nobody, a child of death, a child of Auschwitz', unable to speak except to utter incomprehensible sounds, one of which is attributed to him as his name (Levi, 1987, p. 197). After Henek, a fellow patient, attempts to teach Hurbinek to talk, the group of patients attempt unsuccessfully to interpret the single word of his speech, yet are unable to: 'among us there were speakers of all the languages in Europe; but Hurbinek's word remained secret' (ibid., p. 198), and after his death Levi reports: 'Nothing remains of him: he bears witness through these words of mine' (ibid.). Like the story of Hurbinek, the fictional narrative of Magda and its deployment of tropes of speech, muteness and silencing emphasizes the fact that, as Levi states in *If This Is a Man*, 'The drowned have no story' (ibid., p. 96). Holocaust representation is in this sense inescapably incomplete, a body of work populated heavily by the absence of those whose voices and stories cannot be made present. As Fink's story emphasized the potential of 'traces' to at least indicate the site of those absent voices, however, one might argue that in the silenced cry of Magda an acknowledgement of the absent other is nevertheless made possible, indicating the degree to which Holocaust writing is able to maintain a dialogue with these silences. It is, perhaps, significant that both Fink and Ozick use child characters in their figuration of the absent sites of historical and traumatic knowledge, a topic further examined by Adrienne Kertzer in her chapter in this volume.

Dis/Continuities

From an exploration of some of the significant issues surrounding otherness and the trace in Holocaust literature, I turn now to a consideration of some of the dis/continuities which structure different aspects of this representational project. In addition to the narrative and generic discontinuities explored earlier, issues of temporality form a key concern in literary responses to the Holocaust, as noted by such critics as Susan Gubar in relation to Holocaust poetry,[5] with a particular focus being the degree to which the past is (and can be made) present, in however mediated a fashion. To return to an example from the previous section, Fink's 'Traces', for instance, not only examines the imperative to project the traces of the past into the present, but at the same time emphasizes the irreconcilability of these temporalities, the witness's calm voice and rejection of a glass of water belonging to a different order of events than the horror of the murdered children. Nevertheless, while present and past do not coincide, the two are interwoven throughout; the use of free indirect discourse suggests an instability in the narration which allows it to move constantly into the past:

> 'So, in the last stage, the ghetto was reduced to this one little street?'
>
> Yes, of course. It was a tiny street, Miesna, or Meat, Street. There used to be butcher shops in those stalls and that's why, at the end, the ghetto was called 'the butcher shop ghetto'.
>
> How many people were there? Not many. Maybe eighty. Maybe less. (Fink, 1989, p. 136)

In this example, the narration of the witness's description of Miesna Street in free indirect speech allows a kind of slippage by which these descriptions might be read as occupying the narrative gaze itself, which is suddenly located in the past rather than the present scene of the testimonial exchange. A disorientating sense of oscillation thus punctuates the narrative, highlighting the capacity of Holocaust experience to disrupt the temporality of its survivors,[6] while the conclusion of the tale before the description of the children's deaths intensifies a sense of the narrative's occupation of a kind of suspended present.

Such temporal disruption and distortion – highlighted as a feature of the 'literature of atrocity' by Langer (1975, p. 251) – is evident in a range of different literary works which deal with the experience and legacy of the Holocaust. In Spiegelman's *Maus* ([1996] 2003), Vladek is seen to literally re-enact the movements of his Holocaust experience in the present, reliving the events as he relates them, with events from past and present at times depicted in the same frame, in an articulation at once of the post-traumatic temporality of the survivor and the continued presence of (constructions of) the past in a postmemorial sense.[7] Martin Amis's *Time's Arrow* (1991) deploys an inverted temporality as part of an investigation of the availability (or lack thereof) of Nazi medicine to ethical and cognitive comprehension, while writers like Philip Roth have drawn on devices of alternate history in their post-Holocaust meditations on history and memory, as explored in Chapter 4 in this volume. Haunting is another temporal motif frequently present in texts which explore the aftermath of these events, as, for example, in W. G. Sebald's 2002 novel *Austerlitz*. Fascinating from the perspective of temporality, the eponymous character in *Austerlitz* posits a spatialization of time through which the possibility of recovering lost experiences remains very real:

> I have always resisted the power of time out of some internal compulsion which I myself have never understood, keeping myself apart from so-called current events in the hope, as I now think, said Austerlitz, that time will not pass away, has not passed away, that I can turn back and go behind it, and there I shall find everything as it once was . . . . (Sebald, 2002, p. 144)

A former Kindertransport evacuee who has lost the memory of his former life and family in Prague, Austerlitz is able to re-encounter the experiences of his past via his peregrinations in urban and geographical space. Sebald's novel thus at once offers a fantastic realization of Austerlitz's vision of spatial time, and, on a wider level, dramatizes the investments in images of space and time that populate Holocaust literature and the ambivalent desire for the past's recuperability we often find there. The intensely chronotopic image presented by Sebald likewise underscores the inextricability of images of time and space in Holocaust literature, in which the loss of time and place occurs simultaneously and the experience of deportation and/or exile entails intertwined spatial and temporal trajectories that cannot be undrawn, as recent theorizations of the possibility of 'return' eloquently make clear.[8]

In Sebald's *Austerlitz*, issues of temporal continuity and discontinuity are intricately bound up with questions of postmemory – Marianne Hirsch's concept for the memorially and imaginatively invested relationship borne by children of Holocaust survivors towards the experiences of their parents. Necessitated by the rupture of exile and trauma, by the punctuation of the familial narrative by the caesura of Holocaust experience, postmemory, in Hirsch's words, 'seeks connection' (Hirsch, 1996, p. 664), 'rebuild[ing]' the parental experience through a supplementation of oral narratives and existing documentary traces with imaginative reconstruction, as evident so potently in Spiegelman's graphic novel *Maus* (Spiegelman, [1996] 2003, p. 258). Postmemory texts frequently circulate around the boundary between self and survivor other, particularly as regards psychological conditions associated with first-hand witnessing, such as trauma and survivorhood. This concern with the dis/continuities of second-generation subjectivity is potently explored in Thane Rosenbaum's story 'Cattle Car Complex', in which the protagonist Adam Posner (one of a whole series of Adam Posners who people the collection *Elijah Visible*), a successful lawyer, becomes trapped in an elevator car and descends into panic, overcome by the illusion that he is trapped in one of the cattle-cars of his parents' past. The voice of the Irish night guard who speaks to him through the intercom is transfigured for Adam into a 'strident German' (Rosenbaum, 1996, p. 7), while his Russian driver is interpreted as a liberating Bolshevik (ibid., p. 9). The story's conclusion reads as follows:

> As the elevator doors separated like a curtain, the four men, in one tiny choreographed step, edged closer to the threshold . . . .
>
> Adam was sitting on the floor, dressed in soiled rags. Silvery flecks of stubble dappled his bearded face. Haltingly, he stared at those who greeted him. . . . As he lifted himself to his feet, he reached for a suitcase stuffed with a life's worth of possessions, held together by leather straps fastened like rope. Grabbing his hat and pressing it on his head, Adam emerged, each step the punctuation of an uncertain sentence. His eyes were wide open as he awaited the pronouncement: right or left, in which line was he required to stand? (ibid., p. 11)

The stalling of the elevator in Rosenbaum's story emblematizes the arrested continuity Adam experiences in a structural echoing of traumatic experience itself, an intersection of continuity and discontinuity potently summarized in Adam's motion in the final lines here: 'each step the punctuation of an uncertain sentence'. Adam's movements, the steps by which his walk is strung together as a coherent linkage of space and time, are at the same time caesurae which signal disjunction, while the 'sentence' of his motion is at once a reparative self-expression and a decree of entrapment. The 'threshold' which separates the car from the lobby stands in here for multiple kinds of temporal and interpersonal gulf: the gulf between the descendant of Holocaust survivors and the future-oriented world; but also the unbridgeable gap between past and present, nevertheless bridged (though here with devastating but unavoidable consequences) in the postmemorial consciousness.

This preoccupation with the boundaries of witnessing and of psychological conditions associated with first-hand experience is shared by much Holocaust literature, particularly Holocaust literature of the second and subsequent generations. In Spiegelman's *Maus*, for example, when struggling with the question of his own authority and license to depict the Holocaust, Art is told by his psychotherapist that he too is a survivor ('But you weren't in Auschwitz . . . you were in Rego Park' ([1996] 2003, p. 204, ellipsis in original)), while Anne Michaels' novel *Fugitive Pieces* offers the following depiction of second-generation consciousness in the narration of the character of Ben, another child of survivors:

> My parents' past is mine molecularly. Naomi thinks she can stop the soldier who spat in my father's mouth from spitting into mine, through my father's blood. . . . But I imagine Naomi has a child and I can't stop the writing on its forehead from growing as the child grows. It's not the sight of the number that scares me, even as it bursts across the skin. It's that somehow my watching causes it to happen. ([1996] (1997), p. 280)

In Ben's figuration, memory is literally fluid, as evident in the grotesque imagery of the soldier's spit and also (in an uncomfortable echo of Nazi rhetoric) in the blood, yet this is a source of horror, with the number Ben imagines on his own child's forehead suggesting the definition of the child wholly by the intergenerationally transmitted experience of the camps, rendering memory a curse of victimhood that will be transmitted down the generations.

This sense of the continuity and discontinuity of memory and traumatization extends to literature that is postmemorial in a broader sense, as evident in Nathan Englander's 'What We Talk about When We Talk about Anne Frank', a rewriting of Raymond Carver's story 'What We Talk about When We Talk about Love', in which two couples, during an afternoon of drinking, discuss different perspectives on love in ways that are ultimately ungrounding for their relationships. In Englander's tale, the protagonists are a secular Jewish American couple and an orthodox couple who have emigrated to Israel, and the subjects under discussion are Jewish identity and the Holocaust. Deb, the wife in the secular couple, while bearing no family relationship to the events, is obsessed with the Holocaust, and the four play her game of considering which of their non-Jewish friends would hide them in the event of a 'second Holocaust'. The story concludes with Shoshana (of the orthodox couple) being unable to affirm that her husband Yerucham would save her, were he non-Jewish and she under persecution.

Englander's story raises questions about the role and value of a sense of continuity with the Holocaust in broader cultural memory, where such continuity extends to a problematic centrality of the events in consciousness. In the representation of Deb, for example, he satirizes an American obsession with the Holocaust, as evident in her reaction to Yerucham's telling a story about his survivor-father:

> 'Tell us,' Deb says. And I can see in her eyes that she wants it to be one of those stories of a guy who spent three years hiding inside one of those cannons they use for the circus. And at the end of the war, a Righteous Gentile comes out all joyous and fires him through a hoop and into a tub of water, where he discovers his lost son breathing through a straw. (Englander, 2012, p. 9)

The parodic vocabulary of the circus here underscores the narrator's reading of such fixation as an unseemly spectacularization of historical suffering, yet the function of Holocaust discourse for Deb is also made clear, in terms of its fulfil-ment of redemptive expectations, as the narrator clarifies following the actual unfolding of the story, which does not accord with a redemptive narrative arc: 'Deb looks crestfallen. She was expecting something empowering. Some story with which to educate [their son] Trevor, to reconfirm her belief in the humanity that, from inhumanity, forms' (ibid., p. 11). This statement suggests an essentially conservative and redemptive use of the Holocaust as a means of reinforcing other cultural and ideological continuities, a notion intensified by Yerucham's critique of the mode of secular American Jewishness he identifies in the family of his hosts:

> 'What I'm trying to say . . . is that you can't build Judaism only on the foundation of one terrible crime. It is about this obsession with the Holocaust as a necessary sign of identity. As your only educational tool. Because for the children, there is no connection otherwise. Nothing Jewish that binds.' (Ibid., p. 22)

While Yerucham critiques the function of Holocaust memory in Jewish American discourse as an artificial and one-dimensional means of maintaining Jewish culture, however, he is likewise seen to instrumentalize this past in his description of intermarriage as the current Holocaust and appropriate object of concern for Jews (ibid., p. 24). What emerges is at once a recognition of the inseparability of cultural memory from broader priorities and preoccupations within that specific cultural environment and an acknowledgement of some of the potentially problematic consequences of this phenomenon. In particular, Deb's use of the Holocaust as a touchstone of Jewishness suggests parallels with Terri's consideration of love in Carver's story, where Terri views the violence of her ex-partner, Ed, as a key example of love's magnitude (Carver, [1981] 2003, pp. 114–18). In both cases, a radically negative experience is made into the foun-dation for an ongoing value at the risk of both redeeming and instrumentaliz-ing that experience in distortive ways. The Anne Frank game is to an extent a continuation of these concerns on the narrative's part, validating social bonds through their connection to the weight of historical horror, yet its challenge to the relationship of Shoshana and Yerucham arguably also heightens a sense of the Holocaust as other to conventional social realities and bonds, despite the use of a non-Holocaust text (Carver's story) as a model.

The narrative thus highlights the fact that engagement with the moral dilemmas of the Holocaust is not a kind of identificatory game to be taken lightly, but is rather a process that might prove radically ungrounding. These issues of identification remain a preoccupation of recent Holocaust representations (as, for example, in a novel like Ida Hattemer-Higgins' *The History of History* (2012), in which a young woman's overidentification with two women who killed their children during the war – the persecuted Jew Regina Strauss and the Nazi Magda Goebbels – is gradually identifiable as a flight from more personal issues of culpability), yet questions of identification might also be viewed from the perspective of multidirectionality, the inevitable interconnection of different memorial contexts theorized by Michael Rothberg (2009),[9] a phenomenon explored in Stef Craps' chapter in this volume. An increasingly dominant area of focus within Holocaust studies, the existence of connective or comparative texts which link Holocaust memory to other historical and cultural contexts offers a further field within which the dialectic of continuity and discontinuity remains central.

Englander's narrative at one level raises questions concerning the potentially negative effects of a sense of continuity with the Holocaust – Deb lives in fear of the events' repetition, while Shoshana and Yerucham's relationship is undermined by the application of ethical dilemmas derived from these events. Although the context is profoundly different, such questions also emerge in literature dealing with the impact of perpetration upon subsequent generations – a postmemorial context addressed in Brett Ashley Kaplan and Fernando Herrero-Matoses' chapter in this volume, and examined as a case study for the 'politics of memory' in Richard Crownshaw's chapter – as evident in Bernhard Schlink's story 'Girl With Lizard' (2002), in which an obsession with a painting looted from its Jewish artist prevents the young postwar German protagonist from realizing successful relationships. Interestingly, we find this possibility voiced too in fictions set in a more recent era of German history and memory, as in the 'Micha' section of Rachel Seiffert's 2001 *The Dark Room*, in which Micha's struggles to discover the wartime past of his grandfather lead to his neglecting the needs of his pregnant partner, Mina. That Mina is of Turkish heritage and that her family have experienced racism in Germany raises the additional question of whether continued attention to past atrocities might also take place at the expense of a confrontation of ongoing discrimination in the present. The anxieties about the impact of Holocaust memory in Englander's story thus resonate – though in very different ways – with a wide range of representations of second- and third-generation experience in different cultural contexts.

The questions raised in 'What We Talk About' concerning the Holocaust's relationship to contemporary Jewish identity might also, finally, be linked to an alternative angle of inquiry in Holocaust literature which asks how or whether the Holocaust might be reconciled with the narrative of Jewish history, and in particular with the history of prior Jewish suffering, as Victoria Aarons investigates with regard to lamentation and midrash in her chapter. Explored extensively in the critical work of such figures as David Roskies (1984) and Sidra DeKoven Ezrahi – the latter of whom contends that 'the representation of the Holocaust in art is, essentially, an oscillation and a struggle between continuity and discontinuity with the cultural as well as with the historical past' (Ezrahi, 1980, pp. 3–4) – such questions have formed an aspect of Holocaust literature from its earliest stages, in the ghetto diaries of Chaim Kaplan and others, for instance.[10] More recent works to address these questions include André Schwarz-Bart's *The Last of the Just*, which offers a genealogy of Jewish history and persecution in Europe using a modified version of the legend of the *lamed-vov*, or Just Men, as a structure (Schwarz-Bart, 1961). The last Just Man, Ernie Levy, is killed at Auschwitz in the novel's conclusion, with Ernie's status as 'the last' at once situating the Holocaust as part of a continuing narrative of Jewish persecution and indicating the degree to which existing ways of comprehending Jewish suffering are no longer tenable in the light of this event. The notion of 'dis/continuities' thus presents an umbrella figure for a broad range of issues – including tradition, identification and the boundaries of the postmemorial relationship – that are of key concern, in different ways, to the project of writing the Holocaust.

Complicities

As suggested in the discussion of potentially problematic forms of identification and instrumentalization in Englander's text, questions of cultural and readerly complicity present another key dimension of Holocaust literature, and the final area to be foregrounded in this Introduction. While scholarly attention to questions of complicity gained momentum relatively recently,[11] such questions are not in themselves new ones, as evident from a consideration of the work of Tadeusz Borowski, a major reference point in discussions of complicity and Holocaust literature. Borowski's 'This Way for the Gas, Ladies and Gentleman' is, like the other stories in the collection of this name, told in the first person by a protagonist who shares with the author a first name and position (as Polish political prisoner and camp functionary) in the camp hierarchy. The present-tense narrative relates the protagonist's involvement in the 'processing' of new arrivals at Auschwitz and the appropriation of their possessions. It charts his desensitization to the horrific scenes he participates in, and unflinchingly explores his complicity in the exploitation of other prisoners to enhance his own prospects of survival. Thus, alongside the exploration of other instances of self-serving behaviour (such as that of a mother who disavows her child because 'She is young, healthy, good-looking, she wants to live' (Borowski, [1967] 1976, p. 43)), the protagonist relates his own refusal of empathy: 'For several days the entire camp will talk about "Soznowiec-Będzin". "Soznowiec-Będzin" was a good, rich transport' (ibid., p. 49).

Borowski's emphasis on complicity, radically departing from notions of the absolute innocence and unassailable moral stature of the concentration camp survivor, has proved highly significant to such critics as the philosopher Gillian Rose (1996), who cites him as a counter-example to 'pious' works of literature and art which neither examine critically their own standpoints nor invite a similar process of self-examination in their readers. Borowski's text, by contrast, places an ethical onus on its readership to negotiate their own relationship to the behaviour and perspective of the text's protagonist – a relationship at once of judgement and identification – and in focusing attention thus on the relationship of reader and text, also arguably draws to the fore the questions of readerly exploitation – of drawing (aesthetic) nourishment from the suffering of the textually consumed other – that form an uncomfortable, though certainly distinct, parallel to Tadek's own self-focused activities. In such ways, the evocations of complicity in Borowski's writing have informed productively the work of critics keen to explore dimensions of Holocaust literature which problematize accepted patterns of identification and clear moral demarcations (see, for example, Matthew Boswell (2012); see also Boswell's chapter in this volume), as well as forming one of the key touchstones in a critical tradition arguing in favour of a disruptive Holocaust art.

Such disruptive artworks might include George Tabori's play *The Cannibals* ([1968] 1982), which couples surrealism and formal disruption with a grotesque scenario in which prisoners must decide whether to eat their dead comrade to ensure their own survival; literature dealing with the 'grey zone' identified by Primo Levi (1989)[12] (including material exploring the administration of Nazi policies in the ghetto by members of the *Judenrat* and Jewish police – texts such as Harold and Edith Lieberman's 1973 play *Throne of Straw*); and an emerging literature of perpetration, not least Jonathan Littell's recent novel *The Kindly Ones*, one of the most important works of Holocaust literature in recent years, yet also one of the most controversial, explored in Erin McGlothlin's chapter on the representation of perpetrators in this volume. Written from the perspective of SS officer Maximilien Aue, what makes the novel so challenging is both the degree to which Aue provocatively calls into question the reader's moral complacency ('you should be able to admit to yourselves that you might also have done what I did' (Littell, 2009, p. 20)) and the ways in which his account raises questions about the literary consumption of horror in implicating ways, for example, offering the following comment on a decision to ban soldiers from photographing mass executions:

> Discretion, it seemed, would henceforth be the rule of the day. But the desire to see these things was also human. Leafing through my Plato, I had found the passage of *The Republic* that my reaction in front of the corpses in the Lutsk fortress had brought to mind: *Leontius, the son of Aglaion, coming up one day from the Piraeus, . . . observed, near the executioner, some dead bodies lying on the ground; and he felt a desire to look at them, and at the same time loathing the thought he tried to turn away. For a time he struggled with himself . . . till at length, overcome by the desire, he forced his eyes wide open with his fingers, and running up to the bodies, exclaimed, 'There! you devils! gaze your fill at the beautiful spectacle!'*
> (Ibid., p. 98)

Such analysis compels the reader to contemplate the degree to which their own reading is likewise informed by 'the desire to see these things',[13] while the reference to Plato in the quotation challenges the separability of high-cultural material from such questions, exemplifying the degree to which Aue's intellect and wide array of cultural reference points might be read as implicating broader tenets of Western culture – a concern Theodor Adorno's philosophy influentially highlighted, as examined in David Miller's chapter on post-Holocaust poetry in this volume.

Closely related to questions of readerly complicity are hence issues of a broader complicity of modern culture in these events, whether in terms of the totalizing and reifying project of modernity or the dehumanizing logics of capitalism and consumption. Within this context, the tendency of Holocaust literature as a whole towards a radical undermining of previously held values – or the way in which, in Lawrence Langer's words, Holocaust literature 'usurps the bulwarks of our civilization' (1975, p. 72) – may be considered productive not merely in registering the events' extremity but also in foregrounding the presence of disturbing cultural logics within 'civilization' itself. Such radical undermining thus invites a reconsideration of existing cultural certainties and moral frameworks. The depiction of bodies in Borowski's story is pertinent in this respect; horribly, trampled infants are described as 'naked little monsters with enormous heads and bloated bellies' that the prisoners carry out 'like chickens' (Borowski [1967] 1976, p. 39), while a dead woman is referred to as 'a huge, swollen female corpse' and, more horrifically still, 'the mound of meat' (p. 45). Echoing Sandra Gilbert's notion that the Holocaust presents a key stage in the redefinition of death from 'expiration' to 'termination' (Gilbert, 2007, p. 136), such imagery demonstrates both the protagonist's increasing desensitization to the horrors that confront him and the extent to which a post-Holocaust perspective must grapple to come to terms with these events' attempted reduction of humanity to a solely material level, while also posing questions about the broader cultural trajectories of dehumanization and reification which surround them. Hence, arguably, the painstaking attempts of Tadeusz Różewicz's speaker in 'In the Midst of Life' to reconceive such values as the principle that 'human life has great importance' (1995a, p. 159, l. 41), or the search in 'The Survivor' for 'a teacher and a master' who will 'separate darkness from light' (1995b, p. 157, ll. 22, 25), enabling the post-Holocaust speaker to find new grounds to distinguish between virtue, truth, beauty, courage and their opposites. 'This Way for the Gas' thus highlights the need to redefine the human in the light of these events, which, as noted earlier in the discussion of Delbo, pose a challenge to ethics in their abolition at numerous levels of an apprehension of the alterity (as opposed to merely the objectivized, instrumentalized materiality) of the human other.

Nevertheless, the complicities evoked by Borowski's tale are not merely material and historical; as suggested by the above discussion of the reader's experience, they are also representational. Beyond the use of narrative strategies calculated to draw the reader into the complicitous positions explored – present-tense narration, for example – the text also bears signs of a conflict within its own representational project, insofar as its attempts to blur moral demarcations are undermined by the literary devices deployed. 'This Way for the Gas' deploys a gendered symbolism which appears to counterpoint the protagonist's enmeshment in a 'grey zone' devoid of clear moral distinctions with a series of polarized representations of good and evil. Thus, for example, the female commandant of the women's camp is presented as 'withered, flat-chested, bony, her thin, colourless hair pulled back and tied in a "Nordic" knot' (Borowski, [1967] 1976, p. 41). By contrast, the protagonist later exchanges a gaze with a young woman who has just arrived on the transport:

> Here, standing before me, is a girl, a girl with enchanting blonde hair, with beautiful breasts, wearing a little cotton blouse, a girl with a wise, mature look in her eyes. Here she stands, gazing straight into my face, waiting. And over there is the gas chamber: communal death, disgusting and ugly. (Ibid., p. 44)

The moral opposition here is bluntly made and appears problematically attached to the portrayal of femininity itself, the flat chest and colourless hair of the commandant contrasting against the 'beautiful breasts' and 'enchanting blonde hair' of the victim. Setting aside the problematic symbolic conflation of moral purity and the feminine,[14] one might ask to what extent symbolism is itself a problematic representational structure when applied at the level of character – a structure in which an individual is viewed only as a signifying shortcut to an abstract value or category 'beyond' – in addition to raising questions about the place of the ordering impetus of literary tropes within a literature of the grey zone. The mechanisms of literary representation are in this recognition rendered complicit in the reiteration and/or obscuration of the historical realities they respond to.

It is for this reason, perhaps, that a key strand of Holocaust literature concerns representation in its self-reflexive and self-questioning dimension, with further instances including the 'awkward poetics' identified by Antony Rowland (2005), in which post-Holocaust poetry registers self-consciously its anxieties concerning its own ethical status and representational adequacy; the elaborate framing devices of a novel like Piotr Rawicz's magnificent *Blood from the Sky* ([1964] 2004); and the self-conscious deployment of intertextuality noted by Sue Vice (2000) in her study of Holocaust fiction and linked to such narratives' perceived need to carefully negotiate a proximity to historical actuality via the proxy of documentary writings. Indeed, in a number of Holocaust fictions, the work of writers who were also victims, such as Anne Frank or Bruno Schulz, is invoked in order both to mediate the relationship of the post-Holocaust subject to this history and to self-consciously acknowledge and examine the nature of that mediation – works such as David Grossman's *See Under: Love* (1990) and Jonathan Safran Foer's *Tree of Codes* (2010), for example.[15] Such intertextual reference, however, arguably increasingly takes place less as an anxious or defensive justification of one's avenue of approach to the Holocaust or the legitimacy of the post-Holocaust literary project, and rather as a more commonplace recognition of the Holocaust's availability to post-Holocaust generations solely through its accumulated representations. To link back to some of the issues highlighted in the previous section, this form of acknowledgement might also be read as recognition that this accumulation of representations constitutes its own tradition, a tradition central to the mechanisms by which the Holocaust signifies in literature today and which offers a framework within which explorations of this historical atrocity might occur, as well as presenting a loose set of representational practices and norms for a more recent generation of writers to productively transgress.

Volume Outline

This Introduction has approached the heterogenous body of works we term Holocaust literature through an exploration of three overlapping regions of interpretation – those of traces, dis/continuities and complicities – focusing on several very different short narratives. In each case, the discussion sought to draw out some of the issues in representation provoked by the text and link these to other texts and authors, while relating these analyses to the provisional framework of interpretation sketched out, invoking issues of testimony, alterity, intersubjectivity, im/propriety and the ethics of reading. These issues resurface in different ways in many of the chapters which comprise the body of the Companion, each of which covers a specific topic, theme or genre in order that the heterogeneity of Holocaust literature and the critical angles by which it is approached might find articulation in a volume which nevertheless does not presume to be comprehensive.

The first chapter of the collection, Victoria Aarons' 'A Genre of Rupture: The Literary Language of the Holocaust', examines the Holocaust's compatibility (or lack thereof) with traditional literary forms and structures, exploring the resultant reconfiguration of such structures in the work of a diverse range of writers, including Dan Pagis, Primo Levi, Elie Wiesel, Jerzy Kosinski and Ruth Klüger. Holocaust writing, Aarons suggests, frequently draws upon the framework of pre-existing cultural traditions such as midrash and lamentation, yet at the same time seeks to reconfigure these and other conventions of expression via experimentation at both a generic and a linguistic–syntactical level. Aarons' is followed by three chapters which each address distinct aspects of particular subcategories of Holocaust literature. The first of these is Sue Vice's 'Questions of Truth in Holocaust Memory and Testimony', which examines what the phenomenon of false or embellished testimony – including works by Misha Defonseca, Herman Rosenblat and Binjamin Wilkomirski – reveals about the ways in which testimonial texts circulate, the processes and biases of individual and cultural Holocaust remembrance, and the nature of testimonial truth(s). This is followed by David Miller's 'After Epic: Adorno's Scream and the Shadows of Lyric', which offers a detailed examination of Adorno's writings on the topic of 'poetry after Auschwitz' and their implications regarding the possibilities of the lyric mode. Miller's chapter explicates and contextualizes Adorno's complex pronouncements on these issues, assessing their implications for Holocaust representation and post-Holocaust poetic practice, with key areas of enquiry including the poetry of Paul Celan. Miller's examination of Adorno is followed by my own investigation of the possibilities of radically altered or conflicted forms of realism in post-Holocaust fiction. 'Relationships to Realism in Post-Holocaust Fiction: Conflicted Realism and the Counterfactual Historical Novel' examines precisely what 'realism' might mean in the context of the radical challenge to existing representational paradigms presented by these events, before exploring attempts to revise the realist mode via the genre of the counterfactual historical novel.

The subsequent group of chapters address key thematic concerns in Holocaust literature and criticism. Informed by Jean-François Lyotard's concept of the differend as well as the trauma theory of Cathy Caruth and Shoshana Felman and the philosophy of Emmanuel Levinas, Alain Badiou and others, Michael Bernard-Donals' 'Theory and the Ethics of Holocaust Representation' contends that 'debates that have taken place under the rubric of "Holocaust theory" in the past 30 years are ultimately arguments over *ethics*'. Bernard-Donals explores the imperative that Holocaust representation retain an openness to that which lies beyond understanding and communicability, a fidelity to the radical alterity of both the experiences themselves and the human others with whom we interact. This is followed by a very different examination of questions of knowledge: Adrienne Kertzer's exploration of the boundaries of witnessing and knowing within the specific context of Holocaust literature focused on the experiences of children. In '"Don't You Know Anything?": Childhood and the Holocaust', Kertzer examines a range of texts – including works by Imre Kertész, Nechama Tec, Aharon Appelfeld, Morris Gleitzman and John Boyne – to suggest that configurations of forms of knowledge it is appropriate for child witnesses to possess vary according to the work's intended readership, with innocence in particular playing a different role in child- and adult-oriented texts. Kertzer's chapter on childhood is followed by Brett Ashley Kaplan and Fernando Herrero-Matoses' 'Holocaust Postmemory: W. G. Sebald and Gerhard Richter', which examines the intergenerational response to the Holocaust in the context of German literature and art. Examining the ways in which these figures creatively mediate the after-effects of the Holocaust in Germany via the figure of the familial Nazi, Kaplan and Herrero-Matoses not only demonstrate the productive nature of reading contemporary German literature via the conceptual framework of postmemory, but also illustrate the potential of interdisciplinary approaches to yield additional insights in this endeavour.

The next chapter in the collection, Erin McGlothlin's 'Narrative Perspective and the Holocaust Perpetrator: Edgar Hilsenrath's *The Nazi and the Barber* and Jonathan Littell's *The Kindly Ones*' continues this focus on the contexts of Holocaust perpetration, examining attempts to depict the Holocaust from the perspective of those responsible. Focusing on narratological questions of perspective and focalization, McGlothlin examines the ways in which fiction with a perpetrator-protagonist handles questions of identification, contending that Littell and Hilsenrath's novels at once invite such identification and obscure its possibility, raising further questions regarding the possibility that perpetrators might serve as objects of knowledge and understanding in Holocaust fiction. Such issues are also one area of consideration in Matthew Boswell's chapter 'Holocaust Literature and the Taboo', which investigates more broadly the nature and functioning of taboos in the writing of the Holocaust, including the taboo on fictive Holocaust representation in the early stages of the post-Holocaust era, the privileging of restrained or distanced depictions over more shocking or confrontational ones and the taboo on representation of the consciousness of perpetrators. Contending that representational taboos might in fact be viewed as attempts to evade problematic but significant issues in the cultural response to the Holocaust, Boswell explores the illicit forms of truth and recognition taboo-breaking representations aim at, with key figures in this discussion including Sylvia Plath, Michel Tournier and D. M. Thomas.

The 'Current Research' section comes to a close with two chapters devoted to the broader political and transnational contexts within which Holocaust literature might be appraised. Stef Craps' 'Holocaust Literature: Comparative Perspectives' examines attempts to theorize the Holocaust's relationship to other traumatic histories in the context of an increasingly transnational direction of the critical gaze within memory studies. Analysing closely the work of such scholars as Levy and Sznaider (2006) on 'cosmopolitan memory' and Rothberg (2009) on 'multidirectional memory', Craps examines both the insights and pitfalls of texts that set the Holocaust in dialogue with other histories of violence, offering a corrective to the dominant focus on prose in such investigations in his own consideration of the work of the Native American poet Sherman Alexie. Richard Crownshaw's chapter on the politics of Holocaust representation concludes the section, exploring the notion of a politics of memory and representation via an exploration of post-unification Germany's national politics of remembrance, in order to make the case for the imperative nature of approaches to Holocaust literature that are fully attuned to their contextualizing memorial politics. The fact that a number of the essays draw on examples from German literature and culture in their exploration of questions of (post-)Holocaust memory both exemplifies the recent turn in Holocaust literary studies to the contexts and legacies of perpetration and recalls Cynthia Ozick's statement that the Holocaust – and the imperative to respond to these events – 'belongs' not to Jews but precisely to German history and culture (Ozick, 1988, p. 284).

The chapters thus address a wide range of different angles from which Holocaust literature might be approached, varying in their breadth of focus and precise balance of theoretical and literary–critical material in ways which enable a productive blend of sustained case study and more overarching deliberation. This section is followed by a chapter detailing new directions in Holocaust literary studies, which aims to chart emergent trends in literary analysis at the present moment, and by an Annotated Bibliography which offers useful starting points in secondary reading for students and scholars new to the field, while the Glossary of Major Terms and Concepts provides an accompanying explication of key terminology. The Companion thus aims to offer a wide-ranging and informative approach to Holocaust literature at the present moment that also raises, in productive and thought-provoking ways, further angles of enquiry.

Notes

1. See, likewise, Flanzbaum's comments on Cynthia Ozick's objections to Bernhard Schlink's *The Reader* on the grounds of its lack of realism, contending that such critics 'seem determined to live in the world as it was half a century ago, when few knew about the Holocaust, and writers (both Jewish and not) had a clear investment in seeing that the facts got a full airing' (Flanzbaum, 2011, p. 76).

2. See this volume's 'New Directions' and 'Annotated Bibliography' sections for a more detailed exploration of trajectories of development.
3. Suleiman, 2006, p. 179; see Glossary for an explication of this concept.
4. These issues have been examined with regard to the act of testimony by Giorgio Agamben. See Glossary entry under 'Testimony' for a brief explication of Agamben's ideas on this subject, and entry under 'Witness' for further discussion of Laub's consideration of the Holocaust as an 'event without a witness'.
5. Gubar writes in her study of Holocaust poetry, for example, that 'most of the formal devices I have enumerated buckle time, bringing two moments together: confessional and documentary verse, ecphrasis and antimorphosis, prosopopoeia and lamentation engage the empathic imagination in conveying the dead past of a foreign place into the living present of our native minds' (2003, p. 246).
6. On the temporal dislocations of traumatic experience, see, for example, Caruth, 1995, p. 8.
7. See below, pp. 9–10, for a brief definition of this concept.
8. See, for example, Hirsch and Miller, 2011, pp. 4, 10.
9. It should be noted that the focus of Rothberg's thesis is more on the connections between memories of different traumatic histories than on the relationship between a given history and an experientially distanced individual; as regards the latter, see also Marianne Hirsch's notion of 'affiliative postmemory', elaborated in Hirsch, 2012.
10. See the discussion of ghetto diarists' religious questioning in Patterson, 1999, pp. 118–21.
11. See, for example, Mandel, 2006, pp. 23, 211.
12. See Glossary entry under 'Grey Zone' for a more detailed discussion of this concept.
13. See Adams (2013b), for further discussion of this.
14. This phenomenon is evident in Holocaust discourse more widely, as, for example, in the talismanic status of the mythic tale in which a female prisoner (a dancer or actress in some accounts) disarms and shoots SS officer Schillinger in the undressing room prior to the gas chamber at Auschwitz-Birkenau (for a narration of this episode, see, for example, Greif, 2005, pp. 162–3). Elsewhere, the use of symbolic females as a mechanism for moral and other forms of polarization is perhaps most obviously apparent in Paul Celan's celebrated poem 'Deathfugue', in which the blonde Margarete and the ashen-haired Shulamith dramatize the German and Jewish people respectively (Celan, 2001).
15. See Adams (2013a), for further discussion of this.

Works Cited

Adams, J. (2013a), 'Intertextuality and the trace of the other: spectres of Bruno Schulz', *Symbolism: An International Annual of Critical Aesthetics*, 12/13, 49–68.
—. (2013b), 'Reading (as) violence in Jonathan Littell's *The Kindly Ones*', in J. Adams and S. Vice (eds), *Representing Perpetrators in Holocaust Literature and Film*. London: Vallentine Mitchell, pp. 25–46.
Amis, M. (1991), *Time's Arrow*. London: Penguin.
Borowski, T. [1967] (1976), 'This way for the gas, ladies and gentlemen', in *This Way for the Gas, Ladies and Gentlemen*, trans. B. Vedder. London: Penguin, pp. 29–49.
Boswell, M. (2012), *Holocaust Impiety in Literature, Popular Music and Film*. Basingstoke: Palgrave Macmillan.

Caruth, C. (1995), 'Trauma and experience: introduction', in C. Caruth (ed.), *Trauma: Explorations in Memory*. Baltimore: Johns Hopkins University Press, pp. 3–12.

Carver, R. [1981] (2003), 'What we talk about when we talk about love', in *What We Talk about When We Talk about Love*. London: Vintage, pp. 114–29.

Celan, P. (2001), 'Deathfugue', in *Selected Poems and Prose of Paul Celan*, trans. J. Felstiner. New York: Norton, pp. 31–3.

Delbo, C. (1995a), 'Morning', in *Auschwitz and After*, trans. R. C. Lamont. New Haven: Yale University Press, pp. 62–7.

—. (1995b), 'One day', in *Auschwitz and After*, trans. R. C. Lamont. New Haven: Yale University Press, pp. 24–9.

Englander, N. (2012), 'What we talk about when we talk about Anne Frank', in *What We Talk about When We Talk about Anne Frank*. London: Weidenfeld & Nicolson, pp. 1–32.

Ezrahi, S. DeKoven (1980), *By Words Alone: The Holocaust in Literature*. Chicago and London: Chicago University Press.

Fink, I. (1989), 'Traces', in *A Scrap of Time and Other Stories*, trans. M. Levine and F. Prose. London: Penguin, pp. 135–7.

Flanzbaum, H. (2011), 'Reading the Holocaust: right here, right now', *Holocaust Studies: A Journal of Culture and History*, 17.1, 63–84.

Foer, J. S. (2010), *Tree of Codes*. London: Visual Editions.

Gilbert, S. (2007), *Death's Door: Modern Dying and the Way We Grieve*. New York and London: W. W. Norton.

Greif, G. (2005), *We Wept Without Tears: Testimonies of the Jewish Sonderkommando from Auschwitz*. New Haven and London: Yale University Press.

Grossman, D. (1990), *See Under: Love*, trans. B. Rosenberg. London: Jonathan Cape.

Gubar, S. (2003), *Poetry after Auschwitz: Remembering What One Never Knew*. Bloomington and Indianapolis: Indiana University Press.

Hattemer-Higgins, I. (2012), *The History of History: A Novel of Berlin*. London: Faber and Faber.

Hawthorne, J. (2012), 'The face-to-face encounter in Holocaust narrative', in J. Lothe, S. Rubin Suleiman and J. Phelan (eds), *After Testimony: The Ethics and Aesthetics of Holocaust Narrative*. Columbus: Ohio State University Press, pp. 143–61.

Hirsch, M. (1996), 'Past lives: postmemories in exile', *Poetics Today*, 17.4, 659–86.

—. (2012), *The Generation of Postmemory: Writing and Visual Culture after the Holocaust*. New York: Columbia University Press.

Hirsch, M. and Miller, N. K. (2011), 'Introduction' to M. Hirsch and N. K. Miller (eds), *Rites of Return: Diaspora Poetics and the Politics of Memory*. New York: Columbia University Press, pp. 1–20.

Lang, B. (2000), 'Holocaust genres and the turn to history', in A. Leak and G. Paizis (eds), *The Holocaust and the Text*. Basingstoke: Macmillan, pp. 17–31.

Langer, L. (1975), *The Holocaust and the Literary Imagination*. New Haven and London: Yale University Press.

Laub, D. (1992), 'An event without a witness: truth, testimony and survival', in S. Felman and D. Laub, *Testimony: Crises of Witnessing in Literature, Psychoanalysis and History*. New York and London: Routledge, pp. 75–92.

Levi, P. (1987), *If This Is a Man; The Truce*, trans. S. Woolf. London: Abacus.

—. (1989), 'The grey zone', in *The Drowned and the Saved*, trans. R. Rosenthal. London: Abacus, pp. 22–51.

Levinas, E. (1996), 'Meaning and sense', trans. A. Lingis, rev. S. Critchley and A. T. Peperzak, in A. T. Peperzak, S. Critchley and R. Bernasconi (eds), *Emmanuel Levinas: Basic Philosophical Writings*. Bloomington: Indiana University Press, pp. 33–64.

Levy, D. and Sznaider, N. (2006), *The Holocaust and Memory in the Global Age*, trans. A. Oksiloff. Philadelphia: Temple University Press.

Lieberman, E. and Lieberman, H. [1973] (1982), *Throne of Straw*, in R. Skloot (ed.), *The Theatre of the Holocaust*, vol. 1. Madison: University of Wisconsin Press, pp. 113–96.

Littell, J. (2009), *The Kindly Ones*, trans. C. Mandell. London: Chatto & Windus.

Mandel, N. (2006), *Against the Unspeakable: Complicity, the Holocaust and Slavery in America*. Charlottesville: University of Virginia Press.

Michaels, A. [1996] (1997), *Fugitive Pieces*. London: Bloomsbury.

Orbán, K. (2005), *Ethical Diversions: The Post-Holocaust Narratives of Pynchon, Abish, DeLillo, and Spiegelman*. New York and London: Routledge.

Ozick, C. (1988), 'Roundtable discussion', in B. Lang (ed.), *Writing and the Holocaust*. New York and London: Holmes & Meier, 1988, pp. 277–84.

—. (1991), 'The shawl', in *The Shawl: A Story and a Novella*. London: Jonathan Cape, pp. 10–18.

Pagis, D. (1989), 'Written in pencil in the sealed freightcar', trans. S. Mitchell, in H. Schiff (ed.), *Holocaust Poetry*. London: Fount, p. 180.

Patterson, D. (1999), *Along the Edge of Annihilation: The Collapse and Recovery of Life in the Holocaust Diary*. Seattle: University of Washington Press.

Perec, G. [1988] (1996), *W or the Memory of Childhood*, trans. D. Bellos. London: Harvill Press.

Rawicz, P. [1964] (2004), *Blood from the Sky*, trans. P. Wiles, ed. A. Rudolf. London: Elliott & Thompson.

Rose, G. (1996), *Mourning Becomes the Law: Philosophy and Representation*. Cambridge: Cambridge University Press.

Rosenbaum, T. (1996), 'Cattle car complex', in *Elijah Visible*. New York: St Martin's Griffin, pp. 1–11.

Roskies, D. G. (1984), *Against the Apocalypse: Responses to Catastrophe in Modern Jewish Culture*. Cambridge, MA: Harvard University Press.

Rothberg, M. (2009), *Multidirectional Memory: Remembering the Holocaust in the Age of Decolonization*. Stanford, CA: Stanford University Press.

Rowland, A. (2005), *Holocaust Poetry: Awkward Poetics in the Work of Sylvia Plath, Geoffrey Hill, Tony Harrison and Ted Hughes*. Edinburgh: Edinburgh University Press.

Różewicz, T. (1995a), 'In the midst of life', translator unspecified, in H. Schiff (ed.), *Holocaust Poetry*. London: Fount, pp. 158–60.

—. (1995b), 'The survivor', trans. A. Czerniawski, in H. Schiff (ed.), *Holocaust Poetry*. London: Fount, p. 157.

Schlink, B. (2002), 'Girl with lizard', in *Flights of Love*, trans. J. E. Woods. London: Phoenix, pp. 3–51.

Schwarz-Bart, A. (1961), *The Last of the Just*, trans. S. Becker. London: Secker & Warburg.

Sebald, W. G. (2002), *Austerlitz*, trans. A. Bell. London: Penguin.

Seiffert, R. (2001), *The Dark Room*. London: Heinemann.

Spiegelman, A. [1996] (2003), *The Complete Maus*. London: Penguin.

Stone, D. (2003), *Constructing the Holocaust: A Study in Historiography*. London: Vallentine Mitchell.

Suleiman, S. Rubin (2006), *Crises of Memory and the Second World War*. Cambridge, MA: Harvard University Press.

Tabori, G. [1968] (1982), *The Cannibals*, in R. Skloot (ed.), *The Theatre of the Holocaust*, vol. 1. Madison: University of Wisconsin Press, pp. 197–265.

Vice, S. (2000), *Holocaust Fiction*. London: Routledge.

Current Research

1 A Genre of Rupture: The Literary Language of the Holocaust

Victoria Aarons

Abstract

Holocaust narrative, in drawing from two vital traditions of Jewish expression, midrash and lamentation, constitutes a genre of rupture that creates, extends and responds to the trauma of the Shoah. In doing so, Holocaust texts call upon literary and cultural traditions as a framework for the ongoing response to the devastation of the Holocaust, all the while creating within this responsive framework an interpretative reconfiguration of conventional forms of expression. Such narratives, this chapter argues, produce the effects of disequilibrium and estrangement that represent the enormity of the trauma of the Holocaust, inviting the reader to participate in an ethical act of reading and bearing witness. Such literary modes of representation create a language and a landscape of rupture, of discursive disequilibrium, and of narrative disjunction in an attempt to enact the very conditions they evoke. The convergence of historiography and literary invention in Holocaust writing lends itself to wide-ranging texts that call upon diverse discursive strategies and forms that engage in the strategic performance of rhetorical destabilization. From this subversive impulse, 'a negative rhetoric emerges', a rhetoric of unacceptability and opposition that resists closure and attempts to shape Jewish collective memory, linking personal and collective identities with traumatic history.

In *Holocaust Representation: Art within the Limits of History and Ethics*, Berel Lang argues that Holocaust literature is fashioned by a 'blurring of traditional genres' and that 'this blurring effect reflects two principal sources – the character of the Holocaust as a subject for literary representation and the role of historical and ethical causality in shaping the genres, and thus the forms, of literary discourse' (Lang, 2000, pp. 10, 35). This blurring of otherwise distinct genres and modes is a result of the failure of traditional forms and structures, as well as the perceived failure of ordinary language, to represent adequately the historical and ethical complexities of the Holocaust, to give voice to the felt *experience* of the Holocaust, 'a crime so vast', as Saul Bellow has put it, that it 'brings all Being into Judgment' (2010, p. 439). The enormity of what we have come to think of as the Holocaust – that time between 1933 and 1945, when Nazi Germany put into effect the annihilation of European Jewry – challenges conventional forms of expression and thus defies and reconfigures traditional telling, calling upon writers to seek alternative structures of representation to approximate and extend the scope of the Holocaust and its memory. What emerges through such representation is, to borrow a term from David Roskies, a 'literature of destruction', a literature that both calls upon traditional Jewish responsive and interpretative forms of expression and subverts traditional generic distinctions, paradoxically through which 'one discovers the ultimate value of life' (1989, p. 10). This challenge to received forms of representation makes rupture mimetic, and representation opens up tropically to the willed defiance of the unchangeable experience of trauma. That is, the experience of trauma is thematized by generic subversion in these texts.

Holocaust narratives draw from two vital traditions of Jewish expression as they mediate a post-Holocaust universe: midrash and lamentation. By midrash I refer to the traditional stories that extend themselves through retelling into the interpretative repertoire of Jewish writers, explanations of events and stories that bring them to life in the present, showing their persistent relevance and dramatizing their historical resonance (Aarons, 2005, pp. 40–1). Midrash in Holocaust narratives interpretatively fills in the gaps created by the silences of time and distance. Midrashic stories are openings for moments of continuity and amplification, an invitation to carry the weight of memory into the present. The tradition of midrash offers interpretative, even homiletic, extensions of biblical narratives; as such, it forms the basis of a specifically Jewish hermeneutics, one that extends itself as a methodological principle of interpretation in extending Jewish history and Jewish identity. Lamentation is the second tradition from which Holocaust narratives draw, originating in the Hebrew Book of Lamentations, the prophet Jeremiah's mourning of the destruction of the First Temple in Jerusalem in 586 BCE. In the Book of Lamentations, the prophet assumes the voice of the messenger and transmits memory in a speech act of elegiac reckoning and denunciation. As Roskies proposes, this paradigm 'of destruction and desecration', as the elegiac response to catastrophe, suggests twin archetypal patterns: 'one as literal recall, the other as sacred parody', where historical truth-telling and literary invention engage in the creation of a landscape infused with moral purpose (1984, p. 17). In evoking the two ancient topoi of lamentation and midrash, Holocaust texts simultaneously call upon literary and cultural traditions as a framework for the ongoing response to the devastation of the Holocaust, all the while creating within this responsive framework an interpretative reconfiguration of conventional forms of expression. As James Young suggests, such ancient archetypes are 'invoked' as much as they are 'qualified' and 'recast' (1988, p. 95). Successful Holocaust narratives typically qualify and reshape these archetypal modes of invention in two primary ways: (1) they fuse otherwise discrete genres; and (2) they refigure language and grammatical norms at the level of syntactical arrangement and word choice. These twin conceits of genre and lexicon produce the effects of rupture and estrangement that aim to represent the enormity of the trauma of the Holocaust. Midrash and lamentation function as general modes of perception and expression; they invite the reader into an act of understanding. Disruptions of genre and lexicon both represent and recreate the perceptions and interpretative gestures of midrashic understanding and of its accompanying moral lament.

Holocaust narratives committed to responsible representation create the conditions for discomfort and unease; they create a language and a landscape of rupture, of discursive disequilibrium and of narrative disjunction. To that end, Holocaust novels, memoirs, poems, fables and historical 'imaginings' that attempt, as Elie Wiesel once put it, to bring the reader 'to the other side', must enact the very conditions they evoke (1985, p. 13). Such texts thus engage in the strategic performance of rhetorical destabilization. From this subversive impulse, 'a negative rhetoric emerges', a rhetoric of unacceptability and opposition that resists closure, resists, that is, as Ehud Havazelet puts it in the Holocaust novel *Bearing the Body*, a 'story's consoling shape' (Lang, 2000, p. 18; Havazelet, 2007, p. 132). Such writing creates moments of unease brought about by the subversive disjuncture of expectation and effect. We find this kind of disequilibrium, for example, in Tadeusz Borowski's novella 'This Way for the Gas, Ladies and Gentlemen' ([1959] 1976), whose very title disquietingly juxtaposes civility and barbarity. In this way, Holocaust narratives attempt to upend conventional constructs of language and experience, undoing some of language's palliative, antidotal and redemptive possibilities. As Berel Lang proposes,

[T]he central question to ask in the analysis of Holocaust representation is just how the deepest and most urgent Holocaust art . . . has succeeded in turning an oppositional impulse into its own strength . . . . The pressures exerted . . . are such that the associations of the traditional forms – the developmental order of the novel, the predictability of prosody, the comforting representations of landscape or portrait in painting – are quite inadequate for the images of a subject with the moral dimensions and impersonal will of the Holocaust. Thus the constant turning in Holocaust images to difference: to the use of silence as means and metaphor, to obliqueness in representation . . ., to the uses of allegory and fable and surrealism, to the blurring of traditional genres not just for the sake of undoing them but in the interests of combining certain of their elements that otherwise had been held apart. (2000, pp. 9–10)

Thus writers such as Tadeusz Borowski, Jerzy Kosinski, Isiah Spiegal and, more recently, Cynthia Ozick turn to unconventional means in attempting to represent the Holocaust when traditional forms of literary expression show themselves to be inadequate to its moral enormity. This is not to say that a subject as complex as the Holocaust cannot be known, only that such knowledge requires revised and sometimes extreme modes of representation in its conscientious transmission. As the late Israeli psychologist Dan Bar-On asks, 'How can one "translate" such experiences into ordinary language?' (1998, p. 94). Such a 'translation' is achieved by defamiliarizing language, by making it appear extraordinary, and by refashioning it to rent the fabric of narrative or formal continuity in a conscious break from convention.

Because of the inherent limitations of conventional forms and genres in representing catastrophe, Holocaust narratives draw literary license from dissociation and from various strategies of representational subterfuge, thus effecting in their juncture a 'blurring' of genres to open up the possibilities of interpretation. 'Blurring' is a curious metaphor here. Rather than obscuring or making indistinct its subject, the subversion of convention and its accompanying disruption create a striking clarity in calling forth the experience of rupture. Such strategies of disruption characterize first-hand accounts by Holocaust survivors, those accounts by Elie Wiesel, Ida Fink and Primo Levi, for example. These writers, to borrow the title of one of Wiesel's (2005) novels, testify to 'the time of the uprooted', having been hidden in forests, incarcerated in ghettoes, deported to concentration camps, subjected to death marches. Survivor writing extends beyond direct testimony into the self-consciously strategic revisions of genre and mode. Wiesel's novel *Night* ([1958] 2006) takes its reader through the historical stages of round-up, deportation, incarceration, annihilation and liberation, all the while contextualizing and interpreting those events in the related genres of autobiography, testimony and memoir, all of which merge personal history with meditations on collective significance.

We find a similar generically apposite attempt at the disruption of conventional representation in Primo Levi's turning of the traditional life-affirming prayer of the 'Shema' into a poem about the brutal denial of humanity. Through a harsh syllabic intonation of verse that undercuts the soothing cadences of the lines of the ancient prayer, Levi's poem reinterprets the Shema's reassuring promise of the endurance of the covenant as a receding silhouette by extending the poem into a post-Holocaust present. The poem thus shows the Holocaust as a fundamental deracination of the origins and possibility of Jewish life. The foreboding poetic voice asks us to

> Consider if this is a man
> Who works in the mud
> Who does not know peace
> Who fights for a scrap of bread
> Who dies because of a yes or a no.
> Consider if this is a woman,
> Without hair and without name
> With no more strength to remember,
> Her eyes empty and her womb cold
> Like a frog in winter. (Levi, [1958] 1996, p. 11)

Levi's 'revision' of this biblical text constitutes a midrashic response to the Holocaust's distortion of the basic tenets of a humane world. Levi turns this traditional representation of the endurance of the covenant into its distorted, morbid other. An affirmation of life is modified to become a meditation on death.

Ida Fink's short story, 'The Key Game', is another example of the way Holocaust writing refigures conventional representation to take the reader to the place of traumatic origin. The brief story, which takes place in a family kitchen, takes assumptions about domesticity and child's play and transforms them into games of horror. In the story, the survival of a Jewish family depends on a 3-year-old child's constant rehearsal of a theatrical performance in which he would pronounce his father dead to the soldiers who will inevitably arrive at their door to execute his fate. The juxtaposition of the mother's melodic mimetic simulation of the doorbell's chimes – 'Ding-dong . . . a soft, lovely bell . . . the sound of chimes ringing so musically from his mother's lips' – and the child's ragged, repetitive, deafening pretense of noisily searching for the door key in a futile attempt to afford his father time to conceal himself in a crevasse in the wall creates the anxious conditions of heightened fear, a prelude to ruin (Fink, [1987] 1995b, p. 36). The child never gets it right in the story; there is never enough time for the father to hide. The implication is that history has already prevented the father's escape. This story works by implication, with sparse dialogue and a simple, repetitive event, creating anticipation of collective devastation through the collectivizing anonymity of Fink's characters. Fink's story thus re-enacts traumatic rupture and re-engages the point of its origin, all the while creating in the reader an anxiety of retrospective anticipation, an extreme form of dramatic irony. This vagueness of personalized narrative detail – names, place, time and ethnicity – creates an effect of foreboding through crafted indirection. What is left unsaid evokes precisely what the reader knows to be true, that the Nazis will arrest the father and seize the mother and child. In this way

Fink refigures conventional modes of narrative to achieve an effect of personal and collective disruption and catastrophe.

In these examples, strategic disjunctions are deployed as moments of dislocation within some form of narrative or cultural continuity. In Wiesel's *Night*, the continuity that forms the context of disruption is historical. In Levi's 'Shema', the continuity is biblical. In Fink's 'The Key Game', the continuity is domestic. In all three cases, the associative stability of the familiar is dislocated by the dissociative effect of its narrative and linguistic rupture. The most immediate and provocative Holocaust narratives – poems, stories, novels and imaginative memoirs – attempt to evoke the Holocaust by aligning their modes of representation with historical rupture and trauma. Such 'negative' rhetorical strategies, set in disjunction to the familiar and the consoling, are characteristic not only of survivor writing, but also of the literature of 'second-hand' witnesses, narratives by those who did not experience the events of the Holocaust directly, but who write from a more distanced perspective, a perspective of memory transferred, memory, as Lisa Appignanesi, in her memoir *Losing the Dead*, puts it, that 'cascades through the generations' (2000, p. 8). Holocaust memory and the representation of trauma extend beyond the authorizing source of direct experience. Thus the imagined narratives of post-Holocaust generations, as Alan Berger suggests, 'bear the indelible imprint of the *Shoah*'s cultural, psychic, and theological legacy' (1997, p. 18). At the same time, post-Holocaust generations write as spectators to a history and memory not their own, a memory bequeathed to them with heavy responsibility, both theirs as Jews and not theirs because historically removed. To this end, Marianne Hirsch, in *Family Frames: Photography, Narrative and Postmemory*, provocatively distinguishes memory from 'postmemory':

> Postmemory is a powerful and very particular form of memory precisely because its connection to its object or source is mediated not through recollection but through an imaginative investment and creation. This is not to say that memory itself is unmediated, but that it is more directly connected to the past. (1997, p. 22)

Thus the literary representation of the Holocaust extends beyond survivor testimony. The work of those following generations is part of an ongoing evolution of bearing witness, not only to genocide, but to the survival of its memory and of the cultural life it tried to eradicate. And although post-Holocaust writers, as Henri Raczymow proposes, write from a memory 'shot through with holes', imperfect and fragmentary, these writers are motivated by 'the feeling all of [them] have, deep down, of having missed a train' (1994, p. 105). In other words, the act of representation becomes an attempt to mediate and extend an experience complex and temporally and experientially removed.

Thus, the convergence of historiography and literary invention in Holocaust writing lends itself to wide-ranging texts that call upon diverse discursive strategies. Such works attempt to shape Jewish collective memory, linking personal and collective identities with traumatic history. Throughout the varied corpus of Holocaust literature, we find works that, through the imaginative reconfigurations that engage the Holocaust as a subject of testimony and moral reckoning, attempt to create a particularity of expression to represent the trauma of dispossession. While imaginative investment and a sense of moral purpose are the means by which these writers engage the Holocaust, their work is no less permeated with an abiding sense of the importance of getting history right, of not *misrepresenting* the known facts of history and of testimony. On the one hand, the Holocaust requires a morally engaged response; on the other, the challenges of historical representation make imaginative reconstruction of experience problematic. For example, second-generation Holocaust writer Art Spiegelman, in the graphic novel *MAUS* (1986), will use the genre of the 'comic book' to merge autobiography, biography and history, the conventions of the adopted form defamiliarizing the received weight of each genre in representing the complexity of his family's experience. For this reason, modes of representation become crucial in accounting both for moral conviction and unsettling historical complexity.

The nature of the Holocaust challenges language, just as language attempts to comprehend its history. The character of the Holocaust – its unprecedented, legislated, barbaric pathology, its secreted modes of transport and execution, and its unremitting consequences extending well beyond its chronological end – complicates its telling. As the poet Hyam Plutzik proposes, the utterance 'will dissolve into itself, though in another language' ([1949] 1961a, p. 3). So too the reader of Holocaust narratives, especially if generationally distanced from the events, is arrested by the assault on sensibility exhumed by such narratives of a subject so extreme. Jenni Adams has pointed to 'the continued imperative felt by writers to engage in the project of Holocaust representation', an imperative 'closely linked to the postmemorial compulsion to reimagine Holocaust experiences of previous generations' (2011, p. 173). Thus the complexities of transmission are magnified by the difficulties for readers in locating a fitting response to an art made out of horror.

Thus both writer and reader together are entangled in a complicated and precarious exchange. Both must participate in the transmission of these second-generational texts because there is no disengaged reading of Holocaust narratives. The modes of conventional narration become at times a cautionary challenge, at other times a palpable threat. Such narratives are shaped by a language of pain, 'like a knife in my heart', as one fictionalized Holocaust survivor insists (Newman, 1990, p. 338). The authorial difficulty comes in finding and sustaining a sufficiently searing voice, a wound reopened in the telling. The reader is cautioned implicitly or explicitly not to take comfort from such stories, narratives that are neither redemptive nor hopeful. The Holocaust is uncomfortable topical terrain, and the reader is warned, as this same fictionalized survivor will tell his young interlocutor: 'No happy endings for a nice girl like you' (ibid.). As novelist Cynthia Ozick has argued, any such tendency to find a 'redemptive meaning' in Holocaust literature becomes a failure of moral rectitude, 'a retroactive impulse, an anachronism . . . . [I]t does not suit the events themselves . . . . [N]o promise, no use, no restitution and no redemption can come out of the suffering and destruction of one-third of the Jewish people' (1988, pp. 278–9). Ozick makes clear that there are no conventional narrative solutions, no classic narrative 'arcs' of resolution, redemption, transformation or conversion when writing about the Holocaust. The question remains of what strategies present themselves to the writer for creating a suitable form to perform and extend the burden of testimony in transmitting the legacy of the Shoah. The challenge is in sustaining a narrative that arrests the reader in startled recognition of deep trauma, all the while drawing her or him into a kind of traumatic recall, one representing an experience known second hand. With the Holocaust as subject, we are in two places at once: inside the text and moved by its language, and looking past that language into the horrors of a particular historical moment.

Holocaust writing, as an emergent form of representation, draws upon historical fracture and sets in motion the very rupture and dissociation of which it speaks, 'a traumatic rupture', to borrow a phrase from Joshua Hirsch's study of Holocaust cinematic images (2004, p. 7). This is necessarily a literature and language of extremes. In drawing on discordant tones and restrained, antithetical and often antagonistic impulses, the most pressing Holocaust narratives linguistically reimagine and reconceive the devastation they so urgently perform. In producing a simulacrum of rupture, such narratives create their own equilibrium amid moments of disequilibrium. Certain tropes lend themselves to this shattering effect, as turns of phrase depart from normative syntactical and linguistic expectation, creating a chaos of dislocation. Tropes shape language, and thus constitute strategies for shaping and extending, in a textually material sense, the experience of and response to trauma. The 'troping' of the Holocaust thus draws upon a variety of figures of speech that cause disruption and unease: *personification*, imbuing the inanimate with dissonant and often menacing human characteristics; *aposiopesis*, the deliberate cessation of speech; *polyptoton*, emphasis achieved through a repetition of a word's core with altering forms; *asyndeton*, the coming to a halt of rapid streams of images, phrases and actions; *ellipsis*, the trailing off or omission of subsequent thought or movement; *prosopopoeia*, the reanimation of the dead; *metonymy*, an uneasy substitution of part for whole; *metaphor*, a transformative disturbance of renaming or reconfiguring; *hyperbaton*, the deviation from stable ordering; and *praecisio*, complete and calculated silence. Such interruptions and intentional disorder carry the weight of representation in many of these texts, balanced by a mediating voice of moral authority that remains faithful to history and experience. Thus, as Lang has so aptly suggested, Holocaust literature 'pushes certain features of writing to their limits' (2000, p. 36). In doing so, Holocaust narratives transform disjunction and dissonance into an invitation to a reckoning of conscience, to urgent acts of moral evaluation. These images spill disturbingly beyond the spatial constraints of the confining page. These kinds of rhetorical tropes and their strategic deployment characterize much of Holocaust writing at its most imperative and insistent and make possible its representation of the extreme.

One of the central issues of Holocaust imagery is the moral and historical responsibility of art in aligning itself with historical accuracy. Holocaust narratives must remain faithful to the unfolding of history in the present as well as to history's inevitable recession into the past. Such pressing concerns are derived not only from a moral but also from a discursive condition: how to *talk about* the Holocaust. The representation of any event is, by course, a matter of both mediation and invention. How, then, might Holocaust narratives, in attempting to navigate and expose the historical complexity of the Holocaust, bend language to give voice to the enormity of that history? When a mode of representation exposes its own deficiency in the telling, the manner and method of expression are foregrounded; in other words, the question of testimony depends upon representational choice. The troping of the Holocaust, then, is the refiguring of language, the manipulating of linguistic forms and the midrashic extension of those forms into a discursive future. Tropes create the conditions by which we might individuate and identify the specifics of a history that would otherwise be the stuff of insulated nightmares and solitary suffering, 'reminiscent of pain', like that of Edward Lewis Wallant's Sol Nazerman, a camp survivor relocated amid the impoverished suffering of New York's Harlem in the early 1960s, entombed in the 'horrid silence' of all his dead (Wallant, 1961, pp. 53, 9).

Holocaust writing reanimates the landscape of loss by giving voice to absence; like the tradition of midrash, this reanimation tries to fill in gaps of understanding in the face of trauma and its lamentation. In defiance of silence, such reimagined utterance exacts upon the stillness of death the sound of voice, an intonation of life once lived and thus elegiacally remembered. In summoning an absent voice, such configurations, as Susan Gubar puts it, 'find a language for the staggering horror' (2001, p. 191). Here *prosopopoeia*, a rhetorical trope that recreates the voice of an absent speaker, asserts the presence of the dead by asserting their presence in the text. *Prosopopoeia* conjures an invented or no longer living person, endowing him or her with imagined life for the moment of utterance. Giving voice to the dispossessed through this form of poetic impersonation, as Gubar argues, 'allows the authors who manipulate it to summon the posthumous voice, to conceive of subjectivity enduring beyond the concentration camp, and thereby to suggest that the anguish of the Shoah does not, and will not, dissipate' (ibid., p. 192). In giving voice to the dead, *prosopopoeia* functions metonymically to articulate the plight of the survivor: the living stand in for the dead, as, chiastically, the dead stand in for the living as the 'voice' of collective trauma. Here silence itself becomes a rhetorical trope, invoked at moments of 'inarticulable' terror or loss in order to extract its unburied other. The survivor at the close of Kosinski's *The Painted Bird*, for example, will yearn, 'convincing myself again and again and again that speech was now mine', the regaining of speech a metaphor for bearing witness to both the atrocities suffered and his individual survival (1965, p. 234). Thus, for the survivor, the affirmation of voice, the act of bearing witness, is always an incomplete, unfinished gesture. The lack of punctuation in the reiterative mantra – 'again and again and again' – makes emphatic the necessity for ongoing testimony just as it recalls the endless suffering inflicted. The survivor's is a found voice amid the 'horrid silence' of the dead, its repetition functioning as a memorial to this resisted, horrid silence.

In Dan Pagis's stunningly minimalistic prose poem, 'Written in Pencil in the Sealed Railway-Car', silence is also a metaphor; tropes of omission paradoxically hold absence and presence, voice and silence, and life and death in sharp contrast (1989b, p. 29). Pagis's poem, a fragmented sentence cut off in mid-thought, anticipates the very erasure of life that it enacts. Pagis reanimates the long-since dead only to re-enact that moment of death, turning language against itself, showing the incompletion of representation while embodying the traces of obliteration in the ostensible language of mourning. Pagis dismantles the very language that constructs this moment of 'life'. The truncated promise of a poem reads very simply:

> here in this carload
> i am eve
> with abel my son
> if you see my other son
> cain son of man
> tell him that i

While this incomplete sentence-turned-poem lacks the conventions of punctuation, capitalization and syntax, it does not lack reference. 'Written in Pencil in the Sealed Railway-Car' creates the precise conditions for the occasion of its own utterance, an entreaty unheard but unburied, contained within the sealed confines ('this car'), its impenetrable tomb.

The lack of conventional punctuation and capitalization and the intended deviation from ordinary word order create a tone of disruption and unease, the 'world' turned upside down. Here Pagis will draw upon understated techniques of disjunction, disturbance and interruption in order to disrupt the reader's expectations. The inversion created in the poem's third line – 'with abel my son' – places the emphasis on 'son', on generations collapsing. In this midrashic retelling of the ancient biblical story of the first fratricide, Cain and Abel are archetypal figures. Cain's murderous impulses make Abel the victim, a scapegoat for Cain's covetousness and suspicion, the foundation for familial grief. Pagis develops this theme of foundational violence further through the midrashically reinvented poetic voice of Abel in the poem 'Autobiography': 'My brother invented murder, my parents invented grief, I invented silence' (1989a, p. 5). And in both of these poems, the ironic trope of inexpressibility results from the horror of familial violence. Cain's wilful turning against his brother sets into motion a series of irrevocable events. Cain, 'son of man', is held responsible for the murderous actions motivated by the most base and ignoble of human impulses. Cain intentionally will slay his brother and thus bequeath a calamity of murderous compulsions. As the archetypical sufferer, the found voice of Abel in 'Autobiography' emphasizes his reiterative, prolonged dying: 'you can die once, twice, even seven times, but you can't die a thousand times. I can' (ibid.). In killing his brother, Cain severs himself from all human society; his punishment, appropriately, will be to wander endlessly, without hearth or shelter, cut off from the reassuring embrace of others. It is, after all, 'with abel my son' that the speaker in the poem 'Written in Pencil in the Sealed Railway-Car' is united, although in death. She will not die alone. Pagis's poetic speaker in absentia mourns her own impending death as well as the death of those who accompany her on this transit to hell. She mourns, too, the implied abrogation of the covenant between God and humankind. In this evocation of utterance from an absent speaker, Pagis creates an elegiac gesture that is both midrash and lamentation, interpretation and grief.

The colloquial diction and the simplicity of idiom in 'Written in Pencil in the Sealed Railway-Car' magnify meaning by authenticating the speaking voice. The ellipsis at the poem's close signifies absence, and the poem ends abruptly, a sealed fate. The ellipsis mimetically recreates life and breath cut off. There is no breathing room in the sealed railway-car, and the ending line is a sudden, unexpected cessation of breath. The poem dissolves and, in doing so, its words recede into themselves. In its economy of sound, Pagis's poem creates the conditions of the dispossessed, where even voice is arrested, aborted and abruptly taken away, even murdered. Indeed, this is how tropes of omission work. Such dismantling of syntactical structures creates, in the texture of language, the sensation of menace and desperation, even of extinction. The ellipsis takes away the poem just at the moment of anticipated locution. At the end of Pagis's poem, the speaker is rendered speechless, choked and unable to continue. Her beseeching entreaty – 'tell him that i' – is violently interrupted at the point of the lower-case, diminished first-person. The lack of an ensuing verb halts all further action or movement. Here the *aposiopesis*, a rhetorical figure in which a sentence or phrase is deliberately broken off and left unfinished, recreates the cessation of life. Incompletion here is a means of measuring the unspeakable as inarticulable loss. Represented silence becomes the means by which the poet re-enacts annihilation. In doing so, Pagis constructs an after-image of absence that remains long after the speaker is rendered speechless. In this remarkable poem of grief and generations cut short, understatement creates extremity. The closing ellipsis omits what might have been said and thus what might have been. Thus, we find a rip in the narrative, an opening of the text to history. There is, indeed, something disquieting about language's plasticity in Holocaust writing. Holocaust narratives persist in the idea that voice is remembrance. The poet Hyam Plutzik asks, 'If Moses is dead', 'how then will Aaron speak?' (1961b, p. 37). The persistence of community depends on the persistence of memory, a persistence fulfilled by testimony in the face of loss.

In fashioning a presence where there would otherwise be absence, Holocaust writing defies the 'unspeakable' character of the event, thus attempting to control the uncontrollable. Ultimately, such antitheses, introduced and made emphatic by the oppositional prefix 'un', or 'in', become in their own right tropes of identification and association, 'figures of speech – hyperbole, metaphor – underscoring moral and historical enormity that is not at all immune . . . to description or analysis or to the artistic imagination' (Lang, 2000, p. 5). Such figurative effects clarify experience; they excavate memory, to borrow a recurring trope in Holocaust writing. To this end, Ruth Klüger, child survivor of Theresienstadt, asks us to consider how understanding depends upon recognizable relationships and connections: 'When we ask what something "is like", the language uses an idiom demanding simile or metaphor. We are asking for an association of something we can't know with something recognizable, and we respond with shocks of recognition', or, more precisely, something resembling recognition (2001, p. 11). Such troping, the intentional manipulation of language's associations and connections, simultaneously allows for recognition and disjunction, acknowledgement and surprise, familiarity and alarm, an attempt to create, as Geoffrey Hartman suggests, 'a picture complete enough so that the real might become the intelligible' and its literary depiction 'bearable' (2010, p. 28).

Capitulation to language's inadequacy is symptomatic of the failure of moral reckoning, an indefensible flight of conscience. To say that we cannot articulate the atrocity of the Holocaust is to imply that we cannot judge the motivating conditions and execution of its atrocities. Turning from the subject of the Holocaust, averting one's gaze, cannot be an option. While Elie Wiesel writes of the inevitable inadequacy of language to represent trauma, pain 'so heavy with horror, experienced or anticipated, that words could really not contain it', he cautions, too, that 'not to transmit an experience is to betray it' ([1966] 1982, p. 34; 1985, pp. 13–14). Silence cannot be an option because silence abstains from moral judgement and is too easily replaced by historical amnesia. '[D]igging around in the ruins of memory', as survivor Ida Fink suggests, we create a new language, new structures, a fresh shape to expression, a kaleidoscopic shattering of images and expectations ([1987] 1995a, p. 3). While drawing upon and calling forth a variety of literary traditions and conceits, including lamentation, midrashim, parables, historiography, and modernist and postmodernist literary modes, Holocaust literature, in creating, as Geoffrey Hartman suggests, its 'own rules of engagement . . . enables us to see what otherwise would be too hurtful' and thus immune to active, ethical engagement (2010, p. 36).

Both the structure and the texture of literary works are involved in calling upon dissimilarity and discontinuity to create coherence, that is, to coalesce meaningfully in creating the conditions of their unease. Those larger structural units associated with genre and their relational disposition, as well as the textural intersections and disjunctions that constitute the unfolding and felt sensation of linguistic and syntactic variation – the texture or 'feel' of the language – contribute to the verisimilitude of conditions that invite the reader to enter the forbidding subject of these texts. In finding a language to evoke horrific absence and suffering, a rhetoric of defiance emerges, a range of metaphors, images and figurative effects that create the conditions for entering the narrative space – if only momentarily – of atrocity and loss as well as its obligatory other: the ethical imperative in bearing witness to the Holocaust even as its events recede along the lengthening tracks of history. Thus Holocaust writing might be thought of as its own genre, a genre that 'pushes certain features of writing to their limits', features that deviate from ordinary usage, distorting language so to create a fitting form for its subject (Lang, 2000, p. 36). In the face of the possibility of annihilation, the project of understanding a traumatic experience and refashioning the world in its wake defiantly becomes the motivation for its re-enactment through the revisionary troping of conventional literary forms and cultural narratives.

Because of the necessarily felt presence of history in Holocaust writing, seemingly ordinary linguistic reference becomes significant in the construction of tropes that attempt to define the experience of the Holocaust and make it a 'subject'. When the father of the young narrator in Carl Friedman's *Nightfather* tells his children, 'I have camp', he names a condition that defines him as a survivor ([1991] 1994, p. 2). In drawing upon her father's experiences during the war, Friedman juxtaposes a child's confusion against a parent's indelible past, a diseased legacy he carries with him in his body, a legacy whose stories are passed along intergenerationally, 'stories . . . absorbed . . . through her skin, like medicine or poison', as one of third-generation novelist Julie Orringer's characters, in *The Invisible Bridge*, reveals (Orringer, 2010, p. 596). For the children of the survivor in Friedman's *Nightfather*, 'Camp is not so much a place as a condition', and thus the extrinsic is metonymically made intrinsic ([1991] 1994,

p. 1). As the young narrator explains, her father, no longer imprisoned inside the concentration camp, 'still has camp, especially in his face . . . in his eyes', an affliction she will readily identify in the visage of the caged wolf she happens upon in the zoo, 'with eyes like that' (ibid., p. 2). It is not a congenital condition, nor one inherited by his children – 'we've never had camp', his daughter acknowledges – but one whose countenance and symptoms are distinctly recognizable (p. 2).

'Camp' is no longer extrinsic to the narrator's father. The turning of phrase, the discordant breaking of normative meaning, psychologizes the event, making it a measure of just how transformative, how mutating and mutilating such an experience was and continues to be. 'Camp' remains within the survivor, a condition inscribed. So, too, the Holocaust survivor-father in Art Spiegelman's two-volume graphic novel *MAUS* 'bleeds history' (1986, p. 7). History – the history of the Holocaust and one's individual history as a victim – courses through his body, like blood, spilling over into the next generation. Here history stands as the metonym for the survivor's suffering, for his own blood spilt and, like Edward Lewis Wallant's inconsolable pawnbroker, 'for all his dead', for all those who suffered (1961, p. 278). The very physical description of the pawnbroker suggests that he, too, carries the aggregate of his experiences in his body, as he trudges through the streets of New York, preceded by his own grief, 'his footsteps made ponderous, dragging sounds . . . the great, bulky figure, with its puffy face, its heedless dark eyes . . . dispelled any thought of pleasure . . . the awkward caution of his walk indicated misery on a different scale', a scale measured by the 'blue, cryptic numbers on his arm' (ibid., pp. 4, 247). For Friedman's survivor-character in *Nightfather* to have 'camp' is to collapse cause and effect. The father's experience in the concentration camp causes his continued pain, but the defiant 'misuse' of the term – its figurative grammatical and syntactical turning – reconfigures 'camp' as the effect, the ways in which he is forever altered by the horrors he experienced. Here the trope of camp serves as a metonymic substitution of one word for a totality of anguish. Contained in the simple noun 'camp' is a roster of horrors, a history of misery. In the substitution of one word – the container for the thing contained – we experience a dismantling of the conventional meaning of the word 'camp' in a way that brings about a convergence of individual, collective and historical memory.

The deviation from ordinary usage here is both conceptual and perceptual; language and its associations are reconceived to specify and expand experience, opening up the possibility of interpretation. The term 'camp', like other signifiers of the Shoah, becomes corrupted in language as in history. Never again can 'camp' be thought of in terms of its once normative use: a place of sanctuary, leisure, escape and of its containment within a benevolent natural world. 'Camp' can never again in this discourse be evoked without implicit reference to its corrupted meaning. It is denaturalized of its 'natural' associations.

We find the ghostly presence of such a referent hovering in the background in Philip Roth's 2010 novel *Nemesis*, a novel that parallels the polio outbreak in Newark in that lethal summer of 1944 with the escalation of the war against the Jews in Europe. Here Roth's protagonist, Bucky Cantor, will flee the polio epidemic in Newark along with those children in Weequahic's Jewish section of the city whose families can afford such luxury for the supposed refuge of Camp Indian Hill tucked away in the Poconos. It is here, amid the canopied shelter of the wooded hideaway, that Bucky and the others will be uncovered; the disease will aggressively, perniciously, 'hunt them down', the language evoking the relentless Nazi pursuit of Jews in precarious hiding (Roth, 2010, p. 229). Indeed, pastoral, serene Camp Indian Hill becomes all the more treacherous because of its insidious veneer of asylum. For a Jew in the summer of 1944, Roth reminds us, there is no place to hide. Indeed, the hyperbolized description of the camp exposes its false promises. For not only does an ostensibly beneficent sun and expansive sense of possibility shine on the temporary inhabitants of Edenic Indian Hill, but it is a 'sun . . . too brilliant, the weather too invigorating, the high excitement of the boys beginning their new day unfettered by fear too inspiring' (ibid., p. 177). Roth here creates a skewed landscape, a pastoral scene gone awry. Its excessiveness and exaggerated natural riches – too lush, too green, too fruitful and bountiful, posing far too much of a contrast to the barren, diseased, tainted, inhospitable Newark streets, playgrounds and tenements – shows its nature trove to be, in fact, unnatural, overripe, overabundant, and thus vulnerable to the very conditions it resists; the seeds of corruption are contained within its very landscape. The camp is exposed to the destructive impulses that exist both in nature and without. For polio will find its way to Indian Hill, just as the machinery of Hitler's Final Solution will seek out every Jew in hiding.

The corruption of the natural world and its complicity in malevolence themselves become recurrent tropes in Holocaust narrative. Here the natural world itself is distorted, corrupted by the insidious iniquity of human design. The troping of nature, its turning against itself, characterizes Holocaust narratives as forming a genre of rupture. Making 'nature' the malignant setting for destruction articulates the genre's concern with disruption at the macro-metaphoric level. As in Pagis's poem, where the fundamental Jewish story of Cain and Abel is turned into an allegory of genocide, so in Roth's novel pastoral is turned into a setting for victimization. For much Holocaust writing, counter-intuitively, the natural world morphs into an unnatural landscape of unforeseen dangers. No longer benign or welcoming, previously pastoral nature takes on all-too-human characteristics: menace, predation, murder. The natural order has been broken by human interference, and our illusory, habitual associations of it are ruptured. No longer predisposed to the order of seasons or of time – winter giving way to spring, night to day – the natural order is arrested, time no longer 'measured in months and years', as Ida Fink puts it, 'nor by the rising and setting of the sun' ([1987] 1995a, p. 3). As Elie Wiesel's semi-autobiographical narrator in *Night* laments, 'Never shall I forget that night, the first night in camp, that turned my life into one long night' ([1958] 2006, p. 34). Night, in this context of horror, is not given to the natural turning of the planets, but metaphorically becomes stationary, endless, in defiance of day. Indeed, for the young, incarcerated Wiesel, in the sky 'The stars were only sparks of the fire which devoured us . . . nothing left in the sky but dead stars, dead eyes' (ibid., p. 18). As Primo Levi describes it, in his account of his arrival in the concentration camp, *Survival in Auschwitz*, the natural world was destroyed: 'Dawn came on us like a betrayer; it seemed as though the new sun rose as an ally of our enemies to assist in our destruction' ([1958] 1996, p. 16). Nature itself is complicitous in the destruction, itself an ally of evil: 'Around us everything is hostile. Above us the malevolent clouds chase each other to separate us from the sun' (ibid., p. 42).

The natural world upended, the physical landscape is personified to dispel all hope of relief, as in Arnost Lustig's short story of the ghetto, 'The Lemon', where swallows 'darted across the sullen sky', the firmament 'a shallow, stagnant sea' (1994, pp. 92–3). In Anne Michaels' lyrical novel *Fugitive Pieces*, a Jewish boy hiding in a forest's dense foliage, where 'draping slugs splash like tar across the ferns; black icicles of flesh', is stunned to discover that 'the tree's faint expression is familiar. The face above a uniform' ([1996] 1998, pp. 10, 12). Here the natural world is menacing, threatening and foreboding. So too in Jerzy Kosinski's fantastical, grotesque novel of reiterative cruelty and brutality, *The Painted Bird*, where the natural world is shown to be in collusion with human malice and ill-will, hideously ominous, savage and brutal. The place of hiding for one nameless, vulnerable boy, the forests and countryside of Poland become a grasping terrain of predatory, marauding peril: 'The forest became increasingly dense and forbidding. The slimy striped trunks of snake-colored hornbeams shot straight up into the clouds . . . . The oaks stretched out of their trunks like the necks of starving birds looking for food, and obscured the sun with gloomy branches, casting the pines and poplars and lindens into shadow' (Kosinski, 1965, p. 47). These are shadows in which the earth and its personified demons conspire: 'The wind . . . cracking the brittle twigs . . . tore off the last of the wrinkled leaves, tossing them into the sky' (ibid., p. 11). There is a kind of uncanny symmetry in these descriptions of the natural environment, whose natural elements are vicious and aggressively poised against even their own kind, a metaphor of destructive human aggression and intentionally malevolent design. Animal life itself is distorted in this nightmare world in which a child is relentlessly pursued; life forms become what they are not, transposed, mixed-up, off kilter, all wrong: 'Hens perched owlishly' (ibid.). Tropic substitutions like this more than just amplify ideas; they change the world through unanticipated reference.

In Holocaust writing, understatement and exaggeration intersect, the one creating the other. Understatement and hyperbole are two sides of the same coin, merging in a shared discursive impulse to emphasize through extremity and create a language of reckoning. The blurring effect of mixed genres – folktale, allegory, legend, novel – lends itself to the dismantling and shattering of a world at odds with itself. These magical realist landscapes paradoxically create the effect of stark realism. Eva Hoffman, in *After Such Knowledge*, speaks to her attempts to navigate the storied aspects of her parents' history as revealed to her, the muddled child-vision of fantasy and the real:

> [Those] hypervivid moments summoned by my parents registered themselves as half awful reality, half wondrous fairy tale. A peasant's hut, holding the riddle of life or death; a snowy forest, which confounds the senses and sense of direction. A hayloft in which one sits, awaiting fate, while a stranger downstairs, who is really a good fairy in disguise, is fending off that fate by muttering invocations under her breath and bringing to the hiding place a bowl of soup . . . . [T]hese components of horror became part of a whole generation's store of imagery and narration, the icons and sagas of the post-Holocaust world. (2004, p. 11)

In this merging of history and the imagination, language is reassembled, shackled to history, creating in its wake a world askew. Such narratives, in an attempt to be faithful to history, are fashioned from a language of traumatic rupture in which the perceptions of time and space are irrevocably altered. As Elie Wiesel writes in *The Gates of the Forest*, 'The past became present, everything became confused with everything else: beings lost their identity, objects their proper weight' ([1966] 1982, p. 58). Thus Holocaust narratives, in drawing from the two vital traditions of midrash and lamentation, come together to constitute a genre that creates, extends and responds to the rupture of intense trauma.

The beginning of every story is, as Jonathan Safran Foer observes in the novel *Everything is Illuminated*, 'always an absence', an absence that in a long tradition of Jewish storytelling carries with it the obligation to be filled, to bear witness to the particulars of Jewish history and survival (2002, p. 230). Such moments require one, as Primo Levi cautions in the poem 'Shema', 'to consider', 'to meditate', 'to carve' and 'repeat' the words spoken in truth and in grief, the Shema itself an ancient prayer to 'hear', to bear witness to the unexpected. For, as Susan Sontag suggests, 'Remembering is an ethical act, has ethical value in and of itself. Memory is, achingly, the only relation we can have with the dead' (2003, p. 115). In its individual and communal expression of memory, such literary representation bears witness to atrocity and becomes, ultimately, an affirmation of life, defiantly giving voice where there might otherwise be silence.

Works Cited

Aarons, V. (2005), *What Happened to Abraham? Reinventing the Covenant in American Jewish Fiction*. Newark: University of Delaware Press.

Adams, J. (2011), *Magic Realism in Holocaust Literature*. London: Palgrave Macmillan.

Appignanesi, L. (2000), *Losing the Dead: A Family Memoir*. London: Vintage.

Bar-On, D. (1998), 'Transgenerational aftereffects of the Holocaust in Israel: three generations', in E. Sicher (ed.), *Breaking Crystal: History and Memory after Auschwitz*. Urbana: University of Illinois Press, pp. 91–118.

Bellow, S. (2010), *Saul Bellow: Letters*, ed. B. Taylor. New York: Viking.

Berger, A. (1997), *Children of Job: American Second-Generation Witnesses to the Holocaust*. Albany: State University of New York Press.

Borowski, T. [1959] (1976), 'This way for the gas, ladies and gentlemen', in *This Way for the Gas, Ladies and Gentlemen*, trans. B. Vedder. New York: Penguin, pp. 29–49.

Fink, I. [1987] (1995a), 'A scrap of time', in *A Scrap of Time and Other Stories*, trans. M. Levine and F. Prose. Evanston, IL: Northwestern University Press, pp. 3–10.

—. [1987] (1995b), 'The key game', in *A Scrap of Time and Other Stories*, trans. M. Levine and F. Prose. Evanston, IL: Northwestern University Press, pp. 35–8.

Foer, J. S. (2002), *Everything Is Illuminated*. New York: Perennial.

Friedman, C. [1991] (1994), *Nightfather*, trans. A. and E. Pomerans. New York: Persea Books.

Gubar, S. (2001), 'Prosopopoeia and Holocaust poetry in English: Sylvia Plath and her contemporaries', *The Yale Journal of Criticism*, 14.1, 191–215.

Hartman, G. (2010), 'History writing and the role of fiction', in R. C. Spargo and R. M. Ehrenreich (eds), *After Representation? The Holocaust, Literature, and Culture*. New Brunswick, NJ: Rutgers University Press, pp. 25–40.

Havazelet, E. (2007), *Bearing the Body*. New York: Farrar, Straus and Giroux.

Hirsch, J. (2004), *Afterimage: Film, Trauma, and the Holocaust*. Philadelphia: Temple University Press.

Hirsch, M. (1997), *Family Frames: Photography, Narrative and Postmemory*. Cambridge: Harvard University Press.

Hoffman, E. (2004), *After Such Knowledge: Memory, History, and the Legacy of the Holocaust*. New York: Public Affairs/Perseus.

Klüger, R. (2001), *Still Alive: A Holocaust Girlhood Remembered*. New York: Feminist Press at the City University of New York.

Kosinski, J. (1965), *The Painted Bird*. New York: Houghton Mifflin.

Lang, B. (2000), *Holocaust Representation: Art within the Limits of History and Ethics*. Baltimore: Johns Hopkins University Press.

Levi, P. [1958] (1996), *Survival in Auschwitz: The Nazi Assault on Humanity*, trans. S. Woolf. New York: Touchstone/Simon & Schuster.

Lustig, A. (1994), 'The lemon', in M. Teichman and S. Leder (eds), *Truth and Lamentation: Stories and Poems on the Holocaust*. Urbana and Chicago: University of Illinois Press, pp. 90–106.

Michaels, A. [1996] (1998), *Fugitive Pieces*. New York: Vintage International/Random House.

Newman, L. (1990), 'A letter to Harvey Milk', in J. Antler (ed.), *America and I: Short Stories by American Jewish Women Writers*. Boston: Beacon Press, pp. 324–39.

Orringer, J. (2010), *The Invisible Bridge*. New York: Alfred A. Knopf.

Ozick, C. (1988), 'Roundtable discussion', in B. Lang (ed.), *Writing and the Holocaust*. New York: Holmes & Meier, pp. 277–84.

—. (1989), 'The shawl', in *The Shawl: A Story and Novella*. New York: Knopf, pp. 3–10.

Pagis, D. (1989a), 'Autobiography', in *The Selected Poetry of Dan Pagis*, trans. S. Mitchell. Berkeley: University of California Press, pp. 5–6.

—. (1989b), 'Written in pencil in the sealed railway-car', in *The Selected Poetry of Dan Pagis*, trans. S. Mitchell. Berkeley: University of California Press, p. 29.

Plutzik, H. [1949] (1961a), 'An equation', in *Aspects of Proteus*. New York: Harper & Brothers, p. 3.

—. (1961b), *Horatio: A Poem*. New York: Atheneum.

Raczymow, H. (1994), 'Memory shot through with holes', trans. A. Astro, *Yale French Studies*, 85, 98–105.

Roskies, D. G. (1984), *Against the Apocalypse: Responses to Catastrophe in Modern Jewish Culture*. Cambridge, MA: Harvard University Press.

—. (1989), *The Literature of Destruction: Jewish Responses to Catastrophe*. Philadelphia: Jewish Publication Society.

Roth, P. (2010), *Nemesis*. Boston: Houghton Mifflin Harcourt.

Sontag, S. (2003), *Regarding the Pain of Others*. New York: Farrar, Straus and Giroux.

Spiegelman, A. (1986), *MAUS: A Survivor's Tale*. New York: Pantheon Books.

Wallant, E. L. (1961), *The Pawnbroker*. New York: Harcourt Brace Jovanovich.

Wiesel, E. [1958] (2006), *Night*, trans. M. Wiesel. New York: Hill and Wang.

—. [1966] (1982), *The Gates of the Forest*, trans. F. Frenaye. New York: Schocken Books.

—. (1985), 'Why I write: making no become yes', *New York Times Book Review*, 14 April 1985, 13–14.

—. (2005), *The Time of the Uprooted*, trans. D. Hapgood. New York: Alfred A. Knopf.

Young, J. E. (1988), *Writing and Rewriting the Holocaust: Narrative and the Consequences of Interpretation*. Bloomington: Indiana University Press.

2 Questions of Truth in Holocaust Memory and Testimony

Sue Vice

Abstract

This chapter explores divergent responses to the appearance of inaccuracy and fabrication in survivor testimony, ranging from those who dismiss testimony as a result, to those who see its value to lie precisely in the psychological and proximal factors that underlie such mistakes. It then analyses two categories of Holocaust testimony that pose such questions particularly starkly: these are works which are embellished to a significant degree, or entirely fabricated. A detailed analysis of Herman Rosenblat's account of his boyhood in Buchenwald, *Angel at the Fence: A Love That Survived*, and the cultural factors that produced such embellishment, is placed alongside Bernard Holstein's testimony *Stolen Soul*, the entirely invented status of which is signalled by its literary intertexts. The chapter argues that the study of false and embellished testimonies offers significant insights into the construction and reception of such works. They give evidence for the kinds of narrative clues that might be crucial in considering the status or genre of such a testimony, and the process of cultural debate in the public arena that contributes to their correct description.

The terms 'memory' and 'testimony' might appear to be congruent, since the latter is constituted by means of a subject's recall of facts from the past, but the respects in which they are at odds with each other have particular implications for Holocaust representation and any claim to meaningful remembrance and truth-value. Recent research on autobiographical memory has posited that it is a process susceptible to alteration and suggestion, and is viewed most aptly as a reconstruction of events in the present moment rather than a means of storing or retrieving the past as it was (Fernyhough, 2012, p. 6). Testimony too can be viewed as a phenomenon that is constructed anew in the present moment of each repetition. Henry Greenspan, a psychologist and interviewer of Holocaust survivors, argues that testimony itself is not a static record but an evolving form that brings together elements of its speaker's past and present, as well as responding to the expectations of listeners and interlocutors (1998, p. 167). The instances of embellishment and falsity in testimony that I will analyse in this chapter draw attention to these very processes.

The term 'Holocaust testimony' itself is not a unified one. It refers to a range of phenomena, including interviews with survivors, some conducted almost immediately after the war, others much later; testimony of this kind may be written or filmed, for the sake of repository in such holdings as the National Sound Archive in London, or as part of an aesthetic project, such as Claude Lanzmann's 1985 film *Shoah*. Statements made by survivor-witnesses at war crimes trials may also be described, perhaps more literally, as Holocaust testimony. Although the poet Abraham Sutzkever was one of the very few survivors to testify at the Nuremberg Trials, the trial of Adolf Eichmann took a different form, in which at least 90 survivors were called to the stand. Its placing such testimony centre-stage meant that Eichmann's trial marked the onset of what Annette Wieviorka (2006, p. 57) calls 'the era of the witness', one which is still current. She estimates that there exist 'hundreds of thousands' of such testimonies in their various forms, 'for which no exhaustive bibliography exists' (ibid., p. xi).

Testimony is not only a post-hoc phenomenon, and as such the term is also used to include Holocaust diaries and other contemporary material, almost invariably written by those who did not survive. These include the fragmentary accounts left buried in the crematoria ruins by the Sonderkommando units at Auschwitz, as well as wartime attempts to construct communal bodies of documentation, particularly in the ghettos of occupied Europe. If proximity to the events of the Holocaust is taken into account, in terms of a record made in the immediate wake of events as they unfolded and at the heart of the process of industrialized murder, it is hard to imagine a closer view than these. As James Young argues, the force of Holocaust testimony such as diaries and memoirs is that it is not seen, like other historically based writing, simply to represent or '*stand for*' its epoch, but '*literally* [to] deliver documentary evidence of specific events' (1988, p. 10). Diaries such as the individual ones by writers including Dawid Sierakowiak (1996) and Mary Berg ([1945] 2006) retain a close proximity to events as they occurred to the extent that the diarist's handwriting may itself be visibly altered by the changes and shocks that took place in the moment. Thus the act of writing encodes the event even as the writer's words represent it. Such proximity may offer authenticity rather than accuracy, and it is, as Saul Friedlander claims, precisely the errors of contemporary witnesses that make their documents so significant (1997, p. 2).

In sum, Holocaust testimony is a rich and capacious category used as a legal and historical term as well as to refer to a literary genre and oral utterance. In the twenty-first century, the term most usually refers specifically to published non-fiction accounts of an individual's life in occupied Europe. As Robert Eaglestone (2004) has shown, such works adhere to a surprisingly consistent narrative structure, often buttressed paratextually by the authenticating presence of such documents as maps, photographs and glossaries. This construction of a testimonial template has had the effect that it is both iterable and imitable,[1] leading to the existence of 'Holocaust testimonial novels' (Richardson, 2009), as well as the effect that I discuss later, that of false or embellished testimony which in structural terms fully resembles the real thing. It is just these kinds of concern with falsifiability – alongside those about inaccuracy and fading or unreliable memory – that have made some historians cautious about drawing on testimonial material for any factual purpose. In Lucy Dawidowicz's view, testimony may be 'more hazard than help' to the historian (Wieviorka, 2006, p. xiii). Such a perception entails the insistence that material of a testimonial kind should not be relied upon in isolation, but only in comparison with other sources such as 'wartime diaries, memoirs, published and unpublished testimonies, historical documents, architectural plans, literary works, and much more' (Tec, 2000, p. 87). Yet there has been a turn to survivor-witness accounts even among historians in the years since Hilberg's study was first published in 1961. Friedlander relies explicitly on such testimony in his *Nazi Germany and the Jews*, arguing that the presence in this study of the victims' voices is 'historically essential in itself', in demonstrating both the 'insight' and 'blindness' of those confronted with an 'entirely new and utterly horrifying reality'. That is, the testifiers' errors are not regrettable elements of testimony, but valuable precisely as part of the task of constructing a historical narrative of the Holocaust years, in order 'to put the Nazis' actions into full perspective' (Friedlander, 1997, p. 2).

Other readers may not have such an exclusive interest as these historians in the factual record as it is derived from Holocaust testimony, and attend rather to the psychological, cultural and aesthetic importance of this material. For instance, changes over time in repeatedly delivered testimony, particularly when this takes an oral form, may not be a sign of unreliability or forgetting on the survivor's part, but one element in a more complex process. Such apparent inconsistency may convey how the experience appeared to the testifier in the moment of speaking or writing, and how the narration of memory may change over time.[2] The most famous example of this is an episode recounted by the psychoanalyst Dori Laub, in which a woman relating her experience at Auschwitz for the Fortunoff Video Archive claimed to have witnessed four crematoria chimneys being blown up in the camp rebellion, when in fact only one chimney was destroyed. While historians claimed that this inaccuracy invalidated the entire testimony, Laub argues that, on the contrary, the woman was offering a 'historical truth' in testifying to something 'unimaginable', and 'the number mattered less than the fact of the occurrence' (1992, p. 60). The kind of scepticism about testimony's historical value expressed by Laub's interlocutors also appears in relation to legal testimony, apparently borne out by the overturning in 1993 of a death sentence levied against John Demjanjuk because of survivors' uncertainty in identifying the defendant. Critics have suggested that there are qualities particular to the 'traumatic memory' of the Holocaust that may leave survivors 'possessed by the past' (LaCapra, 2000, p. 90), yet unable to master or articulate it. The division between what Lawrence Langer calls 'common' and 'deep' memory (1991, p. 6) refers to a similar phenomenon: the very words used to describe the Holocaust world have a different meaning in the everyday present. The historian Mark Roseman equally attempts to deconstruct the traditional distinction between factual accuracy and inaccuracy in his account of writing the biography of Marianne Ellenbogen, who survived the war by living in hiding in Germany. Roseman describes the 'complex layers of memory' that characterized Ellenbogen's account and the 'strategies' she adopted in order to 'cope with an unbearable past', the most striking of which included altering the detail of some of the most traumatic elements of her experience (1999, p. 1).

Other examples of the gaps in a text that may succeed in drawing attention to its governing structures include instances of sexual violence; the reluctance to record what Ravenel Richardson (2013) calls 'sexual barter', that is, sexual liaisons, often pragmatic or unwanted, undertaken by – in Richardson's examples – women in an effort to save themselves or others; while other taboo behaviours in these extreme circumstances, ranging from cannibalism to collaboration or betrayal, may be omitted. In an opposite formation, the embellished testimonies that I will explore, in the sense of genuine accounts to which particular incidents have been added, tend to overfill the gaps in their narratives, in ways that equally draw attention to cultural expectations. These include a habit of valuing only the unambiguous virtues of heroic resistance or innocent suffering, in the specific setting of a death camp. False testimonies which are entirely invented represent something rather different, laying bare the overidentification that may result from reading about the Holocaust: yet here the readers in question are most obviously the false or deluded testifiers themselves, whose assiduous researches underlie the fabrication of Holocaust memory.

False and Embellished Testimony

Roseman begins his account of writing Ellenbogen's biography by observing that, 'Whenever we listen to or read the testimony of a Holocaust survivor there is an understandable reluctance to challenge the testimony's accuracy or veracity' (1999, p. 2), while Langer observes in the foreword to his *Holocaust*

Testimonies that the 'factual errors' and 'simple lapses' that sometimes occur in the material he analyses are 'trivial' in the light of 'the complex layers of memory that give birth to the versions of the self' recorded in his book (1991, p. 142). For instance, such features as the expansion or telescoping of time-periods may be an 'accurate' representation of the rememberer's subjective perception at the time, rather than mistakes; other shifts might include the 'adoption' of elements from other sources, including acquaintances' testimonies, or the sudden recall of details in later renditions of the same story (Roseman, 1999, pp. 6–7).[3] Roseman argues that the specific aspects of Ellenbogen's testimony that were altered are not as significant as what the fact of modification itself suggests: an urge to gain a retrospective impression of control over events (ibid., p. 13). As Freud argues, post-traumatic conditions such as shellshock arise from the victim being taken unawares and unprepared for the abrupt occurrence of a life-threatening disaster ([1922] 1950). Yet there are cases, to which I now turn, where the fundamental veracity of the testimony has been shown to be a quality that cannot be taken for granted. In such cases, what is exposed by the exploration of apparently contradictory details is not an alteration over time or the presence of a testifier's psychological coping strategies, but invention and untruth. I will explore separately the embellished and fabricated varieties of false testimony.

Embellished testimony could be seen as a large-scale version of the process of modification that took place in Ellenbogen's case, expanded into the form of a narrative. In the three cases I will mention, the testifier was indeed a Holocaust survivor, but for various reasons felt that the record as it stood was not sufficient. Deli Strummer's testimony *A Reflection of the Holocaust* (1988) recounts her deportation from Vienna and incarceration in several camps, including Theresienstadt, Mauthausen and Auschwitz, but also includes several large-scale alterations to the historical record and to other versions of her life story. Although parts of Strummer's account are based on fact verifiable by means of camp records, the details of her Holocaust experience have altered significantly over the decades of her telling it. The year of Strummer's deportation from Austria and the locations and number of camps she was sent to were subject to change and became more exaggerated. For instance, she could not have narrowly escaped gassing at Mauthausen just before the liberation, as she claims, since the gas chamber there had already been dismantled, nor emerged unscathed from a gas chamber at Auschwitz on several occasions when water instead of gas was turned on, since this was a practical impossibility. Strummer's husband did not die in Dachau, as she describes, but survived the war and the couple later got divorced. Given the number and extent of the changes over time, Langer describes the discrepancies in Strummer's various versions of her story, in spoken, written and filmed testimony, as an 'invented reality' rather than a 'lapse' or retreat from memory (Copeland, 2000, p. F01).[4] While the pathos of Strummer's experience is increased by her miraculous escapes and bereavement, in the case of Martin Gray, who added invented details of his deportation to and escape from Treblinka to a true story of life in the Warsaw Ghetto in his memoir *For Those I Loved*, it is his heroic acts and ability to resist that is emphasized.[5] Both cases make clear the methods by which inaccuracy is exposed, alongside the process of debate in the public realm that may lead to a particular verdict. As in Strummer's case, Gray's memoir revealed the limits of its author's historical knowledge, for instance, in his confusing the two camps at Treblinka (Polak, 2004, pp. 48–50), and repeating details from Jean-François Steiner's novel *Treblinka* ([1966] 1997).

Narrative as well as factual inconsistency is perceptible in Strummer's and Gray's testimonies. Both draw on events that familiarity with other testimonies shows either to be unlikely, or borrowed from elsewhere, and such narrative revelation is even more significant in relation to Herman Rosenblat's 2009 testimony *Angel at the Fence: A True Story of a Love That Survived.*[6] The genesis of Rosenblat's text reveals the kinds of pressure and expectation that might lead to embellishment. In 1996, Rosenblat won a competition run by Oprah Winfrey for 'the most touching love story', in which he described how he was imprisoned in Buchenwald during the war and his life saved by the food thrown to him over the camp fence by a little girl; later in life, he met a young woman, Roma, on a blind date in New York, who turned out to be the 'angel' at the camp fence from Herman's past, and the two fell in love and married. While the detail of the teenage Rosenblat's time in Schlieben, a subcamp of Buchenwald, was true, the meeting with the girl at the fence was an invention. Rosenblat's real-life spouse Roma was, like her husband, a Polish-born Holocaust survivor, but she had spent the war in hiding on a farm with her family near Breslau, over 200 miles from Buchenwald, whose fence was in any case not approachable either by the camp inmates nor from the outside in the way Rosenblat describes. The only public road near the camp was closed to civilians in 1943 (Day, 2009).

For the most part, *Angel at the Fence* relies on Holocaust testimony's standard narrative tropes, including those which draw attention to an acceptable margin of uncertainty between memory and reconstruction. These include providing the detail of reported speech, such as, in Rosenblat's case, dialogue that took place before he was born ([2009] 2013, p. 8), and the interpolation into the present of knowledge that seems likely to have been acquired later, for instance, the teenage boy's ability to distinguish between the two ghettos at Piotrkow (ibid., p. 65), and his father's certainty that the Nazis' aim was to 'destroy all the Jews in the world' (ibid., p. 53). Alongside these features are some that are particular to Rosenblat's narration and its embellished status. From its outset, Rosenblat brings into his testimony a discourse of supernatural maternal protection that prepares the reader for the introduction of his 'angel' narrative: 'It was my mother who ensured that I would survive, who showed me how to keep on living, who promised that an angel would save me and bring light into my life' (ibid., p. 5). Such a statement represents a slippage from reference to Rose Rosenblat's act of ensuring Herman's survival, by refusing to let him stay with her on a transport to Treblinka, into a less concrete, posthumous wish to 'save' her son, a wish that takes on the embodied form of the little girl. The familiar elements of a camp testimony themselves are made to register the anticipation of such a figure, as shown by Rosenblat's emphasis on his hunger and weakness in the days before the girl's appearance (ibid., p. 132).

Indeed, the text as a whole is characterized by the oneiric and visionary, in a way that serves, in hindsight, as an alibi for Rosenblat's invention. During his struggle to survive, Herman frequently takes refuge in dreams, some of which, as he discovers on waking, have real correlatives, while in others his parents return to life and address their son. At his brother Isydor's wedding after the war, Herman claims that, in a way that sounds factual but is clearly imaginary, 'I knew my mother was present at the wedding, looking down on her children reunited' (ibid., p. 198). These moments not only blur history and imagination, but imply that there is a continuum between the two realms. In support of this implication, metaphorical discourse alongside protestations at the event's unlikelihood accompanies the narration of the first sight of the young girl at the fence in Schlieben. Her appearing is described by Herman as a 'miracle' (ibid., p. 137), and as an occurrence that 'fed my will to live on' and 'nourish[ed] my body and soul' (ibid., pp. 138, 147). Such metaphors suggest a hesitancy about the reality of what is being described. On the other hand, the metaphorical discourse of nourishment might suggest that not only did the girl provide Herman with food, but her presence sustained him in less literal ways, by embodying values such as generosity and humanity which implied a link to the legacy of his mother. The narration of Rosenblat's realization, at their date in Coney Island over a decade after the war's end, that Roma was the 'girl at the fence', is equally characterized by a double-voiced and metaphorical discourse that acknowledges unbelievability even as it repudiates it. Herman declares the coincidence of the reunion 'impossible', and enlists the clichés of romantic discourse to an effect the reader must take as literal, in describing the 'shock of recognition' the pair underwent on being introduced, the fact that they were 'fated for one another', and that although it seemed as if they had only just met, 'both knew that wasn't true' (ibid., pp. 223–8).

Although the Holocaust context is crucial for the significance of the couple's later meeting, in *Angel at the Fence* and its reception the Holocaust itself is implicitly subsumed by the romance of the testimony's title. In a reversal that suggests a devolution into what Saul Friedlander (1984) has described as kitsch, it is the postwar encounter leading to Herman and Roma's marriage that casts significance back onto the camp setting. The Holocaust meaning is thus evacuated from the narrative; as implied by the memoir's subtitle, 'A True Story of a Love That Survived', it is not the human survival of genocide but the persistence of a personal relationship in such circumstances that is of importance. Among Herman's earliest words about his parents in *Angel at the Fence* is his conviction that they would be proud their son is 'celebrated as a symbol of the power of love' (Rosenblat, [2009] 2013, p. 5); and he describes his response during the war to Isydor's determination that the brothers should survive Buchenwald by helping each other in observing that, 'That thought helped me survive. Work helped me survive. And one more thing helped me survive: love' (ibid., p. 78). Such statements do double duty as endorsement for the importance of the testimony's romantic invention, and, as if aware of the notion's bathos, imply that other kinds of love are also significant: the testimony portrays parental and particularly fraternal love as crucial to Herman's survival. Indeed, Herman's real story is one of brothers keeping their younger sibling alive, a narrative made subsidiary to the romantic embellishment. At times, a struggle between the actual and invented stories is perceptible in the text, for instance, where a sentence about Herman's memory of his mother has literally to be embellished with an extra clause, where he writes of, 'the benevolent image of my mother as she appeared in my dreams – and of course, my memory of the angel she had sent to me in Schlieben'. This remark is swiftly followed by Herman's acknowledgement that, 'For all its horrors, my survival had taught me what the bond of brotherhood really means', a statement of the real import of his testimony (ibid., p. 178). However, the text's likening of different kinds of love also serves its imposture, by making the 'angel at the fence' appear to be an incarnation of Rose's devotion and that of his older brothers to Herman. While on a transport from Schlieben to Theresienstadt, Herman takes comfort from recalling the

angel at the fence – and my mother coming to me so vividly in my dreams, promising she was watching over me. Surely, this was real. The little girl *had* appeared, as if out of nowhere, at the fence. She *had* fed me when I was starving . . . . Was this a sign that God worked through my dead mother to keep me alive? (Ibid., p. 154)

Here, as elsewhere, the angel is described in factual terms, but the phrasing also seems simply to signify the existence of motherly love, as if it were that and not the little girl which is 'real'. Ambiguity of expression is thus an alibi for Rosenblat's invention.

On the other hand, the episodes concerning the appearance of the angelic girl at Schlieben, and Herman's encounter with her after the war, are narrated without ambiguity. On the first occasion of their encounter, Herman describes how, after half-an-hour's walk in the camp, he reached one of the 'blind spots' in the guards' surveillance of the perimeter fence and states simply, 'that is how I first happened to see the little girl' (ibid., p. 136). Not only is the girl Polish and able to throw Herman an apple over the fence, but, in an intertextual reprise of the child in the red coat from Steven Spielberg's 1993 film *Schindler's List*, she wears a 'red sweater' that offers relief from the 'monochromatic' world of the camp. Conveniently, the young Herman never told anyone about the little girl at the time, and destroyed the notes she wrote to him (ibid., p. 141). Yet a failure to search out evidence for Rosenblat's story supports the historian Kenneth Waltzer's description of a Holocaust 'illiteracy', whether genuine or willed, that enabled the existence of Rosenblat's invention to go unchallenged for over a decade (quoted in Sherman, 2008). We will see this phenomenon writ large in the next example, that of a completely fabricated Holocaust memoir.

There is a disjunction in fabricated testimonies between text and author, in a way that entirely disrupts the 'autobiographical pact' described by Philippe Lejeune (1989) as taking place between author and reader. This is particularly so in the case of Binjamin Wilkomirski, the assumed name of Bruno Doessekker, who claimed to be a Latvian Holocaust orphan, but had in fact suffered the fate of an illegitimate Swiss child whose early years were spent in unsettled circumstances with unsuitable foster-parents. According to Wilkomirski's prize-winning testimony *Fragments: Memories of a Childhood, 1939–1948*, the young boy had been imprisoned in both Majdanek and Auschwitz, then after the war was smuggled into Switzerland and given the papers of a Swiss boy. None of these details was true, except that Wilkomirski's birth name was that of the purportedly vanished Swiss child, Bruno Grosjean. As in the case of Misha Defonseca, whose Holocaust testimony *Surviving with Wolves* ([1997] 2005) became a bestseller in several languages and was made into a film in France (Véra Belmont, 2007), caveats expressed during the process of the testimony's acceptance for publication were either judged to be unverifiable, or were disregarded. The detail of the invention in the case of all the fabricated testimonies I will mention was eventually exposed by means of various investigative strategies instigated by the publishers, including those of a lawyer in the case of *Fragments*, a forensic genealogist for *Surviving with Wolves*, and a private investigator in relation to Bernard Holstein's false testimony *Stolen Soul*. While Defonseca confessed to her invention in 2008 when confronted with the evidence, neither Wilkomirski nor Holstein has relinquished their claim to be Holocaust survivors.

False Holocaust testimony occupies a singular place in any exploration of textual deception, since what is seen as the effrontery of those who create or embellish accounts of survival is judged to have special ethical and political dangers. These include the disparagement of genuine survivor accounts and thus the encouragement of Holocaust denial, while the public controversy that accompanied each of the testimonies' exposure has had the effect of raising anew the question of fiction's role in representing the Holocaust, as if even the customary generic boundaries were not sufficiently strict. For instance, in the wake of *Fragments*' exposure, Jerzy Kosinski's novel *The Painted Bird* was described as if it too were an invented testimony.[7]

An opposite pattern of intertextuality is perceptible in relation to Bernard Holstein's *Stolen Soul*, about its author's purported experiences in Auschwitz as a 9-year-old, in which it is precisely the anterior texts that offer a clue to the testimony's fabricated nature. While *Fragments* draws on such survivor writings as Jona Oberski's fictional *A Childhood* (1983), based on the latter's youthful experience of Bergen-Belsen, and *Surviving with Wolves* on details of the Warsaw Ghetto from Jan Karski's *Story of a Secret State* ([1944] 2011), *Stolen Soul* features material woven together from a range of testimonial and fictional sources. Such material even includes the two earlier false testimonies. In contrast to the other examples in which extra-textually determined inaccuracy revealed an imposture, *Stolen Soul* is an unusual example of a testimony whose invented nature can be perceived in terms of textual evidence alone.[8] For instance, it is beyond coincidence that encounters with nurturing wolves appear in both Defonseca's and Holstein's accounts. Despite its brevity, Holstein's description follows Defonseca's even in terms of small detail. Just as Misha does in *Surviving with Wolves*, Bernard and his companions encounter a pack of wolves in a cave. The transformation typical of lupine mythology, of a 'sovereign' predator into a persecuted victim, and of animal into human (Arnds, 2012), takes place in both testimonies, for Bernard in the form of a hallucination. Although this vision is ostensibly caused by the boy's fever, its description – 'I was on fire, radiating heat, burning' (Holstein, 2004, p. 131) – is also the occasion for an instance of the text's recurrent representation of a fantasy of being killed and burnt:

> Then I was alone, alone in the cave with wolves swarming all around, baring their teeth, screaming, telling me that I had burnt their babies . . . I tried to tell them that I hadn't done anything, that it wasn't my fault, that I hadn't meant to burn their babies, but they didn't hear me because my tongue could not form the words. (Ibid., p. 131)

Holstein interprets his inability to speak as an expression of 'guilt', and this moment is characterized not just by reversal, since the boy imagines being accused by the wolves of murder, but by an oscillation of victim and perpetrator subject-positions. The trio consisting of Bernard and his two companions is reflected in the three wolf-cubs; it is perhaps their vulnerability that prompts the boy's fantasy about the extreme victimization of being killed and cremated. Such a notion coexists with one of wishing for parental protection. In *Surviving with Wolves*, Misha wishes she were one of the wolf pups, 'protected and cherished in their forest lair' (Defonseca, [1997] 2005, p. 134), while in *Stolen Soul* a similar envy is expressed by Erhardt: '"Remember they probably have a mother nearby"' (Holstein, 2004, p. 130). The appearance in Holstein's account of the cubs' parents registers the last stage in the process of the wolves' transformation from predator into nurturer, as well as another detail borrowed from

Defonseca. It is the 'very large, very menacing' male wolf who bares his teeth at the boys, yet later his mate offers them her own vomit as food (ibid., pp. 132–3), just as, in *Surviving with Wolves*, a female wolf regurgitates food for Misha (Defonseca, [1997] 2005, pp. 136–8). Human horror intrudes for Misha when she is left alone by the wolves and thus 'didn't see the danger coming': in this case, a Nazi whose assault on a young Russian girl provokes Misha to stab him to death (ibid., pp. 141–3). In *Stolen Soul*, leaving the 'safety' of the wolves' cave leads the boys 'straight into a German patrol' (Holstein, 2004, p. 134), signalling again the reversal of roles: in both unlikely scenarios, it is not the wolves who are to be feared, but other humans.

Holstein's debt to Wilkomirski's *Fragments* is more extensive but also more general than that to Defonseca's *Surviving with Wolves*. *Stolen Soul* does not reproduce *Fragments'* stylistic innovation of giving priority to the child focalizer over the adult narrator. By contrast, the very gap between adult and child comprehension of the Holocaust world in *Stolen Soul* is related solely in adult terms, as shown in Holstein's description of a state that Wilkomirski presents subjectively – 'We didn't understand [the Auschwitz reality] but we accepted it anyway' (ibid., p. 50) – as well as his use of rhetorical questions: 'how does [a] child deal with the trauma of a premature immersion into the world of adulthood, moreover into a world dominated by sadism, cruelty and deceit?' (ibid., p. 20). In *Fragments*, by contrast, such 'immersion' is a quality of the narration itself. This is clear in the difference between Bernard's simply describing the fact that, as the Holstein family is being taken to the cattle-trucks, 'We had never seen weapons before and were frightened by the sight of them' (ibid., p. 10), and Binjamin's failure to recognize a particular weapon, which is enacted as it is represented. Binjamin addresses a 'soldier' on his arrival at Majdanek:

'What's that funny weapon you've got?' I asked him . . . . Quick as a flash he turned around, just as quickly his arm shot up in the air with the strange thing in his fist, and something whizzed across my face with such burning heat that I thought I'd been cut in two. That's how I learned what a whip is. (Wilkomirski, 2006, p. 37)

This scene of youthful trust betrayed is represented in a stylization of a child-like discourse, with its simple syntax and reduced vocabulary, yet by this means conveys the complex, 'adult' notion of psychic splitting that is the outcome of such violence: 'I thought I'd been cut in two'. In general, *Stolen Soul* appears torn between the extreme and bleak victim status of Binjamin, as shown in Bernard's subjection to brutal treatment including medical experiments alongside the imagery of burning and cremation, and an impulse towards active heroism, as suggested by the boy's recruitment into the camp resistance.

Part of the reason for this conflict lies in the different sources Holstein favoured, as well as the text's internalization of the incompatible survivor stereotypes of abject victim and heroic resister. Alongside *Fragments* and *Surviving with Wolves*, Holstein has adapted particular elements of two real testimonies to suit his purpose: these are Miklos Nyiszli's *Auschwitz: A Doctor's Eyewitness Account* ([1960] 2011) and Olga Lengyel's *Five Chimneys* ([1947] 1995). Although these two testimonies by adult survivors, who were what Robert Jay Lifton (1986, p. 214) calls 'prisoner-doctors', may not seem immediately useful for the construction of Holstein's child protagonist, they furnish the detail necessary to support his account of arriving in the camp, and elements of extreme childhood suffering particularly in relation to medical experiments. While Nyiszli's memoir is about accommodation in order to survive, Lengyel's offers a narrative of resistance. These testimonies are both by Hungarians who were deported late in the war, a time-frame which fits the notion of Bernard's youth and his survival. While Lengyel's account is one of a day-to-day struggle to survive, in which she includes descriptions of the teenage inmates borrowed by Holstein, Nyiszli even appears in *Stolen Soul* as a character, not only offering a clue to the origins of Holstein's account, but literally embodying the doctor's intertextual influence. Holstein has accomplished in *Stolen Soul* what is a second-order, or second-generation, act of borrowing, in a way that advertises its generic links to other fictional works, not just in its reliance on the other two false testimonies, but also because both Nyiszli's and Lengyel's actual testimonies are already well known as the sites of literary borrowing. Martin Amis's *Time's Arrow* (1991), about the life of a Nazi doctor told in reverse, draws on Nyiszli's descriptions of Mengele's experimental procedures as quoted by Lifton, while William Styron's *Sophie's Choice* (1979) recasts the loss of Lengyel's sons in fictional format, drawing on an incident that Holstein likewise covets and reworks.[9]

Holstein's fabricated testimony works by means of collage, and he splices together details from both Lengyel's and Nyiszli's accounts in his version of such events as the liquidation of the Gypsy camp in Auschwitz and negative estimates of its inhabitants (Holstein, 2004, p. 121; Lengyel, [1947] 1995, p. 122; Nyiszli, [1960] 2011, p. 31). Such a methodology is clearest in *Stolen Soul*'s narrative of Bernard's arrival at Auschwitz. From the testimonies on which Holstein has relied, we learn that Nyiszli's 14-year-old daughter was just old enough to be included with the group of prisoners destined for labour (Nyiszli, [1960] 2011, p. 24) while Lengyel herself was selected for work but her sons were both too young and were sent to the gas chambers (Lengyel, [1947] 1995, p. 27). Holstein's text is an amalgamation of the two accounts. Since he is 12, Bernard is old enough to be sent 'to the right' for work, while his younger brother Pieter is consigned to death along with their mother Magda. Magda Holstein cannot follow the precedent of Nyiszli's wife Margareta, nor that of Olga Lengyel, in being sent to work, in part because Bernard has to be a lone survivor in order to avoid any question of corroboration. The struggle related in *Stolen Soul* between Magda Holstein and a guard over the destination of her elder son Bernard, whom she wants to keep with her 'on the left', is indebted to that in Lengyel's account, although its outcome is necessarily different. Lengyel insists that her son Arvad is not yet 12 and should go with his grandmother, a request that is received with unruffled 'acquiescence' on the part of Fritz Klein, the Nazi doctor in charge of selections, and results in the boy's death (ibid., p. 27). This is necessarily altered in Holstein's version, where a 'soldier' demands that Bernard be assigned to the side destined for survival (2004, p. 23).

Most tellingly, Holstein's reliance on the moment of selection in *Five Chimneys* calls upon its overdetermined history as the source of intertextual borrowing. The scene in Lengyel's account in which one of her sons could have remained with his mother is the basis for the much-inflated dilemma in *Sophie's Choice*, where the eponymous protagonist is forced by a Nazi doctor to choose which of her two children to save. What sounds like a subliminal acknowledgement of this rises to the surface of *Stolen Soul* in Holstein's present-day reflection on his mother's actions: 'If she had known the true horror, what would have been her choice for her son, right or left? Could she have made that choice? What would have been my choice?' (ibid., p. 24). The insistent repetition here of Styron's term 'choice' may remind the reader of controversy provoked by that author's recasting of Lengyel's testimony in novelistic form (Vice, 2000, chapter 5). *Stolen Soul* thus offers implicit textual evidence for its generic reclassification as fiction.

Conclusion

The varieties of untruth in Holocaust testimony and memory are not only equally multiple but perhaps also just as significant as the varieties of truth and accuracy. While embellished works could be described as testifying to their authors' and publishers' wish to modify the perceived bleakness or recalcitrance of a Holocaust narrative, as Waltzer says of *The Angel at the Fence* – 'Herman Rosenblat did not believe his own survival was story enough' (Sherman, 2008) – the fabricated examples accomplish a function of the opposite nature. In these cases, the authors have created autobiographies of a specifically Holocaust-related kind, replacing their own experience with a historical calamity. Slavoj Žižek argues that such substitution constitutes an apparently perverse instance of Freud's notion of screen memory, since, instead of conjuring up a reassuring fantasy, here it is the 'very ultimate traumatic experience' of the Holocaust that is used as a 'shield' against real recall (2009, p. 74). Yet the contemporary reception of Holocaust survivors and their stories does possess such compensatory and 'shielding' qualities. For Defonseca, for instance, the legacy of a father who had died in Sonnenburg concentration camp in Poland as a traitor was redeemed by transforming him into a blameless 'racial' victim of the Holocaust.[10]

The process of communal reconsideration of a particular work itself draws attention to the features of a testimony that are considered valuable, and the kinds of detail that might be cause for suspicion. The work of carefully identifying the genre of testimonies and delineating the presence of inaccuracy or falsehood is one reason why invented and embellished examples need not be lamented as a Holocaust denier's gift. Such a process of exploration can be seen as it unfolds in relation to other cases in which invention is suspected but final judgement remains, at the time of writing, suspended. These include two biographies of individuals whose identity has been questioned: Imre Kovács' *Le vengeur* (2006), about a member of the Zionist resistance in Hungary joining the Waffen SS, and Mark Kurzem's *The Mascot* (2007), the account of his father Alex's rediscovery of his Jewish roots and his survival in wartime Belarus as the eponymous 'mascot' of a German battalion.[11] Memoirs by prisoners-of-war who purportedly spent time in Auschwitz have likewise been scrutinized, including Dennis Avey's *The Man Who Broke into Auschwitz* (2011) as well as its precursor and, some argue, its equally embroidered source, John Castle's biography of Charles Coward, *The Password Is Courage* ([1962] 2001).[12] Yet to distinguish between testimonies' genres on the grounds of their accuracy is not necessarily to dismiss them either as worthless texts, in the case of the fabrications, or as valueless eyewitness accounts, in that of the embellished works. Rather, as Tony Kushner argues in relation to elements of unreliability, it is preferable to accept that Holocaust testimony features 'contradictions and mythologies' that emerge from the events' 'chaos and rupture' (2006, p. 283). In the cases of fabrication, it is undeniable that, for instance, Wilkomirski's *Fragments* has become a canonical text in the history of Holocaust literature, precisely by reason of its invented status.[13] The lineaments of testimony's representation of truth and memory are hence most clearly revealed by their appearance in exaggerated and ersatz form.

Notes

1. See Whitehead (2004).
2. See Maiden (2008), and the self-reflexive Bacall-Zwirn and Stark (2000).
3. See also Maiden's analysis of Anita Lasker-Wallfisch's varied accounts of her life in Maiden (2008).
4. As well as her published testimony, Strummer gave regular talks in her home town of Baltimore, recorded an interview for the Yale Fortunoff Archive and is the subject of a film, *From Out of Ashes: The Deli Strummer Story* (2001).
5. See Kushner (2006).
6. See also the novelized version: Penelope Holt's *The Apple: Based on the Herman Rosenblat Holocaust Love Story* (2009).

7. See Finkelstein (2000), which ignores the fictional genre and figural nature of *The Painted Bird*, describing it as a 'purported . . . autobiographical account' and thus a 'hoax' (p. 55).
8. However, it was by the rather different means of being alerted by family members to Holstein's real identity, as an Australian-born Catholic named Bernard Brougham, that the publisher became aware of his fraudulence.
9. See Vice (2000, chapter 5).
10. See Lionel Duroy (2011), for a discussion of these issues.
11. The accuracy of Kovács' memoir has been questioned by the historian László Karsai (personal communication February 2010). Alex Kurzem's claim to keep receiving German reparations payments was upheld after his status was investigated by 'an independent ombudsman': see Moor (2013).
12. Avey's story has been questioned by Guy Walters (2011). See also the discussion of Avey's debt to Coward in Tony Kushner (2013).
13. See, for instance, Eli Park Sorensen's consideration of *Fragments'* legacy (2013).

Works Cited

Amis, M. (1991), *Time's Arrow*. Harmondsworth: Penguin.
Arnds, P. (2012), 'Innocence abducted: youth, war, and the wolf in literary adaptations of the Pied Piper legend from Robert Browning to Michel Tournier', *Jeunesse: Young People, Texts, Cultures*, 4.1, 61–84.
Avey, D. (2011), *The Man Who Broke Into Auschwitz*. London: Hodder and Stoughton.
Bacall-Zwirn, A. and Stark, J. (2000), *No Common Place: The Holocaust Testimony of Alina Bacall-Zwirn*. Omaha: University of Nebraska Press.
Berg, M. [1945] (2006), *The Diary of Mary Berg: Growing Up in the Warsaw Ghetto*, trans. N. Guterman and S. Glass. Oxford: Oneworld.
Castle, J. [1962] (2001), *The Password Is Courage*. London: Souvenir Press.
Copeland, L. (2000), 'Survivor', *Washington Post*, 24 September 2000, [F01].
Day, E. (2009), 'When one extraordinary life is not enough', *Observer*, 15 February 2009, www.theguardian.com/books/2009/feb/15/herman-rosenblat-oprah-winfrey-hoax. Accessed 16 October 2013.
Defonseca, M. [1997] (2005), *Surviving with Wolves: The Most Extraordinary Story of World War II*, with the collaboration of V. Lee and M.-T. Cuny, trans. S. Rose. London: Piatkus.
Duroy, L. (2011), *Survivre Avec Les Loups: La Véritable Histoire de Misha Defonseca*. Paris: XO Editions.
Eaglestone, R. (2004), *The Holocaust and the Postmodern*. Oxford: Oxford University Press.
Fernyhough, C. (2012), *Pieces of Light: The New Science of Memory*. London: Profile.
Finkelstein, N. (2000), *The Holocaust Industry: Reflections on the Exploitation of Jewish Suffering*. London: Verso.
Freud, S. [1922] (1950), *Beyond the Pleasure Principle*, in *The Standard Edition of the Complete Psychological Works of Sigmund Freud*, vol. 18, trans. J. Strachey. London: Hogarth Press, pp. 3–64.
Friedlander, S. (1984), *Reflections of Nazism: An Essay on Kitsch and Death*. New York: Harper and Rowe.
—. (1997), *Nazi Germany and the Jews: The Years of Persecution, 1939–1944*. London: Weidenfeld & Nicolson.
Greenspan, H. (1998), *On Listening to Holocaust Survivors: Recounting and Life History*. New York: Praeger.

Holstein, B. (2004), *Stolen Soul*. Crawley, WA: University of Western Australia Press.

Holt, P. (2009), *The Apple: Based on the Herman Rosenblat Holocaust Love Story*. Rye Brook, NY: York House.

Karski, J. [1944] (2011), *Story of a Secret State: My Report to the World*. London: Penguin.

Kovács, I. (2006), *Le vengeur: à la poursuite des criminels Nazis*, ed. F. Ploquin. Paris: Fayard.

Kurzem, M. (2007), *The Mascot*. London: Rider.

Kushner, T. (2006), 'Holocaust testimony, ethics, and the problem of representation', *Poetics Today*, 27, 275–95.

—. (2013), 'Loose connections? Britain and the "final solution"', in C. Sharples and O. Jensen (eds), *Britain and the Holocaust: Remembering and Representing Genocide*. Basingstoke: Palgrave.

LaCapra, D. (2000), *Writing History, Writing Trauma*. Baltimore: Johns Hopkins University Press.

Langer, L. (1991), *Holocaust Testimonies: The Ruins of Memory*. New Haven: Yale University Press.

Lanzmann, C. (dir) (1985), *Shoah*. DVD. France: Les Films Aleph.

Laub, D. (1992), 'Bearing witness, or the vicissitudes of listening', in S. Felman and D. Laub, *Testimony: Crises of Witnessing in Literature, Psychoanalysis, and History*. London: Routledge, pp. 59–63.

Lejeune, P. (1989), *On Autobiography*. Minneapolis: University of Minnesota Press.

Lengyel, O. [1947] (1995), *Five Chimneys: A Woman Survivor's True Story of Auschwitz*. Chicago: Academy.

Lifton, R. J. (1986), *The Nazi Doctors: Medical Killing and the Psychology of Genocide*. New York: Basic Books.

Maiden, J. (2008), 'Ruptures in remembrance: trauma, utterance and patterns in survivor remembrance', unpublished Ph.D. dissertation, University of Sheffield.

Moor, K. (2013), 'Compensation claim upheld as Holocaust story believed', *Herald-Sun*, 25 July 2013, www.heraldsun.com.au/news/law-order/compensation-claim-upheld-as-holocaust-story-believed/story-fni0fee2–1226685112800. Accessed 17 October 2013.

Nyiszli, M. [1960] (2011), *Auschwitz: A Doctor's Eyewitness Account*, trans. T. Kremer and R. Seaver. Harmondsworth: Penguin.

Oberski, J. (1983), *A Childhood*, trans. R. Manheim. London: Hodder and Stoughton.

Polak, A. (2004), 'The cultural representation of the Holocaust in fiction and other genres', unpublished Ph.D. thesis, University of Sheffield.

Richardson, A. (2009), 'Mapping the lines of fact and fiction in Holocaust testimonial novels', in L. O. Vasvári and S. T. de Zepetnek (eds), *Comparative Central European Holocaust Studies*. West Lafayette, IN: Purdue University Press, pp. 53–66.

Richardson, R. (2013), 'Sexuality and survival during the Holocaust: sexual barter in Eva Roubiková's *We're Alive and Life Goes On: A Theresienstadt Diary* and Renata Laqueur's "Diary from Bergen-Belsen"', talk delivered at the conference 'Trauma and Memory: The Holocaust in Contemporary Culture', University of Portsmouth, July 2013.

Roseman, M. (1999), 'Surviving memory: truth and inaccuracy in Holocaust memory', *Holocaust Studies: A Journal of Culture and History*, 8.1, 1–20.

Rosenblat, H. [2009] (2013), *Angel at the Fence*, unpublished memoir with uncredited ghostwriter S. Margolis, http://pdf.edocr.com/cc90d3b0aebea2ec00843e622e0dbe-aee274a732.pdf. Accessed 12 October 2013.

Sherman, G. (2008), 'Ken Waltzer on Canceled Memoir', *New Republic*, 28 December 2008. www.newrepublic.com/blog/the-plank/ken-waltzer-canceled-memoir-quotwhere-were-the-culture-makersquot. Accessed 16 October 2013.

Sierakowiak, D. (1996), *The Diary of Dawid Sierakowiak: Five Notebooks from the Lodz Ghetto*, trans. K. Turowski. Oxford: Oxford University Press.

Sorensen, E. Park (2013), 'A pathological core of authenticity: rereading the case of Binjamin Wilkomirski's *Bruchstücke*', *Forum for Modern Language Studies*, 49, 79–98.

Spielberg, S. (dir) (1993), *Schindler's List*. DVD. Washington: Amblin Entertainment.

Steiner, J.-F. [1966] (1997), *Treblinka*. Harmondsworth: Penguin.

Strummer, D. (1988), *A Reflection of the Holocaust*. Baltimore: Aurich Press.

Styron, W. (1979), *Sophie's Choice*. New York: Random House.

Tec, N. (2000), 'Diaries and oral history: some methodological considerations', *Religion and the Arts*, 4.1, 87–95.

Vice, S. (2000), *Holocaust Fiction*. London: Routledge.

Walters, G. (2011), 'The curious case of the "break into Auschwitz"', *New Statesman*, 17 November 2011, 15–16.

Whitehead, A. (2004), *Trauma Fiction*. Edinburgh: Edinburgh University Press.

Wieviorka, A. (2006), *The Era of the Witness*, trans. J. Stark. Ithaca: Cornell University Press.

Wilkomirski, B. (2006), *Fragments: Memories of a Childhood, 1939–1948*, trans. C. Brown Janeway. London: Picador.

Young, J. (1988), *Writing and Rewriting the Holocaust*. Bloomington: Indiana University Press.

Žižek, S. (2009), *The Fragile Absolute: Or, Why Is the Christian Legacy Worth Fighting For?* London: Verso.

3 After Epic: Adorno's Scream and the Shadows of Lyric

David Miller

Abstract

This chapter examines the debates and critical trajectories that surround Theodor Adorno's famed assertion concerning the continuing possibility and 'barbarity' of 'poetry after Auschwitz'. Rather than simply accepting or rejecting the assertion on the basis of empirical evidence and literary history, the chapter attempts to trace the underlying tensions and theoretical insights that accumulate and gather force once we understand that Adorno was opening up a debate that strikes at the heart of European literary criticism and the whole framework of generic, historical and ethical assumptions upon which that literary criticism claims to rest. In other words, the chapter seeks to understand Adorno's most famous assertion as a challenge to the notion that literary criticism could ever return to normal after the deeper hell of the death camps.

The debates, counter-statements and arguments that have accumulated around Adorno's claim about the 'impossibility' of 'poetry after Auschwitz' have become as essential to discussions of poetry and the death camps as the core material of the history of the subject itself. Even if one rejects the substantive claim of the statement on the basis that as a matter of simple observed fact we do still 'have' poetry,[1] the troubling insistence of the question of the condition of poetry after Auschwitz nevertheless implies that Adorno's proposition concisely gathers many of the main problems and concerns under its emphatic surface claim. These 'problems' and questions relate not only to the status and content of poetry after the death camps, but also, concomitantly, to what the Holocaust inflicted upon the central claims and undertakings of the European literary inheritance. This literary and cultural inheritance first established and then came to rely upon certain essential procedures and assumptions. The procedures and collective assumptions that permitted 'literary' criticism and the teaching of literature to continue after the war are familiar enough and included, principally, the possibility of a stable literary and historical hermeneutics, the application of trustworthy genre classifications, and intellectual confidence in the explanatory and recuperative powers of literary and cultural criticism. Adorno's claim penetrates right to the core of these issues and undermines any lingering complacency that these essential assumptions may have remained intact after such a catastrophe. That Adorno selects poetry as the central fulcrum of his claims is no accident. For reasons that I will explore more fully later, the nature of lyric poetry interrogates and questions the assembled cultural and historical assumptions that were necessary for European literary 'culture' to re-establish itself after the Holocaust. For example, if the language of lyric poetry is fractured and contaminated after the Holocaust, then any attempted normalization of cultural categories becomes difficult to sustain. One way to approach Adorno's contentious statement, therefore, is to take it as marking the starting point of a necessary questioning of those configurations that have tended to govern what we had once thought of as the main categories and assumptions of our literary history and 'culture'. In other words, it is possible and perhaps necessary to understand Adorno's claim not as a straightforward statement of historical fact that can be either refuted or confirmed by empirical evidence, but rather as a challenge and constant reminder that we must rethink our literary and critical assumptions in the light of the Holocaust.

Approached in this way, Adorno's famous phrase accurately condenses our imprecise but insistent awareness that after the death camps the traditional categories and conceptual arrangements of literary criticism and literary history were either 'changed utterly' (Yeats, 1996, p. 180, l. 15) or completely devastated. Adorno's notorious phrase refuses to simply vanish from our critical concerns because we are still dimly aware that our literary and therefore poetic world has, in truth, been irrevocably altered. Even if one can point to the poets and poetry that surround us today, one is still troubled by questions that are by no means auxiliary: Is what passes for poetry after Auschwitz really what poetry promised to be? Are we capable of encountering what is left of poetic language *as* poetry? Is the poetry that exists after Auschwitz merely the ruins or anguished afterthought of poetry itself? In its urgency to maintain 'culture' after the catastrophe, has an overconfident literary criticism wilfully configured a pale remnant into a flawless poetic garment? Has poetry itself attempted to continue as if all was as it once was? Such questions pertain directly to the practice and theory of literary criticism and literary history and cannot be cancelled or laid to rest by simply pointing to the 'poetry' that exists today. It is worth recalling at this juncture that the statement comes in the closing paragraphs of an essay that deals principally with the failures and ideological complicities of 'cultural criticism' and not with the historical fate of poetry as such. The quotation is from the essay on 'Cultural Criticism and Society' in the collection *Prisms*:

> The critique of culture is confronted with the last stage in the dialectic of culture and barbarism: to write a poem after Auschwitz is barbaric, and that corrodes also the knowledge which expresses why it has become impossible to write poetry today. (Adorno, 1981a, p. 34)

As troubling as it may be, the essay implies that it is not only poetry that is 'impossible' after Auschwitz. The essay clearly suggests concomitantly that what have passed as the apparently stable and seemingly untroubled branches of literary criticism and cultural commentary in the intervening years have been not much more than the groping perambulations of a reanimated intellectual corpse. Adorno's essay clearly shows that it is not only the language of poetry but also the conceptual foundations and ethical assumptions of literary criticism and cultural critique that have been irreparably shattered by the historical catastrophe. In *Minima Moralia*, Adorno is utterly unambiguous on this point. In Aphorism 35, titled 'Back to Culture', he writes: 'The claim that Hitler has destroyed German culture is no more than an advertising stunt of those who want to rebuild it from their telephone desks. Such art and thought as were exterminated by Hitler had long been leading a severed and apocryphal existence, whose last hideouts Fascism swept away' (Adorno, 1974, p. 57).[2] This aphorism, like much else in Adorno's work, is predicated on the assumption that 'culture' is no more immune from the techniques of domination and cruelty than industry or politics are. The claim to be re-establishing a 'culture' that is itself complicit in the most inhuman of crimes is therefore, for Adorno at least, a very dubious boast.

Adorno makes a similar claim in 'Education after Auschwitz', in which he proposes that it is not only the teaching and remembrance of the horrors of the camps that might forestall any possible recurrence of those events. What is more necessary for Adorno (1998) is that the complicit patterns of 'societal' domination and 'reified consciousness' that quickly re-established themselves after the event (of which historical apologia and rationalization are only a part) must be critiqued, challenged and exposed. A failed and defeated literary criticism and a devastated poetic inheritance may seem inauspicious starting points for an attempt to understand what remains of and for poetry after the death camps. Nonetheless, it is my contention that Adorno's severely negative theoretical verdicts were never intended as simple descriptive observations, but function principally as an unswerving theoretical rebuke and challenge to all those who would seek to re-establish traditional literary, cultural and hermeneutic categories after the Holocaust as if the progress of 'culture' remained somehow unimpaired. In what follows, I will trace some of the ramifications and sources of this challenge not only in order to try to better understand what remains of poetry, but also to try to foreground how the critical vocabulary of poetic criticism might respond to it.

The main theoretical source for Adorno's claims about the 'barbarity' and the 'impossibility' of 'poetry after Auschwitz' can be found in Hegel, and specifically in Hegel's *Lectures on Aesthetics*. I give the full quotation here:

> In all these respects art is, and remains for us, on the side of its highest destiny, a thing of the past. Herein it has further lost for us its genuine truth and life, and rather is transferred into our ideas than asserts its former necessity, or assumes its former place, in reality. What is now aroused in us by works of art is over and above our immediate enjoyment, and together with it, our judgment; inasmuch as we subject the content and the means of representation of the work of art and the suitability or unsuitability of the two to our intellectual consideration. (Hegel, 1975, p. 11)

For Hegel, the very existence and rise of philosophical aesthetic theory implies that art has become an 'object' of reflection and judgement for 'us' and it is therefore no longer the essential and spontaneous crucible of our deepest needs and desires. As the 'objective' manifestation of judgement and critical reflection in the world, it is therefore philosophy that occupies the present moment. In other words, the developmental movement of history taken as the phenomenological manifestation of the life of 'World-Spirit' reveals that art has relinquished its sensuous immediacy for us and so is now a matter of critical 'judgement'. Art still exists, but it is now located as the 'past' in relation to the ever-present immediacy of our essential needs. One can see how Adorno accepts the version of a dialectical understanding of history deployed here by Hegel, but radically reverses its conclusions. By means of a further dialectical reversal typical of Adorno's later work,[3] the Holocaust reveals that the 'advanced' movement of history is deadly rather than life affirming.

Adorno was highly critical of Hegel's famous statement in the *Lectures*, that 'art was for us a thing of the past' and denounced it as a result of Hegel's overconfidence in the explanatory and recuperative capabilities of his own philosophical system in the face of historical disaster. In *Minima Moralia* he comments acidly that had Hegel lived, 'Hitler's robot bombs' and crimes would have taken their place beside 'the early death of Alexander and similar images, as just another fact by which the state of the world-spirit manifests itself' (Adorno, 1974, p. 55). This is a significant and curious point and worth pursuing in more detail inasmuch as Adorno seems to have more or less repeated Hegel's claim in respect to poetry being 'a thing of the past' after Auschwitz, while at the same time rejecting Hegel's claim that 'art' was 'a thing of the past' after Napoleon and the French Revolution. Rather than art withering away in positive terms because history has reached a 'higher' stage of development, for Adorno poetry is 'barbaric' because that very dialectical movement has been turned inside out and the movement of history itself has turned deadly – 'progress' is an objective historical fact but it is revealed as domination, alienation and compulsive, and, in the case of the Holocaust, deadly, assimilation. So for Adorno, Hegel is correct about the 'universal' form of history but very wrong about the 'ideal' content of it. Adorno's later lectures titled 'Progress or Regression?', 'Spirit and the Course of the World' and 'Negative Universal History' confirm and elaborate this critical position, and his assertions concerning poetry and Auschwitz must be understood within the context of this critical pattern.[4]

We know that later Adorno continued to rethink this original assertion about 'poetry after Auschwitz' and significantly refashioned and refocused it. There is the now famous passage in *Negative Dialectics* where he states that: 'Perennial suffering has as much right to expression as a tortured man has to scream: hence it may have been wrong to say that after Auschwitz one could no longer write poems' (Adorno, 1981b, p. 326). We see here that Adorno continues his trenchant attack on the idea of a 'progressive' history of humanity outlined previously. He allows for the possibility of the existence of poetry after Auschwitz, but implies that the whole of post-medieval European literary culture, of which poetry was always the central emblem, has been irrevocably exposed as part of a 'tortured' existence. Poetry and the interpretative procedures that justified and disseminated it can no longer remain in the confident domain in which they once resided. It may not be too impertinent, then, to reformulate Adorno's famous phrase and say that therefore as far as poetry is concerned we have the 'impossibility' of hermeneutics after Auschwitz – a 'scream' is what it is. We can see the two salient features of Adorno's analysis: On the one hand, Auschwitz marks a decisive limit or end point, after which the relationship to poetry is qualitatively and unalterably changed. Yet, on the other hand, poetry has 'perennially' and in an ongoing way represented 'suffering' and may continue to do so. If one allows that poetry and the versions of critical commentary that were attached to it are irrevocably altered 'after Auschwitz', then the true force of Adorno's original phrase begins to emerge and one begins to understand why, despite the 'fact' of poetry after Auschwitz, it still haunts literary criticism. What artistic form and linguistic pattern would the 'tortured scream' of which Adorno writes take? How could this 'scream' enter poetic language and not shatter the whole fabric of poetic experience? Is this 'scream' affiliated to any particular literary genre or category above others?

In the two-volume *Notes to Literature*, Adorno offers some clues and possible answers to these questions. In essays such as 'Parataxis', 'Lyric Poetry and Society' and 'Charmed Language', Adorno elaborates three main interlocking categories and patterns of exploration in respect to poetry. These essays offer an exemplary instance of the way one might encounter the challenges that a shattered literary and critical inheritance poses. The title of this book of essays on literature dating from 1958 to 1974 is interesting in itself. The title, both in English and in German, implies a musical accompaniment rather than a critical method or exposition. The idea of a musical accompaniment manages to break with the idea of a systematic interpretation that would explain and then subsume the literary works under its main theses and historical assumptions. The implication is one of a bringing out of the essential qualities of the works by means of a secondary commentary that resembles musical counterpoint. The essays in the volume reflect this approach and allow the essential qualities of the works to stand out rather than interpreting and explaining them as such. Obviously accepting that hermeneutic and cultural security is no longer possible, in the very mode of the commentaries there is a response to the demand for a different and more attuned form of literary commentary after the Holocaust. The difficulties and even the strangeness of the works taken as the subject of the two volumes are made to stand out rather than being explained and simplified. Following the musical analogy, one can say that the main melodies and harmonies of the works are brought out by a sensitive counterpoint that takes its lead from the qualities of the works and not any pre-established order of criticism and conceptual arrangement. The intrinsic mode of the volume, in other words, gestures to one possible answer to the demand of the questions mentioned earlier, in that it implies a much more self-aware and less assertive and encapsulating form of criticism.

The essays offer three interlocking and salient concepts and ideas under which the main approach is achieved. The first of these concepts is 'objectification'. According to this concept, the assumed purified single 'voice' that was previously taken to lie at the heart of lyric poetry has been diminished and even 'devastated by the forces of commerce' (Adorno, 1992a, p. 194), reification and alienation to the point at which the language of lyric must either 'objectify' itself or collapse. Lyric can no longer cling to the subjective impulse that was once its main source of poetic strength. Under the totalizing forces of industrialization and 'progress', any pretence or lingering in the inner subjective 'voice' renders lyric sentiment-laden and insignificant. In other words, the lyric poet as it were, assimilates him or herself, as Adorno writes, to the 'objectification' of language and becomes one with it so that the poet's 'subjectivity turns into objectivity' (1992b, p. 43). In this sense, the assumed centrality of the speaking subject of lyric is annihilated and thus lyric remains true to its truth content, albeit negatively. The language of lyric becomes, as Adorno writes, language as *'writing only'*, and its forms are objectified, brittle and even mechanistic. The specificity and sensuality associated with lyric is therefore abolished. How can the most subjective of poetic forms – asks Adorno elsewhere – survive the 'incapacitation of the subject' (1981b, p. 66)? The absolute commitment to the truth of language demanded of the lyric poet means that the poet becomes assimilated to a language that has itself succumbed to technocratic instrumentalization and the equivalences of commodification. This 'poetic' language therefore no longer emanates from the inner human subject that was supposed to mediate its sensual and expressive resources. The commitment to the 'inner' 'voice' of the subject becomes the double 'objectification' into a language that is itself in the process of becoming utterly 'objectified'.

An additional and connected idea to the concept of 'objectification' is what Adorno terms the 'pathos of metre'. In attempting to maintain the sensuous and sonorous quality of lyric, the poet remains, however submerged, attached to metre inasmuch as this is the echo or inheritance of lyric's attachment to the structures of older forms of song and music. But in a historical period in which the fluid forces of the market and the disintegration and liquidation of social and ethical solidarity have come to dominate, 'free verse' becomes the form under which metre must attempt to covertly maintain itself. Thus, when metre appears it strikes as pathos-laden and a harking back to an earlier moment of true lyric pathos it cannot bring to realization. Metre clings to lyric poetry as a sort of guilt-libel of all it has lost in that it gestures to a more genuine pathos that it ultimately lacks but attempts to maintain – a double pathos, if you will.[5] A further key idea is that of poetic 'anachronism' and 'idiosyncrasy'. Clinging tenuously to a poetic language that might somehow still possess lyric meaning within a general language that has become objectified and impotent, lyric stands out as a curiosity. In attempting to hold out against the forces of advanced industrialization and commodification, lyric poetry could appear as merely nostalgic and pathetic, even a version of outmoded pastoral. But by means of the previously mentioned commitment to its 'objectification' in language, lyric maintains itself. In its most distinct formal qualities, it remains what we could term 'negatively modern' or even something resembling anti-lyric, to go along with Schoenberg's anti-music, Beckett's anti-drama and Proust's anti-novel.[6]

Yet we ought to pause here. Although Adorno makes a general connection between his formulations on 'art after Auschwitz' and the work of Beckett and especially Beckett's *Endgame*, there are some crucial formal and genre questions that need to be considered. As Jacques Derrida makes clear in his work on the poetics of Paul Celan, the disaster and suffering of the death camps has entered the very material or substance of language. The lyric poet after Auschwitz is therefore faced with a double extremity that the dramatist is not, in that the very material with which he or she works is contaminated and poisoned. Beckett's tramps and ragged shadow players may appear as the walking dead, but for all that they remain actors and the mechanisms and props of the stage allow for a representation of sorts, albeit a negative and deeply ironic one. For the poet after Auschwitz, no such material support exists; the very medium of his or her work is the ruined core of language itself. The only conceivable parallel condition in drama would be if Beckett had produced a drama in a bombed out shell-crater rather than a theatre, or simply threw corpses on the stage, or had his audience sit in silence in the local morgue for the evening. In other words, the lyric poet after Auschwitz carries a double burden and works with a ruined substance by definition; this is a burden that other artistic forms do not carry with them. This burden is inherent in the question of the 'tortured scream' because the poisoned language that is then 'objectified' by the poet bears within itself no possibility of commentary or interpretative recuperation. A shattered language can produce no normative or constitutive concepts nor any stable communicative practices capable of conveying an annulled experience. Meaning having been shattered, it carries no possibility of surplus or excess meaning as such. Precisely because of the contagion at the level of substance, no hermeneutics is possible for poetry after Auschwitz. One can then usefully extend Adorno's formulations in order to encounter poetry after Auschwitz as exemplifying and intensifying all these elements to the point at which one can say that such poetry is 'pathos'-laden in its own sense of belatedness; it has internalized its 'anachronistic' condition as part of its self-questioning and it has so 'objectified' itself that the possibilities of meaning have petrified. By extension, one can say, then, that a poetry that does not encounter or acknowledge this post-Holocaust condition, or in fact attempts to evade rather than entering into these forces, is hardly worth the name 'poetry' at all.[7]

A slightly more detailed discussion of a single poet can help to extend and apply these ideas and concepts and also assist in clarifying how they might stand in relation to literary history. The inevitable inclination towards the recuperation of meanings that simultaneously rests upon the acknowledgement that meaning is disintegrating that Adorno identifies as the 'bind' of the modern lyric poet, perhaps explains Adorno's apparently curious association of the work of Celan with 'hermetic poetry'[8] in the *Aesthetic Theory*. Despite Celan's own warnings against linking his work with the hermetic tradition,[9] Adorno persists in maintaining that while Celan's poems may not be hermetic in the full sense, the 'extent' of their association with the hermetic is an open 'question'. The content of this 'question' of the relationship between the hermetic tradition and the work of Celan entails some very instructive concepts and lines of thought for any study of poetry after the Holocaust. Despite the apparent incongruity of the association, part of the answer resides in this question of poetic meaning and the impossibility of rebuilding a systemic literary hermeneutics after Auschwitz. If the allure of hermetic poetry resides in the way it proffers and withholds meaning at one and the same moment and therefore in the way it resists hermeneutic and ideological semantic incorporation, then one can see why it might offer a way of encountering the implicit question of the condition and status of poetic language after Auschwitz in Celan's poetry. As well as the recognized hermetic elements employed by French Symbolism, in Mallarmé and the later Rimbaud, for example, Italian hermetic poets such as Alfonso Gatto saw in the traditions of hermetic writing a way of evading the rising totalitarian manipulations of meaning. In other words, hermetic poetry seems to offer some linguistic and compositional mechanism for sheltering or preserving meaning in the face of the dissolution or repression of artistic expression. Despite this, Celan's own refusal to be classified as part of the hermetic tradition shows the profundity of the issues at stake. In a condition where language itself has been scorched, the resources of literary language that the hermetic poet could once rely upon no longer exist. That which would be shielded or sheltered, or could be taken as residing behind or within the outward contours of hermetic poetic cunning, has itself been shattered and rendered homeless. Following this line of critical thought, in the *Aesthetic Theory* Adorno can offer an understanding of Celan as an 'inverted' or 'negative' hermetic poet. In typical negative dialectical fashion, Celan *is* and *is not* a hermetic poet, or perhaps more problematically, Celan *would* have been a full-blown hermetic poet if the Holocaust had never occurred.

We can see this clearly in Celan's poem 'Tenebrae'. The opening stanzas run:

> We are near, Lord,
> near and at hand.
> Handled already, Lord,
> clawed and clawing as though
> the body of each of us were
> your body, Lord.
> Pray, Lord,
> pray to us,
> we are near.

With the closing stanzas:

> It cast your image into our eyes, Lord.
> Our eyes and our mouths are open and empty, Lord.
> We have drunk, Lord.
> The blood and the image that was in the blood, Lord.
> Pray, Lord.
> We are near. (Celan, 1988)

Here the outward hymnal tonalities and diction are recast to such an extent that any attempts to 'find' a hidden or encoded meaning are utterly demolished. Despite this, the poem still retains a tenuous and fragile connection to the mystical and esoteric poetic hymns of John of the Cross (1542–91). John's most famous poem is the *Dark Night of the Soul* (1578–91) in which the poet mystic describes by means of a rich and obscure symbolism the passage of the soul out of the body to eventual union with God. Celan's poem invokes the 'dark night of the soul' by means of the title, which names the 'shadow' church services of the last three days of Holy Week in which the evening services are 'darkened' by the measured extinguishing of the church candles. In other words, the poem names an accumulating or fully attained darkness by using the outward lyrical resources of Christian religious poetic mysticism. Yet the 'image' and 'blood' of the 'Lord' are arranged in the poem so as to explicitly exclude any possible union with God. The poem inverts the prayer of supplication so that the 'Lord' 'prays' to 'us'. We are 'near' to the 'Lord' not in spiritual consummation but rather in the 'crater' and 'trough' of absolute 'bodily' suffering. The possibility of a deeper or hidden theological meaning that would permit either kataphatic (God projected positively in words or in 'blood' and 'image') or apophatic readings (God conceived only negatively as 'not' like anything on earth such as a 'body') is utterly shattered by this poem. The poetic resources of theological transcendence are retained but turned inwards to reveal the pact with dreadfulness and death-worship that lies at the heart of all such symbolism. We are beyond all either/or in this poetry. The 'image' still 'burns' but we are 'empty' and so the poem both suggests and rejects its own theological and esoteric foundations. What begins in poetic religious mysticism ends in the language of catastrophe and loss – the reverential has become horrific.

This poetic arrangement is intrinsic rather than interpretational to much of Celan's poetry and can also be seen in those poems such as 'Death Fugue' and 'Tübingen, January' (Celan, 1988, pp. 63, 181) that gesture to those cultural achievements of Western and particularly German culture that are held in the highest reverential awe, for example, the fugues of Bach and the later poetic hymns of Hölderlin. Celan's achievement is not a matter of poetic technique or simple inversion or rejection, but rather, his lyric poetry reveals a way of dealing with an artistic language in which meaning is not so much 'hidden' as contaminated and stricken. The poems seem to cling to lyric language while at the same time acknowledging the historical and political 'blood' and brutality that is inherent in the linguistic and cultural system of which they are a part.

In other words, and again following the inversion of Hegel, the Holocaust wrecked the poetic possibilities of Europe to such a degree that the flow of social history itself was ruptured. What comes after this rupture can only be a ghost or shade of what European and in particular German literary culture dreamed it might one day become. The inward collapse of the hermetic procedures and the nullification of the formal patterns of the poetry's own intentions are the result of the 'pressure', the 'shame' and the 'horror' of the Holocaust:

> In the work of the most important contemporary representative of German hermetic poetry, Paul Celan, the experimental content of the hermetic was inverted. His poetry is permeated by the shame of art in the face of suffering that escapes both experience and sublimation. Celan's poems want to speak of the most extreme horror through silence. Their truth content itself becomes negative. They imitate a language beneath the helpless language of human beings, indeed beneath all organic language: It is that of the dead speaking of stones and stars. . . . The language of the lifeless becomes the last possible comfort for a death that is deprived of all meaning. (Adorno, 1997, pp. 319–21)

This tends to imply that what remains, what we have as poetry after the Holocaust, is a ghostly emblem of the poetry we would have had if history had not taken such a 'barbaric' turn. Echoing Adorno's well-known phrase in *Negative Dialectics* that 'philosophy, which once seemed outmoded, remains alive because the moment of its realization was missed' (1981b, p. 3), we can perhaps say that for Adorno, poetry still exists because the chance of its realization was devastated rather than simply 'missed'.

I have used the term 'lyric' because I do not know of any true European 'epic after Auschwitz' – that would surely be 'barbaric'.[10] In *Dialectic of Enlightenment*, Adorno and Horkheimer describe the way that epic narration resembles a dominative technical mastery by using impassive narrative and descriptive techniques to encapsulate the horrors of traumatic experience and render them fit for further social use. The specific example is the passage on the execution of the 'faithless women' in Book 22 of Homer's *Odyssey*, and they then go on to parallel what was once praised by Classicist critics as Homeric 'inhuman composure' with the '*impassibilité*' of the 'realist novel' and the compensatory erotic 'sentimentality' of romance. Epic narration and those subsequent literary forms that are attached to it are, under this analysis, complicit with dominative and compulsively repressive impulses inherent in the progress of civilization (Adorno and Horkheimer, 1997, pp. 78–80).

Adorno's insights about epic narration and realist prose contradict Slavoj Žižek's assertion that it is 'prose' that is impossible after Auschwitz, not 'poetry'. The basis for Žižek's claim is twofold and centres on the mimetic category of prosaic 'description' and expressive poetic category of 'evocation'. Within this distinction, according to Žižek, poetry can 'evoke' or 'allude' to the 'unbearable atmosphere' of the camps in a way that the more direct 'description' of prose never can (2007, pp. 4–6). Under this pattern of analysis, prose can only recoil or disintegrate in the presence of the unbearable reality of the camps.

As suggestive as Žižek's formulation is, it is vulnerable to some obvious criticisms. Žižek's examples tend to contradict his assertion. For example, although it is prose rather than poetry that is 'impossible' after Auschwitz, Žižek uses a 'prose' quotation from a letter rather than a poem from the Russian poet Anna Akhmatova to emphasize his point, and in fact the prose quotation used has nothing to do with the death camps. Again, rather idiosyncratically, Žižek also cites the work of Primo Levi as a support for his proposition on the 'impossibility' of 'prose' after Auschwitz. He specifically cites Levi's *The Periodic Table*, but this collection is a *prose* collection of connected shorter works that in no way can be described as 'poetic' (ibid., pp. 1–7). The obvious example of a prose work 'after Auschwitz' would be Levi's *If This Is a Man*, but curiously it is not mentioned by Žižek. Again, *If This Is a Man* is a complex work and it is not 'epic' in any sense, but it is certainly not a poem or poetic either. In other words, Žižek's argument is contradicted by his examples. Moreover, literary criticism has long recognized that the inwardness, self-consciousness and ironic techniques of Romantic and Modernist fiction rendered the distinction between prosaic 'description' and poetic 'evocation' redundant some decades ago. Although Žižek invokes the name of Adorno, Adorno's connection between epic narration and the so-called objective and clinical observational style of the realist novelists and the rise of political and social brutality falls hard against Žižek's claim. As indicated, Adorno saw the pseudo-scientific techniques and claim to dispassionate 'observation' on behalf of novelists such as Zola, as coincidental with the rise of economic brutality and social indifference. Following the pattern of Adorno's insight, it is precisely 'realistic', explicit, or at its furthest extent even pornographic prose that is most at home with the underlying processes and horrors of the camps.[11] Under Adorno's mode of thought, realist prose would be one of the cultural manifestations of the dominative impulse and hatred of non-identity of which the death camps are the ultimate emblem.

Given these considerations concerning epic, we may also wish to question whether, at the level of form, an epic romance such as Tasso's *La Gerusalemme Liberata* (1581) can actually carry the burden of a poetic reordering of post-traumatic history that is frequently required of it. In Cathy Caruth's influential work *Unclaimed Experience: Trauma, Narrative, and History*, Caruth echoes Freud's reading of the 'double wounding' of the loved one in Tasso's epic romance in order to show how Freud 'turns to literature' in order to expose and identify the way originating catastrophic events are prone to repetition and re-enactment in the minds and actions of those suffering from 'traumatic neurosis' (Caruth, 1996, pp. 1–9). Yet in his analysis, Freud foregrounds the trauma and unconscious guilt of the unwitting perpetrator Tancred, not the 'cry' of the obliterated victim, the dead loved one Clorinda, and it is a very specific form of 'literature' that he selects in order to ground this interpretation. Freud's emphasis in his use of Tasso's epic is repeated by Caruth, and both focus on the way the narrative attempts to explain and encapsulate the 're-enactment' experience of 'traumatic neurosis'. In the epic, Tancred is a guilt-laden but unwitting perpetrator; he is not a survivor or a victim. In order for this narrative to function effectively, the 'cry' of the dead 'beloved' must be contained within the broader narrative frame of the epic 'parable' of Tancred's traumatic experience of guilt through 're-enactment'. Both Freud and Caruth are surely correct in identifying Tasso's main concerns. Yet, how does this analysis cope with or frame the voice of that which has been catastrophically expunged from the world of experience as such by the crime itself, the dead Clorinda? What poetic form can expose and bear witness to her unarticulated anguish and unnecessary death? For Freud and Caruth, Clorinda's 'voice' speaks out through the 'wound' that Tancred inflicts on the tree within which her soul is 'imprisoned' (ibid., pp. 2–5). But we know nothing of the content of this scream or 'cry'. We know only of the use that the epic narration makes of it in the redemptive parable of Tancred's guilt. In other words, Clorinda's 'spirit' is entrapped within the tree in much the same way that her 'cry' is imprisoned, placed or stifled within the overarching narration of Tasso's epic. Clorinda's 'cry' functions within the narrative only to bring to light Tancred's guilt. Yet Clorinda's accusatory 'cry' haunts the epic and in many ways resembles Adorno's claim for poetry as the 'tortured scream' of lyric after Auschwitz. It is the 'cry' of a poetry of suffering that reaches beyond experience as such and it shadows all other attempts to narrate catastrophic trauma. It is the 'cry' of a 'voice' that has been orphaned by a language that was complicit in its suffering. Freud and Caruth may read Tasso accurately, but this very accuracy appears as an attempt to quiet those other poetic murmurs and spectral forms that haunt the whole idea of an epic narration of catastrophic trauma.

Perhaps we can say that after Auschwitz we *have* a poetics of a possible future poetry, but no poetry in any fully present sense.[12] Following this line of argument, we can say that what remains of poetic language after Auschwitz is the tattered remnants of poetry out of which poetry is attempting, step by ghostly step, to fully reappear. In this way, we can conceive of this ruined poetic language after Auschwitz as the allegorical outline of a future poetry that awaits the time of healing and redemption. In this sense, the poetry of the present is the necessary prefiguration and reminder of all that was lost and all that may yet come poetically. We can conceive of poetry after Auschwitz then, as a purgatorial zone of literary meaning, neither the outright inferno of absolute poetic meaninglessness nor the paradise of lyric felicity. As Adorno writes of 'experience after the war', 'memory is to experience after the catastrophe, as the functioning of a machine is to the movements of the body' – a sort of shadow pattern (1974, p. 54). Long before the major catastrophes of European modernity, Dostoevsky's cynical old fool Fedor Karamazov answered his own question concerning the existence of furnaces and 'workshops' in hell for producing 'hooks' for the condemned, with the answer that there are of course, 'no hooks in hell', 'only the shadows of hooks' (Dostoevsky, 1986, p. 24). Like the shadows or outlines of people on the walls of Hiroshima in the aftermath of the dropping of the A-bomb, it may well be that what remains for poetic language after the deeper hell of the death camps are only the shades of lyric. There are no lyrics after Auschwitz, only the shadows of lyrics.

Notes

1. Nelly Sachs, Miklós Radnóti and Paul Celan are three of the most prominent names, but one must be careful not to assume that by simply listing a series of poets and works one can dismiss the deep fracture that has occurred. Well-meaning collections such as Hilda Schiff's *Holocaust Poetry* (2001) run the risk of attempting to normalize or stabilize the disaster of the Holocaust under anthologizing impulses that seek to bracket the catastrophe within habitual literary and cultural categories. The danger of such literary 'normalization' is explained and examined more fully in what follows.
2. It is plausible, therefore, to view some of the most caustic and troubling passages of Adorno's work as constituting an outright attack on all those postwar 'intellectuals' and scholars (Heidegger being only the most prominent) who sought to continue working as 'normal' as if the main currents and 'systems' of European thought could somehow remain guiltless and undamaged by the Holocaust. The most obvious example of this combative strand in Adorno's work is *The Jargon of Authenticity* (1973).
3. Many of the titles and phrases in Adorno's work reveal this determination to reverse and invert all positive conclusions and theoretical suppositions. For example, *Minima Moralia* is an inversion of Aristotle's *Magna Moralia*, 'The Health Unto Death' is an obvious inversion of Kierkegaard's *Sickness Unto Death* and the dedication that opens with the phrase 'the melancholy science' reverses Nietzsche's *The Gay Science*. Both of these examples are from *Minima Moralia*; there are others.
4. See Adorno (2006).
5. See, specifically, Adorno (1992), and also Aphorism 142 of *Minima Moralia*: 'By this does German Song Abide' (Adorno, 1974, p. 221).
6. See Adorno (1992b, p. 40). The examples of Beckett, Proust and Schoenberg can be read as instances of that form of artistic work that extends the internal dynamics of a genre or form to the point at which these dynamics alter and subvert the basic assumptions of the form itself. Needless to say, this type of artistic achievement takes the internal possibilities of artistic form to their generic and modular limits rather than simply rejecting or replacing them outright. This type of 'limit' or 'anti' art is of course one of the major achievements of modernism. It can be differentiated from Surrealism and Dada in that the artistic capabilities are radically extended and deepened rather than simply rejected or refabricated. Adorno seems to imply that the lyric poet must achieve this condition in general while the prose, dramatic and musical artist must achieve it singularly. This tends to confirm the discussion of the question of a 'contaminated poetic language' in the following section of this chapter.
7. For example, very few would now think of the optimistic and sentimental 'light verse' of Edgar Guest (1881–1951) or Nick Kenny (1895–1975) as constituting more than period pieces worthy of only strictly historical analysis.
8. The most prominent figure in hermetic poetry is Salvatore Quasimodo (1901–68). Largely an Italian literary phenomenon with roots in the Neoplatonist thinking and writings of the Renaissance, it stresses obscure, complex and sealed or hidden meanings.

It was taken to be opposed to the commercial and political manipulation of poetic meaning.

9. One of the English translators of Celan, Michael Hamburger, recounts that after being angered by a review in the *Times Literary Supplement* that claimed that his poetry was 'hermetic', Celan inscribed the phrase 'ganz und gar nicht hermetisch' – 'absolutely not hermetic' – into Hamburger's copy of *Die Niemandsrose*. See Hamburger (1988, p. 27), and for further evidence of Celan's disavowal of the term 'hermetic', see also Felstiner (1995, pp. 261–3).

10. William Carlos Williams' *Paterson* (1940–61) and Ezra Pound's *Cantos* (1915–69) are not true epics and the American point of origin tends to exclude them from consideration in any case. Interestingly, the major poetic epics in modern times are probably Ramdhari Singh Dinkar's Hindi epics *Hunkar* (1938) and *Rashmirathi* (1952). Again, the fact of the extra-European point of origin supports the claim.

11. Adorno actually hints at the pornographic quality of the hanging of the 'faithless women' and other death scenes in Homer. See the passage cited by Adorno and Horkheimer in the reference above (p. 75).

12. The title and subtitle of Susan Gubar's (2003) *Poetry after Auschwitz: Remembering What One Never Knew* exemplifies the paradoxical nature of this condition. The whole texture of the book seeks to insist upon the necessity of poetic remembrance and then withdraws this possibly of complete recuperation on the basis that the impairment is too deep. In other words, the paradox is that after the Holocaust, poetry must attempt to resume or take up again that which it knows it cannot achieve and which has already passed into silence. The recourse to photographic images in the book is an index of this wounding of poetic language.

Works Cited

Adorno, T. W. (1973), *The Jargon of Authenticity*, trans. K. Tarnowski and F. Will. London: Routledge and Kegan Paul.

—. (1974), *Minima Moralia: Reflections from a Damaged Life*, trans. E. F. N. Jephcott. London: Verso.

—. (1981a), 'Cultural criticism and society', in *Prisms*, trans. S. Weber and S. Weber Nicholsen. London: MIT Press, pp. 17–34.

—. (1981b), *Negative Dialectics*, trans. E. B. Ashton. London: Continuum.

—. (1992a), 'Charmed language: on the poetry of Rudolf Borchard', in T. W. Adorno, *Notes to Literature Vol. II*, trans. S. Weber Nicholsen. New York: Columbia University Press, pp. 179–93.

—. (1992b), 'On lyric poetry and society', in T. W. Adorno, *Notes to Literature Vol. I*, trans. S. Weber Nicholsen. New York: Columbia University Press, pp. 29–37.

—. (1997), *Aesthetic Theory*, trans. R. Hullot-Kentor, ed. G. Adorno and R. Tiedemann. London: Athlone Press.

—. (1998), 'Education after Auschwitz', in *Critical Models*, trans. H. P. Pickford. New York: Columbia University Press, pp. 191–204.

—. (2006), *History and Freedom: Lectures 1964–1965*, ed. R. Tiedemann, trans. R. Livingstone. London: Polity Press.

Adorno, T. W. and Horkheimer, M. (1997), *Dialectic of Enlightenment*, trans. J. Cumming. London: Verso.

Caruth, C. (1996), *Unclaimed Experience: Trauma, Narrative, and History*. Baltimore: Johns Hopkins University Press.

Celan, P. (1988), 'Deathfugue', 'Tenebrae' and 'Tübingen, January', in *Paul Celan: Selected Poems*, trans. M. Hamburger. London: Penguin, pp. 63, 115, 181, respectively.

Dinkar, R. Singh (2009a), *Hunkar*. New Delhi: Rajkamal Prakashan.

—. (2009b), *Rashmi Rathi*. New Delhi: Lokbharti Prakashan.

Dostoevsky, F. M. (1986), *The Brothers Karamazov*, trans. D. Magarshack. London: Penguin.

Felstiner, J. (1995), *Paul Celan: Poet, Survivor, Jew*. New Haven: Yale University Press.

Gubar, S. (2003), *Poetry after Auschwitz: Remembering What One Never Knew*. Bloomington: Indiana University Press.

Hamburger, M. (1998), *Poems of Paul Celan*. London: Anvil.

Hegel, G. W. F. (1975), 'Introduction', in *Aesthetics: Lectures on Fine Art*, vol. 1, trans. T. M. Knox. Oxford: Clarendon Press, pp. 1–82.

Levi, P. (1986), *The Periodic Table*, trans. R. Rosenthal. London: Abacus.

—. (1987), *If This Is a Man; The Truce*, trans. S. Woolf. London: Abacus.

Pound, E. (1999), *The Cantos*. New York: New Directions.

Schiff, H. (ed.) (2001), *Holocaust Poetry*. Nottinghamshire: Schiff Press.

Williams, W. C. (1995), *Paterson*. New York: New Directions.

Yeats, W. B. (1996), 'Easter 1916', in *The Collected Poems of W. B. Yeats*, ed. R. J. Finneran. New York: Scribner, p.180.

Žižek, S. (2007), *Violence: Six Sideways Reflections*. London: Profile Books.

4 Relationships to Realism in Post-Holocaust Fiction: Conflicted Realism and the Counterfactual Historical Novel

Jenni Adams

Abstract

This chapter explores debates around realism in Holocaust representation. Examining the urgent nature of claims both for and against realism in Holocaust discourse, it traces the growing prevalence of dialectic approaches to this question, outlining the category of 'conflicted realism' and including in this such practices as 'traumatic realism' (Rothberg, 2000), magic realism, the realism of exhaustion and the counterfactual historical novel. Focusing on the latter, it argues that the counterfactual historical novel offers a form of writing in response to the Holocaust which preserves realist possibilities of knowledge and expression while countering problematic aspects of realist discourse such as determinism and the imputed pursuit of transparency and closure. In relation to works by Philip Roth, Michael Chabon, Philip K. Dick and Robert Harris, it examines how counterfactual historical fiction demonstrates the capacities of conflicted realism to renegotiate the mimetic possibilities of historically oriented fiction in ways that respond to key ethical debates regarding Holocaust representation.

Realism as understood here amounts to a representational practice underpinned by the philosophical attitude that, in Matthew Beaumont's words, 'it is possible, through the act of representation, . . . to provide cognitive as well as imaginative access to a material, historical reality that, though irreducibly mediated by human consciousness, and of course, by language, is nonetheless independent of it' (2007, p. 2). These assumptions are, in the term's critical history, often concretized in a set of specific conventions regarding the direction of the mimetic impulse, as Auerbach sums up:

> The serious treatment of everyday reality, the rise of more extensive and socially inferior human groups to the position of subject matter for problematic-existential representation, on the one hand; on the other, the embedding of random persons and events in the general course of contemporary history, the fluid historical background – these, we believe, are the foundations of modern realism. (1953, p. 491)

While, in the context of the Holocaust, what is at issue is precisely not 'everyday reality' in its conventional aspect, the relationship of individual experience to history and the recovery of experiences that are in a profound sense those of marginalization remain key preoccupations. Nevertheless, the issue of realism in (post-)Holocaust representation remains a vexed and contentious one, as a result of both the poststructuralist contentions which challenge the tenability of mimetic aspirations and the specific nature of the event in question.[1]

Even in the testimony of Primo Levi, one of the most 'realist' of Holocaust writers in his commitment to the precise and accurate rendering of Holocaust experience, we can trace an underlying conflict in the notion of mimesis deployed. Levi takes pains to emphasize his pursuit of objectivity and neutrality, speaking of his assumption, for example, of 'the calm, sober language of the witness' (1987, p. 382) and framing his account's purpose – in terms which recall Zola's positioning of the classic realist novel as a kind of experimental projection – as being 'to furnish documentation for a quiet study of certain aspects of the human mind' (ibid., p. 15): in other words, as neutrally presenting an objective reality for the reader's appraisal. This commitment to the possibility of accurately representing experience is coupled with a sense of such representation's imperative nature, with testimony described as both a need and 'an immediate and violent impulse' in Levi's account (ibid.). Nevertheless – and here lies the potential conflict – Levi acknowledges the failure of language in approaching the extremity of Holocaust experience. In an oft-quoted passage, he states:

> Just as our hunger is not that feeling of missing a meal, so our way of being cold has need of a new word. We say 'hunger', we say 'tiredness', 'fear', 'pain', we say 'winter' and they are different things. They are free words, created and used by free men who lived in comfort and suffering in their homes. If the Lagers had lasted longer a new, harsh language would have

been born, and only this language could express what it means to toil the whole day in the wind, with the temperature below freezing . . . . (Ibid., p. 129)

While the envisioning of a 'new, harsh language' maintains faith in the possibility of a mimetic relationship between word and world, the absence of such a language and the consequent gulf between concentrationary and non-concentrationary referential contexts strikes a dissonant note to Levi's earlier pronouncements on the possibility – and necessity – of realism in Holocaust representation. Language's mimetic capabilities – a recurrent preoccupation in more general critiques of realist claims – are thus amplified in their problematic dimension in the context of the Holocaust, a phenomenon also evident, as this chapter will explore, in relation to questions of determinism and redemptive closure.

The contradictory status of realism in Holocaust testimonies like Levi's is echoed to an extent in the approaches of trauma theory. In one sense, the trauma text maintains a mimetic posture in allowing the representation, if not of the event itself, then at least of the traumatic affect through which its unassimilable impact is registered (Caruth, 1995, pp. 154, 155). In a sense, then, trauma theory retains a form of realism among its representational possibilities, merely displacing this from a depiction of the event itself to that of its accompanying affect. Nevertheless, one might also question the extent to which this is indeed mimesis, the claim to reduplication or imitation of an original. Given readings of trauma as missed experience and of testimony as, in Shoshana Felman's words, 'a performative speech act' (1992, p. 5), it might be argued that trauma theory tends instead towards a sense that trauma narratives *present* (rather than representing) the real of trauma in its unmediated and unassimilable primacy, a reading which goes some way to explaining the privileged status of a text like Lanzmann's *Shoah* (in which participants are compelled to re/live rather than merely relate their experiences) within the canon of trauma theory. The complex and belated temporality of trauma, coupled with its alterity regarding structures of language and comprehension, thus complicate the possibility of a realism in conjunction with these events.

Nevertheless, realism remains a necessary dimension of Holocaust representation, as highlighted by Levi's insistence on the imperative nature of attempts to expand the circle of witnessing and ethical reflection through testimony's referential claims. To deny the possibility of historical reference in Holocaust discourse would effectively refuse the possibility of testimony, silencing and isolating survivors and perhaps inadvertently serving the purposes of those who seek to eclipse the presence and availability of these events in cultural memory. Lastly, in contradistinction to ethical arguments against realism (discussed further below) might be asserted its ethical value in its unflinching direction of a gaze upon historical phenomena, however horrific, and its faith in the possibility of a community within which such experience might be conveyed. From this perspective, ethical questions might be raised about poststructuralist emphasis on the unknowability, unrepresentability and incomprehensibility of traumatic historical experience, with the desire to avoid encroaching upon the unassimilable experience of the other at risk of collapsing into a posture of piety insufficiently attentive to questions of empathy and social justice. In short, accounts of realism and the Holocaust must remain conscious of and vigilant against what Rothberg terms 'the postmodern version of the bystander's lament whereby "we didn't know" is transformed into "we can't know"' (2000, p. 140).

Conflicted Realism in Holocaust Discourse

Given the moral seriousness of arguments on both sides of the debate about realism in Holocaust literature, it is perhaps unsurprising that recent critical opinion and literary practice point towards an ongoing mediation between these polarities. Rothberg's concept of traumatic realism, for example, responds to what he terms 'the contradictory nature of the demands for documentation and self-reflexivity made on the literary genre by the historical event' as follows:

> In formulating the concept of *traumatic realism* I seek to preserve these contradictions, while attempting to show that they do not simply undermine the realist project, but can also produce a rejuvenation of realism. . . . Traumatic realism . . . often entails a survival of the claims of realism into a discourse that would otherwise be identified in terms of literary history or style as modernist or even postmodernist. (2000, p. 99)

Rothberg pursues this conception through an analysis of the depiction of the relationship between the extreme and the everyday in the writings of Charlotte Delbo, Ruth Klüger and others, identifying a modification and qualification of realism in writings which nevertheless maintain the strength of their referential claims. In the field of Holocaust fiction, we might trace a number of other forms of a conflicted realism which modifies the concept in the light of Holocaust history and theory. The magic realism of writers like Jonathan Safran Foer (2002), David Grossman (1990) and Markus Zusak (2005) maintains a commitment to history while also both preserving the place of the unrepresentable and radically questioning the forms knowledge and representation may assume in the post-Holocaust era, particularly where these concern the experience of an (often postmemorial) other (Adams, 2011). Novels as diverse as Jonathan Littell's *The Kindly Ones* (2009) and W. G. Sebald's *The Rings of Saturn* (1998) exhibit what might be termed a *realism of exhaustion*, carrying the realist project (in its accumulatory and archival dimensions) to an extreme which serves to problematize precisely these aspects of its practice, as well as their place in the compromised epistemological and representational project of modernity. Such conflicted realism refuses to abandon the mimetic impulse while remaining within its domain in order to work through both its relation to reality and the aspects of the event which render representation susceptible to fetishistic projections of coherence and accessibility;[2] nevertheless, it remains as pragmatically focused on representation's object as on the negotiation and evaluation of its own representational strategies. In this chapter, I examine the possibilities of such conflicted realism in relation to a hitherto largely unrecognized strand in contemporary post-Holocaust fiction: the counterfactual historical novel or alternate history.

The Counterfactual Historical Novel

As Hilary P. Dannenburg writes, '[r]ecent research defines counterfactuals as theoretical alterations or *mutations* of a past sequence of events made in order to construct a different version of reality that counters the events of the "real" or factual world' (2008, p. 110). The counterfactual historical novel proceeds from this logic, positing an alteration at some point in the past – referred to by Karen Hellekson (2001, p. 5) as a 'nexus event' – that changes the course of subsequent events. Perhaps unsurprisingly given its crucial character in determining the direction of subsequent history, the Second World War is a recurrent focus within the genre of counterfactual historical fiction. The majority of these representations – Robert Harris's *Fatherland* (1992), C. J. Sansom's *Dominion* (2012) and Len Deighton's *SS-GB* (1978), for example – are popular rather than literary, though the counterfactual historical mode has crossed over into the terrain of literary fiction with recent works such as Philip Roth's *The Plot Against America* (2004) and Michael Chabon's *The Yiddish Policemen's Union* (2007).[3]

Roth and Chabon's novels are two of the texts discussed in this chapter. Asking the question of whether an anti-Jewish genocide was possible in the United States, *The Plot Against America* takes as its nexus event the election of the anti-Semitic (and anti-interventionist) aviator Charles A. Lindbergh as US president in 1940, the subsequent forging of friendly relations with Nazi Germany, and the escalation of discriminatory measures against Jewish citizens, culminating in riots and pogroms in which one of the neighbours of the narrating 'Philip Roth' is violently killed. *The Yiddish Policemen's Union* occupies a more oblique relationship to the Holocaust in imagining a tentative Jewish settlement in Alaska, a proposal in reality abandoned by Congress in committee stage in 1940 (Rovner, 2011, p. 144; Scanlan, 2011, p. 518), as setting for a detective narrative which examines the possibilities and uncertainties of Diasporic

Jewish identity in a post-Holocaust context. Also under discussion in this chapter are Philip K. Dick's *The Man in the High Castle*, set in an America under the rule of the Axis powers following Allied defeat in the Second World War – a world in which the 'Final Solution' has been extended to Africa with horrific consequences, and in which the Jewish character Frank Frink must disguise his identity in order to escape persecution; and Harris's *Fatherland*, a crime novel set in a victorious Germany in which the crimes uncovered are ultimately those of the nation's wartime history. While all of these novels concern themselves with the Holocaust and are, as I will argue, profoundly post-Holocaust in their negotiation of an ethics of representation, it is important to note that their counterfactual alterations do not concern the reality of the events of the genocide in Europe, instead relating to such issues as the extent to which other societies may also have been susceptible to fascist violence, the implications for Holocaust memory and for other threatened groups of a Nazi victory, and the differing impacts these events may have had on post-Holocaust Jewish culture. Anxieties around the genre of alternative history have often, as Rosenfeld notes, centred around the potential proximity of such fictions to questionable practices of revisionism, especially given the popularity of the Second World War as a locus for counterfactual imaginings (2005, p. 4). Leaving these events intact in their counterfactual interventions offers these writers a means of investigating the capacities of the counterfactual mode to address issues in post-Holocaust representation while sidestepping an uncomfortable proximity to revisionist practices.[4]

Conflicted Realism and the Counterfactual

The conflicted realism of the counterfactual historical novel lies in its combination of the attributes of the realist historical novel with a deviation from history's familiar trajectory. Auerbach lists as one of the key features of the realist novel 'the embedding of random persons and events in the general course of contemporary history' (1953, p. 491); while his approach differs in some respects, Lukács likewise views the aim of the realist novel as the concretization of social and historical forces in the individual human life, making the average individual or 'type' of key importance ([1950] 1972, p. 6). The realist novel's commitment to playing out the macrocosmic movements of history through the microcosm of individual lives is continued into its counterfactual counterpart. This is clearly evident in Roth's novel, where the larger trajectories set in motion by Charles Lindbergh's accession to the presidency are registered through the experiences and interactions of a single family. In one example, prior to the escalation of the government's anti-Jewish measures, Philip and his family visit Washington to see the nation's historical monuments. While there, however, they experience anti-Semitic discrimination, including an incident at the Lincoln Memorial when Philip's father laments the nation's current leadership in contrast to figures like Lincoln and is referred to by fellow visitors as a 'loudmouth Jew'. The subsequent exchange is interesting from the perspective of the realism of the counterfactual historical novel:

> 'To hear words like that in a place like this,' said my father, his choked voice quivering with indignation. 'In a shrine to a man like this!'
>
> Meanwhile Mr Taylor, pointing to the painting, said, 'See there? An angel of truth is freeing a slave.'
>
> But my father could see nothing. 'You think you'd hear that here if Roosevelt was president? People wouldn't dare, they wouldn't dream, in Roosevelt's day . . .,' my father said. 'But now that our great ally is Adolf Hitler, now that the best friend of the president of the United States is Adolf Hitler – why, now they think they can get away with anything. It's disgraceful. It starts with the White House . . .' (Roth, 2004, p. 65, ellipsis in original)

The concretization of the historical moment through the perspective of the family is dramatized in the mise-en-scene of their encounter with the historical monument. Herman's visceral response contrasts with both the monumentalism of Lincoln's 'shrine' and the heavy-handed, abstract religious symbolism of the painting in which 'an angel of truth is freeing a slave', illustrating by contrast the representational potency of detailed and specific depictions of ordinary lives in concretizing wider social and historical forces. Realism's dramatization of historical trajectories through their impact upon the individual is also evident in the novel through the phenomenon John Burt Foster Jr terms 'felt history', which, he states, 'refers to the eloquent gestures and images with which a character or lyric persona registers the direct pressure of events' (1995, p. 273). Roth's reliance at times upon a visceral troping of a Nazi-sympathizing America's impact upon the American Jewish psyche – as, for example, in the loss of Alvin's leg and the fierce physical clash between Alvin and Herman Roth as the program of anti-Semitic disenfranchisement progresses – might thus be read as a central mechanism in the novel's realist pursuit of the macrocosm via the microcosm, the historical via the domestic.

Together with other aspects such as the novel's pursuit of verisimilitude[5] (stated as a key aim by Roth and amplified by the novel's autobiographical positioning and numerous parallels with Roth's childhood as detailed in *The Facts* (1989)), *The Plot Against America*'s deployment of felt history and related use of ordinary individuals as a means for the exploration of more sweeping historical undercurrents partake of the representational project of realism as theorized by Lukács, Auerbach and others. This is a commitment shared by other counterfactual historical novels dealing with Nazism and the Holocaust – in Harris's *Fatherland,* for example, the realist impulse is evident not only in the attempt of the individual, Xavier March, to grapple with and ultimately expose a history of profound horror, but also in the significance of documentation (relating to the Wannsee conference, for example) in Harris's exploration of that history. In Chabon's *The Yiddish Policemen's Union,* questions of personal and cultural redemption become inextricably intertwined, whereas Dick's *The Man in the High Castle* refracts an occupied America after the loss of the Second World War through such characters as contemporary American craftsman Frank Frink and anti-Semitic shopkeeper Robert Childan. Indeed, the counterfactual historical novel, with its particular interest in the far-reaching impact of even minor changes to the historical continuum, has arguably greater reason than the average realist novel for a focus on the microcosm/macrocosm relationship.

Modifications of Realism

The realist refraction of history through the domestic in counterfactual post-Holocaust fiction enables detailed, wide-ranging investigation of fascism and its effect on individual lives. At the same time, however, the counterfactual premise permits a modification of some of realism's more problematic dimensions, dimensions which are arguably more problematic still in the context of Holocaust writing. Realist depictions of history are often rejected, for example, as totalizing and deterministic accounts. While the most extreme form of realist determinism is that espoused by Zola in his theorization of naturalism (Zola, 1963a, p. 166; 1963b), realism in general is commonly associated with a deterministic ethos, as George Becker states:

> [R]ealism insists on the existence of limitations on the efficacy of human personality and endeavor, and it places the boundaries of those limitations rather close at hand. . . . If it makes allowance for random and fortuitous elements in an otherwise causally constituted universe, it generally denies them purpose and is likely to see them as agents of destruction and misfortune rather than of well-being. (1963, p. 36)

In a post-Holocaust context, such determinism may be read as profoundly problematic, as highlighted by Michael André Bernstein, who argues powerfully against the implicit determinism of foreshadowing narrative strategies which hint at the atrocity in discussion of earlier periods. While Bernstein recognizes the temptation to regard the Holocaust as 'the simultaneously inconceivable and yet foreordained culmination of the entire brutal history of European anti-Semitism', he highlights the troubling consequence of such structures of thought and representation in suggesting an implicit blame attaching to the victim for not having recognized and evaded their 'inevitable fate' (1994, pp. 10, 13). In contrast, Bernstein advocates a 'sideshadowing' approach which, attending to 'the unfulfilled or unrealized possibilities of the past' (ibid., p. 3) – the numerous possibilities intrinsic to each historical moment – would recognize the contingency of events as they occurred and resist the temptation to position them as inevitable.

The counterfactual historical novel does partake of a degree of determinism, as Hellekson acknowledges in her linking of the mode to a genetic model of history concerned primarily with causality (2001, p. 2). Nevertheless, in its pursuit of alternative possibilities to those that occurred, counterfactual historical fiction also reinscribes into the appraisal of history a valuable attention to contingency.[6] Chabon's *The Yiddish Policemen's Union*, for example, counters notions of the State of Israel inevitably following from the Holocaust (a reading susceptible to producing problematic interpretations of the ultimate teleological purpose of the genocide) by imagining a world in which the nascent State disintegrates, leaving as the only tentative Jewish state a fragile counterfactual colony in Alaska. Chabon's novel is thus implicitly critical of the ethical consequences resulting from a sense of destiny or teleology in the existence of an individual or people.

Dick's *The Man in the High Castle* offers another key example of the sideshadowing impulse in post-Holocaust counterfactual fiction.[7] Dick's alternative America, which is occupied partly by the Nazis and partly by the Japanese, not only imagines what would have happened had the Axis powers won the war (including an extension of the Holocaust to Africa and America) but counteracts any sense of a binary bifurcation at this point in history through a proliferation of possible postwar worlds.[8] In occupied America, a novel is produced which imagines what would have happened had the Allies won the war, and is indeed produced in part by the I-Ching oracle, which claims it depicts a true reality; nevertheless, this is still not history as we know it. In *The Grasshopper Lies Heavy*, for example, Churchill after the war becomes a kind of dictator responsible for the establishment of concentration camps in South Asia for the imprisonment of Chinese citizens who would prefer US rule after the postwar division of territories. The character Joe Cinnadella summarizes:

. . .'Every eight years the U.S. boots out its leaders, no matter how qualified – but Churchill just stays on. The U.S. doesn't have any leadership like him, after Tugwell. Just nonentities. And the older he gets, the more autocratic and rigid he gets – Churchill, I mean. Until by 1960, he's like some old warlord out of central Asia; nobody can cross him. He's been in power twenty years.' (Dick, [1962] 2001, p. 157)

Dick's novel thus amplifies the sideshadowing possibilities of the counterfactual historical novel in positing a plurality of futures, even following the common outcome of an Allied victory in the Second World War. In the suggestions of a Churchillian dictatorship and the establishment of British-run concentration camps, the novel additionally not only hints towards the overlooked history of British-perpetrated colonial atrocities, but also challenges the moral complacency of Allied nations with a suggestion of their own potential for genocide, oppression and the overriding of democracy. With regard to the Holocaust, such proliferating sideshadowing underscores both the lack of inevitability surrounding these events and the ethical imperative to refuse their solidification into a monumentalized historical past, rather remaining cognizant of the potential for ongoing oppression and violence. Counterfactual post-Holocaust fictions like Dick's thus permit the verisimilitude, specificity and potency of the realist approach to fascism's impact on individual lives, while at the same time radically countering realism's problematically deterministic tendencies in a manner responsive to the crisis of realism precipitated by these events.

One key instance in *The Man in the High Castle*'s exploration of alternative historical realities occurs in the episode in which Mr Tagomi, the head of the Japanese Imperial Trade Mission, slips momentarily into real-world San Francisco. Disorientated by the unfamiliar motor vehicles and expressways of the real-world city, Tagomi stumbles into a café:

> Must obtain respite. Ahead, a dingy lunch counter. Only whites within, all supping. Mr Tagomi pushed open the wooden swinging doors. . . . All stools taken by whites. Mr Tagomi exclaimed. Several whites looked up. *But none departed their places. None yielded their stools to him. They merely resumed supping.*
>
> 'I insist!' Mr Tagomi said loudly to the first white; he shouted in the man's ear.
>
> The man put down his coffee mug and said, 'Watch it, Tojo.' (ibid., p. 223)

On one level, this passage powerfully dramatizes the potentially ethical implications of counterfactual thought in defamiliarizing conventional social hierarchies: Tagomi is brought to experience the arbitrariness of his perceived superiority (as a member of the colonizing nation) through the inverted ethnic hierarchy he encounters. On the level of the slippage, the passage also carries implications regarding the subjectivity of our relationship with reality, as Tagomi goes on to reflect that 'We really do see astigmatically, in fundamental sense: our space and our time creations of our own psyche, and when these momentarily falter – like disturbance of middle ear' (ibid., p. 225).[9] While on one level disturbingly relativistic, the premise does serve to highlight potently a sense of personal responsibility for the historical reality one experiences and either resists or acquiesces to, amplifying the impact of counterfactual historical fiction as a whole in emphasizing the significance and consequence of human agency, as Hellekson (2001, p. 111) has asserted. In a moment in which the otherwise compassionate and sensitive character of Mr Tagomi is compelled towards a recognition of his complicity with fascist oppression, the novel in a powerful statement of post-Holocaust ethics asserts our responsibility for constituting the social and political realities in which we engage.

Multivalence and Closure

Its intervention into the problematic possibilities of determinism is not the only way in which the counterfactual historical novel retains the potential to radically refigure realism in order to reshape its more problematic aspects, both in itself and in the context of Holocaust history.[10] Another aspect of realism often challenged is the mode's propensity towards closure. Catherine Belsey writes that while classic realist narrative 'turns on the creation of enigma through the precipitation of disorder', it ultimately 'moves inevitably towards *closure* which is also disclosure, the dissolution of enigma through the reestablishment of [a familiar] order' (1980, p. 70). Belsey thus views realism as an inherently conservative mode which strives towards the reassertion of the social order, the narrative's closure representing a retreat into the familiar and a refusal to challenge dominant social codes. While Belsey's critique is a broad one, these are issues which also pertain to Holocaust literature in a specific sense given the widespread perception after Adorno that Holocaust literature must find a means of registering the radically disruptive nature of these events and of responding as adequately as possible to Western culture's complicity in the atrocity. Popular representations such as *Schindler's List* have often been found wanting in this respect, offering a form of closure and redemptive resolution that obscures the non-redemptive reality of these events in a fetishistic reassurance of the viewer. Ethical concerns also surround the extent to which this is a sanctioning of complacency and ethical inertia; nothing need change in the viewer's own ethical practice because oppression has been safely overcome – and, moreover, within (in *Schindler's List*) the 'benevolent' space of capitalism, precluding a questioning of broader contexts of dehumanization and enslavement.

From this perspective, the counterfactual post-Holocaust fictions under discussion here make interesting reading, particularly given that a number of these texts – Chabon's and Harris's in particular – deploy plot structures strongly associated with closure, by partaking in the detective genre.[11] In both novels, disclosure does occur – in *Fatherland*, March discovers the truth about the Wannsee conference and the Holocaust, while in Chabon's text, the Messianic plot of the

Verbovers and the US government is unmasked, and the killing of potential Messiah Mendel Shpilman elucidated. The impulse towards disclosure in realist fiction represents, in the context of the Holocaust, a belief in the necessity and possibility of the pursuit of historical truth, yet its teleological trajectory and totalizing force remain questionable. In Chabon and Harris's texts, however, these aspects of closure and disclosure are nevertheless countered by an ultimate open-endedness. Harris's novel closes just after March's discovery of the traces of the buildings at Auschwitz, as the detective, pursued by the state, draws his weapon for the final exchange in which he will presumably die, yet the novel leaves its reader without depicting this outcome. The 'detecting of the Holocaust' in this novel is also undermined by the fact that the fate of the Jews is not hidden at all, is in fact an 'open secret' known (yet unacknowledged) by all; towards the end of the novel, March berates a fellow SS officer who claims not to have known of the genocide:

'I didn't know.' Krebs dropped the notes on the table as if they were contagious. 'I didn't know any of this.'

'Of course you knew! You knew every time someone made a joke about "going East", every time you heard a mother tell her child to behave or they'd go up the chimney. We knew when we moved into their houses, when we took their property, their jobs . . . .' (Harris, [1992] 1993, pp. 357–8)

This moment unpicks the whole logic of the plot in *Fatherland*, the movement towards disclosure becoming instead a slow and dawning recognition of the ordinary citizen's complicity in the state's crimes. While structuring the narrative, the detective plot is gradually positioned as a fetishistic construction positing criminality as deferred in its unmasking and in any case safely projectable onto the monstrous other (here Odilo Globocznik, who is responsible for the series of murders aimed at removing all of those with any knowledge of the Wannsee Conference). While this pertains most obviously to the German populace after the Holocaust, its implications extend beyond this, in terms of both the complicity of Western culture in the modes of thought which manifested themselves in Germany as Nazism and more generally applicable questions of the regard for others. In Chabon's novel, we also find a countering of the possibilities of closure, with the novel ending with Landsman and his ex-wife Bina's decision to break their promise to the US authorities (silence in return for citizenship in Alaska after the end of Jewish settlement rights) and a consequent uncertain future. As regards the detective genre, it might also be asserted that Chabon questions the association of the detective with the upholder of the social order, the conspiracy plot requiring that Landsman unpick the social order even as he seeks the coherence of knowledge.

Multiple Referential Contexts

These novels' post-Holocaust revision of some of the more problematic dimensions of realism in its trajectory towards closure is also expressly linked to their ↓ counterfactual status. The counterfactual historical projection involves a number of superimposed referential domains. As well as a reflection of historical possibility, counterfactual historical fictions are frequently read as a comment upon contemporary society, whether in the form of a displacement of current concerns onto the alternative world or via a dialogue between contemporary society and its counterfactual equivalent. Counterfactual fiction is thus multivalent in its associations, as a consideration of the novels under discussion here will demonstrate.

As Chabon acknowledges in his essay 'Imaginary Homelands', *The Yiddish Policemen's Union* was written in response to his discovery of a 'Say it in Yiddish' phrasebook and his bittersweet response – at once fascination and loss – given the absence of a Yiddish-speaking nation in relation to which it might be used. Speculating on the potential location of such a 'Yiddishland', he states:

> I dreamed of at least two possible destinations. The first one was a modern independent state very closely analogous to the State of Israel . . . – a postwar Jewish homeland created during a time of moral emergency, located presumably, but not necessarily, in Palestine; it could have been in Alaska, or in Madagascar. Here, perhaps, that minority faction of the Zionist movement who favored the establishment of Yiddish as the national language of the Jews were able to prevail over its more numerous Hebraist opponents. (Chabon, 2010, p. 166)

After dwelling at length on this possibility, which became the novel, Chabon at last returns to the second of his possible destinations:

> But there was another destination to which the Weinreichs beckoned, unwittingly but in all the detail that Dover's 'Say It' series required: home, to the 'old country'. To Europe.
>
> In this Europe the millions of Jews who were never killed would have produced grandchildren, and great-grandchildren, and great-great-grandchildren. (Ibid., p. 168)

Behind Chabon's alternative world of Jews in Alaska lies another alternative world, the lost Yiddishland of a Europe which never experienced the Holocaust. In this reckoning, *The Yiddish Policemen's Union* becomes not merely a curious exercise in speculation, but a far more wistful 'what if', an act of mourning for an irrecoverable point of origin and for the generations lost, while the tenuous province-hood of Jewish Sitka enables a displaced and muted rehearsal of these losses. As well as this direction towards the past, however, the novel has also been read as a critical reflection upon present-day US and Israeli politics, as Amelia Glaser states, suggesting that Chabon's 'invention of illegal Jewish settlers outside of Sitka who breed an extreme, latter-day Zionist project is hardly a subtle response to contemporary Israeli policy' (2008, p. 160). Historical conflict between Jewish settlers and Native Alaskans[12] also resonates with the Israeli context, while the US government's support of violent attempts to establish an Israeli state in the novel for their own Messianic reasons (see Chabon, 2007, p. 343) may be read as a critique of the impact of Christian fundamentalism upon US foreign policy in the Middle East.[13]

The Plot Against America has likewise been read as simultaneously a displaced engagement with and working through of the events of the Holocaust and a critique of the contemporary political landscape. As regards the latter, for example, Rosenfeld states:

> Most likely, Roth wanted his novel to serve as a warning about the contemporary dangers facing America in the wake of the terrorist attacks of 9/11 and the war in Iraq. In portraying the United States becoming a fascist-like state under the administration of an ill-qualified, naïve, and incompetent president, Roth offers a not-so-thinly veiled critique of the United States under the administration of President George W. Bush. (2005, pp. 154–5)

Thus the treatment of Jews in the novel echoes fears concerning the treatment of Muslims as the American government exercised heightened restriction upon and surveillance of those it deemed to be threats,[14] with ethnic and religious profiling playing a considerable role in this categorization. Rosenfeld adds in a note the further resonance with the fear that American Jews would be blamed for pro-war lobbying regarding the Iraq war (ibid., p. 440, n. 192), in a reading elicited by the emphasis placed in the novel upon Lindbergh's notorious anti-interventionist speech of 11 September 1941, in which he characterized Jews as agitators for American intervention in the war and as acting in opposition to American interests.[15] Additional readings concern the novel's dialogue with actual American history of the mid-twentieth century, not least in its depiction of anti-Semitic persecution as occupying the place of racism against African Americans during the 1940s, a form of substitution considered troubling by Walter Benn Michaels and others.[16]

These counterfactual historical fictions hence remain open to a range of interpretations, including allegorical approaches which locate their concerns very much in the real world and the present day. *The Man in the High Castle*, written in 1962 and with its world divided between two great (German and Japanese) powers, with nuclear anxieties proliferating, might be read as very much an engagement with the conditions of the Cold War. Even *Fatherland*, ostensibly the least multidirectional of the novels under discussion here, has frequently been read as a response not only to the collapse of the Soviet Union but to the resurgent power of Germany in its centrality to the European Union. Petra Rau contends, for example, that

> For Harris, fascism is quite literally undead, a revenant, the most recent manifestation of a 140-year-old unanswered question, but also somehow the essence of the German soul. In this paranoid reading, the Second World War may have been won on the battlefield but was subsequently lost in the corridors of Brussels. (2013, p. 84)

Precisely because all of these texts have been read as activating so wide a range of referential possibilities, questions might be raised concerning critical attempts to insist upon or exclude any single direction of reading. Thus while Jason Siegel's (2012) contention that Roth does not allegorize post-9/11 America (instead revising historical truth to incorporate a sense of the latent realities which different developments may have actualized more fully) presents a compelling reading, one might argue following Michael Rothberg that there is no reason to resort to an either/or logic[17] in response to a situation that seems in reality to surpass any single perspective or vision. The multiplicity of readings of these works is a firm indication of their historical multivalence, and considered in relation to their generic positioning as counterfactual histories, such multivalence appears less a problem to the interpreter than a characteristic of this narrative mode. Counterfactual histories are ultimately unresolvable in relation to the real; rather than offering *either* an alternative world *or* a reflection of contemporary history, they oscillate between the two. In so doing, such narratives encourage relational thinking and refuse the complacency of a final interpretative stance, resisting the logic of closure frequently associated with the realist novel and considered problematic both in and of itself and in the specific context of the Holocaust.

Transparency

This chapter has thus far argued that counterfactual historical post-Holocaust fictions partake of the techniques of the realist historical novel in refracting historical experience through the concrete perspective of the ordinary individual, while also departing from the more problematic aspects of realism in a post-Holocaust context in their radical rejection of determinism and resistance to closure. The final part of this chapter will consider one further way in which these counterfactual historical works productively refigure the concept of realism: in their rejection of transparency as a goal in favour of more self-conscious rumination on questions of narrative trajectory, genre and plot.

For a summary of charges regarding transparency often levelled at realist fiction, it is instructive to turn again to Belsey, who describes the term 'realism' as especially useful in 'distinguishing between those forms which tend to efface their own textuality, their existence as discourse, and those which explicitly draw attention to it. Realism offers itself as transparent' (1980, p. 51). Although this accusation has been rejected by defenders of realism, who contend that this conception 'at the same time overstates [realism's] mimetic ambitions and dramatically undervalues its ability to exhibit and examine the formal limitations that shape it' (Beaumont, 2007, p. 4),[18] the vocabulary of mimesis does arguably assume a basic faith in the capacity of language to replicate (the appearance of) reality. Like previous angles from which realism has been found wanting, in the context of Holocaust representation the possibility of transparency is especially contentious; as demonstrated in the earlier discussion of Levi, the possibility of a transparent discourse is both central to the possibility of testimony and potentially dangerous in that it might lead to the false assumption that one can grasp and/or falsely identify with another's experience via the medium of discourse. Both the nature of language (as theorized from a poststructuralist perspective) and the specific traumatic extremities of the Holocaust thus stand in opposition to the possibility of transparency.

In considering the development of counterfactual historical fiction as a practice, Rosenfeld cites as significant not only developments in science such as Heisenberg's uncertainty principle and popular awareness of quantum physics, but also developments in postmodern thought, including postmodernism's 'playfully ironic relationship to history' and its exploration of the place of the subjective and relative in historical understanding (2005, p. 7). Counterfactual historical fiction, in its manifestations that draw upon postmodern thought, at least, shares much with the project of historiographic metafiction in calling into question the neutrality and transparency of the discourses through which the past is represented.[19] *The Man in the High Castle*, for example, offers a critique of the notion of historicity which underpins both the fetishization of antiques and wider notions of history. The corporation owner Wyndam-Matson cynically expounds:

> 'Listen. One of those two Zippo lighters was in Franklin D. Roosevelt's pocket when he was assassinated. And one wasn't. One has historicity, a hell of a lot of it. As much as any object ever had. And one has nothing. Can you feel it?' He nudged her. 'You can't. . . .' (Dick, [1962] 2001, p. 66)

Wyndam-Matson's companion demands proof of the lighter's historicity, upon which he produces a document, but exclaims '"That's my point! . . . The paper proves its worth, not the object itself!"' (ibid.). The exchange highlights the inescapably textual nature of history, questioning even the immediacy and self-evidence of the artefact in its exposure of the degree to which discourse functions as the guarantor, itself questionable and tentative, of the historical narrative. The fact that the example chosen is that of the counterfactual assassination of Roosevelt further highlights the connection between the historiographically metafictive episode and the counterfactual project more widely, as an underlying generic undermining of accepted notions (and contents) of history.

The Yiddish Policemen's Union also demonstrates a profoundly self-conscious concern with questions of representation, here focusing specifically on questions of narrative and plot. One potent symbol introduced early on is that of the boundary maven, who plots out with string extensions of the domestic space into the city so observant Jews are able to extend their activities on the Sabbath without transgressing divine law: 'given enough string and enough poles, and with a little creative use of existing walls, fences, cliffs, and rivers, you could tie a circle around pretty much any place and call it an eruv' (Chabon, 2007, p. 110). Given the homonymy of 'plot' as a term for both a charted physical space and a narrative structure (Brooks, 1984, p. 12), the novel's fascination with the image of the *eruv* and the figure of the boundary maven might be read as a self-conscious engagement with the compensatory, fetishistic and/or (depending on one's reading) wholly pragmatic nature of narrative itself, particularly given the focus on the redemptive narrative structures of Messianism and Zionism in the novel. The novel's explorations of the concept of the homeland (symbolized in the *eruv*'s status as an extension of the domestic into less familiar terrain) are thus inextricably tied to its examination of the functions of narrative, with the focus on the failure of the Sitka Settlement as potential homeland carrying interesting implications in this respect. Another passage which closely links representation and spatial mapping reads:

> There was no Permanent Status, no influx of new jewflesh from the bitter corners and dark alleys of Diaspora. The planned housing developments remain lines on blue paper, encumbering some steel drawer.
>
> The Granite Creek Big Macher outlet died about two years ago. Its doors are chained and along its windowless flank where Yiddish and Roman characters once spelled out the name of the store, there is only a cryptic series of holes, domino pips, a Braille of failure. (Chabon, 2007, p. 179)

Here representation is linked to the failure of the hopes of permanent status: the lines in the drawer exist because the housing developments do not; the 'Braille of failure' marks the absence of the characters, which even the aesthetically pleasing assonance of the phrase cannot redeem. Representation is here shown to exist in a compensatory yet fetishistic role, unable to reproduce the real. Nevertheless, while the string and its related signs present an acknowledgement of the extent to which a text (historical or otherwise) is predicated upon an absence, from another perspective this symbolism also inscribes the capacity of the structure of representation to offer a projection of our relationship to a possible world, a relationship which is not necessarily a redemptive one. From this perspective, the counterfactual historical novel offers itself as an alternative homeland, a negotiation of the relationship between the domestic realm of familiar history and another domain in which – for the multiple reasons detailed in this chapter – temporary residence might prove productive. The counterfactual historical novel, where it draws upon its at least partially postmodern heritage, thus combines with its realist aspect self-conscious reflections upon the nature of history and discourse as well as reflections upon its own generic status. This phenomenon is arguably evident too in *The Man in the High Castle*, in which Western assumptions about causality, reason and action are challenged through the emphasis placed upon the I-Ching as an alternative means of negotiating one's historical position.[20] Together with the reconsideration of issues of determinism and closure within the counterfactual historical novel, such possibilities demonstrate the mode's potential value in facilitating a compromised or conflicted realism able to negotiate some of the key conflicting imperatives of Holocaust and post-Holocaust representation.

Notes

1. Robert Eaglestone sees postmodernism and the Holocaust as inextricably linked, with postmodern thought forming a response to this historical context – see Eaglestone (2004).
2. Connections might be drawn here to Gillian Rose's critique in *Mourning Becomes the Law* of the process by which 'Ethical integrity is reclaimed by each generation who must murder their intellectual fathers in order to obtain the licence to practice the profession that they learnt from them' (1996, p. 1); in a statement with interesting implications for the theorization of realism, Rose suggests that 'The unsparing revulsion against the fallen idols and the rush to espouse their formerly degraded "others" perpetuate dualisms in which all the undesirable features of the original term are reinforced and reappear in its ostensibly newly revealed and valorised "other"' (ibid., p. 3).
3. See Rosenfeld (2005, p. 152). Rosenfeld offers a valuable survey of counterfactual historical fiction dealing with Nazism and the Holocaust. For a discussion of alternative histories relating to Hitler specifically, see Butter (2009). Earlier literary counterfactual historical fictions include George Steiner's *The Portage to San Cristobal of A.H.* (1981), which imagines Hitler's escape (and subsequent pursuit) to South America, and Philip Roth's *The Ghost Writer* (1979), in which the imagined survival is that of Anne Frank.
4. It also, perhaps, leaves this chapter open to the counter-argument that none of these texts are really *about* the Holocaust; nevertheless, I hope to demonstrate otherwise in the discussion that follows, as well as foregrounding the significance of conflicted realism as a means of registering and responding to the representational anxieties caused by these events.

5. For discussion of the novel's pursuit of verisimilitude, see Graham (2007, p. 122) and Siegel (2012, pp. 133, 144).
6. See Rovner (2011, p. 142) for a discussion of the 'tension between contingency and determinism' in alternate history.
7. The connection between sideshadowing and counterfactual historical fiction is also noted by Graham (2007, p. 146, n. 4).
8. Dick's chapters towards an uncompleted sequel to the novel (1995b) offer further elaboration of its relationship to the theory of multiple worlds.
9. See Dick (1995a), for a further discussion of some of the philosophical issues around the possibility of multiple worlds and our individual relationship to these.
10. As Niall Ferguson states in relation to historians' attempts to ask similar questions of 'what if?', 'Virtual history is a necessary antidote to determinism' (1998, p. 89).
11. As Belsey states of the Sherlock Holmes stories, '[t]he project of the stories themselves, enigma followed by disclosure, echoes precisely the structure of the classic realist text' (1980, p. 112).
12. See, for example, Chabon (2007, p. 43).
13. For a reading of the novel (and Roth's *The Plot Against America*) along these lines, see Scanlan (2011, p. 506).
14. See ibid., p. 510.
15. The text of Lindbergh's speech, 'Who Are the War Agitators?', is reproduced in Roth (2004, pp. 385–90).
16. Michaels (2006) ultimately views a privileging of antiracist discourse of all kinds in American culture as a means of evading the differing mechanisms of inequality that underlie the more pressing (he suggests) issue of poverty.
17. In *Multidirectional Memory*, Rothberg (2009) contests either/or thinking, arguing instead that different, often intersecting contexts of cultural memory do not exist in an inherently competitive relationship to one another.
18. See also Kearns (1996, p. 4), for the argument that 'realism is not so complacent nor so decorous nor so ingenuous as its recent reputation would suggest'.
19. Historiographic metafiction is Linda Hutcheon's term for postmodern fictions which '[reinstall] historical contexts as significant and even determining, but in so doing, [problematize] the entire notion of historical knowledge' (1988, p. 89). The intersection of another form of conflicted realism, magic realism, with this project is noted and explored in Adams (2011, chapter 1).
20. For an explication of many of these aspects of the I-Ching, as well as a fascinating discussion of his own use of the oracle, see Jung (1968).

Works Cited

Adams, J. (2011), *Magic Realism in Holocaust Literature: Troping the Traumatic Real*. Basingstoke: Palgrave Macmillan.

Auerbach, E. (1953), *Mimesis: The Representation of Reality in Western Literature*, trans. W. R. Trask. Princeton: Princeton University Press.

Beaumont, M. (2007), 'Introduction: reclaiming realism', in M. Beaumont (ed.), *Adventures in Realism*. Oxford: Blackwell, pp. 1–12.

Becker, G. J. (1963), 'Introduction: modern realism as a literary movement', in G. J. Becker (ed.), *Documents of Modern Literary Realism*. Princeton: Princeton University Press, pp. 3–38.

Belsey, C. (1980), *Critical Practice*. London: Routledge.

Bernstein, M. A. (1994), *Foregone Conclusions: Against Apocalyptic History*. Berkeley: University of California Press.

Brooks, P. (1984), *Reading for the Plot*. Oxford: Clarendon Press.

Butter, M. (2009), *The Epitome of Evil: Hitler in American Fiction, 1939–2002*. New York: Palgrave Macmillan.

Caruth, C. (1995), 'Recapturing the past: introduction', in C. Caruth (ed.), *Trauma: Explorations in Memory*. Baltimore: Johns Hopkins University Press, pp. 151–7.

Chabon, M. (2007), *The Yiddish Policemen's Union*. London: Fourth Estate.

—. (2010), 'Imaginary homelands', in *Maps and Legends: Reading and Writing along the Borderlands*. London: Fourth Estate, pp. 157–79.

Craps, S. and Buelens, G. (2011), 'Traumatic mirrorings: Holocaust and colonial trauma in Michael Chabon's *The Final Solution*', *Criticism*, 53.4, 569–86.

Dannenberg, H. P. (2008), *Coincidence and Counterfactuality: Plotting Time and Space in Narrative Fiction*. Lincoln and London: University of Nebraska Press.

Deighton, L. (1978), *SS-GB*. London: Jonathan Cape.

Dick, P. K. (1995a), 'If you find this world bad, you should see some of the others', in L. Sutin (ed.), *The Shifting Realities of Philip K. Dick: Selected Literary and Philosophical Writings*. New York: Pantheon, pp. 233–58.

—. (1995b), 'The two completed chapters of a proposed sequel to *The Man in the High Castle*', in L. Sutin (ed.), *The Shifting Realities of Philip K. Dick: Selected Literary and Philosophical Writings*. New York: Pantheon, pp. 119–34.

—. [1962] (2001), *The Man in the High Castle*. London: Penguin.

Eaglestone, R. (2004), *The Holocaust and the Postmodern*. Oxford: Oxford University Press.

Felman, S. (1992), 'Education and crisis, or the vicissitudes of teaching', in S. Felman and D. Laub, *Testimony: Crises of Witnessing in Literature, Psychoanalysis and History*. New York: Routledge, pp. 1–56.

Ferguson, N. (1998), 'Introduction: virtual history: towards a "chaotic" theory of the past', in N. Ferguson (ed.), *Virtual History: Alternatives and Counterfactuals*. London: Papermac, pp. 1–90.

Foer, J. S. (2002), *Everything Is Illuminated*. Boston: Houghton Mifflin.

Foster, J. B. Jr (1995), 'Magical realism, compensatory vision, and felt history: classical realism transformed in *The White Hotel*', in L. P. Zamora and W. B. Faris (eds), *Magical Realism: Theory, History, Community*. Durham: Duke University Press, pp. 267–83.

Glaser, A. (2008), 'From polylingual to postvernacular: imagining Yiddish in the twenty-first century', *Jewish Social Studies*, 14.3, 150–64.

Graham, T. A. (2007), 'On the possibility of an American Holocaust: Philip Roth's *The Plot Against America*', *Arizona Quarterly*, 63.3, 119–49.

Grossman, D. (1990), *See Under: Love*, trans. B. Rosenberg. London: Jonathan Cape.

Harris, R. [1992] (1993), *Fatherland*. London: Arrow Books.

Hellekson, K. (2001), *The Alternate History: Refiguring Historical Time*. Kent, OH: Kent State University Press.

Hutcheon, L. (1988), *A Poetics of Postmodernism: History, Theory, Practice*. New York and London: Routledge.

Jung, C. G. (1968), 'Foreword' to *The I Ching, or The Book of Changes*, trans. C. F. Baynes, from a previous translation by R. Wilhelm. Princeton: Princeton University Press.

Kearns, K. (1996), *Nineteenth-Century Literary Realism: Through the Looking-Glass*. Cambridge: Cambridge University Press.

Levi, P. (1987), *If This Is a Man; The Truce*, trans. S. Woolf. London: Abacus.

Littell, J. (2009), *The Kindly Ones*, trans. C. Mandell. London: Chatto & Windus.

Lukács, G. [1950] (1972), *Studies in European Realism*. London: Merlin Press.

Michaels, W. B. (2006), 'Plots against America: neoliberalism and antiracism', *American Literary History*, 18.2, 288–302.

Rau, P. (2013), *Our Nazis: Representations of Fascism in Contemporary Literature and Film*. Edinburgh: Edinburgh University Press.

Rose, G. (1996), 'Introduction' to *Mourning Becomes the Law: Philosophy and Representation*. Cambridge: Cambridge University Press, pp. 1–14.

Rosenfeld, G. D. (2005), *The World Hitler Never Made: Alternate History and the Memory of Nazism*. Cambridge: Cambridge University Press.

Roth, P. (1979), *The Ghost Writer*. New York: Farrar, Straus and Giroux.

—. (1989), *The Facts: A Novelist's Autobiography*. London: Jonathan Cape.

—. (2004), *The Plot Against America*. London: Jonathan Cape.

Rothberg, M. (2000), *Traumatic Realism: The Demands of Holocaust Representation*. Minneapolis: University of Minnesota Press.

—. (2009), *Multidirectional Memory: Remembering the Holocaust in the Age of Decolonization*. Stanford, CA: Stanford University Press.

Rovner, A. (2011), 'Alternate history: the case of Nava Semel's *IsraIsland* and Michael Chabon's *The Yiddish Policemen's Union*', *Partial Answers*, 9.1, 131–52.

Sansom, C. J. (2012), *Dominion*. London: Mantle.

Scanlan, M. (2011), 'Strange times to be a Jew: alternative history after 9/11', *MFS: Modern Fiction Studies*, 57.3, 503–31.

Sebald, W. G. (1998), *The Rings of Saturn*, trans. M. Hulse. London: Harvill Press.

Siegel, J. (2012), '*The Plot Against America*: Philip Roth's counter-plot to American history', *MELUS: Multi-Ethnic Literature of the U.S.*, 37.1, 131–54.

Steiner, G. (1981), *The Portage to San Cristobal of A.H.* London: Faber and Faber.

Zola, E. (1963a), 'The experimental novel', in G. J. Becker (ed.), *Documents of Modern Literary Realism*. Princeton: Princeton University Press, pp. 162–96.

—. (1963b), 'Naturalism in the theatre', in G. J. Becker (ed.), *Documents of Modern Literary Realism*. Princeton: Princeton University Press, pp. 197–229.

Zusak, M. (2005), *The Book Thief*. Sydney: Picador.

5 Theory and the Ethics of Holocaust Representation

Michael Bernard-Donals

Abstract

Recently, theorists and philosophers of history have made the case that it is the *extremity* of the event that is Holocaust writing's signal characteristic. It is my contention in this chapter that this is, in fact, an argument about *ethics*. The most significant feature of Holocaust representation is that it radically affects the reading subject's understanding of human subjectivity, of how we engage with one another. It makes us aware of how the material reality of the circumstances in which we are mired – whether or not they are akin to those experienced by those who witnessed the events of the Holocaust – is as much the *result* of our engagements with others as it impinges upon those engagements. In short, representing the events of the Holocaust forces writers to consider the potentially disruptive nature of events, and how that disruption calls for a way of engaging with others – an ethics – in a way that renders us vulnerable, displaced and open to the future.

Elie Wiesel once famously declared that 'a novel about Treblinka is either not a novel or not about Treblinka' (1977, p. 7): for Wiesel, if one is to write about the events, one should leave it to witnesses, and to those forms of representation that make clear the act of witnessing, genres that are testimonial, realist and more or less historically transparent, lest those with a political agenda or an impoverished imagination deny the reality of the events depicted, and, hence, history. But Wiesel's verdict has been rendered moot to a significant degree because the commonplace on which he relied has been significantly challenged by theorists and philosophers (of history and of literature) who see the extremity of the event, its ability to press memory, writing and the subjectivity (or 'personhood') of the writer or the witness to what Jean Amery called the mind's limits, as its signal characteristic. My argument in this chapter will be that debates that have taken place under the rubric of 'Holocaust theory' in the past 30 years are ultimately arguments over *ethics*. The most significant feature of Holocaust representation is that it radically affects the reading subject's understanding of human subjectivity, of how we engage with one another, and of how the material reality of the circumstances in which we are mired – whether or not they are akin to those experienced by those who witnessed the events of the Holocaust – is as much the *result* of our engagements with others as it impinges upon those engagements. In short, representing the events of the Holocaust forces writers to consider the potentially disruptive nature of events, and how that disruption calls for a way of engaging with others – an ethics – in a way that renders us vulnerable, displaced and open to the future.

Holocaust Representation

As I suggested at the outset of this chapter, the most obvious point of contention in Holocaust representation was the appropriateness of representation at all. Theodor Adorno's infamous remark, repeated a number of times in different contexts and in slightly different iterations, that 'to write poetry after Auschwitz is barbaric' (1981, p. 34), has been understood to serve as an injunction not only against Holocaust poetry, but against Holocaust representation more generally. It is consistent with the *bilderverbot*, the biblical prohibition against idolatry found in the second commandment that has been taken in the context of the Shoah to prohibit direct representations of the event. Both of these commonplaces, which underlie Wiesel's problematic assertion about Holocaust novels, fail to capture the fuller significance of the challenges to representation provided by the event of the Shoah. Adorno went on to complicate his assertion:

> If negative dialectics calls for the self-reflection of thinking, the tangible implication is that if thinking is to be true – if it is to be true today, in any case – it must also be a thinking against itself. If thought is not measured by the extremity that eludes the concept, it is from the outset in the nature of the musical accompaniment with which the SS liked to drown out the screams of its victims. (1973, p. 365)

Far from suggesting a prohibition against representation, instead Adorno makes clear an *urgency* of representation: the extremity of the event of the Shoah seems to *demand* a representation, and a thinking, against itself, one that makes visible the extremity, and thereby avoids the 'musical accompaniment' that diverts our attention from it. The same is true of the *bilderverbot*, to which

Miriam Hansen refers in her essay about the 'iconicity' of the images found in Steven Spielberg's film, *Schindler's List*. She cites Claude Lanzmann's charge against the film that it tramples upon the uniqueness of the event, which 'erects a ring of fire around itself, a borderline that cannot be crossed because there is a certain ultimate degree of horror that cannot be transmitted' (Lanzmann, 1994, p. 14). As Hansen points out, the *bilderverbot* makes of the Holocaust an idol, concretizing it into a recognizable object and potentially overriding the event's limits, and what Adorno demands are representations that measure the concept against the extremity that eludes it, 'a type of aesthetic expression that is aware of its problematic status' (1996, p. 302). Representations like Spielberg's, she argues – though she has some significant reservations about the film, as I do – call the Holocaust's status as sacred icon into question.

This argument over the appropriateness of representation also served as the foundation of a long-running disagreement between the philosopher Berel Lang and the historian Hayden White. Lang, like Wiesel and Lanzmann, believed that there was a 'ring of fire' around the event, and that only certain forms of representation can adequately serve as vehicles of its representation. Lang's objection to figurative representations of the Holocaust rests on his understanding that the event was characterized by its dehumanization of its victims. To use a form, such as the novel, that depends so much on the individual point of view of the narrator, to represent an event that was defined by its deindividualization of the victim is 'to misrepresent the subject and thus – where the aspects misrepresented are essential – to diminish it' (Lang, 1991, p. 144). The event's uniqueness warrants only historical writing, or the use of what James Young has called the trope of the eyewitness, writing that represents events 'direct[ly] . . . immediately and unaltered' (quoted in ibid.) by figurative language, conventions of cinematography or accounts that cannot be supported by historical documentation. Interestingly, Lang points to Roland Barthes' notion of intransitive writing, a writing 'that denies the distance among the writer, text, what is written about, and, finally, the reader', writing that doesn't transmit the object or event but in which the writer 'write[s] himself', as the mode most appropriate to the Holocaust (cited in ibid., p. xii). White largely disagrees with Lang, claiming that all representations depend upon figural language, but they agree on at least this one point: he, like Lang, suggests that intransitive writing may respond to Adorno's demand because it attempts to make visible, and to register on the reader, a 'new form of historical reality, a reality that included, among its supposedly unimaginable, unthinkable, and unspeakable aspects, the phenomenon of . . . the Final Solution', realities that are visible and consequential, if not directly or easily representable (1992, p. 50).

The value of the trope of the eyewitness is its ability to make these realities visible in what we tend to think of as the transparent language of the person who was there on the spot. It is in eyewitness testimony, the argument goes, that we see the least aestheticized – and most intransitive – representation of what happened. This argument has been made most strongly, perhaps, by Lawrence Langer, the first American Holocaust theorist who brought Holocaust representation to the attention of the scholarly community in the 1970s and 1980s. In his *Holocaust Testimonies*, Langer examines video-recordings of survivor testimony in Yale University's Fortunoff Archive and builds a case that it is here, in the language of these recordings, that we see most clearly the events of the Shoah. Like Wiesel and Lang, he is suspicious of aestheticized testimonial accounts, and explains that it is only in the unrehearsed oral testimony that we see the 'vast imaginative space separating what [the victim] has endured from our capacity to absorb it' (Langer, 1991, p. 19). Written testimonies, or those that the author has time to linger over, tend to 'eas[e] us into their unfamiliar world through familiar (and hence comforting?) literary devices. The impulse [in written testimonies] is to *portray* reality' (ibid.).

And yet when Langer goes on to analyse the oral testimonies in the Fortunoff Archive, he finds that they are characterized not by transparency but by an opacity brought on by the structure of testimony and witnessing itself. By definition, to witness is to see, to register events in one's experience, if not to understand them. To testify to those events, there must be a transition between the experience of the event and an understanding, and a discursive transmission of, those circumstances. Between seeing the event and providing a testimony of the event, one shifts registers, and what was impressed upon the senses through memory must be expressed, now in memory, in the language of testimony *in such a way that others can see* what the eyewitness saw. The sensual transition is also a temporal one: the event that occurred rushes inevitably into the past, and the language used in the present must also register that movement, that loss. Rather than being the relatively transparent bearer of the events of the Holocaust, as someone like Wiesel or Berel Lang might wish, Langer identifies the structural gap in testimony which, I would argue, makes it most valuable because it indicates the excessiveness of the event, its surplus beyond representation, and the problematic nature of what we call *reality* in the case of the Shoah.

It is just this point about testimony that Jean-François Lyotard takes up in *The Differend*, a book that owes the occasion of its writing to the phenomenon of Holocaust denial in France in the 1970s and 1980s. He likens the events of the Shoah to an earthquake that devastates the instruments used to measure it, and goes on to wonder what happens when a victim of a devastating event is accused of lying about it by dint of her survival. The *differend*, the case 'where the plaintiff is divested of the means to argue and becomes for that reason a victim', is an 'unstable state and instant of language' when 'something which must be able to be put into phrases cannot yet be' (Lyotard, 1988, pp. 9, 13). It is the case when, as with an event such as the Shoah, the name of the event designates a reality that nonetheless is not represented in or by that name. As with the case of testimony, in which the witness must take account of the event's absence as well as its incommensurability with the language that is used to indicate it, Lyotard argues that any statement about the occurrence of an event is both an indication of what happened and an assertion about the impossibility of say-ing what happened: the witness recognizes 'that other aspects which he or she cannot show are possible', that the event includes that which she is incapable of telling (ibid., p. 45). Consequently, far from being the measure of what hap-pened, the eyewitness's testimony marks instead a break between the language used to describe what happened and the material reality of the event. Knowing this, the historian – the reader of testimonies – is cautioned against taking the testimony as a window on the past (what Lyotard calls 'the monopoly over his-tory granted to the cognitive regimen of phrases'), and should instead '[lend] his or her ear to what is not presentable under the rules of knowledge' (ibid., p. 57).

Lyotard's intervention into the arguments over representation and the abil-ity to describe the Shoah accurately – either through the words of the witness or the words of the historian – brings into relief two other significant matters relevant to the intersection of Holocaust representation and theory: the rela-tion of history and memory, and the trauma of the extremity. Since Maurice Halbwachs's work from the middle of the twentieth century was extended by Pierre Nora's *Lieux de Mémoire*, the relation between memory and history has been central to matters of Holocaust representation. Particularly because, as Lyotard makes clear, the Holocaust presents a case where historical documen-tation was both carefully kept and also assiduously destroyed in the closing months of the war, it is largely through memory that we understand what hap-pened, and have a benchmark with which to measure representations of the event. As Yosef Yerushalmi wrote 20 years ago, Jewish history until relatively recently has effectively *been* memory, a cyclical, repetitive, and – at least in its biblical and early modern iterations – incantative superimposition of events. It is testimony, for Yerushalmi, that conveys collective memory, and stands in for the historical past.

Given Lyotard's concerns about the power granted to history through the 'cognitive regimen of phrases' – concerns that such a regimen prevents us from 'lending an ear to what is not presentable under the rules of knowledge' – then it is particularly important to understand what memory presents *beyond* his-torical accounts (or, maybe more accurately, what it presents as a supplement to history). While there is always a distance between recorded history and col-lective memory – what happened, and what a people remembers as meaning-ful – that distance doesn't so much represent a failure of methodology as it does an instance of an event that essentially 'says' more than it indicates. A Polish farmer, interviewed by Claude Lanzmann for his film *Shoah*, remembers that some of the trains that pulled into Treblinka were not cattle-cars but 'Pullmans', passenger trains that contained relatively well-dressed urban Jews. Lanzmann is incredulous, seeing this as one more exaggeration from a bystander who, as is evident from the film, still takes some pleasure in the thought of the Jews' demise. Lanzmann later discovers, interviewing a train engineer responsible for the transports into the camp, that there were, in fact, Pullman cars in some of the trains. Here Lanzmann's memory – which is not a memory at all, but one that has been created for him through the constant repetition of images of boxcar after boxcar full of Jewish victims – stands in stark contradiction to the historical reality. It would be easy to argue that Lanzmann's memory is simply wrong – that, as a 'postmemorial' residue of stories passed down to him by those who were there, something was lost in transmission even though, to Lanzmann, it is *his* understanding of what happened – but I would argue instead that the tension between the historical and the memorial is a discursive sign of the incommensurability of the past and the present: not a sign of failure but rather an instance of the structure of memory and history made visible.

Yerushalmi, among others, makes a useful distinction between the collective and the individual memory – or, more accurately, between *mneme* and *anamnesis*, a distinction that has its foundation in Aristotle's treatise, *On Memory and Recollection*. Like the philosopher David Krell, Yerushalmi thinks of *mneme*, memory, as 'that which is essentially unbroken, continuous', while recollection, *anamnesis*, 'will serve to describe the recollection of that which has been forgotten' (1984, p. 107). The collective memory of the Holocaust, what has been passed down to us both by history and by the testimonies of those who were there, is disrupted by individual memories, *anamnesis*, instances not so much of recollection as forgetting, a flash of memory that doesn't so much fit the continuum of *mneme* but marks a point of discontinuity, an aspect of the event that is disintegrated. Like the material reality that cannot be represented by history, *anamnesis* is here understood to be something like the source of memory, a crux described by Maurice Merleau-Ponty as 'a pit or hollow that opens of itself in the otherwise too solid flesh of the world, a concavity that allows there to be visibility' (1964, p. 193). But it is also 'a certain interiority, a certain absence, a negativity that is not nothing' in a palpable embodiment of ideas. The true problem of memory is that it does 'not . . . restore under the gaze of consciousness a tableau of the self-subsistent past; it . . . ensconce[s] oneself on the horizon of the past and . . . unfold[s] little by little the perspectives contained there until the experiences bounded by that horizon are, as it were, lived anew in their temporal place' (Merleau-Ponty, 2002, p. 30). Memory involves a collapse of time, and involves a bodily 'attempt to reopen time, starting from the implication of the present, and only in the body, being our only permanent means of "adopting a stance"' (ibid., p. 211). It is a mid-point between representing fully a presence of the event in its cultural or collective sense (*mneme*) and the flashing forth in the present of what is altogether lost (*anamnesis*), which is not so much understood as it is felt, a kind of torsion or discomfort, which produces a sense of loss. Memory as crux is both a presence and an absence that limits being and is its guarantor (Krell, 1990, p. 95).

Efforts to represent the events of the Holocaust must take the structural crux of memory seriously, since it has the greatest potential to have an effect upon the viewer or reader that indicates, even if it does not transmit, the historical rupture. But Krell goes even further to suggest that memory is, itself, discursive, that it functions like language. In this Krell is joined by Hayden White, who is most clearly associated with the claim that history, like all representations, functions figurally in a way that displaces the event it is purportedly trying to describe. White took this general claim and applied it to Holocaust historiography at a conference at UCLA in 1990: we can't rule accounts of the Holocaust out of court because they don't adhere to the facts because – as Lyotard tried to make clear – we only understand the facts as facts because we have reached an agreement as to the appropriate narrative of what happened. But White understands discourse, historical discourse included, as functioning by means of figural *displacement*. Memory and history are both discursive operations that *move around* the events, but don't ever pin those events down once and for all; rather, any representation of the event, perhaps most especially an event such as the Shoah (an event that holds such a prominent place in our understanding of history and culture), should make clear just this movement, the movement that troubles the historical commonplaces and realisms that would rule competing claims about the Holocaust out of court, as breaching the 'ring of fire'.

Though all of the complaints about the trope of trauma as applied to the Holocaust are understandable – that it renders all witnesses to the Holocaust as somehow 'damaged'; that it confuses individual traumatic ruptures with broader structures of history; that it introduces notions of sublimity, as Dominick LaCapra notes in the first chapter of *History and Memory after Auschwitz* (1998), that sacralize the event – I think one of the core reasons why it cannot be easily dismissed is because of Cathy Caruth's key insight, namely that trauma indicates the memorial distance between the event as it occurred and the event as it is represented. In *Unclaimed Experience*, she writes that 'the notion of trauma' allows for a 'rethinking of reference [that] is aimed . . . at resituating it in our understanding, that is, at precisely permitting *history* to arise where *immediate understanding* is not' (Caruth, 1996, p. 11), where 'history' here refers to the material reality of events. Citing Freud, Caruth writes that 'the victim of the [terrible event] was never fully conscious during the accident itself: the person gets away, Freud says, "apparently unharmed." . . . A history can be grasped [by the witness] only in the very inaccessibility of its occurrence' (ibid., pp. 17–18). For Caruth, the eyewitness does not remember the traumatic event so much as she 'take[s] leave of it', though it leaves an indelible mark on everything she

109

says including the subject of the narrative of the event. What follows after the 'in-experience' is a profusion of language that erupts after a period of latency, during which the witness had been silent. But this writing or speaking does not disclose events as much as it discloses the *effect* of events upon witnesses. This language does not easily follow the patterns that correspond to the general rules of historical narratives and by itself does not give us a way to adjudicate the competing claims and differences in details one finds from one diary or memoir to another.

In a much-cited essay titled 'Education in Crisis; or, The Vicissitudes of Teaching', Shoshana Felman describes a class she taught at Yale University on testimony. What Felman observed in all the testimony, but particularly the Holocaust testimonies – both written and oral – was consistent with Caruth's observation. Each witness testified to an event 'whose origin cannot be precisely located but whose repercussions, in their very uncontrollable and unanticipated nature, still continue to evolve even in the very process of testimony' (Felman, 1991, pp. 29, 30). Moreover, the trauma that pursues the witness also pursues witnesses to the witnessing. In her seminar at Yale, students experienced what she calls a 'crisis' of witnessing, in which they became profoundly ill at ease with what they were seeing, and broke into an 'endless and relentless talking' about the class. The accident, the 'disaster', whose representations had been read and viewed by the class had, according to Felman, '*passed through the class*' (ibid., p. 52, emphasis in original). Felman argues that, to contend with this memorial break or crisis, her students found a need to fill the abyss of the event with language. So contrary to the assertion that understanding the traumatic nature of Holocaust representation renders those events 'unspeakable' (see, for instance, Naomi Mandel's excellent book, *Against the Unspeakable* (2006), in which she systematically notes the problems with such an assertion), Caruth's and Felman's work indicates that trauma, like the historical instance of the Holocaust, is a *catalyst* for representation, rather than an obstacle to it, though a representation that deeply troubles the subjectivity of the witness.

What I've tried to suggest is that the principal theoretical discussions surrounding the Holocaust over the past 30 years, taken together, suggest that the Shoah, as an event, is not particularly unique – the debate over the uniqueness of the historical event of the Holocaust has, I think, been settled (see Yehuda Bauer's *Rethinking the Holocaust* (2002) and through the recurrence of systematic genocides in the years since 1945) – but that it has thrown into stark relief problems of representation that retrospectively affect how we think about discourse, memory and history. My premise all along has been that the events to which we collectively refer as the Holocaust have reoriented literary critical and theoretical discussions over the past several decades, and while I will not go so far as to claim, with Robert Eaglestone, that the postmodern turn in literary theory since Heidegger is a more or less direct effect of the Holocaust (see *The Holocaust and the Postmodern* (2004), especially its introduction and the chapters on Derrida and Levinas), I would argue that the Holocaust has preoccupied theorists like Levinas, Blanchot, Lyotard, Agamben and Derrida, who take up the matter explicitly in their writing, and people like Jean-Luc Nancy and Alain Badiou, who do not, but who clearly engage with the issues that the events have elicited. Like Maurice Blanchot, in *The Writing of the Disaster*, who very rarely links what he calls 'the disaster of writing' to the Holocaust (always translated with a lower-case 'h'), these theorists see the event (and events as such) as resistant to recuperative memory, to testimony and to representation. Events such as the Holocaust are best understood as 'excessive', as forcing those who encounter them in testimonial accounts or in poems or novels, to see them as altogether other, 'that in me which does not coincide with me' (Blanchot, 1995, p. 23), and which obliges the subject to remain exposed to that otherness, and to be 'put into question' (ibid., p. 28). They do not represent a memory of the event so much as they represent the event as it disintegrates memory, and as a challenge to our inclination to monumentalize that memory – and the event itself – in favour of leaving it alone as it disturbs us and demands some other form of engagement. It is just this ethical demand that is the singular consequence of writing the Holocaust, an ethical turn to which I will devote the remainder of this chapter.

Holocaust Ethics and the Riven Subject

One can clearly see the ethical stakes made visible by the Holocaust in the work of Emmanuel Levinas. Robert Eaglestone (2004) has said that Levinas's conscious attempts to disavow Heidegger's politics without discounting the radical implications of his philosophy had a great deal to do with Levinas's need to engage with the events of the Holocaust, an event that led to the demise of much of his and his wife's family. The opening pages of Levinas's most mature philosophical work, *Otherwise than Being* – which threads together discussions of memory, forgetfulness and history, and their implications for the (witnessing) subject – contain two dedications that in palimpsest lay out his ethical argument. The first dedication is to the six million victims of the Holocaust, and the second (in Hebrew) is to the memory of his and his wife's family who perished in the events. I have made the case elsewhere that it is in these dedications that Levinas gives a palpable presence both to the names that are substituted for the events of history and the effect of the events themselves, to what has been written and what is a 'foreword preceding languages' ([1981] 1998, p. 5). The antecedent or foreword of history – as in the case of the foreword whose language precedes the text – is made present for the witness or reader, but not as knowledge. Events occur in the presence of the witness, the witness sees the

111

events, but what happens *precedes* the witness's ability to say what happened, to transform the event into experience, and to provide a means by which to make it known to others who were not there.

Between the names through which we *know* what happened – the names of the six million, the Holocaust, or even of those individuals closest to us of blessed memory – and the event itself, is the trace, what Maurice Blanchot called 'the disaster', the aporia between the event as such and the speaking of the event as a name. The moment that compels and precedes writing – the event lost to memory – is available through writing *as experience*. Memory dispatches the nuance of what happened to the margins of the narrative that we fix on to recover it, and whatever path we take to try to be mindful of the event is deflected by the name we give it. The failure of the attempt to name them in order to capture the traces of their lives disturbs the narrative and the names themselves, and the individual names force us to realize that those closest among the six million render 'the six million' impossible to recall. The trace of those closest cannot be homogenized and recuperated by (or as) history. Both history and memory refer to a universal past to which Levinas opposes an irrecuperable moment, an anachronism (time out of time) that lies at the heart of human memory and that compels human action. It troubles the speaking subject, the witness to events, and compels him to speak, though *of what* he speaks is sometimes uncertain. The immemorial, the individuals who are lost to history and memory but whose names indicate a trace of that which precedes history, indicates that absence, not as a marker of a person the knowledge of whom is recalled by the invocation of the name, but as a void that compels engagement.

For Levinas, the event, as it is indicated by the trace, is a rupture. The Holocaust serves to make visible the structure of the event *as such*, the extent to which it is impossible to capture historically, and to which it is incumbent upon those who want to engage with it, to take seriously its representations or to write (of) it, to write in a way that lays bare its disastrous nature. The event, though it defies representation, is nonetheless available through writing *as experience*. In *Otherwise than Being*, Levinas turns his attention from the idea of the trace to how the trace is made evident in language: in the saying and the said (*le dire et le dit*). While the two categories reflect different aspects of being, saying is only available by way of the said. Susan Handelman calls saying

> a 'language before language', prior to ontology, 'origin', and representation, an-archic – and so unknowable, or prior to all philosophical consciousness. But this 'saying' necessarily shows and 'betrays itself' in the 'said' – the realm of language as the set of signs which doubles being, which re-presents, synchronizes, names, designates, and which 'consciousness' grasps, manipulates, thematizes, brings to light, remembers, and in which we discuss and define this 'saying'. (1991, p. 233)

Even the simplest discursive operation, in which we liken a word to a synony-mous word – or even a word to itself (as in Levinas's description of substitution, in which 'A is A' reveals a non-identity) – brings to the surface an element of the event, of the real, that falls out of the equation and returns to haunt it (see Levinas, [1981] 1998, p. 114). The closest among the six million and those who are named in loving memory unsay one another; the (French) dedication to memory and the (Hebrew) recitation of the names of the dead can't be made equal. Their juxtaposition produces an element of memory, the 'inflexions of forgotten voices' (ibid., p. 26), that cannot be contained in either; this juxtaposi-tion is potentially horrifying.

Alain Badiou sees the event, this potentially horrifying crux, the moment in which A does not equal A, as that which 'convokes someone to the composition of a subject', a 'something extra', 'something that happens in situations as some-thing that [the subject] and the usual way of behaving in them cannot account for' (2001, p. 41). In the same way that the witness to the events of the Holocaust finds herself in the difficult position of creating a name for events that seem to confound her self-understanding and seem to stand in the way of the utterance that she nonetheless feels compelled to make, the event is not only a rupture of the 'usual way of behaving', but is a rupture of the subject herself. The sub-ject riven by the event is defined by 'a real break (both thought and practiced) in the specific order within which the event took place (be it political, loving, artistic or scientific . . .)' (ibid., p. 42, ellipsis in original). The event – 'irreduc-ible singularities, the 'beyond-the-law' of situations' (ibid., p. 44) – produces in the subject the desire, the fidelity, to hold that moment of rupture open. And rather than see what is presented by the event as producing a large-T 'Truth', or knowledge, or even a set of identities that can be held fast by the name, the sub-ject not only experiences the supplement – the impression – but is 'in excess of himself, because the uncertain course [*trace aléatoire*] of fidelity passes through him, transfixes his singular body and inscribes him, from within time, in an instant of eternity' (ibid., p. 45). The subject in fidelity – through whom, like Felman's students, the event passes – 'is internally and imperceptibly *riven*, or punctured, by this truth that "passes" through that *known* multiple that he [*sic*] is' (ibid., pp. 45–6). The subject in fidelity is a subject riven by the network of multiple possibilities, multiple pasts, the impressions and disorder of the event, and – though this seems counterintuitive – becomes *faithful* to that disorder and discontinuity, 'by linking . . . the known by the not-known'. She 'persevere[s] in the interruption' (ibid., p. 47).

One could argue that this ethical rivenness is related to (though not neces-sarily the same as) trauma, one not brought on so much by the enormity of the event, but by the difficulty inherent in giving voice to an event that is both absent and compelling. The excess that results from the non-coincidence of being – Celan's 'I am you, when I am I' (2001, p. 25, l. 10) – imprints itself on the body as an affective sense of discomfort and of vulnerability. The moment of saying, in which the subject, painfully aware that 'I am I' or 'This is what happened' are impossible equations and utterances, and that what she says can't be made coincident with what has occurred, gives way to an uncontrollable, non- (or extra-) rational speaking; it is a moment of radical exposure, in which the subject incarnates herself as a ruin, the 'ruin . . . of being and time' (Levinas, [1981] 1998, p. 9), the ruins of the essential, self-identical subject. Speaking is not only the ruin of being, but of time as well: history is no longer what happened, but the divergence of what happened from the language in which it could be made known, and it falls to ruins at the moment of saying as well.

It is worth noting here that the physical discomfort associated with saying is represented, in Levinas, as a kind of withdrawal. If 'matter is the very locus of the for-the-other', and 'the way signification shows itself before showing itself as a said in the system of synchronism' is a 'giving [of] his skin' (ibid., p. 77), then saying is a process of turning the self – and the materiality of the self and of the body – inside out. Withdrawal, non-coincidence, is traumatic: saying what one has seen is 'a tearing away of bread from the mouth that tastes it, to give it to the other. Such is the coring out [denucleation] of enjoyment, in which the nucleus of the ego is cored out' (ibid., p. 64). Such a 'trauma theory of language' and subjectivity depends upon the exposure involved in the moment of utterance – the opening of the self, and of history, to the unforeseen. There will always be the risk to the witness that the opening of the self for the other – the act of witnessing – will not be returned in kind; that it will be rebuffed, or misunderstood, or go unheard altogether. There is no redemption that comes automatically with the act of witnessing; 'my substitution for the other (in the first person as the unique, responsible "I") does not constitute in any way a reciprocal demand for the other to substitute her- or himself for me' (Handelman, 1991, p. 258). The witness runs the risk – a risk made apparent years ago by Lyotard as the 'wrong' perpetrated by the deniers in France and made all the more palpable and urgent by the likes of Ernst Zundel in Canada and the Institute for Historical Review in the United States – that either the word will be taken for the event or what she says of the event will be taken as a lie and as an opportunity for persecution (see Levinas, [1981] 1998, p. 126). This makes the act of witnessing all the more disturbing: not only has the witness seen what she has seen, and not only does she admit to a physical discomfort – an illness of ease inside her own skin – in saying what she saw knowing full well that what she says may be ignored, it is also quite possible that she will be persecuted for what she has to say, that it will be taken for a lie, or for bad faith, by people who are themselves shaken by the utterance, the act of witness, by the excessive nature of the 'inflexions and forgotten voices', their fissures and surprises.

In ethical terms, the event of the Shoah has given us a new theory of the riven witness, a vulnerable subject that is never quite at home. According to theorists like Judith Butler, vulnerability is not exceptional but is rather an unavoidable aspect of human experience since the Holocaust. Butler puts it this way, in *Giving an Account of Oneself*:

> [V]iolence is neither a just punishment we suffer nor a just revenge for what we suffer. It delineates a physical vulnerability from which we cannot slip away, which we cannot finally resolve in the name of the subject, but which can provide a way to understand that none of us is fully bounded, utterly separate, but, rather, we are in our skins, given over, in each other's hands, at each other's mercy. (2005, p. 101)

We live in a community of others, others whom we do not know but into whose presence we are plunged, and what we have in common, more than language and certainly more than a 'common humanity', is this vulnerability. The subject occupies a space in which individuals are both with one another and also strangers to one another, and in which subjects are not at home so much as they are in waiting, in expectation of what is to come, because the subject is 'put into question, obsessed (and thus besieged), persecuted, in the very place where he takes place, where, as emigrant, exile, stranger, a guest from the very beginning, he finds himself elected to or taken up by a residence before electing or taking one up' (Derrida, 1999, p. 56). Thus the subject as witness is not free; she is responsible not for 'cultivating a will, but of making use of an unwilled susceptibility as a resource for becoming responsive to the Other' (Butler, 2005, p. 91). The goal of representation should be for writers – subjects as witnesses riven by the event – to engage with the event and with others, endeavouring to maintain an openness to what is beyond understanding, recognizing language's indicative rather than merely verisimilar possibilities, and in so recognizing them understanding that whatever we think we know will inevitably plunge us into an uncertain future in the company of others who share our vulnerability.

This view of post-Holocaust representation – which recognizes the event's impingements upon subjects, the impressions that it leaves upon those subjects, the way in which it compels us to create objects and texts in response to its supplementary nature, and the asocial nature of our engagement with others in response to that supplement, that rivenness – forces subjects to recognize one of Giorgio Agamben's central insights. He writes, in *Remnants of Auschwitz*, referring to the dilemma with which Lyotard opens *The Differend*,

> [T]he paradox here is that if the only one bearing witness to the human is the one whose humanity has been totally destroyed, this means that the identity between human and inhuman is never perfect and that it is not truly possible to destroy the human, that something always *remains*. *The witness is this remnant.* (Agamben, 1999, pp. 133–4)

As susceptible and vulnerable to Others, we are both human and inhuman, vulnerable subjects that 'become human in and through the destitution of [their] humanness' (Butler, 2005, p. 106). In fact, as Adorno wrote, we are *inhuman* precisely to the degree that we refuse to recognize our rivenness, that we refuse to recognize the ways in which we are impinged upon by events. To understand oneself as a riven subject and as a witness, we must also recognize that we are both creatures of will (in which subjects tend to refuse their vulnerability in favour of the will to knowledge) and creatures altogether impinged upon by the supplement, that which is beyond us, but most certainly and unquestionably creatures, imbricated by materiality and violence, and – as Žižek would put it, 'monstrous' (2005, p. 143). To represent the event, then, is – to use Butler's terms – to 'give an account'. It is necessarily writing that recognizes both its limitations and its orientation towards the future through the proliferation of other writing. Butler writes that this kind of writing is 'a kind of showing of oneself, a showing for the purpose of testing whether the account seems right, whether it is understandable by the other, who 'receives' the account through one set of norms or another' (2005, p. 131). But writing as a riven subject is also radically conditional, because – like Derrida's subject put into question and exiled, and like Badiou's notion of exposure – it *dispossesses* the writer: 'I become dispossessed', says Butler, 'in the telling, and in that dispossession an ethical claim takes hold, since no 'I' belongs to itself' (ibid., p. 132). To write as a riven subject, a subject as witness, is to risk one's self, because it involves being haunted by what exceeds knowledge, by what is silent in history, and we are compelled by the urgency of what lies behind and beyond us to continue to write, to continue to act, not knowing just what will become of us and just how we will engage with the others in whose midst we are compelled to act.

Conclusion

What I am suggesting, finally, is that the Holocaust forces us to consider the extent to which the difficult position of the witness – the one who is compelled to give voice to absent memory, to write what seems to stand in the way of language, and what flies in the face of the reasonability of history – displaces the subject, and calls for an ethics that does not attempt to ameliorate that displacement but rather takes it as that which defines us, and which undoes the terms of identification, the 'we', that (in Primo Levi's formulation in the preface to *Survival in Auschwitz*) leads to the Lager (Levi, 1996, p. v). In ethical terms, one of the most significant consequences of this understanding of the riven subject is its asociality. As Badiou puts it, received knowledge – what he calls opinions – is 'the cement of sociality' and 'sustain[s] all human animals, without exception, and we cannot function otherwise' (2001, p. 50). But 'every truth . . .

deposes constituted knowledge, and thus opposes opinions' (ibid.), and so the engagement that is made possible through the encounter with received knowledge works precisely *against* this will to sociality. The displaced subject, then, comes into being – and functions – asocially.

Still, this asocial subject, the subject in fidelity to the event that compels writing, provides a model for the one who writes in the midst of others but who is not dependent upon others, a subject that is who she is *by dint*, rather than in spite, of her rivenness. Such a subject becomes aware of what Jean-Luc Nancy calls her *singularity*, her being-with, in the midst of others and who engages with those others without the need to forge a link of identification with them. If nothing else, the riven subject is haunted not so much by words as by what is beyond them, and this trace, the voices lost to history and memory, compels her to note the strangeness not only of others but also of herself. Recognizing these other others, and the dislocation of the self, also forces us to recognize the multiplicity of possible pasts, and of possible futures, available in writing. Fidelity to the event – the fidelity to writing – compels further writing, further engagement, a 'heterogeneous repetition' which 'opens up an irreducible strangeness of each one of these [engagements with] the other' (Nancy, 2000, p. 6). That passion, that compulsion to write, sets us apart from others, estranges us from them, though we are in the midst of others all the time.

It is this 'with-ness', the sense that we are with others and yet incommensurable with those others and, for that matter, with 'ourselves', that marks the singular dimension of the riven subject, the subject as witness. Jean-Luc Nancy writes that if the idea of 'humanity' – that there is something that we share in common, something worth endeavouring to communicate, something that resides beyond or behind the language of names – is to be valuable, 'this can only be by "being valuable" singularly' (ibid., p. 74), by making clear that the relation of one to the other, the relation of the individual subject to 'society' or to 'humanity' (or even the idea of the 'value' of persons at all) does a certain violence to the individual. We are both ourselves and not ourselves; we are both subjects that have agency and a certain freedom and subjects that are constrained by others in whose midst we reside and who name us and who are named by us. Just as the writer of history and memory understands that there has to be some point of reference for the reader in order for him to understand what happened, some coherence to the narrative, the writer simultaneously is left with the impression that beyond all of that, beyond the words, and the objects, and the writing she herself would do to make sense of it all, is a trace that disturbs the name and compels further writing, a writing *otherwise*. It is this anarchical trace – the event as it precedes and disturbs writing – to which Badiou insists we must have fidelity, and it is just this anarchical trace that Nancy insists is at the crux of history and memory.

Writing the event of the Shoah, then, cannot (only) communicate – convey knowledge – because communication forecloses the event. The disruption of the event, Blanchot's disaster, compels writing that makes visible and (in Badiou's terms) holds open just this exilic position, this out-of-placeness. This kind of writing, in other words, is a kind of *exposure* of the individual as 'an intersection of singularities, the discrete exposition of their simultaneity', and makes clear that 'there is no ultimate language, but instead languages, words, voices' among other languages, words, voices (Nancy, 2000, pp. 85–6). To write the Holocaust in this way – to write it ethically – consists in a kind of 'conversing', . . . [a] crossing through', not a stable process of naming but a 'trans-lation, in the sense of a stretching or spreading out from one origin-of-meaning to another' (ibid., p. 87). Writing of this sort is meant to continue to expose the (riven) subject, and 'to present one thing as another thing, . . . to present the exteriority of the thing, its being-before, its being-with-all-things' (ibid., p. 88). It exposes the 'between' in the phrase 'between us', which, in the end, simply means that it exposes the subject as with others but not of others, as one who has an impression of what, in language, haunts her without knowing precisely what it is. The subject of Holocaust writing, as a riven subject, is not herself but, as a result, is radically open to the anarchy (*an-arche*) of the present.

Works Cited

Adorno, T. W. (1973), *Negative Dialectics*, trans. E. B. Ashton. New York: Seabury.
—. (1981), 'Cultural criticism and society', in *Prisms*, trans. S. Weber and S. Weber Nicholsen. Cambridge: MIT Press, pp. 17–34.
Agamben, G. (1999), *Remnants of Auschwitz*, trans. D. Heller-Roazen. New York: Zone.
Badiou, A. (2001), *Ethics: An Essay on the Understanding of Evil*, trans. P. Hallward. London: Verso.
Bauer, Y. (2002), *Rethinking the Holocaust*. New Haven: Yale University Press.
Blanchot, M. (1995), *The Writing of the Disaster*, trans. A. Smock. Lincoln: University of Nebraska Press.
Butler, J. (2005), *Giving an Account of Oneself*. New York: Fordham University Press.
Caruth, C. (1996), *Unclaimed Experience: Trauma, Narrative, and History*. Baltimore: Johns Hopkins University Press.
Celan, P. (2001), 'In praise of distance' ('Lob der Ferne'), in *Selected Poems and Prose of Paul Celan*, trans. J. Felstiner. New York: W. W. Norton, pp. 24–5.
Derrida, J. (1999), *Adieu, for Emmanuel Levinas*, trans. P.-A. Brault and M. Naas. Stanford, CA: Stanford University Press.
Eaglestone, R. (2004), *The Holocaust and the Postmodern*. Oxford: Oxford University Press.
Felman, S. (1991), 'Education in Crisis; or, the Vicissitudes of Teaching', *American Imago*, 48.1, 13–73.
Handelman, S. (1991), *Fragments of Redemption*. Bloomington: Indiana University Press.
Hansen, M. (1996), '*Schindler's List* is not *Shoah*: the Second Commandment, popular modernism, and public memory', *Critical Inquiry*, 22.2, 292–312.

Krell, D. (1990), *Of Memory, Reminiscing, and Writing*. Bloomington: Indiana University Press.

LaCapra, D. (1998), *History and Memory after Auschwitz*. Ithaca: Cornell University Press.

Lang, B. (1991), *Act and Idea in the Nazi Genocide*. Chicago: University of Chicago Press.

Langer, L. (1991), *Holocaust Testimonies: The Ruins of Memory*. New Haven: Yale University Press.

Lanzmann, C. (1994), 'Why Spielberg has distorted the truth', *Guardian Weekly*, 3 April 1994, 14.

Levi, P. (1996), *Survival in Auschwitz*, trans. S. Woolf. New York: Simon and Schuster.

Levinas, E. [1981] (1998), *Otherwise than Being; or, Beyond Essence*, trans. A. Lingis. Pittsburgh: Duquesne University Press.

Lyotard, J.-F. (1988), *The Differend: Phrases in Dispute*, trans. G. van den Abbeele. Minneapolis: University of Minnesota Press.

Mandel, N. (2006), *Against the Unspeakable: Complicity, the Holocaust, and Slavery in America*. Charlottesville: University of Virginia Press.

Merleau-Ponty, M. (1964), *The Visible and the Invisible*, trans. A. Lingis. Evansville, IL: Northwestern University Press.

—. (2002), *The Phenomenology of Perception*. New York: Routledge.

Nancy, J.-L. (2000), *Being Singular Plural*, trans. A. O'Byrne. Stanford, CA: Stanford University Press.

White, H. (1992), 'Historical emplotment and the problem of truth', in S. Friedlander (ed.), *Probing the Limits of Representation: Nazism and the 'Final Solution'*. Cambridge, MA: Harvard University Press, pp. 37–53.

Wiesel, E. (1977), 'The Holocaust as literary inspiration', in *Dimensions of the Holocaust: Lectures at Northwestern University*. Evanston, IL: Northwestern University Press, pp. 5–19.

Yerushalmi, Y. (1984), *Zakhor: Jewish History and Jewish Memory*. Seattle: University of Washington Press.

Žižek, S. (2005), 'Neighbors and other monsters: a plea for ethical violence', in S. Žižek, E. Santner and K. Reinhard (eds), *The Neighbor: Three Inquiries in Political Theology*. Chicago: University of Chicago Press, pp. 134–90.

6 'Don't You Know Anything?': Childhood and the Holocaust

Adrienne Kertzer

Abstract

What child witnesses are capable of seeing and knowing is a central issue in representations of childhood in the Holocaust. Inspired by the question posed by a child protagonist in Morris Gleitzman's fiction, I contend that the answer to the child's question helps to distinguish Holocaust representations for youth and those for adult readers. Beginning by comparing how child witnesses function in youth literature and adult books, I then examine how fairy tales in writing for young people operate within a pedagogical framework that foregrounds the difference between fairy tales and history. In the third section, I consider how crossover writing challenges even as it confirms distinctions between the ways in which childhood innocence and historical knowledge function in books judged appropriate for youth and those directed towards adults. My final section looks at representative early twenty-first-century Holocaust novels for young people: Monique Polak's *What World Is Left* (2008), Morris Gleitzman's series of Holocaust novels, and John Boyne's *The Boy in the Striped Pajamas: A Fable* ([2006] 2011). By comparing these novels, particularly Gleitzman and Boyne's work, we can trace the continuing debate regarding what is appropriate Holocaust knowledge when the witness is a child.

Defining what children can and should witness is a central issue in representations of childhood in the Holocaust. Roberto Benigni's 1997 film *Life Is Beautiful* participates in this debate when Guido's son Joshua announces 'They make buttons and soap out of us. . . . They cook us in the ovens' (Benigni and

Cerami, [1998] 1999, p. 131). Alarmed by his son's assertion, Guido responds 'Joshua! You fell for it again! And here I thought you were a sharp kid!' (ibid.). What makes this exchange so compelling is that Joshua's witnessing is framed through a voiceover in which the adult Joshua introduces and concludes his father's story, describing it as 'Like a fable' (ibid., p. 1). In a film that is 'Like a fable', how do viewers assess the degree to which as a child Joshua accepted his father's perspective? The film's reliance on fable, a mode now most commonly associated with children's lessons, exemplifies the complex relationship between Holocaust representations for youth and those for adults.[1]

Most Holocaust scholarship about childhood focuses on one or the other: Sue Vice analyses the representation of children in books written 'for an adult readership' (2004, p. 1); Hamida Bosmajian (2002) and Lydia Kokkola (2003) concentrate upon texts written for youth. With a few exceptions (Adams, 2011), the scholarship rarely considers the relationship between books produced for different readers or how the possibilities of crossover literature destabilize attempts to posit secure categories of readers.[2] In contrast, in this chapter, I examine what child witnesses are capable of seeing and knowing in a variety of works directed at different age groups. Driven by the question 'Don't you know anything?', posed repeatedly by 6-year-old Zelda in Morris Gleitzman's *Once* ([2005] 2013, p. 60), I contend that the answer to her question helps define the work's intended readers. My chapter has four sections. Beginning by comparing how child witnesses function in youth literature and adult books, I then examine how fairy tales in writing for young people operate within a pedagogical framework that foregrounds the difference between fairy tales and history. In my third section, I consider how crossover writing challenges even as it confirms distinctions between the ways in which childhood innocence and historical knowledge function in books judged appropriate for youth and those directed towards adults. My final section looks at representative early twenty-first-century Holocaust novels for young people: Monique Polak's *What World Is Left* (2008), Morris Gleitzman's series of Holocaust novels and John Boyne's *The Boy in the Striped Pajamas: A Fable* ([2006] 2011). By comparing these novels, particularly Gleitzman and Boyne's work, we can trace the continuing debate regarding what is appropriate Holocaust knowledge when the witness (a term that I apply to both character and reader) is a child.

Child Witnesses

Although the protagonist in youth literature may begin in a situation of naiveté or ignorance, the framework, often reinforced by the work's paratext, guarantees that the protagonist and implicitly the reader do not remain ignorant. Adult texts also value knowledge, but the kind of knowledge – insight into the failure of representation, the nature of trauma, the impossibility of knowing the past – differs. The treatment of Holocaust knowledge in works of fiction about the *Kindertransport* (the rescue mission that between December 1938 and the beginning of the war in September 1939 brought close to 10,000 children from Germany and German-annexed territories to Great Britain) exemplifies this difference, as I will discuss, but the pattern it reveals is evident in other Holocaust literature as well.

The different value placed on knowledge in child- and adult-aimed Holocaust representations is evident if we look at the narrative function of child witnesses. Adult books increasingly rely upon a very young child as part of an oblique approach to the Holocaust that is quite different from what occurs, for example, in Roberto Innocenti and Christophe Gallaz's picture book *Rose Blanche* ([1985] 1996). The picture-book format implies a text appropriate for children. Such appropriateness requires that the child narrator serve as a witness to Holocaust history, a function reinforced when Innocenti adapts a well-known photograph of a little boy with his hands up during the liquidation of the Warsaw Ghetto.[3] What the child witnesses initiates her journey outside the town, where she discovers a concentration camp. Shocked by the discovery – a shock conveyed by the way the narrative switches at this point from first to third person – Rose Blanche determines to feed the inmates, until they disappear and she is shot. Although her name likely alludes to the young people in the White Rose resistance movement, readers are never informed about the national identity of the soldier who kills her.[4] Resistant to the Nazis like the White Rose students who were executed in 1943, Rose Blanche is more readily emblematic of all child victims of war precisely because readers do not know who killed her.

In contrast, recent adult fiction that examines the traumatic afterlife of the *Kindertransport* problematizes the child's role as witness. In these novels, if there are scenes set in the death and concentration camps, they are deferred, frequently taking place decades later. Thus in W. G. Sebald's *Austerlitz* (2001), the protagonist Jacques Austerlitz only visits Terezin as an adult as part of his quest to understand more about a past that haunts him even as it remains obscured. Four years old when he was placed on a train, Austerlitz has traumatic memories that are clearly connected to his age when he left Prague. An older child might remember more but would not then serve Sebald's interest in exploring the consequences of Austerlitz's trauma.

In a Canadian adult novel, Alison Pick's *Far to Go* (2010), which also uses the *Kindertransport* to explore traumatic memory, Pepik is only 6 years old when he is placed on a train to England. Confused by his feverish state during the journey and his subsequent treatment by his foster-parents, the adult Pepik has next to no memories of the journey or his pre-war childhood (a point Pick reinforces through a narrative structure that devotes only 23 pages to Pepik's experience of the journey and his subsequent life in England). As in much Holocaust fiction, there are lessons, but they differ from the kind found in young people's literature. Adult fiction on the aftermath of the *Kindertransport* often explores the conflict between narrative expectations and Holocaust history. Such lessons are ironized when the narrator, having begun the novel with a warning to readers that the story will not end happily, mocks their disappointment: 'What did you expect? A happy ending?' (Pick, 2010, p. 286).

Since most preadolescent youth who could not escape either through the *Kindertransport* or other means did not survive, *Kindertransport* fiction appeals to adult writers who are interested in exploring the trauma of lost childhood memories. In comparison, the limited ability of *Kindertransport* children to serve as post-1939 witnesses to the Holocaust has made this fiction quite marginal to Holocaust fiction for youth. Adult *Kindertransport* fiction routinely wins literary awards; *Kindertransport* fiction for youth rarely does. One exception to this is Canadian Irene N. Watts's trilogy – *Good-bye Marianne* (1998), *Remember Me* (2000) and *Finding Sophie* (2002). Her work offers a strikingly different approach to the treatment of child witnesses found in either Sebald or Pick. The afterword to *Good-bye Marianne* states that the novel is 'based on factual events' (Watts, 1998, p. 105), that Watts lived at the same address as her fictional protagonist Marianne, and like her, left Berlin on a *Kindertransport*. However, the afterword also reveals an important distinction between Watts and her protagonist: Watts was 7 when she arrived in England, but Marianne is nearly 12. Marianne's age makes her, according to her father, 'old enough to understand what's happening in Germany' (ibid., p. 64). In *Remember Me*, Marianne protects her mother by not writing about what she is really feeling and witnessing. Although she protests at the demands made upon her – 'Why must I be the one to understand?' (Watts, 2000, p. 77) – it is characteristic of Holocaust fiction for young people that Marianne is a child witness who does understand.

During her journey to England, Marianne meets and looks after 7-year-old Sophie. Briefly introduced in the conclusion of *Good-bye Marianne*, Sophie does not reappear until the final novel in the trilogy, when she is nearly 14. In her author's note to *Finding Sophie*, Watts acknowledges that she 'was the same age as Sophie when [she] left Germany' (2002, p. 136). Sophie admits that she remembers little of the train journey; although fragments of memory emerge in the course of the novel, it is evident that Watts uses older children so that they can serve as witnesses, even if their location in Great Britain limits the extent of their witnessing. Younger protagonists would be unable to serve as insightful observers and could not thereby fulfil the educational purpose of Holocaust fiction for the young.

One adult novel that complicates this pattern of child witnessing is Nobel Prize winner Imre Kertész's *Fatelessness* ([1975] 2004). Fourteen years old when he is deported in the summer of 1944, first to Auschwitz and then to Buchenwald and its satellite camp Zeitz, György begins the novel with a sentence that could easily belong to a conventional adolescent story: 'I didn't go to school today' (Kertész, [1975] 2004, p. 3). But the story he tells hardly fits the pattern of youth literature, primarily because György refuses to generalize about the lessons of his experience. Insisting on reporting only what he saw and came to understand, scathing about the metaphorical language that is used by those who did not experience the camps, and focusing on the process whereby the abnormal becomes normal – 'there is a crematorium, naturally' (ibid., p. 126) – he is puzzled when a fellow prisoner jokes that the U on his uniform must stand for '*Unschuldig*', meaning 'innocent' (ibid., p. 142). He cannot comprehend what gratification the inmates derive from calling themselves innocent. In this way, *Fatelessness* resists the usual expectation that the child witness simultaneously loses his innocence and conveys a lesson related to that loss.

Repeatedly György emphasizes that what he learns during his time in the camps is that anything is possible. One aspect of his anger upon his postwar return to Budapest is his inability to convey the truth of his experience to those who were never in the camps, people who are 'in a certain sense . . . mere children' (ibid., p. 248). He is further enraged when others emphasize their and his innocence. Determined to hold on to some sense of freedom, he cannot accept that he was 'neither the cause nor the effect of anything' (ibid., p. 260). Although the novel's irony highlights György's lack of choice, his inability of 'finding any known and . . . rationally acceptable cause for why . . . I happened to be here instead of somewhere else' (ibid., p. 207), he refuses to regard himself as 'merely . . . innocent' (ibid., p. 261). Why should being told that he is innocent make anyone feel better?[5]

Fairy Tales and Holocaust Representation

Another way in which György separates himself from conventional associations between childhood and innocence is through his dismissal of the 'dumb storybooks of [his] childhood' (Kertész, [1975] 2004, p. 164), a dismissal that he immediately troubles when he admits that the rapid deterioration of his body in Buchenwald and Zeitz resembles the accelerated time of a fairy tale. As is evident in Benigni's *Life Is Beautiful* and Pick's *Far to Go*, where the novel's conclusion reveals that the narrator has essentially written a fairy tale for the dying Pepik, fairy tales do not appear only in works for youth. What differs in children's fiction, however, is that part of the knowledge young people learn is the difference between fairy tales and history.

Like Kertész's novel, Nechama Tec's memoir *Dry Tears: The Story of a Lost Childhood* similarly poses questions about the relationship between fairy-tale discourse and Tec's experiences during the war. Eight years old in 1939, not even 14 at the war's end, Tec provides numerous examples of how her guarded optimism kept her going. In one instance, however, she describes her incredulity after being told of the food her father will buy her after the war: 'I listened in amazement and disbelief, as if he were telling me a fairy tale too beautiful to come true' (Tec, [1982] 1984, p. 204). The child is aware that the world she is in has nothing to do with fairy tales.

Andrea Reiter proposes that a primary distinction between children's and adult diaries is that 'The child's interpretation of its perceptions is less guided by logic than by the magical world of the fairy tale' (2006, p. 3). In contrast, Tec's incredulity about fairy tales may well contribute to Edward T. Sullivan's decision to include *Dry Tears* in his Holocaust bibliography *The Holocaust in Literature for Youth: A Guide and Resource Book*. Believing that 'there are plenty of books for all ages that are too didactic, too sensational, that try to evade the horrible truths' (Sullivan, 1999, p. 7), Sullivan may have included *Dry Tears* because Tec's incredulity towards fairy tales fits his requirement for an informative but non-sensational account. And it may be that because memoirs such as Tec's are written in adulthood, they differ from what Reiter finds in children's diaries. Certainly, children's Holocaust fiction that incorporates fairy tales shows little interest in regarding such tales as characteristic of a child's thinking. The young protagonists in Holocaust children's fiction are highly aware of the limitations of fairy-tale analogies.

In numerous North American children's novels, the pedagogical framework extends to paratextual material that reinforces the difference between fairy tale and history. In many of these novels, a young child asks an older person to tell her a fairy tale. In Jane Yolen's *Briar Rose*, the heroine as a child listens to her survivor grandmother tell a version of Sleeping Beauty inflected by her Holocaust experience, but in the author's note Yolen is careful to insist on the distance between fairy tales and Holocaust history: 'Happy-ever-after is a fairy tale notion, not history' (1992, p. 202). In Yolen's *The Devil's Arithmetic*, time travel transports the 13-year-old protagonist Hannah to a Polish shtetl where her warnings about the gas ovens are dismissed as a fairy tale. Although Hannah, like other child protagonists, is a skilled storyteller, Yolen not only foregrounds the difference between children's stories and what Hannah witnesses, but also reinforces this difference through an author's note, 'What Is True about This Book' (Yolen, 1988, p. 167), to ensure that readers recognize the difference.

Lois Lowry's *Number the Stars* similarly includes an afterword that begins, 'How much of Annemarie's story is true? . . . Let me try to tell you' (1989, p. 133). Like many children's novels, *Number the Stars* is highly self-conscious in its use of fairy tales. Annemarie, the 10-year-old Danish Christian protagonist, relies upon fairy tales to control her terror of the Nazi soldiers. When, like the Grimms' Red Riding Hood, she walks through the woods carrying a basket, the basket has material that will help the Resistance escape detection by the guard dogs. Annemarie is fully aware that the woods are 'not like the woods in the story' (ibid., p. 108). But the fairy tale gives her a model of bravery, and in this version, she is lucky enough not to be eaten by wolves. The novel also contrasts with the fairy tale in that Annemarie succeeds precisely because she follows the instructions of her mother, whereas in the Grimm Brothers' version, the wolf defeats the child because she disobeys her mother's orders. Annemarie's mother tells her, 'If the soldiers see you, if they stop you, you must pretend to be nothing more than a little girl' (ibid., p. 105). Her performance of childhood – convincing the Nazi soldiers that she is no more than a silly little girl – ensures her survival, even as her ignorance of the contents of the basket protects her. As Annemarie's uncle tells her, 'it is much easier to be brave if you do not know everything' (ibid., p. 76). Here too, Lowry's plot contrasts with how the heroine's naiveté functions in the Grimms' fairy tale. Knowledge in Holocaust youth literature is paradoxical, simultaneously of great value but also dangerous. Just as Annemarie's survival depends on her not knowing too much, many adults (teachers, parents, writers) conceptualize Holocaust knowledge for the young as an adaptation of the uncle's advice: 'it is much easier to [grow up/become resilient] if you do not know everything'.

Childhood Innocence, Historical Knowledge and Crossover Texts

In contrast to its purpose in Annemarie's story, the innocence of child characters in adult texts often protects readers by limiting their exposure to the genocidal machinery of the Nazis. The innocent child thus functions in contradictory ways: often a symbol of adult incomprehension in books for adults, such incomprehension is of limited utility in young people's reading where the pedagogical framework governing Holocaust literature demands some degree of knowledge. For example, in Aharon Appelfeld's adult novel *Tzili: The Story of a Life*, the adolescent protagonist Tzili is mocked pre-war by the gentile children as 'A Jewish girl without any brains!' ([1983] 1996, p. 2). Early in the novel, the narrator describes Tzili as capable of taking in a conversation about the murder of Jewish residents, 'but not its terrible meaning' (ibid., p. 24). Fifteen at the end of the war, but different from the other survivors not just in the circumstances of her survival but also in that she does not know 'what everyone else already knew' (ibid., p. 130), Tzili can only appreciate the extent of her personal loss: 'everything was gone, gone forever. She would remain alone, alone forever' (ibid., p. 140). This focalization through Tzili's limited comprehension offers readers two options. Either Tzili's simultaneous terror and inability to take it in parallel adults struggling to comprehend the magnitude of the millions murdered, or they provide a way to distance readers who, from their postwar perspective, know what happened, but through the characterization of Tzili can shield themselves from fuller knowledge: 'She guessed that something bad was going to happen, but she didn't know what' (ibid., pp. 40–1). Adult readers presumably know, but the child character's limited perception helps to mute that knowledge.

The fact that Sullivan includes *Tzili* in his Holocaust bibliography may seem surprising until we notice that he glosses *Tzili* as a hopeful story: 'An often anguished story, but not totally bleak' (1999, p. 46). In contrast, Sullivan does not include Louis Begley's *Wartime Lies* (1991), which not only resists the teaching of hopeful lessons, but also is totally indifferent to the premise that reading fiction gives readers insight into Holocaust history. In the novel's opening, the framing narrator foregrounds the invented name of the child protagonist: 'For the sake of an old song, he calls the child Maciek' (Begley, 1991, p. 5). In the conclusion, he reasserts the novel's fictional status: 'Maciek was a child, and our man has no childhood that he can bear to remember; he has had to invent one' (ibid., p. 198). The ending of *Wartime Lies* resembles the conclusion of Pick's *Far to Go*, where the narrator observes that the story she has told 'is just one way it might have happened' (Pick, 2010, p. 308). Such ambiguous admissions do not fit the demands of children's Holocaust fiction. Like Sullivan, who believes that young readers are particularly susceptible to Holocaust revisionists (1999, p. 3), writers of Holocaust fiction for youth rarely regard fiction as merely a way of imagining what 'might have happened'. They prefer to tell readers what did happen. Even John Boyne's *The Boy in the Striped Pajamas* which, as I discuss later, is quite indifferent to what did happen, concludes 'all this happened', albeit 'a long time ago' ([2006] 2011, p. 216).

The premise that children read Holocaust fiction to help them understand what did happen also helps to predict which adult texts will cross over and be marketed for young readers. This is evident in works as different as Anne Frank's *The Diary of a Young Girl: The Definitive Edition* ([1995] 1997), Markus Zusak's *The Book Thief* ([2005] 2006) and Tec's *Dry Tears. The Diary of a Young Girl* has dominated Holocaust literature for children to the extent that we might regard the time-travel novels (Bennett and Gottesfeld, 2001) and picture books (Adler, 1993) produced in response to the *Diary* as a separate subcategory of this literature. Yet when Meyer Levin (1952) initiated the North American acclaim for Frank through his enthusiastic review of her *Diary* in the *New York Times*, he regarded the *Diary* as a work that adults would benefit from reading repeatedly. Although the subsequent play and film contributed to the circulation of the *Diary* as a text that spoke to both young people and adults, the pedagogical apparatus (teachers' guides, lesson plans) that is now available leaves little doubt that it has become a children's text.[6]

The uplifting lesson often ascribed to the *Diary* – 'I still believe in spite of everything that people are truly good at heart' (Frank, [1995] 1997, p. 327) – has been characterized as symptomatic of the Americanization of the Holocaust. Kenneth B. Kidd links the *Diary's* Americanization to its 'juvenilization' (2011,

p. 190); Eric B. Tribunella similarly reads its status among American readers as demonstrating that the 'Americanization of the Holocaust is first and foremost an American *childization* of the Holocaust' (2010, p. 105).[7] Yet adult American fiction often interrogates this version of Frank and critiques the Holocaust knowledge that circulates under her name: for example, Philip Roth's *The Ghost Writer* ([1979] 1980), Shalom Auslander's *Hope: A Tragedy* (2012) and Nathan Englander's 'What We Talk about When We Talk about Anne Frank' (2012). Roth fantasizes the consequences of Frank's survival; Auslander extends this fantasy by imagining the grotesque comic consequences when an elderly Frank hides in an attic; and Englander raises questions about the nature of Holocaust postmemory by imagining contemporary North American Jews wondering who will hide them should the need arise. In contrast to the hopeful lesson children are offered when they are taught Frank's *Diary*, Englander's adult readers find no assurance.

Like Frank's *Diary*, Markus Zusak's *The Book Thief* was not initially categorized as young adult reading. In contrast to how the teaching apparatus for Frank's *Diary* now includes supplementary historical information, in *The Book Thief*, Death claims that the outcome of the Holocaust is so well known that he can ignore readers' expectations regarding suspense: 'I know what happens and so do you' (Zusak, [2005] 2006, p. 243). That Death can assume prior knowledge may well reflect the terms of the novel's original publication for adult readers. However, *The Book Thief* may also be successful as crossover fiction because it fulfils the pedagogical demand of young adult fiction by ensuring that the reader, like the novel's child protagonist, moves from innocence/ignorance to knowledge.

In keeping with the abovementioned demand for historical knowledge, and the practice of carefully delimiting what kind of knowledge is viewed as pedagogically useful, crossover texts marketed for young people tend to limit their depiction of characters' traumas. In *The Book Thief*, Death predicts that Liesel will not recover from the loss of her family and friends: 'That would take decades; it would take a long life' (ibid., p. 546). Given that Liesel does live a long life, and readers do not see the process by which she comes to terms with her traumatic losses, Zusak is as controlled in his attention to trauma as is Nechama Tec. In addition to its treatment of fairy tales, what enables *Dry Tears* to cross over is the restraint with which Tec describes what she observed. While she reports the shock of events such as seeing babies slaughtered in baby carriages, being haunted by the image of her tutor's murdered body whose eyes are missing because the birds have pecked them out, and being unable to tell anyone – 'The scars were too deep' – about the trauma of being left alone in one town when her parents and sister are hiding elsewhere, she never sensationalizes (Tec, [1982] 1984, pp. 29, 39, 116). Her memoir includes details such as an attempted rape and brutal murders, but while Tec acknowledges that such events shocked her into muteness, she chooses not to dwell upon them. Traumatized after she witnesses dead and dying bodies, Tec recalls 'I could not afford to brood over what had happened' (ibid., p. 198) and characterizes her response as one common among adults. There are occasional glimpses of the risks produced by her naiveté, but as Tec observes, 'childhood [was] a luxury Jewish children could no longer afford' (ibid., p. 159), and she gives plentiful examples of the naiveté of adults.

Innocence and Holocaust Knowledge in the Twenty-First Century

Death's claim that readers 'know what happens' (Zusak, [2005] 2006, p. 243) implies that as the Holocaust recedes in time, we can take for granted a familiarity with its history. That this assumption is false can easily be proved. There is plentiful evidence that adults continue to long for amazing stories about young children who were hardly likely to survive, let alone recall what they experienced. Complicating the premise that only child readers need Holocaust knowledge, and in defiance of the reality 'that a mere 11 percent of European Jewish children alive in 1939 survived the war' (Dwork, 1991, p. xi), every few years, bestseller lists are dominated by remarkable child survival stories. The reality that few preadolescent children survived selection in the camps appears to prompt a longing to read about the few who did. Adults may well sense that their stories are 'unbelievable', but then so much about the Holocaust is unbelievable that readers rationalize their incredulity. Their readiness to accept as truthful accounts that subsequently prove to be fictional hints that their knowledge is not as thorough as Zusak's Death assumes. Such readers may scoff at the naive lessons of Holocaust literature for youth, yet in their willingness to celebrate memoirs about survival that prove fraudulent, they demonstrate a reluctance to accept a central component of Holocaust history: the Nazi determination and effectiveness in killing children.[8]

In the case of twenty-first-century Holocaust fiction for youth, the evidence is equally mixed. On the one hand, there are signs of a greater willingness to examine contentious topics such as collaboration. Previously, collaboration might be addressed in an adult memoir subsequently marketed for young adults, as in Tec's *Dry Tears*, but when Canadian Carol Matas published *Daniel's Story* (1993) in conjunction with the children's exhibition of that name at the United States Holocaust Memorial Museum, the museum insisted that she delete reference to the 'Jewish Police' in the Lodz Ghetto. The museum argued that 'the complex moral issues posed by the behavior of Jews forced by the Nazis to administer the ghettos' (Kertzer, 2002, p. 174) exceeded the parameters of children's fiction.[9] In making this case, the museum sided with Primo Levi: 'The young above all demand clarity, a sharp cut . . . they do not like ambiguity' ([1988] 1989, p. 37).

Levi's premise is challenged by the Canadian author Monique Polak in *What World Is Left* (2008). Inspired by her mother's experiences in Terezin, Polak creates Anneke, an adolescent narrator who struggles with her realization that her father creates art enabling the Nazis to fool the Allies that Terezin is a model camp. After the war, Anneke testifies in defence of her father's 'collaboration' in language reminiscent of what Levi ([1988] 1989, pp. 36–69) calls the 'gray zone'. Instructing the Dutch military that they cannot possibly understand what people will do in order to survive, Anneke never resolves her own questions about the ethics of her father's behaviour. Polak's willingness to explore this topic may be grounded in the authority she claims as the daughter of a survivor; such writers often create young protagonists who see and understand much more than their parents assume.[10]

In contrast to the willingness of second-generation authors to depict children who observe and think about what they witness, twenty-first-century authors who have no direct family relationship to Holocaust history are more likely to insist upon the naiveté of their child characters. However, while Morris Gleitzman's four novels – *Once* ([2005] 2013), *Then* ([2008] 2010), *Now* ([2010] 2012a) and *After* (2012b) – and John Boyne's *The Boy in the Striped Pajamas: A Fable* ([2006] 2011) share a dependence on children's adventure intertexts, protagonists of similar age, and a plot that highlights the accidental death of a child whose parents are Nazis, they provide radically different perspectives on innocence and Holocaust knowledge. Gleitzman's child protagonist Felix quickly loses his naiveté, but Boyne's Bruno remains naive to the end. Gleitzman's books work within the comic conventions of young people's writing; in contrast, Boyne's novel follows the parameters of ironic tragedy, and in so doing, contests my chapter's thesis about the treatment of knowledge in young people's writing. While Rachel Falconer refers to *The Boy* as a crossover young adult text (Falconer, 2010b, p.89), thereby signalling that its treatment of innocence and knowledge serves adult readers' needs, *The Boy*'s bestseller success is staunchly grounded in its marketing as appropriate reading for youth.[11] Boyne's sharp deviation from the established pattern of innocence moving to knowledge demands attention.

Both Gleitzman and Boyne are highly self-conscious about writing children's fiction on the Holocaust, and provide notes in which they justify the legitimacy of their work since they are neither survivors nor immediate descendants of survivors. Gleitzman dedicates *Once* to 'all the children whose stories have never been told' ([2005] 2013, n.p.). After briefly identifying himself as the grandson of 'a Jew from Krakow in Poland', he attributes *Once* to his reading of a book about Janusz Korczak, the Polish Jewish doctor who ran an orphanage for Jewish children (ibid., n.p.). His author's notes for both *Once* and its sequel *Then* ([2008] 2010) end by contrasting what he has written with 'the real stories' of the child victims and survivors. What he has written, he implies, can never be as authentic as 'the real stories'.

Boyne similarly believes that 'only the victims and survivors can truly comprehend the awfulness of that time' ([2006] 2011, n.p.). But Boyne goes further by positioning *The Boy* in relation to stories that could not be told because the victims died. Accepting that 'it's presumptuous to assume that from today's perspective one can truly understand the horrors of the concentration camps' (ibid., n.p.), he produces a novel whose very success may well rest on its indifference to key historical facts. Although the novel's subtitle 'A Fable' may justify this indifference, Boyne also grounds his 'fable' in details that leave no doubt about the history that informs his novel. Bruno may not understand what '*Heil Hitler*' means, but he says it (ibid., p. 54). As a result, despite its subtitle, the novel is listed in numerous bibliographical locations as historical fiction.[12]

According to Boyne, the origin of his novel is an image of 'two boys sitting on either side of a fence' (ibid., n.p.). Neither child understands why he is there. Claiming that 'the only respectful way . . . to deal with this subject was through the eyes of a . . . rather naïve child who couldn't possibly understand the terrible things' (ibid., n.p.), he unintentionally evokes the title of an earlier, much more effective Holocaust allegory – Eve Bunting's *Terrible Things: An Allegory of the Holocaust* ([1980] 1993) – that did not require the naive child of a Nazi commandant to make its point. Insisting that his responsibility as a writer is 'to uncover as much emotional truth . . . as he possibly can' (Boyne, [2006] 2011, n.p.), Boyne is less responsible regarding historical probability, such as the premise that the child of a Nazi commandant might spend months chatting with Shmuel, a Jewish boy imprisoned in a death camp. His understandable reluctance to focalize the novel through the experience of a camp inmate results in Shmuel being so dependent upon Bruno that he greets the news of Bruno's departure with sadness that he 'won't have anyone to talk to any more' (ibid., p. 196), which makes one wonder what has happened to the other children Bruno claims to see in the camp. The novel's attention to Bruno's story culminates with Bruno's Nazi commandant father being so traumatized by his realization that his son accidentally died in the death camp he supervises that at the end of the war he doesn't care what the victors do to him. In comparison to these fantastic premises, the plot of *Rose Blanche* resembles stark realism.

Boyne positions himself and his readers as living 'on the other side of the fence' (ibid., n.p.), unable to reach the true comprehension that only the victims and survivors can have. In the final paragraph of his author's note, however, he sets aside the fable premise; Bruno merges with Shmuel as part of the group of child victims who 'didn't live to tell their stories themselves' (ibid., n.p.). Would such victims have remained as innocent as Bruno, whose epiphany in the novel's conclusion that Shmuel is his best friend does not diminish his continuing naive faith in his father's wisdom? Bruno never understands why he and the camp inmates are locked in a room: 'he assumed that it had something to do with keeping the rain out and stopping people from catching colds' (ibid., p. 213). While I cannot claim to know whether children locked in comparable rooms in the death camps remained convinced of adults' good intentions, and I recognize that the novel in keeping with its allegorical coyness does not identify the room as a gas chamber, Boyne's heavy-handed irony unintentionally protects readers from imagining how children crammed into a gas chamber might behave. In the film (Herman, 2009), whose title does not include the subtitle 'A Fable', Bruno and Shmuel are clearly locked in a gas chamber. Although the film's realistic style encourages viewers to share in the family's grief when they realize Bruno's fate, the style further diminishes Boyne's declaration that the story is intended to be a satire of German complacency. Bruno is so obtuse that the novel could as easily be read as a justification of that complacency.

Although the camp setting is undoubtedly Auschwitz, Bruno is incapable of pronouncing either the name of the camp or the words '*Der Fuhrer*'. In an interview with David Fickling (2006) included in the Ember paperback edition, Boyne justifies the omission of the word Auschwitz as a narrative strategy that allows the setting to represent not just 'other camps of the time [but also] other camps after that' (Fickling, [2006] 2011, p. 9). Despite this attempt to universalize the novel's lesson, Boyne defends Bruno's innocence by generalizing how 'people' were shocked postwar to learn of the gas chambers. This is undoubtedly true of some people, but does not justify Boyne's making his central character the son of a Nazi commandant. While Boyne regards Bruno as an example of the 'complacency of people during the late '30s and the 1940s' (ibid., p. 7), he also frames this complacency through reference to 'Hitler's willing executioners' (ibid., p. 8), a phrase from Daniel Jonah Goldhagen's 1996 study *Hitler's Willing Executioners: Ordinary Germans and the Holocaust*. Given that Goldhagen's thesis was that 'ordinary Germans' did know what was going on, the analogy is totally inappropriate. Bruno is not one of Hitler's willing executioners; he is the ultimate innocent child protagonist. The argument for reading the novel as a satire of Germans who claimed postwar that they knew nothing is unpersuasive, as Boyne likely senses since he also justifies Bruno's naiveté by telling Fickling, 'Plus he's a nine-year-old' (ibid., p. 8). The assumption that we agree that 9-year-olds know nothing trumps all.

Morris Gleitzman is much more conventional in moving his child protagonist from naiveté to knowledge. Felix begins *Once* ([2005] 2013) as a child who has lived in an orphanage for over three years. He may be as exceptional as Boyne's Bruno in that he survives while most Jewish children did not, whereas Bruno dies in a death camp and children of Nazi commandants did not. However, in sharp contrast to Boyne's protagonist, Felix begins as a modern Candide, but quickly proceeds to lose his naiveté. He learns that his parents are not coming for him and that the many ways he rationalizes his misfortunes are false, an early example being his realization that the book burning at the convent where he has been hiding was not organized by 'professional librarians [wearing] professional librarian armbands' (ibid., p. 19). I grant that child readers may not question Felix's initially naive conclusions; informed by the nun who is hiding him that the book burners are Nazis, they may share his belief that the threat these 'thugs' pose is only to Jewish books (ibid., p. 23). However, although Felix initially views Nazi behaviour naively – for example, concluding that the half-naked people packed into a truck 'must be farmworkers going on holiday' (ibid., p. 37), and imagining that a soldier will feel horrified when he realizes 'he's shot an innocent kid' (ibid., p. 38) – he gradually realizes that every fanciful story he invents is false.

Gleitzman does not just use Felix's initially naive point of view to ask important questions about bystander and perpetrator behaviour. He also uses the intertext of Richmal Crompton's children's stories to interrogate the power of literature. In order to distract 6-year-old Zelda, who is traumatized by the murder of her parents, Felix begins telling her a story that alludes to the Crompton stories he adores, but she corrects him, informing him that she is not Crompton's William: 'Don't you know anything?' (ibid., p. 61). As his stories increasingly merge Crompton's adventures with genocidal practices – 'Violet Elizabeth and William dig a big hole, like those people over there' (ibid., p. 75) – the children temporarily lose their ability to believe the stories. When they arrive at a ghetto, Felix is no longer able to distract himself with the stories he once took such pleasure in.

Barney, the dentist who is a Korczak-like figure, partly restores Felix's faith in storytelling. He teaches him that stories are beneficial in that they distract people from suffering, but also dangerous in that they are used by the Nazis, who inform Jews that they are going to the countryside to work. At first Felix refuses to believe him: 'That's the stupidest story I've ever heard' (ibid., p. 129). When he realizes the implications of what Barney has told him – his parents are dead; the Jews are being murdered – he longs for his own death, announces that he hates stories, and admits that what he loved about the William stories was their hopefulness.

In a series that gets progressively darker but never quite loses its optimism, Gleitzman repeatedly returns to the necessity and deceitfulness of storytelling. Zelda's question 'Don't you know anything?' resonates in complicated ways, not just leading Felix to think that he doesn't know anything anymore (ibid., p. 70), but also functioning as a challenge to readers who, like him, learn very late in *Once* that Zelda is not Jewish: her father was a Nazi, and her parents have been killed by Polish partisans. Felix struggles with what his responsibilities are to the child of a Nazi, but concludes that Zelda is not responsible for what her father did. In the novel's conclusion, Zelda and a much less naive Felix survive a leap from a death train. However, Zelda dies in the sequel *Then* ([2008] 2010), and in *Now* ([2010] 2012b), Felix's granddaughter (named Zelda after his dead friend) comes to realize that her grandfather is still tormented by Zelda's death.

Enraged by language that ignorantly mirrors Nazi discourse, the elderly Felix lashes out at a child who is bullying his Australian granddaughter: 'Innocent children . . . . Don't you know anything?' (Gleitzman, [2010] 2012b, p. 75). His question suggests that effective Holocaust pedagogy cannot assume readers already know what happened, and that writers still struggle with the tension between the purpose of telling stories – 'To help us know things and feel better about them' (Gleitzman 2012a, p. 198) – and the facts of Holocaust history. Although Boyne's interest in juxtaposing 'an extreme of evil . . . [with] an extreme of innocence' (Fickling, [2006] 2011, p. 6) likely contributes to the novel's bestseller status, his novel does not quite fit Primo Levi's perception that 'we . . . tend to simplify history' (Levi, [1988] 1989, p. 36). Instead *The Boy in the Striped Pajamas: A Fable* shifts attention away from the historical identity of the victims who 'didn't live to tell their stories themselves' (Boyne [2006] 2011, n.p.).

In contrast, Morris Gleitzman, effectively negotiating the tension between the conventions of children's literature and a history that did not end with 'Richmal Crompton's army defeat[ing] the Nazis' ([2008] 2010, p. 196), tells the story of Zelda, a much more plausible victim who didn't live to tell her story herself. Yet despite its occasional comedy, Zelda's story proves difficult to tell. At the end of *Then*, hiding in a hole after Zelda is murdered, Felix vows to serve as her 'evidence' (ibid., p. 196), but it takes nearly 70 years for him to fulfil his promise. In the contemporary setting of *Now*, Felix is once again hiding in a hole in order to survive – this time from the Australian bushfires that destroy his collection of Richmal Crompton. It is in this setting that Felix tells his granddaughter the truth about Zelda. Making her a witness, Gleitzman ensures that she and the young readers who engage with his fiction know something about the Holocaust. Given the continuing debate regarding what is appropriate Holocaust knowledge when the witnesses are children, it is not surprising that Felix takes so long to tell Zelda's story to another child.

Notes

1. For further analysis of *Life Is Beautiful*, see Kertzer (2002, pp. 197–229).
2. Rachel Falconer regards crossover texts as a late twentieth-century phenomenon, particularly characteristic of young adult fiction published between 1997 and 2007 (2010b, p. 87). She provides two definitions: 'children's novels that have crossed over to adult readers rather than the other way round' and works that are published simultaneously 'in dual editions for child and adult markets' (Falconer, 2010a, p. 158). In contrast, Sandra L. Beckett regards crossover as an older practice that 'refers to literature that crosses from child to adult or adult to child' (2011, p. 58). Most Holocaust crossover literature adheres to the latter part of Beckett's definition; it is literature that crosses from adult to child.

3. For further discussion of the photograph in *Rose Blanche*, see Kertzer (2002, pp. 59–61).
4. I do not assume that only adults will recognize the White Rose intertext; as I argue throughout, adult readers are not necessarily better informed about details of Holocaust history.
5. The question *Fatelessness* asks about innocence is rarely to be found in the Holocaust literature marketed in North America.
6. A Google search for 'Anne Frank Lesson Plans' provides 255,000 hits (11 February 2013).
7. Tribunella reads the American interest in mandating education about the Holocaust as part of a concept of maturity that necessitates the 'contrived traumatization of children' (2010, p. xi). His focus on what is American does not sufficiently consider how interest in Holocaust childhood is also apparent elsewhere, as is evident in the international appeal of Anne Frank, Zusak's *The Book Thief*, and John Boyne's *The Boy in the Striped Pajamas: A Fable*.
8. See, for example, Binjamin Wilkomirski's *Fragments: Memories of a Wartime Childhood* ([1995] 1996), published to great acclaim only to have its authenticity subsequently challenged.
9. The Museum clearly regarded *Daniel's Story* as a children's novel although Matas repeatedly pointed out that Daniel, born in 1927, was an adolescent for much of the novel. For a more detailed account of *Daniel's Story*, see Kertzer (2002, pp. 143–93).
10. The child protagonist in Susan Lynn Meyer's *Black Radishes* (2010), a novel based on her father's experiences, is another example of this pattern.
11. A Google search for 'The Boy in the Striped Pajamas Lesson Plans' reveals 94,500 hits (17 June 2013). However, the Ember paperback cover of *The Boy* contests the novel's categorization as children's fiction by announcing 'this isn't a book for nine-year-olds'.
12. For example, the online bookstore of the United States Holocaust Memorial Museum lists the novel as a young adult historical novel.

Works Cited

Adams, J. (2011), *Magic Realism in Holocaust Literature: Troping the Traumatic Real*. New York: Palgrave Macmillan.

Adler, D. A. (1993), *A Picture Book of Anne Frank*, illus. by K. Ritz. New York: Holiday House.

Appelfeld, A. [1983] (1996), *Tzili: The Story of a Life*, trans. D. Bilu. New York: Grove Press.

Auslander, S. (2012), *Hope: A Tragedy*. New York: Riverhead Books-Penguin.

Beckett, S. L. (2011), 'Crossover literature', in P. Nel and L. Paul (eds), *Keywords for Children's Literature*. New York: New York University Press, pp. 58–61.

Begley, L. (1991), *Wartime Lies*. New York. Alfred A. Knopf.

Benigni, R. (dir) (1998), *Life Is Beautiful*. DVD. Montreal: Alliance / Miramax.

Benigni, R. and Cerami, V. [1998] (1999), *Life Is Beautiful*, trans. L. Taruschio. London: Faber and Faber.

Bennett, C. and Gottesfeld, J. (2001), *Anne Frank and Me*. New York: Puffin-Penguin.

Bosmajian, H. (2002), *Sparing the Child: Grief and the Unspeakable in Youth Literature about Nazism and the Holocaust*. New York: Routledge.

Boyne, J. [2006] (2011), *The Boy in the Striped Pajamas: A Fable*. New York: Ember.

Bunting, E. [1980] (1993), *Terrible Things: An Allegory of the Holocaust*, illus. S. Gammell. Philadelphia: Jewish Publication Society.

Dwork, D. (1991), *Children with a Star: Jewish Youth in Nazi Europe*. New Haven: Yale University Press.

Englander, N. (2012), 'What we talk about when we talk about Anne Frank', in *What We Talk about When We Talk about Anne Frank*. New York: Alfred A. Knopf, pp. 1–32.

Falconer, R. (2010a), 'Crossover literature', in D. Rudd (ed.), *The Routledge Companion to Children's Literature*. London: Routledge, pp. 158–60.

—. (2010b), 'Young adult fiction and the crossover phenomenon', in D. Rudd (ed.), *The Routledge Companion to Children's Literature*. London: Routledge, pp. 87–99.

Fickling, D. [2006] (2011), 'An interview with John Boyne', in 'Reader's Guide' section of J. Boyne, *The Boy in the Striped Pajamas: A Fable*. New York: Ember, pp. 4–10.

Frank, A. [1995] (1997), *The Diary of a Young Girl: The Definitive Edition*, ed. O. H. Frank and M. Pressler, trans. S. Massotty. New York: Bantam.

Gleitzman, M. [2008] (2010), *Then*. New York: Henry Holt.

—. (2012a), *After*. London: Puffin-Penguin.

—. [2010] (2012b), *Now*. New York: Henry Holt.

—. [2005] (2013), *Once*. New York: Square Fish-Henry Holt.

Goldhagen, D. J. (1996), *Hitler's Willing Executioners: Ordinary Germans and the Holocaust*. New York: Knopf.

Herman, M. (dir) (2009), *The Boy in the Striped Pajamas*. DVD. Toronto: Maple Pictures.

Innocenti, R. and Gallaz, C. [1985] (1996), *Rose Blanche*. Mankato, MN: Creative Editions-Harcourt, Brace.

Kertész, I. [1975] (2004), *Fatelessness*, trans. T. Wilkinson. New York: Vintage.

Kertzer, A. (2002), *My Mother's Voice: Children, Literature, and the Holocaust*. Peterborough: Broadview Press.

Kidd, K. B. (2011), *Freud in Oz: At the Intersections of Psychoanalysis and Children's Literature*. Minneapolis: University of Minnesota Press.

Kokkola, L. (2003), *Representing the Holocaust in Youth Literature*. New York: Routledge.

Levi, P. [1988] (1989), *The Drowned and the Saved*, trans. R. Rosenthal. New York: Vintage-Random House.

Levin, M. (15 June 1952), 'Life in the secret annex.' *New York Times*, www.nytimes.com/books/97/10/26/reviews/frank-levin.html. Accessed 28 December 2012.

Lowry, L. (1989), *Number the Stars*. New York: Dell.

Matas, C. (1993), *Daniel's Story*. New York: Scholastic.

Meyer, S. L. (2010), *Black Radishes*. New York: Delacorte Press-Random House.

Pick, A. (2010), *Far to Go*. Toronto: House of Anansi Press.

Polak, M. (2008), *What World Is Left*. Victoria, BC: Orca.

Reiter, A. (2006), 'Kinds of testimony: children of the Holocaust', in A. Reiter (ed.), *Children of the Holocaust*. London: Vallentine Mitchell, pp. 1–10.

Roth, P. [1979] (1980), *The Ghost Writer*. New York: Fawcett Crest.

Sebald, W. G. (2001), *Austerlitz*, trans. A. Bell. Toronto: Knopf-Random House.

Sullivan, E. T. (1999), *The Holocaust in Literature for Youth: A Guide and Resource Book*. Lanham, MD: Scarecrow Press.

Tec, N. [1982] (1984), *Dry Tears: The Story of a Lost Childhood*. New York: Oxford University Press.

Tribunella, E. L. (2010), *Melancholia and Maturation: The Use of Trauma in American Children's Literature*. Knoxville: University of Tennessee Press.

Vice, S. (2004), *Children Writing the Holocaust*. New York. Palgrave Macmillan.

Watts, I. N. (1998), *Good-bye Marianne*. Toronto: Tundra.

—. (2000), *Remember Me*. Toronto: Tundra.

—. (2002), *Finding Sophie*. Toronto: Tundra.
Wilkomirski, B. [1995] (1996), *Fragments: Memories of a Wartime Childhood*, trans. C. Brown Janeway. New York: Schocken.
Yolen, J. (1988), *The Devil's Arithmetic*. New York: Viking.
—. (1992), *Briar Rose*. New York: Tor-Tom Doherty.
Zusak, M. [2005] (2006), *The Book Thief*. New York. Alfred A. Knopf.

7 Holocaust Postmemory: W. G. Sebald and Gerhard Richter

Brett Ashley Kaplan and
Fernando Herrero-Matoses

Abstract

This chapter examines several images of Nazis in the work of W. G. Sebald and Gerhard Richter in order to explore what these arresting texts perform. We situate these images within the rubric of postmemory in order to explore how memories of perpetration might work in light of legacies of victimization. While Sebald and Richter are each embedded in diverse literary and painterly contexts, both artists inventively confuse genres to ask ripe and pertinent questions regarding postwar German accumulation of guilt but also of mourning and loss experienced by the generations after those who perpetrated the Nazi genocide. By exploring their work through the lens of postmemory, we wish to retain the ethical difference between victim and perpetrator while examining how residues accrue on both sides. Both Richter and Sebald work in layers. The painter continually overpaints his earlier efforts, leaving a slightly visible trace of the past and working it over and over again; the writer invites us to see the layers of imperial history as distinct yet interconnected moments of traumatization.

In this chapter we explore what some Nazi images perform and how they navigate the troubled terrain of postwar Germany's treatment of the often too familial Nazi past. The German writer W. G. Sebald's novel *Vertigo* (1990) contains a photograph of a young man in Nazi uniform;[1] and several canvasses by the German painter Gerhard Richter including *Uncle Rudi, Aunt Marianne* and *Mr. Heyde* (all painted in 1965) reference the Nazi genocide. When Sebald and Richter pictorially represent and remember their Nazi relatives they open up space for understanding the enduring question of how 'ordinary Germans' could have perpetrated genocide – in all forms of perpetration, from tacit acceptance of an anti-Semitic regime, to refusing to see, to actively murdering civilians, Jewish, queer, Gypsy, communist, resistance fighters and others.

We want to be clear that these images of Sebald and Richter's are not exactly examples of 'Holocaust postmemory' because they principally engage with post-memorial guilt rather than victimization; but it is important to place Holocaust postmemory in conversation with the 'other side', as it were, the subsequent generations of Germans who have these almost literal skeletons in the closet in the form of family connections with Nazis and the shame that that entails. Both Sebald and Richter are obviously anti-Nazi, so for each to choose to represent such striking images begs comparison with how victims' children treat their parents' experiences during the war. In other words, by incorporating these Nazi images into their work, Sebald and Richter explore postmemory using visual imagery in an inverted, through-the-looking-glass sense. The concept of postmemory was developed by Marianne Hirsch, who has defined and redefined the idea of subsequent generations who delve into the past that they themselves did not experience first-hand. Hirsch launched this concept of postmemory especially thinking of the children of Holocaust survivors, but the term has been used variously to describe anyone who struggles to come to terms with the past through intergenerational mediations of this sort. The 'post' refers to the passage of time and the mediation between those who remember the traumatic events of the war and those who engage with the past but who did not necessarily experience it. In *The Generation of Postmemory: Writing and Visual Culture after the Holocaust*, Hirsch (re)defines 'postmemory' by noting that the 'post' 'signals more than a temporal delay and more than a location in an aftermath ... [It] shares the layering and belatedness of ... other "posts", aligning itself with the practices of citation and supplementarity that characterize them' (2012, p. 5). In using the structures of Hirsch's resonant and important concept of postmemory to explore what might be more aptly termed postguilt, we hope to examine what the figure of the familial Nazi performs for subsequent generations whose politics and ethics are so diametrically opposed to those very figures who only occasionally haunt their texts, spectres of the temporal distance between now and then.[2]

Many scholars have narrated the transformations in dealing with the Nazi past in postwar Germany, but to offer a brief summary, and one that leaves much of the complexity and disagreement to the side, the overarching narrative stresses that a shock of silence prevailed in the immediate postwar period about the genocide perpetrated in the name of the supposed glory of the Third Reich. That silence was violently pierced when the generation that includes Sebald came into political consciousness and began agitating for recognition that the so-called denazification process had in fact left many former Nazis in positions of power and that there had never been a reckoning of the moral detritus of genocide. Richter lived through and remembers the war but expressed most visibly this piercing of the silence in the form of paintings of the Baader Meinhof group. Part of the Baader Meinhof cohort's complicated complaint against the powers that reigned in 1970s Germany was precisely that there had been too seamless a transition between fascism and democracy and that this (failed) transition had effectively left Nazis where they had been during Hitler's dictatorship. Richter attempted to recast the debate by repainting photographs of the dead bodies of the Baader Meinhof group. As Kaja Silverman argues, Richter's photo pictures are 'invitations to see double' (2009, p. 169), and Julia Hell and Johannes von Moltke find that 'Richter's paintings evoke more than mnemonic images relating to the RAF. *October 18, 1977* also mobilizes visual memories of the Nazi past' (2005, p. 77). When applied to the Nazi imagery that Fernando Herrero-Matoses discusses in the Richter section of this chapter, this doubling, this double mobilization, is also the doubling of national and familial postmemory. *Uncle Rudi* and the other paintings that address the National Socialist past have generally been read as anomalies, but in *The Nazi Perpetrator*, Paul Jaskot argues that we should refocus attention on how Richter and other contemporary German painters were in fact more consistent in their treatment of Nazism than has previously been underscored. Jaskot finds that 'Richter highlighted how the trace of the past figured in the painted reproduction of the family photo. He conjured up the banal presence of his uncle as a Nazi military officer . . . . For him, the limits of representation marked by the smudged stroke and the ostensibly found subject matter belied issues of remembrance and personal responsibility in the face of atrocities' (Jaskot, 2012, p. 57). Similarly, Sebald has been more concerned with issues of postmemory than many readings would imply. By juxtaposing literature and painting, both thickly embedded in historical consciousness of the after-effects in Germany of the inheritance of genocide, we unspool some of the threads of confrontational representations and what they perform.[3]

Sebald (1944–2001)

W. G. Sebald was born in the small Bavarian town of Wertach im Allgäu in 1944, lived in Sonthofen (also in Bavaria) from 1948 until 1963 and then emigrated to England, where he became a professor in 1970 at the University of East Anglia until his untimely death in a car crash near Norwich in 2001. His novels, *Vertigo* (1990), *The Emigrants* (1992), *The Rings of Saturn* (1995) and *Austerlitz* (2001) have all been translated into multiple languages and reviewed to international acclaim. As many scholars of his rich texts have pointed out, Sebald's works are about the Holocaust but also and equally importantly about a host of other historical traumas.[4] Sebald resides in an awkward place vis-à-vis the history of postwar German silence about the Holocaust and the unravelling of this repression because his novels have consistently engaged with the Nazi past and the history of the genocide of European Jewry, yet when he published a collection of essays, *The Air War and Literature*, in 1999, he argued forcefully for the recognition of German victimization during the Allied air war in 1945.[5] Andreas Huyssen reads this text as 'Sebald's blind spot' and finds that he rewrites earlier memoirs penned by others including descriptions of German victimization during the air war as a 'version of transgenerational traumatization' (2003, p. 150).

Sebald identified in the silence about German victimization during the air war a 'stream of psychic energy that has not dried up to this day, and which has its source in the well-kept secret of the corpses built into the foundations of our state, a secret that bound all Germans together in the postwar years' (2003, p. 13). This striking image of hidden corpses recalls a powerful passage from his novel *The Rings of Saturn* (1995) in which Sebald, while both critiquing Belgian colonial violence in the Congo and reporting on the Polish writer-in-exile Joseph Conrad's critique, finds that Conrad 'now saw the capital of the Kingdom of Belgium, with its ever more bombastic buildings, as a sepulchral monument erected over a hecatomb of black bodies, and all the passers-by in the streets seemed to him to bear that dark Congolese secret within them' (p. 122). In the context of German victimhood, Sebald finds that not only are the bodies of the victims part and parcel with the structures of state power, but they are also a binding force; in the context of his critique of imperialism, Sebald finds the very spectacle of the spoils of Congolese exploitation to cover the bodies of its victims and to call out to flâneurs the secret of these ghosts. The resonance between these crucial moments in *Air War* and *Rings* would seem to align the German victims of the air war with the Congolese murdered, exploited by the likes of Kurtz with his shrunken heads and tortured souls. With the distribution of *Air War*, then, Sebald thus somewhat troubled the impressions scholars and readers might have previously held of him as an author who demonstrated a deep (if sometimes oblique) commitment to grappling with the Holocaust because, as the resonance between Sebald's descriptions of the bodies of the German victims and the bodies of the Congolese underscores, he also aligns German victims of Allied bombing with African victims of colonial violence. Whereas many scholars strive to see the vast melancholia of Sebald's oeuvre as registering principally sadness over the loss of European Jewry,[6] it is also the case that this melancholia can be traced to an understanding of German victimization that troubles this usual reading. Reading Sebald through the lens of postmemory helps to unstick some of these questions because it assumes that he is historically emplotted, first, as anchored in the guilt he will have inherited, but that his novels then work through both this guilt and a resistance to his historical alignment with perpetration.

Through visual imagery, through a photographic record embedded in someone's memorial archive, Sebald explores the postmemory of German families struggling with the Nazis in their past. While Sebald's entire corpus is concerned with postmemories of Nazism and the Holocaust, with the interlocking legacies of colonialism, racism, fascism and totalitarianism, the photograph in *Vertigo* of the young man in uniform is the only Nazi image in all of his novels.[7] This image functions to open up the personal memory of the characters to larger questions of cultural postmemories of perpetration. As with many of the photographs in his novels, the line between the indexical and the metaphorical remains resolutely uncertain. The young Nazi whose shoulders stretch back as his tense gaze looks off to the side, could be the character Seelos Benedikt who is described in the text as a 'non-commissioned officer' (Sebald, 1990, p. 203). While on the one hand, outside of Sebald's novels, Nazi imagery remains ubiquitous (e.g. there are new films featuring fictionalized Nazis every year), on the other hand, finding this young Nazi in this novel, gazing off to the side, shocks, especially following as it does the revelation in *Vertigo* that Sebald's father had 'enlisted in the so-called army of the One Hundred Thousand and was now about to be promoted to quartermaster, [and] could not only look forward to a secure future in the new Reich but could even be said to have attained a certain social position' (ibid., p. 193). Sebald offers his father's involvement in the *Wehrmacht* calmly and without commentary, without handwringing or guilt, and with only a factual notice of the security his father could expect from joining ranks. This security, coupled with the rise in social position that his father's involvement afforded, highlights the pragmatic history of Nazism and downplays the demonic history that is often the most salient attribute of contemporary portrayals of Nazism. In tension with Arendt's argument about the banality of evil (see *Eichmann in Jerusalem*, [1963] 1992), one can speculate that casual inclusions of Nazis in the family, such as Sebald's image in *Vertigo* and Richter's painting *Uncle Rudi*, are actually forceful arguments for reconciling the Nazi with the family tree, for cracking open the often wilful blindness and silence of many German families about the Nazis in their past, for seeing rather than denying the postwar generations' connections to that Nazi past without demonization and its attendant blockage of comprehension. For the families of Holocaust survivors, postmemories often come to subsequent generations as found objects, sometimes as visual archives, sometimes as explicit stories, sometimes in the form of an overwhelming experience of secondary traumatization; for postwar Germans, especially those explicitly opposed to Fascism, negotiating postmemories circulating in various, complex and contradictory ways within their mileux or families can have a similar sense of repression and denial and will likely be inflected not with survivor guilt but with perpetrator guilt, a perhaps much more straightforward ethical position and one which Sebald's focus on German victimization during the Allied air war muddies.

Figure 7.1 Image from W. G. Sebald, *Vertigo* (1990, p. 203),
reproduced by permission of the estate of W. G. Sebald.

In the English edition of *Vertigo*, immediately above the image of the Nazi child, one finds: 'Towards the end of the war, when Seelos Benedikt, who had always been a timorous child, was sent to a school for non-commissioned officers at Rastatt, [his Uncle] Peter's condition deteriorated noticeably' (Sebald, 1990, p. 203). So the boy in the image, tense, anxious, unable or unwilling to look at the camera, could well be Seelos and if so, then the implication is that this engagement with Nazism creates in the already nervous Uncle Peter a worsening condition, a darkening. Sebald continues:

At times he [i.e. Peter] would wander about the village in a cape cut from his charts of the night sky, talking of how one could see the stars by day both from the bottom of a well and from the peaks of the highest mountains, which was probably the consolation he offered himself for the circumstance that now, every evening at the onset of darkness which formerly he had always welcomed, he was beset with so great a fear that he had to cover his ears with his hands or flail about wildly. (Ibid., p. 203)

We are given to understand, then, that Seelos's uncomfortable involvement with Nazism causes Uncle Peter paroxysms of fear. Indeed, Sebald goes on to explain that Peter, after being sent to a hospital in the wake of his refusal to eat, leaves the first night and has 'not been heard of again' (ibid., p. 204). Already unstable and filled with unrealizable architectural dreams (ibid., p. 201), Peter's nephew's turn to Nazism in effect pushes him over the edge. The 'cape cut from his charts of the night sky' that Uncle Peter wears reminds us of Rabbi Loew, regarding the stars and determining that, because disaster is imminent, he must construct a Golem to protect the Jews of Prague.[8] 'The peaks of the highest mountains' resonate with the Alpine landscape of *Vertigo* but also with the Nazi obsession with mountains as they project the supposed glory of the Third Reich.[9] But these mountains also recall Sebald's obsession with snow and its metaphorical vicissitudes.

The final lines of James Joyce's short story, 'The Dead' – 'His soul swooned slowly as he heard the snow falling faintly through the universe and faintly falling, like the descent of their last end, upon all the living and the dead' ([1907] 2001, p. 1685) – echo throughout Sebald's entire oeuvre as he returns repeatedly to snow as a metaphor for both interconnectedness and death. At the beginning of *Rings of Saturn*, Sebald's narrator describes the life of Janine Dakyns, a Flaubert scholar who seems to live in a universe constructed entirely of paper: 'It once occurred to me that at dusk, when all of this paper seemed to gather into itself the pallor of the fading light, it was like snow in the fields, long ago, beneath the ink-black sky' (Sebald, 1995, p. 9). The possible doubling of the night sky recalls this moment in *Vertigo* and had already been introduced at the opening of *Rings* through the narrator's mention of the 'Dog Star', Sirius, which appears single to the eye but is in fact a binary star system. Just as the snow in Joyce's conclusion covers at once the living and the dead and thus brings them closer together than we might have imagined them to be, and just as all the fragments of notes on Flaubert accrete into snow beneath the dark sky, the Dog Star situated there shields its doubled nature. Sebald again links the Dog Star with snow when, a few lines after mentioning it, he adds: 'The iniquity of oblivion blindly scatters her poppyseed and when wretchedness falls upon us one summer's day like snow, all we wish for is to be forgotten' (ibid., p. 24). This resonates powerfully with Joyce and also with the Jewish poet and survivor Paul Celan because the snow reappears here, impossibly on a summer's day, with the black poppyseed – obviously symbolizing forgetting – and the white snow contrasting sharply, setting up the palette of the novel as shading between black, white and grey. Celan's most lauded book of poems, the text that includes 'Todesfuge', is titled *Poppy and Memory* (*Mohn und Gedächtnis* (1952)). While Sebald does not mention Celan, he does include a long visit with one of his and Celan's translators, Michael Hamburger, thus implicitly calling up this brilliant Jewish poet and survivor throughout the text.[10] This also recalls another German postwar artist whose work resonates with Sebald and

Richter's, Anselm Kiefer, who titled one of his texts *The Angel of History (Poppy and Memory)* (*Der Engel der Geschichte (Mohn und Gedächtnis)*). Like Sebald and Richter, Kiefer's art struggles with how to come to terms with the Nazi past and walks a tenuous line between evoking that past through Nazi imagery and deconstructing the imaginaries it conjures.[11] In both postmemorial situations, that of victims and that of perpetrators, mourning for the dead is an inherent part of the incorporation of visual imagery into the multifaceted field of negotiating with the past. The images of Nazis in Sebald and Richter are mournful; and of course this very mournfulness is inherently made problematic by the fact of the subjects of these portraits' perpetration. In part both images ask: how do we mourn the guilty?

In section three of *Rings*, Sebald goes off on a long tangent about herring which includes the following: 'One dependable sign that herring are present is said to be myriads of scales floating on the surface of the water, shimmering like tiny silver tiles by day and sometimes at dusk resembling ashes or snow' (ibid., pp. 55–6). It turns out, although we are not privy to this information until many pages later, that this long discourse on the herring is triggered by the fact that Conrad, about whom Sebald enters into a lengthy discussion, set sail from Lowestoft, and that this is why Sebald finds himself there, thinking of herring. Further, the herring's very shimmer is prefigured in Conrad's *The Secret Sharer*: 'on the shadowy water I could see nothing except a faint phosphorescent flash revealing the glassy smoothness of the sleeping surface' ([1910] 1978, p. 60). In *Rings of Saturn*, the residue of the bodies of the herring themselves recalls snow or ash, thus assimilating two prevalent metaphors that have distinct connotations. Snow relates to the resonance between dead and living and ash cannot help but evoke the Holocaust and precisely the radical impossibility of converse between living and dead – the inability to return. Thus the herring on the one hand connect with the excess of colonial violence that Conrad exposed in *Heart of Darkness* (1898) and the dead in the Holocaust, and on the other, recalling the striking resemblance between Sebald's depiction of German bodies entombed in the very structure of the state and Congolese bodies plastered over by imperial bombast, connect also with German victims of the air war. It is a quintessentially multilayered Sebaldian moment which brings together seemingly diverse aspects; Sebald deepens these resonances further when he remarks that the herring had been a great hope of English scientists who wished that their unusual luminosity would provide an 'organic source of light' (1995, p. 59) but that the attempt had failed, thus creating a 'negligible setback in the relentless conquest of darkness' (ibid.). Clearly, the reference to Conrad emerges in this failed attempt to conquer darkness. But it is also the darkening that offers Sebald a transition to the strange story of George Wyndham Le Strange, a former British soldier who was one of the liberators of Bergen-Belsen and who never recovered from the experience of being among the first in the Allied forces to see first-hand evidence of the Nazi genocide. It is not accidental that the collapse of the metaphors of snow and ash occurs in the context of this seemingly strange and out of place discourse on the herring, precisely because Sebald takes great pains – especially in *Rings* – to place the Holocaust in dialogue with other scenes of violence, genocide, degradation. Thus this moment where the herring collapse ash and snow and recall the heart of darkness and at the same time offer the turning point for Sebald's narrator to include an image of the dead at Bergen-Belsen metaphorically undergirds the larger political argument that seeks to place these moments in tension with one another. Postmemories, then, extend through colonialism, Nazism and the murder of European Jewry, thus on the one hand opening up interpretation of the Nazi genocide to important comparative lenses, but also perhaps placing an ethical strain on reading these histories within their own conditions of possibility.

The darkness that appears below the image of the Nazi in *Vertigo* ('the darkness which formerly he had always welcomed' (Sebald, 1990, p. 203)) sets off in Uncle Peter an immense fear; the darkness that Sebald uses in *Rings* in order to introduce the story of George Wyndham Le Strange is first brought about by 'veils of mist' (1995, p. 59) which then cast a 'grey shadow upon the earth'. Sebald then continues by noting that it was this 'darkening' (ibid.) which reminded him of Le Strange and what he saw at Bergen-Belsen. So one darkening is brought on by the terror of the uncle at the child's immersion in the Nazi world, whereas the other darkening catalyses one of the most direct Holocaust references in all of Sebald's work. One darkening is that of the fear for (not of) the Nazi and the other is the darkening of the vision of the soldier-witness. With the resonance of the 'mist' here, we can wonder whether this traumatic vision is the 'mist that no eye can dispel' that forms the epigraph to Paul Bereyter's section of Sebald's engrossing novel *The Emigrants* (1992). For Le Strange, Bergen-Belsen was this mist and its after-image resides indelibly, causing him to retreat into a profound silence that is never dispelled. These figures of blindness and numbing silence run throughout Sebald's work. And snow as metaphor not only constructs a narrative around the interconnectedness of dead and living, the tissue that binds the Holocaust, colonialism and genocides of all kinds, but also in its associations with mist and darkening deepens these figures of blindness and silence, the eyes unable to take in the horror, the inability to speak it and the indelible mark of the dead on the structures of the living. In a sense, then, by connecting moments of traumatization cross-temporally and cross-culturally, Sebald explores the very structure of postmemories themselves. How does trauma move between the generations? And how do subsequent generations of traumatizers handle the residue of this guilt?

Another snow falls, and other darkening befalls us, as Michael Hamburger (1924–2007, Celan's translator and a friend and translator of Sebald's who he visits as part of the perambulations that constitute *Rings*) writes that when he

147

tried to recall Berlin, 'all I see is a darkened background with a grey smudge in it' (Sebald, 1995, p. 177). With his German-Jewish family, Hamburger had emigrated to England in 1933, but returned to his native Berlin in 1947 and confronted the vast rubble in order to 'search for traces of the life I had lost' (ibid., p. 178); Hamburger finds in Berlin 'millions of bricks . . . and above them the Berlin November sky from which presently the snow would come swirling down – a deathly silent image of the onset of winter' (ibid., p. 179). The darkness of his childhood memories of Berlin (and of course here we think of Benjamin's *Berlin Childhood around 1900* (1938, published 2006)) is Hamburger's self-described 'blind spot' (recalling Huyssen's assessment of Sebald's *Air War*) which he amalgamates as a 'vestigal image' (ibid., p. 178) of these ruins. The darkness of Uncle Peter, fearing for his little Nazi, the darkness that conjures the witness to death at Bergen-Belsen, the darkness of the ruins of Germany at the end of the war; and again, over it all, the snow.

The snow/ash melding of traumatic instants also strikingly appears at the beginning of Alain Resnais and Marguerite Duras's utterly gorgeous film *Hiroshima, mon amour* (1959) wherein the lovers are rendered almost as still lifes, something falling on them – is it ash? snow? – encasing them, isolating them from their surroundings but simultaneously emplotting them in their respective histories: she a French woman who fell in love with a Nazi, he a Japanese man who is marked indelibly by the US bombing of Hiroshima/Nagasaki, playing out their present through their pasts and superimposing one upon the other ceaselessly. Sebald invests the various histories he is at pains to expose with a metaphorical system that encourages a profound understanding of how seemingly geographically and temporally distinct traumas can be seen in surprising and counterintuitive relationship with each other. The Nazi in *Vertigo* inaugurates a trauma for the family, thus smudging the difference between victim and perpetrator in just the same way that Joyce's snow amalgamates living and dead. By now juxtaposing this young Nazi in literature with a painted Nazi uncle, we hope to further explore how German familial postmemories perform politically.

Gerhard Richter (b. 1932)

After a series of black and white paintings such as *Toilet Paper*, *Administrative Building* and *Ferrari* in which he painted banal images copied from magazines and vernacular photographs, in 1965 Gerhard Richter finished three paintings – *Uncle Rudi*, *Aunt Marianne* and *Mr. Heyde* – that mingled personal memory and traumatic events from recent German history. In these three paintings, Richter conflates the formal characteristics of black and white family album imagery and newspaper pictures while smoothly altering their resemblances on the canvases and thus collapsing the visual codes of vernacular photography and the monumentality of history painting by using both aspects explicitly. Confounding artistic genres and blurring the image of the sitters, Richter's paintings become sites of aesthetic inquiry about the difficulty of rendering history as well as offering rhetorical gestures that challenge the limits between personal memory and public recollection. Richter's canvases offer neither personal testimony of history nor its denial. Rather, by destabilizing their pictorial surfaces, Richter's paintings create a visual deferment – what Roland Barthes ([1978] 2002, p. 518) has called an *epojé* of the image – in which psychological identification and historical judgement are both adjourned. Moreover, in suspending and ultimately deferring the viewer's identification and its visual indifference, Richter's paintings of 1965 disregard immediate reception, thus transferring perceptual instability into the viewer's historical and ethical judgement. In this formal and semantic operation, Richter's paintings collapse the distinction between private remembrance and collective recognition, while questioning the displacement from private memory into public history. As Sebald's image of a young Nazi begs to be read both personally and politically, so these paintings question the division between personal and collective memories. Asked about these works, Richter affirms:

> There are personal stories attached to these images, then, but there are historical issues too. If you look at the date of these paintings – 1965 – you see that it was very early for a German artist to be making pictures about World War II that were not simply rhetorical. There were political artists making anti-fascist paintings, but to make a personal image of something connected to the war was almost unheard of. And there you were making pictures that bring that past into the open and very close to home . . . . Maybe that is the main reason why the audience, as well as myself, had to fall back on a strategy of laughter. That's how it worked: people thought it was mischievous and prankish and not too serious and, therefore, it was so much easier to deal with it. (2009, p. 399)

At the edges of remembrance, commemoration and documentation, *Uncle Rudi*, *Mr. Heyde* and *Aunt Marianne* create a visual and psychological uncertainty. This double resistance posits these canvases as spectral images, as images that, as Jacques Derrida has written, always haunt to reappear.[12] By creating an irresolvable visual tension between memory and its suppression, Richter's canvases open an indeterminate space of visual and rhetorical intervention that escapes the overreaching logic of history as concluded past while challenging the neutralizing logic of the art museum as collective archive. Furthermore, by combining aesthetic media with personal and collective memory, Richter's paintings oppose the sentimentalism and nostalgic nature of the family portrait while contesting the monumentalization of painting as mere visual document of recent German history. In their unresolved condition between collective documents and personal reminiscences, Richter's *Uncle Rudi, Aunt Marianne* and *Mr. Heyde* are some of the most striking postmemorial artworks in contemporary German art. Like the photograph of the young Nazi in Sebald's *Vertigo*, these paintings ask questions about postmemory in a counterintuitive vein – about how one mourns a perpetrator in one's midst and about how postwar generations can treat this legacy of guilt and genocide.

Born in Dresden in 1932, Richter studied at the Dresden Fine Arts academy where he was educated in the formal vocabulary of the GDR's realist aesthetics. In 1960 he moved to West Germany where he enrolled in the art school in Düsseldorf. Living in West Germany, Richter encountered the massive circulation of commercial imagery of a capitalistic society and thus faced the Western Neo-Avantgarde, at the time dominated by American pop imagery and Neo-Dadaist artistic practices. In the social and artistic context of Western Germany in the early 1960s, Richter re-examined the conventions of historical realism by appropriating images from mass media – as can be seen in *Ferrari* (1964) and *Motor Boat* (1965) – that he carefully altered, making them both accessible and yet illegible, hence engaging in dialogue with pop-art co-options of consumer culture while problematizing the aesthetic boundaries between photography and painting.

In *Atlas Project* (1962–6), Richter further complicates this aesthetic relationship between photography and the visual homogenization of the modern museum as public archive by creating a series of wall panels in which he challenges the naive redemptory faith in Realism as an artistic ideal for overcoming dramatic historical events. First exhibited at the *Documenta* in Kassel in 1966, these panels juxtaposed mass media photographs with blurred pornographic pictures and photographs from concentration camps. Richter's juxtaposition of conflicting images challenges the genre-boundaries and archival hierarchies between documentary photography, history painting and vernacular public imagery while at a semantic level questioning the legitimacy of either documentary photography or painting in the rendering of history. Moreover, the heterogeneous coexistence of banal images with the literality of pornography and the horror of concentration camps disrupts the contemplation of artworks as mere passive action – what Richter refers to as the Brechtian *distancing effect (Verfremdungseffekt)* – while foregrounding the aesthetic limitations of both painting and photography to properly render recent historical subjects and events. In so doing, Richter's images are eminently ambiguous: they are perceptually and semantically both legible and illegible. In this unresolvable optical uncertainty, Richter's blurred surfaces perform a polysemic gesture that questions the ontological difference between photography and painting, the epistemological difference between memory and history, and the indistinctness between historical document and public commemoration. Art historian Benjamin Buchloh writes:

> In their refusal either to give up painting for photography *tout court* or to accept the supposed lucidity of photography's focused gaze, Richter's photopaintings have consistently opposed the universal presence of that gaze and its ubiquitous instrumentalization of the look . . . . It is in the construction of this dilemma, marked by both the conflict in medium – painting/photography – and the conflict in ideas about representability – the painting's self-referentiality/photography's 'transparency' to the event – that Richter's work testifies to the contemporary difficulties in the production of historical representation in painting. (1989, pp. 93, 95)

Richter's undertaking with the 'representability' of recent German history began in the early 1960s. Starting with *Bombers* (1963), which shows American fighters in the air dropping bombs, Richter moves from what seems a random appropriation of mass-circulated images to the difficult subject of history, thus using visual images to problematize and meditate upon the past. By rejecting the apparent immediacy of documentary photography while embracing the limitations of history painting, Richter's images incarnate what Siegfried Kracauer called memory-images. Kracauer states:

> The meaning of memory-images is linked to their truth content. As long as they are embedded in the uncontrolled life of the drives they are inhabited by a demonic ambiguity; they are opaque like frosted glass that hardly a ray of light can penetrate . . . . All memory-images are bound to be reduced to this type of image, which may rightly be called the last image, since in it alone does the unforgettable persevere. The last image of a person is that person's actual '*history*'. (1993, pp. 425–6)

This intricate relationship between personal memory-images and public history is most explicit in *Uncle Rudi* (1965), an image that recalls powerfully the photograph of a young Nazi in Sebald's *Vertigo*. Appropriated from the family photo album, *Uncle Rudi* shows the handsome and young maternal uncle Rudi who died during the first days of the war, dressed in a winter SS uniform, posing in front of a wall and smiling at the camera. Richter's canvas still retains the conventional pose of usual family pictures while manifesting the artist's presence through the horizontal blurring of the surface of the canvas, which is especially visible on the white building in the background. Rudi's beautiful young face and his cheerful smile increase a sense of nostalgia and mourning of his fate. As Richter recalls, Rudi, who died during the first days of the war, was a favourite of the family and most loved by his mother:

> It was sad when my mother's brothers fell in battle. First one, then the other. I'll never forget how the women screamed. When the postman comes and brings the telegram: 'Fallen for the people and the fatherland' – I remember that very well, even the little details. First we thought it was the other brother who had died. Then we read it again and realized that it wasn't Fred at all, it was the handsome one, Rudi. And the two women screamed again, and much louder. (2009, p. 466)

Uncle Rudi portrays the beloved maternal uncle but also the Nazi in the family. The personal attachment with the subject depicted in the image and the delicate blurring intervenes in the nostalgic yet horrifying personal remembrance, hence transferring the drama of the family story to the history of the nation. As Richter recalls: 'I did want to be a soldier. I was a real little Nazi. When the

Figure 7.2 Gerhard Richter, *Uncle Rudi* (1965), oil on canvas, Lidice Memorial, Czech Republic, reproduced by permission of Gerhard Richter.

soldiers came through the village, I went up to them and wanted to join them. It's a question of upbringing, of course' (ibid., p. 197). In this semantic analogy between the photo-album portrait and the historical image, *Uncle Rudi* conflates Richter's personal remembrance with Modern German public memory.[13] In another interview, Richter further declared: 'Yes, and when I then paint another picture of Uncle Rudi, the little officer, I'm actually watering down the true work of art achieved by those two or three private individuals who put Rudi behind glass and stood him on the sideboard or hung him on the wall. The only sense in which I'm not watering down is that by painting the thing I am giving it rather more universality' (ibid., p. 203).

Uncle Rudi is Richter's second effort (after an attempt in 1962 to paint a portrait of Adolf Hitler) to deal with the images of the Nazi past, and among the early examples of German postwar art to introduce the subject matter of Germany's recent Nazi history into a work of the Neo-Avantgarde.[14] Today exhibited at the Czech Museum of Fine Arts, the painting serves also as a reminder of the Nazi atrocities of Lidice in the Czech Republic and former Czechoslovakia. In its double nature as an intimate and yet public image, *Uncle Rudi* generates a duplicity of memories in which the process of mourning and moral condemnation is simultaneously personal and public, thus revealing collective history to be a fragmentary recollection of private blurred remembrances. This subject of postwar Germany's calculated and restrained relation to the Third Reich in the 1960s as it is explored in *Uncle Rudi* is also the main subject of *Aunt Marianne* and *Mr. Heyde*.

Aunt Marianne is a smudged portrait of Richter's mentally ill aunt, Marianne, as a teenager holding a baby outdoors. Marianne, who had been in medical reclusion since the age of 18, died in a mental hospital during the war; she was a victim of the euthanasia programme. As Richter confirmed years later, the baby she is holding in the picture is the artist himself. Richter recalls: 'Whenever I behaved badly I was told "you will become like crazy Marianne." She, too, died during the time of the war – killed by Nazi doctors who organized a large-scale system of "euthanasia" to deal with the chronically ill, the mentally retarded and the insane' (ibid., p. 40). As in *Uncle Rudi*, *Aunt Marianne* offers an intersection of the family story with the German collective past. In postwar West Germany, *Aunt Marianne* functions as a memory in negative in which State euthanasia practices towards Marianne personify the ideological imposition of political reconciliation with the traumatic past but also the risk of lack of memory of a German generation towards its disturbing past. This double binding process between the intimate drama and the collective paranoia is further increased in *Mr. Heyde*.

Copied from a German newspaper, *Mr. Heyde* shows the capture of former Nazi neurologist Werner Heyde in Frankfurt on 12 November 1959. Heyde had been medically responsible for the Nazi T-4 Euthanasia Program that caused the death of mentally ill and sick citizens in State institutions in Nazi Germany. Despite his involvement in the implementation of the massive Nazi eugenics projects of the 1940s, which included the death of Richter's aunt Marianne, Heyde continued living and working in postwar West Germany under a secret identity as Fritz Sawada until his capture in 1959. Heyde committed suicide in prison days before his trial in November 1964. As Robert Storr affirms, *Mr Heyde* is Marianne's executioner (2002a, p. 4). In this, Richter's images reawaken the personal and collective unsublimated fear and social paranoia of a German postwar generation forced to live in an institutionally imposed reconciliation with the past and at the same time reveals the impossibility of coming-to-terms with that past. In this uneasy historical and psychological circumstance that is simultaneously personal and collective, the State eugenic practices of the Third Reich sideshadow the politically imposed amnesia of the postwar German government towards the past. As Storr writes: 'Together with *Uncle Rudi* and *Aunt Marianne*, *Mr. Heyde* closes the gaps between personal experience and public reality, between a painful guilt-laden past and a present predicated on selective memory – gaps in the fabric of German society and culture kept open by denial and reticence' (ibid., p. 41). In the climax of the miraculous economic policies of Adenauer's West Germany of the 1960s, Richter's paintings of 1965 visually and politically call into question the impossible historical redemption through art while revealing the intricate process of construction of collective memory. In their irresolvable visual and rhetorical ambivalence, Richter's *Uncle Rudi, Aunt Marianne* and *Mr. Heyde* are as much images of remembrance as failed personal and public attempts to aesthetically exorcise the past. These paintings offer postmemorial reflections on the Nazis housed in Richter's family while putting into tension perpetration and victimization by opening up the story of the uncle as perpetrator to that of the aunt as victim. The images invite questions concerning the production of collective memories and public restoration of history and open up to the play of profound readings rather than shutting down interpretation: by placing the collective guilt of postwar Germany into the intimate space of the family, Richter avows the postguilt of his generation; by placing that line in friction with the hint of German victimization, his work highlights the complexity and irresolvability of German postmemorial inheritance.

While Sebald and Richter are each embedded in diverse literary and painterly contexts, both artists inventively confuse genres to ask ripe and pertinent questions regarding postwar German accumulation of guilt but also of mourning and loss experienced by the generations after those who perpetrated the Nazi genocide. By exploring their work through the lens of postmemory, we wish to retain the ethical difference between victim and perpetrator while examining how residues accrue on both sides. Both Richter and Sebald work in layers. The painter continually overpaints his earlier efforts, leaving a slightly visible trace of the past and working it over and over again; the writer invites us to see the layers of imperial history as distinct yet interconnected moments of traumatization that accrue one on top of the other, the bodies of the dead like snow under our feet.

Notes

1. We use the word 'Nazi' admittedly loosely here. I sent the image in Sebald's *Vertigo* to the Militärhistorisches Museum der Bundeswehr and received the following reply: 'It is an army uniform of the Wehrmacht. The soldier has a low rank, Private or Private 1st Class. He has a kind of ribbon on his sleeve (with the unreadable unit on it).' The archivist noted that he could not specify as to whether the soldier was a Nazi or not. The image though, I think, still evokes what has perhaps become a conflation of Wehrmacht soldier with Nazi in our imaginary.
2. For more on victims and perpetrators' legacies see McGlothlin (2006); Kaplan (2007).
3. In addition to Hell and von Moltke (2005), David Ward (2003) has also put Richter into comparison with Sebald, while Will Self (2010) delivered a lecture on Sebald and used Richter's *Uncle Rudi* as a backdrop; see: http://hanskundnani.com/2010/01/12/sebald-and-the-holocaust/
4. See Strathausen (2007); Anderson (2003). The scholarship on Sebald is vast and I can make no attempt to account for it all here; some of this work is insightful: see Anderson (2003 and 2008), Baumgarten (2007), Blumenthal-Barby (2011), Crownshaw (2004), Dean (2003), Denham and McCulloh (2006), Dubow (2007), Lutz (2012), Osborne (2007), Patt et al. (2007), Prager (2005 and 2008), Ryan (2007), Santner (2006) and Strathausen (2007).
5. This was based on a series of lectures delivered in 1997 and published in translation as *On the Natural History of Destruction* (2003).
6. An excellent exception to this is Prager (2005), in which he makes a case for complicating Sebald's levels of empathic identification with Jewish victims.
7. There is an image of Paul Bereyter, in *The Emigrants* (Sebald, 1992, p. 55), looking out of a car with a helmet below the description of his, despite being merely three-quarters Aryan, being called up and serving in the *Wehrmacht*; however, this image bears no Nazi insignia. There are images of the victims of Nazism in *The Rings of Saturn* (Sebald, 1995, pp. 60–1, 97) and a group of photos of British bombers in *On the Natural History of Destruction* (Sebald, 2003, p. 78).
8. See Scholem (1974); and, for a portrayal of the Rabbi divining from the stars, see the 1920 film *The Golem*, directed by Paul Wegener.
9. For more than you ever wanted to know about Nazis and mountains, see Kaplan (2011).
10. For a detailed reading of Celan, see Felstiner (1995).
11. See Kaplan (2007, pp. 107–26).
12. 'This already suffices to distinguish the specter not only from the icon or the idol but also from the image of the image, from the Platonic *Pantasma*, as well as from the simple *simulacrum* of something in general to which it is nevertheless so close and with which it shares, in other respects, more than one feature. . . . Another suggestion: This spectral someone other looks at us, we feel ourselves being looked at by it, outsider of any synchrony, even before and beyond any look at our part, according to an absolute anteriority (which may be on the order of generation, of more than one generation) and asymmetry, according to an absolutely unmasterable disproportion' (Derrida, 1994, p. 7).

13. As Buchloh (1996, p. 74) writes, 'Richter's portrait of his Nazi uncle, however, . . . articulat[es] the difficulties in the context of postfascist Germany of constructing images of historical recollection at all. Indeed, the impediment seems to consist precisely in working through both the pictorial prohibition of the unrepresentable subject (the familial tie to the fascist legacy at large and the fascist legacies of painting) and the necessity of representing this subject within the conventions of painting that traditionally served the purposes of historical recollection.'

14. As Robert Storr (2002a, p. 40) writes, 'On the one hand Uncle Rudi is, for Germans, an immediately recognizable but, after the war, seldom discussed type: "The Nazi in the family." He is not a monster but the average, ordinarily enthusiastic soldier. On the other hand, he was the apple of Richter's mother's eye.'

Works Cited

Anderson, M. M. (2003), 'Edge of darkness', *October*, 106, 102–21.

—. (2008), 'Documents, photography, postmemory: Alexander Kluge, W. G. Sebald, and the German family', *Poetics Today*, 29.1, 129–53.

Arendt, H. [1963] (1992), *Eichmann in Jerusalem: A Report on the Banality of Evil*. New York: Penguin.

Barthes, R. [1978] (2002), 'L' Image', in *Oeuvres Complètes*, vol. 5. Paris: Seuil, pp. 512–19.

Baumgarten, M. (2007), '"Not knowing what I should think": the landscape of postmemory in W. G. Sebald's *The Emigrants*', *Partial Answers: Journal of Literature and the History of Ideas*, 5.2, 267–87.

Benjamin, W. (2006), *Berlin Childhood around 1900*, trans. H. Eiland. Cambridge, MA: Harvard University Press.

Blumenthal-Barby, M. (2011), 'Holocaust and herring: the resuscitation of the silenced in W. G. Sebald's *The Rings of Saturn*', *Monatshefte*, 103.4, 537–58.

Buchloh, B. (1989), 'A note on Gerhard Richter's "October 18, 1977"', *October*, 48, 88–109.

—. (1996), 'Divided memory and post-traditional identity: Gerhard Richter's work of mourning', *October*, 75, 60–82.

Celan, P. (1952), *Mohn und Gedächtnis*. Stuttgart: Deutsche Verlags-Anstalt.

Conrad, J. [1910] (1978), *Heart of Darkness & The Secret Sharer*. New York: Signet Classic.

Crownshaw, R. (2004), 'Reconsidering postmemory: photography, the archive, and post-Holocaust memory in W. G. Sebald's *Austerlitz*', *Mosaic*, 37.4, 215–36.

Dean, T. (2003), 'W. G. Sebald', *October*, 106, 122–36.

Denham, S. and McCulloh, M. (eds) (2006), *W. G. Sebald: History-Memory-Trauma*. Berlin: de Gruyter.

Derrida, J. (1994), *Specters of Marx: The State of Debt, The Work of Mourning and the New International*, trans. P. Kamuf. New York: Routledge.

Dubow, J. (2007), 'Case interrupted: Benjamin, Sebald, and the dialectical image', *Critical Inquiry*, 33.4, 820–36.

Felstiner, J. (1995), *Paul Celan: Poet, Survivor, Jew*. New Haven: Yale University Press.

Hell, J. and von Moltke, J. (2005), 'Unification effects: imaginary landscapes of the Berlin Republic', *Germanic Review*, 80.1, 74–95.

Hirsch, M. (2012), *The Generation of Postmemory: Writing and Visual Culture after the Holocaust*. New York: Columbia University Press.

Huyssen, A. (2003), *Present Pasts: Urban Palimpsests and the Politics of Memory*. Stanford, CA: Stanford University Press.

Jaskot, P. B. (2012), *The Nazi Perpetrator: Postwar German Art and the Politics of the Right*. Minneapolis: University of Minnesota Press, 2012.

Joyce, J. [1907] (2001), 'The dead', in B. Wilkie and J. Hurt (eds), *Literature of the Western World Volume II*. New Jersey: Prentice Hall, pp. 1657–85.

Kaplan, B. (2007), *Unwanted Beauty: Aesthetic Pleasure in Holocaust Representation*. Urbana, IL: University of Illinois Press.

—. (2011), *Landscapes of Holocaust Postmemory*. New York and London: Routledge.

Kracauer, S. (1993), 'Photography', trans. T. Levin, *Critical Inquiry*, 19.3, 421–36.

Lutz, A. (2012), 'Holocaust remembrance in W. G. Sebald's work: melancholy storytelling about an uncanny *Heimat*', *Papers on Language and Literature: A Journal for Scholars and Critics of Language and Literature*, 48.2, 137–71.

McGlothlin, E. (2006), *Second-Generation Holocaust Literature: Legacies of Survival and Perpetration*. Rochester, NY: Camden House.

Osborne, D. (2007), 'Blind spots: viewing trauma in W. G. Sebald's *Austerlitz*', *Seminar: A Journal of Germanic Studies*, 43.4, 517–33.

Patt, L., Bell, V. and Crownshaw, R. (2007), *Searching for Sebald: Photography after W. G. Sebald*. Los Angeles: Institute for Cultural Inquiry and ICI Press.

Prager, B. (2005), 'The good German as narrator: on W. G. Sebald and the risks of Holocaust writing', *New German Critique*, 96, 75–102.

—. (2008), 'On the liberation of perpetrator photographs in Holocaust narratives', in D. Bathrick, B. Prager and M. Richardson (eds), *Visualizing the Holocaust: Documents, Aesthetics, Memory*. Rochester, NY: Camden House, pp. 19–37.

Resnais, A. (dir) (1959), *Hiroshima, Mon Amour*. DVD. New York: Criterion Collection.

—. (2009), *Gerhard Richter: Text: Writings, Interviews and Letters*, ed. D. Elger and H-U. Obrist. London: Thames and Hudson.

Ryan, J. (2007), 'Fulgurations: Sebald and surrealism', *The Germanic Review*, 82.3, 227–49.

Santner, E. (2006), *On Creaturely Life: Rilke, Benjamin, Sebald*. Chicago: Chicago University Press.

Scholem, G. (1974), *Kabbalah*. New York: Dorset Press.

Sebald, W. G. (1990), *Vertigo*, trans. M. Hulse. New York: New Directions.

—. (1992), *The Emigrants*, trans. M. Hulse. New York: New Directions.

—. (1995), *The Rings of Saturn*, trans. M. Hulse. New York: New Directions.

—. (2003), *On the Natural History of Destruction*, trans. Anthea Bell. New York: Random House.

Silverman, K. (2009), *Flesh of My Flesh*. Stanford, CA: Stanford University Press.

Storr, R. (2002a), *Gerhard Richter, 40 Years of Painting*. New York: Museum of Modern Art.

—. (2002b), *Gerhard Richter: October 18, 1977*. New York: Museum of Modern Art.

Strathausen, C. (2007), 'Going nowhere: Sebald's rhizomatic travels', in L. Patt, V. Bell and R. Crownshaw (eds), *Searching for Sebald: Photography after W. G. Sebald*. Los Angeles: Institute for Cultural Inquiry and ICI Press, pp. 472–91.

Ward, D. C. (2003), 'Ghost worlds of the ordinary: W. G. Sebald and Gerhard Richter', *PN Review*, 29.6 [152], 32–6.

Wegener, P. and Boese, C. (dirs) (1920), *The Golem*. DVD. New York: Kino Lorber.

8 Narrative Perspective and the Holocaust Perpetrator: Edgar Hilsenrath's *The Nazi and the Barber* and Jonathan Littell's *The Kindly Ones*

Erin McGlothlin

Abstract

What happens when we read books about the Holocaust that probe the mind of the Nazi perpetrator, a figure that in the contemporary cultural imagination is often regarded as the embodiment of concrete evil? What is our ethical relationship to texts that ask us to imagine the mindset of genocidal murderers and to consider the events of the Holocaust from their point of view? In compelling us to view the Holocaust from the morally questionable perspective of the perpetrator, do such works ask us to betray the Jewish victims whose experience should remain central to our understanding of the event? And how can such works render the mind of the perpetrator without either reducing him to the trope of monster or transforming him into an object of sympathy? How do texts that portray the consciousness of such historically, emotionally and ethically charged figures negotiate the sometimes razor-thin line between insightful provocation and historical bad faith? This chapter will explore the implications of these questions by looking at how the perpetrator's perspective is constructed in Edgar Hilsenrath's *The Nazi and the Barber* and Jonathan Littell's *The Kindly Ones*, two novels noted for their innovative first-person depictions of Holocaust perpetrators.

Since the first texts that have come to be known as Holocaust literature appeared both during and after the events of 1933–45, readers and critics have posed vexing questions about literary representations of Holocaust perpetrators, especially those that frame the horrific events from their perspective. Although we typically associate literature about the Holocaust with the experiences of its victims and survivors, the motivations and actions of the perpetrators are also an important focus of many texts that examine the experience of the Holocaust. For example, the autobiography of Rudolf Höss, the notorious commandant of Auschwitz, which was written in 1947 while Höss was awaiting execution, provides a first-hand account of a perpetrator's experience (Höss, 1958, 1992). Höss's book functions as an important but diametrically opposed counterpart to the memoirs of Auschwitz survivors such as Primo Levi (1959), Ruth Klüger (2001), Charlotte Delbo (1995), Jean Améry (1980), Elie Wiesel (1960) and others by giving its readers a glimpse into the mind of the man who created and administered the death machine of Auschwitz (even if his account is essentially distorted, contradictory and self-serving). However, Höss's text is extraordinary in the canon of Holocaust literature; candid autobiographical accounts by perpetrators, whether prominent or lesser known, are relatively rare, especially in comparison to the profuse number of testimonial narratives by Holocaust survivors. The dearth of autobiographical accounts by perpetrators that narrate first-hand and from the subjective perspective the experience of the individual actor in the collective implementation of mass violence and murder (a point of view that excellent historical studies of Holocaust perpetrators such as Christopher Browning's *Ordinary Men: Reserve Police Battalion 101 and the Final Solution in Poland* (1992), by nature of their method of rigorous historical investigation of the documentary record, cannot reproduce) has left a lacuna in our imagination of the inner workings of individual perpetrators.

Increasingly, this gap has come to be filled not by narrative accounts of actual perpetrators, but by fictional renderings that attempt to frame the Holocaust through the perspective of imagined victimizers, as demonstrated by the popularity and critical acclaim of one of the most recent fictional narratives written in the voice of a perpetrator, Jonathan Littell's *The Kindly Ones* (published in the original French in 2006 and in English translation in 2009). The narrative focalization of the perpetrator, which, as I have argued elsewhere (McGlothlin, 2010, pp. 210–14), was long regarded a taboo perspective by critics of Holocaust literature, has become a more accepted medium through which the post-Holocaust reader can engage imaginatively with the legacy of the Holocaust. While one can justifiably take issue with Aurélie Barjonet's and Liran Razinsky's assertion that *The Kindly Ones* represents a 'rupture within . . . the tradition of Holocaust writing' (2012, p. 9) on account of its supposedly unprecedented representation of the perpetrator's point of view, we have clearly entered a new phase in the literary portrayal of the Holocaust, in which temporal and experiential distance from its actual historical events makes possible particular modes of representation and perspectives that were at one time considered unthinkable. In addition to *The Kindly Ones*, fictional narratives such as Edgar Hilsenrath's *The Nazi and the Barber* (English translation 1971, German original 1977), Michel Tournier's *The Ogre* (French original 1970, English translation 1972), Martin Amis's *Time's Arrow* (1991), Ian MacMillan's *Village of a Million Spirits* (1999), Douglas Skopp's *Shadows Walking* (2010) and Laurent Binet's *HHhH* (French original 2011; English translation 2012) all attempt, to some degree, to enter into the mind of the Nazi perpetrator.

The emerging innovation of literary and artistic engagements with the Holocaust that foreground the perspective of the perpetrator requires an appropriate critical approach and a narrative taxonomy that function as a guide for understanding and reading these texts. One fruitful way to address them is through the methodological approach of narrative theory, which gives us a rich vocabulary and conceptual apparatus for investigating the ways in which the consciousness of a character is constructed through narration. By looking at how texts employ such techniques as voice, or what we designate less technically as narrative perspective, which for the purpose of the present discussion means the point of view of a first-person perpetrator-narrator, and focalization, meaning the ways in which third-person narratives depict events through the consciousness of characters who are perpetrators, one can analyse how texts structure the consciousness and awareness of their Holocaust per-petrators. The representation of the subjective perspective of perpetrators thus mediates to the reader a particular interpretation of the perpetrators' thoughts, motivations, memories and self-image. Such investigation into the narrative construction of the perpetrator's mind can assist us in understanding how we, as readers, are positioned vis-à-vis the perpetrator-protagonist. Chief among the potential problems that arise in the reading of Holocaust texts narrated from the perspective of the victimizer are the narratological issues of unreliable narration and reader identification, both of which provoke a number of criti-cal questions: Can we trust our perpetrator-narrator to tell us the truth about his crimes? And if he is forthcoming about his participation in genocide, can we believe his interpretation of those crimes, especially given that his myopic and often self-serving perspective necessarily excludes a component critical to understanding the scope and nature of the Holocaust, namely the subjective experience of its victims? Moreover, how does autodiegetic narration (or, in the context of texts narrated in the third person, focalization) elicit, by virtue of its narrow and sometimes highly manipulative lens, the reader's sympathies or even identification? If, as Jenni Adams astutely argues, the corpus of Holocaust literature compels a 'conventional pattern of identification . . . in which the reader identifies with the victim' (2011, p. 34), what happens to this structure of identification when the narrator is a perpetrator rather than a victim? Does the type of complex affective attachment on the part of readers to victims and survivors that Gary Weissman documents in his book *Fantasies of Witnessing: Postwar Efforts to Experience the Holocaust* (2004) apply to narratives that feature perpetrators as protagonists? And what happens if, as Suzanne Keen puts it in her insightful study *Empathy and the Novel*, 'the reader connects emotionally with the "wrong character"', one who is 'unsavory', 'nasty', or even 'vicious' (2007, p. 74)? In rendering the mind of the perpetrator, how do such narratives negotiate the risk of allowing or even encouraging their readers to identify with the perpetrator-protagonists? In light of recent fiction that attempts to render the consciousness of Holocaust perpetrators, such questions are of critical ethical importance.

My discussion here will focus on the strategies employed by two novels, Littell's *The Kindly Ones* and Edgar Hilsenrath's *The Nazi and the Barber*, to depict the consciousness of their first-person perpetrator-protagonists. Both texts became media sensations on account of their controversial decision to portray characters who not only support the Nazis' genocide of the European Jews, but also actively commit murder as a part of the Final Solution, and both were hailed in their respective eras as innovative and even transgressive depictions of the Holocaust. In my readings of these two novels, I will analyse the ways in which each protagonist narrates his own history of perpetrating extreme violence and identify in each text particular narrative techniques that function to produce or inhibit the reader's identification with the narrator. My analysis locates in both novels a certain tension at play that revolves around the ethics of identification. On the one hand, each text offers a relatively mimetic and psychologically plausible representation of the consciousness of its violent protagonist, encouraging reader identification on a number of levels.[1] On the other hand, the narratives of violence I analyse also employ particular strategies that at times block the seemingly transparent window into the perpetrators' minds, thus betraying an anxiety about the project of undistorted representation they profess to undertake. Although with their unwavering focus on individual Holocaust perpetrators these texts attempt to provide 'access' to their minds, they also employ what I call 'filtering strategies' in order to alternately compel and foreclose identification, thus drawing the reader directly into the perpetrators' experience and inviting her empathetic response and at the same time deferring any unmediated access to the perpetrators' consciousness. By deftly utilizing such filtering strategies, Littell's and Hilsenrath's novels are able to manipulate carefully the reader's process of identification, allowing it to develop at some junctures in the narrative and retarding it at other points.

Jonathan Littell's *The Kindly Ones* has been dubbed 'the first important work of fiction to narrate the Holocaust from the perpetrator's perspective' (von Koppenfels, 2012, p. 133). However, fully 25 years before its appearance in 2006, Edgar Hilsenrath published *The Nazi and the Barber*, a dazzling satirical novel narrated by Max Schulz, a former member of the SS, who confesses to the reader the genocidal murder he committed during the Second World War. Hilsenrath, a German-Jewish survivor of the Holocaust (he was interned in the Moghilov-Podolsk ghetto in the Transnistria from 1941–4), completed his extraordinary novel in German in 1968. Unable to find a German publisher for his book because of what I have termed the 'narrative transgression' of its first-person depiction of a Holocaust perpetrator (McGlothlin, 2007, pp. 233–5) and its employment of black humour and the grotesque, Hilsenrath published the text first in English translation in 1971; it sold over a million copies within five years and enjoyed a 'resounding echo' in the American press (Braun, 2005, p. 44, my translation). In 1977, after being rejected by over 60 German publishing houses,[2] the novel finally appeared in the original as *Der Nazi und der Friseur* (ibid., p. 46). Initially causing a small scandal in a West German society that preferred not to peer too closely into the psyche of former Nazi criminals, Hilsenrath's novel has since become known as one of the most original works of German literature about the Holocaust and one that, on account of its shocking narrative perspective and its grotesque and even pornographic content, is of particular challenge to readers.

The autodiegetic narrator Max Schulz begins his autobiographical account in *The Nazi and the Barber* with his birth in 1907 in the town of Wieshalle, East Prussia:

> I am Max Schulz, illegitimate though purely Aryan son of Minna Schulz . . . who at the time of my birth was a maid in the house of the Jewish fur dealer Abramowitz. There can be no doubt of my pure Aryan origin, since the family tree of my mother, Minna Schulz, while it does not go back to the Battle of the Teutoburger Forest, nevertheless has roots which reach back to Frederick the Great. Who my father was I cannot tell you with any certainty, but he must definitely have been one of five men: the butcher, Hubert Nagler; the locksmith, Franz Heinrich Wieland; the builder's mate, Hans Huber; the coachman, Wilhelm Hopfenstange; or the butler, Adolf Hennemann. I have had the family trees of my five fathers carefully looked into and I can assure you, the Aryan origin of all five can be certified beyond doubt. (Hilsenrath, 1971, p. 9, ellipsis in original)

With this singular opening passage, Hilsenrath establishes Max's voice in the novel as a picaresque combination of the hyperbolic and the banal, the confessional and the implausible. This particular narratorial configuration draws the reader into Max's idiosyncratic perspective and at the same time alerts her to his likely unreliability, an issue that Max himself addresses head on when he senses the reader's incredulity regarding his authoritative descriptions of his life as an infant: 'This is probably the place where you will ask yourself how it is that I know all this so exactly, but with the best will in the world I can't tell you' (ibid., p. 15). As this quote demonstrates, Max is not remotely interested in giving his readers evidence for his implausible stories. In fact, he pokes fun here at our expectation that he will do so. Furthermore, he fashions his narration in part as a dialogue with an implied reader whom he sets up to reflect back to him a discordant and unreliable image of his function as narrator. After narrating an episode that supposedly takes place shortly after his birth, when his mother, having witnessed the ritual circumcision of the infant son (who was born two minutes after Max) of the town's Jewish barber, tries to castrate her own son, Max exclaims:

> You're probably thinking I'm pulling your leg? Or perhaps that's not what you think, maybe you're just saying to yourself: Max Schulz has a screw loose! He's got a mania that somebody wanted to kill him . . . because he was a bastard . . . and all done under the disguise of a circumcision, executed, as is the custom among Jews, on the eighth day after birth. What is Max Schulz up to? What's he trying to say to me? Who is he trying to blame? His mother? The Jews? Or God? (Ibid., p. 16, ellipsis in original)

Not only does Max figure himself in this passage as the original victim of violence, a claim that conflicts with his self-identification just a few pages earlier as a 'mass-murderer' (ibid., p. 13), but he also models to the reader how she should consume his text: with scepticism as to its veracity and with an awareness of his psychological and narratorial instability. Andreas Graf has written about the 'pathology of the narrative perspective' in *The Nazi and the Barber* (1996, my translation), but this narrative disease is not just an external critical diagnosis of Hilsenrath's text, it is also a condition of which Max himself is aware. Moreover, as evident in the quote, Max even proposes the notion of pathological narration as the appropriate interpretative framework for understanding his story. Beginning with the first sentences of the novel, I argue, Max self-consciously and with surprising adeptness constructs his own elaborate narrative pathology in the form of a markedly self-conscious unreliability that runs the full gamut of James Phelan's taxonomy of unreliable narration (2005, pp. 49–53), ranging from underreporting and misreporting, which have to do with Max's faulty record of the facts, underreading and misreading, which concern the reliability of his perception, and underregarding and misregarding, which relate to his questionable ethical interpretation. Furthermore, key features of Max's diseased narrative include his deliberate manipulation of narrative perspective and his employment of a strategy of obscuration, both of which allow him to withhold from the reader his true relationship to and motivations for his crimes.

In the first of the novel's six books, Max describes his childhood and youth in Wieshalle, focusing in particular on his intense friendship with Itzig

Finkelstein, the son of the Jewish barber, Chaim Finkelstein. Chaim accepts Max as an affiliated member of the Finkelstein family, teaches him Yiddish and Jewish customs, and eventually takes him on, along with Itzig, as an apprentice barber. Itzig and Max are inseparable throughout their time in school and their apprenticeship. However, in the early 1930s, Max is converted to Nazism after attending a speech by Hitler (an event that Hilsenrath satirically locates on the 'Mount of Olives' outside of Wieshalle) and joins the SS. As we then learn in the novel's second book, which takes place after the war, Max goes on to serve during the war first in the mobile killing squad known as *Einsatzgruppe D* (an actual historical unit composed of SS and Gestapo functionaries that from 1941 to 1942 killed over 90,000 civilians, most of whom were Jews, in southern Ukraine and the Crimea) and then in the fictional concentration camp Laubwalde. Max claims to have killed in this camp as many as 10,000 Jewish prisoners (Hilsenrath, 1971, p. 372), a grotesque assertion that is but one example of Max's exaggerated mode of narration. In the third book, Max, on the run as a wanted mass murderer, has himself circumcised and tattooed with an Auschwitz number and then appropriates the identity of Itzig Finkelstein, whom, as Max confesses at the end of the novel, was murdered in Laubwalde by none other than his childhood friend Max. In the last half of Hilsenrath's novel, Max travels as Itzig, under Itzig's name and in Itzig's place to Palestine (a trip financed by a sack of gold teeth looted from his victims in Laubwalde), where he helps found the Jewish state, becomes a model Israeli citizen, marries a Holocaust survivor and composes – even if only mentally – his confessional autobiography – the very text, in fact, that we have been reading all along.

By murdering Itzig, assuming Itzig's identity and living out the life that he brutally robbed of Itzig, Max commits a particularly vituperative act of identity theft, a brutal expropriation of the life of one individual that functions as a synecdoche for both his massacre of multiple victims and the Nazis' project of destroying and effacing from memory millions of European Jews. However, as I have argued elsewhere (McGlothlin, 2007, p. 233), Max's violations not only consist of the crimes he commits in the story world of the text; they also include transgressions he commits as a narrator, particularly his hubristic assumption of the victim's voice and his radical rewriting of his own murderous history as the diametrically opposite tale of survival and heroism. By inserting himself in the position of Itzig's I-narrator, Max vacates the narrative position of the perpetrator and slips into that of the victim. However, this relocation of identity from his old perpetrator-self to an invented survivor-self is not a one-time, unidirectional process. Rather, I argue that Max performs his act of identity theft repetitively and ritualistically throughout his narration, as evident in such frequent utterances as 'I, Itzig Finkelstein, at the time still Max Schulz' (Hilsenrath, 1971, p. 17), 'I, Itzig Finkelstein, alias the mass murderer Max Schulz or vice versa' (ibid., p. 297) and 'I, Itzig Finkelstein or the mass-murderer Max Schulz' (ibid.,

p. 348); with each iterative variant of this statement of cannibalized identity he performatively reproduces his original crime of murder. Moreover, not only does Max's identity go through a complex transformation over the course of the novel, his relationship to his narration changes as well. While Max occupies the position of the autodiegetic narrator for the greater part of the novel, book two, which is set in the immediate postwar period, before Max assumes Itzig's identity, is narrated by a heterodiegetic narrator who focalizes much of the action through Frau Holle, the one-legged widow of one of Max's SS comrades. However, although this book gives us an external perspective of Max, the bulk of the chapter features Max telling Frau Holle about his flight from the Red Army and Polish partisans at the end of the war. In this way, even when Max is patently absent as the diegetic narrator in this part of the novel, he is recuperated as an intradiegetic narrator and thus, in a more alienated fashion, still controls the text's narration. Andreas Graf reads this aberration in the novel's vocal structure as part of its 'pathology of narrative perspective':

> [T]he auctorial narrator of the second book is in all probability identical with the I-narrator of the other books. But his I, his self-confident manner of speaking, is temporarily missing . . . [B]y means of this detour [Max's narration to Frau Holle about his escape] the I-narration finds its way back into the text and thus significantly relativizes the auctorial diegesis, which is degraded to the status of narrative frame. (1996, p. 143, my translation)

Graf argues convincingly that the narrative anomaly of the second book represents a variant, however alienated, of Max's function as a pathological narrator. However, whereas Graf sees this aberrant narration as evidence of a gradual process in which he is able to dissolve, by means of 'a grotesque internally fictitious fiction' (ibid., p. 147, my translation), his two identities as perpetrator and survivor and forge a third, narratively constructed harmonious self, I contend that even on the narrative level, Max practises the same sort of evasion that he utilizes diegetically to circumvent punishment for his crimes. Rather than creating a new, fictive self through the 'therapeutic function of writing' (ibid., my translation), Max manipulates until the end the text's ambiguous narrative perspective, jumping reflexively and repeatedly from one narrative position to the other without either fixing permanently on one of the two poles of identity or forging a third one.

In book four, which chronicles Max's journey by sea from Europe to Palestine, Max displays his slippery vocal identity as well, alternating between the first-person singular and first-person plural and a second-person address to Itzig. However, the referent of the 'you' of the address is ambiguous; at times 'you' designates Max's former friend and his murder victim, with whom Max conducts an imagined, one-sided dialogue. At other times, however, the narrator refers to himself in the second person. Added to this Byzantine vocal structure is the fact that, in those instances in which Max's second-person address is formulated as a self-dialogue, the 'you' to which it is directed is not his Max-self, but rather his newly figured Itzig-self – the self that is produced by his cannibalization of an Other and that seems to reside uncomfortably beside or within his Max-self. In this way, although Max has incorporated Itzig's identity into his own, at the same time, on the level of pronominal reference and in the act of narration, Itzig and Max remain radically unintegrated, a condition made all the more evident by Max's disingenuous second-person address to the deceased Itzig whose identity he has hijacked. Hilsenrath's text thus demonstrates a particularly pathological and almost literal version of Bakhtin's notion of double-voiced discourse (Bakhtin, 1981, p. 324), whereby Max not only claims two speaking selves, one of which has devoured the identity of the other, but also, with his second-person narration, reproduces this cannibalization with his address to himself.

Given the already established vocal promiscuity of *Der Nazi und der Friseur*, it should perhaps not be surprising to us that Max should avail himself of the expanded possibilities for evasion provided by second-person narration, which, as Brian Richardson argues, 'is admirably suited to express the unstable nature and intersubjective constitution of the self' (2006, p. 36) and in particular is adept at 'revealing a mind in flux', 'disclosing the sense of intimate unfamiliarity present' in an addled brain, and indicating 'suppressed subjectivity and silenced speech' (ibid., pp. 35–6). By virtue of its highly constructed, artificial and mutable mode and because, as Richardson argues, 'its very essence is to eschew a fixed essence' (ibid., p. 19), second-person narration seems tailor-made for Max, a narrator who is nothing if not polymorphic and synthetic. The 'you' of his narration in the fourth book is as unstable and protean as the 'I' in the rest of the novel.

In my analysis of *Der Nazi und der Friseur*, the narrative situation thus functions as an analogue to the novel's plot, reproducing on the text's narrative level the interminable processes of equivocal transmutation and escape that Max undergoes as a character. In the end, Max's 'I' is a non-locatable entity, a narrative voice in flight, like the perpetrator himself, from a perspective that would unequivocally pin the self to its murderous autobiography. The pathological 'I' in Hilsenrath's text is, narratively speaking, a moving target, and as such, it functions as a filtering barrier to his consciousness, distorting with its perpetual motion the narrative interface between Max's mind and the reader who wishes to understand his autobiographical construction of his violent history. Rather than compelling the reader's identification with the perpetrator's motives, mindset and worldview, *The Nazi and the Barber* deploys the filtering strategy of Max's non-locatable 'I' to impede the reader's affective attachment to its perpetrator-protagonist. After all, in Hilsenrath's text, there is nary a narrator with whom the reader can identify; Max makes sure that, narratively speaking, there's no there there. In this way, with its heterogenous narrative strategy that exploits the ambiguities of vocal perspective and focalization, Hilsenrath's text self-consciously highlights both its construction of this filter and Max's hubristic assumption of the voice of the victim to narrate his own history of violence.

Jonathan Littell's 2006 novel *Les Bienveillantes*, which appeared in English in 2009 as *The Kindly Ones*, has been credited with providing the most detailed and direct fictional representation of the mind of the Holocaust perpetrator to date with its mimetic, first-person narrative of another Max – in this case, Maximilien Aue, also an SS officer. The superficial resemblance between Hilsenrath's text and Littell's novel remains at the level of the name and military membership, however, for Littell's text avoids Hilsenrath's satirical stance in favour of a more realistic depiction of the SS officer's story. *The Kindly Ones* has won France's Prix Goncourt and the prize of the Académie Française, but reception of the work has been mixed. Critics in France, Germany, the United States and England have both praised and criticized the novel for being the first 'real' attempt at an intimate representation of the perpetrator's mind. Such claims that the novel provides an innovative depiction of the Holocaust perpetrator are prompted not only by Littell's mimetic approach, but also by the apparent absence of a filtering device, such as Hilsenrath's satirical portrayal of the Holocaust through the voice of a radically dissociated I-narrator. However, *The Kindly Ones* also employs some very complex narrative strategies, some of which operate as filtering mechanisms. Chief among these is the novel's prohibitive length of almost 1,000 pages, which, with its sheer mass of repetitive detail and extended discourse, numbs the reader and paradoxically serves at times to screen the narrator's consciousness. Moreover, the novel contains a number of different narrative discourses and epistemologies (which, alongside a documentary-style narration of historical events, include ethical reflections, dreams, fantasies, hallucinations and repressed material) that not only compete with each other for the reader's attention but also to a certain extent contradict each other and call into question the narrator's reliability and truth claims as a whole. Littell's complex narrative approach thus foregrounds its construction of particular filtering strategies in its representation of its perpetrator-protagonist, demonstrating perhaps how fictional narratives of perpetration require a certain intermediary filter as an interface between historical and imaginative discourse.

The first and most prominent of the narrative discourses in the novel is Aue's eyewitness account of his experiences in the war and in the genocide of the Jews. Aue is the ideal figure through which to represent a first-hand account of the Holocaust, for, as a member of the SD branch of the SS, he is a witness to and participant in a number of events: he serves in Ukraine in *Einsatzkommando 4a* and takes part in the mass execution of Jews at Babi Yar; he is present in Stalingrad during the final days of the siege, where he suffers a traumatic head injury and nearly dies; he is charged with improving the survival rate and labour potential of prisoners in a number of camps in occupied Poland, including Auschwitz, in which capacity he interacts with important historical figures such as Heinrich Himmler, Adolf Eichmann and Albert Speer; he is involved in the mass roundups of Hungarian Jews in 1944; he witnesses the death marches from Auschwitz in January 1945; and he experiences the Soviet advance in Pomerania and the fall of Berlin. He thus functions in the narrative as the ideal eyewitness who is present at some of the most important events of the war and the Final Solution. Moreover, for the most part he reports on these historical events honestly and in great detail, referring to himself as 'a veritable memory factory' (Littell, 2009, p. 4). Although he occasionally deflects responsibility for crimes committed during the war and indulges in self-justification, he appears to be as forthcoming as possible about his own participation in the genocide of the Jews without resorting to either sanctimonious contrition or myopic self-pity. As the much older narrating Aue tells us at the beginning of his account: 'I am not pleading *Befehl[s]notstand*, the just-obeying-orders so highly valued by our good German lawyers. What I did, I did with my eyes open, believing that it was my duty and that it had to be done, disagreeable or unpleasant as it may have been' (ibid., p. 18). We are thus dealing with a narrator who not only was witness to what Susan Rubin Suleiman designates 'the two spheres of activity – the killing by the *Einsatzgruppen* (mobile killing units) in the Soviet Union, and the system of the extermination camps in Poland – [that] can be said to constitute the essence of the historical event we know as the Holocaust' (2009, p. 6) but who also, in long ethical and philosophical passages, courageously tries to explain as best he can the how and why of his participation in these crimes. Suleiman argues that 'this combination of participant status with historical reliability, and with what I call moral witnessing, which Aue possesses, is a new phenomenon in fiction' (ibid., p. 5). Thus we, as readers who have heretofore likely observed the events of the Holocaust chiefly through the eyes of the survivor-witnesses, must learn to rely on the perpetrator as our main witness to the events of the Holocaust, a dependence that, while necessary in the context of the novel, is bound to cause anxiety and scepticism.

Littell's text repeatedly underscores Aue's function as the historical eyewitness whose experience is expressed in frequent references to the act of seeing, especially in the first half of the novel, which chronicles Aue's experiences in Ukraine and the Caucasus. In fact, it seems as if Aue himself – both the narrating self from his postwar vantage point and the former self he recounts – regards his primary duty as being to witness, to visually register the events that unfold before his eyes. Just a few pages into his account, he arrives in Lutsk and is forced to view a thousand corpses left behind by the retreating Soviets; this is his first glimpse of mass violence. He describes his reaction thus: 'I wanted to close my eyes, or put my hand over my eyes, and at the same time I wanted to look, to look as much as I could, and by looking, try to understand, this incomprehensible thing, there, in front of me, this void for human thought' (Littell, 2009, p. 34). Later, describing an *Aktion* in which the *Einsatzkommando* shoots a group of about 150 Ukrainian Jews, he admits:

> Now we were killing them. And undeniably, we were killing a lot of people. That seemed atrocious to me, even if it was inevitable and necessary. But one has to confront atrocity; one must always be ready to look inevitability and necessity in the face, and accept the consequences that result from them; closing your eyes is never the answer. (Ibid., p. 81)

Because of Aue's refusal to close his eyes to the atrocities that he observes and then later commits, he is thus able to provide for us an account of events in which there were no Jewish survivors in an eyewitness mode Jason Burke (2009) calls 'narrative photo-realism'.

Aue's narrative mode of historical witnessing and thoughtful reflection, however, while the dominant discourse in Littell's text, comprises only part of the novel. Alongside his painstaking documentary account of the Final Solution exists another narrative, that of Aue's personal and sexual relationships, encompassing in particular his hatred of his mother, his incestuous childhood relationship with his twin sister and his continued obsession with her, and his periodic anonymous and furtive homosexual encounters, which he claims he engages in as a substitute for sex with his sister. In this part of his narration, Aue relates in particularly graphic detail both true and fantasized sexual and violent encounters that become more scatological, erotogenic and grotesque over the course of the novel. This account of Aue's emotional and sexual life, to which the narrator turns recurrently in intervals between descriptions of the larger historical events in which he participates, functions as a counterpart to the historical narrative. However, these interludes occur not just on the level of storytelling; for not only does Aue the narrator suspend his documentary discourse to shift to an account of his personal life, but Aue the actor also periodically withdraws from the historical action and retreats to locations significant for his personal life, such as the south of France, where his mother and stepfather live, and Pomerania, the location of the family estate of his sister's husband. This last locale, to which an entire chapter is devoted near the end of the book, functions as the site of the escalation of the sexual/personal narrative, in which Aue indulges in extended graphic fantasies of his sister, masturbates constantly, and, as he himself describes it, succumbs to 'the demented vision of a perfect coprophagic autarky' (Littell, 2009, p. 886). Much of the criticism of the novel has been directed at this narrative, for reviewers see it as somehow detracting from or even trivializing the larger historical narrative of the Holocaust. At the same time, however, scholarly assessments by Susan Rubin Suleiman and

Liran Razinsky have argued that Littell explicitly turns to the French literary style of excess and transgression in the tradition of Sade, Bataille and Genet as a counterpoint to the larger historical narrative; according to Razinsky, 'historical details are metabolized through Aue's deranged sexuality' (2008, p. 75) and Aue's perspective represents 'a brilliant push to the extreme, *ad absurdum* even, of something of the nature of the Holocaust itself, and of the idea of testimony bound with it' (ibid., p. 80). In this way, Littell's novel performs, on the narrative level, the excess and abjection that characterize the logic of the extreme violence inherent in the genocide.

Alongside these two larger narrative discourses in Littell's novel, namely the historical–documentary and the personal–sexual, I locate a third order of discourse as well: the discourse of dreams, hallucinations and repressed knowledge, which is especially connected to the personal narrative and, like it, gains traction particularly in the latter part of the novel. Not only is Aue shockingly transgressive in his desires, fantasies and sexual proclivities, but he also gradually begins to lose a grip on reality when his fantasies slide into all-out hallucinations, which he narrates as if they were real. The chapter describing his stay in Pomerania, in fact, can be characterized as one long hallucination from which he emerges only sporadically into consciousness. Moreover, his gradual inability to distinguish between reality and fantasy also extends to a limited extent to his memory; although he is able to remember conversations, dates and historical details with apparently perfect recall, with regard to his personal life a few instances occur when he admits to us that some of his memories, especially of his sister, are dubious. Finally, he (and here I refer to both the narrating and the narrated self) represses important knowledge about his personal life altogether; knowledge of which we, as readers, become gradually aware. Chief among these repressions is his brutal murder of his mother and stepfather, which takes place midway through the novel when, on recovery leave for his Stalingrad injury, he visits them in the south of France. Although he is investigated for these crimes throughout the rest of the novel by two persistent Berlin detectives (the furies alluded to in the novel's title), he remains resolutely unaware of the fact that he committed the crime. Moreover, although it finally occurs to him late in the novel that the twin boys who were living with his mother and stepfather during this visit (children they claim are the sons of friends) are actually his sister's children, he never acknowledges the fact that he is likely their father. These instances of hallucinations and repressions thus seriously compromise Aue's status for us as a reliable narrator, at least when it comes to his personal life. But does this unreliability call into question his apparent honesty about his participation in Holocaust crimes? Susan Rubin Suleiman argues that, while the novel flirts with this danger, it does not succumb to it: 'By having Aue – at least the conscious, narrating Aue – remain dissociated from his act [the murder of his mother and stepfather] to the very end, Littell can preserve him as a reliable witness to the Holocaust, even while his memory hole about the family murder demonstrates the human ability to block out unbearable actions' (2009, p. 18). In my opinion, however, the situation is more complex than Suleiman characterizes it, for Aue's murder of his family, while the text's major memory hole, is not the only one, nor do his dissociations remain exclusively in the personal narrative. Rather, as I see it, the discourse of hallucinations occasionally infects the historical eyewitness discourse, which necessarily complicates the larger historical narrative and the documentary effect it produces.

Although most of Aue's hallucinations occur in the personal/sexual narrative, there are a few instances in which they extend to his historical discourse as well, especially to his role as eyewitness. After his head injury in Stalingrad,[3] which is caused by a bullet, he writes that he experiences a new way of seeing that allows him to perceive truths that are not visible to conventional modes of apprehension:

> I had the feeling that the hole in my forehead had opened up a third eye, a pineal eye, one not turned to the sun, not capable of contemplating the blinding light of the sun, but directed at the darkness, gifted with the power of looking at the bare face of death, and of grasping this face behind each face of flesh and blood, beneath the smiles, through the palest, healthiest skin, the most laughing eyes. (Littell, 2009, p. 443)

By attributing his new mode of vision to a pineal, or third, eye, Aue accesses here a number of discourses in both Eastern and Western spiritual traditions that attribute heightened awareness, spiritual and psychological perception and clairvoyance to an inner eye. Aue's pineal eye, which allows him to see 'through the opacity of things' (ibid., p. 470) to their essence, in particular to their dark, almost evil distillate, remains with him throughout the rest of the narrative, and one could argue that it – meaning this change of consciousness that results from his head injury – is what causes his sexual hallucinations, which occur in abundance only in the second half of the novel. Importantly, however, his first extended perception with his pineal eye happens not with his fantasies of his sister, but occurs rather in his historical testimony when, during his recovery leave, he attends a speech given by Hitler, a scene that the narrator describes at length. When Hitler enters the room, Aue is shocked to see him clothed in the ritual garments of the Orthodox Jew, complete with *tallis*, *tefillin* and *peyes*. He notices immediately that he is the only one to perceive Hitler's apparel, for the prominent Nazi leaders present show no special reaction to the speech. Describing his dismay at the time, the narrator writes:

> Maybe, I said to myself, panic-stricken, it's the story of the Emperor's New Clothes: everyone sees how it really is, but hides it, counting on his neighbor

to do the same. No, I reasoned, I must be hallucinating, with a wound like mine, that's entirely possible. Yet I felt perfectly sound of mind. I was far from the platform, though, and the Führer was lit from the side; maybe it was simply an optical illusion? But I still saw it. Maybe my 'pineal eye' was playing a trick on me? But there was nothing dreamlike about it. It was also possible that I had gone mad. (Ibid., p. 467)

This passage raises important questions. What are we to do with this hallucination? What does Aue see here with his pineal eye that can't be penetrated by the gazes of the other observers? Are we to believe that he is really penetrating to Hitler's essence, which in this case would confirm the long-standing rumours of Hitler's possible Jewish ancestry? Or does Littell parody here the novel's dominantly documentary approach by having the narrative break down in its representation of Hitler, the transcendental signifier for Holocaust perpetration in particular and evil in general? I think there may be something to this last question, especially given that, at the end of the novel, in the last days of the war, Littell has Aue bite Hitler's nose as the latter awards the former a German Cross in Gold, an action that either represents Aue's complete breakdown as narrator or character (or both) or Littell's last laugh at our attempts to reconcile such events with the novel's predominantly historical reliability. But aside from these questions and the representation of Hitler in the novel, what is significant here is the novel's characterization of vision and seeing and how Aue transforms from the reliable documentary eyewitness he was in the first part of the novel to a witness who misperceives reality in his search for the essence or meaning behind things. It's unclear, however, whether this transformation of Aue's vision, which serves as a filter to documentary discourse, is inherently detrimental to the goals of the novel. Perhaps the novel suggests here that Aue's altered mode of seeing and the hallucinations it causes allow for a fresh perspective from which we can regard the Holocaust. Or perhaps they offer an alternative to conventional historical discourse, for each mode of vision has its appeal in particular epistemological inquiries; the documentary is important for ascertaining historical truth, while the search for the essential meaning behind historical fact is critical for determining a more existential truth. By having Aue embody both sorts of vision, Littell's novel attempts to travel the roads of both historical truth and imaginative representation, which is a difficult, though not entirely impossible, journey.

In my reading, *The Kindly Ones* thus commences with an apparent absence of filtering strategies and then gradually accumulates them with the extreme friction between the various narrative discourses and with Aue's increasing unreliability as a narrator. Not only does the text vascillate between the documentary–historical and what Daniel Mendelsohn (2009) calls the 'mythic/

sexual', but Aue as a narrator also meanders between these different discursive levels in a movement not dissimilar to Max Schulz's frenetic ping-ponging between vocal positions in *The Nazi and the Barber*. This deviant narrative practice seals Aue's unreliability and causes us to at least question his apparent honesty about his participation in Holocaust crimes. If at first Maximilien Aue, in contrast to Max Schulz, provides an honest and accurate retrospective perspective on his experience (a narrative authority Littell's novel takes pains – along with profuse pages – to establish at the beginning), he gradually loses his status as the narrative's reliable orientation point and ends up, not unlike Max Schulz, dissociated from the narrative perspective he purports to represent. In this way, one might consider Aue's narration, like that of Hilsenrath's narrator, to be pathological. Although I do not endorse Michiko Kakutani's (2009) scathing assessment of Littell's book, I do agree with her assertion that Littell creates in Aue a monster. As the novel constructs it, however, Aue's monstrousness is not a quality that inheres in his identity or behaviour as a Holocaust perpetrator (conduct that is, in the context of *The Kindly Ones*, one of the less shocking experiences in Aue's history); rather, it emerges over the course of the novel in his increasingly aberrant narrative function.

Aue's narratorial decomposition provokes a number of critical questions. Why does our candid narrator, who is forthright about the details of his participation in genocide and other crimes, devolve into an incoherent monster through the process of narrating? In other words, why does Littell, who takes such care to illuminate the consciousness of his protagonist, transform his representation of a perpetrator who is frank about his thoughts and motivations into the overused trope of the perpetrator as incomprehensible Other and mythically insane beast? Why does this much-acclaimed direct view into the mind of the perpetrator automatically degenerate into the obscuration of its object? The question that my reading of Littell's and Hilsenrath's novels raises is ultimately thus: Are the filtering strategies I have identified in *The Nazi and the Barber* and *The Kindly Ones* ineluctable elements in autodiegetic narratives of Holocaust perpetration? One might well posit an answer to this question by imagining a novel that takes a radically opposed approach to that of Littell and Hilsenrath, namely one that reduces all possible distance between the narrator and the reader and encourages rather than frustrates full identification with the perpetrator. Such a text might indeed succeed at historicizing the cultural image of the Holocaust perpetrator, relocating him from the realm of myth into the sphere of human action and responsibility and allowing the reader to imagine that she, too, might, under similar circumstances, become involved in the perpetration of genocide. But such a novel would also run the real risk of encouraging the reader to assume the character's mental framework and to take on not only his ethical values, but also his understanding of his participation in the Holocaust. By conjuring a highly mimetic representation of the perpetrator unmitigated by oppositional formal strategies, such a narrative would be unable to sustain any ethical or critical perspective external to the events he describes. Assuming, of course, that for writers and readers who share an interest in understanding the scope and nature of the Holocaust, including the role of the perpetrators, such an outcome is to be strenuously avoided, strategies for representing perpetrators in a manner that encourages critical reading are indispensable.

As temporal distance from the events of the Holocaust increases, writers have increasingly turned to alternative modes of representation in an attempt to find fresh, heretofore unexamined points of entry into the topic and to puncture the sanctified aura that often characterizes public discourse about the Holocaust. One such innovative approach, as I have demonstrated, is the fictional portrayal of the inner life of perpetrators, a strategy that raises serious questions about the role of reader identification in such transgressive narratives. By utilizing narrative devices that serve to suppress, conceal or camouflage their characters' violent consciousness, these texts effectively impede the kinds of identification initially promised by the intimate rendering of the perpetrators' subjective thoughts. As I argue, the complex operations of revelation and occlusion made possible through filtering techniques allow the texts to involve the reader in carefully controlled exercises in identification. In this way, they enable the reader to engage in complex negotiations with the history of the Holocaust without allowing her to fully and uncritically identify with the perpetrator and his actions and emotions.

Notes

1. Reader identification is a complex issue that can refer to a number of distinct but related phenomena, including the reader's readiness to view the events of the narrative through the eyes of the narrator-protagonist and to exclude alternate points of view, her belief in the narrator's version of the events (an identification that is then related to issues of narrative reliability), the degree of her emotional identification with the narrator's thoughts, feelings and interpretations of the events, and her alignment with the narrator's moral and ethical worldview and his justifications for his own behaviour.
2. Helmut Braun, the original German publisher of *Der Nazi und der Friseur*, gives an excellent overview of its convoluted publication history in German, which he attributes generally to the calcified public discourse about the Holocaust in West Germany in the 1960s and early 1970s and more specifically to a rigid and reflexive philo-Semitism on the part of the German publishing industry.
3. Luc Rasson argues that Aue's experience at Stalingrad effects a decisive shift in his narratorial function, whereby he transforms from a reliable narrator into an unreliable one (2012, p. 107).

Works Cited

Adams, J. (2011), 'Reading (as) violence in Jonathan Littell's *The Kindly Ones'*, in J. Adams and S. Vice (eds), *Representing Perpetrators in Holocaust Literature and Film*. Special issue of *Holocaust Studies: A Journal of Culture and History*, 17.2–3, 27–50.

Améry, J. (1980), *At the Mind's Limits: Contemplations by a Survivor on Auschwitz and Its Realities*, trans. S. Rosenfeld and S. P. Rosenfeld. Bloomington: Indiana University Press.

Bakhtin, M. (1981), 'Discourse in the novel', in *The Dialogic Imagination: Four Essays*, trans. M. Holquist and C. Emerson. Austin: University of Texas Press, pp. 259–422.

Barjonet, A. and Razinsky, L. (2012), 'Introduction', in A. Barjonet and L. Razinsky (eds), *Writing the Holocaust Today: Critical Perspectives on Jonathan Littell's* The Kindly Ones. Amsterdam: Editions Rodopi, pp. 7–16.

Binet, L. (2012), *HHhH*. New York: Farrar, Straus and Giroux.

Braun, H. (2005), 'Entstehungs- und Publikationsgeschichte des Romans *Der Nazi & der Friseur'*, in H. Braun (ed.), *Verliebt in die deutsche Sprache: Die Odyssee des Edgar Hilsenrath*. Berlin: Dittrich Verlag, pp. 41–9.

Browning, C. (1992), *Ordinary Men: Reserve Police Battalion 101 and the Final Solution in Poland*. New York: HarperCollins.

Burke, J. (2009), Review of *The Kindly Ones* by Jonathan Littell, www.guardian.co.uk/books/2009/feb/22/history-holocaust-books-jonathan-littell?INTCMP=SRCH. Accessed 25 October 2013.

Delbo, C. (1995), *Auschwitz and After*, trans. R. C. Lamont. New Haven: Yale University Press.

Graf, A. (1996), 'Mörderisches Ich: zur Pathologie der Erzählperspektive in Edgar Hilsenrath's Roman *Der Nazi und der Friseur'*, in T. Kraft (ed.), *Edgar Hilsenrath: Das Unerzählbare erzählen*. Munich: Piper, pp. 135–49.

Hilsenrath, E. (1971), *The Nazi and the Barber*, trans. A. White. Garden City, NY: Doubleday.

—. [1977] (2004), *Der Nazi und der Friseur*. Munich: Deutscher Taschenbuch Verlag.

Höss, R. (1992), *Death Dealer: The Memoirs of the SS Kommandant at Auschwitz*, ed. S. Paskuly, trans. A. Pollinger. Buffalo, NY: Prometheus Books.

—. (1958), *Kommandant in Auschwitz: Autobiographische Aufzeichnungen*, ed. Martin Broszat. Stuttgart: Deutsche Verlags-Anstalt.

Kakutani, M. (2009), 'Unrepentant and telling of horrors untellable', *New York Times*, 24 February 2009, www.nytimes.com/2009/02/24/books/24kaku.html?_r=0. Accessed 25 October 2013.

Keen, S. (2007), *Empathy and the Novel*. Oxford: Oxford University Press.

Klüger, R. (2001), *Still Alive: A Holocaust Girlhood Remembered*. New York: Feminist Press/City University of New York.

von Koppenfels, M. (2012), 'The infamous "I": notes on Littell and Céline', in A. Barjonet and L. Razinsky (eds), *Writing the Holocaust Today: Critical Perspectives on Jonathan Littell's* The Kindly Ones. Amsterdam: Editions Rodopi, pp. 133–52.

Levi, P. (1959), *If This Is a Man*, trans. S. Woolf. New York: Orion.

Littell, J. (2006), *Les Bienveillantes*. Paris: Gallimard.

—. (2009), *The Kindly Ones*, trans. C. Mandell. New York: Harper.

MacMillan, I. (1999), *Village of a Million Spirits: A Novel of the Treblinka Uprising*. South Royalton, VT: Steerforth.

McGlothlin, E. (2007), 'Narrative transgression in Edgar Hilsenrath's *Der Nazi und der Friseur* and the rhetoric of the sacred in Holocaust discourse', *The German Quarterly*, 80.2, 220–39.

—. (2010), 'Theorizing the perpetrator in Bernhard Schlink's *The Reader* and Martin Amis's *Time's Arrow*', in R. C. Spargo and R. M. Ehrenreich (eds), *After Representation? The Holocaust, Literature, and Culture*. New Brunswick, NJ: Rutgers University Press, pp. 210–30.

Mendelsohn, D. (2009), 'Transgression', *New York Review of Books*, 56.5, 26 March 2009, www.nybooks.com/articles/archives/2009/mar/26/transgression/. Accessed 25 October 2013.

Phelan, J. (2005), *Living to Tell About It: A Rhetoric and Ethics of Character Narration*. Ithaca, NY: Cornell University Press.

Rasson, L. (2012), 'How Nazis undermine their own point of view: irony and reliability in *The Kindly Ones*', in A. Barjonet and L. Razinsky (eds), *Writing the Holocaust Today: Critical Perspectives on Jonathan Littell's* The Kindly Ones. Amsterdam: Editions Rodopi, pp. 97–110.

Razinsky, L. (2008), 'History, excess and testimony in Jonathan Littell's *Les Bienveillantes*', *French Forum*, 33.3, 69–87.

Richardson, B. (2006), *Unnatural Voices: Extreme Narration in Modern and Contemporary Fiction*. Columbus: Ohio State University Press.

Skopp, D. (2010), *Shadows Walking*. [n.p.]: Createspace.

Suleiman, S. Rubin (2009), 'When the perpetrator becomes a reliable witness of the Holocaust: on Jonathan Littell's *Les bienveillantes*', *New German Critique*, 36.1, 1–19.

Tournier, M. (1972), *The Ogre*. New York: Doubleday.

Weissman, G. (2004), *Fantasies of Witnessing: Postwar Efforts to Experience the Holocaust*. Ithaca, NY: Cornell University Press.

Wiesel, E. (1960), *Night*, trans. S. Rodway. New York: Hill and Wang.

9 Holocaust Literature and the Taboo

Matthew Boswell

Abstract

This chapter considers taboos that have developed in and around Holocaust literature, focusing on controversial, fictional responses to the Holocaust, with a particular emphasis on the representation of perpetrators. All of the writers discussed draw on the psychoanalytic theory of Sigmund Freud, and this chapter takes Freud's reading of social taboos as a model for interpreting transgressive forms of historical representation and cultural practice, arguing that the proscription of certain forms of Holocaust representation constitutes an attempt to foreclose responses to the genocide that are particularly difficult to articulate or deal with, such as the 'fascination of Fascism', the ordinariness of perpetrator identities, and ambivalent attitudes towards the dead. It makes a case for the value of novels and poems which engage with truths about our relationship with history that are never straightforwardly empirical, arguing that they are fundamental to what the Germans term 'working through' or 'dealing with' (*Vergangenheitsbewältigung*) the knowledge and cultural legacy of the Holocaust.

Histories of What Cannot Be Said

Described by the experimental psychologist Wilhelm Wundt as 'the oldest unwritten code of law of humanity', a taboo stipulates that certain persons or things are to be avoided: they are off limits, neither to be touched nor named (Freud, [1919] 1938, p. 42). The ways these unwritten laws are made manifest are varied and complex: taboos influence the social and cultural codes that govern individual behaviour, such as ethics; they provide emotive reference points for the media and political propaganda; and they affect individual and group psychology. However, they are never enshrined in formal legislation, which marks the point at which a prohibition ceases to be taboo and instead becomes law. Sigmund Freud's pioneering work in *Totem and Taboo* ([1919] 1938), which draws on Wundt's earlier research, is of particular significance for the psychological understanding of the taboo, exploring the deeply rooted origins of the fears that cause certain subjects and people to become stigmatized in this way. In this study, Freud examines the hold that taboos exerted on primitive societies and 'savage' races, recognizing in their psychic life 'a well-preserved, early stage of our own development' (ibid., p. 15). Paying particular attention to ancient tribal rites and customs, he identifies some of the key characteristics of the taboo, including a paradox at the heart of its symbolic logic:

> Taboo is a Polynesian word, the translation of which provides difficulties for us because we no longer possess the idea which it connotes. . . . For us the meaning of taboo branches off into two opposite directions. On the one hand it means to us sacred, consecrated: but on the other it means uncanny, dangerous, forbidden, and unclean. The opposite for taboo is designated in Polynesian by the word *noa* and signifies something ordinary and generally accessible. Thus something like the concept of reserve inheres in taboo; taboo expresses itself essentially in prohibitions and restrictions. Our combination of 'holy dread' would often express the meaning of taboo. (Ibid., p. 41)

This chapter considers taboos that have developed in and around Holocaust literature. While steering clear of Freudian readings of the unconscious motivations of authors, it recognizes that many controversial literary responses to the Holocaust have stemmed from a considered engagement with Freud's work and with psychoanalysis more broadly. This chapter also draws on Freud's understanding of the taboo as an internally conflicted structure that discloses polarized beliefs about the forbidden object, considering how taboos around Holocaust representation contain traces of this duality and its associated language. And so, for example, while non-victims have been repeatedly exhorted to remember and reflect on the Holocaust, they have also been subject to a forceful ban on representation that echoes the Old Testament commandment outlawing 'graven images', as in the charge made by the survivor and writer Elie Wiesel: 'A novel about Treblinka is either not a novel or not about Treblinka. A novel about Majdanek is about blasphemy. *Is* blasphemy' (1990, p. 7). Wiesel's comments were made at a time, in the late 1970s, when blasphemy was proving exceptionally popular, with the Holocaust and Nazism becoming dominant historical subjects in mainstream literary culture. This chapter will therefore also explore the psychological forces and social formations that tend towards this type of taboo-transgression because, as Freud observes, the unwritten rules associated with the taboo are not made to be broken in any old arbitrary sense: they exist because we already wish to break them:

> If taboo expresses itself mainly in prohibitions it may well be considered self-evident . . . that it is based on a positive, desireful impulse. For what nobody desires to do does not need to be forbidden, and certainly what is expressly forbidden must be an object of desire. ([1919] 1938, p. 115)

Many of the works discussed in this chapter acknowledge that their historical subject matter forms an 'object of desire', often drawing on psychoanalytic interpretations of human behaviour to explore the origins of their will to transgress.

Finally, just as Freud suggests that taboos repress the psychological material of the unconscious, which should be regarded as all the more fundamental for the fact that it is considered unspeakable, this chapter argues that the taboo in Holocaust literature constitutes an attempt to foreclose responses to the Holocaust that are difficult to articulate and deal with. These responses include things like the 'fascination of Fascism' (to paraphrase Susan Sontag (1975)), the ordinariness and even attractiveness of perpetrator identities, and ambivalent attitudes towards the dead. While Holocaust taboos are generally aimed at ensuring that factual historical truths are safeguarded against falsification – Wiesel's mistrust of the Holocaust novel being a case in point – this chapter acknowledges a body of literature that treads a knowingly provocative path between the sacred and the profane in order to engage with another set of equally disturbing truths, yielding illicit meanings, anxieties and forms of knowledge that are never straightforwardly empirical. It makes a case for those 'blasphemous' novels and poems about places like Majdanek and Treblinka precisely because they *are* novels and poems, arguing that texts which might appear, on the surface, to be crude, offensive or factually misleading, are not always as gratuitous or misdirected as they might seem. Rather, they are fundamental to what the Germans term 'working through' or 'dealing with' (*Vergangenheitsbewältigung*) the knowledge and cultural legacy of the Holocaust, helping to construct meaningful relationships between history, individual subjectivities (those of perpetrators, victims and non-victims) and the wider national, political and cultural contexts in which they are written.

In a sense, the Holocaust has always been a taboo subject. During the war, civilians lived alongside a vast infrastructure of camps, ghettos, deportation centres and train lines, yet rarely spoke out. In the prologue to his collection of essays *The Drowned and the Saved*, the Auschwitz survivor Primo Levi writes that the exterminatory system of the *univers concentrationnaire* was 'not a closed universe' ([1986] 1996, p. 5). While recognizing 'the enormity and therefore the non-credibility of what took place in the Lagers', he points to the regular

contact between industrial companies and the camps they supplied with building materials, uniforms, food, poison gas and crematoria ovens (ibid., pp. 2, 5).
Mass murder became tantamount to a 'public secret', illustrating how the taboo
can become an instrument of politics and how forcibly its edicts can be felt in a
terroristic totalitarian system such as National Socialism, where unspoken laws
are just as important as formal legislation.[1]

In the camps themselves, the basic humanity of the victims was also designated taboo, with the prisoners being treated as 'units', tattooed with a number
and never referred to by name. Even after liberation, the extreme dehumanization of the victims extended to the survivors' sense of themselves and their condition *as* victims. Levi identifies the 'feeling of shame or guilt' experienced by
prisoners who had had to endure 'filth, promiscuity and destitution', stealing
food to survive, living for months and years at an 'animal level', and who now
had to live with 'the consciousness of having been diminished' (ibid., p. 56).
Many survivors would not be able to confront their experiences or bear witness until many years later and even those who, like Levi, began writing about
the camps almost straight away, initially found it difficult to find a readership.
When Levi's classic account of his imprisonment in Auschwitz-Birkenau, *If This
Is a Man*, was published in 1947 in a run of 2,500 copies, some 600 unsold copies
were stored in a warehouse in Florence, where they were destroyed by a flood
in 1969 (ibid., p. 137). Levi himself is sanguine about this latency period, ascrib-
ing it to a 'desirable and normal' process whereby 'historical events acquire
their chiaroscuro and perspective only some decades after their conclusion'
(ibid., p. 8). Yet the relative paucity of Holocaust testimony in the immediate
postwar period seems suggestive of traumatic as well as normative memory
processes, with the taboo nature of these memories leaving individual survivors struggling to find the words with which to describe their experiences, and
society reluctant to confront what had happened.

By the mid-1950s cultural recognition of Jewish victimhood had to some
degree broadened following the publication of the English translation of *Anne
Frank: The Diary of a Young Girl* ([1952] 1997) and its socially palatable adaptation
for stage and film. Some years later, major testimonial works from the camps
such as *If This Is a Man* ([1958] 1996) and Wiesel's *Night* ([1958] 1981) were translated into English, and at the landmark trial of Adolf Eichmann in Jerusalem
in 1961 extensive first-hand victim testimony was heard in court and widely
reported by the world's media for the first time. When an American television
mini-series called *Holocaust* was broadcast in 1978, over three decades after the
liberation of the camps, the ultimate taboo was finally lifted, in that the crime
now at least had a name.

The increased public visibility of the Holocaust over these three decades
did not, however, mean that the genocide became entirely free from a relationship with the taboo. With the experience of victimhood increasingly forming

poignant subject matter for films and television programmes, novels, poems and plays, the taboo that surrounded Holocaust representation simply shifted polarities. The victims were no longer ostracized; rather, they spoke with authority from the 'inside' of a genocide that came to be regarded as a taboo subject for those on the 'outside' who were not there, enshrining the Holocaust in a kind of inverse metaphysic whereby hell on earth came to be figured as holy ground. Holocaust taboos in literature thereafter revolved around issues of transgression, aesthetics and representational ethics: if the memory of the Holocaust was authorized through the 'sacred texts' of the witnesses, many believed that the burgeoning 'Holocaust industry', driven by the imaginations of non-victims and corporate profit, constituted a violation that was variously construed as an offence against God or a newly emergent ethical code.

Throughout the 1970s and 1980s Wiesel and other authoritative public figures pointed to the representational inadequacy – indeed, the representational *travesty* – of imaginative literary responses to the genocide. Drawing attention to its unprecedented extremity, they argued that the Holocaust was unique – 'the most radical form of genocide encountered in history', according to Saul Friedlander (1992, p. 3), 'the worst of all crimes to have been or ever to be committed', according to the filmmaker Claude Lanzmann (2007a, p. 30) – and demanded that culture confront its own inadequacy. Employing the metaphysical terminology so often used to inscribe taboos, debate frequently centred on whether silence constituted a more fitting and articulate rendering of this limit event, carrying a weight of meaning that could not be conveyed by language. Even those who did not proscribe literary description of the Holocaust still tended to champion writing that adopted an ethos of anti-representation, where authors avoided vivid description of the most harrowing aspects of the extermination. Friedlander cites Ida Fink's short stories and Lanzmann's documentary *Shoah*, which eschews archival footage, as offering 'a feeling of relative "adequacy" in bringing the reader and viewer to insights about the Shoah':

> A common denominator appears: the exclusion of straight, documentary realism, but the use of some sort of *allusive or distanced realism*. Reality is there, in its starkness, but perceived through a filter: that of memory (distance in time), that of spatial displacement, that of some sort of narrative margin which leaves the unsayable unsaid. (1992, p. 17)

This developing theory of anti-representation modified the earlier dialectic of 'inside' and 'outside', survivor and non-victim, by cutting across the category of authorial biography. Recognizing that non-victims might represent the Holocaust, judgements about representational adequacy now came to rest on the perceived value of different aesthetic strategies, with variants of restrained and respectful anti-representation being set against more experimental or shocking forms of representation. The anti-representation tradition dominated theoretical writing on the Holocaust throughout the latter part of the twentieth century, canonizing the likes of Paul Celan, Aharon Appelfeld and W. G. Sebald, yet this chapter will trace the emergence of a heterogeneous counter-tradition made up of writers who were prepared to represent the Holocaust in more controversial and explicit ways, wilfully exceeding the 'decent' limits of representation in a manner that suggests that creative responses to the Nazi genocide will never be as governable or reverent as we might like. Representational taboos have not prevented these writers from exploring subjects such as memory and identity in the context of the Holocaust; on the contrary, dealing with such taboos has become central to their representational logic, with their postmodern concern with notions of 'truth' meaning that they often find positive value in acts of taboo-transgression.

Death and the Unconscious: 'Daddy' and *The White Hotel*

Sylvia Plath's 'Daddy', published in her posthumous collection *Ariel* (1965), is one of the most notorious works of Holocaust representation by a non-victim. It takes the form of a dramatic monologue spoken by, in Plath's words, 'a girl with an Electra complex. Her father died while she thought he was God' (1989b, p. 293). The speaker's father and husband share a Nazi identity and she links herself to the victims of the Holocaust through variations of the refrain, 'I think I may well be a Jew' (ibid., p. 223). Resonating with episodes in Plath's personal life, including a failed suicide attempt, the death of her German father when she was a child and her marriage to the poet Ted Hughes, 'Daddy' was repeatedly criticized throughout the 1970s and 1980s for indulging in what many took to be an indecent form of emotional plagiarism. Seamus Heaney, for example, wrote that the poem is 'so entangled in biographical circumstances and rampages so permissively in the history of other people's sorrows that it simply overdraws its right to our sympathy' (1988, p. 165). Seeming to lack any reasonable 'objective correlative' (to borrow T. S. Eliot's formulation) between the personal and historical frames of reference, Alvin Rosenfeld doubted that Plath could 'expose the atrocity of the age through exposing self-inflicted wounds' (1988, p. 181).

Although 'Daddy' draws together historical atrocity and authorial biography through the suggestive life story of its speaker, later critics have recognized that the poem is self-evidently not a 'realistic' representation of either sphere. The biographical frameworks of 'confessional poetry' and critiques such as Rosenfeld's assume a very literal set of metaphors, linking personal and historical victimhood with little regard for the impersonality of poetic form or indeed the place of ambiguity in Plath's writing. As Christina Britzolakis notes, 'the elements of caricature, parody, and hyperbole in "Daddy" are so blatant that only a very determined misreading could identify the speaker with the biographical Sylvia Plath' (1999, p. 123). Nonetheless, the poem – and Plath's work more generally – does explore the relationship between subjectivity and history and, without presuming to understand exactly how events such as the Holocaust affected her personally, we might follow the lead of Jacqueline Rose in recognizing that fantasy is 'one of the key terms through which Plath's writing . . . can be thought' (1991, p. 5).

Knowingly risqué, the key 'personal' context for the speaker's violent fantasies ('Every woman adores a Fascist') is the death of her father ('I was ten when they buried you'), who is a 'ghastly' amalgam of taboo figures, being both a godhead and a Nazi (Plath, 1989a, pp. 223, 224, 222). Here Plath's writing is steeped in Freud, drawing on works such as *Mourning and Melancholia* (1917) and *Totem and Taboo* ([1919] 1938). The poem seems to be particularly indebted to the latter, in which Freud recognizes that ancient rituals and fears concerning the dead cannot be adequately explained by theories of mourning, as 'mourning loves to preoccupy itself with the deceased, to elaborate his memory, and preserve it for the longest possible time' ([1919] 1938, p. 98). What Freud terms 'taboos of the dead', on the other hand, are suggestive of a more ambivalent response to death, and specifically to the repression of an unconscious wish for the death of the deceased, something that Freud felt existed 'in almost all cases of intensive emotional allegiance to a particular person' (ibid., pp. 102–3). The taboo of the dead assumes a 'punitive and remorseful character' because of the 'opposition between the conscious grief and the unconscious satisfaction at death' (ibid., p. 104) and 'Daddy' seems to tap into the unconscious of a speaker who both loved and hated her father in this way, enacting the symbolic consummation of a repressed death wish that has to be played out as a fantasy in order for her to achieve psychological liberation.

Psychoanalytic theory thus offers one theoretical inroad into the poem's exploration of the taboos that surround a particular psychological state, grief, linking them to the Oedipal (or, in this case, the Electra) complex, which Freud identifies as 'the nucleus of all the neuroses' (Bernstein, 2002, pp. 137–8). Yet such a reading says very little about historical taboos, or the dead Jews to whom the speaker compares herself, and immediately begs the questions: Does the speaker's ambivalence towards her father's death also inform an unconscious ambivalence towards those killed in the Nazi genocide? If fantasies stem from real experiences, what status do the realities of history have in this poem? And, by extension, if writers really break taboos about the Holocaust in order to confront truths that relate to that event, what truths does 'Daddy' address, beyond those of the individual unconscious?

In turning to such questions, we must first recognize that the issue of historical 'truth' in this poem is a vexed one, not least because it gets all its historical references wrong. Historical space is vague and dehistoricized ('the name of the town is common' (Plath, 1989a, p. 222)) and the speaker keeps getting lost. Her 'Nazi' father is actually an amalgamation of every available Nazi stereotype: he has a 'neat mustache', evoking Hitler, while also being linked to the Luftwaffe and described as a 'Panzer-man' (a member of the tank unit) (ibid., pp. 222, 223). The poem offers no explanation as to how exactly a 'Taroc pack' (ibid., p. 223) would connect the speaker to the Jews and there is a sense that a victim identity is being tried out or self-consciously performed as poem and speaker alike test the limits of what can and cannot be said. Comparisons to the Jews take place at arm's length, with 'I think I may well be a Jew' gradually tapering to 'I may be a bit of a Jew' (ibid.). With no confident hold on either history or its language, the speaker attests to her dumbness and inarticulacy ('the tongue stuck in my jaw', 'I could hardly speak') and feels imprisoned by words which form a 'barb wire snare', entrapping her in her own selfhood ('Ich, ich, ich, ich') (ibid.). Instead of expressing sovereign subjectivity, language acts upon her, positioning her *as* victim, *as* Jew, with the 'obscene' German language becoming 'an engine, an engine' that leads her 'to Dachau, Auschwitz, Belsen' (ibid.).

The speaker's identity is less a form of mastery than a process of subjugation and, set against the perverse pleasures of the unconscious, 'Daddy' identifies socio-linguistic forces that play out on a historical and cultural level. Going beyond the conflict-ridden instincts and drives identified by Freud, the poem challenges identity politics centred purely around personal experience ('ich') by exploring identity as a process or action ('I do, I do') that involves a complex interplay between autonomy and social construction within wider signifying systems (ibid., pp. 223, 224). And these systems, within which and against which the poem is written, seem to be themselves traumatized, informed by the experiences of victims, but in a confused and bewildering way, and engendering a pervasive sense of shock and compulsive repetitions that keep returning us to *that* past. This is registered at the level of the poem's language and form, with the end rhymes of its 'Hieronymus Bosch nursery rhyme' scheme forming their own historical connections ('true' chiming with 'blue' and 'Jew' (ibid., p. 223)) and idiosyncratic digressions (Steiner, 1982, p. 330). The world of the poem – a kind of hell peopled by vampires, devils and perpetrators, a world where the speaker cannot even die – thus enables the coming-into-being of fictional, mythical, transhistorical and intergenerational identities that testify to the continuing presence of past atrocities in oblique and unsettling ways.

With a contrastingly clear sense of its own representative inadequacy, especially in respect of the dead Jews of the Holocaust ('the voices just can't worm through' (Plath, 1989a, p. 224)), 'Daddy' does not seek to illuminate factual historical truths or to supplant testimony. But in challenging cultural taboos of the early 1960s, it anticipates the way that fantasy and psychoanalytic theory would shape works of historical representation by later generations who would become increasingly attentive to the complex links between the unconscious and history. A notable example is D. M. Thomas's *The White Hotel* (1981), which examines the relationship between the Holocaust, fantasy and the unconscious by way of Freud's notion of *Das Unheimliche* ('the uncanny') and the theory of the instincts outlined in *Beyond the Pleasure Principle* ([1920] 1974a), in which Freud posits the idea of a universal struggle between what he terms the 'life instinct' and the 'death instinct'. *The White Hotel* centres on the story of Lisa Erdman, a former opera singer and patient of Freud's in Vienna, who is murdered in Kiev during the massacre at Babi Yar. The novel alternates between erotic poetry, letters and a pastiche of a Freudian case history, while also including third-person narration that draws on factual sources, notably Anatoly Kuznetsov's testimonial work *Babi Yar: A Document in the Form of a Novel* ([1967] 1969), in what was considered by some to be a controversial act of appropriation (Vice, 2000, pp. 38–66). While Freud initially looks to Lisa's childhood to explain her nervous and physical symptoms – and a traumatic sexual assault surfaces late in the novel, when she describes being attacked by sailors for being a 'dirty Jewess' and the daughter of a successful business-man – dreams, portents, fantasies and physical symptoms link Lisa's personal history with the later conflagrations of the Holocaust and the murders at Babi Yar (Thomas, 1982, p. 168). Lisa repeatedly experiences what Freud terms 'the uncanny' – the sense of something seeming both foreign and strangely famil-iar – and as Sue Vice observes, '[h]er "hysterical" symptoms turn out to be real injuries' (2000, p. 38). In *Memories and Hallucinations* (1988), Thomas describes how the early psychoanalytic movement might itself be interpreted as a Jewish response to the burgeoning anti-Semitism of the early twentieth century. He notes that what Freud and his colleagues diagnosed as 'hysteria' was linked, in mythology, to powers of premonition, and asks, 'Might not some of the hyste-rias treated by Freud have been caused by apprehensions of the future rather than suppressions of the past?' (Thomas, 1988, p. 40).

Thomas's novel also draws on *Beyond the Pleasure Principle* and, in writing Lisa's case history, the fictional Freud connects her troubles to his developing theory of the death instinct, noting 'an imperious demand, on the part of some force I did not comprehend, to poison the well of her pleasure at its source' (Thomas, 1982, p. 116). The fully developed theory would postulate a conflict between the life instinct (*Eros*), which is directed towards pleasure and the unification of living substances, and the death instinct (*Thanatos*), which seeks a return to an inorganic state and tends towards self-destruction. For Freud, this conflict characterizes the individual psyche and the evolution of human civilization, governing 'the struggle for life of the human species' ([1930] 1974b, p. 122). In *The White Hotel*, this struggle culminates in the mass murder at Babi Yar, which is marked as a highly symbolic ravine where these instincts are distinctly gendered, with femininity being equated with the life instinct and extreme male violence marking the fullest expression of the death instinct. In one graphic scene, Lisa lies among the dead bodies in the bottom of the valley, having jumped off the ledge with her stepson in an attempt to save their lives. She watches an SS man steal a crucifix from an old woman nearby, with the ambiguous and shifting narrative point of view opening the possibility that this scene is now being focalized through a disembodied and deeply traumatized Lisa, and that she is the old woman who is being described. Sensing the old woman is still alive, the SS man sends 'his jackboot crashing into her left breast' before another man named Demidenko rapes her and assaults her with a bayonet (Thomas, 1982, pp. 219–20). This horrific act represents the wider bodily harm inflicted during the Holocaust, which is described in terms of a universal (read male) propensity towards sexual violence. Thomas follows Freud in suggesting that genocide has its roots in the innate conflicts of the human psyche, which are posited as the founding (and final) truth of human history, regardless of the specific behavioural contexts created by politics, economics and history. As Richard J. Bernstein notes, even though Freud died shortly before the outbreak of the Second World War, he had 'witnessed the cruelty and barbarity of the Nazis' and 'certainly would not have been shocked by the subsequent genocide and massacres that occurred', as he regarded such 'unrestrained orgies of destructiveness' as emanating from man's instinctual nature (2002, p. 149). In *The White Hotel*, Thomas uses a range of techniques, from violent symbolism to erotic lyricism, to figure this conflict in terms of gender and to explode the taboo that would prevent his readers from acknowledging the provocative link between sex and death which, his novel suggests, accounts for the tragic victimhood of both individuals and entire ethnic populations.

The 'New Discourse' and Perpetrator Taboos: *The Ogre* and *The Kindly Ones*

In the West during the postwar decades, as culture became increasingly liberalized and orientated towards social and self-transformation, the influence of Freud remained pervasive. Modernity 'accelerated' into postmodernity, as Chris Jenks puts it, and the period as a whole became characterized by 'the desire to transcend limits – limits that are physical, racial, aesthetic, sexual, national, legal and moral' (2003, p. 8). Robert Gordon draws attention to the way that 'a newly turbid, sexualised idiom for depicting Nazism' emerged in 'the taboo-breaking subcultures of the 1970s, intellectually informed by psychoanalysis and psychosexual analyses of history and ideology from Wilhelm Reich to Herbert Marcuse' (2012, p. 26). This idiom spanned 'high' art and 'low' or trash culture, ranging from the sadomasochistic cinema of *The Night Porter* (Cavani, [1974] 2006) and *Salò, or the 120 Days of Sodom* (1975), to swastika-wearing, leather-clad punk bands such as the Ramones and the Sex Pistols and low-budget exploitation films set in concentration camps with titles such as *SS Experiment, Nazi Love Camp 27* and *Deported Women of the SS Special Sections*.

The trend for literature and film to draw on the powerfully suggestive iconography of Nazism in this way prompted Friedlander to express his concern over what he termed a 'new discourse' about the Third Reich. In *Reflections of Nazism: An Essay on Kitsch and Death* ([1982] 1993), he argues that this discourse gives free reign to 'phantasms, images and emotions', drawing on Michel Foucault's idea that 'power carries an erotic charge' to explain how Hitler and the other distinctly non-sexual males of the Nazi party – memorably described by Foucault as 'lamentable, shabby, puritan young men' and 'a species of Victorian spinsters' – came to be linked with a form of representation that repeatedly figures them in outlandish, sexualized terms (Friedlander, [1982] 1993, pp. 15, 74). One of the key novels cited by Friedlander is Michel Tournier's *The Ogre* ([1970] 1997), which he identifies as 'one of the first major manifestations of this new discourse' (ibid., p. 12). Incorporating elements of magic realism, *The Ogre* is a *bildungsroman* that recounts the life story of the strange, monstrous Abel Tiffauges. A shy and withdrawn schoolboy, Tiffauges lapses into obscurity in middle age as a car mechanic in rural France before undergoing a 'strange liberating process' when held in captivity as a prisoner of war (Tournier, [1970] 1997, p. 173). He eventually ends his days as 'the Ogre of Kaltenborn' who, during the final months of the war, kidnaps Aryan children from local villages and takes them to a Nazi training school in a gothic fortress in East Prussia. Friedlander highlights the novel's fascination with Nazi symbolism and Teutonic mythology. Citing one of the final scenes in the novel, where three of Tiffauges's favourite charges are found dead on the castle terrace, he writes:

> Here is the essence of the frisson: an overload of symbols; a baroque setting; an evocation of a mysterious atmosphere, of the myth and of religiosity enveloping a vision of death announced as a revelation opening out into nothing – nothing but frightfulness and the night. Unless . . . Unless the revelation is that of a mysterious force leading man toward irresistible destruction. (Friedlander, [1982] 1993, pp. 44–5, ellipsis in original)

The Ogre holds tightly to the interpretative anchor of the 'new discourse', with the 'mysterious force' leading its protagonist to destruction being a libido that shapes, and is shaped by, a series of abusive and racially charged power relations. Tiffauges's path to damnation begins with his victimization during his institutionalized childhood in a Catholic boarding school, continues through his marriage to a Jewish wife called Rachel, whom he treats as a sexual object, 'raw flesh' reduced to 'the level of a steak', then culminates in the predatory sexual identity he develops at the training school at Kaltenborn, when he becomes perhaps the ultimate hate figure: a Nazi paedophile (Tournier, [1970] 1997, pp. 8, 9).

In its basic subject matter and mode of narration, which includes the first-person narrative of Tiffauges's 'sinister writings', *The Ogre* transgresses what Erin McGlothlin identifies as 'an unwritten but nevertheless powerful taboo' that 'places the imagination of the consciousness of the perpetrator outside acceptable discourse on the Holocaust' (McGlothlin, 2010, p. 213). Susan Suleiman notes that such writing requires some degree of empathy or imaginative identification on the part of both writer and reader, observing that 'empathy for a perpetrator of genocide – even if it coexists with revulsion and moral condemnation –puts both author and reader on uncomfortable ethical ground, and on uncomfortable aesthetic ground as well' (2009, p. 2). Much like the taboo on imaginative works of Holocaust representation, the taboo against imagining the consciousness of perpetrators becomes evident through the controversies that surround its transgression. Works such as *The Ogre*, Martin Amis's *Time's Arrow* (1991) and Bernhard Schlink's *The Reader* (1997) are all 'scandalous' texts which, in line with Vice's definition, 'provoke controversy by inspiring repulsion and acclaim in equal measure' (2000, p. 1). Suleiman states that, until recently, Robert Merle's novel *Death Is My Trade* (1952), a fictionalized version of the autobiography of Rudolf Höss, the commandant of Auschwitz, was 'the only full-length novel narrated in the voice of a Nazi perpetrator' (2009, p. 1). Regardless of the exact veracity of this claim, the later examples clearly have varying degrees of narrative proximity to the viewpoint of their perpetrator-protagonists, with the distance created by, say, the magic realism of *The Ogre* or the chronological reversal of *Time's Arrow* meaning that there is not always an attempt at *direct* representation of a Nazi mindset.

More recently, however, a novel was published that explores the forbidden ground of perpetrator consciousness in a way that defiantly challenges this representational taboo, incorporating elements of the 'new discourse' and extensive historical scholarship. Written in French by the American-born author Jonathan Littell, *The Kindly Ones* (2006) resembles *The Ogre* in that it draws on mythological narrative structures – Littell's novel takes its title and key plotlines from the *Oresteia*, the trilogy of Greek tragedies by Aeschylus – and sexual deviance is again figured as a defining character trait of a Nazi. The novel is narrated by the cultured, multilingual SS Obersturmbannführer Dr Maximilien Aue, who, despite being married with children, has had homosexual affairs and an incestuous relationship with his sister. In one hallucinatory sequence late in the novel, as his increasingly disturbed state of mind spins out of control, he fantasizes about having sex with a dog and a tree branch, emphatically marking sexual deviance as either a symptom or cause of historical madness.

This is not to say, however, that Aue is wholly 'other' or a Nazi caricature, because unlike the mythical monster Tiffauges, who believes himself to be a magical being whose personal fate affects the entirety of human history, Aue stresses his ordinariness and basic similarity to his imagined readers, whom he terms his 'human brothers' in the novel's opening sentence (Littell, 2009, p. 3). In evidently self-exculpating but frequently persuasive fashion, he regards his being a perpetrator, rather than a victim or war hero, as a matter of historical chance (ibid., p. 592). He believes that his readers, like him, could have found themselves in any of these positions, had they been born in a different time and place, because 'everyone, or nearly everyone, in a given set of circumstances, does what he is told to do' (ibid., p. 20). As Jenni Adams observes, 'Aue insists upon the commonality of his own experience with the potential experience of the reader' and, in doing so, he asserts 'a continuity with his readers' that highlights our 'ethical implication in the narrative' (2011, p. 33). The novel is structurally and thematically informed by a strand of scholarship that runs through landmark studies such as Hannah Arendt's *Eichmann in Jerusalem* ([1963] 1992) and Christopher Browning's *Ordinary Men: Reserve Police Battalion 101 and the Final Solution in Poland* ([1992] 2001): a tradition that seeks to demythologize perpetrators, refuting what James Waller terms the 'mad Nazi theory' and explanations founded in sexual deviance, instead regarding the personalities of perpetrators as being more commonplace or, as Arendt famously put it, 'banal' (Waller, 2007, p. 61). Aue is thus a monumentally divided character, representing both extreme 'otherness' and extreme 'ordinariness'. Noting this duality, critics such as Suleiman and Robert Eaglestone make a helpful distinction between the 'family' strand of the narrative, where Aue is a psychopathic, sexually aberrant murderer, which conforms to an overarching literary and mythological framework, most notably that of the *Oresteia*, and the 'genocidal' strand, which figures Aue as an 'ordinary Nazi' acting as a witness – and, as Suleiman argues, a 'reliable witness', even a 'moral witness' – to a series of meticulously researched historical events (Suleiman, 2009, pp. 5–16; Eaglestone, 2011, p. 23).

Over the course of the novel, Aue's world becomes increasingly bizarre, with the violence and sexual content becoming ever more graphic and outlandish. Traumatized by his wartime experiences and suffering a head injury from the Battle of Stalingrad, he strangles his mother, murders his stepfather with an axe and bites Hitler on the nose, all while being pursued by two German police officers, Weser and Clemens, who represent the Eumenides: the Furies or 'Kindly Ones' from the *Oresteia* who seek to avenge the murder of Clytemnestra by her son, Orestes. For Eaglestone, this fantastical plot shows the 'family' strand winning out, representing a 'swerve' away from the 'genocidal' strand, 'as if the dark sun of the evil of the "ordinary Nazi" is actually too much to bear' (ibid., p. 23). In the final sections, *The Kindly Ones* retreats from the historical and psychological frameworks provided by the likes of Arendt and Browning and figures Aue within the mythic, melodramatic schemata of the 'new discourse', being compelled by mysterious psychosexual forces beyond his control to commit outrageous criminal acts. These episodes are frequently recounted as though they are committed by a sleepwalker or another person. If the taboos on perpetrator perspectives and fictional Holocaust representation are self-evidently challenged – and across some 900 pages Littell exposes the reader to some of the most disturbing episodes in the history of the genocide, from the viewpoint of a perpetrator – there is a sense, following Eaglestone, that another representational impossibility is drawn to the fore, and that the hope of understanding 'ordinary' evil, which *The Kindly Ones* has repeatedly framed as a readerly project of self-examination in light of the atrocities perpetrated by its perpetrator-narrator, is something that we simply cannot or dare not confront. The novel does not substantiate Aue's claim that he is simply 'a man like other men' (Littell, 2009, p. 24), challenging the basis of his hope that through empathetic identification the reader might be drawn into some kind of revelation about his or her own capacity for evil. Instead, the genocidal strand remains a 'dark sun', which is to say a taboo made up of characteristically contradictory elements.

Transgression and Truth

While *The Kindly Ones* offers an approach to representing perpetrators that seems original in every respect, this chapter has suggested that all taboos against Holocaust representation revolve around competing notions of truth and the question of whether different dimensions of the Holocaust can ever be understood, known or revealed. Of course the concept of 'truth' is never stable and singular, and divided responses to taboo-transgression often come to rest on what are at least two very different versions of what is meant by 'truth'. Following Eaglestone, there is 'truth as explanation, corresponding to evidence and states of affairs, and truth as in some way revealing of ourselves, of "who and how we are"', with each existing in a complex relationship to the other (2004, p. 7). Few taboos exist around serious, evidence-based historical studies of the Holocaust, but the claims of this first, more objective kind of truth often form barriers to any exploration of the latter. We have seen that taboos around the literary representation of the Holocaust have been formulated by victims and others with a legitimate interest in preserving the integrity of the public memory of the genocide. But does transgressive literary practice give us access to more 'existential' forms of truth and self-understanding that justify the representational violence and inevitable historical distortion?

In seeking to provide some answers to this question, this chapter has stressed that taboos against Holocaust representation make transgressive literary practice almost inevitable: the very existence of a discourse about the taboo implies that *the transgression has always already been made*. We recall that one of Freud's central insights in *Totem and Taboo* was that taboos would not exist were it not for formations that sought to break them and Wiesel, Friedlander and the theorists of anti-representation recognized that atrocity had long provided a strong stimulus to the artistic imagination. Despite their efforts to safeguard the Holocaust by designating it absolutely 'other', differing in magnitude and nature to all that had come before, the Nazi genocide proved to be no exception, making their cultural 'hysteria' an uncanny portent of the voluminous literary production to come. The evil of the Holocaust has proved to be a source of continuing creative inspiration, with examples ranging from the poetic cycle to the graphic novel, encompassing comedy, satire, allegory, melodrama and tragedy. In the introductory 'Afterward' section of his Holocaust novel *The Painted Bird*, in which he describes the hostile public reaction to his book, the Polish-born author Jerzy Kosinski asks, rhetorically, 'Can the imagination . . . be held prisoner?' (1996, p. 28). The answer, of course, is emphatically no.

But even if the unconscious, the imagination, language and postmodern culture all tend towards taboo-transgression, this does not necessarily mean that such transgressions must be celebrated. While unconscious undercurrents and cultural forces influence creative practice, literary representation is also guided by other, more conscious factors, such as the claims of ethics and justice. Many novels explicitly acknowledge these imperatives. They are in fact central to the representational poetics of *The Kindly Ones*: all the more so, it seems, for the novel's failure to make sense of the atrocities it depicts and the motives of its perpetrator-narrator. Its title, mythological schemata and philosophical meditations all invoke Greek notions of justice and Aue understands that, according to these precepts, 'crime has to do with the deed, not the will'; in the final sentence the Kindly Ones are 'on to' him (Littell, 2009, pp. 592, 975). Yet the claims of justice equally inform taboos *against* representation. James E. Young, for example, links the taboo against the representation of perpetrator consciousness to a concern that such literature might 'reperpetrate' these crimes (1988, p. 209), while others have worried that such writing might seem like a defence of the mindset, with representation being suggestive of commemoration and with it forgiveness. Indeed, many argue that *any* kind of understanding or explanation of the actions of perpetrators constitutes a gesture of assimilation which, by definition, renders criminal acts comprehensible, placing them somewhere on the known spectrum of human behaviour. It is perhaps for this reason that Lanzmann identifies 'an absolute obscenity in the project of understanding', citing Primo Levi's account of the Auschwitz guard who told him, 'here there is no why' (Lanzmann, 2007b, p. 51).

This notion of understanding being 'obscene' – indecent, improper, almost pornographic – leads us to the heart of the conflict that continues to be generated by the literary obsession with evil, suffering and mass death. In the aftermath of the Second World War, the fascination with horror was immediately figured as 'obscene' and made the subject of social taboos. Sebald describes how, after the Allied firestorms, a second-hand bookshop in Hamburg kept photographs of corpses lying in the street under the counter, 'to be fingered and examined in a way usually reserved for pornography' (2004, p. 99). Linking sight to insight and with it a kind of criminal complicity, Lanzmann forcefully resists the 'pornography of representation', rejecting the idea that the Holocaust can ever be exposed or explained. However, this idea has been forcefully opposed, in turn, by historians, writers and survivors who have sought to analyse the genocide in sober, evidence-based terms, believing they must stare the gorgon directly in the eye if they are ever to understand it. In his introduction to *Ordinary Men*, Browning explicitly rejects 'the old clichés that to explain is to excuse, to understand is to forgive', arguing that only by trying to empathize with the perpetrators can any historical study get beyond 'one-dimensional caricature' (2001, p. xviii). Waller makes much the same point in the introduction to *Becoming Evil*, noting that explanation should not be viewed as a moral category, but more straightforwardly as a way of understanding 'the conditions under which many of us could be transformed into killing machines' (2007, p. xvii). In an interview with *The Paris Review*, Levi (1995) describes, *pace* Lanzmann, how his desire to explore the 'why' over and above emotional self-expression is a matter of 'natural hormones', stressing that this analytical impulse does not entail forgiveness, and that he was happy to see Eichmann arrested, tried and executed, even as his 'first reaction was to try to understand him'. These writers and historians suggest that rather than shielding us from obscenity, taboos around Holocaust representation can obscure our understanding of an event that is actually, as the philosopher Gillian Rose puts it in *Mourning Becomes the Law*, 'all too understandable, all too continuous with what we are – human, all too human' (1997, p. 43).

Yet how does all this relate to the more experimental works of fiction discussed in this chapter? We have seen that transparent forms of historical understanding *elude* the narrators of a novel such as *The Kindly Ones* and a poem such as 'Daddy'. Moreover, these texts do not offer documentary case studies exploring why real historical figures committed real evil acts. They are full of ambiguity, uncertainty and unreality. We have seen how the fictional protagonist of *The Kindly Ones* is located in a mythic as well as a historical framework, while Littell makes extensive use of literary devices such as symbolism (eyes, trees), psychoanalytic theory and intertextuality. Perhaps, then, any appreciation of the contribution that imaginative literature might make to the understanding of historical truth must rest on such traits, defining both the value of fiction and the types of truth with which it paradoxically engages. For example, it follows that if there is a 'swerve' away from the genocidal strand of *The Kindly Ones*, then there is equally a swerve *towards* the family strand and with it the questions that are explored in the Greek tragedies on which it is based, such as the possibility of justice and the nature of evil. Rather than constituting an avoidance of truth or the 'why', such a 'swerve' might be regarded as a way of orientating a particular readerly (and literary) relationship to the 'why'.

In *Radical Evil: A Philosophical Interrogation* (2002), Bernstein explores the historical development of different conceptual understandings of evil. He writes:

> I do not believe that there is, or can be, any end to this process; we must always be wary of thinking that we have reached a final resting place. There is . . . something about evil that resists and defies any final comprehension. (Bernstein, 2002, p. 7)

The Kindly Ones proposes something similar, illustrating how literary texts enrich our understanding of concepts such as evil through their explorations of the psychologies and histories of fictional protagonists, drawing on the theoretical writing of the likes of Freud and Arendt, but they never fix it, not least because there is also something about the nature of literary representation and interpretation that resists mastery, final comprehension and definitive endings as well. Without necessarily providing all the answers, a fictional text such as *The Kindly Ones* constitutes a 'thought-adventure', to quote D. H. Lawrence (1997, p. 279), that is open, fluid and dialogic, ensuring that as it evolves, our contemporary understanding of abstract concepts such as evil relates to, and has to do with, the realities of the Holocaust.

But is this enough to mitigate representational violence, gratuitous shock and the risk of causing offence? With the defence of fiction often resting on its capacity to safeguard us against the repetition of historical disasters, perhaps the ultimate question to ask of literary works that have challenged Holocaust taboos is whether, in doing so, they have played, or ever can play, a useful role in confronting the social and psychological formations that allow genocide to take place. If *The Kindly Ones* is the kind of watershed novel that many believe it to be, we might reasonably anticipate a continuation of the 'boom' in perpetrator fiction that has taken place over the past decade (Eaglestone, 2011, p. 15), with novels rising to fill the void that has been left by the observance of the taboo on engaging with perpetrator perspectives. This chapter has demonstrated that the pace of literary engagement with the realities of mass killing is nonetheless slow. How, then, can literature keep up with the rapidly changing nature of global conflict and perpetrator identities? And do readerly processes of empathy and imaginative identification have any broader ethical significance beyond the production of a certain *frisson* and aesthetic gratification? The answers remain unclear, but if breaking taboos around Holocaust representation is part of a process of 'working through' cultural memories of the Holocaust – a process that requires us to consider who we are, what our place in the world is, and also how we are implicated in the violence that our society inflicts on others – then, following Bernstein, this process must always be wary of its own endpoint. By continuing to raise such questions and probing these more 'existential' types of truth in light of the Holocaust, transgressive works of fiction can at least help to ensure that we do not arrive at the kind of dangerous 'final resting place' where the objective truths of mass killing no longer matter.

Note

1. See Robert Eaglestone, 'The Public Secret', presented at the Future of Testimony conference, University of Salford, 2011, forthcoming in J. Kilby and A. Rowland (eds), *The Future of Testimony* (London: Routledge, 2014).

Works Cited

Adams, J. (2011), 'Reading (as) violence in Jonathan Littell's *The Kindly Ones*', in J. Adams and S. Vice (eds), *Representing Perpetrators in Holocaust Literature and Film*. Special issue of *Holocaust Studies: A Journal of Culture and History*, 17.2–3, pp. 27–47.

Amis, M. (1991), *Time's Arrow*. London: Penguin.

Arendt, H. [1963] (1992), *Eichmann in Jerusalem: A Report on the Banality of Evil*. London: Penguin.

Bernstein, R. J. (2002), *Radical Evil: A Philosophical Interrogation*. Cambridge: Polity Press.

Britzolakis, C. (1999), *Sylvia Plath and the Theatre of Mourning*. Oxford: Clarendon Press.

Browning, C. R. [1992] (2001), *Reserve Police Battalion 101 and the Final Solution in Poland*. London: Penguin.

Cavani, L. (dir) [1974] (2006), *The Night Porter*. DVD. Beverly Hills, California: Anchor Bay.

Eaglestone, R. (2004), *The Holocaust and the Postmodern*. Oxford: Oxford University Press.

—. (2011), 'Avoiding evil in perpetrator fiction', in J. Adams and S. Vice (eds), *Representing Perpetrators in Holocaust Literature and Film*. Special issue of *Holocaust Studies: A Journal of Culture and History*, 17.2–3, pp. 13–26.

Frank, A. [1952] (1997), *Anne Frank: The Diary of a Young Girl*, trans. S. Massotty. London: Penguin.

Freud, S. [1919] (1938), *Totem and Taboo*, trans. A. A. Brill. London: Pelican Books.

—. [1920] (1974a), *Beyond the Pleasure Principle*, in *The Standard Edition of the Complete Psychological Works of Sigmund Freud*, vol. 18, trans. under the general editorship of J. Strachey in collaboration with A. Freud, assisted by A. Strachey and A. Tyson. London: Hogarth Press, pp. 1–64.

—. [1930] (1974b), *Civilization and Its Discontents*, in *The Standard Edition of the Complete Psychological Works of Sigmund Freud*, vol. 21, trans. under the general editorship of J. Strachey in collaboration with A. Freud, assisted by A. Strachey and A. Tyson. London: Hogarth Press, pp. 57–146.

Friedlander, S. (1992), 'Introduction' to S. Friedlander (ed.), *Probing the Limits of Representation: Nazism and the Final Solution*. Cambridge, MA: Harvard University Press, pp. 1–21.

—. [1982] (1993), *Reflections of Nazism: An Essay on Kitsch and Death*. Bloomington and Indianapolis: Indiana University Press.

Gordon, R. S. C. (2012), *The Holocaust in Italian Culture, 1944–2010*. Stanford, CA: Stanford University Press.

Heaney, S. (1988), *The Government of the Tongue: The 1986 T. S. Eliot Memorial Lectures and Other Critical Writings*. London: Faber and Faber.

Jenks, C. (2003), *Transgression*. London: Routledge.

Kosinski, J. (1996), *The Painted Bird*. London: Black Swan.

Kuznetsov, A. [1967] (1969), *Babi Yar: A Documentary Novel*, trans. J. Guralsky. London: Sphere Books.

Lanzmann, C. (2007a), 'From the Holocaust to "Holocaust"', in S. Liebman (ed.), *Claude Lanzmann's Shoah: Key Essays*. Oxford: Oxford University Press, pp. 27–36.

—. (2007b), 'Hier ist kein Warum', in S. Liebman (ed.), *Claude Lanzmann's Shoah: Key Essays*. Oxford: Oxford University Press, pp. 51–2.

Lawrence, D. H. (1997), *Kangaroo*. London: Penguin.

Levi, P. (1995), 'The art of fiction no. 140', interview by G. Motala, in *The Paris Review*, 134, www.theparisreview.org/interviews/1670/the-art-of-fiction-no-140-primo-levi. Accessed 15 November 2012.

—. [1958] (1996a), *If This Is a Man*, trans. S. Woolf. London: Abacus.

—. [1986] (1996b), *The Drowned and the Saved*, trans. R. Rosenthal. London: Abacus.

Littell, J. (2009), *The Kindly Ones*, trans. C. Mandell. London: Random House.

McGlothlin, E. (2010), 'Theorizing the perpetrator in Bernhard Schlink's *The Reader* and Martin Amis's *Time's Arrow*', in R. C. Spargo and R. M. Ehrenreich (eds), *After Representation: The Holocaust, Literature, and Culture*. New Brunswick, NJ: Rutgers University Press, pp. 210–30.

Pasolini, P. P. (1975), *Salò, or the 120 Days of Sodom*. DVD. London: BFI Video.

Plath, S. (1989a), 'Daddy', in *Collected Poems*. London: Faber and Faber, pp. 222–4.

—. (1989b), 'Notes: 1962', in *Collected Poems*. London: Faber and Faber, pp. 292–4.

Rose, G. (1997), *Mourning Becomes the Law: Philosophy and Representation*. Cambridge: Cambridge University Press.

Rose, J. (1991), *The Haunting of Sylvia Plath*. London: Virago Press.

Rosenfeld, A. H. (1988), *A Double Dying: Reflections on Holocaust Literature*. Bloomington and Indianapolis: Indiana University Press.

Schlink, B. (1997), *The Reader*, trans. C. Brown Janeway. London: Phoenix.

Sebald, W. G. (2004), *On the Natural History of Destruction*, trans. A. Bell. London: Penguin.

Sontag, S. (1975), 'Fascinating Fascism', *New York Review of Books*, 6 February 1975, pp. 73–105.

Steiner, G. (1982), *Language and Silence: Essays on Language, Literature and the Inhuman*. New York: Atheneum.

Suleiman, S. (2009), 'When the perpetrator becomes a reliable witness of the Holocaust: on Jonathan Littell's *Les Bienveillantes*', *New German Critique*, 36.1, 1–19.

Thomas, D. M. (1982), *The White Hotel*. Harmondsworth: Penguin.

—. (1988), *Memories and Hallucinations*. London: Victor Gollancz.

Tournier, M. [1970] (1997), *The Ogre*. Baltimore: Johns Hopkins University Press.

Vice, S. (2000), *Holocaust Fiction*. London: Routledge.

Waller, J. (2007), *Becoming Evil: How Ordinary People Commit Genocide and Mass Killing*. Oxford: Oxford University Press.

Wiesel, E. [1958] (1981), *Night*, trans. S. Rodway. London: Penguin.

—. (1990), 'The Holocaust as literary inspiration', in *Dimensions of the Holocaust*. Illinois: Northwestern University Press, pp. 5–19.

Young, J. E. (1988), 'Holocaust documentary fiction: the novelist as eyewitness', in B. Lang (ed.), *Writing and the Holocaust*. New York: Holmes and Meier, pp. 200–15.

10 Holocaust Literature: Comparative Perspectives

Stef Craps

Abstract

This chapter discusses attempts to theorize the interrelatedness of the Holocaust and other histories of victimization against the background of, first, the recent broadening of the focus of the field of memory studies from the national to the transnational level, and, secondly, efforts to bridge a disciplinary divide between Jewish and postcolonial studies preventing the Holocaust and histories of slavery and colonial domination from being considered in a common frame. In so doing, it highlights the pitfalls as well as the possibilities of bringing different atrocities into contact, a challenging and often controversial endeavour that holds both perils and promises. Next, it explores the ways in which the Native American writer Sherman Alexie negotiates various comparative perspectives on the Holocaust in 'The Game between the Jews and the Indians Is Tied Going into the Bottom of the Ninth Inning' (1993), a sonnet-length poem that considers Jews and Native Americans as similarly oppressed ethnic minorities, and 'Inside Dachau' (1996), a long, meditative poem that describes a Native American's reflections on visiting a Nazi concentration camp.

The past few years have seen an increasing awareness in academia of the need to think the Holocaust and other historical traumas – such as slavery, colonialism and other genocides – together in order to develop a more comprehensive understanding of the dark underside of modernity and to enable alliances and solidarities that transcend race, ethnicity, nationality, religion and culture. In this chapter, I will discuss attempts to theorize the interrelatedness of the

Holocaust and other histories of victimization against the background of, first, the recent broadening of the focus of the field of memory studies from the national to the transnational level, and, secondly, efforts to bridge a disciplinary divide between Jewish and postcolonial studies preventing the Holocaust and histories of slavery and colonial domination from being considered in a common frame.[1] In so doing, I will highlight the pitfalls as well as the possibilities of bringing different atrocities into contact, a challenging and often controversial endeavour that holds both perils and promises. Next, I will analyse two examples from an important but somewhat overlooked archive of literary texts that employ the strategy of comparison to establish links between the Nazi genocide of the European Jews and other traumatic histories.

As is well known, memory emerged as an urgent topic of debate in the humanities in the 1980s. The past few decades have seen a profusion of important work on memory, leading some to speak of a 'memory boom' (Winter, 2000). A great deal of research has been devoted to 'collective memory', a term developed by Maurice Halbwachs (1992) in the 1920s to denote collectively shared representations of the past, and 'cultural memory', a related concept coined by Jan Assmann (1992) in the 1980s which stresses the role of institutionalized canons of culture in the formation and transmission of collective memories. Early work in memory studies focused on the ways in which memories are shared within particular communities and constitute or reinforce group identity. Very often, most notably in Pierre Nora's monumental *Lieux de mémoire* project ([1984–92] 1996–8), the nation-state has been taken as paradigmatic of such mnemonic communities. In the past few years, however, the transnational and even global dissemination of memory has moved to the centre of attention. The emphasis in memory studies is gradually shifting from static sites of memory to the dynamic movement of memory. With the aid of mass cultural technologies, it has become increasingly possible for people to take on memories of events not 'their own', events that they did not live through themselves and to which they have no familial, ethnic or national tie – a phenomenon which Alison Landsberg (2004) has usefully labelled 'prosthetic memory'.

Arguments about the transnationalization or globalization of memory typically refer to the Holocaust, still the primary, archetypal topic in memory studies. In the second half of the 1990s, for example, Alvin Rosenfeld (1995), Hilene Flanzbaum (1999) and Peter Novick (1999) called attention to the so-called Americanization of the Holocaust. The transnational resonance of the Holocaust did not stop there, however. In *The Holocaust and Memory in the Global Age*, Daniel Levy and Natan Sznaider argue that the global spread of Holocaust discourse has generated a new form of memory, 'cosmopolitan memory', which they define as 'a memory that harbors the possibility of transcending ethnic and national boundaries' (Levy and Sznaider, [2001] 2006, p. 4). In their view, as in Jeffrey Alexander's (2002), the Holocaust has escaped its spatial and temporal particularism to emerge as a common moral touchstone in the wake of the Cold War. The negative memory of the extermination of the Jews can serve as a universal moral norm, they argue, and thus help foster a human-rights culture and advance the cause of global justice.

In the past decade, however, Levy and Sznaider's book and Alexander's essay 'On the Social Construction of Moral Universals' have been accused of being naively optimistic about the consequences of the global dissemination of Holocaust memory.[2] As many commentators have noted, Levy and Sznaider as well as Alexander largely ignore the fact that the Holocaust is often used in ways that do not lead to greater transcultural understanding and the establishment of a universal human-rights culture. A. Dirk Moses, for example, argues that the Holocaust is typically invoked not with the cosmopolitan effect that Levy and Sznaider suppose but 'to express the fear of collective destruction: the apocalypse of genocide', a usage which 'contributes towards terroristic political action in the form of pre-emptive strikes and anticipatory self-defence to forestall feared destruction' (Moses, 2011, p. 91). The employment of 'second Holocaust' rhetoric by Zionists in Israel and George W. Bush's repeated use of Nazi comparisons to rally support for the war in Iraq are cases in point. As Andreas Huyssen (2003) and Miriam Hansen (1996) have noted, Holocaust comparisons can also work as Freudian 'screen memories' – meaning that the Holocaust is remembered in order to repress other instances of historical oppression which are more immediate and closer to home[3] – or simply hinder understanding of specific local histories.[4] Conversely, the comparative argument can be exploited for revisionist ends and serve to relativize, dilute or erase the memory of the Holocaust, as in the *Historikerstreit* of the mid-1980s.[5] Another important criticism that can be levelled both at Levy and Sznaider and at Alexander is that their analysis is marred by Eurocentrism: their work tends to conflate the West with the world and to treat the Holocaust – a genocide that took place in Europe and was committed by Europeans against Europeans – as a unique source of universal moral lessons that cannot be learnt from any other event (A. Assmann and Conrad, 2010).

If the traditional national focus of memory studies is one explanation for why research on the interrelatedness of memories of the Holocaust and other atrocities is a relatively recent phenomenon, another is the gaping disciplinary divide that has long separated Jewish and postcolonial studies. There has been a conspicuous lack of interaction between the two fields, despite a host of shared concerns – after all, both Jewish and postcolonial studies grapple with the legacies of histories of violence perpetrated in the name of racist ideologies and imperialist political projects. In his book *Between Camps: Nations, Cultures and the Allure of Race*, which extends the argument first made in the last chapter of *The Black Atlantic: Modernity and Double Consciousness* (1993) about the need to make connections across black and Jewish diasporic histories, Paul Gilroy asks: 'Why does it remain so difficult for so many people to accept the knotted intersection of histories produced by this fusion of horizons?' (Gilroy, [2000] 2004, p. 78). Bryan Cheyette (2000) addresses just this question in an article in which he explores theoretical impediments that prevent postcolonial studies from incorporating Jewish history into a broader understanding of a colonizing Western modernity. Continuities and overlaps between Jewish and colonial experience have remained underexplored, Cheyette points out, because of the reluctance or inability of many postcolonial theorists to perceive Jews as anything other than part of a supposedly homogeneous, white, 'Judeo-Christian' majoritarian tradition. He gives three reasons to explain postcolonial theory's resistance to breaking down the separate spheres between Jews and other ethnicities: the past complicity of many individual Jews with the colonial enterprise; the history of Zionism, which points to Jewish collusion with colonial practices that continues to this day; and tensions in contemporary black-Jewish relations in the United States over the perceived appropriation of black experience by the Jewish community (i.e. the use of the Holocaust as a screen memory for slavery and segregation).

While Cheyette's focus is on the diffidence shown by postcolonial studies towards Jewish studies, it is fair to say that the feeling is mutual. Indeed, further complicating the dialogue between Jewish and postcolonial studies is a strongly held belief in the uniqueness of the Holocaust among many Jewish studies scholars, most prominently Deborah Lipstadt (1993), Steven Katz (1994), Daniel Goldhagen (1996) and Yehuda Bauer (1978). As Michael Rothberg points out, the proponents of uniqueness typically refuse to consider the Holocaust and other catastrophic histories in a common frame: they 'assiduously search out and refute all attempts to compare or analogize the Holocaust in order to preserve memory of the Shoah from its dilution or relativization' (Rothberg, 2009, p. 9). Critics of uniqueness or of the politics of Holocaust memory, on the other hand, 'often argue . . . that the ever-increasing interest in the Nazi genocide distracts from the consideration of other historical tragedies' (ibid.) – this is, of course, the third reason adduced by Cheyette to explain postcolonial theory's cold-shouldering of Jewish history.[6] In fact, a common critical response to the privileging of the Holocaust is to claim uniqueness or primacy for other histories of suffering, such as African American slavery or the genocide of the Native Americans. While such efforts have helped raise the profile of these relatively neglected histories, they are historically problematic as well as politically and ethically unproductive. Insisting on the distinctiveness and difference of one's own history can indicate a kind of blindness, a refusal to recognize the larger historical processes of which that history is a part. Moreover, claims for the uniqueness of the suffering of the particular victim group to which one belongs tend to deny the capacity for, or the effectiveness of, transcultural empathy.

Though, generally speaking, there has been little interaction between Jewish and postcolonial studies, a number of theorists and historians have long recognized continuities between the history of the European Jews and the history of European colonialism. In the early 1950s, Hannah Arendt ([1951] 2004) put forward the so-called boomerang thesis, according to which European totalitarianism, and Nazism in particular, has its roots in overseas colonialism. At around the same time, Aimé Césaire ([1950] 2000) argued that Nazism should be viewed as the continuation of Europe's treatment of various non-European peoples in the previous centuries. This understanding of Nazism as colonialism revisited on Europe also informs more recent research in the fledgling field of comparative genocide studies by scholars such as Mark Mazower (2008), A. Dirk Moses (2002), David Moshman (2001), Jacques Semelin (2007), Timothy Snyder (2010), Dan Stone (2004) and Jürgen Zimmerer (2005), who have all sought to remove the 'conceptual blockages' (Moses, 2002) in comparing modern atrocities, to move beyond notions of the Holocaust's uniqueness that might inscribe a hierarchy of suffering across modernity, and to elicit the structural continuities and discontinuities between atrocious events.

There has so far been little parallel work by literary and cultural critics; notable exceptions include Michael Rothberg (2009; 2011), Bryan Cheyette (2000), Sam Durrant (2004), Max Silverman (2013), Paul Gilroy ([2000] 2004; 1993), Robert Eaglestone (2008) and Aamir Mufti (2007). A particularly noteworthy intervention is Rothberg's monograph *Multidirectional Memory: Remembering the Holocaust in the Age of Decolonization* (2009), which illuminates what he calls the 'multidirectional' orientation of collective memory. Rothberg offers an alternative to the 'competitive memory' model – shared, as he points out, by many proponents and critics of uniqueness – according to which the capacity to remember historical tragedies is limited and any attention to one tragedy inevitably diminishes our capacity to remember another. Against this framework, which understands collective memory as 'a zero-sum struggle over scarce resources', he suggests that we consider memory as multidirectional, that is, 'as subject to ongoing negotiation, cross-referencing, and borrowing; as productive and not privative' (Rothberg, 2009, p. 3). The concept of multidirectional memory 'draw[s] attention to the dynamic transfers that take place between diverse places and times during the act of remembrance' (ibid., p. 11). Rothberg considers memory to be inherently comparative, but he disputes the idea that comparisons between atrocities inevitably erase the differences between them and imply a false equivalence. In focusing on the Holocaust, he seeks to avoid the twin pitfalls of sacralization and trivialization: the tendency, on the one hand, to emphasize the distinctness of the Holocaust to such an extent that it cannot be compared to anything else; and, on the other, to relativize or dilute its memory by homogenizing very different histories.

Rothberg's specific concern is with the mutually enabling relationship between Holocaust memory and memories of the struggle for decolonization. While Levy and Sznaider and Alexander assume that the Holocaust is central in that it allows other histories of victimization to be articulated, Rothberg maintains that the process is not that simple. Multidirectional memory is not 'a one-way street' (ibid., p. 6): just as the Holocaust has enabled the articulation of other histories, so these other histories have helped shape the way we think about the Holocaust and affected the way Holocaust memory has circulated. In other words, the process is dialogical and multidirectional, not monological and unidirectional. The example that clinches this argument in Rothberg's book is that of Holocaust memory in France. He shows that the Algerian War of Independence (1954–62) helped bring about the conditions in which the Holocaust could be publicly remembered. At the time, many intellectuals pointed out that the colonial violence of the French state in Algeria, and particularly the use of torture and detention camps, echoed the methods of the Nazis. Rothberg contends that, along with the Eichmann trial, the protest against contemporary events in Algeria and in Paris helped enable the emergence of public Holocaust memory in France in the early 1960s.

Besides making a theoretical argument against a logic of competitive memory based on the zero-sum game and a historical argument about the inseparability of memories of the Holocaust and colonial violence, Rothberg also puts forward a political argument in *Multidirectional Memory*. He questions the taken-for-granted link between collective memory and group identity – the assumption that a straight line connects, for example, Jewish memory and Jewish identity or African American memory and African American identity in mutual confirmation. Rothberg rejects the idea that the only kinds of memories and identities that are possible are 'ones that exclude elements of alterity and forms of commonality with others' (ibid., pp. 4–5). Memories do not have exclusive owners; they do not naturally belong to any particular group. Rather, the borders of memory and identity are 'jagged' (ibid., p. 5). Going beyond the 'common sense' of identity politics, Rothberg suggests that the productive, intercultural dynamic of multidirectional memory has the potential to create 'new forms of solidarity and new visions of justice' (ibid.). However, he also recognizes that multidirectional memory can function 'in the interest of violence or exclusion instead of solidarity' (ibid., p. 12). This is often the case, for example, with the invocation of the Holocaust in the context of the Israeli–Palestinian conflict – briefly discussed in the epilogue of his book – which tends to take the form of 'a ritual trading of threats and insults' (ibid., p. 311).

Rothberg returns to the Israeli–Palestinian situation in his article 'From Gaza to Warsaw: Mapping Multidirectional Memory', where he engages with 'some of the more difficult and even troubling cases of multidirectionality' (Rothberg, 2011, p. 524). Even though public memory is structurally multidirectional, he argues, in the sense of always being marked by 'transcultural borrowing, exchange, and adaptation', the politics of multidirectional memory does not therefore come 'with any guarantees' (ibid.). Rothberg sets out to develop 'an ethics of comparison that can distinguish politically productive forms of memory from those that lead to competition, appropriation, or trivialization' (ibid., p. 525). He maps the different forms that public memory can take in politically charged situations, tracing 'a four-part distinction in which multidirectional memories are located at the intersection of an *axis of comparison* (defined by a continuum stretching from equation to differentiation) and an *axis of political affect* (defined by a continuum stretching from solidarity to competition – two complex, composite affects)' (ibid.). Memory discourses that combine differentiation and solidarity offer 'a greater political potential', he maintains, than those that rely on equation and competition (ibid., p. 526). He concludes that 'a radically democratic politics of memory needs to include a differentiated empirical history, moral solidarity with victims of diverse injustices, and an ethics of comparison that coordinates the asymmetrical claims of those victims' (ibid.). The important point this article makes, more explicitly and elaborately than *Multidirectional Memory* (2009), is that not all forms of multidirectionality are to be celebrated as inherently beneficial and politically progressive; indeed, differentiation/solidarity represents only one quadrant on Rothberg's map, a useful tool for navigating the murky waters of comparative memory.

To the extent that literary critics have studied texts that connect the Holocaust to other historical tragedies, they have tended to focus on prose works – mostly novels – that put the Nazi genocide in contact with the horrors of slavery or the violence of the decolonization process. One thinks, for example, of the work of the French Jewish writer André Schwarz-Bart and the British Caribbean author Caryl Phillips analysed by Rothberg in *Multidirectional Memory* (2009), the writings of the African American novelist William Gardner Smith discussed by Gilroy in *Between Camps* ([2000] 2004), and the various novels about the Algerian War of Independence studied by Silverman in *Palimpsestic Memory: The Holocaust and Colonialism in French and Francophone Fiction and Film* (2013).[7] In the remainder of this chapter, however, I will look at how other kinds of mnemonic connections are made in a different literary genre, exploring the ways in which the Native American writer Sherman Alexie negotiates various comparative perspectives on the Holocaust in his poems 'The Game between the Jews and the Indians Is Tied Going into the Bottom of the Ninth Inning' (1993) and 'Inside Dachau' (1996). The former is a sonnet-length poem that, as the title suggests, considers Jews and Native Americans as similarly oppressed ethnic minorities; the latter is a long, meditative poem that describes a Native American's reflections on visiting a Nazi concentration camp. This shift of focus to poetry and to the genocide of the Native Americans is meant to complement the prose- and slavery- or decolonization-centred approaches typically used in the study of transcultural Holocaust literature. However, the reason why I turn to Alexie's work in particular is primarily didactic: it exemplifies a wide range of possible ways to think the Holocaust and other histories of victimization together and thus allows me to conveniently illustrate several of the theoretical perspectives outlined above.

Before I go on to analyse Alexie's poems in some detail, I would like to briefly contextualize them by pointing out that the use of Holocaust rhetoric in relation to Native American history – which comprises genocidal warfare, land theft, ethnic cleansing, disease and cultural destruction – is hardly uncommon among Native American scholars and artists. Indeed, the devastation and suffering inflicted on the indigenous peoples in North America since the arrival of Columbus in the Caribbean in 1492 is widely thought of as a holocaust in its own right and frequently also called that. Many Native American intellectuals refer to this traumatic history as the 'American Holocaust' or the 'American Indian Holocaust'. Like other minorities in the United States, Native Americans use the Holocaust to articulate and demand recognition for their own people's suffering. It suffices to look at the titles of a number of popular studies of Native American history to see how established this practice is: for example, Russell Thornton's *American Indian Holocaust and Survival: A Population History since 1492* (1987), David Stannard's *American Holocaust: Columbus and the Conquest of the New World* (1992) and Ward Churchill's *A Little Matter of Genocide: Holocaust and Denial in the Americas, 1492 to the Present* (1997). One could also point to a frequently cited article by Lilian Friedberg titled 'Dare to Compare: Americanizing the Holocaust' (2000): unlike Novick, Rosenfeld and Flanzbaum, who invoke the phrase 'Americanization of the Holocaust' to designate the process by which the Nazi genocide of the European Jews has moved to the centre of American culture, Friedberg uses it to express her desire for the United States to finally acknowledge its own traumatic genocidal past – the atrocities experienced by the Native Americans – as another holocaustal history. As Friedberg observes, while the Nazi genocide has achieved mainstream recognition in Germany and around the world, the genocide against the indigenous inhabitants of North America continues to be 'denied or dismissed as the inevitable prelude to the rise of the greatest nation on Earth' (Friedberg, 2000, p. 356).

Artists have been no less hesitant than scholars to draw parallels between the genocide of the Native Americans and the Holocaust. Consider, for example, the documentary *American Holocaust: When It's All Over, I'll Still Be Indian* ([2000] 2005) by Joanelle Romero, which compares the Nazi genocide to the US government's treatment of Native Americans and its lasting effect on their culture today. Romero began putting together the film in 1995 and produced a shortened, 29-minute version of it in 2000, in the evidently vain hope of encouraging new funders so that she could complete what she had originally conceived of as a 90-minute documentary. Romero's film shares its main title with a 1996 album by Georgie

Jessup, a singer–songwriter and activist, which contains ten songs describing the plight of the Native Americans. In the field of literature, the anthology *Eating Fire, Tasting Blood: Breaking the Great Silence of the American Indian Holocaust* (2006) is also noteworthy. Edited by MariJo Moore, it brings together Native writers from many different tribal backgrounds from across the Americas who call attention to their traumatic history and protest 'whitewashed' versions of American history which deny, trivialize or normalize the suffering of the Native Americans.

Alexie's work offers a particularly thoughtful and sophisticated engagement with the question of the comparability of the Nazi genocide which goes beyond a straightforward appropriation of Holocaust rhetoric to validate an occluded history of victimization. A poet, novelist and filmmaker, Alexie, who self-identifies as a Spokane/Coeur d'Alene Indian, has self-reflexively invoked the Nazi Holocaust in relation to Native American history from the start of his career. As Nancy Peterson points out in an insightful article that traces these references throughout his work, Alexie's various explorations of the interconnections between Jewish and Native American historical experiences 'reflect a significant ethical engagement with issues attached to genocidal histories and our use of them' (Peterson, 2010, p. 65).[8]

Included in his poetry collection *First Indian on the Moon* (1993), 'The Game between the Jews and the Indians Is Tied Going into the Bottom of the Ninth Inning' is one of Alexie's earliest poems to contemplate the interrelations between the Holocaust and the genocide of the Native Americans, and can be seen as a programmatic prelude to the more extensive, comprehensive, and elaborate treatment of this theme found in the later poem 'Inside Dachau', from his collection *The Summer of Black Widows* (1996). 'The Game' is a multidirectional postmemorial poem that seeks to move beyond a competitive understanding of the relationship between different historical traumas towards a more dialogical, collaborative and inclusive perspective.[9] The speaker is a Native American who is in a love relationship with the addressee, who is Jewish. He wonders whether their intimate touches will evoke traumatic memories of Native American massacres ('Sand Creek, Wounded Knee') in him and of the Holocaust ('Auschwitz, Buchenwald') in his partner. He answers his own question in the negative, adding that

> . . . we will only think of the past
> as one second before
> where we are now, the future
> just one second ahead. (Alexie, 1993, p. 80)

His reluctance to admit such memories of genocide can be accounted for by a desire to fully inhabit and enjoy the present moment of love without distractions or interruptions. However, as Peterson points out, 'there is also the suggestion that history must be bracketed because the lovers might begin to compare their histories and to compete for "most victimized" status' (2010, p. 67). This suggestion is reinforced by the title of the poem, which casts the Jews and the Indians as competing teams in a baseball game that is about to be decided. The game is described as tied, but the eventual outcome can only be a win for one team and a loss for the other. The incongruous and irreverent sports metaphor satirizes the competitive memory model which, it is suggested – baseball being an all-American pastime – the United States imposes on ethnic minorities. Jews and Indians are forced to compete for public visibility and recognition of their respective genocidal histories. Jewish and Native American suffering cannot be remembered together; the collective memory of one group has to win over that of the other, which it inevitably screens out or hides from view. That this pernicious competition is generally seen as having been won convincingly by the Jews is evident in 'Inside Dachau'; in this poem, however, the memory battle is presented as still undecided. Importantly, though, the speaker of the poem goes on to qualify his blanket refusal to accept the burden of his and his partner's traumatic historical memories. In the closing lines he raises the suggestion of a possible alternative to memory competition and comparative victimology:

> but every once in a while
> we can remind each other
> that we are both survivors and children
> and grandchildren of survivors. (Alexie, 1993, p. 80)

The poem ultimately refuses to play the game of competitive memory and resists its presumed inevitability, gesturing instead towards a multidirectional model in which different historical memories enter into dialogue and mutually inform one another rather than cancelling each other out.

This move from competition to multidirectionality can also be found in the longer and more complex poem 'Inside Dachau', Alexie's most sustained and profound comparative engagement with the Holocaust to date. This seven-part poem shares the thematic focus of the earlier poem, bringing memories of the Nazi genocide and the genocide of the Native Americans into contact. It explores what it means to become a responsible witness to the Holocaust, raising difficult questions about how separate histories of mass suffering and their legacies can be brought together in a productive, mutually illuminating manner. The poem interrogates the appropriateness both of using the Holocaust as a metaphor, as a lens through which to look at other histories, and of treating the Holocaust as a radically unique event, incomparable to other atrocities. While it does not shy away from evoking Native American history through Holocaust allusions, thus analogizing these different historical traumas, it ends by embracing a metonymical logic that sets Jewish and Native American experiences alongside one another, preserving the distance between them.

What prompts these reflections and meditations is a visit to the site of the former Nazi concentration camp in Dachau by the speaker and his partner while on a trip to Germany, which is recounted in the first section of the poem.[10] Opening as early as 1933, Dachau was the first concentration camp established by the Nazis. During the next 12 years, an estimated 200,000 people were imprisoned there – two-thirds of them political prisoners, one-third Jews – of whom some 30,000 died there. Dachau holds an important place in American public memory because it was only the second camp to be liberated on the Western front (the first was Ohrdruf, a subcamp of Buchenwald): it was liberated by the US army on 29 April 1945. As a result, it was also one of the first sites where the full scope of the Nazi horrors was exposed to the Western world, through journalistic reports and newsreels. The speaker of the poem and his partner lie to their German hosts about their plans for the day, telling them that they intend to spend their time 'searching for rare albums in [nearby] Munich' (Alexie, 1996, p. 117). It is not entirely clear why the lie is necessary; after all, the German hosts are very open about the Nazi past – they 'always spoke of the camp / as truthfully as they spoke about the seasons' – and admit to feeling guilty about it: 'We are truly ashamed of Dachau' (ibid., p. 118). As Peterson (2010, p. 73) suggests, a possible explanation is that the speaker's initial reasons for wanting to visit the camp – to find inspiration for self-centred poetry about the horrors that took place there – are not entirely honourable:

> Once there, I had expected to feel simple
> emotions: hate, anger, sorrow. That was my plan.
> I would write poetry about how the season
> of winter found a perfect home in cold Dachau.
> I would be a Jewish man who died in the camp.
> I would be the ideal metaphor. (Alexie, 1996, p. 117)

He abandons this plan to take on the identity and assume the voice of a Jewish inmate who died in the camp after realizing that things are not so 'simple' and that his desire for identification is 'selfish'. Indeed, there is a fundamental gap between his experience and that of the Jewish victims that cannot be bridged by metaphor:

> ... I thought it would all be simple
> but there were no easy answers inside the camp.
> The poems still took their forms, but my earlier plans
> seemed so selfish. What could I say about Dachau
> when I had never suffered through any season
> inside its walls? ... (Ibid.)

The speaker questions his ability and his right, as an outsider to this history, to imagine himself in the place of a Holocaust victim. The fact that he is a Native American does not make any difference – in fact, his ethnic background is not even known to the reader at this point in the poem. While we, of course, tend to identify the speaker of a poem with the poet, and are even encouraged to do so in this case by the fact that the speaker's companion is, like Alexie's wife, called Diane, it is not actually made explicit that he is a Native American until the fourth part of the poem, which uses the phrase 'we indigenous people' (ibid., p. 119). Until then, the first-person pronouns that are used could refer to any present-day visitor to Dachau, or, at least, any American visitor (as we will see, one of the couple's German hosts refers to the United States as 'your country' (ibid., p. 118)). In any case, the speaker's ethnicity does not give him the right to conflate his own experience with that of a Jewish Holocaust victim. In so doing, he would be appropriating, exploiting and colonizing the Jewish inmate's experience, erasing its difference, ignoring its historical specificity – an arrogant, insensitive, indeed 'selfish' act.

While the first part of the poem thus warns against conflating distinct historical experiences, it also warns against treating them as unique and incomparable. Mikael, one of the German hosts, asks:

> . . . but what about all the Dachaus
> in the United States? What about the death camps
> in your country? (Ibid.)

This question may well be intended to deflect attention from German to US atrocities – presumably the US government's reservation policy and military massacres – in a manner reminiscent of the conservative position in the *Historikerstreit*; however, as Peterson (2010, p. 73) points out, the ethical issues about the comparability of the Holocaust and Native American history that it leads the speaker to confront will preoccupy him for the rest of the poem. Still in part 1, he acknowledges that Mikael's 'simple questions' are 'ignored, season after season' – meaning that the genocide of the Native Americans continues to be denied – and gloomily reflects:

> Inside Dachau, you might believe winter will never end. You might
>   lose faith in the change of seasons
> because some of the men who built the camps still live in Argentina,
>   in Washington, in Munich.
> They live simple lives. They share bread with sons and daughters
>   who have come to understand the master plan. (Alexie, 1996, p. 118)

Here, and indeed throughout the rest of the poem, the speaker expresses his fear that winter will never end and that regeneration and renewal will remain forever elusive. This fear is based on the observation that the ideology of those who constructed the Nazi camps is being passed along to the next generations, both in Germany and elsewhere in the world. The poem's extensive use of highly repetitive poetic forms – such as the sestina in part 1, the villanelle in parts 3 and 7, and the rondel in part 4 – underlines this sense of hopelessness. The repetition compulsion in which the poem appears to be caught on the formal level, with the same rhymes, words or lines constantly recurring, reflects the speaker's impression that history keeps repeating itself.

He does not acquiesce in this state of affairs, though. The next three sections of the poem go to the root of the problem and examine the role that the memory of the Holocaust can play in perpetuating or confronting the denial – and the resulting continuing perpetration – of other atrocities. In part 2, the speaker notes that by repressing knowledge of atrocities ('we insist / on ignoring the shared fires in our past' (ibid.)), and particularly of our own implication in them ('We attempt to erase our names from the list / that begins and ends with ash' (ibid.)) – like the Germans who claim not to have known about the Holocaust or the Americans who continue to deny what was done to the Native Americans – we ensure that genocides will keep occurring; genocides of which we ourselves may well one day become the victims:

> We ignore the war until we are the last
> standing, until we are the last to persist
> in denial, as we are shipped off to camps
> where we all are stripped, and our dark bodies lit
> by the cruel light of those antique Jew-skinned lamps. (Ibid.)

The speaker is warning us here of what will happen if we persist in whitewashing our own history; if we stop denying, perhaps we have a chance to escape this fate. Both the problem and the solution are captured by the title of part 2, 'history as the home movie'. If we treat history like a home movie, and edit out or fail to record unhappy memories, that means we refuse to confront the dark chapters of our past. These chapters should be made part of our family history, it is suggested, in the sense that we should become as intimately familiar with them as we are with the kinds of events home movies typically record. The title can also be seen to problematize our tendency to narrow history down to our personal history and to ignore the suffering of others.

In part 3, the speaker wonders whether visiting a memorial site such as Dachau can stimulate remembrance and critical reflection. He scrutinizes people's motivations for visiting Dachau, repeatedly asking (using a generic 'we'),

> Why are we here? What have we come to see?
> What do we need to find behind the doors? (Ibid., p. 119)

A possible answer that is offered is that we may be looking for an apology from the perpetrators, bystanders or negationists of the Holocaust. However, it is suggested that that expectation does not suffice and is unsatisfactory. After all, it could be a way of letting ourselves off the hook, of shirking our responsibility to confront our own dark past, which part 2 emphasized. The speaker suddenly adds the question, 'What have we come to see / that cannot be seen in other countries?' and recognizes that 'Every country hides behind a white door' (ibid.). The implication is that visiting sites of trauma in other countries may be a way for people to avoid dealing with disturbing aspects of their own past. The speaker thus criticizes the use of the Holocaust as a screen memory for more discomforting memories of events closer to home. As Friedberg points out:

> In the pathological dynamic of genocidal histories, the perpetrator culture invariably turns its gaze to the horrors registered in the archives and accounts of the 'other guys.' This is why Holocaust studies in the United States focus almost exclusively on the atrocity of Auschwitz, not of Wounded Knee or Sand Creek. (2000, p. 354)

From an American perspective, Dachau is an even more appropriate choice for a screen memory than Auschwitz, as the former was liberated by the Americans, the latter by the Soviets. Hence, visiting Dachau offers Americans an opportunity to see themselves in a heroic, wholly positive light.

However, as part 4 makes clear, it can also have the effect of making the visitor more rather than less aware of the shameful history of their own country and bringing him or her face to face with its continued denial. Provocatively titled 'the american indian holocaust museum', this section of the poem, in which the speaker for the first time explicitly identifies himself as a Native American, circles around three repeated lines:

> What do we indigenous people want from our country?
> We stand over mass graves. Our collective grief makes us numb.
> We are waiting for the construction of our museum. (Alexie, 1996, p. 119)

Part 4 stresses the parallels between Jewish and Native American history. The images of mass graves and, in the next stanza, shoes of the dead that could 'fill a city / to its thirteenth floor' (ibid.) apply to both the Holocaust and the genocide of the Native Americans, and Jews and Native Americans today also share a profound sense of 'collective grief'. However, while Jewish losses are widely acknowledged and publicly commemorated nowadays – for example, through the transformation of Nazi camps into memorial sites and through the foundation, in 1993, of the US Holocaust Memorial Museum in Washington, DC – those suffered by the Native Americans are still officially unrecognized and not taken seriously, as is apparent from the absence of a high-profile museum dedicated to the memory of the victims of colonialism in the United States. The speaker exposes this asymmetry and calls for the establishment of a museum devoted to what the title of this section refers to as the 'american indian holocaust', which could serve the same purpose as the US Holocaust Memorial Museum in making the devastations of Native American history publicly visible.[11]

As Peterson points out, if 'Inside Dachau' had ended here, 'it could be read as primarily interested in developing a comparative suffering framework' to advance the Native American cause, with the Holocaust being used to highlight and demand recognition for the tragic history of indigenous people in the United States (2010, p. 74). However, the poem continues and, in the last few sections, moves towards a more multidirectional understanding of collective memory. This becomes particularly clear in part 6, which juxtaposes Jewish and Native histories both formally and thematically. In fact, this section of the poem can be seen to resume the critique of metaphor that began in part 1 by developing a way of connecting Jewish and Native American experiences without equating them. It is made up of a series of couplets in which the speaker imagines himself to be Jewish in the first line and speaks of being Spokane in the next. The opening stanza, for example, runs as follows:

> If I were Jewish, how would I mourn the dead?
> I am Spokane. I wake. (Alexie, 1996, p. 121)

Each couplet asks a question in the first line, about how a Jewish person would do certain things, and makes a statement in the next, about the speaker being Spokane and therefore acting somewhat differently. As Peterson notes, 'the overall effect' of this structure 'is to locate provocative points of difference and connection' (2010, p. 75). In the first couplet, for example, the speaker establishes a link between different mourning practices – sitting shiva in the Jewish tradition and holding a wake in the Native American one – but refrains from collapsing them into one another. The assumption of easy comparability that underlay the speaker's initial plan for the poem – in which he would be an 'ideal metaphor' for the experience of a Jewish inmate of Dachau – and the whiff of memory competition that hung over part 4 of the poem have given way to an open-ended exploration of points of cross-cultural contact and areas of overlap between Jewish and Native American identities which respectfully acknowledges the gulf that separates the two.

The concluding section of 'Inside Dachau' holds on to the insights gained in the previous section, with the speaker recognizing the limits of his understanding:

> I am not a Jew. I was just a guest
> in that theater which will never close. (Alexie, 1996, p. 22)

As the latter line suggests, the poem does not end happily. The speaker predicts that atrocious events will keep on happening:

> I wonder which people will light fires next
> and which people will soon be turned to smoke. (Ibid., p. 122)

While his reflections lead to a disillusioned perspective, the poem as a whole is not entirely fatalistic. A measure of hope can be found in the agency of the text itself, which performs the very process of cross-cultural mourning whose absence it laments, and which in so doing seeks to transform the reader into an agent of such mourning. As Laura Leibman argues, 'Alexie uses the sequence about visiting Dachau to forge a new identity for the mourner and a new mourning process – one that is active. Through this transformation of readers into agents in mourning, the poet seeks to bring about change' (Leibman, 2005, p. 557). As a textual memorial, Alexie's poem hopes to trigger a form of reflection in its readers in the same way Dachau triggered reflection in the speaker. The invitation it extends to the reader to engage in constructive memory work – by bearing witness to the horrors of the Holocaust, acknowledging the historical traumas of the Native Americans and recognizing the continuing recurrence of genocide – is the poem's modest but valuable attempt to act upon the world in such a way as to help prevent or reduce further violence. Like 'The Game', 'Inside Dachau' thus exemplifies not only the dangers involved in, but also the benefits potentially brought by, adopting a comparative perspective on the Holocaust. As such, it is in line with recent research in the field of comparative memory studies, which is suspicious and critical of overly celebratory accounts of the increasingly transnational circulation of Holocaust memory, but not to the point of altogether abandoning the notion that something positive can come out of it.

Notes

1. For a more detailed study of these two developments, from which this account is drawn, see Craps (2013, chapter 6).
2. For incisive critiques of Levy and Sznaider's and Alexander's arguments, see A. Assmann (2010), A. Assmann and Conrad (2010), Moses (2011), Poole (2010) and the various responses to Alexander's essay included in Alexander et al.'s *Remembering the Holocaust: A Debate* (2009).
3. It can be argued that the enormous amount of attention paid to the Holocaust and the extraordinary importance attached to this event serve to blind Americans and Europeans to certain unpalatable aspects of their own history: the genocide of the Native Americans, slavery and segregation, nuclear warfare and the Vietnam War in the case of the United States; colonial history and collaboration with the Nazis in the case of various European countries. Remembering the Holocaust, so the argument goes, allows these nations to evade these awkward episodes from their own past.

4. See, for example, Neil Levi's (2007) analysis of how, in the Australian context, explicit comparisons of the fate of the Aborigines after settlement with that of the Jews during the Holocaust lead to disavowal or partial remembrance of a traumatic local history.
5. The *Historikerstreit* or Historians' Debate was a controversy over the interpretation of the Holocaust between left-wing and right-wing intellectuals in West Germany. Some conservative historians, led by Ernst Nolte, compared the Holocaust to the crimes of Joseph Stalin in the Soviet Union and to Germany's own losses (the mass expulsions of ethnic Germans from Czechoslovakia and Poland at the end of the Second World War) in order to diminish the importance of the Holocaust and to overcome the singularity of German responsibility for it. Progressive intellectuals, most prominently the philosopher Jürgen Habermas, insisted on the uniqueness of the Holocaust as a defence against this relativistic position, which sought to minimize Nazi crimes.
6. See, for example, Churchill (1997), Stannard (1992), Novick (1999) and Finkelstein and Birn (1998).
7. For additional discussions of prose fiction that connects the Holocaust to other histories of victimization, see Cheyette (2000); Craps (2013, chapters 7 and 8); Craps and Buelens (2011); Mufti (2007); Rothberg et al., eds (2010).
8. For a fine analysis of issues of mourning in Alexie's work, which also devotes considerable attention to 'Inside Dachau', see Leibman (2005).
9. The term 'postmemorial' derives from Marianne Hirsch's concept of postmemory, which she coined, in her book *Family Frames: Photography, Narrative, and Postmemory* (1997), to describe the relationship that children of Holocaust survivors have with their parents' traumatic experiences. More recently, though, Hirsch has expressed her hope that the notion of postmemory can provide 'a useful framework' for 'connective approaches' such as that developed by Rothberg: 'I am interested in exploring affiliative structures of memory beyond the family, and I see this connective memory work as another form of affiliation across lines of difference' (Hirsch, 2012, p. 21). Alexie's poem can be seen to anticipate this intertwining of the multidirectional and the postmemorial.
10. An amateur YouTube video made by an American tourist which combines his personal home video footage of his visit to Dachau with archival images of the same sites gives one a sense of what it is like to visit Dachau today and of what the place looked like in the 1940s (Peppels, 2007).
11. It should be pointed out that the National Museum of the American Indian opened on the Mall in Washington, DC, in 2004, eight years after Alexie published 'Inside Dachau'. However, this museum does not function as the 'american indian holocaust museum' which the poem calls for: rather than documenting genocide, it celebrates the rich history and culture of indigenous peoples throughout the Americas.

Works Cited

Alexander, J. C. (2002), 'On the social construction of moral universals: the "Holocaust" from war crime to trauma drama', *European Journal of Social Theory*, 5.1, 5–85.
Alexander, J. C., Jay, M., Giesen, B., Rothberg, M., Manne, R., Glazer, N., Katz, E. and Katz, R. (2009), *Remembering the Holocaust: A Debate*. Oxford: Oxford University Press.
Alexie, S. (1993), 'The game between the Jews and the Indians is tied going into the bottom of the ninth inning', in *First Indian on the Moon*. New York: Hanging Loose Press, p. 80.

—. (1996), 'Inside Dachau', in *The Summer of Black Widows*. New York: Hanging Loose Press, pp. 117–22.

Arendt, H. [1951] (2004), *The Origins of Totalitarianism*. New York: Schocken.

Assmann, A. (2010), 'The Holocaust – a global memory? extensions and limits of a new memory community', in A. Assmann and S. Conrad (eds), *Memory in a Global Age: Discourses, Practices and Trajectories*. Houndmills: Palgrave Macmillan, pp. 97–117.

Assmann, A. and Conrad, S. (2010), 'Introduction', in A. Assmann and S. Conrad (eds), *Memory in a Global Age: Discourses, Practices and Trajectories*. Houndmills: Palgrave Macmillan, pp. 1–16.

Assmann, J. (1992), *Das kulturelle Gedächtnis: Schrift, Erinnerung, und Identität in den frühen Hochkulturen*. München: C. H. Beck.

Bauer, Y. (1978), *The Holocaust in Historical Perspective*. Seattle: University of Washington Press.

Césaire, A. [1950] (2000), *Discourse on Colonialism*, trans. J. Pinkham. New York: Monthly Review.

Cheyette, B. (2000), 'Venetian spaces: old-new literatures and the ambivalent uses of Jewish history', in S. Nasta (ed.), *Reading the 'New' Literatures in a Postcolonial Era*. Cambridge: Brewer, pp. 53–72.

Churchill, W. (1997), *A Little Matter of Genocide: Holocaust and Denial in the Americas, 1492 to the Present*. San Francisco: City Lights.

Craps, S. (2013), *Postcolonial Witnessing: Trauma Out of Bounds*. Houndmills: Palgrave Macmillan.

Craps, S. and Buelens, G. (2011), 'Traumatic mirrorings: Holocaust and colonial trauma in Michael Chabon's *The Final Solution*', in S. Craps and M. Rothberg (eds), *Transcultural Negotiations of Holocaust Memory*. Special issue of *Criticism: A Quarterly for Literature and the Arts* 53.4, 569–86.

Durrant, S. (2004), *Postcolonial Narrative and the Work of Mourning: J. M. Coetzee, Wilson Harris, and Toni Morrison*. Albany: State University of New York Press.

Eaglestone, R. (2008), '"You would not add to my suffering if you knew what I have seen": Holocaust testimony and contemporary African trauma literature', in S. Craps and G. Buelens (eds), *Postcolonial Trauma Novels*. Special issue of *Studies in the Novel*, 40.1–2, 72–85.

Finkelstein, N. and Birn, R. B. (1998), *A Nation on Trial: The Goldhagen Thesis and Historical Truth*. New York: Metropolitan.

Flanzbaum, H. (ed.) (1999), *The Americanization of the Holocaust*. Baltimore: Johns Hopkins University Press.

Friedberg, L. (2000), 'Dare to compare: Americanizing the Holocaust', *American Indian Quarterly*, 24.3, 353–80.

Gilroy, P. (1993), *The Black Atlantic: Modernity and Double Consciousness*. London: Verso.

—. [2000] (2004), *Between Camps: Nations, Cultures and the Allure of Race*. London: Routledge.

Goldhagen, D. (1996), *Hitler's Willing Executioners: Ordinary Germans and the Holocaust*. New York: Knopf.

Halbwachs, M. (1992), *On Collective Memory*, ed. and trans. L. A. Coser. Chicago: University of Chicago Press.

Hansen, M. Bratu (1996), '*Schindler's List* is not *Shoah*: the second commandment, popular modernism, and public memory', *Critical Inquiry*, 22.2, 292–312.

Hirsch, M. (1997), *Family Frames: Photography, Narrative, and Postmemory*. Cambridge, MA: Harvard University Press.

—. (2012), *The Generation of Postmemory: Writing and Visual Culture after the Holocaust*. New York: Columbia University Press.

Huyssen, A. (2003), *Present Pasts: Urban Palimpsests and the Politics of Memory*. Stanford, CA: Stanford University Press.

Jessup, G. (1996), *American Holocaust*. CD. G. Jessup.

Katz, S. (1994), *The Holocaust in Historical Context, Volume I: The Holocaust and Mass Death before the Modern Age*. New York: Oxford University Press.

Landsberg, A. (2004), *Prosthetic Memory: The Transformation of American Remembrance in the Age of Mass Culture*. New York: Columbia University Press.

Leibman, L. Arnold (2005), 'A bridge of difference: Sherman Alexie and the politics of mourning', *American Literature*, 77.3, 541–61.

Levi, N. (2007), '"No sensible comparison"? the place of the Holocaust in Australia's history wars', *History and Memory*, 19.1, 124–56.

Levy, D. and Sznaider, N. [2001] (2006), *The Holocaust and Memory in the Global Age*, trans. A. Oksiloff. Philadelphia: Temple University Press.

Lipstadt, D. (1993), *Denying the Holocaust: The Growing Assault on Truth and Memory*. New York: Free Press.

Mazower, M. (2008), *Hitler's Empire: Nazi Rule in Occupied Europe*. London: Allen Lane.

Moore, M. (ed.) (2006), *Eating Fire, Tasting Blood: Breaking the Great Silence of the American Indian Holocaust*. New York: Thunder's Mouth.

Moses, A. D. (2002), 'Conceptual blockages and definitional dilemmas in the "racial century": genocides of indigenous peoples and the Holocaust', *Patterns of Prejudice*, 36.4, 7–36.

—. (2011), 'Genocide and the terror of history', in R. Crownshaw (ed.), *Transcultural Memory*. Special issue of *Parallax*, 17.4, 90–108.

Moshman, D. (2001), 'Conceptual constraints on thinking about genocide', *Journal of Genocide Research*, 3.3, 431–50.

Mufti, A. R. (2007), *Enlightenment in the Colony: The Jewish Question and the Crisis of Postcolonial Culture*. Princeton: Princeton University Press.

Nora, P. [1984–92] (1996–8), *Realms of Memory: Rethinking the French Past*, ed. L. D. Kritzman, trans. A. Goldhammer. 3 vols. New York: Columbia University Press.

Novick, P. (1999), *The Holocaust in American Life*. New York: Houghton Mifflin.

Peppels, M. (2007), 'Dachau concentration camp: tribute', *YouTube*, 17 April 2007, http://www.youtube.com/watch?d&v=0ZnAGhwyIfY#! Accessed 23 February 2013.

Peterson, N. J. (2010), '"If I were Jewish, how would I mourn the dead?": Holocaust and genocide in the work of Sherman Alexie', *MELUS*, 35.3, 63–84.

Poole, R. (2010), 'Misremembering the Holocaust: universal symbol, nationalist icon or moral kitsch?', in Y. Gutman, A. D. Brown and A. Sodaro (eds), *Memory and the Future: Transnational Politics, Ethics and Society*. Houndmills: Palgrave Macmillan, pp. 31–49.

Romero, J. (2000) (dir), *American Holocaust: When It's All Over, I'll Still Be Indian*. DVD. Northridge, CA: Spirit World Productions.

Rosenfeld, A. H. (1995), 'The Americanization of the Holocaust', *Commentary*, 99.6, 35–40.

Rothberg, M. (2009), *Multidirectional Memory: Remembering the Holocaust in the Age of Decolonization*. Stanford, CA: Stanford University Press.

—. (2011), 'From Gaza to Warsaw: mapping multidirectional memory', in S. Craps and M. Rothberg (eds), *Transcultural Negotiations of Holocaust Memory*. Special issue of *Criticism: A Quarterly for Literature and the Arts*, 53.4, 523–48.

Rothberg, M., Sanyal, D. and Silverman, M. (eds) (2010), *Nœuds de mémoire: Multidirectional Memory in Postwar French and Francophone Culture*. Special issue of *Yale French Studies*, 118–19.

Semelin, J. (2007), *Purify and Destroy: The Political Uses of Massacre and Genocide*, trans. C. Schoch. New York: Columbia University Press.

Silverman, M. (2013), *Palimpsestic Memory: The Holocaust and Colonialism in French and Francophone Fiction and Film*. New York: Berghahn.

Snyder, T. (2010), *Bloodlands: Europe between Hitler and Stalin*. New York: Basic.

Stannard, D. E. (1992), *American Holocaust: Columbus and the Conquest of the New World*. New York: Oxford University Press.

Stone, D. (2004), 'The historiography of genocide: beyond "uniqueness" and ethnic competition', *Rethinking History*, 8.1, 127–42.

Thornton, R. (1987), *American Indian Holocaust and Survival: A Population History since 1492*. Norman: University of Oklahoma Press.

Winter, J. (2000), 'The generation of memory: reflections on the "memory boom" in contemporary historical studies', *Bulletin of the German Historical Institute*, 27, 69–92.

Zimmerer, J. (2005), 'The birth of the *Ostland* out of the spirit of colonialism: a postcolonial perspective on the Nazi policy of conquest and extermination', *Patterns of Prejudice*, 39.2, 197–219.

11 Depoliticizing and Repoliticizing Holocaust Memory

Richard Crownshaw

Abstract

This chapter will argue the importance of reading literary representations of the Holocaust for their politics of memory. To be more precise, this chapter looks at novels that both represent the ways in which cultures remember the Holocaust and participate in that remembrance. The novels discussed in these case studies, W. G. Sebald's *Austerlitz* (2001) and Bernhard Schlink's novel of 1995, *Der Vorleser* (published as *The Reader* in 1996), have been chosen because of their place in the canon of contemporary Holocaust fiction and will therefore be familiar to most scholars and students of Holocaust literature. It would be beyond the scope of this chapter to offer exhaustive readings of the novels themselves, or of their treatment by critics. What this chapter does do is point to literary–critical tendencies that depoliticize memory texts, and to the ways in which contextualizing literature via a politics of memory can realize more fully the ethical import of the text.

Before a discussion of these novels, it would be useful to define, briefly, what is meant by the politics of memory. Aleida Assmann has defined 'political' memory as a form of top-down, instrumentalized memory that seeks homogeneity (a 'unity of consciousness of the past') rather than heterogeneity (Assmann, 2004, pp. 22–36; 2006a, pp. 211–23; 2008, pp. 51–6). In other words, the consolidation of collective historical understanding can shore up group identity or serve political or ideological agendas through politically authorized and institutionally mediated representations of the past. However, as Jeffrey Olick (2007), among others, reminds us, it is perhaps inaccurate to think of political memory working in this fashion – as the instrumentalization of the past to serve current needs. Rather, the current distribution of memory, no matter how powerfully authorized, must compete with residual memories, which at one time had some political or ideological valency, and is, of course, dependent on the popular subscription of constituencies of memory. Those constituencies are heterogeneous by nature, as are the memories brought to each constituency by its members. What is more, as more recent work on memory studies and Holocaust studies (Rothberg, 2009; Erll, 2011) convincingly argues, memory is subject to the forces and currents of globalization, cannot be contained by cultural or national boundaries and is no longer the exclusive preserve of particular groups. To speak, then, of political memory, is to speak of political intention; to speak of the politics of memory gives a better indication of remembrance as a form of dialogue, competition and negotiation.

The question remains as to how to theorize these negotiations of memory. By way of a preface to the discussion of the political implications of Schlink's novel, the following will establish ways in which memory texts can be depoliticized, and the political and ethical implications of such depoliticization. In interview, W. G. Sebald has projected an idealized reader thus: 'A picture, being visual information, can be contemplated, it does not have to be decoded in time. You can just sit and see it, and the ideal reader for me would be a reader who does not just read the text but sees, who lifts out the perennial wasting which occurs in time' (Bigsby, 2001, p. 156). In other words, Sebald's idealized reader is one who would participate in the memorative projects of his various narrators in their attempt to reconstruct and remember lives, things and places subject to modernity's destructive projects, logics and impulses. That reconstruction and remembrance takes place by way of what remains: textual traces, stranded artefacts, architectural ruins, deserted spaces and ambiguous witnesses. These remnants of modernity constitute Sebald's compendious narratives as the props of his narrators' memory work. As Sebald suggests above, just like the remnants narrativized, his texts themselves are rendered fragile in the face of modernity's ongoing destructive principles. If modernity can be characterized as a process of creative destruction that moves unevenly across its spheres of activity yet inexorably towards a point of oblivion, then, memory is an interruptive force. The idealized reader would participate in the memory work staged by Sebald's texts, transforming those texts into objects of memory.

For Ann Rigney, the novel can act as a 'portable monument', a prop by which individuals can participate in, following Aleida Assmann's (2004) definition of the term, cultural memories of events not directly experienced. The heteroglossic nature of the novel dislocates a series of memories from their original social and historical contexts and recombines them, such is the aesthetic freedom of the form, for the reader's participation and remembrance. If deemed of cultural significance, those memories can be reactivated, reworked and reappropriated, or associated with new ones in the various cultural scenarios of the text's reception and afterlife (Rigney, 2004, pp. 365–89). In many ways, Sebald is suggesting his texts be read as 'portable monuments'.

The following will discuss the ways in which Sebald's novel *Austerlitz* (2001) has had a particularly interesting, 'monumental' afterlife in relation to the discourses of Holocaust Studies. *Austerlitz* is the fictional biography of Jacques Austerlitz, who arrived in England in 1939, aged four-and-a-half, as part of a *Kindertransport* from Prague. He escaped the Holocaust that claimed his parents but forgot his origins and what he had lost. His subsequent life is, for the most part, ruined, haunted by a sense of exile and loss he does not understand, and then by the painful recovery of what he had repressed. What is of significance to this argument is the way in which the text has been read by critics as the literal inscription of the dynamics of the traumatic memory of its protagonist. As Dominick LaCapra would put it, this has been a confusion of structural absence for historical loss, or, to put in other terms, a textual trauma for a historical trauma (2004, pp. 115–27). As Susannah Radstone would argue, this is typical of broader trends in memory and trauma studies that overlook the mediation of objects of memory. This in turn dates back to the academic rise of memory studies as part of a postmodernist rejection of the grand narratives of history in favour of particularized, partial, subjective and embodied experiences (Radstone, 2005, p. 140; 2000, p. 84). The problem, though, lies in the way in which historical experience, given this validation of memory over history, has been stripped of context, overpersonalized: 'the inner world and its very processes has been taken as "the" world' (Radstone, 2005, p. 40). When it comes to objects of memory (memory texts), such as a memoir or monument, these are often taken as direct reflections of the processes of memory and considered, complains Radstone, without due attention to their textual or generic properties, their related discourses or traditions (2008, pp. 30–9), or to the mediating discourses and institutions of the public sphere that authorize these texts and facilitate their articulation of the past (2005, pp. 35–7).

The interplay of image and text in Sebald's work in general and *Austerlitz* in particular makes for unsettled reading, and tempts this kind of conflation of structural (textual) absence or disruption and historical trauma or loss. As Jonathan Long notes, the photographic images found in Sebald's works have a disorientating, doubling effect. The photographs must have been taken by someone in the real world, outside of the text, and yet they are purported to have been taken by a fictional character. The character has 'no extra-textual referent', yet the images do, and, because they do, provide traces of the apparatus and person that produced them in the real world; they provoke an ontological confusion between the textual and the extra-textual, the real and the fictional. The narrative device of having the protagonist, in this case Austerlitz, carry a camera wherever he goes cannot naturalize the images that he produces, nor effect a seamless incorporation of them into the narrative account of his life and memory (Long, 2007, pp. 149–50). That the photographic images consequently flicker, illuminating their reality *and* unreality, conveying the presence *and* absence of their referents suggests a reflection of Austerlitz's own memorative processes of trying to recover his traumatic past. Silke Horstkotte (2004, pp. 271–3, 279, 283–5) develops the ways that a disturbed reading not only reflects Austerlitz's memory but participates in it. In reconstructing the relationship between image and text that has been absent – the provenance of the images being unclear, their illustrative capacity is curtailed – the reader opens up and occupies a third, liminal signifying realm in which different temporalities coincide: the present moment of verbal reference and the return of the past staged by the photographic image. This reflects other moments of the text in which historical artefacts provoke the past's intrusion in the narrator's and narrated subject's present. On the one hand, this coincidence of temporalities is framed by the memorative subjectivity of the narrator and narrated. On the other, the reader is drawn into a liminal realm that exceeds that frame, because the images and text are not identical with themselves and each other. The reality or documentary effect of the images is cast into doubt by their non-correspondence with the verbal text and *vice versa*, even though it was the referential promises of both that provoked the reader into investigating the differences between them. The deconstruction of both orders of signification compounds the ambiguity of the 'imagetext', making it dependent on the reader to fill its 'fantastic gaps' (Horstkotte, 2004) and become the subject of memory (remembering subject) in whom different temporalities coincide.

If, for Horstkotte, the text leaves excessive room for the reader's participation, Amir Eshel (2003) suggests that the photographs which provoke such an excess appear to stand outside, at least temporarily, their narrativization. Before they depart for the last time, Austerlitz gives the narrator the keys to his house and access to his collection of photographs. Those photographs have all the while been illustrating the narrative and will continue to do so. The emplotment of those images has less to do with Austerlitz's unfolding narration of his own life and past and more to do with the narrator's orchestration of their appearance in that life story. The narrator has smuggled them into the narrative before their narrativization becomes apparent. In this 'bricolage' is an attempted defiance of an ordering process found in the act of the literary narrative and the organization of social and cultural processes of modernity that can rationalize violence and subsume the particularities of experience and memory. This has a particular reparative resonance for a German writer, Sebald (and, by implication, his narrator) writing the life of a Jewish subject. For Eshel, the narrator's desire to stave off (modern) time gives rise to a type of narrativity that strives for immediacy, by which Austerlitz and those he stands for can 'transgress the border between textual and transtextual realities' (Eshel, 2003, pp. 81–3, 94).

The emergence of Austerlitz from the text is of course a rhetorical effect of the narrative. Nevertheless, for Horstkotte and now Eshel, the borders of the text are becoming increasingly permeable, and the differences between memory and literature worn thin. Furthermore, the insertion of photographic images disrupts narrative progression, introducing an alternative temporality to the obliviousness of modern time. The reading of images 'relates the spectator to temporality – they make one aware of both the *now* that is frozen in the image and the *now* of the spectatorship, of the reading process', which incorporates the 'time of reading' into the 'narrative's temporal fabric' (ibid.). What, though, is to prevent the time of reading slipping into the time of memory, the temporal convolutions of reading merging with Austerlitz's memorative dynamics? Put another way, readings of *Austerlitz* that move text and memory closer together implicate author and narrator in an appropriation of Jewish memory rendering the text transparent to that memory. What is needed instead in the approach to literary memory-texts is a contextualization of these acts of memory (literary production and consumption), an exploration of the way they can be mediated by questions of identity and identification, and, therefore, an understanding of the political connotations of memory. To illustrate this process, the next section looks at another well-known Holocaust memory text and places its memorative operations in the context of the politics of German memory.

Schlink's novel of 1995 (translated into English in 1996) has attracted a critical consensus that deems it to have reconfigured the perpetrator generation as victims of Nazism, and second-generation Germans as victims of Nazism's legacy (see, for example, Schlant (1999), Bartov (2000), Donahue (2001), LaCapra (2001) and Taberner (2003)). Such an appropriation of victim status is part of a wider discourse of German suffering, prevalent in the 1990s and 2000s, which has often sought to elide or subsume the memory of suffering caused by Germans, or aggregate all those who suffered from 1933 to 1945 – constituting a politics of memory in the service of the construction of a post-unification German identity. However, I will argue that Schlink's novel is not so politically instrumental; rather, it maps out and critiques the proclivities of German remembrance.

To understand Schlink's critical intervention, we need to consider the general structures of German memory. Despite the collapse of difference in the construction of the generalized victim, German cultural memory had historically been directed by the binary thinking that has governed the remembrance and construction of Germany's victims and perpetrators, both in the academic theory and cultural practice of memory. Aleida Assmann's map of German memory is useful here. In 2006, Assmann perceived the persistence of a binary opposition in German cultural memory, in which Germans were remembered as either 'victims' or 'perpetrators', but never both (Assmann, 2006b, p. 190). Memories of German suffering (i.e. the suffering perceived and experienced by the perpetrator generation), according to Assmann, have been the stuff of private, familial, 'communicative' memory, and have not been recognized at an official, commemorative level, which is the preserve of a hegemonic Holocaust memory. Attempts after the immediate postwar period to elevate German suffering from the private and familial to the level of national and official commemoration, via, say, the *Bund der Vetriebenen* (League of Expellees), were deemed by second-generation Germans as revisionist attempts to subsume Holocaust memory by recourse to competing claims of victimization (ibid., p. 192). Denunciations by the so-called 1968ers left no room in the public sphere for empathy for the victims of Allied bombings, expulsions of ethnic Germans from the east, and the Soviet army as it entered German territory. As Assmann notes, it was not until the 1990s that the second generation were able, along with the third generation, to look back not in anger at what their parents and grandparents might have done during the war, but in empathy for what they might have suffered (ibid.). The passing away of the first generation has intensified the memory work of the second and third generations as they anxiously reconstruct the experiences of the first. This turn to empathy is not unproblematic (ibid.). Although the guilt of the first generation is recognized along with its suffering, the inheritance of memory acts as a vicariously confessional experience in which the burden of responsibility lies not so much with those who perpetrated crimes against humanity but with those who confess by proxy (ibid., p. 193). Assmann sees the subsequent proliferation of private, family memories of suffering as part of an inevitable expression of the perspectival, heterogeneous nature of memory itself.

Despite their large-scale distribution by Germany's mass media, Assmann believes that these memories will be and are regulated by an established 'normative framework of memory'. Proliferating in private (as familial and communicative), memories of German suffering, upon entering the public sphere, are integrated into a framework that centres on the Holocaust:

> The norm of German national memory, as established in the 1960s and reconfirmed in the 1980s, is the Holocaust, the recognition and working through of German guilt, involving the assumption of historical responsibility for the atrocities of the Nazi-regime. This is the normative framework into which all other memories have to be integrated. (Ibid., p. 197)

Integrated as such, memories of German suffering and memories of suffering caused by Germans can exist 'side by side' without 'necessarily cancelling each other out' (ibid., p. 198), although the Holocaust will be officially dominant in memory.

Assmann cites the campaign of Erika Steinbach, president of the *Bund der Vetriebenen*, as proof of how this regulatory framework works. Steinbach's personal or family memories of flight – she was born in 1940 – are essentially held in check by a hierarchy of memory. Her family memory will not become nationalized, Assmann predicted in 2006, by her proposed Centre against Expulsions. In its design (based on the United States Holocaust Memorial Museum), exhibitionary contents and structure, and location in Berlin, the centre would vie with the German Memorial to the Murdered Jews of Europe not just to constitute another national memorial, but to constitute *the* German national memorial (Schmitz, 2006, pp. 103–4). On the one hand, the discourse of suffering threatens to invert the hierarchy of German memory. On the other, the academic conceptualization of the hierarchy of memory and suffering may frame and seek to contain the threat of inversion, but, as Helmut Schmitz points out, it is the binary operation of the hierarchy that makes it vulnerable to inversion. Schmitz argues, 'this apparent unevenness between guilt/responsibility and suffering is exactly the issue around which the entire representational discourse of German victim experience circles' (2007, p. 15). Assmann's hierarchy of memory into which the remembrance of German suffering must be integrated effectively reinscribes the binary logic that competitive or revisionist remembrance of German suffering used in the first place as a mechanism to displace Holocaust memory.

A revisionary public–private binary was certainly evident in the 1990s culture of memory, as in, for example, the controversy surrounding Martin Walser's acceptance speech for the Peace Prize of the German Book Trade Fair in Frankfurt (October 1998), and in his literary work itself. Walser complained about the persistence of a left-liberal instrumentalization in Germany of the memory of the Nazi past, forming a culture of contrition rather than national pride (Fuchs, 2008, p. 3; Taberner, 2006, p. 167). Such politically correct memories, argued Walser, could be traced back to the 1960s and the continuing influence of the second generation (the 1968ers). As Bill Niven puts it, 'This generation stands accused of having institutionalised a doctrine of politically correct memory which led to the marginalisation and indeed exclusion of all memory of German suffering, thus making it impossible for the Germans to mourn their losses. Walser's speech undoubtedly triggered in many Germans the feeling that they were victims. Victimisation in the present obstructed empathy with victimhood in the past', that is, Jewish victims of Nazism (Niven, 2006, p. 11). As Niven continues, the accusation uncannily resonated with Nazi conspiracies that placed Jews (figured as perpetrators) at the centre of plots against the nation (ibid.). Indeed, Schmitz argues that in the consequent debate carried out in the media between Ignatz Bubis, then Head of the Central Council of German Jews, and Walser, the position of conspiratorial 'other' was allocated to a representative Bubis. Synecdochally, Bubis stood for a victim's perspective that was deemed inauthentic and outside of the German collective, which now appeared rather Volkish (Schmitz, 2006, p. 102).

In his speech and in the debate that followed, one of Walser's points was that the instrumentalization of Holocaust memory actually serves as the means by which Germans can unburden themselves of historical responsibility, and the routinized mention of Auschwitz the means by which Germans can align themselves with the victims and distance themselves from the perpetrators (ibid., p. 101). Although there is some truth in this, such an accusation rests on a faith in the notion of the 'privacy of conscience', an autonomous realm of authentic memory 'constantly under siege from inauthentic public forms of address' (ibid., pp. 101–2). In other words, according to Walser's theory, Germans could pay lip service to orthodox memory work while retaining their true feelings and memories about the past.

This spurious isolation of private or individual from historical conscience and consciousness separates memory into the authentic ('German') and inauthentic ('Jewish'). This separation of memories is typical of Walser's literature. For example, his semi-autobiographical novel set between 1932 and 1945, *Ein springender Brunnen* (A Springing Fountain, 1998) is conspicuous because it does not mention Auschwitz and is underpinned by an insistence that childhood memory cannot be deformed retrospectively by the political correctness of Holocaust remembrance (Taberner, 2006, p. 167).

The idea of a private, bracketed, enclave of memory can be found more widely in German memory culture, although its construction is not necessarily as revisionist as Walser's psychic topography of remembrance. Anne Fuchs, like Assmann, notes the family as a site of remembrance and of the intergenerational transmission of memory (Fuchs, 2008, p. 4). Like Assmann, she also notes that the family narrative can be exculpatory, romantic and fantastic. Grandchildren indulge in fantasy about the lives of their grandparents, imagining a noble family background and a German tradition unimpaired by the Nazi era (ibid., p. 6). The family romance as a particularly emotional form of memory tends to blur the boundaries between victims and perpetrators, with perpetrators playing the role of the war's victims (ibid.). Fuchs has in mind Harald Welzer's findings in *Opa war kein Nazi* (2002), in which the interviews of three generations of 40 contemporary families showed that while the third generation demonstrated no sympathies for National Socialism and much horror over the Holocaust, they certainly weren't inclined to believe that their grandparents played an integral role in genocidal Nazism (see also Cosgrove and Fuchs, 2006, p. 7, and Wittlinger, 2006, p. 75). That anti-Semites and perpetrators are not recalled leads Niven to argue that 'the memory of German perpetration, guilt, and the suffering of Nazi[ism's] victims' cultivated in the public sphere in the 1980s and 1990s has still not 'percolated down to the level of family memory' (Niven, 2006, p. 20), and, conversely, family memories had been excavated as both a realm of relative innocence of Nazi crimes, and of German suffering. If political, orthodox or institutional memory had not percolated down to and been dominant at the level of family memory, what was remembered at the level of family was percolating upwards into the public sphere, through the proliferation of literary, documentary and historical narratives based on private memories and given exposure and distribution by the mass media. This entry into the public sphere is facilitated in a cultural environment in which uncritical empathy can be the predominant mode of memory transmission (see also ibid.).

In mapping the dynamic politics of memory, the preceding arguments still tend towards reinscribing a binary between public and private, which mobilizes the very categories of memory that have subscribed to notions of the authentic and the inauthentic. Again, following Olick, a critical modelling of the politics of memory would complicate such distinctions between the public and the private, blurring the dividing lines between these realms. Fuchs and Mary Cosgrove draw attention to the fact that studies such as Welzer's, which are the cause of so much academic concern, pay more attention to what is said, neglecting the significance of what remains unsaid: 'The unsaid . . . can function as a powerful transmitter of the unmastered inheritance that is silently passed down the generational line' (Cosgrove and Fuchs, 2006, p. 7). As Fuchs adds, the 'emphatic assertion that "Grandpa wasn't a Nazi" may mean exactly the opposite' (2008, p. 7). Similarly, the repeated assertions on the international stage that Germany is a normal democracy – spectacularly expressed by a national Holocaust memorial – may be ghosted by an 'anxiety of influence' (ibid.). The political distribution of German Holocaust memory at a national (and international) level in memorial form is, then, inextricable from the realm of private or, to use Assmann's terms, familial and communicative memory, and disturbed yet prompted by what might or might not be remembered there.

Despite this inextricability of public and private, the increasing nationalization of Holocaust memory, its political distribution throughout the 1990s and early 2000s, and thereby the highly visible confrontation with the act of perpetration (as opposed to just the remembrance of the victims of the Holocaust), the figure of the German perpetrator, and perpetrator generation, was uncritically reconfigured. Markers of national ownership of the Nazi past in the 1990s and 2000s include the public development of plans for the National Memorial for the Murdered Jews of Europe, the debates surrounding the touring Crimes of the *Wehrmacht* exhibition (1995–9 and 2001), and the publication in German of Daniel Jonah Goldhagen's *Hitler's Willing Executioners* (1996). The *Wehrmacht* exhibition dispelled notions that the regular army had fought a clean war that had nothing to do with genocidal activities in the East. The exhibition made the externalization of responsibility for the Holocaust difficult. The perpetrators were ordinary Germans (in this case ordinary soldiers), not an elite, inner circle of Nazi militarists, politicians, bureaucrats and industrialists. However, the *Wehrmacht* exhibition staged a cathartic reconciliation with the perpetrator generation (Niven, 2002, pp. 143–74). Goldhagen's thesis claimed that anti-Semitism has been endogenous to German society for centuries and that Nazi ideology and policy was simply a catalyst for ordinary Germans to commit genocidal acts. The clumsy ventriloquism of Goldhagen's book that attempted to represent the perpetrator's perspective – a phenomenology of murder – allowed young Germans to note the fact that the perpetrators were supposed to be ordinary, but also enabled them to distance themselves from these caricatured monsters. In other words, the embrace of the past in the public sphere also served to distance that past.

Schmitz's comment on the ownership of past is instructive: 'The turning point here is the issue of guilt' (2006, p. 106). On the one hand, Chancellor Helmut Kohl, in a statement read out on his behalf at the site of Auschwitz-Birkenau during commemorations marking the fiftieth anniversary of the camp's liberation, admitted Germany's guilt and that the darkest chapter in German history had been written there (Marcuse, 2008, p. 379). On the other hand, the institutionalization of memory marked by this and the other events described above, coupled with the shift from the second to the third generation of Germans since the war – the latter's assumption of responsibility for the Nazi past and its vicarious confession of past acts not so much troubled by the guilt and repression experienced by their parents and grandparents – 'opens up the potential for empathising with the "German experience"' (Schmitz, 2006, p. 106). In fact, 'What is remarkable is that the shift from a memory centred on the victims of Nazism to a perpetrator-centred memory occurs, almost antithetically, subsequently to the institutionalisation of the memory of the Holocaust at the heart of contemporary German historical identity' (Schmitz, 2007, p. 4). Institutionally unburdened of a collective historical responsibility for the Nazi past, there are fewer impediments to Germans identifying with victims rather than perpetrators – and this means empathizing with the victims of the Holocaust *and* with those subsuming their place.

What is needed is a reengagement with the perpetrator, because in the complex politics of memory outlined above, the perpetrator has too easily been othered (dehumanized and disowned), too readily declared innocent in the discourse of German suffering, or too easily absolved of guilt (and made available for the discourse of suffering). In other words, conceptions of guilt and innocence, perpetrator and victim are too readily opposed and easily inverted. What is needed is a more complex cultural apprehension of and sustained identification with the figure of the perpetrator to prevent its malleability. Schlink's novel of 1995, contrary to the critical consensus that it transforms perpetrators into the victims of Nazism and the second generation into the victims of the legacies of Nazism – seeks to stage that reengagement. Against this critical consensus, this chapter rereads *The Reader* through Gillian Rose's general critique of postmodern, post-Holocaust philosophy. That critique centres on postmodernism's delegitimization of Holocaust narrative, as if all

228

representation is contaminated by the violent logic of the master narratives that rationalized Auschwitz. For Rose, the argument for the overcoming of representation, in its aesthetic, philosophical and political versions, 'converges with the *inner tendency* of Fascism itself' (1996, p. 41). Only through an 'always contestable and fallible representation' can we know where the representation of fascism converges with the fascism of representation (ibid.). Otherwise, in our Holocaust piety, we render the event ineffable, which is '*to mystify something we dare not understand,* because we fear it may be all too understandable, all too continuous with what we are – human, all too human' (ibid., p. 43).

A strategic identification with a perpetrator, made possible by admitting such a common ground of humanity, would allow us to see where the representation of fascism and the fascism of representation converge. Only by inhabiting, rather than lapsing into, the perpetrator's perspective could we see where the limits and boundaries of that perspective lie. However, how could one identify and empathize with a perpetrator? Surely such an identity would be repellent. Rose imagines the possibility of something like a Nazi *bildungsroman* in which the future allegiances of the protagonist are unknown to the reader, and by the time they are known, the reader has already empathized (ibid., p. 50). A crisis of identification in the reader would signify that empathetic bond. Contrary to the critical consensus, as the following brief reading will argue, *The Reader* attempts to operate in a similar way, in which the narrator-protagonist, Michael, suffers a crisis of identity for having desired a perpetrator, the older Hanna, before he knew her true identity, vicariously establishing for the reader potential bonds of empathy.

If *The Reader* is to inhabit the perspective of the perpetrator in order to scrutinize rather than disavow it, as in Rose's model of the representation of fascism, then the figure of the perpetrator needs to be available to the narrator (and by this proxy, to the reader). Hanna's age (indicating she was not too young to have played an active part in the war), and the way her 1950s body is associated with oblivion (Schlink, 1997, p. 14) raise suspicions about her. If the teenage Michael was not suspicious of her past, Schlink makes sure that we are when Michael narrates the story of his relationship with Hanna retrospectively from his present-day position. The suspicion concerning Hanna's past grows with descriptions of her scrupulous hygiene (ibid., p. 30), and her fondness for uniforms, which attracted her to her postwar job as a tram conductor (ibid., p. 37). These hints of (stereotypical) Nazi leanings are compounded by the suspicious lack of detail about her past, or her unwillingness to reveal very much about it (ibid.). Michael informs us that he had, by the time the affair was in full swing, caught up with his studies since falling ill, including the history of the Third Reich (ibid., p. 39). Given the context, the casual mention of this subject of study is just too conspicuous not to draw the reader's attention. Hints of a stereotyped sadism come with the power games Hanna plays with Michael (ibid., pp. 46–7) and her proclivity for violence – she strikes him when she thought she had been abandoned on a holiday they take together (ibid., pp. 52–3). The hints of stereotypical Nazism (sadism, hygiene) do not seem to fit Rose's model. How can Michael desire such a stereotype, and do not hints of what is to be revealed preclude our vicarious identification with her? However, the stereotypical and the proleptical do suggest the revisionary workings of memory. The narrator is self-conscious and explicit about the revision of the past:

> Why does it make me sad when I think back to that time? Is it a yearning for past happiness – for I was happy in the weeks that followed, in which I really did work like a lunatic and passed the class, and we made love as if nothing else in the world mattered. Is it the knowledge of what came later, and that what came out afterwards had been there all along? (Ibid., p. 35)

Part of the revisionary process is the isolation of certain moments, the mental images that are, as Siegfried Kracauer might put it, 'monogrammatic' (Kracauer, 1995, p. 51). This is an unchanging image into which is distilled all that is valued about the subject. A highly subjective image, suspended above the flux of time, it manages to screen out historical change and other memories. For Michael, the sight of Hanna in his father's study forms one such memory-image: 'It is one of the pictures of Hanna that has stayed with me. I have them stored away, I can project them on a mental screen and watch them, unchanged, unconsumed' (Schlink, 1997, p. 60). Proleptic, stereotypical, or suspended above time, these images do not make Hanna less available. Rather, they suggest that an identification with her has already been made, announcing a consequent crisis of identity on the part of the narrator. The combination of images registers a desire for the Hanna he knew before her trial and the renouncement of that desire through a desperate attempt to other her with cliché and stereotype.

Signs of this crisis of identity are evident in the narration of her trial (in 1965/6), in which, upon seeing her as a defendant, the narrator continues in his attempt to distance himself from her. He 'assumed it was both natural and right that Hanna should be in custody', not because of the charges against her, of which Michael has 'no real knowledge', but because 'in a cell she was out of my world . . . unattainable . . . [a] mere memory' (ibid., pp. 95–6). If we look at Michael's imaginative reconstruction of what Hanna is supposed to have done, that distancing takes an intimate form. Hanna had been a guard, along with four other accused women, at a small satellite camp for Auschwitz, near Cracow. They were indicted with charges for their conduct at the camp, but their main crime was their conduct on a 'death march' west. Michael did not remember the details of the first set of charges, but surviving witnesses (camp inmates) did, and they implicated the accused in selections for the gas chambers at Auschwitz (ibid., pp. 104–5). Hanna's selections were peculiar in that she had

selected 'favourites' among the female prisoners, who received special treatment but had to read to her in the evenings (ibid., pp. 114–15). These tended to
be the 'younger', 'weaker' and more 'delicate' prisoners, who, although saved
from work duty, were still sent to the gas chambers (ibid.). The main charge,
though, was locking the female prisoners who were being marched west in
a village church one night, during which there was an air raid. The women
locked in the church burned to death, all except a mother and daughter (ibid.,
pp. 105–6). The daughter wrote a book of their experiences, which started the
criminal investigation that led to the courtroom proceedings (ibid., p. 104). The
trial fuels a series of fantasies for Michael:

> Hanna by the burning church, hard-faced, in a black uniform, with a riding
> whip. . . . [Hanna] being read to. . . . When the hour was over, she told the
> reader she would be going on the transport to Auschwitz the next morning.
> The reader, a frail creature with a stubble of black hair and shortsighted eyes,
> began to cry. Hanna hit the wall with her hand, two women, also prisoners
> in striped clothing, came in and pulled the reader away. I saw . . . among
> [her prisoners] . . . her screaming face a mask of ugliness . . . [she] helped
> things along with her whip. I saw the church steeple crashing into the roof
> and the sparks flying and heard the desperation of the women. Alongside
> these images [:] . . . Hanna pulling on her stockings in the kitchen, . . . riding
> her bicycle with skirts flying, . . . dancing in front of the mirror, . . . Hanna
> listening to me, talking to me, laughing at me, loving me. Hanna loving me
> with cold eyes and pursed mouth, silently listening to me reading, and at the
> end banging the wall with her hand, talking to me with her face turning into
> a mask. The worst were the dreams in which a hard, imperious, cruel Hanna
> aroused me sexually; I woke from them full of longing and shame and rage.
> And full of fear about who I really was. (ibid., pp. 145–7)

The conflation here of scenes from their postwar love affair with the clichéd
scenes of what he imagines she did as a camp guard eroticize suffering and
position him as the sexualized Jewish victim. The uncertain sense of self that
Michael's fantasies leave him with can be read as an indulgent appropriation
of Jewish identity – the second generation's philo-Semitism as it distanced itself
from the perpetrator generation – *and* another symptom of his crisis of identity
and attempt to distance himself from the object of his desire.

Given the rigidity of the conceptual framework constructed by members
of the second generation in the 1960s by which their parents' generation was
identified wholly in terms of perpetration, it follows that Michael reports
that his university seminar, which followed and analysed Hanna's trial, was
driven by his fellow students' (and their generation's) imputation of collective
guilt to the previous generation: 'The generation that had been served by the

guards and enforcers, or had done nothing to stop them, or had not banished them from its midst as it could have done after 1945, was in the dock, and we explored it, subjected it to trial by daylight, and condemned it to shame' (ibid., p. 89). Although the second generation was alarmed by the legacies of Nazism in German life – Michael cites the Federal Republic's failure to recognize Israel and the fact that old Nazis were still pursuing successful careers in the courts, government and universities – its homogenization of the previous generation was motivated by shame over their ancestors to whom they were emotionally attached rather than by the shouldering of collective responsibility for the past (Donahue, 2001, p. 70). The difficult task of displacing the perpetrator generation embodied by Hanna and the narrator's parents – 'But the finger I pointed at her turned back to me. I had loved her' (Schlink, 1997, p. 168) – was the 'German fate' of his generation (ibid., p. 169). This task is played out in Michael's fantasies of victimhood, which may represent a desperate attempt to gain critical distance on the previous generation using the available cultural rhetoric of philo-Semitism. Distance from the perpetrator is gained by colonizing the victim's identity.

That in turn may explain the general numbness that infects all those who participate in the trial – from defendants to plaintiff (perpetrators and victim), to prosecutors, observers and the judge – who countenance or have countenanced the 'intrusion of horror into daily life' – the atrocities experienced and testified to – which has an 'anaesthetic' effect (ibid., pp. 99–101). This numbing, Michael explains, originates with the camp internees' mode of survival – a cognitive dissociation from daily scenes of brutalization and mass murder and the immanence of death – but which infects victims and perpetrators alike, as well as those who hear their testimony. This universalizing description is one of the novel's more controversial moments, for which critics have charged Schlink with historical relativism (Schlant, 1999, p. 214). However, it is again important to remember the politics of memory – or the political cultures of remembrance. There are two frames of remembrance to bear in mind here: the philo-Semitism of the 1960s, in which the victim's position was occupied to eschew the perpetrator generation; and the framework of the 1990s, in which these events were remembered and narrated (and in which the novel was written). As we have seen, in the 1990s empathy towards the victim gave way to empathy towards the perpetrator and *vice versa*, given the way in which these two figures were opposed and inverted in regimes of memory, allowing a confusion of categories of experience. Michael realizes that his 'fantasized images were poor clichés', which 'undermined my actual memories of Hanna and merged with the images of the camps that I had in my mind' (Schlink, 1997, p. 145). In other words, his imagination reflects the conditions or regimes of remembrance.

Indeed, Michael bemoans that the reservoir of images in cultural circulation at the time of the trial was limited in scope and was unable to correct his fantasies of Hanna: 'The few images derived from Allied photographs and the testimony of survivors flashed on the mind again and again, until they froze into clichés' (ibid., p. 147). The cultural industry of more recent Holocaust representations from the 1970s to the 1990s – *Holocaust, Sophie's Choice* and *Schindler's List* – has simply made those clichés or icons more familiar. Visiting, shortly after the trial, the site of Strutthof concentration camp, Michael 'wanted reality to drive out the clichés' (ibid., p. 148). Revisiting the site of Strutthof before narrating *The Reader*, Michael realizes that the cultural landscape of memory – in this case the memorial topography of Strutthof – 'joined my few already existing images of Auschwitz and Bergen-Belsen, and froze along with them' (ibid., p. 156). The cultural landscape of memory, both in the 1960s and 1990s, resists his desire 'simultaneously to understand Hanna's crime and to condemn it. . . . But it was impossible to do both' (ibid.).

There is much more to say about the novel and other (controversial) episodes of the figuring of the perpetrator, which, given the limitations of space, cannot be dwelt upon in detail. For example: the fact that we never know what Hanna did, that her admission of guilt was facilitated by her desire to keep her illiteracy a secret from the courtroom (or so Michael suspects, as she is accused of submitting a false report to cover up what she and the other guards had done on the forced march) (ibid., pp. 112–13, 124, 125, 128, 145). Hanna's decision to join the SS was also driven (so Michael suspects) by the desire to escape from a previous employer before her illiteracy was discovered; the shame of illiteracy and the shame of being a Nazi become confused (ibid., pp. 131–2; Bartov, 2000; LaCapra, 2001), and she is in effect punished for a social disability more than the crimes she (probably) committed and is thereby a victim of the German instrumentalized legal system and so the legacy of Nazism. Also notable are Michael's failure to enlighten and rehabilitate her with his recordings of his readings from classical German literature sent to her in prison (in other words, his failure to humanize her with Enlightenment thinking – the model of civilization that did nothing to stop the Holocaust in the first place) (Niven, 2003, p. 393), and her suicide on the eve of her release, taking with her to the grave the truth of what she actually did in the Holocaust – a truth she claims, after reading the canon of Holocaust survivor literature, that only the victims of the Holocaust know and understand (Schlink, 1997, p. 215). However, the argument still stands that Schlink has staged an attempt, Michael's, to humanize the perpetrator – to understand and condemn in non-redemptive terms.

That the perpetrator still remains othered and opaque in Schlink's novel, poorly read by its narrator, reflects upon the history of Holocaust memory remembered by this novel – Holocaust memory from the postwar years of Michael's affair with Hanna, the 1960s of the trial, to the 1990s of the novel's narration and publication. More pointedly, the novel points to a contemporary politics of memory that organizes binary oppositions between perpetrators and victims that are all too invertible, leading to the reconfiguration of perpetrators as victims. In Sebald's novel, a politics of memory is implicated if not always realized in the ways in which the novel stages potentially appropriative readings of the protagonist's memory work (by narrator and critic). The textual traumas of Sebald's novel call for a contextualized reading by which the politics of German memory can be navigated.

If the implicit and explicit politics of memory that these two texts represent and in which they participate recall the ways in which memory work is always mediated, they also point to problems in theorizing memory. The individualized acts of remembrance staged by these novels point not just to the need to frame those memories but also to the discrepancy between idiosyncratic practices of memory and theories of collective recollection. As Wulf Kansteiner and Claudio Fogu have argued, the conceptualization of collective memory often elides the difference between institutionalized memory (and the various cultural materials representing that memory) and its multiple addressees or audience(s) that make collective use of institutionalized memory. The standardized academic resort to variations on Maurice Halbwachs's seminal thesis that individual memory is socially framed does not adequately explain the generation of a collective memory through individually held memories. Kansteiner and Fogu argue that a greater differentiation between types of 'social' memory, between the poles of the 'autobiographical' and the 'collective', is needed to prevent the rendering of the collective in terms of individual psychology – particularly when it comes to affective experiences such as trauma (Kansteiner and Fogu, 2006, pp. 288–9). If the politics of memory describes the intended instrumentalization of the past and its negotiation, then, by staging affective and affected acts of individualized memory work, and illuminating their political import, these novels have certainly nuanced social memory. What seems key here are the subject positions of those who remember – be they author, narrator, or implied reader – in nuancing social memory and identifying its politics – and, as LaCapra puts it, the 'transferential relations to the object of study whereby processes active in it are repeated with more or less significant variations' in those who remember, depending on how they identify in relation to the past: a 'survivor, relative of survivors, a former Nazi, a former collaborator, a relative of former Nazis or collaborators, a younger Jew or German distanced from more immediate contact with survival, participation, collaboration' (1996, p. 46). Rather than psychologizing collective memory (*pace* Kansteiner and Fogu), LaCapra's illumination of transferential relations confirms the politicization of remembrance as subjective relations to past events implicate contexts of memory. The emotional bonds to the past dramatized by Schlink and the so-called traumatic imagetexts of Sebald present transferential scenarios and thereby a politics of memory.

Works Cited

Assmann, A. (2004), 'Four formats of memory: from individual to collective constructions of the past', in C. Emden and D. Midgley (eds), *Cultural Memory and Historical
Consciousness in the German Speaking World Since 1500*. Bern: Peter Lang, pp. 19–37.

— (2006a), 'Memory, individual and collective', in R. E. Goodin and C. Tilly (eds), *The
Oxford Handbook of Contextual Political Analysis*. Oxford: Oxford University Press,
pp. 210–24.

— (2006b), 'On the (in)compatability of guilt and suffering in German Memory', trans.
L. Shortt, *German Life and Letters*, 59.2, 187–200.

— (2008), 'Transformations between history and memory', *Social Research*, 75.1, 49–71.

Bartov, O. (2000), *Mirrors of Destruction*. Oxford: Oxford University Press.

Bigsby, C. (2001), 'In conversation with W. G. Sebald', in *Writers in Conversation*. University
of East Anglia, Norwich: Arthur Miller Centre for American Studies, pp. 139–65.

Cosgrove, M. and Fuchs, A. (2006), 'Introduction', in M. Cosgrove, A. Fuchs and G. Grote
(eds), *German Memory Contests: The Quest for Identity in Literature, Film and Discourse
since 1990*. Rochester, NY: Camden House, pp. 1–24.

Donahue, W. C. (2001), 'Illusions of subtlety: Bernhard Schlink's *Der Vorleser* and the
moral limits of Holocaust fiction', *German Life and Letters*, 54.1, 60–81.

Erll, A. (2011), 'Travelling memory', in R. Crownshaw (ed.), *Transcultural Memory*. London
and New York: Routledge.

Eshel, A. (2003), 'Against the power of time: the poetics of suspension in W. G. Sebald's
Austerlitz', *New German Critique*, 88, 71–96.

Fogu, C. and Kansteiner, W. (2006), 'The politics of memory and the poetics of history', in
C. Fogu, W. Kansteiner and R. N. Lebow (eds), *The Politics of Memory in Postwar Europe*.
Durham, NC, and London: Duke University Press, pp. 284–310.

Fuchs, A. (2008), *Phantoms of War in Contemporary German Literature, Films and Discourse*.
Basingstoke and New York: Palgrave Macmillan.

Goldhagen, D. J. (1996), *Hitler's Willing Executioners: Ordinary Germans and the Holocaust*.
New York: Alfred A. Knopf.

Horstkotte, S. (2004), 'Fantastic gaps: photography inserted into narrative in W. G.
Sebald's *Austerlitz*', in C. Emden and D. Midgley (eds), *Science, Technology and the
German Cultural Imagination*. Oxford, Bern, Berlin, Bruxelles, Frankfurt am Main, New
York, Wien: Peter Lang: pp. 269–86.

Kracauer, S. (1995), 'Photography', in T. Levin (ed.), *The Mass Ornament: Weimar Essays*,
trans. T. Levin. Cambridge, MA: Harvard University Press, pp. 47–63.

LaCapra, D. (1996), *Representing the Holocaust: History, Theory, Trauma*. London: Cornell
University Press.

—. (2001), *Writing History, Writing Trauma*. Baltimore: Johns Hopkins University Press.

—. (2004), *History in Transit: Experience, Identity, Critical Theory*. Ithaca: Cornell University
Press.

Long, J. J. (2007), *W. G. Sebald: Image, Archive, Modernity*. Edinburgh: Edinburgh University
Press.

Marcuse, H. (2008), *Legacies of Dachau: The Uses and Abuses of a Concentration Camp, 1933–
2001*. Cambridge: Cambridge University Press.

Niven, W. (2002), *Facing the Nazi Past: United Germany and the Legacy of the Third Reich*.
London and New York: Routledge.

—. (2003), 'Bernhard Schlink's *Der Vorleser* and the problem of shame', *Modern Language
Review*, 98.2, 380–96.

—. (2006), 'Introduction: German victimhood at the turn of the millennium', in B. Niven
(ed.), *Germans as Victims*. Basingstoke: Palgrave Macmillan, pp. 1–25.

Olick, J. (2007), *The Politics of Regret: On Collective Memory and Historical Responsibility*. London and New York: Routledge.

Radstone, S. (2000), 'Screening trauma: *Forrest Gump*, film and memory', in S. Radstone (ed.), *Memory and Methodology*. Oxford: Berg, pp. 79–110.

—. (2005), 'Reconceiving binaries: the limits of memory', *History Workshop Journal*, 59, 134–50.

—. (2008), 'Memory studies: for and against', *Memory Studies*, 1.1, 30–9.

Rigney, A. (2004), 'Portable monuments: literature, cultural memory, and the case of Jeanie Deans', *Poetics Today*, 25.2, 361–96.

Rose, G. (1996), *Mourning Becomes the Law*. Cambridge: Cambridge University Press.

Rothberg, M. (2009), *Multidirectional Memory: Remembering the Holocaust in an Age of Decolonization*. Stanford, CA: Stanford University Press.

Schlant, E. (1999), *The Language of Silence: West German Literature and the Holocaust*. New York and London: Routledge.

Schlink, B. (1997), *The Reader*, trans. C. Brown Janeway. London: Phoenix.

Schmitz, H. (2004), *On Their Own Terms: The Legacy of National Socialism in Post-1990 German Fiction*. Birmingham: University of Birmingham Press.

—. (2006), 'The birth of the collective from the spirit of empathy: from the "Historians' Dispute" to German suffering', in B. Niven (ed.), *Germans as Victims*. Basingstoke: Palgrave Macmillan, pp. 93–108.

—. (2007), 'Introduction: the return of wartime suffering in contemporary German memory culture, literature and film', in H. Schmitz (ed.), *A Nation of Victims? Representation of Wartime Suffering from 1945 to the Present*. Amsterdam and New York: Rodopi, pp. 1–30.

Sebald, W. G. (2001), *Austerlitz*, trans. A. Bell. London: Penguin.

Taberner, S. (2003), 'Introduction', in B. Schlink, *Der Vorleser*, ed. S. Taberner and trans. K. Schödel. London: Bristol Classical Press, pp. 7–38.

—. (2006), 'Representations of German wartime suffering in recent fiction', in B. Niven (ed.), *Germans as Victims*. Basingstoke: Palgrave Macmillan, pp. 164–80.

Welzer, H., Moller, S. and Tschnuggnall, K. (2002), *'Opa war kein Nazi': Nazionalsozialismus und Holocaust in Familiengedächtnis*. Frankfurt/Main: Fischer.

Wittlinger, R. (2006), 'Taboo or tradition? The "Germans as victims" theme in West Germany until the early 1990s', in B. Niven (ed.), *Germans as Victims*. Basingstoke: Palgrave Macmillan, pp. 62–75.

New Directions in Holocaust Literary Studies

Recent analysts of Holocaust literature and culture have noted a profound shift in the kinds of questions being asked of Holocaust representations. As R. Clifton Spargo and Robert M. Ehrenreich state,

> The generation of scholars who first focused on an emerging canon of Holocaust literature – figures such as George Steiner, Lawrence L. Langer, Alvin H. Rosenfeld, and Sidra DeKoven Ezrahi – were faced with the task of defining what Holocaust literature might be. Although this task was initially accomplished by a process of exclusion, asking a series of questions framed in the negative – When was representation inappropriate, and which sorts of representation might be inappropriate? . . . – the legacy of these studies was an emergent critical discourse about the literature of witness and the limits of any representation of atrocity, the impact of which was felt across the discipline of literary studies as well as in other fields in the humanities. (Spargo and Ehrenreich, 2010, p. ix)

While these questions are still relevant today, such critics as Ehrenreich and Spargo have nevertheless begun to chart the emerging resonance of a different set of issues. While an earlier generation of critics focused centrally on questions of representability and appropriateness,[1] they suggest, 'contemporary authors of Holocaust literature and scholars of their work have concentrated with ever greater concern on the cultural context in which such literature is produced' (ibid.). The increasingly self-reflective dimension of both Holocaust literature and criticism is certainly one aspect of the shift in critical and literary sensibilities, as I discuss below; nevertheless, the multifarious nature of developments within the discipline makes the mapping of emergent directions within Holocaust literary studies a complex undertaking. This section of the *Companion* attempts to chart a number of these developments, focusing on a series of key trends within the study of Holocaust literature at the present cultural moment. While the delineation of a small number of key trends inevitably risks a reductive approach, it is nevertheless intended to offer a useful distillation of some of the primary emerging areas of focus and a situation of these areas as regards earlier preoccupations among a first generation of scholars including Lang, Rosenfeld, Langer, Des Pres and others. Reflections on developments in the sphere of Holocaust literary studies will also be contextualized among broader developments in literary theory and criticism.

Part 1: Proximities

New Postmemories

With increasing temporal distance from the Holocaust, emphasis shifted from a sole focus on responses to these events produced by those who experienced or lived through the period of their occurrence to responses created by those who, in a variety of ways, came 'after' the cataclysm and thus necessarily strove to assimilate and comprehend its extremity in more mediated ways. The study of second- and third-generation Holocaust literature has been strongly influenced by Marianne Hirsch's coinage of the terminology of 'postmemory' in the 1990s, a concept which has undergone some development but which in its original incarnation referred to 'the relationship of children of survivors of cultural or collective trauma to the experiences of their parents, experiences that they "remember" only as the stories and images with which they grew up, but that are so powerful, so monumental, as to constitute memories in their own right' (Hirsch, 1999, p. 8). Nevertheless, Hirsch has also implied the wider applicability of the term, describing it, for example, as a possible outcome for all visitors to the United States Holocaust Memorial Museum whatever their personal relationship (or lack of such) to the events themselves (Hirsch, 1996, p. 667). These intimations are further developed and conceptually codified to counter a sense of problematic slippage in Hirsch's delineation of a distinction between 'familial' and 'affiliative' postmemory and examination of the relationship between these structures (Hirsch, 2012). Hirsch's recent work on postmemory also considers the nature of postmemory work in the era of the internet, and emphasizes the commonality between 'affiliative' postmemory, which operates across personal and cultural boundaries, and the multidirectional intersection in memory of diverse histories of trauma and persecution (theorized by such figures as Michael Rothberg and discussed further below), an aspect of postmemory she terms the 'connective'. Like Rothberg, Hirsch attributes to connective postmemory work a potentially ethically valuable dimension, exploring the extent to which it 'might constitute a platform of activist and interventionist cultural and political engagement, a form of repair and redress, inspired by feminism and other movements for social change' (ibid., p. 6).

The parameters of the concept of postmemory have also been investigated by such recent critics as Erin McGlothlin, who in her *Second-Generation Holocaust Literature: Legacies of Survival and Perpetration* (2006) examines the structural congruences between the experiences of the second generation after the Holocaust of both Jewish and German writers. McGlothlin's narratologically informed approach enables a valuable concretization of some of the central features and difficulties of these forms of memory, yielding such critical tools as the notion of 'polychrony' ('a temporal designation that takes into account narratives in which the *then* and the *now* are not clearly and unequivocally delineated' (McGlothlin, 2006, p. 86)), a feature McGlothlin identifies in Art Spiegelman's *Maus*. A range of additional critics who have engaged productively with Hirsch's concept of postmemory and broader issues of memory and the intergenerational include Philippe Codde (2010), Marita Grimwood (2007), Gabriele Schwab (2010), Efraim Sicher (2001), Andrea Liss (1998), Brett Ashley Kaplan (2011) and others.

As well as expanding its scope to inform the study of other contexts than that of Holocaust victimhood, including not only perpetrator contexts but also 'American slavery; the Vietnam War, the Dirty War in Argentina and other dictatorships in Latin America; South African apartheid; Soviet, East European, and Chinese communist terror; the Armenian, the Cambodian, and the Rwandan genocides; the Japanese internment camps in the United States; the stolen generations in aboriginal Australia; the Indian partition; and others' (Hirsch, 2012, p. 19),[2] the concept of postmemory has also consolidated its interdisciplinary status. Elucidated by Hirsch with reference to a range of different cultural productions including museum spaces, installation art, photography and the graphic novel, the concept continues to find a usefully interdisciplinary application. Dora Apel's study *Memory Effects: The Holocaust and the Art of Secondary Witnessing*, which addresses 'secondary witnessing' in photography, installation and conceptual art as well as body art, suggests that art which is itself interdisciplinary offers an appropriate site for postmemory work due to the ungraspable nature of the events themselves (Apel, 2002, p. 4). Apel's theorization highlights the fittingness of both the multidisciplinary nature of postmemorial culture as a whole and of individual instances of postmemory art and literature, suggesting an insightful avenue of approach to the generic intermixing and formal diversity of such literary postmemory texts as Art Spiegelman's *Maus*, magic realist works by writers including Jonathan Safran Foer and Joseph Skibell (as discussed in Adams (2011)), and the novels of W. G. Sebald.

The focus of theorizations of postmemory is also increasingly geographical and spatial, a development consistent with the emphasis placed on the physical 'return' to the sites of one's familial past in such second- and third-generation memoirs as Lisa Appignanesi's *Losing the Dead* (1999) and Daniel Mendelsohn's *The Lost* (2007), as well as fictional explorations of this journey by such figures as Jonathan Safran Foer (2002). In such instances, what Marianne Hirsch and Nancy K. Miller term 'the radical distance that separates the past from the present' (2011, p. 4) is emphasized through its spatial mapping onto the geographical journey undertaken, though such 'sites' can also be more abstract, electronic ones, as Hirsch and Leo Spitzer's essay in the same volume underscores (Hirsch and Spitzer, 2011). On the issue of space and postmemory (here understood in a broader cultural sense), another significant recent reference point is provided by Brett Ashley Kaplan's *Landscapes of Holocaust Postmemory* (2011). Focusing on 'how space and memory connect and how the Holocaust travels through contemporary geographies' (Kaplan, 2011, p. 1), Kaplan's study addresses the multiple intersections of Holocaust postmemory both with literal landscapes (such as the Obersalzberg and the Czech and German landscapes of Susan Silas's *Helmbrechts Walk*) and their representation, and with the political, cultural and psychological landscapes of traumatic history, taking in a range of literary, photographic and artistic works in the process.

Another key development linked to the study of Holocaust postmemory has arguably been the increasing focus on the intergenerational impact of the Holocaust on a cultural rather than familial level, a movement anticipated by the slippage of the term in Hirsch's own usage and its development to assume not only 'familial' but also 'affiliative' forms (Hirsch, 2012). Within such a framework, it is possible to see such phenomena as the 'Americanization of the Holocaust' identified by Flanzbaum (1999), Novick (1999) and others as a post-memorial situation writ large, in which those who did not experience the events and are distant in both time and place from their occurrence nevertheless form an imaginative identification with their conceptions of these traumatic histories. Such an extrapolation is problematic in that it offers the legitimacy of a personal-therapeutic register to a cultural context requiring a more politically nuanced and rigorous analysis, yet it nevertheless contains an element of accuracy in highlighting just how labile the notion of memory has become in the globalized media era. This expansion of the field of postmemory (and indeed, memory itself) is particularly evident in the work of such figures as Alison Landsberg, whose concept of 'prosthetic memory' is elaborated in her 2004 work of that name and offers itself as a revision of the notion of memory in an age of technological reproducibility, globalization and mass culture. According to Landsberg, prosthetic memory 'emerges at the interface between a person and a historical narrative about the past, at an experiential site such as a movie theater or museum. In this moment of contact, an experience occurs through which the person sutures himself or herself into a larger history' (Landsberg, 2004, p. 2). Such 'suturing', according to Landsberg, results in a deeply felt personal 'memory' of the event, and creates conditions for ethical thinking 'by encouraging people to feel connected to, while recognizing the alterity of, the "other"' (ibid., p. 9); in other words, for a sense of empathy and ethical–political solidarity to be fostered across ethnic and cultural differences.

Landsberg's model relies on an application of the term 'memory' to events of which the rememberer has no direct experience, with such an extrapolation made possible by the emphasis on 'experiential sites' which make a form of experience the basis of memory, although what is 'experienced' is nevertheless a representation rather than the historical reality itself. As discussed below, this slippage has been considered problematic by a number of critics. Landsberg's theory depends also on a certain construction of mass culture as a largely positive phenomenon whose ideological biases are not greatly relevant, or are at least vastly overshadowed by its potential to evoke cross-cultural remembering. 'Against the "culture industry" model', she writes, 'I contend that commodification, which is at the heart of mass cultural representations, makes images and narratives widely available to people who live in different places and come from different backgrounds, races, and classes' (ibid., p. 21). Such unconcern about the commercial and ideological interests of mass cultural representations and the extent to which this shapes the forms of engagement individuals are able to have with a traumatic past is echoed by critics like Daniel Levy and Natan Sznaider (discussed below), who in their *The Holocaust and Memory in the Global Age* (2006) depict the globalization of Holocaust memory in optimistic terms and rebut criticism of the sentimentalism and kitschiness of such mass representations as *Schindler's List* with the argument that 'It was precisely these elements . . . that made the Holocaust accessible to a broad public' (Levy and Snaider, 2006, p. 136). These instances of questionable faith in the ethical capacities of the market suggest an ongoing need to counteract both complacency and resignation regarding the impact of capitalism on Western cultural capacities to engage in ethically sensitive and intellectually alert ways with the collective past.

Memory Transmission: New Scrutinies

During the 1990s, theories relating to the traumatic historical event's lack of containment within the parameters of its own witnessing and experiencing were powerfully influential. Alongside Hirsch's notion of postmemory, in which the event spills beyond its original temporal context to exert a determining influence on the experience and memory of subsequent generations, and the extension of this model by such figures as Landsberg, may be placed the model of trauma theory developed by Cathy Caruth, Shoshana Felman and others, which positioned the traumatic event as an occurrence which is not fully experienced as it takes place, due to its unassimilability to existing narrative and experiential schemata. According to the perspectives of trauma theory, the traumatic event is 'missed experience' that can only be experienced and assimilated retrospectively; Felman's theory of testimony, consequently, considers the testimonial situation itself as the site for the event's experiencing (by both speaker and listener) through the process of narration, a kind of performative speech

241

act which brings a knowledge and experience of the event into being – a model of performativity taken up by more recent critics of testimony such as Michael G. Levine (2006). These models of trauma and memory offered a compelling means of conceptualizing the impact of Holocaust experience and were productively applied to literature in a host of critical studies, with one particularly insightful example being Susan Gubar's *Poetry after Auschwitz: Remembering What One Never Knew* (2003), which argues for the efficacy of poetry as a means of representing the Holocaust and its impact precisely due to the capacities of poetic form to mirror the structures of traumatic memory. Nevertheless, models of memory including those of Felman, Caruth, and Landsberg which emphasize the transmissibility of traumatic experience (whether intergenerationally, via reading, or via the testimonial situation) have also been subject to profound and probing scrutiny over recent years as part of an ongoing evaluation of the critical and theoretical discourses of Holocaust memory.

Central in this process of evaluation is the work of the critic Gary Weissman, whose 2004 *Fantasies of Witnessing: Postwar Efforts to Experience the Holocaust* scrutinizes attempts in Holocaust discourse to collapse the boundaries between witnesses and nonwitnesses (Weissman's term) as related to nonwitnesses' desire to experience the Holocaust. Linking such unacknowledged desire to an attempt to make real an increasingly remote and disassociated historical event, as well as an attempt to locate in the event dramatic and significant restagings of our own more abstract or mundane preoccupations, Weissman takes issue in particular with concepts of a broad second or third generation which construe an entire culture (rather than specific descendants of survivors) as heirs to the Holocaust. Hirsch's notion of postmemory is subjected to sceptical analysis, with Weissman arguing, for example, that Hirsch's emphasis on the necessary 'gulf' that separates memory and postmemory is undercut by 'the notion that the difference between memory and postmemory is primarily one of distance rather than substance' (Weissman, 2004, p. 17). Weissman similarly subjects trauma theory to critical examination, arguing of Dori Laub's construction of the Holocaust as an 'event without a witness' that:

> Like Caruth's notion that one can only have memory of events 'fully grasped as they occur' or 'experienced fully at the time,' this postulation raises the question of why being a witness to an event should require a complete and fully accurate perception of 'what happens during an event' – particularly given that most if not all witnessing and remembering is partial, subjective, and imperfect. (Ibid., p. 136)

Weissman's critique of the trauma theory of Caruth et al. joins those of Ruth Leys (2000) and others[3] in directing a powerful scrutiny towards one of the most dominant yet also at times the most rhetorically sweeping critical vocabularies through which Holocaust literature and post-Holocaust culture have been analytically approached.

Holocaust Memory and Metacriticism

Another important recent reference point in the critical examination of perceived technologies of transmission is Amy Hungerford's *The Holocaust of Texts: Genocide, Literature, and Personification* (2003), which critically examines a tendency to conflate texts and individuals in discourse on the Holocaust, to imply that a loss of texts is equivalent to a loss of persons. While Hungerford traces the origins of such personification to a range of factors including deconstructivist notions of the autonomous text (Hungerford, 2003, p. 5), postwar definitions of genocide as including the destruction of culture and artworks as well as human beings (ibid., p. 7), and the 'culture wars' in which 'the highest cultural value is assigned not simply to persons in the humanistic sense but to persons as embodying cultural identities' (ibid., p. 11), the process is also strongly linked to attempts to render the Holocaust transmissible to later generations, an enterprise deemed necessary if the Holocaust is assumed central to Jewish cultural identity. Tracing the logic of personification in the trauma theory of Caruth and Felman (which entails the possibility of trauma's textual transmission, as in the example of Felman's 'traumatized' graduate students (Felman, 1992)), Hungerford identifies a number of dubious ethical corollaries of this position, including the false Holocaust testimony of Binjamin Wilkomirski and Felman's reading of Paul de Man's postwar silence about his writing for a collaborationist newspaper as a form of exculpatory suicide, ultimately highlighting the dangers of this logic of transmissibility:

> The fantasy of the personified text, the fantasy that we can really have another's experience, that we can be someone else, that we can somehow possess a culture we do not practice, elides the gap that imagination – preferable, in my mind, to identification – must fill. (Hungerford, 2003, p. 157)

Noting too that 'the conflation of texts and persons . . . renders the fact of embodiment irrelevant, when embodiment is exactly what situates us in history and makes us vulnerable to oppression' (ibid., p. 21), Hungerford's thought-provoking work offers an important check on the unquestioning adoption of theoretical discourses which, despite their emphasis on the unrepresentable, place a comforting faith in the capacity of texts to contain and transmit memory and experience yet may court ethical and logical pitfalls in the process.

In turning their critical gaze as much on the conceptual tools and rhetorical strategies of other critics and theorists as on literary and cultural representations of the Holocaust themselves, such figures as Hungerford, Weissman and Naomi Mandel (discussed below) also partake in another of the most interesting developments in the literary study of the Holocaust; namely, the construction of Holocaust Studies itself as an object of political and theoretical analysis. This is especially apparent in *Fantasies of Witnessing*, which devotes entire chapters to a critical analysis of the perspectives of such figures as Alfred Kazin and Lawrence Langer, and which is particularly striking in the degree to which the motivations of scholars of Holocaust literature and culture are critiqued. A commitment to 'facing horror' is here read as an assumption of moral superiority over the average reader (Weissman, 2004, pp. 23, 100), the now habitual self-castigation of scholars over their use of the term 'Holocaust' is interpreted as a frustrated attempt to negotiate one's own morally and epistemologically privileged relationship to the events via the search for a specialist term (ibid., p. 25) and Rabbi Irving Greenberg's 'working principle' for those discussing the Holocaust ('No statement, theological or otherwise, should be made that was not credible in the presence of the burning children') is met with the judgement that 'Perhaps no statement better captures the sanctimonious veneration of horror that so often serves to curtail rather than encourage critical thinking about our present-day relationship to the Holocaust' (ibid., p. 215). Such thought-provoking analysis, while threatening to itself in future take the place of the self-castigation which dramatizes the moral stature of the Holocaust critic, promises the valuable disruption of the critical commonplaces into which Holocaust literary studies at the turn of the twenty-first century was in danger of collapsing, with the argument that 'we need to reflect upon what "impels" us to confront the Holocaust, as this shapes our intellectual endeavours in significant ways that may elude conscious understanding' (ibid., p. 129) a profoundly compelling one.

Testimony and Witnessing

Within the context of issues of proximity to the Holocaust, key developments are not confined to questions of the broader cultural and critical response of later generations; further developments are also taking place in the study of testimony and witnessing, with an increasing sensitivity to the specificity of different forms of testimony and their mediation by the particular conditions of their production. This increasing emphasis on particularity is evident from such studies as Zoe Waxman's *Writing the Holocaust: Identity, Testimony, Representation* (2006), which argues in opposition to the treatment of testimony as 'a separate, homogenized, self-contained canon' (p. 1), instead emphasizing the history of the mode's evolution as well as its diversity at any given moment (across ghetto diaries, for example, or women's concentration camp memoirs).

Particularly valuable in Waxman's approach is a critical scrutiny of the questionable preconceptions about testimony which have hitherto led to the neglect of accounts which do not accord with pre-existing assumptions about the victim and her role, such as the notion of the witness as the carrier of universal moral lessons (ibid., p. 6), a configuration with negative implications for those testimonies which raise questions about the possibilities of moral judgement in these circumstances; as well as the assumption that women's testimonies should emphasize female virtues (caring and mothering) and, in the aftermath of Women's Studies, specifically female experiences such as pregnancy (ibid., pp. 123, 128).

Waxman's emphasis on the witness as a social role and her scrutiny of the degree to which the texts of testimony are themselves shaped by these expectations (ibid., p. 158) illustrates the increasing nuance which informs the literary examination of testimony, building substantially on work by such pioneering figures as Lawrence Langer (1991) which considered (particularly oral) testimony as an unmediated conduit of the real. This focus, highlighted as a key area for ongoing research by such critics as Antony Rowland (who emphasizes the need for testimony's literary and performative aspects to be further addressed (2010, p. 114)) also links this work to a wider examination of the nature of witnessing and the cultural status and function of the witness. A particularly noteworthy intervention into this topic is offered by Annette Wieviorka's *The Era of the Witness* (2006), which traces three successive phases in the development of this figure: the deceased witness who testifies to events they did not survive, the emergence of the witness as a social figure (with the Eichmann trial of profound significance here), and the contemporary 'era of the witness'. The development of the social identity of the survivor, Wieviorka argues, transformed the conditions for writing the history of genocide, which was subsequently conceptualized as a victim-focused phenomenon comprised of a collection of individual experiences intended to produce readerly identification (Wieviorka, 2006, p. 88). The 'era of the witness' thus places the witness at the centre of the conception of history (ibid., p. 97), a centrality Wieviorka raises questions about, comparing a juxtaposition of testimonies to an in-depth analytical work of history in concern at the former's apparent eclipsing of the latter (ibid., p. 144). Highlighting the risk that a privileging of testimony and witnessing above historical analysis 'annuls historical narrative' (ibid.), threatening a fragmentation and defocusing of the historical occurrence in its totality, Wieviorka exemplifies a growing unease with an unquestioning prioritization of concepts of memory over those of history, as Richard Crownshaw, in his study *The Afterlife of Holocaust Memory in Contemporary Literature and Culture* (2010), has noted.

While the figure of the witness (and the social investments contained therein) has been an emerging source of critical scrutiny in the aftermath of the emergence of Memory Studies, the discourses through which this figure has been critiqued have in themselves been subjected to sustained examination. This is particularly evident in the recent work of Carolyn J. Dean, whose *Aversion and Erasure: The Fate of the Victim after the Holocaust* (2010) evaluates the reputed surfeit of Jewish memory of suffering, questioning the notion of an 'excess' of memory while acknowledging the contexts within which Holocaust memory has been instrumentalized. Dean ultimately contends that 'The concept of surfeit memory should be recast and envisioned properly as a transformation of victims into aggressors who threaten the tranquillity of those whose memories are acknowledged' (Dean, 2010, p. 181) and goes on to challenge what she terms 'the fashioning of the exemplary victim, typically someone who has a quiet and controlled response to having been victimized and whose testimonial style is thus valorized' as 'a false measure by which to judge all victims' (ibid., p. 182).[4] Critically examining the ethical, conceptual, and ideological frameworks within which notions of witnessing and testimony have taken shape, these critics illustrate an increasing theoretical reflection on the mechanisms which constitute the individual as the bearer of history and shape the conditions for bearing witness.

Unease about the implications of a canonization of testimony at the cost of other forms of historical analysis and inquiry, coupled with growing acknowledgement of testimony's mediation by dominant notions of the witness, her narrative, and her role, might be identified as key factors behind another emerging area of focus in the literary study of testimony: namely, the phenomenon of false testimony, which Antony Rowland interestingly relates to 'increasing attention to the generic nature of testimony' (2010, p. 114). This increasing attention is manifested in the work of such critics as Sue Vice, whose forthcoming *Textual Deceptions* offers an extensive consideration of the motives and mechanisms of literary deception, placing false and embellished Holocaust testimony alongside other instances of literary deception such as gender-based and ethnic 'impersonation' and the false or embellished trauma memoir. Growing attention to ethically questionable forms of testimony is also evident in the recent turn to the examination of perpetrator testimony by such critics as Robert Eaglestone, who contends that 'with due caution, these texts should be examined as more than simply sources to be (warily) mined for historical detail and are, in fact, useful sources for thinking about the affectivity of Holocaust texts and wider cultural and philosophical issues in relation to the Holocaust' (Eaglestone, 2010b, p. 124).

Part 2: License, Prohibition and Play

Transgression

Alongside questions of proximity and witnessing, another emergent issue in Holocaust literary studies is that of transgression, its functions, form and operation. As suggested by the quotation at the opening of this chapter, recent critics of Holocaust literature and culture have noted a movement away from questions of appropriateness in Holocaust discourse. R. Clifton Spargo remarks that 'For reasons having to do perhaps with the recognition of traditions of communal lament but also with the hyper-mediated ethos of modern mass society, the anxiety about representation of the Holocaust began to fade by the early 1990s' (Spargo, 2010a, pp. 6–7). Susanne Rohr and Sophia Komor concur in identifying the mid-1990s as a key moment during and after which a cluster of controversial artworks appeared, provoking an initial outrage that gradually gave way to 'a certain nonchalance' (Rohr and Komor, 2010, p. 9). The new taboo-breaking Holocaust art,[5] according to Rohr and Komor, is a transnational and cross-disciplinary phenomenon in which questions of representability give way to the examination of 'Holocaust *rhetoric*', a notion they elaborate thus:

> The paradigm shift seems to be a movement away from the usual demand for an authentic depiction or for adequate modes of representation. Instead, the new 'scandalous art' reflects the nature and tests the dimensions and limits of a semiotized and mediatized Holocaust, a Holocaust that has, potentially, changed in an ontological sense. This reflecting and testing can also be observed by the way a work of art positions itself within the transnational semiotic Holocaust universe, the way it applies and uses its material, thus respecting, ironizing, attacking or rejecting the existing rules and conventions of representation. (Ibid., p. 10)

This self-reflective trend in Holocaust literature and art is evident in such filmic works as Quentin Tarantino's *Inglourious Basterds* (2009), a self-conscious and troubling engagement with the relationship between cinema and violence, and in such literary texts as Yann Martel's *Beatrice and Virgil* (2010), which explores metafictionally the cultural and material conditions within which writing about the Holocaust takes shape. Belying Berel Lang's claim that 'Holocaust writing characteristically "aspires to the condition of history"' (Lang, 2000, p. 19), this phenomenon has commanded critical attention, with the perceived metacultural dimension to such artworks read as a licensing factor in their transgression.[6] The need to in some sense legitimize transgressive art through an emphasis upon its ethically productive interrogation of the rhetoric and codifications of Holocaust discourse suggests to an extent a continuing hold of the taboo (whether over artists, critics, or both); nevertheless, there is no doubt that the scope of representations is changing – it would be difficult to imagine a work like Jonathan Littell's *The Kindly Ones* appearing 20 years ago, for example.

Another interesting contextualization of the new transgressive art is Spargo's suggestion that the ban on representation was 'either therapeutically overcome in the service of renewing community or efficiently circumvented in the name of the sufferings of the second generation, which now perceived a testimonial imperative in personal events that, while not strictly witnessing to the Holocaust, were nevertheless, in a literal sense, *about* the Holocaust' (Spargo, 2010a, p. 7). This suggests a way of reading Holocaust discourse as an enterprise wholly pervaded by a revised sense of testimony in which writers testify (in whatever genre) to their own relationship to the Holocaust (and that of their present cultural moment), regardless of how distant and mediated that relationship may be, an implication that suggests itself as at once a potentially justificatory mechanism and a statement that, however counter-intuitively, testimony remains the structuring principle and posture of Holocaust literature today.[7]

Recent attempts to theorize transgressive Holocaust art have included Matthew Boswell's 2012 study of Holocaust impiety in literature, popular music and film. Boswell takes as a starting point the philosopher Gillian Rose's critique of the phenomenon of Holocaust piety as entailing a sanctimonious anti-representational posture placing emphasis on the Holocaust's ineffability, yet contends that while such theorists as Rose critique piety, 'they have also tended to distrust artworks that are characterised by opposing qualities such as representational excess, anti-sentimentalism, avant-garde experimentalism or overt historical irreverence' (Boswell, 2012, p. 3). Such artworks – including the poetry of Sylvia Plath and W. D. Snodgrass, the punk and post-punk music of the Ramones, the Sex Pistols, Joy Division and the Manic Street Preachers, and films such as Tarantino's *Inglourious Basterds* and Tim Blake Nelson's *The Grey Zone* – are precisely the object of Boswell's study, which focuses on the degree to which Holocaust impiety, by 'deliberately engineer[ing] a sense of crisis in readers, viewers or listeners by attacking the cognitive and cultural mechanisms that keep our understanding of the Holocaust at a safe distance from our understanding of ourselves', enables productive forms of cultural self-examination to take place, particularly as regards the potential dangers of complicity and/ or moral passivity (ibid., pp. 3, 4). Boswell's study exemplifies the increasingly cross-disciplinary scope of recent considerations of post-Holocaust culture, while also indicating that the roots of the new 'transgressive art' may not be as recently laid as such critics as Spargo, Rohr and Komor suggest.

Critical rejection of the discursive mechanisms of 'Holocaust piety' is likewise embodied in Naomi Mandel's work, which rejects wholeheartedly the rhetoric of 'unspeakability' which dominated Holocaust discourse in its earlier phases. Defining 'the unspeakable' as 'the rhetorical invocation of the limits of language, comprehension, representation, and thought on the one hand, and a deferential gesture toward atrocity, horror, trauma and pain on the other' (Mandel, 2006, p. 4), Mandel highlights the degree to which this taboo in fact serves other functions than those it implicitly lays claim to. While such discourse offers, in Mandel's words, 'the masquerade of rhetorical performance (evoking the unspeakable) as ethical practice (protecting the survivors, respecting the memory of the victims, safeguarding identity, reality, or historical truth)', its object, she argues, is, rather, 'protecting the integrity of its practitioners' (ibid., p. 209). Echoing Boswell's claim that 'The prohibitions of Holocaust piety . . . do not allow for any interrogation of the emergence of genocide in a developed society that in political, cultural and economic terms contained multiple traces of the modern Western world' (Boswell, 2012, p. 9), Mandel argues in favour of more critical modes of self-examination, 'eschew[ing] the moral high ground that the unspeakable so seductively supplies and [embracing] the complicity of our own situation in structures of violence and power' (Mandel, 2006, p. 23).

Ethics

In this way, complicity emerges as a key concept in recent approaches to Holocaust literature, taking the form (as in the work of the critic of South African literature Mark Sanders) of a 'foldedness with the other' (Sanders, 2002, pp. 11–12) which recognizes the mutual implication of one's own and others' actions. In this context, it is perhaps unsurprising that other emerging areas of focus within the study of Holocaust literature include a renewed attention to the figure of the perpetrator (as discussed below) and an increasing emphasis on the ethical (in contrast to more rigid moral frameworks previously applied), as exemplified in such recent work as that of Lothe, Suleiman and Phelan (eds) (2012), which combines attention to the ethics of representation with a focus on narrative theory, Richard Crownshaw's responses to literature and architecture in Crownshaw (2010), and the work of Libby Saxton (2008) on Holocaust film. The movement into focus of 'ethics' at once accords with the broader phenomenon of the 'ethical turn' in the arts and humanities in the last decades of the twentieth century (see Davis and Womack, 2001, for a full elaboration of this) and at the same time may be viewed as a consequence of increasing distance from the events themselves, freeing up both literary and critical-theoretical discourse to pursue more open-ended modes of theorization and enquiry.

Recent examinations of the ethics of Holocaust representation and post-Holocaust thought have frequently concerned the significance of postmodernism and poststructuralist ethical philosophy in this regard. One keynote study in this respect is Robert Eaglestone's *The Holocaust and the Postmodern* (2004) which, focusing on the work of Emmanuel Levinas and Jacques Derrida, argues powerfully for a consideration of postmodern philosophy's 'awareness and consequent rejection of the metaphysics of comprehension', which concept he defines as follows:

> The metaphysics of comprehension can be understood as both the desire for and the methods by and through which Western thought, in many different

ways, comprehends, seizes, or consumes what is other to it and so reduces the other to itself, to the same . . . Postmodernism focuses on the act of comprehending, seizing, covering up, and on the resistance to that act – to the emergence, if only momentarily, of otherness. (Eaglestone, 2004, p. 4)

Such an approach might ultimately be read as an exploration of the complicity of thought and language themselves in totalizing and other-eclipsing structures of comprehension and articulation, in this sense extending the project of cultural and individual self-scrutiny to the most foundational level. Nevertheless, approaches to the Holocaust via postmodern ethics also invite further consideration in terms of their proximity, through an emphasis on unrepresentability via the necessity to avoid encroaching on or illusorily 'grasping' the other's unassimilable experience, to the notion of the 'unspeakable'. From this perspective, one might ask whether a postmodern ethics which focuses concern on the degree to which representations are able to avoid such encroachment even as they ostensibly (though in a bracketed way) 'represent' does not in fact remain focused more on the irreproachability of the representing self than on the other. In this sense, it is arguable that Holocaust studies awaits the theorization of a pragmatic ethics which at once concretizes intimations of complicity and takes the risk of empathic interpersonal connection across experiential gulfs. This qualification aside, the significance of postmodern ethics in the work of such critics as Bernard-Donals (2009), Spargo (2004), Eaglestone (2004) and Orbán (2005), cannot be overstated as a valuable means of interrogating the taken-for-granted structures of discourse which permeate post-Holocaust speech and thought.

Further interesting developments in the consideration of Holocaust literature from an ethical perspective include Brett Ashley Kaplan's re-evaluation of the ethical significance of aesthetic pleasure in the readerly engagement with these works. Kaplan's study may be viewed as part of a wider critical trend (with other key figures here including Elaine Scarry) aimed at reclaiming beauty as a legitimate context within the discussion of art and literature following a widespread suspicion of the concept in the aftermath of fascism's aestheticization of politics.[8] Far from being inappropriate in the context of the Holocaust, she argues, 'beautiful' representations increase our ability to engage with these events – at the levels of survivor writing (beauty making traumatic experience more endurable and aiding its memorialization and communication to others – Delbo, Celan and Semprun being key figures in her argument here), allusive poetic representation, mourning in the visual arts (expanding our understanding and prompting critical thought on the Holocaust and Holocaust representation) and memorial culture. Kaplan's treatment of the latter is particularly interesting, examining the fear of 'aesthetic pollution' (i.e. the concern that the use of aesthetic forms associated with Nazism, such as a monumental aesthetic in memorials, might lead to these artworks being contaminated by a fascist politics). Kaplan argues powerfully against such logic, suggesting that 'by moving beyond the fear of aesthetic pollution, we might produce commemorative sites whose forms will defy the conflation of political with artistic histories' (Kaplan, 2007, p. 163), and exploring the degree to which a logic of contamination and purity resonates with that of Nazism itself. While the notion of the beautiful is often difficult to pinpoint (raising the threat in literary criticism of locating beauty in precisely those representations we find ethically moving), an emergent openness to such questions underscores not only the degree to which Holocaust literature has become an accepted form of engagement with these events and a mode of expression no longer set aside so radically from other forms of literary expression, but also (and relatedly) the lifting of certain taboos and inhibitions regarding the appropriate parameters of critical inquiry in this area. This said, Antony Rowland has recently highlighted the need for further work in the field of testimony specifically upon 'the reception of testimony, linguistic play and readerly pleasure' (Rowland, 2010, p. 115). Coupled with polarized critical reaction to such works as Anne Michaels' poetically rich novels *Fugitive Pieces* and *The Winter Vault*, such commentary may be taken as indicating the still-tentative nature of this research area.

Perpetrators

As mentioned above, renewed attention to the figure of the perpetrator in Holocaust representation forms another key strand of the lifting of prohibitions and taboos within both literature and criticism. A concise summary of the anxieties and imperatives which have structured this question in earlier decades, as well as an indication of the commonality of literary and broader cultural questions of representation in this respect, can be found in the debate during the planning stages about the degree to which perpetrators should be present in the United States Holocaust Memorial Museum. As Edward T. Linenthal comments, while Raul Hilberg felt it necessary for perpetrators to 'speak' in the exhibition, this was controversial among the other parties involved in the decision making: 'this idea threatened to contaminate what for many was commemorative space' (Linenthal, 1995, p. 199). This anxiety that an engagement with the perpetrators might displace or interrupt a victim-focused project with a memorial function was coupled with a concern that the inclusion of Nazi uniforms and iconography might prove perversely appealing for some visitors (ibid.); in both cases, the concerns map onto literature and offer further explanation for the taboo on perpetrator representation, particularly if Holocaust literature is considered as (for many readers) commemorative space. The compromise the museum made in embossing the words of Hitler in a different, less prominent way to those of other cited figures (ibid., p. 200) likewise indicates a fear that to include perpetrator perspectives alongside those of victims would imply ethical equivalence or equivalent demand on visitor attention. Nevertheless, Linenthal's comment on the function of photographs of perpetrators highlights what would become a more dominant argument in calls for the examination of perpetrators (in Holocaust Studies more widely) and their representation (in literary studies): 'The faces of the perpetrators offer visitors the opportunity to reflect on the moral choices made by ordinary people who were not victims' (ibid., p. 210).

This connection between an examination of the perpetrator and the process of cultural and personal ethical self-examination can be identified as a key factor in the 'turn to the perpetrator' not only in literary studies (in the work of such critics as Suleiman (2009), McGlothlin (2010), Eaglestone (2010b), Rau (2013), Gomel (2003), Sanyal (2010), Donahue (2010), Adams and Vice (eds) (2013), and others), but in the humanities and sciences more widely. In historiography, landmark work by Christopher Browning (1992) on the conditions which made participation in atrocity permissible has been built on more recently by such figures as Jan Gross (2003), Olaf Jensen and Claus-Christian Szejnmann (2008); while in the field of social psychology, such critics as Newman and Erber (2002) and Waller (2007) have delved further into the motivating factors behind genocidal violence and complicity, often with an expressly future-oriented aim of aiding in efforts towards genocide prevention. This multidisciplinary and transnational engagement with representations and contexts of perpetration may be linked not only to the 'ethical turn' in the arts and humanities and to increasing temporal distance from the Holocaust, but also, unfortunately, to the enduring relevance of questions of guilt and complicity in relation to ongoing human-rights abuses and neofascist violence in the contemporary political world, including in Europe, as well as the spectacle of trials like those of John Demjanjuk and, in relation to more recent atrocities, Radovan Karadzic, underscoring the ongoing significance of these questions. Furthermore, as many of the artworks gathered in the 2002 exhibition Mirroring Evil make clear, contemporary culture retains, to use Susan Sontag's phrase, a fascination with fascism and a complicity with its economic structures that demands exploration and acknowledgement, even in highly ironized ways. The literary work of such figures as Jonathan Littell (2009), Bernhard Schlink (1997), Laurent Binet (2012), David Grossman (1990), Rachel Seiffert (2001), and Martin Amis (1991), thus does not occur in a context devoid of contemporary resonances of the violence and atrocity they explore, despite the lengthening of the post-Second World War era.

Recent critical work on perpetrators has thus attempted to move beyond a sense of what Claude Lanzmann termed, when refusing to show a film about the Nazi doctor Eduard Wirths, 'the obscenity of understanding' (Lanzmann, 1995), though such critics as Robert Eaglestone (2013) have identified in perpetrator fiction a reluctance to fully abandon such obfuscation. Eaglestone introduces the terminology of the 'swerve' to suggest that while these fictions assume an exploratory attitude towards the motivations and psychological experiences of the perpetrator figure, in reality they steer away from this; in the case of Littell, through the Oresteia plot which at once switches the narrative into a quasi-mythic register and brackets Aue off as an incestuous, matricidal sociopath. While it could be argued in response that the answers to the question of 'why' offered by such texts appear insufficient precisely because the insufficient is depressingly sufficient in terms of the decision to exclude from one's apprehension the reality of another's suffering, such readings raise questions about the degree to which these literary taboos have been fully lifted, as Matthew Boswell and Erin McGlothlin's chapters in this volume, in different ways, observe.

The degree to which perpetrator fictions offer a genuinely explorative and self-questioning approach to perpetrator-protagonists rather than merely trading on their transgressive frisson while evading genuine engagement with these issues – a question that could perhaps have been asked of Holocaust representations themselves in earlier decades, with William Styron's *Sophie's Choice* (1976) being one example here – remains a central point of enquiry within this emerging area of study, with such works as Petra Rau's recent *Our Nazis* (2013) raising key issues in this respect. With a particular interest in genre (including the popular genres of crime/noir and alternate history), Rau draws a clear distinction between 'fascism' and 'Nazis' as they exist in the cultural imagination and the fascism and Nazis of history, with these representations telling us much more about the former than the latter. In particular, Rau addresses the glamorization of fascism as exotic other, contending that this 'often merely cloaks the projection of unconscious desires onto an other, . . . while it simultaneously allows the audience or reader to dramatise and inhabit the fascist longings they habitually disown' (Rau, 2013, p. 10). In addition to such negotiations between cultural self-examination and a more disturbing phenomenon partaking of Sontag's 'fascinating fascism' (Sontag, [1974] 1983) and Friedlander's 'new discourse' combining kitsch and death (Friedlander, 1984), other current and emerging preoccupations in perpetrator representation include questions of gender and abjection (see, for example, Rowland, Brown, and Vice, in Adams and Vice (2013)), popular culture (Boswell, 2012; Rau, 2013), and the functions of perpetrator testimony (see, for example, Eaglestone, 2010b).

Part 3: Intersections and Staged Encounters

Alongside a re-examination of questions of proximity and positionality, an attention to transgressive Holocaust art and an engagement with the figure of the perpetrator, recent years have seen an emerging critical focus upon the interrelation of the memory and representation of the Holocaust with those of other genocides and histories of atrocity. One key and compelling critical framework recently to have emerged within this area is that of Michael Rothberg (2009), who argues against 'zero-sum' approaches which view different cultural memories (e.g. those of colonialism and the Holocaust) as ensnared in a competitive relationship in which remembrance of one history comes at the expense of others. Instead, his theory of 'multidirectional memory' foregrounds the extent to which different cultural memories intersect dialogically, refer to each other, and often permit valuable forms of solidarity or comparative reflection to emerge (while maintaining the specificity and distinctness of the individual contexts in question). Key points of focus in Rothberg's monograph include Hannah Arendt and Aimé Césaire's considerations of Nazi totalitarianism as colonialism revisited upon Europe, French filmic and literary production of the 1960s, the work of André Schwarz-Bart, and the writings of W. E. B. Du Bois following his visit to the site of the Warsaw Ghetto in 1949.

The notion of 'multidirectional memory' goes beyond theorizations of the globalization of Holocaust memory such as those of Daniel Levy and Natan Sznaider (2006), with Rothberg contending that:

> [T]he Holocaust does not simply become a universal moral standard that can then be applied to other histories; rather, some of those *other histories help produce a sense of the Holocaust's particularity*. At the same time, people impacted by the histories of colonialism and decolonization refer to this emergent understanding of the Holocaust as part of a *shared but not necessarily universal* moral and political project. Far from being a floating, universal signifier, the Holocaust emerges in its specificity as part of a multidirectional network of diverse histories of extreme violence, torture, and racist policy. (Rothberg, 2009, p. 244)

Rothberg thus emphasizes the lack of universality of Holocaust memory despite its intersection with a range of memorial contexts, emphasizing too the extent to which the Holocaust does not merely enable the articulation of other contexts of historical suffering, but itself emerges in its particularity through this dialogue. He thus distinguishes his approach from those that stress the Holocaust's provision of a universal moral framework within which all other human-rights abuses may be judged, contending that '[a] more heterogeneous understanding of moral action that recognizes the importance of comparison and generalization while resisting too-easy universalization may not produce a global moral code, but it may produce the grounds for new transnational visions of justice and solidarity that do not reproduce the easily manipulated abstract code of "good" and "evil"' (ibid., p. 265). While, as Rothberg acknowledges, the theory does not encompass all intersections of different cultural and historical memories (with many existing in conflict rather than productive dialogue – memories of the Holocaust and the Israeli–Palestinian conflict, for example), it has proved greatly influential in recent approaches to the Holocaust and other traumatic histories via a connective lens.

Rothberg's theory of multidirectionality crystallizes a recent turn to the connective and/or comparative evident among such critics and theorists as Max Silverman (2013), Stef Craps (2013), Emily Miller Budick (1998), Paul Gilroy (2004), Walter Benn Michaels (1999) and Eric J. Sundquist, whose *Strangers in the Land* (2005) offers an impressively researched and detailed exploration of the relationship between African Americans and Jewish Americans over history, including extensive consideration of the function (and controversy) of the tropes of Exodus and Holocaust in this relationship. As the example of Sundquist's work demonstrates, despite the significance of the essentially optimistic notion of multidirectional memory, research has also focused on contexts in which Holocaust memory forms a site of contrast when used in the articulation of diverse contexts and forms of suffering, in addition to contexts in which Holocaust memory has been instrumentalized. These include considerations of the functioning of Holocaust memory in Israeli political discourse (see, for example, the work of Zertal (2005)) and the aftermath of September 11th, 2001, in which Holocaust memory was utilized in both therapeutic and politically irresponsible ways.[9]

Comparative examinations of Holocaust memory and the memory of other culturally traumatic events do not extend merely to the consideration of more recent events in the context of Holocaust memory, however, but also encompass rereadings of canonical works of literature in the light of the conceptual frameworks derived from Holocaust Studies. Examples include the application of notions of postmemory to a range of additional literary contexts including the literatures of slavery and colonial oppression, in addition to the re-examination of such nineteenth-century works as Conrad's *Heart of Darkness* from a post-Holocaust perspective. Eaglestone, for example, reads both Marlow and Conrad as 'low level genocidal perpetrators' (Eaglestone, 2010a, p. 191) while interpreting Kurtz as a potential whistleblower on a genocidal colonial regime (ibid., p. 199), while Lea Wernick Fridman considers Conrad's text from a different perspective (and indeed, a different direction) as 'a model of literary strategies in the representation of historical horror' that anticipates the strategies of Holocaust writing (Fridman, 2000, p. 2). Sara Guyer's recent work *Romanticism after Auschwitz* (2007) offers another insightful reference point in this context. Guyer examines the recurrence of romantic tropes in post-Holocaust literature, inviting a reconsideration of their original formulations as well as the literatures in which they recur, and contending that 'the romantic lyric and post-Holocaust testimony both are constituted by a rhetoric of survival' (Guyer, 2007, p. 18), where 'a rhetoric of survival' is understood as a rhetoric 'of life and subjectivity beyond possibility or impossibility' (ibid., p. 21). Guyer's work demonstrates the insightful potential of critical attention to the relationship between pre- and post-Holocaust literatures and modes of thought, which remains an area for ongoing enquiry; as Eaglestone (2010a, p. 190) notes, more work could be done in systematically evaluating the significance of post-Holocaust analytical frameworks to contextually diverse literary works, with this being one potential angle for further development in future.

Conclusion

To briefly summarize, Holocaust literary studies in the twenty-first century has seen the emergence of a range of key angles of enquiry including the increasing focus on Holocaust literature produced by those in relationships of lesser proximity to the events themselves; the development, application, and critical scrutiny of new models of memory detached from the immediately experiential; the renewed attention to the concept of the witness and to the generic and contextual conditions of testimony, including troublesome forms of testimony such as perpetrator and false testimony; attention to transgressive aesthetic practice and the representation of perpetrators; the impact of the 'ethical turn' and the negotiation of the significance and ethical valence of poststructuralist thought in this context; the consideration of aesthetic pleasure; the exploration of Holocaust literature as a ground for staging encounters with other contexts of traumatic history; and the self-scrutiny of Holocaust literary studies as a discipline. The latter development in particular might propel the literary scholar working in this area to one of a number of conclusions: the conclusion that the discipline is approaching a kind of late-stage fixation upon its own structures and mechanisms, raising questions about where the interests of literary Holocaust scholars really lie; the concern that the discipline has become excessively codified, necessitating a conscious effort towards the development of new ways of rethinking and reshaping a crowded and perhaps solidified conceptual field; or, more positively, the conclusion that the discipline is at last engaging in a careful and necessary investigation of its own critical standpoints, a process which bodes well for its future intellectual rigour and ethical subtlety. As regards additional areas for enquiry, there is, as noted above, a need for a questioning of postmodern ethical orthodoxies lest these collapse into a form of second-wave piety; areas for further scholarly attention might include the phenomenology of reading about the Holocaust (including questions of identification); representations of the persecution of gay people, members of the Roma and Sinti communities, Communists and other political prisoners, and those targeted via the T-4

Euthanasia Program; multidirectionality *within* the context of the Holocaust (encompassing, for example, further attention to the relationship between the experience and representation of different victim groups); representation of issues of sex and sexuality; and honest reflection on the degree to which the literary–critical engagement with the Holocaust facilitates or merely takes the place of wider possibilities of political and ethical intervention. While the future of Holocaust literary studies is difficult to predict, the extrapolation of current and emerging developments suggests that many of these angles of enquiry may be more fully actualized in future years.

Notes

1. Berel Lang, for example, writing in 1988, usefully summarizes the key preoccupations of the initial wave of Holocaust literary criticism thus: 'What constraints, whether in the use of fact or in the reach of the imagination, are imposed on authors or readers by the subject of the Holocaust? How does that subject shape the perspectives from which it is viewed – the stance, for example, of the "disinterested" scholar, or the assumption of aesthetic distance or "negative capability" in the poet or novelist? Is the enormity of the Holocaust at all capable of literary representation? And what would be the justification for attempting such representation even if it were possible?' (p. 2). For a more extensive outline of some of the key critical perspectives in the initial approach to questions of Holocaust representation, see this volume's Annotated Bibliography.
2. On the extension of issues of intergenerational memory to other contexts beyond that of Holocaust victimhood, see also, for example, Schwab's *Haunting Legacies: Violent Histories and Transgenerational Trauma* (2010).
3. For a useful summary of critiques of the trauma theory of Caruth, Felman et al., see Crownshaw (2010, pp. 4–12).
4. As regards the degree to which, in testimony, '[a] lack of affect is . . . equated with truth', see also Hutton (2005, p. 13).
5. It should also be noted that the 'new taboo-breaking art' does have precedent in earlier disruptions of what Terrence Des Pres famously termed 'Holocaust Etiquette'; see Des Pres's discussion of Holocaust comedy in Des Pres (1988). It should also be noted that while the development in the approach to Holocaust texts is often characterized as a shift from whether the Holocaust should be represented to how it is represented (e.g. Saxton, 2008, p. 2), this pragmatic stance is evident in many earlier appraisals of Holocaust literature and art, such as Lawrence Langer's 1975 work *The Holocaust and the Literary Imagination*. In this sense, it is apparent that the alteration in critical stance, while evident, should not be overstated.
6. This contrasts markedly to earlier critical stances concerning the emergence and recognition of distinct generic and representational structures within Holocaust discourse; Alvin H. Rosenfeld, for example, describes as 'troubling' the notion that 'the "Holocaust Novel" may now be seen as an available subgenre of contemporary fiction, to be written by anyone who is on to and can master the "formula"' (1980, p. 172).
7. There are implications, too, of course, about the changing parameters of witnessing and testimony in this context; see 'New Postmemories' and 'Memory Transmission' sections above.

Another potential way of contextualizing the new 'transgressive Holocaust art' might be to refer back to Geoffrey Hartman's speculation concerning the threat of desensitization: if empathy is exhaustible, Hartman suggests, 'it might indeed be important to retain first impressions, even the painful and shocking ones. They become talismanic: fixed ideas of our once-and-future power to feel. . . . It is in pursuit of such defining memories that we abandon the issue of representational limits and seek to "cut" ourselves, like psychotics who ascertain in this way that they exist. As if only a personal or historical trauma (I bleed, therefore I am) would bond us to life' (1996, p. 152). Like the 'retaining of first impressions', the pursuit of ever more shocking forms of Holocaust art might be read in this context as an attempt to overcome (or negotiate anxiety concerning) desensitization.

On the topic of the 'new transgressive Holocaust art', Dominick LaCapra's assertion that Holocaust representation does not necessarily mean an end to repression is also worthy of note: LaCapra writes that 'In the recent past, the repressed has seemed to return in a complex fashion that has induced renewed disavowal in certain quarters (for example, among revisionist historians) and commodified, commercialized, politically tendentious, and self-interested (if not pornographic) representation in other quarters' (1994, p. 189); reading transgressive art as a complex return of the repressed not necessarily equatable with its working through offers another potentially productive angle on transgression.

8. See Scarry's summary of and refutation of this reaction: 'The banishing of beauty from the humanities in the last two decades has been carried out by a set of political complaints against it. But . . . these political complaints against beauty are themselves incoherent. Beauty is, at the very least, innocent of the charges against it, and it may even be the case that far from damaging our capacity to attend to problems of injustice, it instead intensifies the pressure we feel to repair existing injuries' (1999, p. 57).

9. Examples of the interrelation of these events in cultural memory include Art Spiegelman's collection of comic strips *In the Shadow of No Towers* (2004), which uses a visual and verbal vocabulary of (un)representability drawn from his Holocaust text *Maus* ([1996] 2003) in order to articulate the difficulties in representing 9/11, and the assertion by the novelist Thane Rosenbaum that in the aftermath of 9/11, 'our perception of the Holocaust has changed. It had to, because atrocity now has a new and a different face and name' (2004, pp. 126–7). The 9/11 context also offers more troubling examples of the political instrumentalization of Holocaust memory, both in the US government's justificatory rhetoric for the 'war on terror' and in such controversies as the Ward Churchill affair, as David P. Schulz and G. Michell Reyes (2008) explore. The presence of such contexts of instrumentalization perhaps offers a check on the optimism of theories of multidirectional memory.

Works Cited

Adams, J. (2011), *Magic Realism in Holocaust Literature: Troping the Traumatic Real*. Basingstoke: Palgrave Macmillan.

Adams, J. and Vice, S. (eds) (2013), *Representing Perpetrators in Holocaust Literature and Film*. London: Vallentine Mitchell.

Amis, M. (1991), *Time's Arrow*. London: Jonathan Cape.

Apel, D. (2002), *Memory Effects: The Holocaust and the Art of Secondary Witnessing*. New Brunswick: Rutgers University Press.

Appignanesi, L. (1999), *Losing the Dead*. London: Chatto & Windus.

Berger, A. L. and Berger, N. (eds) (2001), *Second Generation Voices: Reflections by Children of Holocaust Survivors and Perpetrators*. Syracuse, NY: Syracuse University Press.

Bernard-Donals, M. (2009), *Forgetful Memory: Representation and Remembrance in the Wake of the Holocaust*. Albany: State University of New York Press.

Binet, L. (2012), *HHhH*, trans. S. Taylor. London: Harvill Secker.

Boswell, M. (2012), *Holocaust Impiety in Literature, Popular Music and Film*. Basingstoke: Palgrave Macmillan.

Brown, A. (2013), 'Screening women's complicity in the Holocaust: the problems of judgement and representation', in J. Adams and S. Vice (eds), *Representing Perpetrators in Holocaust Literature and Film*. London: Vallentine Mitchell, pp. 69–90.

Browning, C. (1992), *Ordinary Men: Reserve Police Battalion 101 and the Final Solution in Poland*. New York: HarperCollins.

Budick, E. Miller (1998), *Blacks and Jews in Literary Conversation*. Cambridge: Cambridge University Press.

Caruth, C. (ed.) (1995), *Trauma: Explorations in Memory*. Baltimore: Johns Hopkins University Press.

Codde, P. (2010), 'Postmemory, afterimages, transferred loss: first and third generation Holocaust trauma in American literature and film', in S. Komor and S. Rohr (eds), *The Holocaust, Art, and Taboo: Transatlantic Exchanges on the Ethics and Aesthetics of Representation*. Heidelberg: Universitätsverlag Winter, pp. 63–74.

Craps, S. (2013), *Postcolonial Witnessing: Trauma Out of Bounds*. Basingstoke: Palgrave Macmillan.

Crownshaw, R. (2010), *The Afterlife of Holocaust Memory in Contemporary Literature and Culture*. Basingstoke: Palgrave Macmillan.

Davis, T. F. and Womack, K. (eds) (2001), *Mapping the Ethical Turn: A Reader in Ethics, Culture, and Literary Theory*. Charlottesville: University Press of Virginia.

Dean, C. J. (2010), *Aversion and Erasure: The Fate of the Victim after the Holocaust*. Ithaca and London: Cornell University Press.

Des Pres, T. (1988), 'Holocaust *laughter?*', in B. Lang (ed.), *Writing and the Holocaust*. New York and London: Holmes & Meier, pp. 216–33.

Donahue, W. Collins (2010), *Holocaust as Fiction: Bernhard Schlink's 'Nazi' Novels and their Films*. New York: Palgrave Macmillan.

Eaglestone, R. (2004), *The Holocaust and the Postmodern*. Oxford: Oxford University Press.

—. (2010a), 'Reading *Heart of Darkness* after the Holocaust', in R. C. Spargo and R. M. Ehrenreich (eds), *After Representation? The Holocaust, Literature, and Culture*. New Brunswick, NJ: Rutgers University Press, pp. 190–209.

—. (2010b), 'Reading perpetrator testimony', in R. Crownshaw, J. Kilby and A. Rowland (eds), *The Future of Memory*. New York: Berghahn Books, pp. 123–34.

—. (2013), 'Avoiding evil in perpetrator fiction', in J. Adams and S. Vice (eds), *Representing Perpetrators in Holocaust Literature and Film*. London: Vallentine Mitchell, pp. 13–24.

Felman, S. (1992), 'Education and crisis, or the vicissitudes of teaching', in S. Felman and D. Laub, *Testimony: Crises of Witnessing in Literature, Psychoanalysis and History*. New York and London: Routledge, pp. 1–56.

Flanzbaum, H. (ed.) (1999), *The Americanization of the Holocaust*. Baltimore and London: Johns Hopkins University Press.

Foer, J. S. (2002), *Everything Is Illuminated*. Boston: Houghton Mifflin.

Fridman, L. Wernick (2000), *Words and Witness: Narrative and Aesthetic Strategies in the Representation of the Holocaust*. Albany: State University of New York Press.

Friedlander, S. (1984), *Reflections of Nazism: An Essay on Kitsch and Death*, trans. T. Weyr. New York: Harper & Row.

Gilroy, P. (2004), *Between Camps: Nations, Cultures, and the Allure of Race*, 2nd edn. London and New York: Routledge.

Gomel, E. (2003), *Bloodscripts: Writing the Violent Subject*. Columbus: Ohio State University Press.

Grimwood, M. (2007), *Holocaust Literature of the Second Generation*. New York and Basingstoke: Palgrave Macmillan.

Gross, J. T. (2003), *Neighbours: The Destruction of the Jewish Community in Jedwabne, Poland, 1941*. London: Arrow.

Grossman, D. (1990), *See Under: Love*, trans. B. Rosenberg. London: Jonathan Cape.

Gubar, S. (2003), *Poetry after Auschwitz: Remembering What One Never Knew*. Bloomington and Indianapolis: Indiana University Press.

Guyer, S. (2007), *Romanticism after Auschwitz*. Stanford, CA: Stanford University Press.

Hartman, G. (1996), 'Holocaust testimony, art, and trauma', in *The Longest Shadow: In The Aftermath of the Holocaust*. Bloomington and Indianapolis: Indiana University Press, pp. 151–72.

Hirsch, M. (1996), 'Past lives: postmemories in exile', *Poetics Today*, 17.4, 659–86.

—. (1999), 'Projected memory: Holocaust photographs in personal and public fantasy', in M. Bal, J. Crewe and L. Spitzer (eds), *Acts of Memory: Cultural Recall in the Present*. Hanover, NH: University Press of New England, pp. 2–23.

—. (2012), *The Generation of Postmemory: Writing and Visual Culture after the Holocaust*. New York: Columbia University Press.

Hirsch, M. and Miller, N. K. (2011), 'Introduction', in M. Hirsch and N. K. Miller (eds), *Rites of Return: Diaspora Poetics and the Politics of Memory*. New York: Columbia University Press, pp. 1–20.

Hirsch, M. and Spitzer, L. (2011), 'The web and the reunion: http://czernowitz.ehpes. com', in M. Hirsch and N. K. Miller (eds), *Rites of Return: Diaspora Poetics and the Politics of Memory*. New York: Columbia University Press, pp. 59–71.

Hungerford, A. (2003), *The Holocaust of Texts: Genocide, Literature, and Personification*. Chicago and London: University of Chicago Press.

Hutton, M.-A. (2005), *Testimony from the Nazi Camps: French Women's Voices*. London: Routledge.

Jensen, O. and Szejnmann, C.-C. W. (eds) (2008), *Ordinary People as Mass Murderers: Perpetrators in Comparative Perspective*. Basingstoke: Palgrave Macmillan.

Kaplan, B. A. (2007), *Unwanted Beauty: Aesthetic Pleasure in Holocaust Representation*. Urbana and Chicago: University of Illinois Press.

—. (2011), *Landscapes of Holocaust Postmemory*. New York: Routledge.

Kleeblatt, N. (ed.) (2001), *Mirroring Evil: Nazi Imagery / Recent Art*. New Brunswick, NJ: Rutgers University Press; New York: The Jewish Museum.

LaCapra, D. (1994), *Representing the Holocaust: History, Theory, Trauma*. Ithaca and London: Cornell University Press.

Landsberg, A. (2004), *Prosthetic Memory: The Transformation of American Remembrance in the Age of Mass Culture*. New York: Columbia University Press.

Lang, B. (1988), 'Introduction', in B. Lang (ed.), *Writing and the Holocaust*. New York and London: Holmes & Meier, pp. 1–15.

—. (2000), 'Holocaust genres and the turn to history', in A. Leak and G. Paizis (eds), *The Holocaust and the Text*. Basingstoke: Macmillan, pp. 17–31.

Langer, L. (1975), *The Holocaust and the Literary Imagination*. New Haven and London: Yale University Press.

—. (1991), *Holocaust Testimonies: The Ruins of Memory*. New Haven: Yale University Press.

Lanzmann, C. (1995), 'The obscenity of understanding: an evening with Claude Lanzmann', in C. Caruth (ed.), *Trauma: Explorations in Memory*. Baltimore: Johns Hopkins University Press, pp. 200–20.

Laub, D. (1992), 'An event without a witness: truth, testimony and survival', in S. Felman and D. Laub, *Testimony: Crises of Witnessing in Literature, Psychoanalysis and History*. New York and London: Routledge, pp. 75–92.

Levine, M. G. (2006), *The Belated Witness: Literature, Testimony, and the Question of Holocaust Survival*. Stanford, CA: Stanford University Press.

Levy, D. and Sznaider, N. (2006), *The Holocaust and Memory in the Global Age*, trans. A. Oksiloff. Philadelphia: Temple University Press.

Leys, R. (2000), *Trauma: A Genealogy*. Chicago: University of Chicago Press.

Linenthal, E. T. (1995), *Preserving Memory: The Struggle to Create America's Holocaust Museum*. New York: Viking Penguin.

Liss, A. (1998), *Trespassing through Shadows: Memory, Photography and the Holocaust*. Minneapolis: University of Minnesota Press.

Littell, J. (2009), *The Kindly Ones*, trans. C. Mandell. London: Chatto & Windus.

Lothe, J., Suleiman, S. Rubin, and Phelan, J. (eds) (2012), *After Testimony: The Ethics and Aesthetics of Holocaust Narrative for the Future*. Columbus: Ohio State University Press.

Mandel, N. (2006), *Against the Unspeakable: Complicity, the Holocaust and Slavery in America*. Charlottesville: University of Virginia Press.

Martel, Y. (2010), *Beatrice and Virgil*. Edinburgh: Canongate.

McGlothlin, E. (2006), *Second-Generation Holocaust Literature: Legacies of Survival and Perpetration*. Woodbridge: Camden House.

—. (2010), 'Theorizing the perpetrator in Bernhard Schlink's *The Reader* and Martin Amis's *Time's Arrow*', in R. C. Spargo, and R. M. Ehrenreich (eds), *After Representation? The Holocaust, Literature, and Culture*. New Brunswick, NJ: Rutgers University Press, pp. 210–30.

Mendelsohn, D. (2007), *The Lost: A Search for Six of Six Million*. London: HarperCollins.

Michaels, A. [1996] (1997), *Fugitive Pieces*. London: Bloomsbury.

—. (2009), *The Winter Vault*. London: Bloomsbury.

Michaels, W. B. (1999), '"You who never was there": slavery and the new historicism – deconstruction and the Holocaust', in H. Flanzbaum (ed.), *The Americanization of the Holocaust*. Baltimore and London: Johns Hopkins University Press, pp. 181–97.

Newman, L. S. and Erber, R. (2002), *Understanding Genocide: The Social Psychology of the Holocaust*. Oxford: Oxford University Press.

Novick, P. (1999), *The Holocaust and Collective Memory: The American Experience*. London: Bloomsbury.

Orbán, K. (2005), *Ethical Diversions: The Post-Holocaust Narratives of Pynchon, Abish, DeLillo, and Spiegelman*. New York and London: Routledge.

Rau, P. (2013), *Our Nazis: Representations of Fascism in Contemporary Literature and Film*. Edinburgh: Edinburgh University Press.

Rohr, S. (2010), '"Genocide pop": the Holocaust as media event', in S. Komor and S. Rohr (eds), *The Holocaust, Art, and Taboo: Transatlantic Exchanges on the Ethics and Aesthetics of Representation*. Heidelberg: Universitätsverlag Winter, pp. 155–77.

Rohr, S. and Komor, S. (2010), 'Introduction', in S. Komor and S. Rohr (eds), *The Holocaust, Art, and Taboo: Transatlantic Exchanges on the Ethics and Aesthetics of Representation*. Heidelberg: Universitätsverlag Winter, pp. 9–17.

Rosenbaum, T. (2004), 'Art and atrocity in a post-9/11 world', in A. L. Berger and G. L. Cronin (eds), *Jewish American and Holocaust Literature: Representation in the Postmodern World*. Albany: State University of New York Press, pp. 125–36.

Rosenfeld, A. H. (1980), *A Double Dying: Reflections on Holocaust Literature*. Bloomington and Indianapolis: Indiana University Press.

Rothberg, M. (2009), *Multidirectional Memory: Remembering the Holocaust in the Age of Decolonization*. Stanford, CA: Stanford University Press.

Rowland, A. (2010), 'The future of testimony: introduction', in R. Crownshaw, J. Kilby and A. Rowland (eds), *The Future of Memory*. New York: Berghahn Books, pp. 113–21.

—. (2013), 'Reading the female perpetrator', in J. Adams and S. Vice (eds), *Representing Perpetrators in Holocaust Literature and Film*. London: Vallentine Mitchell, pp. 129–43.

Sanders, M. (2002), *Complicities: The Intellectual and Apartheid*. Durham and London: Duke University Press.

Sanyal, D. (2010), 'Reading Nazi memory in Jonathan Littell's *Les Bienveillantes*', *L'Esprit Créateur*, 50.4, 47–66.

Saxton, L. (2008), *Haunted Images: Film, Ethics, Testimony and the Holocaust*. London: Wallflower Press.

Scarry, E. (1999), *On Beauty and Being Just*. Princeton: Princeton University Press.

Schlink, B. (1997), *The Reader*, trans. C. Brown Janeway. London: Weidenfeld & Nicolson.

Schulz, D. P. and Reyes, G. M. (2008), 'Ward Churchill and the politics of public memory', *Rhetoric & Public Affairs*, 11.4, 631–58.

Schwab, G. (2010), *Haunting Legacies: Violent Histories and Transgenerational Trauma*. New York: Columbia University Press.

Seiffert, R. (2001), *The Dark Room*. London: Heinemann.

Sicher, E. (2001), 'The future of the past: countermemory and postmemory in contemporary American post-Holocaust narratives', *History & Memory*, 12.2, 56–91.

Silverman, M. (2013), *Palimpsestic Memory: The Holocaust and Colonialism in French and Francophone Fiction and Film*. New York: Berghahn.

Sontag, S. [1974] (1983), 'Fascinating fascism', in *A Susan Sontag Reader*. London: Penguin, pp. 305–25.

Spargo, R. C. (2004), *The Ethics of Mourning: Grief and Responsibility in Elegiac Literature*. Baltimore: Johns Hopkins University Press.

—. (2010a), 'Introduction: on the cultural continuities of literary representation', in R. C. Spargo and R. M. Ehrenreich (eds), *After Representation? The Holocaust, Literature, and Culture*. New Brunswick, NJ: Rutgers University Press, pp. 1–22.

—. (2010b), 'The Holocaust and the economy of memory, from Bellow to Morrison', in R. C. Spargo and R. M. Ehrenreich (eds), *After Representation? The Holocaust, Literature, and Culture*. New Brunswick, NJ: Rutgers University Press, pp. 137–78.

Spargo, R. C. and Ehrenreich, R. M. (2010), 'Preface' to R. C. Spargo, and R. M. Ehrenreich (eds), *After Representation? The Holocaust, Literature, and Culture*. New Brunswick, NJ: Rutgers University Press, pp. ix–xii.

Spiegelman, A. [1996] (2003), *The Complete Maus*. London: Penguin.

—. (2004), *In the Shadow of No Towers*. New York: Pantheon.

Styron, W. (1976), *Sophie's Choice*. London: Jonathan Cape.

Suleiman, S. Rubin (2006), *Crises of Memory and the Second World War*. Cambridge, MA: Harvard University Press.

—. (2009), 'When the perpetrator becomes a reliable witness of the Holocaust: on Jonathan Littell's *Les bienveillantes*', *New German Critique*, 36.1, 1–19.

Sundquist, E. J. (2005), *Strangers in the Land: Blacks, Jews, Post-Holocaust America*. Cambridge, MA: The Belknap Press of Harvard University Press.

Tarantino, Q. (2009) (dir), *Inglourious Basterds*. DVD. UK: Universal Pictures.

Vice, S. (2013), 'Claude Lanzmann's Einsatzgruppen interviews', in J. Adams and S. Vice (eds), *Representing Perpetrators in Holocaust Literature and Film*. London: Vallentine Mitchell, pp. 47–68.

—. (forthcoming), *Textual Deceptions*. Edinburgh: Edinburgh University Press.

Waller, J. (2007), *Becoming Evil: How Ordinary People Commit Genocide and Mass Killing*, 2nd edn. Oxford: Oxford University Press.

Waxman, Z. V. (2006), *Writing the Holocaust: Identity, Testimony, Representation*. Oxford: Oxford University Press.

Weissman, G. (2004), *Fantasies of Witnessing: Postwar Efforts to Experience the Holocaust*. Ithaca and London: Cornell University Press.

Wieviorka, A. (2006), *The Era of the Witness*, trans. J. Stark. Ithaca: Cornell University Press.

Zertal, I. (2005), *Israel's Holocaust and the Politics of Nationhood*, trans. C. Galai. Cambridge: Cambridge University Press.

Annotated Bibliography

This bibliography aims not to provide an exhaustive list of materials in each of the subcategories listed, but instead to direct readers relatively new to the subject area towards key material and valuable starting points in research. Consequently, the emphasis is on substantial studies addressing the work of multiple authors or drawing overarching conceptual frameworks within which Holocaust literature may be contextualized and understood, rather than on journal articles and studies addressing the work of a single author. For reasons of accessibility and manageability, it is confined to material published in English or in English translation.

Each section of the bibliography is preceded by a short summary giving further information on selected sources of particular significance within the subject area.

Testimony, Witnessing and Trauma

Critical approaches to testimony often draw upon the perspectives of trauma theory, with the work of Cathy Caruth (1995 (ed.), 1996) a key reference point; discussed in greater length elsewhere in this volume,[1] Caruth's approach to trauma, in short, posits the traumatic event as that which was not experienced at the time at which it occurred due to its lack of assimilability to the available narrative and cognitive structures of the self (on the disparity between event and available structures of representation, see also van Alphen, 1997). A number of other key investigations of trauma, literature and history are provided by Hartman (1995) and LaCapra (2001); the latter provides an extensive and theoretically astute exploration of some of the key difficulties posed by traumatic experience to the writing of such events, with a focus in large part upon historiography. It includes examination of the role of the 'middle voice' in representations of traumatic history, the distinctions between absence and loss and between structural and historical trauma, the role of Holocaust testimony in historical understanding, and the issues raised by the Goldhagen debate.[2] For a rigorous example of the critique of contemporary trauma theory, with Caruth's work being subject to particular scrutiny on the grounds of its insistence upon the 'literality' of the trauma's returns, its lack of evidentiary basis, its elision of experiential boundaries, and the accuracy of its interpretation of Freud's writings, see Leys (2000).

Nevertheless, the trauma–theoretical model has informed some of the most influential work on testimony, not least Shoshana Felman and Dori Laub's study *Testimony: Crises of Witnessing in Literature, Psychoanalysis and History*. Felman and Laub here present a series of reflections upon aspects of testimony and trauma as refracted through pedagogical and therapeutic situations as well as literature and theory (including the work of Albert Camus and Paul de Man), advancing a model of testimony as a performative speech act in which the knowledge of the traumatic event comes into being for the first time in the collaborative and supportive dynamic of witness and listener. In emphasizing the significance of this interpersonal dynamic, Felman and Laub position the listener too as a kind of witness to the experience, in witnessing the testimony which allows a previously impossible mode of access to the events; such theorizations of testimony facilitate a reading of trauma itself as transmissible between individuals, as exemplified most strikingly and most controversially in *Testimony* in Felman's description of the vicarious traumatization of her graduate students during the screening of video testimonies. Testimony thus takes on the status of a negotiation between language and the inexpressible, or more precisely, a process through which the inexpressible is able to enter into expression. This conceptual structure is also present to an extent in Giorgio Agamben's conception of testimony in *Remnants of Auschwitz* (1999), which approaches the mode from the starting point of Primo Levi's assertion that it is the Muselmann rather than the survivor who is the true (yet impossible) witness to the events of the Holocaust.[3] Alongside such theoretical readings of the process of witnessing and the role of the witness, recent years have also seen an increasing consideration of the cultural functioning of this figure, as exemplified, for example in Wieviorka (2006) and Dean (2010), discussed in further detail in the 'New Directions' section of this volume.

Among studies of Holocaust testimony, Langer's 1991 work on video testimony presented a milestone in the field, as a landmark study of oral testimony which questioned conventional notions of selfhood, memory and identity through an examination of evidence from the Fortunoff Video Archive. In it, Langer contends that oral testimonies allow a more spontaneous and less mediated form of response to the Holocaust than written testimonies, in which artistic techniques intervene in the generation of artificially coherent and patterned (and hence, in a sense, consolatory) narratives. Through the analysis, various aspects of Holocaust memory are drawn to the fore, including the contrast between deep and common memory, and the notions of anguished memory (which imprisons consciousness), humiliated memory (which shatters the possibility of unitary selfhood), tainted memory (in which the narrative is 'stained by the disapproval of the witness's present moral sensibility' (Langer, 1991, p. 122)), and 'unheroic memory', though the distinction between these forms of memory could at times be clearer. Langer's overall portrayal of the survivor places emphasis on an irreconcilability of Holocaust and non-Holocaust moral and conceptual frameworks and modes of perception, in an approach to survivor experience that might be judged more existentially anguished than therapeutic. Other notable approaches to Holocaust testimony include that of the psychologist Henry Greenspan, whose *On Listening to Holocaust Survivors: Recounting and Life History* (1998) is a sensitive approach to testimony, drawing on numerous and extensive conversations with a small group of survivors, and arguing, ultimately, for a dialogic approach which considers testimony not as a finished story or totality, nor in either diagnostic or celebratory terms, but as an ongoing process which mediates between the construction of meaning (in a number of different registers, and drawing on a number of different sources, narratives and models) and what Greenspan terms the 'dissolution of those meanings within the destruction itself' (Greenspan, 1998, p. 169). While stressing, like Laub, the importance of the listener's presence in the formation of the testimony (though this extends in Greenspan's study to an examination of the ways in which an awareness of listener expectations might lead to particular emphases in the testimony itself), Greenspan is also critical of the despecifi-cizing tendencies of discourses which celebrate 'bearing witness' or attempt a psychologization of the testimonial act in a manner insufficiently attentive to the differences and particularities of each individual survivor (ibid., p. 52), a criticism to which approaches informed by trauma theory are arguably susceptible.

More recent studies of written as opposed to oral testimony include the work of Michael Levine (2006), who develops and applies the notion of testimony as a performative literary mode through which 'untold or unpossessed stories are *unwittingly accessed and unconsciously performed* in the very process of speaking toward another' (Levine, 2006, p. 4), and emphasizes too the corporeal dimensions of this process, through an examination of such works as Art Spiegelman's *Maus*. Andrea Reiter (2000), meanwhile, examines a number of German-language testimonies to concentration camp experience, with a focus on the selection, ordering and presentation of the experiences and the narrative genres deployed. Within the pragmatic testimonial contexts explored, Reiter identifies a reluctance to pursue radically new modes of articulation, noting instead a reliance, for the most part, on pre-existing models. Arguing that 'a form that tried to match the radical novelty of its object would have hindered rather than facilitated communication' (Reiter, 2000, p. 86), Reiter's work thus presents a check to accounts which stress the necessity that narratives of trauma assume radically unconventional forms in order to register the nature of these experiences. In contrast to the discrete body of work examined by Reiter, Zoe Waxman (2006) offers a detailed exploration of various different kinds and contexts of testimony, highlighting their diversity and particularity to the circumstances and contexts of writing, as discussed in greater detail in the 'New

Directions' section of this volume, while Margaret-Anne Hutton (2005) explores French women's testimony with a focus on the construction and impact of various aspects of identity (gendered, political–ideological, class-based, ethnic/religious) in these accounts, and on the textual and epistemological nature of testimony itself. As regards the latter, Hutton emphasizes the influence of both non-literary and literary models and devices in the shaping of the testimonial account, as well as examining the plurality and/or internal division of the testimonial subject. Other notable work on Holocaust testimony includes the 2010 volume *The Future of Memory* (edited by Crownshaw, Kilby and Rowland), which contains extensive reflection on 'the future of testimony' as conceived by such contributors as Antony Rowland, Robert Eaglestone and Sue Vice, as well as incorporating sections on memory and trauma.

Extensive analyses of Holocaust diary-writing – often overlooked in discussions of testimony – are offered by David Patterson (1999), who focuses on Jewish traditions and on the possibilities of the Holocaust diary as a form of spiritual resistance, and Alexandra Garbarini (2006), who situates Holocaust diary-writing within a broader range of cultural and literary contexts, with literary influences, for example, including 'Jewish and non-Jewish writing practices [such as] lamentation literature, autobiography and confession, modern historiography, journalism, jurisprudence, the private diary . . ., and family correspondence' (Garbarini, 2006, pp. 11–12). Patterson highlights the distinction of the diary from the Holocaust memoir, exploring specific generic features of diaries as well as the additional specificities of the Holocaust diary, and suggesting that the latter is distinguished by the presence of a community to whom the diarist is accountable (Patterson, 1999, pp. 21, 23), with other significant features including the 'struggle to recover a trace of the sacred in life' (ibid., p. 24). Garbarini, who focuses largely on unpublished diaries, examines the role of diaries in their writers' attempts to make sense of the persecution they experienced, leading to a consideration of diary-writing as an active mode of response to the Holocaust. Emphasizing the heterogeneity of diary-writers and their experiences and writings, Garbarini nevertheless highlights some illuminating areas of overlap, including diarists' anticipation of contemporary theoretical debates in their consideration of questions of representability and the adequacy of pre-existing narrative forms.

Agamben, G. (1999), *Remnants of Auschwitz: The Witness and the Archive*, trans. D. Heller-Roazen. New York: Zone Books.

van Alphen, E. (1997), *Caught by History: Holocaust Effects in Contemporary Art, Literature, and Theory*. Stanford, CA: Stanford University Press.

Brenner, R. Feldhay (1997), *Writing as Resistance: Four Women Confronting the Holocaust*. University Park: Pennsylvania State University Press.

Caruth, C. (1996), *Unclaimed Experience: Trauma, Narrative and History*. Baltimore: Johns Hopkins University Press.

Caruth, C. (ed.) (1995), *Trauma: Explorations in Memory*. Baltimore: Johns Hopkins University Press.

Crownshaw, R., Kilby, J. and Rowland, A. (eds) (2010), *The Future of Memory*. New York: Berghahn Books.

Dean, C. J. (2010), *Aversion and Erasure: The Fate of the Victim after the Holocaust*. Ithaca and London: Cornell University Press.

Felman, S. and Laub, D. (1992), *Testimony: Crises of Witnessing in Literature, Psychoanalysis and History*. New York: Routledge.

Garbarini, A. (2006), *Numbered Days: Diaries and the Holocaust*. New Haven and London: Yale University Press.

Greenspan, H. (1998), *On Listening to Holocaust Survivors: Recounting and Life History*. Westport, CT: Praeger.

Hartman, G. (1995), 'On traumatic knowledge and literary studies', *New Literary History*, 26.3, 537–63.

Hutton, M.-A. (2005), *Testimony from the Nazi Camps: French Women's Voices*. London: Routledge.

LaCapra, D. (2001), *Writing History, Writing Trauma*. Baltimore: Johns Hopkins University Press.

Langer, L. (1991), *Holocaust Testimonies: The Ruins of Memory*. New Haven: Yale University Press.

Levine, M. G. (2006), *The Belated Witness: Literature, Testimony, and the Question of Holocaust Survival*. Stanford, CA: Stanford University Press.

Leys, R. (2000), *Trauma: A Genealogy*. Chicago: University of Chicago Press.

Matthäus, J. (ed.) (2009), *Approaching an Auschwitz Survivor: Holocaust Testimony and Its Transformations*. New York: Oxford University Press.

Patterson, D. (1999), *Along the Edge of Annihilation: The Collapse and Recovery of Life in the Holocaust Diary*. Seattle: University of Washington Press.

Reiter, A. (2000), *Narrating the Holocaust*, trans. P. Camiller. London and New York: Continuum.

Waxman, Z. V. (2006), *Writing the Holocaust: Identity, Testimony, Representation*. Oxford: Oxford University Press.

Wieviorka, A. (2006), *The Era of the Witness*, trans. J. Stark. Ithaca: Cornell University Press.

Young, J. E. (1987), 'Interpreting literary testimony: a preface to rereading Holocaust diaries and memoirs', *New Literary History*, 18, 403–23.

Holocaust Literature – Companions and Reference Works

Recent decades have witnessed the publication of a number of important reference works providing an impressive breadth of material on Holocaust literature and criticism, a development that perhaps reflects the increasing consolidation and self-reflexivity of the field of Holocaust literary studies. Especially valuable in both its degree of detail and depth and its navigational apparatus is S. Lillian Kremer's two-volume edited encyclopaedia of Holocaust writers. Organized A–Z by Holocaust writer, and containing contributions by over 120 scholars including Andrew Furman, Sara Horowitz, Michael Rothberg, Efraim Sicher, Naomi Sokoloff, Sue Vice, and Ruth Wisse, the text is largely comprised of bio-critical essays of between 1,800 and 8,000 words on more than 300 writers of testimony, poetry, fiction and drama, as well as such theorists as Hannah Arendt. A series of appendices list authors according to genre, literary theme, and the ghettos, camps, events and historical personages referred to in their work, allowing readers to locate relevant material and identify writers who share commonalities with those at the centre of their research. A more concise encyclopaedic work is presented by Riggs (2002), who in a single volume incorporates, in two separate sections, alphabetically ordered entries on 223 writers, and on 307 selected texts. Contributing critics include Robert Eaglestone, Sue Vice, Erin McGlothlin, and Adam Zachary Newton, and additional features include an introduction by James Young, a list of recommended reading, and a chronology. A more recent addition to the field is Alan Rosen's edited companion *Literature of the Holocaust* (2013), which is divided into three parts, the first of which contains essays by Rosen and David Roskies on wartime Holocaust literature, while the second, addressing postwar responses, contains several essays on different national and linguistic (Italian, German, Yiddish, Hebrew, Hungarian, French and English) literatures of the Holocaust, with contributors including Robert Gordon, Stuart Taberner, Leona Toker and S. Lillian Kremer. The final part takes in other contexts and issues including oral memoir, songs of the Holocaust, and questions of anthologization.

Within the specific area of Holocaust fiction, Efraim Sicher's *The Holocaust Novel* (2005) (discussed below) is a wide-ranging study which also incorporates a brief annotated bibliography. Within Holocaust Studies more widely, the 2010 *Oxford Handbook of Holocaust Studies*, edited by Peter Hayes and John K. Roth, is an interdisciplinary volume of value to students new to the subject, with sections on 'Enablers' (necessary contextual conditions for the Holocaust, such as anti-Semitism, nationalism, colonialism and fascism), 'Protagonists' (groups of actors, victims and onlookers), 'Settings' (including discussion of the camps and ghettoes), 'Representations' and 'After-effects' (such as liberation, the State of Israel and the implications for ethics). Holocaust literature is dealt with, if in necessarily rather broad brush-stokes, in the 'Representations' section, which contains essays on diaries, testimonies, literature, films and museums, by critics such as Henry Greenspan, Sara Horowitz, Lawrence Baron, Dora Apel, and James Young, with other contributors to the volume as a whole including Berel Lang, Deborah Lipstadt, Jeffrey Shandler and Michael Berenbaum.

In terms of theoretical material, mention must be made of the important anthology *The Holocaust: Theoretical Readings* (2003), edited by Neil Levi and Michael Rothberg. This volume maps out the major theoretical preoccupations within the study of the Holocaust, including sections on theory emerging from first-hand experience (Levi, Améry, and others), debates about historicization (including extracts from Habermas, Friedlander and Bauman), theorizations of Nazism and anti-Semitism, questions of race and gender, approaches informed by psychoanalysis and trauma theory (Caruth, LaCapra, Laub and others), and questions of religion and ethics (Levinas, Arendt, Agamben, Lyotard), as well as sections on postmemory and on debates concerning the uniqueness or comparability of the Holocaust. While it is the section on 'Literature and Culture after Auschwitz' (incorporating extracts from theorists including Adorno, Howe, Blanchot and Derrida) that most directly addresses questions of the literary impact of these events, the volume as a whole contains a wealth of relevant material which is introduced and juxtaposed insightfully.

Hayes, P. and Roth, J. K. (2010), *The Oxford Handbook of Holocaust Studies*. Oxford: Oxford University Press.

Kremer, S. L. (ed.) (2003), *Holocaust Literature: An Encyclopaedia of Writers and their Work*, 2 vols. New York: Routledge.

Levi, N. and Rothberg, M. (eds) (2003), *The Holocaust: Theoretical Readings*. Edinburgh: Edinburgh University Press.

Riggs, T. (ed.) (2002), *Reference Guide to Holocaust Literature*. Detroit: St. James Press.

Rosen, A. (ed.) (2013), *Literature of the Holocaust*. Cambridge: Cambridge University Press.

Sicher, E. (2005), *The Holocaust Novel*. London: Routledge.

Poetry-, Drama- and Fiction-Specific Studies

Poetry

Among studies of Holocaust poetry, a central place must be accorded to Susan Gubar's excellent 2003 study *Poetry after Auschwitz: Remembering What One Never Knew*, in which Gubar presents a powerful argument for the value and significance of poetry as a means by which to respond to the Holocaust. The study discusses a wide range of poetry, with a focus on specific issues of key concern, including the significance of photographic images, the role of testimony and the documentary, and the motif of prosopopoeia. Significant too are Gubar's reconsideration of notions of identification – often a problematic issue in Holocaust representation – through recourse to Dominick LaCapra's notion of 'empathic unsettlement', and her mapping of the potentialities of poetry onto the particularities of traumatic experience, contending that poetry's potential for fragmentation and eschewal of narrative coherence make it a key mode within the Holocaust's literary representation.

Gubar's willingness to re-examine such commonplaces as the 'no poetry after Auschwitz' dictum associated, often in less than wholly accurate ways, with Adorno, is echoed in different ways by a number of the studies listed here. Examining the work of such poets as Geoffrey Hill, Tony Harrison, Ted Hughes and Sylvia Plath, Antony Rowland (2005) explores the capacity of poetry to live on in the Holocaust's aftermath in 'awkward' forms which self-consciously foreground or interrogate their own representational acts, while R. Clifton

Spargo's examination of elegy, informed by an ethics of alterity, reads such literary mourning 'as both a figure for and expression of an impossible responsibility wherein one refuses to yield the other to the more comfortable freedoms of identity' (Spargo, 2004, p. 274). While not wholly focused on Holocaust poetry, Spargo's study devotes insightful chapters to the work of Sylvia Plath and Randall Jarrell. The work of Sara Guyer approaches the 'after Auschwitz' dilemma[4] from a temporally opposite stance in her examination of the relationship between Romantic and post-Holocaust art, including some particularly insightful discussion of poetry by such figures as Primo Levi and Paul Celan, and tracing the presence in both literatures of what she terms 'a rhetoric of survival', of 'life and subjectivity beyond possibility or impossibility' (Guyer, 2007, p. 21), as well as containing detailed evaluation of the significance of such tropes as prosopopoeia. Key theoretical touchstones include the work of de Man, Derrida, Agamben, Levinas and others.

Moving away from issues of chronology and continuity, such critics as Andrés Nader and Frieda Aaron have contributed substantial works dedicated to the exploration of poetry produced during the period of the Holocaust itself, in the camps and ghettos. Nader's study *Traumatic Verses* (2007), for example, examines German poetry from the camps by both Jewish and non-Jewish writers including Ruth Klüger, Hasso Grabner, Fritz Löhner-Beda and others, examining not only the context and motivations of such poetry, but also what the work reveals about language, extremity, identity, aesthetics and the relationships between these. Nader reads the composition of poetry in the camps as a reassertion of autonomy, a countering of Nazi rhetorics and processes of dehumanization, and advocates a dialogic approach to such poetry, one able 'to show both their situatedness and their representational limits without fetishizing their special status' (Nader, 2007, p. 19). Nader's thought-provoking monograph incorporates, too, a reconsideration of the place of traditional formal structures in poetry, especially the conventions of lyric: in an era liable to view such conventions as irredeemably complicit in the cultural formations that produced the Holocaust, a recognition that 'traditional rhyme and meter are of use to others besides the agents of hegemonic or oppressive structures' (ibid., p. 183) provides a useful check on the purgative logic of such prohibitions. Aaron's *Bearing the Unbearable*, likewise engaging with poetry produced in the events' midst, provides an in-depth analysis of Yiddish and Polish poems composed in camps and ghettoes during the Holocaust by such figures as Abraham Sutzkever and Wladyslaw Szlengel, exploring the role of poetry in giving testimony to the unfolding events, as well as its relationship to questions of faith and morale and issues of resistance.

Other substantial studies of Holocaust poetry include John Felstiner's insightful study of the work of Paul Celan (1998); Walter Kalaidjian's *The Edge of Modernism*, which examines the registering of resonating traumatic histories (including Holocaust history, slavery and domestic trauma) in American poetry, incorporating analysis of poetry by W. G. Snodgrass, Charles Reznikoff, Anthony Hecht, Rachel Blau DuPlessis, and Adrienne Rich; and Harriet Parmet's examination of the work of Sylvia Plath, William Heyen, Gerald Stern and Jerome Rothenberg in *The Terror of Our Days* (2001).

Aaron, F. W. (1990), *Bearing the Unbearable: Yiddish and Polish Poetry in the Ghettos and Concentration Camps*. New York: State University of New York Press.

Ezrahi, S. DeKoven (1992), '"The grave in the air": unbound metaphors in post-Holocaust poetry', in S. Friedlander (ed.), *Probing the Limits of Representation: Nazism and the 'Final Solution'*. Cambridge, MA: Harvard University Press, pp. 259–76.

Felstiner, J. (1998), *Paul Celan: Poet, Survivor, Jew*. New Haven: Yale University Press.

Gubar, S. (2003), *Poetry after Auschwitz: Remembering What One Never Knew*. Bloomington and Indianapolis: Indiana University Press.

Guyer, S. (2007), *Romanticism after Auschwitz*. Stanford, CA: Stanford University Press.

Kalaidjian, W. (2006), *The Edge of Modernism: American Poetry and the Traumatic Past*. Baltimore: Johns Hopkins University Press.

Nader, A. (2007), *Traumatic Verses: On Poetry in German from the Concentration Camps, 1933–45*. Rochester, NY: Camden House, 2007.

Parmet, H. L. (2001), *The Terror of Our Days: Four American Poets Respond to the Holocaust*. Cranbury: Rosemont.

Rowland, A. (2005), *Holocaust Poetry: Awkward Poetics in the Work of Sylvia Plath, Geoffrey Hill, Tony Harrison and Ted Hughes*. Edinburgh: Edinburgh University Press.

Spargo, R. C. (2004), *The Ethics of Mourning: Grief and Responsibility in Elegiac Literature*. Baltimore: Johns Hopkins University Press.

Young, G. (1993), 'The poetry of the Holocaust', in S. S. Friedman (ed.), *Holocaust Literature: A Handbook of Critical, Historical, and Literary Writings*. Westport: Greenwood Press, pp. 547–74.

Drama

Much foundational work within the study of Holocaust drama has been carried out by the critic Robert Skloot, whose two-volume anthology of Holocaust drama – bringing together such key works as *Throne of Straw* by Edith and Harold Lieberman, *The Cannibals* by George Tabori, *Who Will Carry the Word?* by Charlotte Delbo, and the performance piece *The Survivor and the Translator* by Leeny Sack – contains a succession of useful introductions to the field. In his introduction to Volume 1 (1982), Skloot surveys the diversity of perspectives across Holocaust theatre and examines the difficulties of realism in Holocaust drama and the presence of Epic theatrical techniques in a number of the plays anthologized, while also tentatively charting the objectives of Holocaust theatre as being to pay homage to the victims, to educate, to produce an emotional response, to raise moral questions and to draw a lesson. By the time of the publication of Volume 2 (1999), however, it is possible to see the registering of both new and generationally distanced modes of

Holocaust theatre and a negotiation of postmodernism in both secondary criticism and the plays themselves, making Skloot's edited volumes valuable in tracing the development of Holocaust theatre and its interpretation. Skloot's 1988 monograph *The Darkness We Carry: The Drama of the Holocaust*, which devotes chapters to particular themes in Holocaust drama (such as that of choice, or the inversion of victim and perpetrator identities), generic aspects (such as the tenability of tragedy as a mode) and national–contextual specificities (e.g. German writing), also includes a consideration of the responsibilities of dramatist and audience, with the former including a respect for the memory of the victims and an adherence to the historical record. Works under discussion in this study include Rolf Hochhuth's *The Deputy*, Peter Weiss's *The Investigation* and Martin Sherman's *Bent*.

In more recent work, Edward Isser's 1997 study combines chapters devoted to different national contexts (including American, British, German and French Holocaust theatre) with chapters on specific themes (feminism, homosexuality) and particular writers (Arthur Miller, George Tabori and Josef Szajna) in a quest to identify emerging patterns and correlations within Holocaust drama. Like Skloot and other key critics of Holocaust drama such as Plunka (2009), Isser stresses the importance of close adherence to the historical record, and is critical of appropriations of the Holocaust that seek thus to add a sense of moral significance or depth to otherwise unrelated creative endeavours (Isser, 1997, p. 172). Playwrights under discussion include Brecht, Hochhuth, Weiss, Delbo, Gilles Ségal, Josef Szajna and Tony Kushner. Claude Schumacher's 1998 edited volume *Staging the Holocaust* includes essays by Skloot, Schumacher, Hank Greenspan, Dorothy Knowles, and John Ireland; essays address aspects of Holocaust theatre (e.g. questions of justice, the role of the fantastic) and questions of genre, as well as the work of individual playwrights and authors. A notable additional inclusion is a select bibliography of over 200 plays, with accompanying brief summaries. In contrast, situating itself within a range of emerging cultural and critical emphases including the centrality of corporeality and mediatization to contemporary accounts of suffering, the development of the field of Jewish cultural studies, and the use of the Holocaust in articulation of other contexts of historical violence (Patraka, 1999, pp. 12–13), Vivien Patraka's 1999 study *Spectacular Suffering*, examining the public process through which meaning is accorded to the Holocaust, takes a somewhat different and more theoretically grounded approach, attempting to trace what she terms a 'Holocaust performative' within both theatrical representations and museum sites. An examination of theatrical performance which took place during the events themselves is provided in the edited collection of Rovit and Goldfarb (1999), which combines critical essays, documents and memoirs addressing Jewish theatrical performance in Nazi Germany, performances in ghettoes and concentration camps, and theatrical performance at Terezín (with 'theatrical' here interpreted in a broad sense to include activities such as storytelling and musical and dramatic recitation as well as the performance of plays).

The most recent of the studies listed below, Gene Plunka's 2009 work *Holocaust Drama: The Theater of Atrocity*, arguably returns to earlier work by Skloot in its consideration of both the objectives of Holocaust theatre and the value of the art form's immediacy as a mode of Holocaust representation, reading drama as an 'ideal form' of such representation given its capacity to affect audiences 'emotionally, subliminally, or intellectually (sometimes simultaneously) in a direct way that poetry and fiction cannot' (Plunka, 2009, p. 16). Organized thematically in chapters which address such topics as 'Staging the Banality of Evil', 'Marxism and the Holocaust', and 'Holocaust Survivor Memory', Plunka's study analyses over 30 seminal works of Holocaust drama from the United States, Europe and Israel, including works by Weiss, Miller, Hochhuth, Tabori, Sherman and others.

Isser, E. R. (1997), *Stages of Annihilation: Theatrical Representations of the Holocaust*. Madison: Fairleigh Dickinson University Press; London: Associated University Presses.

Patraka, V. M. (1999), *Spectacular Suffering: Theatre, Fascism, and the Holocaust*. Bloomington and Indianapolis: Indiana University Press.

Plunka, G. A. (2009), *Holocaust Drama: The Theater of Atrocity*. Cambridge: Cambridge University Press.

Rovit, R. and Goldfarb, A. (eds) (1999), *Theatrical Performance during the Holocaust: Texts, Documents, Memoirs*. Baltimore and London: Johns Hopkins University Press.

Schumacher, C. (ed.) (1998), *Staging the Holocaust: The Shoah in Drama and Performance*. Cambridge: Cambridge University Press.

Skloot, R. (1988), *The Darkness We Carry: The Drama of the Holocaust*. Madison: University of Wisconsin Press.

Skloot, R. (ed.) (1982), *The Theatre of the Holocaust*, vol. 1. Madison: University of Wisconsin Press.

—. (1999), *The Theatre of the Holocaust*, vol. 2. Madison: University of Wisconsin Press.

Fiction

Much of the material discussed in the 'Holocaust representation – general' section is focused to a large extent upon fiction; nevertheless, here I briefly highlight a few important studies devoted exclusively to the analysis of fictional representation. In terms of early suspicion towards Holocaust fiction, a key point of reference is Wiesel (1977), who denounces the possibility of a work of fiction about the Holocaust as akin to blasphemy, stating that 'A novel about Treblinka is either not a novel or not about Treblinka' (Wiesel, 1977, p. 7). Wiesel refuses Holocaust fiction as a transgression of what he deems both a sacred and a radically irredeemable experience, in addition to offering the argument that the existence of Holocaust fiction may cast doubt on the factuality of the events themselves. From another perspective, Barbara Foley (1982) questions the appropriateness of both realist and irrealist Holocaust fiction on the grounds that the former posits a misleading compatibility of Holocaust experience with conventional generic and ethical norms and teleologies, while the latter risks an evasion of the events' historical specificities; Foley instead advocates the use of the 'pseudohistorical novel', which, in its limited perspective and fictive appeal to a 'putative historical document', 'substitutes historical probabilities for literary ones, and thus insistently reminds the reader of the text's relation to the historical world' (Foley, 1982, p. 351). For examples of a number of further perspectives from the relatively early stages of Holocaust Studies on the possibility or otherwise of fiction about the Holocaust, see the essays collected in Lang's edited volume *Writing and the Holocaust* (1988).

In terms of more recent studies which accept, and write from the position of, the existence and tenability of fictional responses to the Holocaust, a wide-ranging survey of Holocaust novels from a variety of different national and experiential points of origin is offered by Efraim Sicher's 2005 study *The Holocaust Novel*. Addressing work in such categories as writing by survivors, the Jewish American post-Holocaust novel, second-generation writing and postmodern fiction, the study contains detailed discussions of texts including Art Spiegelman's *Maus*, William Styron's *Sophie's Choice*, and Thomas Keneally's *Schindler's List*, as well as works less obviously categorizable as 'Holocaust novels' such as Don DeLillo's *White Noise*. In the context of American fiction, both Alan Berger's *Crisis and Covenant* (1985) and S. Lillian Kremer's *Witness through the Imagination* (1989) analyse the representation of the Holocaust in the work of such writers as Cynthia Ozick, Isaac Bashevis Singer, Bernard Malamud, Saul Bellow and Edward Lewis Wallant. While Berger's study is focused on the ways in which post-Holocaust writers negotiate different modes of relationship to Judaism in the light of these events, Kremer's work analyses a series of representative texts and writers in turn in order to trace common themes and stylistic techniques among them, including a focus not on the Holocaust period itself but on its return via traumatic memory and flashback (Kremer, 1989, p. 358) and a series of recurrent devices such as the use of historical figures and of character types relating to the concentrationary universe, the juxtaposition of the documentary and the symbolic/metaphorical and the inversion of conventional literary forms (ibid., p. 10).

Theoretically focused explorations of fictive representations include Sue Vice's study *Holocaust Fiction* (2000), which examines a series of controversial Holocaust novels written in English by such authors as Martin Amis, D. M. Thomas, Jerzy Kosinski, and Helen Darville (Helen Demidenko), with particular attention to questions of intertextuality, the treatment of time, and the (critically perceived) crucial nature of the relationship between author and narrator; Vice suggests in particular that these 'standard features' of all literature are in this context 'brought to their limit, taken literally, defamiliarized or used self-consciously' (Vice, 2000, p. 4). Holocaust fiction thus registers formally the shock posed by the extremity of these events. Intertextuality is also a key area of discussion in Anne Whitehead's 2004 study *Trauma Fiction*, a work which explores literature dealing with a range of historical contexts, but which includes discussion of Holocaust writing by Anne Michaels, Binjamin Wilkomirski and W. G. Sebald. Examining the ways in which fiction is able to represent trauma by 'mimicking its forms and symptoms' (Whitehead, 2004, p. 3), Whitehead accords a number of techniques prime importance in this process: intertextuality, which can 'suggest the surfacing to consciousness of forgotten or repressed memories' (ibid., p. 85), repetition, which 'suggests the insistent return of the event and the disruption of narrative chronology or progression' (ibid., p. 86), and dispersal or fragmentation of narrative voice. Berger's 1999 *After the End*, which likewise is not focused wholly on the literature of the Holocaust, nevertheless usefully places (post-)Holocaust fiction by Eve Prager, D. M. Thomas and Cynthia Ozick in the context of the notion of the post-apocalyptic, with the latter being its broader thematic concern – one which presents the grounds for an interesting exploration of notions of traumatic representation. Berger considers these post-Holocaust fictions as not only 'after' the events themselves but also 'after', in ways which they must negotiate a response to, the privileged mode of testimony, with intertextual reference playing a key role in these negotiations: 'The urge, the need, to testify to the events of the Shoah remains, but these events now exist not even in personal memory but only through the encounter with texts, particularly the texts of testimony' (Berger, 1999, p. 78). More contentiously, perhaps, Berger also positions the 'return' of testimony in post-Holocaust fiction as a form of traumatic symptom (ibid., p. 79). Other significant contributions to the study of Holocaust fiction include Sara Horowitz's 1997 monograph on the themes of muteness and memory in this body of work, which is discussed in more detail in the following section of this bibliography.

Adams, J. (2011), *Magic Realism in Holocaust Literature: Troping the Traumatic Real*. Basingstoke: Palgrave Macmillan.

Berger, A. L. (1985), *Crisis and Covenant: The Holocaust in American Jewish Fiction*. Albany: State University of New York Press.

Berger, J. (1999), *After the End: Representations of Post-Apocalypse*. Minneapolis: University of Minnesota Press.

Foley, B. (1982), 'Fact, fiction, fascism: testimony and mimesis in Holocaust narratives', *Comparative Literature*, 34.4, 330–60.

Franklin, R. (2011), *A Thousand Darknesses: Lies and Truth in Holocaust Fiction*. Oxford: Oxford University Press.

Horowitz, S. R. (1997), *Voicing the Void: Muteness and Memory in Holocaust Fiction*. Albany: State University of New York Press.

Kremer, S. L. (1989), *Witness through the Imagination: Jewish American Holocaust Literature*. Detroit: Wayne State University Press.

Lang, B. (ed.) (1988), *Writing and the Holocaust*. New York and London: Holmes & Meier.

Sicher, E. (2005), *The Holocaust Novel*. London: Routledge.

Vice, S. (2000), *Holocaust Fiction*. London: Routledge.

Whitehead, A. (2004), *Trauma Fiction*. Edinburgh: Edinburgh University Press.

Wiesel, E. (1977), 'The Holocaust as literary inspiration', in *Dimensions of the Holocaust: Lectures at Northwestern University*. Evanston, IL: Northwestern University Press, pp. 5–19.

Holocaust Literature in General

Foundational Works on Holocaust Representation

Foundational critical works on Holocaust literature include Lawrence Langer's 1975 *The Holocaust and the Literary Imagination*, a groundbreaking and wide-ranging exploration of a series of aspects of what Langer refers to as the 'literature of atrocity', with a focus on themes including the eclipsing of the consciousness of life by that of death, the 'violation of the coherence of childhood' and the 'disruption of chronological time' (Langer, 1975, p. xii). Langer's study, which includes sustained close readings of such individual texts as Wiesel's *Night*, Kosinski's *The Painted Bird*, Schwarz-Bart's *The Last of the Just*, and Jakov Lind's *Soul of Wood*, addresses the diverse ways in which writers have responded to these questions of representation. While much criticism of this period takes a mistrustful stance towards the enterprise of Holocaust fiction, Langer's attitude is a markedly non-moralistic one, prefiguring later critical positions in the assertion that 'The fundamental task of the critic is not to ask whether it should or can be done, since it already has been, but to evaluate *how* it has been done, judge its effectiveness, and analyze its implications for literature and for society' (ibid., p. 22). Other key responses to Holocaust literature from this period include Sidra DeKoven Ezrahi's 1980 study *By Words Alone: The Holocaust in Literature* – another wide-ranging discussion – which identifies a number of strands of the literary response to the Holocaust, including concentrationary realism, survival literature, and Hebraic literature dealing with the relationship between the Holocaust and continuums of Jewish thought, religion, and tradition; and Alvin H. Rosenfeld's *A Double Dying* (1980), which examines ways in which writers of various genres have attempted to meet with the obligations of Holocaust representation, with an initial theoretical chapter followed by a discussion of different modes and genres. Key preoccupations in Rosenfeld's study include 'the need to see Holocaust literature against the history that produced it, a history that reduces the expressive powers of language almost to silence, yet at the same time obligates writers to speech' (1980, p. 8), with the simultaneous impossibility and necessity of representation of key concern. Rosenfeld frames his own study in preliminary terms in the statement that 'Until the primary literature is more widely assimilated, much of the more detailed work that belongs to a secondary literature necessarily will give way to a criticism of broader definition' (ibid., p. 10), highlighting the introductory nature of much of the work on Holocaust literature in the discipline's early stages, while also underscoring the crucial nature of such investigations as a foundation for later studies.

Berel Lang's 1988 edited collection *Writing and the Holocaust*, incorporating essays from such figures as Aharon Appelfeld, George Steiner, Irving Howe and Terrence Des Pres, provides a good example of the preoccupation of much criticism of this early period with questions of limits, prohibitions and obligations – in short, with a *morality* of Holocaust literature, in contract to the ethics privileged in approaches today. Nevertheless, the period also witnessed an increasingly sophisticated approach to questions of history and narrative representation, including work by Geoffrey Hartman, whose 1996 essay collection *The Longest Shadow* includes an interesting reading of Lyotard; James Young, whose *Writing and Rewriting the Holocaust* (1988) incorporates a recognition of the inseparability of Holocaust history from its representation, suggesting a need to 'move beyond the question of whether or not literary and historical accounts of the Holocaust are "perspective ridden" to understand how various literary forms, cultural and religious traditions, and precedent experiences have indeed shaped the Holocaust' (Young, 1988, p. 5), and the seminal collection *Probing the Limits of Representation* (1992), edited by Saul Friedlander. Bringing together essays by historians and literary critics including Hayden White, Dominick LaCapra, Eric Santner and Sidra Ezrahi, much of *Probing the Limits* presents an interdisciplinary grappling with traumatic history in an era of postmodernity, negotiating the challenges posed by postmodern theory to an instinctive attempt on the part of many critics to defend the Holocaust against a number of possibilities of emplotment, namely those of revisionism and other unseemly narrative modes. In many ways, then, these works register the mutual confrontation of literary theory and Holocaust studies.

Holocaust Representation: The Mid-1990s Onwards

The mid to late 1990s saw a series of sophisticated analyses of Holocaust representation, in studies which sought to address particular aspects of representation rather than reprising the often unwieldy overviews of the initial studies. To draw out some works of particular interest, Michael André Bernstein's *Foregone Conclusions* (1994) presents an influential consideration of questions of temporality and causality raised by fictional and non-fictional representations (including biographical studies of Kafka, and Aharon Appelfeld's novel *Badenheim, 1939*) in a powerful argument against narrative treatments of the Holocaust which position the events as inevitable and thereby implicitly blame the victims for not evading their 'fate'.[5] Other notable publications of this period include Sara Horowitz's 1997 study of Holocaust fiction, which considers muteness (evident in such works as Kosinski's *The Painted Bird*) as a key trope in the literary representation of these events, 'central to the idea of Holocaust fiction, to the way imaginative representations of the Shoah address linguistic, ethical, and metaphysical concerns' (Horowitz, 1997, p. 29). James Berger's 1999 monograph *After the End* explores the representation of traumatic history via the concept of the post-apocalyptic, with authors under discussion including the British novelist D. M. Thomas, while the value and significance of experimental and fantastic works of Holocaust literature by such figures as Schwarz-Bart, Appelfeld, Spiegelman, Ozick, Leslie Epstein, and Bruno Schulz is examined in Daniel Schwarz's study *Imagining the Holocaust* (1999). Michael Rothberg's *Traumatic Realism* (2000) offers an important examination of the intersection of realist, modernist and postmodernist strategies in Holocaust representations by Delbo, Klüger, Roth, Spiegelman and others, as discussed more fully in this volume's Glossary (under 'Traumatic realism') and in the essay 'Relationships to Realism in Post-Holocaust Fiction'. Within the sphere of Holocaust fiction, a detailed and wide-ranging companion to the field is presented by Efraim Sicher's *The Holocaust Novel* (2005).

A host of significant edited collections from this period of Holocaust literary studies include *Breaking Crystal: Writing and Memory after Auschwitz* (1998), edited by Efraim Sicher, an important collection of essays, many with an Israeli focus, examining questions of Holocaust writing and memory with particular emphasis on the representational and psychological issues faced by members of the second generation. *Breaking Crystal* incorporates substantial discussion of literature as well as analysis of film and visual art, with contributors including Ilan Avisar, Dan Bar-on, Alan L. Berger, Emily Miller Budick, Ellen S. Fine, Saul Friedlander, Hanna Yablonka and Leon Yudkin. Andrew Leak and George Paizis's *The Holocaust and the Text* (2000) brings together essays on such diverse aspects of Holocaust representation as women's testimony (Anna Hardman), ethical philosophy (Robert Eaglestone), the perspectives of children (Andrea Reiter) and questions of authorial identity (Sue Vice), while the essays collected in Moshe Postone and Eric Santner's *Catastrophe and Meaning* (2003), by major historians, literary critics and others – including Saul Friedlander, Dan Diner, Debórah Dwork, Froma Zeitlin, and Geoffrey Hartman – examine both the Holocaust's relationship to wider historical contexts and trajectories, and its implications regarding subsequent literature and culture and the possibilities and responsibilities of memory. More recent collections of significance include Michael Bernard-Donals and Richard Glejzer's *Witnessing the Disaster: Essays on Representation and the Holocaust* (2003), parts of which address specific texts (including some interesting discussions of Art Spiegelman's *Maus* from James Young and Richard Glejzer), while other essays explore broader and more overarching issues relating to Holocaust representation, knowledge, and ethics, including questions of the tenability of the sublime as a figure for traumatic history and the philosophy of Giorgio Agamben; and Sue Vice's 2003 edited collection *Representing the Holocaust: In Honour of Bryan Burns*, a diverse collection of essays addressing a wide range of literary and cultural representations.

Recent Re-examinations

Recent re-examinations of key questions of Holocaust representation[6] include Robert Eaglestone's illuminating consideration of the relationship between the Holocaust and the postmodern (2004) (with Eaglestone – drawing insightfully on the philosophy of Levinas, Derrida and others, and discussing a range of literary examples including the testimony of Delbo and Levi and the fiction of Anne Michaels, Lily Brett, Emily Prager and Jonathan Safran Foer – reading postmodernism as a mode of response to this history); Amy Hungerford's 2003 scrutiny of tropes of personification in both literary and critical representations; Naomi Mandel's 2006 critique of the notion of the unspeakable in Holocaust discourse of various kinds, and Brett Ashley Kaplan's 2007 re-examination of questions of aesthetic pleasure. Studies which pay particular attention to recent changes in artistic practice (particularly the emergence of a new transgressive Holocaust art, an artistic focus upon the Holocaust's semiotic and mediatized conventions, and an awareness of questions of globalization and multidirectionality) include Komor and Rohr (eds) (2010), a study very much focused on Holocaust representation of the present moment, as examined by such critics as Philippe Codde, Norman Kleeblatt, Hilene Flanzbaum and Andrew S. Gross; and Spargo and Ehrenreich (eds) (2010). The latter juxtaposes essays by eminent scholars including Geoffrey Hartman, Sara Horowitz, Berel Lang, James Young, Michael Bernard-Donals and Robert Eaglestone, likewise attempting to explore the field of Holocaust representation and culture at the present moment and taking in a range of new and emerging perspectives and angles of inquiry such as multidirectional memory (in essays by Michael Rothberg, Eaglestone and Spargo), perpetrators (Erin McGlothlin), and aesthetics (James Young). This volume contains an excellent range of thought-provoking material, including much on the emergent area of the multidirectional (discussed in further detail below).

Other noteworthy recent studies include Matthew Boswell's 2012 examination of 'Holocaust impiety', which shares much with the critical concerns of Komor et al.; Jakob Lothe, Susan Rubin Suleiman and James Phelan's edited collection *After Testimony: The Ethics and Aesthetics of Holocaust Narrative for the Future* (2012), which attempts to scope out a narrative ethics of Holocaust literature for the post-testimonial era, Michael Bernard-Donals' monograph *Forgetful Memory* (2009), and Libby Saxton's *Haunted Images* (2008), notable for its sophisticated examination of an ethics of representation in the context of Holocaust film. From its beginnings in, for the most part, a concern with surveying the field and contending with moral questions of representational limits and prohibitions, the study of Holocaust representation has thus developed into a multifaceted field of overlapping investigations with a focus on ethical self-scrutiny within both literary representations and the critical voices that appraise them. For further discussion on present and emergent preoccupations in Holocaust literary studies, see the 'New Directions' section of this volume.

Children's Literature

While the above discussion has focused primarily on literature for adults, a number of the works listed below address representations aimed either in whole or in part at a child or young adult readership. Central among these is Adrienne Kertzer's *My Mother's Voice: Children, Literature and the Holocaust* (2002), an insightful study addressing a range of questions concerning Holocaust literature for children, including that of the kind of knowledge or lesson such texts are intended to convey, and the role of fairy tales in works by such writers and filmmakers as Roberto Benigni, Jane Yolen and Anne Frank. When discussing the need to mediate between hopeful childhood expectations and the realities of historical horror, Kertzer argues in favour of a double narrative approach, 'one that simultaneously respects our need for hope and happy endings even as it teaches us a different lesson about history' (Kertzer, 2002, p. 75). In another significant work on the representation of the Holocaust in children's literature, Lydia Kokkola (2003) considers the conflict between a perceived etiquette governing Holocaust literature and the conventions of representation for young people, contending that 'Holocaust literature for children can . . . be distinguished by its combination of challenging subject matter, ethical responsibility, and its position outside the normal boundaries of children's literature' (2003, p. 11). Examining the work of such writers as Jane Yolen and Anne Holm, Kokkola's study develops a conceptual framework which includes the notion of 'framed silences' – informational gaps whose presence is nevertheless signalled by the text – a concept relevant to Holocaust representation beyond texts aimed at children. Further substantial works which seek to address the representation of the Holocaust in young people's literature include Bosmajian (2002), while on the topic of Holocaust literature from a child's perspective, see Vice (2004) and Reiter (ed.) (2006).

Adams, J. (2011), *Magic Realism in Holocaust Literature: Troping the Traumatic Real*. Basingstoke: Palgrave Macmillan.
van Alphen, E. (1997), *Caught by History: Holocaust Effects in Contemporary Art, Literature, and Theory*. Stanford, CA: Stanford University Press.

Banner, G. (1999), *Holocaust Literature: Schulz, Levi, Spiegelman, and the Memory of the Offence*. London: Vallentine Mitchell.

Baskind, S. and Omer-Sherman, R. (eds) (2008), *The Jewish Graphic Novel: Critical Approaches*. New Brunswick, NJ, and London: Rutgers University Press.

Berger, J. (1999), *After the End: Representations of Post-Apocalypse*. Minneapolis: University of Minnesota Press.

Bernard-Donals, M. (2009), *Forgetful Memory: Representation and Remembrance in the Wake of the Holocaust*. Albany: State University of New York Press.

Bernard-Donals, M. and Glejzer, R. (eds) (2003), *Witnessing the Disaster: Essays on Representation and the Holocaust*. Madison: University of Wisconsin Press.

Bernstein, M. A. (1994), *Foregone Conclusions: Against Apocalyptic History*. Berkeley and London: University of California Press.

Bosmajian, H. (2002), *Sparing the Child: Grief and the Unspeakable in Youth Literature about Nazism and the Holocaust*. New York and London: Routledge.

Boswell, M. (2012), *Holocaust Impiety in Literature, Popular Music and Film*. Basingstoke: Palgrave Macmillan.

Clendinnen, I. (1999), *Reading the Holocaust*. Cambridge: Cambridge University Press.

Eaglestone, R. (2004), *The Holocaust and the Postmodern*. Oxford: Oxford University Press.

Ezrahi, S. DeKoven (1980), *By Words Alone: The Holocaust in Literature*. Chicago and London: Chicago University Press.

Fridman, L. Wernick (2000), *Words and Witness: Narrative and Aesthetic Strategies in the Representation of the Holocaust*. Albany: State University of New York Press.

Friedlander, S. (ed.) (1992), *Probing the Limits of Representation: Nazism and the 'Final Solution'*. Cambridge, MA: Harvard University Press.

Guyer, S. (2007), *Romanticism after Auschwitz*. Stanford, CA: Stanford University Press.

Hartman, G. H. (1996), *The Longest Shadow: In the Aftermath of the Holocaust*. Bloomington and Indianapolis: Indiana University Press.

Hartman, G. H. (ed.) (1994), *Holocaust Remembrance: The Shapes of Memory*. Oxford: Blackwell.

Horowitz, S. R. (1997), *Voicing the Void: Muteness and Memory in Holocaust Fiction*. Albany: State University of New York Press.

Hungerford, A. (2003), *The Holocaust of Texts: Genocide, Literature, and Personification*. Chicago and London: University of Chicago Press.

Kaplan, B. A. (2007), *Unwanted Beauty: Aesthetic Pleasure in Holocaust Representation*. Urbana and Chicago: University of Illinois Press.

Kertzer, A. (2002), *My Mother's Voice: Children, Literature and the Holocaust*. Peterborough, Ontario: Broadview Press.

Kokkola, L. (2003), *Representing the Holocaust in Children's Literature*. New York: Routledge.

Komor, S. and Rohr, S. (eds) (2010), *The Holocaust, Art, and Taboo: Transatlantic Exchanges on the Ethics and Aesthetics of Representation*. Heidelberg: Universitätsverlag Winter.

Kritzman, L. (ed.) (1995), *Auschwitz and After: Race, Culture, and 'the Jewish Question' in France*. London: Routledge.

LaCapra, D. (1994), *Representing the Holocaust: History, Theory, Trauma*. Ithaca and London: Cornell University Press.

Lang, B. (ed.) (1988), *Writing and the Holocaust*. New York and London: Holmes & Meier.

Langer, L. (1975), *The Holocaust and the Literary Imagination*. New Haven and London: Yale University Press.

—. (1995), *Admitting the Holocaust: Collected Essays*. Oxford: Oxford University Press.

—. (1998), *Preempting the Holocaust*. New Haven and London: Yale University Press.

Leak, A. and Paizis, G. (eds) (2000), *The Holocaust and the Text: Speaking the Unspeakable*. Basingstoke: Macmillan.

Levi, N. and Rothberg, M. (eds) (2003), *The Holocaust: Theoretical Readings*. Edinburgh: Edinburgh University Press.

Lothe, J., Suleiman, S. Rubin and Phelan, J. (eds) (2012), *After Testimony: The Ethics and Aesthetics of Holocaust Narrative for the Future*. Columbus: Ohio State University Press.

Mandel, N. (2006), *Against the Unspeakable: Complicity, the Holocaust and Slavery in America*. Charlottesville: University of Virginia Press.

Miller, J. Hillis (2011), *The Conflagration of Community: Fiction before and after Auschwitz*. Chicago: University of Chicago Press.

Postone, M. and Santner, E. (eds) (2003), *Catastrophe and Meaning: The Holocaust and the Twentieth Century*. Chicago: University of Chicago Press.

Reiter, A. (ed.) (2006), *Children of the Holocaust*. London and Portland, OR: Vallentine Mitchell.

Rosenfeld, A. H. (1980), *A Double Dying: Reflections on Holocaust Literature*. Bloomington and Indianapolis: Indiana University Press.

Rothberg, M. (2000), *Traumatic Realism: The Demands of Holocaust Representation*. Minneapolis: University of Minnesota Press.

Saxton, L. (2008), *Haunted Images: Film, Ethics, Testimony and the Holocaust*. London: Wallflower.

Schlant, E. (1999), *The Language of Silence: West German Literature and the Holocaust*. New York and London: Routledge.

Schwarz, D. R. (1999), *Imagining the Holocaust*. New York: St Martin's Griffin.

Sicher, E. (2005), *The Holocaust Novel*. London: Routledge.

Sicher, E. (ed.) (1998), *Breaking Crystal: Writing and Memory after Auschwitz*. Urbana and Chicago: University of Illinois Press.

Spargo, R. C. and Ehrenreich, R. M. (2010), *After Representation? The Holocaust, Literature, and Culture*. New Brunswick, NJ: Rutgers University Press.

Steiner, G. [1970] (1982), *Language and Silence: Essays on Language, Literature and the Inhuman*. New York: Athenaeum.

Stone, D. (2003), *Constructing the Holocaust: A Study in Historiography*. London: Vallentine Mitchell.

—. (2006), *History, Memory and Mass Atrocity: Essays on the Holocaust and Genocide*. London: Vallentine Mitchell.

Suleiman, S. Rubin (2006), *Crises of Memory and the Second World War*. Cambridge, MA: Harvard University Press.

Vice, S. (2000), *Holocaust Fiction*. London: Routledge.

—. (2004), *Children Writing the Holocaust*. Basingstoke: Palgrave Macmillan.

Vice, S. (ed.) (2003), *Representing the Holocaust: In Honour of Bryan Burns*. London: Vallentine Mitchell.

Whitehead, A. (2004), *Trauma Fiction*. Edinburgh: Edinburgh University Press.

Young, J. E. (1988), *Writing and Rewriting the Holocaust: Narrative and the Consequences of Interpretation*. Bloomington and Indianapolis: Indiana University Press.

—. (1993), *The Texture of Memory: Holocaust Memorials and Meaning*. New Haven and London: Yale University Press.

Gender Issues in Holocaust Representation

While the question of whether gender should form a primary focus in approaches to the Holocaust is one that has been hotly debated, early proponents of the affirmative position include Joan Ringelheim (1984) and Myrna Goldenberg (1990), both of whom highlighted the specificity of women's Holocaust experience (including an added dimension of bodily vulnerability as women exposed to sexual exploitation, for example) and the differences between their strategies of coping and those of men. Specifically, such critics emphasized the collaborative and cooperative bonding between women, drawing a contrast in this respect to relationships between men in the camps. These arguments were controversial given the risk of subordinating the Holocaust to an extraneous gender politics and stereotyping women in ostensibly positive but ultimately traditional and conservative ways; nevertheless, these often polemical interventions usefully highlighted the large-scale omission of gender from most key debates within Holocaust Studies, paving the way for further ongoing inquiry and analysis.

In terms of the subsequent entry of women's testimony into critical consciousness, of prime importance is Rittner and Roth's edited volume *Different Voices* (1993), which brings together primary material by such figures as Livia Bitton-Jackson, Gisela Perl, Olga Lengyel, Sara Nomberg-Przytyk, Charlotte Delbo, Isabella Leitner, and Etty Hillesum, with secondary material and 'voices of reflection' from survivors and others, including Joan Ringelheim (in an essay that reconsiders some of the problematic ideological assumptions underpinning her own earlier research and identifies questions and topics in need of further exploration). While most of the secondary material included might be categorized within the field of historiography, the volume is valuable to literary scholars both contextually and in its marking of a broader willingness within Holocaust Studies as a whole to (re)consider questions of gender. Ofer and Weitzman's edited collection *Women in the Holocaust* (1998) is also weighted towards the historiography of women's experiences; nevertheless, it does additionally contain both personal accounts by female survivor-witnesses and a few essays which take representations as their focus, including Myrna Goldenberg's essay on the memoirs of Auschwitz survivors and Sara Horowitz's analysis of women in Holocaust literature, the latter of which presents an insightful response to questions of gender, including a discussion of the risks of homogenizing female experience or reproducing a patriarchal logic in accounts of women in the Holocaust which focus solely on biological functions such as pregnancy, and ultimately suggesting both the gendered nature of Holocaust experience and the simultaneous irreducibility of that experience to gendered factors. Other contributions to the collection include essays by Gisela Bock and Joan Ringelheim.

More fully focused on questions of representation is Esther Fuchs' 1999 edited collection *Women and the Holocaust: Narrative and Representation*. Encompassing a range of different disciplinary perspectives, including theology, Fuchs' volume contains contributions from such critics as Ronit Lentin, Lawrence Baron, Susan E. Nowak, and Zev Garber, addressing literary, filmic and cultural representations ('narrative' thus being used also in the sense of cultural narrative or (gendered) master narrative), with essays focused on particular themes (e.g. resistance, lesbianism, the Israeli second generation) and particular individuals (e.g. Edith Stein, Nelly Sachs). While not all of the essays included take gender as their central focus, Fuchs herself stresses the importance of a feminist approach to the Holocaust in complicating existing critical assumptions and aiding the articulation of heretofore silenced experiences. Another significant edited collection in this area is Elizabeth Baer and Myrna Goldenberg's *Experience and Expression: Women, the Nazis, and the Holocaust* (2003), which includes essays by S. Lillian Kremer, John K. Roth, Pascale Bos and Rebecca Scherr. Beginning with essays by Roth and Bos on the theoretical framework within which women's Holocaust experience and writing might be approached, the volume incorporates further sections on the experiences of women, the uses of memoirs, and the postwar representation of women's Holocaust experience in art, fiction and film.

Further significant interventions into the field of gender and Holocaust representation include S. Lillian Kremer's important 1999 study *Women's Holocaust Writing: Memory and Imagination,* in which Kremer analyses in detail postwar fiction by female survivors and non-survivors based in America, presenting her readings as one strategy for the recovery of women's responses to the Holocaust (and the gendered particularity of many of the experiences they explore) from obscurity within a male-dominated canon. Like other scholars working within this subject area, Kremer is careful to distance her work from any dubious competitive victimhood which would assert that women or men's suffering was greater, as well as from any homogenization of female experience; rather, she asserts the multiple particularities of women's experiences as one reason for the necessity of such gender-sensitive approaches to Holocaust writing as her own, which takes in the work of (among others) Ilona Karmel, Susan Fromberg Schaeffer, Cynthia Ozick and Norma Rosen. Other substantial studies within this area include Rachel Feldhay Brenner's *Writing as Resistance: Four Women Confronting the Holocaust* (1997), which examines the work of Edith Stein, Simone Weil, Anne Frank, and Etty Hillesum, presenting these writings as modes of resistance to Nazi domination and reassertions of humanist values, as well as locating in them a challenge to the assertions of such theorists as Dori Laub that the witness is unable to understand her experiences at the time; and Judith Tydor Baumel's *Double Jeopardy: Gender and the Holocaust* (1998), which includes discussion of the experiences of ultra-orthodox women (often overlooked or treated marginally in historical accounts) and an essay on the gender issues surrounding the use of Anne Frank's account in pedagogical practice. Margaret-Anne Hutton's work on French women's testimony to concentration camp experience (discussed above in the section on 'Testimony') also contains some useful consideration of other particularities of identity (including class and politics) which influenced the experiences and reflections of female deportees.

Baer, E. R. and Goldenberg, M. (eds) (2003), *Experience and Expression: Women, the Nazis, and the Holocaust*. Detroit: Wayne State University Press.

Baumel, J. Tydor (1998), *Double Jeopardy: Gender and the Holocaust*. London: Vallentine Mitchell.

Brenner, R. Feldhay (1997), *Writing as Resistance: Four Women Confronting the Holocaust*. University Park: Pennsylvania State University Press.

Fuchs, E. (ed.) (1999), *Women and the Holocaust: Narrative and Representation*. Lanham, MD: University Press of America.

Goldenberg, M. (1990), 'Different horrors, same hell', in R. Gottlieb (ed.), *Thinking the Unthinkable: Human Meanings of the Holocaust*. Mahwah, NJ: Paulist Press, pp. 150–66.

Horowitz, S. R. (1994), 'Memory and testimony of women survivors of Nazi genocide', in J. Baskin (ed.), *Women of the Word: Jewish Women and Jewish Writing*. Detroit: Wayne State University Press, pp. 258–82.

Hutton, M.-A. (2005), *Testimony from the Nazi Camps: French Women's Voices*. London: Routledge.

Kremer, S. L. (1999), *Women's Holocaust Writing: Memory and Imagination*. Lincoln: University of Nebraska Press.

Ofer, D. and Weitzman, L. J. (eds) (1998), *Women in the Holocaust*. New Haven and London: Yale University Press.

Ringelheim, J. (1984), 'The unethical and the unspeakable: women and the Holocaust', *Simon Wiesenthal Centre Annual*, 1, 69–87.

Rittner, C. and Roth, J. K. (eds) (1993), *Different Voices: Women and the Holocaust*. New York: Paragon House.

The Representation of Perpetrators

One key debate within this subject area is the question of whether perpetrators and their representation present an appropriate subject for exploration either in Holocaust Studies or in literary culture and art. Concerns were notably highlighted about the latter by Susan Sontag ([1974] 1983) and Saul Friedlander (1984) in the 1970s and 1980s, with both expressing concern about a resurgence of fascination with and fantasmatic investment in imagery of Nazism and fascism. These studies at once raise concern about a literary focus on perpetrators and implicitly suggest the need for a critical vigilance regarding these phenomena. Within the field of historiography, the debate about perpetrators and their representation gained momentum in the 1990s and took the specific form of dispute regarding perpetrator motivations and the nature (or otherwise) of low- and mid-level perpetrators as 'ordinary men'. Important reference points in this debate include Christopher Browning and Daniel Jonah Goldhagen: while Browning takes a social psychological approach in attempting to understand how and why the killers of Reserve Police Battalion 101 participated in mass killings, Goldhagen's visceral and emotive study argues that perpetrators committed murder because they subscribed to a belief system of 'eliminationist antisemitism': in short, simply because they believed the Jews should die. While both Browning and

Goldhagen ostensibly position the motivations of perpetrators as a legitimate object of enquiry, then, the conflict between their positions highlights a resistance to an approach to the perpetrator as a member of the human community (an 'ordinary person') whose motivations can be recognized in their complexity and may necessitate wider self-examination, rather than an ideologically extremist other whose behaviour necessitates no such reflection. In a different register, such resistance is also evident in the argument concerning the 'obscenity of understanding' voiced by the documentary filmmaker Claude Lanzmann.[7] These debates form a backdrop to much of the discussion of the representation of perpetrators in literature, as, too, do the psychological studies of James Waller and others.

In literary criticism, early work on the depiction of Nazi perpetrators includes Rosenfeld's *Imagining Hitler* (1985), which examines the role of Nazism in the US imagination through the lens of popular representations of Hitler.[8] More recent studies include Boswell's 2012 study of 'impious' representations of Nazism and the Holocaust in literature and popular culture, Gomel's *Bloodscripts* (2003), which explores representations of the violent subject, Kleeblatt's *Mirroring Evil* (2001), which accompanied the art exhibition of that name and which includes essays by James Young, Sidra DeKoven Ezrahi and Ernst van Alphen, among others, and Adams and Vice (eds) (2013), which contains essays on a range of depictions in film, literature, and public culture, by such critics as Robert Eaglestone, Lyndsey Stonebridge, Antony Rowland and Matthew Boswell. These and other works (such as Rau, 2013) are discussed further in the 'New Directions' section of this volume. Much of the critical reflection on Jonathan Littell's recent novel *The Kindly Ones* entails a broader consideration of the significance of perpetrator representations in fiction. Suleiman (2009) is a particularly insightful example; see also the contents of Barjonet and Razinsky (eds) (2012). Analysis of the representations of perpetrators in second-generation literature can be found in McGlothlin (2006) and Donahue (2010). While the latter is focused on the work of a single author, the German novelist Bernhard Schlink, I include it here as a counterpoint to the dominant critical tendency to read apparent confrontations of guilt and evocations of wider (including second-generational and readerly) complicity in perpetrator texts as an ethically productive phenomenon; Donahue instead suggests in relation to Schlink that such a blurring of ethical and interpersonal boundaries can in fact facilitate an evasion of specific, historically rooted questions of responsibility, while at the same time permitting a self-congratulatory sense of personal and cultural self-scrutiny to emerge.[9] While these arguments are to a certain extent specific to the cultural contexts Donahue explores, they also demand further negotiation as regards the current valorization within Holocaust Studies of a sense or awareness of complicity as a necessarily productive mode of response to historical violence.

Adams, J. and Vice, S. (eds) (2013), *Representing Perpetrators in Holocaust Literature and Film*. London: Vallentine Mitchell.

Barjonet, A. and Razinsky, L. (eds) (2012), *Writing the Holocaust Today: Critical Perspectives on Jonathan Littell's The Kindly Ones*. Amsterdam: Editions Rodopi.

Boswell, M. (2012), *Holocaust Impiety in Literature, Popular Music and Film*. Basingstoke: Palgrave Macmillan.

Browning, C. (1992), *Ordinary Men: Reserve Police Battalion 101 and the Final Solution in Poland*. New York: HarperCollins.

Butter, M. (2009), *The Epitome of Evil: Hitler in American Fiction, 1939–2002*. New York: Palgrave Macmillan.

Donahue, W. Collins (2010), *Holocaust as Fiction: Bernhard Schlink's 'Nazi' Novels and Their Films*. New York: Palgrave Macmillan.

Friedlander, S. (1984), *Reflections of the Holocaust: An Essay on Kitsch and Death*, trans. T. Weyr. New York: Harper & Row.

Goldhagen, D. J. (1996), *Hitler's Willing Executioners: Ordinary Germans and the Holocaust*. New York: Alfred A. Knopf.

Gomel, E. (2003), *Bloodscripts: Writing the Violent Subject*. Columbus: Ohio State University Press.

Kleeblatt, N. (ed.) (2001), *Mirroring Evil: Nazi Imagery / Recent Art*. New Brunswick, NJ: Rutgers University Press; New York: The Jewish Museum.

Lanzmann, C. (1995), 'The obscenity of understanding: an evening with Claude Lanzmann', in C. Caruth (ed.), *Trauma: Explorations in Memory*. Baltimore: Johns Hopkins University Press, pp. 200–20.

McGlothlin, E. (2006), *Second-Generation Holocaust Literature: Legacies of Survival and Perpetration*. Woodbridge: Camden House.

—. (2010), 'Theorizing the perpetrator in Bernhard Schlink's *The Reader* and Martin Amis's *Time's Arrow*', in R. C. Spargo, and R. M. Ehrenreich (eds), *After Representation? The Holocaust, Literature, and Culture*. New Brunswick, NJ: Rutgers University Press, pp. 210–30.

Rau, P. (2013), *Our Nazis: Representations of Fascism in Contemporary Literature and Film*. Edinburgh: Edinburgh University Press.

Rosenfeld, A. (1985), *Imagining Hitler*. Bloomington: Indiana University Press.

Sontag, S. [1974] (1983), 'Fascinating Fascism', in *A Susan Sontag Reader*. London: Penguin, pp. 305–25.

Suleiman, S. Rubin, (2009), 'When the perpetrator becomes a reliable witness of the Holocaust: on Jonathan Littell's *Les bienveillantes*', *New German Critique*, 36.1, 1–19.

Waller, J. (2007), *Becoming Evil: How Ordinary People Commit Genocide and Mass Killing*, 2nd edn. Oxford: Oxford University Press.

Post-Holocaust Memory and Literature

Given that theorizations of post-Holocaust memory often deploy literary examples in their exploration of the tendencies they trace, secondary material on second- and third-generation literature and more theoretical material dealing with the mechanisms of post-Holocaust memory are here discussed together. The most influential conceptual model in the analysis of second- and third-generation writing is Marianne Hirsch's theory of postmemory (discussed at length elsewhere in this volume),[10] which explores the ways in which the children of

Holocaust survivors create imaginative reconstructions of their families' pasts from a combination of familial narratives, material traces and imaginative elaboration. Hirsch considers postmemory as a mechanism of heteropathic identification, in which identification with the other's experience is qualified by a recognition of their alterity,[11] and also explores the ways in which postmemorial attachment and investment can be either familial (operating within the family) or affiliative (operating across a broader experiential distance) (Hirsch, 1996, 1997, 1999, 2001, 2012). A sense of the conception in its current form can best be gained from a reading of *The Generation of Postmemory* (2012), which also emphasizes the multiculturally 'connective' potential of affiliative postmemory, and includes analysis of a range of literary and artistic works. Other frequent points of reference in theoretical discussions of second-generation memory include the work of Fresco (1984) and Raczymow (1994).

Extensive analysis of literary and artistic works in the light of ideas about second- and third-generation Holocaust memory include Apel (2002) (including discussion of the art of Shimon Attie, Vera Frenkel, Jeffrey Wolin, James Friedman, Susan Silas, Rachel Schreiber and Art Spiegelman) and Berger (1997), which reads second-generation identity as depicted in American literature (including the work of Art Spiegelman, Melvin Jules Bukiet, Thane Rosenbaum and Julie Salomon) with specific reference to orientations towards Judaism. Berger's edited volume (with Naomi Berger) *Second Generation Voices: Reflections by Children of Holocaust Survivors and Perpetrators* (2001) brings together a number of highly self-reflective personal narratives by members of the two 'second generations' referred to in the title, a juxtaposition of contexts of victim and perpetrator postmemory considered problematic by some of the contributing children of survivors (Berger and Berger, 2001, p. 10). Despite the potentially controversial aspect of this juxtaposition, the illuminating nature of such an approach is defended by Erin McGlothlin, who in her 2006 study *Second-Generation Holocaust Literature: Legacies of Survival and Perpetration* explores the structural similarities and qualitative differences between the two postmemorial contexts through an analysis of such works as Rosenbaum's *Elijah Visible*, Spiegelman's *Maus*, Patrick Modiano's *Dora Bruder*, Peter Schneider's *Vati* and Uwe Timm's *In My Brother's Shadow*. A consideration of the descendants of both victims and perpetrators as portrayed in various practices of transgenerational writing, including literature, memoir and testimony by Ruth Klüger, W. G. Sebald, Georges Perec, Toni Morrison, Samuel Beckett, Art Spiegelman, Philippe Grimbert, Ariel Dorfman and Schwab herself, is also offered in Gabriele Schwab's 2010 study *Haunting Legacies: Violent Histories and Transgenerational Trauma*. Deploying a psychoanalytic vocabulary of psychic trauma and the crypt in an exploration of the intergenerational legacies of violence, Schwab's work exemplifies the connective trend in recent work on post-Holocaust memory, contending that 'histories of violence can be put in a dialogical relationship with one another, thus creating a transferential dynamic for those who participate in, witness, or inherit those histories transgenerationally' (Schwab, 2010, p. 29). This connective approach incorporates both victim and perpetrator memory and connects a primary focus on Germany and the Holocaust to a range of other situations of historical violence, including slavery, colonialism, apartheid, post-9/11 torture and 'disappearances' in South American dictatorships.

While the studies detailed above concern themselves primarily with individual instances of and responses to post-Holocaust memory, another body of work concerns itself with the nature of Holocaust memory at a cultural or collective level. American collective memory of the Holocaust, for example, has proved of particular critical interest given the geographical and, in large part, experiential distance of the American nation from these events, with studies by Cole (1999), Novick (1999) and Flanzbaum (ed.) (1999) frequently cited reference points in this respect. Such studies often highlight the Eichmann trial as the key moment in the Holocaust's entry into public discourse, address the current centrality of the Holocaust to American Jewish identity (Novick, 1999, p. 146), examine the commercial embeddedness of Holocaust memory in the United States (Finkelstein, 2003; Cole, 1999, p. 17), and explore the degree to which the centrality of the Holocaust in American culture manifests a screening out of US-perpetrated atrocities such as slavery and the genocide of the Native Americans (Cole, 1999, p. 14). Flanzbaum's 1999 edited collection is essential initial reading within this subject area; essays in this volume examine the presence/centrality of the Holocaust to American culture at the end of the twentieth century as refracted through literature and other forms of cultural presence such as science-fiction television (Jeffrey Shandler) and museums and memorials (James E. Young), with other contributors including Amy Hungerford (on personification in Art Spiegelman and Berel Lang), Andrew Furman (on Thane Rosenbaum), Walter Benn Michaels (on the centrality of the notion of culture to current ideas about the remembrance of historical trauma in US discourse), and Flanzbaum herself on the place of the Holocaust in American poetry. Noteworthy interventions into the consideration of Holocaust memory in the United States also include the work of Alison Landsberg, whose 2004 study *Prosthetic Memory: The Transformation of American Remembrance in the Age of Mass Culture* examines the forms of 'memory' developed in response to the experience of cultural sites and products (the United States Holocaust Memorial Museum or the film *Schindler's List*, for example) relating events of which the viewer has no personal experience.[12] Other areas of particular focus within the approach to national memory of the Holocaust include the German context, with such studies as those of Maier (1997), Niven (2002), Kansteiner (2006), Schlant (1999) and Taberner (2005) significant publications on this topic (the latter two of these are focused on literature, while the others address broader cultural, historiographic and political contexts of memory). Richard Crownshaw's 2010 study

The Afterlife of Holocaust Memory in Contemporary Literature and Culture also contains some excellent readings of the work of W. G. Sebald and Bernhard Schlink in relation to questions of German cultural memory and notions of collective memory more broadly. As regards French memory of the Holocaust, Lawrence Kritzman's edited collection *Auschwitz and After: Race, Culture, and 'the Jewish Question' in France* (1995) is a valuable starting point, containing essays and excerpts from the work of Geoffrey Hartman, Pierre Vidal-Naquet, Susan Rubin Suleiman, Alain Finkielkraut, Emmanuel Levinas and others.

In an era of globalization, questions of post-Holocaust memory of course extend beyond personal and national contexts into a broader field of internationally transmitted and circulated representations and constructions of these events; for an outline of some of the key points of critical response to this phenomenon, see below, particularly the next section's discussion of 'cosmopolitan memory'.

Apel, D. (2002), *Memory Effects: The Holocaust and the Art of Secondary Witnessing.* New Brunswick: Rutgers University Press.

Bal, M., Crewe, J. and Spitzer, L. (eds) (1999), *Acts of Memory: Cultural Recall in the Present.* Hanover and London: University Press of New England.

Berger, A. L. (1997), *Children of Job: American Second-Generation Witnesses to the Holocaust.* Albany: State University of New York Press.

Berger, A. L. and Berger, N. (eds) (2001), *Second Generation Voices: Reflections by Children of Holocaust Survivors and Perpetrators.* Syracuse, NY: Syracuse University Press.

Cole, T. (1999), *Images of the Holocaust: The Myth of the 'Shoah Business'.* London: Duckworth.

Crownshaw, R. (2010), *The Afterlife of Holocaust Memory in Contemporary Literature and Culture.* Basingstoke: Palgrave Macmillan.

Eley, G. (ed.) (2000), *The 'Goldhagen Effect': History, Memory, Nazism – Facing the German Past.* Ann Arbor: University of Michigan Press.

Finkelstein, N. G. (2003), *The Holocaust Industry: Reflections on the Exploitation of Jewish Suffering,* 2nd edn. London and New York: Verso.

Flanzbaum, H. (ed.) (1999), *The Americanization of the Holocaust.* Baltimore and London: Johns Hopkins University Press.

Fresco, N. (1984), 'Remembering the unknown', *International Review of Psychoanalysis,* 11, 417–27.

Hirsch, M. (1996), 'Past lives: postmemories in exile', *Poetics Today,* 17.4, 659–86.

—. (1997), *Family Frames: Photography, Narrative, and Postmemory.* Cambridge, MA: Harvard University Press.

—. (1999), 'Projected memory: Holocaust photographs in personal and public fantasy', in M. Bal, J. Crewe and L. Spitzer (eds), *Acts of Memory: Cultural Recall in the Present.* Hanover, NH: University Press of New England, pp. 2–23.

—. (2001), 'Surviving images: Holocaust photographs and the work of postmemory', *The Yale Journal of Criticism,* 14.1, 5–37.

—. (2012), *The Generation of Postmemory: Writing and Visual Culture after the Holocaust.* New York: Columbia University Press.

Kansteiner, W. (2006), *In Pursuit of German Memory: History, Television, and Politics after Auschwitz.* Athens, OH: University of Ohio Press.

Kaplan, B. A. (2011), *Landscapes of Holocaust Postmemory.* New York: Routledge.

Kritzman, L. (ed.) (1995), *Auschwitz and After: Race, Culture, and 'the Jewish Question' in France*. London: Routledge.

Landsberg, A. (2004), *Prosthetic Memory: The Transformation of American Remembrance in the Age of Mass Culture*. New York: Columbia University Press.

Lennon, J. and Foley, M. (2000), *Dark Tourism: The Attraction of Death and Disaster*. London and New York: Continuum.

Linenthal, E. T. (1995), *Preserving Memory: The Struggle to Create America's Holocaust Museum*. New York: Viking Penguin.

Maier, C. (1997), *The Unmasterable Past: History, Holocaust, and German National Identity*, 2nd edn. Cambridge, MA: Harvard University Press.

McGlothlin, E. (2006), *Second-Generation Holocaust Literature: Legacies of Survival and Perpetration*. Woodbridge: Camden House.

Niven, B. (2002), *Facing the Nazi Past: United Germany and the Legacy of the Third Reich*. London and New York: Routledge.

Novick, P. (1999), *The Holocaust and Collective Memory: The American Experience*. London: Bloomsbury.

Raczymow, H. (1994), 'Memory shot through with holes', *Yale French Studies*, 85, 98–105.

Schlant, E. (1999), *The Language of Silence: West German Literature and the Holocaust*. New York and London: Routledge.

Schwab, G. (2010), *Haunting Legacies: Violent Histories and Transgenerational Trauma*. New York: Columbia University Press.

Taberner, S. (2005), *German Literature of the 1990s and Beyond: Normalization and the Berlin Republic*. Rochester, NY: Camden House.

Webber, J. (ed.) (1994), *Jewish Identities in the New Europe*. London and Washington: Littman Library of Jewish Civilization.

Weissman, G. (2004), *Fantasies of Witnessing: Postwar Efforts to Experience the Holocaust*. Ithaca and London: Cornell University Press.

Holocaust Literature in Dialogue with Other Literary and Cultural Contexts

Given that this emergent area of research is discussed in some detail in the 'New Directions' section of this volume, and that key concepts are elaborated in the volume's Glossary, I will keep the discussion below relatively brief. There has recently been a 'comparative turn' in Holocaust studies that has seen an increasing critical attention to intersections of Holocaust memory and representation with those of other traumatic histories such as slavery, apartheid and colonialism. Work in the late 1990s examining the literary intersection of black and Jewish struggles and identities (e.g. Budick, 1998) has been followed by a range of literary and cultural studies which draw on discourses of globalization as well as such cultural-theoretical works as Paul Gilroy's *Between Camps: Nations, Cultures, and the Allure of Race* ([2000], second edition 2004), which traces a certain continuity of racialized politics between European colonialism and twentieth-century fascism, ultimately arguing against race-based thinking of all kinds (including racial identity politics) in favour of a 'planetary humanism' transcending considerations of colour.

Displaying a certain theoretical confidence in overriding conventional critical injunctions to read every historical event or cultural manifestation within its own specificity, Gilroy's work is often cited as a key reference point by literary and cultural critics who seek to place the Holocaust and other histories of violence and oppression in dialogue. In relation to broad notions of Holocaust memory, Daniel Levy and Natan Sznaider (2006) have argued for the Holocaust's potential role, within an era of 'cosmopolitan' (globalized, and to an extent, decontextualized) memory, as a universal reference point in the promulgation of the discourse of human rights and the identification and judgement of abuses. Contesting the centrality of the Holocaust to such accounts of connective and comparative memory, such critics as Michael Rothberg have, within the context of literary studies, argued in favour of a more 'multidirectional' approach which recognizes the degree to which the memory of other historical conflicts (primarily, in Rothberg's discussion, colonialism and the Algerian War) shapes the memory of the Holocaust as well as *vice versa*. Rothberg's corrective to configurations of the Holocaust as a universal reference point and a dominant and unchanging signifier in comparative and connective representations of history is coupled with a broader revision of what he terms the 'zero-sum' model of historical remembrance in which memory of one event comes at the price of forgetting others (Rothberg, 2009). Further significant studies in this area include that of Max Silverman (2013), which employs the figure of the palimpsest as a means of theorizing the connective nature of memory, while other critical work intersecting with this project includes Marianne Hirsch's recent writing on postmemory (2012), which emphasizes the potential for cross-cultural identifications and engagements within this mode, Gabriele Schwab's work on intergenerational trauma (2010), and Naomi Mandel's study of the unspeakable in both Holocaust discourse and the literature of slavery.

For a more detailed discussion of the recent turn to the comparative and multidirectional within Holocaust studies, see also the 'New Directions' section of this volume.

Budick, E. Miller (1998), *Blacks and Jews in Literary Conversation*. Cambridge: Cambridge University Press.

Craps, S. (2013), *Postcolonial Witnessing: Trauma Out of Bounds*. Basingstoke: Palgrave Macmillan.

Gilroy, P. (2004), *Between Camps: Nations, Cultures, and the Allure of Race*, 2nd edn. London and New York: Routledge.

Hirsch, M. (2012), *The Generation of Postmemory: Writing and Visual Culture after the Holocaust*. New York: Columbia University Press.

Levy, D. and Sznaider, N. (2006), *The Holocaust and Memory in the Global Age*, trans. A. Oksiloff. Philadelphia: Temple University Press.

Mandel, N. (2006), *Against the Unspeakable: Complicity, the Holocaust and Slavery in America*. Charlottesville: University of Virginia Press.

Michaels, W. Benn. (1999), '"You who never was there": slavery and the new historicism – deconstruction and the Holocaust', in H. Flanzbaum (ed.), *The Americanization of the Holocaust*. Baltimore and London: Johns Hopkins University Press, pp. 181–97.

Rothberg, M. (2009), *Multidirectional Memory: Remembering the Holocaust in the Age of Decolonization*. Stanford, CA: Stanford University Press.

Schwab, G. (2010), *Haunting Legacies: Violent Histories and Transgenerational Trauma*. New York: Columbia University Press.

Silverman, M. (2013), *Palimpsestic Memory: The Holocaust and Colonialism in French and Francophone Fiction and Film*. New York: Berghahn.

Sundquist, E. J. (2005), *Strangers in the Land: Blacks, Jews, Post-Holocaust America*. Cambridge, MA: The Belknap Press of Harvard University Press.

Notes

1. See Glossary under 'Trauma'.
2. 'Goldhagen debate' refers to the conflict that ensued upon the publication of Daniel Jonah Goldhagen's study *Hitler's Willing Executioners* (1996), which portrayed 'ordinary Germans' as willing and even enthusiastic participants in anti-Semitic murder, in part as a result of a long history of virulent anti-Semitism in Germany.
3. For a more detailed discussion of both Felman and Laub and Agamben's perspectives on testimony, see entry for 'Testimony' in the Glossary section of this volume.
4. While Guyer's study is not exclusively focused on poetry, I have included it here for its significance in this respect.
5. See Glossary under 'Backshadowing'.
6. A number of the works mentioned in this section of the bibliography are discussed in greater detail in the 'New Directions' section of this volume; for this reason, I avoid going into an extensive degree of detail here.
7. See Glossary under 'Obscenity of understanding' for more on this.
8. For a more recent examination of the Hitler trope in American fiction, see Butter (2009).
9. Donahue writes, for example, of attempts to draw readers into an identification or alignment with perpetrators, that, 'In engaging the subjunctive and the hypothetical, however laudably, we may also, at the same time, be fleeing the unbearably actual and historical. And by privileging an imaginary identification of ourselves with Holocaust perpetrators, we also may be inadvertently endorsing the notion of the moral "undecidability" of their actions. . . . Could this be what lies behind the critical elevation of these "interesting ambiguities"?' (2010, p. 68).
10. See Introduction, Glossary, 'New Directions in Holocaust Literary Studies' and Brett Ashley Kaplan and Fernando Herrero-Matoses' essay on postmemory.
11. For a further discussion of this and other modes of identification, see Glossary under 'Identification'.
12. For a more detailed discussion of Landsberg's work, and potential counter-arguments, see 'New Directions in Holocaust Literary Studies'.

Glossary of Major Terms and Concepts

A feature intended to be of particular benefit to scholars and students new to this subject area, this glossary offers brief explanations of critical terminology often present in discussions of Holocaust literature in order to aid negotiation of critical and theoretical debates.

1.5 Generation

'1.5 generation' is Susan Rubin Suleiman's term to describe 'child survivors of the Holocaust, too young to have had an adult understanding of what was happening to them, and sometimes too young to have any memory of it at all, but old enough to have *been there* during the Nazi persecution of Jews' (2006, p. 179). Suleiman considers the literary imagination to occupy a 'special place . . . in the narratives of child survivors' (ibid., p. 183), with key themes in the literature of this generation including: 'unstable identity and psychological splitting, a preoccupation with absence, emptiness, silence, a permanent sense of loneliness and loss, . . . and, often, an anguished questioning about what it means to be Jewish after the Holocaust', in addition to a preoccupation 'with the question of *how* to tell the story' (ibid., p. 184). In attempting to make sense of their experiences and of the loss of family members, many of whose fates may be unknown, the 1.5 generation are faced at once by the difficulties of trauma and those of postmemory, both negotiating the impact of first-hand experience and attempting to reconstruct in a belated fashion the experiences of those close to them, as well as, in many cases, their own experiences.

Writers whose work might be included in the category of 'writing of the 1.5 generation' include Georges Perec, who escaped the Holocaust in hiding as a child and whose *W or the Memory of Childhood* ([1988] 1996) attempts to reconstruct both his own childhood and, elliptically, the concentration camp universe into which his mother disappeared; other writers who have been placed in this category include Raymond Federman, Louis Begley and Saul Friedlander.

'After Auschwitz'

'After Auschwitz' is a rhetorical trope that refers, at its most basic level, to the aftermath of the Holocaust, but more specifically recalls Theodor Adorno's oft-cited comments regarding the possibility of 'poetry after Auschwitz'. While often linked to claims about the aesthetic impropriety of poetry in the context of atrocity, Adorno's initial comments in fact address the implication of aspects of culture which survive today with the culture that produced the Holocaust, and the impossibility of producing a knowledge of that implication from a position (recalling the Marxist idea of the inextricability of material/economic base and cultural superstructure) complicit with its structures of reification. In the closing passage of 'Cultural Criticism and Society', he writes that:

> The more total society becomes, the greater the reification of the mind and the more paradoxical its effort to escape reification on its own. Even the most extreme consciousness of doom threatens to degenerate into idle chatter. Cultural criticism finds itself faced with the final stage of the dialectic of culture and barbarism. To write poetry after Auschwitz is barbaric. And this corrodes even the knowledge of why it has become impossible to write poetry today. Absolute reification, which presupposed intellectual progress as one of its elements, is now preparing to absorb the mind entirely. Critical intelligence cannot be equal to this challenge as long as it confines itself to self-satisfied contemplation. (Adorno, [1951] 2003a, p. 162)

Exactly what Adorno means by 'reification' is clarified in his comments, in 'Education after Auschwitz', on 'reified consciousness': 'People of such a nature have, as it were, assimilated themselves to things. And then, when possible, they assimilate others to things' ([1967] 2003b, p. 27). 'Reification' for Adorno thus presents a means of describing the way in which capitalism's homogenizing and objectifying reduction of individuals to units of labour – which created the conditions for the treatment of human life during the Holocaust – extends to the notion of the human itself, as deployed interpersonally, in cultural production and thought, and in cultural criticism. The latter are thus complicit in the material conditions of objectification and domination which produced the Holocaust, raising questions about their tenability and autonomy per se as well as the possibility of an art able to respond adequately to these events.

The significance of complicity to Adorno's model of thought in his comments on culture 'after Auschwitz' is taken up by Naomi Mandel in *Against the Unspeakable* (2006), in which she advocates a recognition of complicity as a starting point in post-Holocaust literature and thought: 'To be "after Auschwitz" is to be irrevocably complicit in the culture that produced it; to think "after Auschwitz" is to actively integrate complicity into our ongoing projects of self-articulation' (Mandel, 2006, p. 69) (for more on the significance of 'complicity' as a trope in recent post-Holocaust thinking, see the New Directions section of this volume). For a more extensive and extremely insightful analysis of Adorno and his interpreters' use of the phrase 'after Auschwitz', see Rothberg (2000, chapter 1), while for a discussion of its implications regarding poetic practice, see David Miller's chapter in this volume.

Alterity

'Alterity' is a term meaning 'otherness' and is frequently invoked in approaches to the Holocaust (e.g. Eaglestone, 2004; Orbán, 2005) informed by the ethical philosophy of Emmanuel Levinas. Levinasian ethics is focused on the relationship between self and other, positing an absolute obligation to the other that is instantiated through the act of *facing* (the act, as Alphonso Lingis writes, 'by which alterity breaks into the sphere of phenomena' (1998, p. xix)) and which forms the grounding of subjectivity as such, which comes into being in response to the call of the other (see Critchley, 1999, pp. 64–6). The relationship to alterity is hence one of exposure to, contestation by, and ultimately responsibility for the other, as Levinas articulates in *Otherwise than Being*:

> Responsibility for the other, in its antecedence to my freedom, its antecedence to the present and to representation, is a passivity more passive than all passivity, an exposure to the other without this exposure being assumed, an exposure without holding back, exposure of exposedness, expression, saying. (1998, p. 15)

Levinas's use of the term 'saying' refers precisely to this condition of exposure within which the alterity of the other, and the ethical responsibility and obligation instantiated through this encounter, may be registered; it contrasts with the 'said', which denotes the content of the exchange, or what Simon Critchley terms 'a statement, assertion or proposition of which the truth or falsity may be ascertained' (Critchley, 2002, p. 18). In its focus on the 'saying', Levinasian ethics thus emphasizes the encounter with alterity involved in the act of communication rather than privileging the knowledge which forms its content; it is characterized by a refusal to assimilate the other within the conceptual structures of the self, to subject alterity to the totalizations of knowledge, or to grasp what eludes comprehension, schematization and metaphysical seizure.

For a more extensive discussion of Levinasian and other ethical approaches invoked within the context of Holocaust literature, see Michael Bernard-Donals' chapter in this volume, while for a series of detailed and useful explications of Levinasian ethics, see Davis (1996), Eaglestone (1997) and Critchley (1999). For a critique of Levinasian ethics as founded on what he contends is the ultimately legal rather than ethical principle of responsibility, see Agamben (1999, p. 22). For a discussion of Levinas in the context of postmodern ethics, see Bauman (1993).

Americanization of the Holocaust

The term 'Americanization of the Holocaust' emerged towards the end of the twentieth century to refer to the increasing centrality of the Holocaust to American culture, a phenomenon often read as necessitating special examination given the lack of geographical proximity to the location of the events themselves. While the term often carries pejorative connotations, signifying crass commercial exploitation of the genocide, it is also used in a positive sense by such figures as Michael Berenbaum, one of the shaping forces behind the United States Holocaust Memorial Museum in Washington DC. Berenbaum uses the term to refer to the process by which the Holocaust is assimilated by American culture, assuming relevance to an American public; while this necessitates, in Edward T. Linenthal's words, the history being 'told in a way that would be meaningful to an American audience', the process as envisioned by Berenbaum 'would not require the "dejudaization" of the Holocaust' (1995, pp. 45, 44). In the context of these divergent readings of the phenomenon, Hilene Flanzbaum advocates a careful evaluation of each individual instance of 'Americanization' rather than a recourse to sweeping dismissals or endorsements; in the introduction to an important edited collection on the topic, she writes:

> If the Holocaust, as image and symbol, seems to have sprung loose from its origins, it does not mean we should decry Americanization; rather, the pervasive presence of representations of the Holocaust in our culture demands responsible evaluation and interpretation. The many invocations of the Holocaust for many different purposes call for our sifting, sorting, analysis. (1999, p. 8)

Flanzbaum's measured approach to the phenomenon is evident in her emphasis on contextualizing Jewish American responses to the Holocaust within a sense of broader American values, aesthetics and themes such as universalization; on Steven Spielberg and other Jewish American cultural producers, for example, she writes that 'What they create must automatically bear the imprint of a multicultural but predominantly Gentile America. To expect otherwise is to expect the impossible' (ibid., p. 13).

For additional examinations of the place of the Holocaust in American culture, see also, for example, Novick (1999), Cole (1999) and, more controversially, Finkelstein (2003) (on whom, see *Holocaust Industry*).

Awkward Poetics

'Awkward poetics' is Antony Rowland's term to describe a particular strategy in post-Holocaust poetry (by which term he refers to poetry which engages with the events of the Holocaust but which is written by those who had no personal involvement in these events). If Adorno's famous statements about 'poetry after Auschwitz' imply that poetry after the Holocaust cannot continue as before but must instead register necessary anxieties about its own adequacy and ethics, 'awkward poetics' describes one mode of response to this, namely, a self-reflexive poetry that is attuned to its own problematic status. Rowland identifies such strategies, in different ways, in the work of postwar Anglophone poets such as Sylvia Plath, Tony Harrison and Geoffrey Hill, with one example being the self-scrutinizing admission of Hill's speaker in 'September Song' that while attempting to mark the deportation of an unnamed child, he has in fact 'made an elegy for myself' (see Rowland, 2005, p. 11). Indeed, Hill's work is considered exemplary by Rowland in the 'awkwardness' of its aesthetic strategies. Further strategies of awkward poetics are listed by Rowland as including: 'metrical tension, the anti-elegiac, self-questioning, embarrassed rhetoric, anti-rhetoric, juxtaposition, incongruity, self-declared inadequacies, paradox, minimalism, non-catharsis, heightened tone, hermeneutics, the anti-redemptive, archaisms, anti-objectivism and "stylistic eccentricities"' (ibid., p. 12).

Interestingly, Rowland acknowledges the extent to which awkward poetics could be read as a form of *Holocaust piety* (see separate entry), as 'a pious attempt to register the difficulties of historical representation, a conundrum that the poet then resolves all too easily through self-castigation' (p. 12). Nevertheless, he affirms its value in encouraging reflection as regards the ethical responsibilities of both artist and reader regarding Holocaust representation, contrasting this favourably with popular representations less conducive to ethical self-reflexivity.

Backshadowing

'Backshadowing' is Michael André Bernstein's term to describe a particularly problematic form of foreshadowing (making reference to events yet to come in discussions of a particular historical moment). Foreshadowing implies a deterministic reading of history whereby future events are construed as inevitable; backshadowing, according to Bernstein, intensifies the ethically problematic implications of this by suggesting that individuals at the time should have known that later events lay inevitably in wait, and acted accordingly (with victims of the Holocaust, for example, being implicitly blamed for not escaping the genocide of the European Jews in the years immediately before). As an alternative to foreshadowing and backshadowing narrative structures, Bernstein advocates sideshadowing, which involves a 'gesturing to the side' (1994, p. 1) that recognizes that other outcomes were possible and that the outcomes that ensued resulted from particular acts of human agency and responsibility.

Banality of Evil

The 'banality of evil' is a phrase first used by Hannah Arendt in her response to the 1961 Eichmann trial to refer to the way in which Eichmann's motivations could not be located in notions of the diabolic, of radical evil or of extreme malice, but resisted quantification in these terms, instead appearing wholly absent or utterly mundane. She writes: 'Eichmann was not Iago and not Macbeth, and nothing would have been farther from his mind than to determine with Richard III "to prove a villain". Except for an extraordinary diligence in looking out for his personal advancement, he had no motives at all' (Arendt, [1963] 2006, p. 287), with the Shakespearean references highlighting (in a counterpart to assertions that victims' suffering in the Holocaust resists integration into the plot configurations of tragedy) the difficulties of accounting for perpetrator actions in any adequate way within the inherited literary plots available to us. While Arendt's emphasis on the lack of diabolism or pathologism of Eichmann – on the fact that 'It was sheer thoughtlessness – something by no means identical with stupidity – that predisposed him to become one of the greatest criminals of that period' (ibid., pp. 287–8) – necessarily problematizes the grounds on which judgement is conventionally made, inviting a rethinking of existing notions of justice and guilt (ibid., p. 277), it does not amount to a universalizing exculpation or consequent suggestion that his crimes refuse judgement, with the necessity of judgement of individual moral responsibility remaining imperative.

Arendt's theorization of the 'banality of evil' correlates with a movement in the response to Holocaust perpetrators from an assumption in the immediate postwar period that these actions could only be motivated by extreme psychological pathology to a recognition of the commonality of perpetrators, in term of their psychological functioning, with ordinary citizens who played no role in these events (Waller, 2007) and corresponding claims regarding the value of this recognition in the prevention of future violence. Nevertheless, figurations of pathology have remained an aspect of depictions of perpetrators in literature (often alongside representations of the 'banality' of Holocaust 'evil'), as both Erin McGlothlin and Matthew Boswell (the latter in the context of the taboo) address in their chapters in this volume. For a discussion of the strategies by which literary texts approach and diverge from exploration of the motivations of Holocaust perpetrators and the nature of their 'evil', see under *swerve*, separate entry.

Differend

In Jean-François Lyotard's theorization, 'the differend' is 'the unstable state and instant of language wherein something which must be able to be put into phrases cannot yet be' (1988, p. 13). In other words, the notion of a 'differend' refers to an experience or content which cannot be voiced within a particular genre of discourse, in the way that, for example, an individual testimony of the Holocaust is not able to produce irrefutable positive knowledge of the event in its totality, or a process of killing witnessed only by its victims cannot be identified in the discourse of the living witness. For Lyotard, the status of Auschwitz as differend does not preclude a recognition of its reality and impact, as those concerned about Holocaust denial might fear. Using the analogy of an earthquake so powerful that it destroys the instruments by which the force of earthquakes might be registered, he contends that 'The impossibility of quantitatively measuring it does not prohibit, but rather inspires in the minds of the survivors the idea of a very great seismic force' (ibid., p. 56), adding that:

> [T]he historian must break with the monopoly over history granted to the cognitive regimen of phrases, and he or she must venture forth by lending his or her ear to what is not presentable under the rules of knowledge. Every reality entails this exigency insofar as it entails possible unknown senses. Auschwitz is the most real of realities in this respect. Its name marks the confines wherein historical knowledge sees its competence impugned. It does not follow from that that one falls into non-sense. (Ibid., pp. 57–8)

Lyotard thus advocates a responsibility to the differend and the (im)possibility of its phrasing through an attention to 'that which is not presentable under the rules of knowledge', rather than an obscuration or 'forgetting' of the differend (ibid., p. 142) through the reinforcement or continued privileging of the phrase regimen it exceeds. In the context of the debate surrounding postmodernism and its ethics, the notion of the differend implicitly refutes notions of postmodern philosophy as a relativizing aid to denial, instead emphasizing the ethicity of its refusal to fetishistically shore up the claim to truth of individual discourses (such as history, for example), attending rather to that which they exclude and to the mechanisms of revisionism within this context.

Empathic Unsettlement

Dominick LaCapra introduces the term 'empathic unsettlement' as a means of describing one valuable mode of response to traumatic historical events, primarily in the context of historiography, but also carrying significance beyond this. LaCapra writes:

> I think historiography involves an element of objectification, and objectification may perhaps be related to the phenomenon of numbing in trauma itself. As a counterforce to numbing, empathy may be understood in terms of attending to, even trying, in limited ways, to recapture the possibly split-off, affective dimension of the experience of others. (2001, pp. 39–40)

LaCapra thus raises the possibility that an 'objective' response to historical trauma risks the reproduction of a numbed incapacity to 'work through' the event, positing an all-too-easy closure rather than an attentiveness to and coming-to-terms with the 'unsettlement' the event poses. In his reading, empathic unsettlement entails 'a kind of virtual experience through which one puts oneself in the other's position while recognizing the difference of that position and hence not taking the other's place' and constitutes 'a desirable affective dimension of inquiry which complements and supplements empirical research and analysis' (ibid., p. 78). Such a validation is qualified by the assertion that empathy 'should not be conflated with unchecked identification, vicarious experience, and surrogate victimage' (ibid., p. 40), thereby maintaining a recognition of the other's alterity. The notion of empathic unsettlement has been applied to Holocaust poetry by Susan Gubar (2003); see under *identification*. LaCapra's suggestion that an objective or non-empathic historiography bears parallels to the phenomenon of psychic numbing illustrates his interest in applying psychoanalytic concepts not merely to the subject of historical representation but also to its process; see under *Historikerstreit* for a further example of this.

Facing

See Alterity

Foreshadowing

See Backshadowing

Grey Zone

The 'grey zone' is Primo Levi's phrase for the morally ambiguous region between the clear identities of victims and perpetrators, incorporating prisoners who gained privilege (and thus a better chance of survival) by collaborating with the oppressors' regime, with specific examples being those who took on the role of functionaries in the camps, *Kapos*, members of the *Sonderkommando* (the group of prisoners forced to assist with the killing process itself and the subsequent 'processing' of the bodies), and members of the Jewish Councils in the ghettos, who administered Nazi orders and demands for individuals for deportation. In Levi's essay 'The Grey Zone' in *The Drowned and the Saved*, he examines some of the key instances and motivations of such collaboration (the latter including 'terror, ideological seduction, servile imitation of the victor, myopic desire for any power whatsoever, . . . cowardice, and finally lucid calculation aimed at eluding the imposed orders and order' (1989, p. 28).

Levi's exploration of 'the grey zone' arguably lies in conflict with his strongly felt need to distinguish victims and perpetrators and his moral revulsion at their confusion in discourse about the Holocaust:

> I do not know, and it does not much interest me to know, whether in my depths there lurks a murderer, but I do know that I was a guiltless victim and I was not a murderer. I know that the murderers existed, not only in Germany, and still exist, retired or on active duty, and that to confuse them with their victims is a moral disease or an aesthetic affectation or a sinister sign of complicity; above all, it is precious service rendered (intentionally or not) to the negators of truth. (Ibid., pp. 32–3)

Nevertheless, Levi's point is precisely that the existence of a collaborating victim in 'the grey zone' does not render that person a perpetrator, given the context of the collaboration, in which 'the room for choices (especially moral choices) was reduced to zero' (ibid., p. 33). He thus advocates a suspension of moral judgement in these cases, suggesting that not even those who experienced the camps are in a position to pass judgement on such individuals as the *Sonderkommando* member Filip Müller and the Lodz 'ghetto elder' Chaim Rumkowski. Indeed, Levi's essay on the topic ultimately becomes a site of self-reflection concerning human frailty (ibid., pp. 50–1), implicitly indicating the ethical importance of a recognition of potential complicity, as such critics as Sanders (2002) (in the context of South Africa) and Mandel (2006) (in the context of the Holocaust) have suggested. A further perspective on the reconsideration necessitated by the grey zone is offered by Agamben, who describes this phenomenon as one in which 'good and evil and, along with them, all the metals of traditional ethics reach their point of fusion' (1999, p. 21), requiring philosophy's negotiation of this new ethical territory.

Historikerstreit

The *Historikerstreit* (Historians' Debate) was a 1986 conflict in German historiography which occurred among such figures as Jürgen Habermas, Ernst Nolte, Andreas Hillgruber, Joachim Fest, Eberhard Jäckel, and others, focused on the legitimacy of interpretative approaches to the Holocaust and the Second World War which sought to recontextualize or normalize Nazism's crimes. Hillgruber's book *Zweierlei Untergang* (*Two Kinds of Ruin*) had juxtaposed a strongly identificatory analysis of the collapse of the Eastern Front and the suffering and heroism of the *Wehrmacht* with a brief essay on the Holocaust, suggesting, some commentators felt, a moral equivalence between the two, and indeed a privileging of the former over the latter. Nolte's work argued, as Peter Baldwin summarizes, 'for the Nazi regime to be undemonized, to be reevaluated as a period that may have been unusually . . . horrible, but not one that stood outside the course of historical development, nor one that could not be understood in the terms applicable to other eras and other political systems' (1990, p. 5). This attempt to contextualize the Holocaust included a comparison with Soviet terror, even going so far as to suggest that the Holocaust may have been an 'Asiatic deed' committed in response to the feared actions of the Soviets. These accounts of German history were strongly rejected by the philosopher Jürgen Habermas as attempts to minimize and relativize national crimes as part of 'a new nationalist and conservative search for a usable past', as Charles Maier (1997, p. 2) summarizes, precipitating heated debate among German historians regarding the legitimacy of the new narratives. The debate brought to the fore questions concerning the value, place and appropriate forms of historicization and contextualization as regards recent German history, the dangers of normalization, the place of German victimhood in the history of the Second World War period and the separability or otherwise of questions of historical interpretation from current political concerns. Maier connects the emergence of these questions in the mid-1980s to, among other things, the Bitburg affair (in which President Reagan in 1985 visited a cemetery which included members of the SS as part of a commemoration of the victims of the Second World War), linking what he terms 'Bitburg history' (which involves a blurring of the boundaries between victims and perpetrators, a difficulty surrounding questions of collective responsibility, and a tendency to imply that the horror of the Holocaust is mitigated by the prevalence of other twentieth-century horrors) to the revisionism witnessed during the debate (ibid., pp. 13–16).

The *Historikerstreit* is read in psychoanalytic terms, as a refusal to mourn or work through the cultural legacy of the Holocaust, by Dominick LaCapra (1998, p. 50), a reading of the psychological function of normalizing interpretations of the Holocaust that recalls Eric Santner's notion of *narrative fetishism* (see separate entry), as a response to traumatic disruption in which the need to work through that disruption is disavowed through the application of specific repudiatory narratives.

Holocaust (Shoah, Churban, Jewish Genocide)

'Holocaust' is one of the prevalent commonly accepted terms of reference for the persecution and mass murder of Jews, Roma and Sinti people, homosexuals, and other persecuted groups at the hands of the Nazi regime, with other terms in use including *Shoah* (meaning 'catastrophe') and *Churban*. In an etymological sense, the term 'Holocaust' (from the Greek) means 'burning of the whole', also carrying associations to 'burnt sacrifice', a point that has raised issues of the term's appropriateness for some critics, suggesting an ultimate redemptive meaning or purpose to the genocide (see, for example, Agamben, 1999, pp. 28–31). As regards the naming of the event, it has been customary for critical works on Holocaust literature to begin with both a lengthy discussion of the inadequacy of each potential term for these events and a justification of the term selected. Weissman interprets this practice less as a response to the inadequacies of language and naming than as a search for a privileged relationship to the event on the part of the critic – 'part of the contest . . . over who *really* knows the horror' (2004, p. 25). This critique is echoed by that of Mandel (2006, pp. 42–4), who argues that efforts to protest or avoid the functionalization of the term 'Holocaust' imply an attempt to shun the potential of complicity with this functionalization, when a recognition of such complicity might instead prove ethically productive. Both critics imply that the gesture is ultimately an unhelpful one, and at worst manifests a form of intellectual handwringing which masks a negotiation of a rhetorically constituted ethical posture. Perhaps as a result of such critiques and of the consolidation of the term 'Holocaust' as a signifier for the genocide in English-speaking discourse, recent years have seen a decreasing prevalence of such disquisitions on nomenclature in the openings of critical works.

Holocaust Impiety

See Holocaust Piety

Holocaust Industry

The 'Holocaust industry' is a term most strongly associated with the controversial commentator Norman Finkelstein, who posits the co-option of Holocaust history today as an ideological and commercial construct serving

Israeli political interests as well as the financial interests of American Jewish organizations which, Finkelstein claims, primarily benefit from reparations claims against both Germany and the Swiss banks. The Holocaust industry, Finkelstein contends, is 'built on a fraudulent misappropriation of history for ideological purposes' (2003, p. 61). While Finkelstein's work has been controversial, less polemical recognition of Holocaust memory's connections to commercial and ideological concerns is widespread, particularly in analyses of postmodern Holocaust literature and art which is itself imbued with a recognition of its own commercial embeddedness (see, for example, Kleeblatt, 2001; Komor and Rohr, 2010; Rothberg, 2000, Part III). Aside from literature, art and popular film, however, considerations of issues of appropriation and exploitation must also extend to our practice as academics whose roles depend at least in part upon the appropriation and manipulation of the literary and cultural material issuing from the Holocaust, issues which perhaps require further negotiation in the ongoing consideration of the Holocaust's vulnerability to co-options of various kinds.

Holocaust Piety

'Holocaust piety' is a term coined by the philosopher Gillian Rose (1996) to refer to approaches to the Holocaust which position these events as ineffable, beyond our understanding. Key examples include Elie Wiesel's comparison of Holocaust fiction to 'blasphemy' (1977, p. 7) and Claude Lanzmann's view of the *obscenity of understanding* (see separate entry). Rose's critique of Holocaust piety positions it as a too-easy mystification of a phenomenon which, if confronted, would necessitate too the confrontation of our own capacities for fascist violence (including the violence of representation, which Rose discusses at length). As she states:

> To argue for silence, prayer, the banishment equally of poetry and knowledge, in short, the witness of 'ineffability', that is, non-representability, is *to mystify something we dare not understand*, because we fear that it may be all too understandable, all too continuous with what we are – human, all too human. (Rose, 1996, p. 43)

In her examination of less evasive forms of response to fascist violence, Rose discusses a potential mode of representation which might encourage a problematic form of identification with the perpetrator (and subsequent self-examination) via a 'Nazi *bildungsfilm*' (ibid., p. 50) which might elicit an identificatory crisis in the viewer, a possibility developed in Matthew Boswell's (2012) concept of 'Holocaust impiety', which pertains to forms of representation radically resistant to the 'piety' Rose highlights. 'Holocaust impiety' encompasses a range of strategies such as representational excess, irreverence, dark humour and the assumption or invitation of problematic modes of identification, and is identified in Boswell's study with a diversity of media, including poetry, popular music and film. Its impact, Boswell argues, is to compel a frequently uncomfortable examination of readers'/listeners'/viewers' unacknowledged personal and cultural investments in and continuities with fascism and related structures of thought.

Identification

Identification, the process through which one assumes a personal connection to the experiences of another, is generally considered problematic in the context of the Holocaust, in which the dominant modes of ethical enquiry centre around *alterity* (see separate entry) and in which the events' extremity appears to deny the possibility of their comprehension and assimilation by those who were not involved (see Eaglestone, 2004, pp. 24, 28).

Despite these concerns about identification, however, a number of critics have sought to validate the concept, primarily by contesting generalizations regarding what 'identification' is, breaking the term down into more and less ethically sensitive modes of relation. For example, following Kaja Silverman, Marianne Hirsch advocates a distinction between 'idiopathic' and 'heteropathic' forms of identification, the first of which interiorizes the experiences of the other, while the latter 'does not appropriate or interiorize the other within the self but . . . goes out of one's self and out of one's own cultural norms in order to align oneself, through displacement, with another' (Hirsch, 2012, pp. 85–6). Hirsch considers *postmemory* (see separate entry) to present just such a heteropathic means of identifying with the other's experience, in which a recognition of the irreconcilable distance between the experience of self and other is maintained, even as forms of imaginative investment seek connection. This form of distinction between an appropriative and an ethically engaged form of identification is likewise found in Susan David Bernstein's delineation of 'promiscuous identification', which '[crosses] borders in [the] process of reading without . . . heeding distinctions between the "I" that reads and the autobiographical "I" that is consumed in the act of reading', and 'dissonant identification', which term 'chart[s] the contingencies and liabilities of an engaged reading' (2003, p. 146). Acknowledging that 'Reading through identification is a process that undergirds our textual engagements' (ibid.), Bernstein thus proposes a careful evaluation of individual instances of this phenomenon rather than a wholesale rejection of the process.

A reconsideration of identification is also notably sought by Susan Gubar, who in her study of Holocaust poetry draws on Dominick LaCapra's notion of 'empathic unsettlement' – a form of identification through which one puts oneself in the place of the other while recognizing the difference between these subject positions – in order to explore the modes of relation and investment poetic writing permits (2003, p. 243). Discussing Anne Michaels' lyrical novel *Fugitive Pieces* ([1996] 1997), for example, Gubar writes:

> [I]f, as it is impossible not to suspect, the fugitive pieces of a subjectivity based on empathic identification can be experienced only fleetingly; . . . then the sounds of intimate voices that stop and start in fragmentary bits and parts may be best suited for such an undertaking. The discontinuities and stutters of repetition, the cutting of connectives found in ordinary prose, the blank spaces between stanza-like chapters, . . . the clustering of rhythmic image patterns, the elaboration on and analysis of extended metaphors: all . . . testify to an Otherness that can neither be fully incorporated nor externalized, neither owned nor disowned – only haltingly, sporadically adopted. (Ibid., pp. 256–7)

In this way, Gubar suggests that ethical forms of identification may be facilitated by particular literary forms (in this case, poetry, or lyrical rather than realist fiction), indicating both the multifaceted nature of contemporary critical debate regarding identification, and, arguably, a critical desire to recuperate what is perhaps intuitively felt to be a mode of ethical relation invited by literature from a position of marginalization within a discipline governed by the paradigms of postmodern ethics.

See also under *empathic unsettlement*.

Kitsch

As Saul Friedlander writes, 'Kitsch is adapted to the tastes of the majority, a faithful expression of a common sensibility, of the harmony dear to the petit bourgeois, who see in it a respect for beauty and for the order of things – for the established order and for things as they are' (1984, pp. 25–6). For Friedlander, the intersection of the nostalgic, sentimental, conservative mode of kitsch with themes of death provides the frisson which characterizes both what he identifies as a disturbing 'new discourse' on Nazism (which embodies anew, from the end of the 1960s to more recently, a troubling fantasmatic investment in fascism and its image) and, he suggests, Nazism itself (ibid., p. 26). The 'kitsch of death' juxtaposes the incompatible elements of 'an appeal to harmony, to emotional communion at its simplest and most immediate level' and 'solitude and terror', neutralizing violence through its transformation into 'some sentimental idyll' (ibid., p. 27), and is able to exert its power due to the ubiquitous submergence of culture in kitsch emotion, which Friedlander describes as 'a certain kind of simplified, degraded, insipid, but all the more insinuating romanticism' (ibid., p. 39). Within this mode of analysis, Nazism is figured as an essentially nostalgic mode fixated on the creation of a future society in the image of its romanticized figuration of the past, with the kitschification of death one tool in this collapsing of temporality (ibid., p. 40). Friedlander's work thus invites vigilance regarding the resurgence of kitsch in Holocaust discourse (particularly writing dealing with the representation of fascism) given its potential for a slippage into the reinvocation of a fascist poetics and the corresponding impact of this on the reader, who is, he implies, thereby rendered susceptible to ethically dangerous identificatory and emotional investments.

The notion of kitsch in Holocaust discourse is also relevant in terms of the Holocaust's co-option by commercialized, often sentimentalized, mass-market cultural products such as the Hollywood blockbuster film – see under *Americanization of the Holocaust* and *Holocaust industry* for further discussion of this. More recently, critics such as Susanne Rohr (in her work on 'genocide pop') have traced an emerging phenomenon in Holocaust representation by which self-consciously kitsch or transgressive Holocaust artworks seek to engage self-reflexively with 'the processes of mediatization and Americanization of the historical event' (2010, p. 167), implying that the interrogation of the Holocaust's kitschification is an increasing preoccupation of representations themselves, rather than remaining merely an object of concern for the vigilant literary critic.

Melancholia

See Mourning and Melancholia

Memory

Cosmopolitan

Levy and Sznaider's concept of 'cosmopolitan memory' is intended to express the way in which collective memory in an era of globalization assumes a transnational form in which local concerns are located in dialogue with global issues. Within this context, they view the Holocaust as occupying a particularly significant role, suggesting that memories of these events have become detached from their specific local contexts – in part due to the Holocaust's

Americanization, which led to its becoming 'de-territorialized' (Levy and Sznaider, 2006, p. 153) – to assume the status of universal reference points. Holocaust memory is thus 'a memory that harbors the possibility of transcending ethnic and national boundaries', facilitating 'the formation of transnational memory cultures, which in turn have the potential to become the cultural foundation for global human-rights politics' (ibid., p. 4). In arguing for the ethical potential of a globalized and universalized Holocaust memory (with one specific example being the degree to which this informed international intervention in Kosovo), Levy and Sznaider reject a prevailing critical-theoretical exclusion of universalization as an acceptable stance towards Holocaust memory, implicitly advocating an instrumental and pragmatic approach to memory in which an attention to events in their specificity and complexity is eschewed in favour of a focus on the ethical uses of a universalized (and hence inevitably simplified and decontextualized) mode of memory. One reading of this would be as a prioritization of an ethics oriented towards the future over one oriented towards the past event, though it might also be argued that a universalizing and instrumentalizing approach to past suffering itself forms and informs a present- and future-oriented ethics in troubling ways. See Rothberg's *multidirectional memory* and Silverman's *palimpsestic memory* (separate entries, below) for more nuanced considerations of the interaction of Holocaust memory with the remembrance of and response to other cultural contexts and conflicts.

Deep

The distinction between 'deep memory' and 'common memory' (*mémoire profonde* and *mémoire ordinaire*) was made by Charlotte Delbo and elaborated by Lawrence Langer in *Holocaust Testimonies: The Ruins of Memory* (1991). In Langer's elaboration, 'Deep memory tries to recall the Auschwitz self as it was then; common memory has a dual function: it restores the self to normal pre- and postcamp routines but also offers detached portraits, from the vantage point of today, of what it must have been like then. Deep memory thus suspects *and* depends on common memory, knowing what common memory cannot know but tries nonetheless to express' (1991, p. 6). Thus while common memory pursues and articulates coherence, conventionality and narrative expressibility, deep memory remains other to such rehabilitation, returning to relativize and disrupt attempts to inscribe it within normative frameworks. Within the vocabulary of trauma theory, 'deep memory' may be closely aligned with the unassimilable traumatic memory which can be integrated into narrative order only at the risk of transforming the experience to obscure its traumatic nature.

Langer's approach to the irreconcilability of deep and common memory is, interestingly, a non-therapeutic one; it does not place emphasis on the necessity of reconciliation with the past; the sense that emerges, rather, is of the traumatized subject as inevitably divided in the aftermath of the event.

Forgetful

'Forgetful memory' is a concept developed by Michael Bernard-Donals as a means of articulating the nature of forgetfulness as 'not the absence of but rather an integral element of memory' and exploring the degree to which 'all memory is shot through with moments of forgetfulness, moments that are constitutive of what we can remember as history or remember at all' (2010, p. 119). In this conception, forgetful memory points to the grounding of post-traumatic speech in the 'empty kernel' (ibid., p. 120) residing at the heart of memory, with the involuntary 'flash' of the event in the present signifying not its presence in memory but its status as a foundational absence that elicits a compulsion towards representation.

Multidirectional

Michael Rothberg introduced the term 'multidirectional memory' in his 2009 study of that name to advocate the replacement of what he terms a 'zero-sum' model of memory (in which remembrance of one history or context must always be at the cost of obscuring another) with an understanding of the necessary intersections between different contexts and histories in memory and memorial discourse. Key examples as explored by Rothberg include the complex and interweaving relationship between memories of the Holocaust and those of colonialism and its legacies, including the Algerian war, with Holocaust memory both finding articulation through the response to these events and aiding their recognition and expression, as well as permitting an ethically and politically productive investigation of the relationship between the events on the level of cultural psychology (e.g. in Hannah Arendt and Aimé Césaire's explorations of the Holocaust as a revisiting of the mechanisms and corruptions of colonialism upon Europe itself). Within Rothberg's notion of multidirectionality, Holocaust memory is not subject to universalization but assumes its particularity in a mutually illuminating dialogue with other memorial contexts; the concept thus modifies the unidirectionality of such models as Daniel Levy and Natan Sznaider's consideration of *cosmopolitan memory* (see separate entry). For a more detailed discussion of Rothberg's work, see Stef Craps' chapter in this volume, as well as the brief outline in the 'New Directions' section of this volume.

Palimpsestic

This term is Max Silverman's and is used to describe the nature of memory as a formation in which different times, places and historical contexts are intricately connected, with the image of the palimpsest highlighting 'the superimposition and productive interaction of different inscriptions and the spatialization of time central to the work of memory' (2013, p. 4). It is elaborated in Silverman's 2013 study of that name with reference to postwar French literature and film dealing with the Holocaust, colonialism and the Algerian War. Bearing parallels to Michael Rothberg's concept of *multidirectional memory* in its concern with the interconnection of different memorial contexts, the notion as Silverman theorizes it 'would be a dynamic and open space composed of interconnecting traces of different voices, sites and times, and it would hold out the prospect of new solidarities across the lines of race and nation' (ibid., p. 8). Like Rothberg and other theorists of 'connective memory' such as Hirsch (2012), Silverman (2013) frames his account of memory in ethically and politically optimistic terms, suggesting, for example, that attention to palimpsestic memory might enable it to serve as a model for 'imagining new democratic solidarities' (p. 179).

Postmemory: See *Postmemory* (separate entry)

Prosthetic

'Prosthetic memory' is Alison Landsberg's (2004) term for the form of 'memory' of events not experienced first-hand that is facilitated or imparted by mass cultural media such as popular films and museum spaces. Prosthetic memory emerges experientially (Landsberg maintaining the reality of the experience of history made available through these forms) and contains a bodily dimension, in terms of the viewer's visceral responses to a medium such as film. Landsberg does not consider prosthetic memory to be *inherently* ethical or liberatory, but argues for its ethical potential in facilitating empathy across cultural and temporal differences, thereby at its best compelling the viewer towards ethical and politically progressive thought and action. Commodified experience is therefore considered as a site of potentially ethical orientation towards the past, despite its embeddedness in structures of (particularly in the case of the blockbuster film) capitalist exploitation. The notion of prosthetic memory, together with other theoretical approaches which divorce memory from first-hand experience, has been critiqued on the grounds that it collapses significant experiential differences in the approach to traumatic history; for more details on this critique, see the 'New Directions' section of this volume.

Traumatic: see *Trauma* (separate entry)

Mourning and Melancholia

'Mourning' and 'melancholia' are Freud's terms to describe two different modes of response to loss. While, in Freud's analysis (particularly in the case of melancholia), the loss may take the form not only of bereavement but alternatively the loss of an abstraction, ideal or relationship, in the context of Holocaust representation the loss is most obviously the loss of life and of European Jewish culture that constitute these events, though this vocabulary has also been applied, in a German context, to the loss of Hitler (and the narcissistic investment therein), a loss that could not be mourned by the German populace following the German defeat and the revelation of the extent of Nazi crimes, as explored by Alexander and Margarete Mitscherlich in their study *The Inability to Mourn* (1975). To explicate the distinction between the two, mourning is the painful but non-pathological response to loss in which libidinal investment is gradually withdrawn from the lost object and the individual ultimately comes to an acceptance of the loss, whereas melancholia entails a pathological refusal of the loss via what Freud terms 'an *identification* of the ego with the abandoned object' (1957, p. 249), in which 'love for the object – a love which cannot be given up though the object itself is given up – takes refuge in narcissistic identification' (ibid., p. 251).

Parallels might be drawn between mourning and the process of working through trauma, as a result of which 'one is able to distinguish between past and present and to recall in memory that something happened to one (or one's people) back then while realizing that one is living here and now' (LaCapra, 2001, p. 22), rather than remaining within the immediate possession of the traumatic event; indeed, in his examination of the *Historikerstreit* (see separate entry), LaCapra considers mourning as a mode of working through, and melancholia as a means of acting out, in which the past 'is incorporated rather than introjected' and 'returns as the repressed', being relived in the present moment rather than being recognized as temporally distinct (LaCapra, 1998, p. 45). Given this alignment, LaCapra's contestation of the binary opposition between acting out and working through (he writes, for example, that in the context of trauma, 'acting-out may well be a necessary condition of working-through', and describes the two as 'intimately linked but analytically distinguishable processes' (2001, pp. 70, 71)) carries interesting implications for a consideration of the relationship between mourning and melancholia.

Narrative Fetishism

'Narrative fetishism' is Eric Santner's term to describe, in Santner's words, 'the construction and deployment of a narrative consciously or unconsciously designed to expunge the traces of the trauma or loss that called that narrative into being in the first place' (1992, p. 144). In other words, narrative fetishism is a means by which the need to work through a traumatic past is evaded through the construction of a narrative which denies or evades that need. This is achieved by 'simulating a condition of intactness, typically by situating the site and origin of loss elsewhere' (ibid., p. 144), with one example being the focus of some accounts produced during the German *Historikerstreit* (historians' debate) of the 1980s upon the Soviet threat, depicting the Holocaust as a response to or anticipation of the violence threatened by Stalin. By such manoeuvres, the need to work through the emergence of genocidal fascism in Germany was sidestepped. As suggested in the above summary, narrative fetishism may be contrasted with working through as a means of response to trauma, with Santner clarifying the distinction as follows: the crucial difference between narrative fetishism and working through 'has to do with the willingness or capacity to include the traumatic event in one's efforts to reformulate and reconstitute identity' (ibid., p. 152).

While this example is one drawn from historiography, narrative fetishism can be seen to relate to literary representation as well, and might be applied, for example, to narratives which impose a falsely redemptive closure upon events, implicitly denying the reality that losses remain to be mourned, as is frequently evident in the Hollywood feature film; and narratives which permit unlikely or even impossible 'escapes' from horror (as discussed in Adams, 2011, pp. 146, 155). Rothberg (2000, p. 139) has even considered realism itself as a literary mode susceptible to such fetishism, in that realism, he suggests, seeks to obscure the absence of the real (and in particular the real of trauma): 'Like the fetishist, the realist attempts to use a piece of reality to convert a hole in the real into a real whole.'

Nonwitness

'Nonwitness' is Gary Weissman's term for all individuals who did not experience the Holocaust first-hand. Weissman introduces the term to contest the extension of a discourse of witnessing, victimhood and survival to those other than victims and survivors themselves, through paradigms of postmemory, vicarious witnessing and second-generation survivorhood. He writes: 'the term *nonwitness* stresses that we who were not there did not witness the Holocaust, and that the experience of listening to, reading, or viewing witness testimony is substantially unlike the experience of victimization' (Weissman, 2004, p. 20), and advocates a turning of critical attention to the ways in which Holocaust discourse is shaped by the desires and investments of nonwitnesses. These desires and investments, Weissman suggests, include a wish to experience the Holocaust and to negotiate a privileged position in relation to these events (ibid., pp. 26–7).

Obscenity of Understanding

Claude Lanzmann coined the phrase 'the obscenity of understanding' to articulate his refusal to attempt to integrate the Holocaust into available structures of comprehension, a refusal he explicates as follows:

> I remember when I was working on *Shoah* at the start, I read so many books by reputed academics, for instance George Mosse's book on the formation of the German spirit. It's a very good book. But after you have read it you have to say, 'Well, is it because of all these conditions that the children have been gassed?' This is what I called the obscenity of the project of understanding. (1995, pp. 206–7)

Lanzmann's argument is that an irreconcilable gulf separates any possible delineation of the 'causes' of Nazism (at the level of either mass or individual behaviour) from the effects that ensued, rendering any attempt at 'understanding' an obscene rehabilitation of what in fact defies rationalization. This position is countered by those of such figures as the historian Christopher Browning, who writes, for example, that:

> Explaining is not excusing; understanding is not forgiving. The notion that one must simply reject the acts of the perpetrators and not try to understand them would make impossible not only my history but any perpetrator history that sought to go beyond one-dimensional caricature. (1992, p. 36)

Browning's argument highlights the very real threat of removing the perpetrator from the sphere of human interpretation and judgement if the 'obscenity' of understanding Nazi actions is asserted, recalling Yehuda Bauer's argument of attempts to construe the Holocaust as inexplicable that 'If this were true, then the criminals would become tragic victims of forces beyond human control' (2001, p. 38), and ultimately emphasizing the high ethical and representational stakes of this debate.

Postmemory

'Postmemory' is a concept developed by Marianne Hirsch to refer to the relationship of members of later generations to the traumatic experience of family
members. Of children of Holocaust survivors, Hirsch writes:

> Children of survivors live at a further temporal and spatial remove from that
> decimated world. The distance separating them from the locus of origin is
> the radical break of unknowable and incomprehensible persecution; for those
> born after, it is a break impossible to bridge. Still, the power of mourning and
> memory, and the depth of the rift dividing their parents' lives, impart to
> them something that is akin to memory. (1996, p. 662)

Postmemory thus characterizes the mode of engagement of descendants of survivors with their family members' pasts, in the sense of both their pre-war lives
('that decimated world') and the traumatic experiences which culminated in
their exile from those lives. This mode of engagement draws on material traces
(e.g. photographs) and oral narratives of the past, integrating these into a coherent construction of that past by way of 'imaginative investment and creation':
'postmemory seeks connection. It creates where it cannot recover. It imagines
where it cannot recall' (ibid., pp. 662, 664). Hirsch has suggested that photographs in particular present a powerful medium of postmemory, offering 'a
visual content for our ambivalent longings' (ibid., p. 684), an argument that
perhaps provides an explanation for the significance of photographs, whether
reproduced in the text or merely described, in postmemorial texts such as W. G.
Sebald's *Austerlitz* (2002), Georges Perec's *W, or the Memory of Childhood* ([1988]
1996) and Jonathan Safran Foer's *Everything Is Illuminated* (2002).

For a discussion of the concept of postmemory in relation to more recent
developments in its usage and reach, in addition to critical concerns about the
use of 'memory' as a figure for the relationship to the Holocaust on the part of
non-witnesses, see the 'New Directions' section of this volume.

See also under *Second generation*.

Pre-empting the Holocaust

'Pre-empting the Holocaust' is a problematic critical move identified by
Lawrence Langer in his 1998 work of that name; Langer glosses the concept
thus:

> When I speak of preempting the Holocaust, I mean using – and perhaps
> abusing – its grim details to fortify a prior commitment to an ideal of moral

reality, community responsibility, or religious belief that leaves us with space to retain faith in their pristine value in a post-Holocaust world. (1998, p. 1)

In other words, to pre-empt the Holocaust is to seek and find (because sought) in it confirmation of existing ideologies or frameworks of meaning that the event in fact, in Langer's reading, radically calls into question in its status as 'a reality that escapes the bounds of any philosophy or system of belief that we have cherished since our beginnings' (ibid., pp. 2–3). Examples provided by Langer include Tzvetan Todorov's attempts to recuperate the experience of the concentration camps into a familiar moral framework (in which meaningful distinctions between morality and immorality can yet organize the experiences and behaviours of camp inmates), and Judy Chicago's feminism-informed approach to the events in her *Holocaust Project*, of which Langer states that Chicago's 'feminist beliefs color her conclusions from the beginning' (ibid., p. 13). Langer's approach to the Holocaust is thus, as he himself suggests, 'literalist' rather than 'exemplarist' (the latter denoting the use of the Holocaust as an illuminating example conveying a moral lesson), arguing that 'There is nothing to be learned from a baby torn in two or a woman buried alive' (ibid., p. 10), though one might query whether it is possible to approach any historical event in a manner entirely devoid of prior ideological or conceptual commitments, redemptive or radically otherwise. Nevertheless, Langer's coinage of the term neatly crystallizes critical unease surrounding, for example, Holocaust representations carrying an overtly political stance (as some commentators found of Peter Weiss's play *The Investigation* ([1966] 2000)) or depictions that co-opt the Holocaust into an illustration of (for example) the cooperative and supportive culture of women in contrast to that of men (see, for example, Ringelheim, 1984).

Second Generation

The phrase 'second generation' refers primarily to the children of those who directly experienced the Holocaust. While most often used to refer to the children of survivors, it has also been used to refer to the children of perpetrators, as in Erin McGlothlin's 2006 study of second-generation literature and the edited volume of first-person accounts presented by Berger and Berger (2001). McGlothlin notes that in both cases, '[T]he trauma of the second generation is essentially divorced from the Holocaust experience that engendered it. The signifier remains, but it is unable to locate its referent, resulting in a truncated relationship between experience and affect', adding that 'For the children of survivors, this experience is one of unintegrated trauma and rupture in familial continuity; for the children of perpetrators it is the family's unintegratable history of violation and brutality' (2006, p. 10). It should be noted, however, that in some instances the term 'second generation' has been given a wider application than this, being used to refer to the entire generation of Jews or Germans born after the war, who thus 'inherit' the memory or repression of the Holocaust in a much looser cultural sense. Works like David Grossman's novel *See Under: Love* (1990), for example, have been deemed 'second-generation' texts despite not being written by children of survivors, but rather because of the broader generational identity of their authors and their engagements with issues of postmemory. Questions have been raised about the blurring of experiential boundaries this broadening of the term's application suggests, as discussed further in this volume's 'New Directions' section.

The notion of the second generation has also been qualified in the sense that this overarching concept at times risks homogenizing the experiences of children of survivors across a range of different cultural and familial contexts. As Efraim Sicher states, 'The second-generation perspective seems to have grown to international proportions, except that in each country the second generation has been shaped by the vicissitudes and variations of official discourse on the Holocaust and the shaping of Jewish identity' (2005, p. 171). Sicher's comments offer a useful reminder of the degree to which such categories as the second generation, while expedient in drawing connections between a range of related experiences, nevertheless risk a generalizing approach to the complexities of post-Holocaust memory if applied without sufficient cognizance of the specificities characterizing each individual relationship to these events (on this point, see also Berger, 1997, p. 13).

Beyond the second generation, attention has turned in recent years to the literary work of authors in a third-generational relationship to the Holocaust (i.e. grandchildren of survivors), though critics such as Philippe Codde (2010) have been careful to point out the ways in which this relationship may differ from that of the second generation – Codde notes, for example, that while notions of transmission may be applicable in discussion of the second generation, the third generation sees a more complex mode of relation to these experiences, necessitating different conceptual structures and angles of approach.

See also under *Postmemory*.

Sideshadowing

See Backshadowing

Sublime

The 'sublime' refers to an experience of that which is beyond comprehension, inducing terror and awe through its eclipsing of the formal and ordering strategies of perception and apprehension; for Kant, 'the sublime cannot be contained in any sensible form, but concerns only ideas of reason, which, though no presentation adequate to them is possible, are provoked and called to mind precisely by this inadequacy' (2000, §23); as LaCapra summarizes, the concept of the sublime 'is related to excess or, conversely, lacuna or lack – that which is disconcertingly, perhaps ecstatically other and aporetically beyond (or beneath) any ability to name or to know' (2003, pp. 263–4). The question of the appropriateness of the concept of the sublime to discussions of trauma and the Holocaust is a vexed one. On one level, the sublime offers a means of figuring the degree to which the traumatic historical event exceeds comprehension and resists assimilation to existing mental structures. For Michael Bernard-Donals and Richard Glejzer (2003), the sublime in this way provides an appropriate figure for the impossibility of an ordered, complete and assimilable knowledge of the Holocaust, while for Andrew Slade, the aesthetics of the sublime present a potentially constructive response to trauma, attempting 'to find a way to present the events of terror and death that preserves their terror without reproducing it' (2004, p. 176). Nevertheless, LaCapra himself has highlighted some of the potentially problematic aspects of such a figuration (whether theoretical or artistic), noting the presence of a dimension of the immanent sublime in Nazism itself (2003, p. 264), the degree to which the transfiguration of trauma into the sublime may permit its political appropriation (ibid., p. 265), and the importance of attending to the possibilities of action at a pragmatic level, considerations of agency that may be eclipsed through a sole focus on questions of lacuna, aporia and excess. He writes:

> Without denying one's own implication in the ambivalent 'logic' of the sublime and even recognizing its almost compulsive appeal, one may still insist on the need to develop thought and practice in the transitional civic 'space' or modality that at times seems reduced to a vanishing point in an emphasis on either an immanent or a radically transcendent sublimity. (Ibid, pp. 268–9; see also LaCapra, 2001, p. 93)

Further questions surrounding the adequacy of a discourse of the sublime are noted by Bernard-Donals and Glejzer, who, while ultimately arguing for the validity of such a discourse in a pedagogical context, acknowledge the question of 'whether in speaking of the sublime in relation to the Shoah we are not finding a way to name it, but negatively' (2003, p. 251).

The above outline relates primarily to the function of a discourse of the sublime in relation to questions of trauma; in the context of perpetrators and their narrative representation, Elana Gomel (2003) has also developed the notion of the 'violent sublime' to describe the way in which the self-narratives of violent subjects are shattered and reconfigured by experience outside the capacities of everyday representation, as indicated by a pervasive presence of ellipsis in these self-narratives (see pp. xvi, xxix).

Swerve

The 'swerve' is Robert Eaglestone's vocabulary for the description of a phenomenon by which texts which at first promise to provide insight into the behaviour
and motivations of Holocaust perpetrators ultimately diverge from this endeavour: 'perpetrator fiction, constantly and seemingly unconsciously, appears to
avoid precisely an engagement with the "why" [of perpetration]' (2013, p. 15).
Eaglestone tentatively links such a swerve to the location of evil in precisely the
unspectacular banalities of the genocidal culture and its context, implying that
the nature of evil precludes its functioning as a kind of revelatory content of
the sort readers may desire perpetrator fictions to provide, and also hinting (in
a linking of these everyday banalities to the considerable length and detail of
Littell's *The Kindly Ones*) that evocations of evil in literature might be as much
formal as thematic or characterological.

Testimony

Testimony is the process of bearing witness to an event or situation experienced
at first-hand. In the context of the Holocaust, testimony takes the form of representations produced during the event (such as diaries, letters and drawings) as
well as memoirs and oral accounts given later.

A particularly dominant theory of testimony in recent decades has been
that of Shoshana Felman and Dori Laub, who position it as a 'performative
speech act' that 'addresses what in history is *action* that exceeds any sub-
stantialized significance, and what in happenings is *impact* that dynamically explodes any conceptual reifications and any constative delimitations'
(Felman, 1992, p. 5). In other words, not only does the significance of testimony as an action in which subjectivity is reclaimed and the individual
comes into being as a witness exceed quantification solely in terms of its content; but testimony offers a form in which the event's impact may be made
manifest and registered in ways which otherwise elude both the witness's
and the listener's knowledge and conceptual understanding. The reading of
testimony as a performative act – as a kind of knowledge and subjectivity
that comes into being only in its articulation – is very much central to this
definition, as Felman states: 'In the testimony, language is in process and in
trial, it does not possess itself as a conclusion, as the constatation of a verdict
or the self-transparency of knowledge' (ibid., p. 5). For Felman and Laub, the
witness's inability to grasp the event prior to testifying to it is linked to its
traumatic character, in which the event, as trauma, cannot be registered as
it takes place and thus only belatedly comes into consciousness through its
narration. As Laub summarizes:

> The emergence of the narrative which is being listened to . . . is, therefore, the process and the place wherein the cognizance, the 'knowing' of the event is given birth to. . . . The testimony to the trauma thus includes its hearer, who is, so to speak, the blank screen on which the event comes to be inscribed for the first time. (1992b, p. 57)

Laub's account thus considers the testimonial situation as the privileged (and arguably, the sole) site of working through, via which the witness can regain not only a sense of knowledge of and mastery over the traumatic event, but also a sense of autonomous subjectivity (for more on this idea, and on the notion of the Holocaust as an event without a witness, see also under *witness*).

Another influential, and not unrelated, approach to testimony comes in the work of Giorgio Agamben, who identifies a lacuna at the heart of testimony – namely, that as Levi suggests, the 'true witness' is the drowned or *Muselmann* who has not survived to tell their story (1999, p. 33). Agamben accordingly considers testimony as a bearing witness not to experience but to the impossibility of bearing witness. Linking the content of witnessing to that which is outside language, Agamben figures testimony as a language which does not signify but gives way to a non-signifyingness that indicates its own testimonial impossibility:

> The trace of that to which no one has borne witness, which language believes itself to transcribe, is not the speech of language. The speech of language is born where language is no longer in the beginning, where language falls away from it simply to bear witness: 'It was not light, but was sent to bear witness to the light.' (Ibid., p. 39)

For Agamben, the language of testimony thus bears witness to the trace of that to which no one has borne witness, which he associates with the figure of the desubjectivized and silenced *Muselmann*. Agamben's reading of testimony is closely informed by poststructuralist readings of language and subjectivity, in which language is unable to invoke the real and the subject is constituted in and through language (as in the work of Emile Benveniste), resulting in what Agamben reads as a 'disjunction between the living being and the speaking being that marks its empty place' (ibid, p. 143). Speaking, he suggests, is thus 'a paradoxical act that implies both subjectification and desubjectification, in which the living individual appropriates language in a full expropriation alone, becoming a speaking being only on condition of falling into silence' (ibid, p. 129). In other words, if the assumption of subjectivity through language is at the same time a silencing or occlusion of 'living being' in its non-symbolic aspect, then the act of speech – an assertion of signifyingness and subjectivity – is also marked and informed by non-signifyingness and non-subjectivity. Translating these theorizations into a historically located register, it is in this sense, Agamben argues, that it can be said to be the *Muselmann* that testifies in testimony, by proxy, a reading he elaborates thus:

> Testimony takes place where the speechless one makes the speaking one speak and where the one who speaks bears the impossibility of speaking in his own speech, such that the silent and the speaking, the inhuman and the human enter into a zone of indistinction in which it is impossible to establish the position of the subject . . . and . . . the true witness.
>
> This can also be expressed by saying that *the subject of testimony is the one who bears witness to a desubjectification*. But this expression holds only if it is not forgotten that 'to bear witness to a desubjectification' can only mean there is no subject of testimony . . . and that every testimony is a field of forces incessantly traversed by currents of subjectification and desubjectification. (Ibid., pp. 120–1)

Thus Agamben finds a way of reconciling Levi's assertion that the true witness is the *Muselmann* with the actuality and possibility of Levi's own witnessing – though arguably at the cost of denying the status of testimony as an act of autonomy and self-articulation, and reducing the Holocaust to an exemplary instance of the vexed relationship between language, subjectivity and the real. These issues are, to a lesser extent, shared by Felman and Laub's consideration of testimony, as hinted by the prevalence in their account of the Derridean vocabulary of the performative and the preoccupation here, and in trauma studies more broadly, with the assimilability (or lack thereof) of the real (here, traumatic experience) to the symbolic.

Trauma

In this context, the term 'trauma' is used to denote the psychological impact of extreme experiences. The trauma theory of Cathy Caruth, Shoshana Felman and others – the prevalent discourse of trauma invoked in discussions of Holocaust literature – focuses specifically on the relationship between the precipitating event and available structures of representation, positing that the traumatic event is traumatic not because of any inherent qualities, but because of a discrepancy between that event and the representational structures available to the survivor (van Alphen, 1997, p. 44). Because the event cannot be integrated into the narrative structures of the self, such theory posits, it is not experienced as such and hence returns in the form of post-traumatic symptoms to haunt the survivor after the event itself has taken place. This model of trauma is summarized neatly in Cathy Caruth's statement that:

> The trauma is the confrontation with an event that, in its unexpectedness or horror, cannot be placed within the schemes of prior knowledge . . . and thus continually returns, in its exactness, at a later time. . . . In its repeated imposition as both image and amnesia, the trauma thus seems to evoke the difficult truth of a history that is constituted by the very incomprehensibility of its occurrence. (1995, p. 153)

Trauma is thus constituted as 'missed experience' that can only be recuperated through its integration into the structures of autobiographical knowledge and self-narration, as Dori Laub suggests, considering the testimonial situation as the location for the event's first registering on the part of its survivor in a 'creation of knowledge *de novo*' (1992b, p. 57). Nevertheless, such narrative and cognitive recuperation does risk the event's distortion through the elision of its excessive, traumatic character, as Caruth states:

> The trauma thus requires integration, both for the sake of testimony and for the sake of cure. But on the other hand, the transformation of the trauma into a narrative memory that allows the story to be verbalized and communicated, to be integrated into one's own, and others', knowledge of the past, may lose both the precision and the force that characterizes traumatic recall. (1995, p. 153)

Such a recognition has prompted an openness in trauma studies towards the seeking of forms of articulation which preserve a recognition of the traumatic event's incomprehensibility (something Caruth identifies in the insistence upon the *obscenity of understanding* (see separate entry) underlying the representational project of Lanzmann's *Shoah*).

Trauma theory has been critiqued from a number of different angles. Critics such as Elana Gomel, for example, contend that the discourse of trauma collapses experiential differences, suggesting that if trauma is considered in structural terms (as a relationship between experience and representational possibilities), then 'there is no way to discriminate among morally opposite [i.e. victim and perpetrator] varieties of traumatic discourse' (2003, pp. 167, 179), while Crownshaw (2010, p. 8) highlights the risk of a confusion of historical and structural trauma (on which, see more below) given the structural constitution of both trauma and receptivity to testimony in Caruth's formulation. Others, such as Ruth Leys, have relatedly criticized the way in which Caruth's work 'tends to dilute and generalize the notion of trauma: in her account the experience (or nonexperience) of trauma is characterized as something that can be shared by victims and nonvictims alike' (Leys, 2000, p. 305). Other angles of critique include that of Paul Antze and Michael Lambek, who in their introduction to the 1996 collection *Tense Past: Cultural Essays in Trauma and Memory* query the therapeutic potential of narrative with regard to traumatic events, contending that 'Merely to transfer the story from embodied symptoms to words is not necessarily either to integrate or exorcise it' (Lambek and Antze, 1996, p. xix). Nevertheless, the notion of trauma remains a powerful one within contemporary accounts of the Holocaust and its impact not only on survivors but (via the beleaguered notions of transmission, belatedness and cultural as well as individual applicability) on later generations and broader post-Holocaust cultures.

Within such recent critical and theoretical work, one important distinction made regarding the concept is that drawn by Dominick LaCapra between structural and historical trauma. While '[h]istorical trauma is specific, and not everyone is subject to it', '[e]veryone is subject to structural trauma', which involves such experiences as 'the separation from the (m)other, the passage from nature to culture, . . . the entry into language, [and] the encounter with the "real"' (2001, pp. 78, 79, 77). The collapse or blurring of boundaries between the two is ethically dangerous in that it risks obscuring the specificity of historical trauma and the important distinction between the subject positions of victim, perpetrator and bystander, and also attributing to historical events a misleadingly 'epiphanous, sublime, or sacral quality' (ibid., p. 80). This blurring is a danger LaCapra identifies in literary–theoretical work, citing the work of Blanchot, de Man and Žižek as examples, the latter of whom, LaCapra contends, equates concentration camps with castration anxieties as manifestations of the Lacanian 'real' (ibid., p. 84); and a danger, as highlighted above, identified by Crownshaw in the dominant trauma–theoretical model of Caruth, Felman and others. Specifically, Crownshaw highlights the implication of this model that our receptivity to the trauma of others 'is based not on historical experience . . . but on an ahistorical structural trauma (a lack) at the core of our identity' (2010, p. 8), though at a more general level Caruth et al.'s approach might also be read as vulnerable to a slippage between the trauma of actual historical events and the structural field of that which lies outside the symbolic order.

See also under *Testimony*.

Traumatic Realism

Michael Rothberg identifies two opposed interdisciplinary approaches to the Holocaust: a realist approach, which asserts the availability of these events to knowledge and representation, and an antirealist approach which situates the Holocaust as 'a sublime, unapproachable object beyond discourse and knowledge' (2000, p. 4). His notion of 'traumatic realism' offers a mediation of this opposition, offering a revisioning of realism which seeks to incorporate a recognition of the extreme and of the challenges this poses to conventional categories of representation. Traumatic realist texts, Rothberg contends, 'search for a form of documentation beyond direct reference and coherent narrative but do not fully abandon the possibility for some kind of reference and some kind of narrative (ibid., p. 101); such texts contain a postmodern recognition of their own limits and parameters of articulation, forming 'a realism in which the scars that mark the relationship of discourse to the real are not fetishistically denied, but exposed; a realism in which the claims of reference live on, but so does the traumatic extremity that disables realist representation as usual' (ibid., p. 106).

For further discussion of traumatic realism and of the possibility of a dialectic approach to realism and its other in the aftermath of the Holocaust, see Jenni Adams' chapter in this volume.

Uniqueness Debate

This debate centres around the question of whether the Holocaust can be described as a unique instance of genocide, that is, unparalleled by other atrocities, whether as a result of its scale or, more usually, the intentions which informed it and the manner of its execution. Proponents of the uniqueness argument include Steven T. Katz, who argues that that Holocaust was unprecedented as an instance of genocide, where genocide is defined as applying '*only* when there is an actualized intent, however successfully carried out, to physically destroy an *entire* group (as such a group is defined by the perpetrators)' (Katz, 1994, pp. 128–9). Critics of the uniqueness position include Inge Clendinnen, who contends that the accumulation of recent horrors precludes any attempt to ascribe uniqueness to any single instance of genocide, adding that 'What most disquiets about a too-shrill insistence on the uniqueness of the Holocaust is the danger that, if the Holocaust were indeed to be accepted as unique, it would risk falling out of history – the consultable record of the actions of our species, and the active interrogation of the record – altogether' (1999, pp. 14, 15). From the perspective of Holocaust historiography, Donald Bloxham likewise asserts that '"Uniqueness" is not a word that historians should be comfortable with, for their duty is to examine every historical event in its specificity.' Contending that an assertion of the uniqueness of the Holocaust devalues other instances of genocide, Bloxham argues that 'The concept of "uniqueness" should be recognized for what it originally was before it became an article of faith for some historians and many survivors: a device emerging out of politicized, ahistorical debate' (2003, p. 42).

Perhaps another question of uniqueness relates to whether or not the challenges to representation posed by the Holocaust are specific to this event, or of broader applicability. Of the oft-posited disparity between the Holocaust and conventional vocabularies of representation, James Berger asks, for example: 'Is this not a condition of all representation? Are there not always simultaneously a capacity and inadequacy of symbols to link with the physical world?' (1999, p. 62). Berger's answering comment that 'Representing an apocalypse in history is just like representation in general . . . only more so' (ibid., p. 62, ellipsis in original) implies that the events in question merely pose these challenges in a particularly urgent way, crystallizing and drawing to the fore issues inherent to representation per se, though this issue remains open to debate.

Unspeakability

'Unspeakable' is a rhetorical term used to signify the Holocaust's lack of availability to discourse, and forms one aspect of a common critical or discursive practice which seeks to situate the events as beyond the limit of what may be represented, articulated and known. It is described by Naomi Mandel as 'the rhetorical invocation of the limits of language, comprehension, representation, and thought on the one hand, and a deferential gesture toward atrocity, horror, trauma and pain on the other' (2006, p. 4). In the context of attempts to situate the Holocaust as unrepresentable, one key critical mechanism, as Mandel suggests, is that of trauma theory, which characteristically considers the event as traumatic precisely because of the inability of existing discursive structures to accommodate it (van Alphen, 1997, p. 44). Mandel herself is critical of a rhetoric of the unspeakable, viewing this as a means of evading a pragmatic ethical engagement with the event in favour of a claim to the moral high ground of 'respecting the memory of the victims, safeguarding identity, reality, or historical truth' (2006, p. 209) – a claim that is, in her reading, ultimately self-interested.

Vergangenheitsbewältigung

Vergangenheitsbewältigung is a German term which refers to the enterprise of mastering or coming-to-terms with the (Nazi) past.

Witnessing

The term 'witnessing' refers to the process of being present at, and observing, an event, such that testimony to what ensued can at a later point be given; in some uses of the term, 'witnessing' refers to this process of 'bearing witness' itself. The slippage between these usages may not be considered accidental if one subscribes to Dori Laub's consideration of the Holocaust as 'an event without a witness', with Laub contending that '*the event produced no witnesses*' not only in the sense that the Nazis attempted to leave none among the victims to testify to what had been done, but also in a variety of other respects: the failure of bystanders to assume the role of witness and speak out about the genocide as it was taking place; the impossibility of objective witnessing given the constriction of those 'inside' the event within one of the 'trapping roles' of victim or executioner; the imposition upon the victims of a 'delusional ideology' which 'excluded and eliminated the possibility of an unviolated, unencumbered, and thus sane, point of reference in the witness'; and the dehumanizing dimension to the event (1992a, pp. 80–2). In particular, the isolating and dehumanizing aspects of the event, Laub argues, rendered the victim devoid of 'an other to which one could say "Thou" in the hope of being heard, of being recognized as a subject', and unable to 'say "thou" even to oneself' (ibid., p. 82). This posited impossibility of witnessing in relation to the event itself places added reparative emphasis upon testimony as a process by which the witness is able to come into being as witness and negotiate a possibility of address to self and other: 'the process by which the narrator (the survivor) reclaims his position as a witness: reconstitutes the internal "thou", and thus the possibility of a witness or listener inside himself' (ibid., p. 85). For Laub, then, bearing witness is the process by which the survivor is able to become a witness, assuming through the act of testimony the agency that was denied her during the Holocaust experience itself. As regards the vicissitudes of witnessing, see also under *Testimony* for a discussion of Primo Levi's suggestion that the true witnesses to the Holocaust are those who did not survive, in particular with respect to Giorgio Agamben's elaboration on this.

Another notable application of the notion of witnessing comes in the use of the term to refer to vicarious acts of engagement with Holocaust experience, to a form of encounter mediated by a literary text, image or document, or resulting from familial or other forms of proximity to Holocaust survivors. In his 1997 study *Children of Job*, for example, Alan Berger refers to the children of Holocaust survivors as 'second-generation witnesses'. Acknowledging the dangers of 'substituting the imagination of nonwitnesses for the experience of the survivors' (Berger, 1997, p. 7), he is careful to underline the fact that the second-generation writers he discusses bear witness not in their place of their parents, to their parents' first-hand experiences of the Holocaust, but to their own experience of their parents' remembering:

The makers of this art are not 'rememberers themselves'. Consequently, there is emerging a *paradigm shift* in the shape of Holocaust memory and its representation. Texts written by the contemporary children of Job speak of their own experience of the *Shoah*'s legacy. These texts speak *about* rather than instead of survivors, as this generation seeks to find its own way of shaping the memory and legacy of Auschwitz. (Ibid., p. 20)

Nevertheless, the vocabulary of 'witnessing' arguably risks the collapse of these distinctions, as too does an emphasis on the 'transmission' of memory or testimony, as in statements that the second generation 'have received their parents' testimony and accepted the mission of transmitting it to their own children, the third generation, and to the world at large' (ibid., p. 7). Vocabularies of transmission, while revealing of the degree to which testimony remains the central paradigm through which often radically distinct relationships to the events of the Holocaust must be negotiated, risk construing experience itself as something cut loose from the specificity and subjective rootedness of its experiencing, instead transferrable between individuals via the mechanisms of narrative and the imagination.

The extension of the notion of witnesses to those not present at the time of the events in question has been challenged by such critics as Gary Weissman, who writes that:

I resist these terms because I believe that such a broadening of the term *witness*, as well as similar uses of the terms *memory* and *trauma*, contributes to a wishful blurring of otherwise obvious and meaningful distinctions between the victims and ourselves, and between the Holocaust and our own historical moment. (2004, p. 20)

Weissman thus traces an agenda in the use of these terms, by which later generations seek to construe a closer proximity to the Holocaust than they can in fact legitimately claim; to counteract this experiential blurring and ensure the clarity of distinct categories of witness and representation, he advocates instead the use of the term 'nonwitness' to describe indirect relationships to these events (see separate entry under *nonwitness* for discussion).

For a series of recent re-evaluations of the public role and construction of the witness, see also Dean (2010) and Wieviorka (2006), discussed in more detail in the 'New Directions' section of this volume.

Working Through (and Acting Out): See Mourning and Melancholia

Yizher-Bikher

'Yizkher-bikher' are memorial books commemorating destroyed Jewish communities in Europe. Described by Geoffrey Hartman as 'an unusual example of collective authorship' (1996, p. 31), they are mostly written in Yiddish and bring together surviving documents and records from the community, as well as personal accounts and in some cases maps of the destroyed community. Hartman views the memorial books as a form of history, 'a popular and restitutive genre' (ibid., p. 34), while David Roskies emphasizes the role of the books in a collective working through of the trauma of the Holocaust (1999, p. 61). Yizkher-books can in this sense be considered a form of Holocaust literature, a means of both registering and mourning the communal losses sustained through these events.

Works Cited

Adams, J. (2011), *Magic Realism in Holocaust Literature: Troping the Traumatic Real*. Basingstoke: Palgrave Macmillan.

Adorno, T. [1951] (2003a), 'Cultural criticism and society', trans. S. Weber and S. Weber Nicholsen, in R. Tiedemann (ed.), *Can One Live after Auschwitz? A Philosophical Reader*. Stanford, CA: Stanford University Press, pp. 146–62.

—. [1967] (2003b), 'Education after Auschwitz', trans. H. W. Pickford, in R. Tiedemann (ed.), *Can One Live after Auschwitz? A Philosophical Reader*. Stanford, CA: Stanford University Press, pp. 19–33.

Agamben, G. (1999), *Remnants of Auschwitz: The Witness and the Archive*, trans. D. Heller-Roazen. New York: Zone Books.

van Alphen, E. (1997), *Caught by History: Holocaust Effects in Contemporary Art, Literature, and Theory*. Stanford, CA: Stanford University Press.

Arendt, H. [1963] (2006), *Eichmann in Jerusalem: A Report on the Banality of Evil*. London: Penguin.

Baldwin, P. (1990), 'The *Historikerstreit* in context', in P. Baldwin (ed.), *Reworking the Past: Hitler, the Holocaust, and the Historians' Debate*. Boston: Beacon Press, pp. 3–37.

Bauer, Y. (2001), *Rethinking the Holocaust*. New Haven: Yale University Press.

Bauman, Z. (1993), *Postmodern Ethics*. Oxford: Blackwell.

Berger, A. L. (1997), *Children of Job: American Second-Generation Witnesses to the Holocaust*. Albany: State University of New York Press.

Berger, A. L. and Berger, N. (eds) (2001), *Second Generation Voices: Reflections by Children of Holocaust Survivors & Perpetrators*. Syracuse, NY: Syracuse University Press.

Berger, J. (1999), *After the End: Representations of Post-Apocalypse*. Minneapolis: University of Minnesota Press.

Bernard-Donals, M. (2010), '"If I forget thee, O Jerusalem": the poetry of forgetful memory in Israel and Palestine', in R. C. Spargo and R. M. Ehrenreich (eds), *After Representation? The Holocaust, Literature, and Culture*. New Brunswick, NJ: Rutgers University Press, pp. 119–34.

Bernard-Donals, M. and Glejzer, R. (2003), 'Teaching (after) Auschwitz: pedagogy between redemption and sublimity', in M. Bernard-Donals and R. Glejzer (eds), *Witnessing the Disaster: Essays on Representation and the Holocaust*. Madison: University of Wisconsin Press, pp. 245–61.

Bernstein, M. A. (1994), *Foregone Conclusions: Against Apocalyptic History*. Berkeley: University of California Press.

Bernstein, S. David (2003), 'Promiscuous reading: the problem of identification and Anne Frank's diary', in M. Bernard-Donals and R. Glejzer (eds), *Witnessing the Disaster: Essays on Representation and the Holocaust*. Madison: University of Wisconsin Press, pp. 141–61.

Bloxham, D. (2003), 'Britain's Holocaust memorial days: reshaping the past in the service of the present', in S. Vice (ed.), *Representing the Holocaust: In Honour of Bryan Burns*. London: Vallentine Mitchell, pp. 41–62.

Boswell, M. (2012), *Holocaust Impiety in Literature, Popular Music and Film*. Basingstoke: Palgrave Macmillan.

Browning, C. (1992), 'German memory, judicial interrogation, and historical reconstruction: writing perpetrator history from postwar testimony', in S. Friedlander (ed.), *Probing the Limits of Representation: Nazism and the 'Final Solution'*. Cambridge, MA: Harvard University Press, pp. 22–36.

Caruth, C. (1995), 'Recapturing the past: introduction', in C. Caruth (ed.), *Trauma: Explorations in Memory*. Baltimore: Johns Hopkins University Press, pp. 151–7.

Clendinnen, I. (1999), *Reading the Holocaust*. Cambridge: Cambridge University Press.

Codde, P. (2010), 'Postmemory, afterimages, transferred loss: first and third generation Holocaust trauma in American literature and film', in S. Komor and S. Rohr (eds), *The Holocaust, Art, and Taboo: Transatlantic Exchanges on the Ethics and Aesthetics of Representation*. Heidelberg: Universitätsverlag Winter, pp. 63–74.

Cole, T. (1999), *Images of the Holocaust: The Myth of the 'Shoah Business'*. London: Duckworth.

Critchley, S. (1999), *Ethics, Politics, Subjectivity: Essays on Derrida, Levinas and Contemporary French Thought*. London and New York: Verso.

—. (2002), 'Introduction', in S. Critchley and R. Bernasconi (eds), *The Cambridge Companion to Levinas*. Cambridge: Cambridge University Press, pp. 1–32.

Crownshaw, R. (2010), *The Afterlife of Holocaust Memory in Contemporary Literature and Culture*. Basingstoke: Palgrave Macmillan.

Davis, C. (1996), *Levinas: An Introduction*. Cambridge: Polity Press.

Dean, C. J. (2010), *Aversion and Erasure: The Fate of the Victim after the Holocaust*. Ithaca and London: Cornell University Press.

Eaglestone, R. (1997), *Ethical Criticism: Reading after Levinas*. Edinburgh: Edinburgh University Press.

—. (2004), *The Holocaust and the Postmodern*. Oxford: Oxford University Press.

—. (2013), 'Avoiding evil in perpetrator fiction', in J. Adams and S. Vice (eds), *Representing Perpetrators in Holocaust Literature and Film*. London: Vallentine Mitchell, pp. 13–24.

Felman, S. (1992), 'Education and crisis, or the vicissitudes of teaching', in S. Felman and D. Laub, *Testimony: Crises of Witnessing in Literature, Psychoanalysis and History*. New York and London: Routledge, pp. 1–56.

Finkelstein, N. G. (2003), *The Holocaust Industry: Reflections on the Exploitation of Jewish Suffering*, 2nd edn. London and New York: Verso.

Flanzbaum, H. (1999), 'Introduction: the Americanization of the Holocaust', in H. Flanzbaum (ed.), *The Americanization of the Holocaust*. Baltimore and London: Johns Hopkins University Press, pp. 1–17.

Foer, J. S. (2002), *Everything Is Illuminated*. Boston: Houghton Mifflin.

Freud, S. (1957), 'Mourning and melancholia', in *The Standard Edition of the Complete Psychological Works of Sigmund Freud*, vol. 14, trans. J. Strachey. London: Hogarth Press, pp. 243–58.

Friedlander, S. (1984), *Reflections of the Holocaust: An Essay on Kitsch and Death*, trans. T. Weyr. New York: Harper & Row.

Gomel, E. (2003), *Bloodscripts: Writing the Violent Subject*. Columbus: Ohio State University Press.

Grossman, D. (1990), *See Under: Love*, trans. B. Rosenberg. London: Jonathan Cape.

Gubar, S. (2003), *Poetry after Auschwitz: Remembering What One Never Knew*. Bloomington and Indianapolis: Indiana University Press.

Hartman, G. H. (1996), 'The Weight of What Happened', in *The Longest Shadow: In The Aftermath of the Holocaust*. Bloomington and Indianapolis: Indiana University Press, pp. 27–34.

Hirsch, M. (1996), 'Past lives: postmemories in exile', *Poetics Today*, 17.4, 659–86.

—. (2012), *The Generation of Postmemory: Writing and Visual Culture after the Holocaust*. New York: Columbia University Press.

Kant, I. (2000), *Critique of the Power of Judgement*, trans. P. Guyer and E. Matthews, ed. P. Guyer. Cambridge: Cambridge University Press.

Katz, S. T. (1994), *The Holocaust in Historical Context*, vol. 1: *The Holocaust and Mass Death in the Modern Age*. New York and Oxford: Oxford University Press.

Kleeblatt, N. (ed.) (2001), *Mirroring Evil: Nazi Imagery / Recent Art*. New Brunswick, NJ: Rutgers University Press; New York: The Jewish Museum.

Komor, S. and Rohr, S. (eds) (2010), *The Holocaust, Art, and Taboo: Transatlantic Exchanges on the Ethics and Aesthetics of Representation*. Heidelberg: Universitätsverlag Winter.

LaCapra, D. (1998), *History and Memory after Auschwitz*. Ithaca: Cornell University Press.

—. (2001), *Writing History, Writing Trauma*. Baltimore: Johns Hopkins University Press.

—. (2003), 'Approaching Limit Events: Siting Agamben', in M. Bernard-Donals and R. Glejzer (eds), *Witnessing the Disaster: Essays on Representation and the Holocaust*. Madison: University of Wisconsin Press, pp. 262–304.

Lambek, M. and Antze, P. (1996), 'Introduction: forecasting memory', in P. Antze and M. Lambek (eds), *Tense Past: Cultural Essays in Trauma and Memory*. New York and London: Routledge, pp. xi–xxxviii.

Landsberg, A. (2004), *Prosthetic Memory: The Transformation of American Remembrance in the Age of Mass Culture*. New York: Columbia University Press.

Langer, L. (1991), *Holocaust Testimonies: The Ruins of Memory*. New Haven: Yale University Press.

—. (1998), *Preempting the Holocaust*. New Haven and London: Yale University Press.

Lanzmann, C. (1995), 'The obscenity of understanding: an evening with Claude Lanzmann', in C. Caruth (ed.), *Trauma: Explorations in Memory*. Baltimore: Johns Hopkins University Press, pp. 200–20.

Laub, D. (1992a), 'An event without a witness: truth, testimony and survival', in S. Felman and D. Laub, *Testimony: Crises of Witnessing in Literature, Psychoanalysis and History*. New York and London: Routledge, pp. 75–92.

—. (1992b), 'Bearing witness, or the vicissitudes of listening', in S. Felman and D. Laub, *Testimony: Crises of Witnessing in Literature, Psychoanalysis and History*. New York and London: Routledge, pp. 57–74.

Levi, P. (1989), 'The grey zone', in *The Drowned and the Saved*, trans. R. Rosenthal. London: Abacus, pp. 22–51.

Levinas, E. (1998), *Otherwise than Being, or Beyond Essence*, trans. A. Lingis, with a foreword by R. A. Cohen. Pittsburgh: Duquesne University Press.

Levy, D. and Sznaider, N. (2006), *The Holocaust and Memory in the Global Age*, trans. A. Oksiloff. Philadelphia: Temple University Press.

Leys, R. (2000), *Trauma: A Genealogy*. Chicago: University of Chicago Press.

Linenthal, E. T. (1995), *Preserving Memory: The Struggle to Create America's Holocaust Museum*. New York: Viking Penguin.

Lingis, A. (1998), 'Translator's Preface' to E. Levinas, *Otherwise than Being, or Beyond Essence*, trans. A. Lingis, with a foreword by R. A. Cohen. Pittsburgh: Duquesne University Press, pp. xvii–xlviii.

Lyotard, J.-F. (1988), *The Differend: Phrases in Dispute*, trans. G. van den Abbeele. Minneapolis: University of Minnesota Press.

Maier, C. (1997), *The Unmasterable Past: History, Holocaust, and German National Identity*, 2nd edn. Cambridge, MA: Harvard University Press.

Mandel, N. (2006), *Against the Unspeakable: Complicity, the Holocaust and Slavery in America*. Charlottesville: University of Virginia Press.

McGlothlin, E. (2006), *Second-Generation Holocaust Literature: Legacies of Survival and Perpetration*. Woodbridge: Camden House.

Michaels, A. [1996] (1997), *Fugitive Pieces*. London: Bloomsbury.

Mitscherlich, A. and Mitscherlich, M. (1975), *The Inability to Mourn: The Principles of Collective Behavior*, trans. B. R. Placzek. New York: Grove Press.

Novick, P. (1999), *The Holocaust and Collective Memory: The American Experience*. London: Bloomsbury.

Orbán, K. (2005), *Ethical Diversions: The Post-Holocaust Narratives of Pynchon, Abish, DeLillo, and Spiegelman*. New York and London: Routledge.

Perec, G. [1988] (1996), *W or the Memory of Childhood*, trans. D. Bellos. London: Harvill Press.

Ringelheim, J. (1984), 'The unethical and the unspeakable: women and the Holocaust', *Simon Wiesenthal Centre Annual*, 1, 69–87.

Rohr, S. (2010), '"Genocide pop": the Holocaust as media event', in S. Komor and S. Rohr (eds), *The Holocaust, Art, and Taboo: Transatlantic Exchanges on the Ethics and Aesthetics of Representation*. Heidelberg: Universitätsverlag Winter, pp. 155–77.

Rose, G. (1996), *Mourning Becomes the Law: Philosophy and Representation*. Cambridge: Cambridge University Press.

Roskies, D. G. (1999), *The Jewish Search for a Usable Past*. Bloomington and Indianapolis: Indiana University Press.

Rothberg, M. (2000), *Traumatic Realism: The Demands of Holocaust Representation*. Minneapolis: University of Minnesota Press.

—. (2009), *Multidirectional Memory: Remembering the Holocaust in the Age of Decolonization*. Stanford, CA: Stanford University Press.

Rowland, A. (2005), *Holocaust Poetry: Awkward Poetics in the Work of Sylvia Plath, Geoffrey Hill, Tony Harrison and Ted Hughes*. Edinburgh: Edinburgh University Press.

Sanders, M. (2002), *Complicities: The Intellectual and Apartheid*. Durham and London: Duke University Press.

Santner, E. L. (1992), 'History beyond the pleasure principle: some thoughts on the representation of trauma', in S. Friedlander (ed.), *Probing the Limits of Representation: Nazism and the 'Final Solution'*. Cambridge, MA: Harvard University Press, pp. 143–54.

Sebald, W. G. (2002), *Austerlitz*, trans. A. Bell. London: Penguin.

Sicher, E. (2005), *The Holocaust Novel*. New York and London: Routledge.

Silverman, M. (2013), *Palimpsestic Memory: The Holocaust and Colonialism in French and Francophone Fiction and Film*. New York: Berghahn.

Slade, A. (2004), '*Hiroshima, mon amour*, trauma, and the sublime', in E. A. Kaplan and B. Wang (eds), *Trauma and Cinema: Cross-Cultural Explanations*. Aberdeen and Hong Kong: Hong Kong University Press, pp. 165–81.

Suleiman, S. Rubin (2006), *Crises of Memory and the Second World War*. Cambridge, MA: Harvard University Press.

Waller, J. (2007), *Becoming Evil: How Ordinary People Commit Genocide and Mass Killing*, 2nd edn. Oxford: Oxford University Press.

Weiss, P. [1966] (2000), *The Investigation*, trans. J. Swan and U. Grosbard, rev. R. Cohen, in P. Weiss, *Marat/Sade, The Investigation, and The Shadow of the Body of the Coachman*, ed. R. Cohen. New York: Continuum, pp. 117–298.

Weissman, G. (2004), *Fantasies of Witnessing: Postwar Efforts to Experience the Holocaust*. Ithaca and London: Cornell University Press.

Wiesel, E. (1977), 'The Holocaust as literary inspiration', in *Dimensions of the Holocaust: Lectures at Northwestern University*. Evanston, IL: Northwestern University Press, pp. 5–19.

Wieviorka, A. (2006), *The Era of the Witness*, trans. J. Stark. Ithaca: Cornell University Press.

Index